Lecture Notes in Computer Science   **9910**

Commenced Publication in 1973
Founding and Former Series Editors:
Gerhard Goos, Juris Hartmanis, and Jan van Leeuwen

More information about this series at http://www.springer.com/series/7412

Bastian Leibe · Jiri Matas
Nicu Sebe · Max Welling (Eds.)

Computer Vision – ECCV 2016

14th European Conference
Amsterdam, The Netherlands, October 11–14, 2016
Proceedings, Part VI

 Springer

Editors
Bastian Leibe
RWTH Aachen
Aachen
Germany

Jiri Matas
Czech Technical University
Prague 2
Czech Republic

Nicu Sebe
University of Trento
Povo - Trento
Italy

Max Welling
University of Amsterdam
Amsterdam
The Netherlands

ISSN 0302-9743   ISSN 1611-3349   (electronic)
Lecture Notes in Computer Science
ISBN 978-3-319-46465-7   ISBN 978-3-319-46466-4   (eBook)
DOI 10.1007/978-3-319-46466-4

Library of Congress Control Number: 2016951693

LNCS Sublibrary: SL6 – Image Processing, Computer Vision, Pattern Recognition, and Graphics

Printed on acid-free paper

This Springer imprint is published by Springer Nature
The registered company is Springer International Publishing AG
The registered company address is: Gewerbestrasse 11, 6330 Cham, Switzerland

Foreword

Welcome to the proceedings of the 2016 edition of the European Conference on Computer Vision held in Amsterdam! It is safe to say that the European Conference on Computer Vision is one of the top conferences in computer vision. It is good to reiterate the history of the conference to see the broad base the conference has built in its 13 editions. First held in 1990 in Antibes (France), it was followed by subsequent conferences in Santa Margherita Ligure (Italy) in 1992, Stockholm (Sweden) in 1994, Cambridge (UK) in 1996, Freiburg (Germany) in 1998, Dublin (Ireland) in 2000, Copenhagen (Denmark) in 2002, Prague (Czech Republic) in 2004, Graz (Austria) in 2006, Marseille (France) in 2008, Heraklion (Greece) in 2010, Florence (Italy) in 2012, and Zürich (Switzerland) in 2014.

For the 14th edition, many people worked hard to provide attendees with a most warm welcome while enjoying the best science. The Program Committee, Bastian Leibe, Jiri Matas, Nicu Sebe, and Max Welling, did an excellent job. Apart from the scientific program, the workshops were selected and handled by Hervé Jégou and Gang Hua, and the tutorials by Jacob Verbeek and Rita Cucchiara. Thanks for the great job. The coordination with the subsequent ACM Multimedia offered an opportunity to expand the tutorials with an additional invited session, offered by the University of Amsterdam and organized together with the help of ACM Multimedia.

Of the many people who worked hard as local organizers, we would like to single out Martine de Wit of the UvA Conference Office, who delicately and efficiently organized the main body. Also the local organizers Hamdi Dibeklioglu, Efstratios Gavves, Jan van Gemert, Thomas Mensink, and Mihir Jain had their hands full. As a venue, we chose the Royal Theatre Carré located on the canals of the Amstel River in downtown Amsterdam. Space in Amsterdam is sparse, so it was a little tighter than usual. The university lent us their downtown campuses for the tutorials and the workshops. A relatively new thing was the industry and the sponsors for which Ronald Poppe and Peter de With did a great job, while Andy Bagdanov and John Schavemaker arranged the demos. Michael Wilkinson took care to make Yom Kippur as comfortable as possible for those for whom it is an important day. We thank Marc Pollefeys, Alberto del Bimbo, and Virginie Mes for their advice and help behind the scenes. We thank all the anonymous volunteers for their hard and precise work. We also thank our generous sponsors. Their support is an essential part of the program. It is good to see such a level of industrial interest in what our community is doing!

Amsterdam does not need any introduction. Please emerge yourself but do not drown in it, have a nice time.

October 2016   Theo Gevers
                                                                                                           Arnold Smeulders

Preface

Welcome to the proceedings of the 2016 European Conference on Computer Vision (ECCV 2016) held in Amsterdam, The Netherlands. We are delighted to present this volume reflecting a strong and exciting program, the result of an extensive review process. In total, we received 1,561 paper submissions. Of these, 81 violated the ECCV submission guidelines or did not pass the plagiarism test and were rejected without review. We employed the iThenticate software (www.ithenticate.com) for plagiarism detection. Of the remaining papers, 415 were accepted (26.6 %): 342 as posters (22.6 %), 45 as spotlights (2.9 %), and 28 as oral presentations (1.8 %). The spotlights – short, five-minute podium presentations – are novel to ECCV and were introduced after their success at the CVPR 2016 conference. All orals and spotlights are presented as posters as well. The selection process was a combined effort of four program co-chairs (PCs), 74 area chairs (ACs), 1,086 Program Committee members, and 77 additional reviewers.

As PCs, we were primarily responsible for the design and execution of the review process. Beyond administrative rejections, we were involved in acceptance decisions only in the very few cases where the ACs were not able to agree on a decision. PCs, as is customary in the field, were not allowed to co-author a submission. General co-chairs and other co-organizers played no role in the review process, were permitted to submit papers, and were treated as any other author.

Acceptance decisions were made by two independent ACs. There were 74 ACs, selected by the PCs according to their technical expertise, experience, and geographical diversity (41 from European, five from Asian, two from Australian, and 26 from North American institutions). The ACs were aided by 1,086 Program Committee members to whom papers were assigned for reviewing. There were 77 additional reviewers, each supervised by a Program Committee member. The Program Committee was selected from committees of previous ECCV, ICCV, and CVPR conferences and was extended on the basis of suggestions from the ACs and the PCs. Having a large pool of Program Committee members for reviewing allowed us to match expertise while bounding reviewer loads. Typically five papers, but never more than eight, were assigned to a Program Committee member. Graduate students had a maximum of four papers to review.

The ECCV 2016 review process was in principle double-blind. Authors did not know reviewer identities, nor the ACs handling their paper(s). However, anonymity becomes difficult to maintain as more and more submissions appear concurrently on arXiv.org. This was not against the ECCV 2016 double submission rules, which followed the practice of other major computer vision conferences in the recent past. The existence of arXiv publications, mostly not peer-reviewed, raises difficult problems with the assessment of unpublished, concurrent, and prior art, content overlap, plagiarism, and self-plagiarism. Moreover, it undermines the anonymity of submissions. We found that not all cases can be covered by a simple set of rules. Almost all controversies during the review process were related to the arXiv issue. Most of the reviewer inquiries were resolved by giving the benefit of the doubt to ECCV authors. However, the problem will have to be discussed by the community so that consensus is found on how to handle the issues brought by publishing on arXiv.

Particular attention was paid to handling conflicts of interest. Conflicts of interest between ACs, Program Committee members, and papers were identified based on the authorship of ECCV 2016 submissions, on the home institutions, and on previous collaborations of all researchers involved. To find institutional conflicts, all authors, Program Committee members, and ACs were asked to list the Internet domains of their current institutions. To find collaborators, the Researcher.cc database (http://researcher.cc/), funded by the Computer Vision Foundation, was used to find any co-authored papers in the period 2012–2016. We pre-assigned approximately 100 papers to each AC, based on affinity scores from the Toronto Paper Matching System. ACs then bid on these, indicating their level of expertise. Based on these bids, and conflicts of interest, approximately 40 papers were assigned to each AC. The ACs then suggested seven reviewers from the pool of Program Committee members for each paper, in ranked order, from which three were chosen automatically by CMT (Microsofts Academic Conference Management Service), taking load balancing and conflicts of interest into account.

The initial reviewing period was five weeks long, after which reviewers provided reviews with preliminary recommendations. With the generous help of several last-minute reviewers, each paper received three reviews. Submissions with all three reviews suggesting rejection were independently checked by two ACs and if they agreed, the manuscript was rejected at this stage ("early rejects"). In total, 334 manuscripts (22.5 %) were early-rejected, reducing the average AC load to about 30.

Authors of the remaining submissions were then given the opportunity to rebut the reviews, primarily to identify factual errors. Following this, reviewers and ACs discussed papers at length, after which reviewers finalized their reviews and gave a final recommendation to the ACs. Each manuscript was evaluated independently by two ACs who were not aware of each others, identities. In most of the cases, after extensive discussions, the two ACs arrived at a common decision, which was always adhered to by the PCs. In the very few borderline cases where an agreement was not reached, the PCs acted as tie-breakers. Owing to the rapid expansion of the field, which led to an unexpectedly large increase in the number of submissions, the size of the venue became a limiting factor and a hard upper bound on the number of accepted papers had to be imposed. We were able to increase the limit by replacing one oral session by a poster session. Nevertheless, this forced the PCs to reject some borderline papers that could otherwise have been accepted.

We want to thank everyone involved in making the ECCV 2016 possible. First and foremost, the success of ECCV 2016 depended on the quality of papers submitted by the authors, and on the very hard work of the ACs, the Program Committee members, and the additional reviewers. We are particularly grateful to Rene Vidal for his continuous support and sharing experience from organizing ICCV 2015, to Laurent Charlin for the use of the Toronto Paper Matching System, to Ari Kobren for the use of the Researcher.cc tools, to the Computer Vision Foundation (CVF) for facilitating the use of the iThenticate plagiarism detection software, and to Gloria Zen and Radu-Laurentiu Vieriu for setting up CMT and managing the various tools involved. We also owe a debt of gratitude for the support of the Amsterdam local organizers, especially Hamdi Dibeklioglu for keeping the website always up to date. Finally, the preparation of these proceedings would not have been possible without the diligent effort of the publication chairs, Albert Ali Salah and Robby Tan, and of Anna Kramer from Springer.

October 2016   Bastian Leibe
                                                                 Jiri Matas
                                                                 Nicu Sebe
                                                                 Max Welling

Organization

General Chairs

Theo Gevers — University of Amsterdam, The Netherlands
Arnold Smeulders — University of Amsterdam, The Netherlands

Program Committee Co-chairs

Bastian Leibe — RWTH Aachen, Germany
Jiri Matas — Czech Technical University, Czech Republic
Nicu Sebe — University of Trento, Italy
Max Welling — University of Amsterdam, The Netherlands

Honorary Chair

Jan Koenderink — Delft University of Technology, The Netherlands and KU Leuven, Belgium

Advisory Program Chair

Luc van Gool — ETH Zurich, Switzerland

Advisory Workshop Chair

Josef Kittler — University of Surrey, UK

Advisory Conference Chair

Alberto del Bimbo — University of Florence, Italy

Local Arrangements Chairs

Hamdi Dibeklioglu — Delft University of Technology, The Netherlands
Efstratios Gavves — University of Amsterdam, The Netherlands
Jan van Gemert — Delft University of Technology, The Netherlands
Thomas Mensink — University of Amsterdam, The Netherlands
Michael Wilkinson — University of Groningen, The Netherlands

Workshop Chairs

Hervé Jégou   Facebook AI Research, USA
Gang Hua   Microsoft Research Asia, China

Tutorial Chairs

Jacob Verbeek   Inria Grenoble, France
Rita Cucchiara   University of Modena and Reggio Emilia, Italy

Poster Chairs

Jasper Uijlings   University of Edinburgh, UK
Roberto Valenti   Sightcorp, The Netherlands

Publication Chairs

Albert Ali Salah   Boğaziçi University, Turkey
Robby T. Tan   Yale-NUS College and National University
                             of Singapore, Singapore

Video Chair

Mihir Jain   University of Amsterdam, The Netherlands

Demo Chairs

John Schavemaker   Twnkls, The Netherlands
Andy Bagdanov   University of Florence, Italy

Social Media Chair

Efstratios Gavves   University of Amsterdam, The Netherlands

Industrial Liaison Chairs

Ronald Poppe   Utrecht University, The Netherlands
Peter de With   Eindhoven University of Technology, The Netherlands

Conference Coordinator, Accommodation, and Finance

Conference Office
Martine de Wit   University of Amsterdam, The Netherlands
Melanie Venverloo   University of Amsterdam, The Netherlands
Niels Klein   University of Amsterdam, The Netherlands

Area Chairs

Radhakrishna Achanta	Ecole Polytechnique Fédérale de Lausanne, Switzerland
Antonis Argyros	FORTH and University of Crete, Greece
Michael Bronstein	Universitá della Svizzera Italiana, Switzerland
Gabriel Brostow	University College London, UK
Thomas Brox	University of Freiburg, Germany
Barbara Caputo	Sapienza University of Rome, Italy
Miguel Carreira-Perpinan	University of California, Merced, USA
Ondra Chum	Czech Technical University, Czech Republic
Daniel Cremers	Technical University of Munich, Germany
Rita Cucchiara	University of Modena and Reggio Emilia, Italy
Trevor Darrell	University of California, Berkeley, USA
Andrew Davison	Imperial College London, UK
Fernando de la Torre	Carnegie Mellon University, USA
Piotr Dollar	Facebook AI Research, USA
Vittorio Ferrari	University of Edinburgh, UK
Charless Fowlkes	University of California, Irvine, USA
Jan-Michael Frahm	University of North Carolina at Chapel Hill, USA
Mario Fritz	Max Planck Institute, Germany
Pascal Fua	Ecole Polytechnique Fédérale de Lausanne, Switzerland
Juergen Gall	University of Bonn, Germany
Peter Gehler	University of Tübingen — Max Planck Institute, Germany
Andreas Geiger	Max Planck Institute, Germany
Ross Girshick	Facebook AI Research, USA
Kristen Grauman	University of Texas at Austin, USA
Abhinav Gupta	Carnegie Mellon University, USA
Hervé Jégou	Facebook AI Research, USA
Fredrik Kahl	Lund University, Sweden
Iasonas Kokkinos	Ecole Centrale Paris, France
Philipp Krähenbühl	University of California, Berkeley, USA
Pawan Kumar	University of Oxford, UK
Christoph Lampert	Institute of Science and Technology Austria, Austria
Hugo Larochelle	Université de Sherbrooke, Canada
Neil Lawrence	University of Sheffield, UK
Svetlana Lazebnik	University of Illinois at Urbana-Champaign, USA
Honglak Lee	Stanford University, USA
Kyoung Mu Lee	Seoul National University, Republic of Korea
Vincent Lepetit	Graz University of Technology, Austria
Hongdong Li	Australian National University, Australia
Julien Mairal	Inria, France
Yasuyuki Matsushita	Osaka University, Japan
Nassir Navab	Technical University of Munich, Germany

Sebastian Nowozin	Microsoft Research, Cambridge, UK
Tomas Pajdla	Czech Technical University, Czech Republic
Maja Pantic	Imperial College London, UK
Devi Parikh	Virginia Tech, USA
Thomas Pock	Graz University of Technology, Austria
Elisa Ricci	FBK Technologies of Vision, Italy
Bodo Rosenhahn	Leibniz-University of Hannover, Germany
Stefan Roth	Technical University of Darmstadt, Germany
Carsten Rother	Technical University of Dresden, Germany
Silvio Savarese	Stanford University, USA
Bernt Schiele	Max Planck Institute, Germany
Konrad Schindler	ETH Zürich, Switzerland
Cordelia Schmid	Inria, France
Cristian Sminchisescu	Lund University, Sweden
Noah Snavely	Cornell University, USA
Sabine Süsstrunk	Ecole Polytechnique Fédérale de Lausanne, Switzerland
Qi Tian	University of Texas at San Antonio, USA
Antonio Torralba	Massachusetts Institute of Technology, USA
Zhuowen Tu	University of California, San Diego, USA
Raquel Urtasun	University of Toronto, Canada
Joost van de Weijer	Universitat Autònoma de Barcelona, Spain
Laurens van der Maaten	Facebook AI Research, USA
Nuno Vasconcelos	University of California, San Diego, USA
Andrea Vedaldi	University of Oxford, UK
Xiaogang Wang	Chinese University of Hong Kong, Hong Kong, SAR China
Jingdong Wang	Microsoft Research Asia, China
Lior Wolf	Tel Aviv University, Israel
Ying Wu	Northwestern University, USA
Dong Xu	University of Sydney, Australia
Shuicheng Yan	National University of Singapore, Singapore
MingHsuan Yang	University of California, Merced, USA
Ramin Zabih	Cornell NYC Tech, USA
Larry Zitnick	Facebook AI Research, USA

Technical Program Committee

Austin Abrams	Pulkit Agrawal	Andrea Albarelli
Supreeth Achar	Jorgen Ahlberg	Alexandra Albu
Tameem Adel	Haizhou Ai	Saad Ali
Khurrum Aftab	Zeynep Akata	Daniel Aliaga
Lourdes Agapito	Ijaz Akhter	Marina Alterman
Sameer Agarwal	Karteek Alahari	Hani Altwaijry
Aishwarya Agrawal	Xavier Alameda-Pineda	Jose M. Alvarez

Mitsuru Ambai
Mohamed Amer
Senjian An
Cosmin Ancuti
Juan Andrade-Cetto
Marco Andreetto
Elli Angelopoulou
Relja Arandjelovic
Helder Araujo
Pablo Arbelaez
Chetan Arora
Carlos Arteta
Kalle Astroem
Nikolay Atanasov
Vassilis Athitsos
Mathieu Aubry
Yannis Avrithis
Hossein Azizpour
Artem Babenko
Andrew Bagdanov
Yuval Bahat
Xiang Bai
Lamberto Ballan
Arunava Banerjee
Adrian Barbu
Nick Barnes
Peter Barnum
Jonathan Barron
Adrien Bartoli
Dhruv Batra
Eduardo
   Bayro-Corrochano
Jean-Charles Bazin
Paul Beardsley
Vasileios Belagiannis
Ismail Ben Ayed
Boulbaba Benamor
Abhijit Bendale
Rodrigo Benenson
Fabian Benitez-Quiroz
Ohad Ben-Shahar
Dana Berman
Lucas Beyer
Subhabrata Bhattacharya
Binod Bhattarai
Arnav Bhavsar

Simone Bianco
Hakan Bilen
Horst Bischof
Tom Bishop
Arijit Biswas
Soma Biswas
Marten Bjoerkman
Volker Blanz
Federica Bogo
Xavier Boix
Piotr Bojanowski
Terrance Boult
Katie Bouman
Thierry Bouwmans
Edmond Boyer
Yuri Boykov
Hakan Boyraz
Steven Branson
Mathieu Bredif
Francois Bremond
Stefan Breuers
Michael Brown
Marcus Brubaker
Luc Brun
Andrei Bursuc
Zoya Bylinskii
Daniel Cabrini Hauagge
Deng Cai
Jianfei Cai
Simone Calderara
Neill Campbell
Octavia Camps
Liangliang Cao
Xiaochun Cao
Xun Cao
Gustavo Carneiro
Dan Casas
Tom Cashman
Umberto Castellani
Carlos Castillo
Andrea Cavallaro
Jan Cech
Ayan Chakrabarti
Rudrasis Chakraborty
Krzysztof Chalupka
Tat-Jen Cham

Antoni Chan
Manmohan Chandraker
Sharat Chandran
Hong Chang
Hyun Sung Chang
Jason Chang
Ju Yong Chang
Xiaojun Chang
Yu-Wei Chao
Visesh Chari
Rizwan Chaudhry
Rama Chellappa
Bo Chen
Chao Chen
Chao-Yeh Chen
Chu-Song Chen
Hwann-Tzong Chen
Lin Chen
Mei Chen
Terrence Chen
Xilin Chen
Yunjin Chen
Guang Chen
Qifeng Chen
Xinlei Chen
Jian Cheng
Ming-Ming Cheng
Anoop Cherian
Guilhem Cheron
Dmitry Chetverikov
Liang-Tien Chia
Naoki Chiba
Tat-Jun Chin
Margarita Chli
Minsu Cho
Sunghyun Cho
TaeEun Choe
Jongmoo Choi
Seungjin Choi
Wongun Choi
Wen-Sheng Chu
Yung-Yu Chuang
Albert Chung
Gokberk Cinbis
Arridhana Ciptadi
Javier Civera

James Clark
Brian Clipp
Michael Cogswell
Taco Cohen
Toby Collins
John Collomosse
Camille Couprie
David Crandall
Marco Cristani
James Crowley
Jinshi Cui
Yin Cui
Jifeng Dai
Qieyun Dai
Shengyang Dai
Yuchao Dai
Zhenwen Dai
Dima Damen
Kristin Dana
Kostas Danilidiis
Mohamed Daoudi
Larry Davis
Teofilo de Campos
Marleen de Bruijne
Koichiro Deguchi
Alessio Del Bue
Luca del Pero
Antoine Deleforge
Hervé Delingette
David Demirdjian
Jia Deng
Joachim Denzler
Konstantinos Derpanis
Frederic Devernay
Hamdi Dibeklioglu
Santosh Kumar Divvala
Carl Doersch
Weisheng Dong
Jian Dong
Gianfranco Doretto
Alexey Dosovitskiy
Matthijs Douze
Bruce Draper
Tom Drummond
Shichuan Du
Jean-Luc Dugelay

Enrique Dunn
Zoran Duric
Pinar Duygulu
Alexei Efros
Carl Henrik Ek
Jan-Olof Eklundh
Jayan Eledath
Ehsan Elhamifar
Ian Endres
Aykut Erdem
Anders Eriksson
Sergio Escalera
Victor Escorcia
Francisco Estrada
Bin Fan
Quanfu Fan
Chen Fang
Tian Fang
Masoud Faraki
Ali Farhadi
Giovanni Farinella
Ryan Farrell
Raanan Fattal
Michael Felsberg
Jiashi Feng
Michele Fenzi
Andras Ferencz
Basura Fernando
Sanja Fidler
Mario Figueiredo
Michael Firman
Robert Fisher
John Fisher III
Alexander Fix
Boris Flach
Matt Flagg
Francois Fleuret
Wolfgang Foerstner
David Fofi
Gianluca Foresti
Per-Erik Forssen
David Fouhey
Jean-Sebastien Franco
Friedrich Fraundorfer
Oren Freifeld
Simone Frintrop

Huazhu Fu
Yun Fu
Jan Funke
Brian Funt
Ryo Furukawa
Yasutaka Furukawa
Andrea Fusiello
David Gallup
Chuang Gan
Junbin Gao
Jochen Gast
Stratis Gavves
Xin Geng
Bogdan Georgescu
David Geronimo
Bernard Ghanem
Riccardo Gherardi
Golnaz Ghiasi
Soumya Ghosh
Andrew Gilbert
Ioannis Gkioulekas
Georgia Gkioxari
Guy Godin
Roland Goecke
Boqing Gong
Shaogang Gong
Yunchao Gong
German Gonzalez
Jordi Gonzalez
Paulo Gotardo
Stephen Gould
Venu M. Govindu
Helmut Grabner
Etienne Grossmann
Chunhui Gu
David Gu
Sergio Guadarrama
Li Guan
Matthieu Guillaumin
Jean-Yves Guillemaut
Guodong Guo
Ruiqi Guo
Yanwen Guo
Saurabh Gupta
Pierre Gurdjos
Diego Gutierrez

Ajmal Mian
Tomer Michaeli
Ondrej Miksik
Anton Milan
Erik Miller
Gregor Miller
Majid Mirmehdi
Ishan Misra
Anurag Mittal
Daisuke Miyazaki
Hossein Mobahi
Pascal Monasse
Sandino Morales
Vlad Morariu
Philippos Mordohai
Francesc Moreno-Noguer
Greg Mori
Bryan Morse
Roozbeh Mottaghi
Yadong Mu
Yasuhiro Mukaigawa
Lopamudra Mukherjee
Joseph Mundy
Mario Munich
Ana Murillo
Vittorio Murino
Naila Murray
Damien Muselet
Sobhan Naderi Parizi
Hajime Nagahara
Nikhil Naik
P.J. Narayanan
Fabian Nater
Jan Neumann
Ram Nevatia
Shawn Newsam
Bingbing Ni
Juan Carlos Niebles
Jifeng Ning
Ko Nishino
Masashi Nishiyama
Shohei Nobuhara
Ifeoma Nwogu
Peter Ochs
Jean-Marc Odobez
Francesca Odone

Iason Oikonomidis
Takeshi Oishi
Takahiro Okabe
Takayuki Okatani
Carl Olsson
Vicente Ordonez
Ivan Oseledets
Magnus Oskarsson
Martin R. Oswald
Matthew O'Toole
Wanli Ouyang
Andrew Owens
Mustafa Ozuysal
Jason Pacheco
Manohar Paluri
Gang Pan
Jinshan Pan
Yannis Panagakis
Sharath Pankanti
George Papandreou
Hyun Soo Park
In Kyu Park
Jaesik Park
Seyoung Park
Omkar Parkhi
Ioannis Patras
Viorica Patraucean
Genevieve Patterson
Vladimir Pavlovic
Kim Pedersen
Robert Peharz
Shmuel Peleg
Marcello Pelillo
Otavio Penatti
Xavier Pennec
Federico Pernici
Adrian Peter
Stavros Petridis
Vladimir Petrovic
Tomas Pfister
Justus Piater
Pedro Pinheiro
Bernardo Pires
Fiora Pirri
Leonid Pishchulin
Daniel Pizarro

Robert Pless
Tobias Pltz
Yair Poleg
Gerard Pons-Moll
Jordi Pont-Tuset
Ronald Poppe
Andrea Prati
Jan Prokaj
Daniel Prusa
Nicolas Pugeault
Guido Pusiol
Guo-Jun Qi
Gang Qian
Yu Qiao
Novi Quadrianto
Julian Quiroga
Andrew Rabinovich
Rahul Raguram
Srikumar Ramalingam
Deva Ramanan
Narayanan Ramanathan
Vignesh Ramanathan
Sebastian Ramos
Rene Ranftl
Anand Rangarajan
Avinash Ravichandran
Ramin Raziperchikolaei
Carlo Regazzoni
Christian Reinbacher
Michal Reinstein
Emonet Remi
Fabio Remondino
Shaoqing Ren
Zhile Ren
Jerome Revaud
Hayko Riemenschneider
Tobias Ritschel
Mariano Rivera
Patrick Rives
Antonio Robles-Kelly
Jason Rock
Erik Rodner
Emanuele Rodola
Mikel Rodriguez
Antonio
    Rodriguez Sanchez

Gregory Rogez
Marcus Rohrbach
Javier Romero
Matteo Ronchi
German Ros
Charles Rosenberg
Guy Rosman
Arun Ross
Paolo Rota
Samuel Rota Bulò
Peter Roth
Volker Roth
Brandon Rothrock
Anastasios Roussos
Amit Roy-Chowdhury
Ognjen Rudovic
Daniel Rueckert
Christian Rupprecht
Olga Russakovsky
Bryan Russell
Emmanuel Sabu
Fereshteh Sadeghi
Hideo Saito
Babak Saleh
Mathieu Salzmann
Dimitris Samaras
Conrad Sanderson
Enver Sangineto
Aswin Sankaranarayanan
Imari Sato
Yoichi Sato
Shin'ichi Satoh
Torsten Sattler
Bogdan Savchynskyy
Yann Savoye
Arman Savran
Harpreet Sawhney
Davide Scaramuzza
Walter Scheirer
Frank Schmidt
Uwe Schmidt
Dirk Schnieders
Johannes Schönberger
Florian Schroff
Samuel Schulter
William Schwartz

Alexander Schwing
Stan Sclaroff
Nicu Sebe
Ari Seff
Anita Sellent
Giuseppe Serra
Laura Sevilla-Lara
Shishir Shah
Greg Shakhnarovich
Qi Shan
Shiguang Shan
Jing Shao
Ling Shao
Xiaowei Shao
Roman Shapovalov
Nataliya Shapovalova
Ali Sharif Razavian
Gaurav Sharma
Pramod Sharma
Viktoriia Sharmanska
Eli Shechtman
Alexander Shekhovtsov
Evan Shelhamer
Chunhua Shen
Jianbing Shen
Li Shen
Xiaoyong Shen
Wei Shen
Yu Sheng
Jianping Shi
Qinfeng Shi
Yonggang Shi
Baoguang Shi
Kevin Shih
Nobutaka Shimada
Ilan Shimshoni
Koichi Shinoda
Takaaki Shiratori
Jamie Shotton
Matthew Shreve
Abhinav Shrivastava
Nitesh Shroff
Leonid Sigal
Nathan Silberman
Tomas Simon
Edgar Simo-Serra

Dheeraj Singaraju
Gautam Singh
Maneesh Singh
Richa Singh
Saurabh Singh
Vikas Singh
Sudipta Sinha
Josef Sivic
Greg Slabaugh
William Smith
Patrick Snape
Jan Sochman
Kihyuk Sohn
Hyun Oh Song
Jingkuan Song
Qi Song
Shuran Song
Xuan Song
Yale Song
Yi-Zhe Song
Alexander
    Sorkine Hornung
Humberto Sossa
Aristeidis Sotiras
Richard Souvenir
Anuj Srivastava
Nitish Srivastava
Michael Stark
Bjorn Stenger
Rainer Stiefelhagen
Martin Storath
Joerg Stueckler
Hang Su
Hao Su
Jingyong Su
Shuochen Su
Yu Su
Ramanathan Subramanian
Yusuke Sugano
Akihiro Sugimoto
Libin Sun
Min Sun
Qing Sun
Yi Sun
Chen Sun
Deqing Sun

Ganesh Sundaramoorthi
Jinli Suo
Supasorn Suwajanakorn
Tomas Svoboda
Chris Sweeney
Paul Swoboda
Raza Syed Hussain
Christian Szegedy
Yuichi Taguchi
Yu-Wing Tai
Hugues Talbot
Toru Tamaki
Mingkui Tan
Robby Tan
Xiaoyang Tan
Masayuki Tanaka
Meng Tang
Siyu Tang
Ran Tao
Dacheng Tao
Makarand Tapaswi
Jean-Philippe Tarel
Camillo Taylor
Christian Theobalt
Diego Thomas
Rajat Thomas
Xinmei Tian
Yonglong Tian
YingLi Tian
Yonghong Tian
Kinh Tieu
Joseph Tighe
Radu Timofte
Massimo Tistarelli
Sinisa Todorovic
Giorgos Tolias
Federico Tombari
Akihiko Torii
Andrea Torsello
Du Tran
Quoc-Huy Tran
Rudolph Triebel
Roberto Tron
Leonardo Trujillo
Eduard Trulls
Tomasz Trzcinski

Yi-Hsuan Tsai
Gavriil Tsechpenakis
Chourmouzios Tsiotsios
Stavros Tsogkas
Kewei Tu
Shubham Tulsiani
Tony Tung
Pavan Turaga
Matthew Turk
Tinne Tuytelaars
Oncel Tuzel
Georgios Tzimiropoulos
Norimichi Ukita
Osman Ulusoy
Martin Urschler
Arash Vahdat
Michel Valstar
Ernest Valveny
Jan van Gemert
Kiran Varanasi
Mayank Vatsa
Javier Vazquez-Corral
Ramakrishna Vedantam
Ashok Veeraraghavan
Olga Veksler
Jakob Verbeek
Francisco Vicente
Rene Vidal
Jordi Vitria
Max Vladymyrov
Christoph Vogel
Carl Vondrick
Sven Wachsmuth
Toshikazu Wada
Catherine Wah
Jacob Walker
Xiaolong Wang
Wei Wang
Limin Wang
Liang Wang
Hua Wang
Lijun Wang
Naiyan Wang
Xinggang Wang
Yining Wang
Baoyuan Wang

Chaohui Wang
Gang Wang
Heng Wang
Lei Wang
Linwei Wang
Liwei Wang
Ping Wang
Qi Wang
Qian Wang
Shenlong Wang
Song Wang
Tao Wang
Yang Wang
Yu-Chiang Frank Wang
Zhaowen Wang
Simon Warfield
Yichen Wei
Philippe Weinzaepfel
Longyin Wen
Tomas Werner
Aaron Wetzler
Yonatan Wexler
Michael Wilber
Kyle Wilson
Thomas Windheuser
David Wipf
Paul Wohlhart
Christian Wolf
Kwan-Yee Kenneth Wong
John Wright
Jiajun Wu
Jianxin Wu
Tianfu Wu
Yang Wu
Yi Wu
Zheng Wu
Stefanie Wuhrer
Jonas Wulff
Rolf Wurtz
Lu Xia
Tao Xiang
Yu Xiang
Lei Xiao
Yang Xiao
Tong Xiao
Wenxuan Xie

Lingxi Xie
Pengtao Xie
Saining Xie
Yuchen Xie
Junliang Xing
Bo Xiong
Fei Xiong
Jia Xu
Yong Xu
Tianfan Xue
Toshihiko Yamasaki
Takayoshi Yamashita
Junjie Yan
Rong Yan
Yan Yan
Keiji Yanai
Jian Yang
Jianchao Yang
Jiaolong Yang
Jie Yang
Jimei Yang
Michael Ying Yang
Ming Yang
Ruiduo Yang
Yi Yang
Angela Yao
Cong Yao
Jian Yao
Jianhua Yao
Jinwei Ye
Shuai Yi
Alper Yilmaz
Lijun Yin
Zhaozheng Yin

Xianghua Ying
Kuk-Jin Yoon
Chong You
Aron Yu
Felix Yu
Fisher Yu
Lap-Fai Yu
Stella Yu
Jing Yuan
Junsong Yuan
Lu Yuan
Xiao-Tong Yuan
Alan Yuille
Xenophon Zabulis
Stefanos Zafeiriou
Sergey Zagoruyko
Amir Zamir
Andrei Zanfir
Mihai Zanfir
Lihi Zelnik-Manor
Xingyu Zeng
Josiane Zerubia
Changshui Zhang
Cheng Zhang
Guofeng Zhang
Jianguo Zhang
Junping Zhang
Ning Zhang
Quanshi Zhang
Shaoting Zhang
Tianzhu Zhang
Xiaoqun Zhang
Yinda Zhang
Yu Zhang

Shiliang Zhang
Lei Zhang
Xiaoqin Zhang
Shanshan Zhang
Ting Zhang
Bin Zhao
Rui Zhao
Yibiao Zhao
Enliang Zheng
Wenming Zheng
Yinqiang Zheng
Yuanjie Zheng
Yin Zheng
Wei-Shi Zheng
Liang Zheng
Dingfu Zhou
Wengang Zhou
Tinghui Zhou
Bolei Zhou
Feng Zhou
Huiyu Zhou
Jun Zhou
Kevin Zhou
Kun Zhou
Xiaowei Zhou
Zihan Zhou
Jun Zhu
Jun-Yan Zhu
Zhenyao Zhu
Zeeshan Zia
Henning Zimmer
Karel Zimmermann
Wangmeng Zuo

Additional Reviewers

Felix Achilles
Sarah Adel Bargal
Hessam Bagherinezhad
Qinxun Bai
Gedas Bertasius
Michal Busta
Erik Bylow
Marinella Cadoni

Dan Andrei Calian
Lilian Calvet
Federico Camposeco
Olivier Canevet
Anirban Chakraborty
Yu-Wei Chao
Sotirios Chatzis
Tatjana Chavdarova

Jimmy Chen
Melissa Cote
Berkan Demirel
Zhiwei Deng
Guy Gilboa
Albert Gordo
Daniel Gordon
Ankur Gupta

Contents – Part VI

Poster Session 7

Poster Session 6 (Continued)

Spatio-Temporally Consistent Correspondence for Dense Dynamic Scene Modeling

Dinghuang Ji$^{(\boxtimes)}$, Enrique Dunn, and Jan-Michael Frahm

The University of North Carolina at Chapel Hill, Chapel Hill, USA
{jdh,dunn,jmf}@cs.unc.edu

Abstract. We address the problem of robust two-view correspondence estimation within the context of dynamic scene modeling. To this end, we investigate the use of local spatio-temporal assumptions to both identify and refine dense low-level data associations in the absence of prior dynamic content models. By developing a strictly data-driven approach to correspondence search, based on bottom-up local 3D motion cues of local rigidity and non-local coherence, we are able to robustly address the higher-order problems of video synchronization and dynamic surface modeling. Our findings suggest an important relationship between these two tasks, in that maximizing spatial coherence of surface points serves as a direct metric for the temporal alignment of local image sequences. The obtained results for these two problems on multiple publicly available dynamic reconstruction datasets illustrate both the effectiveness and generality of our proposed approach.

Keywords: Two-View correspondences · Motion consistency

1 Introduction

Dynamic 3D scene modeling addresses the estimation of time-varying geometry from input imagery. Existing motion capture techniques have typically addressed well-controlled capture scenarios, where aspects such as camera positioning, sensor synchronization, and favorable scene content (*i.e.*, fiducial markers or "green screen" backgrounds) are either carefully designed *a priori* or controlled online. Given the abundance of available crowd-sourced video content, there is growing interest in estimating dynamic 3D representations from uncontrolled video capture. Whereas multi-camera static scene reconstruction methods leverage photoconsistency across spatially varying observations, their dynamic counterparts must address photoconsistency in the spatio-temporal domain. In this respect, the main challenges are (1) finding a common temporal reference frame across independent video captures, and (2) meaningfully propagating temporally

---

Electronic supplementary material The online version of this chapter (doi:10. 1007/978-3-319-46466-4_1) contains supplementary material, which is available to authorized users.

B. Leibe et al. (Eds.): ECCV 2016, Part VI, LNCS 9910, pp. 3–18, 2016.
DOI: 10.1007/978-3-319-46466-4_1

4   D. Ji et al.

varying photo-consistency estimates across videos. These two correspondence problems – temporal correspondence search among unaligned video sequences and spatial correspondence for geometry estimation – must be solved jointly when performing dynamic 3D reconstruction on uncontrolled inputs.

In this work, we address both of these challenges by enforcing the geometric consistency of optical flow measurements across spatially registered video segments. Moreover, our approach builds on the thesis that *maximally consistent geometry is obtained with minimal temporal alignment error*, and *vice versa*. Towards this end, we posit that it is possible to recover the spatio-temporal overlap of two image sequences by maximizing the set of consistent spatio-temporal correspondences (that is, by maximizing the completeness of the estimated dynamic 3D geometry) among the two video segments.

In practice, our approach addresses the spatio-temporal two-view stereo problem. Taking as input two unsynchronized video streams of the same dynamic scene, our method outputs a dense point cloud corresponding to the evolving shape of the commonly observed dynamic foreground. In addition to outputting the observed 3D structure, we estimate the temporal offset of a pair of input video streams with a constant and known ratio between their frame rates. An overview of our framework is shown in Fig. 1. Our framework operates within local temporal windows in a strictly data-driven manner to leverage the low-level concepts of local rigidity and non-local geometric coherence for robust model-free structure estimation. We further illustrate how our local spatio-temporal assumptions can be built to successfully address problems of much larger scope, such as content-based video synchronization and object-level dense dynamic modeling.

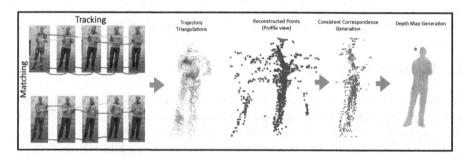

Fig. 1. Overview of the proposed approach for dense dynamic scene reconstruction from two input video streams.

2   Related Work

For static environments, very robust structure-from motion (SfM) systems [1–3] and multi-view stereo (MVS) approaches[4] have shown much success in recovering scene geometry with high accuracy on a large variety of datasets. Modeling non-static objects with this framework, however, is considerably more difficult because the assumptions driving correspondence detection and 3D point triangulation in rigid scenarios cannot be directly applied to moving objects. To address these challenges, a wide array of dynamic scene reconstruction techniques have been introduced in the computer vision literature, in capture situations that are controlled or uncontrolled, synchronized or unsynchronized, single-view or multi-view, and model-based or model-free.

In general, highly controlled image capture scenarios have shown considerable success for non-static scene capture because they are able to leverage more powerful assumptions w.r.t. appearance and correspondence of scene elements. For example, Joo et al. [5,6] used a large-scale rig of 480 synchronized cameras arranged along a sphere to obtain high-quality, dense reconstructions of moving objects within the capture environment. For more general applications, Kim et al. [7] designed a synchronized, portable, multi-camera system specifically tailored for dynamic object capture. Jiang et al. [8] and Taneja et al. [9] further proposed probabilistic frameworks to model outdoor scenes with synchronized handheld cameras. Mustafa et al. [10] introduced a general approach to dynamic scene reconstruction from multiple synchronized moving cameras without prior knowledge or limiting constraints on the scene structure. These works, and others [11–17], clearly indicate the strong potential for non-rigid reconstruction in general capture scenarios, and they highlight in particular the usefulness of multiple synchronized video streams toward this end. In this paper, we build on these works by automatically recovering the temporal alignment of unsynchronized video streams as part of the dense, dynamic reconstruction process.

Single-view video capture can be considered as a dynamic reconstruction scenario inherently lacking the benefits of multi-view synchronization. On this front, the monocular method of Russell et al. [18] is most germane to our approach. The authors employ automatic segmentation of rigid object subparts, for example 3D points on the arms, legs, and torso of a human, and solve the dynamic reconstruction problem by jointly computing hierarchical object segmentation and sparse 3D motion. Their notion of *spatial consistency* of rigid subparts is an important contribution that we leverage in our approach to unsynchronized multi-view reconstruction. A key distinction is that our method utilizes multiple camera views to recover relative object translation in the static surrounding environment, which is not completely recoverable using monocular input alone.

Despite the large amount of crowd-sourced video data available on the Internet (for example, multiple video uploads from a live concert), relatively little research has focused on dynamic 3D reconstruction from unsynchronized, concurrent capture. To our knowledge, Zheng et al. [19] were the first to propose a solution to this interesting reconstruction task. The authors introduced a dictionary learning method to simultaneously solve the problem of video synchronization and sparse 3D reconstruction. In this method, the frame offsets of multiple videos are obtained by sparse representation of the triangulated 3D shapes, and the shapes are iteratively refined with updated sequencing information. However,

this approach is not automatic, relying heavily on manually labeled correspondences on the rigid bodies, and the resulting reconstructions are relatively sparse
(*i.e.*, they represent a human using only 15 3D points). Their extended version
[20], further asserts that both outlier correspondences and reduced/small temporal overlap will hinder the accuracy of the temporal alignment. In contrast to
Zheng *et al.* [19], our work aims to jointly recover dense object geometry and
temporal information in an unsupervised manner.

In the past, multi-view geometric reasoning has been employed for the general problem of video synchronization. These methods are related to the video
synchronization aspect our work, but they do not provide dense 3D geometry.
For example, Basha *et al.* [21,22] proposed methods for computing partial order-
ings for a subset of images by analyzing the movement of dynamic objects in the
images. There, dynamic objects are assumed to move closely along a straight
line within a short time period, and video frames are ordered to form a consistent motion model. Tuytelaars *et al.* [23] proposed a method for automatically
synchronizing two video sequences of the same event. They do not enforce any
constraints on the scene or cameras, but rather rely on validating the rigidity of
at least five non-rigidly moving points among the video sequences, matched and
tracked throughout the two sequences. In [24], Wolf and Zomet propose a strategy that builds on the idea that every 3D point tracked in one sequence results
from a linear combination of the 3D points tracked in the other sequence. This
approach works with articulated objects, but requires that the cameras are static
or moving jointly. Finally, Pundik *et al.* [25] introduced a novel formulation of
low-level temporal signals computed from epipolar lines. The spatial matching
of two such temporal signals is given by the fundamental matrix relating each
pair of images, without requiring pixel-wise correspondences.

3   Spatio-Temporal Correspondence Assessment

Our goal is to analyze two spatially-registered video sub-sequences of equal
length, in order to determine the largest set of spatio-temporally consistent pixel
correspondences belonging to a commonly observed dynamic foreground object.
In particular, we are interested in building two-view correspondence-based visual
3D tracks spanning the entire length of the sub-sequences and assessing the validity of the initial correspondences in terms of the geometric properties of the 3D
tracks. Our goal has two complimentary interpretations: (1) to develop a spatio-
temporal correspondence filtering mechanism, and (2) to provide a measure of
local spatio-temporal consistency among video sub-sequences in terms of the size
of the valid correspondence set. We explore both these interpretations within the
context of video synchronization and dense dynamic surface modeling.

3.1   Notation

Let $\{\mathcal{I}_i\}$ and $\{\mathcal{I}'_j\}$ denote a pair of input image sequences, where $1 \leq i \leq M$
and $1 \leq j \leq N$ are the single image indices. For each image $\mathcal{I}_k \in \{\mathcal{I}_i\} \cup \{\mathcal{I}'_j\}$, we

first obtain via structure-from-motion (SfM) a corresponding camera projection matrix, $\mathbf{P}(\mathcal{I}_k) = \mathbf{K}_k \left[\mathbf{R}_k | - \mathbf{R}_k \mathbf{C}_k \right]$, where $\mathbf{K}$, $\mathbf{R}$, and $\mathbf{C}$ respectively denote the camera's intrinsic parameter matrix, external rotation matrix, and 3D position. Let $\mathbf{F}_{ij}$ denote the fundamental matrix relating the camera poses for images $\mathcal{I}_i$ and $\mathcal{I}'_j$. Furthermore, let $\mathcal{O}_i$ and $\mathcal{O}'_j$ denote optical flow fields for corresponding 2D points in consecutive images $(e.g., \mathcal{I}_i \rightarrow \mathcal{I}_{i+1}$ and $\mathcal{I}'_j \rightarrow \mathcal{I}'_{j+1})$ in each of the two input sequences. Finally, let $\mathbf{x}_{ip}$ and $\mathbf{X}_{ip}$ denote the 2D pixel position and the 3D world point, respectively, for pixel p in image $\mathcal{I}_i$ (and similarly $\mathbf{x}'_{jp}$ and $\mathbf{X}'_{jp}$ for image $\mathcal{I}'_j$).

3.2 Pre-processing and Correspondence Formulation

Spatial Camera Registration. Our approach takes as input two image streams capturing the movements of a dynamic foreground actor, under the assumption of sufficient visual overlap that enables camera registration to a common spatial reference defined by a static background structure. Inter-sequence camera registration is carried out in a pre-processing step using standard SfM methods [15] over the aggregated set of frames, producing a spatial registration of the individual images from each stream. Since the goal of this stage is simply image registration of the two sequences, the set of input images for SfM can be augmented with additional video streams or crowd-sourced imagery for higher-quality pose estimates; however, this is not necessarily required for our method to succeed.

Dynamic Foreground Segmentation. SfM simultaneously recovers the camera poses for the input images and reconstructs the 3D structure of the static background. The first step in our method is to build a reliable dynamic foreground mask for each image using the available 3D SfM output. At first blush, it seems that this task can be accomplished by simply reprojecting the SfM 3D points into each image and aggregating these projections into a background mask. However, this approach is less effective for automatic foreground segmentation primarily because it does not account for spurious 3D point triangulations of the dynamic foreground object. Hence, to identify the non-static foreground points in an image, we adopt a three-stage process: First, we perform RANSAC-based dominant 3D plane fitting on the SfM point cloud, under the assumption that large planar structures will be part of the background. We iteratively detect dominant planes until we have either included over 70 % of available points or the estimated inlier rate of the current iteration falls below a pre-defined threshold. Second, for the remaining reconstructed 3D points not belonging to a dominant plane, we identify their set of nearest 3D neighbors and measure the photoconsistency of this set with their corresponding color projections into the image under consideration. We measure the normalized cross correlation (NCC) of these samples and threshold values above 0.8 as background and below 0.5 as foreground. Third, we perform a graph-cut optimization to determine a global foreground-background segmentation, where we use the points on the dominant planes along with photoconsistent reprojections as initial background seeds, while the non-photoconsistent pixels are considered foreground seeds. Figure 2 illustrates an example of our segmentation output.

Correspondence Search Space. Consider two temporally corresponding image frames $\mathcal{I}_i$ and $\mathcal{I}_j'$. For a given pixel position $\mathbf{x}_{ip}$ contained within the dynamic foreground mask of image $\mathcal{I}_i$, we can readily compute a correspondence $\mathbf{x}_{jp}'$ in image $\mathcal{I}_j'$ by searching for the most photoconsistent candidate along the epipolar line $\mathbf{F}_{ij}\mathbf{x}_{ip}$. We can further reduce the candidate set $\Omega(\mathbf{x}_{ip}, \mathbf{F}_{ij}) \in \mathcal{I}_j'$ by only considering points along the epipolar line contained within the foreground mask of $\mathcal{I}_j'$ (Fig. 3(a) and (b)). In this manner, we have $\Omega(\mathbf{x}_{ip}, \mathbf{F}_{ij}) = \{\mathbf{x}_{jq}' \mid \mathbf{x}_{ip}\mathbf{F}_{ij}\mathbf{x}_{jq}' = 0\}$. Henceforth, we shall omit the dependence on the pre-computed camera geometry and segmentation estimates from our notation, denoting the set of candidate matches for a given pixel as $\Omega(\mathbf{x}_{ip})$. We measure NCC w.r.t. the reference pixel $\mathbf{x}_{ip}$ using 15×15 patches along the epipolar line, and all patches with a NCC value greater than 0.8 are deemed potential correspondences. Once $\Omega(\mathbf{x}_{ip})$ is determined, its elements $\mathbf{x}_{jq}'$ are sorted in descending order of their photoconsistency value. Figure 3(c) and (d) provides an example of our epipolar correspondence search for an image pair.

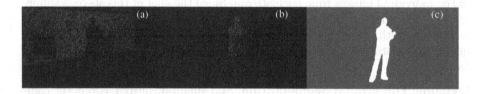

Fig. 2. (a) Background mask that has high color consistency. (b) Foreground mask with low color consistency. (c) Segmented result.

3.3 Assesment and Correction Mechanisim

Based on the example shown in Fig. 3, we propose a method to discern wrong correspondences and correct them with an alternative pixel matches. The steps of our method are as follows:

Step ❶: Building Motion Tracks. The set of 2D feature points $\{\mathbf{x}_{ip}\}$ and currently selected corresponding points $\{\mathbf{x}_{jq}'\}$ are updated with optical flow motion vectors computed between neighboring frames using the approach of Brox et al. [26]. Thus we have $\{\mathbf{x}_{i+1,p}\} = \{\mathbf{x}_{i,p}\} + \mathcal{O}_i$ and $\{\mathbf{x}_{j+1,q}'\} = \{\mathbf{x}_{jq}'\} + \mathcal{O}_j'$. We select the video with the higher frame rate as the target sequence, which will be temporally sampled according to the frame rate ratio α among the sequences. The reference sequence will be used at its native frame rate. Hence, given a temporal window of W frames, the reference video frames and their features will be denoted, respectively, by $\mathcal{I}_i$ and $\{\mathbf{x}_{i,p}\}$, where $1 \leq i \leq W$, denotes the frame index. Accordingly, the frames and features in the target video frames will be denoted by $\mathcal{I}_j'$ and $\{\mathbf{x}_{j+w*\alpha,q}'\}$, where j corresponds to the temporal frame offset

Fig. 3. (a) Local features in reference image. (b) Corresponding points are found along the epipolar lines in the target image. In (c) and (d) Red stars: Feature point in reference frame. Blue stars: Matched feature points in the target frame. Green circles: Points with highest NCC values. (c), the point with the highest NCC value is actually the correct correspondence. (d), the green circle is indicating the wrong match. The other candidate is the correct correspondence and should be used for triangulation.

between the two sequences, and $0 \leq w < W$. The size of the temporal window must strike a balance between building informative 3D tracks for spatial analysis and maintaining the reliability of the chain of estimated dense optical flows.

The initial set of correspondence estimates $\{\mathbf{x}_{ip}\}$, $\{\mathbf{x}'_{jq}\}$ are temporally tracked through successive intra-sequence optical flow estimates, and their updated locations are then used for two-view 3D triangulation. Namely, for each point $\mathbf{x}_{ip}$ selected at frame p, we have a 3D track $\mathbf{T}_i = \{\mathbf{X}_{iw}\}$ comprised of $1 \leq w \leq W$ 3D positions determined across the temporal sample window.

Step ❷: Enforcing Local Rigidity. Local rigidity assumes a pair of nearby 3D points in the scene will maintain a constant Euclidean distance throughout our temporal observation window. Assuming a correct spatio-temporal inter-sequence registration and accurate intra-sequence optical flow estimates, deviations from this assumption are attributed to errors in the initial correspondence estimation. More specifically, tracks having incorrect initial correspondences will present inconsistent motion patterns. Accordingly, the key component of our rigidity estimation is the scope of our locality definition. To this end, we use the appearance-based super-pixel segmentation method proposed in [27] to define relatively compact local regions aligned with the observed edge structure. The SLIC scale parameter is adaptively set such that the total of superpixels contained within the initial segmentation mask is 30. The output of this over-segmentation of the initial frame in the reference sequence is a clustering of our 3D tracks into disjoints partitions $\{\mathcal{C}_c\}$, where $1 \leq c \leq 30$.

Having defined disjoint sets of 3D tracks, we independently evaluate the rigidity of each track cluster. We measure this property in terms of the largest consensus set of constant pairwise distances across successive frames. Although this set can be identified through exhaustive evaluation of all pairwise track distances, we instead take a sampling approach for efficiency. We iteratively select one of the tracks in $\mathcal{C}_c$ and compare the temporal consistency against all other tracks. We then store the track with the largest support within $\mathcal{C}_c$. An outline of our sampling method is presented in Algorithm 1. Our local rigidity criteria decides if two trajectories are consistent based on the accumulated temporal variation of point-wise distance of two 3D tracks over time:

$$\sum_{i=2}^{W} \left| \|\mathbf{X}_{m,i-1} - \mathbf{X}_{n,i-1}\|_2 - \|\mathbf{X}_{m,i} - \mathbf{X}_{n,i}\|_2 \right|, \; \mathbf{T}_n, \mathbf{T}_m \in \mathcal{C}_c \qquad (1)$$

Once the consensus track set has been identified, all its members are considered inliers to the rigidity assumption, while all tracks not belonging to the consensus set are labeled as outliers.

Algorithm 1. SAMPLING FOR LOCAL RIGIDITY TRACK CONCENSUS

Input: 3D trajectories $\mathbf{T}_i(m)$, $1 \leq m \leq |\mathcal{C}_i(c)|$
Output: Inliers trajectories set $\{\hat{\mathcal{C}}_i(c)\}$

1 iterations $= 0$
2 $\hat{\mathcal{C}}_i(c) = NULL$
3 **while** *iterations* $\leq |\mathcal{C}_i(c)|/5$ **do**
4      $\mathcal{C}'_i(c) = NULL$
5   Draw a random trajectories $\mathbf{T}_i(m)$
6   **for** $k \in [1, \|\mathcal{C}_i(c)\|]$ **do**
7   decide if $\mathbf{T}_i(m)$ and $\mathbf{T}_i(k)$ are consistent
8   **if** *consistent* **then**
9   add k into $\mathcal{C}'_i(c)$; **if** $\mathcal{C}'_i(c) = \mathcal{C}_i(c)$ **then**
10   return
11   **if** $\mathcal{C}'_i(c) \geq \hat{\mathcal{C}}_i(c)$ **then**
12         $\hat{\mathcal{C}}_i(c) = \mathcal{C}'_i(c)$

Step ❸: Enforcing Structural Coherence. Local rigidity in isolation is unable to determine systematic errors caused by motion correlation among content having similar appearance. A particular challenge is the presence of poorly textured and (nearly) static scene elements, as both appearance and motion cues are ill-defined in this scenario. For example, in Fig. 5(a), some correspondences are located on the left leg, while the true correspondences should be on the right leg. In order to make our correspondence estimation more robust, we further enforce the assumption of geometric coherence within local structure estimates deemed to be locally rigid. We consider two types of non-local coherence violations:

1. **Track-Bundle Consistency.** 3D Tracks emanating from a common compact image region should also correspond to a compact set of 3D trajectories. We

observe that small subsets of inlier (*i.e.*, mutually rigid) 3D tracks can be spatially disjoint from the remaining tracks belonging to the same initial cluster (Fig. 5(b)). We measure this behavior by analyzing the results of individual pairwise 3D point sampling used in step ❷for rigidity consensus estimation. We aggregate all the sampled $N = \|\mathcal{C}_c\|$ pairwise rigid distances of the inlier set into a single vector $S_c \in \mathbf{R}^N$ and sort the elements by increasing distance. We then scan for an inflection point depicting the largest pairwise deviation among successive bins in S_c and threshold on both the relative magnitude and the percentile of the inflection point location within the histogram. Inflection points found in the top and bottom 10 % quantiles are to be discarded. If an inflection point is found in the histogram, the corresponding distance value is used as a distance consistency threshold. Tracks exhibiting an average distance to other tracks greater than the consistency threshold are removed from the inlier set $\mathcal{C}_c$. Figure 4 illustrates the behavior of the distance histogram for different 3D track bundle scenarios. The above framework operates under the assumption that locally inconsistent tracks represent a small fraction of a cluster's track bundle.

2. **Inter-Cluster Consistency.** The scenario where the majority (or all) of the mutually rigid tracks within a cluster are structured outliers is extremely uncommon but cannot be identified through track-bundle consistency (Fig. 5(c)). To address this challenge, we impose thresholds on the spatial divergence between the average 3D positions of a given track and a fixed global 3D reference representative of the estimated structure across the entire image. We define this reference to be the 3D centroid of the 3D tracks of all other clusters. This approach is aimed at identifying gross outliers within the context of a single foreground dynamic object and is to be considered a special-purpose noise filtering technique. In practice, 3D tracks away from the moving body are identified and singled out as correspondence outliers.

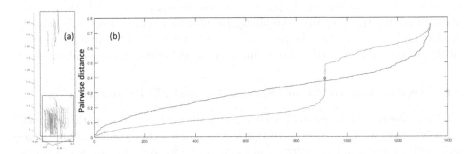

Fig. 4. In (a), trajectories from wrong correspondences deviate away from the inlier trajectories (outlined in blue). (b) The sorted pairwise distance array of all inliers has no abrupt gradient in the middle, sorted pairwise distance array of all trajectories will have those cutting edge when outlier trajectories are present.

Fig. 5. Corresponding points in image pairs. Red dots (crosses): Feature (inlier) points within one super-pixel in the reference frame. Blue dots (crosses): Correspondence (inlier) points found in the target frame. In (a), outliers on the left leg are detected because they located in different rigid parts. In (b), outliers on the right waist are removed because they are far away from majority of other trajectories. In (c), correct correspondences are the minority (there might be repetitive correspondences in the target frame). The wrong correspondences are removed by the depth constraints.

Step ❹: Track Correction. The set of 3D tracks determined to be outliers by our preceding validation steps are assumed to occur due to an outlier feature correspondence $\mathbf{x}_{ip} \leftrightarrow \mathbf{x}_{jq}$. Accordingly, to correct this erroneous initial assignment, we revisit the sorted set of correspondence candidates $\Omega(\mathbf{x}_{ip})$ lying on the epipolar line. We will replace the initial assignment with the next-most photo-consistent element of $\Omega(\mathbf{x}_{ip})$ and evaluate the local rigidity of the updated 3D track across the temporal sampling window. We can now modify the correspondence to regenerate the 3D track (i.e. step ❶) and re-run our original rigidity sampling procedure (i.e. step ❷) over the entire cluster to account for possible changes to the consensus set. In practice, it is more efficient to verify the rigidity of each updated track against a small sample of the current consensus/inlier (i.e. locally rigid) set of tracks. The process is repeated until each original feature has either (1) been determined to be an inlier or (2) exhausted the candidate set.

3.4   Applications to Stream Sequencing and 3D Reconstruction

We have described a framework to determine and enhance the spatio-temporal consistency of two-view pixel correspondences across a time window. Our image-wide active correspondence correction framework effectively maximizes the number of locally consistent 3D tracks. The relevance of this functionality lies in the insight that, given an unknown temporal offset between two spatial overlapping video sequences, scanning a short video segment from one sequence over the entirety of the other sequence can be used to identify the temporal offset between those sequences. Figure 6(b) shows the average correspondences with different offsets (computed over 50 consecutive frames from one of our datasets), we can see our method obtain the highest value on the 0 offset point, which means accurate alignment. The criteria to determine alignment is, intuitively, the offset resulting maximal locally rigid (e.g. inlier) 3D tracks. Conversely, determining a robust and dense set of inter-sequence correspondences, directly provides the observed 3D geometry given knowledge of the imaging geometry. A straightforward way to generate depthmaps under our framework is to perform bi-linear 2D interpolation on each sequence frame for all inlier 3D tracks. Figure 6(a), illustrates the depthmap generated by our approach without any post-processing corrections.

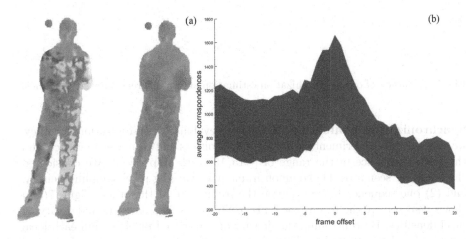

Fig. 6. (a) show depth map generated from raw correspondences (Left) and the corrected correspondences (Right). (b)Average correspondences with different offsets(red curve), the green boundary should the plus minus standard deviation.

4   Experiments

Experimental Setup. All reported experiments considered a temporal window size of $W = 6$, and unless stated otherwise, the initial correspondence set is comprised of all putative pixel correspondences along the epipolar line with an NCC value above 0.8. We evaluated our method on three datasets: the ETH juggler [28], the CMU bat [5], and the UNC juggler [19]. For the ETH dataset (6 cameras) and the UNC dataset (4 cameras), we select the pair of cameras having the smallest baseline. For the CMU dataset, we select two neighboring cameras facing the front of the players. The CMU dataset provides reconstructed 3D points which are used as ground truth to evaluate the accuracy of our estimated 3D triangulations and depth maps. The UNC dataset is not synchronized; hence, we adopt the synchronized result from [19] as sequencing ground truth. Details for each of the three considered datasets are provided in Table 1.

Table 1. Composition of our datasets.

Name	# Video frames	GT 3D Points	Synchronized	Moving Cameras	Outdoor Scene
ETH	200	No	Yes	Yes	Yes
CMU	160	Yes	Yes	No	No
UNC	150	No	No	Yes	Yes

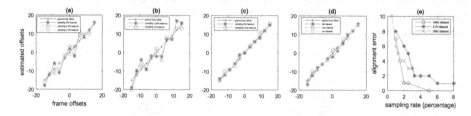

Fig. 7. Accuracy of our synchronization estimation across different datasets scenarios.

Synchronization Evaluation. In order to evaluate synchronization accuracy, we carried out experiments with temporal offsets between the reference and the target sequence in the range of $[-15, 15]$ with step size 3. We considered the following scenarios: (1) common frame with varying pixel sampling density, and (2) one sequence having double the frame rate of the other. Figure 7(a-c) shows respectively the results for ETH, UNC, and CMU datasets under varying pixel densities. By controlling the density of considered pixels within each local neighborhood (i.e. SLIC-based superpixel segmentation) we can directly control the computational burden of our sampling rigidity framework. Alternatively, we may perform KLT-based feature selection. For efficiency reasons, we simply select in these experiments a fixed number of random pixels as features for correspondence analysis within a local neighborhood $\mathcal{C}_c$. We experimented with pixel densities of 2 %, 2.5 %, and 3.3 %. The results illustrated in Fig. 7(a-c) highlight the positive effect of increased pixel densities towards synchronization

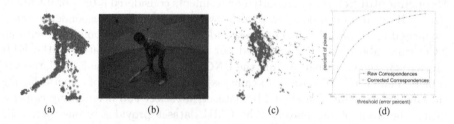

Fig. 8. Results of corrected point cloud on the CMU dataset. Left: Blue 3D points depict the originally reconstructed 3D points from initial correspondences, while red points denote the 3D points obtained through corrected correspondences. Left middle: Corresponding reference image. Right center: A side view of the same structure. Right: Accuracy for both original and corrected point sets.

Fig. 9. Qualitative results illustrating the effectiveness of our correspondence correction functionality.

accuracy. We observe that, in addition to segments exhibiting reduced motion or poorly textured content, repetitive motion was a source of synchronization ambiguity leading to potential errors. Figure 7(d) shows the alignment results with the target sequence at twice the frame rate of reference sequence. We use 3.3 %, 1.25 %, and 5 % sampling density, and the results are very close to the equal-frame-rate test, with a decrease in average accuracy of 9 %. In Fig. 7(e) we show more synchronization results with variable sampling rates for video streams.

Dense Modeling Evaluation. We explored the effectiveness of our correspondence correction functionality when applied for 3D reconstruction. Given that the CMU dataset provides groundtruth 3D structure values, we include the reconstruction error of our 3D reconstructions. In Fig. 8(a) and (c), we show the front and back view of the estimated 3D points. We observe our method's ability to effectively remove outlier 3D structure. In Fig. 8(d), we quantitatively evaluate the accuracy of our depth map, in terms of the percentage of pixels falling within variable accuracy thresholds. Figure 9 shows some qualitative comparisons of our interpolated depth maps obtained from correspondence-corrected 3D points against the depthmaps interpolated from raw correspondence output (e.g. in the absence of corrections). Since [10] does not consider motion consistency nor temporal alignment, their depth maps correspond to "raw correspondences" in our method given synchronized input frames.

5 Discussion and Conclusion

We have presented a local spatio-temporal correspondence verification and correction method, and used it to develop a bottom-up solution for video synchronization and dense dynamic modeling. The underlying assumption of local geometric consistency as a guide for spatio-temporal overlap has been proven to be informative across an expanded spatio-temporal scope. We used recent freely available datasets for dynamic 3D reconstruction and these considered a single dynamic element. The multi-body dynamics would be naturally included into our framework as, beyond the attainability of SFM-based camera registration, we only make assumptions on local rigidity and cross-view photo-consistency. Future improvements to our framework include extending the scope of our temporal window through the adoption of robust feature-based tracking frameworks able to sustain and recover tracks across extended periods. Moreover, we will continue to explore more robust structure and synchronization frameworks that leverage our proposed consistency assessment framework as low-level functional building block.

References

1. Agarwal, S., Snavely, N., Simon, I., Seitz, S., Szeliski, R.: Building rome in a day. In: Proceedings of ICCV (2012)
2. Heinly, J., Schonberger, J., Dunn, E., Frahm, J.M.: Reconstructing the world* in six days *(as captured by the yahoo 100 million image dataset). In: Proceedings of CVPR (2015)
3. Wu, C.: Towards linear-time incremental structure from motion. In: 3DV, pp. 127–134 (2013)
4. Furukawa, Y., Ponce, J.: Towards internet-scale multi-view stereo. In: Proceedings of CVPR 1434 (2010)
5. Joo, H., Park, H., Sheikh, Y.: Map visibility estimation for large scale dynamic 3d reconstruction. In: Proceedings of CVPR (2014)

6. Joo, H., Liu, H., Tan, L., Gui, L., Nabbe, B., Matthews, I., Kanade, T., Nobuhara, S., Sheikh, Y.: Panoptic studio: A massively multiview system for social motion capture. In: Proceedings of ICCV (2015)
7. Kim, H., Sarim, M., Takai, T., Guillemaut, J., Hilton, A.: Dynamic 3d scene reconstruction in outdoor environments. In: Proceedings of 3DPVT (2010)
8. Jiang, H., Liu, H., Tan, P., Zhang, G., Bao, H.: 3d reconstruction of dynamic scenes with multiple handheld cameras. In: Proceedings of ECCV (2012)
9. Taneja, A., Ballan, L., Pollefeys, M.: Modeling dynamic scenes recorded with freely moving cameras. In: Proceedings of ECCV (2010)
10. Mustafa, A., Kim, H., Guillemaut, J., Hilton, A.: General dynamic scene reconstruction from multiple view video. In: Proceedings of ICCV (2015)
11. Oswald, M., Cremers, D.: A convex relaxation approach to space time multi-view 3d reconstruction. In: International Conference on Computer Vision (ICCV) Workshops, pp. 291–298 (2013)
12. Oswald, M., Stühmer, J., Cremers, D.: Generalized connectivity constraints for spatio-temporal 3d reconstruction. In: European Conference on Computer Vision (ECCV) pp. 32–46. IEEE (2014)
13. Djelouah, A., Franco, J.S., Boyer, E., Le Clerc, F., Pérez, P.: Sparse multi-view consistency for object segmentation. Pattern Anal. Mach. Intell. (PAMI) $37(9)$, 1890–1903 (2015)
14. Letouzey, A., Boyer, E.: Progressive shape models. In: Conference on Computer Vision and Pattern Recognition (CVPR), pp. 190–197. IEEE (2012)
15. Wu, C., Varanasi, K., Liu, Y., Seidel, H.P., Theobalt, C.: Shading-based dynamic shape refinement from multi-view video under general illumination. In: International Conference on Computer Vision (ICCV), pp. 1108–1115. IEEE (2011)
16. Guan, L., Franco, J.S., Pollefeys, M.: Multi-view occlusion reasoning for probabilistic silhouette-based dynamic scene reconstruction. Int. J. Comput. Vis. (IJCV) $90(3)$, 283–303 (2010)
17. Cagniart, C., Boyer, E., Ilic, S.: Probabilistic deformable surface tracking from multiple videos. In: European Conference on Computer Vision (ECCV), pp. 326–339. Springer, Heidelberg (2010)
18. Russell, C., Yu, R., Agapito, L.: Video pop-up: Monocular 3d reconstruction of dynamic scenes. In: Proceedings of ECCV (2014)
19. Zheng, E., Ji, D., Dunn, E., Frahm, J.: Sparse dynamic 3d reconstruction from unsynchronized videos. In: Proceedings of ICCV, pp. 4435–4443 (2015)
20. Zheng, E., Ji, D., Dunn, E., Frahm, J.: Self-expressive dictionary learning for dynamic 3d reconstruction. arXiv preprint (2014). arXiv:1605.06863
21. Basha, T., Moses, Y., Avidan, S.: Photo sequencing. In: Proceedings of ECCV (2012)
22. Basha, T., Moses, Y., Avidan, S.: Space-time tradeoffs in photo sequencing. In: Proceedings of ICCV (2013)
23. Tuytelaars, T., Gool, L.: Synchronizing video sequences. In: Proceedings of CVPR, pp. 762–768 (2004)
24. Wolf, L., Zomet, A.: Wide baseline matching between unsynchronized video sequences. Int. J. Comput. Vis. 68, 43–52 (2006)
25. Pundik, D., Moses, Y.: Video synchronization using temporal signals from epipolar lines. In: Proceedings of ECCV, pp. 15–28 (2010)
26. Brox, T., Bruhn, A., Papenberg, N., Weickert, J.: High accuracy optical flow estimation based on a theory for warping. In: Proceedings of ECCV (2004)

27. Achanta, R., Shaji, A., Smith, K., Lucchi, A., Fua, P., Susstrunk, S.: Slic super-pixels compared to state-of-the-art superpixel methods. Trans. PAMI **34**, 2274 (2012)

28. Ballan, L., Brostow, G.J., Puwein, J., Pollefeys, M.: Unstructured video-based rendering: Interactive exploration of casually captured videos. ACM Trans. Graph. **29**, 87 (2010). ACM

3D Image Reconstruction from X-Ray Measurements with Overlap

Maria Klodt$^{(\boxtimes)}$ and Raphael Hauser

Mathematical Institute, University of Oxford, Oxford, UK
{klodt,hauser}@maths.ox.ac.uk

Abstract. 3D image reconstruction from a set of X-ray projections is an important image reconstruction problem, with applications in medical imaging, industrial inspection and airport security. The innovation of X-ray emitter arrays allows for a novel type of X-ray scanners with multiple simultaneously emitting sources. However, two or more sources emitting at the same time can yield measurements from overlapping rays, imposing a new type of image reconstruction problem based on nonlinear constraints. Using traditional linear reconstruction methods, respective scanner geometries have to be implemented such that no rays overlap, which severely restricts the scanner design. We derive a new type of 3D image reconstruction model with nonlinear constraints, based on measurements with overlapping X-rays. Further, we show that the arising optimization problem is partially convex, and present an algorithm to solve it. Experiments show highly improved image reconstruction results from both simulated and real-world measurements.

Keywords: Image reconstruction · Medical imaging · X-ray · Overlap

1 Introduction

Reconstructing a three-dimensional image from a set of two-dimensional projections is a typical inverse problem. Applications of X-ray image reconstruction include medical imaging, industrial inspection and airport security. This paper addresses the problem of reconstructing a 3D image from a set of 2D X-ray projections with overlapping measurements. Traditionally, X-ray tomography is based on a single moving source following specific positions around the object or person to be scanned, for example the source moves around the reconstruction domain. In this type of set-up, images are taken sequentially, which implies that overlapping rays cannot occur. However, when using an emitter array, several sources can emit X-rays simultaneously [1,2]. This new type of X-ray scanning can lead to a new form of measurements: overlapping X-rays where rays from more than one emitter reach the same detector at the same time.[1]

Since measurements are usually undersampled, i.e. the number of measurements is less than the number of unknowns, prior information about the image

---

[1] Certain aspects described in this publication have been filed for patent protection.

© Springer International Publishing AG 2016
B. Leibe et al. (Eds.): ECCV 2016, Part VI, LNCS 9910, pp. 19–33, 2016.
DOI: 10.1007/978-3-319-46466-4_2

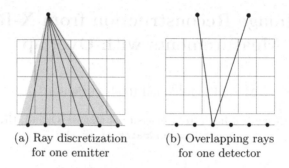

(a) Ray discretization   (b) Overlapping rays
    for one emitter   for one detector

Fig. 1. Scanner set-up with a set of X-ray emitters above the reconstruction domain, and a flat panel detector below (schematic 2D view). (a): A finite set of rays is modeled for each emitter, connecting the emitter source positions with the center of each detector pixel, which discretizes the emitter cone (blue). (b): If multiple sources emit simultaneously, it can occur that two or more rays reach the same detector at the same time, yielding a nonlinear overlapping measurement. (Color figure online)

to be reconstructed can help to improve the image reconstructions. Sparsity priors about the image are widely used. In compressed sensing research it has been shown that minimizing the L1 norm subject to linear constraints can yield sparse solutions for certain classes of reconstruction problems [3,4]. For medical images, the Total Variation (TV) norm has been shown to provide a suitable sparsity prior, e.g. for magnetic resonance imaging (MRI) [5,6] and X-ray computed tomography (CT) [7]. The arising reconstruction problem is closely related to another Computer Vision problem: 3D surface reconstruction from 2D photographs. Instead of X-rays, minimizing the TV norm on ray constraints can also be based on visual rays, e.g. to impose silhouette consistency in 3D multi-view reconstruction [8]. Other related applications include X-ray image reconstruction with shape priors [9] and segmentation of CT reconstructions [10].

The relevant literature on sparse reconstruction mainly considers linear constraints. In most related work on nonlinear compressed sensing the nonlinearity is due to noise [11,12]. Other recent works considering nonlinearity in compressed sensing include a generalization to quasi-linear compressed sensing [11] and compressed sensing with quadratic constraints [13]. More recent works on compressed sensing consider more general constraints [14], where a restricted isometry property for nonlinear measurements is defined as the distance to a linearized version.

Measurements from overlapping rays yield a different type of nonlinearity. In a set-up where multiple sources (partially) emit simultaneously, using image reconstruction from linear constraints requires the scanner to be designed such that the emitter cones do not overlap. This restriction to small emitter cones and small stand-off distances (distances between emitters and reconstruction domain) highly constrains the scanner geometry. In particular, hand-held devices where the distance from sources to detectors cannot be positioned exactly are constrained to unnecessarily small collimation angles, in order to guarantee that no rays overlap. An appropriate handling of overlap is therefore essential to improve robustness with respect to varying emitter and detector positions. It allows for larger emitter collimation angles of the device, which is necessary for accurate 3D image reconstructions.

In this paper an image reconstruction problem arising from measurements with overlapping X-rays is derived, and an algorithm to solve it is presented. The main contributions are:

– derivation of a new model for image reconstruction from X-ray measurements with overlap, which arises from a novel type of multi-source X-ray scanners,
– proof that the arising optimization problem is partially convex,
– a novel optimization method to solve 3D X-ray image reconstruction from measurements with overlap,
– demonstrated practicability of the method by comparison to ground truth from simulated data, as well as practicability under real-world conditions using real X-ray measurements. Experiments show both quantitatively and visually improved results compared to traditional linear reconstruction.

The outline of the paper is as follows: Sect. 2 briefly reviews X-ray image reconstruction from sequential measurements, yielding linear constraints. Section 3 presents a novel formulation of an image reconstruction problem based on nonlinear constraints from overlapping rays. The section further presents an algorithm to solve the arising optimization problem. Section 4 gives details on the implementation. Section 5 shows experiments with overlapping X-rays based on simulated as well as real-world measurements. Section 6 concludes the paper.

2   X-Ray Image Reconstruction with Linear Constraints

The scanner set-up considered in this paper consists of a set of emitters which are located above the region to reconstruct and a rectangular panel of detector pixels located below the region. The X-rays emitted from the conoidal sources are discretized as a finite set of rays connecting each detector pixel center with the emitter source positions. We further assume a three-dimensional region of interest in which the object to reconstruct is located, discretized to a Cartesian grid of n voxels. A schematic two-dimensional view of the rays for one emitter is depicted in Fig. 1(a).

Assuming homogenuous material per voxel, no ray scattering, no noise, and no overlap, the *Beer-Lambert* law decribes the relation of material properties and radiation intensity I_{Ej} at the emitter and radition intensity I_{Dj} at the detector:

$$I_{Dj} = I_{Ej} \exp \left(\sum_{i=1}^{n} -\xi_{ij} x_i \right) \tag{1}$$

for measurements $j = 1, \ldots, m$. Here, ξ_{ij} is the distance that the ray corresponding to measurement j traverses through voxel i. Reformulation of (1) yields a sparse linear system of equations

$$\log\left(\frac{I_{Dj}}{I_{Ej}}\right) = \sum_{i=1}^{n} -\xi_{ij}x_i \Leftrightarrow Ax = b \tag{2}$$

where $A \in \mathbb{R}^{m \times n}$ with $a_{ij} = -\xi_{ij}$ is a matrix projecting the 3D image x to the 2D projections b, depending on scanner geometry and grid discretization. The measurements are stacked to vector $b \in \mathbb{R}^m$ with $b_j = \log(I_{Dj}/I_{Ej})$, and the (unknown) densities x_i per voxel are stacked to vector $x \in \mathbb{R}^n$. Hence, each column of A corresponds to a voxel index i, and each row corresponds to a measurement j. Furthermore, A is sparse, because in general, each ray intersects only a small number of voxels, implying that most of the entries a_{ij} are zero.

Usually, the measurements are undersampled, i.e. $m \ll n$, and prior information about the unknown x can help to recover the solution. In the context of compressed sensing one is interested in the sparsest solution which can be represented by the reconstruction problem

$$\min \|x\|_1 \quad \text{s.t.} \quad Ax = b. \tag{3}$$

It has been shown that for certain matrices, minimizing the L1 norm can yield sparse solutions for $Ax = b$, i.e. x with few non-zero elements [3,4].

3   Nonlinear Measurements with Overlapping Rays

The standard X-ray image reconstruction model (3) based on linear constraints is obtained from sequential exposures of X-ray sources, i.e. no rays overlap. However, if multiple X-ray sources emit simultaneously, it can occur that two or more rays reach the same detector at the same time (see Fig. 1(b)). We will see that the measurements of overlapping rays are not linear anymore, however we can show that they are convex. In this section we will derive a convex formulation of the arising reconstruction problem, and propose a forward-backward splitting algorithm to optimize it.

3.1   A Model for X-Ray Image Reconstruction with Overlap

If two rays reach the same detector at the same time the intensity at measurement j sums up to

$$\frac{I_{Dj}}{I_{Ej}} = \exp\left(\sum_{i=1}^{n} -\xi_{ij1}x_i\right) + \exp\left(\sum_{i=1}^{n} -\xi_{ij2}x_i\right) \tag{4}$$

where each of the two terms on the right-hand side corresponds to the attenuation along one ray, and equal emitter intensities I_{Ej} are assumed for the simultaneously active emitters. A more general formulation for p rays simultaneously reaching measurement j is given by

$$\frac{I_{Dj}}{I_{Ej}} = \sum_{k=1}^{p} \exp\left(\sum_{i=1}^{n} -\xi_{ijk}x_i\right) := \psi_j(x) \tag{5}$$

where the coefficients ξ_{ijk} correspond to the length of the intersection between voxel i and the ray from emitter k to the detector corresponding to measurement j. Assuming again that we are interested in a sparse reconstruction x, minimization with L1 prior yields

$$\min_{x} \|x\|_1 \quad \text{s.t.} \quad \sum_{k=1}^{p} \exp\left(\sum_{i=1}^{n} -\xi_{ijk}x_i\right) = b_j, \quad \forall j = 1, \ldots, m \qquad (6)$$

with measurements $b_j = I_{Dj}/I_{Ej}$. The coefficients $-\xi_{ijk}$ can be represented with sparse vectors $r_{jk} \in \mathbb{R}^n$:

$$r_{jk} = \left(-\xi_{1jk}, \ldots, -\xi_{njk}\right)^{\top}, \; j = 1, \ldots, m, k = 1, \ldots, p. \qquad (7)$$

Allowing for noise in the data constraint term, we propose the following least squares formulation of (6):

$$\min_{x} \left\{ \|x\|_1 + \frac{1}{2\mu} \sum_{j=1}^{m} \left(\sum_{k=1}^{p} \exp\left(\sum_{i=1}^{n} -\xi_{ijk}x_i\right) - b_j\right)^2 \right\} \qquad (8)$$

with regularization parameter $\mu > 0$ which provides a balance between sparsity prior and data fidelity term. The formulation (8) corresponds to an optimization problem of the form

$$\min_{x} \left\{ f(x) + g(x) \right\} \qquad (9)$$

with convex non-differentiable $f : \mathbb{R}^n \to \mathbb{R}$:

$$f(x) = \|x\|_1 \qquad (10)$$

and partially convex, differentiable $g : \mathbb{R}^n \to \mathbb{R}$:

$$g(x) = \frac{1}{2\mu} \sum_{j=1}^{m} \left(\sum_{k=1}^{p} \exp\left(\sum_{i=1}^{n} -\xi_{ijk}x_i\right) - b_j\right)^2. \qquad (11)$$

Theorem 1. *Let $\hat{x}$ be a minimizer that fulfils the measurements (5). The function $g(x)$ is partially convex for $0 \leq x \leq \hat{x}$.*

Theorem 2. *The gradient ∇g is Lipschitz continuous for all $x \geq 0$ with Lipschitz constant $L = \frac{1}{\mu} 2mp^2 \xi_{max}^2$. Here, ξ_{max} denotes the maximum value of all ξ_{ijk}:*

$$\xi_{max} := \max\left\{\xi_{ijk} \,|\, i \in \{1, \ldots, n\}, j \in \{1, \ldots, m\}, k \in \{1, \ldots, p\}\right\} \qquad (12)$$

which is bounded by the maximum intersection length of a ray with a voxel. For a voxel size h this is $\xi_{max} \leq \sqrt{3}h$.

Proofs for Theorems 1 and 2 are provided in the appendix.

3.2 Optimization with Forward-Backward Splitting

An optimization problem of the form (9) can be solved using the first-order forward-backward splitting update sequence for $t = 0, 1, 2, \ldots$ and $x^0 = 0$:

$$x^{t+1} = \text{prox}_{\lambda f}(x^t - \lambda \nabla g(x^t)) \qquad (13)$$

with convergence rate $\mathcal{O}(1/t)$ and step size $\lambda = 1/L$ [15]. Note that due to the generally high dimension of the reconstruction problem, second-order optimization is infeasible, as the Hessian matrix has dimension n^2. It has been shown in [15] that the update sequence (13) converges to a minimum of (9), if f is a lower semicontinuous convex function, and g is convex, differentiable and has a Lipschitz continuous gradient. The proximal operator $\text{prox}_{\lambda f} : \mathbb{R}^n \to \mathbb{R}^n$ is defined as

$$\text{prox}_{\lambda f}(x) = \underset{u}{\text{argmin}} \left\{ f(u) + \tfrac{1}{2\lambda} \|u - x\|_2^2 \right\}. \qquad (14)$$

For the L1 ball $f(x) = \|x\|_1$ it can be computed analytically and is given by the "soft thresholding operator" [16]:

$$\text{prox}_{\lambda f}(x) = \begin{cases} x - \lambda, & x > \lambda \\ 0, & |x| \le \lambda \\ x + \lambda, & x < -\lambda \end{cases} \qquad (15)$$

For a recent overview of proximal operators and algorithms, see for example [17].

For an optimization of (8), the initialization of x should be smaller than a minimizer $\hat{x}$, because g is partially convex for $x \le \hat{x}$. Knowing that the densities x cannot be negative, we chose the lower bound $x^0 = 0$. Furthermore, the step sizes λ have to be chosen such that $x \le \hat{x}$ is assured for all t. We determine the step sizes λ using a backtracking line search algorithm [18], while here we have to ensure the constraint $x \le \hat{x}$. Although in general, $\hat{x}$ is unknown, the measurements b are given with $b_j = \psi_j(\hat{x})$, and hence we constrain the line search by

$$\psi_j(x) \ge b_j \text{ for all } j = 1, \ldots, m. \qquad (16)$$

We propose the following forward-backward splitting algorithm to minimize (8):

Input:

$b \in \mathbb{R}^m$: vector of measurements
$r_{jk} \in \mathbb{R}^n$: sparse vectors of intersection lengths of rays and voxels
$c \in (0, 1)$: line search control parameter
$L = \frac{1}{\mu} 2mp^2 \xi_{max}^2$: Lipschitz constant for g

Initialize $x^0 = 0$.
Iterate for $t = 0, 1, 2, \ldots$:

1. *Compute search direction:*

$$\nabla g(x^t) = \frac{1}{\mu} \sum_{j=1}^m \left(\sum_{k=1}^p e^{r_{jk}^T x^t} - b_j \right) \left(\sum_{k=1}^p r_{jk} e^{r_{jk}^T x^t} \right) \qquad (17)$$

2. *Backtracking line search:*

$$\lambda = 1/L \tag{18}$$

$$x^{new} = \text{prox}_{\lambda f}(x^t - \lambda \nabla g(x^t)) \tag{19}$$

$$\text{while } \exists j \in \{1, \ldots, m\} : \psi_j(x^{new}) < b_j :$$

$$\lambda \leftarrow \lambda c \tag{20}$$

$$x^{new} = \text{prox}_{\lambda f}(x^t - \lambda \nabla g(x^t)) \tag{21}$$

3. *Update x:* $x^{t+1} = x^{new}$.

4   Implementation

To compute the projection vectors r_{jk}, the intersection lengths ξ_{ijk} of each voxel with each ray have to be computed. The choice of an efficient algorithm is crucial to the performance of the method to avoid a computation time of $O(mn)$ for m rays and n voxels. Efficient methods that can be used include line rastering algorithms used for ray tracing in computer graphics applications. We implemented the algorithm of [19] which is based on traversing only those voxels whith non-zero intersection length for each ray.

As regularization term we implemented the discrete version of the isotropic Total Variation (TV) norm, which has been shown to provide a suitable sparsity prior for X-ray image reconstruction [5]. On a discrete three-dimensional grid it is given by:

$$\|x\|_{TV} = \sum_{i,j,k} |(\nabla x)_{i,j,k}| \tag{22}$$

with

$$|(\nabla x)_{i,j,k}| = \frac{1}{h}\sqrt{(x_{i,j,k} - x_{i+1,j,k})^2 + (x_{i,j,k} - x_{i,j+1,k})^2 + (x_{i,j,k} - x_{i,j,k+1})^2}$$

where h denotes the spacing in the grid, and here i, j, k denote the indices of the discrete locations in the image domain.

5   Experiments with Overlapping X-Rays

This experimental section aims to investigate how overlapping of X-rays affects the reconstruction accuracy, and which amount of overlap is tolerable in order to be able to recover the 3D image. The proposed method is tested for both simulated data and real X-ray measurements, which allows to both draw conclusions about reconstruction errors where a ground truth is available, and observing the behaviour of the method under real-world conditions including noise.

Since this paper is based on a novel type of reconstruction problem, we compare to a reconstruction based on non-overlapping measurements only, where we eliminate all measurements b_j and corresponding vectors r_{jk} where the number of rays per measurement is ≥ 2. This non-overlapping case yields a reconstruction

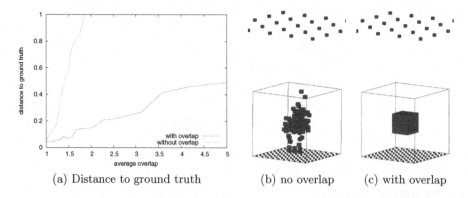

(a) Distance to ground truth   (b) no overlap   (c) with overlap

Fig. 2. Reconstruction of a cube from simulated data. (a): Reconstruction error measured as distance to ground truth for increasing amount of overlap $\bar{p}$, i.e. the average number of rays per measurement. (b),(c): Reconstruction and scanner geometry for average overlap of $\bar{p} \approx 2$. Emitter positions are shown above the reconstruction domain, detectors below. (b): reconstruction from non-overlapping measurements only, (c): reconstruction with overlap.

problem of type (3), and can be optimized using a standard image reconstruction algorithm based on linear constraints [20].

The distance $d(x)$ of a reconstruction x to the reference $\hat{x}$ is measured by

$$d(x) = \|x - \hat{x}\|_2 / \|\hat{x}\|_2. \tag{23}$$

5.1   Reconstruction from Simulated Data

Figure 2(a) shows reconstruction errors for simulated measurements of a three-dimensional cube, comparing the proposed method with overlap to the linear reconstruction from non-overlapping measurements only. The x-axis shows increasing amount of average overlap $\bar{p}$ which we define as the average number of rays per measurement, i.e. the average number of rays reaching the same detector pixel at the same time. We compute measurements with overlap by varying the number of exposures, i.e. the number of simultaneously emitting sources. Overlapping rays then result from randomly chosen simultaneously active emitters. Hence, an overlap of $\bar{p} = 1$ corresponds to sequential exposures. The rest of the experimental set-up is not changed during the experiment. The y-axis shows the relative distance $d(x)$ of the reconstruction x to the ground truth $\hat{x}$, computed by (23). For increasing amount of overlap, the reconstruction from non-overlapping constraints is based on fewer measurements, resulting in an empty volume reconstructed. Thus, for $x \approx 0$ the plot reaches $d(x) \approx 1$, which can be seen in the graph. While both methods yield increasing reconstruction errors for increasing amount of overlap, the proposed method with handling of overlap yields significantly smaller reconstruction errors compared to reconstructions from non-overlapping measurements only.

The scanner geometry used for this experiment is visualized in Fig. 2(b) and (c): The reconstruction domain of $20{\times}20{\times}20$ voxels is visualized by the grid bounding box, above, $5{\times}5$ emitters are located with a stand-off distance of 20 voxels, and directly below the domain, a panel of $10{\times}10$ detectors. The binary test object $\hat{x}$ consists of cube of density $\hat{x}_i = 1$ and size $6{\times}6$ located in the center of the domain. Outside the cube, the test object has density $\hat{x}_i = 0$. Inside the bounding boxes are thresholded versions of the reconstructed densities, i.e. all voxels with $x_i \geq 0.5$, that have been reconstructed from the set-up with average overlap of $\bar{p} \approx 2$. Figure 2(b) shows the reconstruction from non-overlapping measurements only, using optimization with linear constraints. Figure 2(c) shows the reconstruction from all measurements, including overlap, using the proposed method. The results show that also by visual comparison, the method with overlap yields a clearly better reconstruction.

5.2 Reconstruction from Real-World Measurements

The experiments with real X-ray measurements have been taken using a similar general scanner set-up as the simulated data: Above the reconstruction domain, a rectangular array of X-ray emitters is located, and directly below, a flat panel detector of $512{\times}512$ pixels and size $13{\times}13$ cm^2. Two different test objects were measured and reconstructed: The data set "letters" consists of two wooden letters, stacked on top of each other, and measurements were taken from $14{\times}13{=}182$ equally spaced emitter positions. The data set "polecat" is the skull of a polecat, measured from $13{\times}9{=}117$ different emitter positions. Overlapping rays are simulated from the sequential measurements by adding detector images of randomly chosen emitter positions. Hence, the intensities of two or more different sources are accumulated in the measurements.

Figure 3(a) and (b) show the distance to the reconstruction from sequential measurements for increasing amount of overlap. The reconstruction with overlap is compared to the reconstruction which rejects the overlapping measurements, for the two data sets. All reconstructions are computed from the same geometry of emitters, detectors and grid dimension. The only parameter that is varying during one experiment is the number of simultaneously emitting X-ray sources, which determines the average amount of overlap per measurement. Again, the x-axis shows the average amount of overlap per measurement, while the y-axis shows the distance to the reconstruction from sequential measurements, measured by (23). Since a ground truth is not available for the real data, we consider the respective reconstruction from sequential exposures as reference $\hat{x}$, which corresponds to a reconstruction with overlap of $\bar{p} = 1$.

The two graphs allow to observe how much the reconstruction quality decreases with increasing amount of overlap. As in the case of simulated measurements, again we observe that increasing amount of overlap increases reconstruction errors, while the proposed method to handle overlapping rays clearly outperforms the reconstruction from non-overlapping measurements only. This is also visible in the images of reconstructed densities shown in the figure. The images show one slice of the reconstructed 3D densities, for an average overlap

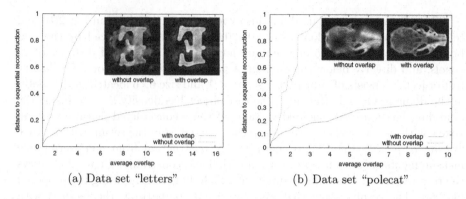

(a) Data set "letters"   (b) Data set "polecat"

Fig. 3. Reconstruction from real X-ray measurements, for the two data sets "letters" and "polecat". Reconstruction errors for increasing amount of overlap are measured as distance to the respective reconstruction from sequential measurements. The images in the top right corners show reconstructions for an average overlap of $\bar{p} \approx 2$, comparing linear reconstruction from non-overlapping measurements to the proposed method with handling of overlap.

of $\bar{p} \approx 2$, using measurements from non-overlapping measurements only, and the proposed method with overlap.

Figure 4(a) shows two of the 182 detector images measured for the data set "letters". The two images can be added to obtain overlapping measurements, shown in Fig. 4(b). Due to the limited field of view of each emitter cone, not all measurements in Fig. 4(b) are overlapping. Only a part of the image, where the two emitter cones intersect, contains measurements with two overlapping rays, the other pixels have overlap of 1. Note that pixels outside any of the emitter cones are considered not visible and are excluded from the measurements.

Figure 4(c) shows the 3D surface of reconstructed densities, thresholded at $x \geq 0.035$, computed from sequential measurements, i.e. overlap of 1.

Figure 5 shows two different slices of the reconstructed densities, for increasing amount of average overlap $\bar{p}$. The first image with overlap of $\bar{p} = 1$ corresponds to sequential exposures. The reconstructions were computed on a voxel volume of dimension $512 \times 512 \times 20$. While the x- and y-axes have the same dimension as the detector panel, we chose a significantly smaller resolution of the z-axis, because it corresponds to the main orientation of rays, which implies reduced recoverability along the z-axis. The slices shown in the figure are along the z-axis, and thus parallel to the detector panel. Note that the reconstruction is capable to clearly seperate the two letters from each other in the different slices, although they are overlayed in all of the projections (see Fig. 4). The experiment shows that up to an average overlap of $\bar{p} \approx 2$, the method is capable to recover almost the same image quality compared to sequential exposures.

Figure 6(a) shows measurements at the detector for one of the 117 images of the "polecat" data set. Figure 6(b) shows the logarithm of the ratio of emitter and detector intensities. The dark spots on the right part of the visible

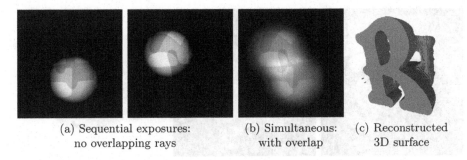

(a) Sequential exposures:	(b) Simultaneous:	(c) Reconstructed
no overlapping rays	with overlap	3D surface

Fig. 4. Two of 182 detector images from sequential (a) and simultaneous (b) exposures. Scanned were two stacked wooden letters, images taken from above. (c): 3D view of reconstructed densities, thresholded at $x \geq 0.035$.

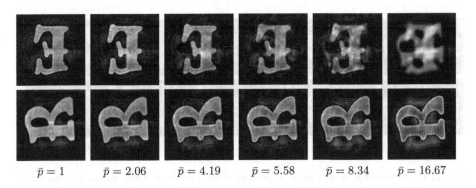

$\bar{p} = 1$	$\bar{p} = 2.06$	$\bar{p} = 4.19$	$\bar{p} = 5.58$	$\bar{p} = 8.34$	$\bar{p} = 16.67$

Fig. 5. Slices of reconstructed densities for the data set "letters", using varying amount of average overlap $\bar{p}$. First row: slice 5 of 20, second row: slice 19 of 20.

area correspond to points where the detector measures zero intensity. Possible reasons for no measurements include defective detector pixels, and low emitter intensity in combination with dense material which attenuates all the radiation. Figure 6(c) shows the 3D surface of reconstructed densities, thresholded at $x \geq 0.2$, computed from sequential measurements, i.e. overlap of 1.

Figure 7 shows two different slices of the 3D reconstructed densities of the "polecat" data set. The grid consists of 512×512×20 voxels, and the overlap of $\bar{p} = 1$ corresponds to sequential exposures. Again, the slices are along the horizontal axis, i.e. parallel to the detector panel and vertical to the main direction of rays. The results show that, similar to the observation of the "letters" data set, an average overlap of $\bar{p} \approx 2$ is tolerable to recover almost the same image quality compared to sequential exposures.

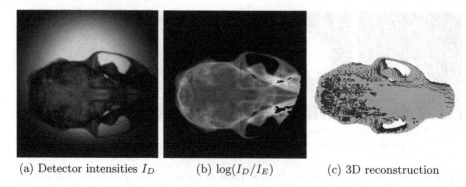

(a) Detector intensities I_D (b) $\log(I_D/I_E)$ (c) 3D reconstruction

Fig. 6. Data set "polecat". (a): Measurements at the detector for one of 117 views. (b): Log-ratio of detector and emitter intensities. (c): 3D surface of reconstructed densities, thresholded at $x \geq 0.2$.

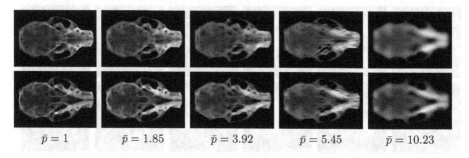

$\bar{p} = 1$ $\bar{p} = 1.85$ $\bar{p} = 3.92$ $\bar{p} = 5.45$ $\bar{p} = 10.23$

Fig. 7. Reconstructed densities of a polecat skull with increasing amount of average overlap $\bar{p}$. First row: slice 9 of 20, second row: slice 12 of 20.

5.3   Computation Time

Reconstruction from linear constraints is faster than the proposed reconstruction with handling of overlapping rays. One of the reasons is that step sizes for the linear constraints can be computed analytically, while the convex constraints need a backtracking line search to compute step sizes. Furthermore, the computation of the exponential function in the data constraints of overlapping rays is time consuming. In our experiments, the method with overlap is approximately 5 times slower than the corresponding reconstruction from non-overlapping measurements, which we consider a tolerable factor given the highly improved reconstruction results.

In medical applications, the computation time for the reconstruction is generally not a limiting factor, but the total exposure time is, as the patient is moving. This is where the method with overlap has major advantages, as in certain cases the time budget does not allow for taking sufficiently many sequential exposures to acquire data without overlap.

6   Conclusions

This paper has presented a practicable method to solve a novel type of optimization problem arising from overlapping X-rays. The method is based on modelling nonlinear constraints in sparse reconstruction. A new type of image reconstruction problem has been formulated, based on nonlinear constraints from overlapping X-ray measurements. Moreover, it has been proved that the arising optimization problem is partially convex. Results have shown that the proposed method improves reconstruction accuracies compared to linear constraints, using both simulated and real-world measurements. Experiments show that the method is capable to recover nearly the same image quality compared to sequential exposures up to an average overlap of ∼2.

The proposed method has a potential impact on X-ray scanner designs, because it allows to handle measurements from overlapping X-rays, where traditional X-ray image reconstruction from linear constraints cannot cope with. This novelty highly increases robustness with respect to stand-off distances and emitter collimation angles, allowing now for a new class of hand-held X-ray scanning devices. Furthermore it allows for more flexibility in the design of X-ray scanner geometry.

Acknowledgements. We thank Adaptix Ltd for providing the X-ray measurements used in the experiments. This work was partly supported by Adaptix Ltd and EPSRC.

A   Proof of Theorems

Proof of Theorem 1 (convexity of g). Let $\psi(x)$ defined as in (5). The convexity of

$$\psi_j(x) = \sum_{k=1}^{p} \exp\left(\sum_{i=1}^{n} -\xi_{ijk} x_i\right) \tag{24}$$

follows from convexity of the exponential function. For all $x, y \in \mathbb{R}^n$ with $0 \le x_i \le \hat{x}_i$ and $0 \le y_i \le \hat{x}_i$ for $i = 1, \ldots, n$ and $\lambda \in [0, 1]$

$$g(\lambda x + (1 - \lambda)y) = \frac{1}{2\mu} \sum_{j=1}^{m} (\psi_j(\lambda x + (1 - \lambda)y) - b_j)^2 \tag{25}$$

$$\le \frac{1}{2\mu} \sum_{j=1}^{m} (\lambda \psi_j(x) + (1 - \lambda)\psi_j(y) - b_j)^2 \tag{26}$$

$$\le \lambda \frac{1}{2\mu} \sum_{j=1}^{m} (\psi_j(x) - b_j)^2 + (1 - \lambda) \frac{1}{2\mu} \sum_{j=1}^{m} (\psi_j(y) - b_j)^2 \tag{27}$$

$$= \lambda g(x) + (1 - \lambda)g(y) \tag{28}$$

where (26) follows from the monotonicity of the square function for positive values, and (27) follows from convexity of ψ_j for all $j = 1, \ldots, m$.   □

Proof of Theorem 2 (Lipschitz continuity of ∇g). We will show $|g''| \leq L$ for all $x_i \geq 0$ with $i = 1, \ldots, n$ which implies Lipschitz continuity of ∇g. The first and second derivatives of g are given by:

$$\frac{\partial g}{\partial x_{i_1}} = \frac{1}{\mu} \sum_{j=1}^{m} \left(\sum_{k=1}^{p} \exp \left(\sum_{i=1}^{n} -\xi_{ijk} x_i \right) - b_j \right) \left(\sum_{k=1}^{p} -\xi_{i_1 jk} \exp \left(\sum_{i=1}^{n} -\xi_{ijk} x_i \right) \right) \tag{29}$$

$$\frac{\partial^2 g}{\partial x_{i_1} \partial x_{i_2}} = \frac{1}{\mu} \sum_{j=1}^{m} \left[\sum_{k=1}^{p} -\xi_{i_2 jk} \exp \left(\sum_{i=1}^{n} -\xi_{ijk} x_i \right) \sum_{k=1}^{p} -\xi_{i_1 jk} \exp \left(\sum_{i=1}^{n} -\xi_{ijk} x_i \right) \right.$$
$$\left. + \left(\sum_{k=1}^{p} \exp \left(\sum_{i=1}^{n} -\xi_{ijk} x_i \right) - b_j \right) \left(\sum_{k=1}^{p} \xi_{i_1 jk} \xi_{i_2 jk} \exp \left(\sum_{i=1}^{n} -\xi_{ijk} x_i \right) \right) \right]. \tag{30}$$

The upper bound $L = \frac{1}{\mu} 2mp^2 \xi_{max}^2$ on g'' derives from $\xi_{ijk} \in [0, \xi_{max}]$ as follows:

$$\left| \frac{\partial^2 g}{\partial x_{i_1} \partial x_{i_2}} \right| = \left| \frac{1}{\mu} \sum_{j=1}^{m} \left(\left(\sum_{k=1}^{p} -\xi_{i_2 jk} e^{r_{jk}^\top x} \right) \left(\sum_{k=1}^{p} -\xi_{i_1 jk} e^{r_{jk}^\top x} \right) \right. \right.$$
$$\left. \left. + \left(\sum_{k=1}^{p} e^{r_{jk}^\top x} - \sum_{k=1}^{p} e^{r_{jk}^\top \hat{x}} \right) \left(\sum_{k=1}^{p} \xi_{i_1 jk} \xi_{i_2 jk} e^{r_{jk}^\top x} \right) \right) \right| \tag{31}$$

$$\leq \frac{1}{\mu} \sum_{j=1}^{m} \left(\left| \sum_{k=1}^{p} -\xi_{i_2 jk} e^{r_{jk}^\top x} \right| \left| \sum_{k=1}^{p} -\xi_{i_1 jk} e^{r_{jk}^\top x} \right| \right.$$
$$\left. + \left| \sum_{k=1}^{p} e^{r_{jk}^\top x} - \sum_{k=1}^{p} e^{r_{jk}^\top \hat{x}} \right| \left| \sum_{k=1}^{p} \xi_{i_1 jk} \xi_{i_2 jk} e^{r_{jk}^\top x} \right| \right) \tag{32}$$

$$\leq \frac{1}{\mu} \sum_{j=1}^{m} \left(\left(\sum_{k=1}^{p} \xi_{i_2 jk} \right) \left(\sum_{k=1}^{p} \xi_{i_1 jk} \right) + p \left(\sum_{k=1}^{p} \xi_{i_1 jk} \xi_{i_2 jk} \right) \right) \tag{33}$$

$$\leq \frac{1}{\mu} \sum_{j=1}^{m} 2p^2 \xi_{max}^2 = \frac{1}{\mu} 2mp^2 \xi_{max}^2 := L. \tag{34}$$

while (32) follows from the triangle inequality and (33) follows from the fact that $\xi_{ijk} \geq 0$ and $\exp(r_{jk}^\top x) \in (0, 1]$. □

References

1. Gonzales, B., Spronk, D., Cheng, Y., Tucker, A.W., Beckman, M., Zhou, O., Lu, J.: Rectangular fixed-gantry CT prototype: Combining CNT x-ray sources and accelerated compressed sensing-based reconstruction. IEEE Access **2**, 971–981 (2014)
2. Chen, D., Song, X., Zhang, Z., Li, Z., She, J., Deng, S., Xu, N., Chen, J.: Transmission type flat-panel x-ray source using zno nanowire field emitters. Appl. Phys. Lett. **107**(24), 243105 (2015)

3. Candes, E.J., Romberg, J., Tao, T.: Stable signal recovery from incomplete and inaccurate measurements. Comm. Pure Appl. Math. **59**, 1207–1223 (2006)
4. Donoho, D.L.: Compressed sensing. IEEE Trans. Inf. Theor. **52**, 1289–1306 (2006)
5. Lustig, M., Donoho, D.L., Santos, J.M., Pauly, J.M.: Compressed sensing MRI. IEEE Sig. Process. Mag. **25**(2), 72–82 (2007)
6. Ma, S., Yin, W., Zhang, Y., Chakraborty, A.: An efficient algorithm for compressed mr imaging using total variation and wavelets. In: IEEE Conference on Computer Vision and Pattern Recognition (CVPR) (2008)
7. Yan, M., Vese, L.A.: Expectation maximization and total variation based model for computed tomography reconstruction from undersampled data. In: Proceedings of SPIE vol. 7961 Medical Imaging 2011: Physics of Medical Imaging (2011)
8. Kolev, K., Cremers, D.: Integration of multiview stereo and silhouettes via convex functionals on convex domains. In: Forsyth, D., Torr, P., Zisserman, A. (eds.) ECCV 2008. LNCS, vol. 5302, pp. 752–765. Springer, Heidelberg (2008). doi:10.1007/978-3-540-88682-2_57
9. Serradell, E., Romero, A., Leta, R., Gatta, C., Moreno-Noguer, F.: Simultaneous correspondence and non-rigid 3d reconstruction of the coronary tree from single x-ray images. In: International Conference on Computer Vision (ICCV), pp. 850–857. IEEE Computer Society (2011)
10. Kim, H., Thiagarajan, J.J., Bremer, P.: A randomized ensemble approach to industrial ct segmentation. In: International Conference on Computer Vision (ICCV), pp. 1707–1715. IEEE (2015)
11. Ehler, M., Fornasier, M., Sigl, J.: Quasi-linear compressed sensing. Multiscale Model. Simul. **12**(2), 725–754 (2014)
12. Needell, D., Tropp, J.A.: Cosamp: Iterative signal recovery from incomplete and inaccurate samples. Commun. ACM **53**(12), 93–100 (2010)
13. Li, X., Voroninski, V.: Sparse signal recovery from quadratic measurements via convex programming. SIAM J. Math. Anal. **45**(5), 3019–3033 (2013)
14. Blumensath, T.: Compressed sensing with nonlinear observations and related nonlinear optimisation problems. IEEE Trans. Inf. Theor. **59**(6), 3466–3474 (2013)
15. Combettes, P.L., Wajs, V.R.: Signal recovery by proximal forward-backward splitting. Multiscale Model. Simul. **4**(4), 1168–1200 (2005)
16. Donoho, D.L., Johnstone, I.M.: Minimax estimation via wavelet shrinkage. Ann. Stat. **26**(3), 879–921 (1998)
17. Parikh, N., Boyd, S.: Proximal algorithms. Found. Trends Optim. **1**(3), 127–239 (2014)
18. Beck, A., Teboulle, M.: A fast iterative shrinkage-thresholding algorithm for linear inverse problems. SIAM J. Img. Sci. **2**(1), 183–202 (2009)
19. Amanatides, J., Woo, A.: A fast voxel traversal algorithm for ray tracing. Eurographics **87**, 3–10 (1987)
20. Chambolle, A., Pock, T.: A first-order primal-dual algorithm for convex problems with applications to imaging. J. Math. Imaging Vis. **40**(1), 120–145 (2011)

DeeperCut: A Deeper, Stronger, and Faster Multi-person Pose Estimation Model

Eldar Insafutdinov[1(✉)], Leonid Pishchulin[1], Bjoern Andres[1],
Mykhaylo Andriluka[1,2], and Bernt Schiele[1]

[1] Max Planck Institute for Informatics, Saarbrücken, Germany
eldar@mpi-inf.mpq.de
[2] Stanford University, Stanford, USA

Abstract. The goal of this paper is to advance the state-of-the-art of articulated pose estimation in scenes with multiple people. To that end we contribute on three fronts. We propose (1) improved body part detectors that generate effective bottom-up proposals for body parts; (2) novel image-conditioned pairwise terms that allow to assemble the proposals into a variable number of consistent body part configurations; and (3) an incremental optimization strategy that explores the search space more efficiently thus leading both to better performance and significant speed-up factors. Evaluation is done on two single-person and two multi-person pose estimation benchmarks. The proposed approach significantly outperforms best known multi-person pose estimation results while demonstrating competitive performance on the task of single person pose estimation (Models and code available at http://pose.mpi-inf.mpg.de).

1 Introduction

Human pose estimation has recently made dramatic progress in particular on standard benchmarks for single person pose estimation [1,2]. This progress has been facilitated by the use of deep learning-based architectures [3,4] and by the availability of large-scale datasets such as "MPII Human Pose" [2]. In order to make further progress on the challenging task of multi-person pose estimation we carefully design and evaluate several key-ingredients for human pose estimation.

The first ingredient we consider is the generation of body part hypotheses. Essentially all prominent pose estimation methods include a component that detects body parts or estimates their position. While early work used classifiers such as SVMs and AdaBoost [1,5–7], modern approaches build on different flavors of deep learning-based architectures [8–11]. The second key ingredient are pairwise terms between body part hypotheses that help grouping those into valid human pose configurations. In earlier models such pairwise terms were essential for good performance [1,5,6]. Recent methods seem to profit less from such pairwise terms due to stronger unaries [8,10,11]. Image-conditioned pairwise terms [7,9] however have the promise to allow for better grouping. Last but not least, inference time is always a key consideration for pose estimation models. Often, model complexity has to be treated for speed and thus many

© Springer International Publishing AG 2016
B. Leibe et al. (Eds.): ECCV 2016, Part VI, LNCS 9910, pp. 34–50, 2016.
DOI: 10.1007/978-3-319-46466-4_3

Fig. 1. Sample multi-person pose estimation results by the proposed *DeeperCut*.

models do not consider all spatial relations that would be beneficial for best performance.

In this paper we contribute to all three aspects and thereby significantly push the state of the art in multi-person pose estimation. We use a general optimization framework introduced in our previous work [10] as a test bed for all three key ingredients proposed in this paper, as it allows to easily replace and combine different components. Our contributions are three-fold, leading to a novel multi-person pose estimation approach that is deeper, stronger, and faster compared to the state of the art [10]:

- "deeper": we propose strong body part detectors based on recent advances in deep learning [12] that – taken alone – already allow to obtain competitive performance on pose estimation benchmarks.
- "stronger": we introduce novel image-conditioned pairwise terms between body parts that allow to push performance in the challenging case of multi-people pose estimation.
- "faster": we demonstrate that using our image-conditioned pairwise along with very good part detection candidates in a fully-connected model dramatically reduces the run-time by 2–3 orders of magnitude. Finally, we introduce a novel incremental optimization method to achieve a further 4x run-time reduction while improving human pose estimation accuracy.

We evaluate our approach on two single-person and two multi-person pose estimation benchmarks and report the best results in each case. Sample multi-person pose estimation predictions by the proposed approach are shown in Fig. 1.

Related work. Articulated human pose estimation has been traditionally formulated as a structured prediction task that requires an inference step combining local observations of body joints with spatial constraints. Various formulations have been proposed based on tree [6,13–15] and non-tree models [16,17]. The goal of the inference process has been to refine observations from local part detectors into coherent estimates of body configurations. Models of this type have been increasingly superseded by strong body part detectors [18–20], which has been reinforced by the development of strong image representations based on convolutional networks. Recent work aimed to incorporate convolutional detectors into part-based models [9] or design stronger detectors by combining the detector output with location-based features [21].

Specifically, as we suggest in [10], in the presence of strong detectors spatial reasoning results in diminishing returns because most contextual information can be incorporated directly in the detector. In this work we elevate the task to a new level of complexity by addressing images with multiple potentially overlapping people. This results in a more complex structured prediction problem with a variable number of outputs. In this setting we observe a large boost from conducting inference on top of state-of-the-art part detectors.

Combining spatial models with convnets allows to increase the receptive field that is used for inferring body joint locations. For example [11] iteratively trains a cascade of convolutional parts detectors, each detector taking the scoremap of all parts from the previous stage. This effectively increases the depth of the network and the receptive field is comparable to the entire person. With the recent developments in object detection newer architectures are composed of a large number of layers and the receptive field is large automatically. In this paper, we introduce a detector based on the recently proposed deep residual networks [12]. This allows us to train a detector with a large receptive field [11] and to incorporate intermediate supervision.

The use of purely geometric pairwise terms is suboptimal as they do not take local image evidence into account and only penalize deviation from the expected joint location. Due to the inherent articulation of body parts the expected location can only approximately guide the inference. While this can be sufficient when people are relatively distant from each other, for closely positioned people more discriminative pairwise costs are essential. Two prior works [7,9] have introduced image-dependent pairwise terms between connected body parts. While [7] uses an intermediate representation based on poselets our pairwise terms are conditioned directly on the image. [9] clusters relative positions of adjacent joints into $T = 11$ clusters, and assigns different labels to the part depending on which cluster it falls to. Subsequently a CNN is trained to predict this extended set of classes and later an SVM is used to select the maximum scoring joint pair relation.

Single person pose estimation has advanced considerably, but the setting is simplified. Here we focus on the more challenging problem of multi-person pose estimation. Previous work has addressed this problem as sequence of person detection and pose estimation [22–24]. [22] use a detector for initialization and reasoning across people, but rely on simple geometric body part relationships and only reason about person-person occlusions. [24] focus on single partially occluded people, and handle multi-person scenes akin to [6]. In [10] we propose to jointly detect and estimate configurations, but rely on simple pairwise terms only, which limits the performance and, as we show, results in prohibitive inference time to fully explore the search space. Here, we innovate on multiple fronts both in terms of speed and accuracy.

2 DeepCut Recap

This section summarizes *DeepCut* [10] and how unary and pairwise terms are used in this approach. *DeepCut* is a state-of-the-art approach to multi-person pose estimation based on integer linear programming (ILP) that jointly estimates poses of all people present in an image by minimizing a joint objective. This objective aims to jointly partition and label an initial pool of body part candidates into consistent sets of body-part configurations corresponding to distinct people. We use *DeepCut* as a general optimization framework that allows to easily replace and combine different components.

Specifically, *DeepCut* starts from a set D of *body part candidates*, i.e. putative detections of body parts in a given image, and a set C of *body part classes*, e.g., head, shoulder, knee. The set D of part candidates is typically generated by body part detectors and each candidate $d \in D$ has a *unary score* for every body part class $c \in C$. Based on these unary scores *DeepCut* associates a cost or reward $\alpha_{dc} \in \mathbb{R}$ to be paid by all feasible solutions of the pose estimation problem for which the body part candidate d is a body part of class c.

Additionally, for every pair of distinct body part candidates $d, d' \in D$ and every two body part classes $c, c' \in C$, the *pairwise term* is used to generate a cost or reward $\beta_{dd'cc'} \in \mathbb{R}$ to be paid by all feasible solutions of the pose estimation problem for which the body part d, classified as c, and the body part d', classified as c', belong to the same person.

With respect to these sets and costs, the pose estimation problem is cast as an ILP in two classes of 01-variables: Variables $x : D \times C \to \{0, 1\}$ indicate by $x_{dc} = 1$ that body part candidate d is of body part class c. If, for a $d \in D$ and all $c \in C$, $x_{dc} = 0$, the body part candidate d is suppressed. Variables $y : \binom{D}{2} \to \{0, 1\}$ indicate by $y_{dd'} = 1$ that body part candidates d and d' belong to the same person. Additional variables and constraints described in [10] link the variables x and y to the costs and ensure that feasible solutions (x, y) well-define a selection and classification of body part candidates as body part classes as well as a clustering of body part candidates into distinct people.

The *DeepCut* ILP is hard and hard to approximate, as it generalizes the minimum cost multicut or correlation clustering problem which is APX-hard [25, 26]. Using the branch-and-cut algorithm [10] to compute constant-factor approximative feasible solutions of instances of the *DeepCut* ILP is not necessarily practical. In Sect. 5 we propose an incremental optimization approach that uses branch-and-cut algorithm to incrementally solve several instances of ILP, which results into 4–5x run-time reduction with increased pose estimation accuracy.

3 Part Detectors

As argued before, strong part detectors are an essential ingredient of modern pose estimation methods. We propose and evaluate a deep fully-convolutional human body part detection model drawing on powerful recent ideas from semantic segmentation, object classification [12,27,28] and human pose estimation [10,11,20].

3.1 Model

Architecture. We build on the recent advances in object classification and adapt the extremely deep Residual Network (ResNet) [12] for human body part detection. This model achieved excellent results on the recent ImageNet Object Classification Challenge and specifically tackles the problem of vanishing gradients by passing the state through identity layers and modeling residual functions. Our best performing body part detection model has 152 layers (c.f. Sect. 3.2) which is in line with the findings of [12].

Stride. Adapting ResNet for the sliding window-based body part detection is not straight forward: converting ResNet to the fully convolutional mode leads to a 32 px stride which is too coarse for precise part localization. In [10] we show that using a stride of 8 px leads to good part detection results. Typically, spatial resolution can be recovered by either introducing up-sampling *deconvolutional* layers [27], or blowing up the convolutional filters using the *hole algorithm* [28]. The latter has shown to perform better on the task of semantic segmentation. However, using the *hole algorithm* to recover the spatial resolution of ResNet is infeasible due to memory constraints. For instance, the 22 residual blocks in the conv4 bank of ResNet-101 constitute the major part of the network and running it at stride 8 px does not fit the net into GPU memory[1]. We thus employ a hybrid approach. First, we remove the final classification as well as average pooling layer. Then, we decrease the stride of the first convolutional layers of the conv5 bank from 2 px to 1 px to prevent down-sampling. Next, we add holes to all 3x3 convolutions in conv5 to preserve their receptive field. This reduces the stride of the full CNN to 16 px. Finally, we add deconvolutional layers for 2x up-sampling and connect the final output to the output of the conv3 bank.

Receptive field size. A large receptive field size allows to incorporate context when predicting locations of individual body parts. [8,11] argue about the importance of large receptive fields and propose a complex hierarchical architecture predicting parts at multiple resolution levels. The extreme depth of ResNet allows for a very large receptive field (on the order of 1000 px compared to VGG's 400 px [4]) without the need of introducing complex hierarchical architectures. We empirically find that re-scaling the original image such that an upright standing person is 340 px high leads to best performance.

Intermediate supervision. Providing additional supervision addresses the problem of vanishing gradients in deep neural networks [11,29,30]. In addition

---

[1] We use NVIDIA Tesla K40 GPU with 12 GB RAM.

to that, [11] reports that using part scoremaps produced at intermediate stages as inputs for subsequent stages helps to encode spatial relations between parts, while [31] use spatial fusion layers that learn an implicit spatial model. ResNets address the first problem by introducing identity connections and learning residual functions. To address the second concern, we make a slightly different choice: we add part loss layers inside the conv4 bank of ResNet. We argue that it is not strictly necessary to use scoremaps as inputs for the subsequent stages. The activations from such intermediate predictions are different only up to a linear transformation and contain all information about part presence that is available at that stage of the network. In Sect. 3.2 we empirically show a consistent improvement of part detection performance when including intermediate supervision.

Loss functions. We use sigmoid activations and cross entropy loss function during training [10]. We perform location refinement by predicting offsets from the locations on the scoremap grid to the ground truth joint locations [10].

Training. We use the publicly available ResNet implementation (Caffe) and initialize from the ImageNet-pre-trained models. We train networks with SGD for 1M iterations, starting with the learning rate lr=0.001 for 10k, then lr=0.002 for 420k, lr=0.0002 for 300k and lr=0.0001 for 300k. This corresponds to roughly 17 epochs of the MPII [2] train set. Finetuning from ImageNet takes two days on a *single* GPU. Batch normalization [32] worsens performance, as the batch size of 1 in fully convolutional training is not enough to provide a reliable estimate of activation statistics. During training we switch off collection of statistics and use the mean and variance that were gathered on the ImageNet dataset.

3.2 Evaluation of Part Detectors

Datasets. We use three public datasets: "Leeds Sports Poses" (LSP) [1] (person-centric (PC) annotations); "LSP Extended" (LSPET) [15]; "MPII Human Pose" ("Single Person") [2] consisting of 19185 training and 7247 testing poses. To evaluate on LSP we train part detectors on the union of MPII, LSPET and LSP training sets. To evaluate on MPII Single Person we train on MPII *only*.

Evaluation measures. We use the standard "Percentage of Correct Keypoints (PCK)" evaluation metric [8,33,34] and evaluation scripts from the web page of [2]. In addition to PCK at fixed threshold, we report "Area under Curve" (AUC) computed for the entire range of PCK thresholds.

Results on LSP. The results are shown in Table 1. ResNet-50 with 8 px stride achieves 87.8 % PCK and 63.7 % AUC. Increasing the stride size to 16 px and up-sampling the scoremaps by 2x to compensate for the loss on resolution slightly drops the performance to 87.2 % PCK. This is expected as up-sampling cannot fully compensate for the information loss due to a larger stride. Larger stride minimizes memory requirements, which allows for training a deeper ResNet-152. The latter significantly increases the performance (89.1 vs. 87.2 % PCK, 65.1 vs. 63.1 % AUC), as it has larger model capacity. Introducing intermediate supervision further improves the performance to 90.1 % PCK and 66.1 % AUC, as it constraints

Table 1. Pose estimation results (PCK) on LSP (PC) dataset.

Setting	Head	Sho	Elb	Wri	Hip	Knee	Ank	PCK	AUC
ResNet-50 (8 px)	96.9	90.3	85.0	81.5	88.6	87.3	84.8	87.8	63.7
ResNet-50 (16 px + 2x up-sample)	96.7	89.8	84.6	80.4	89.3	86.4	82.8	87.2	63.1
ResNet-101 (16 px + 2x up-sample)	96.9	91.2	85.8	82.6	90.9	**90.2**	85.9	89.1	64.6
ResNet-152 (16 px + 2x up-sample)	97.4	91.7	85.7	82.4	90.1	89.2	86.9	89.1	65.1
+ intermediate supervision	97.4	**92.7**	**87.5**	**84.4**	**91.5**	89.9	87.2	90.1	**66.1**
DeepCut [10]	97.0	91.0	83.8	78.1	91.0	86.7	82.0	87.1	63.5
Wei et al. [11]	**97.8**	92.5	87.0	83.9	**91.5**	90.8	**89.9**	**90.5**	65.4
Tompson et al. [8]	90.6	79.2	67.9	63.4	69.5	71.0	64.2	72.3	47.3
Chen & Yuille [9]	91.8	78.2	71.8	65.5	73.3	70.2	63.4	73.4	40.1
Fan et al. [35]	92.4	75.2	65.3	64.0	75.7	68.3	70.4	73.0	43.2

the network to learn useful representations in the early stages and uses them in later stages for spatial disambiguation of parts.

The results are compared to the state of the art in Table 1. Our best model significantly outperforms *DeepCut* [10] (90.1 % PCK vs. 87.1 % PCK), as it relies on deeper detection architectures. Our model performs on par with the recent approach of Wei et al. [11] (90.1 vs. 90.5 % PCK, 66.1 vs. 65.4 AUC). This is interesting, as they use a much more complex multi-scale multi-stage architecture.

Results on MPII Single Person. The results are shown in Table 2. ResNet-152 achieves 87.8 % PCK$_h$ and 60.0 % AUC, while intermediate supervision slightly improves the performance further to 88.5 % PCK$_h$ and 60.8 % AUC. Comparing the results to the state of the art we observe significant improvement over *DeepCut* [10] (+5.9 % PCK$_h$, +4.2 % AUC), which again underlines the

Table 2. Pose estimation results (PCK$_h$) on MPII Single Person.

Setting	Head	Sho	Elb	Wri	Hip	Knee	Ank	PCK$_h$	AUC
ResNet-152	96.3	94.1	88.6	83.9	87.2	82.9	77.8	87.8	60.0
+ intermediate supervision	96.8	**95.2**	**89.3**	84.4	**88.4**	**83.4**	78.0	**88.5**	60.8
DeepCut [10]	94.1	90.2	83.4	77.3	82.6	75.7	68.6	82.4	56.5
Tompson et al. [8]	95.8	90.3	80.5	74.3	77.6	69.7	62.8	79.6	51.8
Carreira et al. [36]	95.7	91.7	81.7	72.4	82.8	73.2	66.4	81.3	49.1
Tompson et al. [20]	96.1	91.9	83.9	77.8	80.9	72.3	64.8	82.0	54.9
Wei et al. [11]	**97.8**	95.0	88.7	84.0	**88.4**	82.8	**79.4**	**88.5**	**61.4**

importance of using extremely deep model. The proposed approach performs on par with the best know result by Wei et al. [11] (88.5 vs. 88.5 % PCK$_h$) for the maximum distance threshold, while slightly loosing when using the entire range of thresholds (60.8 vs. 61.4 % AUC). We envision that extending the proposed approach to incorporate multiple scales as in [11] should improve the performance. The model trained on the union of MPII, LSPET and LSP training sets achieves 88.3 % PCK$_h$ and 60.7 % AUC. The fact that we use the same trained model on both LSP and MPII benchmarks and achieve similar performance demonstrates the generality of the proposed approach.

4   Image-Conditioned Pairwise Terms

As discussed in Sect. 3, a large receptive field for the CNN-based part detectors allows to accurately predict the presence of a body part at a given location. However, it also contains enough evidence to reason about locations of other parts in the vicinity. We draw on this insight and propose to also use deep networks to make pairwise part-to-part predictions. They are subsequently used to compute the pairwise probabilities and show significant improvements for multi-person pose estimation.

4.1   Model

Our approach is inspired by the body part location refinement described in Sect. 3. In addition to predicting offsets for the current joint, we directly regress from the current location to the relative positions of all other joints. For each scoremap location $k = (x_k, y_k)$ that is marked positive w.r.t the joint $c \in C$ and for each remaining joint $c' \in C \setminus c$, we define a relative position of c' w.r.t. c as a tuple $t^k_{cc'} = (x_{c'} - x_k, y_{c'} - x_k)$. We add an extra layer that predicts relative position $o^k_{cc'}$ and train it with a smooth L$_1$ loss function. We thus perform *joint* training of body part detectors (cross-entropy loss), location regression (L$_1$ loss) and pairwise regression (L$_1$ loss) by linearly combining all three loss functions. The targets t are normalized to have zero mean and unit variance over the training set. Results of such predictions are shown in Fig. 2.

We then use these predictions to compute pairwise costs $\beta_{dd'cc'}$. For any pair of detections (d, d') (Fig. 3) and for any pair of joints (c, c') we define the following quantities: locations l_d, l'_d of detections d and d' respectively; the offset prediction $o^d_{cc'}$ from c to c' at location d (solid red) coming from the CNN and similarly the offset prediction $o^{d'}_{c'c}$ (solid turquoise). We then compute the offset between the two predictions: $\hat{o}_{dd'} = l_{d'} - l_d$ (marked in dashed red). The degree to which the prediction $o^d_{cc'}$ agrees with the actual offset $\hat{o}_{dd'}$ tells how likely d, d' are of classes c, c' respectively and belong to the same person. We measure this by computing the distance between the two offsets $\Delta_f = \|\hat{o}_{dd'} - o^d_{cc'}\|_2$, and the absolute angle $\theta_f = |\angle(\hat{o}_{dd'}, o^d_{cc'})|$ where f stands for forward direction, i.e. from d to d'. Similarly, we incorporate the prediction $o^{d'}_{c'c}$ in the backwards direction by computing $\Delta_b = \|\hat{o}_{d'd} - o^{d'}_{c'c}\|_2$ and $\theta_b = |\angle(\hat{o}_{d'd}, o^{d'}_{c'c})|$. Finally, we

Fig. 2. Visualizations of regression predictions. Top: from left shoulder to the right shoulder (green), right hip (red), left elbow (light blue), right ankle (purple) and top of the head (dark blue). Bottom: from right knee to the right hip (green), right ankle (red), left knee (dark blue), left ankle (light blue) and top of the head (purple). Longer-range predictions, such as e.g. shoulder – ankle may be less accurate for harder poses (top row, images 2 and 3) compared to the nearby predictions. However, they provide enough information to constrain the search space in the fully-connected spatial model. (Color figure online)

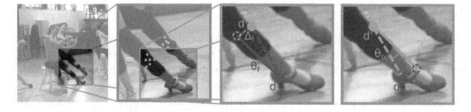

Fig. 3. Visualization of features extracted to score the pairwise. See text for details. (Color figure online)

define a feature vector by augmenting features with exponential terms: $f_{dd'cc'} = (\Delta_f, \theta_f, \Delta_b, \theta_b, \exp(-\Delta_f), \ldots, \exp(-\theta_b))$.

We then use the features $f_{dd'cc'}$ and define logistic model:

$$p(z_{dd'cc'} = 1 | f_{dd'cc'}, \omega_{cc'}) = \frac{1}{1 + \exp(-\langle \omega_{cc'}, f_{dd'cc'} \rangle)}. \tag{1}$$

where $K = (|C| \times (|C| + 1))/2$ parameters $\omega_{cc'}$ are estimated using ML.

4.2 Sampling Detections

Location refinement NMS. *DeepCut* samples the set of detections D from the scoremap by applying non-maximum suppression (NMS). Here, we utilize location refinement and correct grid locations with the predicted offsets before applying NMS. This pulls detections that belong to a particular body joint

Table 3. Effects of proposed pairwise and unaries on the pose estimation performance (AP) on MPII Multi-person Val.

Unary	Pairwise	Head	Sho	Elb	Wri	Hip	Knee	Ank	AP	time [s/frame]
DeepCut [10]	*DeepCut* [10]	50.1	44.1	33.5	26.5	33.0	28.5	14.4	33.3	259220
DeepCut [10]	this work	68.3	58.3	47.4	38.9	45.2	41.8	31.2	47.7	1987
this work	this work	70.9	59.8	53.1	44.4	50.0	46.4	39.5	52.3	1171
+ location refinement before NMS		70.3	61.6	52.1	43.7	50.6	47.0	40.6	52.6	578

towards its true location thereby increasing the density of detections around that location, which allows to distribute the detection candidates in a better way.

Splitting of part detections. *DeepCut* ILP solves the clustering problem by labeling each detection d with a single part class c and assigning it to a particular cluster that corresponds to a distinct person. However, it may happen that the same spatial location is occupied by more than one body joint, and therefore, its corresponding detection can only be labeled with one of the respecting classes. A naive solution is to replace a detection with n detections for each part class, which would result in a prohibitive increase in the number of detections. We simply split a detection d into several if more than one part has unary probability that is higher than a chosen threshold s (in our case $s = 0.4$).

4.3 Evaluation of Pairwise

Datasets and evaluation measure. We evaluate on the challenging public "MPII Human Pose" ("Multi-Person") benchmark [2] consisting of 3844 training and 1758 testing groups of multiple overlapping people in highly articulated poses with a variable number of parts. We perform all intermediate experiments on a validation set of 200 images sampled uniformly at random and refer to it as MPII Multi-Person Val. We report major results on the full testing set, and on the subset of 288 images for the direct comparison to [10]. The AP measure [10] evaluating consistent body part detections is used for performance comparison. Additionally, we report median running time per frame measured in seconds[2].

Table 4. Effects of different versions of the pairwise terms on the pose estimation performance (AP) on MPII Multi-person Val.

Setting	Head	Sho	Elb	Wri	Hip	Knee	Ank	AP	time [s/frame]
bi-directional + angle	70.3	61.6	52.1	43.7	50.6	47.0	40.6	52.6	578
uni-directional + angle	69.3	58.4	51.8	44.2	50.4	44.7	36.3	51.1	2140
bi-directional	68.8	58.3	51.0	42.7	51.1	46.5	38.7	51.3	914

Evaluation of unaries and pairwise. The results are shown in Table 3. Baseline *DeepCut* achieves 33.3 % AP. Using the proposed pairwise significantly

---

[2] Run-time is measured on a single core Intel Xeon 2.70 GHz.

improves performance achieving 47.7 % AP. This clearly shows the advantages of using image-conditioned pairwise to disambiguate the body part assignment for multiple overlapping individuals. Remarkably, the proposed pairwise dramatically reduce the run-time by two orders of magnitude (1987 vs. 259220 s/frame). This underlines the argument that using strong pairwise in the fully-connected model allows to significantly speed-up the inference. Using additionally the proposed part detectors further boosts the performance (52.3 vs. 47.7 % AP), which can be attributed to better quality part hypotheses. Run-time is again almost halved, which clearly shows the importance of obtaining high-quality part detection candidates for more accurate and faster inference. Performing location refinement before NMS slightly improves the performance, but also reduces the run-time by 2x: this allows to increase the density of detections at the most probable body part locations and thus suppresses more detections around the most confident ones, which leads to better distribution of part detection candidates and reduces confusion generated by the near-by detections. Overall, we observe significant performance improvement and dramatic reduction in run-time by the proposed *DeeperCut* compared to the baseline *DeepCut*.

Ablation study of pairwise. An ablation study of the proposed image-conditioned pairwise is performed in Table 4. Regressing from both joints onto the opposite joint's location and including angles achieves the best performance of 52.6 % AP and the minimum run-time of 578 s/frame. Regressing from a single joint only slightly reduces the performance to 51.1 % AP, but significantly increases run-time by 4x: these pairwise are less robust compared to the bi-directional, which confuses the inference. Removing the angles from the pairwise features also decreases the performance (51.3 vs. 52.6 % AP) and doubles run-time, as it removes the information about body part orientation.

5 Incremental Optimization

Solving one instance of the *DeepCut* ILP for all body part candidates detected for an image, as suggested in [10] and summarized in Sect. 2, is elegant in theory but disadvantageous in practice:

Firstly, the time it takes to compute constant-factor approximative feasible solution by the branch-and-cut algorithm [10] can be exponential in the number of body part candidates in the worst case. In practice, this limits the number of candidates that can be processed by this algorithm. Due to this limitation, it does happen that body parts and, for images showing many persons, entire persons are missed, simply because they are not contained in the set of candidates.

Secondly, solving one instance of the optimization problem for the entire image means that no distinction is made between part classes detected reliably, e.g. head and shoulders, and part classes detected less reliably, e.g. wrists, elbows and ankles. Therefore, it happens that unreliable detections corrupt the solution.

To address both problems, we solve not one instance of the *DeepCut* ILP but several, starting with only those body part classes that are detected most reliably and only then considering body part classes that are detected less reliably. Concretely, we study two variants of this incremental optimization approach which are defined in Table 5. Specifically, the procedure works as follows:

For each subset of body part classes defined in Table 5, an instance of the *DeepCut* ILP is set up and a constant-factor approximative feasible solution computed using the branch-and-cut algorithm. This feasible solution selects, labels and clusters a subset of part candidates, namely of those part classes that are considered in this instance. For the next instance, each cluster of body part candidates of the same class from the previous instance becomes just one part candidate whose class is fixed. Thus, the next instance is an optimization problem for selecting, labeling and clustering body parts that have not been determined by previous instances. Overall, this allows us to start with more part candidates consistently and thus improve the pose estimation result significantly.

Table 5. As the run-time of the DeepCut branch-and-cut algorithm limits the number of part candidates that can be processed in practice, we split the set of part classes into subsets, coarsely and finely, and solve the pose estimation problem incrementally.

	Stage 1	Stage 2	Stage 3
2-stage	head, shoulders	hips, knees	
	elbows, wrists	ankles	
3-stage	head	elbows	hips, knees
	shoulders	wrists	ankles

5.1   Evaluation of Incremental Optimization

Results are shown in Table 6. Single stage optimization with $|D| = 100$ part detection candidates achieves 52.6 % AP (best from Table 3). More aggressive NMS with radius of 24 px improves the performance (54.5 vs. 52.6 % AP), as it allows to better distribute detection candidates. Increasing $|D|$ to 150 slightly improves the performance by +0.6 % AP, but significantly increases run-time (1041 vs. 596 s/frame). We found $|D| = 150$ to be maximum total number of detection candidates (11 per part) for which optimization runs in a reasonable time. Incremental optimization of 2-stage inference slightly improves the performance (56.5 vs. 55.1 % AP) as it allows for a larger number of detection candidates per body part (20) and leverages typically more confident predictions of the upper body parts in the first stage before solving for the entire body. Most importantly, it halves the median run-time from 1041 to 483 s/frame. Incremental optimization of 3-stage inference again almost halves the run-time to 271 s/frame while noticeably improving the human pose estimation performance for all body parts but elbows achieving 57.6 % AP. These results clearly demonstrate the advantages of the proposed incremental optimization. Splitting the detection candidates that simultaneously belong to multiple body parts with

Table 6. Performance (AP) of different hierarchical versions of *DeeperCut* on MPII Multi-person Val.

Setting	Head	Sho	Elb	Wri	Hip	Knee	Ank	AP	time [s/frame]
1-stage optimize, 100 det, nms 1x	70.3	61.6	52.1	43.7	50.6	47.0	40.6	52.6	578
1-stage optimize, 100 det, nms 2x	71.3	64.1	55.8	44.1	53.8	48.7	41.3	54.5	596
1-stage optimize, 150 det, nms 2x	74.1	65.6	56.0	44.3	54.4	49.2	39.8	55.1	1041
2-stage optimize	75.9	66.8	58.8	46.1	54.1	48.7	42.4	56.5	483
3-stage optimize	78.3	69.3	58.4	47.5	55.1	49.6	42.5	57.6	271
+ split detections	**78.5**	**70.5**	**59.7**	**48.7**	**55.4**	**50.6**	**44.4**	**58.7**	**270**
DeepCut [10]	50.1	44.1	33.5	26.5	33.0	28.5	14.4	33.3	259220

high confidence slightly improves the performance to 58.7 % AP. This helps to overcome the limitation that each detection candidate can be assigned to a single body part and improves on cases where two body parts overlap thus sharing the same detection candidate. We also compare the obtained results to *DeepCut* in Table 6 (last row). The proposed *DeeperCut* outperforms baseline *DeepCut* (58.7 vs. 33.3 % AP) by almost doubling the performance, while run-time is reduced dramatically by 3 orders of magnitude from the infeasible 259220 s/frame to affordable 270 s/frame. This comparison clearly demonstrates the power of the proposed approach and dramatic effects of better unary, pairwise and optimization on the overall pose estimation performance and run-time.

5.2   Comparison to the State of the Art

We compare to others on MPII Multi-Person Test and WAF [22] datasets.

Results on MPII Multi-person. For direct comparison with *DeepCut* we evaluate on the same subset of 288 testing images as in [10]. Additionally, we provide the results on the entire testing set. Results are shown in Table 7. *DeeperCut* without incremental optimization already outperforms *DeepCut* by a large margin (66.2 vs. 54.1 % AP). Using 3-stage incremental optimization further improves the performance to 69.7 % AP improving by a dramatic 16.5 % AP over the baseline. Remarkably, the run-time is reduced from 57995 to 230 s/frame, which is an improvement by two orders of magnitude. Both results underline the importance of strong image-conditioned pairwise terms and incremental optimization to maximize multi-person pose estimation performance at the reduced run-time. A similar trend is observed on the full set: 3-stage optimization improves over a single stage optimization (59.4 vs. 54.7 % AP). We observe that the performance on the entire testing set is over 10 % AP lower compared to the subset and run-time is doubled. This implies that the subset of 288 images is easier compared to the full testing set. We envision that performance differences between *DeeperCut* and *DeepCut* on the entire set will be

Table 7. Pose estimation results (AP) on MPII Multi-person.

Setting	Head	Sho	Elb	Wri	Hip	Knee	Ank	AP	time [s/frame]
subset of 288 images as in [10]									
DeeperCut (1-stage)	83.3	79.4	66.1	57.9	63.5	60.5	49.9	66.2	1333
DeeperCut	**87.5**	**82.8**	**70.2**	**61.6**	**66.0**	**60.6**	**56.5**	**69.7**	**230**
DeepCut [10]	73.4	71.8	57.9	39.9	56.7	44.0	32.0	54.1	57995
full set									
DeeperCut (1-stage)	73.7	65.4	54.9	45.2	52.3	47.8	40.7	54.7	2785
DeeperCut	**79.1**	**72.2**	**59.7**	**50.0**	**56.0**	**51.0**	**44.6**	**59.4**	485
Faster R-CNN [37] + unary	64.9	62.9	53.4	44.1	50.7	43.1	35.2	51.0	1

at least as large as when compared on the subset. We also compare to a strong two-stage baseline: first each person is pre-localized by applying the state-of-the-art detector [37] following by NMS and retaining rectangles with scores at least 0.8; then pose estimation for each rectangle is performed using *DeeperCut* unary only. Being significantly faster (1 s/frame) this approach reaches 51.0 % AP vs. 59.4 % AP by *DeeperCut*, which clearly shows the power of joint reasoning by the proposed approach.

Table 8. Pose estimation results (mPCP) on WAF dataset.

Setting	Head	U Arms	L Arms	Torso	mPCP	AOP
DeeperCut nms 3.0	**99.3**	**83.8**	**81.9**	**87.1**	**86.3**	**88.1**
DeepCut [10]	**99.3**	81.5	79.5	**87.1**	84.7	86.5
Ghiasi et al. [38]	-	-	-	-	63.6	74.0
Eichner & Ferrari [22]	97.6	68.2	48.1	86.1	69.4	80.0
Chen & Yuille [24]	98.5	77.2	71.3	88.5	80.7	84.9

Results on WAF. Results using the official evaluation protocol [22] assuming mPCP and AOP evaluation measures and considering detection bounding boxes provided by [22] are shown in Table 8. *DeeperCut* achieves the best result improving over the state of the art *DeepCut* (86.3 vs. 84.7 % mPCP, 88.1 vs. 86.5 % AOP). Noticeable improvements are observed both for upper (+2.3 % mPCP) and lower (+2.4 % mPCP) arms. However, overall performance differences between *DeeperCut* and the baseline *DeepCut* are not as pronounced compared to MPII Multi-Person dataset. This is due to the fact that actual differences are washed out by the peculiarities of the mPCP evaluation measure: mPCP assumes that people are pre-detected and human pose estimation performance is evaluated only for people whose upper body detections match the ground truth. Thus, a pose estimation method is not penalized for generating multiple body pose predictions, since the only pose prediction is considered whose upper body bounding box best matches the ground truth. We thus re-evaluate the competing approaches [10,24] using the more realistic AP evaluation measure[3]. The results are shown in Table 9. *DeeperCut* significantly improves over *DeepCut* (82.0 vs. 76.2 % AP). The largest boost in performance is achieved for head (+16.0 % AP) and wrists (+5.2 % AP): *DeeperCut* follows incremental optimization strategy by first solving for the most reliable body parts, such as head and shoulders, and then using the obtained solution to improve estima-tion of harder body parts, such as wrists. Most notably, run-time is dramatically reduced by 3 orders of magnitude from 22000 to 13 s/frame. These results clearly show the advantages of the proposed approach when evaluated in the real-world detection setting. The proposed *DeeperCut* also outperforms [24] by a large mar-gin. The performance difference is much more pronounced compared to using *m*PCP evaluation measure: in contrast to *m*PCP, AP penalizes multiple body pose predictions of the same person. We envision that better NMS strategies are likely to improve the AP performance of [24].

Table 9. Pose estimation results (AP) on WAF dataset.

Setting	Head	Sho	Elb	Wri	AP	time [s/frame]
DeeperCut	**92.6**	**81.1**	**75.7**	**78.8**	**82.0**	13
DeepCut [10]	76.6	80.8	73.7	73.6	76.2	22000
Chen & Yuille [24]	83.3	56.1	46.3	35.5	55.3	-

6 Conclusion

In this paper we significantly advanced the state of the art in articulated multi-person human pose estimation. To that end we carefully re-designed and thor-oughly evaluated several key ingredients. First, drawing on the recent advances in deep learning we proposed strong extremely deep body part detectors that – taken alone – already allow to obtain state of the art performance on stan-dard pose estimation benchmarks. Second, we introduce novel image-conditioned pairwise terms between body parts that allow to significantly push the perfor-mance in the challenging case of multi-people pose estimation, and dramatically reduce the run-time of the inference in the fully-connected spatial model. Third, we introduced a novel incremental optimization strategy to further reduce the run-time and improve human pose estimation accuracy. Overall, the proposed improvements allowed to almost double the pose estimation accuracy in the chal-lenging multi-person case while reducing the run-time by 3 orders of magnitude.

---

[3] We used publicly-available pose predictions of [24] for all people in WAF dataset.

References

1. Johnson, S., Everingham, M.: Clustered pose and nonlinear appearance models for human pose estimation. In: BMVC 2010
2. Andriluka, M., Pishchulin, L., Gehler, P., Schiele, B.: 2d human pose estimation: New benchmark and state of the art analysis. In: CVPR 2014
3. Krizhevsky, A., Sutskever, I., Hinton, G.E.: Imagenet classification with deep convolutional neural networks. In: NIPS 2012
4. Simonyan, K., Zisserman, A.: Very deep convolutional networks for large-scale image recognition. In: CoRR 2014
5. Andriluka, M., Roth, S., Schiele, B.: Discriminative appearance models for pictorial structures. In: IJCV 2011
6. Yang, Y., Ramanan, D.: Articulated human detection with flexible mixtures of parts. In: PAMI 2013
7. Pishchulin, L., Andriluka, M., Gehler, P., Schiele, B.: Poselet conditioned pictorial structures. In: CVPR 2013
8. Tompson, J.J., Jain, A., LeCun, Y., Bregler, C.: Joint training of a convolutional network and a graphical model for human pose estimation. In: NIPS 2014
9. Chen, X., Yuille, A.: Articulated pose estimation by a graphical model with image dependent pairwise relations. In: NIPS 2014
10. Pishchulin, L., Insafutdinov, E., Tang, S., Andres, B., Andriluka, M., Gehler, P., Schiele, B.: Deepcut: Joint subset partition and labeling for multi person pose estimation. In: CVPR 2016
11. Wei, S.E., Ramakrishna, V., Kanade, T., Sheikh, Y.: Convolutional pose machines. In: CVPR 2016
12. He, K., Zhang, X., Ren, S., Sun, J.: Deep residual learning for image recognition. In: CVPR 2016
13. Ramanan, D.: Learning to parse images of articulated objects. In: NIPS 2006
14. Jiang, H., Martin, D.R.: Global pose estimation using non-tree models. In: CVPR 2009
15. Johnson, S., Everingham, M.: Learning effective human pose estimation from inaccurate annotation. In: CVPR 2011
16. Tran, D., Forsyth, D.: Improved human parsing with a full relational model. In: Daniilidis, K., Maragos, P., Paragios, N. (eds.) ECCV 2010, Part IV. LNCS, vol. 6314, pp. 227–240. Springer, Heidelberg (2010). doi:10.1007/978-3-642-15561-1_17
17. Wang, F., Li, Y.: Beyond physical connections: Tree models in human pose estimation. In: CVPR 2013
18. Pishchulin, L., Andriluka, M., Gehler, P., Schiele, B.: Strong appearance and expressive spatial models for human pose estimation. In: ICCV 2013
19. Gkioxari, G., Arbelaez, P., Bourdev, L., Malik, J.: Articulated pose estimation using discriminative armlet classifiers. In: CVPR 2013
20. Tompson, J., Goroshin, R., Jain, A., LeCun, Y., Bregler, C.: Efficient object localization using convolutional networks. In: CVPR 2015
21. Ramakrishna, V., Munoz, D., Hebert, M., Andrew Bagnell, J., Sheikh, Y.: Pose machines: Articulated pose estimation via inference machines. In: Fleet, D., Pajdla, T., Schiele, B., Tuytelaars, T. (eds.) ECCV 2014, Part II. LNCS, vol. 8690, pp. 33–47. Springer, Heidelberg (2014). doi:10.1007/978-3-319-10605-2_3
22. Eichner, M., Ferrari, V.: We are family: Joint pose estimation of multiple persons. In: Daniilidis, K., Maragos, P., Paragios, N. (eds.) ECCV 2010, Part I. LNCS, vol. 6311, pp. 228–242. Springer, Heidelberg (2010). doi:10.1007/978-3-642-15549-9_17

23. Ladicky, L., Torr, P.H., Zisserman, A.: Human pose estimation using a joint pixel-wise and part-wise formulation. In: CVPR 2013
24. Chen, X., Yuille, A.: Parsing occluded people by flexible compositions. In: CVPR 2015
25. Bansal, N., Blum, A., Chawla, S.: Correlation clustering. In: ML 2004
26. Demaine, E.D., Emanuel, D., Fiat, A., Immorlica, N.: Correlation clustering in general weighted graphs. In: Theoretical Computer Science 2006
27. Long, J., Shelhamer, E., Darrell, T.: Fully convolutional networks for semantic segmentation. In: CVPR 2015
28. Chen, L.C., Papandreou, G., Kokkinos, I., Murphy, K., Yuille, A.L.: Semantic image segmentation with deep convolutional nets and fully connected crfs. In: ICLR 2015
29. Szegedy, C., Liu, W., Jia, Y., Sermanet, P., Reed, S., Anguelov, D., Erhan, D., Vanhoucke, V., Rabinovich, A.: Going deeper with convolutions. In: CVPR 2015
30. Lee, C.Y., Xie, S., Gallagher, P., Zhang, Z., Tu, Z.: Deeply-supervised nets. In: AISTATS 2015
31. Pfister, T., Charles, J., Zisserman, A.: Flowing convnets for human pose estimation in videos. In: ICCV 2015
32. Ioffe, S., Szegedy, C.: Batch normalization: Accelerating deep network training by reducing internal covariate shift. In: CoRR 2015
33. Sapp, B., Taskar, B.: Multimodal decomposable models for human pose estimation. In: CVPR 2013
34. Toshev, A., Szegedy, C.: Deeppose: Human pose estimation via deep neural networks. In: CVPR 2014
35. Fan, X., Zheng, K., Lin, Y., Wang, S.: Combining local appearance and holistic view: Dual-source deep neural networks for human pose estimation. In: CVPR 2015
36. Carreira, J., Agrawal, P., Fragkiadaki, K., Malik, J.: Human pose estimation with iterative error feedback. In: CVPR 2016
37. Ren, S., He, K., Girshick, R., Sun, J.: Faster R-CNN: Towards real-time object detection with region proposal networks. In: NIPS 2015
38. Ghiasi, G., Yang, Y., Ramanan, D., Fowlkes, C.: Parsing occluded people. In: CVPR 2014

Resonant Deformable Matching: Simultaneous Registration and Reconstruction

John Corring[✉] and Anand Rangarajan

Department of Computer and Information Science and Engineering,
University of Florida, Gainesville, USA
{corring,anand}@cise.ufl.edu

Abstract. In the past decade we have seen the emergence of many efficient algorithms for estimating non-rigid deformations registering a template to target features. Registration of density functions is particularly popular. In contrast to the success enjoyed by the density function representation, we have not seen similar success with the signed distance function representation. Resonant deformable matching (RDM) simultaneously estimates a non-rigid deformation and a set of unknown target normal directions by registering fields comprising signed distance and probability density information. Resonance occurs as the reconstruction estimate comes into agreement with the registered template. We perform experiments probing two problems: point-set registration and normal estimation. RDM compares favorably to top tier point registration and graph algorithms in terms of registration and reconstruction metrics.

1 Introduction

Many problems in computer vision require us to determine ***correspondences*** between similar sets of features. However, we are often faced with scenarios where it is very difficult to even define what a correspondence between two objects should be—no natural map, moreover bijection, may exist at all—often due to mismatched representations. Work focused on determining point correspondences for matching organized features has been abundant, as we highlight below, but there remains a clear need for handling mismatched representations. This work provides a solution for the mismatched case where the template consists of oriented points and the target consists of points, under the assumption that both template and target are drawn from outlines of shapes.

Given a set of point-features, correspondences can be obtained via ***registration***. In this approach, sparse feature sets are often first converted into scalar field representations. Then non-rigid matching of the template field with that of the target yields dense point to point correspondences. For example, point features can be converted into a probability density function representation [1–3]. Registration is obtained by deforming the template density onto the target using regularized spatial deformations [4,5]. Implicit shape representations are not restricted to probability density functions estimated from sets of features.

© Springer International Publishing AG 2016
B. Leibe et al. (Eds.): ECCV 2016, Part VI, LNCS 9910, pp. 51–68, 2016.
DOI: 10.1007/978-3-319-46466-4_4

Implicit representations abound in the literature [6–8]. The signed distance function (SDF) is an example in which the sign encodes interior/exterior properties with the absolute value encoding the distance to the nearest point in the set of curves (surfaces) [9–11]. Contrast this with the unsigned distance function which lacks interior/exterior information. Surprisingly, there is little work on matching template and target SDFs. We address the technical reasons for this now.

The signed distance $b_S : \mathbb{R}^d \to \mathbb{R}$ for an open set S satisfies $|\nabla b_S| = 1$: $b_S|_{\partial S} = 0$ with b_S continuously differentiable across the set boundary. The first technical problem we encounter in matching SDFs is the choice of a distance measure between them. Far away from the shape boundary (in the *far field*) SDFs take large values. This renders many standard distances useless, like L^p or W^p. The second problem we encounter is that SDFs are usually not available in closed form, in sharp contrast to parametric density representations. This implies that closed form distances between SDFs are elusive. Third, note that matching is extremely difficult to perform within the space of SDFs. For $\phi \in \mathcal{H}$ to maintain the properties of SDFs, we see that $\left|\left(\nabla|_{\phi(x)}b_S\right)\phi'|_x\right| = 1$, implying that $\phi'|_x \in \mathbb{O}(d)$ for all $x \in \mathbb{R}^d$—restricting $\mathcal{H}$ to rigid transformations. The difficulty of managing this constraint is related to the *reinitialization* problem in level-set methods [12–14] where ϕ is the (instantaneous) motion of an interface represented by a level set function. The complex wave representation [15] of shape is a parametric representation with aspects of the signed distance that avoids these issues. When the target is given as points (from ∂S) the problem of estimating the target SDF remains. Estimating an SDF from a sparse set of features is the *very difficult problem* of curve (or surface) **reconstruction** [16–19]. In this paper we use reconstruction in the following sense—consistent assignment of normal vectors to points. Dense normal estimation provides useful data for constructing a surface [20, 21]. The representation that we use allows us to construct surfaces via extraction of a zero level-set, as in Figs. 1 and 2.

Our approach integrates registration and reconstruction from a deformable template viewpoint, hence *Resonant Deformable Matching*. A complex scalar field representation is utilized wherein the squared **magnitude** of the field is proportional to the probability density whereas the **phase** of the field is related to the signed distance (corresponding to implicit curves in 2D and surfaces in 3D). Using a representation with both signed distance and probability information allows us to penalize geometric mismatches in a weighted fashion that preserves the advantages of density fields. During registration, the target signed distance information is *simultaneously* estimated along with the spatial deformation. The advantages of our approach relative to previous work are as follows: (i) our approach employs both probability density and signed distance information for improved registration; (ii) we derive a closed form distance between template and target functions that distinguishes oriented point-sets in the feature space; (iii) reconstruction of the target is achieved during the matching process, which can lead to improved registration; (iv) RDM outperforms competing point and field-based methods on registration and template-based normal estimation.

2   Previous Work

Field based methods make a specific choice of representation that is consistent among all point-sets and shapes being matched. Kernel Correlation [1] and gmmreg [2] use Parzen-window densities, employing correlation and L^2-distance objectives respectively. Matching distributions [22] allows singular measures to be matched. A crossover between the density and distance fields in [23] utilized distance transforms yielding a density field which is matched by a geodesic distance. In these works the unifying theme is a field that organizes in terms of *uncertainty*. SDFs, which organize in terms of *geometry*, have also been used for non-rigid registration in [10] where a variational approach leads to a *grid-based* PDE-method that performs distortion on the field. In [24] the signed distance values in the near-field of curves are viewed as random variables with a Gaussian-Kernel based probability model, and the mutual information is minimized using free-form deformations of the domain of the signed distance. Signed-distance registration techniques also have a natural outgrowth towards segmentation through shape-prior approaches [25, 26] to registering shapes to images.

Point-based methods feature explicit estimation of correspondence, possibly in a soft or probabilistic fashion. Coherent Point Drift (CPD) [27] and TPS-RPM [28] are two standard-bearers. TPS-RPM alternates between estimating the (soft) correspondence and a TPS deformation. CPD uses a similar formulation, but also imposes additional constraints (arising from motion coherence theory) on the deformation. RPM-LNS [29] imposes symmetric neighborhood structures to preserve local shape while allowing global deformation.

Graph matching methods have also been employed for point registration [30]. Local and global relations can be encoded in graphs, yielding a powerful structure for correspondence estimation. While graph matching is a computationally hard problem, algorithms for structured graphs and relaxation techniques show promise for point matching [31–33]. When a planar shape is available as a silhouette a cyclic graph emerges and elastic matching can be done quickly [34]. Manifolds induce *Laplace-Beltrami* eigenfunctions [35], providing a canonical basis from which to perform matching from a joint coordinate perspective [36] or a function mapping perspective [37]. These methods all rely on *equivalent organization of source and target*. While organization elevates the richness of the matching techniques available, it also presents a difficulty: these methods require a level footing between template and target. Estimating a graph or mesh from points can be very challenging.

Point feature organization can be viewed from many perspectives: computational geometric methods [17], psychological gestalt principles [38–40], clustering [41, 42], and level-set methods [18, 19] all organize points in some sense. Shape representations are typically chosen to engender a desired organizational aspect of shapes [43]. Through a multi-valued function or a distributional representation, different aspects of shapes can be embodied in fields that interact predictably [7, 8, 15]. These works provide a spectrum of organizational principles that can be used to temper the difficulty of the point matching problem. **In this work we obtain a reconstruction while matching**, which means that no target structure needs to be estimated before matching. Few works touting simultaneous matching and reconstruction are currently available [44,45].

3   Complex Wave Mixtures and Signed Distance Functions

In [15], the complex-valued field—or wave representation of shape was introduced. It was used to compress closed curves with PCA (exploiting linearity of the representation) and classify oriented point-sets using reconstruction error as a distance metric. Here, we prove interesting properties of this shape representation for the purposes of curve reconstruction and as a feature function before proceeding to showcasing simultaneous matching and reconstruction. Consider a point-set augmented with directional information at each point. That is, let $\mathcal{S} = \{(m_a, \nu_a)\}_{a=1}^M$, where ν_a is a normal associated with the point m_a. We may use S to denote the set underlying the oriented point-set $\mathcal{S}$, with each $m_a \in \partial S$ and ν_a pointing in the outward direction from S. We refer to this as an **oriented point-set** [15,20]. The complex field we use extends the standard Gaussian Parzen window density to a square-root of a density by using the normal information, written (unnormalized) as

$$\psi_{\mathcal{S}}(x) = \sum_{a=1}^M e^{-\frac{\|x - m_a\|^2}{2\sigma^2} + i\frac{\nu_a^T(x - m_a)}{\lambda}}. \tag{1}$$

λ controls the frequency of the wave: the lower the value of λ the higher the spatial frequency. The wave oscillates along the normal near a point feature but integrates information from different wavefronts in the far field (near and far are a function of σ, λ). The squared magnitude of $\psi(x)$ encodes probability density information. Zero level-sets of the phase now carry *shape geometry* information.

The mixture in (1) has similarities to the Gabor filter or wavelet—well known to vision researchers and mathematicians [46–48]. This allows us to leverage the mathematical literature to prove useful properties of this representation, such as proof of injectivity below which follows a similar argument for a related Gabor system [48]. Gabor systems are families of *time-frequency* translates of an admissible function. The use of Gabor wavelets for function approximation has been studied in the past [46,47], but the connection linking the phase of a square-root density estimator to signed distance functions (and static Hamilton-Jacobi equations [49]) is subtle and less well-known.

In contrast to the unsigned distance function, the signed distance is smooth across shape boundaries (providing a reconstruction) with the sign of the distance indicating whether a location is inside or outside the shape. When we fit Parzen window density estimators to a point-set, we can obtain an approximate unsigned distance function at every point. The relation $G(x) \approx C_R e^{-\frac{R^2(x)}{2\sigma^2}}$ holds (with C_R being a normalization constant), where the approximate unsigned distance function $R(x)$ approaches the true distance pointwise as σ decreases toward zero [50].

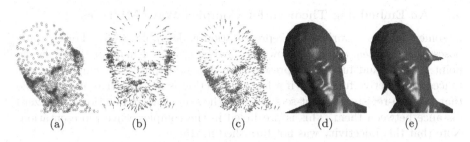

(a)   (b)   (c)   (d)   (e)

Fig. 1. An example of **surface reconstruction** by RDM. (a) and (b) are the inputs to RDM, the points in (a) are the target and the oriented point-set in (b) is the template. (c) shows the estimated normal vectors from *RDM* and the true normal vectors. 99 % of the normal vectors are recovered to within $\pi/4$ angular error. (d) shows the reconstructed surface (the zero level set of the phase of ψ) from the true normal vectors and (e) the reconstructed surface from RDM. The protrusions from the ears are due to mis-oriented normals in the high curvature area near the ear lobe.

For oriented point-sets the relation is

$$\psi_S(x) \approx \Psi_S = e^{-\frac{b_S^2(x)}{2\sigma^2} + i\frac{b_S(x)}{\lambda}} \tag{2}$$

where $b_S(x)$ is the SDF. For a fixed S, the approximation becomes more accurate as $\sigma, \lambda \to 0$. Note that the magnitude is agnostic to the sign of the distance whereas the phase carries the sign but is modular due to the wrapped nature of the phase. We refer to this as a ***modular distance function*** since phase unwrapping is required to obtain a global SDF. Note that *we do not require or use phase unwrapping* in this paper. Two key advantages to using the modular distance function in lieu of the signed distance function are: (i) the modulus decays as we approach the far-field, handling the far-field issue mentioned above, (ii) Equation (2) allows us to derive distances in closed form.

3.1 Relationship Between Signed Distances and Complex Wave Mixtures

To solidify the claim made in Eq. (2), first note that $||\Psi_S||^2 < \infty$. $|\Psi_S(x)|^2 = |\exp\{-\frac{b_S^2(x)}{2\sigma^2} + ib_S(x)/\lambda\}|^2$ is dominated by its concave envelope $\overline{\Psi}_S$, which has $||\overline{\Psi}_S||^2 \leq \frac{((2\pi\sigma^2)^{d/2}+1)\pi^{d/2}\,\mathrm{diam}(S)^d}{\Gamma(\frac{d}{2}+1)}$, by an application of volumes of revolution. $||\Psi_S|| \geq (2\pi\sigma^2)^{d/2}$ as $d(x,p) > d(x,S)$ for all $p \in S$.

Then, note that as $\sigma \to 0$ that $\langle\exp\{-\frac{||x-m||^2}{2\sigma^2} + i\frac{v^T(x-m)}{\lambda}\}, \Psi^{\sigma,\lambda}\rangle \to 0$ whenever $m \notin \partial S$. And as $\lambda \to 0$ destructive interference causes $\langle\exp\{-\frac{||x-m||^2}{2\sigma^2} + i\frac{v^T(x-m)}{\lambda}\}, \Psi^{\sigma,\lambda}\rangle \to 0$ by an application of the stationary phase expansion [51]. This means that as σ, λ shrink, the only significant coefficients of the Gabor Transform of Ψ_S come from atoms centered on the boundary, oriented in the outward normal direction. More evidence supporting the substitution of the signed distance by the complex wave mixture is provided in Sect. 4.2.

3.2   An Embedding Theorem for Complex Wave Mixtures

In some contexts, invariance of representation is desirable [36,37]. For the purposes of *deformable matching*, however, having a $1-$to-1 mapping between the point features and function representation is a prerequisite for employing distances as objective functions: if a feature function is not injective, it is possible that two non-registered point-sets result in the same feature functions, with zero distance between them. This is precluded in the complex wave representation. Note that this injectivity was not furnished in [15].

Theorem 1. ψ. *is an injective map from finite sets of oriented points to* L^2. *Any metric on* L^2 *distinguishes oriented point sets under this representation.*

Proof. Let $\mathcal{A} = \{(m_a, \nu_a)\}_{a=1}^{A}, \mathcal{B} = \{(q_b, \omega_b)\}_{b=1}^{B}$ be distinct oriented point-sets. We will show that $\psi_{\mathcal{A}} - \psi_{\mathcal{B}}$ is not identically zero. Suppose that m_1 (a location in $\mathcal{A}$, with index 1 by reordering) is on the convex hull of $K = \{m_a\}_{a=1}^{A} \cup \{q_b\}_{b=1}^{B}$. Without loss of generality assume $m_1 = 0$. Let $\mathcal{C} = \mathcal{A} \cup \mathcal{B} \setminus (m_1, \nu_1)$. Then

$$\psi_{\mathcal{A}} - \psi_{\mathcal{B}} = \exp\{-\frac{||x||^2}{2\sigma^2}\} \left(\exp\{i\frac{\nu_1^T x}{\lambda}\} + \sum_{(r,\gamma)\in\mathcal{C}} h_{(r,\gamma)}(x) \exp\{\frac{x^T r}{\sigma^2}\} \right) \quad (3)$$

where each $h_{(r,\gamma)} = [-1]^{(r,\gamma)\in\mathcal{B}} \exp\{-\frac{||r||^2}{2\sigma^2} + i\frac{\gamma^T(x-r)}{\lambda}\}$. Since m_1 is on the convex hull, there is a ray $\{\kappa p\}_{\kappa>0}$ in the Voronoi cell of m_1 (relative to K). So there is a κ sufficiently large, so that $\left| \sum_{(r,\gamma)\in\mathcal{A}\cup\mathcal{B}\setminus\{m_1,\nu_1\}} h_{(r,\gamma)}(x) \exp\{\frac{\kappa p^T r}{\sigma^2}\} \right| < \epsilon/2$, so $|\psi_{\mathcal{A}}(\kappa p) - \psi_{\mathcal{B}}(\kappa p)|^2 > \exp\{-||\frac{\kappa p}{\sigma}||^2\}(1-\epsilon) > 0$. If an oriented point-set has multiple oriented points with the same location (but distinct normals at these oriented points) we can use the injectivity of the Fourier Transform [52] to show that the sum of trigonometric polynomials (for the duplicated locations) is nonvanishing. Thus, the above argument holds even in that case. If d is a metric on L^2 it is nonzero on distinct functions, distinguishing oriented point-sets. □

4   Complex Wave Registration and Normal Estimation

In registration, we seek a transformation of the template objects onto the target objects. We denote the transformation of the positions as $\{\phi(m_a)\}_{a=1}^{M}$ where $\phi \in \mathcal{H}$ is an element of the set of non-rigid transformations (assumed to be from the thin-plate spline family in the experiments). We depart from standard registration techniques as in our case the transformation of not only the template centers $\{m_a\}_{a=1}^{M}$, but also the template normals $\{\nu_a\}_{a=1}^{M}$, is carried out under the action of ϕ. The appropriate transformation is the Jacobian, ϕ', of the deformation ϕ. Note that $\phi' : \mathbb{R}^d \to \mathbb{R}^d$ is the derivative of the deformation with respect to the spatial variable, *not the parameters of the deformation*. ϕ acts on (m_a, ν_a) by

$$\phi \cdot (m_a, \nu_a) = (\phi(m_a), \phi'|_{m_a} \nu_a), \quad \text{with} \quad (\phi'|_{m_a})_{i,j} = \frac{\partial \phi^{(i)}}{\partial x_j}\bigg|_{m_a}, \quad (4)$$

and $\phi \cdot \mathcal{S} = \{\phi \cdot (m_a, \nu_a)\}_{a=1}^N$. We can write the transformed template as

$$\psi_{\phi \cdot \mathcal{S}}(x) = \sum_{a=1}^M e^{-\frac{\|x - \phi(m_a)\|^2}{2\sigma^2}} e^{i \frac{(\phi' | m_a \nu_a)^T (x - \phi(m_a))}{\lambda}}. \tag{5}$$

Note that the centers and normals have been transformed via the action of the non-rigid deformation ϕ but the location variable x remains intact. This allows us to define a distance between template and target functions in terms of a feature-space domain integral, which we will minimize w.r.t. ϕ. Note that we actually minimize a regularized version of this distance since large deformations can bring very different point-sets into register. We discuss the specifics of the distance below. First, we address the representational mismatch.

4.1 Introducing Normal Variables for the Target

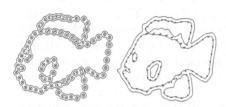

Fig. 2. An example of **curve reconstruction** by RDM. **Left:** The target points are shown in black ×'s, with the level-sets of the unsigned distance function shown as contours. **Right:** After RDM estimates target normal vectors, the level sets of the phase of $\psi_{\mathcal{T}(W)}$ are shown. Abutting point-sets make this particular reconstruction problem difficult, because choosing opposite orientations for nearby points goes against most normal estimation regularizers. See also Sect. 5.2.

Oriented point-set matching assumes an additional feature: normal directions for each point of the *template* and the *target*. *Template normals* are estimated offline: a standard approach to estimation involves the fitting of curves and surfaces to the template features followed by a sampling of the curves (or surfaces) into an oriented point-set. We assume template curves (surfaces) do not self-intersect in order to preserve normal uniqueness. This leaves the target normals. To recover a reconstruction of the surface underlying the target point-set, we augment the objective with variables for the target normals $W = \{\omega_i\}_{i=1}^N$.

This normal estimation component has **no counterpart** in the density matching literature. Adding these parameters does not increase overfitting of ϕ, since the parameterization of ϕ is independent of the normals. We discuss the effect of this simultaneous fitting and estimating below.

To summarize, first we assume that we are in possession of an oriented template point-set $\mathcal{S}$. This template point-set is deformed onto an un-oriented (and un-organized) target point-set $\mathcal{T}$ via the action of a non-rigid deformation minimizing (8). Since the target point-set is un-organized, we estimate a set of target normals at each point during the matching process, thereby obtaining an oriented target point-set denoted $\mathcal{T}(W) = \{(q_i, \omega_i)\}_{i=1}^N$. This simultaneous matching and reconstruction approach is enabled by a closed-form distance measure between template and target complex wave mixtures.

4.2   Choosing a Suitable Distance Function

Minimizing $D(\psi_{\phi \cdot S}, \psi_{T(W)})$ w.r.t. ϕ and W is a difficult optimization problem regardless of the choice of D—symmetries and local minima stand in the way. In the literature, we have seen different choices (geodesic distance on S^∞ [23], Cauchy-Schwarz [3], Kullback-Leibler [53]) as well as different choices for the Parzen kernel (Gaussian [2], Schrödinger [50]). This cross product space of distances, kernels and algorithms is an active area of research.

We use the L^2 distance. The L^2 distance for density function registration was studied in [2] as a specialization of the density power divergence [54]. It strikes a balance between robustness to sampling and computability. L^2 is robust to small Gaussian perturbations in the location parameters: $\mathbb{E}_{\boldsymbol{\delta}} \left[||\psi_S - \psi_{S+\boldsymbol{\delta}}||^2 \right] \to 0$ as $\text{var}(\boldsymbol{\delta}) \to 0$ by Fubini's theorem [52]. While behavior under resampling is harder to examine theoretically, a certain amount of robustness is borne out in Sect. 5.2. Now, note that if $||\psi_S - \psi_T||^2 < \epsilon$ then $||\psi_S/C_S - \psi_T/C_T||^2 < \epsilon'$ (C_S, C_T are normalization constants), and so $1 - \epsilon'/2 < |\langle \psi_S/C_S, \psi_T/C_T \rangle|$. Continuing the line of reasoning in Sect. 3.1, if we pass to the normalized versions of Ψ_S and Ψ_T then we see that the signed distances b_S and b_T must be approximately aligned in the near field (of S and T). Otherwise, destructive interference would cause cancellations in the product field, decreasing the correlation.

We evaluate the squared L_2 distance between the deformed template and target complex wave mixtures, subsequently minimized w.r.t. the unknown matching and normal parameters. The action of the spatial non-rigid deformation results in deformed template points *and* normals. Contrast this to the typical density matching situation in which only the template points are deformed. The squared L_2 distance between the deformed template $\psi_{\phi \cdot S}$ and target $\psi_{T(W)}$, $D(\psi_{\phi \cdot S}, \psi_{T(W)})$, is given by

$$\int_{\mathbb{R}^D} |\sum_{a=1}^{M} e^{-\frac{||x - \phi(m_a)||^2}{2\sigma^2} + i\frac{\phi \cdot \nu_a^T (x - \phi(m_a))}{\lambda}} - \sum_{b=1}^{N} e^{-\frac{||x - q_b||^2}{2\sigma^2} + i\frac{\omega_b^T (x - q_b)}{\lambda}}|^2 dx \qquad (6)$$

where the target wave mixture has been specified for the oriented point-set $T(W) = \{(q_b, \omega_b)\}_{b=1}^{N}$. Note that their cardinalities M and N can differ. When evaluating the L_2 distance, we are required to determine the inner product between terms which may differ in their location and frequency (with common scale and frequency parameters σ and λ respectively).

The inner product, denoted $I_{(m,\nu)}^{(q,\omega)} = \langle \psi_{(m,\nu)}, \psi_{(q,\omega)} \rangle$, is given by the integral

$$\int_{\mathbb{R}^D} e^{\frac{-||x-m||^2 - ||x-q||^2}{2\sigma^2} + i\frac{\nu^T (x-m) - \omega^T (x-q)}{\lambda}} dx = \frac{e^{-\frac{||m-q||^2}{4\sigma^2} - \frac{\sigma^2 ||\nu-\omega||^2}{4\lambda^2} + i\frac{(\nu+\omega)^T (m-q)}{2\lambda}}}{(2\pi\sigma^2)^{\frac{D}{2}}}.$$
$$(7)$$

If $m = q$, then the spatial term goes to 1 and weights the Gaussian corresponding to the frequency term heavily. If $m \approx q + \delta\omega^\perp$ this weighting is dampened, but we obtain constructive interference provided the normals ν and ω are aligned. When the normals are not aligned, we get destructive interference. This can either force the normal estimates in line with the template or influence the template movement, and prevent unnecessary local rotation of the template normals.

The objective function minimized in this work is therefore

$$\mathcal{E}(\phi, W) = D(\psi_{\phi \cdot S}, \psi_{T(W)}) + \beta L(\phi). \tag{8}$$

In (8), ϕ and W are the desired spatial deformation and target normal set respectively. Additionally, β is a regularization parameter and L a suitable spline regularization (chosen to be the thin plate spline bending energy). Assuming a set of fixed centers $\{p_b\}_{b=1}^{P}$ on the template, the thin plate spline [4] maps the location $x \in \mathbb{R}^D$ to the location $A(x) + \sum_{b=1}^{P} \mathbf{C}_b^T K(x - p_b)$ where A is an affine transformation, K is the thin-plate spline kernel and $\{\mathbf{C}_b\}_{b=1}^{P}$ is the set of spline parameters. The mapping is linear in each $\mathbf{C}_b$ and A and therefore so is ϕ'. The regularization term in (8) becomes $\beta \operatorname{tr} (\mathbf{C}^T \mathbf{KC})$ where $\mathbf{C}$ is the $P \times D$ matrix of spline coefficients, and $\mathbf{K}_{ij} = K(p_i - p_j)$ is the Gram matrix of the set of control points.

We can characterize the asymptotic behavior of our matching objective. Examining the wave mixture, we see that the wave flattens out as $\lambda \to \infty$— eventually approaching 1. This intuitively results in the Gabor tending to the Gaussian. This is made more precise in the following Proposition, essentially a consequence of the dominated convergence theorem [52].

Proposition 1. *Let* $\{m_a, \nu_a\}_{a=1}^{M}$, $\{q_b, \omega_b\}_{b=1}^{N}$ *be a pair of oriented point-sets. As* $\lambda \to \infty$ *the objective function* (6) *converges to*

$$\int_{\mathbb{R}^D} |\sum_{a=1}^{M} e^{-\frac{\|x - m_a\|^2}{2\sigma^2}} - \sum_{i=1}^{N} e^{-\frac{\|x - \phi \cdot q_i\|^2}{2\sigma^2}}|^2 dx. \tag{9}$$

with $\phi \cdot$ *acting by restriction to the first coordinate of Eq.* (4).

4.3   Gradient Computation and Optimization Details

We derive the gradient for the TPS parameterization discussed above. The penalty term is easy to differentiate with respect to $\mathbf{C}$:

$$\partial_{\mathbf{C}} \beta \operatorname{tr} \mathbf{C}^T \mathbf{KC} = 2\beta \mathbf{KC} \tag{10}$$

by differentiating the trace and using the symmetry of $\mathbf{K}$. The derivative of the inner product with respect to the parameters $\mathbf{C}$ is

$$\partial_{\mathbf{C}} I_{(q,\omega)}^{\phi_{\mathbf{C}} \cdot (m,\nu)} = \partial_{\phi_{\mathbf{C}}(m)} I_{(q,\omega)}^{\phi_{\mathbf{C}} \cdot (m,\nu)} \frac{\partial \phi_{\mathbf{C}}(m)}{\partial \mathbf{C}} + \partial_{\phi_{\mathbf{C}} \cdot \nu} I_{(q,\omega)}^{\phi_{\mathbf{C}} \cdot (m,\nu)} \frac{\partial [\phi_{\mathbf{C}} \cdot \nu]}{\partial \mathbf{C}}. \tag{11}$$

Recall that $\phi_{\mathbf{C}}$ acts on the normal ν at point m by $\phi_{\mathbf{C}} \cdot \nu = \phi'_{\mathbf{C}}|_m \nu$ [55] where $\phi'_{\mathbf{C}}|_m$ is the Jacobian at m. Note that now $\frac{\partial}{\partial \mathbf{C}} \phi_{\mathbf{C}}$ is the derivative w.r.t. the TPS parameters, *not the spatial variable*. We use ∂. and $\frac{\partial}{\partial}$ interchangeably. Let $\mathbf{R} \in \mathbb{R}^{P \times N}$ be given by $\mathbf{R}_{ij} = K(p_i - m_j)$, the kernel matrix pairing template and control points. Then $\frac{\partial}{\partial \mathbf{C}}[\phi_{\mathbf{C}}(m_j)]^a = \mathbf{R}_j e_a$ (the superscript a indicates the ath coordinate, $e_a \in \mathbb{R}^d$ the ath basis row vector) with $\mathbf{R}_j$ the jth column of $\mathbf{R}$. Differentiating,

$$\frac{\partial[\phi_{\mathbf{C}}(m_j)]^a}{\partial \mathbf{C}} = \mathbf{R}_j e_a, \quad [\frac{\partial I_{(q,\omega)}^{\phi_{\mathbf{C}}\cdot(m,\nu)}}{\partial \phi_{\mathbf{C}}(m)}]^a = \left[-\frac{\phi_{\mathbf{C}}(m) - q}{2\sigma^2} + i\frac{\phi_{\mathbf{C}} \cdot \nu + \omega}{2\lambda}\right]^a I_{(q,\omega)}^{\phi_{\mathbf{C}}\cdot(m,\nu)}.$$
(12)

When applying the entire gradient update (through all points), this is simply an outer product of the derivatives of the inner product and $\mathbf{R}$.

The second term in Eq. (11) is not typically seen in the point matching literature. We must differentiate $\phi'_{\mathbf{C}}|_{m_j}\nu$ with respect to $\mathbf{C}$, where $'$ denotes differentiation with respect to the domain variable. Denote by $[\mathbf{R}']^k$ the matrix of derivatives in the kth coordinate of the kernel function at each point in the template set. Then

$$[\phi'_{\mathbf{C}}|_{m_j}\nu_j]^a = \left[[\mathbf{R}_j']^{a^T}\mathbf{C}\right]\nu_j, \quad \text{and so} \quad \partial_{\mathbf{C}}[\phi'_{\mathbf{C}}|_{m_j}\nu_j]^a = ([\mathbf{R}_j']^a)\nu_j^T,$$

by treating $\mathbf{C}$ as a scalar-valued form acting on $([\mathbf{R}_j']^a, \nu)$. So the second term in Eq. (11) is

$$\frac{\partial I_{(q,\omega)}^{\phi_{\mathbf{C}}(m_j,\nu_j)}}{\partial \mathbf{C}} = I_{(q,\omega)}^{\phi_{\mathbf{C}}(m_j,\nu_j)} \sum_{a=1}^{D} \left(\left[-\sigma^2 \frac{\phi_{\mathbf{C}} \cdot \nu_j - \omega}{2\lambda^2} + i\frac{q - m}{2\lambda}\right]^a [\mathbf{R}_j']^a\right)\nu_j^T. \quad (13)$$

The descent direction for the TPS parameters is given by

$$\nabla_{\mathbf{C}} D = 2 \sum_{i=1}^{M} \sum_{j=1}^{M} \left[\partial_{\phi_{\mathbf{C}}(m_i)} I_{(m_j,\nu_j)}^{\phi_{\mathbf{C}}(m_i,\nu_i)} \frac{\partial \phi_{\mathbf{C}}(m_i)}{\partial \mathbf{C}} + \partial_{\phi_{\mathbf{C}} \cdot \nu_i} I_{(m_j,\nu_j)}^{\phi_{\mathbf{C}}(m_i,\nu_i)} \frac{\partial[\phi_{\mathbf{C}} \cdot \nu_i]}{\partial \mathbf{C}}\right]$$
$$- 2 \sum_{i=1}^{M} \sum_{j=1}^{N} \left[\partial_{\phi_{\mathbf{C}}(m_i)} I_{(q_j,\omega_j)}^{\phi_{\mathbf{C}}(m_i,\nu_i)} \frac{\partial \phi_{\mathbf{C}}(m_i)}{\partial \mathbf{C}} + \partial_{\phi_{\mathbf{C}} \cdot \nu_i} I_{(q_j,\omega_j)}^{\phi_{\mathbf{C}}(m_i,\nu_i)} \frac{\partial[\phi_{\mathbf{C}} \cdot \nu_i]}{\partial \mathbf{C}}\right].$$
(14)

To complete the picture, we return to the principal themes of this work—simultaneous registration and reconstruction. Recall that we began by pointing out that there was a paucity of literature on non-rigid SDF matching in comparison to density matching. We zeroed in on the difficulty of estimating SDFs as the main reason. Rather than estimate an SDF for the target point-set with the aid of a deformed template, we chose to estimate target normals as we deformed the template. To do this, we apply the descent direction for each ω_i in terms of combinations of $\partial_{\omega_i} I_{(q_j,\omega_j)}^{\phi_{\mathbf{C}}(m_i,\nu_i)}$ during each round. Further details of the optimization algorithm are provided below. To obtain the signed distance from these normals one may use previously developed methods (e.g. [20,21]) or use the phase of the resulting wave-function directly (see Figs. 1 and 2). The result is an integrated probability density and SDF approach to simultaneous deformable template matching and multiple curve (or surface) reconstruction.

5   Experiments

We compare with the state of the art in density field matching (such as gmmreg, abbreviated to GMM) [2], generalized function matching (diffeomorphic measure matching abbreviated DIFF) [22], point-based matching (CPD) [27], and graph-matching (FGM-U) [32]. While other methods [10,56] are appropriate for further comparison, handling the asymmetry in representation is not possible in their current formulation. The corresponding results are indicated by the appropriate marker and color combinations (see legend in Fig. 5). We investigate the performance of RDM on a variety of datasets and conditions, outlined below.

Parameter Configuration: The following parameters are used in the experiments below unless explicitly stated otherwise. In all of the following experiments the data sets are scaled to $[0,1]^2$ before matching. We use a common initial scale parameter ($\sigma = .1$ for both GMM and RDM) throughout. Two initializations with decreasing σ values are used for both GMM and RDM (DIFF uses 2 reinitializations). CPD estimates scaled progressively during matching, so no reinitialization is performed. For RDM $\beta = .0075$ for 2d, for GMM $\beta = .01$, for CPD $\beta = 2, \lambda = 2$ (different parameters). For FGM-U Delaunay triangulation was used for graph construction, and 101 iterations at 100 scales were executed for path following. GMM, DIFF, and RDM use MATLAB®'s function fminunc (set to use a quasi-newton solver—BFGS iterations) for optimization. Unless otherwise noted, the error measure is mean Euclidean distance to correspondent.

5.1   Synthetic Normal Recovery, Warps, and Occlusions

This subsection consists of two sets of experiments. First, we compared our algorithm to a pipeline approach to normal estimation:

1. Register a template point-set to a target by an estimated deformation.
2. Let the deformation act on the normal vectors of the template.
3. Use a nearest-neighbor approach to infer normal vectors onto the corresponding points in the target set.

We used GMM as the matching algorithm. A single curve (a body curve consisting of 80 points) from the multi-curve GatorBait dataset was used. For synthetic deformation, a diffeomorphism is fit to point perturbations by solving a 3d flow problem [5]. Therefore relative normal orientations are preserved. The deformation level corresponds to $\sup_{x \in \mathbb{R}^D} ||\phi(x) - x||$ (evaluated on the test points). Results are shown in Fig. 3. In this experiment GMM and RDM only used a single initialization. This experiment shows that a gain in normal recovery is obtained by using RDM instead of imposing template structure *after* matching.

In the second set of experiments, we tested the performance of our algorithm in the 2d and 3d synthetic settings against 4 other methods: CPD, DIFF, FGM-U, and GMM. For 2d we used a point-set consisting of 5 curves (see Fig. 2) from the aforementioned dataset, while for 3d the Stanford bunny and TOSCA datasets were used. We create the target by randomly perturbing points lying along a grid and solving for a TPS with identity affine component. *No information about the target normal vectors is known beforehand.* After registration, the mean distance to the corresponding point, average error, is recorded. For the occlusion trials, an approximate fixed deformation level is used, .3 in norm for 2d and .15 in 3d. Robustness to outliers and noise is also studied. For these experiments FGM-U was run at 50 scales, due to runtime limitations. One can see from Fig. 4 that FGM-U struggles with nonrigid deformation. A plot showing the percentage of recovered normal orientations is included as well.

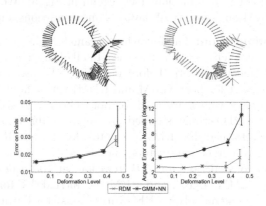

Fig. 3. Top: the *recovered normal vectors* for **GMM+NN** (left) and **RDM** (right) and the True normals (both) are attached at the points. **Bottom:** Average error and the median angle error between corresponding normal vectors for RDM and GMM+NN. 50 trials per level were performed.

5.2 Non-synthetic Matching Experiments

We perform intra-class matching experiments on the TOSCA [57], FAUST [58], and Gatorbait datasets. TOSCA and FAUST represent the 3d performance gauge on real matching experiments. We chose the GatorBait dataset because it has *multiple corresponding parts* which many 2d and 3d point-sets and meshes lack. The same statistic as above—average error to correspondent—is collected for the sets with known correspondence. We present recall (percentage of correct correspondences within a threshold) for matching pose 0 to poses 1, 2, 4, and 5 (smaller deformations) of the FAUST training registrations over all 10 subjects and present comparisons with GMM and CPD. For TOSCA we match the first cat, dog, and gorilla to the remaining poses. We have foregone benchmark comparisons here because in the large deformation regime extrinsic matching is prone to local minima, and we restrict the comparisons to relative performance among other extrinsic matching techniques. We use these datasets as a baseline for comparison with GMM and CPD.

The GatorBait dataset does not have known correspondences. Furthermore, it consists of nearly abutting curves (see Fig. 2)—organizing points into their

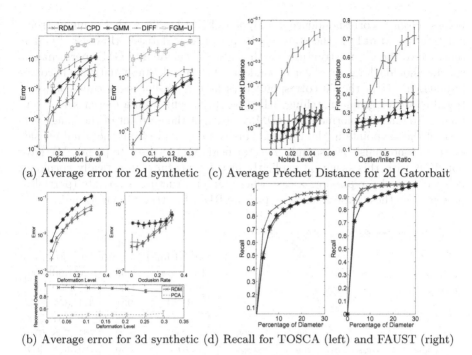

(a) Average error for 2d synthetic (c) Average Fréchet Distance for 2d Gatorbait

(b) Average error for 3d synthetic (d) Recall for TOSCA (left) and FAUST (right)

Fig. 4. Experimental comparison of RDM, GMM, CPD, DIFF, and FGM. (a) The GatorBait Dataset is deformed as explained in Sect. 5.1. The left plot shows robustness to moderate deformation levels and the right plot shows robustness to occlusion (dropping points in a randomly placed disc). (b) The same experiments are carried out in 3d on the Stanford Bunny. We also report the percentage of normal vectors recovered to within a cone of $\pi/3$ radians. (c) The Fréchet distances (sum over the parts) between the registered template and the target curves are reported. On the left the target has added noise of the indicated standard deviation and on the right outliers are added. (d) Recall graphs for a subset (See Sect. 5.2) of TOSCA and FAUST.

appropriate curve components is made much harder by the existence of neighborhood points on different curves. The *Fréchet Distance* [59] between corresponding parts in the final registration and the target is recorded. This allows us to measure how accurately *each part* of the template is matched to the target. The first fish species is used as the template and matched to 23 other species. We also perturb the fish with noise and add outliers as uniformly drawn additional points. See Fig. 4 for results. For large 3d datasets, DIFF and FGM were found to be impractical from a runtime perspective (for a runtime comparison see Fig. 5). For the GatorBait dataset, FGM was not competitive.

5.3 CMU House Dataset

The CMU House dataset consists of a sequence of image frames and keypoints. The task is to perform point-matching and recover correspondences between

points. From a correspondence standpoint, FGM-U [32] with Delaunay triangulation (FGM-del) is the state of the art on this dataset. However, FGM is
sensitive to the graph structure—with 2-nearest neighbors FGM's performance
suffers. Should a large set of correspondences be needed, graph matching becomes
impractical—even the 30 correspondences here represent significant computational effort for graph matching. RDM would benefit from a denser set of keypoints. To initialize normals for RDM, we extract the gradient of the image I at
each of the keypoints in the frames. This is a departure from the usual consideration of 'normals'—we sample a vector field (∇I) at discrete points. We have
not dealt with this situation explicitly in the text, but syntactically speaking,
it is valid. It also represents a case where target structure is already (partially)
present—for these experiments we provide RDM the true target normal.

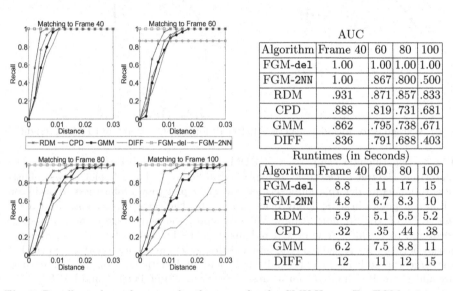

AUC				
Algorithm	Frame 40	60	80	100
FGM-del	1.00	1.00	1.00	1.00
FGM-2NN	1.00	.867	.800	.500
RDM	.931	.871	.857	.833
CPD	.888	.819	.731	.681
GMM	.862	.795	.738	.671
DIFF	.836	.791	.688	.403
Runtimes (in Seconds)				
Algorithm	Frame 40	60	80	100
FGM-del	8.8	11	17	15
FGM-2NN	4.8	6.7	8.3	10
RDM	5.9	5.1	6.5	5.2
CPD	.32	.35	.44	.38
GMM	6.2	7.5	8.8	11
DIFF	12	11	12	15

Fig. 5. Recall graphs and area under the curve for the CMU House. For FGM, triangulation yields excellent matches but nearest-neighbor graphs are poor. All experiments
run on an AMD X2 B22 with 8 Gb of RAM. We report AUC and runtimes in the table.

6   Conclusion and Future Work

Deformable template matching with RDM is done by minimizing the closed form
squared L^2 distance between template and target wave mixtures augmented with
a standard regularization on the spatial transformation (done in practice via
standard nonlinear optimization software implementing quasi-Newton methods).
When only the template normals are available at runtime, they can be estimated
for the target set during the registration. This provides normal estimates.

In this work we proved injectivity of the representation, derived the gradient term for optimization, showed that RDM can outperform standard normal

transfer by registration, and highlighted the registration accuracy of RDM. We plan to extend RDM to the case where neither point-set is accurately oriented and to evaluate the reconstruction accuracy of RDM against other unsupervised and semi-supervised methods in future work. We are also exploring alternative deformation models for the oriented point-set transformation setting.

References

1. Tsin, Y., Kanade, T.: A correlation-based approach to robust point set registration. In: Pajdla, T., Matas, J. (eds.) ECCV 2004. LNCS, vol. 3023, pp. 558–569. Springer, Heidelberg (2004). doi:10.1007/978-3-540-24672-5_44
2. Jian, B., Vemuri, B.C.: Robust point set registration using Gaussian mixture models. IEEE Trans. Pattern Anal. Mach. Intell. (PAMI) 33(8), 1633–1645 (2011)
3. Hasanbelliu, E., Sanchez Giraldo, L., Principe, J.C.: Information theoretic shape matching. IEEE Trans. Pattern Anal. Mach. Intell. (PAMI) 36(12), 2436–2451 (2014)
4. Wahba, G.: Spline Models for Observational Data, vol. 59. SIAM, Philadelphia (1990)
5. Camion, V., Younes, L.: Geodesic interpolating splines. In: Figueiredo, M., Zerubia, J., Jain, A.K. (eds.) EMMCVPR 2001. LNCS, vol. 2134, pp. 513–527. Springer, Heidelberg (2001). doi:10.1007/3-540-44745-8_34
6. Gorelick, L., Galun, M., Sharon, E., Basri, R., Brandt, A.: Shape representation and classification using the Poisson equation. IEEE Trans. Pattern Anal. Mach. Intell. (PAMI) 28(12), 1991–2005 (2006)
7. Charon, N., Trouvé, A.: The varifold representation of nonoriented shapes for diffeomorphic registration. SIAM J. Imaging Sci. 6(4), 2547–2580 (2013)
8. Guler, R., Tari, S., Unal, G.: Screened Poisson hyperfields for shape coding. SIAM J. Imaging Sci. 7(4), 2558–2590 (2014)
9. Osher, S., Sethian, J.A.: Fronts propagating with curvature-dependent speed: algorithms based on Hamilton-Jacobi formulations. J. Comput. Phys. 79(1), 12–49 (1988)
10. Paragios, N., Rousson, M., Ramesh, V.: Non-rigid registration using distance functions. Comput. Vis. Image Underst. (CVIU) 89(2), 142–165 (2003)
11. Osher, S., Fedkiw, R.: Level-Set Methods and Dynamic Implicit Surfaces, vol. 153. Springer Science & Business Media, New York (2006)
12. Sussman, M., Smereka, P., Osher, S.: A level set approach for computing solutions to incompressible two-phase flow. J. Comput. Phys. 114(1), 146–159 (1994)
13. Gomes, J., Faugeras, O.: Reconciling distance functions and level-sets. J. Vis. Commun. Image Represent. 11(2), 209–223 (2000)
14. Estellers, V., Zosso, D., Lai, R., Osher, S., Thiran, J., Bresson, X.: An efficient algorithm for level-set method preserving distance function. IEEE Trans. Image Process. (TIP) 21(12), 4722–4734 (2012)
15. Corring, J., Rangarajan, A.: Shape from phase: an integrated level-set and probability density shape representation. In: International Conference on Pattern Recognition (ICPR), IAPR, pp. 46–51 (2014)
16. Hoppe, H., DeRose, T., Duchamp, T., McDonald, J., Stuetzle, W.: Surface reconstruction from unorganized points. Spec. Interest Group Graph. Interact. Techn. (SIGGRAPH) 26(2), 71–78 (1992)

17. Edelsbrunner, H.: Shape reconstruction with Delaunay complex. In: Lucchesi, C.L., Moura, A.V. (eds.) LATIN 1998. LNCS, vol. 1380, pp. 119–132. Springer, Heidelberg (1998). doi:10.1007/BFb0054315

18. Zhao, H.K., Osher, S., Merriman, B., Kang, M.: Implicit and nonparametric shape reconstruction from unorganized data using a variational level-set method. Comput. Vis. Image Underst. (CVIU) **80**(3), 295–314 (2000)

19. Mullen, P., de Goes, F., Desbrun, M., Cohen-Steiner, D., Alliez, P.: Signing the unsigned: Robust surface reconstruction from raw pointsets. Comput. Graph. Forum **29**(5), 1733–1741 (2010)

20. Kazhdan, M., Bolitho, M., Hoppe, H.: Poisson surface reconstruction. Proceedings of the Fourth Eurographics Symposium on Geometry Processing (SGP), vol. 7, pp. 61–70 (2006)

21. Manson, J., Petrova, G., Schaefer, S.: Streaming surface reconstruction using wavelets. Comput. Graph. Forum **27**(5), 1411–1420 (2008)

22. Glaunes, J., Trouvé, A., Younes, L.: Diffeomorphic matching of distributions: A new approach for unlabelled point-sets and sub-manifolds matching. In: IEEE Conference on Computer Vision and Pattern Recognition (CVPR), vol. 2, pp. 712–718. IEEE (2004)

23. Deng, Y., Rangarajan, A., Eisenschenk, S., Vemuri, B.C.: A Riemannian framework for matching point clouds represented by the Schrödinger distance transform. In: IEEE Conference on Computer Vision and Pattern Recognition (CVPR), pp. 3756–3761. IEEE (2014)

24. Huang, X., Paragios, N., Metaxas, D.N.: Shape registration in implicit spaces using information theory and free form deformations. IEEE Trans. Pattern Anal. Mach. Intell. (PAMI) **28**(8), 1303–1318 (2006)

25. Leventon, M.E., Grimson, W.E.L., Faugeras, O.: Statistical shape influence in geodesic active contours. In: IEEE Conference on Computer Vision and Pattern Recognition (CVPR), pp. 316–323. IEEE (2000)

26. Rousson, M., Paragios, N.: Shape priors for level set representations. In: Heyden, A., Sparr, G., Nielsen, M., Johansen, P. (eds.) ECCV 2002. LNCS, vol. 2351, pp. 78–92. Springer, Heidelberg (2002). doi:10.1007/3-540-47967-8_6

27. Myronenko, A., Song, X.: Point set registration: coherent point drift. IEEE Trans. Pattern Anal. Mach. Intell. (PAMI) **32**(12), 2262–2275 (2010)

28. Chui, H., Rangarajan, A.: A new point matching algorithm for non-rigid registration. Comput. Vis. Image Underst. (CVIU) **89**(2), 114–141 (2003)

29. Zheng, Y., Doermann, D.: Robust point matching for non-rigid shapes by preserving local neighborhood structures. IEEE Trans. Pattern Anal. Mach. Intell. (PAMI) **28**(4), 643–649 (2006)

30. Gold, S., Rangarajan, A.: A graduated assignment algorithm for graph matching. IEEE Trans. Pattern Anal. Mach. Intell. (PAMI) **18**(4), 377–388 (1996)

31. Zhou, F., de la Torre, F.: Factorized graph matching. In: IEEE Conference on Computer Vision and Pattern Recognition (CVPR), pp. 127–134. IEEE (2012)

32. Zhou, F., de la Torre, F.: Deformable graph matching. In: IEEE Conference on Computer Vision and Pattern Recognition (CVPR), pp. 2922–2929. IEEE (2013)

33. Kezurer, I., Kovalsky, S.Z., Basri, R., Lipman, Y.: Tight relaxation of quadratic matching. Comput. Graph. Forum **34**(5), 115–128 (2015)

34. Schmidt, F.R., Farin, D., Cremers, D.: Fast matching of planar shapes in sub-cubic runtime. In: IEEE International Conference on Computer Vision (ICCV), pp. 1–6. IEEE (2007)

35. Lévy, B.: Laplace-Beltrami eigenfunctions: towards an algorithm that "understands" geometry. In: IEEE International Conference on Shape Modeling and Applications, pp. 13–21. IEEE (2006)
36. Kovnatsky, A., Bronstein, M.M., Bronstein, A.M., Glashoff, K., Kimmel, R.: Coupled quasi-harmonic bases. Comput. Graph. Forum **32**(2), 439–448 (2013)
37. Ovsjanikov, M., Ben-Chen, M., Solomon, J., Butscher, A., Guibas, L.: Functional maps: a flexible representation of maps between shapes. ACM Trans. Graph. (TOG) **31**(4), 30:1–30:11 (2012)
38. Guy, G., Medioni, G.: Inferring global perceptual contours from local features. In: IEEE Conference on Computer Vision and Pattern Recognition (CVPR), pp. 786–787. IEEE (1993)
39. Mordohai, P., Medioni, G.: Tensor voting: a perceptual organization approach to computer vision and machine learning. Synth. Lect. Image Video Multimedia Process. **2**(1), 1–136 (2006)
40. Boyer, K.L., Sarkar, S.: Perceptual Organization for Artificial Vision Systems. vol. 546. Springer Science & Business Media (2012)
41. Pauly, M., Gross, M.H., Kobbelt, L.: Efficient simplification of point-sampled surfaces. In: IEEE Visualization, pp. 163–170 (2002)
42. Zelnik-Manor, L., Perona, P.: Self-tuning spectral clustering. In: Advances in Neural Information Processing Systems (NIPS), pp. 1601–1608 (2004)
43. Kimia, B.B., Tannenbaum, A.R., Zucker, S.W.: Shapes, shocks, and deformations I: the components of two-dimensional shape and the reaction-diffusion space. Int. J. Comput. Vis. (IJCV) **15**(3), 189–224 (1995)
44. Mjolsness, E., Gindi, G., Anandan, P.: Optimization in model matching and perceptual organization. Neural Comput. **1**(2), 218–229 (1989)
45. Cho, M., Lee, K.M.: Progressive graph matching: Making a move of graphs via probabilistic voting. In: IEEE Conference on Computer Vision and Pattern Recognition (CVPR), pp. 398–405. IEEE (2012)
46. Daubechies, I.: The wavelet transform, time-frequency localization and signal analysis. IEEE Trans. Inf. Theory (IT) **36**(5), 961–1005 (1990)
47. Lee, T.S.: Image representation using 2D Gabor wavelets. IEEE Trans. Pattern Anal. Mach. Intell. (PAMI) **18**(10), 959–971 (1996)
48. Heil, C., Ramanathan, J., Topiwala, P.: Linear independence of time-frequency translates. Proc. Am. Math. Soc. (AMS) **124**(9), 2787–2795 (1996)
49. Aubert, G., Kornprobst, P.: Mathematical Problems in Image Processing: Partial Differential Equations and the Calculus of Variations. Applied Mathematical Sciences, vol. 147. Springer (2006)
50. Sethi, M., Rangarajan, A., Gurumoorthy, K.: The Schrödinger distance transform (SDT) for point-sets and curves. In: IEEE Conference on Computer Vision and Pattern Recognition (CVPR), pp. 198–205. IEEE (2012)
51. Wong, R.: Asymptotic Approximations of Integrals. Society for Industrial and Applied Mathematics (2001)
52. Folland, G.B.: Real analysis, 2nd edn. Pure and Applied Mathematics (New York). John Wiley & Sons Inc., New York (1999). Modern techniques and their applications, A Wiley-Interscience Publication
53. Wang, Y., Woods, K., McClain, M.: Information-theoretic matching of two point sets. IEEE Trans. Image Process. (TIP) **11**(8), 868–872 (2002)
54. Basu, A., Harris, I.R., Hjort, N.L., Jones, M.: Robust and efficient estimation by minimising a density power divergence. Biometrika **85**(3), 549–559 (1998)
55. Spivak, M.: A comprehensive introduction to differential geometry, 3rd edn, vol. 1–5. Publish or Perish (1999)

56. Siddiqi, K., Shokoufandeh, A., Dickinson, S.J., Zucker, S.W.: Shock graphs and shape matching. Int. J. Comput. Vis. (IJCV) **35**(1), 13–32 (1999)
57. Bronstein, A.M., Bronstein, M.M., Kimmel, R.: Numerical Geometry of Non-Rigid Shapes. Monographs in Computer Science. Springer (2009)
58. Bogo, F., Romero, J., Loper, M., Black, M.J.: FAUST: Dataset and evaluation for 3D mesh registration. In: IEEE Conference on Computer Vision and Pattern Recognition (CVPR), pp. 3794–3801. IEEE, June 2014
59. Veltkamp, R.C.: Shape matching: similarity measures and algorithms. In: IEEE International Conference on Shape Modeling and Applications (SMI), pp. 188–197. IEEE (2001)

Unsupervised Learning of Visual Representations by Solving Jigsaw Puzzles

Mehdi Noroozi$^{(\boxtimes)}$ and Paolo Favaro

Institute of Informatics, University of Bern, Bern, Switzerland
{noroozi,paolo.favaro}@inf.unibe.ch

Abstract. We propose a novel unsupervised learning approach to build features suitable for object detection and classification. The features are pre-trained on a large dataset without human annotation and later transferred via fine-tuning on a different, smaller and labeled dataset. The pre-training consists of solving jigsaw puzzles of natural images. To facilitate the transfer of features to other tasks, we introduce the *context-free network* (CFN), a siamese-ennead convolutional neural network. The features correspond to the columns of the CFN and they process image tiles independently (i.e., free of context). The later layers of the CFN then use the features to identify their geometric arrangement. Our experimental evaluations show that the learned features capture semantically relevant content. We pre-train the CFN on the training set of the ILSVRC2012 dataset and transfer the features on the combined training and validation set of Pascal VOC 2007 for object detection (via fast RCNN) and classification. These features outperform all current unsupervised features with 51.8 % for detection and 68.6 % for classification, and reduce the gap with supervised learning (56.5 % and 78.2 % respectively).

Keywords: Unsupervised learning · Image representation learning · Self-supervised learning · Feature transfer

1 Introduction

Visual tasks, such as object classification and detection, have been successfully approached through the supervised learning paradigm [1,10,23,33], where one uses labeled data to train a parametric model. However, as manually labeled data can be costly, unsupervised learning methods are gaining momentum.

Recently, Doersch *et al.* [9], Wang and Gupta [36] and Agrawal *et al.* [2] have explored a novel paradigm for unsupervised learning called *self-supervised learning*. The main idea is to exploit different labelings that are freely available besides or within visual data, and to use them as intrinsic reward signals to learn general-purpose features. [9] uses the relative spatial co-location of patches in images as a label. [36] uses object correspondence obtained through tracking in videos, and [2] uses ego-motion information obtained by a mobile agent such as the Google car [7]. The features obtained with these approaches have been successfully transferred to classification and detections tasks, and their performance is very encouraging when compared to features trained in a supervised manner.

© Springer International Publishing AG 2016
B. Leibe et al. (Eds.): ECCV 2016, Part VI, LNCS 9910, pp. 69–84, 2016.
DOI: 10.1007/978-3-319-46466-4_5

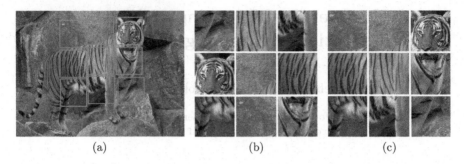

(a)   (b)   (c)

Fig. 1. Learning image representations by solving jigsaw puzzles. (a) The image from which the tiles (marked with green lines) are extracted. (b) A puzzle obtained by shuffling the tiles. Some tiles might be directly identifiable as object parts, but others are ambiguous (*e.g.*, have similar patterns or belong to the background) and their localization is much more reliable when all tiles are jointly evaluated. In contrast, with reference to (c), determining the relative position between the central tile and the top two tiles from the left can be very challenging [9]. (Color figure online)

A fundamental difference between [9] and [2,36] is that the former method uses single images as the training set and the other two methods exploit multiple images related either through a temporal or a viewpoint transformation. While it is true that biological agents typically make use of multiple images and also integrate additional sensory information, such as ego-motion, it is also true that single snapshots may carry more information than we have been able to extract so far. This work shows that this is indeed the case. We introduce a novel self-supervised task, the *jigsaw puzzle reassembly* problem (see Fig. 1), which builds features that yield high performance when transferred to detection and classification tasks.

We argue that solving jigsaw puzzles can be used to teach a system that an object is made of parts and what these parts are. The association of each separate puzze tile to a precise object part might be ambiguous. However, when all the tiles are observed, the ambiguities might be eliminated more easily because the tile placement is mutually exclusive. This argument is supported by our experimental validation. Training a jigsaw puzzle solver takes about 2.5 days compared to 4 weeks of [9]. Also, there is no need to handle chromatic aberration or to build robustness to pixelation. Moreover, the features are highly transferrable to detection and classification and yield the highest performance to date for an unsupervised method. In object classification these features lead to the best accuracy (38.1 %) when compared to other existing features trained via self-supervised learning on the ILSVRC2012 dataset [8]. Moreover, these features used as pre-training in the Fast R-CNN pipeline [14] achieve 51.8 % mAP for detection and 68.6 % for classification on PASCAL VOC 2007. This performance is close to that obtained in the supervised case by AlexNet [23] (56.5 % mAP for detection and 78.2 % in classification).

2   Related Work

This work falls in the area of *representation/feature learning*, which is an unsupervised learning problem [3]. Representation learning is concerned with building intermediate representations of data useful to solve machine learning tasks. It also involves *transfer learning* [37], as one repurposes features that have been learned by solving the jigsaw puzzle to other tasks such as object classification and detection. In our experiments we do so via the *pre-training + fine-tuning* scheme, as in prior work [2]. Pre-training corresponds to the feature learning that we obtain with our jigsaw puzzle solver. Fine-tuning is instead the process of updating the weights obtained during pre-training to solve another task (object classification or detection).

Unsupervised Learning. There is a rich literature in unsupervised learning of visual representations [5]. Most techniques build representations by exploiting general-purpose priors such as smoothness, sharing of factors, factors organized hierarchically, belonging to a low-dimension manifold, temporal and spatial coherence, and sparsity. In this work we represent objects as a collection of parts (tiles) and design features to separate two factors: appearance and arrangement (geometry) of the parts.

Because of the relevance to contemporary research and to this work, we discuss mainly methods in deep learning. In general one can group unsupervised learning methods into: probabilistic, direct mapping (autoencoders), and manifold learning ones. Probabilistic methods divide variables of a network into observed and latent ones. Learning is then associated with determining model parameters that maximize the likelihood of the latent variables given the observations. A family of popular probabilistic models is the *Restricted Boltzmann Machine* (RBM) [16,34], which makes training tractable by imposing a bipartite graph between latent and observed variables. Unfortunately, these models become intractable when multiple layers are present and are not designed to produce features in an efficient manner. The direct mapping approach focuses on the latter aspect and is typically built via *autoencoders* [6,17,26]. Autoencoders specify explicitly the feature extraction function (encoder) in a parametric form as well as the mapping from the feature back to the input (decoder). These direct mappings are trained by minimizing the reconstruction error between the input and the output produced by the autoencoder (obtained by applying the encoder and decoder sequentially). A remarkable example of a very large scale autoencoder is the work of Le *et al.* [24]. Their results showed that robust human and cat faces as well as human body detectors could be built without human labeling.

If the data structure suggests that data points might concentrate around a manifold, then *manifold learning* techniques can be employed [4,31]. This representation allows to map directly smooth variations of the factors to smooth variations of the observations. Some of the issues with manifold learning techniques are that they might require computing nearest neighbors (which scales quadratically with the number of samples) and that they need a sufficiently high density of samples around the manifold (and this becomes more difficult to achieve with high-dimensional manifolds).

Self-supervised Learning. This learning strategy is a recent variation on the unsupervised learning theme that exploits labeling that comes for "free" with the data [2,9,36]. We make a distinction between labels that are easily accessible and are associated with a non-visual signal (for example, ego-motion [2], but also one could consider audio, text and so on), and labels that are obtained from the structure of the data [9,36]. Our work relates to the latter case as we simply re-use the input images and exploit the pixel arrangement as a label.

Doersch *et al.* [9] train a convolutional network to classify the relative position between two image patches. One tile is kept in the middle of a 3×3 grid and the other tile can be placed in any of the other 8 available locations (up to some small random shift). In Fig. 1(c) we show an example where the relative location between the central tile and the top-left and top-middle tiles is ambiguous. In contrast, the jigsaw puzzle problem is solved by observing all the tiles at the same time. This allows the trained network to intersect all ambiguity sets and possibly reduce them to a singleton.

The method of Wang and Gupta [36] builds a metric to define similarity between patches. Three patches are used as input, where two patches are matched via tracking in a video and the third one is arbitrarily chosen. The main advantage of this method is that labeling requires just using a tracking method (they use SURF interest points to detect initial bounding boxes and then tracking via the KCF method [15]). The matched patches will have some intraclass variability due to changes in illumination, occlusion, viewpoint, pose, occlusions, and clutter factors. However, the choice of the third frame is crucial to learn non trivial features. If the third frame is too easily distinguishable (e.g., the color histogram is different) then the features might learn a simple shortcut.

The method proposed by Agrawal *et al.* [2] exploits labeling (egomotion) provided by other sensors. The advantage is that this labeling is freely available in most cases or is quite easy to obtain. They show that egomotion is a useful supervisory signal when learning features. They train a siamese network to estimate egomotion from two image frames and compare it to the egomotion measured with odometry sensors. The trained features will build an invariance similar to that of Wang and Gupta [36]. However, because the task is to determine egomotion, the learned features may need to exploit correspondence across the two input frames and thus may focus on their similarities (such as color and texture), which might not generalize well to a category. In contrast, the jigsaw puzzle approach ignores similarities between tiles (such as color and texture), as they do not help their localization, and focuses instead on their differences. In Fig. 2 we illustrate this concept with two examples: Two cars that have different colors and two dogs with different fur patterns. The features learned to solve puzzles in one (car/dog) image will apply also to the other (car/dog) image as they will be invariant to patterns shared across parts. The ability of the jigsaw puzzle solver to cluster together object parts can be seen in the top 16 activations shown in Fig. 4 and in the image retrieval samples in Fig. 5.

Fig. 2. Most of the shape of these 2 pairs of images is the same (two separate instances within the same categories). However, some low-level statistics are different (color and texture). The jigsaw puzzle solver learns to ignore such statistics when they do not help the localization of parts. (Color figure online)

Jigsaw Puzzles. Jigsaw puzzles have been associated with learning since their inception. They were introduced in 1760 by John Spilsbury as a pretext to help children learn geography. The first puzzle was a map attached to a wooden board, which was then sawed in pieces corresponding to countries [35]. Studies in Psychonomic show that jigsaw puzzles can be used to assess visuospatial processing in humans [30]. Indeed, the *Hooper Visual Organization Test* [18] is routinely used to measure an individual's ability to organize visual stimuli. This test uses puzzles with line drawings of simple objects and requires the patient to recognize the object without moving the tiles. Instead of using jigsaw puzzles to assess someone's visuospatial processing ability, in this paper we propose to use jigsaw puzzles to develop a visuospatial representation of objects.

There is also a sizeable literature on solving jigsaw puzzles computationally (see, for example, [12, 28, 29]). However, these methods rely on the shape of the tiles or on texture especially in the proximity of the borders of the tiles. These are cues that we avoid when training the jigsaw puzzle solver, as they do not carry information that can generalize well to a part detector.

Recently, a new data initialization technique for training convolutional neural networks by Krähenbühl *et al.* [22] has been applied to [2,9,36] with a remarkable increase in performance for object detection on PASCAL VOC 2007. The performance of the method of Doersch *et al.* [9] gains considerably with this data initialization method, and goes from 46.6 % mAP to 51.1 % mAP, which however is still below our 51.8 % mAP performance. Moreover, our training time is quite low: [9] takes 4 weeks while our method takes only 2.5 days (for completeness, [36] takes 1 week and [2] takes 10 h).

3   Solving Jigsaw Puzzles

In the following sections we describe how we cast the jigsaw puzzle task so that features suitable for object detection and classification are implicitly learned.

3.1   The Jigsaw Puzzle Task

In the jigsaw task, the input data is a collection of identical square tiles from an image and the labels are permutations of these tiles taken from a predefined

---

Algorithm 1. Generation of the *maximal* Hamming distance permutation set

---

Output: P

1: $\bar{P} \leftarrow$ all permutations $[\bar{P}_1, \ldots, \bar{P}_{9!}]$ \\ $\bar{P}$ *is a* $9 \times 9!$ *matrix*

2: $P \leftarrow \emptyset$

3: $j \sim \mathcal{U}[1, 9!]$ \\ *uniform sample out of* $9!$ *permutations*

4: $i \leftarrow 1$

5: **repeat**

6:     $P \leftarrow [P \; \bar{P}_j]$ \\ *add permutation* $\bar{P}_j$ *to* P

7:     $\bar{P} \leftarrow [\bar{P}_1, \ldots, \bar{P}_{j-1}, \bar{P}_{j+1}, \ldots]$ \\ *remove* $\bar{P}_j$ *from* $\bar{P}$

8:     $D \leftarrow$ Hamming$(P, \bar{P})$ \\ D *is an* $i \times (9! - i)$ *matrix*

9:     $\bar{D} \leftarrow \mathbf{1}^T D$ \\ $\bar{D}$ *is a* $1 \times (9! - i)$ *row vector*

10:     $j \leftarrow \arg\max_k \bar{D}_k$ \\ $\bar{D}_k$ *denotes the* k-*th entry of* $\bar{D}$

11:     $i \leftarrow i + 1$

12: **until** $i \leq 100$

---

set $\mathcal{S}$. For example, an image is divided in a 3×3 grid, where each tile corresponds to a number from 1 to 9 (see Fig. 3). A permutation is an ordering of the tiles, *e.g.*, $(9, 4, 6, 8, 3, 2, 5, 1, 7)$. We generate the set $\mathcal{S}$ via the greedy algorithm shown in Algorithm 1 and never change it during or after training. A factor that was found important to learn transferrable features is the Hamming distance between the permutations (*i.e.*, the number of different tile locations between 2 permutations $S_1, S_2 \in \mathcal{S}$ divided by 9). From our experimental validation, the average Hamming distance seems to control the difficulty of the jigsaw puzzle reassembly task, and to also correlate with the object detection performance. In Table 4 we compare 3 choices for the Hamming distance: minimal, middle and maximal. For the minimal and middle case, the $\arg\max_k$ function at line 10 is replaced by $\arg\min_k$ and uniform sampling respectively. From those tests we can see that large Hamming distances are desirable.

Although there are $9! = 362,880$ possible permutations with 9 tiles, it turns out that it is not necessary to consider the whole space of permutations. We have found out experimentally that increasing the cardinality of $\mathcal{S}$ beyond 100 does not improve any performance. Indeed, by setting $|\mathcal{S}| = 1000$ the CFN-9(middle) (3×3 grid with middle case for the Hamming distance) can solve puzzles with an accuracy of 85 %, achieves the classification performance of 38 % on ILSRVC 2012 [8] with all layers locked (see Table 2), and takes 2.5 days to train (notice that only the last layer changes with the size of $\mathcal{S}$ and the training dataset size does not change). Thus, in all the experiments below we fix $|\mathcal{S}| = 100$.

3.2 The Context-Free Architecture

Jigsaw puzzles can be solved by matching low-level statistics (*e.g.*, structural patterns or texture) close to the boundaries of adjacent tiles, that is, by ignoring the inner contents of the tiles. While these are cues that humans often use to solve jigsaw puzzles, they do not lead to a complete representation of the global object, which is necessary for object classification. Thus, here we present a network that delays the computation of statistics across different tiles (see Fig. 3). The network first computes features based only on the pixels within each tile (one row on the

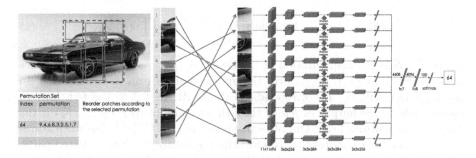

Fig. 3. Context Free Network. The figure illustrates how a puzzle is generated and solved. We randomly crop a 225×225 pixel window from image (red dashed box), divide it into a 3 × 3 grid, and randomly pick a 64 × 64 pixel tiles from each 75 × 75 pixel cell. These 9 tiles are reordered via a randomly chosen permutation from a predefined permutation set and are then fed to the CFN. The task is to predict the index of the chosen permutation (technically, we define as output a probability vector with 1 at the 64-th location and 0 elsewhere). CFN is a siamese-ennead CNN. For simplicity, we do not indicate the max-pooling and ReLU layers. These shared layers are implemented exactly as in AlexNet [23]. The only difference is that we set the stride of the first layer to 2 instead of 4. (Color figure online)

right-hand side of Fig. 3). Then, it finds the parts arrangement just by using these features (*fc7* and *fc8* in Fig. 3). The objective is to force the network to learn features that are as representative and discriminative as possible of each object part for the purpose of determining their relative location.

Towards this goal we build a siamese-ennead convolutional network (see Fig. 3) where each row up to the first fully connected layer (*fc6*) uses the AlexNet architecture [23] with shared weights. Similar schemes were used in prior work [2,9,36]. The outputs of all *fc6* layers are concatenated and given as input to *fc7*. All the layers in the rows share the same weights up to and including *fc6*.

We call this architecture the *context-free network* (CFN) because the data flow of each patch is explicitly separated until the fully connected layer and context is handled only in the last fully connected layers. We verify that this architecture performs as well as AlexNet in the classification task on the ILSVRC2012 dataset [8]. In this test we resize the input images to 225 × 225 pixels, split them into a 3 × 3 grid and then feed the full 75 × 75 tiles to the network. We find that the CFN achieves 57.1 % top-1 accuracy while AlexNet achieves 57.4 % top-1 accuracy (see Table 2). Thus, limiting the receptive field of *fc6* to a tile does not significantly affect the performance in classification.

3.3 Training the CFN

The output of the CFN can be seen as the conditional probability density function (pdf) of the spatial arrangement of object parts (or scene parts) in a part-based model, *i.e.*,

$$p(S|A_1, A_2, \ldots, A_9) = p(S|F_1, F_2, \ldots, F_9) \prod_{i=1}^{9} p(F_i|A_i) \tag{1}$$

where $S \in \mathcal{S}$ is the configuration of the tiles, $\{A_i\}_{i=1,\ldots,9}$ form the appearance of an object, and $\{F_i\}_{i=1,\ldots,9}$ form the intermediate feature representation. In our CFN (see Fig. 3), A_i corresponds to the RGB tile fed to the i-th row, F_i corresponds to the output of $fc6$ in the i-th row, and $p(S|F_1, F_2, \ldots, F_9)$ is the output of the softmax layer. Our objective is to train the CFN so that the features F_i have semantic attributes that can identify the relative position between parts.

Given the limited amount of data that we can use to build an approximation of this very high-dimensional pdf, close attention must be paid to the training strategy. One problem is when the CFN learns to associate each appearance A_i to an absolute position. In this case, the features F_i would carry no semantic meaning, but just information about an arbitrary 2D position. This problem could happen if we generate just 1 jigsaw puzzle per image. Then, the CFN could learn to cluster patches only based on their absolute position in the puzzle, and not on their textural/structural content. If we write the configuration S as a list of tile positions $S = (L_1, \ldots, L_9)$ then in this case the conditional pdf $p(S|F_1, F_2, \ldots, F_9)$ would factorize into independent terms

$$p(L_1, \ldots, L_9 | F_1, F_2, \ldots, F_9) = \prod_{i=1}^{9} p(L_i|F_i) \tag{2}$$

where each tile location L_i is fully determined by the corresponding feature F_i. The CFN would not have learned the correlation between different tiles.

To avoid these issues we feed multiple jigsaw puzzles of the same image to the CFN (an average of 69 out of 100 possible puzzle configurations) and make sure that the tiles are shuffled as much as possible by choosing configurations with sufficiently large average Hamming distance. In this way the same tile would have to be assigned to multiple positions (possibly all 9) thus making the mapping of features F_i to any absolute position equally likely.

As mentioned earlier on, we also leave a random gap between the tiles to discourage the CFN from learning low-level statistics. This was also done in [9]. During training we resize each input image until either the height or the width matches 256 pixels and preserve the original aspect ratio. Then, we crop a random region from the resized image of size 225×225 and split it into a 3×3 grid of 75×75 pixels tiles. We then extract a 64×64 region from each tile by introducing random shifts and feed them to the network. Thus, we have an average gap of 11 pixels between the tiles. However, the gaps may range from a minimum of 0 pixels to a maximum of 22 pixels.

No color dropping or filling image channels with noise was needed. We used Caffe [21] and modified the code to choose random image patches and permutations during the training time. This allowed us to keep the dataset small (1.3 M images from ImageNet) and the training efficient, while the CFN could see an average of 69 different puzzles per image (that is about 90 M different jigsaw puzzles).

3.4   Implementation Details

We use stochastic gradient descent without batch normalization [19] on one Titan X GPU. The training uses 1.3M color images of 256×256 pixels and mini-batches with a batch size of 256 images. We preserve the aspect ratio of the original images by resizing them until the smallest between their height and width matches 256 pixels. Then, the other dimension is cropped to 256 pixels. The training converges after 350K iterations with a basic learning rate of 0.01 and takes 59.5 h in total ($\sim$2.5 days). If we take $122\% = \frac{3072\text{cores@}1000\,\text{Mhz}}{2880\text{cores@}875\,\text{Mhz}} = \frac{6,144\text{GFLOPS}}{5,040\text{GFLOPS}}$ as the best possible performance ratio between the Titan X and the Tesla K40 (used for [9]) we can predict that the CFN would have taken $\sim$72.5 h ($\sim$3 days) on a Tesla K40. We compute that on average each image is used $350\,\text{K} \times 256/1.3\,\text{M} \simeq 69$ times.

3.5   CFN Filter Activations

Some recent work has devoted efforts towards the visualization of CNNs to better understand how they work and how we can exploit them [20,25,32,38]. Some of these works and also Google Inceptionism[1] aim at obtaining the input image that best represents a category according to a given neural network. This has shown that CNNs retain important information about the categories. Here instead we analyze the CFN by considering the units at each layer as object part detectors as in [13]. We extract 1M patches from the ImageNet validation set (20 randomly sampled 64×64 patches) and feed them as input to the CFN. At each layer (conv1, conv2, conv3, conv4, conv5) we consider the outputs of one channel and compute their ℓ_1 norm. We then rank the patches based on the ℓ_1 norm and select the top 16 ones that belong to different images. Since each layer has several channels, we hand-pick the 6 most significant ones. In Fig. 4 we show the top-16 activation patches for only 6 channels per layer. These activations show that the CFN features correspond to patterns sharing similar shapes and that there is a good correspondence based on object parts (in particular see the conv4 activations for dog parts). Some channels seem to be good face detectors (see conv3, but the same detectors can be seen in other channels, not shown, in conv4 and conv5) and others seem to be good texture detectors (*e.g.*, grass, water, fur). In Fig. 4(f) we also show the filters of the conv1 layer of the CFN. Because of the green-magenta bias, our conv1 filters seem to be also sensitive to chromatic aberration [9]. However, it appears as though this bias does not affect the performance when features are transferred to detection and classification tasks (see next section).

---

[1] See http://googleresearch.blogspot.co.uk/2015/06/inceptionism-going-deeper-into-neural.html.

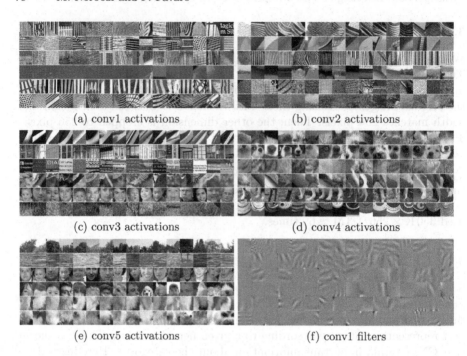

(a) conv1 activations

(b) conv2 activations

(c) conv3 activations

(d) conv4 activations

(e) conv5 activations

(f) conv1 filters

Fig. 4. Visualization of the top 16 activations for 6 units of the conv1, conv2, conv3, conv4, conv5 layers in our CFN. (f) we show the filters of conv1, which show a green-magenta bias. The selection of the top activations is identical to the visualization method of Girshick *et al.* [13], except that we compute the average response rather than the maximum. We show some of the most significant units. We can see that in the first (a) and second (b) layers the filters specialize on different types of textures. On the third layer (c) the filters become more specialized and we have a first face detector (later layers will also have face detectors in some units) and some part detectors (*e.g.*, the bottom corner of the butterflies wing). On the fourth layer (d) we have already quite a number of part detectors. We purposefully choose all the dog part detectors: head top, head center, neck, back legs, and front legs. Notice the intraclass variation of the parts. Lastly, the fifth convolutional layer (e) has some other part detectors and some scene part detectors. (Color figure online)

4 Experiments

We evaluate our learned features by using transfer learning [37] on the object classification task on ImageNet and as pre-trained weights for classification and detection tasks on PASCAL VOC 2007 [11]. We also perform a novel experiment to understand whether semantic classification is useful to solve jigsaw puzzles, and thus to see how much object classification and jigsaw puzzle reassembly tasks are related. We take the pre-trained AlexNet and transfer its features to solve 3×3 jigsaw puzzles with permutations generated with the middle case Hamming distance (which is used by the CFN-9(middle) in later sections). We also use the same locking scheme as in [37] to see the transferability of features at

Table 1. Transfer learning of AlexNet from a classification task to the jigsaw puzzle reassembly problem. The j-th column indicates that all layers from conv1 to conv-j were locked and all subsequent layers were randomly initialized and retrained. Notice how the first 4 layers provide very good features for solving puzzles. This shows that object classification and the jigsaw puzzle problems are related.

	🔒 conv1	🔒 conv2	🔒 conv3	🔒 conv4	🔒 conv5
AlexNet [23]	88	87	86	83	74

Table 2. Comparison of classification results on validation set of ImageNet 2012.

	🔒 conv1	🔒 conv2	🔒 conv3	🔒 conv4	🔒 conv5
CFN	**57.1**	**56.0**	**52.4**	**48.3**	**38.1**
Doersch *et al.* [9]	53.1	47.6	48.7	45.6	30.4
Wang and Gupta [36]	51.8	46.9	42.8	38.8	29.8
Random	48.5	41.0	34.8	27.1	12.0

different layers. The performance is shown in Table 1. Compared to the maximum accuracy of the CFN-9(middle) (88 %) we can see that semantic training is quite helpful towards recognizing object parts. Indeed, the performance is very high up to conv4. Finally, we also compare the CFN features with those of [9, 36] both qualitatively and quantitatively on image retrieval.

4.1 ImageNet Classification

Yosinski *et al.* [37] have shown that the last layers of AlexNet are specific to the task and dataset used for training, while the first layers are general-purpose. In the context of transfer learning, this transition from general-purpose to task-specific determines where in the network one should extract the features. In this section we try to understand where this transition occurs in the CFN. We repurpose the CFN, [9, 36] to the classification task on the ImageNet 2012 dataset [8] and Table 2 summarizes the results on the validation set. The analysis consists of training each network with the labeled data from ImageNet 2012 by locking a subset of the layers and by initializing the unlocked layers with random values. If we train AlexNet we obtain the reference maximum accuracy of 57.4 %. Our method achieves 38.1 % when only fully connected layers are trained, which is 7.0 % higher than the next best performing algorithm [9]. There is a significant improvement (from 38.1 % to 48.3 %) when the conv5 layer is also trained. This shows that the conv5 layer starts to be specialized in the jigsaw puzzle reassembly task.

4.2 Pascal VOC 2007 Classification and Detection

We use the CFN features for object detection, with Fast R-CNN [14], and classification tasks on PASCAL VOC 2007. For both tasks we use the same baseline

80   M. Noroozi and P. Favaro

Table 3. Results on PASCAL VOC 2007 Detection and Classification. The results of the other methods are taken from Pathak *et al.* [27].

Method	Pretraining time	Supervision	Classification	Detection
Krizhevsky*et al.* [23]	3 days	1000 class labels	**78.2 %**	**56.8 %**
Wang and Gupta [36]	1 week	motion	58.4 %	44.0 %
Doersch *et al.* [9]	4 weeks	context	55.3 %	46.6 %
Pathak *et al.* [27]	14 h	context	56.5 %	44.5 %
CFN-9(max)	2.5 days	context	**68.6 %**	**51.8 %**

Table 4. Object detection results on Pascal VOC 2007 for different configurations of the CFN. We compare the 2×2 grid (trained on all 24 permutations) and 3×3 grid with different average Hamming distances. We can see that the 3×3 grid achieves better results. Moreover, the average Hamming distance between permutations has a direct impact on the performance of the learned features.

CFN-4	CFN-9(min)	CFN-9(middle)	CFN-9(max)	CFN-sup
49.8 %	51.0 %	51.2 %	**51.8 %**	**56.3 %**

used by Krähenbühl *et al.* [22]. Because our fully connected layers are different from those used in Fast R-CNN, we select one row of the CFN (up to `conv5`), copy only the weights of the convolutional layers, and fill the fully connected layers with Gaussian random weights with mean 0.1 and standard deviation 0.001. The results are summarized in Table 3.

We evaluate the impact of different configurations on the detection task in Table 4. We consider two cases for the CFN pre-trained with the jigsaw puzzle task: one based on a 2×2 grid (denoted `CFN-4`) and one based on a 3×3 grid (denoted `CFN-9`). The average performance shows that `CFN-9` learns better features. We also analyze the impact of the average Hamming distance between permutations on the detection task. We generate 3 cases for the average Hamming distance: .45 (`CFN-9(min)`), .67 (`CFN-9(middle)`), and .88 (`CFN-9(max)`). As shown in Table 4 the feature map extracted from `CFN-9(max)` is the best performing one. We also use as a reference the CFN pre-trained on ImageNet with labels and call it `CFN-Sup` in Table 4. This test is done only to show the full potential of the network when trained in a supervised manner for classification. Indeed, we get 56.3 % mAP for detection which is almost the same as that of AlexNet (56.5 % mAP). `CFN-9(max)` features achieve 51.8 % mAP in detection, and 68.6 % in classification, thus outperforming all other methods and reducing the gap with features obtained with supervision.

4.3   Image Retrieval

We also evaluate the features qualitatively (see Fig. 5) and quantitatively (see Fig. 6) for image retrieval with a simple image ranking.

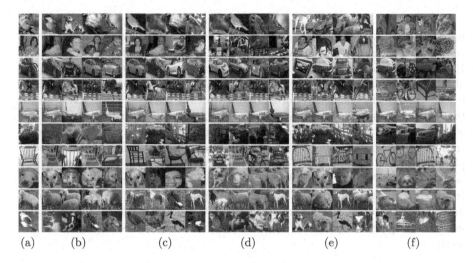

Fig. 5. Image retrieval (qualitative evaluation). (a) query images; (b) top-4 matches with AlexNet; (c) top-4 matches with the CFN; (d) top-4 matches with Doersch *et al.* [9]; (e) top-4 matches with Wang and Gupta [36]; (f) top-4 matches with AlexNet with random weights.

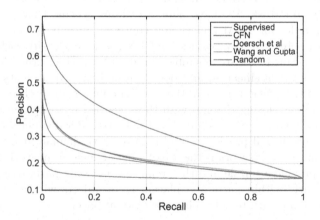

Fig. 6. Image retrieval (quantitative evaluation). We compare the precision-recall for image retrieval on the PASCAL VOC 2007. The ranking of the retrieved images is based on the inner products between normalized features extracted from a pre-trained AlexNet, the CFN, Doersch *et al.* [9], Wang and Gupta [36] and from AlexNet with random weights. The performance of CFN and [9] are very similar when using this simple ranking metric. When the metric is instead learned with two fully connected layers, then we see that CFN features yield a clearly higher performance than all other features from self-supervised learning methods (see Table 2).

We find the nearest neighbors (NN) of pool5 features using the bounding boxes of the PASCAL VOC 2007 *test* set as query and bounding boxes of the *trainval* set as the retrieval entries. We discard bounding boxes with fewer than 10K pixels inside. In Fig. 5 we show some examples of image retrievals (top-4) obtained by ranking the images based on the inner product between normalized features of a query image and normalized features of the retrieval set. We can see that the features of the CFN are very sensitive to objects with similar shape and often these are within the same category. In Fig. 6 we compare CFN with the pre-trained AlexNet, [9,36] and AlexNet with random weights. The precision-recall plots show that [9] and CFN features perform equally well. However, the real potential of CFN features is demonstrated when the feature metric is learned. In Table 2 we can see how CFN features surpass other features trained in an unsupervised way by a good margin. In that test the dataset (ImageNet) is more challenging because there are more categories and the bounding box is not used.

5   Conclusions

We have introduced the *context-free* network (CFN), a CNN whose features can be easily transferred between detection/classification and jigsaw puzzle reassembly tasks. The network is trained in an unsupervised manner by using the jigsaw puzzle as a *pretext* task. We have built a training scheme that generates, on average, 69 puzzles for 1.3 M images and converges in only 2.5 days. The key idea is that by solving jigsaw puzzles the CFN learns to identify each tile as an object part and how parts are assembled in an object. The learned features are evaluated on both classification and detection and the experiments show that we outperform the previous state of the art. More importantly, the performance of these features is closing the gap with those learned in a supervised manner. We believe that there is a lot of untapped potential in self-supervised learning and in the future it will provide a valid help to costly human annotation. One possible extension to this work is the use of a hierarchical-framework where each tile can also provide a puzzle and thus represent not only parts within objects, but also subparts within parts and placement of objects within a scene. The puzzle solver could learn to solve all these cases at once.

Acknowledgements. We thank Philipp Krähenbühl for his assistance with the experiments on Pascal VOC 2007 and for kindly evaluating our CFN weights on his configuration for classification with Pascal VOC 2007.

References

1. Agrawal, P., Girshick, R., Malik, J.: Analyzing the performance of multilayer neural networks for object recognition. In: Fleet, D., Pajdla, T., Schiele, B., Tuytelaars, T. (eds.) ECCV 2014. LNCS, vol. 8695, pp. 329–344. Springer, Heidelberg (2014). doi:10.1007/978-3-319-10584-0_22

2. Agrawal, P., Carreira, J., Malik, J.: Learning to see by moving. In: ICCV (2015)
3. Barlow, H.B.: Unsupervised learning. Neural Comput. 1, 295–311 (1989)
4. Belkin, M., Niyogi, P.: Laplacian eigenmaps for dimensionality reduction and data representation. Neural Comput. 15, 1373–1396 (2003)
5. Bengio, Y., Courville, A., Vincent, P.: Representation learning: a review and new perspectives. PAMI 35(8), 1798–1828 (2013)
6. Boulard, H., Kamp, Y.: Auto-association by multilayer perceptrons and singular value decomposition. Biol. Cybern. 59, 291–294 (1988)
7. Chen, D.M., Baatz, G., Koser, K., Tsai, S.S., Vedantham, R., Pylvanainen, T., Roimela, K., Chen, X., Bach, J., Pollefeys, M., Girod, B., Grzeszczuk, R.: City-scale landmark identification on mobile devices. In: CVPR (2011)
8. Deng, J., Dong, W., Socher, R., Li, L.J., Li, K., Fei-Fei, L.: Imagenet: A large-scale hierarchical image database. In: CVPR (2009)
9. Doersch, C., Gupta, A., Efros, A.A.: Unsupervised visual representation learning by context prediction. In: ICCV (2015)
10. Donahue, J., Jia, Y., Vinyals, O., Hoffman, J., Zhang, N., Tzeng, E., Darrell, T.: Decaf: a deep convolutional activation feature for generic visual recognition. In: ICML (2014)
11. Everingham, M., Eslami, S.M.A., Gool, L.V., Williams, C.K.I., Winn, J., Zisserman, A.: The pascal visual object classes challenge: A retrospective. IJCV (2014)
12. Freeman, H., Garder, L.: Apictorial jigsaw puzzles: the computer solution of a problem in pattern recognition. IEEE Trans. Electron. Comput. EC–13, 118–127 (1964)
13. Girshick, R., Donahue, J., Darrell, T., Malik, J.: Rich feature hierarchies for accurate object detection and semantic segmentation. In: CVPR (2014)
14. Girshick, R.: Fast r-cnn. In: ICCV (2015)
15. Henriques, J.F., Caseiro, R., Martins, P., Batista, J.: High-speed tracking with kernelized correlation filters. PAMI (2015)
16. Hinton, G.E., Sejnowski, T.J.: Learning and relearning in boltzmann machines. In: Parallel Distributed Processing: Explorations in the Microstructure of Cognition, vol. 1 (1986)
17. Hinton, G.E., Zemel, R.S.: Autoencoders, minimum description length and helmholtz free energy. NIPS (1993)
18. Hooper, H.: The Hooper Visual Organization Test. Western Psychological Services, Los Angeles (1983)
19. Ioffe, S., Szegedy, C.: Batch normalization: accelerating deep network training by reducing internal covariate shift. In: ICML (2015)
20. Jason, Y., Jeff, C., Anh, N., Thomas, F., Hod, L.: Understanding neural networks through deep visualization. In: Deep Learning Workshop, ICML (2015)
21. Jia, Y., Shelhamer, E., Donahue, J., Karayev, S., Long, J., Girshick, R., Guadarrama, S., Darrell, T.: Caffe: Convolutional architecture for fast feature embedding. ACM-MM (2014)
22. Krähenbühl, P., Doersch, C., Donahue, J., Darrell, T.: Data-dependent initializations of convolutional neural networks. In: ICLR (2016)
23. Krizhevsky, A., Sutskever, I., Hinton, G.E.: Imagenet classification with deep convolutional neural networks. NIPS (2012)
24. Le, Q., Ranzato, M., Monga, R., Devin, M., Chen, K., Corrado, G., Dean, J., Ng, A.: Building high-level features using large scale unsupervised learning. In: ICML (2012)

25. Mahendran, A., Vedaldi, A.: Understanding deep image representations by inverting them. In: CVPR (2015)
26. Olshausen, B.A., Field, D.J.: Sparse coding with an overcomplete basis set: a strategy employed by v1? Vision Research (1997)
27. Pathak, D., Krähenbühl, P., Donahue, J., Darrell, T., Efros, A.A.: Context encoders: feature learning by inpainting. In: CVPR (2016)
28. Pomeranz, D., Shemesh, M., Ben-Shahar, O.: A fully automated greedy square jigsaw puzzle solver. In: CVPR (2011)
29. Pomeranz, D.: Solving the square jigsaw problem. Ph.D. thesis, Ben-Gurion University of the Negev (2012)
30. Richardson, J., Vecchi, T.: A jigsaw-puzzle imagery task for assessing active visuospatial processes in old and young people. Behavior Research Methods, Instruments, & Computers (2002)
31. Roweis, S.T., Saul, L.K.: Nonlinear dimensionality reduction by locally linear embedding. Science (2000)
32. Simonyan, K., Vedaldi, A., Zisserman, A.: Deep inside convolutional networks: Visualising image classification models and saliency maps. In: ICLR (2014)
33. Simonyan, K., Zisserman, A.: Two-stream convolutional networks for action recognition in videos. NIPS (2014)
34. Smolensky, P.: Information processing in dynamical systems: Foundations of harmony theory. Parallel Distributed Processing (1986)
35. Tybon, R.: Generating Solutions to the Jigsaw Puzzle Problem. Ph.D. thesis, Griffith University (2004)
36. Wang, X., Gupta, A.: Unsupervised learning of visual representations using videos. In: ICCV (2015)
37. Yosinski, J., Clune, J., Bengio, Y., Lipson, H.: How transferable are features in deep neural networks? NIPS (2014)
38. Zeiler, M.D., Fergus, R.: Visualizing and understanding convolutional networks. In: Fleet, D., Pajdla, T., Schiele, B., Tuytelaars, T. (eds.) ECCV 2014. LNCS, vol. 8689, pp. 818–833. Springer, Heidelberg (2014). doi:10.1007/978-3-319-10590-1_53

COCO Attributes: Attributes for People, Animals, and Objects

Genevieve Patterson[1]([⊠]) and James Hays[2]

[1] Microsoft Research, Cambridge, USA
gen@microsoft.com
[2] Georgia Institute of Technology, Atlanta, USA
hays@gatech.edu

Abstract. In this paper, we discover and annotate visual attributes for the COCO dataset. With the goal of enabling deeper object understanding, we deliver the largest attribute dataset to date. Using our COCO Attributes dataset, a fine-tuned classification system can do more than recognize object categories – for example, rendering multi-label classifications such as "sleeping spotted curled-up cat" instead of simply "cat". To overcome the expense of annotating thousands of COCO object instances with hundreds of attributes, we present an Economic Labeling Algorithm (ELA) which intelligently generates crowd labeling tasks based on correlations between attributes. The ELA offers a substantial reduction in labeling cost while largely maintaining attribute density and variety. Currently, we have collected 3.5 million object-attribute pair annotations describing 180 thousand different objects. We demonstrate that our efficiently labeled training data can be used to produce classifiers of similar discriminative ability as classifiers created using exhaustively labeled ground truth. Finally, we provide baseline performance analysis for object attribute recognition.

Keywords: Dataset creation · Attributes · Crowdsourcing · Multilabel recognition

1 Introduction

Traditionally, computer vision algorithms describe objects by giving each instance a categorical label (e.g. cat, Barack Obama, bedroom, etc.). However, category labels provide a limited approximation of the human understanding of natural images. This categorical model has some significant limitations: (1) We have no way to express *intra*-category variations, e.g. "fresh apple" vs. "rotten apple." (2) A categorical representation alone cannot help us to understand the state of objects relative to other objects in a scene. For example, if there are two people arguing in a scene, knowing that they are both 'people' won't help us understand who is angry or who is guilty. (3) The categorical model prevents researchers from responding to complex questions about the contents of a

© Springer International Publishing AG 2016
B. Leibe et al. (Eds.): ECCV 2016, Part VI, LNCS 9910, pp. 85–100, 2016.
DOI: 10.1007/978-3-319-46466-4_6

natural scene. This final limitation is a particular obstacle in Visual Question Answering [1] or the Visual Turing Test [2].

To alleviate these limitations, we aim to add semantic visual attributes [3,4] to objects. The space of attributes is effectively infinite but the majority of possible attributes (e.g., "This man's name is John.", "This book has historical significance.") are not interesting to us. We are interested in finding attributes that are likely to visually distinguish objects from each other (not necessarily along categorical boundaries). In this paper, we expand on the type of attributes introduced by Farhadi et al.

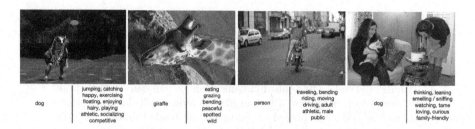

| dog | jumping, catching happy, exercising floating, enjoying hairy, playing athletic, socializing competitive | giraffe | eating grazing bending peaceful spotted wild | person | traveling, bending riding, moving driving, adult athletic, male public | dog | thinking, leaning smelling / sniffing watching, tame loving, curious family-friendly |

Fig. 1. *Examples from COCO Attributes.* In the figure above, images from the COCO dataset are shown with one object outlined in white. Under the image, the COCO object label is listed on the left, and the COCO Attribute labels are listed on the right. The COCO Attributes labels give a rich and detailed description of the context of the object.

Outline: In Sect. 3, we explain how we determine which attributes to include in our dataset. To determine the attribute taxonomy for COCO, we implement a crowd-in-the-loop content generation system. Section 4 illustrates the burden of taking a naíve approach to attribute labeling. In that section we exhaustively label all of our discovered attributes for a subset of 6500 object instances. This 'exhaustive' sub-dataset is then used to bootstrap our economic labeling pipeline described in Sect. 5. Section 6 presents some baseline classification results on COCO Attributes.

The COCO dataset contains 500,000 images and 2M individually annotated objects. Given the scale of this dataset, it is economically infeasible to annotate all attributes for all object instances. The Economic Labeling Algorithm (ELA) introduced in Sect. 5 approximates the exhaustive annotation process. The ELA selects a subset of attributes that is likely to contain all of the positive labels for a novel image. By labeling the attributes most likely to be positive first, we are able to reduce the number of annotations required without greatly sacrificing overall label recall. We annotate objects from 29 of the most-populated COCO object categories with nearly 200 discovered attributes.

Currently, our COCO Attributes dataset comprises 84,044 images, 188,426 object instances, 196 object attributes, and 3,455,201 object-attribute annotation pairs. The objects in the dataset vary widely, from cars to sandwiches to cats and dogs. In Sect. 3 we employ proven techniques, such as text-mining, image comparison tasks, and crowd shepherding, to find the 196 attributes we later use to label the dataset [5–9].

Our contribution is straightforward — we obtain attribute labels for thousands of object instances at a reasonable cost. For the sake of estimating an upper bound on the cost of annotating attributes across the COCO dataset, let us assume several figures relating to the number of annotations and cost per annotation using the widely employed Amazon Mechanical Turk platform (AMT).

Let's assume that crowd workers are asked to annotate 50 images per human intelligence task (HIT). Our dataset contains approximately 200 visual attributes. For COCO Attributes, we annotate attributes for a subset of the total COCO dataset, approximately 180,000 objects across 29 object categories. The cost of exhaustively labeling 200 attributes for all of the object instances contained in our dataset would be: 180k objects × 200 attributes)/50 images per HIT × ($0.07 pay per HIT + $0.014 Amazon fee) = $60,480. If we annotate each attribute for the top 10 % of object instances mostly likely to contain a particular attribute, the overall annotation cost would drop to a reasonable $6,048. But how do we discover the most informative and characteristic attributes for each object in the COCO dataset? We present our answer to this question in Sect. 5.

To verify the quality of the COCO Attributes dataset, we explore attribute classification. In Sect. 6, we show that a CNN finetuned on our ELA labeled training set to predict multi-label attribute vectors performs similarly to classifiers trained on exhaustively labeled instances.

2 Related Work

To our knowledge, no attribute dataset has been collected containing both the number of images and the number of object attributes as our COCO Attributes dataset. Existing attribute datasets concentrate on either a small range of object categories or a small number of attributes.

One notable exception is the Visual Genome dataset introduced in Krishna et al. [10], which also aims to provide a dataset of complex real-world interactions between objects and attributes. Visual Genome contains myriad types of annotations, all of which are important for deeper image understanding. For COCO Attributes, we focus on making the largest attribute dataset we possibly can. In that regard we have been able to collect more than double the number of object-attribute pair annotations. COCO Attributes and the Visual Genome dataset together open up new avenues of research in the vision community by providing non-overlapping attribute datasets. Creating COCO Attributes is an experiment in economically scalling up attribute annotation as demonstrated in attribute literature such as the CUB 200 dataset [11], the SUN Attribute dataset [8], Visual Genome, and other well-cited works of attribute annotation [12,13].

Initial efforts to investigate attributes involved labeling images of animals with texture, part, and affordance attributes [3,4,14]. These attributes were chosen by the researchers themselves, as the interesting attributes for animals were clear at the time of publication. COCO dataset images are more complicated than those in Farhadi et al. [14]. They often have multiple objects, object occlusions, and complicated backgrounds. Attributes are necessary to differentiate objects in COCO scenes or describe the variety in instances of the same category. As a result, the COCO Attributes are more detailed and descriptive than those in earlier datasets.

Other attribute datasets have concentrated on attributes relating to people. Kumar et al. [15] and Liu et al. [16] introduced datasets with face attributes and human activity affordances, respectively. The influential Poselets dataset [17] labeled human poses and has been crucial for the advancement of both human pose and attribute estimation.

Vedaldi et al. [18] used a specialized resource for collecting attributes. They collected a set of discriminative attributes for airplanes by consulting hobbyist and expert interest websites. It is possible that the best method for collecting high-quality attributes is to use a more sophisticated crowd, reserving the general-expertise crowd to label the dataset. We explore bootstrapping the attribute discovery process by mining discriminative words from a corpus of descriptive text written by language 'experts' — novels and newspapers. Similar methods have been demonstrated successfully in [5,12,13]. We use the descriptive words found in these texts to seed a crowd pipeline that winnows the large variety of seed words down to the attributes that visually describe the COCO objects.

Several datasets have collected attributes for the purpose of making visual search more tractable. The Whittlesearch [19] dataset contains 14,658 shoe images with 10 instance-level relative attributes. Parikh and Grauman [20] show that predicted attributes can be used to better describe the relative differences between objects of the same and different categories. This paper furthers the attribute annotation and recognition research begun in those papers by concentrating on scaling up the size of the attribute dataset.

A number of past projects sought to bootstrap dataset annotation using active learning [21–24]. The ELA method presented in Sect. 5 takes a different approach. The ELA is also iterative, exploiting correlation and information gain in a partially labeled training set, but does not use an intermediate classifier. The ELA uses no visual classification.

Vijayanarasimhan and Grauman [21] and Patterson et al. [24] show that the crowd in combination with active learning can rapidly converge on a visual phenomena. However, these active learning systems may be missing the most visually unusual examples. While we seek to annotate COCO Attributes with maximum efficiency, we choose not to make the visual approximation inherently imposed by an active learning pipeline.

Admittedly, our Efficient Labeling Algorithm (ELA) has the possible bias that may occur when we label a subset of the total number of attributes. Section 5 describes the trade-offs among visual diversity, label accuracy, and annotation cost.

We identify additional cost-saving annotation strategies by imitating successes in multi-class recognition [25,26]. Deng et al. define the Hierarchy and Exclusion (HEX) graph, which captures semantic relationships between object labels [26]. HEX graphs describe whether a pair of labels are mutually exclusive, overlap, or subsume one or the other. In Deng et al. HEX graphs are used for object classification. We use the hierarchy of the COCO objects to inform our economic labeling algorithm (ELA), described in Sect. 5.

This paper introduces a large new dataset and a novel way to cheaply collect annotations without introducing visual bias. In Sect. 3, we use the crowd to curate our collection of attributes. Section 4 presents a baseline for exhaustive annotation. Section 5 introduces the ELA and shows how we improve on the cost of the exhaustive baseline. Section 5 demonstrates that a dataset collected with the ELA protocol has similar annotation density to an exhaustively labeled dataset. Section 6 contrasts classifiers trained on ELA generated labels and exhaustive labels to show that labeling bias is minimal. Finally, Sect. 6 compares recognizing attributes individually or in a multilabel setting.

3 Attribute Discovery

The first stage of creating the COCO Attributes dataset is determining a taxonomy of relevant attributes. For COCO Attributes, we search for attributes for all of the object categories contained under the COCO super-categories of Person, Vehicle, Animal, and Food. These categories are person, bicycle, car, motorcycle, airplane, bus, train, truck, boat, bird, cat, dog, horse, cow, sheep, elephant, bear, zebra, giraffe, banana, apple, orange, broccoli, carrot, hot dog, pizza, donut, cake, and sandwich. We must determine the attributes that would be useful for describing these objects.

When annotating the COCO objects, we will use a universal taxonomy of attributes versus a category specific taxonomy. Objects from all categories will be annotated with all attributes. Of course, some attributes won't occur at all for certain categories (we didn't observe any "furry" cars), but other attributes like "shiny" manifest across many categories. Certain attributes may have very different visual manifestation in different categories, e.g. an "saucy" pizza and an "saucy" person don't necessarily share the same visual features. We aim to find a large corpus of attributes that will describe both specific categories and often be applicable to several unrelated categories.

Asking Amazon Mechanical Turk (AMT) workers to describe the objects from scratch might result in terms that do not generalize well to other objects in the same hierarchical group or are too common to be discriminative, for example 'orange' does not help us describe the difference between oranges. To bootstrap the attribute discovery process, we mine a source of English text likely to contain descriptive words – the New York Times Annotated Corpus [27]. This corpus contains all of the articles published by the NYT from 1987–2008. We extract all adjectives and verbs occurring within five words of one of our object words. This results in hundreds of descriptive words. Unfortunately, not all of these candidate attributes describe visually recognizable phenomena.

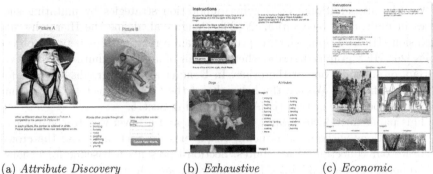

(a) *Attribute Discovery*
User Interface (UI).

(b) *Exhaustive*
Annotation UI.

(c) *Economic*
Annotation UI.

Fig. 2. Amazon Mechanical Turk (AMT) Task Interfaces used in the creation of COCO Attributes.

In order to filter the attributes mined from the NYT corpus, and indeed add a few new ones, we design an AMT Human Intelligence Task (HIT). Our attribute discovery HIT, shown in Fig. 2a, encourages AMT workers to submit visual attributes by asking them to discriminate between two images. In this experiment, we show workers two randomly selected COCO objects from the same category. The worker types in several words that describe one of the images but not the other. To help focus our workers and guide them to make better suggestions, we show a random subsampling of the attributes discovered via the NYT corpus or submitted in previous HITs.

In the end, approximately 300 unique terms were submitted by AMT workers to describe the 29 different categories. The authors manually condensed the combined list of NYT corpus attributes and AMT worker attributes. Attributes that do not refer to a visual property were also removed, e.g. 'stolen' or 'unethical'. The final attribute list comprises 196 attributes.

4   Exhaustive Annotation

In annotating our attributes we would like to avoid asking redundant questions (e.g. asking if a person is "sitting" when they're already labeled as "standing"). To intelligently avoid these situations we need to understand the correlations among attributes. We first build an exhaustively annotated dataset that has a ground truth label obtained via the crowd for every possible object-attribute pair. Our exhaustively labeled dataset serves as a training set for the ELA method we will introduce in Sect. 5. A portion of the exhaustively labeled set is set aside as a validation set to measure the performance of the ELA.

To create the exhaustively labeled part of the COCO Attributes dataset, we employ the annotation UI shown in Fig. 2b for AMT. The object instances in this part of the dataset were chosen as follows: for all categories we exhaustively annotate 10 % of object instances that are larger than 32 × 32 px. AMT workers are shown 10 images per HIT and 20 possible attributes subsampled from the total 196. Workers are asked to check all attributes that apply to the object outlined in white. The attributes are roughly grouped by type, such as action word, emotion, surface property, etc.

To improve annotation quality, we implement several quality control techniques. We require that workers complete an annotation quiz in order to begin working on HITs. The quiz looks identical to the UI in Fig. 2b. The worker is required to score 90 % recall of the attributes present in that HIT. Labels are repeated by three workers in order to establish a consensus value for each label. Workers are discarded if their work is checked by the authors and found to be poor. The authors completed > 4,000 annotations. Workers are flagged for a check when they disagree too frequently with the authors' or trusted worker annotations. We define "too frequently" as disagreeing more often than a standard deviation away from the average disagreement of trusted workers. Trusted workers are established by the author's manual review.

We annotate a total of 20,112 object instances with all 196 attributes (5000 person instances and approximately 500 instances of every other object). If two of the three annotations for an attribute are positive, we consider it a true positive.

Responding to comments from our workers, we pay $0.10 per exhaustive annotation HIT. In total, this portion of the dataset cost: 20112 images × 196 attributes)/avg. 196 annotations per HIT × ($0.10 pay per HIT + $0.02 Amazon fee) × 3 workers repeat each annotation ≈ $7,240. If we continued this annotation policy to annotate the remaining 'person', 'animal', 'vehicle', and 'food' objects from COCO (285k instances), the total annotation cost would be **$102,600**. Using the ELA, we will be able to accomplish this task for only **$26,712**. That is the price of labeling the remaining 265 K object instances, querying 10 % of the attributes, and using our ELA MTurk HIT that shows 50 images per task (265k object × 20 attributes/50 images per HIT × $0.084 Amazon Fee × 3 workers = $26,712).

5   Economic Labeling

Attributes in many domains are sparse. With 196 attributes, we find that across all 29 object categories, the average number of positive attributes per object is 9.35. Ideally, we could identify the most likely attributes that are positive for each object and only ask the AMT workers to annotate (or verify) those attributes. Annotating a new dataset with a huge number of possible attributes would then be relatively inexpensive. Unfortunately, we do not possess an oracle capable of identifying the perfect set of attributes to ask about.

Without the benefit of an attribute oracle, we apply a method of selecting attributes that are likely to be positive for a given object instance. We begin with the set of COCO Attributes A. For an unlabeled object, we calculate the probability $P(a_i = 1|y)$ that an attribute $a_i \in A$ is true given the category y. Equation (3) calculates this likelihood as the mean of the probability of that attribute in all observations of the object category $\mathcal{I}_y$ (Eq. 1) and the probability of that attribute in the sibling object categories x that are part of the same super category S as y (Eq. 2). The object super categories and their child relationships are defined as part of the COCO dataset.

$$P(a_i = 1|\mathcal{I}_y) = \frac{N^1_{a_i,\mathcal{I}_y}}{N_{\mathcal{I}_y}} \tag{1}$$

To avoid a zero count for a rare attribute for object category y, we count the occurrences of a_i in all instances $\mathcal{I}_x$ of the sibling categories x of y, for $x \in S$. The hierarchical super-category S contains K sub-categories.

$$P(a_i = 1|\mathcal{I}_S) = \frac{\sum_{x=1}^K N^1_{a_i,\mathcal{I}_x}}{\sum_{x=1}^K N_{\mathcal{I}_x}} \tag{2}$$

We calculate the probability of a_i given y by the average of $P(a_i = 1|\mathcal{I}_y)$ and $P(a_i = 1|\mathcal{I}_S)$.

$$P(a_i = 1|y) = \frac{1}{2} * (P(a_i = 1|\mathcal{I}_y) + P(a_i = 1|\mathcal{I}_S)) \tag{3}$$

For example, Eq. 3 would calculate the probability of 'glazed' given 'donut' by calculating the percent of images where 'glazed' and 'donut' or 'glazed' and <other food category> were present for the same object in the set of exhaustively labeled examples. If an attribute such as 'dirty' never co-occurs with 'horse', Eq. 3 uses just the percent of images where 'dirty' co-occurred with any other animal category like 'cat' and 'dog'.

To select the most likely attribute for the object instance $\hat{a}$, given the set all of the labeled instances of category $\mathcal{I}_y$, we use by Eq. (4).

$$\hat{a} = \arg\max_{a_i \in A} P(a_i = 1|y) \tag{4}$$

Essentially, our economic labeling algorithm follows these steps: (1) Obtain an exhaustively annotated training set T. (2) For each object instance $\mathcal{I}_j$ in the unlabed dataset $\mathcal{D}$, label the most likely attribute from T calculated using Eq. (3). (3) Select the subset of labeled object instances from T that share the object category y of $\mathcal{I}_j$. (4) Annotate the attribute $\hat{a}$ (Eq. (4)) for object $\mathcal{I}_j$. (5) Repeat this process until each object in $\mathcal{D}$ has at least N attributes labeled, resulting in the labeled attribute dataset $\mathcal{D}'$. After the first round of labeling, step (3) is slightly changed so that y represents all object instances of category y that also share the attributes labeled in the previous iterations $\hat{a}_{n-1}$. This process is more precisely described in Algorithm 1.

There is one stage of the ELA that presents a tricky problem. What should be done if the subset of T returned by the function MatchingSubset in Algorithm 1 is empty? We explore four possible alternatives for overcoming the problem of an uninformative subset.

Our four alternative varieties of the AltMatchingMethod method are only used if either the matching subset is empty or the remaining attributes from

Input: Dataset $\mathcal{D}$ of unlabeled images, fully labeled training set $\mathcal{T}$, labels to annotate A
Output: Labeled dataset $\mathcal{D}'$

```
 1 for I_j ∈ D do
 2                                          ▷ I_j is an unlabeled image from D
 3     while NumLabels(I_j) < N do
 4                                          ▷ Repeat annotation until N labels are acquired
 5         D_S = MatchingSubset(I_j, D)
 6         if isEmpty(D_S) then
 7           | D_S = AltMatchingMethod(I_j, D)
 8         end
 9         Q_n = SelectAttributeQuery(D_S)
10         I_j[n] = Annotate(Q_n)
11     end
12 end
13 return D'
```

Algorithm 1. Economic Labeling Algorithm (ELA)

the matching subset have no positive labels. Otherwise, the ELA continues to ask for annotation of the most popular attributes in decreasing order. For our experiments, we also deemed a matching subset to be "empty" if it contained fewer than 5 matching instances.

The first alternative is the Random method, which randomly selects the next attribute to label from the set of unlabeled attributes. The second strategy is the Population method, which proceeds to query the next most popular attribute calculated from the whole labeled set $\mathcal{T}$.

Our third alternative, Backoff, retreats backward through the previously calculated subsets until a subset with a positive attribute that has not been labeled is found. For example, if a dog instance is annotated first with 'standing' and then with 'not furry', there may be no matching dog instances in the training that have both of those labels. The Backoff method would take the subset of training instances labeled 'dog' and 'standing', calculate the second most popular attribute after 'furry', and ask about that second most popular attribute. The Backoff method is similar to the Population method except that the Population method effectively backs off all the way to the beginning of the decision pipeline to decide the next most popular attribute.

The fourth method we explore is the Distance method. This alternative uses the current subset of annotated attributes as a feature vector and finds the 100 nearest neighbors from the set $\mathcal{T}$, given only the subset of currently labeled attributes. For example, if a partially labeled example had 10 attributes labeled, the nearest neighbors would be calculated using the corresponding 10-dimensional feature vector. The next most popular attribute is selected from the set of nearest neighbors.

In order to compare these alternative methods, we split our exhaustively labeled dataset into test and train sets. We use 19k object instances for the training set and 1k object instances for test. The object instances are randomly selected from all 29 object categories. In our simulation, we use the ELA methods to generate the annotated attributes for the test set. For each object instance in the test set, we begin by knowing the category and super-category labels. For example, given a test image we might know that it is a 'dog' and an 'animal'.

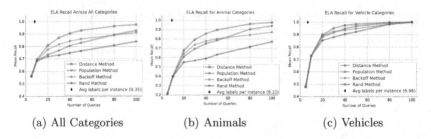

(a) All Categories   (b) Animals   (c) Vehicles

Fig. 3. *Mean Recall Comparison of Alternative ELA methods.* (a) plots the mean recall of the test dataset alternatively labeled with each ELA method and stopped for a range of query limits. All categories were included in this comparison. The Distance method is the clear winner, obtaining 80 % recall for only 20 attribute queries, approximately 10 % of the total number of attributes. (b) and (c) show the mean recall across all test instances of their type of category. The vehicle categories achieve a higher recall with fewer queries than the animal categories. This may be due to the smaller subset of attributes relevant to vehicles than to animals.

We proceed by following the steps of the ELA up to a limit of N attribute queries. We determine the response to each query by taking the ground truth value from the test set. In this way we simulate 3 AMT workers responding to an attribute annotation query and taking their consensus. After N queries, we calculate the recall for that instance by comparing the number of positive attribute annotations in the ELA label vector to the exhaustive label vector. If we use the ELA to label a 'dog' instance up to 20 queries and obtain 8 positive attributes, but the ground truth attribute vector for that dog has 10 positive attributes, then the recall for that instance is 0.8.

We compare the four alternative methods in Fig. 3. Each method is tested on 1k object instances, and the mean recall score averages the recall of all test instances. In all of the plots in Fig. 3, the four methods preform approximately the same for the first 10 attribute queries. This is to be expected as none of the methods will perform differently until the partially labeled instances become sufficiently distinctive to have no matching subsets in the training set.

After approximately 10 queries, the methods begin to diverge. The Random method shows linear improvement with the number of queries. If these plots were extrapolated to 196 queries, the Random method would achieve a recall of 1.0 at query 196. The other methods improve faster, approaching perfect recall much sooner. The Backoff method initially out-performs the population method, indicating that at early stages querying the popular attributes from a more specific subset is a better choice than querying the most popular attributes overall. This distinction fails to be significant after more queries are answered.

The best performing method is the Distance method. This method comes closer to selecting the best subset of attribute queries both for the full hierarchy and for the animal and vehicle sub-trees. The success of the Distance method indicates that the most likely next attribute for a given image may be found by looking at examples that are similar but not exactly the same as a given object.

Based on the Distance method results in Fig. 3, we use a different number of attribute queries per object type to annotate COCO Attributes. We ask enough questions to ensure that each object type's attributes have mean recall of 80 %, e.g. 30 for animals, 17 for vehicles, etc. We ask for 20 attributes on average according to Fig. 3a.

To further examine the performance of the ELA with the Distance method, we plot a selection of per attribute recall scores in Fig. 4. The attributes in Fig. 4 are sorted by ascending population in the dataset. One would expect the more popular attributes to have higher recall than the less popular attributes for a lower number of attribute queries. This is not strictly the case however. 'Stretching', for example, is a popular attribute, but does not obtain higher than 0.9 recall until 100 queries. This indicates that 'stretching' is not strongly correlated with other attributes in the dataset. Conversely, even at 20 attribute queries many of the rarer attributes still have a reasonable chance of being queried.

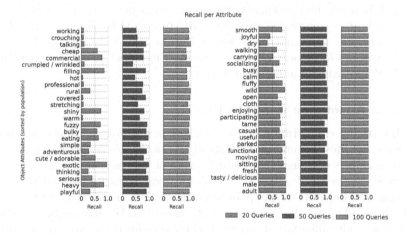

Fig. 4. *Mean Recall Across all Categories for 50 Attributes.* This plot shows the recall of the ELA-Distance method for annotating 50 randomly selected attributes from the full set of 196. The recall is calculated across all instances of the exhaustively labeled test set. The attributes are sorted by their popularity in the exhaustively labeled dataset. Mean chance recall is 0.092, and varies from 0.03 to 0.1 across attributes. The ELA beats chance recall for all attributes.

We also attempt hybrid versions of the methods described above. We repeat the simulation shown in Fig. 3 by first annotating the top 10 most popular attributes, and then continuing with the alternate methods. In this way we might be able to to discover unusual objects early, thus making our method more robust. However, the performance of the hybrid methods were barely different than that shown in Fig. 3.

Figure 4 shows where the ELA does cause a bias by missing the "tail" of rare attributes with too few attribute queries. But this is not a *visual* bias linked

Fig. 5. *Examples from COCO Attributes.* These are positive examples of the listed attributes from the dataset. Examples such as the man cuddling a horse or the dog riding a surfboard shows how this dataset adds important context to image that would otherwise be lost by only listing the objects present in an image.

to a particular feature or classifier as would be the case with an active learning approach. It would be problematic if dataset errors were linked to a particular feature and future approaches were implicitly penalized for being different from that feature. The ELA and visual active learning could be used together, but in this paper we focus only on characterizing the potential bias incurred by a non-visual approximate annotation method.

Attribute Annotation using the ELA

For ELA attribute annotation, we ask workers to label one attribute at a time. We cannot use the UI from Fig. 2b. Instead we ask the AMT workers to select all positive examples of a single attribute for a set of images from a given category, example shown in Fig. 2c. We elect to ask for fewer annotations per HIT in the ELA stage (50 object-attribute pairs) than in the exhaustive stage (200 object-attribute pairs). This choice was made to lessen worker fatigue and improve performance. The difference in worker performance for the exhaustive and ELA HITs is discussed more in the supplemental materials.

Thus far we have collected approximately 3.4M object-attribute pairs. Apart from the exhaustive labels we used to bootstrap ELA annotation, we have collected at least 20 attributes for 24,492 objects at a cost of **$2,469** ($\sim$ 24k objects $\times$ 20 attributes/50 attributes per HIT $\times$ 3 repeat workers $\times$ \$0.084 per HIT). If we used the exhaustive annotation method, this would have cost **$8,817**.

In the end, the COCO Attributes dataset has a variety of popular and rare attributes. 75 % of attributes have more than 216 positive examples in the dataset, 50 % have more than 707, and 25 % have more than 2511. Figure 5 shows some qualitative examples from COCO Attributes.

6   Attribute Classification

Ultimately, attribute labels are only useful if visual classifiers can be built from them. To verify the detectability of our attributes, we trained independent clas-

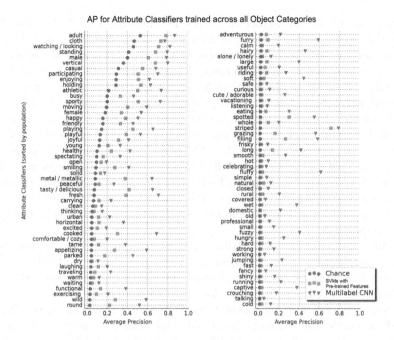

Fig. 6. *Average Precision vs. Chance.* Performance is shown for 100 randomly selected attributes. Attribtues are sorted in descending order by their population in the dataset. Each yellow square represents an SVM that was trained using pre-trained CNN features to recognize that particular attribute. Each blue triangle represents the AP for that attribute calculated on the full multi-label test set predictions of our fine-tuned CNN. (Color figure online)

sifiers for each attribute, agnostic of object category. Figure 6 shows AP scores of 100 randomly selected attribute classifiers.

To train the attribute classifiers, features for each object instance's bounding box were extracted using the pre-trained Caffe hybridCNN network released with the publication of the Places Dataset [28,29]. For the features used in these classifiers, we take the output of the final fully connected layer, randomly subsample 200 dimensions, and apply power normalization as per the recommendations of [30]. We then train a linear SVM using a set of object instances that have 20 or more attributes annotated with the ELA. Subsampling the FC7 activations to 200D actually leads to higher performance than using all activations (4096D), with an average increase of 0.012 AP across all attribute classifiers. Chance is calculated as the ratio of true positives to total training examples for each attribute.

As a counterpoint to recognizing attributes in isolation, we trained a multi-label CNN to simultaneously predict all attributes for a novel test image. We created this network by fine-tuning the BVLC reference network from the Caffe library [29]. Our attribute network uses a sigmoid cross-entropy loss layer instead of a softmax layer to optimize for multi-label classification, as suggested by previous research in multi-label and attribute classification [31–33]. The fine-tuning was accomplished with SGD with momentum slightly higher than the reference net, but with learning rate lower and regularization stronger to account for the sparsity of positive labels in the training set. This network is trained with a the full, multi-label attribute vector for each object in the train and test sets. Unlabeled attributes are assumed to be negative after 20 rounds of ELA.

In Fig. 6 the objects in the training set for all classifiers shown are members of the COCO 'train2014' set, and test instances are members of the 'val2014' set. In order to compare the individual SVMs and the multilabel CNN, we used the same training and test sets for all classifiers. The train/test sets were composed of 50k object instances labeled with the ELA with 20 or more attributes. All unlabeled attributes were assumed false for both the SVMs and CNN. The train/test set split was 30k/20k and contained instances from COCO train and val sets respectively.

Figure 6 compares the per attribute AP over the test set predictions from our multi-label CNN to the independent SVMs trained independently for each attribute. This plot shows that exploiting the correlations between attributes often improves classifier performance for the CNN compared to the independent SVMs, especially for rarer attributes. Overall attributes the mean chance score is 0.08 AP, mean SVM performance is 0.18 AP, and mean CNN performance is 0.35 AP. This experiment shows the benefits of exploiting multilabel co-occurrence information with a 0.17 mAP over using pre-trained features.

7   Future Work

Work on COCO Attributes is ongoing. Workers are continuously submitting new ELA HITs for the remaining 'person', 'animal', 'vehicle', and 'food' instances from the COCO dataset. The set of objects could easily be expanded to comprise more of the COCO categories. More categories would necessitate more attributes, but our attribute discovery process combined with the ELA are capable of scaling up the annotation effort effectively. Further analysis of alternative selection methods could result in improved recall for low numbers of attribute queries. This economical annotation method begs to be used on larger dataset annotation efforts.

References

1. Antol, S., Agrawal, A., Lu, J., Mitchell, M., Batra, D., Lawrence Zitnick, C., Parikh, D.: VQA: visual question answering. In: Proceedings of the IEEE International Conference on Computer Vision, pp. 2425–2433 (2015)
2. Geman, D., Geman, S., Hallonquist, N., Younes, L.: Visual turing test for computer vision systems. Proc. Natl. Acad. Sci. **112**(12), 3618–3623 (2015)
3. Farhadi, A., Endres, I., Hoiem, D., Forsyth, D.: Describing objects by their attributes. In: CVPR (2009)
4. Lampert, C.H., Nickisch, H., Harmeling, S.: Learning to detect unseen object classes by between-class attribute transfer. In: CVPR (2009)

5. Rohrbach, M., Stark, M., Szarvas, G., Gurevych, I., Schiele, B.: What helps where-
and why? semantic relatedness for knowledge transfer. In: 2010 IEEE Conference
on Computer Vision and Pattern Recognition (CVPR), pp. 910–917. IEEE (2010)
6. Deng, J., Krause, J., Fei-Fei, L.: Fine-grained crowdsourcing for fine-grained
recognition. In: IEEE Conference on Computer Vision and Pattern Recognition
(CVPR), June 2013
7. Branson, S., Wah, C., Schroff, F., Babenko, B., Welinder, P., Perona, P., Belongie,
S.: Visual recognition with humans in the loop. In: Daniilidis, K., Maragos, P.,
Paragios, N. (eds.) ECCV 2010. LNCS, vol. 6314, pp. 438–451. Springer, Heidelberg
(2010). doi:10.1007/978-3-642-15561-1_32
8. Patterson, G., Hays, J.: Sun attribute database: discovering, annotating, and recognizing scene attributes. In: 2012 IEEE Conference on Computer Vision and Pattern
Recognition (CVPR), pp. 2751–2758. IEEE (2012)
9. Dow, S., Kulkarni, A., Klemmer, S., Hartmann, B.: Shepherding the crowd yields
better work. In: Proceedings of the ACM 2012 Conference on Computer Supported
Cooperative Work, pp. 1013–1022. ACM (2012)
10. Krishna, R., Zhu, Y., Groth, O., Johnson, J., Hata, K., Kravitz, J., Chen, S.,
Kalantidis, Y., Li, L.J., Shamma, D.A., et al.: Visual genome: connecting language and vision using crowdsourced dense image annotations. arXiv preprint
arXiv:1602.07332 (2016)
11. Wah, C., Branson, S., Welinder, P., Perona, P., Belongie, S.: The Caltech-UCSD
Birds-200-2011 Dataset. Technical report CNS-TR-2011-001, California Institute
of Technology (2011)
12. Berg, T.L., Berg, A.C., Shih, J.: Automatic attribute discovery and characterization from noisy web data. In: Daniilidis, K., Maragos, P., Paragios, N. (eds.)
ECCV 2010. LNCS, vol. 6311, pp. 663–676. Springer, Heidelberg (2010). doi:10.
1007/978-3-642-15549-9_48
13. Parikh, D., Grauman, K.: Interactively building a discriminative vocabulary of
nameable attributes. In: CVPR (2011)
14. Farhadi, A., Endres, I., Hoiem, D.: Attribute-centric recognition for cross-category
generalization. In: CVPR (2010)
15. Kumar, N., Berg, A., Belhumeur, P., Nayar, S.: Attribute and simile classifiers for
face verification. In: ICCV (2009)
16. Liu, J., Kuipers, B., Savarese, S.: Recognizing human actions by attributes. In:
CVPR (2011)
17. Bourdev, L., Maji, S., Malik, J.: Describing people: a poselet-based approach to
attribute classification. In: 2011 International Conference on Computer Vision, pp.
1543–1550. IEEE (2011)
18. Vedaldi, A., Mahendran, S., Tsogkas, S., Maji, S., Girshick, R., Kannala, J., Rahtu,
E., Kokkinos, I., Blaschko, M.B., Weiss, D., et al.: Understanding objects in detail
with fine-grained attributes. In: 2014 IEEE Conference on Computer Vision and
Pattern Recognition (CVPR), pp. 3622–3629. IEEE (2014)
19. Kovashka, A., Parikh, D., Grauman, K.: Whittlesearch: image search with relative
attribute feedback. In: The IEEE Conference on Computer Vision and Pattern
Recognition (CVPR) (2012)
20. Parikh, D., Grauman, K.: Relative attributes. In: ICCV (2011)
21. Vijayanarasimhan, S., Grauman, K.: Large-scale live active learning: training
object detectors with crawled data and crowds. In: 2011 IEEE Conference on Computer Vision and Pattern Recognition (CVPR), pp. 1449–1456. IEEE (2011)
22. Abramson, Y., Freund, Y.: Active learning for visual object recognition. Technical
report, UCSD (2004)

23. Collins, B., Deng, J., Li, K., Fei-Fei, L.: Towards scalable dataset construction: an active learning approach. In: Forsyth, D., Torr, P., Zisserman, A. (eds.) ECCV 2008. LNCS, vol. 5302, pp. 86–98. Springer, Heidelberg (2008). doi:10.1007/978-3-540-88682-2_8

24. Patterson, G., Van Horn, G., Belongie, S., Perona, P., Hays, J.: Tropel: crowdsourcing detectors with minimal training. In: Third AAAI Conference on Human Computation and Crowdsourcing (2015)

25. Deng, J., Russakovsky, O., Krause, J., Bernstein, M.S., Berg, A., Fei-Fei, L.: Scalable multi-label annotation. In: Proceedings of the SIGCHI Conference on Human Factors in Computing Systems, pp. 3099–3102. ACM (2014)

26. Deng, J., Ding, N., Jia, Y., Frome, A., Murphy, K., Bengio, S., Li, Y., Neven, H., Adam, H.: Large-scale object classification using label relation graphs. In: Fleet, D., Pajdla, T., Schiele, B., Tuytelaars, T. (eds.) ECCV 2014. LNCS, vol. 8689, pp. 48–64. Springer, Heidelberg (2014). doi:10.1007/978-3-319-10590-1_4

27. Sandhaus, E.: The new york times annotated corpus. Linguist. Data Consortium Philadelphia 6(12), e26752 (2008)

28. Zhou, B., Lapedriza, A., Xiao, J., Torralba, A., Oliva, A.: Learning deep features for scene recognition using places database. In: Advances in Neural Information Processing Systems, pp. 487–495 (2014)

29. Jia, Y., Shelhamer, E., Donahue, J., Karayev, S., Long, J., Girshick, R., Guadarrama, S., Darrell, T.: Caffe: convolutional architecture for fast feature embedding. In: Proceedings of the ACM International Conference on Multimedia, pp. 675–678. ACM (2014)

30. Razavian, A.S., Azizpour, H., Sullivan, J., Carlsson, S.: CNN features off-the-shelf: an astounding baseline for recognition. arXiv preprint arXiv:1403.6382 (2014)

31. Shankar, S., Garg, V.K., Cipolla, R.: Deep-carving: discovering visual attributes by carving deep neural nets. In: Proceedings of the IEEE Conference on Computer Vision and Pattern Recognition, pp. 3403–3412 (2015)

32. Gong, Y., Jia, Y., Leung, T., Toshev, A., Ioffe, S.: Deep convolutional ranking for multilabel image annotation. arXiv preprint arXiv:1312.4894 (2013)

33. Guillaumin, M., Mensink, T., Verbeek, J., Schmid, C.: TagProp: discriminative metric learning in nearest neighbor models for image auto-annotation. In: 2009 IEEE 12th International Conference on Computer Vision, pp. 309–316. IEEE (2009)

Temporally Robust Global Motion Compensation by Keypoint-Based Congealing

S. Morteza Safdarnejad$^{(\boxtimes)}$, Yousef Atoum, and Xiaoming Liu

Michigan State University, East Lansing, USA
safdarne@egr.msu.edu, atoumyou@msu.edu, liuxm@cse.msu.edu

Abstract. Global motion compensation (GMC) removes the impact of camera motion and creates a video in which the background appears static over the progression of time. Various vision problems, such as human activity recognition, background reconstruction, and multi-object tracking can benefit from GMC. Existing GMC algorithms rely on sequentially processing consecutive frames, by estimating the transformation mapping the two frames, and obtaining a composite transformation to a global motion compensated coordinate. Sequential GMC suffers from temporal drift of frames from the accurate global coordinate, due to either error accumulation or sporadic failures of motion estimation at a few frames. We propose a temporally robust global motion compensation (TRGMC) algorithm which performs accurate and stable GMC, despite complicated and long-term camera motion. TRGMC densely connects pairs of frames, by matching local keypoints of each frame. A joint alignment of these frames is formulated as a novel keypoint-based congealing problem, where the transformation of each frame is updated iteratively, such that the spatial coordinates for the start and end points of matched keypoints are identical. Experimental results demonstrate that TRGMC has superior performance in a wide range of scenarios.

Keywords: Global motion compensation · Congealing · Motion panorama

1 Introduction

Global motion compensation (GMC) removes the impact of *intentional* and *unwanted* camera motion in the video, transforming the video to have *static* background with the only motion coming from foreground objects. As a related problem, video stabilization removes *unwanted* camera motion, such as vibration, and generates a video with a *smooth* camera motion. The term "global motion compensation" is also used in video coding literature, where background motion is estimated roughly to enhance the video compression performance [1,2].

GMC is an essential module for processing videos from *non-stationary* cameras, which are abundant due to emerging mobile sensors, e.g., wearable cameras, smartphones, and camera drones. First, the resultant *motion panorama* [3], as if virtually generated by a static camera, is by itself appealing for visual perception. More importantly, many vision tasks may benefit from GMC. For instance,

© Springer International Publishing AG 2016
B. Leibe et al. (Eds.): ECCV 2016, Part VI, LNCS 9910, pp. 101–119, 2016.
DOI: 10.1007/978-3-319-46466-4_7

Fig. 1. Schematic diagrams of proposed TRGMC and existing sequential GMC algorithms, and resultant motion panorama for a video shot by panning the camera up and down. Background continuity breaks easily in the case of the sequential GMC [10].

dense trajectories [4] are shown to be superior when camera motion is compensated [5]. Otherwise, camera motion interferes with human motion, rendering the analysis problem very challenging. GMC allows reconstruction of a "stitched" background [6], and subsequently segmentation of foreground [7,8]. This helps multi-object tracking by mitigating the unconstrained problem of tracking multiple in-the-wild objects, to tracking objects with a static background [9].

In existing GMC works [10–12], frames are transformed to a global motion-compensated coordinate (GMCC), by *sequentially* processing input frames. For a pair of consecutive frames, the mapping transformation is estimated, and by accumulating the transformations, a *composite* global transformation of each frame to the GMCC is obtained. However, the sequential processing scheme causes frequent GMC failures for multiple reasons: (1) Sequential GMC is only as strong as the *weakest* pair of consecutive frames. A single frame with high blur or dominant foreground motion can cause the rest of the video to fail. (2) Generally, multiple planes exist in the scene. The common assumption of a single homography will accumulate residual errors into remarkable errors. (3) Even if the error of consecutive frames is in a sub-pixel scale, due to the *multiplication* of several homography matrices, the error can be significant over time [6]. These problems are especially severe when processing long videos and/or the camera motion becomes more complicated. E.g., when the camera pans to left and right repeatedly, or severe camera vibration exists, the GMC error is obvious by exhibiting discontinuity on the background (see Fig. 1 for an example).

To address the issues of sequential GMC, we propose a temporally robust global motion compensation (TRGMC) algorithm which by *joint* alignment of input frames, estimates accurate and temporally consistent transformations to GMCC. The result can be rendered as a motion panorama that maintains perceptual realism despite complicated camera motion (Fig. 1). TRGMC densely connects pairs of frames, by matching local keypoints via keypoint descriptors.

Joint alignment (a.k.a. congealing) of these frames is formulated as an optimization problem where the transformation of each frame is updated iteratively, such that for each *link* interconnecting a keypoint pair, the spatial coordinates of two end points are identical. This novel *keypoint-based congealing*, built upon succinct keypoint coordinates instead of high-dimensional appearance features, is the core of TRGMC. Joint alignment not only leads to the temporal consistency of GMC, but also improves GMC stability by using redundancy of the information. This improved stability is crucial for GMC, especially in the presence of considerable foreground motion, motion blur, non-rigid motion like water, or low-texture background. The joint alignment scheme also provides capabilities such as coarse-to-fine alignment, i.e., alignment of the keyframes followed by non-keyframes, and appropriate weighting of keypoints matches, which cannot be naturally integrated into sequential GMC. Our quantitative experiments reveal that TRGMC pushes the alignment error close to human performance.

2 Prior Work

TRGMC is related to many techniques in different aspects. We first review them and then compare our work with existing GMC algorithms.

Firstly, homography estimation from keypoint matches is crucial to many vision tasks, e.g., image stitching, registration, and GMC. Its main challenge is the false matches due to appearance ambiguities. Methods are proposed to either be robust to outliers, such as RANSAC [13–16] and reject false matches [17,18], or probabilistically combine appearance similarities and keypoint matches [10,19]. *All methods estimate a homography for a frame pair.* In contrast, we jointly estimate homographies of *all frames* to a global coordinate, which leverages the redundant background matches over time to better handle outliers.

Image stitching (IS) and panoramic image mosaicing share similarity with GMC. IS aims to minimize the distortions and ghosting artifact in the overlap region. Recent works focus on different challenges, e.g., multi-plane scenes [20–25], the parallax issue [26–28], and motion blur [29]. In these works, input images have much less overlap than GMC. On the other hand, video mosaicing takes in a video which raster scans a wide angle *static* scene, and produces a single *static* panoramic image [30–32]. When the camera path forms a 2D scan [30] or a 360° rotation [32], global refinement is performed via bundle adjustment (BA) [33], which ensures an artifact-free panoramic image. Although a byproduct of TRGMC is a similar static reconstruction of the scene, TRGMC focuses on efficient generation of an appealing video, for a *highly dynamic* scene. While one may use BA to estimate camera pose and then transformation between frames, our experiments reveal that BA is not reliable for videos with foreground motion and is less efficient than TRGMC. Hence, image/video mosaicing and GMC have different application scenarios and challenges.

Another related topic is the panoramic video [34–38]. For instance, Perazzi et al. [35] create a panoramic video from an array of stationary cameras by generalizing parallax-tolerant image stitching to video stitching. While these works focus on stitching *multiple* synchronized videos, GMC creates a motion panorama from a *single non-stationary* camera. Unlike GMC, video panoramas do not require the resultant video to have a stationary background.

Video stabilization (VS) is a closely related but different problem. TRGMC can be re-purposed for VS, but not vice versa, due to the accuracy requirement. Given the accurate mapping to a global coordinate using TRGMC, VS would mainly amount to cropping out a smooth sequence of frames and handling rendering issues such as parallax. Among different categories of VS, 2D VS methods calculate consecutive warping between the frames and have similarities with *sequential* GMC, but any estimation error will not cause severe degradation in VS as long as it is smoothed. While TRGMC targets *long-term staticness of the background*, VS mainly cares about *smoothing* of camera motion, not *removing* it. In other words, TRGMC imposes a stronger constraint on the result. This strict requirement differentiates TRGMC also from Re-Cinematography [39].

Congealing aims to jointly align a stack of images from one object class, e.g., faces and letters [40–43]. Congealing iteratively updates the transformations of all images such that the entropy [40] or Sum of Squared Differences (SSD) [44] of the images, is minimized. However, despite many extensions of congealing [45–49], almost all prior work define the energy based on the *appearance features* of two images. Our experiments on GMC show that appearance-based congealing is inefficient and sensitive to initialization and foreground motion. Therefore, we propose a novel keypoint-based congealing algorithm minimizing the SSD of corresponding *keypoint coordinates*. Further, most prior works apply to a spatially cropped object such as faces, while we deal with complex video frames with dynamic foreground and moving background, at a higher spatial-temporal resolution. Note that [46] uses a heuristic local feature based algorithm to rigidly align object class images. In contrast we formulate the joint alignment of keypoints as an optimization problem and solve it in a principal way.

There are a few existing sequential GMC works, where the main problem is to accurately estimate a homography transformation between consecutive frames, given challenges such as appearance ambiguities, multi-plane scene, and dominant foreground [3,10,12]. Bartoli et al. [11] first estimate an approximate 4-degree-of-freedom homography, and then refine it. Sakamoto et al. [32] generate a 360° panorama from an image sequence. Assuming a 5-degree-of-freedom homography, all the homographies are optimized jointly to prevent error accumulation. In contrast, TRGMC employs an 8-degree-of-freedom homography. Although using homography in the case of considerable camera translation and large depth variation results in parallax artifacts, using a higher degrees-of-freedom homography than prior works allows TRGMC to better handle camera panning, zooming, and translation. Safdarnejad et al. [10] incorporate edge matching into a probabilistic framework that scores candidate homographies. Although [10,12] improve the robustness to foreground, error accumulation and failure in a single frame pair still deteriorate the overall performance. Thus, TRGMC targets robustness of the GMC in terms of both the presence of foreground and long-term consistency by joint alignment of frames.

3   Proposed TRGMC Algorithm

The core of TRGMC is the novel keypoint-based congealing algorithm. Our method relies on densely interconnecting the input frames, regardless of their temporal offset, by matching the detected SURF keypoints at each frame using SURF descriptors [50]. We refer to these connections, shown in Fig. 2, as *links*. Frames are initialized to their approximate spatial location by only 2D translation (Sect. 3.4). We rectify the keypoint matches such that majority of the links have end points on the background region. Then the congealing applies appropriate transformation to each frame and the links connected to it, such that the spatial coordinates of the end-points of each link are as similar as possible. In Fig. 2, this translates to having the links as parallel to the $t-$axis as possible.

For efficiency and robustness, TRGMC processes an input video in two stages. Stage one selects and jointly aligns a set of keyframes. The keyframes are frozen, and then stage two aligns each remaining frame to its two encompassing keyframes. The remainder of this section presents the details of the algorithm.

3.1   Formulation of Keypoint-Based Congealing

Given a stack of N frames $\{\mathbf{I}^{(i)}\}$, with indices $i \in \mathbb{K} = \{k_1, ..., k_N\}$, the keypoint-based congealing is formulated as an optimization problem,

$$\min_{\{\mathbf{p}_i\}} \epsilon = \sum_{i \in \mathbb{K}} [\mathbf{e}_i(\mathbf{p}_i)]^\mathsf{T} \Omega^{(i)} [\mathbf{e}_i(\mathbf{p}_i)], \tag{1}$$

where $\mathbf{p}_i$ is the transformation parameter from frame i to GMCC, $\mathbf{e}_i(\mathbf{p}_i)$ collects the pair-wise alignment errors of frame i relative to all the other frames in the stack, and $\Omega^{(i)}$ is a weight matrix.

We define the alignment error of frame i as the SSD between the spatial coordinates of the endpoints of all links connecting frame i to the other frames, instead of the SSD of appearance [44]. Specifically, as shown in Fig. 3, we denote coordinates of the start and the end point of each link k connecting frame i to the frame $d_k^{(i)} \in \mathbb{K}\backslash\{i\}$ as $(x_k^{(i)}, y_k^{(i)})$ and $(u_k^{(i)}, v_k^{(i)})$, respectively. For simplicity, we omit the frame index i in $\mathbf{p}_i$. Thus, the error $\mathbf{e}_i(\mathbf{p})$ is defined as,

$$\mathbf{e}_i(\mathbf{p}) = [\boldsymbol{\Delta}\mathbf{x}_i(\mathbf{p})^\mathsf{T}, \boldsymbol{\Delta}\mathbf{y}_i(\mathbf{p})^\mathsf{T}]^\mathsf{T}, \tag{2}$$

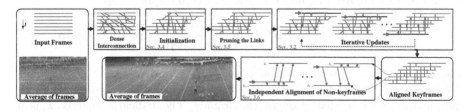

Fig. 2. Flowchart of the TRGMC algorithm.

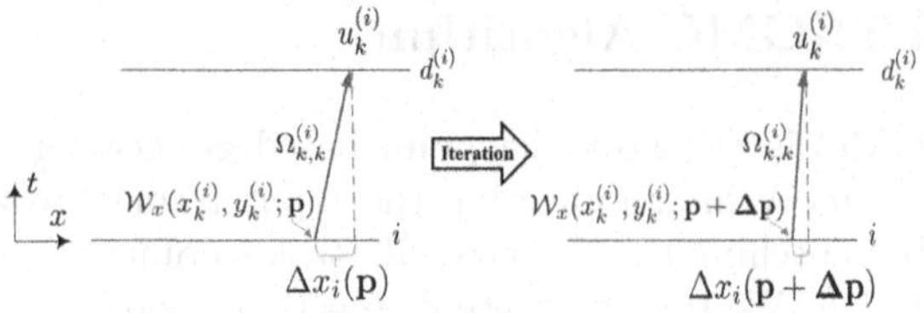

Fig. 3. The notation used in TRGMC.

where $\Delta\mathbf{x}_i(\mathbf{p}) = \mathbf{w}_x^{(i)} - \mathbf{u}^{(i)}$ and $\Delta\mathbf{y}_i(\mathbf{p}) = \mathbf{w}_y^{(i)} - \mathbf{v}^{(i)}$, are the errors in $x-$ and $y-$ axes. The vectors $\mathbf{w}_x^{(i)} = [\mathcal{W}_x(x_k^{(i)}, y_k^{(i)}; \mathbf{p})]$ and $\mathbf{w}_y^{(i)} = [\mathcal{W}_y(x_k^{(i)}, y_k^{(i)}; \mathbf{p})]$ denote the x and $y-$ coordinates of $(x_k^{(i)}, y_k^{(i)})$ warped by the parameter $\mathbf{p}$, respectively. The vectors $\mathbf{u}^{(i)} = [u_k^{(i)}]$ and $\mathbf{v}^{(i)} = [v_k^{(i)}]$ denote the coordinates of the end points and $\mathbf{x}^{(i)} = [x_k^{(i)}]$ and $\mathbf{y}^{(i)} = [y_k^{(i)}]$ denote the coordinates of the start points. If N_i links emanate from frame i, $\mathbf{e}_i$ is a $2N_i-$dim vector. $\Omega^{(i)}$ is a diagonal matrix of size $2N_i \times 2N_i$ which assigns a weight to each element in $\mathbf{e}_i$. The parameter $\mathbf{p}$ has 2, 6, or 8 elements for the cases of 2D translation, affine transformation, or homography, respectively. In this paper, we focus on homography transformation which is a projective warp model, parameterized as,

$$\begin{bmatrix} \mathcal{W}_x(x_k^{(i)}, y_k^{(i)}; \mathbf{p}) \\ \mathcal{W}_y(x_k^{(i)}, y_k^{(i)}; \mathbf{p}) \\ 1 \end{bmatrix} = \overbrace{\begin{bmatrix} p_1 & p_2 & p_3 \\ p_4 & p_5 & p_6 \\ p_7 & p_8 & 1 \end{bmatrix}}^{\mathbf{p}} \begin{bmatrix} x_k^{(i)} \\ y_k^{(i)} \\ 1 \end{bmatrix}. \tag{3}$$

Although the homography model assumes the planar scene and this assumption may be violated in real world [27], we identify the problem of temporal robustness to be more fundamental for GMC than the inaccuracies due to a *single* homography. Also, videos for GMC are generally swiped through the scene with high overlap, thus the discontinuity resulted from this assumption is minor.

3.2 Optimization solution

Equation 1 is a non-linear optimization problem and difficult to minimize. Following [44], we linearize this equation by taking the first-order Taylor expansion around $\mathbf{p}$. Starting from an initial $\mathbf{p}$, the goal is to estimate $\Delta\mathbf{p}$ by,

$$\underset{\Delta\mathbf{p}}{\operatorname{argmin}} \, [\mathbf{e}_i(\mathbf{p}) + \frac{\partial\mathbf{e}_i(\mathbf{p})}{\partial\mathbf{p}} \Delta\mathbf{p}]^{\mathsf{T}} \Omega^{(i)} [\mathbf{e}_i(\mathbf{p}) + \frac{\partial\mathbf{e}_i(\mathbf{p})}{\partial\mathbf{p}} \Delta\mathbf{p}] + \gamma\Delta\mathbf{p}^{\mathsf{T}}\mathcal{I}\Delta\mathbf{p}, \tag{4}$$

where $\Delta\mathbf{p}^{\mathsf{T}}\mathcal{I}\Delta\mathbf{p}$ is a regularization term, with a positive constant γ setting the trade-off. We observe that without this regularization, parameter estimation may lead to distortion of the frames. The indicator matrix $\mathcal{I}$ is a diagonal matrix specifying which elements of $\Delta\mathbf{p}$ need a constraint. We use

$\mathcal{I} = diag([1, 1, 0, 1, 1, 0, 1, 1])$ to specify that there is no constraint on the translation parameters of the homography, but the rest of parameters should remain small.

By setting the first-order derivative of Eq. 4 to zero, the solution for $\Delta\mathbf{p}$ is,

$$\Delta\mathbf{p} = \mathbf{H}_R^{-1} \frac{\partial\mathbf{e}_i(\mathbf{p})^{\mathsf{T}}}{\partial\mathbf{p}} \Omega^{(i)} \mathbf{e}_i(\mathbf{p}), \tag{5}$$

$$\mathbf{H}_R = \frac{\partial\mathbf{e}_i(\mathbf{p})^{\mathsf{T}}}{\partial\mathbf{p}} \Omega^{(i)} \frac{\partial\mathbf{e}_i(\mathbf{p})}{\partial\mathbf{p}} + \gamma\mathcal{I}. \tag{6}$$

Using the chain rule, we have $\frac{\partial\mathbf{e}_i(\mathbf{p})}{\partial\mathbf{p}} = \frac{\partial\mathbf{e}_i(\mathbf{p})}{\partial\mathcal{W}} \frac{\partial\mathcal{W}}{\partial\mathbf{p}}$. Knowing that the mapping has two components as $\mathcal{W} = (\mathcal{W}_x, \mathcal{W}_y)$, and the first half of $\mathbf{e}_i$ only contains x components and the rest only y components, we have,

$$\frac{\partial\mathbf{e}_i(\mathbf{p})}{\partial\mathcal{W}} = \begin{bmatrix} \mathbf{1}_{N_i} & \mathbf{0}_{N_i} \\ \mathbf{0}_{N_i} & \mathbf{1}_{N_i} \end{bmatrix}, \tag{7}$$

where $\mathbf{1}_{N_i}$ (or $\mathbf{0}_{N_i}$) is a N_i−dim vector with all elements being 1 (or 0). For homography transformation, $\frac{\partial\mathcal{W}}{\partial\mathbf{p}} = \frac{\partial(\mathcal{W}_x, \mathcal{W}_y)}{\partial(p_1, p_2, p_3, p_4, p_5, p_6, p_7, p_8)}$ is given by,

$$\frac{\partial\mathcal{W}}{\partial\mathbf{p}} = \begin{bmatrix} \mathbf{w}_x^{(i)} & \mathbf{w}_y^{(i)} & \mathbf{1}_{N_i} & \mathbf{0}_{N_i} & \mathbf{0}_{N_i} & \mathbf{0}_{N_i} & -\mathbf{u}^{(i)}\mathbf{w}_x^{(i)} & -\mathbf{u}^{(i)}\mathbf{w}_y^{(i)} \\ \mathbf{0}_{N_i} & \mathbf{0}_{N_i} & \mathbf{0}_{N_i} & \mathbf{w}_x^{(i)} & \mathbf{w}_y^{(i)} & \mathbf{1}_{N_i} & -\mathbf{v}^{(i)}\mathbf{w}_x^{(i)} & -\mathbf{v}^{(i)}\mathbf{w}_y^{(i)} \end{bmatrix}. \tag{8}$$

At each iteration, and for each frame i, $\Delta\mathbf{p}$ is calculated and the start points of all the links emanating from frame i are updated accordingly. Similarly, for all links with end points on frame i, the end point coordinates are updated.[1]

We use the SURF [50] algorithm for keypoint detection with a low detection threshold, $\tau_s = 200$, to ensure sufficient keypoints are detected even for low-texture backgrounds. We use the nearest-neighbor ratio method [51] to match the keypoints descriptors and form links between each pair of keyframes.

Keyframe selection. We select keyframes at a constant step of Δf, i.e., from every Δf frames, only one is selected. Based on the experimental results, as a trade-off between accuracy and efficiency, we use $\Delta f = 10$ in TRGMC.

3.3 Weight assignment

We have defined all parameters in the problem formulation, except the weights of links, $\Omega^{(i)}$. We consider two factors in setting $\Omega^{(i)}$. Firstly, the keypoints detected at larger scales are more likely to be from background matches, since they cover coarser information and larger image patches. Thus, to be robust to foreground,

---

[1] In algorithm implementation, it is important to store the original coordinates of the detected keypoints and apply the *composite* transformations accumulated in all the iterations to update the coordinates of the start and end points of the links. Otherwise, accumulation of numerical errors will harm the performance.

the early iterations should emphasize links from larger-scale keypoints, which forms a coarse-to-fine alignment. We normalize the scales of all keypoints such that the maximum is 1, and denote the minimum of the normalized scales of the two keypoints comprising the link k as s_k. Then, $\Omega_{k,k}^{(i)}$ is set proportional to s_k.

Secondly, for each frame i, the links may be made either to all the previous frames, denoted as *backward* scheme, or both the previous and upcoming frames, denoted as *backward-forward* scheme. The former is for real-time applications, whereas the latter for offline video processing. These schemes are implemented by assigning different weights to backward and forward links,

$$\Omega_{k,k}^{(i)} = \begin{cases} (\beta.s_k)^{r^q}; & \text{if } d_k^{(i)} < i \quad \text{(Backward links)} \\ (\alpha.s_k)^{r^q}; & \text{if } d_k^{(i)} > i \quad \text{(Forward links)} \end{cases} \tag{9}$$

where $0 < \alpha, \beta < 1$, q is the iteration index, and $0 < r < 1$ is the rate of change of the weights. Note that the alignment errors in x and $y-$axes have the same weights, i.e., $\Omega_{k+N_i,k+N_i}^{(i)} = \Omega_{k,k}^{(i)}$. After a few iterations, the weights of all the links will be restored to 1. In the backward scheme, we set $\alpha = 0$.

3.4 Initialization

Initialization speeds up the alignment and decreases the false keypoint matches. The objective is to roughly place each frame at the appropriate coordinates in the GMCC. For initialization, we align the frames based only on rough estimation of translation without considering rotation, skew, or scale. We use the average of the motion vectors in matching two consecutive frames as the translation. Using this simple initialization, even if the camera has in-plane rotation, estimated 2D translations are zero, which is indeed correct and does not cause any problem for TRGMC. Given the estimated translation, approximate overlap area of each pair of frames is calculated, and only the keypoints inside the overlap area are matched, reducing number of false matches due to appearance ambiguities.

3.5 Outlier handling

Links may become outliers for two reasons: (i) the keypoints reside on foreground objects not consistent with camera motion; (ii) false links between different physical locations are caused by the low detection threshold and similar appearances.

In order to prune the outliers, we assume that the motion vectors of background matches, i.e., background links, have consistent and smooth patterns, caused by camera motion such as pan, zoom, tilt, whereas, the outlier links will exhibit arbitrary pattern, inconsistent with the background pattern. Specifically, we use Ma et al. [17] method to prune outlier links by imposing a smoothness constraint on the motion vector field[2]. This method outperforms RANSAC if the set of keypoint matches contains a large proportion of outliers. Since keyframes have larger relative time difference than consecutive frames, the foreground motion

---

[2] We use the implementation provided by the authors and the default parameters.

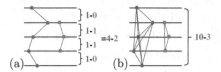
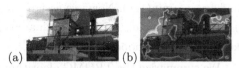

Fig. 4. Comparison of the ratios of background-foreground matches for (a) sequential GMC and (b) TRGMC.

Fig. 5. (a) The input frame, (b) the reliability map, with the red color showing higher reliability. (Color figure online)

is accentuated and more distinguishable from camera motion. This helps with better pruning of the foreground links. At each stage that the keypoints from a pair of frames are matched to form the links, we perform the pruning.

Congealing of an image stack also increases the proportion of background matches over the outliers - another way to suppress outliers. The keypoints on background are more likely to form longer range matches than the foreground ones, due to non-rigid foreground motion. Hence, when $\binom{N}{2}$ combinatorial pairs of frames are interconnected, there are a lot more background matches (Fig. 4).

3.6 Alignment of Non-keyframes

The keyframes alignment provides a set of temporally consistent motion compensated frames, which are the basis for aligning non-keyframes. We refer to keyframes and non-keyframes with superscripts i and j, respectively. For a non-keyframe j between the keyframes k_i and k_{i+1}, its alignment is a special case of Eq. 1, with indices $\mathbb{K} = \{j\}$, and the destination of the links $d_k^{(j)} \in \{k_i, k_{i+1}\}$, i.e., only $\mathbf{p}_j$ of frame j is updated while the keyframes remain fixed. Each non-keyframe between keyframes k_i and k_{i+1} is aligned independently.

However, given the small time offset between j and $d_k^{(j)}$, the observed foreground motion may be hard to discern. Also, frame j is linked only to two keyframes, thus there is no redundancy of background information to improve robustness to foreground motion. So, we handle outlier handling by assigning higher weights to links that are more likely to be connected to the background.

For each keyframe i, we quantify how well the links emanating from frame i are aligned with other keyframes. If the alignment error is small, i.e., $\epsilon_k^{(i)} = |\mathcal{W}_x(x_k^{(i)}, y_k^{(i)}; \mathbf{p}) - u_k^{(i)}| + |\mathcal{W}_y(x_k^{(i)}, y_k^{(i)}; \mathbf{p}) - v_k^{(i)}| < \tau$, the link k is more likely on the background of frame i and thus, more reliable for aligning non-keyframes. We create a *reliability map* for each keyframe i, denoted as $\mathbf{R}^{(i)}$ (Fig. 5). For each link k with $\epsilon_k^{(i)} < \tau$, a Gaussian function with $\mu_k = (x_k^{(i)}, y_k^{(i)})$ and $\sigma_k = cs_k$ is superposed on $\mathbf{R}^{(i)}$, where the constant c is 20. We define,

$$\mathbf{R}_{m,n}^{(i)} = \left\lceil \left\lfloor \sum_{k \in \mathbb{B}_i} e^{-\frac{\left(m-x_k^{(i)}\right)^2 + \left(n-y_k^{(i)}\right)^2}{2\sigma_k^2}} \right\rfloor_1 \right\rceil_\eta , \quad (10)$$

where $\mathbb{B}_i = \{k|\epsilon_k^{(i)} < \tau\}$, $\eta > 0$ is a small constant (set to 0.1), $\lceil x \rceil_\eta = \max(x, \eta)$ and $\lfloor x \rfloor_1 = \min(1, \eta)$. Now, we assign the weight of the links connecting frame j to the keyframe $d_k^{(j)}$ at the coordinate $(u_k^{(j)}, v_k^{(j)})$, as the reliability map of the keyframe at the endpoint, $\Omega_{k,k}^{(j)} = \left(\mathbf{R}_{u_k^{(j)}, v_k^{(j)}}^{(a)}\right)^{r^q}$, where $a = d_k^{(j)}$.

We summarize the TRGMC algorithm in Algorithm 1.

Algorithm 1. TRGMC Algorithm

Data: A set of input frames $\{\mathbf{I}^{(m)}\}_{m=1}^M$
Result: A set of homography matrices $\{\mathbf{p}_m\}_{m=1}^M$
/* Align keyframes (Sec. 3.2)   */
1 Specify $\mathbb{K} = \{k_1, ..., k_N\}$ and initialize (Sec. 3.4);
2 Match keypoints of all frames $i \in \mathbb{K}$ densely;
3 Prune links (Sec. 3.5) and set weights (Eqn. 9);
4 Store links' start and end coordinates in $(\mathbf{x}_i, \mathbf{y}_i)$ and $(\mathbf{u}_i, \mathbf{v}_i)$;
5 **repeat**
6   **forall** $i \in \mathbb{K}$ **do**
7   Compute $\Delta\mathbf{p}_i$ (Eqn. 5), update $\mathbf{p}_i$, $\mathbf{x}_i$ and $\mathbf{y}_i$;
8   Update $(\mathbf{u}_m, \mathbf{v}_m)$ according to $\mathbf{p}_i$ for $m \in \mathbb{K}\backslash\{i\}$;
9   Update weights (Eqn. 9);
10     $q \leftarrow q + 1$;
11 **until** $q < T_1$ or $\left(\frac{1}{N}\sum_{i\in\mathbb{K}} \|\Delta\mathbf{p}_i\|^2 > \tau_1\right)$;
/* Align non-keyframes (Sec. 3.6)   */
12 Compute reliability map $\mathbf{R}^{(i)}$ for $i \in \mathbb{K}$;
13 **for** $i = 1 : N - 1$ **do**
14   **forall** $j \in \{k_i + 1, ..., k_{i+1} - 1\}$ **do**
15   Match keypoints in j with $d^{(j)} \in \{k_i, k_{i+1}\}$;
16   Prune links (Sec. 3.5) and set weights $\Omega_{k,k}^{(j)}$;
17   Store links' coordinates in $(\mathbf{x}_j, \mathbf{y}_j)$ and $(\mathbf{u}_j, \mathbf{v}_j)$;
18   **repeat**
19   Compute $\Delta\mathbf{p}_j$ (Eqn. 5), update $\mathbf{p}_j$, $\mathbf{x}_j$ and $\mathbf{y}_j$;
20   Update weights (Eqn. 9), $q \leftarrow q + 1$;
21   **until** $q < T_2$ or $\left(\|\Delta\mathbf{p}_j\|^2 > \tau_2\right)$;

---

4 Experimental Results and Applications

We now present qualitative and quantitative results of the TRGMC algorithm and discuss how different computer vision applications will benefit from TRGMC.

4.1   Experiments and results

Baselines and details. We choose three sequential GMC algorithms as the baselines for comparison: MLESAC [15] and HEASK [19] both based on our own implementation, and RGMC [10] based on the authors' Matlab code available online. TRGMC is implemented in Matlab and is available for download.[3] Denoting the video frames of $w \times h$ pixels, we set the parameters as $\gamma = 0.1wh$, $T_1 = 300$, $\tau_1 = 5 \times 10^{-4}$, $T_2 = 50$, $\tau_2 = 10^{-4}$, $r = 0.7$, $\tau = 1$, $\Delta f = 10$, and $\beta = 1$. For the backward-forward scheme we set $\alpha = 1$ and for the backward scheme $\alpha = 0$.

Datasets and metric. We form a dataset composed of 40 challenging videos from SVW [52] and 15 videos from UCF101 [53], termed "quantitative dataset". SVW is an extremely unconstrained dataset including videos of amateurs practicing sports, and is also captured by amateurs via smartphone. In addition, we form another "qualitative dataset" with 200 *unlabeled* videos from SVW, in challenging categories of boxing, diving, and hockey.

To compare GMC over different temporal distances of frames, for each video of length M frames in the quantitative dataset, we manually align all 10 possible pairs from the 5-frame set, $\mathbb{F} = \{1, 0.25M, 0.5M, 0.75M, M\}$, as long as they are overlapping, and specify the background regions. For this, a GUI is developed for a labeler to match 4 points on each frame pair, and fine tune them up to a half-pixel accuracy, until the background difference is minimized. Then, the labeler selects the foreground regions which subsequently identify the background region. Similar to [10], we quantify the consistency of two warped frames $\mathbf{I}^{(i)}(\mathbf{p}_i)$ and $\mathbf{I}^{(j)}(\mathbf{p}_j)$ (0 to 1 grayscale pixels) via the background region error (BRE),

$$\mathrm{BRE}(i,j) = \frac{1}{\|\mathbf{M_B}\|_1}\||(\mathbf{I}^{(i)}(\mathbf{p}_i) - \mathbf{I}^{(j)}(\mathbf{p}_j))| \odot \mathbf{M_B}\|_1, \qquad (11)$$

where $\odot$ is element-wise multiplication and $\mathbf{M_B}$ is the background mask for the intersection of two warped frames.

Quantitative evaluation. Average of BRE over all the temporal frames pairs is shown in Table 1. TRGMC outperform all the baseline methods with considerable margin. The *backward-forward (BF)* scheme has a slightly better accuracy

Table 1. Comparison of GMC algorithms on quantitative dataset (*GT: Ground truth, BF: Backward-Forward, B: Backward).

Algorithm	MLESAC	HEASK	RGMC	TRGMC		GT*
Setting	–	–	–	BF*	B*	–
Avg. BRE	0.116	0.110	0.097	**0.058**	0.060	0.038
Efficiency (s/f)	0.17	7.47	3.47	0.64	0.41	–

---

[3] http://cvlab.cse.msu.edu/project-trgmc.html.

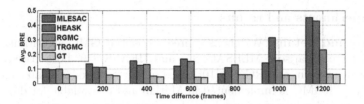

Fig. 6. Average BRE of frame pairs versus the time difference between the two frames.

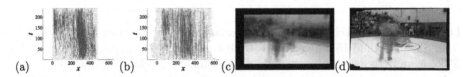

Fig. 7. Top view of the frames and links (a) before and (b) after TRGMC. The parallel links in (b) show successful *spatial* alignment of keypoints. For better visibility, we show up to 15 links emanated per frame. Average of frames (c) before and (d) after TRGMC.

Fig. 8. Composite image formed by overlaying the frame n on frame 1 for several videos after TRGMC. Left to right, n is equal to 144, 489, 912, 93, respectively. In the overlap region the difference between the frames is shown.

than the *backward (B)* scheme, and is also more stable based on our visual observation. Thus, we use BF as the default scheme for TRGMC.

To illustrate how the accumulation of errors over time affects the final error, Fig. 6 summarizes the average error versus the time difference between the frames in $\mathbb{F}$. This shows that TRGMC error is almost constant over a wide temporal distance between the frames. Thus, even if a frame is not aligned accurately, the error is not propagating to all the frames after that. However, in sequential GMC, the error increases as the time difference increases.

Qualitative evaluation. While quantitative results are comprehensive, the number of videos is limited by the labeling cost. Thus, we further compare TRGMC and the best performing baseline, RGMC, on the larger qualitative dataset. The resultant motion panoramas were *visually* investigated and categorized into three cases: good, shaking, and failed (i.e., considerable background discontinuity). The comparison in Table 2 again shows the superiority of TRGMC.

Figure 7 shows the *links* of a sample video processed by TRGMC, and the average frames, before and after processing. Initialization module is disable for generating this figure to better illustrate how well the spatial coordinate of the

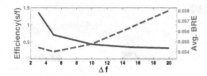

Fig. 9. Error and efficiency vs. the keyframe selection step, Δf.

Table 2. Comparison of GMC algorithms on qualitative dataset.

Alg.\Perfromance	Good	Shaking	Failed
RGMC	64 %	33 %	3 %
TRGMC	**93 %**	5 %	2 %

keypoints are aligned, resulting in links parallel to the $t-$ axis. Figure 8 shows a composite image formed by overlaying the last frame (or a far apart frame with enough overlap) on frame 1 for several videos, after TRGMC. In the overlap region, difference between the two frames is shown, to demonstrate how well the background region matches for the frames with large temporal distances.

Computational efficiency. Table 1 also presents the average time for processing one frame for each method, on a PC with an Intel i5-3470@3.2 GHz CPU, and 8 GB RAM. While obtaining considerably better accuracy than HEASK or RGMC, TRGMC is on average 15 times faster than HEASK and 7 times faster than RGMC. MLESAC is ~3 times faster than TRGMC, but with twice the error. For TRGMC, the backward scheme is 50 % faster than forward-backward, since it has approximately half the links of BF.

Accuracy vs. efficiency trade-off. Figure 9 presents the error and efficiency results for a set of 5 videos versus the keyframe selection step, Δf. For this set, the ground truth error is 0.049. As a sweet spot in the error and efficiency trade-off, we use $\Delta f = 10$ for TRGMC. This figure also justifies the two stage processing scheme in TRGMC, as processing frames at a low selection step Δf, is costly in terms of efficiency, but only improves the accuracy slightly.

4.2   TRGMC applications

Motion panorama. By sequentially reading input frames, applying the transformation found by TRGMC, and overlaying the warped frames on a sufficiently large canvas, a motion panorama is generated. Furthermore, it is possible to reconstruct the background using the warped frames *first* (as will be discussed later), and overlay the frames on that, to create a more impressive panorama. Figure 10 shows a few exemplar panoramas and the camera motion trajectory.

Background reconstruction. Background reconstruction is important for removing occlusions, or detecting foreground [6]. To reconstruct the background, a weighted average scheme is used to weight each frame by the *reliability map*, $\mathbf{R}^{(i)}$, which assigns higher weights to background. Since the minimum value of $\mathbf{R}^{(i)}$ is a positive constant η, if no reliable keyframe exists at a coordinate, all the frames will have equal weights. Specifically, the background is reconstructed by $\mathbf{B} = \frac{\sum_{i \in \mathbb{K}} \mathbf{R}^{(i)}(\mathbf{p}_i) \mathbf{I}^{(i)}(\mathbf{p}_i)}{\sum_{i \in \mathbb{K}} \mathbf{R}^{(i)}(\mathbf{p}_i)}$, where $\mathbf{R}^{(i)}(\mathbf{p}_i)$ and $\mathbf{I}^i(\mathbf{p}_i)$ are the reliability map and

Fig. 10. Temporal overlay of frames from different videos processed by TRGMC. Trajectory of the center of image plane over time is overlaid on each plot to show the camera motion pattern, where color changes from blue to red with progression of time. (Color figure online)

Fig. 11. Background reconstruction results. Compare the left image with Fig. 10, middle image with Fig. 7, and right image with Fig. 8.

(a)   (b)

Fig. 12. Segmented fore-   **Fig. 13.** Dense trajectories of the (a) original video, ground overlaid on the input.   and (b) TRGMC-processed video.

the input frame warped using the transformation $\mathbf{p}_i$. Using our scheme, reconstructed background in Fig. 11 is sharper and less impacted by the foreground.

Foreground segmentation. The reliable background reconstruction result $\mathbf{B}$ along with the GMC result of frame $\mathbf{I}^{(i)}$, e.g., $\mathbf{p}_i$, can be easily used to segment the foreground by thresholding the difference, $|\mathbf{B} - \mathbf{I}^{(i)}(\mathbf{p}_i)|$ (Fig. 12).

Human action recognition. State of the art human action recognition heavily relies on analysis of human motion. GMC helps to suppress camera motion and magnify human motion, making the motion analysis more feasible, which is clearly shown by the dense trajectories [4] in Fig. 13.

Multi-object Tracking (MOT). When appearance cues for tracking are ambiguous, e.g., tracking players in team sports like football, motion cues gain extra significance [54,55]. MOT is comprised of two tasks, data association by assigning each detection a label, and trajectory estimation – both highly affected by camera motion. TRGMC can be applied to remove camera motion and thus, revive the power of tracking algorithms relying on motion cues. To verify the impact of TRGMC, we manually label the locations of all players in 566 frames of a football video and use this ground truth detection results to study how MOT using [56] benefits from TRGMC. Figure 14 compares the trajectories of players over time with and without applying TRGMC. Comparing number of

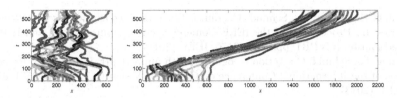

Fig. 14. Multi-player tracking using [56] for a football video with camera panning to the right, before (left) and after processing by TRGMC (right).

label switches qualitatively demonstrates improvement of a challenging MOT scenario using TRGMC. Also, the Multi-Object Tracking Accuracy [57] for the original video and the video processed by TRGMC are 63.79 % and 84.23 %, respectively.

5 Conclusions and Discussions

We proposed a temporally robust global motion compensation (TRGMC) algorithm by joint alignment (congealing) of frames, in contrast to the common sequential scheme. Despite complicated camera motions, TRGMC can remove the *intentional* camera motion, such as pan, as well as *unwanted* motion due to vibration on handheld cameras. Experiments demonstrate that TRGMC outperforms existing GMC methods, and applications of TRGMC.

The enabling assumption of TRGMC is that the camera motion in the direction of the optical axis is negligible. For instance, TRGMC will not work properly on a video from a wearable camera of a pedestrian, since in the global coordinate the upcoming frames grow in size and cause computational and rendering problems. The best results are achieved if the optical center of the camera has negligible movement, making a homography-based approximation of camera motion appropriate. However, if the optical center moves in the perpendicular direction to the optical axis (e.g., a camera following a swimmer), TRGMC still works well, but results will be visually degraded by the parallax effect.

Acknowledgement. This work was partially supported by TechSmith Corporation.

References

1. He, Y., Feng, B., Yang, S., Zhong, Y.: Fast global motion estimation for global motion compensation coding. In: Proceedings of the IEEE International Symposium on Circuits and Systems (ISCAS), vol. 2, pp. 233–236. IEEE (2001)
2. Smolić, A., Vatis, Y., Schwarz, H., Wiegand, T.: Long-term global motion compensation for advanced video coding. In: ITG-Fachtagung Dortmunder Fernsehseminar, pp. 213–216 (2003)
3. Bartoli, A., Dalal, N., Bose, B., Horaud, R.: From video sequences to motion panoramas. In: Proceedings of the Conference Motion and Video Computing Workshops, pp. 201–207. IEEE (2002)

4. Wang, H., Klaser, A., Schmid, C., Liu, C.L.: Action recognition by dense trajectories. In: Proceedings of the IEEE Conference on Computer Vision and Pattern Recognition (CVPR), pp. 3169–3176. IEEE (2011)

5. Wang, H., Schmid, C.: Action recognition with improved trajectories. In: Proceedings of the International Conference on Computer Vision (ICCV), pp. 3551–3558. IEEE (2013)

6. Monari, E., Pollok, T.: A real-time image-to-panorama registration approach for background subtraction using pan-tilt-cameras. In: Proceedings of the IEEE Conference on Advanced Video and Signal Based Surveillance (AVSS), pp. 237–242. IEEE (2011)

7. Sun, Y., Li, B., Yuan, B., Miao, Z., Wan, C.: Better foreground segmentation for static cameras via new energy form and dynamic graph-cut. In: Proceedings of the International Conference on Pattern Recognition (ICPR), vol. 4, pp. 49–52. IEEE (2006)

8. Wan, C., Yuan, B., Miao, Z.: A new algorithm for static camera foreground segmentation via active coutours and GMM. In: Proceedings of the International Conference on Pattern Recognition (ICPR), pp. 1–4. IEEE (2008)

9. Solera, F., Calderara, S., Cucchiara, R.: Learning to divide and conquer for online multi-target tracking. arXiv preprint arXiv:1509.03956 (2015)

10. Safdarnejad, S.M., Liu, X., Udpa, L.: Robust global motion compensation in presence of predominant foreground. In: Proceedings of the British Machine Vision Conference (BMVC) (2015)

11. Bartoli, A., Dalal, N., Horaud, R.: Motion panoramas. Comput. Animation Virtual Worlds 15(5), 501–517 (2004)

12. Déniz, O., Bueno, G., Bermejo, E., Sukthankar, R.: Fast and accurate global motion compensation. Pattern Recogn. 44(12), 2887–2901 (2011)

13. Fischler, M.A., Bolles, R.C.: Random sample consensus: a paradigm for model fitting with applications to image analysis and automated cartography. ACM Commun. 24(6), 381–395 (1981)

14. Chum, O., Matas, J., Kittler, J.: Locally optimized RANSAC. In: Michaelis, B., Krell, G. (eds.) DAGM 2003. LNCS, vol. 2781, pp. 236–243. Springer, Heidelberg (2003). doi:10.1007/978-3-540-45243-0_31

15. Torr, P.H., Zisserman, A.: MLESAC: a new robust estimator with application to estimating image geometry. Comput. Vis. Image Underst. 78(1), 138–156 (2000)

16. Tordoff, B.J., Murray, D.W.: Guided-MLESAC: faster image transform estimation by using matching priors. IEEE Trans. Pattern Anal. Mach. Intell. 27(10), 1523–1535 (2005)

17. Ma, J., Zhao, J., Tian, J., Yuille, A.L., Tu, Z.: Robust point matching via vector field consensus. IEEE Trans. Image Process. 23(4), 1706–1721 (2014)

18. Li, X., Hu, Z.: Rejecting mismatches by correspondence function. Int. J. Comput. Vis. 89(1), 1–17 (2010)

19. Yan, Q., Xu, Y., Yang, X., Nguyen, T.: HEASK: Robust homography estimation based on appearance similarity and keypoint correspondences. Pattern Recogn. 47(1), 368–387 (2014)

20. Szpak, Z.L., Chojnacki, W., van den Hengel, A.: Robust multiple homography estimation: An ill-solved problem. In: Proceedings of the IEEE Conference on Computer Vision and Pattern Recognition (CVPR), pp. 2132–2141. IEEE (2015)

21. Zuliani, M., Kenney, C.S., Manjunath, B.: The multiRANSAC algorithm and its application to detect planar homographies. In: Proceedings of the International Conference on Image Processing (ICIP), vol. 3, pp. III–153. IEEE (2005)

22. Toldo, R., Fusiello, A.: Robust multiple structures estimation with J-Linkage. In: Forsyth, D., Torr, P., Zisserman, A. (eds.) ECCV 2008. LNCS, vol. 5302, pp. 537–547. Springer, Heidelberg (2008). doi:10.1007/978-3-540-88682-2_41

23. Ma, J., Chen, J., Ming, D., Tian, J.: A mixture model for robust point matching under multi-layer motion. PloS One **9**(3), e92282 (2014)

24. Uemura, H., Ishikawa, S., Mikolajczyk, K.: Feature tracking and motion compensation for action recognition. In: Proceedings of the British Machine Vision Conference (BMVC), pp. 1–10 (2008)

25. Gao, J., Kim, S.J., Brown, M.S.: Constructing image panoramas using dual-homography warping. In: Proceedings of the IEEE Conference on Computer Vision and Pattern Recognition (CVPR), pp. 49–56. IEEE (2011)

26. Lin, W.Y., Liu, S., Matsushita, Y., Ng, T.T., Cheong, L.F.: Smoothly varying affine stitching. In: Proceedings of the IEEE Conference on Computer Vision and Pattern Recognition (CVPR), pp. 345–352. IEEE (2011)

27. Zaragoza, J., Chin, T.J., Tran, Q.H., Brown, M.S., Suter, D.: As-projective-as-possible image stitching with moving dlt. IEEE Trans. Pattern Anal. Mach. Intell. **36**(7), 1285–1298 (2014)

28. Lin, C.C., Pankanti, S.U., Ramamurthy, K.N., Aravkin, A.Y.: Adaptive as-natural-as-possible image stitching. In: Proceedings of the IEEE Conference Computer Vision and Pattern Recognition (CVPR), pp. 1155–1163. IEEE (2015)

29. Li, Y., Kang, S.B., Joshi, N., Seitz, S.M., Huttenlocher, D.P.: Generating sharp panoramas from motion-blurred videos. In: Proceedings of the IEEE Conference on Computer Vision and Pattern Recognition (CVPR), pp. 2424–2431. IEEE (2010)

30. Sawhney, H.S., Hsu, S., Kumar, R.: Robust video mosaicing through topology inference and local to global alignment. In: Burkhardt, H., Neumann, B. (eds.) ECCV 1998. LNCS, vol. 1407, pp. 103–119. Springer, Heidelberg (1998). doi:10.1007/BFb0054736

31. Shum, H.Y., Szeliski, R.: Construction and refinement of panoramic mosaics with global and local alignment. In: Proceedings of the International Conference on Computer Vision (ICCV)

32. Sakamoto, M., Sugaya, Y., Kanatani, K.: Homography optimization for consistent circular panorama generation. In: Chang, L.-W., Lie, W.-N. (eds.) PSIVT 2006. LNCS, vol. 4319, pp. 1195–1205. Springer, Heidelberg (2006). doi:10.1007/11949534_121

33. Triggs, B., McLauchlan, P.F., Hartley, R.I., Fitzgibbon, A.W.: Bundle adjustment — a modern synthesis. In: Triggs, B., Zisserman, A., Szeliski, R. (eds.) IWVA 1999. LNCS, vol. 1883, pp. 298–372. Springer, Heidelberg (2000). doi:10.1007/3-540-44480-7_21

34. El-Saban, M., Izz, M., Kaheel, A., Refaat, M.: Improved optimal seam selection blending for fast video stitching of videos captured from freely moving devices. In: Proceedings of the International Conference on Image Processing (ICIP), pp. 1481–1484. IEEE (2011)

35. Perazzi, F., Sorkine-Hornung, A., Zimmer, H., Kaufmann, P., Wang, O., Watson, S., Gross, M.: Panoramic video from unstructured camera arrays. In: Computer Graphics Forum, vol. 34, pp. 57–68. Wiley Online Library (2015)

36. Zeng, W., Zhang, H.: Depth adaptive video stitching. In: Proceedings of the IEEE Conference on Computer and Information Science (ICIS), pp. 1100–1105. IEEE (2009)

37. Jiang, W., Gu, J.: Video stitching with spatial-temporal content-preserving warping. In: Proceedings of the IEEE Conference on Computer Vision and Pattern Recognition Workshops (CVPRW), pp. 42–48. IEEE (2015)

38. Ibrahim, M.T., Hafiz, R., Khan, M.M., Cho, Y., Cha, J.: Automatic reference selection for parametric color correction schemes for panoramic video stitching. In: Bebis, G., Boyle, R., Parvin, B., Koracin, D., Fowlkes, C., Wang, S., Choi, M.-H., Mantler, S., Schulze, J., Acevedo, D., Mueller, K., Papka, M. (eds.) ISVC 2012. LNCS, vol. 7431, pp. 492–501. Springer, Heidelberg (2012). doi:10.1007/978-3-642-33179-4_47

39. Gleicher, M.L., Liu, F.: Re-cinematography: Improving the camerawork of casual video. ACM Trans. Multimedia Comput. Commun. Appl. (TOMM) 5(1), 2 (2008)

40. Learned-Miller, E.G.: Data driven image models through continuous joint alignment. IEEE Trans. Pattern Anal. Mach. Intell. 28(2), 236–250 (2006)

41. Liu, X., Tong, Y., Wheeler, F.W.: Simultaneous alignment and clustering for an image ensemble. In: Proceedings of the International Conference on Computer Vision (ICCV), pp. 1327–1334. IEEE (2009)

42. Tong, Y., Liu, X., Wheeler, F.W., Tu, P.: Automatic facial landmark labeling with minimal supervision. In: Proceedings of the IEEE Conference on Computer Vision and Pattern Recognition (CVPR). IEEE (2009)

43. Liu, X., Tong, Y., Wheeler, F.W., Tu, P.H.: Facial contour labeling via congealing. In: Daniilidis, K., Maragos, P., Paragios, N. (eds.) ECCV 2010. LNCS, vol. 6311, pp. 354–368. Springer, Heidelberg (2010). doi:10.1007/978-3-642-15549-9_26

44. Cox, M., Sridharan, S., Lucey, S., Cohn, J.: Least squares congealing for unsupervised alignment of images. In: Proceedings of the IEEE Conference on Computer Vision and Pattern Recognition (CVPR), pp. 1–8. IEEE (2008)

45. Huang, G., Mattar, M., Lee, H., Learned-Miller, E.G.: Learning to align from scratch. In: Advances in Neural Information Processing Systems (NIPS), pp. 764–772 (2012)

46. Lankinen, J., Kämäräinen, J.K.: Local feature based unsupervised alignment of object class images. In: Proceedings of the British Machine Vision Conference (BMVC), vol. 1 (2011)

47. Lucey, S., Navarathna, R., Ashraf, A.B., Sridharan, S.: Fourier Lucas-Kanade algorithm. IEEE Trans. Pattern Anal. Mach. Intell. 35(6), 1383–1396 (2013)

48. Cox, M., Sridharan, S., Lucey, S., Cohn, J.: Least-squares congealing for large numbers of images. In: Proceedings of the International Conference on Computer Vision (ICCV), pp. 1949–1956. IEEE (2009)

49. Shokrollahi Yancheshmeh, F., Chen, K., Kamarainen, J.K.: Unsupervised visual alignment with similarity graphs. In: Proceedings of the IEEE Conference Computer Vision and Pattern Recognition (CVPR), pp. 2901–2908. IEEE (2015)

50. Bay, H., Tuytelaars, T., Gool, L.: SURF: speeded up robust features. In: Leonardis, A., Bischof, H., Pinz, A. (eds.) ECCV 2006. LNCS, vol. 3951, pp. 404–417. Springer, Heidelberg (2006). doi:10.1007/11744023_32

51. Lowe, D.G.: Distinctive image features from scale-invariant keypoints. Int. J. Comput. Vis. 60(2), 91–110 (2004)

52. Safdarnejad, S.M., Liu, X., Udpa, L., Andrus, B., Wood, J., Craven, D.: Sports videos in the wild (SVW): a video dataset for sports analysis. In: Proceedings of the International Conference on Automatic Face and Gesture Recognition (FG), pp. 1–7. IEEE (2015)

53. Soomro, K., Zamir, A.R., Shah, M.: UCF101: A dataset of 101 human actions classes from videos in the wild. arXiv preprint arXiv:1212.0402 (2012)

54. Lezama, J., Alahari, K., Sivic, J., Laptev, I.: Track to the future: spatio-temporal video segmentation with long-range motion cues. In: Proceedings of the IEEE Conference on Computer Vision and Pattern Recognition (CVPR). IEEE (2011)

55. Dicle, C., Camps, O., Sznaier, M.: The way they move: tracking multiple targets with similar appearance. In: Proceedings of the International Conference on Computer Vision (ICCV), pp. 2304–2311. IEEE (2013)
56. Andriyenko, A., Schindler, K., Roth, S.: Discrete-continuous optimization for multi-target tracking. In: Proceedings of the IEEE Conference on Computer Vision and Pattern Recognition (CVPR), pp. 1926–1933. IEEE (2012)
57. Bernardin, K., Stiefelhagen, R.: Evaluating multiple object tracking performance: the CLEAR MOT metrics. J. Image Video Process. **2008**, 1 (2008)

Salient Deconvolutional Networks

Aravindh Mahendran[(✉)] and Andrea Vedaldi

Department of Engineering Science, University of Oxford, Oxford, UK
{aravindh,andrea}@robots.ox.ac.uk

Abstract. Deconvolution is a popular method for visualizing deep convolutional neural networks; however, due to their heuristic nature, the meaning of deconvolutional visualizations is not entirely clear. In this paper, we introduce a family of reversed networks that generalizes and relates deconvolution, backpropagation and network saliency. We use this construction to thoroughly investigate and compare these methods in terms of quality and meaning of the produced images, and of what architectural choices are important in determining these properties. We also show an application of these generalized deconvolutional networks to weakly-supervised foreground object segmentation.

Keywords: DeConvNets · Deep convolutional neural networks · Saliency · Segmentation

1 Introduction

Despite the success of modern Convolutional Neural Networks (CNNs), there is a limited understanding of *how* these complex black-box models achieve their performance. Methods such as *deconvolutional networks* (DeConvNets) have been proposed to *visualize* image patterns that strongly activate any given neuron in a CNN [25] and therefore shed some light on the CNN structure. However, the DeConvNet construction is partially heuristic and so are the corresponding visualizations. Simonyan *et al.* [16] noted similarities with their *network saliency* method which partially explains DeConvNets, but this interpretation remains incomplete.

This paper carries a novel and systematic analysis of DeConvNets and closely related visualization methods such as network saliency. Our first contribution is to extend DeConvNet to a general method for architecture reversal and visualization. In this construction, the reversed layers use selected information extracted by the forward network, which we call *bottleneck information* (Sect. 2). We show that backpropagation is a special case of this construction which yields a reversed architecture, SaliNet, equivalent to the network saliency method of Simonyan *et al.* (Sect. 2.1). We also show that the *only* difference between

---

Electronic supplementary material The online version of this chapter (doi:10.1007/978-3-319-46466-4_8) contains supplementary material, which is available to authorized users.

© Springer International Publishing AG 2016
B. Leibe et al. (Eds.): ECCV 2016, Part VI, LNCS 9910, pp. 120–135, 2016.
DOI: 10.1007/978-3-319-46466-4_8

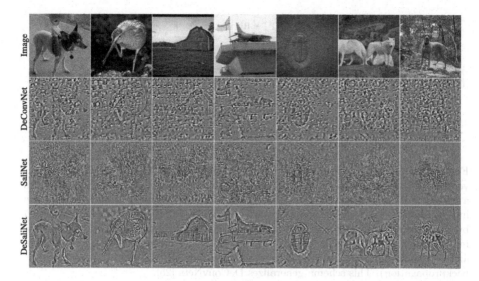

Fig. 1. From top row to bottom: Original image, DeConvNet, SaliNet and our DeSaliNet visualizations from the fc8 layer in AlexNet (just before the softmax operation). The maximally active neuron is visualized in each case. DeSaliNet results in crisper visualizations. They suppress the background while preserving edge information. Best viewed on screen.

DeConvNet and SaliNet is a seemingly innocuous change in the reversal of Rectified Linear Units (ReLU; Sect. 2.2). However, this change has a *very significant* effect on the results: the SaliNet response is well localized but lacks structure, whereas the DeConvNet response accurately reproduces the image boundaries and object shapes, but is less localized (Fig. 1). We also show that the two methods can be combined in order to simultaneously obtain structure and localization (DeSaliNet). DeSaliNet is also similar to results recently obtained by [17].

We then move to the important question of whether deconvolutional architectures are useful for visualizing neurons. Our answer is partially negative, as we find that the output of reversed architectures is mainly determined by the bottleneck information rather than by which neuron is selected for visualization (Sect. 3.3). In the case of SaliNet and DeSaliNet, we confirm that the output is selective of any recognizable foreground object in the image, but the class of the selected object cannot be specified by manipulating class-specific neurons.

Having established the dominance of bottleneck information, we draw an analogy between that and phase information in the Fourier transform (Sect. 3.4) and show the importance of polarity information in reversed architectures.

Finally, we quantitatively test the ability of SaliNet and DeSaliNet to identify generic foreground objects in images (Sect. 3.5). Combined with GrabCut, we achieve near state-of-the-art segmentation results on the ImageNet segmentation task of [4], while using off-the-shelf CNNs pretrained from a *largely disjoint subset* of ImageNet and with only image-level supervision.

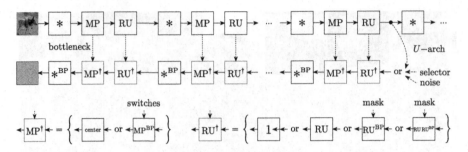

Fig. 2. The top row shows a typical CNN obtained by repeating short chains of convolution (∗), max pooling (MP) and ReLU (RU) operators. The middle row shows a generic "deconvolution" architecture, in which information flows backward to the image using the convolution transpose $\ast^{BP}$ operator. Different variants are obtained by: (i) choosing a different input (U-architecture, feature selector, or noise), (ii) choosing a variant of backward ReLU $RU^{\dagger}$ (1, ReLU, ReLU backpropagation, or hybrid), and (iii) choosing a variant of backward max pooling $MP^{\dagger}$ (unpool to centre or MP backpropagation). This schema generalizes DeConvNets [25].

Related Work. DeConvNets were originally proposed as a method for unsupervised feature learning [26,27] and later applied to visualization [25]. There are several CNN visualizations alternative to DeCovnNets. Some recent ones such as [24] build on the idea of *natural* (regularized) pre-images introduced in [13], which in turn are based on prior contributions that applied pre-images to representations such as HOG [21], SIFT [22], BoVW [2,7], as well as early neural networks [6,9,10,12,20,23]. A related line of work [1] is to learn a second neural network to act as the inverse of the original one. Several authors characterize properties of CNNs and other models by generating images that confuse them [14,18,19]. Our DeSaliNet architecture is also similar to the work of [17].

Recently, DeConvNets have also been proposed as a tool for semantic image segmentation; for example,[5,15] interpolate and refine the output of a fully-convolutional network [11] using a deconvolutional architecture. In this paper, inspired by [16], we apply reversed architectures for foreground object segmentation, although as a by-product of visualization and in a weakly-supervised transfer-learning setting rather than as a specialized segmentation method.

2   A Family of Deconvolutional Architectures

Given an image $\mathbf{x} \in \mathcal{X}$, a deep CNN extracts a feature vector or representation

$$\phi : \mathbf{x} \mapsto \phi_L \circ \cdots \circ \phi_1(\mathbf{x}) \tag{1}$$

using a sequence of L linear and non-linear layers ϕ_i (Fig. 2.top). Typical layers include convolution, ReLU, max pooling, and local contrast normalization.

The goal is to associate to ϕ a corresponding architecture $\phi^{\dagger}$ that reverses in some sense the computations and produces an image as output. While such reversed architectures have several uses, here we focus on the problem of *visualizing* deep networks: by looking at the images produced by $\phi^\dagger$, we hope to gain some insights about the forward network ϕ. This method was popularized by the work of Zeiler and Fergus in [25], where a particular construction called DeConvNet was shown to produce surprisingly crisp renderings of neural activations. However, given the heuristic nature of some choices in DeConvNets, it is difficult to precisely characterize the meaning of these results.

In order to explore this point, we consider here a generalization of the DeConvNet construction. To this end, each layer ϕ_i is associated with a corresponding layer $\phi_i^\dagger$ that reverses input $\mathbf{x}$ and output $\mathbf{y}$ (Fig. 2 middle row). We also allow the reverse layer to be influenced by auxiliary information $\mathbf{r}$ computed by the forward layer. For instance, in DeConvNet, the reverse max pooling layer requires the "setting of the pooling switches" computed in the forward pass. Thus a layer ϕ_i and its reverse $\phi_i^\dagger$ are maps:

$$\text{forward } \phi_i : \mathbf{x} \mapsto (\mathbf{y}, \mathbf{r}), \qquad \text{reversed } \phi_i^\dagger : (\hat{\mathbf{y}}, \mathbf{r}) \mapsto \hat{\mathbf{x}}. \tag{2}$$

The $\hat{\ }$ symbol emphasizes that, in the backward direction, the tensors $\hat{\mathbf{x}}$ and $\hat{\mathbf{y}}$ have the same shape as $\mathbf{x}$ and $\mathbf{y}$ in the forward pass, but different values.

Since the auxiliary information $\mathbf{r}$ is a function of the input $\mathbf{r} = \pi(\mathbf{x})$, one can always let $\mathbf{r} = \mathbf{x}$ without loss of generality; however, the interesting case is when the auxiliary information is limited and $\mathbf{r}$ is an *information bottleneck*. For example, the pooling switches $\mathbf{r}$ in DeConvNet contain much less information than the input data $\mathbf{x}$. In Fig. 2 these bottlenecks are denoted by dotted arrows.

The question then is how can we build reverse layers $\phi^\dagger$? Next, we show that back-propagation provides a general construction for reverse layers, which only in some cases corresponds to the choice in DeConvNet.

2.1   SaliNet: Network Saliency as a Deconvolutional Architecture

The *network saliency* method of Simonyan et al. [16] characterizes which pixels of an image are most responsible for the output of a CNN. Given an image $\mathbf{x}_0$ and a network $\phi(\mathbf{x}_0)$, saliency is obtained as the derivative of the (projected) CNN output $S(\phi, \mathbf{x}_0, \mathbf{p})$ with respect to the image:

$$S(\phi, \mathbf{x}_0, \mathbf{p}) = \frac{\partial}{\partial \mathbf{x}} \langle \mathbf{p}, \phi(\mathbf{x}) \rangle \Big|_{\mathbf{x}=\mathbf{x}_0}. \tag{3}$$

Since the CNN output $\phi(\mathbf{x})$ is in general a vector or tensor, the latter is transformed into a scalar by linear projection onto a constant tensor $\mathbf{p}$ before the derivative is computed. In practice, $\mathbf{p}$ is usually a one-hot tensor that selects an individual neuron in the output. In this case, the value of a pixel in the saliency map $S(\phi, \mathbf{x}_0, \mathbf{p})$ answers the question: "how much would the neuron response $\langle \mathbf{p}, \phi(\mathbf{x}_0) \rangle$ change by slightly perturbing the value of that pixel in the image $\mathbf{x}_0$?"

Saliency is computed from (1) and (3) using the chain rule:

$$\text{vec } S(\phi, \mathbf{x}_0, \mathbf{p}) = \text{vec } \mathbf{p}^\top \times \frac{\partial \text{ vec } \phi_L}{\partial \text{ vec } \mathbf{x}_L^\top} \times \cdots \times \frac{\partial \text{ vec } \phi_1}{\partial \text{ vec } \mathbf{x}_0^\top}. \tag{4}$$

Here the vec operator stacks tensors into vectors and allows us to use a simple matrix notation for the derivatives.

The *Back Propagation* (BP) algorithm is the same as computing the products (4) from left to right; this reduces to a chain of derivatives in the form of (3), one for each layer, where $\mathbf{p}$ is replaced with the derivative $\hat{\mathbf{y}}$ obtained from the layer above. In this manner, BP provides a general way to define a reverse of any layer ϕ_i:

$$\phi_i : \mathbf{x} \mapsto \mathbf{y} \quad \text{BP-reversed becomes} \quad \phi_i^{\mathrm{BP}} : (\mathbf{x}, \hat{\mathbf{y}}) \mapsto \frac{\partial}{\partial \mathbf{x}} \langle \hat{\mathbf{y}}, \phi_i(\mathbf{x}) \rangle. \quad (5)$$

We denote the BP-reversed of a layer with the symbol ϕ_i^{BP}. Any CNN toolbox can compute BP-reversed for any layer as it contains code for back-propagation. Note also that the BP-reversed layer is *a linear map* in the argument $\hat{\mathbf{y}}$, even if the forward layer is not linear in $\mathbf{x}$. In this manner, one can compute backpropagation, and therefore the saliency map $S(\phi, \mathbf{x}_0, \mathbf{p})$ of [16], by using a "deconvolutional" architecture of the type of Fig. 2, where layers are reversed using the BP Eq. (5). We call this architecture *SaliNet*.

The BP-reversed layer ϕ_i^{BP} takes as input both $\mathbf{x}$ and $\hat{\mathbf{y}}$, whereas from our discussion above we would like to replace $\mathbf{x}$ with a bottleneck $\mathbf{r}$. Formally, using the definition (2), we rewrite the BP-reversed layer $\phi_i^{\mathrm{BP}}(\mathbf{x}, \hat{\mathbf{y}})$ as $\phi_i^{\dagger}(\hat{\mathbf{y}}, \mathbf{r})$ where $\mathbf{r} = \pi(\mathbf{x})$ projects the data $\mathbf{x}$ onto the smallest possible bottleneck. Note that this does not change the meaning of a BP-reversed layer, but it does characterizes how much auxiliary information it requires. The latter is easy to find in an abstract sense,[1] but it is much more instructive to derive it for concrete layer types, which we do below for common layers.

Affine layers. A *fully connected layer* ϕ_{fc} simply multiplies the data $\mathbf{x}$ by a matrix A and adds a bias b. Given that the data $\mathbf{x} \in \mathbb{R}^{H \times W \times C}$ is a 3D tensor of height H and width W and C feature channels, we use the vec operator to write this in terms of matrices[2] as $\phi_{\mathrm{fc}} : \mathrm{vec}\, \mathbf{y} = A\, \mathrm{vec}\, \mathbf{x} + b$. *Linear convolution* ϕ_* can conveniently be defined in the same way, by replacing matrix A with a matrix $\rho(F)$ constructed by "sliding" a bank of filters F, giving $\phi_* : \mathrm{vec}\, \mathbf{y} = \rho(F)\, \mathrm{vec}\, \mathbf{x} + b$. Using (5), the BP-reversed layers are obtained by transposing the respective matrices:

$$\phi_{\mathrm{fc}}^{\mathrm{BP}} : \mathrm{vec}\, \hat{\mathbf{x}} = A^{\top} \mathrm{vec}\, \hat{\mathbf{y}}, \qquad \phi_*^{\mathrm{BP}} : \mathrm{vec}\, \hat{\mathbf{x}} = \rho(F)^{\top} \mathrm{vec}\, \hat{\mathbf{y}}. \quad (6)$$

The layer ϕ_*^{BP} is often called *deconvolution* and gives the name to DeConvNets.

Note that the computation of these layers does not require any information from the forward pass, so the bottleneck $\mathbf{r}$ is empty. This is due to linearity and explains why in Fig. 2 there are no dashed arrows connecting convolutional layers.

---

[1] Let $\mathbf{x}' \sim \mathbf{x}''$ be equivalent whenever functions $\phi_i^{\mathrm{BP}}(\mathbf{x}', \cdot) = \phi_i^{\mathrm{BP}}(\mathbf{x}'', \cdot)$ are the same. It is easy to check that this defines an equivalence relation. Then the smallest possible bottleneck $\pi : \mathbf{x} \mapsto \mathbf{r} \in \mathcal{X}/\sim$ projects $\mathbf{x}$ into its equivalence class.

[2] This is slightly more general than usual as it specifies a different bias for each output dimension instead for each output feature channel.

Rectified linear Unit (ReLU or RU). ReLU and its BP-reversed layer are given by

$$\phi_{\mathrm{RU}}(\mathbf{x}) = \max\{\mathbf{x}, 0\}, \qquad \phi_{\mathrm{RU}}^{\mathrm{BP}}(\mathbf{x}, \hat{\mathbf{y}}) = \phi_{\mathrm{RU}}^{\dagger}(\hat{\mathbf{y}}, \mathbf{r}) = \hat{\mathbf{y}} \odot \mathbf{r}, \quad \mathbf{r} = [\mathbf{x} > 0], \quad (7)$$

where max is computed element-wise, $\odot$ is the element-wise product, and $[\mathbf{x} > 0]$ is a mask (binary tensor) with a 1 for every positive element of $\mathbf{x}$ and 0 otherwise. Hence the *bottleneck information for ReLU is the mask*. Note that $\phi_{\mathrm{RU}}^{\mathrm{BP}}(\mathbf{x}, \hat{\mathbf{y}})$ is not the reversal used by DeConvNets [16,25] and this choice changes the output significantly.

Max Pooling (MP). Let x_{uc} be the element of tensor $\mathbf{x}$ at spatial location $u \in \Omega$ and feature channel c. MP is obtained by computing the maximum of x_{vc} over a small spatial neighbourhood $v \in N(u) \subset \Omega$ corresponding to u:

$$[\phi_{\mathrm{MP}}(\mathbf{x})]_{uc} = \max_{v \in N(u)} x_{vc} = x_{s(u|c,\mathbf{x}),c} \quad \text{where} \quad s(u|c, \mathbf{x}) = \operatorname*{argmax}_{v \in N(u)} x_{vc}. \quad (8)$$

Here $v = s(u|\mathbf{x}, c)$ tells which element x_{vc} of the input is associated by max to each element y_{uc} of the output and is informally called a *setting of the pooling switches*. A short derivation from (5) shows that the BP-reversed is given by

$$[\phi_{\mathrm{MP}}^{\mathrm{BP}}(\mathbf{x}, \hat{\mathbf{y}})]_{vc} = [\phi_{\mathrm{MP}}^{\dagger}(\hat{\mathbf{y}}, \mathbf{r})]_{vc} = \sum_{u \in s^{-1}(v|c,\mathbf{x})} \hat{y}_{uc}, \qquad \mathbf{r} = s(\cdot|\cdot, \mathbf{x}). \quad (9)$$

Hence the *bottleneck information for MP is the setting of the pooling switches*.

2.2 Deconvolutional Architectures

BP-reversal is only one way of defining reversed layers in a deconvolutional architecture. Here, we consider three variations. The **first variation** is whether the reversed max-pooling layers are the BP-reversed ones $\phi_{\mathrm{MP}}^{\mathrm{BP}}$, with pooling switches as bottleneck, or whether they simply unpool to the center of each neighborhood, with empty bottleneck. The **second variation** is whether the reversed ReLU units are the BP-reversed ones $\phi_{\mathrm{RU}}^{\mathrm{BP}}$, with the ReLU mask as bottleneck, or whether they are simply replaced with the identity function 1, with empty bottleneck. The **third variation** is whether the reversed ReLU units are, as in DeConvNets, also composed with a second ReLU. We will see that, while this choice seems arbitrary, it has a very strong impact on the results as it preserves the polarity of neural activations. Overall, we obtain eight combinations, summarized in Fig. 3, including three notable architectures: DeConvNet, SaliNet, and the hybrid DeSaliNet. Note that only SaliNet has an immediate interpretation, which is computing the derivative of the forward network.

Affine layers, max pooling, and ReLU cover all the layer types needed to reverse architectures such as VGG-VD, GoogLeNet, Inception and ResNet.[3] AlexNet includes *local response normalization* (LRN) layers, which in DeConvNet are reversed as the identity. As discussed in the supplementary material, this has little effect on the results.

---

[3] In all cases we deal with the network only till the layer before the softmax.

3   Experiments

Experiments thoroughly investigate the family of deconvolutional architectures
identified in Sect. 2. Section 3.1 tests eight possible network architectures and
identifies DeConvNet, SaliNet, and DeSaliNet as interesting cases for further
exploration. Section 3.2 compares the architectures in terms of clarity of the
generated images. Section 3.3 investigates whether visualizations provide useful
information about neurons, and Sect. 3.4 looks at the effect of the bottleneck
information. Finally, Sect. 3.5 evaluates these techniques on a practical application: segmentation of foreground objects.

Several experiments are shown here for a few representative images, but many
more examples are provided in the supplementary material.[4]

3.1   Overview of Deconvolutional Architectures

The first experiment compares the eight deconvolutional architectures of Fig. 3.
This is done by "reversing" the computations obtained when a network ϕ is
evaluated on an image $\mathbf{x}_0$ (in the example, the "trilobite" image of Fig. 1). Here
the forward network $\mathbf{y} = \phi(\mathbf{x}_0)$ is AlexNet [8] truncated at the last max-pooling

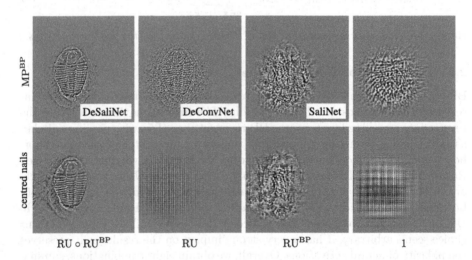

Fig. 3. Visualizations of VGG-16 using the *trilobite* image of Fig. 1 using eight deconvolutional architectures. The architectures are used to visualize the maximally-firing
neuron in the *pool5_3* layer and the full output image is shown (localization is mostly
due to the finite support of the neuron). From top to bottom we change the MP† reverse
and from left to right the RU† reverse. Here all methods use the identity as the reverse
LRN†.

---

[4] To improve the clarity of visualization images $\mathbf{x} = \phi^\dagger(\mathbf{p})$ in print, their real valued
ranges are remapped using the expression $\sigma(\mathbf{x}/(-\log(99)a))$ where a is the 0.5 %
quantile in vec I.

layer (pool5). The input $\mathbf{p}$ to the reversed network $\phi^{\dagger}(\mathbf{p})$ is the one-hot tensor selecting the pool5 neuron y_{uc} that is maximally excited by $\mathbf{x}_0$.

We can make the following observations. First, as in [16], SaliNet computes a fuzzy saliency map. Likewise, matching the results of [25], the result of DeConvNet has structure, in the sense that object edges are recovered.

Second, we compare the left four deconvolutional architectures to the right ones, which differ by the use of the ReLU units in the backward direction. We note that adding these units is *necessary* in order to recover the image edges. In particular, by modifying SaliNet in this manner, DeSaliNet produces an image with structure.

Third, using pooling switches (top row) slightly improves the clarity of the results compared to unpooling to center (bottom row). Even so, we note that the image structure can still be clearly recognized in the bottom-left image, using unpooling to center complemented by the hybrid $\mathrm{RU} \circ \mathrm{RU}^{\mathrm{BP}}$ as reverse ReLU. In fact, this image is arguably crisper than the DeConvNet result. This suggests that, perhaps unexpectedly, the ReLU polarity (captured by RU in the backward direction) is more important that the MP switches. It also shows that the ReLU masks (captured by $\mathrm{RU}^{\mathrm{BP}}$) significantly improve the sharpness of the results.

So far the LRN layers in AlexNet have been reversed using the identity, as in DeConvNet; however, the original saliency method by [16] uses the BP-reversed $\mathrm{LRN}^{\mathrm{BP}}$. In the supplementary material we show that this has a minor impact on the result, with slightly sharper results for the DeConvNet solution. Therefore, in the rest of the manuscript, DeConvNet and DeSaliNet use identity, while SaliNet, in keeping with the original saliency method by [16], uses $\mathrm{LRN}^{\mathrm{BP}}$.

3.2   Generated Image Quality

A first striking property of DeSaliNet is the clarity of resulting visualizations compared to the other architectures (e.g. Figs. 1, 3, 4, 6). While sharper visualizations than SaliNet are expected given the results in [16], the gap with DeConvNet is somewhat unexpected and particularly strong for deep layers (e.g. Fig. 1) and deeper architectures (e.g. Fig. 6). DeConvNet results appear to be less sharp than the ones shown in [25], which could be due to the fact that they used a custom version of AlexNet, whereas we visualize off-the-shelf versions of AlexNet and VGG-VD. Unfortunately, it was not possible to obtain a copy of their custom AlexNet to verify this hypothesis.

3.3   Meaning and Selectivity of the Deconvolutional Response

Visualizations obtained using reversed architectures such as DeConvNets are meant to characterize the *selectivity of neurons* by finding which visual patterns cause a neuron to fire strongly. However, we will see here that this interpretation is fragile.

Consider the i-th neuron $[\phi(\mathbf{x})]_i = \langle \mathbf{e}_i, \phi(\mathbf{x}) \rangle$ in the output layer of a (truncated) CNN architecture, where $\mathbf{e}_i$ is an indicator vector. In order to characterize

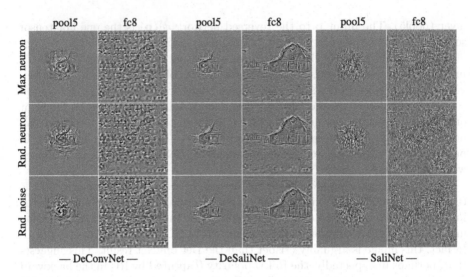

Fig. 4. *Lack of neuron selectivity.* The bottleneck information **r** is fixed to the one computed during the forward pass $\phi(\mathbf{x})$ through AlexNet and the output of $\phi^{\dagger}(\mathbf{e}, \mathbf{r})$ is computed by choosing **e** as: the most active neuron (top row), a second neuron at random (middle), or as a positive random mixture of all neurons (bottom row). Results barely differ, particularly for the deeper layers. See Fig. 1 for the original house input image **x**. Best viewed on screen.

this neuron, Zeiler and Fergus [25] search a large collection of images to find an image $\mathbf{x}^{*}$ that causes $\phi_i(\mathbf{x}^{*})$ to respond strongly. Thus, even before the deconvolutional network $\phi^{\dagger}(\mathbf{e}_i, \mathbf{r})$ is applied, the image $\mathbf{x}^{*}$ is already representative of the neuron. The application of $\phi^{\dagger}$ then *refines* this information by highlighting which regions in $\mathbf{x}^{*}$ are most responsible for this activation.

While this sounds simple, there is a subtle complication. Note in fact that the deconvolutional architecture $\phi^{\dagger}(\mathbf{e}_i, \mathbf{r})$ is a function both of the neuron indicator $\mathbf{e}_i$ as well as the bottleneck information **r** extracted from the forward pass of $\mathbf{x}^{*}$ through $\phi(\mathbf{x})$. In the deconvolution process, $\mathbf{e}_i$ is a direct specification of the neuron to be visualized. The other parameter, **r**, can also be considered a specification of the same neuron, although a fairly indirect one, because it is extracted from an image $\mathbf{x}^{*}$ that happens to excite the neuron strongly. Then the question is whether the deconvolutional response can be interpreted as a *direct* characterization of a neuron or not. This is answered next.

Lack of neuron selectivity. If the output of $\phi^{\dagger}(\mathbf{e}_i, \mathbf{r})$ is a direct characterization of the i-th neuron, we would expect the generated image to *meaningfully change* as the input $\mathbf{e}_i$ to the deconvolutional network changes.

In Fig. 4, DeConvNet, DeSaliNet, and SaliNet are used to visualize the responses of different neurons at the center of the image. The reversed function $\phi^{\dagger}(\mathbf{e}, \mathbf{r})$ is evaluated by keeping **r** fixed (as obtained from the forward pass $\phi(\mathbf{x}_0)$) and by replacing **e** with either: the indicator vector $\mathbf{e}^{*}$ of the neuron

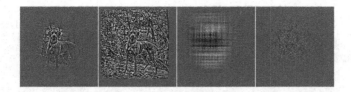

Fig. 5. *Effect of finite neuron support.* From left to right: Visualization from VGG-16 pool5_3 using DeSaliNet; the same result after $x^{0.1}$ renormalization; visualization without any bottleneck information as in Fig. 3-bottom right; the same visualization without bottleneck information but with randomized filter weights for the $*^{BP}$ operators. The re-normalization reveals that the true receptive field of pool5 is much larger and that the sides are not discarded but simply weakened in the deconvolution process.

that has the maximal response, a second random neuron e' that still generates a non-zero image, and a random non-negative vector e. It can be noted that, particularly in deeper layers, the response changes very little with different choices of e.

A clear difference between images from different depths (e.g. pool5 vs fc8 in Figs. 4 and 6) is the extent of the response, which however corresponds to the neuron support and depends on the architecture and not on the learned network weights or data. This is further confirmed in Fig. 5 by considering a network with random weights. There, it is also shown that renormalizing the image intensities reveals the full neuron support, which is only partially suppressed in the visualization, and in a manner which is architecture-dependent rather than weight or data dependent.

We conclude that the reversed architectures $\phi^\dagger(e, r)$ are mainly dependent on the bottleneck information r rather than the neuron selector e. Hence, they provide poor direct characterizations of neurons, particularly of deep ones.

Note that methods such as [13,16,24], which visualize individual neurons by activation maximization, are not affected by this problem. There are two reasons: first, they start from random noise, such that the bottleneck information r is *not* primed by a carefully-selected reference image x_0; secondly, they iteratively update the bottleneck information, drifting away from the initial value.

Foreground object selectivity. SaliNet is an equivalent implementation of the network saliency technique of Simonyan et al. [16], which showed that the deepest class-specific neurons (in fc8) in an architecture such as AlexNet are strongly selective for the foreground object in an image. However, in the previous section we have shown the apparently contradictory result that this response depends very weakly on the choosen class-specific neuron.

To clarify this point, in Figs. 1 and 6 we observe that SaliNet and DeSaliNet *are indeed* selective for the foreground object in the image; however, the information *comes mainly from the bottleneck* r and not from which specific neuron is selected. In other words, SaliNet and DeSaliNet emphasize whatever foreground object is detected by the network in the forward pass, regardless of which neuron

| | ─── VGG-VD Pool5_3 ─── | | | ─── VGG-VD FC8 ─── | | |
| Image | DeConvNet | SaliNet | DeSaliNet | DeConvNet | SaliNet | DeSaliNet |

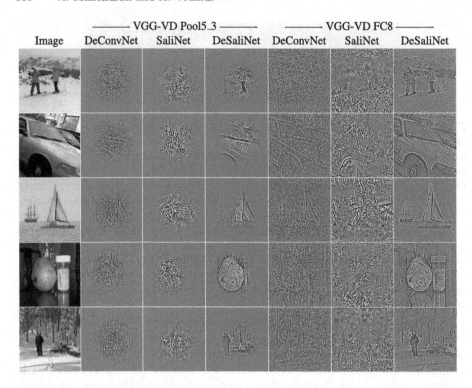

Fig. 6. *Foreground object selectivity.* This figure compares the response of DeConvNet, SaliNet, and DeSaliNet by visualizing the most active neuron in Pool5_3 and FC8 of VGG-VD. SaliNet and DeSaliNet tend to emphasize more foreground objects (see e.g. the faces of people), whereas DeConvNet's response is nearly uniform. Note that the apparent spatial selectivity of Pool5_3 is due to the finite support of the neuron and is content independent. Best viewed on screen.

is specified as input to the reversed architecture. The main difference between SaliNet and DeSaliNet, as observed before, is that the latter produces a much more localized and crisp response

Compared to SaliNet and DeSaliNet, DeConvNet fails to produce a clearly selective signal from these very deep neurons, generating a rather uniform response. We conclude that saliency, in the sense of foreground object selectivity, requires not only the max pooling switches (available in all three architectures), but also the ReLU masks (used only by SaliNet and DeSaliNet).

Informativeness of bottleneck. In order to characterize the amount of information contained in the bottleneck, we used the method of [3] to train a network that acts as the inverse of another. However, while the inverse network of [3] operates only from the output of the direct model, here we modified it by using different amounts of bottleneck information as well. The reconstruction error of these "informed" inverse networks illustrates importance of the bottleneck information. We found that inverting with the knowledge of the ReLU rectification

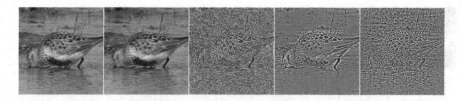

Fig. 7. *Analogy with phase information in Fourier Transform.* From left to right: The original image, the inverse Fourier transform of the Fourier transform of the original image, the inverse Fourier transform but after randomizing the amplitude of the spectrum, DeSaliNet $\phi^\dagger(\mathbf{p}, \mathbf{r})$ with positive random input $(\mathbf{p})$ and DeConvNet with positive random input $(\mathbf{p})$. Best viewed on screen.

Table 1. Mean Intersection over Union (IoU) and Mean Per-Pixel (PP) accuracy for different segmentation methods on the dataset of [4].

Method	CNN	PP	IoU	CNN	PP	IoU	Method	PP	IoU
SaliNet	AlexNet	82.82	57.07	VGG-16	82.45	56.33	Baseline	78.97	46.27
DeSaliNet	AlexNet	82.31	55.57	VGG-16	83.29	56.25	Guillaumin *et al.* [4]	84.4	57.3
DeConvNet	AlexNet	75.85	48.26	VGG-16	76.52	48.16	Baseline of [4]	73.4	24.0

masks and the MP pooling switches has 15 % lower $L2$ reconstruction error (on validation images) compared than using pooling switches alone, and 46 % lower than using the rectification masks alone. Finally, pooling switches alone have 36 % lower $L2$ error than using only rectification masks.

3.4 Dominance of "phase" Information

If a message emerges from the previous sections, it is that the response of all reversed architectures $\phi^\dagger(\mathbf{e}, \mathbf{r})$ is *dominated by the bottleneck information* $\mathbf{r}$. As seen in Sect. 2, the bottleneck information comprises (1) the setting of the pooling switches in the Max Pool units and (2) the setting of the masks in the ReLU units.

Interestingly, this information does not code for the intensity of the neural activations, but rather for their spatial location and polarity. We argue that this information is somewhat similar to phase information in the Fourier transform and related representations. To explain this analogy, consider the Fourier transform $X(\omega_x, \omega_y) = \mathcal{F}[\mathbf{x}](\omega_x, \omega_y) \in \mathbb{C}$ of image $\mathbf{x}$; a well known result is that if one replaces the modulus of the Fourier transform with a random signal but preserves the phase, then the reconstructed image $\hat{\mathbf{x}} = \mathcal{F}^{-1}[|Y(\omega_x, \omega_y)|e^{i\angle X(\omega_x, \omega_y)}]$ still contains the structure (edges) of $\mathbf{x}$ and very little of $\mathbf{y}$ is recognizable. In fact the resulting image, an example of which is shown in Fig. 7, is not dissimilar from the output of DeConvNet and DeSaliNet.

In the Fourier transform, changing the phase of a spectral component $Ae^{j(\omega x + \theta)}$ by $\Delta\theta$ amounts to shifting it by $-\Delta\theta/\omega$. Furthermore, negating the signal is equivalent to a phase shift of π. In the deconvolutional architectures, the max pooling switches record the location of filter activations, whereas the ReLUs

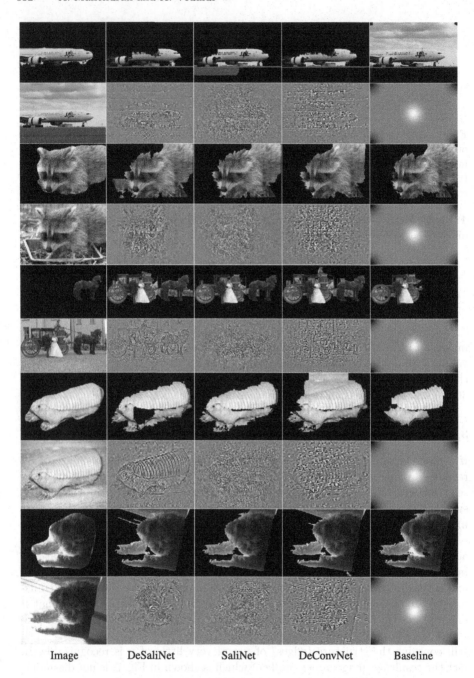

Image   DeSaliNet   SaliNet   DeConvNet   Baseline

Fig. 8. Segmentation results (random selection). For each image, the top row shows the GrabCut segmentation and the bottom row shows the output of the corresponding deconvolutional network derived from AlexNet

applied in the backward direction contribute to reconstructing the polarity. More precisely, in the forward pass the ReLU block computes $y = \max\{0, x\}$. In the backward direction, the signal $\hat{y}$ is propagated towards the input as follows:

$$\hat{x} = \max\{\hat{y}, 0\} \text{ (in DeConvNet)}, \quad \hat{x} = \max\{\hat{y}, 0\} \odot [x > 0] \text{ (in DeSaliNet)}.$$

(10)

We see that both constructions guarantee that the polarity of the backward signal $\hat{x}$ is the same as the polarity of the forward signal y, which is non-negative. In fact, DeConvNet guarantees that $y\hat{x} \geq 0$, and DeSaliNet adds the guarantee that $y = 0 \Rightarrow \hat{x} = 0$. The first condition is stronger in term of preserving the polarity, and as seen in Fig. 3 it is necessary to obtain a clear reconstruction of the image edges.

3.5 Objectness for Free: Weakly-Supervised Salient Object Segmentation

In this section we demonstrate that pre-trained CNNs reversed using SaliNet and DeSaliNet can accurately segment generic foreground objects. To this end, we consider the benchmark dataset of [4] consisting of 4276 ImageNet images annotated with the binary mask of the foreground objects. Notably, the object categories in this benchmarks are partially disjoint from the ones in the ImageNet ILSVRC data used to pre-train the CNNs: of the 445 synsets present in the segmentation benchmark data only 215 of them overlap with the 1000 ILSVRC classes.

In order to perform segmentation, we improve the setup of [16]. Given an image $\mathbf{x}$, the CNN $\phi(\mathbf{x})$ is evaluated until the last layer before softmax (FC8 in AlexNet[5] and VGG-VD), recording the bottleneck information $\mathbf{r}$. Rather than resizing the image to the standard network input size, the CNN is applied in a fully convolutional manner [11]. The tensor $\mathbf{e}^*$ is set to the indicator of the channel that contains the maximally-activated neuron in FC8, the L^∞ norm of each RGB triplet in the output $\hat{\mathbf{x}} = \phi^\dagger(\mathbf{e}^*, \mathbf{r})$ of the reversed architecture is computed, and the resulting saliency map is used in GrabCut to segment the object as in [16]. Besides the ILSVRC data used to pre-train the CNN and 98 segmented images for validating the design choices above, there is no further training. For segmentation, this is a weakly-supervised setting as no object bounding boxes or segmentations are used for training.

Table 1 and Fig. 8 compare the three reversed architectures and the method of [4], which uses a combination of segment transfer from VOC2010 data, label propagation, bounding box annotations for 60k training images, and class label annotations for all images. It also compares a simple baseline obtained by assuming as a saliency map a fixed Gaussian blob (Fig. 8), similar but much better than the analogous baseline in [4].

---

[5] For DeSaliNet, the LRN layers in AlexNet are reversed using BP-reversal LRN^{BP} instead of the identity, which was found to be slightly superior in terms of IoU performance.

DeSaliNet and SaliNet performed about as well, much better than the baseline, and nearly as well as the method of [4], despite using weak supervision and a training set that, for the most part, contains different classes from the test set. This suggests that CNN learn the appearance of generic objects, which SaliNet and DeSaliNet can extract efficiently. DeConvNet did not perform better than the Gaussian baseline confirming its lack of foreground selectivity (Sect. 3.3).

Somewhat surprisingly, VGG-VD did not perform better than AlexNet, nor DeSaliNet better than SaliNet, despite achieving in general much sharper saliency maps. Qualitatively, it appears that GrabCut prefers a more diffuse saliency map as opposed to a sharper one that focuses on the object boundaries, which may create "holes" in the segmentation. In fact, GrabCut improves dramatically even the weak Gaussian baseline.

4   Discussion

In this paper we have derived a general construction for reversed "deconvolutional" architectures, showed that BP is an instance of such a construction, and used this to precisely contrast DeConvNet and network saliency. DeSaliNet produces convincingly sharper images that network saliency while being more selective to foreground objects than DeConvNet.

We showed that the sharpness of generated images depends mainly on the polarization enforced by reversed ReLU units, followed by the ReLU unit masks, and with a secondary contribution from the max pooling switches. Some of these ideas may be transferable to other applications of deconvolution such as the U-architecture of [15] for semantic segmentation. We also showed that bottleneck information (pooling switches and ReLU masks) dominates the output of deconvolutional architectures which questions their utility in characterizing individual neurons.

Acknowledgements. We gratefully acknowledge the support of ERC StG IDIU for Andrea Vedaldi and of BP for Aravindh Mahendran.

References

1. Bishop, C.M.: Neural Networks for Pattern Recognition. Clarendon Press, Oxford (1995)
2. d'Angelo, E., Alahi, A., Vandergheynst, P.: Beyond bits: reconstructing images from local binary descriptors. In: Proceedings of ICPR, pp. 935–938 (2012)
3. Dosovitskiy, A., Brox, T.: Inverting visual representations with convolutional networks. In: Proceedings of CVPR (2016)
4. Guillaumin, M., Küttel, D., Ferrari, V.: Imagenet auto-annotation with segmentation propagation. IJCV **110**(3), 328–348 (2014)
5. Hong, S., Noh, H., Han, B.: Decoupled deep neural network for semi-supervised semantic segmentation. In: Proceedings of NIPS, pp. 1495–1503 (2015)
6. Jensen, C.A., Reed, R.D., Marks, R.J., El-Sharkawi, M., Jung, J.B., Miyamoto, R., Anderson, G., Eggen, C.: Inversion of feedforward neural networks: algorithms and applications. Proc. IEEE **87**(9), 1536–1549 (1999)

7. Kato, H., Harada, T.: Image reconstruction from bag-of-visual-words. In: Proceedings of CVPR (2014)
8. Krizhevsky, A., Sutskever, I., Hinton, G.E.: Imagenet classification with deep convolutional neural networks. In: Proceedings of NIPS (2012)
9. Lee, S., Kil, R.M.: Inverse mapping of continuous functions using local and global information. IEEE Trans. Neural Netw. 5(3), 409–423 (1994)
10. Linden, A., Kindermann, J.: Inversion of multilayer nets. In: Proceedings of International Conference on Neural Networks (1989)
11. Long, J., Shelhamer, E., Darrell, T.: Fully convolutional networks for semantic segmentation. In: Proceedings of CVPR, pp. 3431–3440 (2015)
12. Lu, B.L., Kita, H., Nishikawa, Y.: Inverting feedforward neural networks using linear and nonlinear programming. IEEE Trans. Neural Netw. 10(6), 1271–1290 (1999)
13. Mahendran, A., Vedaldi, A.: Understanding deep image representations by inverting them. In: Proceedings of CVPR (2015)
14. Nguyen, A., Yosinski, J., Clune, J.: Deep neural networks are easily fooled: high confidence predictions for unrecognizable images. In: Proceedings of CVPR (2015)
15. Noh, H., Hong, S., Han, B.: Learning deconvolution network for semantic segmentation. In: Proceedings of ICCV, pp. 1520–1528 (2015)
16. Simonyan, K., Vedaldi, A., Zisserman, A.: Deep inside convolutional networks: visualising image classification models and saliency maps. In: ICLR (2014)
17. Springenberg, J.T., Dosovitskiy, A., Brox, T., Riedmiller, M.: Striving for simplicity: the all convolutional net. In: ICLR Workshop (2015)
18. Szegedy, C., Zaremba, W., Sutskever, I., Bruna, J., Erhan, D., Goodfellow, I.J., Fergus, R.: Intriguing properties of neural networks. In: ICLR (2014)
19. Tatu, A., Lauze, F., Nielsen, M., Kimia, B.: Exploring the representation capabilities of the HOG descriptor. In: ICCV Workshop (2011)
20. Várkonyi-Kóczy, A.R., Rövid, A.: Observer based iterative neural network model inversion. In: IEEE International Conference on Fuzzy Systems (2005)
21. Vondrick, C., Khosla, A., Malisiewicz, T., Torralba, A.: HOGgles: visualizing object detection features. In: Proceedings of ICCV (2013)
22. Weinzaepfel, P., Jégou, H., Pérez, P.: Reconstructing an image from its local descriptors. In: Proceedings of CVPR (2011)
23. Williams, R.J.: Inverting a connectionist network mapping by back-propagation of error. In: Proceedings of CogSci (1986)
24. Yosinksi, J., Clune, J., Nguyen, A., Fuchs, T., Lipson, H.: Understanding neural networks through deep visualization. In: ICML Deep Learning Workshop (2015)
25. Zeiler, M.D., Fergus, R.: Visualizing and understanding convolutional networks. In: Fleet, D., Pajdla, T., Schiele, B., Tuytelaars, T. (eds.) ECCV 2014. LNCS, vol. 8689, pp. 818–833. Springer, Heidelberg (2014). doi:10.1007/978-3-319-10590-1_53
26. Zeiler, M.D., Krishnan, D., Taylor, G.W., Fergus, R.: Deconvolutional networks. In: Proceedings of CVPR (2010)
27. Zeiler, M.D., Taylor, G.W., Fergus, R.: Adaptive deconvolutional networks for mid and high level feature learning. In: Proceedings of ICCV (2011)

Visualizing Image Priors

Tamar Rott Shaham$^{(\boxtimes)}$ and Tomer Michaeli

Technion—Israel Institute of Technology, Haifa, Israel
stamarot@campus.technion.ac.il, tomer.m@ee.technion.ac.il

Abstract. Image priors play a key role in low-level vision tasks. Over the years, many priors have been proposed, based on a wide variety of principles. While different priors capture different geometric properties, there is currently no unified approach to interpreting and comparing priors of different nature. This limits our ability to analyze failures or successes of image models in specific settings, and to identify potential improvements. In this paper, we introduce a simple technique for visualizing image priors. Our method determines how images should be deformed so as to best conform to a given image model. The deformed images constructed this way, highlight the elementary geometric structures to which the prior resonates. We use our approach to study various popular image models, and reveal interesting behaviors, which were not noticed in the past. We confirm our findings through denoising experiments. These validate that the structures we reveal as 'optimal' for a specific prior are indeed better denoised by this prior.

1 Introduction

Image priors play a fundamental role in many low-level vision tasks, such as denoising, deblurring, super-resolution, inpaiting, and more [1–9]. Over the years, many priors have been proposed, based on a wide variety of different principles. These range from priors on derivatives [2,10], wavelet coefficients [11,12], filter responses [13,14], and small patches [1,15], to nonparametric models that rely on the tendency of patches to recur within and across scales in natural images [16–19].

Different priors capture different geometric properties. For example, it is known that the total variation (TV) regularizer [10] prefers boundaries with limited curvature [20], whereas the local self-similarity prior [21] prefers straight edges and sharp corners (structures which look the same at different scales). However, generally, characterizing the behavior of complex image priors (*e.g.,* trained models) is extremely challenging. This limits our ability to interpret failures or successes in specific settings, as well as to identify possible model improvements.

In this paper, we present a simple technique for visualizing image priors. Given an image model, our method determines how images should be deformed so that they become more plausible under this model. That is, for any input image, our algorithm produces a geometrically 'idealized' version, which better

© Springer International Publishing AG 2016
B. Leibe et al. (Eds.): ECCV 2016, Part VI, LNCS 9910, pp. 136–153, 2016.
DOI: 10.1007/978-3-319-46466-4_9

| (a) Input | (b) BM3D | (c) Shrinkage Fields | (d) Total Variation | (e) Multi-Layer Perceptron |

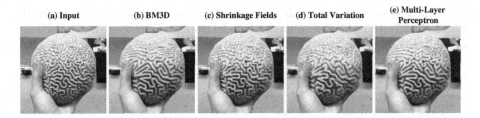

Fig. 1. Visualizing image priors. Our algorithm determines how images should be deformed so as to better comply with a given image model (exemplified here on a Brain Coral image). The deformed images give insight into the elementary geometric features to which the prior resonates. As can be seen, different image models (BM3D [17], Shrinkage Fields [22] with pairwise cliques, Total Variation [10], Multi-Layer Perceptron [4]) have quite different geometric preferences.

conforms to the prior we wish to study. Figure 1 shows several example outputs of our algorithm. As can be seen, our idealization process nicely highlights the elementary features to which different priors resonate, and thus gives intuition into their geometric preferences.

Our approach is rather general and, in particular, can be used to visualize generative models (*e.g.,* fields of experts [14]), discriminative models (*e.g.,* deep nets [4]), nonparametric models (*e.g.,* nonlocal means [16]), and any other image model that has an associated denoising algorithm. In fact, the 'idealized' images produced by our method have a nice interpretation in terms of the associated denoiser: Their geometry is not altered if we attempt to 'denoise' them (treating them as noisy images). We thus refer to our 'idealized' images as *Geometric Eigen-Modes* (GEMs) of the prior.

Figure 2 illustrates how GEMs encode geometric preferences of image models. For example, since the TV prior [10] penalizes for large gradients, a TV-GEM is a deformed image in which the gradient magnitudes are smaller. Similarly, the wavelet sparsity prior [11] penalizes for non-zero wavelet coefficients. Therefore, a wavelet-GEM is a deformed image in which the wavelet coefficients are sparser. Finally, the internal KSVD model [15] assumes the existence of a dictionary over which all patches in the image admit a sparse representation. Thus, a KSVD-GEM is a deformed image for which there exists a dictionary allowing better sparse representation of the image patches.

We use our approach to study several popular image models and observe various interesting phenomena, which, to the best of our knowledge, were not pointed out in the past. First, unsurprisingly, we find that all modern image priors prefer large structures over small ones. However, the preferred shapes of these large objects, differ among priors. Specifically, most internal priors (*e.g.,* BM3D [17], internally-trained KSVD [15], cross-scale patch recurrence [19]) prefer straight edges and sharp corners. On the other hand, externally trained models (*e.g.,* EPLL [1], multi-layer perceptorn [4]), are much less biased towards straight borders, and their preferred shapes of corners are rather round. But we also find a few surprising exceptions to this rule. For example, it turns out that nonlocal means (NLM) [16], which is an internal model, rather resonates to curved edges, similarly to external priors. Another interesting exception is the fields of experts (FoE) prior [14], an externally-trained model which turns out to prefer straight *axis-aligned* edges.

Fig. 2. GEMs better conform to the prior. (a) The internal KSVD model [15] assumes that each patch in the image can be sparsely represented over some dictionary. (b) A KSVD-GEM is a deformed image in which the diversity between patches is smaller, so that the sparsity assumption holds better. Namely, for the KSVD-GEM, there exists a dictionary over which each patch can be sparsely represented *with better accuracy*. Note how less atoms are invested in representing the fine details in this dictionary. (c) The wavelet sparsity prior [11] penalizes the ℓ_1 norm of the wavelet coefficients of the image (we use the Haar wavelet for illustration). (d) A wavelet-GEM is a deformed image in which the wavelet coefficients have a smaller ℓ_1 norm, and are thus sparser. (e) The TV prior penalizes the ℓ_1 norm of the gradient magnitude. (f) A TV-GEM is a deformed image in which the gradient magnitude is smaller (and so has a smaller ℓ_1 norm).

The behaviors we reveal are often impossible to notice visually in standard image recovery experiments on natural images (*e.g.,* denoising, deblurring, super-resolution). However, they turn out to have significant effects on the PSNR in such tasks. We demonstrate this through several denoising experiments. As we show, structures predicted by our approach to be most 'plausible', can indeed be recovered from their noisy versions significantly better than other geometric features. So, for example, we show how the FoE model indeed performs significantly better in denoising an axis-aligned square, than in denoising a rotated one.

1.1   Related Work

There are various approaches to interpreting and visualizing image models. However, most methods are suited only to specific families of priors, and are thus of limited use when it comes to *comparing* between models of different nature.

Moreover, existing visualizations are typically indirect, and hard to associate to the reaction of the model to real natural images.

Analytic Characterization: Certain models can be characterized analytically. One example is the TV regularizer [10], which has been shown to preserve convex shapes as long as the maximal curvature along their boundary is smaller than their perimeter divided by their area [20]. Another example is sparse representations over multiscale frames (*e.g.,* wavelets [23], bandlets [24], curvelets [25], etc.). For instance, contourlets have been shown to provide optimally sparse representations for objects that are piecewise smooth and have smooth boundaries [26] (*i.e.,* functions that are C^2 except for discontinuities along C^2 curves). However, general image priors (especially trained models), are extremely difficult to analyze mathematically.

Patch Based Models: Many parametric models have been used for small image patches, including independent component analysis (ICA) [27], products of experts [28], Gaussian mixture models (GMMs) [1], sparse representation over some dictionary [15], and more. Those models are usually visualized by plotting the basic elements which comprise them. Namely, the independent components in ICA, the dictionary atoms in sparse representations, the top eigenvectors of the Gaussians' covariances in GMM, etc.

Markov Random Fields: These models use Gibbs distributions over filter responses [13,14,29–31]. The filters (as well as their potentials) are typically learned from a collection of training images. Those priors can be visualized by drawing samples from the learned model using Markov-chain Monte Carlo (MCMC) simulation [29]. Another common practice is to plot the learnt filters. However, as discussed in [32], those filters are often nonintuitive and difficult to interpret. Indeed, as we show in Sect. 3, our visualization reveals certain geometric preferences of the MRF models [14,22,31], which were not previously pointed out.

Deep Networks: These architectures are widely used in image classification, but are also gaining increasing popularity in low-level vision tasks, including in denoising [4], super-resolution [33], and blind deblurring [34]. Visualizing feature activities at different layers has been studied mainly in the context of convolutional networks, and was primarily used to interpret models trained for classification [35,36]. Features in the first layer typically resemble localized Gabor filters at various orientations, while deeper layers capture structures with increasing complexity.

Patch Recurrence: Patch recurrence is known as a dominant property of natural images. A technique for revealing and modifying variations between repeating structures in an image was recently presented in [37]. This method determines how images should be deformed so as to increase the patch repetitions within them. Although presented in the context of image editing, this method can in fact be viewed as a special case of our proposed approach, where the prior being visualized enforces patch-recurrence within the image. Here, we use the same concept, but to visualize *arbitrary* image priors.

In contrast to previous approaches, which visualize filters, atoms, or other building blocks of the model, our approach rather visualizes the model's effect on images. As we illustrate, in many cases this visualization is significantly more informative.

2   Algorithm

Suppose we are given a probability model $p(x)$ for natural images. To visualize what geometric properties this model captures, our approach is to determine how images should be deformed so that they become more likely under this model. That is, for any input image y, we seek an idealized version $x \approx \mathcal{T}\{y\}$, for some piecewise-smooth deformation $\mathcal{T}$, such that $\log p(x)$ is maximal. More specifically, we define the idealizing deformation $\mathcal{T}$ as the solution to the optimization problem

$$\underset{x,\mathcal{T}}{\arg\min}\ \underbrace{-\log p(x)}_{\text{log-prior}} + \underbrace{\lambda \Phi(\mathcal{T})}_{\text{smoothness}} + \underbrace{\tfrac{1}{2\sigma^2}\|\mathcal{T}\{y\} - x\|^2}_{\text{fidelity}}. \tag{1}$$

The log-prior term forces the image x to be highly plausible under the prior $p(x)$. The smoothness term regularizes the deformation $\mathcal{T}$ to be piecewise smooth. Finally, the fidelity term ensures that the deformed (idealized) input image $\mathcal{T}\{y\}$ is close to x. The parameters σ and λ control the relative weights of the different terms, and as we show in Sect. 2.2, can be used to control the scales of features captured by the visualization.

We use nonparametric deformations, so that the transformation $\mathcal{T}$ is defined as

$$\mathcal{T}\{y\}(\xi, \eta) = y(\xi + u(\xi, \eta), \eta + v(\xi, \eta)) \tag{2}$$

for some flow field (u, v). We define the smoothness term to be the robust penalty

$$\Phi(\mathcal{T}) = \iint \sqrt{\|\nabla u(\xi, \eta)\|^2 + \|\nabla v(\xi, \eta)\|^2 + \varepsilon^2}\, d\xi d\eta, \tag{3}$$

where $\nabla = (\frac{\partial}{\partial \xi}, \frac{\partial}{\partial \eta})$ and ε is a small constant. This penalty is commonly used in the optical flow literature [38] and is known to promote smooth flow fields while allowing for sharp discontinuities at objects boundaries.

To solve the optimization problem (1), we use alternating minimization. Namely, we iterate between minimizing the objective w.r.t. the image x while holding the deformation $\mathcal{T}$ fixed, and minimizing the objective w.r.t. $\mathcal{T}$ while holding x fixed.

x-step: The smoothness term in (1) does not depend on x, so that this step reduces to

$$\underset{x}{\arg\min}\ \tfrac{1}{2\sigma^2}\|\mathcal{T}\{y\} - x\|^2 - \log p(x). \tag{4}$$

This can be interpreted as computing the maximum a-posteriori (MAP) estimate of x from a "noisy signal" $\mathcal{T}\{y\}$, assuming additive white Gaussian noise with

---

Input: Image y, denoising function `Denoise()`
Output: Idealizing transformation $\mathcal{T}$, idealized image y^{GEM}
Initialize $\mathcal{T}^0$ to be the identity mapping.
for $k = 1, \ldots, K$ **do**
  $\quad x^k \leftarrow \text{Denoise}(\mathcal{T}^{k-1}\{y\})$ /* tuned for noise level σ */
  $\quad \mathcal{T}^k \leftarrow \text{OpticalFlow}(y, x^k)$ /*with regularization parameter $2\lambda\sigma^2$ */
end
$\mathcal{T} \leftarrow \mathcal{T}^K$
$y^{\text{GEM}} \leftarrow \mathcal{T}\{y\}$

Algorithm 1. Geometric prior visualization.

Fig. 3. Schematic illustration of the algorithm. In each iteration, the current corrected image $\mathcal{T}\{y\}$ is "denoised" to obtain an updated image x. Then, the deformation $\mathcal{T}$ is updated to be that which best maps the input y to the new x. This results in a new corrected image $\mathcal{T}\{y\}$. The iterations are shown for the FoE model [14]. Photo courtesy of Mickey Weidenfeld.

variance σ^2. Thus, x is obtained by "denoising" the current $\mathcal{T}\{y\}$ using the prior $p(x)$.

$\mathcal{T}$-**step:** The log-likelihood term in (1) does not depend on $\mathcal{T}$, so that this step boils down to solving

$$\arg\min_{\mathcal{T}} \|\mathcal{T}\{y\} - x\|^2 + 2\lambda\sigma^2 \cdot \Phi(\mathcal{T}). \tag{5}$$

This corresponds to computing the optical flow between the current image x and the input image y, where the regularization weight is $2\lambda\sigma^2$. To solve this problem we use the iteratively re-weighted least-squares (IRLS) algorithm proposed in [39] (using an L_2 data-term in place of their L_1 term).

Therefore, as summarized in Algorithm 1, our algorithm iterates between denoising the current deformed image, and warping the input image to match the denoised result. Intuitively, when the denoiser is applied on the image, it modifies it to be more plausible according to the prior $p(x)$. This modification introduces slight deformations, among other effects. The role of the optical flow stage is to capture only the geometric modifications, which are those we wish to study. This process is illustrated in Fig. 3.

Note that typical optical flow methods work coarse-to-fine to avoid getting trapped in local minima (the flow computed in each level is interpolated to provide an initialization for the next level). In our case, however, this is not needed because the flow changes very slowly between consecutive iterations of

Algorithm 1. Thus, in each iteration, we simply use the flow from the previous iteration as initialization.

2.1 Alternative Interpretation: Geometric Eigen-Modes

Our discussion so far assumed generative models for whole images. However, many image enhancement algorithms do not explicitly rely on such probabilistic models. Some methods only model the local statistics of small neighborhoods (patches), either by learning from an external database [1], or by relying on the recurrence of patches within the input image itself [16,17]. Other approaches are discriminative [4], directly learning the desired mapping from input degraded images to output clean images. In all these cases, there is no explicit definition of a probability density function $p(x)$ for whole images, so that the optimization problem (1) is not directly applicable. Nevertheless, note that Algorithm 1 can be used even in the absence of a probability model $p(x)$, as all it requires is the availability of a denoising algorithm. To understand what Algorithm 1 computes when the denoising does not correspond to MAP estimation, it is insightful to examine how the flow $\mathcal{T}$ evolves along the iterations.

Collecting the two steps of Algorithm 1 together, we see that the deformation evolves as $\mathcal{T}^{k+1} = \texttt{OpticalFlow}(y, \texttt{Denoise}(\mathcal{T}^k\{y\}))$. Therefore, the algorithm converges once the transformation $\mathcal{T}$ satisfies

$$\mathcal{T} = \texttt{OpticalFlow}(y, \texttt{Denoise}(\mathcal{T}\{y\})). \tag{6}$$

This implies that after convergence, denoising $\mathcal{T}\{y\}$ does not introduce geometric deformations anymore. In other words, the output $y^{\text{GEM}} = \mathcal{T}\{y\}$ has the same geometry as its denoised version $\texttt{Denoise}(y^{\text{GEM}})$. To see this, note that condition (6) states that the image $\texttt{Denoise}(y^{\text{GEM}})$ is related to y by the deformation $\mathcal{T}$. But, recall that the image y^{GEM} itself is also related to y by the deformation $\mathcal{T}$. This is illustrated in Fig. 4.

From the discussion above we conclude the image y^{GEM} produced by our algorithm has the property that *its geometry is not altered by the denoiser*. We therefore call y^{GEM} a *Geometric Eigen-Mode (GEM)* of the prior, associated with image y. Because GEMs are not geometrically modified by the denoiser, the local geometric structures seen in a GEM are precisely those structures which are best preserved by the denoiser. This makes GEMs very informative for studying the geometric preferences of image priors.

2.2 Controlling the Visualization Strength

Recall that the parameters λ and σ control the relative weights of the three terms in Problem[1] (1). To tune the strength of the visualization, we can vary the weight of the log-prior term, which affects the extent to which the 'idealized'

---

[1] Strictly speaking, this interpretation is valid only if our denoiser performs MAP estimation. However, the intuition is the same also for arbitrary denoisers.

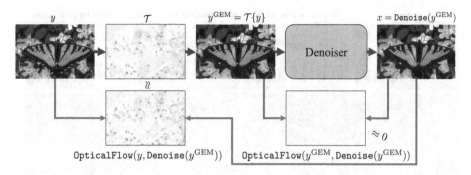

Fig. 4. Denoising a GEM does not change its geometry. The GEM y^{GEM} is obtained by warping the image y with the 'idealizing' flow field $\mathcal{T}$. 'Denoising' y^{GEM}, results in an image with the same geometry as y^{GEM} itself. That is, the optical flow between $\texttt{Denoise}(y^{\text{GEM}})$ and y^{GEM} is zero, and optical flow between $\texttt{Denoise}(y^{\text{GEM}})$ and y is equal to $\mathcal{T}$ (like the transformation between y^{GEM} itself and y). The results are shown for the multi-layer perceptron (MLP) model [4].

image complies with the prior. This requires varying σ while keeping the product $\lambda\sigma^2$ fixed. Figure 5 shows BM3D-GEMs with several different strengths. As we increase the weight of the log-prior term, smaller and smaller features get deformed so that the prior is better satisfied. This effect is clearly seen in the small arcs, the mandrill's pupils, and the delicate textures on the mandrill's fur.

3   Experiments

We used our algorithm on images from [40,41] and from the Web to study a variety of popular priors [1,4,10,14–17,22,31]. Some denoising methods work only on grayscale images. So, for fair comparison, we always determined the idealizing deformation based on the grayscale version of the input image, and then used this deformation to warp the color image itself. In all our experiments we used 50 iterations, $\sigma = 25/50$ and λ in the range $[0.5 \times 10^{-4}, 3 \times 10^{-4}]$ (for gray values in the range $[0, 255]$). Some denoisers do not accept σ as input, like nonlocal means and TV. We tuned those methods' parameters to perform best in the task of removing noise of variance σ^2 from noisy images.

Figure 6 shows visualization results for BM3D [17], FoE [14], EPLL [1] and TV [10]. As can be seen, common to all these models is that they prefer large structures over small ones. Indeed, note how the small yellow spots on the butterfly, the small arcs in the colosseum, the small black spots on the Dalmatians, and the small white spots on the owl, are all removed in the idealization process (the flow shrinks them until they disappear). The remaining large structures, on the other hand, are distorted quite differently by each of the models.

BM3D [17] is an internal model, which relies on comparisons between patches within the image. As can be seen in Fig. 6, BM3D clearly prefers straight edges connected at sharp corners. Moreover, it favors textures with straight thin

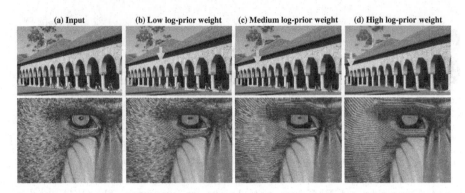

Fig. 5. Controlling the visualization strength. (a) Input images Arcs and Mandril. (b)–(d) BM3D-GEMs with varying strengths, obtained by tuning the log-prior weight in Problem (1). The effect is obtained by increasing σ while decreasing λ so that the product $\lambda\sigma^2$ is kept fixed. We used $\sigma = 20, 30, 50$ in (b), (c), (d), and $\lambda\sigma^2 = 0.128$. As the log-prior weight increases, smaller structures get deformed (*e.g.*, the small arcs and the mandril's pupils and fur).

threads (see the owl's head). This can be attributed to the fact that the patch repetitions in those structures are strong. In fact, as we show in Fig. 7, straight edges and sharp corners are also favored by other internal patch-recurrence models, including internally-trained KSVD [15] and the cross-scale patch recurrence prior of [19].

The FoE model [14] expresses the probability of natural images in terms of filter responses. As can be seen in Fig. 6, FoE resonates to straight *axis-aligned* edges connected at right-angle corners. This surprising behavior cannot be predicted by examining the models' filters, and to the best of our knowledge, was not reported in the past. Note that FoE is an external model that was trained on a collection of images [41]. Therefore, an interesting question is whether its behavior is associated to the statistics of natural images, or rather to some limitation of the model. A partial answer can be obtained by examining the visualizations of EPLL [1], another external model which was trained on the same image collection [41]. As observed in Fig. 6, EPLL also has a preference to straight edges, but its bias towards horizontal and vertical edges is much weaker than that of FoE (a small bias can be noticed on the butterfly's wings, on the flowers behind the butterfly, and on the Dalmatians' spots). This suggests that the excessive tendency of FoE to axis-aligned structures is rather related to a limitation of the model, as we further discuss below. We also note that, unlike FoE, the optimal shapes of corners in EPLL are rather round.

Finally, as seen in Fig. 6, the TV prior exhibits a very different behavior. As opposed to all other priors, which prefer straight edges over curved ones, TV clearly preserves curved edges as long as their curvature is not too large. This phenomenon has been studied analytically in [20].

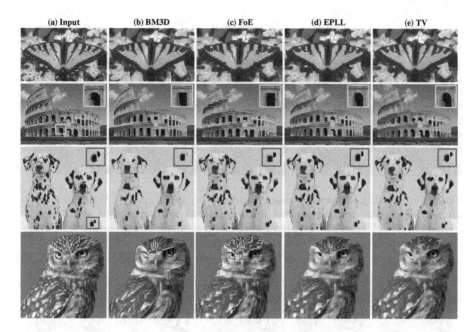

Fig. 6. Visualizing popular image priors. (a) Input images Flower, Colosseum, Dalmatians, and Owl. (b)–(e) Geometric idealization w.r.t. to the BM3D [17], FoE [14], EPLL [1] and TV [10] priors with $\sigma = 50$ and $\lambda = 0.7 \times 10^{-4}$. Note how different elementary structures are preferred by each of the models.

Internal Models: We next compare between several internal models, which rely on the tendency of patches to repeat within and across scales in natural images [42]. Figure 7 shows visualizations for four such methods: BM3D [17], KSVD [15] (trained internally on the input image), the cross-scale patch recurrence model[2] of [19], and NLM [16]. As can be seen, the GEMs of all these priors have increased redundancy: Edges are deformed to be straighter, stripes are deformed to have constant widths, etc. However, close inspection also reveals interesting differences between the GEMs. Most notably, the NLM method seems to reduce the curvature of edges, but does not entirely straightens them. This may be caused by the fact that it uses a rather localized search window for finding similar patches (15×15 pixels in this experiment). Another noticeable phenomenon, is the thin straight threads appearing in the cross-scale patch recurrence visualization. Those structures are locally self-similar (namely, they look the same at different scales of the image), and are thus preserved by this prior.

External Models: While internal models share a lot in common, external methods exhibit quite diverse phenomena. Figure 8 shows visualizations for several

---

[2] This model was presented in [19] in the context of blind deblurring. To use for denoising, we removed the blur-kernel estimation stage and forced the kernel to be a delta function.

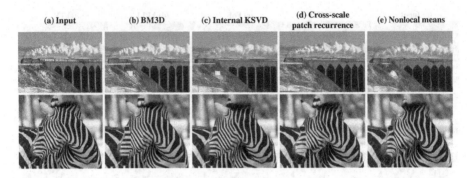

Fig. 7. Comparing internal image models. (a) Input images Train and Zebra (courtesy of Mickey Weidenfeld). (b)–(e) Geometric idealization w.r.t. the BM3D [17], internal KSVD [15], cross-scale patch recurrence [19], and nonlocal means [16] models using $\sigma = 25$ and $\lambda = 2 \times 10^{-4}/3.6 \times 10^{-4}$ for Train/Zebra.

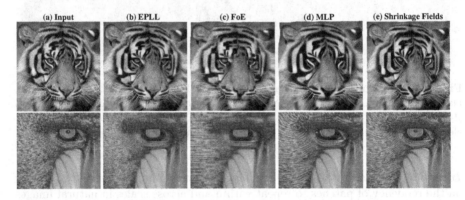

Fig. 8. Comparing external image models. (a) Input images Tiger and Mandril. (b)–(e) Geometric idealization w.r.t. the EPLL [1], FoE [14], multi-layer perceptron (MLP) [4], and Shrinkage Fields [22] models with $\sigma = 25$ and $\lambda = 2 \times 10^{-4}$.

external models, which were all trained on the same dataset [41]: EPLL [1], FoE [14], multi-layer perceptron (MLP) [4], and Shrinkage Fields [22] (an MRF-based model with 7×7 filters). As can be seen, all these models seem to prefer edges with small curvatures. However, apart for FoE, none of them prefers sharp corners. Moreover, the typical shapes of the optimal low-curvature edges differ substantially among these methods. An additional variation among external methods, is that they resonate differently to textures, as can be seen on the mandril's fur. In the EPLL GEM, the fur is deformed to look smoother, while in all other GEMs, the fur is deformed to exhibit straight strokes.

MRF Models: As mentioned above, the FoE model has a surprising preference to straight axis-aligned edges, significantly more than other external methods trained on the same dataset. This suggests that the FoE model either has limited representation power (*e.g.*, due to the use of 5×5 filters as opposed to the

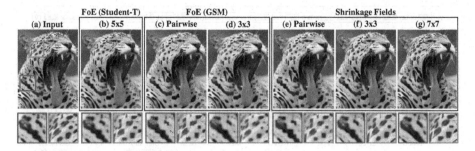

Fig. 9. Comparing MRF image models. (a) Input Jaguar image. (b) GEM of the FoE model with Student-T potentials [14]. (c)–(d) GEMs of FoE model with GSM potentials [31], (e)–(g) GEMs of the Shrinkage Fields model [22]. In all cases $\sigma = 25$ and $\lambda = 2 \times 10^{-4}$.

8×8 patches used in EPLL, or due to the use of Student-T clique potentials), or the learning procedure has converged to a sub-optimal solution. To study this question, Fig. 9 compares the FoE model with [31], an MRF model with Gaussian scale mixture (GSM) clique potentials, and with Shrinkage Fields [22], a discriminative approach which is roughly based on a cascade of several MRF models. The Shrinkage Fields architecture allows efficient training with far larger image crops, than what is practically possible in the FoE model. As can be seen, when using pairwise cliques (horizontal and vertical derivatives), the GSM MRF and Shrinkage Fields also tend to prefer axis-aligned edges. However, this tendency decreases as the filter sizes are increased. With 3×3 filters, in both the GSM MRF and Shrinkage Fields this behavior is already weaker than in the 5×5 FoE model. And for Shrinkage Fields with 7×7 filters, this phenomenon does not exist at all. We confirm this observation in denoising experiments below. While FoE and Shrinkage Fields differ in a variety of aspects (not only the choice of filter sizes), our experiment suggests that MRF models *can* achieve a decent degree of rotation invariance, even with small filters. However, this seems to require large training sets to achieve without intervention. Note that imposing rotation invariance on the filters, has been shown to be beneficial in [32].

3.1 Denoising Experiments

The geometric preferences revealed by our visualizations are very hard, if not impossible, to visually perceive by the naked eye in conventional image recovery experiments on natural images (*e.g.,* denoising, deblurring, super-resolution, etc.). This raises the question: To what extent do these geometric preferences affect the recovery error in such tasks? To study this question, we performed several denoising experiments.

Denoising GEMs: We begin by examining how much easier it is for denoising methods to remove noise from the GEM of an image, than from the image itself. Intuitively, since GEMs contain structures that best conform to the prior,

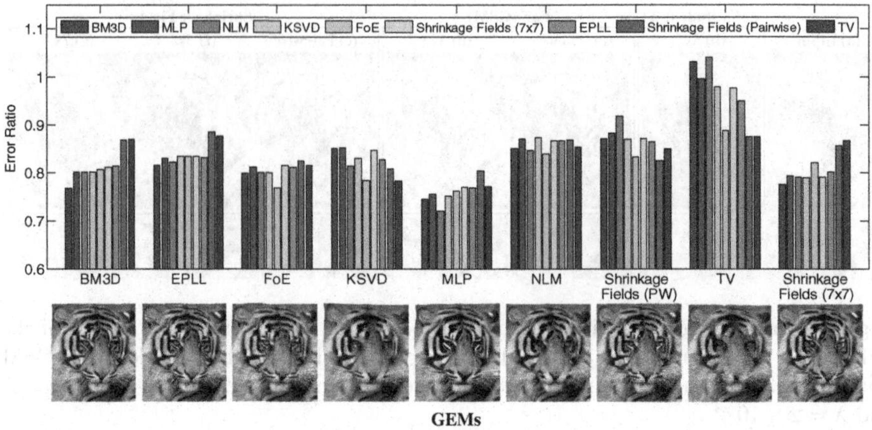

 Fig. 10. Denoising GEMs. We added noise to the GEMs corresponding to various priors, and then denoised each of them using various denoising methods. For each denoiser, we report the ratio between the MSE it achieves in denoising the GEM, and the MSE it achieves in denoising the original image. Each color corresponds to a different denoiser, and each group of bars corresponds to a different GEM.

denoising a GEM should be an easier task. Denote by y_p^{GEM} the GEM of image y according to prior p (*e.g.*, p $\in$ {'BM3D', 'MLP', ... }). We define the *error ratio*

$$r_{p,q}(y) = \frac{MSE_q(y_p^{GEM})}{MSE_q(y)}, \quad (7)$$

where $MSE_q(y_p^{GEM})$ and $MSE_q(y)$ denote the mean square errors (MSEs) attained in recovering the images y_p^{GEM} and y, respectively, from their noisy versions, based on prior q. An error ratio smaller than 1 indicates that recovering y_p^{GEM} with prior q leads to better MSE than recovering y itself with prior q.

Figure 10 shows the error ratios attained by 9 different denoising methods (colored bars), on the 9 GEMs of the corresponding priors (groups of bars) for the tiger image of Fig. 8(a). As can be seen, all the denoisers attain an error ratio smaller than 1 on the GEMs corresponding to their prior (namely $r_{p,p}(y) < 1$ for all p). Moreover, almost all the denoisers attain error ratios smaller than 1 also on the GEMs corresponding to *other* priors[3]. This suggests that the geometric structures that are optimal for one prior are usually quite good also for other priors.

This experiment further highlights several interesting behaviors. BM3D and NLM perform very poorly on the TV-GEM. This illustrates that an image with low total-variation (the TV-GEM) does not necessarily have strong patch rep-

---

[3] Note that some denoisers perform better on the GEMs of other priors than on their own GEM. This is because GEMs are not optimized to minimize the MSE in denoising tasks. Their construction also takes into account a penalty on the deformation smoothness.

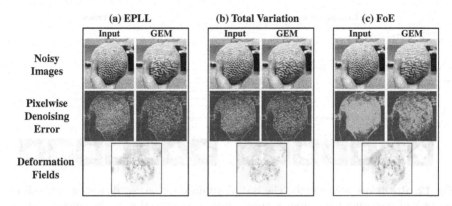

Fig. 11. Pixelwise RMSE. We compare between the pixelwise RMSE (averaged over 50 noise realizations) attained in denoising an image and its GEM. Results are shown alongside the deformation field for (a) EPLL [1], (b) Total variation [10] and (c) FoE [14]. As can be seen, a significant RMSE improvement is achieved in regions which undergo a large deformation.

etitions (as required by the BM3D and NLM denoisers). Shrinkage Fields with pairwise cliques and TV perform very similarly on all the GEMS, and quite differently from all other methods. This may be associated to the fact that they are the only priors based on derivatives. Another distinctive group is MLP, Shrinkage Fields (7×7) and EPLL, which perform similarly on all the GEMs. Common to these methods, is that they are all based on external models trained on the same dataset.

Pixelwise MSE: We next visualize which pixels in a GEM contribute the most to the improved ability to denoise it. Figure 11 shows the pixelwise root-MSE (RMSE) attained in denoising the Brain Coral image and its GEM (using the GEM's prior), averaged over 50 noise realizations. As can be seen, the largest RMSE improvement occurs at regions which are strongly deformed. Those regions are precisely the places which did not comply with the model initially, and were 'corrected' in the GEM.

Rotation Invariance: Our visualizations in Figs. 6, 8, and 9, revealed an interesting preference to axis aligned edges for some of the priors (especially FoE). To verify whether our observations are correct, we plot in Fig. 12 the RMSE that different methods attain in denoising images of rotated squares. As predicted by our visualizations, among external models, the FoE prior indeed has the least degree of rotation invariance, followed by Shrinkage Fields with pairwise cliques. The RMSE of these two methods drops significantly as the angle of the square approaches 0. It can be seen that EPLL also has a slight tendency to axis-aligned edges, while Shrinkage Fields (7×7) is almost entirely indifferent to the square's angle. These behaviors align with our conclusions from Figs. 8 and 9. We note, however, that MLP also seems to perform slightly better in denoising axis-aligned squares, a behavior that we could not clearly see in the

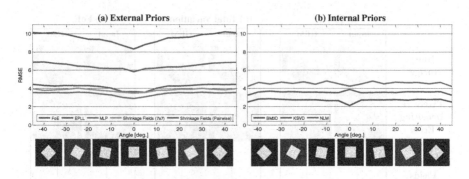

Fig. 12. Rotation invariance. The RMSE attained by various denoising methods in the task of removing noise from a noisy square, as a function of the square's angle. (a) Methods based on external priors. (b) Methods based on internal priors.

GEM of Fig. 8. The internal models, shown in Fig. 12(b), are almost completely insensitive to the square's angle, which aligns with the behaviors we observed in the GEMs of Fig. 7. The singular behaviors at angles 0 and 45 are related to the fact that these are the only two angles in which the rotated square does not involve interpolation artifacts.

4   Conclusions

We presented an algorithm for visualizing the geometric preferences of image priors. Our method determines how an image should be deformed so as to best comply with a given image model. Our approach is generic and can be used to visualize arbitrary priors, providing a useful means to study and compare between them. Applying our method on several popular image models, we found various interesting behaviors that are impossible to see using any other visualization technique. Although we demonstrated our approach in the context of visualizing *geometric* properties of image models, our framework can be easily generalized to other types of transformations (*e.g.,* color mappings). This only requires replacing the optical-flow stage in our algorithm accordingly. Our visualizations can be used to analyze failures and successes of image models in specific settings, and may thus help to identify potential model improvements, which are of great importance in image enhancement tasks.

Acknowledgements. This research was supported in part by the Ollendorff Foundation and the Horev and Alon Fellowships.

References

1. Zoran, D., Weiss, Y.: From learning models of natural image patches to whole image restoration. In: IEEE International Conference on Computer Vision, pp. 479–486 (2011)

2. Levin, A.: Blind motion deblurring using image statistics. In: Advances in Neural Information Processing Systems, pp. 841–848 (2006)
3. Elad, M., Starck, J.L., Querre, P., Donoho, D.L.: Simultaneous cartoon and texture image inpainting using morphological component analysis (MCA). Appl. Comput. Harmonic Anal. **19**(3), 340–358 (2005)
4. Burger, H.C., Schuler, C.J., Harmeling, S.: Image denoising: can plain neural networks compete with BM3D? In: IEEE Conference on Computer Vision and Pattern Recognition (CVPR), pp. 2392–2399 (2012)
5. Zontak, M., Mosseri, I., Irani, M.: Separating signal from noise using patch recurrence across scales. In: IEEE Conference on Computer Vision and Pattern Recognition (CVPR), pp. 1195–1202 (2013)
6. Sun, J., Sun, J., Xu, Z., Shum, H.Y.: Image super-resolution using gradient profile prior. In: IEEE Conference on Computer Vision and Pattern Recognition (CVPR), pp. 1–8 (2008)
7. Yang, J., Wright, J., Huang, T.S., Ma, Y.: Image super-resolution via sparse representation. IEEE Trans. Image Process. **19**(11), 2861–2873 (2010)
8. Levin, A., Zomet, A., Weiss, Y.: Learning how to inpaint from global image statistics. In: Proceedings of Ninth IEEE International Conference on Computer Vision, pp. 305–312 (2003)
9. Bertalmio, M., Sapiro, G., Caselles, V., Ballester, C.: Image inpainting. In: Proceedings of the 27th Annual Conference on Computer Graphics and Interactive Techniques, pp. 417–424 (2000)
10. Rudin, L.I., Osher, S., Fatemi, E.: Nonlinear total variation based noise removal algorithms. Phys. D: Nonlinear Phenom. **60**(1), 259–268 (1992)
11. Donoho, D.L.: De-noising by soft-thresholding. IEEE Trans. Inf. Theory **41**(3), 613–627 (1995)
12. Portilla, J., Strela, V., Wainwright, M.J., Simoncelli, E.P.: Image denoising using scale mixtures of Gaussians in the wavelet domain. IEEE Trans. Image Process. **12**(11), 1338–1351 (2003)
13. Zhu, S.C., Mumford, D.: Prior learning and Gibbs reaction-diffusion. IEEE Trans. Pattern Anal. Mach. Intell. **19**(11), 1236–1250 (1997)
14. Roth, S., Black, M.J.: Fields of experts: a framework for learning image priors. In: IEEE Conference on Computer Vision and Pattern Recognition (CVPR), vol. 2, pp. 860–867 (2005)
15. Elad, M., Aharon, M.: Image denoising via sparse and redundant representations over learned dictionaries. IEEE Trans. Image Process. **15**(12), 3736–3745 (2006)
16. Buades, A., Coll, B., Morel, J.M.: A non-local algorithm for image denoising. In: IEEE Computer Society Conference on Computer Vision and Pattern Recognition (CVPR), vol. 2, pp. 60–65 (2005)
17. Dabov, K., Foi, A., Katkovnik, V., Egiazarian, K.: Image denoising with block-matching and 3D filtering. In: Electronic Imaging, p. 606414 (2006)
18. Glasner, D., Bagon, S., Irani, M.: Super-resolution from a single image. In: International Conference on Computer Vision (ICCV) (2009)
19. Michaeli, T., Irani, M.: Blind deblurring using internal patch recurrence. In: Fleet, D., Pajdla, T., Schiele, B., Tuytelaars, T. (eds.) ECCV 2014. LNCS, vol. 8691, pp. 783–798. Springer, Heidelberg (2014). doi:10.1007/978-3-319-10578-9_51
20. Bellettini, G., Caselles, V., Novaga, M.: The total variation flow in $\mathbb{R}^N$. J. Differ. Eqn. **184**(2), 475–525 (2002)
21. Freedman, G., Fattal, R.: Image and video upscaling from local self-examples. ACM Trans. Graph. (TOG) **30**(2), 12 (2011)

22. Schmidt, U., Roth, S.: Shrinkage fields for effective image restoration. In: IEEE Conference on Computer Vision and Pattern Recognition (CVPR), pp. 2774–2781 (2014)
23. Mallat, S.: A wavelet tour of signal processing: the sparse way (2008)
24. Candes, E.J., Donoho, D.L.: Curvelets: a surprisingly effective nonadaptive representation for objects with edges. Technical report, DTIC Document (2000)
25. Starck, J.L., Candès, E.J., Donoho, D.L.: The curvelet transform for image denoising. IEEE Trans. Image Process. **11**(6), 670–684 (2002)
26. Candès, E.J., Donoho, D.L.: New tight frames of curvelets and optimal representations of objects with piecewise $C^\in$ singularities. Commun. Pure Appl. Math. **57**(2), 219–266 (2004)
27. Hyvärinen, A., Oja, E.: Independent component analysis: algorithms and applications. Neural Netw. **13**(4), 411–430 (2000)
28. Hinton, G.E.: Products of experts. In: Ninth International Conference on Artificial Neural Networks, vol. 1, pp. 1–6 (1999)
29. Geman, S., Geman, D.: Stochastic relaxation, Gibbs distributions, and the Bayesian restoration of images. IEEE Trans. Pattern Anal. Mach. Intell. **6**, 721–741 (1984)
30. Freeman, W.T., Pasztor, E.C., Carmichael, O.T.: Learning low-level vision. Int. J. Comput. Vision **40**(1), 25–47 (2000)
31. Schmidt, U., Gao, Q., Roth, S.: A Generative perspective on MRFs in low-level vision. In: IEEE Conference on Computer Vision and Pattern Recognition (CVPR), pp. 1751–1758. IEEE (2010)
32. Weiss, Y., Freeman, W.T.: What makes a good model of natural images? In: IEEE Conference on Computer Vision and Pattern Recognition (CVPR), pp. 1–8 (2007)
33. Dong, C., Loy, C.C., He, K., Tang, X.: Learning a deep convolutional network for image super-resolution. In: Fleet, D., Pajdla, T., Schiele, B., Tuytelaars, T. (eds.) ECCV 2014. LNCS, vol. 8692, pp. 184–199. Springer, Heidelberg (2014). doi:10. 1007/978-3-319-10593-2_13
34. Schuler, C.J., Hirsch, M., Harmeling, S., Schölkopf, B.: Learning to Deblur. IEEE Trans. Pattern Anal. Mach. Intell. **38**(7), 1439–1451 (2015)
35. Zeiler, M.D., Fergus, R.: Visualizing and understanding convolutional networks. In: Fleet, D., Pajdla, T., Schiele, B., Tuytelaars, T. (eds.) ECCV 2014. LNCS, vol. 8689, pp. 818–833. Springer, Heidelberg (2014). doi:10.1007/978-3-319-10590-1_53
36. Zeiler, M.D., Krishnan, D., Taylor, G.W., Fergus, R.: Deconvolutional networks. In: IEEE Conference on Computer Vision and Pattern Recognition (CVPR), pp. 2528–2535 (2010)
37. Dekel, T., Michaeli, T., Irani, M., Freeman, W.T.: Revealing and modifying nonlocal variations in a single image. ACM Trans. Graph. (TOG) **34**(6), 227 (2015)
38. Brox, T., Bruhn, A., Papenberg, N., Weickert, J.: High accuracy optical flow estimation based on a theory for warping. In: Pajdla, T., Matas, J. (eds.) ECCV 2004. LNCS, vol. 3024, pp. 25–36. Springer, Heidelberg (2004). doi:10.1007/ 978-3-540-24673-2_3
39. Liu, C.: Beyond pixels: exploring new representations and applications for motion analysis. Ph.D. thesis, Citeseer (2009)
40. Rubinstein, M., Gutierrez, D., Sorkine, O., Shamir, A.: A Comparative study of image retargeting. ACM Trans. Graph. **29**(6) 160:1–160:10 (2010). (Proc. SIGGRAPH Asia)

41. Martin, D., Fowlkes, C., Tal, D., Malik, J.: A Database of human segmented natural images and its application to evaluating segmentation algorithms and measuring ecological statistics. In: Proceedings of the 8th International Conference on Computer Vision, vol. 2. 416–423, July 2001
42. Zontak, M., Irani, M.: Internal statistics of a single natural image. In: IEEE Conference on Computer Vision and Pattern Recognition (CVPR), pp. 977–984 (2011)

Exploiting Semantic Information and Deep Matching for Optical Flow

Min Bai[✉], Wenjie Luo[✉], Kaustav Kundu, and Raquel Urtasun

Department of Computer Science, University of Toronto, Toronto, Canada
{mbai,wenjie,kkundu,urtasun}@cs.toronto.edu

Abstract. We tackle the problem of estimating optical flow from a monocular camera in the context of autonomous driving. We build on the observation that the scene is typically composed of a static background, as well as a relatively small number of traffic participants which move rigidly in 3D. We propose to estimate the traffic participants using instance-level segmentation. For each traffic participant, we use the epipolar constraints that govern each independent motion for faster and more accurate estimation. Our second contribution is a new convolutional net that learns to perform flow matching, and is able to estimate the uncertainty of its matches. This is a core element of our flow estimation pipeline. We demonstrate the effectiveness of our approach in the challenging KITTI 2015 flow benchmark, and show that our approach outperforms published approaches by a large margin.

Keywords: Optical flow · Low-level vision · Deep learning · Autonomous driving

1 Introduction

Despite many decades of research, estimating dense optical flow is still an open problem. Large displacements, texture-less regions, specularities, shadows, and strong changes in illumination continue to pose difficulties. Furthermore, flow estimation is computationally very demanding, as the typical range for a pixel's potential motion can contain more than 30K possibilities. This poses many problems for discrete methods, therefore most recent methods rely on continuous optimization [1,2].

In this paper, we are interested in computing optical flow in the context of autonomous driving. We argue that strong priors can be exploited in this context to make estimation more robust (and potentially faster). In particular, we build on the observation that the scene is typically composed of a static background, as well as a relatively small number of traffic participants which move rigidly in 3D. To exploit such intuition, we need to reliably identify the independently moving objects, and estimate their motion. Past methods typically attempt to segment the objects based solely on motion. However, this is a chicken and egg problem:

M. Bai and W. Luo have equally contributed to this work.

© Springer International Publishing AG 2016
B. Leibe et al. (Eds.): ECCV 2016, Part VI, LNCS 9910, pp. 154–170, 2016.
DOI: 10.1007/978-3-319-46466-4_10

an accurate motion estimation is necessary for an accurate motion segmentation, yet the latter also circularly depends upon the former.

In contrast, we propose an alternative approach in this paper which relies solely on exploiting semantics to identify the potentially moving objects. Note that semantic segmentation is not sufficient as different vehicles might move very differently, yet form a single connected component due to occlusion. Instead, we exploit instance-level segmentation, which provides us with a different segmentation label for each vehicle. Given the instance segmentations, our approach then formulates the optical flow problem as a set of epipolar flow estimation problems, one for each moving object. The background is considered as a special object whose motion is solely due to the ego-car. This contrasts current epipolar flow approaches [3,4], which assume a static scene wherein only the observer can move. As shown in our experimental evaluation, this results in much better flow estimates for moving objects. Since we formulate the problem as a set of epipolar flow problems, the search space is reduced from a 2D area to a 1D search along the epipolar lines. This has benefits both in terms of the computational complexity, as well as the robustness of our proposed approach. We refer the reader to Fig. 1 for an illustration of our approach.

The success of our approach relies on accurate fundamental matrix estimation for each moving object, as well as accurate matching. To facilitate this, our second contribution is a new convolutional net that learns to perform flow matching, and is able to estimate the uncertainty of its matches. This allows us to reject outliers, leading to better estimates for the fundamental matrix of each moving object. We smooth our predictions using semi-global block matching [5], where each match from the convolutional net is restricted to lie on its epipolar line. We post-process our flow estimate using left-right consistency to reject outliers, followed by EpicFlow [1] for the final interpolation. Additionally, we take advantage of slanted plane methods [4] for background flow estimation to increase smoothness for texture-less and saturated regions.

We demonstrate the effectiveness of our approach in the challenging KITTI 2015 flow benchmark [6], and show that our approach outperforms all published approaches by a large margin. In the following, we first review related work, and discuss our convolutional net for flow estimation. We then present our novel approach that encodes flow as a collection of rigidly moving objects, follow by our experimental evaluation.

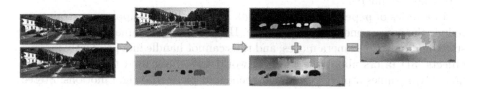

Fig. 1. Full pipeline of our approach. We take the input image, segment the potentially moving vehicles from the background, estimate the flow individually for every object and the background, and combine the flow for the final result.

2   Related Work

The classical approach for optical flow estimation involves building an energy model, which typically incorporates image evidence such as gradient consistency [7,8], warping [9], or matches [1] as unary terms. Additionally, there is a pairwise term to encourage smoothness. There are various methods for energy minimization and embedding of additional priors. This section summarizes several major categories.

The study of [2] shows that classical approaches to optical flow estimation are mainly gradient based methods [7,8]. Unfortunately, these are typically unsuitable for estimating large displacements (often encountered in traffic scenes) due to inconsistent image patch appearances. Both coarse-to-fine strategies [10] as well as inference at the original image resolution are employed [11,12]. EpicFlow [1] is a global approach that is very often used to interpolate sparse flow fields taking into account edges [13]. As shown in our experiments, its performance can be improved even further when augmented with explicit reasoning about moving objects.

Many approaches formulate flow as inference in a Markov random field (MRF) [14–18]. Message passing or move making algorithms are typically employed for inference. One of the most successful optical flow methods in the context of autonomous driving is DiscreteFlow [17], which reduces the search space by utilizing only a small number of proposals. These are shared amongst neighbors to increase matching performance and robustness. An MRF is then employed to encourage smoothness. After some post processing, the final flow is interpolated using EpicFlow [1]. [19] segments images using superpixels and approximates flow of each superpixel as homographies of 3D planes. Unlike our method, these methods do not exploit the fact that the background is static and only a few objects move.

Concurrent to our work, [20] also employs semantics to help optical flow. In particular, they identify three classes of components: static planar background, rigid moving objects, and elements for which a compact motion model cannot be defined. A different model is then adapted for each of the three classes to refine DiscreteFlow [17]. An affine transformation and a smooth deformation is fitted to moving vehicles, and homographies are fitted to planar backgrounds. In contrast, we use a stronger 3D epipolar motion constraint for both foreground vehicles and the entire static background. Our experiments shows that this results in much better flow estimates.

In a series of papers, Yamaguchi et al. [3,4] exploited epipolar constraints to reduce the correspondence search space. However, they assume that the scene is static and only the camera moves, and thus cannot handle independently moving objects. 3D priors about the physical world have been used to estimate scene flow. [21] assumes a piecewise planar scene and piece-wise rigid motions. Stereo and temporal image pairs are used to track these moving planes by proposing their position and orientation. [6] tracks independently moving objects by clustering super-pixels. However, both [6,21] require two cameras.

Our approach is also related to multibody flow methods (e.g., [22–24]), which simultaneously segment, track, and recover structure of 3D scenes with moving objects. However, [22] requires noiseless correspondences, [23] uses a stereo setup, and [24] has a simple data term which, unlike our approach, does not exploit deep learning.

Recent years have seen a rise in the application of deep learning models to low level vision. In the context of stereo, [25] uses a siamese network to classify matches between two input patches as either a match or not. Combined with smoothing, it achieves the best performance on the KITTI stereo benchmark. Similarly, [26] uses convolutional neural nets (CNNs) to compute the matching cost at different scales. Different CNN architectures were investigated in [27]. Luo et al. [28] exploited larger context and trained the network to produce a probability distribution over disparities, resulting in better matching. Deep learning has also been used for flow estimation [29]. They proposed a convolution-deconvolution network (i.e., FlowNet) which is trained end-to-end, and achieves good results in real-time.

3   Deep Learning for Flow Estimation

The goal of optical flow is to estimate a 2D vector encoding the motion between two consecutive frames for each pixel. The typical assumption is that a local region (e.g., image patch) around each pixel will look similar in both frames. Flow algorithms then search for the pixel displacements that produce the best score. This process is referred to as matching. Traditional approaches adopt hand-crafted features, such as SIFT [30], DAISY [31], census transform [32] or image gradients to represent each image patch. These are matched using a simple similarity score, e.g., via an inner product on the feature space. However, these features are not very robust. Flow methods based on only matching perform poorly in practice. To address this, sophisticated smoothing techniques have been developed [1,3,13,17].

Deep convolutional neural networks have been shown to perform extremely well in high-level semantic tasks such as classification, semantic segmentation, and object detection. Recently, they have been successfully trained for stereo matching [25,28], producing state-of-the-art results in the challenging KITTI benchmark [33]. Following this trend, in our work we adopt a deep convolution neural network to learn feature representations that are tailored to the optical flow estimation problem.

3.1   Network Architecture

Our network takes two consecutive frames as input, and processes them in two branches of a siamese network to extract features. The two branches are then combined with a product layer to create a matching score for each possible displacement. We refer the reader to Fig. 2 for an illustration of our convolutional net.

In particular, our network uses 9 convolutional layers, where each convolution is followed by batch normalization [34] and a rectified non-linear unit (ReLU). We use 3×3 kernels for each convolution layer. With a stride of one pixel and no pooling, this gives us a receptive field size of 19×19. The number of filters for each convolution layer varies. As shown in Fig. 2, we use the following configuration for our network: 32, 32, 64, 64, 64, 128, 128, 128. Note that although our network has 9 layers, the number of parameters is only around 620K. Therefore, our network is much smaller than networks used for high-level vision tasks, such as AlexNet or VGG which have 60 and 135 millions parameters, respectively. As our last layer has 128 filters, the dimension of our feature vector for each pixel is also 128.

3.2   Learning

To train the network, we use small image patches extracted at random from the set of pixels for which ground truth is available. This strategy is beneficial, as it provides us with a diverse set of training examples (as nearby pixels are very correlated). Furthermore, it is more memory efficient. Let $\mathcal{I}$ and $\mathcal{I}'$ be two images captured by the same camera at two consecutive times. Let (x_i, y_i) be the image coordinates of the center of the patch extracted at random from $\mathcal{I}$, and let (f_{x_i}, f_{y_i}) be the corresponding ground truth flow. We use a patch of size 19×19, since this is the size of our total receptive field. Since the magnitude of (f_{x_i}, f_{y_i}) can be very large, we create a larger image patch in the second image $\mathcal{I}'$. Including the whole search range is computationally very expensive, as this implies computing 30K scores. Instead, we reduce the search space and construct two training examples per randomly drawn patch, one that searches in the horizontal direction and another in the vertical direction, both centered on the ground truth point $(x + f_{x_i}, y + f_{y_i})$. The horizontal training example is shown in Fig. 2. Thus, their size is $19 \times (19 + R)$ and $(19 + R) \times 19$, respectively. Note that this poses no problem as we use a convolutional net. In practice, we use $R = 200$. We find the network performance is not very sensitive to this hype-parameter.

As we do not use any pooling and a stride of one, the siamese network outputs a single feature vector from the left branch and $(1 + R)$ feature vectors from the right branch corresponding to all candidate flow locations. Note that by construction, the ground truth is located in the middle of the patch extracted in $\mathcal{I}'$. The matching network on top then computes the corresponding similarity score for each possible location. We simply ignore the pixels near the border of the image, and do not use them for training.

We learn the parameters of the model by minimizing cross entropy, where we use a soft-max over all possible flow locations. We thus optimize:

$$\min_{\mathbf{w}} \sum_{i=1}^{N} \sum_{s_i} p_i^{GT}(s_i) \log p_i(s_i, \mathbf{w}).$$

where $\mathbf{w}$ are the parameters of the network, and N is the total number of training examples. N is double the number of sample patches, as we generate two training

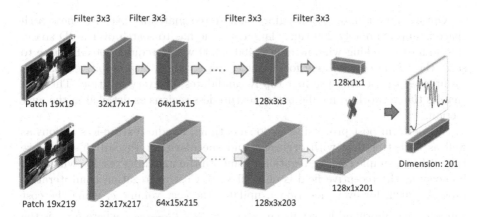

Fig. 2. Network Overview: A siamese convolutional net is followed by a product layer that computes a score for each displacement. During training, for each pixel we compute a softmax over a horizontal or vertical 1D displacement, and minimize cross-entropy.

examples for each patch. In practice, we generate 22 million training examples from the 200 image pairs. Further, s_i is the ground truth location index for patch i in the second image. Recall that the second image patch was of size $(19 + R)$ or $(R + 19)$. Finally, p_i^{GT} is the target distribution, and p_i is the predicted distribution for patch i according to the model (i.e., output of the soft-max).

Note that when training neural nets, p^{GT} is typically assumed to be a delta function with non-zero probability mass only for the correct hypothesis. Here, we use a more informative loss, which penalizes depending on the distance to the ground truth configuration. We thus define

$$p_i^{GT}(s_i) = \begin{cases} \lambda_1 \text{ if } s_i = s_i^{GT} \\ \lambda_2 \text{ if } |s_i - s_i^{GT}| = 1 \\ \lambda_3 \text{ if } |s_i - s_i^{GT}| = 2 \\ 0 \quad \text{o.w.} \end{cases}.$$

This allows the network to be less strict in discriminating patches within 3-pixels from the ground truth. In practice we choose $\lambda_1 = 0.5$, $\lambda_2 = 0.2$ and $\lambda_3 = 0.05$.

3.3 Inference

In contrast to training where we select small image patches, during inference we need to evaluate all the pixels for first image frame. Using the same routine as for learning would result in as many forward passes as the number of pixels in the image, which is computationally very expensive. Instead, following stereo approaches [25,28], we can efficiently compute the feature vector for all pixels with the siamese network using only one forward pass. Similar trick was also used when training FastRCNN [35], where features for all regions proposal are computed by one forward pass.

Optical flow is more challenging than stereo matching because the search space is approximately 200 times larger, as one has to search over a 2D space. A standard searching window of size 400×200 would require $300\,\text{GB}$ space to store the whole cost volume for a single image, which is prohibitive. Instead, we propose to use only the first top-K candidates for every location. This also enables the network to handle better texture-less regions as detailed in the next section.

We perform post processing to do smoothing, handle texture-less regions as well as to better deal with occlusion and specularities. Toward this goal, we first utilize a simple cost aggregation to smooth the matching results, which can be noisy as the receptive field is only 19×19. Cost aggregation is an iterative process which, for every location i, updates the cost volume c_i using the cost values of neighborhood locations i.e., $c_i^t(s_i) = \frac{\sum_{j \in \mathcal{N}(i)} c_j^{t-1}(s_i)}{N}$, where $\mathcal{N}(i)$ is the set of neighbor locations of i, $c_i^t(s_i)$ is the cost volume at location i during the t-th aggregation iteration, s_i is the flow configuration id, and $c_i^0(s_i)$ is the raw output from our network. Note that applying cost aggregation multiple times is equivalent to performing a weighted average over a larger neighborhood. In practice, we use 4 iterations of cost aggregation and a 5×5 window size. Due to the fact that we only store top-K configurations in our cost volume to reduce memory usage, neighboring locations have different sets of label ids. Thus we perform cost aggregation on the union of label sets, and store only the top-K results after aggregation as final results $c_i^T(s_i)$. Note that one can interpret $c_i^T(s_i)$ as a score of the network's confidence. We thus threshold the cost $c_i^T(s_i)$ to select the most confident matches. The threshold is selected such that on average 60% of the locations are estimated as confident. This simple thresholding on the cost aggression allows us to eliminate most specularities and shadows. In texture-less regions, the sparse top-K predicted matches sets of neighboring pixels have very little overlap. Combined with cost aggregation, scores of erroneous matches decrease through the aggregation iterations, thus eliminating erroneous matches. Another possible solution would be using uncertainty estimation by computing the entropy at each pixel. However, our experiments show that selecting top-K combined with simple thresholding works much better than thresholding the entropy. In practice, we used $K = 30$ as it balances memory usage and performance.

4   Object-Aware Optical Flow

In this section, we discuss our parameterization of the optical flow problem as a result of projection of 3D scene flow. In particular, we assume that the world encountered in autonomous driving scenarios consists of independently moving rigid objects. The ego-car where the camera is located is a special object, which is responsible for the optical flow of the static background.

Our approach builds on the observation that if the 3D motion of an object is rigid, it can be parameterized with a single transformation. This is captured by the fundamental matrix, which we denote by $F \in \mathcal{R}^{3 \times 3}$ with $\text{rank}(F) = 2$. Let

$\mathcal{I}$ and $\mathcal{I}'$ be two images captured by a single camera at two consecutive times, then for any point in a rigidly moving object the following well-known epipolar constraint holds

$$\tilde{p}_i'^{\top} F \tilde{p}_i = 0$$

where $p_i = (x_i, y_i)$ and $p_i' = (x_i', y_i')$ are the projection of a 3D point p_i into the two images, and $\tilde{p} = (x, y, 1)$ is p in homogeneous coordinates. Further, the line defined by $l_i' = F_i \tilde{p}_i$ is the epipolar line in $\mathcal{I}'$ corresponding to point p, passing through both the epipole in $\mathcal{I}'$ and p_i'.

4.1 Segmenting Traffic Participants

Since only pixels belonging to one independently moving vehicle obey the same epipolar constraint, it is necessary to obtain a segmentation of the scene into independently moving objects. This is traditionally done by clustering the motion estimates. In this paper we take an alternative approach and use semantics to infer the set of potential traffic participants. Towards this goal, we exploit instance-level segmentation which segments each traffic participant into a different component. Note that we aim at an upper bound on the number of moving objects, as some of the vehicles might be parked.

To compute instance-level segmentations we exploit the approach of [36], which uses a multi-resolution CNN follow by a fully connected conditional random field to create a global labeling of the scene in terms of instances. Since only labelled training data for *cars* was available, the method is unable to detect vans and trucks. This results in high precision but lower recall. To partially alleviate this shortcoming, we augment the instance segmentation results with extra segmentations which are computed by performing 3D detection [37] follow by CAD model fitting. In particular, we simply go over all CAD models and select the one which best aligns with the 3D box, following the technique in [38]. Since this process has higher recall but lower precision than the instances of [36], we only add new segmentation masks if they do not overlap with the previously computed masks. We refer the reader to Fig. 3 for an example. This process provides us with a segmentation of the scene in terms of rigidly moving objects. We now discuss how to estimate flow for each moving object as well as for the background.

4.2 Foreground Flow Estimation

Our first goal is to reliably estimate the fundamental matrix describing the motion of each moving object. We consider this motion to be the combination of the vehicle's motion and the motion of the ego-car, that is to be the 3D motion whose projection we observe as optical flow. This is a challenging task, as moving objects can be very small and contain many specularities. We take advantage of the fact that our convolutional net outputs an uncertainty estimate, and only use the most confident matches for this task. In particular, we use RANSAC with the 8 point algorithm [39] to estimate the fundamental matrix of each moving object independently. We then

Fig. 3. Top left: KITTI image. **Top right**: Instance segmentation masks overlaid on input image. **Bottom left**: Car segmentation masks from [36]. **Bottom right**: Segmentation instances augmented by 3D detection [37] follow by CAD model fitting [38].

choose the hypothesis with smaller median squared error, where error is defined as the shortest distance between each matching point and its epipolar line.

Following [3], we consider the optical flow $u_p = (u_x, u_y)$ at point p to decompose into its rotational and translational components. Thus

$$u_{p_k} = u_w(p_k) + u_v(p_k, Z_{p_k})$$

where $u_w(p)$ is the component of the flow of pixel p due to rotation, and $u_v(p, Z_p)$ is the component of the flow from the translation of the object relative to the camera. Note that the direction Z here is perpendicular to the image plane of $\mathcal{I}'$. If the rotation is small, the rotational component can be linearized. We estimate the linear coefficients using matched point pairs, with the additional constraint that the point $p + u_w(p)$ must lie on the epipolar line in the second image.

Upon application of the aforementioned linear transformation to $\mathcal{I}$, the image planes of the image patches corresponding to the object are now parallel, and related to each other only by a relative translation. This reduces the problem to either an epipolar contraction or epipolar expansion, where matching point pairs both lie on the same epipolar line. Therefore, the search for a matching point is reduced to a 1D search along the epipolar line. The flow at a given point is then parameterized as the disparity along the epipolar line between its rectified coordinates and its matching point.

To smooth our results, we exploit semi-global block matching (SGM) [5]. In particular, we parameterized the problem using disparity along the epipolar line as follows:

$$E(d) = \sum_{p_k} C'(p_k, d_{p_k}) + \sum_{p_k, p'_k \in \mathcal{N}} S(d_{p_k}, d_{p'_k})$$

with $C'(p_k, d_{p_k})$ being the matching similarity score computed by our convolutional net with local cost aggregation to increase robustness to outliers. Note that the vz-ratio parameterization of disparity in [3] is unsuitable for foreground objects, as it relies on a significant relative motion in the z-direction (perpendicular to the image plane). This assumption is often violated by foreground vehicles, such as those crossing an intersection in front of the static observer. We use a standard smoothing term

$$S(d_{\mathrm{p}_k}, d_{\mathrm{p}'_k}) = \begin{cases} \lambda_1 \text{ if } |d_{\mathrm{p}_k} - d_{\mathrm{p}'_k}| = 1 \\ \lambda_2 \text{ if } |d_{\mathrm{p}_k} - d_{\mathrm{p}'_k}| > 1 \\ 0 \quad \text{otherwise} \end{cases}$$

with $\lambda_2 > \lambda_1 > 0$. In practice, $\lambda_2 = 256$ and $\lambda_1 = 32$. After SGM, we use left-right consistency check to filter out outliers. The output is a semi-dense flow estimate.

Occasionally, the fundamental matrix estimation for an object fails due to either too few confident matches or too much noise in the matches. In this case, we directly use the network's matching to obtain a flow-field. Finally, we use the edge-aware interpolation of EpicFlow [1] to interpolate the missing pixels by performing one step of variational smoothing. This produces a fully dense flow-field for all objects.

4.3   Background Flow Estimation

To estimate the background flow, we mostly follow Yamaguchi et al. [3]. However, we make two significant changes which greatly improve its performance. First, we restrict the matches to the areas estimated to be background by our semantic segmentation. We use RANSAC and the 8-point algorithm with SIFT to estimate the fundamental matrix. Note that this simple approach is sufficient as background occupies most of the scene. Similar to the foreground, the flow u_{p} at a point p is considered to be a sum of a rotational and a translational component: $u_{\mathrm{p}} = u_{\mathrm{w}}(\mathrm{p}) + u_{\mathrm{v}}(\mathrm{p}, Z_{\mathrm{p}})$. Again, we linearize the rotational component. To find the matching point p' for p, we search along the epipolar line l', and parameterize the displacement vector as a scalar disparity.

Further, the disparity at point p_i can be written as

$$d(\mathrm{p}, Z_{\mathrm{p}}) = |\mathrm{p} + u_{\mathrm{w}}(\mathrm{p}) - \mathrm{o}'| \frac{\frac{v_z}{Z_{\mathrm{p}}}}{1 - \frac{v_z}{Z_{\mathrm{p}}}}$$

where v_z is the forward (Z) component of the ego-motion, o' is the epipole and $\omega_{\mathrm{p}} = \frac{v_z}{Z_{\mathrm{p}}}$.

We use SGM [5] to smooth the estimation. However, we parameterize the flow in terms of the vz-ratio instead of directly using disparity as in the case of foreground flow estimation. We perform inference along 4 directions and aggregate the results. Finally, we post process the result by checking left-right consistency to remove outliers. This provides us with a semi-dense estimate of flow for the background pixels.

Unfortunately, no matches are found by the matching pair process in occluded regions such as portions of road or buildings that disappear from view as the vehicle moves forward. An additional significant improvement over [3] is a 3D geometry-inspired extrapolation. Let $\delta_{\mathrm{p}} = |\mathrm{p} + u_{\mathrm{w}}(\mathrm{p}) - \mathrm{o}'|$ be the distance between the point p and o'. For a planar surface in the 3D world, δ_{p} is inversely proportional to Z_{p}. Since v_z is constant for all points after the linearized rotational flow component $u_{\mathrm{w}}(\mathrm{p})$ is removed, the vz-ratio is also proportional to δ_{p}. For each point p where the vz-ratio is not estimated, we search along the line segment joining p to o' to collect a set of up to 50 vz-ratios at pixels p', and calculate their associated $\delta_{p'}$. We take advantage of semantic information to exclude points belonging to moving foreground vehicles. Using this set, we fit a linear model which we use to estimate the missing vz-ratio at p.

We employ a slanted plane model similar to MotionSLIC [3] to compute a dense and smooth background flow field. This assumes that the scene is composed of small, piece-wise planar regions. In particular, we model the vz-ratios of the pixels in each superpixel with a plane defined as $\frac{v_z}{Z_p} = A(x - x_c) + B(y - y_c) + C$. Here, (A, B, C) are the plane parameters, and (x_c, y_c) are the coordinates of the center of the superpixel. We simultaneously reason both about the assignments of pixels to planes, the plane parameters, and the types of boundaries between superpixels (i.e., co-planar, hinge, occlusion). Inference is simply performed by block coordinate descent.

5   Experimental Evaluation

We evaluated our approach on the KITTI Optical Flow 2015 benchmark [33], which consists of 200 training and 200 testing image pairs. There are a number of challenges including specularities, moving vehicles, sensor saturation, large displacements and texture-less regions. The benchmark error metric is the percentage of pixels whose error exceeds 3 px or 5 % (whichever is greater) from the ground truth flow. We refer to (Fl-fg) and (Fl-bg) as the error evaluated only on the foreground and background pixels respectively, while (Fl-all) denotes the average error across all pixels. In this section, we first analyze our method's performance in comparison with the state-of-the-art. Additionally, we explore the impact of various stages of our pipeline.

We trained our siamese convolutional network for 100k iterations using stochastic gradient descend with Adam [40]. We used a batch size of 128 and an initial learning rate of 0.01 with a weight decay of 0.0005. We divided the learning rate by half at iterations 40K, 60K and 80K. Note that since we have 22 million training examples, the network converges before completing one full epoch. This shows that 200 images are more than enough to train the network. Training takes 17 h on an NVIDIA-Titan Black GPU. However, performance improves only slightly after 70k iterations.

Comparison to the State-of-the-Art: We first present our results[1] on the KITTI Optical Flow 2015 test set, and compare our approach to published monocular approaches that exploit a single temporal image pair as input. As shown in Table 1, our approach significantly outperforms all published approaches. Our approach is particularly effective on the background, outperforming MotionSLIC [3]. Moreover, our method's foreground performance is very close to the leading foreground estimation technique DiscreteFlow [17]. As we

---

[1] We exploit the instances of [41] for our submission to the evaluation server.

will see in our analysis section, our method has a clear potential to exceed DiscreteFlow [17] in foreground also. The test set images are fairly correlated, as many pairs are taken from the same sequence. To provide further analysis, we also computed results on the training set, where we average results over 5 folds. For each fold, 160 images are used for training, and the remaining 40 are used for testing. The same improvements as with the test set can be seen in Table 2.

Influence of Instance Segmentation: Table 3 shows performance when using [41] and [36] to create the instance segmentations. We also explore augmenting them by fitting CAD models with [38] to the 3D detections of [37]. Note that

Table 1. KITTI Flow 2015 Test Set: we compare our results with top scoring published monocular methods that use a single image pair as input

Method	Non occluded px			All px		
	Fl-bg	Fl-fg	Fl-all	Fl-bg	Fl-fg	Fl-all
HS [2]	30.49%	50.59%	34.13%	39.90%	53.59%	42.18%
DeepFlow [12]	16.47%	31.25%	19.15%	27.96%	35.28%	29.18%
EpicFlow [1]	15.00%	29.39%	17.61%	25.81%	33.56%	27.10%
MotionSLIC [3]	6.19%	64.82%	16.83%	14.86%	66.21%	23.40%
DiscreteFlow [17]	9.96%	**22.17%**	12.18%	21.53%	**26.68%**	22.38%
SOF [20]	8.11%	23.28%	10.86%	14.63%	27.73%	16.81%
Ours	**5.75%**	22.28%	**8.75%**	**8.61%**	26.69%	**11.62%**

Table 2. KITTI Flow 2015 Training Set: we compare our results with the state-of-the-art by averaging performance over 5 different splits of the KITTI training dataset into training/testing.

Method	Non occluded px			All px		
	Fl-bg	Fl-fg	Fl-all	Fl-bg	Fl-fg	Fl-all
EpicFlow [1]	16.14%	28.75%	18.66%	27.28%	31.36%	28.09%
MotionSLIC [3]	6.32%	64.88%	17.97%	15.45%	65.82%	24.54%
DiscreteFlow [17]	10.86%	**20.24%**	12.71%	22.80%	**23.32%**	22.94%
Ours	**6.21%**	21.97%	**9.35%**	**9.38%**	24.79%	**12.14%**

Table 3. Flow estimation with various instance segmentation algorithms

Method	Non occluded px			All px		
	Fl-bg	Fl-fg	Fl-all	Fl-bg	Fl-fg	Fl-all
[41]	**6.17%**	25.30%	9.98%	**9.31%**	28.11%	12.69%
[36]	6.18%	24.61%	9.82%	9.35%	27.31%	12.54%
[41] augmented with [37]	**6.17%**	22.06%	**9.35%**	**9.31%**	25.08%	12.15%
[36] augmented with [37]	6.21%	**21.97%**	**9.35%**	9.38%	**24.79%**	**12.14%**

a combination of segmentation and detection is beneficial. A limiting factor of our foreground flow estimation performance arises when we missed moving vehicles when estimating our instances. Using our 5 folds on the training set, we explore what happens when we have perfect objects masks. Towards this goal, we first examine the foreground flow estimation performance only on our detected vehicle masks. The left half of Table 4 shows that within the vehicle masks we detect, our flow estimation is significantly more accurate than our competitors in the same regions. Moreover, the right half of the same table shows that the same is true within the ground truth object masks. Thus, if the instances were further improved (e.g., by incorporating temporal information when computing them) our method can be expected to achieve a significant improvement over the leading competitors. It is thus clear that our current bottleneck is in the accuracy of the masks.

Table 4. Foreground flow estimation within detected object masks and within ground truth masks

Method	Within detected object masks		Within ground truth object masks	
	Non-occ px error %	All px error %	Non-occ px error %	All px error %
EpicFlow [1]	26.77 %	29.93 %	28.75 %	31.36 %
DiscreteFlow [17]	18.76 %	22.42 %	20.24 %	23.32 %
Ours	**15.91 %**	**19.72 %**	**15.42 %**	**18.62 %**

Estimating Fundamental Matrix: Having an accurate fundamental matrix is critical to the success of our method. While the strong epipolar constraint offers great robustness to outliers, it can also cause many problems if it is wrongly estimated. We now compare different matching algorithms employed to compute the fundamental matrices, and use the rest of our pipeline to estimate flow. As shown in Table 5, selecting only confident matches from our network to estimate the fundamental matrix is significantly better than using the flow field estimations from other algorithms, including DiscreteFlow.

Table 5. Foreground flow estimation errors when F is estimated from various sources

Source for matches for F estimation	Non-occluded px error %	All px error %
EpicFlow [1]	25.02 %	27.58 %
DiscreteFlow [17]	23.40 %	26.05 %
Our Matching Network	**21.97 %**	**24.79 %**

Qualitative Analysis: Figure 4 shows qualitative results, where each column depicts the original image, the network most confident estimates, the 3D detections of [37], our final instance segmentations, our final flow field and its errors. Our convolutional net is able to predict accurate results for most regions in the image. It leaves holes in regions including texture-less areas like the sky, occlusion due the motion of car and specularites on windshield. The 3D detector is able to detect almost all cars, regardless of their orientation and size. Our final object masks used to label foreground objects are very accurate and contain many cars of different sizes and appearances. Note that different shades represents distinct car instances whose fundamental matrices are estimated separately. As shown in the last two rows, we produce very good overall performance.

Fig. 4. Examples of successful flow estimations. Within each group, from top to bottom: first frame of input image, confident flow produced by our network, 3D car detection results, instance segmentation output augmented by 3D car detection, final flow field, and flow field error.

Failure Modes: Our technique has several failure modes. If a car is not segmented, the estimation of flow defaults to using the epipolar constraint of the background. This happens particularly often with trucks and vans, as we do not have training examples of these types of vehicles to train our segmentation and detection networks. Figure 5(a) shows an example where a van is not segmented. By coincidence, its true epipolar lines are almost identical with those calculated using the background fundamental matrix. As such, its flow estimation is still mostly correct. If object masks contain too many background pixels (which are outliers from the perspective of foreground fundamental matrix estimation), our algorithm can also fail. This is commonly associated with objects identified by the 3D object detector rather than the instance-segmentation algorithm, as the 3D detection box might be misaligned with the actual vehicle. Moreover, fitting CAD models to monocular images is not a trivial task. The right-most car in Fig. 5(b) is such an example. The other failure mode of our approach is wrong estimation of the fundamental matrix, which can happen when the matches are very sparse or contain many outliers. Figure 5(c) shows such an example, where the fundamental matrix of the left-most car is incorrectly estimated due to the sparseness in confident matching results (showing in the second row).

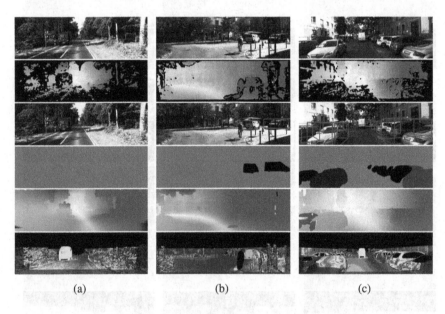

      (a)   (b)   (c)

Fig. 5. Failure cases for our algorithm.

6 Conclusion

We have proposed an approach to monocular flow estimation in the context of autonomous driving which builds on the observation that the scene is composed of a static background as well a relatively small number of traffic participants (including the ego-car). We have shown how instance-level segmentation and 3D object detection can be used to segment the different vehicles, and proposed a new convolutional network that can accurately match patches. Our experiments showed that we can outperform the state-of-the-art by a large margin in the challenging KITTI 2015 flow benchmark. In the future, we plan to estimate the different traffic participants by reasoning temporally when doing instance-level segmentation.

Acknowledgements. This work was partially supported by ONR-N00014-14-1-0232, Samsung, and NSERC.

References

1. Revaud, J., Weinzaepfel, P., Harchaoui, Z., Schmid, C.: EpicFlow: edge-preserving interpolation of correspondences for optical flow. In: CVPR (2015)
2. Sun, D., Roth, S., Black, M.: A quantitative analysis of current practices in optical flow estimation and the principles behind them. IJCV **106**(2), 115–137 (2013)
3. Yamaguchi, K., Mcallester, D., Urtasun, R.: Robust monocular epipolar flow estimation. In: CVPR (2013)
4. Yamaguchi, K., McAllester, D., Urtasun, R.: Efficient joint segmentation, occlusion labeling, stereo and flow estimation. In: Fleet, D., Pajdla, T., Schiele, B., Tuytelaars, T. (eds.) ECCV 2014. LNCS, vol. 8693, pp. 756–771. Springer, Heidelberg (2014). doi:10.1007/978-3-319-10602-1_49
5. Hirschmuller, H.: Stereo processing by semigloabl matching and mutual information. In: PAMI (2008)
6. Menze, M., Geiger, A.: Object scene flow for autonomous vehicles. In: CVPR (2015)
7. Lucas, B., Kanade, T.: An iterative image registration technique with an application to stereo vision. In: CVPR (2015)
8. Horn, B., Schunck, B.: Determining optical flow. Artif. Intell. **17**, 185–203 (1981)
9. Papenberg, N., Bruhn, A., Brox, T., Didas, S., Weickert, J.: Highly accurate optical flow computation with theoretically justified warping. IJCV **67**(2), 141–158 (2006)
10. Sun, D., Roth, S., Black, M.J.: Secrets of optical flow estimation and their principles. In: CVPR (2010)
11. Bruhn, A., Weickert, J., Schnoerr, C.: Lucas/Kanade meets Horn/Schunck: combining local and global optic flow methods. IJCV **61**(3), 211–231 (2004)
12. Weinzaepfel, P., Revaud, J., Harchaoui, Z., Schmid, C.: DeepFlow: large displacement optical flow with deep matching. In: ICCV (2013)
13. Weinzaepfel, P., Revaud, J., Harchaoui, Z., Schmid, C.: DeepFlow: large displacement optical flow with deep matching. In: ICCV, Sydney, Australia, December 2013
14. Yang, H., Lin, W., Lu, J.: DAISY filter flow: a generalized discrete approach to dense correspondences. In: CVPR (2014)
15. Bao, L., Yang, Q., Jin, H.: Fast edge-preserving PatchMatch for large displacement optical flow. In: CVPR (2014)
16. Lempitsky, V., Roth, S., Rother, C.: FusionFlow: discrete-continuous optimization for optical flow estimation. In: CVPR (2008)

17. Menze, M., Heipke, C., Geiger, A.: Discrete optimization for optical flow. In: Gall, J., Gehler, P., Leibe, B. (eds.) GCPR 2015. LNCS, vol. 9358, pp. 16–28. Springer, Heidelberg (2015). doi:10.1007/978-3-319-24947-6_2
18. Lei, C., Yang, Y.H.: Optical flow estimation on coarse-to-fine region-trees using discrete optimization. In: ICCV (2009)
19. Yang, J., Li, H.: Dense accurate optical flow estimation with piecewise parametric model. In: CVPR (2015)
20. Sevilla-Lara, L., Sun, D., Jampani, V., Black, M.: Optical flow with semantic segmentation and localized layers. In: CVPR (2016)
21. Vogel, C., Schindler, K., Roth, S.: 3D scene flow estimation. IJCV 115(1), 1–28 (2015)
22. Vidal, R., Ma, Y., Soatto, S., Sastry, S.: Two-view multibody structure from motion. IJCV 68(1), 7–25 (2006)
23. Zhang, G., Jia, J., Bao, H.: Simultaneous multi-body stereo and segmentation. In: ICCV (2011)
24. Roussos, A., Russell, C., Garg, R., Agapito, L.: Dense multibody motion estimation and reconstruction from a handheld camera. In: ISMAR (2012)
25. Zbontar, J., LeCun, Y.: Computing the stereo matching cost with a convolutional neural network. In: CVPR, June 2015
26. Chen, Z., Sun, X., Wang, L., Yu, Y., Huang, C.: A deep visual correspondence embedding model for stereo matching costs. In: ICCV, pp. 972–980 (2015)
27. Zagoruyko, S., Komodakis, N.: Learning to compare image patches via convolutional neural networks. In: CVPR, pp. 4353–4361 (2015)
28. Luo, W., Schwing, A., Urtasun, R.: Efficient deep learning for stereo matching. In: CVPR, July 2016
29. Dosovitskiy, A., Fischer, P., Ilg, E., Hausser, P., Hazirbas, C., Golkov, V., Smagt, P., Cremers, D., Brox, T.: FlowNet: learning optical flow with convolutional networks. In: ICCV (2015)
30. Lowe, D.: Distinctive image features from scale-invariant keypoints. IJCV 60(2), 91–110 (2004)
31. Tola, E., Lepetit, V., Fua, P.: DAISY: an efficient dense descriptor applied to wide baseline stereo. In: PAMI (2010)
32. Zabih, R., Woodfill, J.: Non-parametric local transforms for computing visual correspondence. In: Eklundh, J.-O. (ed.) ECCV 1994. LNCS, vol. 801, pp. 151–158. Springer, Heidelberg (1994). doi:10.1007/BFb0028345
33. Geiger, A., Lenz, P., Urtasun, R.: Are we ready for autonomous driving? The KITTI vision benchmark suite. In: Proceedings of CVPR (2012)
34. Ioffe, S., Szegedy, C.: Batch normalization: accelerating deep network training by reducing internal covariate shift. arXiv preprint arXiv:1502.03167 (2015)
35. Girshick, R.: Fast r-cnn. In: ICCV, pp. 1440–1448 (2015)
36. Zhang, Z., Fidler, S., Urtasun, R.: Instance-level segmentation with deep densely connected MRFs. In: CVPR (2016)
37. Chen, X., Kundu, K., Zhang, Z., Ma, H., Fidler, S., Urtasun, R.: Monocular 3D object detection for autonomous driving. In: CVPR (2016)
38. Fidler, S., Dickinson, S., Urtasun, R.: 3D object detection and viewpoint estimation with a deformable 3D cuboid model. In: NIPS (2012)
39. Hartley, R.: In defence of the eight-point algorithm. In: PAMI (1997)
40. Kingma, D., Ba, J.: Adam: a method for stochastic optimization. arXiv preprint arXiv:1412.6980 (2014)
41. Ren, M., Zemel, R.: End-to-end instance segmentation and counting with recurrent attention. arXiv preprint arXiv:1605.09410 (2016)

Similarity Registration Problems for 2D/3D Ultrasound Calibration

Francisco Vasconcelos$^{(\boxtimes)}$, Donald Peebles, Sebastien Ourselin, and Danail Stoyanov

University College London, London, UK
{v.vasconcelos,d.peebles,s.ourselin,danail.stoyanov}@ucl.ac.uk

Abstract. We propose a minimal solution for the similarity registration (rigid pose and scale) between two sets of 3D lines, and also between a set of co-planar points and a set of 3D lines. The first problem is solved up to 8 discrete solutions with a minimum of 2 line-line correspondences, while the second is solved up to 4 discrete solutions using 4 point-line correspondences. We use these algorithms to perform the extrinsic calibration between a pose tracking sensor and a 2D/3D ultrasound (US) curvilinear probe using a tracked needle as calibration target. The needle is tracked as a 3D line, and is scanned by the ultrasound as either a 3D line (3D US) or as a 2D point (2D US). Since the scale factor that converts US scan units to metric coordinates is unknown, the calibration is formulated as a similarity registration problem. We present results with both synthetic and real data and show that the minimum solutions outperform the correspondent non-minimal linear formulations.

Keywords: Calibration · Similarity registration · Ultrasound · Medical imaging

1 Introduction

Ultrasound (US) is a low-cost and real-time medical imaging technique in minimally invasive surgery and in percutaneous procedures. It observes information under the surface, so it is used to locate invisible details about vessels, nerves, or tumours. By tracking the pose of a 2D ultrasound probe (2D US) we can render 3D reconstructions from a collection of 2D slices [1], while a tracked 3D probe (3D US) is able to build large and detailed 3D models from a set of 3D scans [2]. Both 2D US and 3D US can also be used to guide other tracked medical instruments, such as biopsy needles [3], and fuse data with other imaging modalities such as endoscopes.

Freehand 3D ultrasound generally refers to the extrinsic calibration between a hand-held US probe and a pose tracking device. This calibration aims at determining the rigid transformation between the US scan and the tracked marker as well as the scale factor that converts the US scan to metric coordinates, i.e. a similarity transformation. This is usually achieved by scanning a known calibration object (phantom) immersed in either water or a tissue mimicking

© Springer International Publishing AG 2016
B. Leibe et al. (Eds.): ECCV 2016, Part VI, LNCS 9910, pp. 171–187, 2016.
DOI: 10.1007/978-3-319-46466-4_11

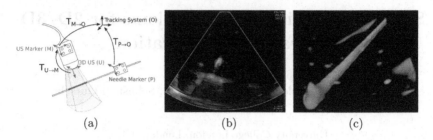

(a)   (b)   (c)

Fig. 1. (a) Scanning a tracked needle with a US probe; (b) a 2D US probe detects a cross section of the needle; (c) a 3D US detects a line segment.

gel. Since the speed of sound in water is different than in tissue, sometimes an alcoholic solution is used to obtain a more realistic US scale. A multitude of calibration phantoms with different shapes have been proposed in the literature [4], including intersecting wires [5], a single plane [6,7], a stylus [1,8,9], and 3D printed objects [10]. Although these methods focus on 2D US calibration, some extensions to 3D US using similar phantoms have been proposed as well [11,12] (Fig. 1).

In this paper we focus on using a tracked needle as the calibration phantom. Our main motivation is towards assisted guidance and motion analysis in fetal interventions that require the extraction of *in utero* samples with a biopsy needle. It thus becomes a practical solution to use the same needle as a calibration object, avoiding the need to introduce new objects in the operating room and the additional burden of their sterilization. The tracked needle is detected by the pose tracking system as a 3D line, and it is scanned either as a line (3D US) or as a point (2D US). By scanning the needle under different poses, we formulate the 3D US calibration as the similarity registration between two sets of 3D lines and the 2D US calibration as the similarity registration between co-planar 3D points and 3D lines.

In this paper we propose a minimal solver to the similarity registration between two sets of 3D lines. We will also show that the registration between co-planar 3D points and 3D lines is a sub-problem of the same formulation and therefore the same minimal solver can be applied. Additionally, we show that this minimal solution can be easily generalised to the registration of any combination of plane, line, and point correspondences. We also present an alternative simplified minimal solver to the similarity registration between a set of co-planar points and a set of 3D lines. We apply the minimal solutions to the calibration of a 2D US and a 3D US with a pose tracking sensor and perform validation with both synthetic and real data.

2   Related Work

Freehand US calibration using a tracked linear target was proposed in [1]. However, this method is initialized with a non-minimal linear solution and is only meant for calibration of 2D US probes. Furthermore, it assumes that the US probe produces an anisotropic image, i.e. it has different scaling factors along the x and y axes of the image. An alternative method [13] extends this calibration procedure to 3D US and shows that assuming an isotropic model (single scale factor) produces better calibration results for curvilinear shaped probes. In this paper we assume that the US scans are isotropic. In some contexts, it is possible to assume that the scale factor is known, and the calibration problem becomes the Euclidean registration between the US probe and the phantom target. In the 2D US case this problem becomes equivalent to the extrinsic calibration between a camera and a laser *rangefinder* [14]. In the 3D US case, with the appropriate phantom (e.g. 3 known 3D points) the absolute pose of the probe can be recovered in each calibration scan, and thus it can be formulated as the standard hand-eye problem [15,16]. In this paper, however, we consider that the scale is always unknown.

Estimating the similarity transformation (rigid pose and scale) between two coordinate frames gained recent attention due to its application in the registration of different Structure-from-Motion (SfM) sequences. If the same scene is recovered in two different monocular SfM runs, the scale of each reconstruction can be arbitrarily different. Therefore, to produce extended and more detailed 3D maps from independent SfM runs both the rigid pose and the scale must be recovered. If correspondences between SfM sequences are not available, one can use an extension of the ICP algorithm [17] to handle unknown scale [18]. If 2D-3D point correspondences are available, this is called the generalised pose and scale problem [19,20], and is solved by extending the *PnP* formulation [21–23] to handle the alignment of image rays from multiple view points. A closely related contribution estimates a similarity transformation from pairwise point correspondences between two generalised cameras [24].

In the case of 3D US calibration, we are interested in the similarity registration between two sets of 3D lines. Different algorithms have been proposed to the euclidean registration between sets of lines [25,26]. One possible approach to solve the similarity registration problem would be to first estimate the unknown scale factor independently, e.g. by computing the ratio of orthogonal distances between all pairs of lines in both sets, and then use any of the previously mentioned euclidean registration algorithms. We found that this approach is extremely unstable with noisy measurements and thus we focus on the joint estimation of all similarity parameters. Non-minimal linear algorithms and non-linear refinement methods have been proposed to solve the registration of two sets of 3D lines for different non-rigid configurations, including the similarity transformation [27]. However, and to the best of our knowledge, a minimal closed-form solution for the similarity registration of two sets of lines have not been proposed in the literature.

The 2D US calibration problem is the similarity registration between a set of 3D lines and a set of co-planar points. This is a particular case of the pose and scale problem [19] when the 3D points are co-planar, and therefore this method could be adapted to solve this problem. However, the co-planarity of points introduces further simplifications, and as we will show in this paper, this problem can be minimally solved with a much more compact set of equations.

Our strategy to solve both registration problems is to convert them to an equivalent registration between a set of 3D points and a set of 3D planes. Although this strategy has been described in the context of euclidean registration [28], it is also valid for non-rigid registration.

Minimal solutions are a well established topic in computer vision literature [29–33]. In most cases they require solving a system of polynomial equations, which can be achieved using Grobner basis methods [30,33,34]. Although these methods provide a general framework to build numeric polynomial solvers, they require a certain amount of symbolic manipulation that often requires a case-by-case analysis. To address this issue an automatic generator of polynomial solvers have been proposed [32]. In this paper we develop minimum solutions using the action matrix method as presented in [34].

3   2D/3D US Model

US probes emit a set of acoustic beams that are partially reflected whenever they cross a medium interface with a change in acoustic impedance. The time response of the echo reflections enables the formation of a spatial grayscale map representing the different acoustic impedances within the US scanning field of view. Note that US beams have a varying width (Fig. 2(a)) which might induce undesired out of focus distortions. In an analogous way to most camera calibration models, we assume that the scanned region is always focused and thus each scene point reflects a beam along a single straight line.

US image formation depends on the probe construction. Linear 2D US probes (Fig. 2(b)) emit parallel beams and thus there are two scale factors involved: s_y depends on the speed of sound in the propagation medium, while s_x is a fixed parameter that depends on the physical distance between beam emitters. These probes usually operate with high frequency acoustic signals (4–16 MHz) and are used for short range scans (e.g. musculoskeletal imaging). The calibration of these

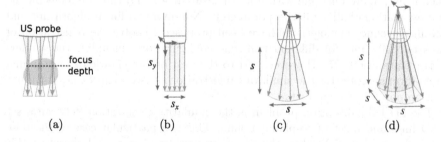

Fig. 2. US probe models: (a) US emitted beams have a varying width. If we assume that the scanned region is focused, beams are approximated by a straight line. (b) linear 2D US (c) Curvilinear 2D US (d) curvilinear 3D US.

probes cannot be represented with a similarity transformation and we discard it from further analysis in this paper. Curvilinear 2D US probes (Fig. 2(c)) emit beams in radial directions that intersect in a single point, forming a planar bundle of lines. In this case, the speed of sound in the propagation medium affects the scan scale isotropically. The curvilinear 3D US (Fig. 2(d)) is a generalization of the curvilinear 2D US, emitting a 3D bundle of beams. Curvilinear probes usually operate with lower frequency signals (2–8 MHz) and are more suitable to long range scans (e.g. obstetrics, cardiac imaging).

4   Problem Statement

Consider a hand-held curvilinear 3D US probe whose pose is tracked by a rigidly attached marker (Fig. 3). In each frame the tracking system determines the transformation $T_{M \to O}$ from the marker coordinate system (M) to a fixed frame O. The freehand 3D US calibration consists in determining the unknown similarity transformation A that maps 3D points $\mathbf{X}_i$ in the US volume to 3D points $\mathbf{P}_i$ represented in M.

$$\mathbf{P}_i = A\mathbf{X}_i \qquad (1)$$

The similarity A is defined by a rotation R, a translation $\mathbf{t}$ and a scale factor s that converts the 3D US volume to metric coordinates, and is represented as

$$A = \begin{pmatrix} S & t \\ 0 & 1 \end{pmatrix} \qquad (2)$$

where $S = sR$ is a scaled rotation matrix such that

$$S^\mathsf{T}S = SS^\mathsf{T} = \begin{pmatrix} s^2 & 0 & 0 \\ 0 & s^2 & 0 \\ 0 & 0 & s^2 \end{pmatrix} \qquad (3)$$

The calibration procedure consists in capturing a tracked needle in the 3D US volume under different poses. The needle is previously calibrated by determining

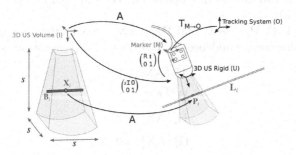

Fig. 3. 3D US calibration problem. The similarity transformation A maps points $\mathbf{X}_i$ in the 3D US volume (red) to points $\mathbf{P}_i$ in the marker reference frame (green). A can be decomposed as a uniform scaling transformation followed by a rigid transformation. (Color figure online)

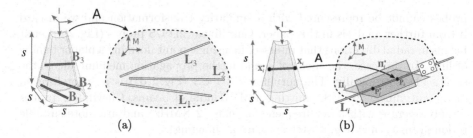

Fig. 4. (a) The 3D US calibration is formulated as the similarity registration between lines $\mathbf{B}_i$ and lines $\mathbf{L}_i$; (b) Each line $\mathbf{L}_i$ can be re-defined as two intersecting planes $\mathbf{\Pi}_i$, $\mathbf{\Pi}_i^*$, while each line $\mathbf{B}_i$ can be redefined as two points $\mathbf{X}_i$, $\mathbf{X}_i^*$.

its two endpoints in the reference frame M and then it is represented in each acquisition as a 3D line $\mathbf{L}_i$. The needle is also detected as a 3D line $\mathbf{B}_i$ in the 3D US volume. The calibration problem is thus formulated as the 3D similarity registration between two sets of lines (Fig. 4(a)).

5   3D US Calibration Solution

In this section we derive a minimal solution for the calibration of a 3D US probe. We start by re-stating it as the similarity registration between 3D points and 3D planes, and then derive a linear and a minimal solution for this problem. The calibration of a 2D US is presented in Sect. 6 as a particular case of the 3D US problem.

5.1   3D US Calibration as Point-Plane Registration

Ramalingam et al. showed that any 3D registration problem involving 3D planes, lines and/or points can be re-stated as the registration between 3D planes and 3D points [28]. In our calibration problem this can be achieved by defining each needle line $\mathbf{L}_i$ as two intersecting planes $\mathbf{\Pi}_i$, $\mathbf{\Pi}_i^*$ and each line $\mathbf{B}_i$ as two points $\mathbf{X}_i$, $\mathbf{X}_i^*$ (Fig. 4(b)).

Given that both $\mathbf{P}_i = \mathbf{A}\mathbf{X}_i$ and $\mathbf{P}_i^* = \mathbf{A}\mathbf{X}_i^*$ are contained in planes $\mathbf{\Pi}_i$ and $\mathbf{\Pi}_i^*$, each line-line correspondence $(\mathbf{L}_i, \mathbf{B}_i)$ puts 4 linear constraints on $\mathbf{A}$

$$\mathbf{\Pi}_i^{\mathsf{T}}\mathbf{A}\mathbf{X}_i = 0 \tag{4}$$

$$\mathbf{\Pi}_i^{*\mathsf{T}}\mathbf{A}\mathbf{X}_i = 0 \tag{5}$$

$$\mathbf{\Pi}_i^{\mathsf{T}}\mathbf{A}\mathbf{X}_i^* = 0 \tag{6}$$

$$\mathbf{\Pi}_i^{*\mathsf{T}}\mathbf{A}\mathbf{X}_i^* = 0 \tag{7}$$

Note that the same reasoning can be applied to any combination of plane, point, and line correspondences (planes are defined by 3 points, and points are defined as the intersection of 3 planes), and thus the remainder of this section equally applies to these problems as well.

5.2 Linear Solution

The similarity matrix A has 13 linear parameters and for N line-line correspondences we can stack instances of the Eqs. 4, 5, 6 and 7) to form a linear system
with $4N$ equations and 13 unknowns. This linear system can be solved with
SVD decomposition using at least 3 correspondences, determining A up to a
scale factor. The correct scale of A can be recovered by setting the homogeneous
parameter to 1. Note, however, that with noisy line measurements Eq. 3 is not
satisfied and thus the linear solution for A is generally not a similarity. The linear
estimation can be projected to a similarity using QR decomposition of matrix S
and forcing its upper triangular component to be a scaled identity matrix (using
the mean of its diagonal elements as scale s)

$$S = sR = R \begin{pmatrix} s\ 0\ 0 \\ 0\ s\ 0 \\ 0\ 0\ s \end{pmatrix} \tag{8}$$

5.3 Minimal Solution

Equation 3 puts 5 quadratic constraints on matrix A and therefore only 7 linear
constraints are required to compute its 13 parameters. This can be achieved with
a minimum of 2 line-line correspondences. Note that with 2 correspondences
we have 8 linear constraints. To solve the problem minimally we should either
discard one of the linear equations or partially solve the complete linear system,
leaving 6 up to scale unknowns undetermined. We found the latter option to be
numerically more stable. The linear system with 7 equations and 13 unknowns
is partially solved using SVD decomposition, generating a 6D solution subspace
for A

$$A = aA_a + bA_b + cA_c + dA_d + eA_e + fA_f \tag{9}$$

where a, b, c, d, e, f are the remaining 6 unknowns.

Equation 3 can be written as the following system of 10 quadratic equations

$$
\begin{array}{ll}
c_1{}^T c_1 - c_2{}^T c_2 = 0 & r_1{}^T r_1 - r_2{}^T r_2 = 0 \\
c_1{}^T c_1 - c_3{}^T c_3 = 0 & r_1{}^T r_1 - r_3{}^T r_3 = 0 \\
c_1{}^T c_2 = 0 & r_1{}^T r_2 = 0 \\
c_1{}^T c_3 = 0 & r_1{}^T r_3 = 0 \\
c_2{}^T c_3 = 0 & r_2{}^T r_3 = 0
\end{array}
\tag{10}
$$

where c_i is the ith column of S and r_i is the ith row of S. Substituting Eq. 9
into Eq. 10 generates a system of 10 quadratic equations in the 6 unknowns a,
b, c, d, e, f. Note that this polynomial system is the same solved in [19] for the
Generalised Pose and Scale Problem.

This polynomial system is solved with the action matrix method [34]. Since
the quadratic constraints determine A up to scale we set $f = 1$. We expand the
polynomial system by multiplying all equations by a, b, c, d and form a cubic

system with 47 linearly independent equations and 55 monomials. Using LU decomposition, we reduce the system to 5 equations in 13 monomials

$$\left(\mathsf{C}_{5\times5}\;\mathsf{B}_{5\times8}\right)\begin{pmatrix}\mathbf{m}_C\\\mathbf{m}_B\end{pmatrix} = 0 \tag{11}$$

with

$$\mathbf{m}_C = \begin{pmatrix} b^3 & ab^2 & be & bd & bc \end{pmatrix}^{\mathsf{T}} \tag{12}$$

$$\mathbf{m}_B = \begin{pmatrix} b^2 & ab & e & d & c & b & a & 1 \end{pmatrix}^{\mathsf{T}} \tag{13}$$

When a polynomial system is presented in this format, it can be solved with the action matrix method if matrix $\mathsf{C}_{5\times5}$ is invertible and also if there is a monomial w such that $w\mathbf{m}_B$ is a linear combination of $\mathbf{m}_B$. In our calibration problem $\mathsf{C}_{5\times5}$ is generally invertible, and for $w = b$ we can build a 8×8 matrix M such that

$$\mathsf{M}\mathbf{m}_B = b\mathbf{m}_B \tag{14}$$

The 8 solutions to $\mathbf{m}_B$ that verify this constraint are the eigen vectors of M, from which we can extract 8 solutions for a, b, c, d, e and recover 8 solutions for A using Eq. 9. The correct scale of A is recovered in the same way as explained in Sect. 5.2.

6   2D US Calibration Solution

If we consider the same calibration problem with a curvilinear 2D US probe instead, each needle acquisition is detected as a single point $\mathbf{X}_i$ that belongs to the US scanning plane. For the sake of continuity with the previous section, we still treat the image coordinates $\mathbf{X}_i$ of the 2D US as 3D co-planar points, for an arbitrarily fixed scanning plane $\boldsymbol{\Delta}$. Note that calibrating a curvilinear 2D US aims at determining the same 7 parameters as in the 3D US case. Therefore the calibration problem becomes the 3D similarity registration between a set of co-planar points $\mathbf{X}_i$ and a set of lines $\mathbf{L}_i$ Fig. (5(a)).

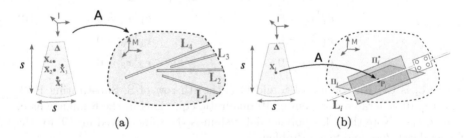

(a)   (b)

Fig. 5. (a) The 2D US calibration is formulated as the similarity registration between co-planar points $\mathbf{P}_i$ and lines $\mathbf{L}_i$; (b) each line $\mathbf{L}_i$ can be re-defined as two intersecting planes $\boldsymbol{\Pi}_i$, $\boldsymbol{\Pi}_i^*$.

Each point-line correspondence puts 2 linear constraints on matrix A (Eqs. 4 and 5), and therefore this problem can be minimally solved using 4 point-line correspondences. The same minimal solution described in Sect. 5.3 can be used in this case, since the co-planarity of points X_i is not a degenerate configuration. We observed that some particular choices for the scanning plane Δ (e.g. $z = 0$) result in matrix $C_{5 \times 5}$ being singular and thus the polynomial system becomes numerically unstable. We found out through simulation that defining Δ as the plane $z = k$, with $k > 0$ generally produces an invertible matrix $C_{5 \times 5}$ and the polynomial system is solvable.

On the other hand, the linear solution described in Sect. 5.2 will not solve the 2D US problem, as the system will always be rank deficient. This can only be achieved with the additional elimination of parameters in the linear equations. These simplifications also lead to an alternative minimal solution for the 2D US case. Both methods are described in the remainder of this section.

6.1   Linear Solution

If we define the scanning plane Δ as $z = 0$, the 2D US points have the format $X_i = \begin{pmatrix} x_i & y_i & 0 & 1 \end{pmatrix}^{\mathsf{T}}$ and the linear equations do not put any constraints on the third column of S. The linear equations for each acquisition become

$$\Pi_i{}^{\mathsf{T}} \bar{A} \begin{pmatrix} x_i & y_i & 1 \end{pmatrix}^{\mathsf{T}} = 0 \tag{15}$$

$$\Pi_i^{*\mathsf{T}} \bar{A} \begin{pmatrix} x_i & y_i & 1 \end{pmatrix}^{\mathsf{T}} = 0 \tag{16}$$

with

$$\bar{A} = \begin{pmatrix} \bar{S} & t \\ 0 & 1 \end{pmatrix} \tag{17}$$

$$\bar{S} = \begin{pmatrix} c_1 & c_2 \end{pmatrix} \tag{18}$$

where c_1 and c_2 are the first two columns of S. The linear system is thus reduced to 10 unknown parameters and can be solved with a minimum of 5 point-line correspondences. Note that analogously to the 3D US case (Eq. 3), $\bar{A}$ must verify the following constraint

$$\bar{S}\bar{S}^{\mathsf{T}} = \begin{pmatrix} s^2 & 0 \\ 0 & s^2 \end{pmatrix} \tag{19}$$

and with noisy measurements the linear solution must be forced to this format using its QR decomposition

$$\bar{S} = R \begin{pmatrix} s & 0 \\ 0 & s \\ 0 & 0 \end{pmatrix} \tag{20}$$

The third column of S can then be extracted by multiplying the third column of rotation R by s.

6.2 Alternative Minimal Solution (2D US Only)

This problem can be minimally solved with 7 linear constraints (4 point-line correspondences). Since in this case there are only 10 linear parameters, we can generate a 3D linear solution subspace

$$\bar{\mathsf{A}} = a\bar{\mathsf{A}}_a + b\bar{\mathsf{A}}_b + c\bar{\mathsf{A}}_c \tag{21}$$

Equation 19 is re-written as the following system

$$\begin{aligned} \mathbf{c}_1{}^\mathsf{T}\mathbf{c}_1 - \mathbf{c}_2{}^\mathsf{T}\mathbf{c}_2 &= 0 \\ \mathbf{c}_1{}^\mathsf{T}\mathbf{c}_2 &= 0 \end{aligned} \tag{22}$$

Substituting Eq. 21 into Eq. 22 we generate a system of 2 quadratic homogeneous equations in the 3 unknowns a, b, c. Using the same procedure from Sect. 5.3 we use monomial multiplication and LU decomposition to re-write this system as

$$\left(\mathsf{C}_{2\times2}\,\mathsf{B}_{2\times4}\right)\begin{pmatrix}\mathbf{m}_C \\ \mathbf{m}_B\end{pmatrix} = 0 \tag{23}$$

with

$$\mathbf{m}_C = \left(ab^2\ b^2\right)^\mathsf{T} \tag{24}$$

$$\mathbf{m}_B = \left(ab\ b\ a\ 1\right)^\mathsf{T} \tag{25}$$

We solve this system using eigen decomposition of the action matrix, yielding up to 4 solutions.

7 Degenerate Cases

The degenerate configurations for both 3D US and 2D US calibration are closely related to the ones described for the pose and scale problem [19]. If the needle is moved without rotation (lines $\mathbf{L}_i$ are parallel) there is an ambiguity in translation. This implies that fixing the needle and scanning with the US probe in different positions is a degenerate case, however, the inverse scenario of fixing the US probe while moving the needle is generally not a degenerate case. If the needle motion is a pure rotation around itself (lines $\mathbf{L}_i$ intersect in a single point) there is an ambiguity in scale. This is analogous to pose estimation with monocular pinhole cameras. If lines $\mathbf{L}_i$ are co-planar, the point detections $\mathbf{X}_i$ of a 2D US are co-linear and there is a rotation ambiguity around the axis defined by these points. This, however, is not generally a degenerate case in 3D US calibration unless only 2 line correspondences are available, since it falls under either one of the two previously mentioned cases. Therefore, the similarity between two sets of co-planar lines can only be estimated from a minimum of 3 correspondences.

8   Iterative Refinement

The closed-form solutions can be refined with Levenberg-Marquardt iterative optimization [35], however, there is no consensus on the most appropriate residue metric for 3D line registration [27]. In all our experiments we perform iterative refinement by minimizing the euclidean orthogonal distance between the 3D lines $\mathbf{L}_i$ and the projected 3D points from the US image $\mathbf{P}_i = \mathbf{A}\mathbf{X}_i$. The refined solution is parametrised by the translation $\mathbf{t}$, 3 rotation parameters ($\mathbf{R}$ is represented as a unit norm quaternion), and the scale factor s. For the 3D US the optimization problem is

$$\min_{\mathbf{R},\mathbf{t},s} \sum_{i=1}^{N} d(\mathbf{L}_i, \mathbf{P}_i)^2 + d(\mathbf{L}_i, \mathbf{P}_i^*)^2 \tag{26}$$

where $d(\mathbf{L}_i, \mathbf{P}_i)$ represents the euclidean distance between line $\mathbf{L}_i$ and point $\mathbf{P}_i$. For the 2D US problem the last term of the minimization is ignored.

9   Experimental Results

We test the calibration algorithms both in simulation and with real data. For the 3D US calibration we test the linear solution from Sect. 5.2 (**3line3D**) and the minimum solution from Sect. 5.3 (**2line3D**), while for the 2D US we test the linear solution from Sect. 6.1 (**5point2D**), the general minimal solution from Sect. 5.3 (**2line3D**), and the simplified minimum solution from Sect. 6.2 (**4point2D**). All algorithms are tested within a RANSAC framework [36] with outlier threshold of 5 mm, followed by iterative refinement.

With both synthetic and real data, the 3D US lines $\mathbf{B}_i$ are obtained by sampling points from 2D slices with different angles (Fig. 6). This is is a practical solution since we can directly define the points $\mathbf{X}_i$ and $\mathbf{X}_i^*$ to input in Eqs. 4, 5, 6 and 7. The needle tracking measurements (lines $\mathbf{L}_i$) are converted to two intersecting planes $\mathbf{\Pi}_i$ and $\mathbf{\Pi}_i^*$ such that $\mathbf{\Pi}_i$ intersects both $\mathbf{L}_i$ and the origin of

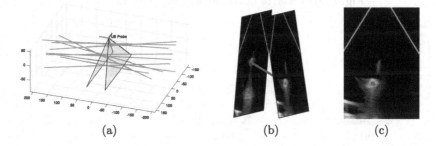

(a)   (b)   (c)

Fig. 6. The needle detections in 3D are obtained by sampling 2D slices: (a) simulated set-up with a fixed 3D US scanner and random needle poses in green; (b) 3D US line acquisition; 2D US point acquisition. (Color figure online)

the US attached marker reference frame M, and Π_i^* is orthogonal to Πi. Note that this approach degenerates when the needle is aligned with the origin of M and therefore this should be taken into account when positioning the needle during calibration.

All plots in this section are represented with Matlab boxplot function: the central mark is the median, the box limits are the 25th and 75th percentiles, the whiskers are the maximum and minimum inliers, and individual crosses are outliers.

9.1   Simulation

We simulate a 2D/3D US probe with a scale factor $s = 0.24$ in a fixed position. 50 line segments with 400 mm are generated at random poses within the field of view of the US. Gaussian noise is added to the US points along the 2D slices ($\sigma = 1$ pixel) and also to the extreme points of the line segments $\mathbf{L}_i$ ($\sigma = 1$mm) to simulate tracking error. In each trial, we calibrate the US by sampling N random line segments. N varies between 3 and 10 for the 3D US case, and between 5 and 10 for the 2D US case. For each value N we perform 100 trials. The calibration results are compared against of rotation (R_{GT}), translation (t_{GT}), and scale factor (s_{GT}) and are presented in Figs. 7 and 8. The rotation error is measured as the angle displacement of the residual rotation $\mathsf{R}^\mathsf{T}\mathsf{R}_{GT}$, the

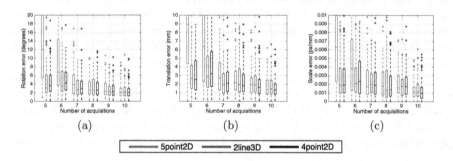

Fig. 7. 2D US error distributions with synthetic data

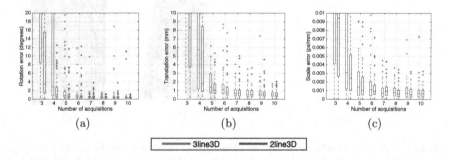

Fig. 8. 3D US error distributions with synthetic data

translation error as $\|\mathbf{t}_{GT} - \mathbf{t}\|$ and the scale error as $|s_{GT} - s|$. As expected, the minimal solutions perform better than the linear solutions with a low number of input acquisitions and converge to the same result as the number of acquisitions grow. Also not surprisingly, 3D US performs better that 2D US for the same number of acquisitions, given that it has twice as much linear constraints. In the case of 2D US, the two alternative minimum solutions have similar performance.

9.2   Real Data

Our calibration method is tested using the set-up displayed in Fig. 9(a) that includes a GE Voluson E10 machine with a eM6C probe (3D US) and a 333 mm length metal needle. Both instruments are tracked by the infrared camera system Optitrack V120 Trio. Experiments were conducted in a container filled with water at room temperature. We use the same probe for both for 2D US and 3D US data acquisition. For the 2D US we just choose a single 2D slice from the 3D US volume at a specified angle. The needle is manually segmented as a point in each 2D slice. Unlike in the simulation experiment, in this calibration procedure both the needle and the 3D US probe are moved between acquisitions.

To validate the calibration accuracy we use an x-shaped wire phantom Fig. 9(b) whose point intersection can be measured as a single point in the US scan. We use this phantom to measure the projection reconstruction accuracy (PRA) of our calibration results, i.e., the difference in mm between the intersection point $\mathbf{AX}$ according to the calibrated US measurement and the same point $\mathbf{P}$ measured by the tip of the tracked needle. We performed 10 acquisitions of the wire phantom in order to cover different regions of the US scan. Figures 10(a) and 10(b) display the distribution of PRA results for all trials. Each distribution contains 200 error measurements (20 trials × 10 phantom scans). In the 2D US results we only display the results for one of the minimal solutions, since as we've seen in simulation the results from both approaches are very similar.

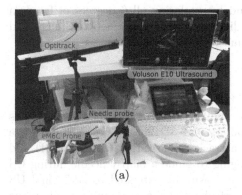 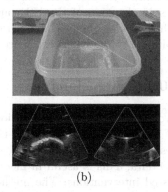

(a)   (b)

Fig. 9. (a) Calibration set-up with a tracked 3D US probe and a tracked needle; (b) validation using a cross wire pattern that defines a known 3D point in the tracker reference frame.

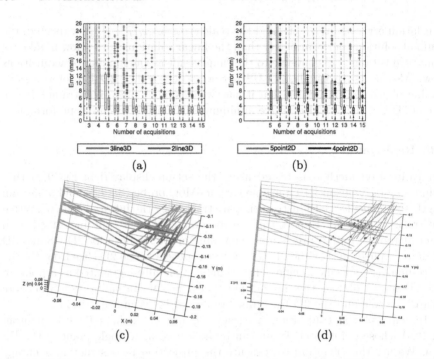

Fig. 10. Validation results: (a) projection reconstruction accuracy (PRA) with 3D US; (b) PRA with 2D US (c) sample registration result with 3D US projected lines in red and needle tracking measurements in green (d) sample registration result with 2D US projected points in red and needle tracking measurements in green (Color figure online)

The US calibration converges to a solution with an error between 2 and 3 mm within a total scanning radius of 120 mm. Since in each trial we select random needle poses, close to degenerate configurations can be chosen and result in outlier results. This can be avoided in practice by scanning the needle in a spread region of the US volume, and by exploring all 6 degrees of freedom while moving the needle. Overall, the difference in accuracy between linear and minimal solutions is even more pronounced than in simulation.

10   Conclusions

We propose a minimum solution to the similarity registration between two sets of 3D lines, and between co-planar points and 3D lines. These solutions are tested to calibrate a US probe using a tracked line target with both 3D and 2D data. This is useful in medical imaging to guide a biopsy needle during US based interventions. The method can be easily be extended to additional US calibration problems using other types of phantoms, e.g. scanning single plane target leads to the similarity registration between co-planar lines and 3D planes (2D US) or between two sets of 3D planes (3D US). In other computer vision domains this algorithm can potentially be used as an extension of the pose and scale problem to the alignment of line-based and/or plane-based SfM sequences.

Acknowledgements. This work was supported through an Innovative Engineering for Health award by the Wellcome Trust [WT101957] and an Engineering and Physical Sciences Research Council (EPSRC) [NS/A000027/1].

References

1. Khamene, A., Sauer, F.: A novel phantom-less spatial and temporal ultrasound calibration method. In: Duncan, J.S., Gerig, G. (eds.) MICCAI 2005. LNCS, vol. 3750, pp. 65–72. Springer, Heidelberg (2005). doi:10.1007/11566489_9
2. Brattain, L.J., Howe, R.D.: Real-time 4D ultrasound mosaicing and visualization. In: Fichtinger, G., Martel, A., Peters, T. (eds.) MICCAI 2011. LNCS, vol. 6891, pp. 105–112. Springer, Heidelberg (2011). doi:10.1007/978-3-642-23623-5_14
3. Stoll, J., Ren, H., Dupont, P.: Passive markers for tracking surgical instruments in real-time 3-D ultrasound imaging. IEEE Trans. Med. Imaging **31**(3), 563–575 (2012)
4. Mercier, L., Lang, T., Lindseth, F., Collins, L.D.: A review of calibration techniques for freehand 3-D ultrasound systems. Ultrasound Med. Biol. **31**(2), 143–165 (2005)
5. Chen, T.K., Thurston, A.D., Ellis, R.E., Abolmaesumi, P.: A real-time freehand ultrasound calibration system with automatic accuracy feedback and control. Ultrasound Med. Biol. **35**(1), 79–93 (2009)
6. Prager, R., Rohling, R., Gee, A., Berman, L.: Rapid calibration for 3-D freehand ultrasound. Ultrasound Med. Biol. **24**(6), 855–869 (1998)
7. Najafi, M., Afsham, N., Abolmaesumi, P., Rohling, R.: A closed-form differential formulation for ultrasound spatial calibration: single wall phantom. Ultrasound Med. Biol. **41**(4), 1079–1094 (2015)
8. Muratore, D.M., Galloway Jr., R.L.: Beam calibration without a phantom for creating a 3-D freehand ultrasound system. Ultrasound Med. Biol. **27**(11), 1557–1566 (2001)
9. Hsu, P.W., Treece, G.M., Prager, R.W., Houghton, N.E., Gee, A.H.: Comparison of freehand 3-D ultrasound calibration techniques using a stylus. Ultrasound Med. Biol. **34**(10), 1610–1621 (2008)
10. Najafi, M., Afsham, N., Abolmaesumi, P., Rohling, R.: A closed-form differential formulation for ultrasound spatial calibration: multi-wedge phantom. Ultrasound Med. Biol. **40**(9), 2231–2243 (2014)
11. Bergmeir, C., Seitel, M., Frank, C., Simone, R., Meinzer, H.P., Wolf, I.: Comparing calibration approaches for 3D ultrasound probes. Int. J. Comput. Assist. Radiol. Surg. **4**(2), 203–213 (2009)
12. Hummel, J., Kaar, M., Hoffmann, R., Bhatia, A., Birkfellner, W., Figl, M.: Evaluation of three 3D US calibration methods. In: Proceedings of SPIE, vol. 8671, pp. 86712I–86712I-8 (2013)
13. Vasconcelos, F., Peebles, D., Ourselin, S., Stoyanov, D.: Spatial calibration of a 2D/3D ultrasound using a tracked needle. Int. J. Comput. Assist. Radiol. Surg. **11**(6), 1091–1099 (2016)
14. Zhang, Q., Pless, R.: Extrinsic calibration of a camera and laser range finder (improves camera calibration). In: 2004 IEEE/RSJ International Conference on Intelligent Robots and Systems (IROS 2004), Proceedings, vol. 3, pp. 2301–2306. IEEE (2004)

15. Horaud, R., Dornaika, F.: Hand-eye calibration. Int. J. Robot. Res. **14**(3), 195–210 (1995)
16. Thompson, S., Stoyanov, D., Schneider, C., Gurusamy, K., Ourselin, S., Davidson, B., Hawkes, D., Clarkson, M.J.: Hand-eye calibration for rigid laparoscopes using an invariant point. Int. J. Comput. Assist. Radiol. Surg. **11**(6), 1071–1080 (2016)
17. Zhang, Z.: Iterative point matching for registration of free-form curves and surfaces. Int. J. Comput. Vis. **13**(2), 119–152 (1994)
18. Du, S., Zheng, N., Xiong, L., Ying, S., Xue, J.: Scaling iterative closest point algorithm for registration of m-D point sets. J. Vis. Commun. Image Rep. **21**(56), 442–452 (2010). Special issue on Multi-camera Imaging, Coding and Innovative Display
19. Ventura, J., Arth, C., Reitmayr, G., Schmalstieg, D.: A minimal solution to the generalized pose-and-scale problem. In: The IEEE Conference on Computer Vision and Pattern Recognition (CVPR), June 2014
20. Sweeney, C., Fragoso, V., Höllerer, T., Turk, M.: gDLS: a scalable solution to the generalized pose and scale problem. In: Fleet, D., Pajdla, T., Schiele, B., Tuytelaars, T. (eds.) ECCV 2014. LNCS, vol. 8692, pp. 16–31. Springer, Heidelberg (2014). doi:10.1007/978-3-319-10593-2_2
21. Haralick, R.M., Lee, D., Ottenburg, K., Nolle, M.: Analysis and solutions of the three point perspective pose estimation problem. In: IEEE Computer Society Conference on Computer Vision and Pattern Recognition, Proceedings CVPR 1991, pp. 592–598, June 1991
22. Quan, L., Lan, Z.: Linear N-point camera pose determination. IEEE Trans. Pattern Anal. Mach. Intell. **21**(8), 774–780 (1999)
23. Lepetit, V., Moreno-Noguer, F., Fua, P.: EPnP: an accurate O(n) solution to the PnP problem. Int. J. Comput. Vis. **81**(2), 155–166 (2009)
24. Sweeney, C., Kneip, L., Hollerer, T., Turk, M.: Computing similarity transformations from only image correspondences. In: The IEEE Conference on Computer Vision and Pattern Recognition (CVPR), June 2015
25. Zhang, Z., Faugeras, O.D.: The first BMVC 1990 determining motion from 3D line segment matches: a comparative study. Image Vis. Comput. **9**(1), 10–19 (1991)
26. Kamgar-Parsi, B., Kamgar-Parsi, B.: Algorithms for matching 3D line sets. IEEE Trans. Pattern Anal. Mach. Intell. **26**(5), 582–593 (2004)
27. Bartoli, A., Sturm, P.: The 3D line motion matrix and alignment of line reconstructions. In: Proceedings of the 2001 IEEE Computer Society Conference on Computer Vision and Pattern Recognition (CVPR 2001), vol. 1. p. I-287–I-292 (2001)
28. Ramalingam, S., Taguchi, Y., Marks, T.K., Tuzel, O.: $P2\pi$: a minimal solution for registration of 3D points to 3D planes. In: Daniilidis, K., Maragos, P., Paragios, N. (eds.) ECCV 2010. LNCS, vol. 6315, pp. 436–449. Springer, Heidelberg (2010)
29. Nister, D.: An efficient solution to the five-point relative pose problem. IEEE Trans. Pattern Anal. Mach. Intell. **26**(6), 756–770 (2004)
30. Stewenius, H.: Gröbner basis methods for minimal problems in computer vision. Ph.D. thesis, Lund University (2005)
31. Stewénius, H., Nistér, D., Oskarsson, M., Åström, K.: Solutions to minimal generalized relative pose problems. In: Workshop on Omnidirectional Vision, vol. 1, p. 3 (2005)
32. Kukelova, Z., Bujnak, M., Pajdla, T.: Automatic generator of minimal problem solvers. In: Forsyth, D., Torr, P., Zisserman, A. (eds.) ECCV 2008. LNCS, vol. 5304, pp. 302–315. Springer, Heidelberg (2008). doi:10.1007/978-3-540-88690-7_23

33. Kukelova, Z., Bujnak, M., Pajdla, T.: Polynomial eigenvalue solutions to minimal problems in computer vision. IEEE Trans. Pattern Anal. Mach. Intell. **34**(7), 1381–1393 (2012)
34. Byröd, M., Josephson, K., Åström, K.: Fast and stable polynomial equation solving and its application to computer vision. Int. J. Comput. Vis. **84**(3), 237–256 (2009)
35. Marquardt, D.W.: An algorithm for least-squares estimation of nonlinear parameters. J. Soc. Indust. Appl. Math. **11**(2), 431–441 (1963)
36. Fischler, M.A., Bolles, R.C.: Random sample consensus: a paradigm for model fitting with applications to image analysis and automated cartography. Commun. ACM **24**(6), 381–395 (1981)

Adaptive Signal Recovery on Graphs via Harmonic Analysis for Experimental Design in Neuroimaging

Won Hwa Kim[1(✉)], Seong Jae Hwang[1], Nagesh Adluru[4],
Sterling C. Johnson[3], and Vikas Singh[1,2]

[1] Department of Computer Sciences, University of Wisconsin, Madison, WI, USA
wonhwa@cs.wisc.edu
[2] Department of Biostatistics and Medical Informatics,
University of Wisconsin, Madison, WI, USA
[3] GRECC, William S. Middleton VA Hospital, Madison, WI, USA
[4] Waisman Center, Madison, WI, USA
http://pages.cs.wisc.edu/~wonhwa

Abstract. Consider an experimental design of a neuroimaging study, where we need to obtain p measurements for each participant in a setting where $p'(< p)$ are cheaper and easier to acquire while the remaining $(p - p')$ are expensive. For example, the p' measurements may include demographics, cognitive scores or routinely offered imaging scans while the $(p - p')$ measurements may correspond to more expensive types of brain image scans with a higher participant burden. In this scenario, it seems reasonable to seek an "adaptive" design for data acquisition so as to minimize the cost of the study without compromising statistical power. We show how this problem can be solved via harmonic analysis of a band-limited graph whose vertices correspond to participants and our goal is to fully recover a multi-variate signal on the nodes, given the full set of cheaper features and a partial set of more expensive measurements. This is accomplished using an adaptive query strategy derived from probing the properties of the graph in the frequency space. To demonstrate the benefits that this framework can provide, we present experimental evaluations on two independent neuroimaging studies and show that our proposed method can reliably recover the true signal with only partial observations directly yielding substantial financial savings.

1 Introduction

Consider an experimental design setting which involves a cohort $\mathcal{S}$ comprised of N individuals (or examples) in total. We are allowed to obtain a maximum of p

This research was supported by NIH grants AG040396, and NSF CAREER award 1252725, UW ADRC AG033514, UW ICTR 1UL1RR025011, UW CPCP AI117924, UW CIBM 5T15LM007359-14 and Waisman Core Grant P30 HD003352-45.

Electronic supplementary material The online version of this chapter (doi:10. 1007/978-3-319-46466-4_12) contains supplementary material, which is available to authorized users.

© Springer International Publishing AG 2016
B. Leibe et al. (Eds.): ECCV 2016, Part VI, LNCS 9910, pp. 188–205, 2016.
DOI: 10.1007/978-3-319-46466-4_12

measurements (or features) for each participant (or example) in $\mathcal{S}$. Depending on the application, these p measurements may be variously interpreted — for example, in a machine learning experiment, we may have p distinct numerical preferences a user assigns to each item whereas in computer vision, the measurements may reflect p specific requests for supervision or indication on each image in $\mathcal{S}$ [1–4]. In a neuroscience experiment, the cohort corresponds to individual subjects — the p measurements will denote various types of imaging and clinical measures we can acquire. Of course, independent of the application, the "cost" of measurements is quite variable: while features such as gender and age of a participant have negligible cost, requesting a user to rate an image in abstract terms, "How natural is this image on a scale of 1 to 5?", may be more expensive. In neuroimaging, acquiring some clinical and cognitive measures is cheap, whereas certain image scans can cost several thousands of dollars [5,6].

In the past, when datasets were smaller, these issues were understandably not very important. But as we move towards acquiring and annotating large scale datasets in machine learning and vision [7–9], the cost implications can be substantial. For instance, if the budget for a multi-modal brain imaging study involving several different types of image scans for $\sim$200 subjects is \$3M+ and we know *a priori* which type of inference models will finally be estimated using this data, it seems reasonable to ask if "adaptive" data acquisition can bring down costs by 25 % with negligible deterioration in statistical power. While experiment design concepts in classical statistics provide an excellent starting point, they provide little guidance in terms of practical technical issues one faces in addressing the question above. Outside of a few recent works [10–12], this topic is still not extensively studied within mainstream machine learning and vision.

In this paper, we study a natural form of the experimental design problem in the context of an important brain imaging application. Assume that we have access to a cohort $\mathcal{S}$ of n subjects. In principle, we can acquire p measurements for each participant. But all p measures are not easily available — say, we start only with a *default* set of p' measures for each subject which may be considered as "inexpensive". This yields a matrix of size $N \times p'$. We are also provided the remaining set of $(p - p')$ measurements but only for a small subset $\mathcal{S}'$ of n' subjects — possibly due to the associated expense of the measurement. We can, if desired, acquire these additional $(p - p')$ measures for each individual participant in $\mathcal{S}\backslash\mathcal{S}'$, but at a high per-individual cost. Our goal is to eventually estimate a statistical model that has high fidelity to the "true" model estimated using the full set of p measures/features for the full cohort $\mathcal{S}$. The key question is whether we can design an adaptive query strategy that minimizes the overall cost we incur and yet provides high confidence in the parameter estimates we obtain. The problem statement is quite general and models experimental design considerations in numerous scientific disciplines including systems biology and statistical genomics where an effective solution can drive improvements in efficiency.

1.1 Related Work

There are three distinct areas of the literature that are loosely related to the development described in this paper. At the high level, perhaps the most closely related to our work is *active learning* which is motivated by similar cost-benefit considerations, but in terms of minimizing the number of queries (seeking the label of an example) [13]. Here, one starts with a pool of unlabeled data and picks a few examples at random to obtain their labels. Then, we repeatedly fit a classifier to the labeled examples seen so far and query the unlabeled example that is most uncertain or likely to decrease overall uncertainty. This strategy is generally successful though may asymptotically converge to a sub-optimal classifier [14]. Adaptive query strategies have been presented to guarantee that the hypothesis space is fully explored and to obtain theoretically consistent results [15,16]. Much of active learning focuses on learning discriminative classifiers; while the Bayesian versions of active learning can, in principle, be applied to far more general settings, it is not clear whether such formulations can be adapted for the stratified cost structure we encounter in the motivating example above and for general parameter estimation problems where the likelihood expressions are not computationally 'nice'.

Within the statistics literature, the problem of experiment design has a rich history going back at least four decades [17–19], and seeks to formalize how one deals with the non-deterministic nature of physical experiments. In contrast to the basic setting here and even data-driven measures of merit such as D-optimality [20,21], experiment design concepts such as the Latin hypercube design [22] intentionally assume very little about the relationship between input features and the output labels. Instead, with d features, such procedures will generate a space-filling design so that each of the dimensions is divided into equal levels — the calculated configuration merely provides a selection of inputs at which to compute the output of an experiment to achieve specific goals. Despite a similar name, the goals of these ideas are quite different from ours.

Within machine learning and vision, papers related to collaborative filtering (and matrix completion) [23–26] share a number of technical similarities to the development in our work. For instance, one may assume that in a matrix of size $N \times p$ (subjects × measurements), the first p' columns are fully observed whereas multiple rows in the remaining $(p - p')$ columns are missing. This clearly yields a matrix completion problem; unfortunately, the setup lies far from incoherent sampling and the matrix versions of restricted isometry property (RIP) that make the low-rank completion argument work in practice [27,28]. This observation has been made in recent works where collaborative filtering was generalized to the graph domain [29] and where random sampling was introduced for graphs in [30]. However, these approaches, which will serve as excellent baselines, do not exploit the band-limited nature of measurements in frequency space. Separately, matrix completion within an adaptive query setting [31,32] yields important theoretical benefits but so far, no analogs for the graph setting exist.

The contribution of this paper is to provide a harmonic analysis inspired algorithm to estimate band-limited signals that are defined on graphs. It turns out that such solutions directly yield an efficient procedure to conduct adaptive queries for designing experiments involving stratified costs of measurements, i.e., where the first subset of measures is free whereas the second set of $(p - p')$ measures is expensive and must be requested for a small fraction of participants. Our framework relies on the design of an efficient decoder to recover the band-limited original signal involving multiple channels which was only partially observed. In order to accomplish these goals, the paper makes the following contributions.

(i) We propose a novel sampling and signal recovery strategy on a graph that is derived via harmonic analysis of the graph.
(ii) We show how a band-limited multi-variate signal on a graph can be reconstructed with only a few observations via a simple optimization scheme.
(iii) We provide an extensive set of experiments on *two independent datasets* which demonstrate that our framework works well in estimating expensive image-derived measurements based on (a) a partial set of observations (involving less expensive image-scan data) and (b) a full set of measurements on only a small fraction of the cohort.

2 Preliminaries: Linear Transforms in Euclidean and Non-euclidean Spaces

Well known signal transforms in the forward/inverse directions such as the wavelet and Fourier transforms (in non-Euclidean space) are fundamental to our proposed framework. These transforms are well understood in the Euclidean setting, however, their analogues in non-Euclidean spaces have not been studied until recently [33]. We provide a brief overview of these transforms in both Euclidean and non-Euclidean spaces.

2.1 Continuous (Forward) Wavelet Transform

The Fourier transform is a fundamental tool for frequency analyses of a signal by transforming the signal $f(x)$ into the frequency domain as

$$\hat{f}(\omega) = \langle f, e^{j\omega x} \rangle = \int f(x) e^{-j\omega x} \mathrm{d}x \tag{1}$$

where $\hat{f}(\omega)$ is the resultant Fourier coefficient. Wavelet transform is similar to the Fourier transform, but it uses a different type of oscillating basis function (i.e., mother wavelet). Unlike Fourier basis (i.e., $\sin()$) with infinite support, a wavelet ψ is a localized function with finite support. One can define a mother wavelet $\psi_{s,a}(x) = \frac{1}{s}\psi(\frac{x-a}{s})$ with *scale* and *translation* properties, controlled by s and a respectively. Here, changing s controls the dilation and varying a controls the location of ψ. Using $\psi_{s,a}$ as bases, a wavelet transform of a function $f(x)$ results in wavelet coefficients $\mathcal{W}_f(s, a)$ at scale s and at location a as

$$\mathcal{W}_f(s, a) = \langle f, \psi \rangle = \frac{1}{s} \int f(x) \psi^*(\frac{x - a}{s}) \mathrm{d}x \tag{2}$$

where ψ^* is the complex conjugate of ψ [34].

Interestingly, ψ_s is localized not only in the original domain but also in the frequency domain. It behaves as a band-pass filter covering different bandwidths corresponding to scales s. These band-pass filters *do not* cover the low-frequency components, therefore an additional low-pass filter ϕ, a scaling function, is typically introduced. A transform with the scaling function ϕ results in a low-pass filtered representation of the original function f. In the end, filtering at multiple scales s of the wavelet offers a multi-resolution view of the given signal.

2.2   Wavelet Transform in Non-euclidean Spaces

Defining a wavelet transform in the Euclidean space is convenient because of the regularity of the domain (i.e., a regular lattice). In this case, one can easily define the shape of a mother wavelet in the context of an application. However, in non-Euclidean spaces (e.g., graphs that consists of a set of vertices and edges with arbitrary connections), an implementation of a mother wavelet becomes difficult due to the ambiguity of dilation and translation. Due to these issues, the classical definition of the wavelet transform has not been suitable for analyses of data in non-Euclidean spaces until recently when [33,35] proposed wavelet and Fourier transforms in non-Euclidean spaces.

The key idea in [33] for constructing a mother wavelet ψ on the nodes of a graph is simple. Instead of defining it in the original domain where the properties of ψ are ambiguous, we define a mother wavelet in a dual domain where its representation is clear and then transform it back to the original domain. The core ingredients for such a construction are (1) a set of "orthonormal" bases that provide the means to transform a signal between a graph and its dual domain (i.e., an analogue of the frequency domain) and (2) a kernel function $h()$ that behaves as a band-pass filter determining the shape of ψ. Utilizing these ingredients, a mother wavelet is first constructed as a kernel function in the frequency domain and then localized in the original domain using a δ function and the orthonormal bases. Such an operation will implement a mother wavelet ψ on the original graph. Defining a kernel function in the 1-D frequency domain is simple, and one can rely on spectral graph theory to obtain the orthonormal bases of a graph [33] which can be used for graph Fourier transform.

A graph $\mathcal{G} = \{\mathcal{V}, \mathcal{E}\}$ is formally defined by a vertex set $\mathcal{V}$ with N number of vertices and a edge set $\mathcal{E}$ with edges that connect the vertices. Such a graph is generally represented by an adjacency matrix $\mathcal{A}_{N \times N}$ where each element a_{ij} denotes the connection between ith and jth vertices by a corresponding edge weight. Another matrix that summarizes the graph, a degree matrix $\mathcal{D}_{N \times N}$, is a diagonal matrix where the ith diagonal is the sum of edge weights connected to the ith vertex. A graph Laplacian is then defined from these two matrices as $\mathcal{L} = \mathcal{D} - \mathcal{A}$, which is a self-adjoint and positive semi-definite operator. The matrix $\mathcal{L}$ can be decomposed into pairs of eigenvalues $\lambda_l \geq 0$ and corresponding eigenvectors χ_l where $l = 0, 1, \cdots, N - 1$. The orthonormal bases χ can be used as analogues of Fourier bases in the Euclidean space to define the graph Fourier transform of a function $f(n)$ defined on the vertices n as

$$\hat{f}(l) = \sum_{n=1}^{N} \chi_l^*(n)f(n) \quad \text{and} \quad f(n) = \sum_{l=0}^{N-1} \hat{f}(l)\chi_l(n) \tag{3}$$

where the forward transform yields the graph Fourier coefficient $\hat{f}(l)$ and the inverse transform reconstructs the original function $f(n)$. If the signal $f(n)$ lies in the spectrum of the first k number of χ_l in the dual space, we say that $f(n)$ is k band-limited. Just like in the conventional Fourier transform, this graph Fourier transform offers a mechanism to transform a signal on graph vertices back and forth between the original and the frequency domain.

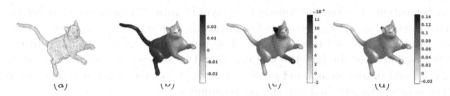

Fig. 1. Examples of bases functions on a graph. (a) Cat shaped graph, (b) A graph Fourier basis χ_2, (c) Graph wavelet bases ψ_1 at two different locations (ear and paw), (d) Graph wavelet basis ψ_4 as in (c). Notice that wavelet bases in (c) and (d) are localized while χ_2 is spread all over the mesh.

Using the graph Fourier transform, a mother wavelet ψ is implemented by first defining a kernel function $h()$ and then localizing it by a Dirac delta function δ_n in the original graph through the inverse graph Fourier transform. Since $\langle \delta_n, \chi_l \rangle = \chi_l^*(n)$, the mother wavelet $\psi_{s,n}$ at vertex n at scale s is defined as

$$\psi_{s,n}(m) = \sum_{l=0}^{N-1} h(s\lambda_l)\chi_l^*(n)\chi_l(m). \tag{4}$$

Here, using the scaling property of Fourier transform [36], the scale s can be defined as a parameter in the kernel function $h()$ independent from the bases χ. Representative examples of a graph Fourier basis and graph wavelet bases are shown in Fig. 1. A cat shaped graph is given in Fig. 1(a), and one of its graph Fourier basis χ_2 is shown in (b). Also, graph wavelets at two different scales (i.e., dilation) at two different locations (ear and paw) are shown in Fig. 1(c) and (d). Notice that χ in Fig. 1(b) is diffused all over the graph, while the wavelet bases in (c) and (d) are localized with finite support.

Once the bases ψ are defined, the wavelet transform of a function f on graph vertices at scale s follows the classical definition of the wavelet transform:

$$\mathcal{W}_f(s,n) = \langle f, \psi_{s,n} \rangle = \sum_{l=0}^{N-1} h(s\lambda_l)\hat{f}(l)\chi_l(n) \tag{5}$$

resulting in wavelet coefficients $\mathcal{W}_f(s,n)$ at scale s and location n. This transform offers a multi-resolution view of signals defined on graph vertices by multi-resolution filtering. Our framework, to be described shortly, will utilize the definition of the mother wavelet in (4) for data sampling strategy on graphs as well as the graph Fourier transform for signal recovery.

3   Adaptive Sampling and Signal Recovery on Graphs

Suppose there exists a band-limited signal (of p channels/features) defined on graph vertices, and we have limited access to the observation on only a few of the vertices in the graph. Our goal is to estimate the entire signal using only the partial observations. Since the signal is band-limited, we do not need to sample every location in the native domain (i.e., Nyquist rate). Unfortunately, we do not have powerful sampling theorems for graphs. In this regime, in order to recover the original signal, we need an efficient sampling strategy for the data. In the following, we describe how the vertices should be selected for accurate recovery of the band-limited signal and propose a novel decoder working in a dual space that is more efficient than alternative techniques.

3.1   Graph Adaptive Sampling Strategy

In order to derive a random sampling of the data measurement on a graph (i.e., signal measurement on vertices), we first need to assign a probability distribution p on the graph nodes. This probability tells us which vertices are more likely to be sampled for measurements, and needs to satisfy the definition of a probability distribution as $\sum_{n=1}^{N} \mathsf{p}(n) = 1$ where $\mathsf{p} > 0$. The construction of p is based on how the energy spreads over the graph vertices, given the graph structure. It means that it is easier to reconstruct a given signal with limited number of bases at some vertices than other vertices, and prioritizing those vertices for sampling will yield better estimation of the original signal.

In order to define the probability distribution p over the vertices, we make use of the eigenvalues and eigenvectors from spectral graph theory to describe the energy propagation on the graph. In [30], the authors show how well a δ_n can be reconstructed at a vertex n with k number of eigenvectors and normalize them to construct a probability distribution as

$$\mathsf{p}(n) = \frac{1}{k} ||V_k^T \delta_n||_2^2 = \frac{1}{k} \sum_{l=0}^{k-1} \chi_l(n)^2 \tag{6}$$

where V_k is a matrix with column vectors as $V_k = [\chi_0 \cdots \chi_{k-1}]$. Their solution puts the same weight on each eigenvector to compute the distribution, assuming that the signal is uniformly distributed in the k-band (i.e., the spectrum of the first k eigenvectors). Such a strategy uses the graph Fourier bases to reconstruct a delta function, which typically is not desirable in many applications since Fourier bases suffers from ringing artifacts. Moreover, in many cases, the signal may be localized even within the k-band, and it necessitates a scaling (i.e., filtering) of the signal at multiple scales in the frequency domain.

Interestingly, it turns out that the definition of p above can be viewed entirely via a non-Euclidean wavelet expansion described in Sect. 2. Recall that a mother wavelet $\psi_{s,n}$ is implemented by localizing a wavelet operation at scale s as in (4). It constructs a mother wavelet at scale s localized at n as a unit energy propagating from n to neighboring vertices as a diminishing wave function. When we look at $\psi_{s,n}(n)$, the self-effect of a mother wavelet at vertex n is written as

$$\psi_n(s,n) = \sum_{l=0}^{N-1} h(s\lambda_l)\chi_l(n)^2. \tag{7}$$

At the high level, (7) tells us how much of the unit energy is maintained at n itself at scale s. Notice that (7) is a kernelized version of (6) using a kernel function $h()$. Depending on the design of the kernel function $h()$, we may interpret it as robust graph-based signatures such as heat-kernel signature (HKS) [37], wave kernel signature (WKS) [38], global point signature (GPS) [39] and wavelet kernel descriptor (WKD) [40], which were introduced in computer vision literature for detecting interest points on graphs and mesh segmentation.

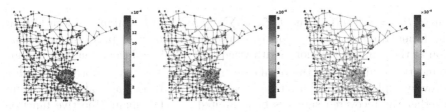

Fig. 2. Sampling probability distribution p_s in different scales derived from "Meyer" wavelet on Minnesota graph. Left: at scale $s = 1$, Middle: at scale $s = 2$, Right: at scale $s = 3$.

Our idea is to make use of the wavelet expansion to define a probability distribution at scale s as

$$p_s(n) = \frac{1}{Z_s}\psi_n(s,n) = \frac{1}{Z_s}\sum_{l=0}^{N-1} h(s\lambda_l)\chi_l(n)^2 \tag{8}$$

where $Z_s = \sum_{n=1}^{N}\psi_n(s,n)$. Then p_s is used as a sampling probability distribution which drives how we adaptively query the measurements at the unobserved vertices. Depending on application purposes, $h()$ can be designed as any known filters for wavelets such as Morlet, Meyer, difference of Gaussians (DOG) and so on. Examples of p_s using Meyer wavelet are shown in Fig. 2.

Our formulation in (8) is especially useful when we know the distribution of λ prior to the analysis by imposing higher weights on the band where signal is concentrated. We also work with only k eigenvectors when a full diagonalization of $\mathcal{L}$ is expensive. We will see that this observation is important in the next Section, where we utilize a low dimensional space spanned by the k eigenvectors for an efficient solver, while other methods require the full eigenspectrum.

3.2 Recovery of a Band-Limited Signal in a Dual Space

Consider a setting where we observe only a partial signal $y \in \mathbb{R}^{m \times p}$ of a full signal $f \in \mathbb{R}^{N \times p}$ where $m \ll N$, and our goal is to recover the original signal f given y. Suppose that our budget allows querying m vertices (to acquire measurements) in the setting phase. Let the locations where we observe the signal be denoted as $\Omega = \{\omega_1, \cdots, \omega_m\}$ yielding $y(i) = f(\omega_i)$, $\forall i \in \{1, 2, \cdots, m\}$. Now the question is how Ω should be selected for optimal (or high fidelity) recovery of f. Our framework uses the strategy described in Sect. 3.1 to sample data according to a sampling probability. Based on the m samples (observations), we can build a projection operator $M_{m \times N}$ (i.e., a sampling matrix) yielding $Mf = y$ as

$$M_{i,j} = \begin{cases} 1 & \text{if} \quad j = \omega_i \\ 0 & \text{o.w.} \end{cases} \tag{9}$$

Using the ideas described above, a typical decoder would solve for an estimation g of the original signal f using a convex problem as

$$g^* = \arg \min_{g \in \mathbb{R}^n} ||\mathcal{P}_\Omega^{-\frac{1}{2}}(Mg - y)||_2^2 + \gamma g^T h(\mathcal{L})g \tag{10}$$

where $\mathcal{P}_\Omega = \text{diag}(\mathsf{p}(\Omega))$ and $h(\mathcal{L}) = \sum_{l=0}^{N-1} h(\lambda_l)\chi_l\chi_l^T$. Taking a close look at the formulation above, it prioritizes minimizing the error between an estimation at the sampled locations (with weights of $\frac{1}{\sqrt{\mathsf{p}_\Omega}}$), and the remaining missing elements are filled in by the regularizer representing graph smoothness. Such a recovery explained in [30] has three weaknesses. (1) It does not take into account whether the recovered signal is band-limited. (2) The main objective function (i.e., the first term) in (10) suggests that it does not matter whether the estimated elements in the unsampled locations are correct. (3) Finally, the analytic solution to the above problem is not easily obtainable without the regularizer or when the regularizer is not full rank. This becomes computationally problematic in real cases when the given graph is large, since the filtering operation in (10) requires a full eigendecomposition of the graph Laplacian $\mathcal{L}$.

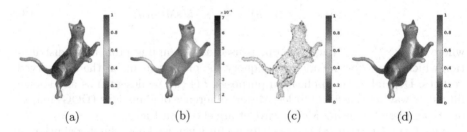

(a)   (b)   (c)   (d)

Fig. 3. A toy example of our framework on a cat mesh ($N = 3400$). (a) Band-limited random signal in $[0, 1]$ with noise, (b) Sampling probability p_1 derived from (8), (c) Sampled signal at $m = 340$ locations out of 3400, (d) Recovered signal using our method with only $k = 50$.

To deal with the problems above, we propose to encode the band-limited nature of the recovered signal as a constraint. Our framework solves for a solution to (10) entirely in a dual space by projecting the problem to a low dimensional space where we search for a solution of size $k \ll N$.

Let $\hat{g}(l) = \sum_{n=1}^{N} g(n)\chi_l(n)$ be the graph Fourier transform of a function g and $\hat{g}_k$ be the first k coefficients, then reformulating the model in (10) using $g = V_k\hat{g}_k$ (assuming that g is k-band limited) yields

$$\hat{g}_k^* = \arg\min_{\hat{g}_k \in \mathbb{R}^k} ||\mathcal{P}_\Omega^{-\frac{1}{2}}(MV_k\hat{g}_k - y)||_2^2 + \gamma(V_k\hat{g}_k)^T h(\mathcal{L})V_k\hat{g}_k. \tag{11}$$

An analytic solution to this problem can be achieved by taking the derivative of (11) and setting it to 0. The optimal solution $\hat{g}_k^*$ must satisfy the condition

$$(V_k^T M^T \mathcal{P}_\Omega^{-1} MV_k + \gamma V_k^T h(\mathcal{L})V_k)\hat{g}_k^* = V_k^T M^T \mathcal{P}_\Omega^{-1} y \tag{12}$$

which reduces to

$$(V_k^T M^T \mathcal{P}_\Omega^{-1} MV_k + \gamma h(\Lambda_k))\hat{g}_k^* = V_k^T M^T \mathcal{P}_\Omega^{-1} y \tag{13}$$

where Λ_k is a $k \times k$ diagonal matrix where the diagonals are the first k eigenvalues of $\mathcal{L}$. Using the optimal $\hat{g}_k^*$, we can easily recover a low-rank estimation $g^* = V_k\hat{g}_k^*$ that reconstructs f. Notice that we only need to find a solution of a much smaller dimension which is significantly more efficient. Moreover, the filtering operation $h()$ in the regularizer in (12) becomes much simpler, and concurrently the solution natively maintains the k-band limited property of the original signal.

A toy example demonstrating this idea is shown in Fig. 3. Given a cat mesh with $N = 3400$ vertices, we first define a random signal $f \in [0, 1]$ that is band-limited in the spectrum of $\mathcal{L}$ with Gaussian noise of $N(0, 0.1)$. We take p_1 for the sampling distribution and sample $m = 340$ (10 % of the total) vertices without replacement. Our estimation g using only $k = 50$ bases is shown in Fig. 3(d), where the error between the true f and g is extremely small despite using such little data to begin with. We also can see that our method is robust to noise.

4   Experiment Design in Neuroimaging

In this section, we present proof of principle experimental results on two different neuroimaging studies: **(1)** the Human Connectome Project (HCP) dataset and **(2)** Wisconsin Registry for Alzheimer's Prevention (WRAP) dataset. In both studies, we demonstrate the performance of our method in estimating expensive neuroimage-derived measurements at regions of interests (ROI) in the brain using **(1)** a set of p' less expensive measures of all p measures available to the full cohort $\mathcal{S}$ of N subjects and **(2)** a set of $(p - p')$ expensive measures available to a small cohort subset $\mathcal{S}'$ which includes m subjects. Given these datasets, the goal of these experiments is to see if we can get accurate estimates of the $(p - p')$ expensive measures of the *full cohort* $\mathcal{S}$ of N subjects in a way that statistical power for the follow-up analysis is not greatly compromised.

4.1 Experimental Setup

We compare the performance of our method with two other state-of-the-art methods, (1) Collaborative filtering by Rao et al. [29] and (2) Random sampling of band-limited signals by Puy et al. [30]. For all three methods: (a) We derived adjacency matrices $\mathcal{A}$ using data from the full set $\mathcal{S}$ of N samples and p' economical measures (i.e., more widely available and/or less expensive modalities) and the radial basis function $\exp(-||x - y||^2/\sigma^2)$. We then constructed normalized graph Laplacians $\mathcal{L} = \mathcal{D}^{-1/2}(\mathcal{D} - \mathcal{A})\mathcal{D}^{-1/2}$ used in our framework. (b) We set $h(\lambda_l) = \lambda_l^4$ for $h(\mathcal{L})$ for the filtering operation in the regularizer and set $\gamma = 0.01$ in (11). (c) We show estimation results of the $(p - p')$ expensive measures using $R \in \{20, 40, 60\}\%$ of total N samples for both studies and assess the ℓ_2-norm error of the difference between the estimated and observed measures. Because of the stochastic nature of the sampling step, we ran the estimation 100 times and use the average of the corresponding errors for comparisons. In addition, we also compare the predicted values of the $(p - p')$ neuroimaging measures at each ROI (averaged across subjects) against true values and the estimates of the other two baseline methods. For example, given a cohort of $N = 100$ subjects, suppose we have full data for $p' = 10$ low-cost measurements. Then, the goal is to acquire the $p - p' = 5$ measurements on only $m = 20$ subjects (i.e., 20 % of the cohort) and estimate the $(p - p')$ measurements on the remaining $N - m$ subjects.

4.2 Prediction on the Human Connectome Project

Dataset. The diffusion weighted MR images (DW-MRI) from HCP ([42]) were acquired on custom built hardware using advanced pulse sequences [43] and for a *lengthy* scan time ($\sim$1 h). It allows estimating microstructural properties of the brain, accurate reconstruction of the white matter pathways ([44]) (e.g., see Fig. 4) which form a crucial component in mapping the structural connectome of the human brain [45–48]. Typically, such an acquisition of DW-MRI is not feasible in many research sites due to limitations of hardware and software. On the other hand, the set of non-imaging measurements are cheaper and easier to acquire. Hence the ability to predict such high quality diffusion metrics (e.g. fractional anisotropy (FA)) from only a small sample of the DW-MRI scans and the non-imaging measurements has value. HCP provides several categories of non-imaging covariates for the subjects [49] covering factors spanning several different categories. (The full list of covariates is given in the appendix.) We demonstrate the performance of our model on the task of FA prediction in 17 widely studied fiber bundles (shown in Fig. 4) [41,50] using 27 variables related to cognition, demographics, education and so on.

Results. Given the full cohort $\mathcal{S}$ of $N = 487$ subjects from the HCP dataset with the selected $p' = 27$ low-cost covariates, we recovered high-cost FA measures in $p - p' = 17$ ROIs (i.e. pathways) using p' covariates and the FA values from $m \ll N$ participants. The p' measures were used to construct $\mathcal{L}$ with $\sigma = 5$ and $k = 100$ for generating the sampling distribution p for our framework.

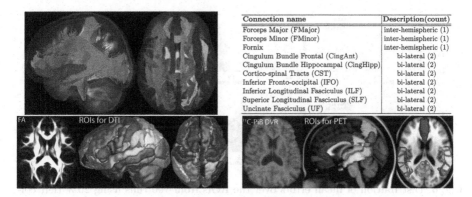

Connection name	Description(count)
Forceps Major (FMajor)	inter-hemispheric (1)
Forceps Minor (FMinor)	inter-hemispheric (1)
Fornix	inter-hemispheric (1)
Cingulum Bundle Frontal (CingAnt)	bi-lateral (2)
Cingulum Bundle Hippocampal (CingHipp)	bi-lateral (2)
Cortico-spinal Tracts (CST)	bi-lateral (2)
Inferior Fronto-occipital (IFO)	bi-lateral (2)
Inferior Longitudinal Fasciculus (ILF)	bi-lateral (2)
Superior Longitudinal Fasciculus (SLF)	bi-lateral (2)
Uncinate Fasciculus (UF)	bi-lateral (2)

Fig. 4. Top: The 17 major white matter pathways analyzed in the HCP study [41], Bottom: ROIs and measures analyzed in the WRAP study (Left: A sample FA map and the 162 gray matter ROIs for DTI, Right: Sample ^{11}C PiB DVR map and the 16 gray matter ROIs).

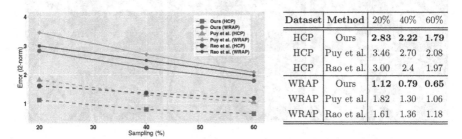

Dataset	Method	20%	40%	60%
HCP	Ours	**2.83**	**2.22**	**1.79**
HCP	Puy et al.	3.46	2.70	2.08
HCP	Rao et al.	3.00	2.4	1.97
WRAP	Ours	**1.12**	**0.79**	**0.65**
WRAP	Puy et al.	1.82	1.30	1.06
WRAP	Rao et al.	1.61	1.36	1.18

Fig. 5. Sampling ratio versus error plot (left) on the HCP dataset (dashed lines) and the WRAP dataset (straight lines). The corresponding values are in the table on the right. (Color figure online)

We analyzed three cases by sampling 20%, 40%, 60% of the total population according to p for m observations to predict FA on N subjects.

Figure 5 (dashed lines) summarizes the overall estimation errors using $R = \{20, 40, 60\}\%$ samples of the total population. For all three methods, the errors decreased with an increase in sample size, and our method (red) consistently outperformed the other two methods (blue and green). When we look at the distribution of errors, shown in the top row of Fig. 6, the center of the error distribution using our framework (red) is far lower than the other methods (blue and green). Anatomical specificity of the estimation measures (using 40% samples) is illustrated on the top panel of Fig. 7 where the location of spheres represents the position of the ROIs and their sizes and colors correspond to the mean errors. As seen in Fig. 7, our method (top-left) clearly has smaller and blue spheres compared to the other methods (middle and right). The quantitative error for individual ROIs used for the spheres are provided in left table of Table 1, and

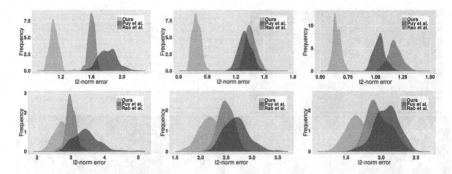

Fig. 6. Distribution of mean errors over the ROIs from 100 runs using 20 % (left column), 40 % (middle column) and 60 % (right column) samples on the HCP (top row) and the WRAP dataset (bottom row). Ours (red) show the lower errors than Puy et al. (green) and Rao et al. (blue). (Color figure online)

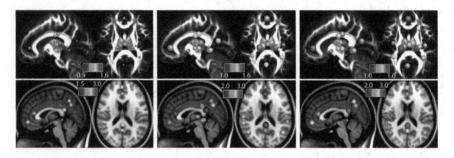

Fig. 7. Spherical representations of the prediction errors (ℓ_2-norm) in the HCP study (top) and in the WRAP study (bottom). Left: errors using Ours, Middle: errors using Puy et al., Right: errors using Rao et al. The spheres are centered at the center-of-mass of the specific bundle/regional volumes, and the radius of the spheres are proportional to the prediction error. (Color figure online)

the predicted FA for all ROIs (averaged across subjects) are presented in Fig. 8. For all 17 FA measures, with 40 % sampling, we see that our results (blue) are closest to the ground truth (red) while other methods under/over estimate. (Additional results shown in supplement.) When the ℓ_2−norm error is small, we expect results from downstream statistical analysis (e.g., p-values) will be accurate since the distributions of measurements are closer to the true sample distribution.

4.3 Prediction on a Preclinical Alzheimer's Disease Project

Dataset. Alzheimer's disease (AD) is known as a disconnection syndrome [51,52] because connectivity disruption can impede functional communication between brain regions, resulting in reduced cognitive performance [53,54]. Currently, positron emission tomography (PET) using radio-chemicals such as [11]C

Pittsburgh compound B (PiB) is important in mapping functional AD pathology. Distribution volume ratios (DVR) of PiB in the brain offer a good measure of the plaque pathology which is considered specific to AD. Unfortunately these PET scans are costly and involve lengthy procedures. WRAP dataset consists of participants in preclinical stages of AD [54,55] and contains 140 samples with both *low-cost* FA measures and *high-cost* PiB DVR (examples shown in Fig. 4). Utilizing the FA values over the entire set of subjects and a partial observation of the PiB measures from a fraction of the population, we investigate the performance of our model for the recovery of PiB measures.

Remark. From a neuroimaging perspective, predicting PiB measures accurately enough for actual scientific analysis is problematic. Utilizing a modality (e.g., cerebrospinal fluid) will be more appropriate for predicting PiB measures, and such results are available on the project homepage. The results below demonstrate that such a prediction task yields results numerically feasible compared to baseline strategies although not directly deployable for neuroscientific studies.

Results. For this set of experiments, we selected $p' = 17$ pathways with most reliable FA measures to construct a graph with $N = 140$ vertices (i.e., subjects). Utilizing the graph and a partial set of PiB DVR measurements from $m \ll N$ participants (20 %, 40 % and 60 % of the total population), we predicted the expensive PiB DVR values on 16 ROIs over the whole subjects. To define $\mathcal{L}$ and p, we used $\sigma = 3$ and $k = 50$. As shown in Fig. 5 in straight lines, our estimation (red) yields the smallest error compared to [30] (green) and [29] (blue) for all three sampling cases. The bottom row in Fig. 6 shows that the centers of error distribution using our algorithm (red) have lower errors than those of other methods (green and blue). As seen in the bottom panel of Fig. 7, similar to the HCP results in Sect. 4.2, we observe smaller errors in every ROI, where the actual region-wise errors are given in the right table of Table 1. Figure 8 presents the predicted regional PiB DVR values against the ground truth where our prediction in blue are consistently closer to the ground truth in red. Additional results using 20 % and 60 % of the subjects are presented in the appendix.

Table 1. Region-wise mean ℓ_2-norm of 100 runs of HCP-FA (left) and PiB DVR (right) with 40% samples. Errors from our method are the lowest shown in bold.

HCP ROIs	Ours	Puy et al.	Rao et al.
FMajor	**1.15**	1.93	1.70
FMinor	**1.21**	1.99	1.75
Fornix	**1.20**	1.84	1.65
LCingAnt	**0.95**	1.49	1.33
LcingHipp	**1.17**	1.87	1.65
LCST	**1.25**	2.06	1.82
LIFO	**1.14**	1.87	1.65
LILF	**1.16**	1.90	1.68
LSLF	**1.08**	1.77	1.56
LUnc	**0.99**	1.61	1.42
RCingAnt	**0.93**	1.48	1.32
RcingHipp	**1.20**	1.92	1.71
RCST	**1.25**	2.07	1.83
RIFO	**1.11**	1.82	1.61
RIFL	**1.12**	1.83	1.62
RSLF	**1.04**	1.69	1.50
RUnc	**1.05**	1.70	1.50

PiB ROIs	Ours	Puy et al.	Rao et al.
Angular_L	**2.89**	3.42	2.98
Angular_R	**2.73**	3.20	2.82
Cingulum_Ant_L	**3.19**	3.73	3.30
Cingulum_Ant_R	**3.18**	3.78	3.32
Cingulum_Post_L	**3.29**	4.10	3.49
Cingulum_Post_R	**3.20**	4.03	3.43
Frontal_Med_Orb_L	**2.90**	3.44	3.05
Frontal_Med_Orb_R	**3.08**	3.66	3.24
Precuneus_L	**2.88**	3.45	3.03
Precuneus_R	**3.03**	3.61	3.15
SupraMarginal_L	**2.43**	3.09	2.67
SupraMarginal_R	**2.51**	3.13	2.70
Temporal_Mid_L	**2.47**	3.13	2.68
Temporal_Mid_R	**2.59**	3.22	2.78
Temporal_Sup_L	**2.42**	3.14	2.68
Temporal_Sup_R	**2.52**	3.21	2.75

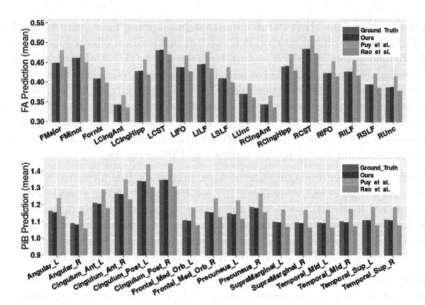

Fig. 8. Average estimations of the HCP-FA in the fiber bundle (top) and the WRAP PiB DVRs (bottom) using 40 % samples. For each measurement, the bars from the left to right are the measurements of the ground truth, ours, Puy et al. and Rao et al. Ours most closely estimate the actual ground truth values of all the measurements. (Color figure online)

5   Conclusion

In this paper, we presented an adaptive sampling scheme for signals defined on a graph. Using a dual space of these measurements obtained via a non-Euclidean wavelet transform, we show how signals can be recovered with high fidelity based on a stratified set of partial observations on the nodes of a graph. We demonstrated the application of this core technical development on accurately estimating diffusion imaging and PET imaging measures from two independent neuroimaging studies, so that one can perform standard analysis just as if the measurements were acquired directly. We presented experimental results demonstrating that our framework can provide accurate recovery using observations from only a small fraction of the full samples. We believe that this ability to estimate unobserved data based on a partial set of measurements can have impact in numerous computer vision and machine learning applications where acquisitions of large datasets often involve varying degrees of stratified human interaction. Many real experiments involve entities that have intrinsic relationships best captured as a graph. Mechanisms to exploit the properties of these graphs using similar formulations as those presented in this work may have important practical and immediate ramifications for many experimental design considerations in numerous scientific domains.

References

1. Blum, A.L., Langley, P.: Selection of relevant features and examples in machine learning. Artif. Intell. **97**(1), 245–271 (1997)
2. Biswas, A., Parikh, D.: Simultaneous active learning of classifiers & attributes via relative feedback. In: CVPR, pp. 644–651 (2013)
3. Jayaraman, D., Grauman, K.: Zero-shot recognition with unreliable attributes. In: NIPS, pp. 3464–3472 (2014)
4. Lughofer, E.: Hybrid active learning for reducing the annotation effort of operators in classification systems. Pattern Recognit. **45**(2), 884–896 (2012)
5. Hancock, C., Bernal, B., Medina, C., et al.: Cost analysis of diffusion tensor imaging and MR tractography of the brain. Open J. Radiol. 2014 (2014)
6. Saif, M.W., Tzannou, I., Makrilia, N., et al.: Role and cost effectiveness of PET/CT in management of patients with cancer. Yale J. Biol. Med. **83**(2), 53–65 (2010)
7. Prasad, A., Jegelka, S., Batra, D.: Submodular meets structured: finding diverse subsets in exponentially-large structured item sets. In: NIPS, pp. 2645–2653 (2014)
8. Deng, J., Dong, W., Socher, R., et al.: Imagenet: a large-scale hierarchical image database. In: CVPR, pp. 248–255 (2009)
9. Vijayanarasimhan, S., Grauman, K.: Large-scale live active learning: training object detectors with crawled data and crowds. IJCV **108**(1–2), 97–114 (2014)
10. Deng, J., Russakovsky, O., Krause, J., et al.: Scalable multi-label annotation. In: SIGCHI, pp. 3099–3102. ACM (2014)
11. Bragg, J., Weld, D.S., et al.: Crowdsourcing multi-label classification for taxonomy creation. In: AAAI (2013)
12. Read, J., Bifet, A., Holmes, G., et al.: Scalable and efficient multi-label classification for evolving data streams. Mach. Learn. **88**(1–2), 243–272 (2012)
13. Settles, B.: Active learning literature survey. University of Wisconsin, Madison vol. 52(55–66), p. 11 (2010)
14. Dasgupta, S.: Analysis of a greedy active learning strategy. In: NIPS, pp. 337–344 (2004)
15. Beygelzimer, A., Dasgupta, S., Langford, J.: Importance weighted active learning. In: ICML, pp. 49–56. ACM (2009)
16. Dasgupta, S., Hsu, D.: Hierarchical sampling for active learning. In: ICML, pp. 208–215. ACM (2008)
17. Winer, B.J., Brown, D.R., Michels, K.M.: Statistical Principles in Experimental Design. McGraw-Hill, New York (1971)
18. Lentner, M.: Generalized least-squares estimation of a subvector of parameters in randomized fractional factorial experiments. Ann. Math. Stat. **40**, 1344–1352 (1969)
19. Myers, J.L.: Fundamentals of Experimental Design. Allyn & Bacon, Boston (1972)
20. Mitchell, T.J.: An algorithm for the construction of D-optimal experimental designs. Technometrics **16**(2), 203–210 (1974)
21. De Aguiar, P.F., Bourguignon, B., Khots, M., et al.: D-optimal designs. Chemometr. Intell. Lab. Syst. **30**(2), 199–210 (1995)
22. Park, J.S.: Optimal Latin-hypercube designs for computer experiments. J. Stat. Plann. Infer. **39**(1), 95–111 (1994)
23. Su, X., Khoshgoftaar, T.M.: A survey of collaborative filtering techniques. Adv. Artif. Intell. **2009**, 4: 2 (2009)
24. Dabov, K., Foi, A., Katkovnik, V., et al.: Image denoising by sparse 3-D transform-domain collaborative filtering. Image Process. **16**(8), 2080–2095 (2007)

25. Yu, K., Zhu, S., Lafferty, J., et al.: Fast nonparametric matrix factorization for large-scale collaborative filtering. In: SIGIR, pp. 211–218. ACM (2009)
26. Srebro, N., Salakhutdinov, R.R.: Collaborative filtering in a non-uniform world: learning with the weighted trace norm. In: NIPS, pp. 2056–2064 (2010)
27. Juditsky, A., Nemirovski, A.: On verifiable sufficient conditions for sparse signal recovery via ℓ1 minimization. Math. Program. **127**(1), 57–88 (2011)
28. Krahmer, F., Ward, R.: Stable and robust sampling strategies for compressive imaging. Image Process. **23**(2), 612–622 (2014)
29. Rao, N., Yu, H.F., Ravikumar, P.K., et al.: Collaborative filtering with graph information: consistency and scalable methods. In: NIPS (2015)
30. Puy, G., Tremblay, N., Gribonval, R., et al.: Random sampling of bandlimited signals on graphs. Appl. Comput. Harmonic Anal. (2016)
31. Kumar, S., Mohri, M., Talwalkar, A.: Sampling methods for the Nyström method. JMLR **13**(1), 981–1006 (2012)
32. Krishnamurthy, A., Singh, A.: Low-rank matrix and tensor completion via adaptive sampling. In: NIPS, pp. 836–844 (2013)
33. Hammond, D., Vandergheynst, P., Gribonval, R.: Wavelets on graphs via spectral graph theory. Appl. Comput. Harmonic Anal. **30**(2), 129–150 (2011)
34. Mallat, S.: A Wavelet Tour of Signal Processing. Academic press, San Diego (1999)
35. Coifman, R., Maggioni, M.: Diffusion wavelets. Appl. Comput. Harmonic Anal. **21**(1), 53–94 (2006)
36. Haykin, S., Veen, B.V.: Signals and Systems. Wiley, New York (2005)
37. Bronstein, M.M., Kokkinos, I.: Scale-invariant heat kernel signatures for non-rigid shape recognition. In: CVPR, pp. 1704–1711. IEEE (2010)
38. Aubry, M., Schlickewei, U., Cremers, D.: The wave kernel signature: a quantum mechanical approach to shape analysis. In: ICCV Workshops, pp. 1626–1633. IEEE (2011)
39. Rustamov, R.M.: Laplace-Beltrami eigen functions for deformation invariant shape representation. In: Eurographics Symposium on Geometry Processing, Eurographics Association, pp. 225–233 (2007)
40. Kim, W.H., Chung, M.K., Singh, V.: Multi-resolution shape analysis via non-euclidean wavelets: applications to mesh segmentation and surface alignment problems. In: CVPR, pp. 2139–2146. IEEE (2013)
41. Varentsova, A., Zhang, S., Arfanakis, K.: Development of a high angular resolution diffusion imaging human brain template. Neuroimage **91**, 177–186 (2014)
42. Van Essen, D.C., Smith, S.M., Barch, D.M., et al.: The WU-Minn human connectome project: an overview. Neuroimage **80**, 62–79 (2013)
43. Setsompop, K., Cohen-Adad, J., Gagoski, B., et al.: Improving diffusion MRI using simultaneous multi-slice echo planar imaging. Neuroimage **63**(1), 569–580 (2012)
44. Jbabdi, S., Sotiropoulos, S.N., Haber, S.N., et al.: Measuring macroscopic brain connections in vivo. Nature Neurosci. **18**(11), 1546–1555 (2015)
45. Sporns, O., Tononi, G., Kötter, R.: The human connectome: a structural description of the human brain. PLoS Comput. Biol. **1**(4), e42 (2005)
46. Van Essen, D.C., Ugurbil, K.: The future of the human connectome. Neuroimage **62**(2), 1299–1310 (2012)
47. Toga, A.W., Clark, K.A., Thompson, P.M., et al.: Mapping the human connectome. Neurosurgery **71**(1), 1 (2012)
48. Sporns, O.: The human connectome: origins and challenges. Neuroimage **80**, 53–61 (2013)
49. Herrick, R., McKay, M., Olsen, T., et al.: Data dictionary services in XNAT and the human connectome project. Front. Neuroinform. **8**, 65 (2014)

50. Kim, W.H., Kim, H.J., Adluru, N., et al.: Latent variable graphical model selection using harmonic analysis: applications to the human connectome project (HCP). In: CVPR. IEEE (2016)
51. Brier, M.R., Thomas, J.B., Ances, B.M.: Network dysfunction in Alzheimer's disease: refining the disconnection hypothesis. Brain connectivity 4(5), 299–311 (2014)
52. Delbeuck, X., Van der Linden, M., Collette, F.: Alzheimer's disease as a disconnection syndrome? Neuropsychol. Rev. 13(2), 79–92 (2003)
53. Geschwind, N.: Disconnexion syndromes in animals and man. In: Geschwind, N. (ed.) Selected Papers on Language and the Brain. Boston Studies in the Philosophy of Science, vol. 16, pp. 105–236. Springer, Amsterdam (1974)
54. Kim, W.H., Adluru, N., Chung, M.K., et al.: Multi-resolution statistical analysis of brain connectivity graphs in preclinical Alzheimer's disease. Neuroimage 118, 103–117 (2015)
55. Kim, W.H., Singh, V., Chung, M.K., et al.: Multi-resolutional shape features via non-Euclidean wavelets: applications to statistical analysis of cortical thickness. Neuroimage 93, 107–123 (2014)

A Benchmark for Automatic Visual Classification of Clinical Skin Disease Images

Xiaoxiao Sun, Jufeng Yang$^{(\boxtimes)}$, Ming Sun, and Kai Wang

College of Computer and Control Engineering, Nankai University, Tianjin, China
yangjufeng@nankai.edu.cn

Abstract. Skin disease is one of the most common human illnesses. It pervades all cultures, occurs at all ages, and affects between 30 % and 70 % of individuals, with even higher rates in at-risk. However, diagnosis of skin diseases by observing is a very difficult job for both doctors and patients, where an intelligent system can be helpful. In this paper, we mainly introduce a benchmark dataset for clinical skin diseases to address this problem. To the best of our knowledge, this dataset is currently the largest for visual recognition of skin diseases. It contains 6,584 images from 198 classes, varying according to scale, color, shape and structure. We hope that this benchmark dataset will encourage further research on visual skin disease classification. Moreover, the recent successes of many computer vision related tasks are due to the adoption of Convolutional Neural Networks(CNNs), we also perform extensive analyses on this dataset using the state of the art methods including CNNs.

Keywords: Skin disease image · Computer aided diagnosis · Image classification · CNNs · Hand-crafted features

1 Introduction

Skin disease is one of the most common illnesses in human daily life. It pervades all cultures, occurs at all ages, and affects between 30 % and 70 % of individuals [1]. There are tens of millions of people affected by it every day. Skin disease is twofold, i.e. skin infection and skin neoplasm, in which thousands of skin conditions have been described [2]. Skin disease has a major adverse impact on quality of life and many are associated with significant psychosocial mobility. However, only a small proportion of people can recognize these diseases without access to a field guide. Moreover, there are many over-the-counter (OTC) drugs to treat the frequently-occurring skin diseases in daily life. In this case, correctly recognizing the skin diseases becomes very important for people who need to make a choice about these medicines. If people want to make a preliminary self diagnosis, it is undisputed that a visual recognition system will be useful for assisting them even if it is not perfect. For example, if an accurate skin disease classifier is developed, a user can submit a photo of recently skin condition to query a diagnosis. Surprisingly, there exists few research using computer vision techniques to recognize many common skin diseases based on ordinary photographical images.

© Springer International Publishing AG 2016
B. Leibe et al. (Eds.): ECCV 2016, Part VI, LNCS 9910, pp. 206–222, 2016.
DOI: 10.1007/978-3-319-46466-4_13

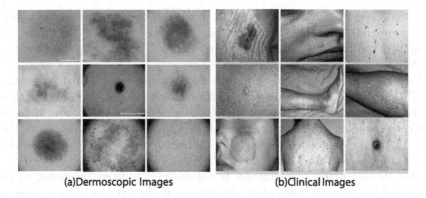

(a)Dermoscopic Images   (b)Clinical Images

Fig. 1. Examples of dermoscopic and clinical images. (a) Dermoscopic images are acquired through a digital dermatoscope, which have relatively low levels of noise and consistent background illumination. (b) Clinical images are collected via various sources, most of which are captured with digital cameras and cell phones

Despite there are some related applications, the problem of recognizing skin diseases has not been fully solved by the computer vision community. In contrast to object or scene classification, skin disease image has no distinctive spatial layout, as we can label a bird with its body and head or an outdoor scene with sky region and house. For example, it's difficult for us to find an accurate description of scattered red eczema. Besides, there are many challenges, including low contrast between lesion and surrounding skin, irregular and fuzzy borders, fragmentation or variegated coloring inside the lesion, etc., which make it hard to recognize skin diseases.

Most previous works on recognition of skin disease are restricted to dermoscopic images [3,4], which are acquired through a digital dermatoscope. A dermatoscope is a special device for dermatologists to use to look at skin lesions that acts as a filter and magnifier [5]. As a result, dermoscopic images have low level of noise and are always with unique lighting. We show some examples of dermoscopic images in Fig. 1(a). On the other hand, clinical skin disease images are collected via a variety of sources, most of which are acquired using digital cameras and cell phones. Examples are shown in Fig. 1(b). We have found some work based on clinical disease images [5,6]. However, all these work are built on small datasets which only contain very few species and are not publicly available. The absence of benchmark datasets is a barrier to a more dynamic development of this research area. As a consequence, in this paper, we introduce a new, publicly available dataset for real-world skin disease images recognition. This dataset contains 6,584 images of 198 fine-grained skin disease categories.

As is well known, image classification is one of the most fundamental problems of computer vision, and has been studied for many years. Large-scale annotated image datasets have been instrumental for driving progress in object recognition over the last decade. These datasets contain a wide variety of basic-level classes, such as different kinds of animals and inanimate objects. Significant progress has been made in the past few years in object classification as researchers compete on the ImageNet Large Scale Visual Recognition Challenge (ILSVRC).

Compared to generic object classification, fine-grained visual categorization [7–11] aims to classify categories which belong to the same basic-level class. In recent years, fine-grained recognition has been demonstrated in many domains with corresponding datasets, including birds [12,13], flowers [14,15], leaves [16], dogs [17,18], and cars [19]. A variety of methods have been developed for classifying fine-grained categories [7,11,20–23].

Skin disease image classification is naturally considered belonging to the problem of fine-grained visual object classification. However, in contrast to scene classification or object classification, it has own characteristics different from the existing fine-grained classification work, because it's a difficult problem that push the limits of the visual abilities for both human and computers. Clinically, the diagnosis of any particular skin condition is made by gathering pertinent information regarding the presenting skin lesion(s), including the location, symptoms, duration, arrangement (solitary, generalized, annular, linear), morphology (macules, papules, vesicles), and color (red, blue, brown, black, white, yellow) [24]. In addition, the diagnosis of many conditions often requires more complicated information.

In order to validate the usefulness of our proposed dataset and inspire the computer vision community to carry out more meaningful research in this field, we perform a lot of basic experiments employing both hand-crafted features and deep features to establish a baseline performance on the dataset. On the other hand, recently deep learning has enabled robust and accurate feature learning, which in turn produces the state-of-the-art performance on many computer vision related tasks. In this work, we want to find out whether or not applying CNNs to skin disease classification provides advantages over hand-crafted features.

Our contributions are summarized as follows. First, we collect a novel and large scale benchmark dataset for skin disease image recognition. Second, we evaluate the performance of skin disease classification using CNNs as well as hand-engineered features. Extensive experimental results show that using the existing CNN model does not outperform manually crafted visual features. On the other hand, we hope this can promote future research on skin disease classification with deep learning.

2   Related Work

Our work is closely related to image classification on both dermoscopic and clinical images, and convolutional neural networks.

2.1   Dermoscopic Images Recognition

Present works on skin disease image classification are twofold, that is, dermoscopic and clinical image recognition. First, we introduce the representative works on dermoscopic images.

Dermoscopic images have been mostly used in computer aided diagnosis, which is a technique of visualizing lesions by directing light onto the skin. Because dermoscopic images have bright illumination conditions, it is clear enough for recognition. Besides, the viewpoint is basically invariable and background clutter is very limited. All these characteristics make the processing of dermoscopic images easier, which further result that the computer vision studies based on dermoscopic images are much more than work based on clinical images.

Some work have focused on developing different components of dermoscopic image recognition, including segmentation [25], detection [26] and classification [3,27], etc. Gonzalez-Castro *et al.* [3] introduce a color texture descriptor and apply it to classify images of nevi into benign lesions and melanoma. Celebi *et al.* [27] present a methodological approach for the classification of dermoscopy images. The approach involves border detection, feature extraction, and SVM classification with model selection. Kasmi and Mokrani [28] introduce an algorithm that extracts the characteristics of ABCD (asymmetry, border irregularity, colour and dermoscopic structure) attributes to build a binary classifier, again distinguishing melanoma from benign nevus.

The popular datasets of dermoscopic images used in recent works are shown in Table 1. There is no doubt that these studies have developed the diagnosis of skin diseases. However, their applications are limited due to the specialized medical equipments and requirement for expert knowledge. Different from the mentioned datasets, in this paper, we build a large scale clinical image dataset to encourage further research which could be applied in real life scenes.

2.2   Clinical Image Recognition

Some efforts have been made to classify clinical skin disease images [35–37]. Concretely, Glaister *et al.* [5] propose a segmentation algorithm based on texture distinctiveness (TD) to locate skin lesions in photographs. They introduce a joint statistical TD metric and a texture-based region classification algorithm,

Table 1. Statistics of recent datasets of dermoscopic images. Also, the representative work employing these datasets are listed here.

Dataset	[29]	[27]	[30]	[31]	[32]	[33]	[34]	[25]	[28]
Classes#	2	2	6	2	3	2	2	2	2
Images#	527	596	320	1097	945	241	200	208	200
Year	2000	2007	2011	2012	2013	2015	2015	2015	2016
Available?	Y	N	Y	N	Y	N	Y	N	N

which captures the dissimilarity between learned representative texture distributions. Alcón *et al.* [38] describe an automatic system for inspection of pigmented skin lesions and discriminating between malignant an benign lesions. The system includes a dedicated image processing system for feature extraction and classification, and patient-related data decision support machinery for calculating a personal risk factor. It has been shown that their algorithm is capable of recreating controlled lighting conditions and correcting for uneven illumination.

Moreover, Razighi *et al.* [6,39,40] heavily rely on human-in-the-loop and high level knowledge in their work. They use human provided information with a random forest or bayesian framework. The aforementioned interaction information comes from questions designed in advance. For example, the answer to a binary question like: Is the object red? can be regarded as the presence of tag *Red*, that can be used as a visual feature to improve the final classification result. They include 10 questions and 37 possible binary answers/tags in their system.

Typically, the previous works focusing on clinical skin disease images are commonly built on a small size datasets. To the best of our knowledge, the largest dataset contains 2309 images from only 44 different diseases, and it is not publicly available to the community.

2.3   Convolutional Neural Networks

In recent years, Convolutional Neural Networks (CNNs) have achieved great empirical successes in many computer vision tasks, such as image classification [41], object detection [42], scene recognition [43], and fine-grained classification [23,44,45]. It is now possible to train a very deep network [46] on large collections of images with the help of the increasing computational power of GPU.

Skin diseases have the similar characteristics with objects in fine-grained classification, that is, lesion areas in skin disease images show large intra-class variation and small inter-class variation. Therefore, CNNs are also supposed to make sense in skin disease recognition. On the other hand, skin disease images are different from conventional fine-grained object images in some degrees. For example, some current works in fine-grained classification employ bounding box of objects of interest to help recognition, while it's more difficult label bounding box in skin disease images, or to distinguish lesions from background. Furthermore, objects always have specific shapes and parts, resulting a massive of part based methods to train fine-grained part models in CNNs. However, choosing parts of lesion is almost impossible when skin disease images are applied.

3   Our Dataset

Several datasets have been used for skin disease studies [6,37]. Concretely, Razeghi *et al.* [37] collect two subsets in their work, which contain 90 and 706 images from 3 and 7 different skin diseases, respectively. In another work of the same team [6], they acquire a new dataset containing 2,309 visual similar images

Table 2. Statistics of the existing clinical skin disease datasets. In [6,37], the authors add a question and answer bank into their datasets, which is used to provide human-computer interaction in the systems. Note that none of current datasets are publicly available. For comparison, we also show information of our work in the last two columns, which expand both the dataset size and the number of categories.

Dataset	$[37]$-1st	$[37]$-2nd	[6]	SD-128	SD-198
Classes#	3	7	44	128	198
Images#	90	706	2309	5619	6584
Year	2012	2012	2013	2016	2016
Available?	N	N	N	Y	Y

of skin conditions from 44 different diseases. The authors argue that the lesions are manually segmented using a bounding box in their dataset, and the dataset has a question and answer bank for help classification. Unfortunately, both of the mentioned datasets are not publicly available.

In this work, we present a new clinical skin disease dataset, namely SD-198. To the best of our knowledge, it is the largest available skin disease database, whether clinical or dermoscopic images are mentioned. The statistics of the existing skin disease datasets are shown in Table 2.

Our SD-198 dataset contains 198 different diseases from different types of eczema, acne and various cancerous conditions. There are 6,584 images in total. We also choose the classes with more than 20 image samples as a subset, namely SD-128. In general, overall classification can be improved when less categories and more samples are applied, which is verified in our experiments. Examples of images in our dataset can be found in Fig. 2.

3.1 Image Collection and Annotation

Collection. The images are downloaded from the DermQuest[1], which is an online medical resource for dermatologists and healthcare professionals with an interest in dermatology. It contains an extensive clinical images shared by the wide dermatology community. The images are submitted by patients or dermatologists.

The website contains 729 species of skin lesions in total, which include all kinds of conditions that affect the integumentary system, i.e., the organ system that encloses the body and includes skin, hair, nails, and related muscle and glands [47]. We execute a statistical analysis of these skin lesion categories, and remove the species that rarely appear in real life or that have less than 10 samples.

We initially have collected more than 10,000 clinical skin disease images. In order to keep balance of categories, we remove some samples from the subsets whose images are sufficient so as to each category has 60 images at most. Then,

---

[1] https://www.dermquest.com.

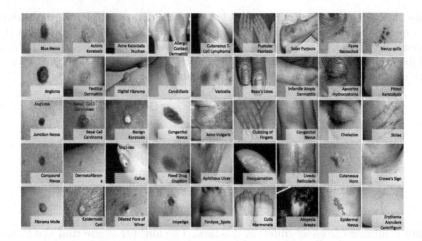

Fig. 2. Here we show some examples of our SD-198 dataset, each of which is selected from different classes. In another word, none of the images listed here have the same class label. However, it's difficult to distinguish these skin disease images, because some of them have the extremely same color and shape. For example, the five images in the first column belong to different categories, while finding the differences among these images are challenging. (Color figure online)

we further drop the duplicate images and low-quality images. Finally, we get a dataset containing 6,584 images from 198 different categories.

Annotation. The ground truth annotations of the images in our collected dataset are obtained from DermQuest, since each image has been recognized by experts and labeled with the name of its class. Because the clinical case notes and diagnosis quizzes on the website are reviewed by an international editorial board comprised of renowned dermatologists, the labels obtained for our dataset are considered reliable. Despite that, in order to ensure the label quality of our dataset, we have invited two professionals to review our dataset.

3.2 Properties of Dataset

Not only our dataset is larger than previous datasets, but also has superior performance. We will introduce the properties of the proposed dataset in this section.

Scale. This paper aims to provide a large-scale clinical skin disease benchmark dataset. To the best of our knowledge, its size is about 3 to 10 times as the reported scale of the previous datasets. It contains 198 categories which have covered all of the common skin diseases. We hope the dataset with 6,584 well-labeled clinical skin disease images can promote the vision research in this area.

Diversity. All images are from the real scene with variance in color, exposure, illumination and level of details. That is to say the images may be taken by any configuration of equipments or in a variety of environments. Therefore, hopefully the future works based on our benchmark dataset will be easier to be applied into practices. The mentioned diversities mainly include:

(1) Species Diversity: Skin lesion images in our dataset contain: eczema, psoriasis, acne vulgaris, pruritus, alopecia areata, decubitus ulcer, urticaria, scabies, impetigo, abscess, bacterial skin diseases, viral warts, molluscum, melanoma and non-melanoma skin cancer, which have covered most of the common skin diseases. Figure 3 shows the statistics of the number of images in each class.

We also show some images in Fig. 4. For example, in Fig. 4(a), the first row is angioma, and the second row contains four kinds of diseases. In the third row, images of acne vulgaris and guttate psoriasis are in green and yellow boxes, respectively. Figure 4(b) also contains three kinds of diseases. Due to space limitation, we do not show all classes. However, one can already find the species diversity of clinical skin disease images in these figures.

(2) Appearance Diversity: In real life, clinicians and dermatologists determine whether a lesion is a melanoma by a certain criteria, that is ABCD criteria (asymmetry, border irregularity, colour and diameter or differential structures). The criteria is proposed by Friedman *et al.* [48], which has been widely adopted through the previous works, especially in dermoscopic image recognition.

Compared to dermoscopic images, there are different meanings of ABCD in clinical skin disease images. We summarize ABCD's conventional meanings and refine them to apply to clinical images in our dataset. In Fig. 4(b), we show some examples of clinical images based on ABCD criteria. The images in the same row represent the A-asymmetry, B-border irregularity, and C-multiple colors,

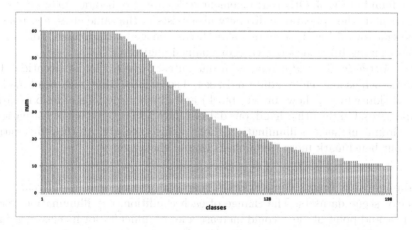

Fig. 3. Statistics of the numbers of images for each class in our SD-128 and SD-198 datasets. Note that each category of SD-128 contains more than 20 samples, while SD-198 has some categories whose samples are between 10 and 20.

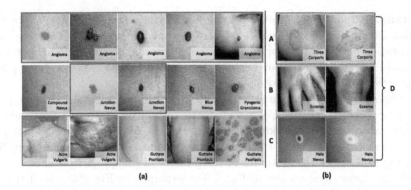

Fig. 4. Species diversity and appearance diversity of our proposed dataset. If I tell you that the images in the first row of (a) belong to the same class, do you think the images in the next row are from the same class? The answer is no. Moreover, the third row of (a) show that different shooting distance and illumination have a big influence on the appearance of skin diseases. In (b) we show some examples with the ABCD criteria. Note that these mentioned diversities, as well as attribute diversity, contribute to making automatic recognition of clinical skin disease image a challenging work. (Color figure online)

respectively. The D-diameter is difficult to be judged by images, but we can see from Fig. 4(b) that it varies greatly among different diseases.

Skin diseases in our dataset show that they have different appearances from an ABCD perspective, which includes arrangement (solitary, generalized, annular, and linear), color (red, blue, brown, black, white, and yellow), border (well defined, poorly defined), shape(circular, strip, and irregular). Most of these styles can be found in Fig. 4. Other arrangement styles are also included in our dataset. In particular, the appearance diversity also exists in the same class, e.g. images in the first row of Fig. 4(a) contain skin disease images with different colors and shapes, coming from the same category named angioma.

(3) Attribute Diversity: Images in our dataset cover a lot of situations for patients such as age (child, adult, old), sex, disease site (hand, feet, head, nails), color of skin(white, yellow, brown, black) and different periods of lesions(early, middle, late). On the other hand, our dataset have also covered a lot of situations for environment, such as illumination, shooting distance, etc. All these diversities make our benchmark more comprehensive and challenging.

Challenge and Lack. Our dataset is a special images dataset different from object or scene datasets. The change of each condition, e.g. illumination, focal distance, and point of view, could increase a lot of difficulty for its classification. For example, the images with yellow boxes in the third row of Fig. 4(a) are from the same category named guttate psoriasis. The images from left to right are with different illumination and shooting distance leading to big differences among them. Furthermore, pathological changes in different periods and different colors of skin of the patients all make a large intra-class variation. There are some diseases with low color contrast of foreground(lesion) and background(health skin), which are hard to recognize.

Of course, our dataset also has disadvantages. Details of dermatosis marks need stronger professional knowledge than other object and scene datasets. Considering the differences between clinical skin disease and fine-grained object images, e.g. birds and dogs, it's difficult for us to label part annotations in skin disease images. Besides, as Fig. 3 shows, our dataset shows imbalance among different categories. We try to collect the same number of samples, while some diseases rarely appear in real life.

4   Clinical Skin Disease Classification

In order to establish a baseline performance on our proposed dataset and evaluate the performance of different features, we design experiments for two aspects: (a) comparing the influence of different baseline features; (b) evaluating some existing methods whose aim is fine-grained classification. In all of the experiments, we randomly select half images from each class as the training set and the rest as testing set. We introduce our implementation details in the next paragraph. In addition, we present the color and texture features for classification and analyze their influences.

4.1   Hand-Crafted Features Based Classification

Implementation Details. We first investigate how conventional computer vision methods are used to recognize clinical skin disease images. We employ seven kinds of texture and color features and utilize LIBSVM, a popular library for support vector machine, to build some baseline algorithms. We use these algorithms to measure the classification accuracy on our dataset. Then, we evaluate our dataset using some existing work with their hand-tuned features and off-the-shelf frameworks. SIFT and Color Names features are extracted following the routine of [49]. HOG and LBP features are obtained by employing VLFeat [50].

Baseline Approaches. Two representative works [49,51] are included in this paper. Then, their performance on our proposed benchmark dataset are evaluated. While these methods are designed to classify fine-grained object or natural scene images, skin disease images are also sensitive to texture and color cues, which are employed in these tools.

In detail, Goering et al. [49] compute a global representation using the whole image. Feature types are the same as commonly used for fine-grained classification, i.e. bag-of-visual words with SIFT and Color Names, but with additional spatial pyramid pooling. Furthermore, they apply GrabCut segmentation to estimate the foreground. This algorithm performs iterative segmentation with a conditional Markov random field, where unary potentials are modeled with a Gaussian mixture model re-estimated in each iteration, and pairwise potentials

Table 3. Classification performance with different hand-engineered features on both of our datasets, i.e. SD-198 and SD-128. Each of the first seven methods is built with a popular off-the-shelf feature, using SVM as its classifier. On the other hand, the last two methods are designed for similar vision tasks, i.e. fine-grained object classification and natural scene classification, respectively.

Num	Features	Features dimension	Classifier	SD-198 %	SD-128 %
1	SIFT	21000	SVM	25.85	29.40
2	HOG	12400	SVM	12.78	14.17
3	LBP	23200	SVM	15.46	17.09
4	Color Histogram	768	SVM	4.19	5.59
5	Color Names(CN)	21000	SVM	20.20	20.32
6	Gist	512	SVM	16.49	17.52
7	Gabor	4000	SVM	10.14	11.37
Num	Methods	Features dimension	Methods or features	SD-198 %	SD-128 %
8	[49]	21000	SIFT+CN+SVM	52.19	53.29
9	[51]	4200	Spatial Pyramid	22.45	24.45

are added to favor strong image edges. Lazebnik *et al.* [51] have presented a holistic approach for image categorization based on a modification of pyramid match kernels. They repeatedly subdivide an image and compute histograms of image features over the resulting subregions, showing promising results on scene databases.

Results and Analysis. To establish a baseline performance on our dataset, we evaluate the features mentioned in Table 3. The experimental results show that texture features play a more important role than color features in this dataset. We find that the colors of foreground and background are extremely the same in some skin disease images. On the other hand, the lesions often present different textures and shapes, such as annular, linear, concave and convex shapes.

Furthermore, there are different skin disease categories sharing very similar shapes, and their color cures are slightly different, e.g. neurofibroma and apocrine hydrocystoma. Considering these cases, the off-the-shelf tool [49], performs best in this configuration, although it's designed for fine-grained object recognition. Note that, the influence of background clutter is significant in this method.

4.2 Deep Features Based Classification

Implementation Details. In our experiments, we extract deep convolutional features from a CNN model pre-trained on ImageNet. Due to the skin classes in our dataset, we change the original 1000-way fc8 classification layer to a new 198-way fc8 layer, whose weights are randomly initialized by a Gaussian function. We set fine-tuning learning rates as proposed by CaffeNet CNN, and initialize the global rate to a tenth of the initial ImageNet learning rate. In addition, during

Table 4. The average classification accuracy with different models of convolutional neural networks.ft indicates that the corresponding model is fine-tuned with our training samples

Method	SD-198[%]	SD-128[%]
CaffeNet	42.31	42.83
CaffeNe+ft	46.69	47.38
VGG	37.91	39.27
VGG+ft	50.27	52.15

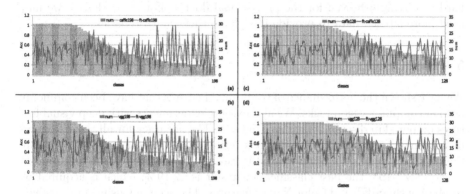

Fig. 5. Accuracy for each class with different models. (a) The performance of CaffeNet on SDC-198. (b) The performance of VGGNet on SDC-198. (c) The performance of CaffeNet on SDC-128. (d) The performance of VGGNet on SDC-128. For each figure, the secondary Y-axis(right) represents the number of testing image.

the training process, we drop the learning rate by a factor of 10. Furthermore, we independently fine-tune the ImageNet pre-trained CNN for classification on ground truth crops of each region warped to the 227×227 network input size. At test time, we extract features from the test images using the network fine-tuned on the training set of our skin disease images. Meanwhile, we also fine-tune a very deep CNN architecture, i.e. VGGNet [52] with 16 layers, to extract deep features.

Results and Analysis. We fine-tune the pre-trained CNN model, and compare it with the original CaffeNet by showing the results of using the SVM as a classifier. We extract deep features from the last layer of CaffeNet and obtain a 4096 dimensional feature representation. For both of our skin disease datasets, i.e. SD198 and SD-128, half images of each class are used for fine-tuning the model. From Table 4, we can draw a conclusion that the fine-tuned VGGNet gets significant promotion, which is mainly benefited from our lager-scale well-labeled dataset.

To further analyze their performance, we also calculate the accuracy for each class of the CNN models. Figure 5(a, b) show the classification results on SD-198, and Fig. 5(c, d) show the classification results on SD-128. It's shown that the accuracies have bigger fluctuation when the number of images of each class decreases. For these classes, the skin diseases have a relatively low morbidity in our daily life. Furthermore, we observe these classes, including stomatitis, histiocytosis-X, lymphangioma-circumscriptum, pomade-acne, etc., and find they share a common point that the corresponding images usual carry strong landmarks of lesions. For example, the region of skin disease is a saliency area. On the other hand, we find the classes has accuracy close to 0, which almost are hard to distinguish even for the professional doctor. For these classes, we may need more labeled data to provide in-sight to their characteristics.

5   Discussion

We have shown the performance of traditional features that have been commonly used in computer vision tasks. We also execute experiments with deep visual features on our skin disease benchmark dataset. The accuracy for all these features have been showed in Tables 3 and 4, respectively. In this section, we will compare the best performance of hand-crafted features with the deep visual features.

For SDC-198, the best classification result is 52.19 %, which is acquired by combining the SIFT and Color Names features. The accuracy using a pre-trained and fine-tuned VGGNet is 50.27 %. It is interesting to find that the performance

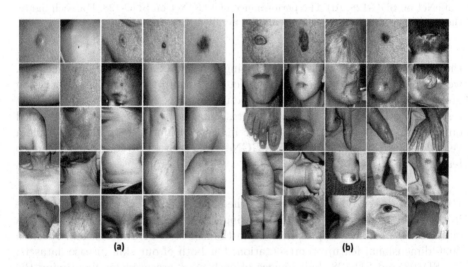

(a)   (b)

Fig. 6. Examples of classification results on our proposed benchmark dataset. (a) Images are correctly classified by [49] and wrongly classified by VGGNet. (b) Images are correctly classified by deep network and wrongly classified by [49] (Color figure online)

of hand-crafted features is better than deep visual features for the skin disease classification.

In order to investigate the reason, in Fig. 6(a), we show some representative images which have been correctly classified by [49] and wrongly classified by VGGNet. We also show the images in the opposite situation in Fig. 6(b). Useful observation can be draw from the presented images. First, images in (a) always have a cleaner background than the disease images in (b), and second, the appearance of lesions in (a) is much simpler than (b). Since [49] has applied a segmentation procedure with GrabCut to estimate the foreground, it's reasonable that this algorithm outperforms CNNs when both of them are applied to images in (a). For example, consider the images in the first row of both (a) and (b), these images are corresponding to skin diseases such as dermatofibroma, basal cell carcinoma, angioma, seborrheic keratosis and blue nevus etc. Compared to images in (a), the lesions in (b) are surrounded with more hair, which will weaken the segmentation employed in [49]. Moreover, CNNs have shown advantages in finding structure and semantic information. Images in (b) include more cues about the location of lesion, e.g. mouth, foot, eye, hand, etc., perform better with powerful VGGNet.

6 Conclusion

In this paper, we raise a challenging problem of automatic visual classification of clinical skin disease images. The absence of benchmark datasets is a barrier to a more dynamic development of this research area. We build a new and challenging clinical skin disease images dataset, including 6,584 real-world images from 198 categories. Each sample in our benchmark is well labeled. We intend to release the dataset to the community to promote the related research. Furthermore, we also evaluate the performance of different features to establish a baseline performance on our dataset.

Acknowledgements. This work was supported by the National Natural Science Foundation of China (No. 61301238, 61201424), China Scholarship Council (No. 2015 06205024) and the Natural Science Foundation of Tianjin, China (No.14ZCDZGX00831).

References

1. Hay, R.J., Johns, N.E., Williams, H.C., Bolliger, I.W., et al.: The global burden of skin disease in 2010: an analysis of the prevalence and impact of skin conditions. J. Invest. Dermatol. **134**(6), 1527–1534 (2014)
2. Lynch, P.J., Edwards, L.: Genital Dermatology. Churchill Livingstone, New York (1994)
3. Gonzalez-Castro, V., Debayle, J., Wazaefi, Y., Rahim, M., Gaudy-Marqueste, C., Grob, J.J., Fertil, B.: Automatic classification of skin lesions using color mathematical morphology-based texture descriptors. In: QCAV, p. 953409 (2015)

4. Badano, A., Revie, C., Casertano, A., Cheng, W.C., Green, P., Kimpe, T., Krupinski, E., Sisson, C., Skrøvseth, S., Treanor, D., et al.: Consistency and standardization of color in medical imaging: a consensus report. J. Digit. Imaging **28**(1), 41–52 (2015)
5. Glaister, J., Wong, A., Clausi, D., et al.: Segmentation of skin lesions from digital images using joint statistical texture distinctiveness. IEEE Trans. Biomed. Eng. **61**(4), 1220–1230 (2014)
6. Razeghi, O., Zhang, Q., Qiu, G.: Interactive skin condition recognition. In: ICME, pp. 1–6 (2013)
7. Yao, B., Khosla, A., Fei-Fei, L.: Combining randomization and discrimination for fine-grained image categorization. In: CVPR, pp. 1577–1584 (2011)
8. Wang, J., Yang, J., Yu, K., Lv, F., Huang, T., Gong, Y.: Locality-constrained linear coding for image classification. In: CVPR, pp. 3360–3367 (2010)
9. Branson, S., Wah, C., Schroff, F., Babenko, B., Welinder, P., Perona, P., Belongie, S.: Visual recognition with humans in the loop. In: Daniilidis, K., Maragos, P., Paragios, N. (eds.) ECCV 2010. LNCS, vol. 6314, pp. 438–451. Springer, Heidelberg (2010). doi:10.1007/978-3-642-15561-1_32
10. Farrell, R., Oza, O., Zhang, N., Morariu, V., Darrell, T., Davis, L.S., et al.: Birdlets: Subordinate categorization using volumetric primitives and pose-normalized appearance. In: ICCV, pp. 161–168 (2011)
11. Chai, Y., Lempitsky, V., Zisserman, A.: Symbiotic segmentation and part localization for fine-grained categorization. In: ICCV, pp. 321–328 (2013)
12. Welinder, P., Branson, S., Mita, T., Wah, C., Schroff, F., Belongie, S., Perona, P.: Caltech-UCSD birds 200 (2010)
13. Wah, C., Branson, S., Welinder, P., Perona, P., Belongie, S.: The caltech-UCSD birds-200-2011 dataset (2011)
14. Nilsback, M.E., Zisserman, A.: Automated flower classification over a large number of classes. In: ICVGIP, pp. 722–729 (2008)
15. Angelova, A., Zhu, S., Lin, Y.: Image segmentation for large-scale subcategory flower recognition. In: WACV, pp. 39–45 (2013)
16. Kumar, N., Belhumeur, P.N., Biswas, A., Jacobs, D.W., Kress, W.J., Lopez, I.C., Soares, J.V.: Leafsnap: a computer vision system for automatic plant species identification. In: Fitzgibbon, A., Lazebnik, S., Perona, P., Sato, Y., Schmid, C. (eds.) ECCV 2012, Part II. LNCS, vol. 7573, pp. 502–516. Springer, Heidelberg (2012)
17. Parkhi, O.M., Vedaldi, A., Zisserman, A., Jawahar, C.: Cats and dogs. In: CVPR, pp. 3498–3505 (2012)
18. Khosla, A., Jayadevaprakash, N., Yao, B., Li, F.F.: Novel dataset for fine-grained image categorization: Stanford dogs. In: CVPRW (2011)
19. Yang, L., Luo, P., Change Loy, C., Tang, X.: A large-scale car dataset for fine-grained categorization and verification. In: CVPR, June 2015
20. Duan, K., Parikh, D., Crandall, D., Grauman, K.: Discovering localized attributes for fine-grained recognition. In: CVPR, pp. 3474–3481 (2012)
21. Yao, B., Bradski, G., Fei-Fei, L.: A codebook-free and annotation-free approach for fine-grained image categorization. In: CVPR, pp. 3466–3473 (2012)
22. Yang, S., Bo, L., Wang, J., Shapiro, L.G.: Unsupervised template learning for fine-grained object recognition. In: NIPS, pp. 3122–3130 (2012)
23. Krause, J., Jin, H., Yang, J., Fei-Fei, L.: Fine-grained recognition without part annotations. In: CVPR (2015)
24. Wolff, K., Johnson, R.A., Suurmond, D.: Color Atlas and Synopsis of Clinical Dermatology. Mcgraw-hill Medical Pub. Division, New York (2005)

25. Maglogiannis, I., Delibasis, K.K.: Enhancing classification accuracy utilizing glob-
    ules and dots features in digital dermoscopy. Comput. Methods Programs Biomed.
    118(2), 124–133 (2015)
26. Celebi, M.E., Iyatomi, H., Schaefer, G., Stoecker, W.V.: Lesion border detection
    in dermoscopy images. Comput. Med. Imaging Graph. **33**(2), 148–153 (2009)
27. Celebi, M.E., Kingravi, H.A., Uddin, B., Iyatomi, H., Aslandogan, Y.A., Stoecker,
    W.V., Moss, R.H.: A methodological approach to the classification of dermoscopy
    images. Comput. Med. Imaging Graph. **31**(6), 362–373 (2007)
28. Kasmi, R., Mokrani, K.: Classification of Malignant Melanoma and Benign Skin
    Lesions: implementation of automatic ABCD rule. IET Image Process. **10**(6), 448–
    455 (2016)
29. Argenziano, G., Soyer, H.P., De Giorgi, V., Piccolo, D., Carli, P., Delfino, M., et al.:
    Interactive Atlas of Dermoscopy (Book and CD-ROM), pp. 1–10. EDRA Medical
    Publishing & New Media (2000)
30. Abbas, Q., Fondón, I., Rashid, M.: Unsupervised skin lesions border detection
    via two-dimensional image analysis. Comput. Methods Programs Biomed. **104**(3),
    1–15 (2011)
31. Wazaefi, Y., Paris, S., Fertil, B.: Contribution of a classifier of skin lesions to the
    dermatologist's decision. In: IPTA, pp. 207–211 (2012)
32. Sadeghi, M., Lee, T.K., McLean, D., Lui, H., Atkins, M.S.: Detection and analy-
    sis of irregular streaks in dermoscopic images of skin lesions. IEEE Trans. Med.
    Imaging **32**(5), 849–861 (2013)
33. Barata, C., Emre Celebi, M., Marques, J.S.: Melanoma detection algorithm based
    on feature fusion. In: EMBC, pp. 2653–2656 (2015)
34. Mendonça, T., Ferreira, P.M., Marques, J.S., Marcal, A.R., Rozeira, J.: PH 2-A
    dermoscopic image database for research and benchmarking. In: EMBC, pp. 5437–
    5440 (2013)
35. Glaister, J.L.: Automatic segmentation of skin lesions from dermatological pho-
    tographs. MSc Dissertation, Dept. Systems Design Eng., University of Waterloo,
    Ontario, Canada (2013)
36. Cho, D.S., Haider, S., Amelard, R., Wong, A., Clausi, D.A.: Quantitative features
    for computer-aided melanoma classification using spatial heterogeneity of eume-
    lanin and pheomelanin concentrations. In: ISBI, pp. 59–62 (2015)
37. Razeghi, O., Qiu, G., Williams, H., Thomas, K.: Skin lesion image recognition
    with computer vision and human in the loop. In: Medical Image Understanding
    and Analysis (MIUA), Swansea, UK, pp. 167–172 (2012)
38. Alcón, J.F., Ciuhu, C., Ten Kate, W., Heinrich, A., Uzunbajakava, N., Krekels,
    G., Siem, D., De Haan, G.: Automatic imaging system with decision support for
    inspection of pigmented skin lesions and melanoma diagnosis. IEEE J. Sel. Top.
    Sign. Proces. **3**(1), 14–25 (2009)
39. Razeghi, O., Fu, H., Qiu, G.: Building skin condition recogniser using crowd-
    sourced high level knowledge. In: Medical Image Understanding and Analysis
    (MIUA), Birmingham, UK, pp. 225–230 (2013)
40. Razeghi, O., Qiu, G.: 2309 skin conditions and crowd-sourced high-level knowledge
    dataset for building a computer aided diagnosis system. In: ISBI, pp. 61–64 (2014)
41. Krizhevsky, A., Sutskever, I., Hinton, G.E.: Imagenet classification with deep con-
    volutional neural networks. In: NIPS, pp. 1097–1105 (2012)
42. Girshick, R., Donahue, J., Darrell, T., Malik, J.: Rich feature hierarchies for accu-
    rate object detection and semantic segmentation. In: CVPR, pp. 580–587 (2014)
43. Zhou, B., Lapedriza, A., Xiao, J., Torralba, A., Oliva, A.: Learning deep features
    for scene recognition using places database. In: NIPS, pp. 487–495 (2014)

44. Xiao, T., Xu, Y., Yang, K., Zhang, J., Peng, Y., Zhang, Z.: The application of two-level attention models in deep convolutional neural network for fine-grained image classification. In: CVPR, pp. 842–850 (2014)
45. Zhang, N., Donahue, J., Girshick, R., Darrell, T.: Part-based R-CNNs for fine-grained category detection. In: Fleet, D., Pajdla, T., Schiele, B., Tuytelaars, T. (eds.) ECCV 2014. LNCS, vol. 8689, pp. 834–849. Springer, Heidelberg (2014). doi:10.1007/978-3-319-10590-1_54
46. Simonyan, K., Zisserman, A.: Very deep convolutional networks for large-scale image recognition. In: ICLR (2015)
47. Marks, J.G., Miller, J.J.: Lookingbill and Marks' Principles of Dermatology, pp. 7–10. Elsevier Health Sciences (2013)
48. Friedman, R.J., Rigel, D.S., Kopf, A.W.: Early detection of malignant melanoma: the role of physician examination and self-examination of the skin. CA Cancer J. Clin. **35**(3), 130–151 (1985)
49. Goering, C., Rodner, E., Freytag, A., Denzler, J.: Nonparametric part transfer for fine-grained recognition. In: CVPR, pp. 2489–2496 (2014)
50. Vedaldi, A., Fulkerson, B.: VLFeat: an open and portable library of computer vision algorithms (2008). http://www.vlfeat.org/
51. Lazebnik, S., Schmid, C., Ponce, J.: Beyond bags of features: spatial pyramid matching for recognizing natural scene categories. In: CVPR, vol. 2, pp. 2169–2178 (2006)
52. Simonyan, K., Zisserman, A.: Very deep convolutional networks for large-scale image recognition. CoRR abs/1409.1556 (2014)

Deep Learning 3D Shape Surfaces Using Geometry Images

Ayan Sinha[1(✉)], Jing Bai[2], and Karthik Ramani[1]

[1] Purdue University, West Lafayette, USA
{sinha12,ramani}@purdue.edu
[2] Beifang University of Nationalities, Yinchuan, China
bai58@purdue.edu

Abstract. Surfaces serve as a natural parametrization to 3D shapes. Learning surfaces using convolutional neural networks (CNNs) is a challenging task. Current paradigms to tackle this challenge are to either adapt the convolutional filters to operate on surfaces, learn spectral descriptors defined by the Laplace-Beltrami operator, or to drop surfaces altogether in lieu of voxelized inputs. Here we adopt an approach of converting the 3D shape into a *'geometry image'* so that standard CNNs can directly be used to learn 3D shapes. We qualitatively and quantitatively validate that creating geometry images using authalic parametrization on a spherical domain is suitable for robust learning of 3D shape surfaces. This spherically parameterized shape is then projected and cut to convert the original 3D shape into a flat and regular geometry image. We propose a way to implicitly learn the topology and structure of 3D shapes using geometry images encoded with suitable features. We show the efficacy of our approach to learn 3D shape surfaces for classification and retrieval tasks on non-rigid and rigid shape datasets.

Keywords: Deep learning · 3D Shape · Surfaces · CNN · Geometry images

1 Introduction

The ground-breaking accuracy obtained by convolutional neural networks (CNNs) for image classification [16] marked the advent of deep learning methods for various vision tasks such as video recognition, human and hand pose tracking using 3D sensors, image segmentation and retrieval [9,13,27]. Researchers have tried to adapt the CNN architecture for 3D non-rigid as well as rigid shape analysis.

The lack of a unified shape representation has led researchers pursuing deformable and rigid shape analysis using deep learning down different routes. One strategy for learning rigid shapes is to represent a shape as a probability

Electronic supplementary material The online version of this chapter (doi:10.1007/978-3-319-46466-4_14) contains supplementary material, which is available to authorized users.

ⓒ Springer International Publishing AG 2016
B. Leibe et al. (Eds.): ECCV 2016, Part VI, LNCS 9910, pp. 223–240, 2016.
DOI: 10.1007/978-3-319-46466-4_14

distribution on a 3D voxel grid [20,32]. Other approaches quantify some measure of local or global variation of surface coordinates relative to a fixed frame of reference [26]. These representations based on voxels or surface coordinates are *extrinsic* to the shape, and can successfully learn shapes for classification or retrieval tasks under rigid transformations (rotations, translations and reflections). However, they will naturally fail to recognize isometric deformation of a shape, say the deformation of a standing person to a sitting person. Invariance to isometry is a necessary property for robust non-rigid shape analysis. This is substantiated by the popularity of the *intrinsic* shape signatures for 3D deformable shape analysis in the geometry community [31]. Hence, CNN-based deformable shape analysis methods propose the use of geodesic convolutional filters as patches or model spectral-CNN's using the eigen decomposition of the Laplace-Beltrami operator to derive robust shape descriptors [1,6,19]. In summary, the vision community has focussed on extrinsic representation of 3D shapes suitable for learning rigid shapes, whereas the geometry community has focussed on adapting CNN's to non-Euclidean manifolds using intrinsic shape properties for creating optimal descriptors. A method to unify these two complementary approaches has remained elusive.

Here we propose a 3D shape representation that serves to learn rigid as well as non-rigid objects using intrinsic or extrinsic descriptors input to standard CNNs. Instead of adapting the CNN architecture to support convolution on surfaces, we adopt the alternate approach of molding the 3D shape surface to fit a planar structure as required by CNNs. The traditional approach to create a planar surface parametrization is to first cut the surface into disk-like charts, then piecewise parameterize them in the plane followed by stitching them together into a texture atlas [18]. This approach fails to preserve the connectivity between different surfaces, vital for holistic shape analysis. In contrast, we create a planar parametrization by introducing a method to transform a general mesh model into a flat and completely regular 2D grid, which we term 'geometry image', following

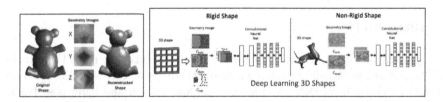

Fig. 1. Left Shape representation using geometry images: The original teddy model to the left is reconstructed (right) using geometry image representation corresponding to the X, Y and Z coordinates (center), **Right** Learning 3D shape surfaces using geometry images: Our approach to learn shapes using geometry images is applicable to rigid (left) as well as non-rigid objects undergoing isometric transformations (right). The geometry image encode local properties of shape surfaces such as principal curvatures (C_{min}, C_{max}). Topology of a non-zero genus surface is accounted for by using a topological mask (C_{top}) as in the bookshelf example.

[11] (see Fig. 1 left). The traditional approach to create a geometry image has critical limitations for learning 3D shape surfaces (see Sect. 2). We validate that an intermediate shape representation for creating geometry images in the form of an authalic parametrization on a spherical domain overcomes these limitations and is able to efficiently learn 3D shape surfaces for subsequent analysis. To this end, we develop a robust method for authalic spherical parametrization applicable to general 3D shapes. We use this parametrization to encode suitable intrinsic or extrinsic features of a 3D shape for 3D shape tasks. This encoded spherical parametrization is converted to a completely regular geometry image of a desired size. We demonstrate the use of these geometry images to directly learn shapes using a standard CNN architecture to classify and retrieve shapes. In summary our main contributions are: (1) robust authalic parametrization of general 3D shapes for creating geometry images, and (2) a procedure to learn 3D surfaces using a geometry image representation which encodes suitable features for rigid or non-rigid shape tasks (see Fig. 1 right).

Our article is organized as follows. Section 2 rationalizes our choice of parametrization. Section 3 discusses our parametrization method. Section 4 is devoted to learning shapes using geometry images and CNNs followed by results in Sect. 5.

2 Frame of Reference and Related Work

In this section we first validate that authalic parametrization on a spherical domain has key advantages over alternate surface parametrization techniques in the context of learning shapes using geometry images. We briefly overview existing techniques and point the readers to [7] for a good overview of surface parametrization.

Why spherical parametrization?: Geometry images as the name suggests are a particular kind of surface parametrization wherein the geometry is resampled into a regular 2D grid akin to an image. Geometry images are advantageous for learning shapes using CNNs over free boundary or disc parameterizations as every pixel encodes desired shape information. This reduces memory and learning complexity in CNNs as the need to abstract the mask of inside/outside shape boundary is obviated. The traditional approach to create a geometry image is to cut the surface into a disc using a network of cut paths and then map the disc boundary to a square [11]. However, defining consistent *a priori* cuts over a range of shapes in a class is a hard problem. A natural solution to overcome this limitation is a data-driven approach to learn a shape over several cuts. This is computationally inefficient for cuts defined *a priori*. Another assumption of [11] is that the surface cut into a disc maps well onto a square. Different cuts lead to variation in geometry image boundaries [22], and hence, learning them requires the CNN to learn maps between image boundaries in addition to image pixels. These two limitations of traditional geometry images are overcome by geometry images created by first parameterizing a 3D shape over a spherical domain, then sampling onto an octahedron and finally cutting the octahedron along its edges to output a flat and regular geometry image. This is because: (1) Cuts are defined *a posteriori* to the parametrization. This enables us to efficiently create many geometry images for a given shape by sampling several cuts and feed it as input to data driven learning techniques such as CNNs. (2) Spherical symmetry allows creating a regular geometry image boundaries without discontinuities. The symmetry enables us to implicitly inform the CNN that the geometry image is derived from a spherical domain via padding. Although spherical parametrization is only applicable to genus zero surfaces, we propose a heuristic extension to higher genus surface models using a topological mask.

Why authalic parametrization?: There are two strategies for spherical parametrization of a 3D shape: (a) Authalic or area conserving, (b) Conformal or angle conserving. Although, methods for conformal (angle preserving) mesh parametrization abound [4,12,25], there is relatively less work on authalic (area preserving) mesh parametrization. This is because a conformal parametrization preserves local shape, which is useful to the graphics community for feature oriented applications such as texture mapping. However, an authalic parametrization of a shape is more compatible with the notion of convolving surface patches with constant size (equi-areal) filters. Also, conformal parametrization induces severe distortion to elongated shape structures common in deformable shape models [34]. The necessity of authalic parametrization arises from the fact that the number of training samples and learning parameters in the CNN sometimes limit the input resolution of the geometry images. Under the constraint of resolution, authalic geometry images encode more information about the shape as compared to conformal geometry images (see Fig. 2). Note that a mapping that is both conformal and authalic is isometric, and must have zero Gaussian curvature everywhere. This is rare in the context of general 3D mesh models and one must choose one or the other. There exist only a handful of methods in literature that authalically parameterize a shape on a spherical domain. Dominitz and Tannenbaum [5] and Zhao et al. [34] use optimal transport for area-preserving mapping. Although efficient to

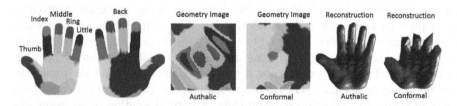

Fig. 2. Authalic vs Conformal parametrization: (Left to right) 2500 vertices of the hand mesh are color coded in the first two plots. A 64× 64 geometry image is created by uniformly sampling a parametrization, and then interpolating the nearby feature values. Authalic geometry image encodes all tip features. Conformal parametrization compress high curvature points to dense regions [12]. Hence, finger tips are all mapped to a very small regions. The fourth plot shows that the resolution of geometry image is insufficient to capture the tip feature colors in conformal parametrization. This is validated by reconstructing shape from geometry images encoding x, y, z locations for both parametrizations in final two plots. (Color figure online)

implement, these methods introduce smoothing and sharp edges get lost [29]. This is a critical drawback for CAD-like objects which contain several sharp edges. A method that implicitly corrects area distortion by penalizing large triangle sizes is proposed in [8]. However, our experiments indicate that this approach fails to work in a practical setting. A method similar in spirit to ours uses Lie advection to iteratively minimize the planar areal distortion of a parametrization [35]. However, the method frequently introduces singularities and triangle flips, highly undesirable for coherent 3D shape representation and analysis.

Why geometry images?: As discussed previously, current methods employing deep learning for 3D rigid shape analysis such as ShapeNets [32], VoxNet [20], DeepPano [26] are extrinsic representations and are not suitable for analyzing non-rigid shapes undergoing isometric deformations. Another bottleneck in voxel based approaches is that the 3rd extra dimension introduces a large computational overhead. Consequently, the voxel grid is restricted to a relatively low resolution. Also, active voxels interior to the shape are less useful if the boundary surface is well defined. Methods using CNN for 3D non-rigid shape analysis such as [1,19] focus on deriving robust shape descriptors suitable for local shape correspondence. The potential of CNN's to automatically learn hierarchical abstractions of a shape from raw input features is not realized by these approaches. In contrast to all approaches, the pixels in geometry images can encode either extrinsic or intrinsic surface property as suitable for the task at hand. A standard CNN then automatically learn discriminative abstractions of the 3D shape, useful for shape classification or retrieval.

3 Authalic Parametrization of 3D Shapes

We briefly discuss preprocessing steps to transform erroneous or high genus mesh models into a genus zero topology. These steps ensure that parametrization techniques from discrete differential geometry literature are applicable to a shape of arbitrary topology. A surface mesh, M is represented as V, F, E wherein V is the set of vertex coordinates, F the set of faces and E the set of edges constituting all faces. With abuse of notation, we term mesh models following the Euler characteristic to be accurate, given by:

$$2 - 2m = |V| - |E| + |F| \tag{1}$$

where $|x|$ indicates the cardinality of feature x and m is the genus of the surface. If a mesh model is not accurate, a heuristic but accurate procedure is discussed in the supplementary material to transform it into an accurate mesh. In our experiments we perform this procedure only for models in the Princeton ModelNet [32] benchmark. If the genus of an accurate mesh model is evaluated to be non-zero, we propose another heuristic in the supplementary material to convert the mesh into a genus-0 surface. This genus-0 shape serves as input to the authalic parametrization procedure. Note that a non genus-0 shape has an associated topological geometry image informing the holes in the original shape.

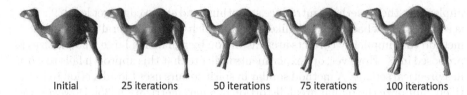

Initial   25 iterations   50 iterations   75 iterations   100 iterations

Fig. 3. Progression of our authalic spherical parametrization algorithm: Individual plots display the shape reconstructed from the geometry image corresponding to a spherical parametrization. The area distortion associated with the geometry image, and hence the spherical parametrization, progressively decreases with more iterations given an initial spherical parametrization.

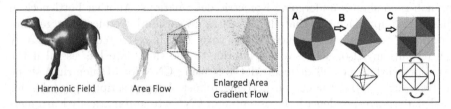

Fig. 4. Left Left: Harmonic field corresponding to area distortion on sphere displayed on the original mesh. Center: Area restoring flow on the spherical domain mapped onto the original mesh as a quiver plot. Right: Enlarged plot of area restoring flow. **Right**: Explanation of geometry image construction from a spherical parametrization: The spherical parametrization (A) is mapped onto an octahedron (B) and then cut along edges (4 colored dashed edges in line plot below) to output a flat geometry image (C). The colored edges share the same color coding as the one in the octahedron. Also the half-edges on either side of the midpoint of colored edges correspond to the same edge of the octahedron. (Color figure online)

Our method for authalic spherical parametrization takes as input any spherically parameterized mesh and iteratively minimizes the areal distortion (see Fig. 3) in 3 steps described in detail below and outputs a bijective map onto the surface of a sphere. We use the spherical parametrization suggested in [10] for initialization due to its speed and ease of implementation. We evaluated different initial parameterizations [25] and our experiments indicate that our method is robust to initialization. We now detail the 3 steps:

(1) At every iteration we first evaluate a scalar harmonic field corresponding to the areal distortion ratio of vertices in the original mesh and spherical mesh by solving a Poisson equation. Mathematically, we solve

$$\nabla^2 g = \delta h \tag{2}$$

where g is a function defined on the vertex set V, ∇^2 transforms to the Laplacian operator, L (see supplement) for a closed mesh surface [14], and δh is the areal distortion ratio wherein each element of the vector is defined as $\delta h_u = \frac{A_u^s}{A_u} - 1$. A_u^s is the spherical triangular area associated with the Voronoi region around vertex u and A_u is the triangular area associated with vertex u on the mesh model. Equation 2 now becomes

$$Lg = \delta h \qquad (3)$$

The scalar field g is evaluated using the above equation at every iteration for the vector δh (see Fig. 4 left). Due to the sparsity of L, Eq. 3 can be efficient evaluated at every iteration using the preconditioned bi-conjugate gradient method. However, we precalculate the pseudoinverse of L once, and use it for every iteration. This saves the overall computational time. Note, k-rank approximation ($k \approx 300$) of the pseudoinverse when $|V|$ is large does not noticeably affect the final result.

(2) We then evaluate the gradient field of the harmonic function on the original mesh. This field is indicative of the required vertex displacements on the spherical mesh so as to decrease the areal distortion ratio. Consider a face f_{uvw} in the original mesh with its three corners lying at u, v, w. Let n be a unit normal vector perpendicular to the plane of the triangle. The gradient vector ∇g for each face is solved as [33]:

$$\begin{bmatrix} v - u \\ w - v \\ n \end{bmatrix} \nabla g = \begin{bmatrix} g_v - g_u \\ g_w - g_v \\ 0 \end{bmatrix}$$

A unique gradient vector for each vertex is obtained as weighted mean of incident angle of each face at the vertex and the corresponding gradient value as done in [35]:

$$\nabla g_u = \frac{1}{\sum_{f_{uvw}} c_{vw}^u} \sum_{f_{uvw}} c_{vw}^u \nabla g(f_{uvw}) \qquad (4)$$

f_{uvw} are the faces in the one ring neighborhood of vertex u and c_{vw}^u is the angle subtended at vertex u by the edge vw. Figure 4 shows the gradient low field using a quiver plot on the mesh model.

(3) We finally displace the vertices on the original mesh and then map these displacements onto the spherical mesh using barycentric mapping, i.e., vertex displacements on the original mesh serve as proxy to determine the corresponding displacements on the spherical mesh. Barycentric mapping is possible because the original and spherical mesh have the same triangulation. Each vertex in the original mesh is (hypothetically) displaced by:

$$v = v + \rho \nabla g_v \qquad (5)$$

where ρ is a small parameter value. A large value of ρ leads to a large displacement of the vertex and may displace it beyond the its 1-neighborhood. This causes triangle flips and the error propagates through iterations. However, a small value of ρ leads to large convergence time. We empirically set ρ equal to 0.01 in all our experiments which achieves the right tradeoff between number of iterations to convergence and accuracy. The barycentric coordinates of displaced vertices are evaluated with respect to triangles in the one-ring, and the triangle with all coordinates less than 1 is naturally chosen as the destination face. The vertex in the spherical mesh is then mapped to the corresponding destination face with the same barycentric weights. In contrast to [35] which operates directly on the spherical mesh domain, the indirect mapping procedure has the following advantages: (1) The vertex displacements minimizing areal distortion are constrained to be on the input mesh, which in turn ensure the mapped displacements onto the spherical domain are well behaved. (2) The constraint that the vertices remain on the mesh model minimize triangle flips and alleviate the need for an expensive retriangulation procedure after each iteration. The iterations continue until convergence. In practice we stop the iterations after the all areal distortion ratios fall below a threshold or the maximum number of iterations has been reached. The maximum number of iterations is set to 100. Supplementary material provides a pseudo code of the above procedure and MATLAB code for creating geometry images are available at: https://github.com/sinhayan/learning_geometry_images. Next, we discuss the geometry image and its application to deep learning.

4   Deep Learning Shapes Using Geometry Image

In this section we briefly discuss the creation of a geometry image with desirable surface properties encoded in the pixels to learn 3D shapes. We also discuss our CNN architecture for shape classification and retrieval.

4.1   Geometry Image and Descriptors

The spherical parametrization maps the surface of the mesh onto a sphere. We then project this spherical surface onto an octahedron and cut it to obtain a square, thus creating a geometry image. We consider spherical triangular area when sampling from sphere to octahedron, so that the authalic parametrization is respected, and hence, the areas are preserved after projection onto a octahedron. The advantage of mapping the surface onto an octahedron over other regular polyhedra such as a tetrahedron or cube is that the signals can be linearly interpolated onto a regular square grid [22]. For brevity, we skip details on the spherical area sampling for projecting points on the sphere onto an octahedron and refer readers to [22] for details. The edges of the octahedron cut to flatten the polyhedron are shown in Fig. 4 right. Observe the reflective symmetry of the geometry image along the vertical, horizontal and diagonal axes shown in Fig. 4 right. Due to this symmetry, we can create replicates without any discontinuities along any edge or corner of the image (see Fig. 5 right). This property is useful for implicitly informing a deep learning model about the warped mesh the image represents, further explained below. The procedure of creating the geometry image is visually elucidated in Fig. 4 right. Additionally, a MATLAB implementation is provided in supplementary material. Having obtained a geometry image from a mesh model, we next discuss encoding the pixel values with local surface property descriptors. There exist several possibilities of which we enumerate a few:

1. Principal curvatures: The two principal curvatures, κ_1 and κ_2 measure the degree by which the surface bends in orthogonal directions at a point. They are in effect the eigenvalues of the shape tensor at a given point.
2. Gaussian Curvature: The Gaussian curvature κ is defined as the product of the principal curvatures at a point on the surface, $\kappa = \kappa_1\kappa_2$. Gaussian curvature is an intrinsic descriptor. The sign of Gaussian curvature indicates whether a point is elliptic ($\kappa > 0$), hyperbolic ($\kappa < 0$) or flat ($\kappa = 0$)
3. Heat kernel signature [31]: The heat kernel, h_t is the solution to the differential equation $\frac{\delta h_t}{\delta t} = -\Delta h_t$ (h_t is the heat kernel). The heat kernel signature (HKS) at the point is the amount of untransferred heat after time t, given by

$$h_t(u, u) = \sum_{i \geq 0} e^{-t\lambda_i} \Phi_i(u)\Phi_i(u) \tag{6}$$

Where λ and Φ are the eigenvalues and eigenvectors of the Laplace-Beltrami operator. The heat kernel is invariant under isometric transformations and stable under small perturbations to the isometry, such as small topological changes or noise, i.e., is intrinsic. Additionally, the time parameter t in the HKS controls the scale of the signature with large t representing increasingly global properties, i.e. its a multiscale signature. Variants of the heat kernel include the GMS [28], GPS [23]which differ in the weighting of the eigenvalues. Figure 5 left discusses the difference between intrinsic HKS and point coordinates which are extrinsic in the context of analyzing articulated shapes. The invariance of intrinsic descriptors to articulations of a deformable object such as a hand is further demonstrated in Fig. 5 center. In our experiments we use the HKS for non-rigid shape analysis and the two principal curvatures for rigid-shape analysis.

4.2   Convolutional Neural Net

We discuss four aspects of learning rigid and non-rigid shapes using geometry images created using the authalic parametrization method discussed in the previous section as input to a CNN, i.e., encoding a property, padding the image, robustness to cut and the CNN architecture which takes geometry images as inputs and performs shape analysis tasks.

(1) **Encoded Property:** After parameterizing the shape, we are interested in encoding the geometry image with a suitable property. These are the RGB pixel values in images which are fed as input to a CNN. Unlike traditional deep architectures, CNN's have the attractive property of weight sharing reducing the number of variables to be learned. The principle of weight sharing in convolutional filters extensively applied to image processing is

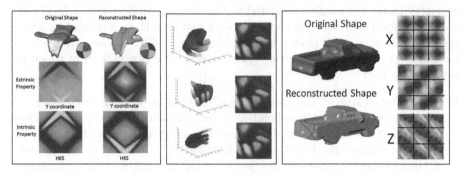

Fig. 5. Left Intrinsic vs. Extrinsic properties of shapes. Top left: Original shape. Top Right: Reconstructed shape from geometry image with cut edges displayed in red. The middle and bottom rows show the geometry image encoding the y coordinates and HKS, respectively of two spherical parameterizations (left and right). The two spherical parameterizations are symmetrically rotated by 180 degrees along the Y-axis. The geometry images for Y-coordinate display an axial as well as intensity flip. Whereas, the geometry images for HKS only display an axial flip. This is because HKS is an intrinsic shape signature (geodesics are persevered) whereas point coordinates on a shape surface are not. **Center** Intrinsic descriptors (here the HKS) are invariant to shape articulations. **Right** Padding structure of geometry images: The geometry images for the 3 coordinates are replicated to produce a 3× 3 grid. The center image in each grid corresponds to the original geometry image. Observe no discontinuities exist along the grid edges.

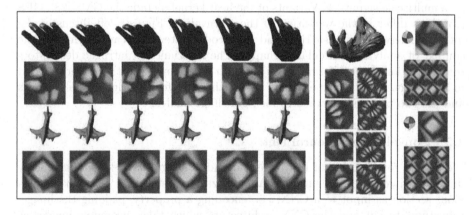

Fig. 6. Left Geometry images created by fixing the polar axis of a hand (top) and aeroplane (bottom), and rotating the spherical parametrization by equal intervals along the axis. The cut is highlighted in red. **Center** Four rotated geometry images for a different cut location highlighted in red. The plots to the right show padded geometry images wherein the similarity across rotated geometry images are more evident and the five finger features coherently visible **Right** Changing the viewing direction for a cut inverts the geometry image. The similarity in geometry images for the two diametrically opposite cuts emerges when we pad the image in a 3×3 grid (Color figure online)

applicable to learning 3D shapes using geometry images as well. This is because shapes like images are composed of atomic features and have a natural notion of hierarchy. However, we encode different features in the pixels of the geometry image for rigid and non-rigid shapes as it helps a CNN to discriminatively learn shape surfaces. The Gaussian curvature is the most atomic and intrinsic property suitable for non-rigid shape analysis. The heat kernel signature too can be interpreted as an extension to gaussian curvature [31]. We use the HKS for our experiments on non-rigid datasets as it enforces long-range consistency to geometry images. In rigid shape analysis, the principal curvatures serve as the atomic local descriptors for points on a surface. Although, the intrinsic HKS can be used for rigid shape analysis, HKS has a high computational cost unsuitable for large datasets like the Princeton Shape Benchmark.

(2) **Padding:** We now have a geometry image with a suitably encoded property. It is naturally beneficial to inform the CNN that this flat geometry image stems from a compact manifold. The spherical symmetry of our parametrization allows us to implicitly inform the CNN about the genus-0 surface via padding. There are no edge and corner discontinuities if we connect replicates of a geometry image along each of the 4 edges of the image which are rotated by 180 degrees (or flipped once along the x-axis and y-axis each). This is due to spherical symmetry and orientation of edges in the derived octahedral parametrization. This is visually illustrated for the geometry images encoding the x, y, and z coordinates of the mesh model in Fig. 5 right. No subsequent layer in the CNN is padded so as to not distort this information.

(3) **Cut:** Recall that the octahedral edges cut to create a geometry image are dependent on the orientation of the spherical parametrization. We implicitly inform the CNN that different cuts resulting in slightly different geometry images stem from the same shape. When the shape is known to be upright as in the Princeton shape benchmark, we realign north pole of the derived spherical parametrization to be coincident with the highest point along the centroid axis to make the north pole to be approximately co-located for the same class of shapes. The directed axis connecting the north and south pole can be thought of as a viewing direction of the sphere, and hence the geometry image. Rotation around this polar axis of the sphere will result in different cuts of the octahedron and hence slightly different geometry images which are rotationally related. This rotational relationship between geometry images for the same object is learnt by rotating the spherical parametrization in equal intervals about the polar axis for a shape (see Fig. 6 left). This is analogous to the procedure of augmenting data by rotation along the gravity direction as done in voxel based approaches such as [20, 30, 32] to create models in arbitrary poses, and hence, remove pose ambiguity. The rotational variance along the polar axis for geometry images of upright objects can be further resolved by incorporating an additional feature map in CNN architecture as the geometry image encoding the angle between a vertex normal and the gravity direction [9]. When there is no information about

orientation of the shape, we naturally set multiple radial axes of the sphere to be the directed polar axes (we set six orthogonal directed axes of the sphere to be the polar axes in our experiments with non-rigid datasets) and then rotate the sphere by equal intervals along each polar axes to holistically augment the training data along different viewing directions of the spherical parametrization. Figure 6 left and center show the rotated geometry images for an articulated hand for two different polar cutting axes. Observe that although the geometry images appear very different for the two cuts, they are functionally related as they are just projections along different viewing directions of spherical parametrization onto the flat geometry image. For example there are 5 primary features in both geometry images corresponding to the 5 fingers and their relative locations are similar in both images. The mild stretch variations among geometry images would not appear if the parametrization was isometric. Indeed, the accuracy of our approach stems from the power of CNNs to automatically abstract these similarity in patterns robust against different cut locations in the augmented data across articulations of a deformable object or variations of objects in a class.

(4) **Resolution and architecture:** There are two determining factors for the resolution of a geometry image: (i) The number of training samples (ii) Features in the mesh model. Currently there are no large databases for non-rigid shapes, and hence, a large resolution will lead to a large number of weight parameters to be learnt in the CNN. Although we have large databases for rigid shapes, the number of geometry features (eg. protrusion, corners etc.) in rigid shapes is typically much lower compared to images and even articulated objects. We set the size of the geometry image to be 56×56 for all our experiments on rigid and non-rigid datasets which balances the number of weights to be learnt in CNN and capturing relevant features of a mesh model. The number of layers in CNN is determined by the size of the training database. Hence, we choose a relatively shallow architecture for non-rigid database compared to the rigid database. The precise architecture of the CNNs are discussed in the supplementary section.

5   Experiments

In this section we first compare our parametrization scheme. Then we discuss results for 3D shape analysis tasks on rigid as well as non-rigid datasets.

Authalic parametrization: We compare our authalic spherical parametrization scheme to other area correcting methods. We qualitatively adjudge the parametrization in terms of the geometry image created from the corresponding spherical parameterizations on some prototypical meshes. The methods compared to are the lie advection based method in [35], and the penalty-term based method proposed in [8], both of which are iterative methods. For fair comparison, the maximum number of iterations was fixed to 100 for all methods along with suggested parameter settings. Figure 7 left shows the comparison. We observe that our method is the only method to consistently complete the shape while

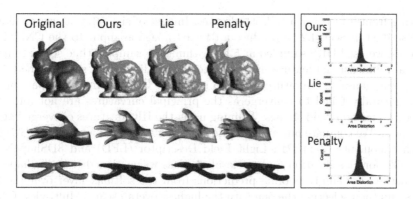

Fig. 7. Left Comparison of authalic surface parametrization methods in terms of shape reconstruction using geometry image. Left to Right: Original mesh model, Our authalic parametrization, Lie advection based method in [35], Penalty based method proposed in [8]. **Right** Top to Bottom: Area distortion viewed as a histogram over triangles for ours, [8,35].

keeping extraneous noise at a minimum. For example no method apart from ours is able to complete the bunny's ears or completely reveal all 5 fingers. This validates our approach in the context of geometry image creation and authalic spherical parametrization in general. Next we quantitatively evaluate the accuracy of our authalic parametrization by comparing the area distortion across all triangles in all 148 shapes in TOSCA database. The distortion metric is δhA. Figure 7 right shows area distortion as a histogram as done in [35]. A perfect authalic parametrization would manifest as a delta function in this plot. Hence we evaluate the variance of these three approaches. Observe that our method has the sharpest peak and the variance is evaluated to be 9.8e-8 for our method compared to 5.2e-7 for [35] and 2.65e-7 for [8], i.e., lowest among all.

Non-rigid shapes: We evaluated our approach for surface based intrinsic learning of shapes on two datasets. We used 200 shapes from the McGill 3D shape benchmark consisting of articulated as well as non-articulated shapes from 10 classes (20 in each class). To test the robustness of our approach, we also evaluated our approach on the challenging SHREC-11 [17] database of watertight meshes consisting of 20 shapes from 30 classes (600 in total). For each of the 2 databases, we performed classification tasks on 2 splits: (1) 10 randomly chosen shapes from each class were used for training and 10 were test (2) 16 randomly chosen shapes were in the train set and the rest were test cases. Due to the small size of the database, we kept our CNN relatively shallow (3 convolutional, 1 fully connected layer and a classification layer) so as to limit the number of training parameters. We augment the data in order to be robust to cut location by inputting 36 geometry images for a shape created by (1) fixing the six directed intersections of the three orthogonal coordinate axes with the spherical parametrization as the polar axes and then (2) creating a geometry image for each incremental rotation of the sphere along the polar axes by 60 degrees starting from 0 to cover a full 360 degrees. Images of size 56×56 were padded as described in Sect. 4.2 to produce a 64×64 image as input to the CNN. For features, we used HKS sampled at 5 logarithmically sampled time scales to produce a 5 dimensional feature map. Due to the small training sample, the CNN using only gaussian curvature failed to converge. CNNs using principal curvatures naturally failed to converge as the principal curvatures are not intrinsic properties for non-rigid shapes. Training using the HKS features converged after 30 epochs. We compare our approach to 4 other methods: ShapeGoogle (SG)[2], Zerkine moments (Zer) [21], Light Field Descriptor (LFD) and 3DShapeNets (SN) [32] for classification and retrieval. A class was assigned to each shape in our method by simply pooling predictions from the softmax layer over the 36 views and then selecting the one with the highest overall score. Multi-view CNN architecture [30] can be directly employed for a more principled way to pool and learn across different cuts within the CNN architecture itself, which we wish to investigate in the future when larger non-rigid databases are available. We trained a linear SVM classifier for SG, LFD and Zer methods.[1] We see that our method significantly outperforms all other methods on both splits for the 2 databases (Table 1) indicating that our geometry image representation was able to *learn* the shape structure of each class. Our method performs significantly better than SN [32] on these benchmarks because voxels capture extrinsic shape information, and hence, confuse shape articulations. It performs better than SG [2] because of the same reason that CNNs outperform bag of feature (BOF) based approaches on image tasks, i.e., CNNs are better able to automatically abstract relevant information for tasks than BOFs. We also quantitatively validate that authalic parametrization is more suitable for shape analysis compared to conformal (Conf) parametrization [12] or Spharm (Sph) [24] which minimizes length distortion. Performance of authalic parametrization is a lot higher than others for non-rigid shapes, as expected because the other two parameterizations do not robustly capture elongated protrusions. We use the L2 distance to measure the similarity between all pairs of testing samples and retrieval accuracy was measured in terms of mean average precision (MAP) as standard in literature. The penultimate 48-dimensional activation vector in the fully connected layer was used for measuring the retrieval accuracy of our method. We perform best in all but one dataset, i.e., 2nd to SG for SHREC2, inspite our feature vector being $1/50^{th}$ the size of SG. This highlights that our method can be used to output highly informative shape signatures. Figure 8 shows precision-recall curves for the 4 splits.

Rigid shapes: We evaluate our approach for surface-based learning of 3D shape classification on the two versions of the large scale Princeton ModelNet dataset: ModelNet40 and ModelNet10 consisting of 40 and 10 classes respectively following the protocol of [32]. We use four feature maps encoded in geometry images: 2 principal curvatures, topological mask along with a height field encoded as angle to the positive gravity direction. Additionally, each spherical parametriza-

---

[1] Note we do not report the scores for SG on Mcgill because the author provided implementation failed on several shapes and produced spurious results.

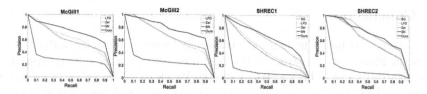

Fig. 8. Precision recall curves for shape retrieval on non-rigid datasets

Table 1. Classification/Retrieval accuracy of our method compared to 4 other methods and compared to 2 other surface parameterizations.

Database	SG [2]	Zer [21]	LFD [3]	SN [32]	Conf [12]	Sph [24]	Ours
McGill1	NA	63.0/0.64	75.0/0.67	65.0/0.29	55.0/0.36	62.0/0.35	**83.0/0.75**
Mcgill2	NA	57.5/0.69	72.5/0.68	57.2/0.28	80.0/0.58	82.5/0.58	**92.5/0.72**
SHREC1	62.6/**0.65**	43.3/0.47	56.7/0.50	52.7/0.10	60.6/0.45	59.0/0.65	**88.6/ 0.65**
SHREC2	70.8/**0.74**	50.8/0.64	65.8/0.65	48.4/0.13	85.0/0.45	82.5/0.66	**96.6**/0.72

Table 2. Classification/Retrieval accuracies of our method on the ModelNet40 and ModelNet10 database compared to 5 other 3D learning methods and two alternate surface parameterizations.

Database	VN [20]	DP [26]	LFD [3]	SN [32]	SH [15]	Conf [12]	Sph [24]	Ours
ModelNet10	**92.0**/NA	85.5/**84.1**	79.8/49.8	83.5/69.2	79.9/45.9	78.2/67.4	79.9/65.2	88.4/74.9
ModelNet40	83.0/NA	77.6/**76.8**	75.4/40.9	77.3/49.9	68.2/34.4	75.6/46.2	75.9/44.8	**83.9**/51.3

tion is augmented by incrementally shifting by 30 degrees along the centroid axes described in Sect. 4.2 to create 12 replicates. The size and structure of the geometry image is the same as the ones used for non-rigid testing. Supplementary material validates technical parameter settings on the ModelNet10 dataset. Table 2 shows the classification accuracies (same method as non-rigid) and retrieval results (MAP %) relative to 5 methods (VN is VoxNet, DP is DeepPano, SH is spherical harmonic) and 2 alternate parameterizations. We employ the procedure in [32] to use the L2 distance between the penultimate 96-dimensional activation vectors in the fully connected layer for retrieval. We achieve the best classification accuracy on ModelNet40 dataset. Our MAP retrieval is second only to Deep-Pano on both splits, however our classification accuracies are higher suggesting the a panoramic representation may be more suitable for retrieval with high intra-class discrimination, whereas geometry images are highly robust for classification. Our method performs better than SN [32] on these benchmarks because (i) encoding local principal curvatures in geometry images is analogous to pixel intensities in images, which suit CNN's architecture. (ii) Learning is harder for voxel locations compared to surface properties. Indeed training required about 3 hours on the ModelNet40 benchmark compared to 2 days for SN [32].

6 Conclusion

We introduce geometry images for intrinsically learning 3D shape surfaces. Our geometry images are constructed by combining area correcting flows, spherical parameterizations and barycentric mapping. We show the potential of geometry images to flexibly encode surface properties of shapes and demonstrate its efficacy for analyzing both non-rigid and rigid shapes. Furthermore, our work serves as a general validation of surface based representations for shape understanding. In the future we wish to build upon these insights for generative modeling of 3D shapes using geometry images instead of traditional images using deep learning. We believe that deep learning using geometry images can potentially spark a closer communion between the 3D vision and geometry community.

Acknowledgements. This work was partially supported by the NSF Award No.1235232 from CMMI as well as the Donald W. Feddersen Chaired Professorship from Purdue School of Mechanical Engineering. Dr. Jing Bai was supported by the National Natural Science Foundation of China (No. 61163016) and by the China Scholarship Council. Any opinions, findings, and conclusions or recommendations expressed in this material are those of the authors and do not necessarily reflect the views of the sponsors.

References

1. Boscaini, D., Masci, J., Melzi, S., Bronstein, M.M., Castellani, U., Vandergheynst, P.: Learning class-specific descriptors for deformable shapes using localized spectral convolutional networks. Comput. Graph. Forum **34**, 13–23 (2015)
2. Bronstein, A.M., Bronstein, M.M., Guibas, L.J., Ovsjanikov, M.: Shape google: geometric words and expressions for invariant shape retrieval. ACM Trans. Graph. (TOG) **30**(1), 1 (2011)
3. Chen, D.-Y., Tian, X.-P., Shen, Y.-T., Ouhyoung, M.: On visual similarity based 3D model retrieval. Comput. Graph. Forum **22**(3), 223–232 (2003)
4. Desbrun, M., Meyer, M., Alliez, P.: Intrinsic parameterizations of surface meshes. Comput. Graph. Forum **21**, (2002)
5. Dominitz, A., Tannenbaum, A.: Texture mapping via optimal mass transport. IEEE Trans. Vis. Comput. Graph. **16**(3), 419–433 (2010)
6. Fang, Y., Xie, J., Dai, G., Wang, M., Zhu, F., Xu, T., Wong, E.: 3D deep shape descriptor. In: Proceedings of the IEEE Conference on Computer Vision and Pattern Recognition, pp. 2319–2328 (2015)
7. Floater, M.S., Hormann, K.: Surface parameterization: a tutorial and survey. Advances in Multiresolution for Geometric Modelling, pp. 157–186. Springer, Heidelberg (2005)
8. Friedel, I., Schröder, P., Desbrun, M.: Unconstrained spherical parameterization. J. Graph. Tools **12**(1), 17–26 (2007)
9. Girshick, R., Donahue, J., Darrell, T., Malik, J.: Rich feature hierarchies for accurate object detection and semantic segmentation. In: IEEE Conference on Computer Vision and Pattern Recognition (CVPR), pp. 580–587. IEEE (2014)
10. Gotsman, C., Gu, X., Sheffer, A.: Fundamentals of spherical parameterization for 3D meshes. In: Proceedings of the 2006 Symposium on Interactive 3D Graphics and Games, 14–17 March 2006, pp. 28–29 (2003)

11. Gu, X., Gortler, S.J., Hoppe, H.: Geometry images. In: Proceedings of the 29th Annual Conference on Computer Graphics and Interactive Techniques, SIG-GRAPH 2002, pp. 355–361. ACM, New York (2002)
12. Gu, X., et al.: Genus zero surface conformal mapping and its application to brain surface mapping. IEEE Trans. Medical Imaging (2003)
13. Karpathy, A., Toderici, G., Shetty, S., Leung, T., Sukthankar, R., Fei-Fei, L.: Large-scale video classification with convolutional neural networks. In: Proceedings of International Computer Vision and Pattern Recognition (CVPR 2014) (2014)
14. Kazhdan, M., Bolitho, M., Hoppe, H.: Poisson surface reconstruction. In: Proceedings of the Fourth Eurographics Symposium on Geometry Processing, SGP 2006, pp. 61–70. Eurographics Association, Aire-la-Ville (2006)
15. Kazhdan, M., Funkhouser, T., Rusinkiewicz, S.: Rotation invariant spherical harmonic representation of 3D shape descriptors, June 2003
16. Krizhevsky, A., Sutskever, I., Hinton, G.E.: Imagenet classification with deep convolutional neural networks. In: Pereira, F., Burges, C., Bottou, L., Weinberger, K. (eds.) Advances in Neural Information Processing Systems, vol. 25, pp. 1097–1105 (2012)
17. Laga, H.T., Schreck, A., Ferreira, A., Godil, I.P., Meshes, W., Lian, Z., Godil, A., Bustos, B., Daoudi, M., Hermans, J., Kawamura, S., Kurita, Y., Lavou, G., Nguyen, H.V., Ohbuchi, R., Ohkita, Y., Ohishi, Y., Porikli, F., Reuter, M., Sipiran, I., Smeets, D., Suetens, P., Tabia, H.: SHREC 2011 Track: shape retrieval on non-rigid 3D (2011)
18. Lévy, B., Petitjean, S., Ray, N., Maillot, J.: Least squares conformal maps for automatic texture atlas generation. ACM Trans. Graph. **21**(3), 362–371 (2002)
19. Masci, J., Boscaini, D., Bronstein, M.M., Vandergheynst, P.: Shapenet: Convolutional neural networks on non-euclidean manifolds. arXiv preprint arXiv:1501.06297 (2015)
20. Maturana, D., Scherer, S.: Voxnet: a 3D convolutional neural network for real-time object recognition. In: Signal Processing Letters (2015)
21. Novotni, M., Klein, R.: Shape retrieval using 3D zernike descriptors. Comput. Aided Design **36**, 1047–1062 (2004)
22. Praun, E., Hoppe, H.: Spherical parametrization and remeshing. In: ACM Transactions on Graphics (TOG), vol. 22, pp. 340–349. ACM (2003)
23. Rustamov, R.M.: Laplace-beltrami eigen functions for deformation invariant shape representation. Proceedings of the Fifth Eurographics Symposium on Geometry Processing, SGP 2007, pp. 225–233, Aire-la-Ville (2007)
24. Shen, L., Makedon, F.: Spherical mapping for processing of 3-D closed surfaces. In: Image and Vision Computing (2006)
25. Shen, L., Makedon, F.: Spherical mapping for processing of 3D closed surfaces. Image Vis. Comput. **24**(7), 743–761 (2006)
26. Shi, B., Bai, S., Zhou, Z., Bai, X.: DeepPano: deep panoramic representation for 3-D shape recognition. IEEE Signal Process. Lett. **22**(12), 2339–2343 (2015)
27. Sinha, A., Choi, C., Ramani, K.: DeepHand: robust hand pose estimation by completing a matrix imputed with deep features. In: The IEEE Conference on Computer Vision and Pattern Recognition (CVPR), June 2016
28. Sinha, A., Ramani, K.: Multi-scale kernels using random walks. Comput. Graphics Forum **33**(1), 164–177 (2014)
29. Solomon, J., de Goes, F., Studios, P.A., Peyré, G., Cuturi, M., Butscher, A., Nguyen, A., Du, T., Guibas, L.: Convolutional wasserstein distances: efficient optimal transportation on geometric domains. ACM Transactions on Graphics (Proceeding SIGGRAPH 2015) (2015)

30. Su, H., Maji, S., Kalogerakis, E., Learned-Miller, E.G.: Multi-view convolutional neural networks for 3D shape recognition. In: Proceeding ICCV (2015)
31. Sun, J., Ovsjanikov, M., Guibas, L.: A concise and provably informative multi-scale signature based on heat diffusion. In: Proceedings of the Symposium on Geometry Processing, SGP 2009, pp. 1383–1392, Aire-la-Ville (2009)
32. Wu, Z., Song, S., Khosla, A., Yu, F., Zhang, L., Tang, X., Xiao, J.: 3D ShapeNets: a deep representation for volumetric shapes. In: Proceedings of the IEEE Conference on Computer Vision and Pattern Recognition, pp. 1912–1920 (2015)
33. Yu, Y., Zhou, K., Xu, D., Shi, X., Bao, H., Guo, B., Shum, H.-Y.: Mesh editing with poisson-based gradient field manipulation. ACM Trans. Graph. **23**(3), 644–651 (2004)
34. Zhao, X., Su, Z., Gu, X.D., Kaufman, A., Sun, J., Gao, J., Luo, F.: Area-preservation mapping using optimal mass transport. IEEE Trans. Visual Comput. Graphics **19**(12), 2838–2847 (2013)
35. Zou, G., Hu, J., Gu, X., Hua, J.: Authalic parameterization of general surfaces using lie advection. IEEE Trans. Visual Comput. Graphics **17**(12), 2005–2014 (2011)

Deep Image Retrieval: Learning Global Representations for Image Search

Albert Gordo$^{(\boxtimes)}$, Jon Almazán, Jerome Revaud, and Diane Larlus

Computer Vision Group, Xerox Research Center Europe, Meylan, France
{Albert.Gordo,Jon.Almazan,Jerome.Revaud,Diane.Larlus}@xrce.xerox.com

Abstract. We propose a novel approach for instance-level image retrieval. It produces a global and compact fixed-length representation for each image by aggregating many region-wise descriptors. In contrast to previous works employing pre-trained deep networks as a black box to produce features, our method leverages a deep architecture trained for the specific task of image retrieval. Our contribution is twofold: (i) we leverage a ranking framework to learn convolution and projection weights that are used to build the region features; and (ii) we employ a region proposal network to learn which regions should be pooled to form the final global descriptor. We show that using clean training data is key to the success of our approach. To that aim, we use a large scale but noisy landmark dataset and develop an automatic cleaning approach. The proposed architecture produces a global image representation in a single forward pass. Our approach significantly outperforms previous approaches based on global descriptors on standard datasets. It even surpasses most prior works based on costly local descriptor indexing and spatial verification. Additional material is available at www.xrce.xerox. com/Deep-Image-Retrieval.

Keywords: Deep learning · Instance-level retrieval

1 Introduction

Since their ground-breaking results on image classification in recent ImageNet challenges [29,50], deep learning based methods have shined in many other computer vision tasks, including object detection [14] and semantic segmentation [31]. Recently, they also rekindled highly semantic tasks such as image captioning [12,28] and visual question answering [1]. However, for some problems such as *instance-level image retrieval*, deep learning methods have led to rather underwhelming results. In fact, for most image retrieval benchmarks, the state of the art is currently held by conventional methods relying on local descriptor matching and re-ranking with elaborate spatial verification [30,34,58,59].

Recent works leveraging deep architectures for image retrieval are mostly limited to using a pre-trained network as local feature extractor. Most efforts have been devoted towards designing image representations suitable for image retrieval on top of those features. This is challenging because representations for

© Springer International Publishing AG 2016
B. Leibe et al. (Eds.): ECCV 2016, Part VI, LNCS 9910, pp. 241–257, 2016.
DOI: 10.1007/978-3-319-46466-4_15

retrieval need to be compact while retaining most of the fine details of the images. Contributions have been made to allow deep architectures to accurately represent input images of different sizes and aspect ratios [5,27,60] or to address the lack of geometric invariance of convolutional neural network (CNN) features [15,48].

In this paper, we focus on *learning* these representations. We argue that one of the main reasons for the deep methods lagging behind the state of the art is the lack of supervised learning for the specific task of instance-level image retrieval. At the core of their architecture, CNN-based retrieval methods often use local features extracted using networks pre-trained on ImageNet for a classification task. These features are learned to distinguish between different semantic categories, but, as a side effect, are quite robust to intra-class variability. This is an undesirable property for instance retrieval, where we are interested in distinguishing between particular objects – even if they belong to the same semantic category. Therefore, learning features for the specific task of instance-level retrieval seems of paramount importance to achieve competitive results.

To this end, we build upon a recent deep representation for retrieval, the regional maximum activations of convolutions (R-MAC) [60]. It aggregates several image regions into a compact feature vector of fixed length and is thus robust to scale and translation. This representation can deal with high resolution images of different aspect ratios and obtains a competitive accuracy. We note that all the steps involved to build the R-MAC representation are differentiable, and so its weights can be learned in an end-to-end manner. Our **first contribution** is thus to use a *three-stream Siamese network* that explicitly optimizes the weights of the R-MAC representation for the image retrieval task by using a triplet ranking loss (Fig. 1).

To train this network, we leverage the public Landmarks dataset [6]. This dataset was constructed by querying image search engines with names of different landmarks and, as such, exhibits a very large amount of mislabeled and false positive images. This prevents the network from learning a good representation. We propose an automatic cleaning process, and show that on the cleaned data learning significantly improves.

Our **second contribution** consists in learning the pooling mechanism of the R-MAC descriptor. In the original architecture of [60], a rigid grid determines the location of regions that are pooled together. Here we propose to predict the location of these regions given the image content. We train a region proposal network with bounding boxes that are estimated for the Landmarks images as a by-product of the cleaning process. We show quantitative and qualitative evidence that region proposals significantly outperform the rigid grid.

The combination of our two contributions produces a novel architecture that is able to encode one image into a compact fixed-length vector in a single forward pass. Representations of different images can be then compared using the dot-product. Our method significantly outperforms previous approaches based on global descriptors. It even outperforms more complex approaches that involve keypoint matching and spatial verification at test time.

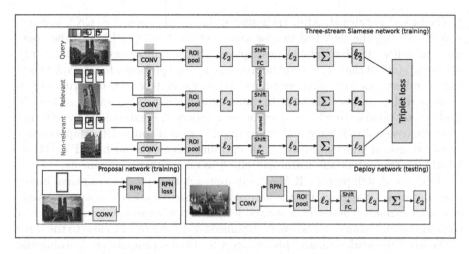

Fig. 1. Summary of the proposed CNN-based representation tailored for retrieval. At training time, image triplets are sampled and simultaneously considered by a *triplet-loss* that is well-suited for the task (top). A *region proposal network* (RPN) learns which image regions should be pooled (bottom left). At test time (bottom right), the query image is fed to the learned architecture to efficiently produce a *compact global image representation* that can be compared with the dataset image representations with a simple dot-product.

Finally, we would like to refer the reader to the recent work of Radenovic *et al.* [47], concurrent to ours and published in these same proceedings, that also proposes to learn representations for retrieval using a Siamese network on a geometrically-verified landmark dataset.

The rest of the paper is organized as follows. Section 2 discusses related works. Sections 3 and 4 present our contributions. Section 5 validates them on five different datasets. Finally Sect. 6 concludes the paper.

2 Related Work

We now describe previous works most related to our approach.

Conventional image retrieval. Early techniques for instance-level retrieval are based on bag-of-features representations with large vocabularies and inverted files [37,44]. Numerous methods to better approximate the matching of the descriptors have been proposed, see *e.g.* [24,35]. An advantage of these techniques is that spatial verification can be employed to re-rank a short-list of results [39,44], yielding a significant improvement despite a significant cost. Concurrently, methods that aggregate the local image patches have been considered. Encoding techniques, such as the Fisher Vector [40], or VLAD [25], combined with compression [22,42,46] produce global descriptors that scale to larger databases at the cost of reduced accuracy. All these methods can be combined with other post-processing techniques such as query expansion [3,8,9].

CNN-based retrieval. After their success in classification [29], CNN features were used as off-the-shelf features for image retrieval [6,48]. Although they out-perform other standard global descriptors, their performance is significantly below the state of the art. Several improvements were proposed to overcome their lack of robustness to scaling, cropping and image clutter. [48] performs region cross-matching and accumulates the maximum similarity per query region. [5] applies sum-pooling to whitened region descriptors. [27] extends [5] by allowing cross-dimensional weighting and aggregation of neural codes. Other approaches proposed hybrid models involving an encoding technique such as FV [41] or VLAD [15,38], potentially learnt as well [2] as one of their components.

Tolias *et al.* [60] propose R-MAC, an approach that produces a global image representation by aggregating the activation features of a CNN in a fixed layout of spatial regions. The result is a fixed-length vector representation that, when combined with re-ranking and query expansion, achieves results close to the state of the art. Our work extends this architecture by discriminatively learning the representation parameters and by improving the region pooling mechanism.

Fine-tuning for retrieval. Babenko *et al.* [6] showed that models pre-trained on ImageNet for object classification could be improved by fine-tuning them on an external set of Landmarks images. In this paper we confirm that fine-tuning the pre-trained models for the retrieval task is indeed crucial, but argue that one should use a good image representation (R-MAC) and a ranking loss instead of a classification loss as used in [6].

Localization/Region pooling. Retrieval methods that ground their descriptors in regions typically consider random regions [48] or a rigid grid of regions [60]. Some works exploit the center bias that benchmarks usually exhibit to weight their regions accordingly [5]. The spatial transformer network of [21] can be inserted in CNN architectures to transform input images appropriately, including by selecting the most relevant region for the task. In this paper, we would like to bias our descriptor towards interesting regions without paying an extra-cost or relying on a central bias. We achieve this by using a proposal network similar in essence to the Faster R-CNN detection method [49].

Siamese networks and metric learning. Siamese networks have commonly been used for metric learning [55], dimensionality reduction [17], learning image descriptors [53], and performing face identification [7,20,56]. Recently triplet networks (i.e. three stream Siamese networks) have been considered for metric learning [19,62] and face identification [51]. However, these Siamese networks usually rely on simpler network architectures than the one we use here, which involves pooling and aggregation of several regions.

3 Method

This section introduces our method for retrieving images in large collections. We first revisit the R-MAC representation (Sect. 3.1) showing that, despite its handcrafted nature, all of its components consist of differentiable operations.

From this it follows that one can learn the weights of the R-MAC representation in an end-to-end manner. To that aim we leverage a three-stream Siamese network with a triplet ranking loss. We also describe how to learn the pooling mechanism using a region proposal network (RPN) instead of relying on a rigid grid (Sect. 3.2). Finally we depict the overall descriptor extraction process for a given image (Sect. 3.3).

3.1   Learning to Retrieve Particular Objects

R-MAC revisited. Recently, Tolias *et al.* [60] presented R-MAC, a global image representation particularly well-suited for image retrieval. The R-MAC extraction process is summarized in any of the three streams of the network in Fig. 1 (top). In a nutshell, the convolutional layers of a pre-trained network (*e.g.* VGG16 [54]) are used to extract activation features from the images, which can be understood as local features that do not depend on the image size or its aspect ratio. Local features are max-pooled in different regions of the image using a multi-scale rigid grid with overlapping cells. These pooled region features are independently ℓ_2-normalized, whitened with PCA and ℓ_2-normalized again. Unlike spatial pyramids, instead of concatenating the region descriptors, they are sum-aggregated and ℓ_2-normalized, producing a compact vector whose size (typically $256 - 512$ dimensions) is independent of the number of regions in the image. Comparing two image vectors with dot-product can then be interpreted as an approximate many-to-many region matching.

One key aspect to notice is that *all these operations are differentiable*. In particular, the spatial pooling in different regions is equivalent to the *Region of Interest* (ROI) pooling [18], which is differentiable [13]. The PCA projection can be implemented with a shifting and a fully connected (FC) layer, while the gradients of the sum-aggregation of the different regions and the ℓ_2-normalization are also easy to compute. Therefore, one can implement a network architecture that, given an image and the precomputed coordinates of its regions (which depend only on the image size), produces the final R-MAC representation in a single forward pass. More importantly, *one can backpropagate through the network architecture to learn the optimal weights of the convolutions and the projection.*

Learning for particular instances. We depart from previous works on fine-tuning networks for image retrieval that optimize classification using cross-entropy loss [6]. Instead, we consider a ranking loss based on image triplets. It explicitly enforces that, given a query, a relevant element to the query and a non-relevant one, the relevant one is closer to the query than the other one. To do so, we use a three-stream Siamese network in which the weights of the streams are shared, see Fig. 1 top. Note that the number and size of the weights in the network (the convolutional filters and the shift and projection) is independent of the size of the images, and so we can feed each stream with images of different sizes and aspect ratios.

Let I_q be a query image with R-MAC descriptor q, I^+ be a relevant image with descriptor d^+, and I^- be a non-relevant image with descriptor d^-.

We define the ranking triplet loss as

$$L(I_q, I^+, I^-) = \frac{1}{2} \max(0, m + \|q - d^+\|^2 - \|q - d^-\|^2), \qquad (1)$$

where m is a scalar that controls the margin. Given a triplet with non-zero loss, the gradient is back-propagated through the three streams of the network, and the convolutional layers together with the "PCA" layers – the shifting and the fully connected layer – get updated.

This approach offers several advantages. First and foremost, we directly optimize a ranking objective. Second, we can train the network using images at the same (high) resolution that we use at test time[1]. Last, learning the optimal "PCA" can be seen as a way to perform discriminative large-margin metric learning [63] in which one learns a new space where relevant images are closer.

3.2 Beyond Fixed Regions: Proposal Pooling

The rigid grid used in R-MAC [60] to pool regions tries to ensure that the object of interest is covered by at least one of the regions. However, this uniform sampling poses two problems. First, as the grid is independent of the image content, it is unlikely that any of the grid regions accurately align with the object of interest. Second, many of the regions only cover background. This is problematic as the comparison between R-MAC signatures can be seen as a many-to-many region matching: image clutter will negatively affect the performance. Note that both problems are coupled: increasing the number of grid regions improves the coverage, but also the number of irrelevant regions.

We propose to replace the rigid grid with region proposals produced by a Region Proposal Network (RPN) trained to localize regions of interest in images. Inspired by the approach of Ren *et al.* [49], we model this process with a fully-convolutional network built on top of the convolutional layers of R-MAC (see bottom-left part of Fig. 1). This allows one to get the region proposals at almost zero cost. By using region proposals instead of the rigid grid we address both problems. First, the region proposals typically cover the object of interest more tightly than the rigid grid. Second, even if they do not overlap exactly with the region of interest, most of the proposals do overlap significantly with it (see Sect. 5.3), which means that increasing the number of proposals per image not only helps to increase the coverage but also helps in the many-to-many matching.

The main idea behind an RPN is to predict, for a set of candidate boxes of various sizes and aspects ratio, and at all possible image locations, a score describing how likely each box contains an object of interest. Simultaneously, for each candidate box it performs regression to improve its location. This is achieved by a fully-convolutional network consisting of a first layer that uses 3×3 filters, and two sibling convolutional layers with 1×1 filters that predict, for each candidate box in the image, both the *objectness* score and the regressed location. Non-maximum

---

[1] By contrast, fine-tuning networks such as VGG16 for classification using high-resolution images is not straightforward.

suppression is then performed on the ranked boxes to produce k final proposals per image that are used to replace the rigid grid.

To train the RPN, we assign a binary class label to each candidate box, depending on how much the box overlaps with the ground-truth region of interest, and we minimize an objective function with a multi-task loss that combines a classification loss (log loss over object vs background classes) and a regression loss (smooth ℓ_1 [13]). This is then optimized by backpropagation and stochastic gradient descent (SGD). For more details about the implementation and the training procedure of the RPNs, we refer the reader to [49].

We note that one could, in principle, learn the RPN and the ranking of the images simultaneously. However, preliminary experiments showed that correctly weighting both losses was difficult and led to unstable results. In our experiments, we first learn the R-MAC representation using a rigid grid, and only then we fix the convolutional layers and learn the RPN, which replaces the rigid grid.

3.3 Building a Global Descriptor

At test time, one can easily use this network to represent a high-resolution image. One feeds the image to the network, which produces the region proposals, pools the features inside the regions, embeds them into a more discriminative space, aggregates them, and normalizes them. All these operations happen in a single forward pass (see bottom-right part of Fig. 1). This process is also quite efficient: we can encode approximately 5 high-resolution (i.e. 724 pixels for the largest side) images per second using a single Nvidia K40 GPU.

4 Leveraging Large-Scale Noisy Data

To train our network for instance-level image retrieval we leverage a large-scale image dataset, the **Landmarks** dataset [6], that contains approximately 214K images of 672 famous landmark sites. Its images were collected through textual queries in an image search engine without thorough verification. As a consequence, they comprise a large variety of profiles: general views of the site, close-ups of details like statues or paintings, with all intermediate cases as well, but also site map pictures, artistic drawings, or even completely unrelated images, see Fig. 2.

We could only download a subset of all images due to broken URLs. After manual inspection, we merged some classes together due to partial overlap. We also removed classes with too few images. Finally, we meticulously removed all classes having an overlap with the Oxford 5k, Paris 6k, and Holidays datasets, on which we experiment, see Sect. 5. We obtained a set of about 192,000 images divided into 586 landmarks. We refer to this set as **Landmarks-full**. For our experiments, we use 168,882 images for the actual fine-tuning, and the 20,668 remaining ones to validate parameters.

Cleaning the Landmarks dataset. As we have mentioned, the Landmarks dataset present a large intra-class variability, with a wide variety of views and

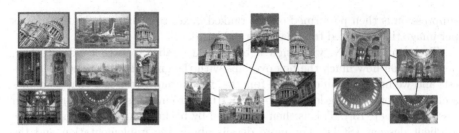

Fig. 2. Left: random images from the "St Paul's Cathedral" landmark. Green, gray and red borders resp. denote prototypical, non-prototypical, and incorrect images. **Right**: excerpt of the two largest connected components of the pairwise matching graph (corresponding to outside and inside pictures of the cathedral). (Color figure online)

profiles, and a non-negligible amount of unrelated images (Fig. 2). While this is not a problem when aiming for classification (the network can accommodate during training for this diversity and even for noise), for instance-level matching we need to train the network with images of the same particular object or scene. In this case, variability comes from different viewing scales, angles, lighting conditions and image clutter. We pre-process the Landmarks dataset to achieve this as follows.

We first run a strong image matching baseline within the images of each landmark class. We compare each pair of images using invariant keypoint matching and spatial verification [32]. We use the SIFT and Hessian-Affine keypoint detectors [32,33] and match keypoints using the first-to-second neighbor ratio rule [32]. This is known to outperform approaches based on descriptor quantization [43]. Afterwards, we verify all matches with an affine transformation model [44]. This heavy procedure is affordable as it is performed offline only once at training time.

Without loss of generality, we describe the rest of the cleaning procedure for a single landmark class. Once we have obtained a set of pairwise scores between all image pairs, we construct a graph whose nodes are the images and edges are pairwise matches. We prune all edges which have a low score. Then we extract the connected components of the graph. They correspond to different profiles of a landmark; see Fig. 2 that shows the two largest connected components for St Paul's Cathedral. In order to avoid any confusion, we only retain the largest connected component and discard the rest. This cleaning process leaves about 49,000 images (divided in 42,410 training and 6382 validation images) still belonging to one of the 586 landmarks, referred to as **Landmarks-clean**.

Bounding box estimation. Our second contribution (Sect. 3.2) is to replace the uniform sampling of regions in the R-MAC descriptor by a learned ROI selector. This selector is trained using bounding box annotations that we automatically estimate for all landmark images. To that aim we leverage the data obtained during the cleaning step. The position of verified keypoint matches is a meaningful cue since the object of interest is consistently visible across the

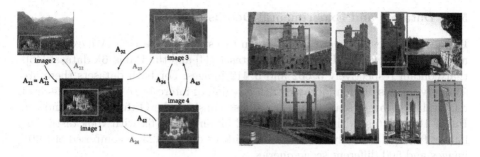

Fig. 3. Left: the bounding box from image 1 is projected into its graph neighbors using the affine transformations (blue rectangles). The current bounding box estimates (dotted red rectangles) are then updated accordingly. The diffusion process repeats through all edges until convergence. **Right**: initial and final bounding box estimates (resp. dotted red and plain green rectangles). (Color figure online)

landmark's pictures, whereas distractor backgrounds or foreground objects are varying and hence unmatched.

We denote the union of the connected components from all landmarks as a graph $S = \{V_S, E_S\}$. For each pair of connected images $(i, j) \in E_S$, we have a set of verified keypoint matches with a corresponding affine transformation A_{ij}. We first define an initial bounding box in both images i and j, denoted by B_i and B_j, as the minimum rectangle enclosing all matched keypoints. Note that a single image can be involved in many different pairs. In this case, the initial bounding box is the geometric median of all boxes[2], efficiently computed with [61]. Then, we run a diffusion process, illustrated in Fig. 3, in which for a pair (i, j) we predict the bounding box B_j using B_i and the affine transform A_{ij} (and conversely). At each iteration, bounding boxes are updated as: $B'_j = (\alpha - 1)B_j + \alpha A_{ij}B_i$, where α is a small update step (we set $\alpha = 0.1$ in our experiments). Again, the multiple updates for a single image are merged using geometric median, which is robust against poorly estimated affine transformations. This process iterates until convergence. As can be seen in Fig. 3, the locations of the bounding boxes are improved as well as their consistency across images.

5   Experiments

We now present our experimental results. We start by describing the datasets and experimental details (Sect. 5.1). We then evaluate our proposed ranking network (Sect. 5.2) and the region proposal pooling (Sect. 5.3). Finally, we compare our results to the state of the art (Sect. 5.4).

---

[2] Geometric median is robust to outlier boxes compared to *e.g.* averaging.

5.1 Datasets and Experimental Details

Datasets. We evaluate our approach on five standard datasets. We experiment mostly with the **Oxford 5k** building dataset [44] and the **Paris 6k** dataset [45], that contain respectively 5, 062 and 6, 412 images. For both datasets there are 55 query images, each annotated with a region of interest. To test instance-level retrieval on a larger-scale scenario, we also consider the **Oxford 105k** and the **Paris 106k** datasets that extend Oxford 5k and Paris 6k with 100k distractor images from [44]. Finally, the INRIA **Holidays** dataset [23] is composed of 1,491 images and 500 different scene queries.

Evaluation. For all datasets we use the standard evaluation protocols and report mean Average Precision (mAP). As is standard practice, in Oxford and Paris one uses only the annotated region of interest of the query, while for Holidays one uses the whole query image. Furthermore, the query image is removed from the dataset when evaluating on Holidays, but not on Oxford or Paris.

Experimental details. Our experiments use the very deep network (VGG16) of Simonyan *et al.* [54] pre-trained on the ImageNet ILSVRC challenge as a starting point. All further learning is performed on the Landmarks dataset unless explicitly noted. To perform fine-tuning with classification [6] we follow standard practice and resize the images to multiple scales (shortest side in the $[256 - 512]$ range) and extract random crops of 224×224 pixels. This fine-tuning process took approximately 5 days on a single Nvidia K40 GPU. When performing fine-tuning with the ranking loss, it is crucial to mine hard triplets in an efficient manner, as random triplets will mostly produce easy triplets or triplets with no loss. As a simple yet effective approach, we first perform a forward pass on approximately ten thousand images to obtain their representations. We then compute the losses of all the triplets involving those features (with margin $m = 0.1$), which is fast once the representations have been computed. We finally sample triplets with a large loss, which can be seen as hard negatives. We use them to train the network with SGD with momentum, with a learning rate of 10^{-3} and weight decay of $5 \cdot 10^{-5}$. Furthermore, as images are large, we can not feed more than one triplet in memory at a time. To perform batched SGD we accumulate the gradients of the backward passes and only update the weights every n passes, with $n = 64$ in our experiments. To increase efficiency, we only mine new hard triplets every 16 network updates. Following this process, we could process approximately 650 batches of 64 triplets per day on a single K40 GPU. We processed approximately 2000 batches in total, *i.e.*, 3 days of training. To learn the RPN, we train the net for 200k iterations with a weight decay of $5 \cdot 10^{-5}$ and a learning rate of 10^{-3}, which is decreased by a factor of 10 after 100k iterations. This process took less than 24 h.

5.2 Influence of Fine-Tuning the Representation

In this section we report retrieval experiments for the baselines and our ranking loss-based approach. All results are summarized in Table 1. First of all, as can

Table 1. Comparison of R-MAC [60], our reimplementation of it and the learned versions fine-tuned for classification on the full and the clean sets (C-Full and C-Clean) and fine-tuned for ranking on the clean set (R-Clean). All these results use the initial regular grid with no RPN.

Dataset	PCA	R-MAC		Learned R-MAC		
		[60]	Reimp.	C-Full	C-Clean	R-Clean
Oxford 5k	PCA Paris	66.9	66.9	-	-	-
	PCA Landmarks	-	66.2	74.8	75.2	81.1
Paris 6k	PCA Oxford	83.0	83.0	-	-	-
	PCA Landmarks	-	82.3	82.5	83.2	86.0

be seen in the first and second columns, the accuracy of our reimplementation of R-MAC is identical to the one of the original paper. We would also like to highlight the following points:

PCA learning. R-MAC [60] learns the PCA on different datasets depending on the target dataset (*i.e.* learned on Paris when evaluating on Oxford and vice versa). A drawback of this is that different models need to be generated depending on the target dataset. Instead, we use the Landmarks dataset to learn the PCA. This leads to a slight decrease in performance, but allows us to have a single universal model that can be used for all datasets.

Fine-tuning for classification. We evaluate the approach of Babenko *et al.* [6], where the original network pre-trained on ImageNet is fine-tuned on the Landmarks dataset on a classification task. We fine-tune the network with both the complete and the clean versions of Landmarks, denoted by *C-Full* and *C-Clean* in the table. This fine-tuning already brings large improvements over the original results. Also worth noticing is that, in this case, cleaning the dataset seems to bring only marginal improvements over using the complete dataset.

Fine-tuning for retrieval. We report results using the proposed ranking loss (Sect. 3.1) in the last column, denoted by *R-Clean*. We observe how this brings consistent improvements over using the less-principled classification fine-tuning. Contrary to the latter, we found of paramount importance to train our Siamese network using the clean dataset, as the triplet-based training process is less tolerant to outliers. Figure 4 (left) illustrates these findings by plotting the mAP obtained on Oxford 5k at several training epochs for different settings. It also shows the importance of initializing the network with a model that was first fine-tuned for classification on the full landmarks dataset. Even if *C-Full* and *C-Clean* obtain very similar scores, we speculate that the model trained with the full Landmark dataset has seen more diverse images so its weights are a better starting point.

Image size. R-MAC [60] finds important to use high resolution images (longest side resized to 1024 pixels). In our case, after fine-tuning, we found no noticeable

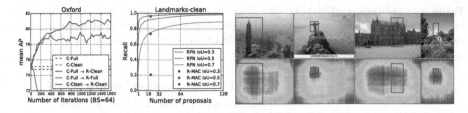

Fig. 4. Left: evolution of mAP when learning with a rank-loss for different initializations and training sets. **Middle**: landmark detection recall of our learned RPN for several IoU thresholds compared to the R-MAC fixed grid. **Right**: heat-map of the coverage achieved by our proposals on images from the Landmark and the Oxford 5k datasets. Green rectangles are ground-truth bounding boxes. (Color figure online)

Table 2. Proposals network. mAP results for Oxford 5k and Paris 6k obtained with a fixed-grid R-MAC, and our proposal network, for an increasingly large number of proposals, before and after fine-tuning with a ranking-loss. The rigid grid extracts, on average, 20 regions per image.

Dataset	Model	Grid	# Region Proposals					
			16	32	64	128	192	256
Oxford 5k	C-Full	74.8	74.9	75.3	75.3	76.4	76.7	76.8
	R-Clean	81.1	81.5	82.1	82.6	82.8	83.1	83.1
Paris 6k	C-Full	82.5	81.8	82.8	83.4	84.0	84.1	84.2
	R-Clean	86.0	85.4	86.2	86.7	86.9	87.0	87.1

difference in accuracy between 1024 and 724 pixels. All further experiments resize images to 724 pixels, significantly speeding up the image encoding and training.

5.3   Evaluation of the Proposal Network

In this section we evaluate the effect of replacing the rigid grid of R-MAC with the regions produced by the proposal network.

Evaluating proposals. We first evaluate the relevance of the regions predicted by our proposal network. Figure 4 (middle) shows the detection recall obtained in the validation set of Landmarks-Clean for different IoU (intersection over union) levels as a function of the number of proposals, and compares it with the recall obtained by the rigid grid of R-MAC. The proposals obtain significantly higher recall than the rigid grid even when their number is small. This is consistent with the quantitative results (Table 2), where 32–64 proposals already outperform the rigid regions. Figure 4 (right) visualizes the proposal locations as a heat-map on a few sample images of Landmarks and Oxford 5k. It clearly shows that the proposals are centered around the objects of interest. For the Oxford 5k images, the query boxes are somewhat arbitrarily defined. In this case, as expected, our proposals naturally align with the entire landmark in a query agnostic way.

Table 3. Accuracy comparison with the state of the art. Methods marked with an [a] use the full image as a query in Oxford and Paris instead of using the annotated region of interest as is standard practice. Methods with a [b] manually rotate Holidays images to fix their orientation. [c] denotes our reimplementation. We do not report QE results on Holidays as it is not a standard practice.

| | Method | Dim. | Datasets | | | | |
			Oxf5k	Par6k	Oxf105k	Par106k	Holidays
Global descriptors	Jégou & Zisserman [26]	1024	56.0	-	50.2	-	72.0
	Jégou & Zisserman [26]	128	43.3	-	35.3	-	61.7
	Gordo et al. [16]	512	-	-	-	-	79.0
	Babenko et al. [6]	128	55.7[a]	-	52.3[a]	-	75.9/78.9[b]
	Gong et al. [15]	2048	-	-	-	-	80.8
	Babenko & Lempitsky [5]	256	53.1	-	50.1	-	80.2[c]
	Ng et al. [36]	128	59.3[a]	59.0[a]	-	-	83.6
	Paulin et al. [38]	256K	56.5	-	-	-	79.3
	Perronnin & Larlus [41]	4000	-	-	-	-	84.7
	Tolias et al. [60]	512	66.9	83.0	61.6	75.7	85.2[c]/86.9[c,b]
	Kalantidis et al. [27]	512	68.2	79.7	63.3	71.0	84.9
	Arandjelovic et al. [2]	4096	71.6	79.7	-	-	83.1/87.5[b]
	Previous state of the art		71.6 [2]	83.0 [60]	63.3 [27]	75.7 [60]	84.9 [27]
	Ours	512	**83.1**	**87.1**	**78.6**	**79.7**	**86.7/89.1[b]**
Matching /Spatial verif./QE	Chum et al. [8]		82.7	80.5	76.7	71.0	-
	Danfeng et al. [10]		81.4	80.3	76.7	-	-
	Mikulik et al. [35]		84.9	82.4	79.5	77.3	75.8[b]
	Shen et al. [52]		75.2	74.1	72.9	-	76.2
	Tao et al. [57]		77.8	-	-	-	78.7
	Deng et al. [11]		84.3	83.4	80.2	-	84.7
	Tolias et al. [58]		86.9	85.1	85.3	-	81.3
	Tolias et al. [60]	512	77.3	86.5	73.2	79.8	-
	Tolias & Jégou [59]		**89.4**	82.8	84.0	-	-
	Xinchao et al. [30]		73.7	-	-	-	89.2
	Kalantidis et al. [27]	512	72.2	85.5	67.8	79.7	-
	Azizpour et al. [4]		79.0	85.1	-	-	**90.0**
	Previous state of the art		89.4 [59]	86.5 [60]	85.3 [58]	79.8 [60]	90.0 [4]
	Ours + QE	512	89.1	**91.2**	**87.3**	86.8	-

Retrieval results. We now evaluate the proposals in term of retrieval performance, see Table 2. The use of proposals improves over using a rigid grid, even with a baseline model only fine-tuned for classification (*i.e.* without ranking loss). On Oxford 5k, the improvements brought by the ranking loss and by the proposals are complementary, increasing the accuracy from 74.8 mAP with the C-Full model and a rigid grid up to 83.1 mAP with ranking loss and 256 proposals per image.

5.4   Comparison with the State of the Art

Finally we compare our results with the current state of the art in Table 3. In the first part of the table we compare our approach with other methods that also compute global image representations without performing any form of spatial verification or query expansion at test time. These are the closest methods to ours, yet our approach significantly outperforms them on all datasets – in one case by more than 15 mAP points. This demonstrates that a good underlying representation is important, but also that using features learned for the particular task is crucial.

In the second part of Table 3 we compare our approach with other methods that do not necessarily rely on a global representation. Many of these methods have larger memory footprints (*e.g.* [4,10,59,60]) and perform a costly spatial verification (SV) at test time (*e.g.* [30,35,60]). Most of them also perform query expansion (QE), which is a comparatively cheap strategy that significantly increases the final accuracy. We also experiment with average QE [9], which has a negligible cost (we use the 10 first returned results), and show that, despite not requiring a costly spatial verification stage at test time, our method is on equal foot or even improves the state of the art on most datasets. The only methods above us are the ones of Tolias and Jégou [59] (Oxford 5k) and Azizpour *et al.* [4] (Holidays). However, they are both hardly scalable as they require a lot of memory storage and a costly verification ([59] requires a slow spatial verification that takes more than 1 s per query, excluding the descriptor extraction time). Without spatial verification, the approach of Tolias and Jégou [59] achieves 84.8 mAP in 200 ms. In comparison, our approach reaches 89.1 mAP on Oxford 5k for a runtime of 1 ms per query and 2 kB data per image. Other methods such as [10,52,58] are scalable and obtain good results, but perform some learning on the target dataset, while in our case we use a single universal model.

6   Conclusions

We have presented an effective and scalable method for image retrieval that encodes images into compact global signatures that can be compared with the dot-product. The proposed approach hinges upon two main contributions. First, and in contrast to previous works [15,41,48], we *deeply* train our network for the specific task of image retrieval. Second, we demonstrate the benefit of predicting and pooling the likely locations of regions of interest when encoding the images. The first idea is carried out in a Siamese architecture [17] trained with a ranking loss while the second one relies on the successful architecture of region proposal networks [49]. Our approach very significantly outperforms the state of the art in terms of retrieval performance when using global signatures, and is on par or outperforms more complex methods while avoiding the need to resort to complex pre- or post-processing.

References

1. Antol, S., Agrawal, A., Lu, J., Mitchell, M., Batra, D., Zitnick, C.L., Parikh, D.: VQA: visual question answering. In: ICCV (2015)
2. Arandjelovic, R., Gronat, P., Torii, A., Pajdla, T., Sivic, J.: NetVLAD: CNN architecture for weakly supervised place recognition. In: CVPR (2016)
3. Arandjelovic, R., Zisserman, A.: Three things everyone should know to improve object retrieval. In: CVPR (2012)
4. Azizpour, H., Razavian, A., Sullivan, J., Maki, A., Carlsson, S.: Factors of transferability for a generic convnet representation. TPAMI **PP**(99), 1 (2015)
5. Babenko, A., Lempitsky, V.S.: Aggregating deep convolutional features for image retrieval. In: ICCV (2015)
6. Babenko, A., Slesarev, A., Chigorin, A., Lempitsky, V.: Neural codes for image retrieval. In: Fleet, D., Pajdla, T., Schiele, B., Tuytelaars, T. (eds.) ECCV 2014, Part I. LNCS, vol. 8689, pp. 584–599. Springer, Heidelberg (2014). doi:10.1007/978-3-319-10590-1_38
7. Chopra, S., Hadsell, R., Lecun, Y.: Learning a similarity metric discriminatively, with application to face verification. In: CVPR (2005)
8. Chum, O., Mikulik, A., Perdoch, M., Matas, J.: Total recall II: Query expansion revisited. In: CVPR (2011)
9. Chum, O., Philbin, J., Sivic, J., Isard, M., Zisserman, A.: Total recall: automatic query expansion with a generative feature model for object retrieval. In: ICCV (2007)
10. Danfeng, Q., Gammeter, S., Bossard, L., Quack, T., Van Gool, L.: Hello neighbor: accurate object retrieval with k-reciprocal nearest neighbors. In: CVPR (2011)
11. Deng, C., Ji, R., Liu, W., Tao, D., Gao, X.: Visual reranking through weakly supervised multi-graph learning. In: ICCV (2013)
12. Frome, A., Corrado, G.S., Shlens, J., Bengio, S., Dean, J., Ranzato, M.A., Mikolov, T.: DeViSE: a deep visual-semantic embedding model. In: NIPS (2013)
13. Girshick, R.: Fast R-CNN. In: CVPR (2015)
14. Girshick, R., Donahue, J., Darrell, T., Malik, J.: Rich feature hierarchies for accurate object detection and semantic segmentation. In: CVPR (2014)
15. Gong, Y., Wang, L., Guo, R., Lazebnik, S.: Multi-scale orderless pooling of deep convolutional activation features. In: Fleet, D., Pajdla, T., Schiele, B., Tuytelaars, T. (eds.) ECCV 2014, Part VII. LNCS, vol. 8695, pp. 392–407. Springer, Heidelberg (2014). doi:10.1007/978-3-319-10584-0_26
16. Gordo, A., Rodríguez-Serrano, J.A., Perronnin, F., Valveny, E.: Leveraging category-level labels for instance-level image retrieval. In: CVPR (2012)
17. Hadsell, R., Chopra, S., Lecun, Y.: Dimensionality reduction by learning an invariant mapping. In: CVPR (2006)
18. He, K., Zhang, X., Ren, S., Sun, J.: Spatial pyramid pooling in deep convolutional networks for visual recognition. In: Fleet, D., Pajdla, T., Schiele, B., Tuytelaars, T. (eds.) ECCV 2014, Part III. LNCS, vol. 8691, pp. 346–361. Springer, Heidelberg (2014). doi:10.1007/978-3-319-10578-9_23
19. Hoffer, E., Ailon, N.: Deep metric learning using triplet network. In: Feragen, A., Pelillo, M., Loog, M. (eds.) SIMBAD 2015. LNCS, vol. 9370, pp. 84–92. Springer, Heidelberg (2015). doi:10.1007/978-3-319-24261-3_7
20. Hu, J., Lu, J., Tan, Y.P.: Discriminative deep metric learning for face verification in the wild. In: CVPR (2014)

21. Jaderberg, M., Simonyan, K., Zisserman, A., Kavukcuoglu, K.: Spatial transformer networks. In: NIPS (2015)
22. Jégou, H., Chum, O.: Negative evidences and co-occurences in image retrieval: The benefit of PCA and whitening. In: Fitzgibbon, A., Lazebnik, S., Perona, P., Sato, Y., Schmid, C. (eds.) ECCV 2012, Part II. LNCS, vol. 7573, pp. 774–787. Springer, Heidelberg (2012). doi:10.1007/978-3-642-33709-3_55
23. Jegou, H., Douze, M., Schmid, C.: Hamming embedding and weak geometric consistency for large scale image search. In: Forsyth, D., Torr, P., Zisserman, A. (eds.) ECCV 2008, Part I. LNCS, vol. 5302, pp. 304–317. Springer, Heidelberg (2008). doi:10.1007/978-3-540-88682-2_24
24. Jégou, H., Douze, M., Schmid, C.: Improving bag-of-features for large scale image search. IJCV (2010)
25. Jégou, H., Douze, M., Schmid, C., Pérez, P.: Aggregating local descriptors into a compact image representation. In: CVPR (2010)
26. Jégou, H., Zisserman, A.: Triangulation embedding and democratic aggregation for image search. In: CVPR (2014)
27. Kalantidis, Y., Mellina, C., Osindero, S.: Cross-dimensional weighting for aggregated deep convolutional features. In: arXiv preprint arXiv:1512.04065 (2015)
28. Karpathy, A., Joulin, A., Fei-Fei, L.: Deep fragment embeddings for bidirectional image-sentence mapping. In: NIPS (2014)
29. Krizhevsky, A., Sutskever, I., Hinton, G.: ImageNet classification with deep convolutional neural networks. In: NIPS (2012)
30. Li, X., Larson, M., Hanjalic, A.: Pairwise geometric matching for large-scale object retrieval. In: CVPR (2015)
31. Long, J., Shelhamer, E., Darrell, T.: Fully convolutional networks for semantic segmentation. In: CVPR (2015)
32. Lowe, D.G.: Distinctive image features from scale-invariant keypoints. IJCV (2004)
33. Mikolajczyk, K., Schmid, C.: Scale & affine invariant interest point detectors. IJCV (2004)
34. Mikulík, A., Perdoch, M., Chum, O., Matas, J.: Learning a fine vocabulary. In: Daniilidis, K., Maragos, P., Paragios, N. (eds.) ECCV 2010, Part III. LNCS, vol. 6313, pp. 1–14. Springer, Heidelberg (2010). doi:10.1007/978-3-642-15558-1_1
35. Mikulik, A., Perdoch, M., Chum, O., Matas, J.: Learning vocabularies over a fine quantization. IJCV (2013)
36. Ng, J.Y.H., Yang, F., Davis, L.S.: Exploiting local features from deep networks for image retrieval. In: CVPR workshops (2015)
37. Nister, D., Stewenius, H.: Scalable recognition with a vocabulary tree. In: CVPR (2006)
38. Paulin, M., Douze, M., Harchaoui, Z., Mairal, J., Perronin, F., Schmid, C.: Local convolutional features with unsupervised training for image retrieval. In: ICCV (2015)
39. Perdoch, M., Chum, O., Matas, J.: Efficient representation of local geometry for large scale object retrieval. In: CVPR (2009)
40. Perronnin, F., Dance, C.: Fisher kernels on visual vocabularies for image categorization. In: CVPR (2007)
41. Perronnin, F., Larlus, D.: Fisher vectors meet neural networks: a hybrid classification architecture. In: CVPR (2015)
42. Perronnin, F., Liu, Y., Sánchez, J., Poirier, H.: Large-scale image retrieval with compressed fisher vectors. In: CVPR (2010)

43. Philbin, J., Isard, M., Sivic, J., Zisserman, A.: Descriptor learning for efficient retrieval. In: Daniilidis, K., Maragos, P., Paragios, N. (eds.) ECCV 2010, Part III. LNCS, vol. 6313, pp. 677–691. Springer, Heidelberg (2010). doi:10.1007/978-3-642-15558-1_49

44. Philbin, J., Chum, O., Isard, M., Sivic, J., Zisserman, A.: Object retrieval with large vocabularies and fast spatial matching. In: CVPR (2007)

45. Philbin, J., Chum, O., Isard, M., Sivic, J., Zisserman, A.: Lost in quantization: Improving particular object retrieval in large scale image databases. In: CVPR (2008)

46. Radenovic, F., Jegou, H., Chum, O.: Multiple measurements and joint dimensionality reduction for large scale image search with short vectors-extended version. ICMR (2015)

47. Radenovic, F., Tolias, G., Chum, O.: CNN image retrieval learns from BoW: unsupervised fine-tuning with hard examples. In: Leibe, B., et al. (eds.) ECCV 2016, Part I. LNCS, vol. 9905, pp. 3–20. Springer, Heidelberg (2016)

48. Razavian, A.S., Azizpour, H., Sullivan, J., Carlsson, S.: CNN features off-the-shelf: an astounding baseline for recognition. In: CVPR Deep Vision Workshop (2014)

49. Ren, S., He, K., Girshick, R., Sun, J.: Faster R-CNN: towards real-time object detection with region proposal networks. In: NIPS (2015)

50. Russakovsky, O., Deng, J., Su, H., Krause, J., Satheesh, S., Ma, S., Huang, Z., Karpathy, A., Khosla, A., Bernstein, M., Berg, A.C., Fei-Fei, L.: Imagenet large scale visual recognition challenge. IJCV (2015)

51. Schroff, F., Kalenichenko, D., Philbin, J.: FaceNet: a unified embedding for face recognition and clustering. In: CVPR (2015)

52. Shen, X., Lin, Z., Brandt, J., Wu, Y.: Spatially-constrained similarity measurefor large-scale object retrieval. TPAMI (2014)

53. Simo-Serra, E., Trulls, E., Ferraz, L., Kokkinos, I., Fua, P., Moreno-Noguer, F.: Discriminative learning of deep convolutional feature point descriptors. In: ICCV (2015)

54. Simonyan, K., Zisserman, A.: Very deep convolutional networks for large-scale image recognition. In: ICLR (2015)

55. Song, H.O., Xiang, Y., Jegelka, S., Savarese, S.: Deep metric learning via lifted structured feature embedding. In: CVPR (2016)

56. Sun, Y., Chen, Y., Wang, X., Tang, X.: Deep learning face representation by joint identification-verification. In: NIPS (2014)

57. Tao, R., Gavves, E., Snoek, C.G., Smeulders, A.W.: Locality in generic instance search from one example. In: CVPR (2014)

58. Tolias, G., Avrithis, Y., Jégou, H.: Image search with selective match kernels: aggregation across single and multiple images. IJCV (2015)

59. Tolias, G., Jégou, H.: Visual query expansion with or without geometry: refining local descriptors by feature aggregation. PR (2015)

60. Tolias, G., Sicre, R., Jégou, H.: Particular object retrieval with integral max-pooling of CNN activations. In: ICLR (2016)

61. Vardi, Y., Zhang, C.H.: The multivariate L1-median and associated data depth. In: Proceedings of the National Academy of Sciences (2004)

62. Wang, J., Song, Y., Leung, T., Rosenberg, C., Wang, J., Philbin, J., Chen, B., Wu, Y.: Learning fine-grained image similarity with deep ranking. In: CVPR (2014)

63. Weinberger, K.Q., Saul, L.K.: Distance metric learning for large margin nearest neighbor classification. JMLR (2009)

Building Scene Models by Completing and Hallucinating Depth and Semantics

Miaomiao Liu[1]([✉]), Xuming He[1], and Mathieu Salzmann[2]

[1] Data61, CSIRO, and ANU, Canberra, Australia
miaomiao.liu@data61.csiro.au, xuming.he@anu.edu.au
[2] CVLab, EPFL, Lausanne, Switzerland
mathieu.salzmann@epfl.ch

Abstract. Building 3D scene models has been a longstanding goal of computer vision. The great progress in depth sensors brings us one step closer to achieving this in a single shot. However, depth sensors still produce imperfect measurements that are sparse and contain holes. While depth completion aims at tackling this issue, it ignores the fact that some regions of the scene are occluded by the foreground objects. Building a scene model would therefore require to hallucinate the depth behind these objects. In contrast with existing methods that either rely on manual input, or focus on the indoor scenario, we introduce a fully-automatic method to jointly complete and hallucinate depth and semantics in challenging outdoor scenes. To this end, we develop a two-layer model representing both the visible information and the hidden one. At the heart of our approach lies a formulation based on the Mumford-Shah functional, for which we derive an effective optimization strategy. Our experiments evidence that our approach can accurately fill the large holes in the input depth maps, segment the different kinds of objects in the scene, and hallucinate the depth and semantics behind the foreground objects.

1 Introduction

Building 3D models of real scenes has been a longstanding goal of computer vision. While impressive results can be achieved with multi-view and video-based approaches [1–4], the progress of depth sensors and their decreasing prices make them an attractive alternative, able to capture 3D in a single shot [5]. Unfortunately, even the best depth sensors still provide imperfect measurements. In particular, these measurements are often sparse and contain large holes due to various factors, such as reflective surfaces or too-distant portions of the scenes.

Overcoming these limitations has therefore recently become a popular research topic. For instance, *depth super-resolution* [6–11] tackles the sparseness issue and attempts to densify the observed depth data. Typically, however, existing methods assume that the measurements are regularly spaced, and are

Electronic supplementary material The online version of this chapter (doi:10.1007/978-3-319-46466-4_16) contains supplementary material, which is available to authorized users.

B. Leibe et al. (Eds.): ECCV 2016, Part VI, LNCS 9910, pp. 258–274, 2016.
DOI: 10.1007/978-3-319-46466-4_16

thus ill-suited to handle large holes. By contrast, *depth completion* or *inpainting* [12,13] are designed to handle irregular measurements and fill holes in the input depth maps by leveraging RGB image information, or fusing multiple depth measurements [14]. These methods, however, simply complete the observed data. As a consequence, they are ill-suited to build a model of a scene, where one is *not* interested in modeling the foreground objects. To address this problem, one should truly *hallucinate* the depth behind the observed foreground objects.

Only little work has been done to tackle the task of depth hallucination from a noisy depth map and its corresponding RGB image [12,13,15,16], and existing methods typically work under additional assumptions. For example, [12,13] rely on a user-defined foreground mask to hallucinate the background depth. The method in [15] relies on a layered depth model simply assuming that each layer is a smoothly varying surface, thus not considering semantics or image information. While [16] exploits image and semantics, it relies on CAD models to represent the foreground objects. Furthermore, both methods were designed for the indoor scenario, and are thus ill-suited to handle complex outdoor scenes.

By contrast, in this paper, we introduce a fully automatic approach to performing depth completion and hallucination for general (outdoor) scenes in a single shot. To this end, we develop a two-layer scene model accounting for the visible information and the hidden one. In each layer, we jointly estimate the depth and the semantics of the scene. Not only does this let us leverage depth to detect the foreground objects, but it also allows us to exploit the dependencies between depth and semantics to improve completion and hallucination. As evidenced by Fig. 1, our approach lets us accurately fill the large holes in the input depth maps, segment the different kinds of objects observed in the scene, and hallucinate the depth and semantics behind the foreground objects.

Specifically, we rely on the assumptions that depth is piecewise planar, semantics piecewise constant, and that the discontinuities of both modalities should largely coincide. We show that these assumptions can be formalized with a single Mumford-Shah functional. We then formulate the task of jointly completing and hallucinating depth and semantics as a discrete-continuous optimization problem whose variables encode a foreground-background mask and two layers of depth and semantics information: one for the data that is visible in the image/depth map and one for the data that is hidden behind the foreground. Following an alternating optimization strategy, we show that each type of variables has an elegant solution; the discrete ones can be computed via simple thresholding, and the continuous ones via a primal-dual algorithm implemented on the GPU. Altogether, this provides us with an effective framework to build scene models from a single noisy depth map and its corresponding RGB image despite the presence of undesirable foreground objects.

We demonstrate the effectiveness of our approach on two datasets, *i.e.*, KITTI [17] and Stixel [18]. Our experiments evidence that our method can produce accurate models of complex outdoor scenes without requiring any manual intervention. This, we believe, constitutes a significant step towards making 3D scene modeling in real, dynamic environments practical.

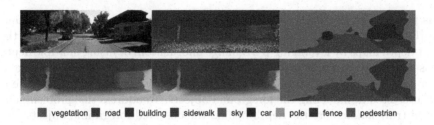

vegetation ■ road ■ building ■ sidewalk ■ sky ■ car ■ pole ■ fence ■ pedestrian

Fig. 1. Our approach. Given an input RGB image and a noisy, incomplete depth map, we complete and hallucinate depth and semantic to produce a complete scene model. First row: Input RGB image, incomplete depth measurements, estimated semantics; Second row: completed depth for the visible layer, hallucinated depth and semantics for the hidden layer. (Color figure online)

2   Related Work

With access to depth sensors becoming easier everyday, increasingly many methods rely on depth as input for various applications, such as autonomous driving [17], augmented reality [19] and personal robotics [20]. Unfortunately, depth sensors are not perfect; they typically produce relatively sparse measurements with large holes.

Depth super-resolution attempts to overcome the sparseness issue by generating a high-resolution depth map from a low-resolution one. This is typically achieved via Markov Random Fields [6,7,12], bilateral filtering [21], layered representations [22], patch-based approaches [10,11], or depth transfer [8,9]. These approaches, however, inherently assume to have access to regularly-spaced depth measurements, and thus cannot handle large holes in depth maps.

By contrast, depth completion techniques have been designed to work with irregular measurements and to fill in large holes. In this context, Liu et al. [23] combine a modified fast matching method with guided filtering to inpaint Kinect depth maps. In [24], image segmentation is exploited to complete range data. Herrera et al. [25] propose an MRF with second-order prior to inpaint piece-wise planar depth maps. In [26], depth completion is formulated within a total variation framework where image cues guide the completion process. A different approach to depth completion consists of treating a depth map as an intensity image, and rely on standard image inpainting algorithms, such as [27,28]. All the above-mentioned methods focus on depth completion form a single view and aim at completing the visible scene information only. By contrast, some approaches have proposed to exploit multiple views [14,29] and thus can handle the fact that parts of the scene are hidden in some views, albeit not all of them. Similarly, great progress has been made in building complete scene models by fusing multiple noisy depth maps [30–32]. These methods, however, assume to have access to multiple input depth images.

Only little work has been done on the problem of building a complete scene model in one shot, despite the presence of occluding objects. Guo and Hoiem [33]

focus on semantic labeling of unseen surfaces without depth information. In the context of stereo matching, Bleyer et al. [34] introduce a method that hallucinates depth in the regions that are occluded in one view, but not in both. In [12,13], while the goal is indeed to replace the depth of foreground objects with that of the background, the methods assume to be given a perfect foreground mask, defined by a user. As a consequence, these approaches truly perform depth completion, albeit without the knowledge of the RGB intensity behind the foreground mask. By contrast, [15,16] work without any manual input. However, in both cases, the methods were designed for the indoor scenario, and are thus ill-suited to model complex outdoor scenes, which are typically much more challenging.

In this paper, we introduce a fully-automatic approach to jointly completing and hallucinating depth and semantics. A key component of our approach is the use of a Mumford-Shah functional [35], which defines a non-convex energy function that encourages piece-wise constant solutions. Strekalovskiy and Cremers [36] develop a real-time primal-dual algorithm for minimizing the Mumford-Shah functional with a single variable, which we use and extend in this paper. Furthermore, our work relies on the piece-wise planar world assumption [37]. Despite its simplicity, it has been widely adopted in modeling outdoor man-made scenes [38,39]. Our work also relates to 3D scene understanding, where joint semantics and depth prediction has been explored, e.g., [40]. However, to the best of our knowledge existing methods do not recover hidden surfaces.

3 Our Approach

Given partial depth measurements and a corresponding intensity image, our goal is to produce a complete scene model with background depth and semantics at every pixel, including those that are hidden by foreground objects. To this end, we need to simultaneously perform depth completion, reason about semantics, and hallucinate the background scene behind the foreground objects.

To achieve this, we introduce a two-layer scene representation modeling the visible information and the hidden one. Each layer consists of two modalities: depth and semantics. The resulting model is encoded by a discrete-continuous optimization problem. In Sect. 4, we develop an optimization procedure to minimize the corresponding energy, thus allowing us to jointly complete and hallucinate depth and semantics.

3.1 A Visible Layer for Semantics-Aware Depth Completion

We first focus on modeling the scene that is visible in the input data. We assume that the underlying scene is piecewise planar and the corresponding semantic label map piecewise constant. Furthermore, we rely on the intuition that the depth discontinuities are often aligned with the boundaries of semantic classes, which lets us exploit the semantics to further regularize depth completion.

Let I be an input image of size $m \times n$ and $\mathbf{x} \in \Omega$ denote a pixel location on the two dimensional image plane Ω. We associate each pixel with two variables encoding depth value and semantic label, respectively. The semantic label

$\mathbf{s}^v(\mathbf{x}) \in \mathbb{R}^L$ is represented as an L-dimensional vector for L classes. As for depth, in this work, we make use of a disparity-based representation.[1] The motivation behind this is the following: Let $y^v(\mathbf{x}) \in \mathbb{R}$ be the disparity value at pixel $\mathbf{x}$. This disparity value can be equivalently encoded by plane parameters $\mathbf{u}^v(\mathbf{x}) \in R^3$, since we can write $y^v(\mathbf{x}) = \mathbf{p}(\mathbf{x})^T \mathbf{u}^v(\mathbf{x})$, where $\mathbf{p}(\mathbf{x}) = (\mathbf{x}^T, 1)^T$ is the homogeneous coordinate representation of $\mathbf{x}$. Then, our piecewise planar assumption of the depth map, which is equivalent to a piecewise planar assumption of the disparity map, can be encoded by a piecewise *constant* assumption on the plane parameters. This therefore allows us to define a unified Mumford-Shah functional on $\mathbf{u}^v$ and $\mathbf{s}^v$, which simultaneously encodes our two initial assumptions.

The Mumford-Shah functional [35] was originally introduced to compute a piecewise smooth approximation of observed data. In our context, let us denote by $\{y^o(\mathbf{x})\}_{\mathbf{x} \in \Omega}$ the incomplete disparity measurements, with disparity observation mask $\{d(\mathbf{x})\}_{\mathbf{x} \in \Omega}$, where $d(\mathbf{x}) = 1$ if the disparity measurement at pixel location $\mathbf{x}$ is valid, and 0 otherwise. Furthermore, let $\mathbf{s}^o(\mathbf{x})$ be a noisy label probability distribution at pixel $\mathbf{x}$, obtained by any image-based semantic labeling method. Our goal therefore is for our visible layer to fit the observed data, and thanks to our change of variable, that both $\mathbf{u}^v$ and $\mathbf{s}^v$ are piecewise constant while having their discontinuities aligned. This can be expressed by a coupled Mumford-Shah functional of the form

$$E_v(\mathbf{u}^v, \mathbf{s}^v) = E_d(\mathbf{u}^v, \mathbf{s}^v) + E_{r,v}(\mathbf{u}^v, \mathbf{s}^v), \tag{1}$$

where $E_d(\mathbf{u}^v, \mathbf{s}^v)$ is the data fidelity term, and $E_{r,v}(\mathbf{u}^v, \mathbf{s}^v)$ denotes the regularization term that jointly encodes the piecewise constant and aligned discontinuities assumptions. We now describe these two energy terms in details.

Data term. The data term encourages the disparity and semantic label predictions to be consistent with the incomplete disparity measurements and the noisy semantic label probabilities. This can be expressed as

$$E_d(\mathbf{u}^v, \mathbf{s}^v) = \sum_{\mathbf{x} \in \Omega} d \cdot (\mathbf{p}^T \mathbf{u}^v - y^o)^2 + \eta_d \sum_{\mathbf{x} \in \Omega} \|\mathbf{s}^v - \mathbf{s}^o\|^2 . \tag{2}$$

where η_d is a weight that balances the influence of depth and semantics.

Regularization term. The regularization term encourages both $\mathbf{u}^v$ and $\mathbf{s}^v$ to be piecewise constant while having their discontinuities aligned. Following the Mumford-Shah formalism, we express this as

$$E_{r,v}(\mathbf{u}^v, \mathbf{s}^v) = \eta_{rv} \sum_{\mathbf{x} \in \Omega} \min(\alpha_1 \|\mathbf{K}\mathbf{u}^v\|^2 + \|\mathbf{K}\mathbf{s}^v\|^2, \lambda_1) , \tag{3}$$

where η_{rv} and α_1 are parameters controlling the strength of the smoothness and of the coupling between the two modalities and λ_1 is the truncation parameter.

---

[1] Note that using disparity instead of depth does not really come at any loss of generality, since they simply are the inverse of each other, up to a constant. If provided with depth measurements for the image pixels, one can therefore easily convert them to pseudo-disparities.

Here, we further rely on the oriented gradient operator $\mathbf{K}$ of [26], which computes an image-adaptive gradient for each channel of $\mathbf{u}^v$ and $\mathbf{s}^v$. More specifically, the oriented gradient operator $\mathbf{K}$ at location $\mathbf{x}$ is defined by $T_I(\mathbf{x})\nabla$, where T_I is an image-based anisotropic diffusion tensor. This tensor is defined as

$$T_I = \exp(-\beta|\nabla I|^\gamma)\mathbf{n}\mathbf{n}^T + \mathbf{n}^\perp\mathbf{n}^{\perp T}, \tag{4}$$

where $\mathbf{n} = \frac{\nabla I}{|\nabla I|}$ and $\mathbf{n}^\perp$ is the normal vector to the image gradient. Note that T_I is a symmetric matrix, and hence $\mathbf{K} = T_I(\mathbf{x})\nabla$ is a linear operator.

3.2 Adding a Hidden Layer for Depth and Semantics Hallucination

Recall that our goal is to produce a complete scene model from incomplete depth measurements. While the functional introduced in the previous section can complete the missing depth it still only represents the visible information. As such, it is unable to infer the scene depth and semantics behind the foreground objects. To address this limitation, we incorporate a hidden layer that focuses on modeling and hallucinating the depth and semantics of the background scene.

Formally, we split the semantic class set $\mathcal{L}$ into two subsets, one for the foreground classes $\mathcal{L}_f$ and the other for the background ones $\mathcal{L}_b$. At each pixel location $\mathbf{x}$, we introduce two additional variables, $\mathbf{u}^h(\mathbf{x}) \in \mathbb{R}^3$ and $\mathbf{s}^h(\mathbf{x}) \in \mathbb{R}^L$, which encode the (potentially occluded) disparity value and semantic label at the hidden scene layer at $\mathbf{x}$. Furthermore, we define a binary variable $m(\mathbf{x})$ indicating the foreground class mask (i.e., where the hidden layer is invisible). In other words, for the pixels where $m(\mathbf{x}) = 1$, there are neither disparity measurements nor semantic predictions for the hidden layer variables $\mathbf{u}^h(\mathbf{x})$ and $\mathbf{s}^h(\mathbf{x})$. Note that this binary variable is not strictly necessary, since this information can be extracted from the semantics variables. However, as will be discussed in Sect. 4, introducing it makes the resulting problem easier to optimize.

To hallucinate the depth and semantics of the hidden scene layer, we rely on the following assumptions/constraints: In the parts of the image that correspond to foreground, (1) the hidden layer should be jointly piecewise constant in $\mathbf{u}^h$ and $\mathbf{s}^h$; (2) given training data, the hidden layer variables should follow the data statistics; (3) In the parts of the image that correspond to background, the visible and hidden layers should agree; (4) The mask and the visible semantics should be coherent. Below, we formalize these assumptions by defining a corresponding set of energy terms and linear constraints.

(1) Piecewise constancy. Similarly to the visible layer, we define a regularization term $E_{r,h}(\mathbf{u}^h, \mathbf{s}^h, m)$ that encourages $\mathbf{u}^h$ and $\mathbf{s}^h$ to be piecewise constant and have aligned discontinuities. Here, however, we only enforce this term on the foreground regions, i.e., where $m(\mathbf{x}) = 1$. This can be expressed as

$$E_{r,h}(\mathbf{u}^h, \mathbf{s}^h, m) = \eta_{rh} \sum_{\mathbf{x}} m \cdot \min(\alpha_2\|\nabla\mathbf{u}^h\|^2 + \|\nabla\mathbf{s}^h\|^2, \lambda_2), \tag{5}$$

where η_{rh} and α_2 are parameters controlling the strength of the smoothness and of the coupling between the two modalities, and λ_2 is the truncation parameter.

As there are no image cues for the hidden layer in the foreground regions, we use the standard gradient to penalize the discontinuities.

(2) Training data statistics. Given training data, we compute an average disparity map for each background class $k \in \mathcal{L}_b$, denoted by $\{y_k^s(\mathbf{x})\}_{\mathbf{x}\in\Omega}$. We refer the reader to Sect. 5 for the details of this process. We then encourage the disparity and semantics of the hidden layer to be consistent with this statistics, which can be expressed as

$$E_s(\mathbf{u}^h, \mathbf{s}^h, m) = \eta_s \sum_{\mathbf{x}} m \cdot \sum_{k\in\mathcal{L}_b} \mathbf{s}_k^h (\mathbf{p}^T \mathbf{u}^h - y_k^s)^2 \,. \tag{6}$$

where η_s is a weight defining the influence of this term.

(3) Agreement between the two layers. These constraints can be directly expressed as

$$\mathbf{u}^h(\mathbf{x}) = \mathbf{u}^v(\mathbf{x}), \quad \mathbf{s}^h(\mathbf{x}) = \mathbf{s}^v(\mathbf{x}), \quad \forall \mathbf{x} \mid m(\mathbf{x}) = 0 \,, \tag{7}$$

(4) Coherent mask and visible semantics. We encourage the mask and the visible semantics to agree by penalizing the discrepancy between the total probability mass of foreground classes predicted by $\mathbf{s}^v$ and the mask variable at every pixel. This can be written as

$$E_c(\mathbf{s}^v, m) = \eta_c \sum_{\mathbf{x}} \Big(\sum_{k\in\mathcal{L}_f} \mathbf{s}_k^v - m + b \Big)^2 \,. \tag{8}$$

where η_c is a weighting parameter and b is a bias for the foreground mask.

Altogether, our two-layer approach to completing and hallucinating depth and semantics can be expressed as the discrete-continuous optimization problem

$$\min_{\mathbf{u}^v,\mathbf{s}^v,\mathbf{u}^h,\mathbf{s}^h,m} E_d + E_{r,v} + E_{r,h} + E_s + E_c \tag{9}$$

$$\text{s.t.} \quad \mathbf{u}^h(\mathbf{x}) = \mathbf{u}^v(\mathbf{x}), \ \mathbf{s}^h(\mathbf{x}) = \mathbf{s}^v(\mathbf{x}) \quad \forall \mathbf{x} \mid m(\mathbf{x}) = 0$$

$$\sum_k \mathbf{s}_k^v(\mathbf{x}) = 1, \ \mathbf{s}_j^v(\mathbf{x}) \ge 0, \ \sum_k \mathbf{s}_k^h(\mathbf{x}) = 1, \ \mathbf{s}_j^h(\mathbf{x}) \ge 0, \quad \forall \mathbf{x}, j$$

$$m(\mathbf{x}) \in \{0, 1\}, \quad \forall \mathbf{x}$$

where E_d, $E_{r,v}$, $E_{r,h}$, E_s, E_c are defined in Eqs. (2), (3), (5), (6) and (8), respectively. The first two constraints come from Eq. (7), and the third and fourth ones encode the simplex domain of probability distributions, and the fifth one the binary nature of the foreground mask m.

4   Optimizing Our Two-Layer Model

The optimization problem encoding our two-layer problem, defined in Eq. (9), is challenging to solve, since it has a large number of coupled discrete and continuous variables. Fortunately, given the disparity and semantics, optimizing the mask is straightforward; the optimal mask value at each pixel can be computed in a closed form. Furthermore, when the mask variables are given, the energy functional decomposes into two subproblems: one for the visible layer, and one for the hidden one. These subproblems correspond to multi-modal versions of the Mumford-Shah functional. An efficient first-order primal-dual algorithm was introduced by [36] to tackle the single-modality case. We show that this algorithm can be extended to address the multi-modal scenario.

We therefore adopt an alternating procedure to minimize Eq. (9). This procedure consists of three steps repeated iteratively. In the first and second step, we optimize w.r.t. the visible and hidden layer, respectively, and, in the third step, we update the mask variables. Since our procedure decreases the energy functional in every cycle, it converges to a local minimum. Below, we first review the first-order primal-dual algorithm of [36] for solving the Mumford-Shah functional and then discuss the solution to each step of our minimization strategy.

Primal-Dual Algorithm for the Mumford-Shah Functional. The primal-dual algorithm in [36] aims to solve a non-convex optimization problem of form

$$\min_{\mathbf{y}} D(\mathbf{y}) + R(\mathbf{A}\mathbf{y}) , \qquad (10)$$

where $D(\cdot)$ usually denotes a data fidelity term, and $R(\cdot)$ is the regularization term encouraging piecewise smoothness in the Mumford-Shah functional. Let $\mathbf{A}$ denote a linear operator, which can be the gradient operator ∇, or an oriented gradient operator $\mathbf{K}$ additionally encoding image gradient information.

The primal-dual formulation introduces a dual variable $\mathbf{q}$ and solves the equivalent saddle-point problem

$$\min_{\mathbf{y}} \max_{\mathbf{q}} \ D(\mathbf{y}) + < \mathbf{q}, \mathbf{A}\mathbf{y} > -R^*(\mathbf{q}). \qquad (11)$$

where R^* is the conjugate of the regularization term. Following the fast Mumford-Shah method of [36], the primal-dual update equations can be written as

$$\mathbf{q}^{n+1} = prox_{\sigma_n, R^*}(\mathbf{q}^n + \sigma_n \mathbf{A}\bar{\mathbf{y}}^n), \quad \mathbf{y}^{n+1} = prox_{\tau_n, D}(\mathbf{y}^n - \tau_n \mathbf{A}^{-1}\mathbf{q}^{n+1}), (12)$$

$$\theta_n = \frac{1}{\sqrt{1 + 4\tau_n}}, \ \tau_{n+1} = \theta_n \tau_n, \ \sigma_{n+1} = \frac{\sigma_n}{\theta_n}. \qquad (13)$$

$$\bar{\mathbf{y}}^{n+1} = \mathbf{y}^{n+1} + \theta_n(\mathbf{y}^{n+1} - \mathbf{y}^n), \qquad (14)$$

where $prox_{.,.}(\cdot)$ denotes the proximal operator. The convergence [41] of this primal-dual procedure for a convex problem depends on the parameter values τ and σ, which must satisfy $\tau\sigma\|\mathbf{A}\|^2 \leq 1$. For non-convex functional, [36] shows the algorithm generates a bounded solution with empirically convergence.

Our procedure uses a similar primal-dual procedure to optimize the subproblems corresponding to the visible and hidden layers. These subproblems have a specific functional form for D and R. Moreover, they rely on two modalities, $\mathbf{u}$ and $\mathbf{s}$. Below, we develop our algorithms for the visible and hidden layers, respectively. We only provide the formulation of D and R as in Eq. (10) and refer the reader to the supplementary for the details of the proximal operators.

4.1 Optimization w.r.t. the Visible Layer s^v, u^v

In this step, we fix the variables in the hidden layer u^h, s^h and the foreground mask m, and optimize the subproblem defined on the visible layer. We also relax the consistent constraints of Eq. (9) at this step. We will enforce the constraints after optimizing w.r.t the visible and hidden layer. The resulting subproblem can thus be written as

$$\min_{u^v, s^v} \quad E_d(u^v, s^v) + E_{r,v}(u^v, s^v) + E_c(s^v, m). \tag{15}$$

Note that the subproblem objective can be written in the standard Mumford-Shah functional form when it is optimized w.r.t. either u^v or s^v. Therefore, to optimize this subproblem with the primal-dual algorithm, we further divide the task into two steps.

Optimizing u^v with fixed s^v. By fixing the semantic variable s^v, we can write the objective in Eq. (15) in the standard Mumford-Shah form, with

$$D_{u^v}(u^v) = \sum_{\mathbf{x}} \|d(\mathbf{p}^T u^v - y^o)\|^2 , \tag{16}$$

$$R_{u^v}(\mathbf{K}u^v) = \eta_{rv} \sum_{\mathbf{x} \in \Omega} \min(\alpha_1 \|\mathbf{K}u^v\|^2 + e_{uv}, \lambda_1) , \tag{17}$$

where $e_{uv} = \|\mathbf{K}s^v\|^2$. Here, $\|\mathbf{K}u\|^2 := \sum_j \|\mathbf{K}u_j\|^2$ denotes the Euclidean norm, where u_j is the j-th channel in the multi-channel variable u.

Optimizing s^v with fixed u^v. We then fix the disparity variable u^v, and write the objective in Eq. (15) in the standard form, which yields

$$D_{s^v}(s^v) = \sum_{\mathbf{x}} \eta_d \|(s^v - s^o)\|^2 + \eta_c \sum_{\mathbf{x}} (\mathbf{f}^T s^v - m + b)^2 , \tag{18}$$

$$R_{s^v}(\mathbf{K}s^v) = \eta_{rv} \sum_{\mathbf{x} \in \Omega} \min(\alpha_1 e_{sv} + \|\mathbf{K}s^v\|^2, \lambda_1) , \tag{19}$$

where $e_{sv} = \|\mathbf{K}u^v\|^2$, and $\mathbf{f}$ is a binary vector with 1s in the position corresponding to the foreground classes and 0 everywhere else.

4.2 Optimization w.r.t. the Hidden Layer s^h, u^h

Let us now fix the disparity and semantics of the visible layer u^v, s^v and the foreground mask m, and optimize the functional w.r.t. the hidden layer variables u^h, s^h. We consider the following equivalent subproblem

$$\min_{u^h, s^h} \quad E_s(u^h, s^h, m) + E_{r,h}(u^h, s^h, m) + E_p(u^h, s^h) \tag{20}$$

Where $E_p(\cdot)$ is a regularization term with the following form:

$$E_p(u^h, s^h) = \gamma_{uh} \sum_{\mathbf{x}} (1 - m)(\mathbf{p}^T u^h - \mathbf{p}^T u^v)^2 + \gamma_{sh} \sum_{\mathbf{x}} (1 - m)(s^h - s^v)^2 \tag{21}$$

Here γ_{uh} and γ_{sh} are large weights (usually 1000), and we essentially use a soft version of consistency constraints to regularize the problem, which empirically produces a more stable optimization step. Similar to the visible layer, we divide the optimization of this subproblem into two steps.

Optimizing u^h with fixed s^h. Fixing the semantic variable s^h, and writing the objective in Eq. (20) in the standard form yields

$$D_{\mathbf{u}^h}(\mathbf{u}^h) = \gamma_{uh} \sum_{\mathbf{x}} (1 - m)(\mathbf{p}^T\mathbf{u}^h - \mathbf{p}^T\mathbf{u}^v)^2 + m\,\eta_s \sum_{j} s_j^h(\mathbf{p}^T\mathbf{u}^h - y_j^s)^2 \,, \quad (22)$$

$$R_{\mathbf{u}^h}(\nabla\mathbf{u}^h) = \eta_{rh} m \min(\alpha_2\|\nabla\mathbf{u}^h\|^2 + e_{uh}, \lambda_2) \,, \quad\quad\quad (23)$$

where $e_{uh} = \|\nabla s^h\|^2$.

Optimizing s^h with fixed u^h. We then fix the disparity variable u^h, and write the objective in Eq. (20) in the standard form, which yields

$$D_{\mathbf{s}^h}(\mathbf{s}^h) = \gamma_{sh} \sum_{\mathbf{x}} (1 - m)(s^h - s^v)^2 + m\,\eta_s \sum_{j} s_j^h(\mathbf{p}^T\mathbf{u}^h - y_j^s)^2 \,, \quad (24)$$

$$R_{\mathbf{s}^h}(\nabla\mathbf{s}^v) = \eta_{rh} m \sum_{\mathbf{x}\in\Omega} \min(\alpha_2 e_{sh} + \|\nabla s^v\|^2, \lambda_2) \,, \quad\quad (25)$$

where $e_{sh} = \|\nabla\mathbf{u}^h\|^2$.

4.3 Adding Constraints and Updating the Foreground Mask m

After computing the visible and hidden variables without the constraints, we now project them onto the constraint set defined in Eq. (9). The projection onto the consistent constraint set is computed as $\mathbf{s}^v = \mathbf{s}^h = \frac{\mathbf{s}^v + \mathbf{s}^h}{2}$ and $\mathbf{u}^v = \mathbf{u}^h = \frac{\mathbf{u}^v + \mathbf{u}^h}{2}$. For semantics $\mathbf{s}^v, \mathbf{s}^h$, we then project them onto the probability simplex.

Given the semantic and disparity variables in the visible and hidden layers, the foreground mask variables are decoupled into a set of independent variables for each location $\mathbf{x}$. The problem can then be re-written as

$$\min_{m} \sum_{\mathbf{x}} w(\mathbf{x}) m(\mathbf{x}) \,, \quad \text{s.t.} \quad m(\mathbf{x}) \in \{0, 1\}, \quad\quad (26)$$

where the weight $w(\mathbf{x})$ is given by

$$w(\mathbf{x}) = \eta_{rh} \cdot \min(\alpha_2\|\nabla\mathbf{u}^h\|^2 + \|\nabla\mathbf{s}^h\|^2, \lambda_2) + \eta_s \sum_{j} s_j^h(\mathbf{p}^T\mathbf{u}^h - y_j^s)^2 + \eta_c(1 - 2(\mathbf{f}^T\mathbf{s}^v + b)). \quad (27)$$

Ultimately, $m(\mathbf{x}) = 1$ if $w(\mathbf{x}) < 0$, and 0 otherwise.

5 Experiments

To demonstrate the effectiveness of our approach, we evaluated our method on two publicly available outdoor datasets: KITTI [17] and Stixel [18]. Below, we discuss our results on both datasets.

5.1   Experimental Setup

Initialization. We used SLIC [42] to produce an over-segmentation of the image, and fit a plane to each superpixel using the corresponding sparse depth observations. The resulting plane parameters are used as initialization for $\mathbf{u}^v$ for each pixel in the superpixels. For large holes where no observations were available in the superpixels, we initialized the plane parameters to zero.

We adopted the FCN-32s model [43] followed by smoothing via a fully-connected CRF [44], which allowed us to initialize $\mathbf{s}^v$ and foreground mask $\mathbf{m}$, as well as provides the observations $\mathbf{s}^o$. We initialize $\mathbf{u}^h$ and $\mathbf{s}^h$ from $\mathbf{u}^v$ and $\mathbf{s}^v$ and set the foreground regions to 0.

Ground-truth for the hidden layer. To the best of our knowledge, no ground-truth is available for the hidden layer variables. In order to provide a quantitative evaluation, we generated the ground truth in two different ways: (1) Manual annotation. We first annotated the hidden semantic labels, based on which we then filled in the hidden depth using the planes fitted to the superpixels around the true foreground mask. (2) Image and depth composition. We overlaid an object from an image (foreground image) on a background image of unoccluded scene. Since the camera intrinsics are roughly the same for both images, the depth map would be consistent after adding the object in the same location as in the foreground image.

Co-occurence statistics. To obtain the class-dependent disparity statistics $\{y_k^s\}$ in Eq. (6), we followed the intuition that semantics are often highly correlated with image location, which was exploited, for example, in [45] for depth prediction. To this end, we follow a superpixel-based approach. For each superpixel j in the test image, we take the plane parameters of the corresponding pixels in all the training images. For each class k, we then cluster these plane parameters, and take the cluster center with largest size. We finally generate y_k^s as the disparity obtained from the plane parameters of this center.

Baselines. Note that our scene model consists of two layers. For the visible layer, depth estimation translates to the usual depth completion problem. We therefore compare the results of our visible layer with the of the classical method of [28], and with the more recent technique of [26].

For the hidden layer, since no other has tackled the outdoor scenario in a fully-automatic manner, we rely on the following two-stage strategy. We first generate a foreground mask using the state-of-the-art semantic labeling method, FCN-32s model [43], followed by a smoothing with a fully-connected CRF [44]. Let us denote by *Fg-Mask* this foreground mask and by *Bg-Mask* the remaining image pixels. In Bg-Mask, the appearance is known, and thus the same depth completion methods as before can be employed. In Fg-Mask, however, no appearance information about the background is available. We therefore apply the technique of [27] to inpaint this area, which, to the best of our knowledge, remains the most mature method when it comes to depth completion without intensity information. This yields two baselines, which we will refer to as Baseline-1 (semantic segmentation followed by [28] + [27]) and Baseline-2 (semantic segmentation

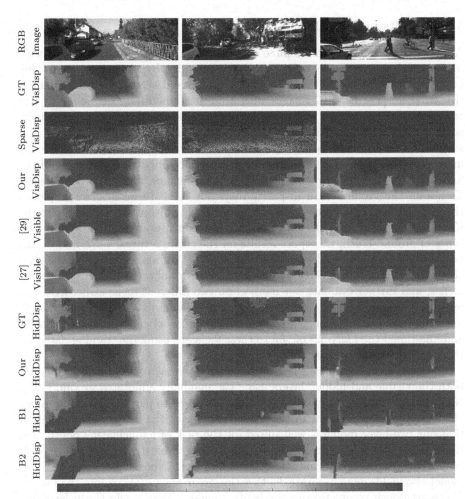

Fig. 2. Qualitative results on the KITTI dataset. For the disparity values, red denotes large values, and blue denotes small disparity values. **From top to bottom:** RGB image, ground-truth visible disparity map, sparse observations with large holes, our completed disparity map, two baselines for the visible layer, ground truth disparity for the hidden layer, our disparity for the hidden layer, and two baselines for the hidden layer. Note that our method can remove the foreground as well as accurately fill in the background disparity behind the foreground objects. Compared to the baselines, our approach can better complete the disparity for the visible and hidden layers. (Color figure online)

followed by [26] + [27]). To compare the different algorithms, we make use of the following metrics:1) *visible-rmse*: the-root-mean-square-error (rmse) for the entire depth map; 2)*hidden-rmse*: the rmse for the depth map hallucinated underneath the ground truth foreground mask.

5.2 Results on KITTI

As a first dataset, we utilized three subsets of the KITTI data annotated with semantic labels and/or disparity maps, and provided by (i) Ladický et al. [46], i.e., 60 aligned images, with dense disparity map and accurate semantic labels; (ii) Xu et al. [47], i.e., 107 images with accurate semantic labels; and (iii) Ros et al. [48], i.e., 146 images with accurate semantic labels. Note that only Ladický et al. [46] provide ground-truth disparity maps. However, this subset is constrained in terms of the scene types it depicts, i.e. mostly residential areas. To make our evaluation more meaningful, we therefore only used 40 images of the first subset as test images, complemented by 14 images from the other subsets. To obtain the ground-truth disparity maps for these 14 images, we employed the MC-CNN-acrt stereo matching algorithm [49], which ranks at the top in the KITTI stereo challenge. To avoid biasing our conclusions with these different types of ground-truth, we report results on the entire set, $test - 54$, and on the two subsets, $sub - 40$ and $sub - 14$, respectively. We also partitioned the data according to Manhattan (MH: 35 images) vs Non-Manhattan (NMH: 19 images) scenes, and further evaluate our method on two different scene structures. The remaining images from the three subsets were split into 200 for training and 59 for validation. For semantics, we mapped different label annotations to 9 classes and fine-tuned the FCN-32s of [43] to these 9 classes using the training data. We then define *car* and *pedestrian* as foreground classes.

In Table 1, we compare the results of our approach with the baselines for both the visible and hidden layers using the manually annotated ground truth. Note that we outperform the baselines in most cases. In particular, our approach yields a large improvement in the hidden regions of the image. This evidences that our two-layer model is well-suited for the task of hallucinating depth, and thus constitutes a significant step towards being able to build scene models despite the presence of occluding foreground objects. Note that the fact that our model also yields more accurate depth estimates in the visible regions than state-of-the-art depth completion methods also suggests that it effectively leverages the visible information. Additionally, we created a test set of 14 images using the composition strategy described in the previous section, which gives us access to the ground-truth hidden depth. Note that the 14 images were chosen to respect the scene type ratio of the original test data. The resulting hidden-rmse of our method is 7.72, which is superior to Baseline-1 (9.76) and Baseline-2 (10.94). Figure 2 provides a qualitative comparison of our results with the ground truth and the baselines.

In Table 2, we show the results of our semantics labeling estimates for the hidden regions. Here, since no baseline is available for this task, we only report the results of our approach. These results show that, while hallucinating small classes, such as fence and poles, remains challenging, our model yields good accuracy on the more common and larger classes. Note that effectively handling the small classes in outdoor semantic labeling is known to be difficult even when leveraging visible information. Finally, we observed that the semantic labeling accuracy in the visible layer did not significantly change compared to our initialization. In particular, we obtained

Table 1. Depth estimation. Quantitative comparison with several baselines for the visible and hidden depth, respectively.

Visible-rmse	Test-54	Sub-40	Sub-14	MH	NMH	Hidden-rmse	Test-54	Sub-40	sub-14	MH	NMH
Ours	**5.15**	**5.53**	**4.07**	**4.88**	5.66	Ours	**10.56**	**10.43**	**11.08**	**10.1**	**13.4**
[28]	5.42	5.67	4.68	5.49	**5.28**	Baseline-1	13.29	11.85	17.92	11.7	21.4
[26]	5.38	5.60	4.77	5.41	5.34	Baseline-2	12.53	11.37	16.34	11.3	19.1

Table 2. Estimating hidden semantics. Per-class and overall accuracy of our approach.

Veg	Road	Building	Sky	Sidewalk	Polar	Fence	Class-avg.	Pixel-avg.
73.6	51.52	85.07	16.64	16.97	3.61	0.51	35.42	50.08

88.51 % per pixel accuracy and 67.28 % average per class accuracy. In Fig. 3, we provided the qualitative results for semantic segmentation on KITTI dataset.

To further illustrate the effect of our approach on the visible semantics, we initialized our algorithm with the results of FCN-32s only. The per-pixel and per-class accuracies of FCN-32s were 87.86 % and 69.98 %, respectively. Our method improved the per-pixel accuracy to 88.5 % and left the per-class one virtually unchanged (69.81 %). This also resulted in an improved visible-rmse of 5.01.

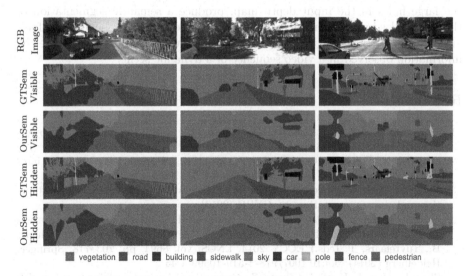

vegetation   road   building   sidewalk   sky   car   pole   fence   pedestrian

Fig. 3. Qualitative results for semantic segmentation on the KITTI dataset. From top to bottom: RGB image, ground truth results and our results, ground truth disparity for the hidden layer, our disparity for the hidden layer, Baseline 1 and Baseline 2, ground truth semantics for the hidden layer, and our estimated semantics for the hidden layer. (Color figure online)

5.3   Results on Stixel

As a second experiment, we employed the Stixel dataset. This dataset contains 500 images with corresponding noisy depth (disparity) maps and semantics, partitioned into 300 training images and 200 test images. Note that the disparity provided in this dataset was computed using a semi-global matching algorithm. Since ground-truth disparity is only partially available for this dataset, it is therefore not possible to generate the ground-truth disparity for the foreground mask as before. We therefore only provide a qualitative comparison of our approach with the baselines. There are 5 semantic classes in the dataset. We define *car* and *pedestrian* as the foreground class. The qualitative results of this dataset are shown in the Supplementary Material (Fig. 4). Note that, again, we can see that our approach produces more accurate disparity maps.

6   Conclusion

We have introduced a fully-automatic approach to jointly completing and hallucinating depth and semantics from an incomplete depth map and an RGB image. To this end, we have developed a two-layer model, encoding both the visible information and the information hidden behind the foreground objects. Furthermore, we have designed an effective strategy to optimize our two-layer model. Our experiments have evidenced that our approach can accurately fill the large holes in the input depth map, produce a semantic segmentation of the observed scene, and hallucinate the depth and semantics behind the foreground objects. In the future, we plan to extend our method to accumulate the information observed in a video sequence of a dynamic scene.

References

1. Snavely, N., Seitz, S.M., Szeliski, R.: Modeling the world from internet photo collections. In: IJCV (2008)
2. Cornelis, N., Leibe, B., Cornelis, K., Van Gool, L.: 3d urban scene modeling integrating recognition and reconstruction. In: IJCV (2008)
3. Hane, C., Zach, C., Cohen, A., Angst, R., Pollefeys, M.: Joint 3d scene reconstruction and class segmentation. In: CVPR (2013)
4. Kundu, A., Li, Y., Dellaert, F., Li, F., Rehg, J.M.: Joint semantic segmentation and 3d reconstruction from monocular video. In: Fleet, D., Pajdla, T., Schiele, B., Tuytelaars, T. (eds.) ECCV 2014. LNCS, vol. 8694, pp. 703–718. Springer, Heidelberg (2014). doi:10.1007/978-3-319-10599-4_45
5. Shao, L., Han, J., Kohli, P., Zhang, Z.: Computer vision and machine learning with RGB-D sensors. Springer, Heidelberg (2014)
6. Diebel, J., Thrun, S.: An application of markov random fields to range sensing. In: NIPS (2005)
7. Park, J., Kim, H., Tai, Y.W., Brown, M., Kweon, I.: High quality depth map upsampling for 3d-tof cameras. In: ICCV (2011)

8. Aodha, O.M., Campbell, N.D.F., Nair, A., Brostow, G.J.: Patch based synthesis for single depth image super-resolution. In: Fitzgibbon, A., Lazebnik, S., Perona, P., Sato, Y., Schmid, C. (eds.) ECCV 2012. LNCS, vol. 7574, pp. 71–84. Springer, Heidelberg (2012). doi:10.1007/978-3-642-33712-3_6
9. Hornácek, M., Rhemann, C., Gelautz, M., Rother, C.: Depth super resolution by rigid body self-similarity in 3d. In: CVPR (2013)
10. Kiechle, M., Hawe, S., Kleinsteuber, M.: A joint intensity and depth co-sparse analysis model for depth map super-resolution. In: ICCV (2013)
11. Lu, S., Ren, X., Liu, F.: Depth enhancement via low-rank matrix completion. In: CVPR (2014)
12. Wang, L., Jin, H., Yang, R., Gong, M.: Stereoscopic inpainting: Joint color and depth completion from stereo images. In: CVPR (2008)
13. Doria, D., Radke, R.J.: Filling large holes in lidar data by inpainting depth gradients. In: CVPR Workshops (2012)
14. Dolson, J., Baek, J., Plagemann, C., Thrun, S.: Upsampling range data in dynamic environments. In: CVPR (2010)
15. Zach, C.: Dual decomposition for joint discrete-continuous optimization. In: AISTATS (2013)
16. Geiger, A., Wang, C.: Joint 3D object and layout inference from a single RGB-D image. In: Gall, J., Gehler, P., Leibe, B. (eds.) GCPR 2015. LNCS, vol. 9358, pp. 183–195. Springer, Heidelberg (2015). doi:10.1007/978-3-319-24947-6_15
17. Geiger, A., Lenz, P., Urtasun, R.: Are we ready for autonomous driving? the kitti vision benchmark suite. In: CVPR (2012)
18. Scharwächter, T., Enzweiler, M., Franke, U., Roth, S.: Stixmantics: a medium-level model for real-time semantic scene understanding. In: Fleet, D., Pajdla, T., Schiele, B., Tuytelaars, T. (eds.) ECCV 2014. LNCS, vol. 8693, pp. 533–548. Springer, Heidelberg (2014). doi:10.1007/978-3-319-10602-1_35
19. Glocker, B., Izadi, S., Shotton, J., Criminisi, A.: Real-time rgb-d camera relocalization. In: ISMAR (2013)
20. Rusu, R.B., Holzbach, A., Diankov, R., Bradski, G., Beetz, M.: Perception for mobile manipulation and grasping using active stereo. In: IEEE-RAS International Conference on Humanoid Robots (2009)
21. Yang, Q., Yang, R., Davis, J., Nistér, D.: Spatial-depth super resolution for range images. In: CVPR (2007)
22. Shen, J., Cheung, S.: Layer depth denoising and completion for structured-light rgb-d cameras. In: CVPR (2013)
23. Liu, J., Gong, X., Liu, J.: Guided inpainting and filtering for kinect depth maps. In: ICPR (2012)
24. Bhavsar, A.V., Rajagopalan, A.N.: Range map superresolution-inpainting, and reconstruction from sparse data. CVIU 116(4), 572–591 (2012)
25. Herrera C., D., Kannala, J., Ladický, L., Heikkilä, J.: Depth map inpainting under a second-order smoothness prior. In: Kämäräinen, J.-K., Koskela, M. (eds.) SCIA 2013. LNCS, vol. 7944, pp. 555–566. Springer, Heidelberg (2013). doi:10.1007/978-3-642-38886-6_52
26. Ferstl, D., Reinbacher, C., Ranftl, R., Rüther, M., Bischof, H.: Image guided depth upsampling using anisotropic total generalized variation. In: ICCV (2013)
27. Criminisi, A., Perez, P., Toyama, K.: Object removal by exemplar-based inpainting. In: CVPR (2003)
28. Levin, A., Lischinski, D., Weiss, Y.: Colorization using optimization. In: TOG (2004)

29. Schuon, S., Theobalt, C., Davis, J., Thrun, S.: Lidarboost: Depth superresolution for tof 3d shape scanning. In: CVPR (2009)
30. Izadi, S., Kim, D., Hilliges, O., Molyneaux, D., Newcombe, R., Kohli, P., Shotton, J., Hodges, S., Freeman, D., Davison, A., et al.: Kinectfusion: real-time 3d reconstruction and interaction using a moving depth camera. In: ACM UIST (2011)
31. Sturm, J., Engelhard, N., Endres, F., Burgard, W., Cremers, D.: A benchmark for the evaluation of rgb-d slam systems. In: IROS (2012)
32. Zhou, Q.Y., Koltun, V.: Dense scene reconstruction with points of interest. In: TOG (2013)
33. Guo, R., Hoiem, D.: Beyond the line of sight: labeling the underlying surfaces. In: Fitzgibbon, A., Lazebnik, S., Perona, P., Sato, Y., Schmid, C. (eds.) ECCV 2012. LNCS, vol. 7576, pp. 761–774. Springer, Heidelberg (2012). doi:10.1007/978-3-642-33715-4_55
34. Bleyer, M., Rother, C., Kohli, P., Scharstein, D., Sinha, S.: Object stereo joint stereo matching and object segmentation. In: CVPR (2011)
35. Mumford, D., Shah, J.: Optimal approximations by piecewise smooth functions and associated variational problems. Commun. Pure Appl. Math. 42, 577–685 (1989)
36. Strekalovskiy, E., Cremers, D.: Real-time minimization of the piecewise smooth mumford-shah functional. In: Fleet, D., Pajdla, T., Schiele, B., Tuytelaars, T. (eds.) ECCV 2014. LNCS, vol. 8690, pp. 127–141. Springer, Heidelberg (2014). doi:10.1007/978-3-319-10605-2_9
37. Faugeras, O.D., Lustman, F.: Motion and structure from motion in a piecewise planar environment. Int. J. Pattern Recogn. Artif. Intell. 2(3), 4010–4017 (1988)
38. Baillard, C., Zisserma, A.: Automatic reconstruction of piecewise planar models from multiple views. In: CVPR (1999)
39. Gallup, D., Frahm, J.M., Pollefeys, M.: Piecewise planar and non-planar stereo for urban scene reconstruction. In: CVPR (2010)
40. Ladický, L., Sturgess, P., Russell, C., Sengupta, S., Bastanlar, Y., Clocksin, W., Torr, P.H.: Joint optimization for object class segmentation and dense stereo reconstruction. In: IJCV (2012)
41. Chambolle, A., Pock, T.: A first-order primal-dual algorithm for convex problems with applications to imaging. J. Math. Imaging Vis. 40, 120–145 (2011)
42. Achanta, R., Shaji, A., Smith, K., Lucchi, A., Fua, P., Suesstrunk, S.: Slic superpixels compared to state-of-the-art superpixel methods. In: PAMI (2012)
43. Long, J., Shelhamer, E., Darrell, T.: Fully convolutional networks for semantic segmentation. In: CVPR (2015)
44. Krähenbühl, P., Koltun, V.: Efficient inference in fully connected crfs with gaussian edge potentials. In: NIPS (2011)
45. Liu, B., Gould, S., Koller, D.: Single image septh estimation from predicted semantic labels. In: CVPR (2010)
46. Ladický, L., Shi, J., Pollefeys, M.: Pulling things out of perspective. In: CVPR (2014)
47. Xu, P., Davoine, F., Bordes, J.B., Zhao, H., Denœux, T.: Multimodal information fusion for urban scene understanding. Mach. Vis. Appl. 27, 331 (2014)
48. Ros, G., Ramos, S., Granados, M., Bakhtiary, A., Vazquez, D., Lopez, A.M.: Vision-based offline-online perception paradigm for autonomous driving. In: WACV (2015)
49. Zbontar, J., LeCun, Y.: Stereo matching by training a convolutional neural network to compare image patches. JMLR 17, 1–32 (2016)

Weakly Supervised Learning of Heterogeneous Concepts in Videos

Sohil Shah[1]($\boxtimes$), Kuldeep Kulkarni[2], Arijit Biswas[3], Ankit Gandhi[4],
Om Deshmukh[4], and Larry S. Davis[1]

[1] University of Maryland, College Park, MD, USA
sohilas@umd.edu
[2] Arizona State University, Tempe, AZ, USA
[3] Amazon Development Center India, Bangalore, India
[4] Xerox Research Centre India, Bangalore, India

Abstract. Typical textual descriptions that accompany online videos are 'weak': i.e., they mention the important heterogeneous concepts in the video but not their corresponding spatio-temporal locations. However, certain location constraints on these concepts can be inferred from the description. The goal of this paper is to present a generalization of the Indian Buffet Process (IBP) that can (a) systematically incorporate heterogeneous concepts in an integrated framework, and (b) enforce location constraints, for efficient classification and localization of the concepts in the videos. Finally, we develop posterior inference for the proposed formulation using mean-field variational approximation. Comparative evaluations on the Casablanca and the A2D datasets show that the proposed approach significantly outperforms other state-of-the-art techniques: 24 % relative improvement for pairwise concept classification in the Casablanca dataset and 9 % relative improvement for localization in the A2D dataset as compared to the most competitive baseline.

1 Introduction

Watching and sharing videos on social media has become an integral part of everyday life. We are often intrigued by the textual description of the videos and attempt to fast-forward to the segments of interest without watching the entire video. However, these textual descriptors usually do not specify the exact segment of the video associated with a particular description. For example, someone describing a movie clip as "head-on collision between cars while Chris Cooper is driving" neither provide the time-stamps for the collision or driving events nor the spatial locations of the cars or Chris Cooper. Such descriptions are referred to as 'weak labels'. For efficient video navigation and consumption, it is

This work was done at Xerox Research Center India. Sohil and Kuldeep were interns.

Electronic supplementary material The online version of this chapter (doi:10. 1007/978-3-319-46466-4_17) contains supplementary material, which is available to authorized users.

important to automatically determine the spatio-temporal locations of these concepts (such as 'collision' or 'cars'). However, it is prohibitively expensive to train concept-specific models for all concepts of interest in advance and use them for localization. This shortcoming has triggered a great amount of interest in *jointly* learning concept-specific classification models as well as localizing concepts from multiple weakly labeled images [1–3] or videos [4,5].

Video descriptions include concepts which may refer to persons, objects, scenes and/or actions and thus a typical description is a combination of heterogeneous concepts. In the running example, extracted heterogeneous concepts are 'car' (object), 'head-on collision' (action), 'Chris Cooper' (person) and 'driving' (action). Learning classifiers for these heterogeneous concepts along with localization is an extremely challenging task because: (a) the classifiers for different kinds of concepts are required to be learned simultaneously, e.g., a face classifier, an object classifier, an action classifier etc., and (b) the learning model must take into account the spatio-temporal location constraints imposed by the descriptions while learning these classifiers. For example, the concepts 'head-on collision' and 'cars' should spatio-temporally co-occur at least once and there should be at least one car in the video.

Recently there has been growing interest to jointly learn concept classifiers from weak labels [1,5]. Bojanowski *et al.* [5] proposed a discriminative clustering framework to jointly learn person and action models from movies using weak supervision provided by the movie scripts. Since weak labels are extracted from scripts, each label can be associated with a particular shot in the movie, which may last only for a few seconds, i.e., the labels are well localized and that makes the overall learning easier. However, in real world videos, one does not have access to such shot-level labels but only to video-level labels. Therefore in our work, we do not assume availability of such well localized labels, and tackle the more general problem of learning concepts from weaker video-level labels. The framework in [5], when extended to long videos, does not give satisfactory results (see Sect. 4). Such techniques, which are based on a linear mapping from features to labels and model background using only a single latent factor, are usually inadequate to capture all the inter-class and intra-class variations. Shi *et al.* [1] jointly learn object and attribute classifiers from images using weakly supervised Indian Buffet Process (IBP). Note that IBP [6,7] allows observed features to be explained by a countably infinite number of latent factors. However, the framework in [1] is not designed to handle heterogeneous concepts and location constraints, which leads to a significant degradation in performance (Sect. 4.3). [8] and [9] propose IBP based cross-modal categorization/query image retrieval models which learn semantically meaningful abstract features from multimodal (image, speech and text) data. However, these unsupervised approaches do not incorporate any location constraints which naturally arise in the weakly supervised setting with heterogeneous labels.

We propose a novel Bayesian Non-parametric (BNP) approach called WSC-SIIBP (Weakly Supervised, Constrained &Stacked Integrative IBP) to jointly learn heterogeneous concept classifiers and localize these concepts in videos. BNP models are a class of Bayesian models where the hidden structure that may have generated the observed data is not assumed to be fixed. Instead, a framework is provided that allows the complexity of the model to increase as more data is observed [10]. Specifically, we propose:

1. A novel generalization of IBP which for the first time incorporates weakly supervised spatio-temporal location constraints and heterogeneous concepts in an integrated framework.
2. Posterior inference of WSC-SIIBP model using mean-field approximation.

We assume that the weak video labels come in the form of tuples: in the running example, the extracted heterogeneous concept tuples are ({car, head-on collision}, {Chris Cooper, driving})[1]. We perform experiments on two video datasets (a) the Casablanca movie dataset [5] and (b) the A2D dataset [11]. We show that the proposed approach WSC-SIIBP outperforms several state-of-the-art methods for heterogeneous concept classification and localization in a weakly supervised setting. For example, WSC-SIIBP leads to a relative improvement of 7 %, 5 % and 24 % on person, action and pairwise classification accuracies, respectively, over the most competitive baselines on the Casablanca dataset. Similarly, the relative improvement on localization accuracy is 9 % over the next best approach on the A2D dataset.

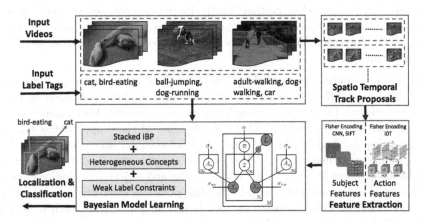

Fig. 1. Pipeline of WSC-SIIBP. Multiple videos with heterogeneous weak labels are provided as input and localization and classification of the concepts are performed in these videos.

---

[1] Extracting concept tuples is an interesting research problem but beyond the scope of this paper.

2   Related Work

In this section, we discuss relevant prior work in two broad categories.

Weakly Supervised Learning: Localizing concepts and learning classifiers from weakly annotated data is an active research topic. Researchers have learned models for various concepts from weakly labeled videos using Multi-Instance Learning (MIL) [12,13] for human action recognition [14], visual tracking [15] etc. Cour *et al.* [16] uses a novel convex formulation to learn face classifiers from movies and TV series using multimodal features which are obtained from finely aligned screenplay, speech and video data. In [4,17], the authors propose discriminative clustering approaches for aligning videos with temporally ordered text descriptions or predefined tags and in the process also learn action classifiers. In our approach, we consider weak labels which are neither ordered nor aligned to any specific video segment. [18] proposes a method for learning object class detectors from real world web videos known to contain only the target class by formulating the problem as a domain adaptation task. [19] learns weakly supervised object/action classifiers using a latent-SVM formulation where the objects or actions are localized in training images/videos using latent variables. We note that - both [18,19] consider only a single weak label per video and, unlike our approach, do not jointly learn the heterogeneous concepts. The authors in [20,21] use dialogues, scene and character identification to find an optimal mapping between a book and movie shots using shortest path or CRF approach. However, these approaches neither jointly model heterogeneous concepts nor spatio-temporally localized them. Although [22] proposes a discriminative clustering model for coreference resolution in videos, only faces are considered in their experiments.

Heterogeneous concept learning: There are prior works on automatic image [23–26] and video [27–29] caption generation, where models are trained on pairs of image/video and text that contain heterogeneous concept descriptions to predict captions for novel images/videos. While most of these approaches rely on deep learning methods to learn a mapping between an image/video and the corresponding text description, [25] uses MIL to learn visual concept detectors (spatial localization in images) for nouns, verbs and adjectives. However, none of these approaches spatio-temporally localize points of interests in videos. Perhaps the available video datasets are not large enough to train such a weakly supervised deep learning model.

To the best of our knowledge there is no prior work that jointly classifies and localizes heterogeneous concepts in weakly supervised videos.

3   WSC-SIIBP: Model and Algorithm

In this section, we describe the details of WSC-SIIBP (see Fig. 1 for the pipeline). We first introduce notations and motivate our approach in Sects. 3.1 and 3.2 respectively. This is followed by Sect. 3.3 where we introduce stacked non-parametric graphical model - IBP and its corresponding posterior computation.

In Sects. 3.4 and 3.5, we formulate an extension of the stacked IBP model which can generalize to heterogeneous concepts as well as incorporate the constraints obtained from weak labels. In Sect. 3.6, we briefly describe the inference procedure using truncated mean-field variational approximation and summarize our entire algorithm. Finally, we discuss how one can classify and localize concepts in new test videos using WSC-SIIBP.

3.1 Notation

Assume we are given a set of weakly labeled videos denoted by $\mathbf{\Lambda} = \{(i, \Gamma^{(i)})\}$, where i indicates a video and $\Gamma^{(i)}$ denotes the heterogeneous weak labels corresponding to the i-th video. Although the proposed approach can be used for any number of heterogeneous concepts, for readability, we restrict ourselves to two concepts and call them subjects and actions. We also have a closed set of class labels for these heterogeneous concepts: for subjects $\mathcal{S} = (s_1, \ldots, s_{K_s})$ and for actions $\mathcal{A} = (a_1, \ldots, a_{K_a})$. Let $K_s = |\mathcal{S}|$, $K_a = |\mathcal{A}|$, $\Gamma^{(i)} = \{(s_l, a_l) : s_l \in \mathcal{S} \cup \emptyset, a_l \in \mathcal{A} \cup \emptyset, 1 \leq l \leq |\Gamma^{(i)}|\}$, $\emptyset$ indicate that the corresponding subject or action class label is not present and $M = |\mathbf{\Lambda}|$ represents the number of videos. The video-level annotation simply indicates that the paired concepts $\Gamma^{(i)}$ can occur anywhere in the video and at multiple locations.

Assume that N_i spatio-temporal tracks are extracted from each video i where each track j is represented as an aggregation of multiple local features, $\mathbf{x}_j^{(i)}$. The spatio-temporal tracks could be face tracks, 3-D object proposals or action proposals (see Sect. 4.1 for more details). We associate the jth track in video i to an infinite binary latent coefficient vector $\mathbf{z}_j^{(i)}$ [1,6]. Each video i is represented by a bag of spatio-temporal tracks $\mathbf{X}^{(i)} = \{\mathbf{x}_j^{(i)}, j = 1, \ldots, N_i\}$. Similarly, $\mathbf{Z}^{(i)} = \{\mathbf{z}_j^{(i)}, j = 1, \ldots, N_i\}$.

3.2 Motivation

Our objective is to learn (a) a mapping between each of the N_i tracks in video i and the labels in $\Gamma^{(i)}$ and (b) the appearance model for each label identity such that the tracks from new test videos can be classified. To achieve these objectives, it is important for any model to discover the latent factors that can explain similar tracks across a set of videos with a particular label. In general, the number of latent factors are not known apriori and must be inferred from the data. In Bayesian framework, IBP treats this number as a random variable that can grow with new observations, thus letting the model to effectively explain the unbounded complexity in the data. Specifically, IBP defines a prior distribution over an equivalence class of binary matrices of bounded rows (indicating spatio-temporal tracks) and infinite columns (indicating latent coefficients). To achieve our goals, we build on IBP and introduce the WSC-SIIBP model which can effectively learn the latent factors corresponding to each heterogeneous concept and utilize prior location constraints to reduce the ambiguity in learning through the knowledge of other latent coefficients.

3.3   Indian Buffet Process (IBP)

The spatio-temporal tracks in the videos $\mathbf{\Lambda}$ are obtained from an underlying generative process. Specifically, we consider a stacked IBP model [1] as described below.

- For each latent factor $k \in 1 \ldots \infty$,
    1. Draw an appearance distribution with mean $\mathbf{a}_k \sim \mathcal{N}(0, \sigma_A^2 \mathbf{I})$
- For each video $i \in 1 \ldots M$,
    1. Draw a sequence of i.i.d. random variables, $v_1^{(i)}, v_2^{(i)} \cdots \sim \text{Beta}(\alpha, 1)$
    2. Construct the prior on the latent factors, $\pi_k^{(i)} = \prod_{t=1}^k v_t^{(i)}, \forall k \in 1 \ldots \infty$,
    3. For j^{th} subject track in i^{th} video, where $j \in 1 \ldots N_i$,
        (a) Sample state of each latent factor, $z_{jk}^{(i)} \sim \text{Bern}(\pi_k^{(i)})$,
        (b) Sample track appearance, $\mathbf{x}_j^{(i)} \sim \mathcal{N}\left(\mathbf{z}_j^{(i)}\mathbf{A}, \sigma_n^2 \mathbf{I}\right)$

where α is the prior controlling the sparsity of latent factors, σ_A^2 and σ_n^2 are the prior appearance and noise variance shared across all factors, respectively. Each $\mathbf{a}_k$ forms k^{th} row of $\mathbf{A}$ and the value of the latent coefficient $z_{jk}^{(i)}$ indicates whether data $\mathbf{x}_j^{(i)}$ contains the kth latent factor or not. In the above model, we have used stick-breaking construction [30] to generate the $\pi_k^{(i)}$s.

Posterior: Now, we describe how the posterior is obtained for the above graphical model. Let $\mathbf{Y} = \left\{\pi^{(1)} \ldots \pi^{(M)}, \mathbf{Z}^{(1)} \ldots \mathbf{Z}^{(M)}, \mathbf{A}\right\}$ and $\mathbf{\Theta} = \left\{\alpha, \sigma_A^2, \sigma_n^2\right\}$ denote hidden variables and prior parameters, respectively. $\mathbf{X}$ denotes the concatenation of all the spatio-temporal tracks in all M videos, $\left\{\mathbf{X}^{(1)} \ldots \mathbf{X}^{(M)}\right\}$. Given prior distribution $\Psi(\mathbf{Y}|\mathbf{\Theta})$ and likelihood function $p(\mathbf{x}_j^{(i)}|\mathbf{Y}, \mathbf{\Theta})$, the posterior probability is given by,

$$p(\mathbf{Y}|\mathbf{X}, \mathbf{\Theta}) = \frac{\Psi(\mathbf{Y}|\mathbf{\Theta}) \prod_{i=1}^M \prod_{j=1}^{N_i} p(\mathbf{X}_j^{(i)}|\mathbf{Y}, \mathbf{\Theta})}{p(\mathbf{X}|\mathbf{\Theta})}$$

$$\Psi(\mathbf{Y}|\mathbf{\Theta}) = \prod_{k=1}^{\infty} \left(\prod_{i=1}^M p(\pi_k^{(i)}|\alpha) \prod_{j=1}^{N_i} p(z_{jk}^{(i)}|\pi_k^{(i)})\right) p(\mathbf{a}_{k.}|\sigma_A^2).$$

(1)

where $p(\mathbf{X}|\mathbf{\Theta})$ is the marginal likelihood. For simplicity, we denote $p(\mathbf{Y}|\mathbf{X}, \mathbf{\Theta})$ as $q(\mathbf{Y})$. Apart from the significance of inferring $\mathbf{Z}^{(i)}$ for identifying track-level labels, inferring prior $\pi_k^{(i)}$ for each video helps to identify video-level labels, while the inference of appearance model $\mathbf{A}$ will be used to classify new test samples (see Sect. 3.6). Thus, learning in our model requires computing the full posterior distribution over $\mathbf{Y}$.

Regularized posterior: We note that it is difficult to infer the regularized posterior distributions using (1). However, it is known [31,32] that the posterior distribution in (1) can also be obtained as the solution $q(\mathbf{Y})$ of the following optimization problem,

$$\min_{q(\mathbf{Y})} \quad \text{KL}\left(q(\mathbf{Y})\|\Psi(\mathbf{Y}|\mathbf{\Theta})\right) - \sum_{i=1}^M \sum_{j=1}^{N_i} \int \log p(\mathbf{x}_j^{(i)}|\mathbf{Y}, \mathbf{\Theta})q(\mathbf{Y})d\mathbf{Y} \quad s.t. \quad q(\mathbf{Y}) \in P_{prob}$$

(2)

where KL(.) denotes the Kullback-Liebler divergence and P_{prob} is the probability simplex. As we will see later, this procedure enables us to learn the posterior distribution using a constrained optimization framework.

3.4 Integrative IBP

Our objective is to model heterogeneous concepts (such as subjects and actions) using a graphical model. However, the IBP model described above can not handle multiple concepts because it is highly unlikely that the subject and the action features can be explained by the same statistical model. Hence, we propose an extension of stacked IBP for heterogeneous concepts, where different concept types are modeled using different appearance models.

Let the subject and action types corresponding to the spatio-temporal track j in video i be denoted by $\mathbf{x^s}_j^{(i)}$ and $\mathbf{x^a}_j^{(i)}$, respectively, with each having different dimensions D^e ($e \in \{s, a\}$)[2]. Unlike the IBP model, $\mathbf{X^s}_j^{(i)}$ and $\mathbf{X^a}_j^{(i)}$ are now represented using two different gaussian noise models $\mathcal{N}(\mathbf{z}_j^{(i)} \mathbf{A}^s, \sigma_{ns}^2 \mathbf{I})$ and $\mathcal{N}(\mathbf{z}_j^{(i)} \mathbf{A}^a, \sigma_{na}^2 \mathbf{I})$ respectively where σ_{ne}^2 denotes prior noise variance and $\mathbf{A}^e$ are $K \times D^e$ matrices ($K \to \infty$). The mean of the subject and action appearance models for each latent factor are also sampled independently from gaussian distributions of different variances σ_{Ae}^2. The new posterior probability is given by,

$$
\tilde{q}(\mathbf{Y}) = \frac{\Psi(\mathbf{Y}|\Theta) \prod_{i=1}^{M} \prod_{j=1}^{N_i} \prod_{e \in \{s,a\}} p(\mathbf{x}_j^{e^{(i)}} | \mathbf{Z}, \mathbf{A}^e, \Theta)}{p(\mathbf{X}|\Theta)}
$$

$$
\Psi(\mathbf{Y}|\Theta) = \prod_{k=1}^{\infty} \left(\prod_{i=1}^{M} p(\pi_k^{(i)}|\alpha) \prod_{j=1}^{N_i} p(z_{jk}^{(i)}|\pi_k^{(i)}) \right) \prod_{e \in \{s,a\}} p(\mathbf{a}_k^e | \sigma_{Ae}^2 \mathbf{I}).
$$

(3)

3.5 Integrative IBP with Constraints

Although the graphical model described above is capable of handling heterogeneous features, the location constraints inferred from the weak labels still need to be incorporated into the graphical model. As motivated in Sect. 1, the concepts 'head-on collision' and 'cars' should spatio-temporally co-occur at least once and there should be at least one car in the full video. Imposing these location constraints in the inference algorithm can lead to more accurate parameter estimation of the graphical model and faster convergence of the inference procedure. These constraints can be generalized as follows,

1. Every label tuple in $\Gamma^{(i)}$, is associated with at least one spatio-temporal track (i.e., the event occurs in the video).
2. Spatio-temporal tracks should be assigned a label only from the list of weak labels assigned to the video. Concepts present in the video but not in the label will be subsumed in the background models.

---

[2] We often use e as a replacement for s and a throughout the paper.

Ideally, in the case of noiseless labels, these constraints should be strictly followed. However, we assume that real-world labels could be noisy and noise is independent of the videos. Hence, we allow constraints to be violated but penalize the violations using additional slack variables.

We associate the first K_s and the following K_a latent factors (the rows of $\mathbf{A}$) to the subject and action classes in $\mathcal{S}$ and $\mathcal{A}$ respectively. The inferred values of their corresponding latent coefficients in $\mathbf{z}_j^{(i)}$ are used to determine the presence/absence of the associated concept in a particular spatio-temporal track. The remaining unbounded number of latent factors are used to explain away the background tracks from unknown action and subject classes in a video. With these assignments, we enforce the following constraints on latent factors which are sufficient to satisfy the conditions mentioned earlier.

To satisfy 1, we introduce the following constraints, $\forall i \in 1 \ldots M$, and $\forall j \in 1 \ldots N_i$,

$$\sum_{j=1}^{N_i} z_{js}^{(i)} z_{ja}^{(i)} \geq 1 - \xi_{(s,a)}^{(i)}, \quad \forall (s,a) \in \Gamma^{(i)}, \tag{4}$$

$$\sum_{j=1}^{N_i} z_{js}^{(i)} \geq 1 - \xi_{(s,\emptyset)}^{(i)}, \quad \forall (s,\emptyset) \in \Gamma^{(i)}, \tag{5}$$

$$\sum_{j=1}^{N_i} z_{ja}^{(i)} \geq 1 - \xi_{(\emptyset,a)}^{(i)}, \quad \forall (\emptyset,a) \in \Gamma^{(i)}, \tag{6}$$

where ξ is the slack variable, z_{js} and z_{ja} are the latent factor coefficients corresponding to subject class s and action class a respectively.

To satisfy 2, we use the following constraints, $\forall i \in 1 \ldots M$ and $\forall j \in 1 \ldots N_i$,

$$z_{js}^{(i)} = 0, \text{if } \nexists (s,\emptyset) \in \Gamma^{(i)} \text{ and } \nexists (s,a) \in \Gamma^{(i)}, \forall a \in \mathcal{A}, \tag{7}$$

$$z_{ja}^{(i)} = 0, \text{if } \nexists (\emptyset,a) \in \Gamma^{(i)} \text{ and } \nexists (s,a) \in \Gamma^{(i)}, \forall s \in \mathcal{S}. \tag{8}$$

The constraints defined in (4)–(8) have been used in the context of discriminative clustering [5,22]. However, our model is the first to use these constraints in a Bayesian setup. In their simplest form, they can be enforced using the point estimate of z e.g., MAP estimation. However, $\mathbf{Z}^{(i)}$ is defined over the entire probability space. To enforce the above constraints in a Bayesian framework, we need to account for the uncertainty in $\mathbf{Z}^{(i)}$. Following [33,34], we define effective constraints as an expectation of the original constraints in (4)–(8), where the expectation is computed w.r.t. the posterior distribution in (3) (see supplementary material for the expectation constraints). The proposed graphical model, incorporating heterogeneous concepts as well as the location constraints provided by the weak labels, is shown in Fig. 2.

We restrict the search space for the posterior distribution in Eq. (3) by using the expectation constraints. In order to obtain the regularized posterior distribution of the proposed model, we solve the following optimization problem under these expectation constraints,

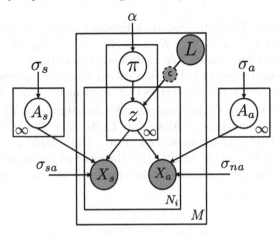

Fig. 2. WSC-SIIBP: Graphical Model using two heterogeneous concepts, subjects and actions. Each video (described by video-level labels L) is independently modeled using latent factor prior π and contains N_i tracks. Each track is represented using subject and action features X_s and X_a respectively, which are modeled using Gaussian appearance models A_s and A_a. z are the binary latent variables indicating the presence or absence of the latent factors in each track. c denotes the set of location constraints extracted from the video labels.

$$\min_{\tilde{q}(\mathbf{Y}),\xi^{(i)}} \mathrm{KL}\left(\tilde{q}(\mathbf{Y})\|\tilde{\Psi}(\mathbf{Y}|\Theta)\right) - \sum_{i=1}^{M}\sum_{j=1}^{N_i} \int \left(\sum_{e\in\{s,a\}} \log p\left(\mathbf{X}^{\mathbf{e}(i)}_j|\mathbf{Y},\Theta\right)\right)\tilde{q}(\mathbf{Y})d\mathbf{Y}$$

$$+ C\sum_{i=1}^{M}\sum_{J\in\Gamma^{(i)}} \xi^{(i)}_J \quad s.t. \quad \tilde{q}(\mathbf{Y}) \in P_{prob} \tag{9}$$

3.6 Learning and Inference

Note that the variational inference for true posterior $\tilde{q}(\mathbf{Y})$ (in Eq. (3)) is intractable over the general space of probability functions. To make our problem easier to solve, we establish *truncated* mean-field variational approximation [30] to the desired posterior $\tilde{q}(\mathbf{Y})$, such that the search space P_{prob} is constrained by the following tractable parametrised family of distributions,

$$\tilde{w}(\mathbf{Y}) = \prod_{i=1}^{M}\left(\prod_{k=1}^{K_{max}} p(v^{(i)}_k|\tau^{(i)}_{k1},\tau^{(i)}_{k2}) \prod_{j=1}^{N_i} p(z^{(i)}_{jk}|\nu^{(i)}_{jk})\right) \prod_{k=1}^{K_{max}} \prod_{e\in\{s,a\}} p(\mathbf{a}^e_k|\mathbf{\Phi}^e_k,\sigma^2_{ke}\mathbf{I}). \tag{10}$$

where $p(v^{(i)}_k|\tau^{(i)}_{k1},\tau^{(i)}_{k2}) = \mathrm{Beta}(v^{(i)}_k;\tau^{(i)}_{k1},\tau^{(i)}_{k2})$, $p(z^{(i)}_{jk}|\nu^{(i)}_{jk}) = \mathrm{Bern}(z^{(i)}_{jk};\nu^{(i)}_{jk})$ and $p(\mathbf{a}^e_k|\mathbf{\Phi}^e_k,\sigma^2_{ke}\mathbf{I}) = \mathcal{N}(\mathbf{a}^e_k;\mathbf{\Phi}^e_k,\sigma^2_{ke}\mathbf{I})$. In Eq. (10), we note that all the latent variables are modeled independently of all other variables, hence simplifying the inference procedure. The truncated stick breaking process of $\pi_k^{(i)}$'s is bounded at K_{max}, wherein $\pi_k = 0$ for $k > K_{max} \gg K_s + K_a + K_{bg}$. K_{bg} indicates the number of latent factors chosen to explain background tracks.

The optimization problem in Eq. (9) is solved using the posterior distribution from Eq. (10). We obtain the parameters (see supplementary material for details) σ_{ke}^2, $\boldsymbol{\Phi}^{\mathbf{e}}_k$, $\tau_{ke}^{(i)}$ and $\nu_{jk}^{(i)}$ for the optimal posterior distribution $\tilde{q}(\mathbf{Y})$ using iterative update rules as summarized in Algorithm 1. We note that this algorithm is similar to other IBP learning algorithms [1,30]. The complexity of Algorithm 1 is $\mathcal{O}(MN_{max}D_{max}K_{max})$, the same as [1]. The mean of binary latent coefficients z_{jk}, denoted by ν_{jk}, has an update rule which will lead to several interesting observations.

$$\nu_{jk}^{(i)} = \frac{L_k^{(i)}}{1 + e^{-\zeta_{jk}^{(i)}}}. \tag{11}$$

$$\zeta_{jk}^{(i)} = \sum_{j=1}^{k} \left(\Psi(\tau_{j1}^{(i)}) - \Psi(\tau_{j1}^{(i)} + \tau_{j2}^{(i)}) \right) - \mathcal{L}_k - \sum_{e \in \{s,a\}} \frac{1}{2\sigma_{ne}^2} \left(D^e \sigma_{ke}^2 + \boldsymbol{\Phi}^{\mathbf{e}}_k \boldsymbol{\Phi}^{\mathbf{e}T}_k \right)$$

$$+ \sum_{e \in \{s,a\}} \frac{1}{\sigma_{ne}^2} \boldsymbol{\Phi}^{\mathbf{e}}_k \left(\mathbf{x}_j^{(i)} - \sum_{l \neq k} \nu_{jl}^{(i)} \boldsymbol{\Phi}^{\mathbf{e}}_l \right)^T + C \underbrace{\sum_{\substack{J \in \Gamma^{(i)} \\ J=(k,a)}} \mathbb{I}_{\left\{ \sum_{l=1}^{N_i} \nu_{lk}^{(i)} \nu_{la}^{(i)} < 1 \right\}} \nu_{ja}^{(i)}}_{(i)} \tag{12}$$

$$+ C \overbrace{\sum_{\substack{J \in \Gamma^{(i)} \\ J=(s,k)}} \mathbb{I}_{\left\{ \sum_{l=1}^{N_i} \nu_{ls}^{(i)} \nu_{lk}^{(i)} < 1 \right\}} \nu_{js}^{(i)}}^{(ii)} + C \overbrace{\mathbb{I}_{\left\{ \sum_{l=1}^{N_i} \nu_{lk}^{(i)} < 1, k \leq K_a + K_s \right\}}}^{(iii)}.$$

where $\Psi(.)$ is the digamma function, $\mathbb{I}$ is an indicator function, $L_k^{(i)}$ is an indicator variable and $\mathcal{L}_k$ is a lower bound for $\mathbb{E}_{\tilde{w}}[\log(1 - \prod_{j=1}^{k} v^{(i)})]$. The $L_k^{(i)}$ indicates whether a concept (action/subject) k is part of the ith video label set $\Gamma^{(i)}$ or not. If $L_k^{(i)} = 0$, all the corresponding binary latent coefficients $z_{jk}^{(i)}$, $j = \{1, \ldots, N_i\}$, are forced to 0, which is equivalent to enforcing the constraints in Eq. (7) and (8). Note that the value of $\nu_{jk}^{(i)}$ increases with $\zeta_{jk}^{(i)}$. The terms (i)-(iii) in the update rule for $\zeta_{jk}^{(i)}$ (Eq. (12)), which are obtained due to the location constraints in Eq. (4)–(6), act as the coupling terms between $\nu_{je}^{(i)}$'s. For example, for any action concept, term (ii) suggests that if the location constraints are not satisfied, better localization of all the coupled subject concepts (high value of $\nu_{js}^{(i)}$) will drive up the value of $\zeta_{ja}^{(i)}$. This implies that the strong localization of one concept can lead to better localization of other concepts.

The hyperparameter σ_{ne}^2 and σ_{Ae}^2 can be set apriori or estimated from data. Similar to the maximization step of EM algorithm, their empirical estimation can easily be obtained by maximizing the expected log-likelihood (see supplementary material).

Algorithm 1. Learning Algorithm of WSC-SIIBP

1: **Input:** data $\Lambda = \{(i, \Gamma^{(i)})\}_{i \in 1 \ldots M}$, constant α, K_{max}, C
2: **Output:** distribution $p(\mathbf{v}), p(\mathbf{Z}), p(\mathbf{A}^s), p(\mathbf{A}^a)$ and hyper-parameters $\sigma_{ns}^2, \sigma_{na}^2, \sigma_{As}^2$ and σ_{Aa}^2
3: **Initialize:** $\tau_{k1}^{(i)} = \alpha, \tau_{k2}^{(i)} = 1, \nu_{jk}^{(i)} = 0.5, \Phi_k^s = \Phi_k^a = 0, \sigma_{ks}^2 = \sigma_{ka}^2 = \sigma_{ns}^2 = \sigma_{na}^2 = \sigma_{As}^2 = \sigma_{Aa}^2 = 1$
4: **repeat**
5:     **repeat**
6:         update σ_{ke}^2 and $\Phi^e{}_k.$, $\forall 1 \leq k \leq K_{max}, e \in \{s, a\}$;
7:         update $\tau_{k1}^{(i)}$ and $\tau_{k2}^{(i)}$, $\forall 1 \leq k \leq K_{max}$ and $i \in 1$ to M;
8:         update $\nu_{jk}^{(i)}$ using Equation (11) and (12), $\forall 1 \leq k \leq K_{max}, 1 \leq j \leq N_i$ and $i \in 1$ to M;
9:     **until** T iterations or $\frac{\|L(t-1)-L(t)\|}{L(t)} \leq 1e^{-3}$
10:     update the hyperparameters $\sigma_{As}^2, \sigma_{Aa}^2, \sigma_{ns}^2, \sigma_{na}^2$
11: **until** T' iterations or $\frac{\|L(t'-1)-L(t')\|}{L(t')} \leq 1e^{-4}$

Given the input features $\mathbf{X_s}$ and $\mathbf{X_a}$, the inferred latent coefficients $\nu_{je}^{(i)}$ estimate presence/absence of associated classes in a video. One can classify each spatio-temporal track by estimating the track-level labels using $L_j^* = \arg\max_k \nu_{jk}$. Here the maximization is over the latent coefficients corresponding to either the subject or action concepts depending upon the label which we are interested in extracting. For the concept localization task in a video with label pair (s, a), the best track in the video is selected using $j^* = \arg\max_j \nu_{js} \times \nu_{ja}$.

Test Inference: Although the above formulation is proposed for concept classification and localization in a given set of videos (transductive setting), the same algorithm can also be applied to unseen test videos. The latent coefficients for the tracks of test videos can be learned alongside the training data except that the parameters $\sigma_{ke}^2, \Phi^e{}_k., \sigma_{Ae}^2$ and σ_{ne}^2 are updated only using training data. In the case of free annotation, i.e., absence of labels for test video i, we run the proposed approach by setting $L_k^{(i)} = 1$ in Eq. (11), indicating that the tracks in a video i can belong to any of the classes in $\mathcal{S}$ or $\mathcal{A}$ (i.e., no constraints as defined by (4)–(8) are enforced).

4   Experimental Results

In this section, we present an evaluation of WSC-SIIBP on two real-world databases: Casablanca movie and A2D dataset, which represent typical 'in-the-wild' videos with weak labels on heterogeneous concepts.

4.1   Datasets

Casablanca dataset: This dataset, introduced in [5], has 19 persons (movie actors) and three action classes (sitdown, walking, background). The heterogeneous concepts used in this dataset are persons and actions. The Casablanca movie is divided into shorter segments of duration either 60 or 120 s. We manually annotate all the tracks in each video segment which may contain multiple persons and actions. Given a video segment and the corresponding video-level labels (extracted from all ground truth track labels), our algorithm maps each of these labels to one or more tracks in that segment, i.e., converts the weak labels to strong labels. Our main objective of evaluation on this dataset is to compare the performance of various algorithms in classifying tracks from videos of varying length.

For our setting, we consider face and action as the two heterogeneous concepts and thus it is required to extract the face and the corresponding action track features. We extract 1094 facial tracks from the full 102 min Casablanca video. The face tracks are extracted by running the multi-view face detector from [35] in every frame and associating detections across frames using point tracks [36]. We follow [37] to generate the face track feature representations: Dense rootSIFT features are extracted for each face in the track followed by PCA and video-level Fisher vector encoding. The action tracks corresponding to 1094 facial tracks are obtained by extrapolating the face bounding-boxes using linear transformation [5]. For action features, we compute Fisher vector encoding on dense trajectories [38] extracted from each action track.

On an average, each 60 s. segment contains 11 face-action tracks and 4 face-action annotations while each 120 s. video contains 21 tracks and 6 annotations. Note that, our experimental setup is more difficult compared to the experimental setting considered in [5]. In [5], the Casablanca movie is divided into numerous bags based on the movie script, where on average each segment is of duration 31 s. containing only 6.27 face-action tracks.

A2D dataset: This dataset [11] contains 3782 YouTube videos (on average 7–10 s. long) covering seven objects (bird, car etc.) performing one of nine actions (fly, jump etc.). The heterogeneous concepts considered are objects and actions. This dataset provides the bounding box annotations for every video label pair of object and action. Using the A2D dataset, we aim to analyze the track localization performance on weakly labeled videos as well as the track classification accuracy on a held-out test dataset.

We use the method proposed in [39] to generate spatio-temporal object track proposals. For computational purpose, we consider only 10 tracks per video and use the Imagenet pretrained VGG CNN-M network [40] to generate object feature representation. We extract convolutional layer conv-4 and conv-5 features for each track image followed by PCA and video-level Fisher vector encoding. In this dataset, the corresponding action tracks are kept similar to the object tracks (proposals) and the action features are extracted using the same approach as used for the Casablanca dataset.

4.2 Baselines

We compare WSC-SIIBP to several state-of-the-art approaches using the same features.

1. **WS-DC** [5]: This approach uses similar weak constraints as in (4)–(6), but in a discriminative setup where the constraints are incorporated in a biconvex optimization framework.
2. **WS-SIBP** [1]: This is a weakly supervised stacked IBP model which does not consider integrative framework for heterogeneous data and only enforces constraints equivalent to (7)–(8). For each spatio-temporal track, the features extracted for heterogeneous concepts are concatenated while using this approach.
3. **WS-S / WS-A**: This is similar to WS-SIBP except that instead of concatenating features from multiple concepts they are treated independently in two different IBP. WS-S(WS-A) is used to model only the person/object(action) features.
4. **WS-SIIBP**: This model integrates WS-SIBP with heterogeneous concepts.
5. **WSC-SIBP**: This model is similar to WS-SIBP, but unlike WS-SIBP, it additionally enforces the location constraints obtained from weak labels.

Implementation details: For each dataset, the Fisher encoded features are PCA reduced to an appropriate dimension, D^e. We select the best feature length and other algorithm specific hyper-parameters for each algorithm using cross-validation on a small set of input videos. For the IBP based models, the cross-validation range for hyper-parameters are $K_{max} := K_a + K_s : 10 : K_a + K_s + 100$, $\alpha := 3K_{max} : 10 : 4K_{max}$ and $C := 0 : 0.5 : 5$. For all IBP based models, the parameters D^e, α, K_{max} and C are set as 32, 100, 30 and 0.5 respectively for the Casablanca dataset and as 128, 160, 50 and 5 respectively for the A2D dataset. For WS-DC, D^e is set as 1024.

4.3   Results on Casablanca

The track-level classification performance is compared in Fig. 3. From Figs. 3a and d, it can be seen that WSC-SIIBP significantly outperforms other methods for person and action classification in almost all of the scenarios. For instance, in the 120 s video segments, person classification improves by 4 % (relative improvement is 7 %) compared to the most competitive approach WS-SIIBP. We also compare pairwise label accuracy to gain insight into the importance of the constraints in eq (4)–(6). For any given track with non-background person and action label, the classification is assumed to be correct only if both person and action labels are correctly assigned. Even in this scenario WSC-SIIBP performs 8.1 % better (24 % relative improvement) than the most competitive baseline. Since we combine the heterogeneous concepts along with location constraints in an integrated framework, WSC-SIIBP outperforms all other baselines. The weak results of WS-DC in pairwise classification, though surprising, can be attributed to their action classification results which are significantly biased towards one particular action 'sitdown' (Fig. 3d, note that WS-DC performs very poorly in 'walking' classification). Indeed, it should be noted that nearly 40 % and 89 % of person and action labels respectively belong to the background class. Thus, for fair evaluation of both background and non-background classes, we also plot the recall of background class against the recall of nonbackground classes for person and action classification in Fig. 3b, c, e and f. These curves were obtained by simultaneously computing recall for background and non-background classes over a range of threshold values on score, ν. The mean average precision (mAP) of WSC-SIIBP along with all other baselines are plotted in Fig. 3g and h. The mAP values also clearly demonstrate the effectiveness of the proposed approach. From the performance of WS-SIIBP (integrative concepts, no constraints) and WSC-SIBP (no integrative concepts, constraints) (Fig. 3a and d), it is clear that the improvement in performance in the WSC-SIIBP can be attributed to both addition of integrative concepts and the location constraints.

Effect of constraints (7), (8): We note that, regardless of other differences, every weakly supervised IBP model considered here enforces constraints (7), (8). However, these constraints are not part of the original WS-DC. To make a fair comparison between WS-DC and WSC-SIIBP, we analyze the effect of these constraints in Fig. 3i. Although, these additional constraints improve WS-DC performance, they do not supersede the performance of WSC-SIIBP. Further we

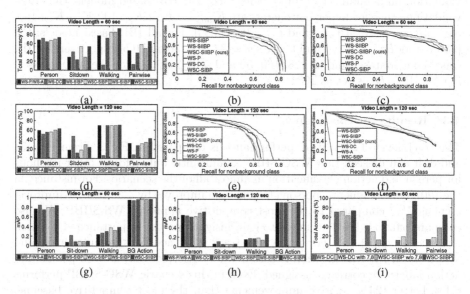

Fig. 3. Comparison of results for the Casablanca movie dataset. (a) Classification accuracy for 60 s. segments. (b) Recall for background vs non-background class (60 s, person). (c) Recall for background vs non-background (60 s., action). (d) Classification accuracy for 120 s. segments. (e) Recall for background vs non-background class (120 s., person). (f) Recall for background vs non-background (120 s., action). (g),(h) Mean Average Precision for 60, 120 s. segments. (i) Classification accuracy obtained with and without constraints (7) and (8)

observe that these constraints have improved the performance of all the weakly supervised IBP models.

4.4   Results on A2D

First, we evaluate localization performance on the full A2D dataset. We experiment with 37,820 tracks extracted from 3,782 videos with around 5000 weak labels. For every given object-action label pair our algorithm selects the best track from the corresponding video using the approach outlined in Sect. 3.6. The localization accuracy is measured by calculating the average IoU (Intersection over Union) of the selected track (3-D bounding box) with the ground truth bounding box. The class-wise IoU accuracy and the mean IoU accuracy for all classes are tabulated in Tables 1 and 2 respectively. In this task WSC-SIIBP also leads to a relative improvement of 9 % above the next best baseline. We also evaluate how accurately the extracted object proposals match with the ground truth bounding boxes to estimate an upper bound on the localization accuracy (referred as Upper Bound in Tables 1 and 2). In this case, the track maximizing the average IoU with the ground truth annotation is selected and the corresponding IoU is reported. We plot the correct localization accuracy with varying IoU thresholds in Fig. 4a, which also shows the effectiveness of the proposed approach. Figure 4b–4c shows some qualitative track localization results using the proposed approach on the selected frame.

Test Inference: We evaluate the classification performance on held-out test samples using the same train/test partition as in [11]. We consider two setups for the evaluation, (a) using video-level labels for the test samples and (b) free annotation where no test video labels are provided. The proposed approach is compared with GT-SVM, which is a fully supervised linear SVM that uses ground truth bounding boxes and their corresponding strong labels during training. The results are tabulated in Table 3. Note that the performance of WSC-SIIBP is close to that of the fully supervised setup.

(a)   (b)   (c)

Fig. 4. (a) Correct localization accuracy at various IOU thresholds. (b) and (c) Qualitative results: green boxes show the concept localization using our proposed approach.

Table 1. Per class mean IoU on A2D dataset.

	adult	baby	ball	bird	car	cat	dog	climb	crawl	eat	fly	jump	roll	run	walk
WSC-SIIBP	28.4	43.6	9.8	37.8	37.4	40.8	42.0	37.5	47.6	46.1	24.5	29.4	50.9	25.6	37.2
Upper Bound	39.9	53.9	16.4	48.2	48.7	52.8	51.4	50.0	59.2	57.2	33.9	41.0	59.1	38.1	47.9

Table 2. Average IoU comparison with other approaches on A2D dataset.

	Random	WS-P	WS-A	WS-SIBP	WS-SIIBP	WSC-SIBP	WSC-SIIBP	Upper Bound
IoU	25.5	29.7	30.43	31.1	31.55	31.69	**34.38**	45.05

Table 3. mAP classification test accuracy on A2D dataset.

	WSC-SIIBP		GT-SVM	
Setup	Obj	Act	Obj	Act
Using video Labels	94.77	90.68	98.20	94.92
Free Annotation	76.62	64.77	85.18	73.26

5   Conclusion

We developed a Bayesian non-parametric approach that integrates the Indian Buffet Process with heterogeneous concepts and spatio-temporal location constraints arising from weak labels. We report experimental results on two recent datasets containing heterogeneous concepts such as persons, objects and actions and show that our approach outperforms the best state of the art method. In future work, we will extend the WSC-SIIBP model to additionally localize audio concepts from speech input and develop an end-to-end deep neural network for joint feature learning and Bayesian inference.

Acknowledgments. The work of L.S. Davis was supported by the US Office of Naval Research under grant N000141612713.

References

1. Shi, Z., Yang, Y., Hospedales, T.M., Xiang, T.: Weakly supervised learning of objects, attributes and their associations. In: Fleet, D., Pajdla, T., Schiele, B., Tuytelaars, T. (eds.) ECCV 2014. LNCS, vol. 8690, pp. 472–487. Springer, Heidelberg (2014). doi:10.1007/978-3-319-10605-2_31
2. Leung, T., Song, Y., Zhang, J.: Handling label noise in video classification via multiple instance learning. In: 2011 IEEE International Conference on Computer Vision (ICCV), pp. 2056–2063. IEEE (2011)
3. Oquab, M., Bottou, L., Laptev, I., Sivic, J.: Is object localization for free? weakly-supervised learning with convolutional neural networks. In: Proceedings of the IEEE Conference on Computer Vision and Pattern Recognition (2015)

4. Bojanowski, P., Lajugie, R., Bach, F., Laptev, I., Ponce, J., Schmid, C., Sivic, J.: Weakly supervised action labeling in videos under ordering constraints. In: Fleet, D., Pajdla, T., Schiele, B., Tuytelaars, T. (eds.) ECCV 2014. LNCS, vol. 8693, pp. 628–643. Springer, Heidelberg (2014). doi:10.1007/978-3-319-10602-1_41

5. Bojanowski, P., Bach, F., Laptev, I., Ponce, J., Schmid, C., Sivic, J.: Finding actors and actions in movies. In: 2013 IEEE International Conference on Computer Vision (ICCV), pp. 2280–2287. IEEE (2013)

6. Ghahramani, Z., Griffiths, T.L.: Infinite latent feature models and the indian buffet process. Adv. Neural Inf. Proces. Syst. **18**, 475–482 (2005)

7. Griffiths, T.L., Ghahramani, Z.: The indian buffet process: an introduction and review. J. Mach. Learn. Res. **12**, 1185–1224 (2011)

8. Ozdemir, B., Davis, L.S.: A probabilistic framework for multimodal retrieval using integrative indian buffet process. In: Advances in Neural Information Processing Systems, pp. 2384–2392 (2014)

9. Yildirim, I., Jacobs, R.A.: A rational analysis of the acquisition of multisensory representations. Cogn. Sci. **36**(2), 305–332 (2012)

10. Gershman, S.J., Blei, D.M.: A tutorial on bayesian nonparametric models. J. Math. Psychol. **56**(1), 1–12 (2012)

11. Xu, C., Hsieh, S.H., Xiong, C., Corso, J.J.: Can humans fly? action understanding with multiple classes of actors. In: Proceedings of the IEEE Conference on Computer Vision and Pattern Recognition, pp. 2264–2273 (2015)

12. Zhang, C., Platt, J.C., Viola, P.A.: Multiple instance boosting for object detection. Adv. Neural Inf. Process. Syst. **7**, 1417–1424 (2005)

13. Andrews, S., Tsochantaridis, I., Hofmann, T.: Support vector machines for multiple-instance learning. In: Proceedings of Advances in Neural Information Processing Systems, pp. 561–568 (2002)

14. Ali, S., Shah, M.: Human action recognition in videos using kinematic features and multiple instance learning. Pattern Anal. Mach. Intell. IEEE Trans. **32**(2), 288–303 (2010)

15. Babenko, B., Yang, M.H., Belongie, S.: Visual tracking with online multiple instance learning. In: IEEE Conference on Computer Vision and Pattern Recognition, CVPR 2009, pp. 983–990. IEEE (2009)

16. Cour, T., Jordan, C., Miltsakaki, E., Taskar, B.: Movie/Script: alignment and parsing of video and text transcription. In: Forsyth, D., Torr, P., Zisserman, A. (eds.) ECCV 2008. LNCS, vol. 5305, pp. 158–171. Springer, Heidelberg (2008). doi:10.1007/978-3-540-88693-8_12

17. Bojanowski, P., Lagugie, R., Grave, E., Bach, F., Laptev, I., Ponce, J., Schmid, C.: Weakly-supervised alignment of video with text. In: ICCV, IEEE (2015)

18. Prest, A., Leistner, C., Civera, J., Schmid, C., Ferrari, V.: Learning object class detectors from weakly annotated video. In: 2012 IEEE Conference on Computer Vision and Pattern Recognition (CVPR), pp. 3282–3289. IEEE (2012)

19. Bilen, H., Namboodiri, V.P., Van Gool, L.J.: Object and action classification with latent window parameters. Int. J. Comput. Vis. **106**(3), 237–251 (2014)

20. Tapaswi, M., Bauml, M., Stiefelhagen, R.: Book2movie: Aligning video scenes with book chapters. In: Proceedings of the IEEE Conference on Computer Vision and Pattern Recognition, pp. 1827–1835 (2015)

21. Zhu, Y., Kiros, R., Zemel, R., Salakhutdinov, R., Urtasun, R., Torralba, A., Fidler, S.: Aligning books and movies: towards story-like visual explanations by watching movies and reading books. In: Proceedings of the IEEE International Conference on Computer Vision, pp. 19–27 (2015)

22. Ramanathan, V., Joulin, A., Liang, P., Fei-Fei, L.: Linking people in videos with "their" names using coreference resolution. In: Fleet, D., Pajdla, T., Schiele, B., Tuytelaars, T. (eds.) ECCV 2014. LNCS, vol. 8689, pp. 95–110. Springer, Heidelberg (2014). doi:10.1007/978-3-319-10590-1_7

23. Karpathy, A., Fei-Fei, L.: Deep visual-semantic alignments for generating image descriptions. In: Proceedings of the IEEE Conference on Computer Vision and Pattern Recognition, pp. 3128–3137 (2015)

24. Xu, K., Ba, J., Kiros, R., Cho, K., Courville, A., Salakhudinov, R., Zemel, R., Bengio, Y.: Show, attend and tell: Neural image caption generation with visual attention. In: Proceedings of The 32nd International Conference on Machine Learning, pp. 2048–2057 (2015)

25. Fang, H., Gupta, S., Iandola, F., Srivastava, R.K., Deng, L., Dollár, P., Gao, J., He, X., Mitchell, M., Platt, J.C., et al.: From captions to visual concepts and back. In: Proceedings of the IEEE Conference on Computer Vision and Pattern Recognition, pp. 1473–1482 (2015)

26. Sun, C., Gan, C., Nevatia, R.: Automatic concept discovery from parallel text and visual corpora. In: Proceedings of the IEEE International Conference on Computer Vision, pp. 2596–2604 (2015)

27. Venugopalan, S., Rohrbach, M., Donahue, J., Mooney, R., Darrell, T., Saenko, K.: Sequence to sequence-video to text. In: Proceedings of the IEEE International Conference on Computer Vision, pp. 4534–4542 (2015)

28. Rohrbach, A., Rohrbach, M., Schiele, B.: The long-short story of movie description. In: Gall, J., Gehler, P., Leibe, B. (eds.) GCPR 2015. LNCS, vol. 9358, pp. 209–221. Springer, Heidelberg (2015). doi:10.1007/978-3-319-24947-6_17

29. Cho, K., Courville, A., Bengio, Y.: Describing multimedia content using attention-based encoder-decoder networks. Multimedia IEEE Trans. 17(11), 1875–1886 (2015)

30. Doshi, F., Miller, K., Gael, J.V., Teh, Y.W.: Variational inference for the indian buffet process. In: International Conference on Artificial Intelligence and Statistics, pp. 137–144 (2009)

31. Wainwright, M.J., Jordan, M.I.: Graphical models, exponential families, and variational inference. Found. Trends Mach. Learn. 1(1–2), 1–305 (2008)

32. Zellner, A.: Optimal information processing and bayes's theorem. Am. Stat. 42(4), 278–280 (1988)

33. Zhu, J., Chen, N., Xing, E.P.: Bayesian inference with posterior regularization and applications to infinite latent svms. J. Mach. Learn. Res. 15(1), 1799–1847 (2014)

34. Ganchev, K., Graça, J., Gillenwater, J., Taskar, B.: Posterior regularization for structured latent variable models. J. Mach. Learn. Res. 11, 2001–2049 (2010)

35. Zhu, X., Ramanan, D.: Face detection, pose estimation and landmark estimation in the wild. In: IEEE Conference on Computer Vision and Pattern Recognition (CVPR) (2012)

36. Everingham, M., Sivic, J., Zisserman, A.: Hello! my name is buffy-automatic naming of characters in tv video. In: BMVC. vol. 2. 6 (2006)

37. Parkhi, O.M., Simonyan, K., Vedaldi, A., Zisserman, A.: A compact and discriminative face track descriptor. In: 2014 IEEE Conference on Computer Vision and Pattern Recognition (CVPR), pp. 1693–1700. IEEE (2014)

38. Wang, H., Schmid, C.: Action recognition with improved trajectories. In: 2013 IEEE International Conference on Computer Vision (ICCV), pp. 3551–3558. IEEE (2013)
39. Oneata, D., Revaud, J., Verbeek, J., Schmid, C.: Spatio-temporal object detection proposals. In: Fleet, D., Pajdla, T., Schiele, B., Tuytelaars, T. (eds.) ECCV 2014. LNCS, vol. 8691, pp. 737–752. Springer, Heidelberg (2014). doi:10.1007/978-3-319-10578-9_48
40. Chatfield, K., Simonyan, K., Vedaldi, A., Zisserman, A.: Return of the devil in the details: delving deep into convolutional nets. In: British Machine Vision Conference (2014)

Learning Semantic Deformation Flows with 3D Convolutional Networks

M. Ersin Yumer[1(✉)] and Niloy J. Mitra[2]

[1] Adobe Research, San Jose, CA, USA
yumer@adobe.com
[2] University College London, London, UK
n.mitra@cs.ucl.ac.uk

Abstract. Shape deformation requires expert user manipulation even when the object under consideration is in a high fidelity format such as a 3D mesh. It becomes even more complicated if the data is represented as a point set or a depth scan with significant self occlusions. We introduce an end-to-end solution to this tedious process using a volumetric Convolutional Neural Network (CNN) that learns deformation flows in 3D. Our network architectures take the voxelized representation of the shape and a semantic deformation intention (*e.g.*, make more sporty) as input and generate a deformation flow at the output. We show that such deformation flows can be trivially applied to the input shape, resulting in a novel deformed version of the input without losing detail information. Our experiments show that the CNN approach achieves comparable results with state of the art methods when applied to CAD models. When applied to single frame depth scans, and partial/noisy CAD models we achieve ~60 % less error compared to the state-of-the-art.

1 Introduction

Shape deformation is a core component in 3D content synthesis. This problem has been well studied in graphics where low level, expert user manipulation is required [2,36]. It is acknowledged that this is an open and difficult problem, especially for deformations that follow semantic meaning, where very sparse high level information (*e.g.*, make this shoe more durable) need to be extrapolated to a complex deformation. One way to solve this problem using traditional editing paradigms is through highly customized template matching [44], which does not scale. In this paper, we introduce a novel volumetric CNN, end-to-end trained for learning deformation flows on 3D data, which generalizes well to low fidelity models as well.

CNNs have been shown to outperform hand-crafted features and domain knowledge engineered methods in many fields of computer vision. Promising applications to classification [23], dense segmentation [26], and more recently direct synthesis [8] and transformation [39,43] have been demonstrated.

Electronic supplementary material The online version of this chapter (doi:10.1007/978-3-319-46466-4_18) contains supplementary material, which is available to authorized users.

© Springer International Publishing AG 2016
B. Leibe et al. (Eds.): ECCV 2016, Part VI, LNCS 9910, pp. 294–311, 2016.
DOI: 10.1007/978-3-319-46466-4_18

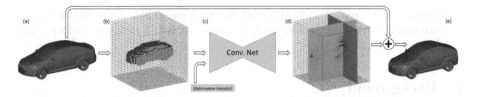

Fig. 1. Our 3D convolutional network (c) takes a volumetric representation (b) of an object (a) and high-level deformation intentions as input and predicts a deformation flow (d) at the output. Applying the predicted deformation flow to the original object yields a high quality novel deformed version (e) that displays the high-level transformation intentions (In this illustration, the car is deformed to be more compact).

Encouraged by these advances, we propose using the reference shape's volumetric representation, and high-level deformation intentions (*e.g.,* make the shape more sporty) as input to our 3D convolutional neural network, where both channels get mixed through fully connected layers and is consequently 'upconvolved'[1] into a volumetric deformation flow at the output. When such a deformation flow is applied to the original reference shape, it yields a deformed version of the shape that displays the high-level deformation intentions (Fig. 1).

We train and test end-to-end networks for four different object categories: cars, shoes, chairs, and airplanes with five high-level relative attribute based deformation controls for each category. In addition to Yumer *et al.* [44]'s dataset (referred to as the SemEd dataset), we also use additional data for the same categories from ShapeNet [3,35]. We use more than 2500 unique shapes for each category, which yields in ~2.5M training pairs with additional data types (point set and depth scan), as well as data augmentation.

We introduce two novel deformation flow CNN architectures. We compare with state of the art semantic deformation methods, as well as a data-driven baseline and two direct shape synthesis CNN baselines where the output is replaced with volumetric representation of the deformed shape instead of the deformation flow in our architectures. Even though the ultimate goal is generating a deformed version of the shape, we opt to learn a deformation flow instead of directly learning to generate the shape in volumetric format. We show that our deformation flow approach results in ~70 % less error compared to such direct synthesis approaches using the same CNN architectures. Moreover, we quantitatively and qualitatively show that deformation flow based CNN perform significantly better than the state-of-the-art semantic deformation [44]: we achieve ~60 % less error on depth scans and noisy/partial CAD models.

Our main contributions are:

– Introducing the first 3D volumetric generative network that learns to predict per-voxel dense 3D deformation flows using explicit high level deformation intentions.

---

[1] *Upconvolution* in our context is unpooling followed by convolution. Refer to Sect. 3.1 for more details.

– Demonstrating semantic 3D content deformation exploiting structural compatibility between volumetric network grids and free-form shape deformation lattices.

2 Background

3D Deep Learning. 3D ShapeNets [40] introduced 3D deep learning for modeling shapes as volumetrically discretized (*i.e.*, in voxel form) data, and showed that intuitive 3D features can be learned directly in 3D. Song *et al.* [37] introduced an amodal 3D object detector method for RGB-D images using a two 3D convolutional networks both for region proposal and object recognition. Maturana and Scherer demonstrated the use of 3D convolutional networks in object classification of point clouds [30] and landing zone detection [29], specifically from range sensor data. 3D feature extraction using fully connected autoencoders [10,41] and multi-view based CNNs [38] are also actively studied for classification and retrieval. Although volumetric convolution is promising for feature learning, due to the practically achievable resolution of the voxel space prevents high quality object synthesis [40]. We circumvent this by learning a deformation flow instead of learning to generate the transformed object directly. Such deformation flows exhibit considerably less high frequency details compared to the shape itself, and therefore are more suitable to be generated by consecutive convolution and upsampling layers.

Generative Learning. There has been several recent methods introduced to generate or alter objects in images using deep networks. Such methods generally utilize 3D CAD data by applying various transformations to objects in images in order to synthesize controlled training data. Dosovitskiy *et al.* [8] introduced a CNN to generate object images from a particular category (chairs in their case) via controlling variation including 3D properties that affect appearance such as shape and pose. Using a semi-supervised variational autoencoder [20], Kingma *et al.* [19] utilized class labels associated to part of the training data set to achieve visual analogies via controlling the utilized class labels. Similar to the variational autoencoder [20], Kulkarni *et al.* [24] introduced the deep convolutional inverse graphics network, which aims to disentangle the object in the image from viewing transformations such as light variations and depth rotations. Yang *et al.* [43] introduced a recurrent neural network to exploit the fact that content identity and transformations can be separated more naturally by keeping the identity constant across transformation steps. Note that the generative methods mentioned here tackle the problem of separating and/or imposing transformations in the 2D image space. However, such transformations act on the object in 3D, whose representation is naturally volumetric. As the applied transformation gets more severe, the quality and sharpness of the generated 2D image diminishes. On the other hand, our volumetric convolution based deformation flow applies the transformation in 3D, therefore does not directly suffer from the discrepancy between 2D and 3D data.

3D Deformation. 3D shape deformation is an actively studied research area, where many energy formulations that promote smoothness and minimize shear on manifolds have been widely used (see [2] for an extensive review). With the increasing availability of 3D shape repositories, data-driven shape analysis and synthesis methods have been recently receiving a great deal of attention. Mitra et al. [31] and Xu et al. [42] provide extensive overviews of related techniques. These methods aim to decipher the geometric principles that underlie a product family in order to enable deformers that are customized for individual models, thereby expanding data-driven techniques beyond compositional modeling [12, 44,46]. Yumer et al. [44,46] present such a method for learning statistical shape deformation handles [45] that enable 3D shape deformation. The problem with such custom deformation handles are two folds: (1) Limited generalization due to dependency on correct registration of handles between template and the model, (2) Being capable to only operate on fully observed data (e.g., complete 3D shapes) and not generalizing well for partially observed data (e.g., depth scans, range sensor output). We circumvent the registration problem by training an end-to-end volumetric convolutional network for learning a volumetric deformation field. We show that our method outperforms the previous methods when the input is partially observed by providing experiments on depth sensor data.

Relative Attributes. We incorporate explicit semantic control of the deformation flow using relative attributes [4,32,33,44]. Relative attributes have been demonstrated useful for high level semantic image search [22], shape assembly [4], and human body shape analysis [1]. Recently, Yumer et al. [44] showed that relative attributes can be directly used in a shape editing system to enable semantic deformation (e.g., make this car sportier) using statistical shape deformation handles. We use their system to generate training data with CAD models. We show that our end-to-end method generalizes better compared to [44], especially for low quality, higher variance, and incomplete data (e.g., partial shapes, depth sensor output).

3   Approach

3.1   Network Architectures

Convolutional neural networks are known to perform well in learning input-output relations given sufficient training data. Hence, we are motivated to introduce an end-to-end approach for semantically deforming shapes in 3D (e.g., deform this shoe to be more comfortable). This is especially useful for raw and incomplete data such as depth scans, which previous methods have not addressed. One might think that a complete network to generate the deformed shape at the output of the network is a better solution. While this is a reasonable thought, the resulting shape will be missing high frequency details due to the highest resolution that is achievable with a volumetric network. Results from such a network fail to capture intricate shape details (see Sect. 5 for comparison).

Dense Prediction with CNNs. Krizhevsky *et al.* [23] showed that convolutional neural networks trained with backpropagation [25] perform well for image classification in the wild. This paved the way to recent advancements in computer vision where CNNs have been applied to computer vision problems at large by enabling end-to-end solutions where feature engineering is bypassed. Rather, features are learned implicitly by the network, optimizing for the task and data at hand. Our volumetric convolution approach is similar to CNNs that operate in 2D and generate dense prediction (*i.e.*, per pixel in 2D). To date, such CNNs have been mainly used in semantic segmentation [11,14,26], key point prediction [16], edge detection [13], depth inference [9], optical flow prediction [7], and content generation [8,34,39]. Below, we introduce our 3D convolutional network architecture that derives inspiration from these recent advances in dense prediction approaches.

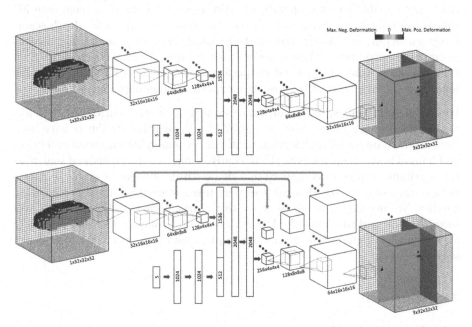

Fig. 2. Top: Volumetric convolutional encoder (red)'s third set of filter responses ($128^*4 \times 4 \times 4$) are fully connected to a layer of 1536 neurons, which are concatenated with the 512 codes of deformation indicator vector (green). After three fully connected layer mixing, convolutional decoder part (**blue**) generates a volumetric deformation flow ($3^*32 \times 32 \times 32$). Bottom: We add all filter responses from the encoder part to the decoder part at corresponding levels. (Only the far faces of input - output volume discretization is shown. The deformation flow is computed in the entire volume, where only two slices are shown for visual clarity. Arrows indicate fully connected layers, whereas convolution and upconvolution layers are indicated with appropriate filters.) (Color figure online)

3D Deformation Flow CNN Architecture. We propose two network architectures for learning deformation flows (Fig. 2). Our first network architecture (Fig. 2-top) integrates ideas from Tatarchenko *et al.* [39] where explicit control over transformation parameters (deformation attributes in our case) are fed into the network as a separate input channel. Each element of the input channel demarcates the deformation indicator based on the semantic attribute: 0: generate a deformation flow to decrease this attribute, 1.0: generate a deformation flow to increase this attribute, and 0.5: keep this attribute same. This simpler architecture is easier and faster to train, but fails to capture some of the sharp details in the deformation flow when the structure is volumetrically thin (Fig. 3).

Our second network architecture introduces additional feature maps from the encoder part of the network, as well as upconvolving coarse predictions added to the corresponding resolution layers in the decoder part (analogous to Long *et al.* [26] and Dosovitskiy *et al.* [7] but in 3D). This approach performs better at reconstructing higher frequency details in the deformation flow due to the low level features introduced at corresponding layers. As such, it enables us to perform subtle deformations that are not possible with the first architecture. Figure 3 shows that this architecture captures the shoe sole thickness transformation that corresponds to a 'more durable' deformation.

In the following parts of this paper, we denote the first and second architecture with F1-32 and F2-32. Additionally, we compare with a lower resolution, easier to train version of the networks denoted by F1-16 and F2-16, where 16 denotes the lower volumetric resolution at the input and output ($16 \times 16 \times 16$ instead of $32 \times 32 \times 32$). These low resolution variations are architecturally identical to the ones in Fig. 2 except the fact that the volumetric encoder and the decoder have one less number of layers but same number of convolution filters. For comparison purposes, we also train direct volumetric content synthesis versions of high resolution networks by replacing the deformation flow at the output with the voxelized deformed target shape ($1^*32 \times 32 \times 32$) and denote these variations as: S1-32 and S2-32.

We use leaky rectified nonlinearities [28] with negative slope of 0.2 after all layers. For both convolution and upconvolution layers, we use $5 \times 5 \times 5$ filters. After each convolution layer we use a $2 \times 2 \times 2$ max pooling layer, whereas

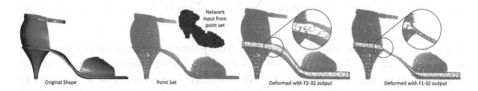

Original Shape   Point Set   Deformed with F2-32 output   Deformed with F1-32 output

Fig. 3. Our 3D convolutional network takes a volumetric representation of an object ('the point set' in this example) and high-level deformation intentions as input ('durable' in this example) and predicts a deformation flow that can be used to deform the underlying object. Note that the our F2-32 architecture gracefully deforms all parts of the object, whereas the simpler F1-32 might miss the thin regions.

upconvolution layers use an unpooling layer preceding them. Following [8], we simply replace each entry of a feature map with a $2 \times 2 \times 2$ block with entry value at the top left corner and zeros everywhere else. Hence, each upconvolution results in doubled height, width and depth of the feature map. In our second architecture (Fig. 2-bottom), these upconvolved feature maps are concatenated with the corresponding feature maps from the encoder part of the CNN, resulting in doubled the number of feature maps compared to the simpler network illustrated in Fig. 2-top.

3.2   Deformation Flow Computation

Since the volumetric convolution is computed in a regular 3D grid, it conforms naturally to free-form deformation (FFD) using lattices [6,36]. FFD embeds a shape in a lattice space and enables the embedded shape to be deformed using the FFD lattice vertices, which act as control points in the local volumetric deformation coordinate system. The FFD lattice vertices are defined at the voxel centers of the last layer of the CNN (Fig. 4), since the prediction is per voxel.

Formally, the local lattice space for each deformation volume is given by 64 control points, whose position are denoted with $\mathbf{P}_{ijk}$, are the vertices of 27 sub-deformation volumes. Deformed positions of arbitrary points in the center sub-deformation lattice can be directly computed using control point positions:

$$\mathbf{P}(u,v,w) = \sum_{i=0}^{3}\sum_{j=0}^{3}\sum_{k=0}^{3}\mathbf{P}_{ijk}B_i(u)B_j(v)B_k(w) \quad \begin{matrix} 0<u<1 \\ 0<v<1 \\ 0<w<1 \end{matrix} \quad (1)$$

where $B_n(x)$ is a Bernstein polynomial of degree n [21], that acts as a blending function. For the sake of completeness, we include a detailed formulation of Bernstein polynomials in our supplementary material.

Since our data is in the form of *undeformed-deformed* shape or point set pairs, we first compute a binary voxel mask for the *undeformed* shape as network input, and a deformation flow for each pair as network output for the training dataset. To compute the deformation flow, we solve the following optimization problem to compute the deformed lattice vertex positions for the input-output pairs:

$$\underset{\mathbf{d}'\in\mathcal{D}}{\arg\min}\ \sum_i l(\mathbf{p}'_i - \mathbf{F}(\mathbf{p}_i)). \quad (2)$$

where $\mathbf{p}'_i$ and $\mathbf{p}_i$ are the *deformed* and *undeformed* positions of points in the shape or point set data, $\mathbf{d}'$ is the deformation lattice vertex position in the deformed state, and $\mathcal{D}$ is the set of all deformation lattice vertices. $\mathbf{F}$ is the FFD deformation flow operator applied on the undeformed positions using Eq. 1. The deformation lattice vertices are the voxel centers in the network output (Fig. 4). Hence, the deformation flow vector in $\mathbb{R}^3$ for each voxel is given by $\mathbf{v} = \mathbf{d}' - \mathbf{d}$, where $\mathbf{d}$ is the undeformed lattice vertex position.

One can argue that instead of computing the deformation flow a priori and using an Euclidean loss on the dense deformation flow as we do, an alternative is to deform the input shape using the deformation flow at each forward pass, and compute an Euclidean loss over points in the deformed positions of the shape or point cloud. The problem with such an optimization is that only a sparse number of voxels contribute to the deformation. In our approach, the non-contributing voxel values are set to zero to enforces correct dense prediction. We experimented with both, and observed that dense deformation flow Euclidean loss resulted in ~5x faster convergence, without any performance difference on test sets.

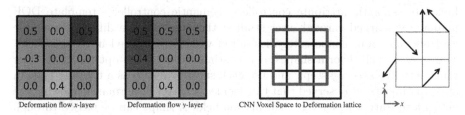

Fig. 4. CNN voxels to FFD lattice illustrated with a 2D example for clarity. The flow values predicted for each voxel (left), correspond to the deformation lattice vertices (middle), which result in the deformation vectors applied to the control points (right).

Deformation of the Shape using the Predicted Flow. At test time, we use the trained network to predict a volumetric deformation flow for the input shape or point set. We apply the flow to the deformation lattice vertices where the input is embedded, which results in the final deformed shape/range scan.

4 Implementation and Training Details

4.1 Training Data Generation

We build eight datasets (four object classes × two data types) from two sources: (1) ShapeNet [3], (2) SemEd [44]. We train and test on three different data types: 3D shapes in mesh representation, point sets sampled directly on the shape, and simulated single frame depth scans from a kinect sensor [15] in point cloud representation. The four object classes we include are: Cars, Shoes, Chairs, Airplanes. Note that a network is trained per object class.

3D Shapes. We collect 2500 shapes from ShapeNet for each category[2] in addition to the data provided by Yumer et al. [44] for each category. We randomly separate ~20 % from each group to be used as tests.

Point Sets and Simulated Depth Scans. One of the powerful aspects of our method is that, it can gracefully handle low fidelity and incomplete data. We achieve this by sampling points on the shape set and also simulating single view depth scans for the shapes mentioned above from arbitrary viewpoints

---

[2] We collect additional data from 3D Warehouse where ShapeNet counts fall short.

and include these in the training set as well. Note that for the simulated scans, only the input of the training pair changes such that the network is trained to predict complete deformation flow from single viewpoint depth scans in order to correctly deform the points.

Undeformed-Deformed Pairs. We generate deformed shapes using the method introduced by Yumer et al. [44]. Their approach semantically deforms shapes by first fitting a class dependent template to the shape, and subsequently deforming the shape using the template whose degrees of freedom (DOF) are linked to semantic attribute controllers. Semantic controller - template DOF mapping is learned through user studies: they provide five different semantic controllers for four shape categories, all of which are utilized in our networks. Yumer et al. [44] deform shapes at a continuous scale. We opt to divide their range into five *severity* steps, and use each successive step as a training pair. In our experiments we observed that this yielded a better performance allowing the network to learn a less severe deformation field. A shape can be passed through the network multiple times by using the output from the previous step as the input, resulting in more severe deformation (Fig. 5). Note that, their dependency on customized deformation templates and correct registration of template labels for successful deformation limits the variety of shapes they can operate on. Their system will mostly fail to fit correct templates to depth scans and point sets (refer to Sect. 5 for details of such experiments). We therefore utilize the following strategy to generate the deformed counter part for point sets and depth scans: (1) register the nearest point on the shape for each point in the simulated depth scan, (2) deform the original shape with Yumer et al. [44], (3) transform each point in the depth scan to a deformed position by using the relative distance to the corresponding nearest point on the shape.

Data Augmentation. We utilize two data augmentations to increase the robustness of the network, and to provide additional training data: (1)part removal from input, (2) translation and rotation transforms. Note that part removal only applied to the input (*i.e.,* the network is trained to predict the full deformation flow), whereas transformations are applied to both the input and the output (*i.e.,* the network is expected to predict the flow both at globally and locally correct positions relative to the shape data) We assume that the object up direction is known, which is available in both data sources we utilize, and easy to obtain for shapes where such information is not available a priori. Therefore, the rotation transformation applies only to in-plane rotation on the ground.

Training Data Statistics. Table 1 show detailed statistics of the datasets used both in training. Although the number of shapes in each category we use in training is ~2000, this quickly multiplies: each category has 5 different semantic deformation modes, and 5 different severity steps, yielding 25 input-output pairs for each shape. Moreover, we simulated depth scans from 6 arbitrary views for each shape, and apply 7 random data augmentations. This results in ~2.5 million input-output training pairs per object category.

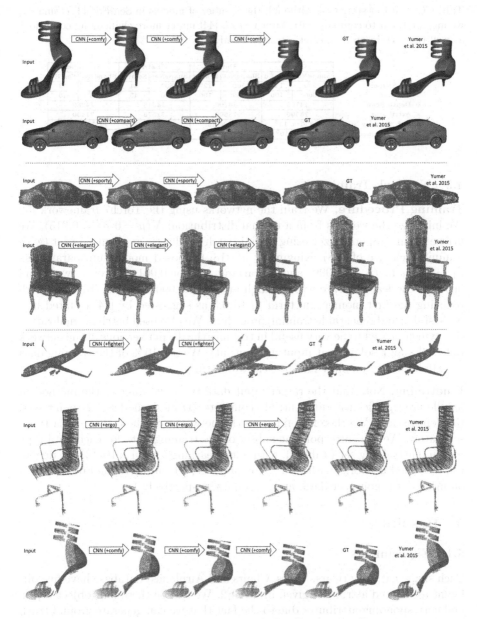

Fig. 5. Results using our finetuned networks (F2-32{-fm, -fp, -fs}) for 3D shapes in mesh representation (grey), point sets (red), and depth scan data (blue). Note that the shape is processed through the network a few number of times to achieve the desired deformation effect. Comparisons with Yumer *et al.* [44] show that our method achieves similar results for high quality mesh data. On the other hand, both for point sets and depth scans, our method outperforms Yumer *et al.* [44] significantly. For additional visual comparisons, please refer to our supplementary material. (Color figure online)

Table 1. Dataset statistics. Although the number of models in SemEd [44] is smaller, we include them to compare with Yumer *et al.* [44] under more challenging conditions as well (*e.g.*, train on ShapeNet – test on SemEd).

	Cars		Shoes		Chairs		Airplanes	
	ShapeNet	SemEd	ShapeNet	SemEd	ShapeNet	SemEd	ShapeNet	SemEd
All Shapes	2500	131	2500	127	2500	61	2500	53
Training	2000	100	2000	100	2000	45	2000	40
+ Depth Scan	14700		14700		14315		14280	
× Attributes	73500		73500		71575		71400	
× Def. Severity Steps	$\sim350 \times 10^3$		$\sim350 \times 10^3$		$\sim350 \times 10^3$		$\sim350 \times 10^3$	
× Data Augmentation	$\sim2.5 \times 10^6$		$\sim2.5 \times 10^6$		$\sim2.5 \times 10^6$		$\sim2.5 \times 10^6$	

4.2 Network Training

Training Procedure. We train the networks using the Torch7 framework [5]. We initialize the weights from a normal distribution: $\mathcal{N}(\mu = 0, \sigma^2 = 0.015)$. We utilize Adam [18] optimizer using a mini-batch stochastic gradient descent (with a mini-batch size of 128). Kingma *et al.* [18] proposed momentum parameters $\beta_1 = 0.9$ and $\beta_2 = 0.999$, and a learning rate of 0.001. However, we found out that the learning rate was too high and used 0.0002 instead. Together with reducing the first momentum term β_1 to 0.5 as suggested by [34] resulted in a more stable and repeatable training procedure. We also used batch normalization [17], which proved to be very useful in training the deeper versions of the network ($32 \times 32 \times 32$ resolution at input and output). We use 10 % of the training data for validation, to monitor and prevent overfitting.

Finetuning. Note that the target input data types we want to the method to handle are significantly different: (1) complete 3D mesh models, (2) point sets, (3) depth scans. We therefore finetune the networks on these three data types separately. We use corresponding subset of the training data for each data type within our training set (Table 1), with a low learning rate (1×10^{-6}). We denote the finetuned networks with '-fm', '-fp', and '-fs', which correspond to finetuned on mesh data, point set data, and scan data, respectively.

5   Results

5.1   Experiments

Each shape category (Cars, Shoes, Chairs and Airplanes) database have five different associated attributes given in Table 2. We choose these four object types, and corresponding attributes due to the fact that we can generate ground truth data for comparison and training using Yumer *et al.* 's method [44]. We train the multiple network architectures as introduced in Sect. 3.1 for these four shape categories: two low resolution deformation flow networks (F1-16, F2-16), two deformation flow networks (F1-32, F2-32), and an additional data type specific finetuned version (F2-32{-fm, -fp, -fs}).

Baselines. In addition to comparing our method with Yumer *et al.* [44], we also introduce three baseline methods which we compare with our deformation

Table 2. Mesh deformation error [voxelized space edge length $\times 10^{-2}$]. In each row: Lowest error - best performance. Highest error.

	[44]	kNN	S1-32	S2-32	F1-16	F2-16	F1-32	F2-32	F2-32-fm
Car-luxurious	0.0	7.43	9.45	8.10	4.54	3.72	1.93	1.13	0.82
Car-sporty	0.0	10.4	15.8	12.0	7.02	5.45	3.76	2.65	1.83
Car-compact	0.0	11.6	13.7	11.6	6.52	5.82	3.54	2.49	1.79
Car-muscular	0.0	6.98	9.21	7.90	4.28	3.26	1.87	1.07	0.77
Car-modern	0.0	6.43	10.2	8.67	5.78	4.23	2.04	1.02	0.79
Shoe-fashionable	0.0	9.64	15.4	14.2	7.43	7.21	4.32	3.24	3.20
Shoe-durable	0.0	4.28	4.71	4.28	4.78	4.34	0.23	0.21	0.19
Shoe-comfy	0.0	7.45	13.5	12.5	6.93	6.87	3.97	3.10	2.45
Shoe-feminine	0.0	10.4	15.3	13.2	8.29	7.64	4.81	4.06	3.50
Shoe-active	0.0	7.43	14.2	13.8	7.26	7.12	4.20	3.57	3.07
Chair-comfy	0.0	8.43	9.12	8.10	7.05	6.18	4.15	3.20	2.01
Chair-ergonomic	0.0	8.02	10.6	9.12	7.43	6.01	3.28	3.01	1.98
Chair-elegant	0.0	9.11	9.10	8.52	6.18	5.43	3.05	2.29	2.00
Chair-antique	0.0	0.24	9.58	8.54	0.45	0.49	0.10	0.08	0.10
Chair-sturdy	0.0	4.10	4.51	4.24	4.80	3.34	2.30	2.20	1.49
Airplane-fighter	0.0	14.3	14.2	13.8	10.5	9.54	6.32	5.90	5.06
Airplane-fast	0.0	16.5	13.4	12.6	9.67	8.75	5.71	4.88	4.27
Airplane-stealth	0.0	7.84	10.6	9.47	8.43	7.86	5.61	4.83	3.30
Airplane-sleek	0.0	8.59	9.41	9.02	7.40	7.02	6.04	5.31	3.29
Airplane-civilian	0.0	12.7	15.3	11.6	6.73	6.12	5.23	5.47	4.01

flow based approach: two direct synthesis network baselines (S1-32, S2-32), and a nearest neighbor baseline (demarcated as kNN in results Tables 2, 3, and 4). The synthesis baselines replace the last layer of the networks with voxelized representation of the deformed model instead of the deformation flows. We then use marching cubes [27] for reconstructing a surface mesh representation for the deformed shape. For the kNN baseline, we build three databases each registering training inputs for one data type (mesh, point set, depth scan) to the corresponding deformation flows. We include all rotation and translation augmentations introduced in Sect. 4. At test time, we find the k nearest neighbors to the input using average nearest point Euclidean distance (for meshes we use randomly sampled points on the shape), blend the corresponding deformation flows of the k neighbors proportionally weighted by their inverse distance to the input. We experimented with various k between 3 and 25, however we report our results using $k = 15$ which performed best. More details on the kNN and synthesis CNN baselines can be found in our supplementary material.

Table 3. Point set deformation test error [voxelized space edge length $\times 10^{-2}$]. In each row: Lowest error - best performance. Highest error.

	[44]	kNN	S1-32	S2-32	F1-16	F2-16	F1-32	F2-32	F2-32-fp
Car-luxurious	2.12	7.43	9.88	8.27	4.50	3.70	1.86	1.17	0.76
Car-sporty	1.98	10.4	13.9	11.6	7.43	5.60	3.68	2.59	1.90
Car-compact	0.96	11.6	14.1	12.0	6.60	5.62	3.62	2.32	1.84
Car-muscular	1.24	6.98	9.76	7.63	4.74	3.31	1.97	1.11	0.72
Car-modern	1.57	6.43	10.9	8.75	5.75	4.10	2.43	1.18	0.75
Shoe-fashionable	2.23	9.64	14.3	14.8	7.81	7.93	4.51	2.99	2.60
Shoe-durable	0.31	4.28	4.40	4.44	4.76	4.55	0.22	0.25	0.21
Shoe-comfortable	2.76	7.45	13.1	12.2	6.63	6.25	4.24	3.42	2.33
Shoe-feminine	3.20	10.4	15.8	12.9	8.97	7.70	4.19	4.64	3.28
Shoe-active	3.25	7.43	13.1	13.0	7.76	7.25	4.01	3.70	3.36
Chair-comfortable	2.54	8.43	9.77	8.35	7.24	6.21	4.28	3.47	2.24
Chair-ergonomic	2.36	8.02	10.2	8.93	7.67	6.43	3.65	3.23	2.10
Chair-elegant	2.71	9.11	9.65	8.80	6.34	5.22	3.69	2.75	2.54
Chair-antique	0.06	0.24	9.90	8.71	0.66	0.60	0.12	0.09	0.12
Chair-sturdy	1.32	4.10	4.75	4.41	4.48	3.12	2.37	2.25	1.25
Airplane-fighter	5.67	14.3	13.4	13.2	11.4	9.70	6.20	5.64	4.96
Airplane-fast	5.21	16.5	15.7	12.4	9.07	8.72	5.67	4.70	4.41
Airplane-stealth	3.78	7.84	11.3	9.76	8.86	7.89	5.74	4.65	3.20
Airplane-sleek	4.02	8.59	9.73	9.47	7.61	6.90	6.23	5.10	3.68
Airplane-civilian	4.85	12.7	14.6	11.2	6.40	6.34	5.53	5.20	4.36

Ground Truth. As mentioned in Sect. 4, Yumer *et al.* [44] cannot deform the shape when their deformation template does not register correctly. This is a major problem for point sets and depth scans. hence we generate the deformed counter part for these input types by using the underlying 3D shape mesh: (1) register the nearest point on the shape for each point in the simulated depth scan, (2) deform the original shape with Yumer *et al.* [44], (3) transform each point in the depth scan to a deformed position by using the relative distance to the corresponding nearest point on the shape. The point sets are sampled directly on the shape, whereas depth scans are simulated by using a virtual kinect sensor [15].

Deformation Test Error. We compute the test error relative to the network input 3D volume edge length. We report average Euclidean error comparing point positions with respect to the ground truth (for the mesh representation we compute the error using randomly sampled points on the mesh since mesh vertices might be sparse and inconsistently distributed). Tables 2, 3, and 4 show all results for the mesh, point set, and depth scan data, respectively.

Table 4. Depth scan deformation test error [voxelized space edge length $\times 10^{-2}$]. In each row: Lowest error - best performance. Highest error.

	[44]	kNN	S1-32	S2-32	F1-16	F2-16	F1-32	F2-32	F2-32-fs
Car-luxurious	13.5	11.2	10.2	9.70	4.99	4.23	2.34	1.40	1.18
Car-sporty	15.4	14.5	14.2	12.7	7.86	6.25	4.02	2.66	2.04
Car-compact	19.6	15.3	14.6	13.1	7.21	6.09	3.94	2.89	2.01
Car-muscular	15.0	11.6	10.5	8.50	5.19	4.28	2.40	1.50	0.95
Car-modern	12.7	9.30	11.4	9.42	5.82	5.09	2.40	1.36	0.98
Shoe-fashionable	14.8	11.2	14.9	13.5	7.94	8.51	4.87	3.45	3.08
Shoe-durable	0.52	4.99	4.80	4.67	4.81	4.42	0.32	0.20	0.20
Shoe-comfortable	16.4	8.86	13.2	11.5	6.92	6.75	4.41	3.87	2.86
Shoe-feminine	11.9	12.8	15.6	12.7	9.44	7.98	4.53	4.84	3.70
Shoe-active	13.5	9.30	12.6	12.4	8.03	7.59	4.28	3.89	3.51
Chair-comfortable	11.5	9.97	10.8	9.51	9.30	6.70	4.60	4.06	3.07
Chair-ergonomic	10.6	9.75	11.6	9.03	8.57	6.87	3.41	3.74	2.74
Chair-elegant	9.05	10.2	12.0	8.75	7.36	5.98	3.87	3.12	3.18
Chair-antique	0.09	0.21	8.52	8.40	0.98	0.56	0.29	0.14	0.16
Chair-sturdy	10.8	5.40	6.10	5.69	5.33	4.10	3.03	2.89	1.90
Airplane-fighter	18.7	13.5	14.1	12.7	12.5	10.5	6.93	5.33	5.23
Airplane-fast	14.1	15.6	15.8	12.0	9.96	9.82	6.26	4.94	4.78
Airplane-stealth	15.2	9.78	12.0	10.6	9.50	8.90	5.91	4.47	3.45
Airplane-sleek	13.6	10.4	11.4	11.0	7.93	7.54	6.98	5.39	3.79
Airplane-civilian	12.4	14.1	12.5	12.5	8.05	7.02	6.68	5.61	4.52

5.2 Discussions

We present average deformation error results on all test datasets in Tables 2, 3, and 4 for mesh, point set, and depth scan data separately. Note that these tables show aggregated error from both ShapeNet and SemEd (Table 1 (shapes that were not used for training)). Specifically, Cars: 500 ShapeNet + 31 SemEd, Shoes: 500 ShapeNet + 27 SemEd, Chairs: 500 ShapeNet + 16 SemEd, and Airplanes: 500 ShapeNet + 13 SemEd mesh models were used in the tests. Point sets also used the same models resulting in the same number of test subjects, whereas depth scans used twice the number of input by generating test date from two randomly chosen sensor locations around each shape. We challenge our method by training only on ShapeNet dataset and testing on SemEd (this is more challenging because the previous work we compare with [44] is trained on SemEd and utilizes a mixture of experts approach). We present detailed comparison of this additional experiment in our supplementary material, where our method outperformed the comparison similarly as in Tables 2, 3, and 4.

For the mesh representation deformation (Table 2), Yumer *et al.* 's [44] results are null, since their method is used to compute ground truth, and complete shapes are the ideal case. Our finetuned network (F2-32-fm) performs best among the convolutional network approaches, and outperforms the kNN baseline as well. Note that, the synthesis network baselines (S1-32, S2-32) are not as good as the kNN baseline in most cases. Note also that, kNN results for point sets are the same with kNN for mesh data since kNN for mesh also uses the points sampled on the shape as described in Sect. 5.1.

When there is a considerable amount of uncertainty is existent in the input (such as point set or depth scan input type), our method outperforms the results of [44] (Tables 3, and 4). Moreover, since depth scans incorporate a significant amount of missing data (Fig. 5), Yumer *et al.* [44] is not able to generate plausible deformations due to their template matching step failing to fit correspondences.

Figure 5 shows visual results for all three data types. Our method achieves similar results to that of Yumer *et al.* [44] with respect to the ground truth for the mesh data type. Note the significant loss of deformation quality with the previous work for point set and depth scan data. Our method gracefully generates deformation flows that meaningfully deform such low fidelity data. Table 4 shows that deformation using our best performing network (F2-32-fs) achieves ∼5× less error compared to the four benchmark methods (Yumer *et al.* [44], kNN, S1-32, S2-32). Refer to our supplemental material for visual comparisons with kNN and synthesis network baselines.

Robustness to Noise and Partial Data. We further test our method by introducing noise and partially missing parts to the input (Fig. 6(a–c)). To add noise, we randomly select a point on the surface from a uniform distribution and generate a sphere that has a radius drawn from $\mathcal{N}(d/20, d/100)$, where d is the diagonal of the shape bounding box. The number of spheres added affects the amount of noise, which is measured in added voxel percentage in the voxelized representation of the shape. For introducing missing parts (Fig. 6(b)), we randomly select a point on the surface from a uniform distribution and remove polygons from the shape to match the percentage of missing voxels required. Figure 6(d–e) show the results of this experiment on 1000 randomly selected shapes from our test data, with 1000 randomly selected deformation indications from a uniform distribution. Figure 6 shows that the CNN methods are more robust to noise in general, with our flow based networks outperforming other methods including the synthesis networks.

Limitations. Our deformation flow is continuous in the voxel grid, and this introduces some limitations when the optimal deformation can only be achieved with a discontinuous flow. An example of this can be observed in the airplanes dataset with the 'fighter' deformation indicator. The airplane wings stretch significantly whereas the sides of the fuselage where the wings attach does not stretch with it in the original deformation. Our deformation for such extreme discontinuity requirements is not as good as globally continuous cases as seen in Table 2.

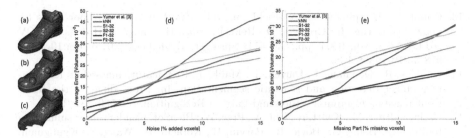

Fig. 6. Right: Example augmentation on test data: (a) original shape, (b) noise, (c) missing parts. (d) Noise vs. Average test error, (e) Missing data vs. Average test error. Both noise and missing data percentages are measured with respect to the original input's voxelized representation number of filled voxels.

References

1. Allen, B., Curless, B., Popović, Z.: The space of human body shapes: reconstruction and parameterization from range scans. ACM Trans. Graph. **22**, 587–594 (2003)
2. Botsch, M., Sorkine, O.: On linear variational surface deformation methods. IEEE TVCG **14**(1), 213–230 (2008)
3. Chang, A.X., Funkhouser, T., Guibas, L., Hanrahan, P., Huang, Q., Li, Z., Savarese, S., Savva, M., Song, S., Su, H., et al.: Shapenet: an information-rich 3d model repository. arXiv preprint arXiv:1512.03012 (2015)
4. Chaudhuri, S., Kalogerakis, E., Giguere, S., Funkhouser, T.: Attribit: content creation with semantic attributes. In: Proceedings of the 26th Annual ACM Symposium on User Interface Software and Technology, pp. 193–202. ACM (2013)
5. Collobert, R., Kavukcuoglu, K., Farabet, C.: Torch7: a matlab-like environment for machine learning. In: BigLearn, NIPS Workshop. No. EPFL-CONF-192376 (2011)
6. Coquillart, S.: Extended free-form deformation: a sculpturing tool for 3D geometric modeling. ACM SIGGRAPH Comput. Graph. **24**, 187–196 (1990). ACM
7. Dosovitskiy, A., Fischer, P., Ilg, E., Hausser, P., Hazirbas, C., Golkov, V., van der Smagt, P., Cremers, D., Brox, T.: Flownet: learning optical flow with convolutional networks. In: Proceedings of the IEEE International Conference on Computer Vision, pp. 2758–2766 (2015)
8. Dosovitskiy, A., Tobias Springenberg, J., Brox, T.: Learning to generate chairs with convolutional neural networks. In: Proceedings of the IEEE Conference on Computer Vision and Pattern Recognition, pp. 1538–1546 (2015)
9. Eigen, D., Puhrsch, C., Fergus, R.: Depth map prediction from a single image using a multi-scale deep network. In: Advances in Neural Information Processing Systems, pp. 2366–2374 (2014)
10. Fang, Y., Xie, J., Dai, G., Wang, M., Zhu, F., Xu, T., Wong, E.: 3d deep shape descriptor. In: Proceedings of the IEEE Conference on Computer Vision and Pattern Recognition, pp. 2319–2328 (2015)
11. Farabet, C., Couprie, C., Najman, L., LeCun, Y.: Learning hierarchical features for scene labeling. IEEE Trans. Pattern Anal. Mach. Intell. **35**(8), 1915–1929 (2013)
12. Fish, N., Averkiou, M., Van Kaick, O., Sorkine-Hornung, O., Cohen-Or, D., Mitra, N.J.: Meta-representation of shape families. ACM Trans. Graph. **33**(4), 34–1 (2014)

13. Ganin, Y., Lempitsky, V.: N^4-Fields: neural network nearest neighbor fields for image transforms. In: Cremers, D., Reid, I., Saito, H., Yang, M.-H. (eds.) ACCV 2014. LNCS, vol. 9004, pp. 536–551. Springer, Heidelberg (2015). doi:10.1007/978-3-319-16808-1_36

14. Girshick, R., Donahue, J., Darrell, T., Malik, J.: Rich feature hierarchies for accurate object detection and semantic segmentation. In: Proceedings of the IEEE Conference on Computer Vision and Pattern Recognition, pp. 580–587 (2014)

15. Gschwandtner, M., Kwitt, R., Uhl, A., Pree, W.: BlenSor: blender sensor simulation toolbox. In: Bebis, G., Boyle, R., Parvin, B., Koracin, D., Wang, S., Kyungnam, K., Benes, B., Moreland, K., Borst, C., DiVerdi, S., Yi-Jen, C., Ming, J. (eds.) ISVC 2011. LNCS, vol. 6939, pp. 199–208. Springer, Heidelberg (2011). doi:10.1007/978-3-642-24031-7_20

16. Hariharan, B., Arbeláez, P., Girshick, R., Malik, J.: Hypercolumns for object segmentation and fine-grained localization. In: Proceedings of the IEEE Conference on Computer Vision and Pattern Recognition, pp. 447–456 (2015)

17. Ioffe, S., Szegedy, C.: Batch normalization: accelerating deep network training by reducing internal covariate shift. arXiv preprint arXiv:1502.03167 (2015)

18. Kingma, D., Ba, J.: Adam: a method for stochastic optimization. arXiv preprint arXiv:1412.6980 (2014)

19. Kingma, D.P., Mohamed, S., Rezende, D.J., Welling, M.: Semi-supervised learning with deep generative models. In: Advances in Neural Information Processing Systems, pp. 3581–3589 (2014)

20. Kingma, D.P., Welling, M.: Stochastic gradient vb and the variational auto-encoder. In: ICLR (2014)

21. Korovkin, P.: Bernstein polynomials. In: Hazewinkel, M. (ed.) Encyclopedia of Mathematics. Springer (2001). ISBN: 978-1-55608-010-4

22. Kovashka, A., Parikh, D., Grauman, K.: Whittlesearch: image search with relative attribute feedback. In: IEEE CVPR, pp. 2973–2980 (2012)

23. Krizhevsky, A., Sutskever, I., Hinton, G.E.: Imagenet classification with deep convolutional neural networks. In: Advances in Neural Information Processing Systems, pp. 1097–1105 (2012)

24. Kulkarni, T.D., Whitney, W.F., Kohli, P., Tenenbaum, J.: Deep convolutional inverse graphics network. In: Advances in Neural Information Processing Systems, pp. 2530–2538 (2015)

25. LeCun, Y., Boser, B., Denker, J.S., Henderson, D., Howard, R.E., Hubbard, W., Jackel, L.D.: Backpropagation applied to handwritten zip code recognition. Neural Comput. **1**(4), 541–551 (1989)

26. Long, J., Shelhamer, E., Darrell, T.: Fully convolutional networks for semantic segmentation. In: Proceedings of the IEEE Conference on Computer Vision and Pattern Recognition, pp. 3431–3440 (2015)

27. Lorensen, W.E., Cline, H.E.: Marching cubes: a high resolution 3d surface construction algorithm. In: ACM SIGGRAPH Computer Graphics, vol. 21, pp. 163–169. ACM (1987)

28. Maas, A.L., Hannun, A.Y., Ng, A.Y.: Rectifier nonlinearities improve neural network acoustic models. In: Proceedings of ICML, vol. 30, p. 1 (2013)

29. Maturana, D., Scherer, S.: 3d convolutional neural networks for landing zone detection from lidar. In: 2015 IEEE International Conference on Robotics and Automation (ICRA), pp. 3471–3478. IEEE (2015)

30. Maturana, D., Scherer, S.: Voxnet: A 3d convolutional neural network for real-time object recognition. In: 2015 IEEE/RSJ International Conference on Intelligent Robots and Systems (IROS), pp. 922–928. IEEE (2015)

31. Mitra, N.J., Wand, M., Zhang, H., Cohen-Or, D., Bokeloh, M.: Structure-aware shape processing. In: Eurographics STARs, pp. 175–197 (2013)
32. Parikh, D., Grauman, K.: Interactively building a discriminative vocabulary of nameable attributes. In: IEEE CVPR, pp. 1681–1688. IEEE (2011)
33. Parikh, D., Grauman, K.: Relative attributes. In: IEEE Conference on Computer Vision, pp. 503–510. IEEE (2011)
34. Radford, A., Metz, L., Chintala, S.: Unsupervised representation learning with deep convolutional generative adversarial networks. arXiv preprint arXiv:1511.06434 (2015)
35. Savva, M., Chang, A., Hanrahan, P.: Semantically-enriched 3d models for common-sense knowledge. In: Proceedings of the IEEE Conference on Computer Vision and Pattern Recognition Workshops, pp. 24–31 (2015)
36. Sederberg, T.W., Parry, S.R.: Free-form deformation of solid geometric models. ACM SIGGRAPH Comput. Graph. **20**(4), 151–160 (1986)
37. Song, S., Xiao, J.: Deep sliding shapes for amodal 3d object detection in rgb-d images. arXiv preprint arXiv:1511.02300 (2015)
38. Su, H., Maji, S., Kalogerakis, E., Learned-Miller, E.: Multi-view convolutional neural networks for 3d shape recognition. In: Proceedings of the IEEE International Conference on Computer Vision, pp. 945–953 (2015)
39. Tatarchenko, M., Dosovitskiy, A., Brox, T.: Single-view to multi-view: reconstructing unseen views with a convolutional network. arXiv preprint arXiv:1511.06702 (2015)
40. Wu, Z., Song, S., Khosla, A., Yu, F., Zhang, L., Tang, X., Xiao, J.: 3d shapenets: a deep representation for volumetric shapes. In: Proceedings of the IEEE Conference on Computer Vision and Pattern Recognition, pp. 1912–1920 (2015)
41. Xie, J., Fang, Y., Zhu, F., Wong, E.: Deepshape: deep learned shape descriptor for 3d shape matching and retrieval. In: Proceedings of the IEEE Conference on Computer Vision and Pattern Recognition, pp. 1275–1283 (2015)
42. Xu, K., Kim, V.G., Huang, Q., Kalogerakis, E.: Data-driven shape analysis and processing. Computer Graphics Forum (to appear)
43. Yang, J., Reed, S.E., Yang, M.H., Lee, H.: Weakly-supervised disentangling with recurrent transformations for 3d view synthesis. In: Advances in Neural Information Processing Systems, pp. 1099–1107 (2015)
44. Yumer, M.E., Chaudhuri, S., Hodgins, J.K., Kara, L.B.: Semantic shape editing using deformation handles. ACM Trans. Graph. (TOG) **34**(4), 86 (2015)
45. Yumer, M.E., Kara, L.B.: Co-abstraction of shape collections. ACM Trans. Graph. (TOG) **31**(6), 166 (2012)
46. Yumer, M.E., Kara, L.B.: Co-constrained handles for deformation in shape collections. ACM Trans. Graph. (TOG) **33**(6), 187 (2014)

Recurrent Instance Segmentation

Bernardino Romera-Paredes$^{(\boxtimes)}$ and Philip Hilaire Sean Torr

Department of Engineering Science, University of Oxford, Oxford, UK
bernard@robots.ox.ac.uk, philip.torr@eng.ox.ac.uk

Abstract. Instance segmentation is the problem of detecting and delineating each distinct object of interest appearing in an image. Current instance segmentation approaches consist of ensembles of modules that are trained independently of each other, thus missing opportunities for joint learning. Here we propose a new instance segmentation paradigm consisting in an end-to-end method that learns how to segment instances sequentially. The model is based on a recurrent neural network that sequentially finds objects and their segmentations one at a time. This net is provided with a spatial memory that keeps track of what pixels have been explained and allows occlusion handling. In order to train the model we designed a principled loss function that accurately represents the properties of the instance segmentation problem. In the experiments carried out, we found that our method outperforms recent approaches on multiple person segmentation, and all state of the art approaches on the Plant Phenotyping dataset for leaf counting.

Keywords: Instance segmentation · Recurrent neural nets · Deep learning

1 Introduction

Instance segmentation, the automatic delineation of different objects appearing in an image, is a problem within computer vision that has attracted a fair amount of attention. Such interest is motivated by both its potential applicability to a whole range of scenarios, and the stimulating technical challenges it poses.

Regarding the former, segmenting at the instance level is useful for many tasks, ranging from allowing robots to segment a particular object in order to grasp it, to highlighting and enhancing the outline of objects for the partially sighted, wearing "smart specs" [1]. Counting elements in an image has interest in its own right [2] as it has a wide range of applications. For example, industrial processes that require the number of elements produced, knowing the number of people who attended a demonstration, and counting the number of infected and healthy blood cells in a blood sample, required in some medical procedures such as malaria detection [3].

Electronic supplementary material The online version of this chapter (doi:10. 1007/978-3-319-46466-4_19) contains supplementary material, which is available to authorized users.

B. Leibe et al. (Eds.): ECCV 2016, Part VI, LNCS 9910, pp. 312–329, 2016.
DOI: 10.1007/978-3-319-46466-4_19

Instance segmentation is more challenging than other pixel-level learning problems such as semantic segmentation, which deals with classifying each pixel of an image, given a set of classes. There, each pixel can belong to a set of predefined groups (or classes), whereas in instance segmentation the number of groups (instances) is unknown *a priori*. This difference exacerbates the problem: where in semantic segmentation one can evaluate the prediction pixel-wise, instance segmentation requires the clustering of pixels to be evaluated with a loss function *invariant to the permutation* of this assignment (i.e. it does not matter if a group of "person" pixels is assigned to be person "1" or person "2"). That leads to further complexities in the learning of these models. Hence, instance segmentation has remained a more difficult problem to solve.

Most approaches proposed for instance level segmentation are based on a pipeline of modules whose learning process is carried out independent of each other. Some of them, such as [4,5], rely on a module for object proposal, followed by another one implementing object recognition and segmentation on the detected patches. A common problem with such piecewise learning methods is that each module does not learn to accommodate itself to the outputs of other modules. Another drawback is that in such cases, it is often necessary to define an independent loss function for each module, which places a burden on the practitioner to decide on convenient representations of the data at intermediate stages of the pipeline.

These issues led us to take a different route and develop a fresh and *end-to-end* model able to learn the whole instance-segmentation process. Due to the magnitude of the task, in this study we focus on the problem of *class-specific* instance segmentation. That is, we assume that the model segments instances that belong to the *same* class, excluding classification stages. The solution to this problem is useful in its own right, for example to segment and to count people in images [6], but we consider that this is also the first step towards general semantic learning systems that can segment and classify different kinds of instances.

The approach we propose here is partially inspired by how humans count elements in a scene. It is known, [7,8], that humans count sequentially, using accurate spatial memory in order to keep track of the accounted locations. Driven by this insight, our purpose is to build a learning model capable of segmenting the instances of an object in an image sequentially, keeping current state in an internal memory. In order to achieve this, we rely on recurrent neural networks (RNNs), which exhibit the two properties discussed: the ability to produce sequential output, and the ability to keep a state or memory along the sequence.

Our primary contributions, described in this paper, are 1. the development of an *end-to-end* approach for *class specific* instance segmentation, schematized in Fig. 1, based on RNNs containing convolutional layers, and 2. the derivation of a principled loss function for this problem. We assess the capabilities of our model by conducting two experiments; one on segmentation of multiple people, and the other on plant-leaves segmentation and counting.

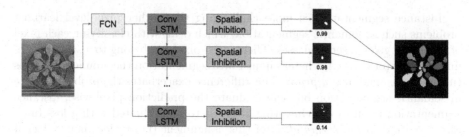

Fig. 1. Diagram of Recurrent Instance Segmentation (RIS).

2 Background

The work presented here combines several research areas. In this section we summarize the main developments in these areas.

2.1 Instance Segmentation Models

Instance segmentation can be formulated as the conjunction between semantic segmentation and object detection, for example in [9], the authors proposed a model that integrates information obtained at pixel, segment, and object levels. This is because instance segmentation requires the capacity of object detection approaches to separate between instances, and the ability of semantic segmentation methods to produce pixel-wise predictions, and hence a delineation of the shape of the objects. The progress of instance segmentation methods is thus limited by the advances made in both object detection and semantic segmentation.

A recent breakthrough in object detection is the Region-based CNN (R-CNN) [10]. This approach consists in using a region proposal method to produce a large set of varied sized object proposals from an image, then extracting features for each of them by means of a CNN, and finally classifying the resultant feature vectors. Several approaches for instance segmentation build on this method. Two of them are [4,5], which both use multiscale combinatorial grouping [11] as a region proposal method to extract candidates, followed by a region refinement process. In the former work [4], the authors perform non-maximum suppression on the candidates, in order to remove duplicates, and then they combine the coarse information obtained by the CNN with superpixels extracted from the image in order to segment the instances. In the latter work [5], the output is refined by means of exemplar-based shape prediction and graph-cut. These approaches have produced state of the art results in instance segmentation. However, they suffer a common drawback that we want to avoid: they consist in an ensemble of modules that are trained independently of each other.

Semantic segmentation methods have seen a significant improvement recently, based first on the work in [12] which proposed a fully convolutional network that produces pixel-wise predictions, followed by the works in [13,14] that improve the delineation of the predicted objects by using Conditional Random Fields (CRFs). The work in [15] builds an instance segmentation model standing on these previous approaches. This is based on predicting pixel-wise instances locations by a network, and then applying a clustering method as a post-processing step, where the number of clusters (instances) is predicted by another CNN. A problem with this approach is that it is not optimizing a direct instance segmentation measure, but it relies on a surrogate loss function based on pixel distances to object positions.

One problem associated to instance segmentation is related to the lack of an order among the instances in images (e.g. which instance should be the first to be segmented). Several works [16–18] aim to overcome this problem by inferring and exploiting depth information as a way to order the instances. They model that by means of a Markov Random Field on the top of a CNN. One advantage of this approach is that occlusion between objects is explicitly modeled. A disadvantage is that this approach is not beneficial when instances appear at a similar depth, for example, an image containing a sport team with many players together.

Unlike previous approaches, we propose a new paradigm for instance segmentation based on learning to segment instances sequentially, *letting the model decide* the order of the instances for each image.

2.2 Recurrent Neural Networks

Recurrent neural networks (RNNs) are powerful learning models. Their power resides in their capacity to keep a state or memory, in which the model is able to store what it considers relevant events towards minimizing a given loss function. They are also versatile, as they can be applied to arbitrary input and output sequence sizes. These two properties have led to the successful application of RNNs to a wide range of tasks such as machine translation [19], handwriting recognition [20] and conversational models [21], among others.

RNNs are also useful for obtaining variable length information from static images. One such example is DRAW [22], which is a variational auto-encoder for learning how to generate images, in which both the encoder and the decoder are RNNs, so that the image generation process is sequential. Image captioning is another application which has benefited from the use of RNNs on images. Examples of these are [23–25], which are based on using a CNN for obtaining a meaningful representation of the image, which is then introduced into an RNN that produces one word at each iteration. Another example, involving biological images, is in [26], where the authors explore a combination of convolutional layers and LSTMs in order to predict for each protein the subcellular compartment it belongs to. In [27] the authors use an RNN to predict a bounding box delimiting one human face at each iteration. This approach shares some of our motivations. The main difference between both approaches is that they consider a regression problem, producing at each iteration a set of scalars that specify the bounding box where the instance is, whereas we consider a pixel-wise classification problem. In [28], the authors present several recurrent structures to track and segment objects in videos. Finally, it is worth mentioning the approach in [29] despite not being an RNN, which consists in a greedy sequential algorithm for learning several objects in an image.

2.3   Attention Based Models

Attention based approaches consist in models that have the capability of deciding at each time which part of the input to look at in order to perform a task. They have recently shown impressive performance in several tasks like image generation [22], object recognition [30], and image caption generation [31]. These approaches can be divided into two main categories: hard, and soft attention mechanisms. Hard attention mechanisms are those that decide which part of the instance process at a time, totally ignoring the remainder [32]. On the contrary, soft attention mechanisms decide at each time a probability distribution over the input, indicating the attention that each part must receive. The latter are wholly differentiable, thus they can be optimized by backpropagation [33].

Our approach resembles attention models in the sense that in both cases the model selects different parts of the same input in successive iterations. Attention based models are different from our approach in which they apply attention mechanisms as a means to an end task (e.g. image caption generation or machine translation), whereas in our approach, attention to one instance at each time is the end target we aim for.

3   Segmenting One Instance at a Time

In this section we describe the inference process that our approach performs, as well as the structural elements that compose it.

The process at inference stage is depicted in Fig. 1, and can be described as follows: an image with height h and width w, $\mathbf{I} \in \mathbb{R}^{h \times w \times c}$ (c is usually 3, or 4 if including depth information) is taken as input of a fully convolutional network, such as the one described in [12]. This is composed of a sequence of convolutional and max-pooling layers that preserve the spatial information in the inner representations of the image. The output of that network, $\mathbf{B} \in \mathbb{R}^{h' \times w' \times d}$, represents the d-dimensional features extracted for each pixel, where the size of this map may be smaller than the size of the input image, $h' \leq h$, $w' \leq w$, due to the subsampling effect of the described network. This output $\mathbf{B}$ will be the input to the RNN in all iterations in the sequence. At the beginning of the sequence, the initial inner state of the RNN, $\mathbf{h_0}$, is initialized to 0. After the first iteration, the RNN produces the segmentation of one of the instances in the image (any of them), together with an indicator that informs about the confidence of the prediction in order to have a stopping condition. Simultaneously, the RNN updates the inner state, $\mathbf{h_1}$, to account for the recent segmented instance. Then, having again as inputs $\mathbf{B}$, and as inner state $\mathbf{h_1}$, the model outputs another segmented instance and its confidence score. This process keeps iterating until the confidence score drops below a certain level in which the model stops, ideally having segmented all instances in the image.

The sequential nature of our model allows to deal with common instance segmentation problems. In particular it can implicitly model occlusion, as it can segment non-occluded instances first, and keep in its state the regions of the image that have already been segmented in order to detect occluded objects.

Another purpose of the state is to allow the model to consider potential relationships from different instances in the image. For example, if in the first iteration an instance of a person embracing something is segmented, and this information is somehow kept in the state, then in subsequent iterations, it might increase the plausibility of having another person being embraced by the first one.

The structure of our approach is composed of a fully convolutional network, followed by an RNN, a function to transform the state of the RNN into the segmentation of an instance and its confidence score, and finally the loss function that evaluates the quality of the predictions and that we aim to optimize. The first of these components, the fully convolutional network, is used in a similar manner as explained in [12]. In the following we describe in detail the remaining three components.

3.1   Convolutional LSTM

Long short-term memory (LSTM) networks [34] have stood out over other recurrent structures because they are able to prevent the vanishing gradient problem. Indeed, they are the chosen model in most works reviewed in Sect. 2.2 in which they have achieved outstanding results. In this section we build on top of the LSTM unit, but we perform some changes in its structure to adapt it to the characteristics of our problem.

In the problem we have described, we observe that the input to the model is a map from a lattice (in particular, an image), and the output is also a map from a lattice. Problems with these characteristics, such as semantic segmentation [12,14] and optical flow [35], are often tackled using structures based on convolutions, in which the intermediate representations of the images preserve the spatial information. In our problem, we can see the inner state of recurrent units as a map that preserves spatial information as well. That led us to convolutional versions of RNNs, and in particular to convolutional long short-term memory (ConvLSTM) units.

A ConvLSTM unit is similar to an LSTM one, the only difference being that the fully connected layers in each gate are replaced by convolutions, as specified by the following update equations:

$$
\begin{aligned}
\mathbf{i_t} &= \text{Sigmoid}\left(\text{Conv}\left(\mathbf{x_t}; \mathbf{w_{xi}}\right) + \text{Conv}\left(\mathbf{h_{t-1}}; \mathbf{w_{hi}}\right) + \mathbf{b_i}\right) \\
\mathbf{f_t} &= \text{Sigmoid}\left(\text{Conv}\left(\mathbf{x_t}; \mathbf{w_{xf}}\right) + \text{Conv}\left(\mathbf{h_{t-1}}; \mathbf{w_{hf}}\right) + \mathbf{b_f}\right) \\
\mathbf{o_t} &= \text{Sigmoid}\left(\text{Conv}\left(\mathbf{x_t}; \mathbf{w_{xo}}\right) + \text{Conv}\left(\mathbf{h_{t-1}}; \mathbf{w_{ho}}\right) + \mathbf{b_o}\right) \\
\mathbf{g_t} &= \text{Tanh}\;\;\left(\text{Conv}\left(\mathbf{x_t}; \mathbf{w_{xg}}\right) + \text{Conv}\left(\mathbf{h_{t-1}}; \mathbf{w_{hg}}\right) + \mathbf{b_g}\right) \\
\mathbf{c_t} &= \mathbf{f_t} \odot \mathbf{c_{t-1}} + \mathbf{i_t} \odot \mathbf{g_t} \\
\mathbf{h_t} &= \mathbf{o_t} \odot \text{Tanh}(\mathbf{c_t})
\end{aligned}
\tag{1}
$$

where $\odot$ represents the element-wise product operator, $\mathbf{i_t}, \mathbf{f_t}, \mathbf{o_t}, \mathbf{g_t} \in \mathbb{R}^{h' \times w' \times d}$ are the gates, and $\mathbf{h_t}, \mathbf{c_t} \in \mathbb{R}^{h' \times w' \times d}$ represents the memory of the recurrent unit, being d the amount of memory used for each pixel (in this paper we assume that the number of channels in the recurrent unit is the same as the number of channels produced by the previous FCN). Each of the filter weights ($\mathbf{w}$ terms) has dimensionality $d \times d \times f \times f$, where f is the size of the filter, and each of the bias terms (**b** terms) is a d-dimensional vector repeated across height and width. We refer to the diagrams and definitions presented in [34] for a detailed explanation of the LSTM update equations, from which Eq. (1) follows. We also provide a diagram illustrating Eq. (1) in the Appendix Sect. B. Note that a primary aspect of keeping a memory or state is to allow our model to keep account of the pixels of the image that have already been segmented in previous iterations of the process. This can be naturally done by applying convolutions to the state. We can also stack two or more ConvLSTM units with the aim of learning more complex relationships.

The advantages of ConvLSTM with respect to regular LSTM go hand in hand with the advantages of convolutional layers with respect to linear layers: they are suitable for learning filters, useful for spatially invariant inputs such as images, and they require less memory for the parameters. In fact the memory required is independent of the size of the input. A similar recurrent unit has been recently proposed in [36] in the context of weather forecasting in a region.

3.2   Attention by Spatial Inhibition

The output produced by our model at time t is a function $r(\cdot)$ of the hidden state, $\mathbf{h_t}$. This function produces two outputs, $r(\cdot) : \mathbb{R}^{h' \times w' \times d} \to \{[0,1]^{h \times w}, [0,1]\}$. The first output is a map that indicates which pixels compose the object that is segmented in the current iteration. The second output is the estimated probability that the current segmented candidate is an object. We use this output as a stopping condition. In the following we describe these two functions, supporting our presentation on a schematic view of $r(\cdot)$, which is given in Fig. 2.

The function that produces the first output can be described as a sequence of layers which have the aim of discriminating one, and only one instance, filtering out everything else. Firstly we use a convolutional layer which maps the d channels of the hidden state to 1 output channel, using 1×1 filters. This is followed by a log-softmax layer, $f_{\mathrm{LSM}}(\mathbf{x})_i = \log \left(\frac{\exp(x_i)}{\sum_j \exp(x_j)} \right)$, which normalizes the input across all pixels, and then applies a logarithm. As a result, each pixel value can be in the interval $(-\infty, 0]$, where the sum of the exponentiation of all values is 1. This leads to a competing mechanism that has the potential of inhibiting pixels that do not belong to the current instance being segmented. Following that, we use a layer which adds a learned bias term to the input data. The purpose of this layer is to learn a threshold, b, which filters the pixels that will be selected for the present instance. Then, a sigmoid transformation is applied pixel-wise. Hence, the resultant pixel values are all in the interval $[0, 1]$, as required. Finally, we upsample the resultant $h' \times w'$ map back to the original size of the input image, $h \times w$. In order to help understand the effect of these layers, we visualize in Sect. A in the Appendix, the inner representations captured by the model at different stages of the described pipeline.

The function which encodes the relationship between the current state $\mathbf{h_t}$ and the confidence of the predicted candidate consists simply of a max-pooling and a linear layer, followed by a sigmoid function.

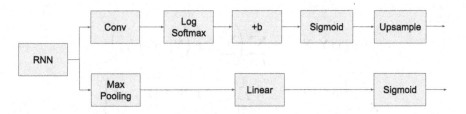

Fig. 2. Diagram of the spatial inhibition module.

3.3 Loss Function

Choosing a loss function that accurately reflects the objective we want to achieve is key for any model to be able to learn a given task. In order to present the loss function that we use, let us first add some notation.

At training stage we are provided with the training set composed of labeled images. We denote image i as $\mathbf{I}^{(i)} \in \mathbb{R}^{h \times w \times c}$, where for simplicity we consider the same size $(h \times w \times c)$ for all images. Its annotation $\mathbf{Y}^{(i)} = \left\{ \mathbf{Y}_1^{(i)}, \mathbf{Y}_2^{(i)}, \dots, \mathbf{Y}_{n_i}^{(i)} \right\}$, is a set of n_i masks, $\mathbf{Y}_t^{(i)} \in \{0,1\}^{h \times w}$, for $t \in \{1, \dots, n_i\}$, containing the segmentation of each instance in the image. One point to note about the labels is that the dimension of the last index, n_i, depends on the image i, because each image may have a different number of instances.

Our model predicts both a sequence of masks, $\hat{\mathbf{Y}}^{(i)} = \left\{ \hat{\mathbf{Y}}_1^{(i)}, \hat{\mathbf{Y}}_2^{(i)}, \dots, \hat{\mathbf{Y}}_{\hat{n}_i}^{(i)} \right\}$, for image i, where $\hat{\mathbf{Y}}_{\hat{t}}^{(i)} \in [0,1]^{h \times w}$, $\hat{t} \in \{1, \dots, \hat{n}_i\}$, and a confidence score associated to those masks $\mathbf{s}^{(i)} = \left\{ s_1^{(i)}, s_2^{(i)}, \dots, s_{\hat{n}_i}^{(i)} \right\}$. At inference time, the number of elements predicted, $\hat{n}_i$, depends on the confidence values, $\mathbf{s}^{(i)}$, so that the network stops producing outputs after time t when $s_t^{(i)} < 0.5$. At training time we can predefine the length of the predicted sequence. Given that we know the length, n_i, of the i-th ground truth annotation, we set the length of the predicted sequence to be $\hat{n}_i = n_i + 2$, so that the network can learn when to stop. In any case, the number of elements in the predicted sequence, $\hat{n}_i$, is not necessarily equal to the elements in the corresponding ground truth set, n_i, given that our model could underestimate or overestimate the number of objects.

One way to represent the scenario is to arrange the elements in $\mathbf{Y}$ and $\hat{\mathbf{Y}}$ (where we omit hereafter the index of the image, i, for the sake of clarity) in a bipartite graph, in which each edge between $\mathbf{Y}_t$, $t \in \{1, \dots n\}$, and $\hat{\mathbf{Y}}_{\hat{t}}$, $\hat{t} \in \{1, \dots \hat{n}\}$, has a cost associated to the intersection over union between $\mathbf{Y}_t$ and $\hat{\mathbf{Y}}_{\hat{t}}$. A similarity measure between $\mathbf{Y}$ and $\hat{\mathbf{Y}}$ can be defined as the maximum sum of the intersection over union correspondence between the elements in $\mathbf{Y}$ and the elements in $\hat{\mathbf{Y}}$:

$$\max_{\delta \in \mathcal{S}} f_{\text{Match}}(\hat{\mathbf{Y}}, \mathbf{Y}, \delta), \tag{2}$$

where

$$f_{\text{Match}}\left(\hat{\mathbf{Y}}, \mathbf{Y}, \delta\right) = \sum_{\hat{t}=1}^{\hat{n}} \left(\sum_{t=1}^{n} f_{\text{IoU}}\left(\hat{\mathbf{Y}}_{\hat{t}}, \mathbf{Y}_{t}\right) \delta_{\hat{t},t} \right), \quad (3)$$

$$\mathcal{S} = \left\{ \delta \in \{0,1\}^{\hat{n} \times n} : \begin{array}{l} \sum\limits_{\hat{t}=1}^{\hat{n}} \delta_{\hat{t},t} \leq 1, \forall t \in \{1 \ldots n\} \\ \sum\limits_{t=1}^{n} \delta_{\hat{t},t} \leq 1, \forall \hat{t} \in \{1 \ldots \hat{n}\} \end{array} \right\}, \quad (4)$$

and $f_{\text{IoU}}(\hat{\mathbf{y}}, \mathbf{y}) = \frac{\langle \hat{\mathbf{y}}, \mathbf{y} \rangle}{\|\hat{\mathbf{y}}\|_1 + \|\mathbf{y}\|_1 - \langle \hat{\mathbf{y}}, \mathbf{y} \rangle}$, used in [37], is a relaxed version of the inter-section over union (IoU) that allows the input to take values in the continuous interval $[0, 1]$.

The elements in δ determine the optimal matching between the elements in $\mathbf{Y}$ and $\hat{\mathbf{Y}}$, so that $\hat{\mathbf{Y}}_{\hat{t}}$ is assigned to $\mathbf{Y}_t$ if and only if $\delta_{\hat{t},t} = 1$. The constraint set $\mathcal{S}$, defined in Eq. (4), impedes one ground truth instance being assigned to more than one of the predicted instances and vice versa. It may be the case that prediction $\hat{\mathbf{Y}}_{\hat{t}}$ remains unassigned if and only if $\sum_{t=1}^{n} \delta_{\hat{t},t} = 0$, or that the ground truth $\mathbf{Y}_t$ is not covered by any prediction if and only if $\sum_{\hat{t}=1}^{\hat{n}} \delta_{\hat{t},t} = 0$. The optimal matching, δ, can be found out efficiently by means of the Hungarian algorithm, in a similar vein as in [27]. The coverage loss described in [38] has a similar form, where the predictions were discrete, and the problem was posed as an integer program.

End-to-end learning is possible with this loss function, as it is the point-wise minimum of a set of continuous functions (each of those functions corresponding to a possible matching in $\mathcal{S}$). Thus, a direction of decrease of the loss function at a point can be computed by following two steps: 1. Figuring out which function in the set $\mathcal{S}$ achieves the minimum at that point. 2. Computing the gradient of that function. Here, the Hungarian algorithm is employed in the described first step to find out the function that achieves the minimum at the point. Then, the gradient of that function is computed. The details of this process are shown in Sect. D in the Appendix.

We now need to account for the confidence scores $\mathbf{s}$ predicted by the model. To do so, we consider that the ideal output is to predict $s_t = 1$ if the number of instances t segmented so far is equal or less than the total number of instances n, otherwise s_t should be 0. Taking this into account, we propose the following loss function:

$$\ell(\hat{\mathbf{Y}}, \mathbf{s}, \mathbf{Y}) = \min_{\delta \in \mathcal{S}} - \sum_{\hat{t}=1}^{\hat{n}} \sum_{t=1}^{n} f_{\text{IoU}}\left(\hat{\mathbf{Y}}_{\hat{t}}, \mathbf{Y}_{t}\right) \delta_{\hat{t},t} + \lambda \sum_{t=1}^{\hat{n}} f_{\text{BCE}}\left([t \leq n], s_t\right), \quad (5)$$

where $f_{\text{BCE}}(a, b) = -\left(a\log(b) + (1 - a)\log(1 - b)\right)$ is the binary cross entropy, and the Iverson bracket $[\cdot]$ is 1 if the condition within the brackets is true, and 0 otherwise. Finally, λ is a hyperparameter that ponders the importance of the second term with respect to the first one.

4 Experiments

We perform two kinds of experiments, in which we study the capabilities of our approach to both segment and count instances. In the first experiment we focus on multi-instance subject segmentation, and in the second we focus on segmenting and counting leaves in plants. Before presenting those results, we first describe the implementations details that are common to both experiments.

4.1 Implementation Details of Our Method

We have implemented our approach using the Lua/Torch deep learning framework [39]. The code and models are publicly available[1].

The recurrent stage is composed of two ConvLSTM layers, so that the output of the first ConvLSTM acts as the input for the second one. This stage is followed by the spatial inhibition module which produces a confidence score together with an instance segmentation mask. The resultant prediction is evaluated according to the loss function defined in Eq. (5), where we set $\lambda = 1$.

At training stage, the parameters of the recurrent structure are learned by backpropagation through time. In order to prevent the exploding gradient effect, we clipped the gradients so that each of its elements has a maximum absolute value of 5. We use the Adam optimization algorithm [40] for training the whole network, setting the initial learning rate to 10^{-4}, and multiplying it by 0.1 when the training error plateaus. We use neither dropout nor ℓ_2 regularization, as we did not observe overfitting in preliminary experiments. In the same way as in [14], we have used one image per batch.

The weights of the recurrent structure are initialized at random, sampling them uniformly from the interval $[-0.08, 0.08]$ with the exception of the bias terms in the forget gate, $\mathbf{b_f}$ in Eq. (1). They have been initialized to 1 with the aim of allowing by default to backpropagate the error to previous iterations in the sequence.

We perform curriculum learning by gradually increasing the number of objects that are required to be segmented from the images. That is, at the beginning we use only 2 recurrent iterations, so that the network is expected to learn to extract at most 2 objects per image, even when there are more. Once the training procedure converges, we increment this number, and keep iterating the process.

At inference time we assign a pixel to an instance if the predicted value is higher than 0.5. Nevertheless, we observe that the predicted pixels values in $\hat{\mathbf{Y}}$ are usually saturated, that is, they are either very close to 0 or very close to 1. Although uncommon, it might happen that the same pixel is assigned to more than one instance in the sequence. Whenever that is the case, we assign the pixel to the instance belonging to the earlier iteration. Finally, the produced sequence terminates whenever the confidence score predicted by the network is below 0.5.

---

[1] Available at http://romera-paredes.com/ris.

4.2 Multiple Person Segmentation

We assess the quality of our approach for detecting and segmenting individual subjects in real images. Multiple person segmentation is extremely challenging because people in pictures present high variations such as different posture, age, gender, clothing, location and depth within the scene, among others.

In order to learn this task, we have integrated our model on the FCN-8s network developed in [12]. The FCN-8s network is composed of a series of layers and adding skips that produce, as a result, an image representation whose size is smaller than the original image. This is followed by an upsampling layer that resizes the representation back to the original image size. We modify this structure by putting the ConvLSTM before this upsampling layer, which is integrated into the subsequent spatial inhibition module, as shown in Fig. 2. Following other works such as [12,14] we add padding and/or resize the input image so that the resultant size is 500×500. As a consequence, the size of the input of the ConvLSTM layers, as well as their hidden states have dimensionality $64 \times 64 \times 100$, where 100 is the number of features extracted for each pixel. All gates ($\mathbf{i_t}$, $\mathbf{f_t}$, $\mathbf{o_t}$, and $\mathbf{g_t}$ in Eq. 1) of both ConvLSTM layers use 1×1 convolutions.

For training we used the MSCOCO dataset [41], and the training images of the Pascal VOC 2012 dataset. We first fixed the weights of the FCN-8s except for the last layer, and then learned the parameters of that last layer, together with the ConvLSTM and the spatial inhibition module, following the procedure described in Sect. 4.1. Then we fine-tuned the whole network using a learning rate of 10^{-6} until convergence.

We observed that the predictions obtained by recurrent instance segmentation (RIS), while promising, were coarse with respect to the boundaries of the segmented subjects. That is expected, as the ConvLSTM operates on a low resolution representation of the image. In order to amend this, we have used a CRF as a post-processing method over the produced segments. We call this approach RIS+CRF.

We compare these two approaches with the recent instance segmentation methods presented in [4,5,15], already introduced in Sect. 2.1. We also compare to a baseline consisting in performing proposal generation from the semantic segmentation result produced by the FCN-8s of [12]. We have use Faster R-CNN [42] as the proposal generation method. Following previous works, we measure the predictive performance of the methods with respect to the Pascal VOC 2012 validation set, using two standard metrics: average precision (AP^r) on the predicted regions having over 0.5 IoU overlapping with ground truth masks, denoted as $AP^r(0.5)$; and averaging the AP^r for different degrees of IoU overlapping, from 0.1 to 0.9, denoted as $AP^r Ave$. We show the results in Table 1. We observe that RIS achieves comparable results to state of the art approaches. When using CRF as a post-processing method the results improve, outperforming the competing methods. We also provide some qualitative results in Fig. 3, and more extensively in Sect. C in the Appendix.

Table 1. Multiple person segmentation comparison with state of the art approaches on the PASCAL VOC 2012 validation set. First row: using AP^r metric at 0.5 IoU. Second row: averaging AP^r metric from 0.1 to 0.9 IoU (gaps indicate unreported results).

	Baseline	[5]	[4]	[15]	RIS	RIS+CRF
$AP^r(0.5)$	45.8	48.3	47.9	48.8	46.7	**50.1**
$AP^r Ave$	39.6			42.9	41.9	**43.7**

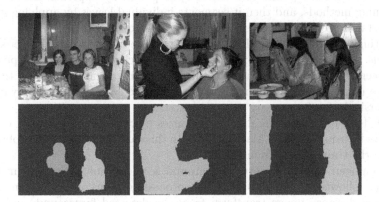

Fig. 3. Instance segmentation for detecting people using RIS+CRF. Input images taken from the VOC Pascal 2012 dataset. Best viewed in colour. (Color figure online)

4.3 Plants Leaf Segmentation and Counting

Automatic leaf segmentation and counting are useful tasks for plant phenotyping applications that can lead to improvements in seed production and plant breeders processes. In this section we use the Computer Vision Problems in Plant Phenotyping (CVPPP) dataset [43,44]. In particular, we utilize the A1 subset of plants, which is the biggest subset available, and contains 161 top-down view images, having 500×530 size each, as the one shown in Fig. 1, Left. The training set is composed of 128 of those images, which have annotations available. The remaining 33 images are left out for testing purposes. All these images are challenging because they present a high range of variations, with occasional leaf occlusions, varied backgrounds, several slightly blurred images due to a lack of focus, and complex leaf shapes.

The limited number of training images has driven us to augment the data by considering some valid transformations of the images. We apply two transformations: rotating the image by a random angle, and flipping the resultant image with a probability of 0.5.

We learn the fully convolutional network from scratch. Its structure is composed by a sequence of 5 convolutional layers, each of them followed by a rectified linear unit. The first convolution learns 30 9×9 filters, and the following four learn 30 3×3 filters each. This sequence of convolutions produces a $100 \times 106 \times 30$ representation of the image, which is the input to the recurrent stage of the model. In the stack of two ConvLSTMs we have set all gates to have 3×3 convolutional layers.

We compare our method with several approaches submitted to the CVPPP challenges on both leaf segmentation and counting. These are:

- IPK Gatersleben [45]: Firstly, it segments foreground from background by using 3D histograms and a supervised learning model. Secondly, it identifies the leaves centre points and leaves split points by applying unsupervised learning methods, and then it segments individual leaves by applying graph-based noise removal, and region growing techniques.
- Nottingham [46]: Firstly, SLIC is applied on the image in order to get super-pixels. Then the plant is extracted from the background. The superpixels in the centroids of each leaf are identified by finding local maxima on the distance map of the foreground. Finally, leaves are segmented by applying the watershed transform.
- MSU [46]: It is based on aligning instances (leaves) with a given set of templates by using Chamfer Matching [47]. In this case the templates are obtained from the training set ground truth.
- Wageningen [48]: It performs foreground segmentation using a neural network, followed by a series of image processing transformations, including inverse distance image transform from the detected foreground, and using the watershed transform to segment leaves individually.
- PRIAn [49]: First, a set of features is learned in an unsupervised way on a log-polar representation of the image. Then, a support vector regression model is applied on the resultant features in order to predict the number of leaves.

These competing methods are explicitly designed to perform well in this particular plant leaf segmentation and counting problems, containing heuristics that are only valid on this domain. On the contrary, the applicability of our model is broad.

Table 2. Results obtained on the CVPPP dataset according to the measures: Difference in Count (DiC), absolute Difference in Count ($|DiC|$), and Symmetric Best Dice (SBD). Reported mean and standard deviation (in parenthesis).

	IPK	Nottingham	MSU	Wageningen	PRIAn	RIS	RIS+CRF
$DiC \longrightarrow 0$	−1.9	−3.6	−2.3	−0.4	0.8	**0.2**	**0.2**
	(2.5)	(2.4)	(1.6)	(3.0)	(1.5)	**(1.4)**	**(1.4)**
$|DiC|\downarrow$	2.6	3.8	2.3	2.2	1.3	**1.1**	**1.1**
	(1.8)	(2.0)	(1.5)	(2.0)	(2.0)	**(0.9)**	**(0.9)**
$SBD(\%) \uparrow$	**74.4**	68.3	66.7	71.1	–	56.8	66.6
	(4.3)	(6.3)	(7.6)	(6.2)		(8.2)	(8.7)

The results obtained are shown in Table 2, using the measures reported by the CVPPP organization in order to compare the submitted solutions. These are

Difference in Count (DiC) which is the difference between the predicted number of leaves and the ground truth, $|DiC|$, which is the absolute value of DiC averaged across all images, and Symmetric Best Dice (SBD), which is defined in [46], and provides a measure about the accuracy of the segmentation of the instances. Regarding leaf counting, we observe that our approach significantly outperforms the competing ad hoc methods that were designed for this particular problem. With regard to segmentation of leaves, our approach obtains comparable results with respect to the competitors, yet it does not outperform any approach. We hypothesize that despite the data augmentation process we follow, the amount of original images available for training is too small as to learn how to segment a wide variety of leaf shapes from scratch. This scarcity of training data has a smaller impact in the competing methods, given that they contain heuristics and prior information about the problem.

We have also visualized, in Fig. 4, a representation of what the network keeps in memory as the sequence is produced. The column denoted as $\kappa(\mathbf{h}_t)$ shows a summary function of the hidden state $\mathbf{h}$ of the second ConvLSTM layer. The summary function consists of the sum of the absolute values across channels for each pixel. The column denoted as $\hat{\mathbf{Y}}_t$ corresponds to the output produced by the network. We observe that as time advances, the state is modified to take into account parts of the image that have been visited. We also inspected the value of the cell, that is $\mathbf{c}_t$ in Eq. (1), but we have not observed any clear clues.

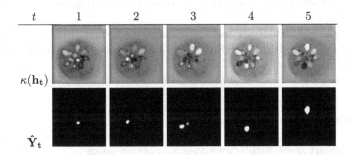

Fig. 4. Representation of the state, $\kappa(\mathbf{h}_t)$ (the sum of the absolute values across channels), and the output, $\hat{\mathbf{Y}}_t$, of a sequence produced by our model.

5 Discussion

In this paper we have proposed a new instance segmentation paradigm characterized by its sequential nature. Similarly to what human beings do when counting objects in a scene, our model proceeds sequentially, segmenting one instance of the scene at a time. The resulting model integrates in a single pipeline all the required functions to segment instances. These functions are defined by a set of parameters that are jointly learned end-to-end. A key aspect in our model is the use of a recurrent structure that is able to track visited areas in the image as well as to handle occlusion among instances. Another key aspect is the definition of a loss function that accurately represents the instance segmentation objective we aim to achieve. The experiments carried out on multiple person segmentation and leaf counting show that our approach outperforms state of the art methods. Qualitative results show that the state in the recurrent stage contains information regarding the visited instances in the sequence.

The primary objective of this paper is to show that learning end-to-end instance segmentation is possible by means of a recurrent neural network. Nevertheless, variations of some architectural choices could lead to even better results. We tried a variety of other alternatives, such as adding the sum of the prediction masks as an extra input into the recurrent unit. We also tried alternatives to f_{IoU} in Eq. (3), such as log-likelihood. The results obtained in either case were not better than the ones achieved by the model described in Sect. 3. The analysis of these and other alternative architectures is left for future work.

There are several extensions that can be carried out in our approach. One is allowing the model to classify the segmented instance at each time. This can be done by generalizing the loss function in Eq. (5). Another extension consists in integrating the CRF module as a layer in the end-to-end model, such as in [14]. Another interesting line of research is investigating other recurrent structures that could be as good or even better than ConvLSTMs for instance segmentation. Finally, the extension of this model for exploiting co-occurrence of objects, parts of objects, and attributes, could be a promising research direction.

Acknowledgments. This work was supported by the EPSRC, ERC grant ERC-2012-AdG 321162-HELIOS, HELIOS-DFR00200, EPSRC grant Seebibyte EP/M013774/1 and EPSRC/MURI grant EP/N019474/1.
Thanks to Siddharth Narayanaswamy for proofreading this work.

References

1. VA-ST: Smart specs. http://www.va-st.com/smart-specs
2. Arteta, C., Lempitsky, V., Noble, J.A., Zisserman, A.: Learning to detect partially overlapping instances. In: Computer Vision and Pattern Recognition (CVPR), pp. 3230–3237. IEEE (2013)
3. Trager, W., Jensen, J.B.: Human malaria parasites in continuous culture. Science **193**(4254), 673–675 (1976)
4. Hariharan, B., Arbeláez, P., Girshick, R., Malik, J.: Simultaneous detection and segmentation. In: Fleet, D., Pajdla, T., Schiele, B., Tuytelaars, T. (eds.) ECCV 2014. LNCS, vol. 8695, pp. 297–312. Springer, Heidelberg (2014). doi:10.1007/978-3-319-10584-0_20
5. Chen, Y.T., Liu, X., Yang, M.H.: Multi-instance object segmentation with occlusion handling. In: Proceedings of the IEEE Conference on Computer Vision and Pattern Recognition (CVPR), pp. 3470–3478 (2015)
6. Vineet, V., Warrell, J., Ladicky, L., Torr, P.H.: Human instance segmentation from video using detector-based conditional random fields. In: British Machine Vision Conference (BMVC), pp. 1–11 (2011)

7. Dehaene, S., Cohen, L.: Dissociable mechanisms of subitizing and counting: neuropsychological evidence from simultanagnosic patients. J. Exp. Psychol. Hum. Percept. Perform. **20**(5), 958 (1994)

8. Porter, G., Troscianko, T., Gilchrist, I.D.: Effort during visual search and counting: insights from pupillometry. Q. J. Exp. Psychol. **60**(2), 211–229 (2007)

9. Ladický, Ľ., Sturgess, P., Alahari, K., Russell, C., Torr, P.H.S.: What, where and how many? Combining object detectors and CRFs. In: Daniilidis, K., Maragos, P., Paragios, N. (eds.) ECCV 2010. LNCS, vol. 6314, pp. 424–437. Springer, Heidelberg (2010). doi:10.1007/978-3-642-15561-1_31

10. Girshick, R., Donahue, J., Darrell, T., Malik, J.: Rich feature hierarchies for accurate object detection and semantic segmentation. In: Computer Vision and Pattern Recognition (CVPR), pp. 580–587. IEEE (2014)

11. Arbelaez, P., Pont-Tuset, J., Barron, J., Marques, F., Malik, J.: Multiscale combinatorial grouping. In: 2014 IEEE Conference on Computer Vision and Pattern Recognition (CVPR), pp. 328–335. IEEE (2014)

12. Long, J., Shelhamer, E., Darrell, T.: Fully convolutional networks for semantic segmentation. In: Proceedings of the IEEE Conference on Computer Vision and Pattern Recognition (CVPR), pp. 3431–3440 (2015)

13. Liang-Chieh, C., Papandreou, G., Kokkinos, I., Murphy, K., Yuille, A.: Semantic image segmentation with deep convolutional nets and fully connected CRFs. In: International Conference on Learning Representations (ICLR) (2015)

14. Zheng, S., Jayasumana, S., Romera-Paredes, B., Vineet, V., Su, Z., Du, D., Huang, C., Torr, P.H.: Conditional random fields as recurrent neural networks. In: IEEE International Conference on Computer Vision (ICCV) (2015)

15. Liang, X., Wei, Y., Shen, X., Yang, J., Lin, L., Yan, S.: Proposal-free network for instance-level object segmentation. arXiv preprint arXiv:1509.02636 (2015)

16. Tighe, J., Niethammer, M., Lazebnik, S.: Scene parsing with object instances and occlusion ordering. In: Computer Vision and Pattern Recognition (CVPR), pp. 3748–3755. IEEE (2014)

17. Yang, Y., Hallman, S., Ramanan, D., Fowlkes, C.C.: Layered object models for image segmentation. IEEE Trans. Pattern Anal. Mach. Intell. **34**(9), 1731–1743 (2012)

18. Zhang, Z., Schwing, A.G., Fidler, S., Urtasun, R.: Monocular object instance segmentation and depth ordering with CNNs. In: IEEE International Conference on Computer Vision (ICCV), pp. 2614–2622 (2015)

19. Bahdanau, D., Cho, K., Bengio, Y.: Neural machine translation by jointly learning to align and translate. arXiv preprint arXiv:1409.0473 (2014)

20. Graves, A., Schmidhuber, J.: Offline handwriting recognition with multidimensional recurrent neural networks. In: Advances in Neural Information Processing Systems (NIPS), pp. 545–552 (2009)

21. Vinyals, O., Le, Q.: A neural conversational model. arXiv preprint arXiv:1506.05869 (2015)

22. Gregor, K., Danihelka, I., Graves, A., Wierstra, D.: Draw: a recurrent neural network for image generation. In: Proceedings of the 32nd International Conference on Machine Learning (ICML) (2015)

23. Donahue, J., Anne Hendricks, L., Guadarrama, S., Rohrbach, M., Venugopalan, S., Saenko, K., Darrell, T.: Long-term recurrent convolutional networks for visual recognition and description. In: Proceedings of the IEEE Conference on Computer Vision and Pattern Recognition (CVPR), pp. 2625–2634 (2015)

24. Karpathy, A., Fei-Fei, L.: Deep visual-semantic alignments for generating image descriptions. In: Proceedings of the IEEE Conference on Computer Vision and Pattern Recognition (CVPR), pp. 3128–3137 (2015)
25. Vinyals, O., Toshev, A., Bengio, S., Erhan, D.: Show and tell: a neural image caption generator. In: Conference on Computer Vision and Pattern Recognition (CVPR), pp. 3156–3164 (2015)
26. Sønderby, S.K., Sønderby, C.K., Nielsen, H., Winther, O.: Convolutional LSTM networks for subcellular localization of proteins. In: Dediu, A.-H., Hernández-Quiroz, F., Martín-Vide, C., Rosenblueth, D.A. (eds.) AlCoB 2015. LNCS, vol. 9199, pp. 68–80. Springer, Heidelberg (2015). doi:10.1007/978-3-319-21233-3_6
27. Stewart, R., Andriluka, M.: End-to-end people detection in crowded scenes. arXiv preprint arXiv:1506.04878 (2015)
28. Pavel, M.S., Schulz, H., Behnke, S.: Recurrent convolutional neural networks for object-class segmentation of rgb-d video. In: International Joint Conference on Neural Networks (IJCNN), pp. 1–8. IEEE (2015)
29. Williams, C.K., Titsias, M.K.: Greedy learning of multiple objects in images using robust statistics and factorial learning. Neural Comput. **16**(5), 1039–1062 (2004)
30. Ba, J., Mnih, V., Kavukcuoglu, K.: Multiple object recognition with visual attention. In: International Conference on Learning Representations (ICLR) (2015)
31. Xu, K., Ba, J., Kiros, R., Cho, K., Courville, A., Salakhudinov, R., Zemel, R., Bengio, Y.: Show, attend and tell: neural image caption generation with visual attention. In: Proceedings of the 32nd International Conference on Machine Learning (ICML), pp. 2048–2057 (2015)
32. Mnih, V., Heess, N., Graves, A., et al.: Recurrent models of visual attention. In: Advances in Neural Information Processing Systems (NIPS), pp. 2204–2212 (2014)
33. Hermann, K.M., Kocisky, T., Grefenstette, E., Espeholt, L., Kay, W., Suleyman, M., Blunsom, P.: Teaching machines to read and comprehend. In: Advances in Neural Information Processing Systems (NIPS), pp. 1693–1701 (2015)
34. Hochreiter, S., Schmidhuber, J.: Long short-term memory. Neural Comput. **9**(8), 1735–1780 (1997)
35. Dosovitskiy, A., Fischery, P., Ilg, E., Hazirbas, C., Golkov, V., van der Smagt, P., Cremers, D., Brox, T., et al.: Flownet: learning optical flow with convolutional networks. In: IEEE International Conference on Computer Vision (ICCV), pp. 2758–2766. IEEE (2015)
36. Xingjian, S., Chen, Z., Wang, H., Yeung, D.Y., Wong, W.k., Woo, W.c.: Convolutional lstm network: a machine learning approach for precipitation nowcasting. In: Advances in Neural Information Processing Systems (NIPS), pp. 802–810 (2015)
37. Krähenbühl, P., Koltun, V.: Parameter learning and convergent inference for dense random fields. In: Proceedings of the 30th International Conference on Machine Learning (ICML), pp. 513–521 (2013)
38. Silberman, N., Sontag, D., Fergus, R.: Instance segmentation of indoor scenes using a coverage loss. In: Fleet, D., Pajdla, T., Schiele, B., Tuytelaars, T. (eds.) ECCV 2014. LNCS, vol. 8689, pp. 616–631. Springer, Heidelberg (2014). doi:10.1007/978-3-319-10590-1_40
39. Collobert, R., Kavukcuoglu, K., Farabet, C.: Torch7: a matlab-like environment for machine learning. In: BigLearn, NIPS Workshop. Number EPFL-CONF-192376 (2011)
40. Kingma, D., Ba, J.: Adam: a method for stochastic optimization. arXiv preprint arXiv:1412.6980 (2014)

41. Lin, T.-Y., Maire, M., Belongie, S., Hays, J., Perona, P., Ramanan, D., Dollár, P., Zitnick, C.L.: Microsoft COCO: common objects in context. In: Fleet, D., Pajdla, T., Schiele, B., Tuytelaars, T. (eds.) ECCV 2014. LNCS, vol. 8693, pp. 740–755. Springer, Heidelberg (2014). doi:10.1007/978-3-319-10602-1_48
42. Ren, S., He, K., Girshick, R., Sun, J.: Faster R-CNN: towards real-time object detection with region proposal networks. In: Advances in Neural Information Processing Systems (NIPS), pp. 91–99 (2015)
43. Minervini, M., Abdelsamea, M.M., Tsaftaris, S.A.: Image-based plant phenotyping with incremental learning and active contours. Ecol. Inform. 23, 35–48 (2014)
44. Minervini, M., Fischbach, A., Scharr, H., Tsaftaris, S.A.: Finely-grained annotated datasets for image-based plant phenotyping. Pattern Recognition Letters Special Issue on Fine-grained Categorization in Ecological Multimedia (2015)
45. Pape, J.-M., Klukas, C.: 3-D histogram-based segmentation and leaf detection for rosette plants. In: Agapito, L., Bronstein, M.M., Rother, C. (eds.) ECCV 2014. LNCS, vol. 8928, pp. 61–74. Springer, Heidelberg (2015). doi:10.1007/978-3-319-16220-1_5
46. Scharr, H., Minervini, M., French, A.P., Klukas, C., Kramer, D.M., Liu, X., Luengo Muntion, I., Pape, J.M., Polder, G., Vukadinovic, D., Yin, X., Tsaftaris, S.A.: Leaf segmentation in plant phenotyping: a collation study. Mach. Vision Appl. 27, 585–606 (2016)
47. Barrow, H.G., Tenenbaum, J.M., Bolles, R.C., Wolf, H.C.: Parametric correspondence and chamfer matching: two new techniquesfor image matching. Technical report, DTIC Document (1977)
48. Yin, X., Liu, X., Chen, J., Kramer, D.M.: Multi-leaf tracking from fluorescence plant videos. In: 2014 IEEE International Conference on Image Processing (ICIP), pp. 408–412. IEEE (2014)
49. Giuffrida, M.V., Minervini, M., Tsaftaris, S.A.: Learning to count leaves in rosette plants. In: British Machine Vision Conference (CVPPP Workshop). BMVA Press (2015)

Individualness and Determinantal Point Processes for Pedestrian Detection

Donghoon Lee[1], Geonho Cha[1], Ming-Hsuan Yang[2], and Songhwai Oh[1(✉)]

[1] Electrical and Computer Engineering and ASRI,
Seoul National University, Seoul, Korea
{donghoon.lee,geonho.cha}@cpslab.snu.ac.kr, songhwai@snu.ac.kr
[2] Electrical Engineering and Computer Science,
University of California, Merced, USA
mhyang@ucmerced.edu

Abstract. In this paper, we introduce individualness of detection candidates as a complement to objectness for pedestrian detection. The individualness assigns a single detection for each object out of raw detection candidates given by either object proposals or sliding windows. We show that conventional approaches, such as non-maximum suppression, are sub-optimal since they suppress nearby detections using only detection scores. We use a determinantal point process combined with the individualness to optimally select final detections. It models each detection using its quality and similarity to other detections based on the individualness. Then, detections with high detection scores and low correlations are selected by measuring their probability using a determinant of a matrix, which is composed of quality terms on the diagonal entries and similarities on the off-diagonal entries. For concreteness, we focus on the pedestrian detection problem as it is one of the most challenging problems due to frequent occlusions and unpredictable human motions. Experimental results demonstrate that the proposed algorithm works favorably against existing methods, including non-maximal suppression and a quadratic unconstrained binary optimization based method.

Keywords: Determinantal point process · Individualness · Object detection · Pedestrian detection

1 Introduction

The goal of object detection is to locate objects from one known category in an image. It is essential for a number of vision tasks, such as visual tracking, scene understanding, and action recognition, to name a few. In visual tracking, tracking-by-detection is an effective approach which locates target objects in an image sequence by associating detections [1]. By learning about object locations

Electronic supplementary material The online version of this chapter (doi:10.1007/978-3-319-46466-4_20) contains supplementary material, which is available to authorized users.

© Springer International Publishing AG 2016
B. Leibe et al. (Eds.): ECCV 2016, Part VI, LNCS 9910, pp. 330–346, 2016.
DOI: 10.1007/978-3-319-46466-4_20

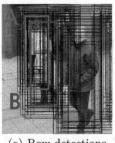  

   (a) Raw detections   (b) NMS   (c) Proposed method

Fig. 1. Pedestrian detection results from the INRIA dataset. (a) Raw detections in black boxes using a sliding window method. (b) Detection results from a typical non-maximum suppression method. (c) Detection results from the proposed algorithm. Raw detection boxes A and B represent different pedestrians.

in the image, we can better understand what is happening in the scene [2]. Object detection is also applied to action recognition by finding specific items related to an action of interest [3].

The general framework for object detection is to test image patches given by either a sliding window method or object proposals using a trained classifier. A number of object detectors have been developed which can reliably detect objects if they are well separated [4–7]. However, while it is desirable to report a single detection for each object, a sliding window method and object proposals entail a large number of raw detection responses around a true object as shown in Fig. 1(a). Redundant detection responses are usually suppressed using a simple greedy algorithm, such as non-maximum suppression (NMS), based on the detection scores as shown in Fig. 1(b).

It is known to be difficult to detect heavily occluded objects using the above-mentioned framework. This can be attributed to the fact that a detector is trained to distinguish between target classes, and not designed to differentiate between intra-class objects. For example, a detector reports detections A and B as shown in Fig. 1(a). Since the detected bounding boxes are heavily overlapped, we examine whether these are false positives or negatives. During NMS, one of the detections, e.g., A, is likely to be suppressed, based on the confidence scores of these two detections. Therefore, the NMS scheme inevitably generates false negatives when multiple detections occur in proximity (i.e., in crowded scenes). On the other hand, if some prior information about two detections is available, e.g., detected objects have different identities, this issue can be alleviated. In fact, the false rejection significantly affects the detection accuracy, as the recall of raw detections in the dataset used in this paper is about 90 %, while it drops to about 50 % after final detections are selected by NMS. Therefore, it is an important task to select raw detections properly.

In this paper, we propose an algorithm based on *individualness* and a *determinantal point process* (DPP) for accurate detection which can be applied to any object detector. The proposed individualness is complementary to objectness for detection. While objectness is used to generate a set of detection candidates, individualness finds the relationship between candidates to obtain the final detection. We define individualness using the correlation between feature vectors, which describes the appearance and spatial information of detection results enclosed by bounding boxes. For concreteness, we focus on detecting multiple pedestrians in crowded scenes as it is one of the most challenging problems with numerous applications.

A DPP is a random process used to model particles with repulsive interactions in theoretical quantum physics [8]. It prohibits co-occurrences of highly correlated quantum states. This property is well suited for the task in this work to reject redundant detections. To apply a DPP, the quality and diversity factors need to be defined. They are used to compute the unary score (quality) and the pair-wise correlation (diversity) of detections. Based on these two factors, we can select an optimal subset of detections as shown in Fig. 1(c).

The contributions of this paper are summarized as follows. First, the problem in the existing detection framework, which naively selects final detections from a pool of detection candidates, is addressed. Second, a DPP is introduced to enhance the detection accuracy with a novel design of the quality term and the diversity feature. Finally, while finding the optimal subset of detections using a DPP is NP-hard, we show that a simple and efficient greedy algorithm performs favorably against existing pedestrian detection methods on the INRIA [5], PETS 2009 [9], and EPFL Terrace [10] datasets. On the PETS 2009 dataset with a deformable part model (DPM) detector, the proposed method achieves the accuracy rate of 41.9 % and precision rate of 99.0 %, while NMS achieves 23.2 % accuracy and 98.2 % precision. In addition, it takes less than 30 ms to process an image containing more than 300 detection candidates from over 30 pedestrians.

2   Related Work

Pedestrian Detection Methods. For completeness, we briefly discuss pedestrian detectors used in this paper. The HOG [5] features are computed by dividing an image patch into cells and blocks. Each block consists of cells and is represented by a histogram of gradients. Histograms from all blocks are concatenated into a single feature vector. Based on HOG features, an SVM classifier is trained and used to classify each sliding window in a test image for pedestrian detection. A deformable part model (DPM) [6] is developed based on HOG features. It learns a classifier for each body part and finds a pedestrian by considering body part detection scores and their spatial configuration. The DPM achieves higher accuracy in pedestrian detection but requires heavier computational load than the HOG based method.

A boosting-based detector is developed using different color spaces and gradients [11] where subregions or aggregated pixels of different channels work as a weak classifier. This multi-channel based detector has been shown to perform more efficiently and accurately than HOG-based approaches. The faster R-CNN [12] method has been developed recently. This deep learning approach is developed based on object proposals rather than sliding windows [5,6,11].

Merging Detection Results. We note that all the above-mentioned methods use NMS schemes to eliminate multiple detections around a true object including the state-of-the-art detector [12]. Given a set of detected bounding boxes within a region, NMS finds the one with the highest score and discards all the other neighboring detections. Typically, a neighboring detection is defined by thresholding on the overlap area ratio of bounding boxes. As stated in Sect. 1, NMS is likely to generate false positives or negatives when objects are close to each other.

Recently, numerous approaches have been proposed in order to address the discussed problems of NMS. In [13], it is shown that the localization accuracy of a bounding box is not strongly correlated to the score of a detection box when the score is high. To address this problem, a regression model is constructed to learn location statistics of raw detections with respect to the ground truth bounding boxes. However, a regression model needs to be trained for each detector. In addition, the performance of this method depends on the characteristics of the training data. The NMS scheme can also be integrated into deep learning models [14]. However, the parameters of NMS remain fixed during the training.

The task of NMS can be formulated as an optimization problem. In [15], a quadratic unconstrained binary optimization (QUBO) algorithm is proposed to replace NMS. The objective of QUBO is to find a binary vector where each element indicates whether the corresponding detection should be suppressed from a pool of candidate detections. The objective function consists of unary and pairwise terms. The unary term measures the confidence that a candidate detection truly represents a pedestrian and the pairwise term penalizes an overlap between a pair of candidate detections. The objective function is solved using a greedy algorithm. The main drawback of QUBO is that it approximates the distribution of raw detections, i.e., the distance between pedestrians, using a quadratic objective function. In Sect. 3.5, we show the limitations of QUBO in real world scenarios with comparisons to the proposed method.

A method based on affinity propagation clustering (APC) [16] is proposed. APC is a clustering algorithm which aims to find exemplars, such that the sum of similarities between exemplars and cluster members is maximized. However, APC is not naturally suitable for object detection since it does not explicitly penalize close exemplars which can be duplicated detections from the same object. Although this method can be improved by adding a repelling function which penalizes close exemplars, the detection accuracy is not notably increased compared to NMS.

3 Proposed Algorithm

The proposed detection process is a two-stage framework, which consists of objectness and individualness parts as shown in Fig. 2. The objectness part returns a set of detection candidates with their scores. Then, the individualness part analyzes candidates using their appearances, relative locations, and sizes. The final detection is obtained by merging objectness (detection score) and

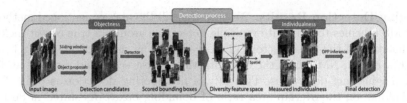

Fig. 2. Flow chart of the proposed detection framework.

individualness (similarity between detection candidates) into a single objective function. In this paper, we propose to use a DPP to model their relationships.

3.1 Determinantal Point Process Formulation

Let N be the number of items and $\mathcal{Y} = \{1, 2, .., N\}$ be the corresponding index set. Each item i is represented by its quality q_i and similarity S_{ij} to another item j. A DPP aims to select high quality items while avoiding highly correlated items simultaneously. Let $Y \subset \mathcal{Y}$ be an index set of the selected items. Using their qualities and similarities, we compute a positive-semidefinite kernel matrix $L_Y = [L_{ij}]_{i,j \in Y}$, where

$$L_{ij} = q_i q_j S_{ij}. \tag{1}$$

To ensure the positive-semidefinite property, S_{ij} is usually computed by an inner product of each item's descriptor vector, which is called a diversity feature. Then, a DPP measures the probability, $\mathcal{P}_L(Y)$, of the selected indices using the determinant of L_Y. In other words, a DPP seeks to find the most probable subset by solving the following optimization problem:

$$Y^* = \arg\max_{Y \subset \mathcal{Y}}(\det(L_Y)) = \arg\max_{Y \subset \mathcal{Y}}(\prod_{i \in Y} q_i^2)\det(S_Y), \tag{2}$$

where $S_Y = [S_{ij}]_{i,j \in Y}$ and Y^* is the optimal subset of item indices. Generally, the problem is NP-hard because all possible subsets have to be examined [17]. Fortunately, the problem is log-submodular which can be well approximated by a simple greedy algorithm [8].

The implicit meaning of the determinantal probability measure can be explained by the following example. With a subset $Y = \{i, j\}$,

$$\mathcal{P}_L(Y) \propto \begin{vmatrix} L_{ii} & L_{ij} \\ L_{ji} & L_{jj} \end{vmatrix} = \begin{vmatrix} q_i^2 & q_i q_j S_{ij} \\ q_i q_j S_{ij} & q_j^2 \end{vmatrix}. \tag{3}$$

The diagonal entries are computed without a similarity term because the correlation to itself is always one. The determinant is decreased when $|S_{ij}|$ increases. Therefore, a DPP tends to pick uncorrelated items in these cases. On the other hand, higher quality items increase the determinant, and thus a DPP tends to pick high-quality items in such cases. As a consequence, an appropriate design of the quality term and the diversity feature plays an important role. In this work, we use a DPP for the detection problem by using each raw detection as an item and Y^* as the final detection set.

3.2   Quality Term

The quality term indicates the value of an item. For the pedestrian detection problem, it can be described by a detection score. However, the original scores are independently obtained from each image patch. Therefore, they do not contain information of neighboring detections or the scene. We propose a simple, yet effective scheme to re-score each detection.

Let $\mathbf{s}^o = \{s_1^o, s_2^o, ..., s_N^o\}$ be set of scores for N raw detections. One common factor that degrades the detection accuracy is a wrong detection with a high confidence score, as it can potentially suppress neighboring true detections. The problem is worsened when the bounding box of the wrong detection is large. Figure 3(a) shows an example of wrong detections from a detector. In order to deal with this problem, we penalize unnecessarily large raw detections. As such, we count the number of other raw detections inside a bounding box. Figure 3(b) shows the number of raw detections inside a ground truth bounding box from the INRIA dataset. It shows that a bounding box with a small number of raw detections is more likely to contain ground truth detections. Based on this observation, we re-score each detection as $s_i^c = s_i^o \exp(-\lambda n_i)$, where n_i is the number of raw detections inside the current bounding box and λ is a constant. Another advantage of the proposed re-scoring function is that it favorably yields tight bounding boxes as discussed in Sect. 4.

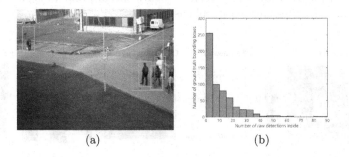

(a)   (b)

Fig. 3. (a) Detection results show that a detector can return wrong detections with large bounding boxes. These wrong detections may suppress other true detections. (b) The number of raw detections inside a ground truth bounding box (INRIA dataset).

Additionally, we can use prior information when it is available. For a fixed camera environment, such as the PETS 2009 and EPFL Terrace datasets, and numerous practical surveillance applications, the height of a pedestrian at each location in an image does not vary significantly. Let (x_i, y_i) be the image coordinate location and h_i be the height of detection i, which is the height of its bounding box. Given a training set, we can find coefficients of the following relationship to estimate the expected height of a person at different locations:

$$\widetilde{h}_i = ax_i + by_i + c. \tag{4}$$

Then, we re-score each detection based on the assumption that the height distribution of people is Gaussian, i.e., $s_i^p = s_i^c \frac{1}{\sqrt{2\pi\sigma^2}} \exp\left(-\frac{(h_i - \bar{h}_i)^2}{2\sigma^2}\right)$. The re-scored detection score, $\mathbf{s} = \{s_1, s_2, ..., s_N\}$, is obtained by using s_i^p when prior information is available, otherwise s_i^c. The quality term $\mathbf{q}$ is represented as follows:

$$\mathbf{q} = \alpha\mathbf{s} + \beta, \tag{5}$$

where α and β are weights for the quality term. The weights are needed to balance the detection score of different detectors, e.g., an average detection score of a DPM detector is about 0.7 while an ACF detector is about 33.2 from the INRIA dataset. We find these parameters using the pattern search algorithm [18], which maximizes the detection performance on a training set.

3.3 Individualness and Diversity Feature

Individualness aims to determine whether two image patches originated from the same object (person) or not. It might be reminiscent of the person re-identification problem in a multi-camera environment. However, this problem is different and difficult for two reasons. First, the overlapping region of two image patches contains exactly the same information. Therefore, the distance between two image patches in a feature space tends to be closer. Second, we mainly deal with occluded people while the person re-identification problem typically takes image patches of well-separated people as inputs.

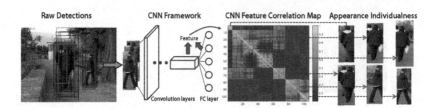

Fig. 4. Measuring the appearance individualness of each detection box using a CNN. The goal is to give a high correlation score to the bounding boxes around a single person (blue boxes), while giving a low correlation score when there is a different person. (color figure online)

We tackle this problem by measuring the correlation of feature descriptors from bounding boxes. The feature descriptor should be insensitive to new background pixels and scale variations around a single person as shown in blue detection boxes in Fig. 4, while being sensitive to a new pedestrian as shown in red detection boxes in Fig. 4. Toward this goal, we consider features from convolutional neural network (CNN) layers. The CNN features are translation and scale invariant due to multiple max-pooling operations. Figure 4 shows the correlation between CNN features of different bounding boxes using a pre-trained network

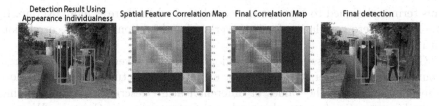

Fig. 5. The result of DPP inference. It is more robust to detect pedestrians by combining appearance and spatial information.

for image classification [12]. Overall, the correlation matrix is block diagonal and the correlation between different individuals is low. This observation encourages us to use the CNN feature, denoted as ϕ_i for the i-th detection, for the individualness.

While highly effective, the sole use of CNN features to measure the individualness is not robust. As shown in Fig. 4, there can be duplicated clusters for a single pedestrian or ambiguous clusters between nearby pedestrians. Consequently, there may be a wrong inference from the DPP algorithm as shown in Fig. 5. In this example, the shapes inside two boxes around a boy on the right-hand side are significantly different although a large portion of the smaller bounding box is included in the larger box. The difference misleads the CNN feature to have a low correlation between these two boxes (see the CNN feature correlation map in Fig. 4). On the other hand, in the case of the woman in the middle, the CNN features fail to ignore new background pixels. To overcome this problem, we additionally consider the spatial location of each detection box.

The spatial individualness is designed to give high correlation to multiple detection boxes around a single pedestrian. Let φ_i be the spatial individualness vector of the i-th detection and let π_i denote a set of pixel indices belonging to the detection box. We propose an efficient form as follows:

$$\varphi_i^k = \frac{1}{\sqrt{|\pi_i|}} \begin{cases} 1 & \text{if } k \in \pi_i \\ 0 & \text{otherwise} \end{cases}, \tag{6}$$

where φ_i^k is the k-th entry of $\varphi_i \in [0,1]^n$, n is the number of pixels in an input image, and $|\pi_i|$ is the number of pixels in the i-th detection box. The square root of $|\pi_i|$ is used for normalization so that φ_i is unit norm. Although the dimension of φ_i is as large as the size of the image, $\varphi_i^\top \varphi_j$ can be computed easily as follows:

$$\varphi_i^k \varphi_j^k = \frac{1}{\sqrt{|\pi_i||\pi_j|}} \begin{cases} 1 & \text{if } k \in \pi_i \cap \pi_j \\ 0 & \text{otherwise} \end{cases}. \tag{7}$$

Furthermore, φ_i itself does not have to be stored in the memory since only detection sizes and the overlap area are required

$$\varphi_i^\top \varphi_j = \frac{|\pi_i \cap \pi_j|}{\sqrt{|\pi_i||\pi_j|}} \in [0,1]. \tag{8}$$

This term is designed to increase the correlation when there is more overlap. It also satisfies zero correlation for non-overlapping detections and the correlation with itself is one.

Given individualness features ϕ_i and φ_i, there are several schemes to merge them into a single diversity feature. For example, a structured DPP [19] is performed by averaging the values of different feature descriptors. However, this method is restrictive because the number of features must be the same. We propose a more general and effective way to design a diversity feature and construct a positive semi-definite similarity matrix S directly. Let S^c and S^s denote the similarity matrices constructed from ϕ_i and φ_i, respectively. In other words, $S^c_{ij} = \phi_i^\top \phi_j$ and $S^s_{ij} = \varphi_i^\top \varphi_j$. We then merge them into a single matrix using an operation that preserves the positive semi-definite property.

In this paper, two different ways are considered. First, from the Schur-product theorem [20], $S = S^c \circ S^s$ is a positive semi-definite matrix where $\circ$ is a Hadamard product or an element-wise product of matrices. For pedestrian detection, we find this approach is not suitable, as the correlation between items becomes too small when multiplying values within $[0, 1]$. Second, any positive combination of positive semi-definite matrices is also positive semi-definite. Therefore, we construct S as follows:

$$S = wS^c + (1 - w)S^s, \qquad (9)$$

where $0 \le w \le 1$ can determine the relative importance of each feature descriptor. This formulation implies that the diversity feature is a concatenation of ϕ_i and φ_i. We set w as 0.8 throughout the paper in order to make sure that the correlation between items that are spatially separated is low enough. In the next section, we discuss how to efficiently solve (2) given the proposed quality term and similarity matrix.

3.4 Mode Finding

As mentioned earlier, the problem of finding the exact solution to (2) is NP-hard [17]. Since $\mathcal{P}_L(Y)$ is log-submodular, greedy mode finding approaches for DPPs perform well in numerous machine learning applications [8]. Using a similar idea, our algorithm iteratively adds the j^*-th detection to the final solution set Y^* if j^* maximizes $\mathcal{P}_L(Y^* \cup \{j^*\})$ among the remaining detection candidates. Once j^* is added to the Y^*, we delete j^* from the candidate detection set $\mathcal{Y}$. The algorithm terminates when the candidate detection set is empty or there is no more detection which increases $\mathcal{P}_L(Y)$ by $(1 + \epsilon)$ times the previous value of $\mathcal{P}_L(Y)$. The main steps of the proposed algorithm are summarized in Algorithm 1. Note that although there exists an approximate algorithm [21] for this problem, we use Algorithm 1, which has a formal guarantee for monotone submodular problems [8], since it is fast and works well in practice.

Algorithm 1. A greedy algorithm for solving (2)
___
1: INPUT : $\mathbf{q}$, S, $\mathcal{Y}$, ϵ
2: OUTPUT : Y^*
3: $Y^* = \emptyset$
4: **while** $\mathcal{Y} \neq \emptyset$ **do**
5:      $j^* = \arg\max_{j \in \mathcal{Y}} (\prod_{i \in Y^* \cup \{j\}} q_i^2) \det(S_{Y^* \cup \{j\}})$
6:      $Y = Y^* \cup \{j^*\}$
7:      **if** $P_L(Y)/P_L(Y^*) > 1 + \epsilon$ **then**
8:          $Y^* \leftarrow Y$
9:          delete j^* from $\mathcal{Y}$
10:     **else**
11:         break
12:     **end if**
13: **end while**
___

3.5   Relationship to Quadratic Unconstrained Binary Optimization

The objective function of quadratic unconstrained binary optimization can be converted to a similar form using the DPP objective function as follows:

$$\max_x x^\top L x = \max_Y \sum_{i,j} (L_Y)_{ij}, \tag{10}$$

where x is a binary vector and Y is a set of non-zero indices in x. In other words, QUBO finds Y that maximizes the sum of all elements in a submatrix L_Y, while a DPP seeks to maximize the determinant of L_Y. This leads to two key differences. First, QUBO cannot deal with positively correlated items. By (1), those items have positive entries in L_Y. Therefore, QUBO blindly selects them all to maximize the objective function. On the other hand, the DPP is well-defined for both positively and negatively correlated items. Second, QUBO penalizes highly correlated items more than DPP, which is not suitable to detect occluded pedestrians. We show this by an illustrative example that we face often during the experiments. Let there be two pedestrians in an image, and a detector reports a detection for each of them which constructs $L_Y = \begin{bmatrix} 2 & -0.8 \\ -0.8 & 1.4 \end{bmatrix}$. We set off-diagonal entries as -0.8 to represent overlapped detections. The first pedestrian has higher detection score, which usually indicates that the second pedestrian is occluded by the first pedestrian. In this case, QUBO and DPP work differently. By Algorithm 1, the first pedestrian is picked (QUBO uses a similar greedy algorithm). Then, QUBO does not pick the second detection since $-0.8 - 0.8 + 1.4 = -0.2 < 0$ while a DPP selects both detections since $\det(L_Y) = 2.16 > 2$. Moreover, QUBO ignores the elements of the previously selected items while DPP considers the whole matrix to select a new item. For instance, if the first element of L_Y is 1.5, DPP does not pick the second item, since $\det(L_Y)$ becomes 1.46. The additional consideration enables a DPP to deal with more complex relationships between items. In Sect. 4, we demonstrate that the proposed method outperforms both NMS and QUBO for detecting pedestrians.

Fig. 6. Number of pedestrians and their overlap ratio for each evaluated dataset. The pedestrian overlap ratio of an image is defined by dividing the summation of overlapped bounding box regions by the summation of all bounding box areas. The numbers are calculated based on the ground truth data. Note that the y-axis is log-scale.

4   Experiments

We first discuss the experimental settings for evaluating the proposed and existing methods, and then present the empirical results. More results are available in the supplementary material. All the source code and annotated datasets will be made available to the public[1].

4.1   Experimental Settings

We evaluate the proposed algorithm with comparisons to other methods on the INRIA [5], PETS 2009 [9], and EPFL Terrace [10] datasets. Figure 6 shows the number of pedestrians per image and the average overlap ratio of pedestrians of these datasets, where the average overlap ratio is defined by $\frac{\sum_{i,j} |\pi_i \cap \pi_j|}{\sum_i |\pi_i|}$, and π_i is the same as in Sect. 3.3.

The INRIA dataset contains a relatively small number of well-separated pedestrians as it is designed to measure the effectiveness of a detector. We use 288 images in the test set for evaluation. For the PETS 2009 dataset, we use the walking sequence (S1.L1) of 190 frames and the dataset contains at most 33 people in a frame. This sequence results in a significant number of overlaps between people because the set is originally designed for the pedestrian density estimation. The height of a pedestrian on the image coordinate gradually decreases to half of the maximum height as a pedestrian moves from the lower right corner to the upper left corner of the image. To reliably detect small pedestrians at the upper left corner, we have resized each image from 768×576 pixels to 1440×1080 pixels in all experiments. We have randomly selected 50 frames from another sequence with the same viewpoint for learning parameters. The EPFL Terrace dataset has 5,010 frames at a frame rate of 25 fps and there are at most seven people in a frame. We use every 25th frame from Sequence-1 of Camera-3, resulting in a total of 201 frames for evaluation. It is recorded from a relatively short distance, therefore, sometimes the height of a person is taller than the height of the image.

---

[1] http://cpslab.snu.ac.kr/software.

To measure detection performance, we compare the results from each evaluated algorithm to the ground truths. Let d_e be the detection reported by an algorithm and d_g be the ground truth detection. Each detection d_e is declared as a true positive when d_e satisfies the PASCAL 2012 detection criteria [22]. Since multiple detections on a single object should be false positives except one, we run the Hungarian algorithm using area ratios as costs to find the best matching between detections and ground truths.

4.2 Evaluation Results

The quantitative detection performance of the proposed algorithm is reported in Table 1 and Fig. 7. It contains results of three detectors: DPM [6], ACF [11], and faster R-CNN [12], using the original source codes. For fair comparisons, we apply NMS using [22] to define neighboring detections for all detectors. The results show that the proposed algorithm performs favorably against NMS for all detectors and datasets. The improvement of the detection accuracy is most

Table 1. Pedestrian detection results. We report results by setting a false positive per image (FPPI) to 0.1. (TP = number of true positives, FP = number of false positives, FN = number of false negatives, Accuracy = TP/(TP + FP + FN), and Precision = TP/(TP + FP).)

		DPM + NMS	DPM + DPP	ACF + NMS	ACF + DPP	RCNN + NMS	RCNN + DPP
INRIA	TP	409	481	391	475	521	523
	FP	29	29	29	29	29	29
	FN	180	108	198	114	68	66
	Accuracy	66.2	**77.8**	63.3	**76.9**	84.3	**84.6**
	Precision	93.4	**94.3**	93.1	**94.2**	94.7	**94.7**
PETS 2009	TP	1017	1836	633	967	69	137
	FP	19	19	19	19	19	19
	FN	3348	2529	3732	3398	4296	4228
	Accuracy	23.2	**41.9**	14.4	**22.1**	1.6	**3.1**
	Precision	98.2	**99.0**	97.1	**98.1**	78.4	**87.8**
EPFL Terrace	TP	525	579	467	590	580	594
	FP	20	20	20	20	20	20
	FN	192	138	250	127	137	123
	Accuracy	71.2	**78.6**	63.4	**80.1**	78.7	**80.6**
	Precision	96.3	**96.7**	95.9	**96.7**	96.7	**96.7**

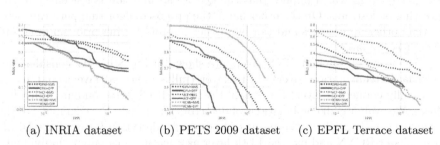

(a) INRIA dataset   (b) PETS 2009 dataset   (c) EPFL Terrace dataset

Fig. 7. Detection error tradeoff curves for different detectors and datasets. The x-axis is false positive per image (FPPI). The lower the curve is better.

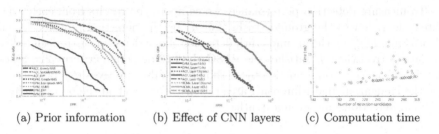

(a) Prior information   (b) Effect of CNN layers   (c) Computation time

Fig. 8. (a) Comparison to greedy NMS, non-greedy NMS, and QUBO, including the effect of the prior information, on the PETS 2009 dataset. (b) The effect of different CNN features. (c) The computation time of the proposed algorithm.

noticeable on the PETS dataset. This is because the problem of selecting a correct set of individual raw detections becomes more important when there are frequent occlusions due to crowded pedestrians. It is also interesting to see that the detection accuracy of the RCNN detector outperforms other detectors on the INRIA dataset while it is less effective on the PETS dataset. This can be explained by noting that the object proposal method tends to generate boxes on a group of overlapping pedestrians instead of boxes on individuals, even when a large number of proposals are used. Note that the proposed algorithm do not use any prior information in (4) for this experiment.

In addition to the basic greedy NMS, which is still used in many state-of-the-art detectors, we also report results from other methods in Fig. 8(a). Instead of [22], the ACF detector often uses a different criteria, $\frac{area(d_g \cap d_e)}{min(area(d_g), area(d_e))} >$ 0.65, for NMS (denoted as the Specialized NMS). Compared to this criteria, the proposed algorithm generates more accurate results. The non-greedy NMS method examines all pairs of detections. In other words, a detection can suppress other detections after being suppressed, whereas in the greedy NMS, a detection can be eliminated before it can suppress other detections. Therefore, non-greedy NMS tends to give a small number of false positives while it is computationally expensive. Nevertheless, the results by the non-greedy NMS are worse than those by optimization based algorithms. The accuracy of QUBO is similar to non-greedy NMS which implies that the QUBO formulation is less effective for detecting pedestrians. On the other hand, the proposed algorithm performs better than other approaches and can be further improved using prior information when it is available.

The effects of different CNN layers are shown in Fig. 8(b). We consider the 13-th layer (convolution layer), 14-th layer (fully-connected layer), and 15-th layer (fully-connected layer) features of the faster R-CNN to compute individualness. We evaluate all combinations of detectors and layers. For example, DPM, Layer14(fc) in Fig. 8(b) is the result of feeding raw detection boxes of the DPM to the faster RCNN and use the 14-th layer as a feature to compute individualness. The results show that the detection accuracy is not sensitive to the selected features from different layers. Feature combinations of two or more layers are not

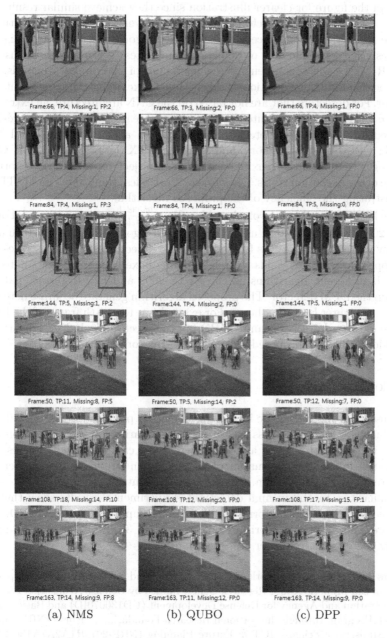

(a) NMS   (b) QUBO   (c) DPP

Fig. 9. Some detection results from the EPFL Terrace and PETS 2009 datasets. A green box is a true positive, a blue box is a false positive, and a red box is a missing detection. (a) Results from the DPM detector using NMS. (b) Results from the DPM detector using QUBO. (c) Results from the DPM detector using DPP. (Color figure online)

shown in the figure for clearer illustration since they achieve similar results. We use the 4,096-dimensional vector from the 14-th layer as the diversity feature ϕ.

The run time performance of the proposed algorithm is shown in Fig. 8(c) with respect to the number of detection candidates in the scene. We use the faster R-CNN code which generates a maximum of 300 object proposals. The run time includes the execution of Algorithm 1, excluding the time spent by a detector. For detectors that are not based on the CNN architecture, an extra time of 248 ms is needed to compute the convolutional features (image patch resizing and feed forward) of 300 detection candidates on a machine with Intel Xeon 2.3 GHz CPU, 128 GB memory, and GeForce GTX Titan X D5 12 GB GPU. For images that have the maximum number of object proposals, we report the average of the execution times. On average, it takes less than 30 ms on MATLAB, demonstrating the efficiency of the proposed algorithm.

The localization accuracy of a bounding box, $\frac{|d_e \cap d_g|}{|d_e|}$, is also measured. For the PETS 2009 dataset, it is 0.81 using the proposed algorithm, while it is 0.76 using NMS by averaging the results from all matched detections. It demonstrates that the proposed algorithm yields tighter bounding boxes. Figure 9 shows detection results by different algorithms on the PETS 2009 and EPFL Terrace datasets based on the DPM detector. The proposed algorithm generate accurate detection results and tighter bounding boxes. For example, at the 84-th frame of the EPFL Terrace dataset, both NMS and QUBO fail to detect an occluded pedestrian in the middle while the proposed algorithm returns correct detections.

5   Conclusions

We present an algorithm for improving detection performance by introducing individualness. Individualness measures the similarity between detection candidates while the objectness aims to generate the candidates with scores. The appearance and spatial information of each detection candidate are considered to compute individualness. Then, a determinantal point process combines the score and similarities to obtain final detections. Experimental results show that the proposed algorithm outperforms non-maximum suppression and QUBO. Furthermore, the proposed algorithm takes less than 30 ms to process an image with 300 detections from over 30 pedestrians.

Acknowledgements. The work of D. Lee, G. Cha, and S. Oh is supported in part by a grant to Bio-Mimetic Robot Research Center funded by Defense Acquisition Program Administration and Agency for Defense Development (UD130070ID) and Basic Science Research Program through the National Research Foundation of Korea (NRF) funded by the Ministry of Science, ICT & Future Planning (NRF-2015R1A2A1A15052493). The work of M.-H. Yang is supported in part by the NSF CAREER grant #1149783, and gifts from Adobe and Nvidia.

References

1. Andriluka, M., Roth, S., Schiele, B.: People-tracking-by-detection and people-detection-by-tracking. In: Proceeding of the IEEE Computer Vision and Pattern Recognition (2008)
2. Li, L.J., Socher, R., Fei-Fei, L.: Towards total scene understanding: classification, annotation and segmentation in an automatic framework. In: Proceeding of the IEEE Computer Vision and Pattern Recognition (2009)
3. Yao, B., Jiang, X., Khosla, A., Lin, A.L., Guibas, L., Fei-Fei, L.: Human action recognition by learning bases of action attributes and parts. In: Proceeding of the IEEE International Conference on Computer Vision (2011)
4. Viola, P., Jones, M.: Rapid object detection using a boosted cascade of simple features. In: Proceeding of the IEEE Computer Vision and Pattern Recognition (2001)
5. Dalal, N., Triggs, B.: Histograms of oriented gradients for human detection. In: Proceeding of the IEEE Computer Vision and Pattern Recognition (2005)
6. Felzenszwalb, P.F., Girshick, R.B., McAllester, D., Ramanan, D.: Object detection with discriminatively trained part-based models. IEEE Trans. Pattern Anal. Mach. Intell. $32(9)$, 1627–1645 (2010)
7. Girshick, R., Donahue, J., Darrell, T., Malik, J.: Rich feature hierarchies for accurate object detection and semantic segmentation. In: Proceeding of the IEEE Computer Vision and Pattern Recognition (2014)
8. Kulesza, A., Taskar, B.: Determinantal point processes for machine learning. arXiv preprint arXiv:1207.6083 (2012)
9. Ferryman, J., Shahrokni, A.: PETS2009: dataset and challenge. In: Winter-PETS (2009)
10. Fleuret, F., Berclaz, J., Lengagne, R., Fua, P.: Multicamera people tracking with a probabilistic occupancy map. IEEE Trans. Pattern Anal. Mach. Intell. $30(2)$, 267–282 (2008)
11. Dollár, P., Appel, R., Belongie, S., Perona, P.: Fast feature pyramids for object detection. IEEE Trans. Pattern Anal. Mach. Intell. $36(8)$, 1532–1545 (2014)
12. Ren, S., He, K., Girshick, R., Sun, J.: Faster R-CNN: towards real-time object detection with region proposal networks. In: Advances in Neural Information Processing Systems, pp. 91–99 (2015)
13. Liu, S., Lu, C., Jia, J.: Box aggregation for proposal decimation: last mile of object detection. In: Proceeding of the IEEE International Conference on Computer Vision, pp. 2569–2577 (2015)
14. Wan, L., Eigen, D., Fergus, R.: End-to-end integration of a convolution network, deformable parts model and non-maximum suppression. In: Proceeding of the IEEE Conference on Computer Vision and Pattern Recognition, pp. 851–859 (2015)
15. Rujikietgumjorn, S., Collins, R.T.: Optimized pedestrian detection for multiple and occluded people. In: Proceeding of the IEEE Computer Vision and Pattern Recognition (2013)
16. Rothe, R., Guillaumin, M., Gool, L.V.: Non-maximum suppression for object detection by passing messages between windows. In: Proceeding of the IEEE Asian Conference on Computer Vision (2014)
17. Çivril, A., Magdon-Ismail, M.: On selecting a maximum volume sub-matrix of a matrix and related problems. Theoret. Comput. Sci. $410(47)$, 4801–4811 (2009)
18. Meinshausen, N., Bickel, P., Rice, J.: Efficient blind search: optimal power of detection under computational cost constraints. Ann. Appl. Stat. 38–60 (2009)

19. Kulesza, A., Taskar, B.: Structured determinantal point processes. In: Advances in neural information processing systems, pp. 1171–1179 (2010)
20. Schur, J.: Bemerkungen zur theorie der beschränkten bilinearformen mit unendlich vielen veränderlichen. J. 1 für die reine und Angewandte Mathematik **140**, 1–28 (1911)
21. Gillenwater, J., Kulesza, A., Taskar, B.: Near-optimal MAP inference for determinantal point processes. In: Advances in Neural Information Processing Systems (2012)
22. Everingham, M., Gool, L.V., Williams, C.K.I., Winn, J., Zisserman, A.: The PASCAL visual object classes challenge 2012 (VOC2012) results (2012)

3D

Real-Time 3D Reconstruction and 6-DoF Tracking with an Event Camera

Hanme Kim$^{(\boxtimes)}$, Stefan Leutenegger, and Andrew J. Davison

Department of Computing, Imperial College London, London, UK
{hanme.kim,s.leutenegger,a.davison}@imperial.ac.uk

Abstract. We propose a method which can perform real-time 3D reconstruction from a single hand-held event camera with no additional sensing, and works in unstructured scenes of which it has no prior knowledge. It is based on three decoupled probabilistic filters, each estimating 6-DoF camera motion, scene logarithmic (log) intensity gradient and scene inverse depth relative to a keyframe, and we build a real-time graph of these to track and model over an extended local workspace. We also upgrade the gradient estimate for each keyframe into an intensity image, allowing us to recover a real-time video-like intensity sequence with spatial and temporal super-resolution from the low bit-rate input event stream. To the best of our knowledge, this is the first algorithm provably able to track a general 6D motion along with reconstruction of arbitrary structure including its intensity and the reconstruction of grayscale video that exclusively relies on event camera data.

Keywords: 6-DoF tracking · 3D reconstruction · Intensity reconstruction · Visual odometry · SLAM · Event-based camera

1 Introduction

Event cameras offer a breakthrough new paradigm for real-time vision, with potential in robotics, wearable devices and autonomous vehicles, but it has proven very challenging to use them in most standard computer vision problems. Inspired by the superior properties of human vision [2], an event camera records not image frames but an asynchronous sequence of per-pixel intensity changes, each with a precise timestamp. While this data stream efficiently encodes image dynamics with extremely high dynamic range and temporal contrast, the lack of synchronous intensity information means that it is not possible to apply much of the standard computer vision toolbox of techniques. In particular, the multi-view correspondence information which is essential to estimate motion and structure is difficult to obtain because each event by itself carries little information and no signature suitable for reliable matching.

Approaches aiming at simultaneous camera motion and scene structure estimation therefore need also to jointly estimate the intensity appearance of the scene, or at least a highly descriptive function of this such as a gradient map.

© Springer International Publishing AG 2016
B. Leibe et al. (Eds.): ECCV 2016, Part VI, LNCS 9910, pp. 349–364, 2016.
DOI: 10.1007/978-3-319-46466-4_21

So far, this has only been successfully achieved in the reduced case of pure camera rotation, where the scene reconstruction takes the form of a panorama image.

In this paper we present the first algorithm which performs joint estimation of 3D scene structure, 6-DoF camera motion and up to scale scene intensity from a single hand-held event camera moved in front of an unstructured static scene. Our approach runs in real-time on a standard PC. The core of our method is three interleaved probabilistic filters, each estimating one unknown aspect of this challenging Simultaneous Localisation and Mapping (SLAM) problem: camera motion, scene log intensity gradient and scene inverse depth. From pure event input our algorithm generates various outputs including a real-time, high bandwidth 6-DoF camera track, scene depth map for one or multiple linked keyframes, and a high dynamic range reconstructed video sequence at a user-chosen frame-rate.

1.1 Event-Based Cameras

The event camera or silicon retina is gradually becoming more widely known by researchers in computer vision, robotics and related fields, in particular since the release as a commercial device for researchers of the Dynamic Vision Sensor (DVS) [14] shown in Fig. 1(c). The pixels of this device asynchronously report log intensity changes of a pre-set threshold size as a stream of asynchronous events, each with pixel location, polarity, and microsecond-precise timestamp. Figure 1 visualises some of the main properties of the event stream; in particular the almost continuous response to very rapid motion and the way that the output data-rate depends on scene motion, though in practice almost always dramatically lower than that of standard video. These properties offer the potential to overcome the limitations of real-world computer vision applications, relying on conventional imaging sensors, such as high latency, low dynamic range, and high power consumption.

Recently, cameras have been developed that interleave event data with conventional intensity frames (DAVIS [3]), or per-event intensity measurement (ATIS [21]). Our framework could be extended to make use of these image measurements this would surely make joint estimation easier. However, in a persistently dynamic motion, they may not be useful. Also, they partially break the appeal and optimal information efficiency of a pure event-based data stream. We therefore believe that first solving the hardest problem of not relying on standard image frames will be useful on its own and provides the insights to make best use of additional measurements if they are available.

1.2 Related Work

Early published work using event cameras focused on tracking moving objects from a fixed point of view, successfully showing the superior high speed measurement and low latency properties [6,8]. However, work on tracking and reconstruction of more general, previously unknown scenes with a freely moving event camera, which we believe is the best place to take full advantage of its remarkable

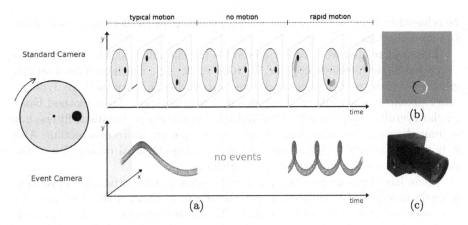

Fig. 1. Event-based camera: (a): in contrast to standard video frames shown in the upper graph, a stream of events from an event camera, plotted in the lower graph, offers no redundant data output, only informative pixels or no events at all. Red and blue dots represent positive and negative events respectively (this figure was recreated inspired by the associated animation of [19]: https://youtu.be/LauQ6LWTkxM?t=35s). (b): image-like visualisation by accumulating events within a time interval — white and black pixels represent positive and negative events respectively. (c): the first commercial event camera, DVS128, from iniLabs Ltd. (Color figure online)

properties, has been limited. The clear difficulty is that most methods normally used in tracking and mapping, such as feature detection and matching or whole image alignment, cannot be directly applied to its fundamentally different visual measurement stream.

Cook et al. [7] proposed an interacting network which interprets a stream of events to recover different visual estimate 'maps' of scenes such as intensity, gradient and optical flow while estimating global rotating camera motion. More recently, Bardow et al. [1] presented an optical flow and intensity estimation using an event camera which allows any camera motion as well as dynamic scenes.

An early 2D SLAM method was proposed by Weikersdorfer et al. [24] which tracks a ground robot pose while reconstructing a planar ceiling map with an upward looking DVS camera. Mueggler et al. [19] presented an onboard 6-DoF localisation flying robot system which is able to track its relative pose to a known target even at very high speed. To investigate whether current techniques can be applied to a large scale visual SLAM problem, Milford et al. [16] presented a simple visual odometry system using a DVS camera with loop closure built on top of the SeqSLAM algorithm using events accumulated into frames [17].

In a much more constrained and hardware-dependent setup, Schraml et al. [22] developed a special 360° rotating camera that consists of a pair of dynamic vision line sensors which creates 3D panoramic scenes aided by its embedded encoders and stereo event streams. Combined with an active projector, Matsuda et al. [15] showed that high quality 3D object reconstruction can be achievable which is better than for laser scanners or RGB-D cameras in some specific situations.

The most related work to our method is the simplified SLAM system based on probabilistic filtering proposed by Kim *et al.* [12], which estimates spatial gradients which are then integrated to reconstruct high quality and high dynamic range planar scenes while tracking global camera rotation. Their method has a similar overall concept to ours with multiple interacting probabilistic filters, but is limited to pure rotation camera motion and panorama reconstruction. Also it is not completely real-time because of the computational complexity of the particle filter used in their tracking algorithm.

There have been no previous published results on estimating 3D depth from a single moving event camera. Most researchers working with event cameras have assumed that this problem is too difficult, and attempts at 3D estimation have combined an event camera with other sensors: a standard frame-based CMOS camera [5], or an RGB-D camera [23]. These are, of course, possible practical ways of using an event camera for solving SLAM problems. However, we believe that resorting to standard sensors discards many of the advantages of processing the efficient and data-rick pure event stream, as well as introducing extra complication including synchronisation and calibration problems to be solved. One very interesting approach if the application permits is to combine two event cameras in a stereo setup [4]. The nicest part of that method is the way that stereo matching of events can be achieved based on coherent timestamps.

Our work in this paper was inspired by a strong belief that depth estimation from a single moving event camera must be possible, because if the device is working correctly and recording all pixel-wise intensity changes then all of the information present in a standard video stream must be available in principle, at least up to scale. In fact, the high temporal contrast and dynamic range of event pixels means that much more information should be present in an event stream than in standard video at the same resolution. In particular, the results of Kim *et al.* [12] on sub-pixel tracking and super-resolution mosaic reconstruction from events gave a strong indication that the accurate multi-view correspondence needed for depth estimation is possible. The essential insight to extending Kim *et al.*'s approach towards getting depth from events is that once the camera starts to translate, if two pixels have the same intensity gradient, the one which is closer to the camera move past the camera faster and therefore emit more events than the farther one. This is the essential mechanism built into our probabilistic filter for inverse depth.

2   Method

Following many recent successful SLAM systems such as PTAM [13], DTAM [20], and LSD-SLAM [10], which separate the tracking and mapping components based on the assumption that the current estimate from one component is accurate enough to lock for the purposes of estimating the other, the basic structure of our approach relies on three interleaved probabilistic filters. One tracks the global 6-DoF camera motion; the second estimates the log intensity gradients in a keyframe image — a representation which is also in parallel upgraded into a full image-like intensity map. Finally the third filter estimates the inverse depths of a keyframe. It should be noted that we essentially separate the mapping part into two, i.e. the gradient and inverse depth estimations, considering fewer number of events caused by parallax while almost all events carry gradient information. We also build a textured semi-dense 3D point cloud from selected keyframes with their associated reconstructed intensity and inverse depth estimate. We do not use an explicit bootstrapping method as we have found that, starting from scratch, alternating estimation very often lead to convergence.

2.1 Preliminaries

We denote an event as $\mathbf{e}(u, v) = (u, v, p, t)^{\top}$ where u and v are pixel location, p is polarity and t is microsecond-precise timestamp — our event-based camera has the fixed pre-calibrated intrinsic matrix K and all event pixel locations are pre-warped to remove radial distortion. We also define two important time intervals τ and τ_c, as in [12], which are the time elapsed since the most recent previous event from *any pixel* and at *the same pixel* respectively.

2.2 Event-Based Camera 6-DoF Tracking

We use an Extended Kalman Filter (EKF) to estimate the global 6-DoF camera motion over time with its state $\mathbf{x} \in \mathbb{R}^6$, which is a minimal representation of the camera pose c with respect to the world frame of reference w, and covariance matrix $\mathsf{P_x} \in \mathbb{R}^{6 \times 6}$. The state vector is mapped to a member of the Lie group $\mathbf{SE}(3)$, the set of 3D rigid body transformations, by the matrix exponential map:

$$\mathsf{T}_{wc} = \exp\left(\sum_{i=1}^{6} \mathbf{x}_i \mathsf{G}_i\right) = \begin{pmatrix} \mathsf{R}_{wc} & \mathbf{t}_w \\ \mathbf{0}^{\top} & 1 \end{pmatrix}, \tag{1}$$

where G is the Lie group generator for $\mathbf{SE}(3)$, $\mathsf{R}_{wc} \in \mathbf{SO}(3)$, and $\mathbf{t}_w \in \mathbb{R}^3$. The basic idea is to find (assuming that the current log intensity and inverse depth estimates are correct) the camera pose which best predicts a log intensity change consistent with the event just received, as shown in Fig. 2(a).

Motion Prediction. We use a 6-DoF (translation and rotation) constant position motion model for motion prediction; the variance of the prediction is proportional to the time interval:

$$\mathbf{x}^{(t|t-\tau)} = \mathbf{x}^{(t-\tau|t-\tau)} + \mathbf{n}, \tag{2}$$

$$\mathsf{P_x}^{(t|t-\tau)} = \mathsf{P}_{\mathbf{x}}^{(t-\tau|t-\tau)} + \mathsf{P_n}, \tag{3}$$

where each component of $\mathbf{n}$ is independent Gaussian noise in all six axes i.e. $\mathbf{n}_i \sim \mathcal{N}(0, \sigma_i^2 \tau)$, and $\mathsf{P_n} = \mathrm{diag}(\sigma_1^2 \tau, \ldots, \sigma_6^2 \tau)$.

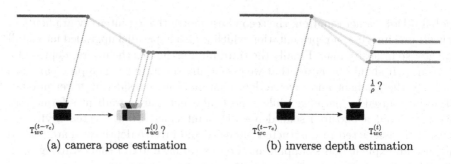

(a) camera pose estimation   (b) inverse depth estimation

Fig. 2. Camera pose and inverse depth estimation. (a): based on the assumption that the current log intensity estimate (shown as the colour of the solid line) and inverse depth estimate (shown as the geometry of the solid line) are correct, we find current camera pose $\mathbf{T}_{wc}^{(t)}$ most consistent with the predicted log intensity change since the previous event at the same pixel at pose $\mathbf{T}_{wc}^{(t-\tau_c)}$ compared to the current event polarity. (b): similarly for inverse depth estimation, we assume that the current reconstructed log intensity and camera pose estimate are correct, and find the most probable inverse depth consistent with the new event measurement. (Color figure online)

Measurement Update. We calculate the value of a measurement $z_{\mathbf{x}}$ given an event $\mathbf{e}(u, v)$, the current keyframe pose $\mathbf{T}_{wk}$, the current camera pose estimate $\mathbf{T}_{wc}^{(t)}$, the previous pose estimate $\mathbf{T}_{wc}^{(t-\tau_c)}$, where the previous event was received at *the same pixel*, and a reconstructed image-like log intensity keyframe with inverse depth by taking a log intensity difference between two corresponding ray-triangle intersection points, $\mathbf{p}_w^{(t)}$ and $\mathbf{p}_w^{(t-\tau_c)}$, as shown in Fig. 3:

$$z_{\mathbf{x}} = \pm C \,, \tag{4}$$

$$h_{\mathbf{x}}(\mathbf{x}^{(t|t-\tau)}) = \mathbf{I}_l\left(\mathbf{p}_w^{(t)}\right) - \mathbf{I}_l\left(\mathbf{p}_w^{(t-\tau_c)}\right) \,, \tag{5}$$

$$\text{where } \mathbf{I}_l(\mathbf{p}_w) = (1 - a - b)\mathbf{I}_l(\mathbf{v}_0) + a\mathbf{I}_l(\mathbf{v}_1) + b\mathbf{I}_l(\mathbf{v}_2) \,. \tag{6}$$

Here $\pm C$ is a known event threshold — its sign is decided by the polarity of an event. $\mathbf{I}_l$ is a log intensity value based on a reconstructed log intensity keyframe, and $\mathbf{v}_0$, $\mathbf{v}_1$, and $\mathbf{v}_2$ are three vertices of an intersected triangle. To obtain a corresponding 3D point location $\mathbf{p}_w$ in the world frame of reference, we use ray-triangle intersection [18] which yields a vector $(l, a, b)^{\top}$ where l is the distance to the triangle from the origin of the ray and a, b are the barycentric coordinates of the intersected point which is then used to calculate an interpolated log intensity.

In the EKF framework, the camera pose estimate and its uncertainty covariance matrix are updated by the standard equations at every event using:

$$\mathbf{x}^{(t|t)} = \mathbf{x}^{(t|t-\tau)} + \mathbf{W}_{\mathbf{x}}\nu_{\mathbf{x}} \,, \tag{7}$$

$$\mathbf{P}_{\mathbf{x}}^{(t|t)} = \left(\mathbf{I}_{6\times6} - \mathbf{W}_{\mathbf{x}}\frac{\partial h_{\mathbf{x}}}{\partial \mathbf{x}^{(t|t-\tau)}}\right)\mathbf{P}_{\mathbf{x}}^{(t|t-\tau)} \,, \tag{8}$$

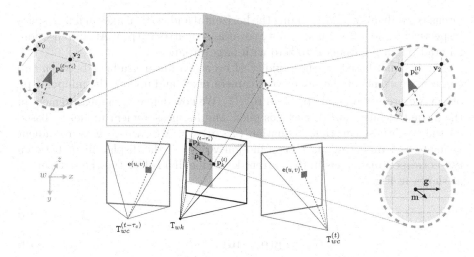

Fig. 3. Basic geometry for; **tracking** and **inverse depth estimation**: we find two corresponding ray-triangle intersection points, $\mathbf{p}_w^{(t)}$ and $\mathbf{p}_w^{(t-\tau_c)}$, in the world frame of reference using a ray-triangle intersection method [18] to compute the value of a measurement — a log intensity difference between two points given an event $\mathbf{e}(u,v)$, the current keyframe pose $\mathbf{T}_{wk}$, the current camera pose estimate $\mathbf{T}_{wc}^{(t)}$, the previous pose estimate $\mathbf{T}_{wc}^{(t-\tau_c)}$, the reconstructed log intensity and inverse depth keyframe, **gradient estimation**: we project two intersection points onto the current keyframe, $\mathbf{p}_k^{(t)}$ and $\mathbf{p}_k^{(t-\tau_c)}$, to find a displacement vector between them, which is then used to calculate a motion vector $\mathbf{m}$ to compute the value of a measurement $(\mathbf{g} \cdot \mathbf{m})$ at a midpoint $\hat{\mathbf{p}}_k$ based on the brightness constancy and the linear gradient assumption.

where the innovation $\nu_{\mathbf{x}}$ and Kalman gain $\mathbf{W}_{\mathbf{x}}$ are defined by the standard EKF definitions. The measurement uncertainty is a scalar variance $\sigma_{\mathbf{x}}^2$, and we omit the Jacobian $\frac{\partial h_{\mathbf{x}}}{\partial \mathbf{x}^{(t|t-\tau)}}$ derivation due to the space limitation.

2.3 Gradient Estimation and Log Intensity Reconstruction

We now use the updated camera pose estimate to incrementally improve the estimates of the log intensity gradient at each keyframe pixel based on a pixel-wise EKF. However, because of the random walk nature of our tracker which generates a noisy motion estimate, we first apply a weighted average filter to the new camera pose estimate. To reconstruct super resolution scenes by harnessing the very high speed measurement property of the event camera, we use a higher resolution for keyframes than for the low resolution sensor. This method is similar to the one in [12], but we model the measurement noise properly to get better gradient estimate, and use a parallelisable reconstruction method for speed.

Pixel-Wise EKF Based Gradient Estimation. Each pixel of the keyframe holds an independent gradient estimate $\mathbf{g}(\mathbf{p}_k) = (g_u, g_v)^\top$, consisting of log intensity gradients g_u and g_v along the horizontal and vertical axes in image space respectively, and a 2×2 uncertainty covariance matrix $\mathbf{P_g}(\mathbf{p}_k)$. At initialisation, all gradients are initialised to zero with large variances.

We assume, based on the rapidity of events, a linear gradient between two consecutive events at the same event camera pixel, and update the midpoint $\hat{\mathbf{p}}_k$ of the two projected points $\mathbf{p}_k^{(t)}$ and $\mathbf{p}_k^{(t-\tau_c)}$. We now define $z_\mathbf{g}$, a measurement of the instantaneous *event rate* at this pixel, and its measurement model $h_\mathbf{g}$ based on the brightness constancy equation $(\mathbf{g} \cdot \mathbf{m})\tau_c = \pm C$, where $\mathbf{g}$ is a gradient estimate and $\mathbf{m} = (m_u, m_v)^\top$ is a motion vector — the displacement between two corresponding pixels in the current keyframe divided by the elapsed time τ_c as shown in Fig. 3:

$$z_\mathbf{g} = \pm \frac{C}{\tau_c} \,, \tag{9}$$

$$h_\mathbf{g} = (\mathbf{g}(\hat{\mathbf{p}}_k) \cdot \mathbf{m}) \,, \tag{10}$$

$$\text{where} \quad \mathbf{m} = \frac{\mathbf{p}_k^{(t)} - \mathbf{p}_k^{(t-\tau_c)}}{\tau_c} \,. \tag{11}$$

The current gradient estimate and its uncertainty covariance matrix at that pixel are updated independently in the same way as in the measurement update of our tracker following the standard EKF equations.

The Jacobian $\frac{\partial h_\mathbf{g}}{\partial \mathbf{g}(\hat{\mathbf{p}}_k)^{(t-\tau_c)}}$ of the measurement function with respect to changes in gradient is simply (m_u, m_v), and the measurement noise $\mathbf{N_g}$ is:

$$\mathbf{N_g} = \frac{\partial z_\mathbf{g}}{\partial C} P_C \left(\frac{\partial z_\mathbf{g}}{\partial C} \right)^\top = \frac{\sigma_C^2}{\tau_c^2} \,, \tag{12}$$

where σ_C^2 is the sensor noise with respect to the event threshold.

Log Intensity Reconstruction. Along with the pixel-wise EKF based gradient estimation method, we perform interleaved absolute log intensity reconstruction running on a GPU. We define our convex minimisation function as:

$$\min_{I_l} \left\{ \int_\Omega \|\mathbf{g}(\mathbf{p}_k) - \nabla I_l(\mathbf{p}_k)\|_{\epsilon_d}^h + \lambda \|\nabla I_l(\mathbf{p}_k)\|_{\epsilon_r}^h \, d\mathbf{p}_k \right\} \,. \tag{13}$$

Here the data term represents the error between estimated gradients $\mathbf{g}(\mathbf{p}_k)$ and those of a reconstructed log intensity $\nabla I_l(\mathbf{p}_k)$, and the regularisation term enforces smoothness, both under a robust Huber norm. This function can be written using the Legendre Fenchel transformation [11] as follows:

$$\min_{I_l} \max_{\mathbf{q}} \max_{\mathbf{p}} \{ \langle \mathbf{p}, \mathbf{g} - \nabla I_l \rangle - \frac{\epsilon_d}{2} \|\mathbf{p}\|^2 - \delta_\mathbf{p}(\mathbf{p})$$

$$+ \langle \mathbf{q}, \nabla I_l \rangle - \frac{\epsilon_r}{2\lambda} \|\mathbf{q}\|^2 - \delta_\mathbf{q}(\mathbf{q}) \} \,, \tag{14}$$

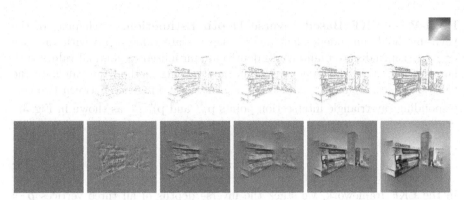

Fig. 4. Typical temporal progression (left to right) of gradient estimation and log intensity reconstruction as a hand-held camera browses a 3D scene. The colours and intensities on the top row represent the orientations and strengths of the gradients of the scene (refer to the colour chart in the top right). In the bottom row, we see these gradient estimates upgraded to reconstructed intensity images. (Color figure online)

where we can solve by maximising with respect to $\mathbf{p}$:

$$\mathbf{p}^{(n+1)} = \frac{\frac{\mathbf{p}^{(n)}+\sigma_{\mathbf{p}}(\mathbf{g}-\nabla I_l)}{1+\sigma_{\mathbf{p}}\epsilon_d}}{\max\left(1, \left|\frac{\mathbf{p}^{(n)}+\sigma_{\mathbf{p}}(\mathbf{g}-\nabla I_l)}{1+\sigma_{\mathbf{p}}\epsilon_d}\right|\right)}, \tag{15}$$

maximising with respect to $\mathbf{q}$:

$$\mathbf{q}^{(n+1)} = \frac{\frac{\mathbf{q}^{(n)}+\sigma_{\mathbf{q}}\nabla I_l}{1+\frac{\sigma_{\mathbf{q}}\epsilon_r}{\lambda}}}{\max\left(1, \frac{1}{\lambda}\left|\frac{\mathbf{q}^{(n)}+\sigma_{\mathbf{q}}\nabla I_l}{1+\frac{\sigma_{\mathbf{q}}\epsilon_r}{\lambda}}\right|\right)}, \tag{16}$$

and minimising with respect to I_l:

$$I_l^{(n+1)} = I_l^{(n)} - \sigma_{I_l}(\operatorname{div}\mathbf{p}^{(n+1)} - \operatorname{div}\mathbf{q}^{(n+1)}). \tag{17}$$

We visualise the progress of gradient estimation and log intensity reconstruction over time during hand-held event camera motion in Fig. 4.

2.4 Inverse Depth Estimation and Regularisation

We now use the same camera pose estimate as in the gradient estimation and a reconstructed log intensity keyframe to incrementally improve the estimates of the inverse depth at each keyframe pixel based on another pixel-wise EKF. As in camera pose estimation, assuming that the current camera pose estimate and reconstructed log intensity are correct, we aim to update the inverse depth estimate to best predict the log intensity change consistent with the current event polarity as shown in Fig. 2(b).

Pixel-Wise EKF Based Inverse Depth Estimation. Each pixel of the keyframe holds an independent inverse depth state value $\rho(\mathbf{p}_k)$ with variance $\sigma^2_{\rho(\mathbf{p}_k)}$. At initialisation, all inverse depths are initialised to nominal values with large variances. In the same way as in our tracking method, we calculate the value of a measurement z_ρ which is a log intensity difference between two corresponding ray-triangle intersection points $\mathbf{p}_w^{(t)}$ and $\mathbf{p}_w^{(t-\tau_c)}$ as shown in Fig. 3:

$$z_\rho = \pm C \ , \tag{18}$$

$$h_\rho = \mathbf{I}_l \left(\mathbf{p}_w^{(t)} \right) - \mathbf{I}_l \left(\mathbf{p}_w^{(t-\tau_c)} \right) \ . \tag{19}$$

In the EKF framework, we stack the inverse depths of all three vertices $\rho = (\rho_{\mathbf{v}_0}, \rho_{\mathbf{v}_1}, \rho_{\mathbf{v}_2})^\top$ which contribute to the intersected 3D point and update them with their associated 3×3 uncertainty covariance matrix at every event in the same way of the measurement update of our tracker following the standard EKF equations. The measurement noise $\mathbf{N}_\rho$ is a scalar variance σ^2_ρ, and we omit the Jacobian $\frac{\partial h_\rho}{\partial \rho^{(t-\tau_c)}}$ derivation due to the space limitation.

Inverse Depth Regularisation. As a background process running on a GPU, we perform inverse depth regularisation on keyframe pixels with high confidence inverse depth estimate whenever there has been a large change in the estimates. We penalise deviation from a spatially smooth inverse depth map by assigning each inverse depth value the average of its neighbours, weighted by their respective inverse variances as described in [9]. If two adjacent inverse depths are different more than 2σ, they do not contribute to each other to preserve discontinuities due to occlusion boundaries. We visualise the progress of inverse depth estimation and regularisation over time as event data is captured during hand-held event camera motion in Fig. 5.

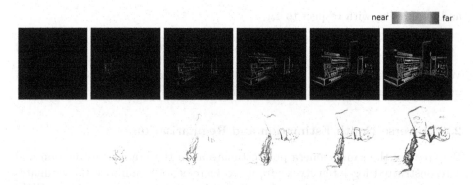

Fig. 5. Typical temporal progression (left to right) of inverse depth estimation and regularisation as a hand-held camera browses a 3D scene. The colours on the top row represent the different depths of the scene (refer to the colour chart in the top right and the associated semi-dense 3D point cloud on the bottom row). (Color figure online)

3 Experiments

Our algorithm runs in real-time on a standard PC with typical scenes and motion speed, and we have conducted experiments both indoors and outdoors. We recommend viewing our video[1] which illustrates all of the key results in a better form than still pictures and in real-time.

3.1 Single Keyframe Estimation

We demonstrate the results from our algorithm as it tracks against and reconstructs a single keyframe in a number of different scenes. In Fig. 6, for each scene we show column by column an image-like view of the event streams, estimated gradient map, reconstructed intensity map with super resolution and high dynamic range properties, estimate depth map and semi-dense 3D point cloud. The 3D reconstruction quality is generally good, though we can see that there are sometimes poorer quality depth estimates near to occlusion boundaries and where not enough events have been generated.

3.2 Multiple Keyframes

We evaluated the proposed method on several trajectories which require multiple keyframes to cover. If the camera has moved too far away from the current keyframe, we create a new keyframe from the most recent estimation results and reconstruction. To create a new keyframe, we project all 3D points based on the current keyframe pose and the estimated inverse depth into the current camera pose, and propagate the current estimates and reconstruction only if they have high confidence in inverse depth. Figure 7 shows one of the results in a semi-dense 3D point cloud form constructed based on generated keyframes each consisting of reconstructed super-resolution and high dynamic range intensity and inverse depth map. The bright RGB 3D coordinate axes represent the current camera pose while the darker ones show all keyframe poses generated in this experiment.

3.3 Video Rendering

Using our proposed method, we can turn an event-based camera into a high speed and high dynamic range artificial camera by rendering video frames based on ray-casting as shown in Fig. 8. Here we choose to render at the same low resolution as event-based input.

3.4 High Speed Tracking

We evaluated the proposed method on several trajectories which include rapid motion (e.g. shaking hand). The top graph in Fig. 9 shows the estimated camera pose history, and the two groups of the insets below show an image-like event

---

[1] https://youtu.be/yHLyhdMSw7w.

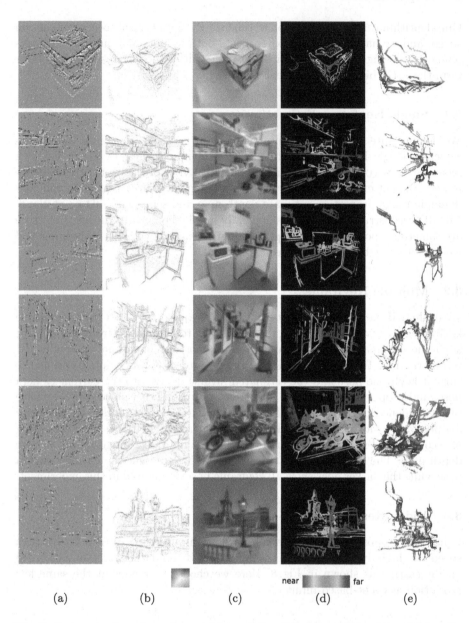

near ■■■■ far

(a)   (b)   (c)   (d)   (e)

Fig. 6. Demonstrations in various settings of the different aspects of our joint estimation algorithm. (a) visualisation of the input event stream; (b) estimated gradient keyframes; (c) reconstructed intensity keyframes with super resolution and high dynamic range properties; (d) estimated depth maps; (e) semi-dense 3D point clouds.

Fig. 7. 3D point cloud of an indoor scene constructed from multiple keyframes, showing keyframe poses with their intensity and depth map estimates. (Color figure online)

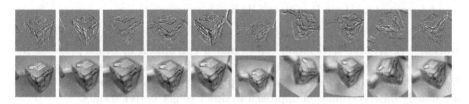

Fig. 8. Our proposed method can render HDR video frames at user-chosen time instances and resolutions by ray-casting the current reconstruction. This is the same scene as in the first row of Fig. 6.

visualisation, a rendered video frame showing the quality of our tracker, and a motion blurred standard camera video frame as a reference of rapid motion. Our current implementation is not able to process this very high event-rate (up to 1 M events per second in this experiment) in real-time, but we believe it is a simple matter of engineering to run at this extremely high rate in real-time in the near future.

3.5 Discussion

Our results so far are qualitative, and we have focused on demonstrating the core novelty of our approach in breaking through to get joint estimation of depth, 6-DoF motion and intensity from pure event data with general motion and unknown general scenes. There are certainly still weakness in our current approach, and while we believe that it is remarkable that our approach of three interleaved filters, each of which operates as if the results of the others are correct, works at all, there is plenty of room for further research. It is clear that the interaction of these estimation processes is key, and in particular that the relatively slow convergence of inverse depth estimates tends to cause poor

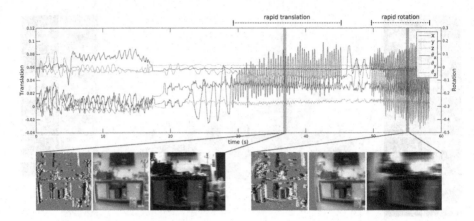

Fig. 9. The top graph shows the estimated camera pose history, and the two groups of the insets below show an image-like event visualisation, a rendered video frame showing the quality of our tracker, and a motion blurred standard camera video frame as a reference of rapid motion (up to 5 Hz in this experiment).

tracking, then data association errors and a corruption of other parts of the estimation process. We will investigate this further, and may need to step back from our current approach of real-time pure event-by-event processing towards a partially batch estimation approach in order to get better results.

4   Conclusions

To the best of our knowledge, this is the first 6-DoF tracking and 3D reconstruction method purely based on a stream of events with no additional sensing, and it runs in real-time on a standard PC. We hope this opens up the door to practical solutions to the current limitations of real-world SLAM applications. It is worth restating that the measurement rate of the event-based camera is on the order of a microsecond, its independent pixel architecture provides very high dynamic range, and the bandwidth of an event stream is much lower than a standard video stream. These superior properties of event-based cameras offer the potential to overcome the limitations of real-world computer vision applications relying on conventional imaging sensors.

Acknowledgements. Hanme Kim was supported by an EPSRC DTA scholarship and the Qualcomm Innovation Fellowship 2014. We thank Jacek Zienkiewicz, Ankur Handa, Patrick Bardow, Edward Johns and other colleagues at Imperial College London for many useful discussions.

References

1. Bardow, P., Davison, A.J., Leutenegger, S.: Simultaneous optical flow and intensity estimation from an event camera. In: Proceedings of the IEEE Conference on Computer Vision and Pattern Recognition (CVPR) (2016)

2. Boahen, K.: Neuromorphic Chips. Scientific American (2005)
3. Brandli, C., Berner, R., Yang, M., Liu, S.C., Delbruck, T.: A 240 × 180 130 dB 3 μs latency global shutter spatiotemporal vision sensor. IEEE J. Solid-State Circ. (JSSC) 49(10), 2333–2341 (2014)
4. Carneiro, J., Ieng, S., Posch, C., Benosman, R.: Event-based 3D reconstruction from neuromorphic retinas. J. Neural Netw. 45, 27–38 (2013)
5. Censi, A., Scaramuzza, D.: Low-latency event-based visual odometry. In: Proceedings of the IEEE International Conference on Robotics and Automation (ICRA) (2014)
6. Conradt, J., Cook, M., Berner, R., Lichtsteiner, P., Douglas, R., Delbruck, T.: A pencil balancing robot using a pair of AER dynamic vision sensors. In: IEEE International Symposium on Circuits and Systems (ISCAS) (2009)
7. Cook, M., Gugelmann, L., Jug, F., Krautz, C., Steger, A.: Interacting maps for fast visual interpretation. In: Proceedings of the International Joint Conference on Neural Networks (IJCNN) (2011)
8. Delbruck, T., Lichtsteiner, P.: Fast sensory motor control based on event-based hybrid neuromorphic-procedural system. In: IEEE International Symposium on Circuits and Systems (ISCAS) (2007)
9. Engel, J., Sturm, J., Cremers, D.: Semi-dense visual odometry for a monocular camera. In: Proceedings of the International Conference on Computer Vision (ICCV) (2013)
10. Engel, J., Schöps, T., Cremers, D.: LSD-SLAM: large-scale direct monocular SLAM. In: Fleet, D., Pajdla, T., Schiele, B., Tuytelaars, T. (eds.) ECCV 2014. LNCS, vol. 8690, pp. 834–849. Springer, Heidelberg (2014). doi:10.1007/978-3-319-10605-2_54
11. Handa, A., Newcombe, R.A., Angeli, A., Davison, A.J.: Applications of the Legendre-Fenchel transformation to computer vision problems. Technical report DTR11-7, Imperial College London (2011)
12. Kim, H., Handa, A., Benosman, R., Ieng, S.H., Davison, A.J.: Simultaneous mosaicing and tracking with an event camera. In: Proceedings of the British Machine Vision Conference (BMVC) (2014)
13. Klein, G., Murray, D.W.: Parallel tracking and mapping for small AR workspaces. In: Proceedings of the International Symposium on Mixed and Augmented Reality (ISMAR) (2007)
14. Lichtsteiner, P., Posch, C., Delbruck, T.: A 128 × 128 120 dB 15 μs latency asynchronous temporal contrast vision sensor. IEEE J. Solid-State Circ. (JSSC) 43(2), 566–576 (2008)
15. Matsuda, N., Cossairt, O., Gupta, M.: MC3D: motion contrast 3D scanning. In: Proceedings of the IEEE International Conference on Computational Photography (ICCP) (2015)
16. Milford, M., Kim, H., Leutenegger, S., Davison, A.J.: Towards visual SLAM with event-based cameras. In: The Problem of Mobile Sensors: Setting Future Goals and Indicators of Progress for SLAM Workshop in Conjunction with Robotics: Science and Systems (RSS) (2015)
17. Milford, M., Kim, H., Mangan, M., Leutenegger, S., Stone, T., Webb, B., Davison, A.J.: Place recognition with event-based cameras and a neural implementation of SeqSLAM. In: The Innovative Sensing for Robotics: Focus on Neuromorphic Sensors Workshop at the IEEE International Conference on Robotics and Automation (ICRA) (2015)
18. Möller, T., Trumbore, B.: Fast, minimum storage ray/triangle intersection. J. Graph. Tools 2(1), 21–28 (1997)

19. Mueggler, E., Huber, B., Scaramuzza, D.: Event-based, 6-DOF pose tracking for high-speed maneuvers. In: Proceedings of the IEEE/RSJ Conference on Intelligent Robots and Systems (IROS) (2014)
20. Newcombe, R.A., Lovegrove, S., Davison, A.J.: DTAM: dense tracking and mapping in real-time. In: Proceedings of the International Conference on Computer Vision (ICCV) (2011)
21. Posch, C., Matolin, D., Wohlgenannt, R.: A QVGA 143 dB dynamic range frame-free PWM image sensor with lossless pixel-level video compression and time-domain CDS. IEEE J. Solid-State Circ. (JSSC) **46**(1), 259–275 (2011)
22. Schraml, S., Belbachir, A.N., Bischof, H.: Event-driven stereo matching for real-time 3D panoramic vision. In: Proceedings of the IEEE Conference on Computer Vision and Pattern Recognition (CVPR) (2015)
23. Weikersdorfer, D., Adrian, D.B., Cremers, D., Conradt, J.: Event-based 3D SLAM with a depth-augmented dynamic vision sensor. In: Proceedings of the IEEE International Conference on Robotics and Automation (ICRA) (2014)
24. Weikersdorfer, D., Hoffmann, R., Conradt, J.: Simultaneous localization and mapping for event-based vision systems. In: International Conference on Computer Vision Systems (ICVS) (2013)

Single Image 3D Interpreter Network

Jiajun Wu[1]([✉]), Tianfan Xue[1],
Joseph J. Lim[1,2], Yuandong Tian[3], Joshua B. Tenenbaum[1],
Antonio Torralba[1], and William T. Freeman[1,4]

[1] Massachusetts Institute of Technology, Cambridge, USA
jiajunwu@mit.edu
[2] Stanford University, Stanford, USA
[3] Facebook AI Research, Menlo Park, USA
[4] Google Research, Cambridge, USA

Abstract. Understanding 3D object structure from a single image is an important but difficult task in computer vision, mostly due to the lack of 3D object annotations in real images. Previous work tackles this problem by either solving an optimization task given 2D keypoint positions, or training on synthetic data with ground truth 3D information.

In this work, we propose 3D INterpreter Network (3D-INN), an end-to-end framework which sequentially estimates 2D keypoint heatmaps and 3D object structure, trained on both real 2D-annotated images and synthetic 3D data. This is made possible mainly by two technical innovations. First, we propose a Projection Layer, which projects estimated 3D structure to 2D space, so that 3D-INN can be trained to predict 3D structural parameters supervised by 2D annotations on real images. Second, heatmaps of keypoints serve as an intermediate representation connecting real and synthetic data, enabling 3D-INN to benefit from the variation and abundance of synthetic 3D objects, without suffering from the difference between the statistics of real and synthesized images due to imperfect rendering. The network achieves state-of-the-art performance on both 2D keypoint estimation and 3D structure recovery. We also show that the recovered 3D information can be used in other vision applications, such as image retrieval.

Keywords: 3D structure · Single image 3D reconstruction · Keypoint estimation · Neural network · Synthetic data

1 Introduction

Deep networks have achieved impressive performance on 1,000-way image classification [19]. However, for any visual system to parse objects in the real world,

---

J. Wu and T. Xue are equal contributions.

Electronic supplementary material The online version of this chapter (doi:10. 1007/978-3-319-46466-4_22) contains supplementary material, which is available to authorized users.

© Springer International Publishing AG 2016
B. Leibe et al. (Eds.): ECCV 2016, Part VI, LNCS 9910, pp. 365–382, 2016.
DOI: 10.1007/978-3-319-46466-4_22

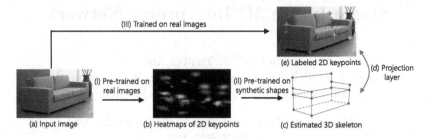

Fig. 1. An abstraction of the proposed 3D INterpreter Network (3D-INN).

it needs not only to assign category labels to objects, but also to interpret their intra-class variation. For example, for a chair, we are interested in its intrinsic properties such as its *style, height*, leg *length*, and seat *width*, and extrinsic properties such as its *pose*.

In this paper, we recover these object properties from a single image by estimating 3D structure. Instead of a 3D mesh or a depth map [2,9,16,18,32,40, 50], we represent an object via a 3D skeleton [47], which consists of keypoints and the connections between them (Fig. 1c). Being a simple abstraction, the skeleton representation preserves the structural properties that we are interested in. In this paper, we assume one pre-defined skeleton model for each object category (*e.g.* chair, sofa, and human).

The main challenge of recovering 3D object structure from a single RGB image is the difficulty in obtaining training images with ground truth 3D geometry, as manually annotating 3D structures of objects in real images is labor-intensive and often inaccurate. Previous methods tackle this problem mostly in two ways. One is to directly recover a 3D skeleton from estimated 2D keypoint locations by minimizing its reprojection error. This method uses no training data in 3D reconstruction, thus it is not robust to noisy keypoint estimation, as shown in experiments (Sect. 4). The other is to train on synthetically rendered images of 3D objects [23,41], where complete 3D structure is available. However, the statistics of synthesized images are often different from those of real images, possibly due to lighting, occlusion, and shape details, making models trained mostly on synthetic data hard to generalize well to real images.

In this paper, we propose 3D INterpreter Network (3D-INN), an end-to-end framework for recovering 3D object skeletons, trained on both real 2D-labeled images and synthetic 3D objects. Our model has two major innovations. First, we introduce a *Projection Layer*, a simple renderer which calculates 2D keypoint projections from a 3D skeleton at the end of the network (Fig. 1d). This enables 3D-INN to predict 3D structural parameters that minimizes the error in the 2D space with labeled real images, without requiring 3D object annotations.

Second, we further observe that training with real images only under a projection layer is not enough due to the fundamental ambiguity in 2D-to-3D mapping. In other words, the algorithm might recover an unnatural 3D geometry whose projection matches the 2D image, because the projection layer only requires the 3D prediction to be plausible in 2D. We therefore incorporate synthetic

3D objects into training data, in order to encode the knowledge of "plausible shapes". To this end, our model is designed to first predict keypoint locations (Fig. 1-I) and then to regress 3D parameters (Fig. 1-II). We pre-train the former part with 2D-annotated real images and the latter part with synthetic 3D data, and then train the joint framework end-to-end with the projection layer (Fig. 1-III). We choose heatmaps of keypoints (Fig. 1b) as an intermediate representation between two components to resolve the domain adaptation issue between real and synthetic data.

Several experiments demonstrate the effectiveness of 3D-INN. First, the proposed network achieves state-of-the-art performance on various keypoint localization datasets (FLIC [35] for human bodies, CUB-200-2011 [51] for birds, and our new dataset, Keypoint-5, for furniture). We then evaluate our network on IKEA [25], a dataset with ground truth 3D object structures and viewpoints. On 3D structure estimation, 3D-INN shows its advantage over a optimization-based method [61] when keypoint estimation is imperfect. On 3D viewpoint estimation, it also performs better than the state-of-the-art [41]. We further evaluate 3D-INN, in combination with detection frameworks [11], on the popular benchmark PASCAL 3D+ [53]. Though our focus is not on pose estimation, 3D-INN achieves results comparable to the state-of-the-art [41,49]. At last, we show qualitatively that 3D-INN has wide vision applications including 3D object retrieval.

Our contributions include (1) introducing an end-to-end 3D INterpreter Network (3D-INN) with a projection layer, which can be trained to predict 3D structural parameters using only 2D-annotated images, (2) using keypoint heatmaps to connect real and synthetic worlds, strengthening the generalization ability of the network, and (3) state-of-the-art performance in 2D keypoint and 3D structure and viewpoint estimation.

2 Related Work

Single image 3D reconstruction.   Previous 3D reconstruction methods mainly used object representations based on depth or meshes, or based on skeletons or pictorial structure. Depth-/mesh-based models can recover detailed 3D object structure from a single image, either by adapting existing 3D models from a database [2,3,8,15,16,36,39,40,59], or by inferring from its detected 2D silhouette [18,32,50].

In this paper, we choose to use a skeleton-based representation, exploiting the power of abstraction. The skeleton model can capture geometric changes of articulated objects [1,47,57], like a human body or the base of a swivel chair. Typically, researchers recovered a 3D skeleton from a single image by minimizing its projection error on the 2D image plane [12,22,27,33,55,62]. Recent work in this line [1,61] demonstrated state-of-the-art performance. In contrast to them, we propose to use neural networks to predict a 3D object skeleton from its 2D keypoints, which is more robust to imperfect detection results and can be jointly learned with keypoint estimators.

Our work also connects to the traditional field of vision as inverse graphics [14,21] and analysis by synthesis [5,20,52,58], as we use neural nets to decode latent 3D structure from images, and use a projection layer for rendering. Their approaches often required supervision for the inferred representations or made over-simplified assumptions of background and occlusion in images. Our 3D-INN learns 3D representation without using 3D supervision, and generalizes to real images well.

2D keypoint estimation. Another line of related work is 2D keypoint estimation. During the past decade, researchers have made significant progress in estimating keypoints on humans [35,56] and other objects [38,51]. Recently, there have been several attempts to apply convolutional neural networks to human keypoint estimation [7,29,44,48], which all achieved significant improvement. Inspired by these work, we use 2D keypoints as our intermediate representation, and aim to recover 3D skeleton from them.

3D viewpoint estimation. 3D viewpoint estimation seeks to estimate the 3D orientation of an object from a single image [53]. Some previous methods formulated it as a classification or regression problem, and aimed to directly estimate the viewpoint from an image [10,41]. Others proposed to estimate 3D viewpoint from detected 2D keypoints or edges in the image [24,49,62]. While the main focus of our work is to estimate 3D object structure, our method can also predict its 3D viewpoint.

Training with synthetic data. Synthetic data are often used to augment the training set [30,37,40]. Su *et al.* [40] attempted to train a 3D viewpoint estimator using a combination of real and synthetic images, while Sun *et al.* [42] and Zhou *et al.* [60] also used a similar strategy for object detection and matching, respectively. Huang *et al.* [16] analyzed the invariance of convolutional neural networks using synthetic images. For image synthesis, Dosovitskiy *et al.* [9] trained a neural network to generate new images using synthetic images.

In this paper, we combine real 2D-annotated images and synthetic 3D data for training 3D-INN to recover a 3D skeleton. We use heatmaps of 2D keypoints, instead of (often imperfectly) rendered images, from synthetic 3D data, so that our algorithm has better generalization ability as the effects of imperfect rendering are minimized. Yasin *et al.* [57] also proposed to use both 2D and 3D data for training, but they uses keypoint location, instead of heatmaps, as the intermediate representation that connects 2D and 3D.

3   Methods

We design a deep convolutional network to recover 3D object structure. The input to the network is a single image with an object of interest at its center, which can be obtained by state-of-the-art object detectors [34]. The output of the network is a 3D object skeleton, including its 2D keypoint locations, 3D structural parameters, and 3D poses (see Fig. 3). In the following, we will describe our 3D skeleton representation (Sect. 3.1), network architecture (Sect. 3.2), and training strategy (Sect. 3.3).

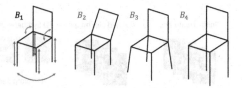

Fig. 2. A simplification of our skeleton model and base shapes for chairs

3.1   3D Skeleton Representation

As discussed in Sect. 1, we use skeletons as our 3D object representation. A skeleton consists of a set of keypoints as well as their connections. For each object category, we manually design a 3D skeleton characterizing its abstract 3D geometry.

There exist intrinsic ambiguities in recovering 3D keypoint locations from a single 2D image. We resolve this issue by assuming that objects can only have constrained deformations [47]. For example, chairs may have various leg lengths, but for a single chair, its four legs are typically of equal length. We model these constraints by formulating 3D keypoint locations as a weighted sum of a set of base shapes [18]. The first base shape is the mean shape of all objects within the category, and the rest define possible deformations and intra-class variations. Figure 2 shows an simplification of our skeleton representation for chairs: the first is the mean shape of chairs, the second controls how the back bends, and the last two are for legs. The weight for each base shape determines how strong the deformation is, and we denote these weights as the *internal parameters* of an object.

Formally, let $\mathcal{Y} \in \mathbb{R}^{3 \times N}$ be a matrix of 3D coordinates of all N keypoints. Our assumption is that the 3D keypoint locations are a weighted sum of base shapes $B_k \in \mathbb{R}^{3 \times N}$, or $\mathcal{Y} = \sum_{k=1}^{K} \alpha_k B_k$, where $\{\alpha_k\}$ is the set of internal parameters of this object and K is the number of base shapes.

Further, let $\mathcal{X} \in \mathbb{R}^{2 \times N}$ be the corresponding 2D coordinates. Then the relationship between the observed 2D coordinates $\mathcal{X}$ and the internal parameters $\{\alpha_k\}$ is

$$\mathcal{X} = P(R\mathcal{Y} + T) = P(R \sum_{k=1}^{K} \alpha_k B_k + T), \tag{1}$$

where $R \in \mathbb{R}^{3 \times 3}$ (rotation) and $T \in \mathbb{R}^3$ (translation) are the external parameters of the camera, and P is a projective transformation. P only depends on the focal length f under the central projection we assuming.

Therefore, to recover the 3D structural information of an object in a 2D image, we only need to estimate its internal parameters ($\{\alpha_k\}$) and the external viewpoint parameters (R, T, and f). In the following section, we discuss how we design a neural network for this task, and how it can be jointly trained with real 2D images and synthetic 3D objects.

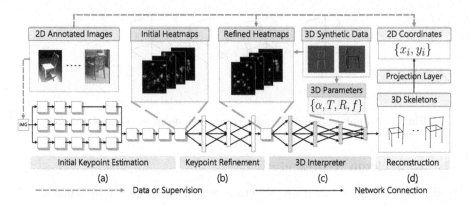

Fig. 3. 3D-INN takes a single image as input and reconstructs the detailed 3D structure of the object in the image (*e.g.*, human, chair, *etc.*). The network is trained independently for each category, and here we use chairs as an example. **(a)** Estimating 2D keypoint heatmaps with a multi-scale CNN. **(b)** Refining keypoint locations by considering the structural constraints between keypoints. This is implicitly enforced with an information bottleneck which yields cleaner heatmaps. **(c)** Recovered 3D structural and camera parameters $\{\alpha, T, R, f\}$. **(d)** The projection layer maps reconstructed 3D skeletons back to 2D keypoint coordinates. (Color figure online)

3.2   Architecture of 3D-INN

Our network consists of three components: first, a keypoint estimator, which localizes 2D keypoints of objects from 2D images by regressing to their heatmaps (Fig. 3a and b, blue part); second, a 3D interpreter, which infers internal 3D structural and viewpoint parameters from the heatmaps (Fig. 3c, red part); third, a projection layer, mapping 3D skeletons to 2D keypoint locations so that real 2D-annotated images can be used as supervision (Fig. 3d, yellow part).

Keypoint Estimation. The keypoint estimation component consists of two steps: initial estimation (Fig. 3a) and keypoint refinement (Fig. 3b).

The network architecture for initial keypoint estimation is inspired by the pipeline proposed by Tompson *et al.* [44,45]. The network takes multi-scaled images as input and estimates keypoint heatmaps. Specifically, we apply Local Contrast Normalization (LCN) on each image, and then scale it to 320×240, 160×120, and 80×60 as input to three separate scales of the network. The output is k heatmaps, each with resolution 40×30, where k is the number of keypoints of the object in the image.

At each scale, the network has three sets of 5×5 convolutional (with zero padding), ReLU, and 2×2 pooling layers, followed by a 9×9 convolutional and ReLU layer. The final outputs for the three scales are therefore images with resolution 40×30, 20×15, and 10×7, respectively. We then upsample the outputs of the last two scales to ensure they have the same resolution (40×30). The outputs from the three scales are later summed up and sent to a Batch Normalization layer and three 1×1 convolution layers, whose goal is to regress to target heatmaps. We found that Batch Normalization is critical for convergence, while Spatial Dropout, proposed in [44], does not affect performance.

The second step of keypoint estimation is keypoint refinement, whose goal is to implicitly learn category-level structural constraints on keypoint locations after the initial keypoint localization. The motivation is to exploit the contextual and structural knowledge among keypoints (*e.g.*, arms cannot be too far from the torso). We design a mini-network which, like an auto-encoder, has information bottleneck layers, enforcing it to implicitly model the relationship among keypoints. Some previous works also use this idea and achieve better performance with lower computational cost in object detection [34] and face recognition [43].

In the keypoint refinement network, We use three fully connected layers with widths $8,192$, $4,096$, and $8,192$, respectively. After refinement, the heatmaps of keypoints are much cleaner, as shown in Fig. 5 and Sect. 4.

3D Interpreter. The goal of our 3D interpreter is to infer 3D structure and viewpoint parameters, using estimated 2D heatmaps from earlier layers. While there are many different ways of solving Eq. 1, our deep learning approach has clear advantages. First, traditional methods [13,47] that minimize the reprojection error consider only one keypoint hypothesis, and is therefore not robust to noises in keypoint detection. In contrast, our framework uses soft heatmaps of keypoint locations, as shown in Fig. 3c, which is more robust when some keypoints are invisible or incorrectly located. Further, our algorithm only requires a single forward propagation during testing, making it more efficient than the most previous optimization-base methods.

As discussed in Sect. 3.1, the set of 3D parameters we estimate consists of $S = \{\alpha_i, R, T, f\}$, with which we are able to recover the 3D object structure using Eq. 1. As shown in Fig. 3c, we use four fully connected layers as our 3D interpreter, with widths $2,048$, 512, 128, and $|S|$, respectively. The Spatial Transformer Network [17] also explored the idea of learning rotation parameters R with neural nets, but our network can also recover structural parameters $\{\alpha_i\}$. Note that our representation for latent parameters may also be naturally extended to other types of abstract 3D representations.

Projection Layer. The last component of the network is a projection layer (Fig. 3d). The projection layer takes estimated 3D parameters as input, and computes projected 2D keypoint coordinates $\{x_i, y_i\}$ using Eq. 1. As all operations are differentiable, the projection layer enables us to use 2D-annotated images as ground truth, and run back-propagation to update the entire network.

3.3 Training Strategy

A straightforward training strategy is to use real 2D images as input, and their 2D keypoint locations as supervision for the output of the projection layer. Unfortunately, experiments show that the network can hardly converge using this training scheme, due to the high-dimensional search space and the ambiguity in the 3D to 2D projection.

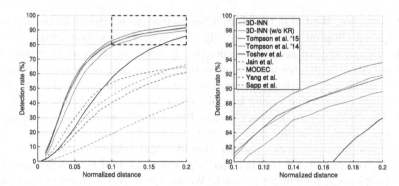

Fig. 4. PCK curves on the FLIC dataset. 3D-INN performs consistently better than other methods. Without keypoint refinement, it is comparable to Tompson *et al.* [44]. A zoomed view of the dashed rectangle is shown on the right.

We therefore adopt an alternative three-step training strategy: first, training the keypoint estimator (Fig. 3a and b) using real images with 2D keypoint heatmaps as supervision; second, training the 3D interpreter (Fig. 3c) using synthetic 3D data as there are no ground truth 3D annotations available for real images; and third, training the whole network using real 2D images with supervision on the output of the projection layer at the end.

To generate synthetic 3D objects, for each object category, we first randomly sample structural parameters $\{\alpha_i\}$ and viewpoint parameters P, R and T. Then we calculate 3D keypoint coordinates using Eq. 1. To model deformations that cannot be captured by base shapes, we add Gaussian perturbation to 3D keypoint locations of each synthetic 3D object, whose variance is 1 % of its diagonal length. Examples of synthetic 3D shapes are shown in Fig. 3c. Note that we are not rendering these synthesized objects, as we are only using heatmaps of keypoints, rather than rendered images, as training input.

4 Evaluation

We evaluate our entire framework, 3D-INN, as well as each component within. In this section, we present both qualitative and quantitative results on 2D keypoint estimation (Sect. 4.1) and 3D structure recovery (Sect. 4.2).

4.1 2D Keypoint Estimation

Data. For 2D keypoint estimation, we evaluate our algorithm on three image datasets: FLIC [35] for human bodies, CUB-200-2011 [51] for birds, and a new dataset Keypoint-5 for furniture. Specifically, FLIC is a challenging dataset containing $3,987$ training images and $1,016$ test images, each labeled with 10 keypoints of human bodies. The CUB-200-2011 dataset was originally proposed for fine-grained bird classification, but with labeled keypoints of bird parts. It has

5, 994 images for training and 5, 794 images for testing, each coming with up to 15 keypoints.

We also introduce a new dataset, Keypoint-5, which contains five categories: bed, chair, sofa, swivel chair, and table. There are 1, 000 to 2, 000 images in each category, where 80 % are for training and 20 % for testing. For each image, we asked three workers on Amazon Mechanical Turk to label locations of a pre-defined category-specific set of keypoints; we then, for each keypoint, used the median of the three responses as ground truth.

Metrics. To quantitatively evaluate the accuracy of estimated keypoints on FLIC (human body), we use the standard Percentage of Correct Key-points (PCK) measure [35] to be consistent with previous works [35,44,45]. We use the evaluation toolkit and results of competing methods released by the Tompson et al. [44]. On CUB-200-2011 (bird) and the new Keypoint-5 (furni-ture) dataset, following the convention [26,38], we evaluate results in Percentage of Correct Parts (PCP) and Average Error (AE). PCP is defined as the percent-age of keypoints localized within 1.5 times of the standard deviation of annota-tions. We use the evaluation code from [26] to ensure consistency. Average error is computed as the mean of the distance, bounded by 5, between a predicted keypoint location and ground truth.

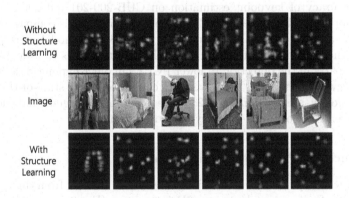

Without Structure Learning

Image

With Structure Learning

Fig. 5. 2D keypoint predictions from a single image, where each color corresponds to a keypoint. The keypoint refinement step cleans up false positives and produces more regulated predictions. (Color figure online)

Table 1. Keypoint estimation results on CUB-200-2011, measured in PCP (%) and AE. Our method is comparable to Mdshift [38] (better in AE but worse in PCP), and better than all other algorithms.

Method	Poselets [6]	Consensus [4]	Exemplar [26]	Mdshift [38]	3D-INN	Human
PCP (%)	27.47	48.70	59.74	**69.1**	66.7	84.72
Average error	2.87	2.13	1.80	1.39	**1.35**	1.00

Table 2. Keypoint estimation results of 3D-INN and Tompson *et al.* [44] on Keypoint-5, measured in PCP (%) and AE. 3D-INN is consistently better in both measures. We retrained the network in [44] on Keypoint-5.

	Method	Bed	Chair	Sofa	Swivel chair
PCP	3D-INN	**77.4**	**87.7**	**77.4**	**78.5**
	Tompson *et al.* [44]	76.2	85.3	76.9	69.2
AE	3D-INN	**1.16**	**0.92**	**1.14**	**1.19**
	Tompson *et al.* [44]	1.20	1.02	1.19	1.54

Results. For 2D keypoint detection, we only train the keypoint estimator in our 3D-INN (Fig. 3a and b) using the training images in each dataset. Figure 4 shows the accuracy of keypoint estimation on the FLIC dataset. On this dataset, we employ a fine-level network for post-processing, as suggested by [44]. Our method performs better than all previous methods [35,44,45,48,56] at all precisions. Moreover, the keypoint refinement step improves results significantly (about 2 % for a normalized distance ≥ 0.15), without which our framework has similar performance with [44]. Such improvement is also demonstrated in Fig. 5, where the heatmaps after refinement are far less noisy.

The accuracy of keypoint estimation on CUB-200-201 dataset is listed in Table 1. Our method is better than [26] in both metrics, and is comparable to the state-of-the-art [38]. Specifically, compared with [38], our model more precisely estimates the keypoint locations for correctly detected parts (a lower AE), but miss more parts in the detection (a lower PCP). On our Keypoint-5 dataset, our model achieves higher PCPs and lower AEs compared to the state-of-the-art [44] for all categories, as shown in Table 2. These experiments in general demonstrate the effectiveness of our model on keypoint detection.

4.2 Structural Parameter Estimation

For 3D structural parameter estimation, we evaluate 3D-INN from three different prospectives. First, we evaluate our 3D interpreter (Fig. 3c alone) against the optimization-based method [61]. Second, we test our full pipeline on the IKEA dataset [25], where ground truth 3D labels are available. We show qualitative results on three datasets: Keypoint-5, IKEA, and SUN [54] at last.

Comparing with an optimization-based method. We first compared our 3D interpreter (Fig. 3c) with the state-of-the-art optimization-based method that directly minimizing re-projection error (Eq. 1) on the synthetic data.

We first tested the effectiveness of our 3D interpreter (Fig. 3c) on synthetic data. We compare our trained 3D interpreter against the state-of-the-art method on directly minimizing re-projection error (Eq. 1). Since most optimization based methods only consider the parallel projection, we extend the one by Zhou *et al.* [61] as follows. We first uses their algorithm to get an initial guess of internal parameters and viewpoints, and then applying a simple gradient descent method to refine it considering perspective distortion.

We generate synthetic data for this experiment, using the scheme described in Sect. 3.3. Each data point contains the 2D keypoint heatmaps of an object, and its corresponding 3D keypoint locations and viewpoint, which we would like to estimate. We also add different levels of salt-and-pepper noise to heatmaps to evaluate the robustness of both methods. We generated 30,000 training and 1,000 testing cases. Because the analytical solution only takes keypoint coordinates as input, we convert heatmaps to coordinates using argmax.

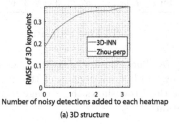 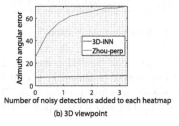

(a) 3D structure   (b) 3D viewpoint

Fig. 6. Plots comparing our method against an analytic solution on synthetic heatmap. (a) The accuracy of 3D structure estimation; (b) The accuracy of 3D viewpoint estimation.

For both methods, we evaluate their performance on both 3D structure recovery and 3D viewpoint estimation. For 3D structure estimation, we compare their accuracies on 3D keypoint estimation ($\mathcal{Y}$ in Sect. 3.1); for 3D viewpoint estimation, we evaluate errors in azimuth angle, following previous work [41]. As the original algorithm by Zhou et al. [61] was mainly designed for the parallel projection and comparatively clean heatmaps, our 3D interpreter outperforms it in the presence of noise and perspective distortion, as shown in Fig. 6.

Evaluating the full pipeline. We now evaluate 3D-INN on estimating 3D structure and 3D viewpoint. We use the IKEA dataset [25] for evaluation, as it provides ground truth 3D mesh models and the associated viewpoints for testing images. We manually label ground truth 3D keypoint locations on provided 3D meshes, and calculate the root-mean-square error (RMSE) between estimated and ground truth 3D keypoint locations.

As IKEA only have no more than 200 images per category, we instead train 3D-INN on our Keypoint-5, as well as one million synthetic data points, using the strategy described in Sect. 3.3. Note that, first, we are only using no more than 2,000 real images per category for training and, second, we are testing the trained model on different datasets, avoiding the possible dataset bias [46].

The left half of Fig. 7 shows RMSE-Recall curve of both our algorithm and the optimization-based method described above (Zhou-perp [61]). The y-axis shows the recall — the percentage of testing samples under a certain RMSE threshold. We test two versions of our algorithm: with fine-tuning (3D-INN) and without

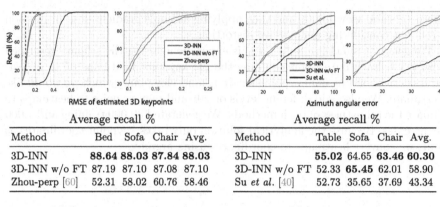

Method	Bed	Sofa	Chair	Avg.
3D-INN	**88.64**	**88.03**	**87.84**	**88.03**
3D-INN w/o FT	87.19	87.10	87.08	87.10
Zhou-perp [60]	52.31	58.02	60.76	58.46

(a) Structure estimation

Method	Table	Sofa	Chair	Avg.
3D-INN	**55.02**	64.65	**63.46**	**60.30**
3D-INN w/o FT	52.33	**65.45**	62.01	58.90
Su et al. [40]	52.73	35.65	37.69	43.34

(b) Pose estimation

Fig. 7. Evaluation on the IKEA dataset [25]. (a) The accuracy of structure estimation. RMSE-Recall curved is shown in the first row, and zoomed-views of the dashed rectangular regions are shown on the right. The third row shows the average recall on all thresholds. (b) The accuracy of pose estimation.

fine-tuning (3D-INN w/o FT). Both significantly outperform the optimization-based method [61], as [61] is not designed for multiple keypoint hypothesis and perspective distortion, while our 3D-INN can deal with them. Also, finetuning improves the accuracy of keypoint estimation by about 5 % under the RMSE threshold 0.15.

Table 3. Joint object detection and viewpoint estimation on PASCAL 3D+ [53]. Following previous work, we use Average Viewpoint Precision (AVP) as our measure, which extends AP so that a true positive should have both a correct bounding box and a correct viewpoint (here we use a 4-view quantization). Both V&K [49] and our algorithm (3D-INN) use R-CNN [11] for object detection, and others use their own detection algorithm. VDPM [53] and DPM-VOC+VP [31] are trained on PASCAL VOC 2012, V&K [49] is trained on PASCAL 3D+, Su et al. [41] is trained on PASCAL VOC 2012, together with synthetic 3D CAD models, and 3D-INN is trained on Keypoint-5.

Category	VDPM [53]	DPM-VOC+VP [31]	Su et al. [41]	V&K [49]	3D-INN
Chair	6.8	6.1	15.7	**25.1**	23.1
Sofa	5.1	11.8	18.6	43.8	**45.8**

Though we focus on recovering 3D object structure, as an extension, we also evaluate 3D-INN on 3D viewpoint estimation. We compare it with the state-of-the-art viewpoint estimation algorithm by Su et al. [41]. The right half of Fig. 7 shows the results (recall) in azimuth angle. As shown in the table, 3D-INN outperforms Su et al. [41] by about 40 % (relative), measured in average

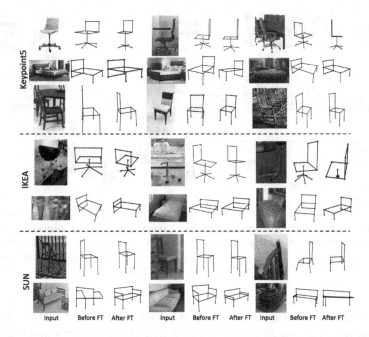

Fig. 8. Qualitative results on Keypoint-5, IKEA, and SUN databases. For each example, the first one is the input image, the second one is the reconstruct 3D skeleton using the network before fine-tuning, and third one is using the network after fine-tuning. The last column shows failure cases.

Training: beds, Test: chairs   Training: sofas, Test: chairs

Fig. 9. Qualitative results on chairs using networks trained on sofas or beds. In most cases models provide reasonable output. Mistakes are often due to the difference between the training and test sets, *e.g.*, in the third example, the model trained on beds fails to estimate chairs facing backward.

recall. This is mainly because it is not straightforward for Su *et al.* [41], mostly trained on (cropped) synthesized images, to deal with the large number of heavily occluded objects in the IKEA dataset.

Although our algorithm assumes a centered object in an input image, we can apply it, in combination with an object detection algorithm, on images where object locations are unknown. We evaluate the results of joint object detection and viewpoint estimation on PASCAL 3D+ dataset [53]. We use the standard R-CNN [11] for object detection, and our 3D-INN for viewpoint estimation. Table 3 shows that our model is comparable with the state-of-the-art [49], and ourperforms other algorithms with a significant margin. Note that all the other

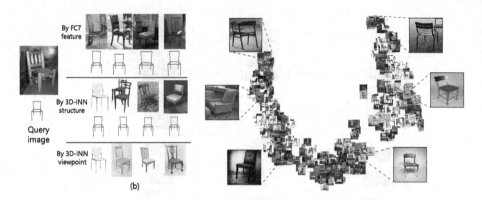

(b)

Fig. 10. Retrieval results in different feature spaces. 3D-INN helps to retrieve objects with similar 3D structures or similar viewpoints.

Fig. 11. Object graph visualization based on learned object representations: we visualize images using t-SNE [28] on predicted 3D viewpoint by 3D-INN.

algorithms are trained on either PASCAL VOC or PASCAL 3D+, while our algorithm is trained on Keypoint-5, which indicates that our learned model is not suffering much from the dataset bias problem [46].

Qualitative results on benchmarks. At last, we show qualitative results on Keypoint-5, IKEA, and the SUN database [54] in Fig. 8. When the image is clean and objects are not occluded, our algorithm can recover 3D object structure and viewpoint with high accuracy, while fine-tuning can further helps to improve the results (see chairs at row 1 column 1, and row 4 column 1). Our algorithm is also robust of partial occlusion, demonstrated by the IKEA bed at row 5 column 1. One major failure case is when the object is heavily cropped in the input image (see the last column in row 4 to 7), as the 3D object skeleton becomes hard to infer.

When 3D-INN is used in combination with detection models, it needs to deal with imperfect detection results. Here, we also evaluate 3D-INN on noisy input, specifically, on images with an object from a different but similar category. Figure 9 shows the recovered 3D structures of chairs using a model trained either on sofas or beds. In most cases 3D-INN still provides reasonable output, and the mistakes are mostly due to the difference between training and test sets, *e.g.*, the model trained on beds does not perform well on chairs facing backward, because there are almost no beds with a similar viewpoint in the training set.

5 Applications

Our inferred latent parameters, as a compact and informative representation of objects in images, have wide applications. In this section, we demonstrate representative ones including image retrieval and object graph construction.

Image Retrieval. Using estimated 3D structural and viewpoint information, we can retrieve images based on their 3D configurations. Figure 10 shows image retrieval results using FC7 features from AlexNet [19] and using the 3D structure and viewpoint learned by 3D-INN. Our retrieval database includes all testing images of chairs and sofas in Keypoint-5. In each row, we sort the best matches of the query image, measured by Euclidean distance in a specific feature space. We retrieve images in two ways: *by structure* uses estimated internal structural parameters ($\{\alpha_i\}$ in Eq. 1), and *by viewpoint* uses estimated external viewpoint parameters (R in Eq. 1).

Object Graph. Similar to the retrieval task, we visualize all test images for chairs in Keypoint-5 in Fig. 11, using t-SNE [28] on estimated 3D viewpoints. Note the smooth transition from the chairs facing left to those facing right.

6   Conclusion

In this paper, we introduced 3D INterpreter Network (3D-INN), which recovers the 2D keypoint and 3D structure of a (possibly deformable) object given a single image. To achieve this goal, we used 3D skeletons as an abstract 3D representation, incorporated a projection layer to the network for learning 3D parameters from 2D labels, and employed keypoint heatmaps to connect real and synthetic data. Empirically, we showed that 3D-INN performs well on both 2D keypoint estimation and 3D structure and viewpoint recovery, comparable to or better than the state-of-the-arts. Further, various applications demonstrated the potential of the skeleton representation learned by 3D-INN.

Acknowledgement. This work is supported by NSF Robust Intelligence 1212849 and NSF Big Data 1447476 to W.F., NSF Robust Intelligence 1524817 to A.T., ONR MURI N00014-16-1-2007 to J.B.T., Shell Research, and the Center for Brain, Minds and Machines (NSF STC award CCF-1231216). The authors would like to thank Nvidia for GPU donations. Part of this work was done during Jiajun Wu's internship at Facebook AI Research.

References

1. Akhter, I., Black, M.J.: Pose-conditioned joint angle limits for 3d human pose reconstruction. In: CVPR (2015)
2. Aubry, M., Maturana, D., Efros, A., Russell, B., Sivic, J.: Seeing 3d chairs: exemplar part-based 2d–3d alignment using a large dataset of cad models. In: CVPR (2014)
3. Bansal, A., Russell, B.: Marr revisited: 2d–3d alignment via surface normal prediction. In: CVPR (2016)
4. Belhumeur, P.N., Jacobs, D.W., Kriegman, D.J., Kumar, N.: Localizing parts of faces using a consensus of exemplars. IEEE TPAMI **35**(12), 2930–2940 (2013)
5. Bever, T.G., Poeppel, D.: Analysis by synthesis: a (re-) emerging program of research for language and vision. Biolinguistics **4**(2–3), 174–200 (2010)

6. Bourdev, L., Maji, S., Brox, T., Malik, J.: Detecting people using mutually consistent poselet activations. In: Daniilidis, K., Maragos, P., Paragios, N. (eds.) ECCV 2010. LNCS, vol. 6316, pp. 168–181. Springer, Heidelberg (2010). doi:10.1007/978-3-642-15567-3_13

7. Carreira, J., Agrawal, P., Fragkiadaki, K., Malik, J.: Human pose estimation with iterative error feedback. In: CVPR (2016)

8. Choy, C.B., Xu, D., Gwak, J., Chen, K., Savarese, S.: 3d-r2n2: a unified approach for single and multi-view 3D object reconstruction. In: Leibe, B., Matas, J., Sebe, N., Welling, M. (eds.) ECCV 2006, Part VIII. LNCS, vol. 9912, pp. 1–17. Springer, Heidelberg (2016)

9. Dosovitskiy, A., Tobias Springenberg, J., Brox, T.: Learning to generate chairs with convolutional neural networks. In: CVPR (2015)

10. Fidler, S., Dickinson, S.J., Urtasun, R.: 3d object detection and viewpoint estimation with a deformable 3d cuboid model. In: NIPS (2012)

11. Girshick, R., Donahue, J., Darrell, T., Malik, J.: Rich feature hierarchies for accurate object detection and semantic segmentation. In: CVPR (2014)

12. Hejrati, M., Ramanan, D.: Analysis by synthesis: 3d object recognition by object reconstruction. In: CVPR (2014)

13. Hejrati, M., Ramanan, D.: Analyzing 3d objects in cluttered images. In: NIPS (2012)

14. Hinton, G.E., Ghahramani, Z.: Generative models for discovering sparse distributed representations. Philos. Trans. R. Soc. London B: Biol. Sci. 352(1358), 1177–1190 (1997)

15. Hu, W., Zhu, S.C.: Learning 3d object templates by quantizing geometry and appearance spaces. IEEE TPAMI 37(6), 1190–1205 (2015)

16. Huang, Q., Wang, H., Koltun, V.: Single-view reconstruction via joint analysis of image and shape collections. ACM SIGGRAPH 34(4), 87 (2015)

17. Jaderberg, M., Simonyan, K., Zisserman, A., Kavukcuoglu, K.: Spatial transformer networks. In: NIPS (2015)

18. Kar, A., Tulsiani, S., Carreira, J., Malik, J.: Category-specific object reconstruction from a single image. In: CVPR (2015)

19. Krizhevsky, A., Sutskever, I., Hinton, G.E.: Imagenet classification with deep convolutional neural networks. In: NIPS (2012)

20. Kulkarni, T.D., Kohli, P., Tenenbaum, J.B., Mansinghka, V.: Picture: a probabilistic programming language for scene perception. In: CVPR (2015)

21. Kulkarni, T.D., Whitney, W.F., Kohli, P., Tenenbaum, J.B.: Deep convolutional inverse graphics network. In: NIPS (2015)

22. Leclerc, Y.G., Fischler, M.A.: An optimization-based approach to the interpretation of single line drawings as 3d wire frames. IJCV 9(2), 113–136 (1992)

23. Li, Y., Su, H., Qi, C.R., Fish, N., Cohen-Or, D., Guibas, L.J.: Joint embeddings of shapes and images via cnn image purification. ACM SIGGRAPH Asia 34(6), 234 (2015)

24. Lim, J.J., Khosla, A., Torralba, A.: FPM: fine pose parts-based model with 3D CAD models. In: Fleet, D., Pajdla, T., Schiele, B., Tuytelaars, T. (eds.) ECCV 2014. LNCS, vol. 8694, pp. 478–493. Springer, Heidelberg (2014). doi:10.1007/978-3-319-10599-4_31

25. Lim, J.J., Pirsiavash, H., Torralba, A.: Parsing ikea objects: fine pose estimation. In: ICCV (2013)

26. Liu, J., Belhumeur, P.N.: Bird part localization using exemplar-based models with enforced pose and subcategory consistency. In: ICCV (2013)

27. Lowe, D.G.: Three-dimensional object recognition from single two-dimensional images. Artif. Intell. **31**(3), 355–395 (1987). Elsevier
28. Van der Maaten, L., Hinton, G.: Visualizing data using t-sne. JMLR **9**(11), 2579–2605 (2008)
29. Newell, A., Yang, K., Deng, J.: Stacked hourglass networks for human pose estimation. arXiv preprint arXiv:1603.06937 (2016)
30. Peng, X., Sun, B., Ali, K., Saenko, K.: Exploring invariances in deep convolutional neural networks using synthetic images. CoRR, abs/1412.7122 2 (2014)
31. Pepik, B., Stark, M., Gehler, P., Schiele, B.: Teaching 3d geometry to deformable part models. In: CVPR (2012)
32. Prasad, M., Fitzgibbon, A., Zisserman, A., Van Gool, L.: Finding nemo: deformable object class modelling using curve matching. In: CVPR (2010)
33. Ramakrishna, V., Kanade, T., Sheikh, Y.: Reconstructing 3D human pose from 2D image landmarks. In: Fitzgibbon, A., Lazebnik, S., Perona, P., Sato, Y., Schmid, C. (eds.) ECCV 2012. LNCS, vol. 7575, pp. 573–586. Springer, Heidelberg (2012). doi:10.1007/978-3-642-33765-9_41
34. Ren, S., He, K., Girshick, R., Sun, J.: Faster R-CNN: towards real-time object detection with region proposal networks. In: NIPS (2015)
35. Sapp, B., Taskar, B.: Modec: multimodal decomposable models for human pose estimation. In: CVPR (2013)
36. Satkin, S., Lin, J., Hebert, M.: Data-driven scene understanding from 3D models. In: BMVC (2012)
37. Shakhnarovich, G., Viola, P., Darrell, T.: Fast pose estimation with parameter-sensitive hashing. In: ICCV (2003)
38. Shih, K.J., Mallya, A., Singh, S., Hoiem, D.: Part localization using multi-proposal consensus for fine-grained categorization. In: BMVC (2015)
39. Shrivastava, A., Gupta, A.: Building part-based object detectors via 3d geometry. In: ICCV, pp. 1745–1752 (2013)
40. Su, H., Huang, Q., Mitra, N.J., Li, Y., Guibas, L.: Estimating image depth using shape collections. ACM TOG **33**(4), 37 (2014)
41. Su, H., Qi, C.R., Li, Y., Guibas, L.: Render for cnn: viewpoint estimation in images using cnns trained with rendered 3d model views. In: ICCV (2015)
42. Sun, B., Saenko, K.: From virtual to reality: fast adaptation of virtual object detectors to real domains. In: BMVC (2014)
43. Taigman, Y., Yang, M., Ranzato, M., Wolf, L.: Web-scale training for face identification. In: CVPR (2015)
44. Tompson, J., Goroshin, R., Jain, A., LeCun, Y., Bregler, C.: Efficient object localization using convolutional networks. In: CVPR (2015)
45. Tompson, J.J., Jain, A., LeCun, Y., Bregler, C.: Joint training of a convolutional network and a graphical model for human pose estimation. In: NIPS (2014)
46. Torralba, A., Efros, A.A.: Unbiased look at dataset bias. In: CVPR (2011)
47. Torresani, L., Hertzmann, A., Bregler, C.: Learning non-rigid 3d shape from 2d motion. In: NIPS (2003)
48. Toshev, A., Szegedy, C.: Deeppose: human pose estimation via deep neural networks. In: CVPR, pp. 1653–1660 (2014)
49. Tulsiani, S., Malik, J.: Viewpoints and keypoints. In: CVPR (2015)
50. Vicente, S., Carreira, J., Agapito, L., Batista, J.: Reconstructing pascal voc. In: CVPR (2014)
51. Wah, C., Branson, S., Welinder, P., Perona, P., Belongie, S.: The Caltech-UCSD Birds-200-2011 Dataset. Technical report. CNS-TR-2011-001, California Institute of Technology (2011)

52. Wu, J., Yildirim, I., Lim, J.J., Freeman, B., Tenenbaum, J.: Galileo: perceiving physical object properties by integrating a physics engine with deep learning. In: NIPS (2015)
53. Xiang, Y., Mottaghi, R., Savarese, S.: Beyond pascal: a benchmark for 3d object detection in the wild. In: WACV (2014)
54. Xiao, J., Hays, J., Ehinger, K., Oliva, A., Torralba, A.: Sun database: large-scale scene recognition from abbey to zoo. In: CVPR (2010)
55. Xue, T., Liu, J., Tang, X.: Example-based 3d object reconstruction from line drawings. In: CVPR (2012)
56. Yang, Y., Ramanan, D.: Articulated pose estimation with flexible mixtures-of-parts. In: CVPR (2011)
57. Yasin, H., Iqbal, U., Krüger, B., Weber, A., Gall, J.: A dual-source approach for 3d pose estimation from a single image. In: CVPR (2016)
58. Yuille, A., Kersten, D.: Vision as bayesian inference: analysis by synthesis? Trends Cogn. Sci. 10(7), 301–308 (2006)
59. Zeng, A., Song, S., Nießner, M., Fisher, M., Xiao, J.: 3dmatch: learning the matching of local 3d geometry in range scans. arXiv preprint arXiv:1603.08182 (2016)
60. Zhou, T., Krähenbühl, P., Aubry, M., Huang, Q., Efros, A.A.: Learning dense correspondence via 3d-guided cycle consistency. In: CVPR (2016)
61. Zhou, X., Leonardos, S., Hu, X., Daniilidis, K.: 3d shape reconstruction from 2d landmarks: a convex formulation. In: CVPR (2015)
62. Zia, M.Z., Stark, M., Schiele, B., Schindler, K.: Detailed 3d representations for object recognition and modeling. IEEE TPAMI 35(11), 2608–2623 (2013)

Dual Structured Light 3D Using a 1D Sensor

Jian Wang[1], Aswin C. Sankaranarayanan[1(✉)], Mohit Gupta[2],
and Srinivasa G. Narasimhan[1]

[1] Carnegie Mellon University, Pittsburgh, USA
{jianwan2,saswin}@andrew.cmu.edu, srinivas@cs.cmu.edu
[2] University of Wisconsin-Madison, Madison, USA
mohitg@cs.wisc.edu

Abstract. Structured light-based 3D reconstruction methods often illuminate a scene using patterns with 1D translational symmetry such as
stripes, Gray codes or sinusoidal phase shifting patterns. These patterns
are decoded using images captured by a traditional 2D sensor. In this
work, we present a novel structured light approach that uses a 1D sensor with simple optics and no moving parts to reconstruct scenes with
the same acquisition speed as a traditional 2D sensor. While traditional
methods compute correspondences between columns of the projector
and 2D camera pixels, our 'dual' approach computes correspondences
between columns of the 1D camera and 2D projector pixels. The use
of a 1D sensor provides significant advantages in many applications that
operate in short-wave infrared range (0.9–2.5 microns) or require dynamic
vision sensors (DVS), where a 2D sensor is prohibitively expensive and
difficult to manufacture. We analyze the proposed design, explore hardware alternatives and discuss the performance in the presence of ambient
light and global illumination.

Keywords: Structured light · Dual photography

1 Introduction

Structured light (SL) [9] is one of the most popular techniques for 3D shape
acquisition. An SL system uses active illumination, typically via a projector, to
obtain robust correspondences between pixels on the projector and a camera,
and subsequently, recovers the scene depth via triangulation. In contrast to passive techniques like stereo, the use of active illumination enables SL systems to
acquire depth even for textureless scenes at a low computational cost.

The simplest SL method is point scanning [7], where the light source illuminates a single scene point at a time, and the camera captures an image. Correspondence between camera and projector pixels is determined by associating

Electronic supplementary material The online version of this chapter (doi:10.
1007/978-3-319-46466-4_23) contains supplementary material, which is available to
authorized users.

© Springer International Publishing AG 2016
B. Leibe et al. (Eds.): ECCV 2016, Part VI, LNCS 9910, pp. 383–398, 2016.
DOI: 10.1007/978-3-319-46466-4_23

the brightest pixel in each acquired image to the pixel illuminated by the projector. However, this approach requires a large number (N^2) of images to obtain a depth map with $N \times N$ pixels. In order to reduce the acquisition time, stripe scanning technique was proposed where the light source emits a planar sheet of light [1,5,25]. Consider a scene point that lies on the emitted light plane. Its depth can be estimated by finding the intersection between the light plane, and the ray joining the camera center and the camera pixel. This is illustrated in Fig. 1(a). We can further reduce the acquisition time by using more sophisticated temporal coding techniques; for example, binary codes [19], Gray codes [12,22] and sinusoidal phase shifting [26].

Underlying all these methods is the idea that, for a calibrated camera-projector pair, we only need to measure disparity, i.e., a 1D displacement map. Thus, we need to perform coding along only one dimension of the projector image plane, thereby achieving significant speed-ups over point-scanning systems. For example, several structured light patterns have a 1D translational symmetry, i.e., in the projected patterns, all the pixels within a column (or a row) have the same intensities.[1] This is illustrated in Fig. 1(a). *For such patterns with 1D translational symmetry, conventional structured light systems can be thought of as using a 1D projector, and a 2D sensor.*

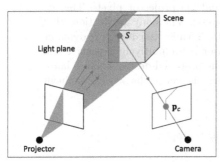
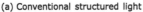
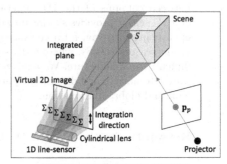

(a) Conventional structured light   (b) Dual structured light (DualSL)

Fig. 1. DualSL compared with traditional SL. Depth from SL can be obtained by performing ray-plane triangulation. For traditional SL, the ray is from camera pixel, and plane is formed by center of projection and a column of the projector. In DualSL, ray is from projector pixel, and plane is formed by a line sensor pixel with cylindrical optics.

In this paper, we present a novel SL design called *DualSL* (Dual Structured Light) that uses *a 2D projector and a 1D sensor, or a line-sensor.* DualSL comprises of a novel optical setup where pixels on the line-sensor integrates light along

---

[1] An exception is 'single-shot' structured light techniques that use patterns with 2D intensity variations, for example, sparse 2D grid of lines [20], 2D color encoded grids [21], 2D pseudo-random binary code [27], and 2D random dots (used in the first generation Microsoft Kinect depth sensing cameras [16]).

columns of the image focused by the objective lens, as shown in Fig. 1(b). As a consequence, the DualSL design can be interpreted as the optical dual [23] of a traditional SL system, i.e., we *find correspondences between columns of the camera and pixels on the projector.* In contrast, in conventional SL, we find correspondences between pixels of the camera and columns of the projector.

Why use a 1D sensor for structured light? The use of a line-sensor, instead of a 2D sensor, can provide significant advantages in many applications where a 2D sensor is either expensive or difficult to obtain. For example, the typical costs for sensors in shortwave infrared (SWIR; 900 nm–2.5 μm) is \$0.10 per pixel [8]; hence, a high-resolution 2D sensor can be prohibitively expensive. In this context, a system built using a 1D line-sensor, with just a few thousand pixels, can have a significantly lower cost. A second application of DualSL is in the context of dynamic vision sensors (DVS) [14], where each pixel has the capability of detecting temporal intensity changes in an asynchronous manner. It has been shown that the use of a DVS with asynchronous pixels can reduce the acquisition time of line striping based structured light by up to an order of magnitude [4,15]. However, the additional circuit at each pixel for detecting temporal intensity changes and enabling asynchronous readout leads to sensors that are inherently complex and have a poor fill-factor (around 8.1 % for commercially available units [6,11]), and low resolution (e.g., 128 × 128). In contrast, a 1D DVS sensor [18] can have a larger fill-factor (80 % for the design in [18]), and thus, a significantly higher 1D resolution (e.g., 2048 pixels), by moving the per-pixel processing circuit to the additional space available both above and below the 1D sensor array.

Our contributions are as follows:

- **SL using a line-sensor.** We propose a novel SL design that utilizes a line-sensor and simple optics with no moving parts to obtain the depth map of the scene. This can have significant benefits for sensing in wavelength regimes where sensors are expensive as well as sensing modalities where 2D sensors have low fill-factor, and thus poor resolution (e.g., dynamic vision sensors).
- **Analysis.** We analyze the performance of DualSL and show that its performance in terms of temporal resolution is the same as a traditional SL system.
- **Validation via hardware prototyping.** We realize a proof-of-concept hardware prototype for visible light to showcase DualSL, propose a procedure to calibrate the device, and characterize its performance.

2   DualSL

In this section, we describe the principle underlying DualSL, and analyze its performance in terms of the temporal resolution of obtaining depth maps.

2.1   Design of the Sensing Architecture

The optical design of sensing architecture, adapted from [28], is shown in Fig. 2. The setup consists of an objective lens, a cylindrical lens, and a line-sensor. The line-sensor is placed on the image plane of the objective lens, so that the scene is perfectly in focus along the axis of the line-sensor. A cylindrical lens is placed in between the objective lens and the sensor such that its axis is aligned with that of the line-sensor. The cylindrical lens does not perturb light rays along the x-axis (axis parallel to its length). This results in the scene being in focus along the x-axis. Along the y-axis (perpendicular to the length of the cylindrical lens), the position and focal length of the cylindrical lens are chosen to ensure that its aperture plane is focused at the image plane. Hence, the scene is completely defocused along the y-axis, i.e., each line-sensor pixel integrates light along the y-axis. This is illustrated in Fig. 2(bottom-row). Further, for maximum efficiency in gathering light, it is desirable that the aperture of the objective lens is magnified/shrunk to the height of the line-sensor.

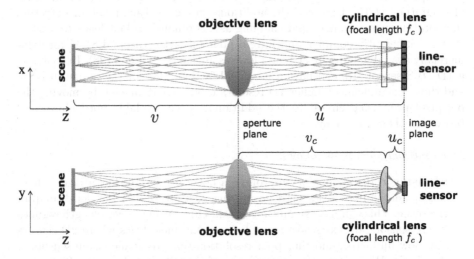

Fig. 2. Design of the sensing architecture visualized as ray diagrams along two orthogonal axes. The line-sensor is placed at the image plane of the objective lens. A cylindrical lens is placed in front of the line-sensor such that its axis is aligned with that of the line-sensor. The cylindrical lens does not perturb light rays along the x-axis (top-row); this results in the scene being in focus along the x-axis. Along the y-axis (bottom-row), the cylindrical lens brings the aperture plane into focus at the image plane. Hence, the scene is completely defocused along the y-axis, i.e., each line-sensor pixel integrates light along the y-axis.

Determining the parameters of the cylindrical lens. The focal length, f_c, of the cylindrical lens and its distance to the line-sensor, u_c, can be derived from the desiderata listed above. Given the aperture diameter of the objective lens D, the sensor-lens distance u, the height H of the line-sensor pixels, and the length of the line-sensor L, we require the following constraints to be satisfied:

$$\frac{1}{u_c} + \frac{1}{u - u_c} = \frac{1}{f_c} \qquad \text{(focusing aperture plane onto image plane)}$$

$$\frac{D}{H} = \frac{u - u_c}{u_c} \qquad \text{(magnification constraints)}$$

Putting them together, we can obtain the following expressions for u_c and f_c:

$$u_c = \frac{H}{D + H} u, \quad f_c = \frac{HD}{(D + H)^2} u. \tag{1}$$

The last parameter to determine is the height of the cylindrical lens which determines the field-of-view along the axis perpendicular to the line-sensor. For a symmetric field-of-view, we would require the height of the cylindrical lens to be greater than $\frac{D}{D+H}(L + H)$.

Remark. It is worth noting here that line-sensors are often available in form-factors where the height of the pixels H is significantly greater than the pixel pitch. For example, for the prototype used in this paper, the pixel height is $1\,\mathrm{mm}$ while the pixel pitch is $14\,\mu\mathrm{m}$. This highly-skewed pixel aspect ratio allows us to collect large amounts of light at each pixel with little or no loss of resolution along the x-axis. Further, such tall pixels are critical to ensure that the parameters' values defined in (1) are meaningful. For example, if $D \approx H$, then $u_c = u/2$ and $f_c = u/4$. Noting that typical values of flange distances are $17.5\,\mathrm{mm}$ for C-mount lenses and $47\,\mathrm{mm}$ for Nikkor lenses, it is easily seen that the resulting values for the position and the focal length are reasonable.

Scene to sensor mapping. The sensor architecture achieves the following scene-to-sensor mapping. First, the objective lens forms a virtual 2D image of the scene, $I(m, n)$.[2] Second, the effect of the cylindrical lens is to completely defocus the virtual image along one direction. Hence, the measurements on the line-sensor are obtained by projecting the virtual image along a direction perpendicular to the axis of the line-sensor. Specifically, each pixel of the line-sensor integrates the virtual image along a line, i.e., the measurement made by a pixel x on the line sensor is the integration of intensities observed along a line with a slope b/a:

$$i(x) = \int_\alpha I(x + a\alpha, b\alpha) d\alpha.$$

The slope b/a is controlled by the axis of the line-sensor/cylindrical lens. An important feature of this design is that the *pre-image* of a line-sensor pixel is a plane. Here pre-image of a pixel is defined as the set of 3D world points that are imaged at that pixel; for example, in a conventional perspective camera, the pre-image of a pixel is a ray. As we will demonstrate shortly, this property will be used by the DualSL system for acquiring 3D scans of a scene.

---

[2] For simplicity, the image formation is described while ignoring the effects of pixelation and quantization.

2.2   3D Scanning Using the DualSL Setup

We obtain 3D scans of the scene by obtaining correspondences between projector and line-sensor pixels. Suppose that pixel (m, n) of the projector corresponds to pixel x on the line-sensor. We can obtain the 3D scene point underlying this correspondence by intersecting the pre-image of the projector pixel, which is a line in 3D, with the pre-image of the line-sensor pixel — a plane in 3D. As long as the line and the plane are not parallel, we are bound to get a valid intersection, which is the 3D location of the scene point. For simplicity, we assume that the projector and line-sensor are placed in a rectified left-right configuration; hence, we can choose $a = 0$ and $b = 1$ to integrate vertically (along "columns") on the virtual 2D image.

Obtaining projector-camera correspondences. The simplest approach for obtaining correspondences is to illuminate each pixel on the projector sequentially, and capturing an image with the 1D sensor for each projector pixel location. For each projector pixel, we can determine its corresponding line-sensor pixel by finding the pixel with the largest intensity. Assuming a projector with a resolution of $N \times N$ pixels, we would need to capture N^2 images from the line-sensor. Assuming a line-sensor with N pixels, this approach requires N^3 pixels to be read out at the sensor.

We can reduce the acquisition time significantly by using temporal coding techniques, similar to the use of binary/Gray codes in traditional SL (see Fig. 3). In the DualSL setup, this is achieved as follows. We project each row of every SL pattern sequentially.[3] Given that the row has N pixels, we can find projector-camera correspondences using a binary/Gray code with $\log_2(N)$ projector patterns. For this scanning approach, we would require to read out $\log_2(N)$ frames for each row. Given that the projector has N rows, and the sensor has N pixels, a total of $N^2 \log_2(N)$ pixels will need to be read out at the sensor.

2.3   Analysis of Temporal Resolution

We now show that the temporal resolution of DualSL is the same as that of a traditional SL setup for synchronous-readout sensor, i.e. a conventional sensor. For this analysis, we assume that the goal is to obtain an $N \times N$-pixels depth map. The temporal resolution is defined in terms of the time required to acquire a single depth map. We assume that in a sensor, all pixels share one analog-to-digital converter (ADC). We also assume that the bottleneck in all cases is the ADC rate of the camera. This assumption is justified due to the operating speed of projectors (especially laser projectors) being many orders of magnitude greater than cameras. Hence, the number of pixels to be read out divided by ADC rate is temporal resolution of the system.

---

[3] It would be desirable to scan along epipolar lines of the projector-camera setup, since this avoids illuminating multiple scene points that lie on the pre-image of the same sensor pixel. However, this would be hard in non-rectified setups and hence, row-scanning is a simpler and effective alternative.

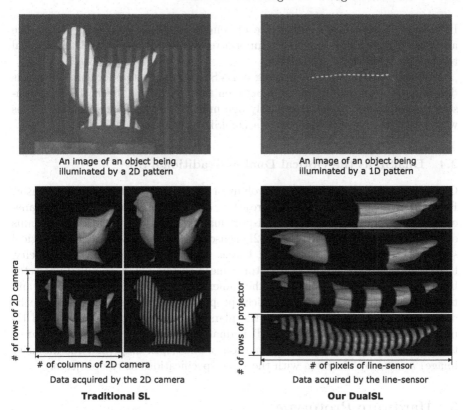

Fig. 3. 3D scanning using (left) traditional SL and (right) DualSL. For each setup, we show (top-row) the scene being illuminated by the projector, observed using an auxiliary camera, as well as (bottom-row) measurements made by the cameras. Here the auxiliary camera is not required for triangulation; it is used only for visualization purposes. For the traditional SL setup, these are simply images acquired by the 2D sensor. For DualSL, we stack together 1D measurements made for the same Gray code into individual image.

Line striping. The simplest instance of a traditional SL setup is to illuminate projector columns, one at a time. For each projector column, we read out an $N \times N$-pixels image at the camera. Hence, for a total of N projector columns, we read out N^3 pixels at the ADC. DualSL has an identical acquisition time, equivalent to the readout of N^3 pixels per depth map, when we sequentially scan each projector pixel.

Binary/Gray codes. As mentioned earlier, by scanning one projector-row at a time and using binary/Gray temporal codes, we can reduce the acquisition time to the readout of $N^2 \log_2(N)$ pixels per depth map. This readout time is identical to the amount required for a traditional SL system when using binary/Gray coding of the projector columns, where $\log_2(N)$ images, each with $N \times N = N^2$ pixels, are captured.

In essence, with appropriate choice of temporal coding at the projector, the acquisition time and hence, the temporal resolution, of the DualSL is identical to that of a traditional SL system.

For asynchronous readout using a DVS sensor, the temporal resolution is determined by the minimum time between two readouts. Current 1D DVS sensors typically support approximately one million readouts per second [2]. This would be the achievable limit with a DualSL system using DVS.

2.4   DualSL as the Optical Dual of Traditional SL

Consider a traditional SL system involving a 1D projector and a 2D image sensor. Recall that all pixels in a single projector columns are illuminated simultaneously. Let us consider the light transport matrix $\mathcal{L}$ associated with the columns of the projector and pixels on the 2D sensor. Next, let us consider the optical setup whose light transport is $\mathcal{L}^T$. Under principles of Helmholtz reciprocity, this corresponds to the dual projector-camera system where the dual-projector has the same optical properties as the camera in the traditional SL system, and the dual-camera has the same optical properties as the projector. Hence, the dual-camera integrates light along the planes originally illuminated by the 1D projector in the traditional setup. This dual architecture is the same as that of the DualSL setup and enables estimation of the depth map (and the intensity image) as seen by a camera with the same specifications as the projector.

3   Hardware Prototype

In this section, we present the specifications of our DualSL hardware prototype, shown in Fig. 4(a). The hardware prototype consists of a 50 mm F/1.8 objective lens, a 15 mm cylindrical lens, a Hamamatsu S11156-2048-01 line-sensor, and a DMD-based projector built using DLP7000 development kit and ViALUX STAR CORE optics. The line-sensor has 2048 pixels, each of size 14 μm × 1 mm. The projector resolution is 768 × 1024 pixels.

We implemented a slightly different optical design from the ray diagrams shown in Fig. 2. To accommodate the cylindrical lens in the tight spacing, we used a 1:1 relay lens to optically mirror the image plane of the objective lens. This provided sufficient spacing to introduce the cylindrical lens and translational mounts to place it precisely. The resulting schematic is shown in Fig. 4(b). Zemax analysis of this design shows that the spot-size has a RMS-width of 25 μm along the line-sensor and 3.7 mm perpendicular to the line-detector. Given that the height of the line-detector pixel is 1 mm, our prototype loses 73 % of the light. This light loss is mainly due to sub-optimal choice of optical components.

Calibration. The calibration procedure is a multi-step process with the eventual goal of characterizing the light ray associated with each projector pixel, and the plane associated with each line-sensor pixel.

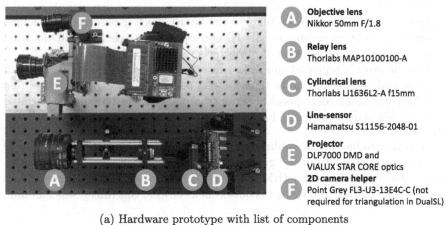

(a) Hardware prototype with list of components

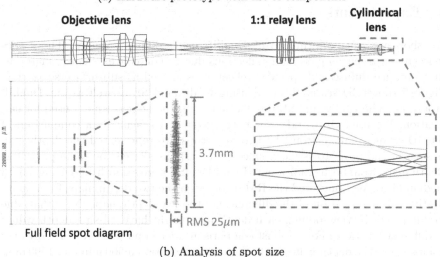

(b) Analysis of spot size

Fig. 4. Our hardware prototype. We used a 1:1 relay lens to mirror the image plane of the objective lens to provide more space to position the cylindrical lens. The spot-size of the resulting setup has a RMS-width of 25 μm along the axis of the line-sensor and 3.7 mm across.

- We introduce a helper 2D camera whose intrinsic parameters are obtained using the MATLAB Camera Calibration Toolbox [3].
- The projector is calibrated using a traditional projector-camera calibration method [13]. In particular, we estimate the intrinsic parameters of the projector as well as the extrinsic parameters (rotation and translation) with respect to the helper-camera's coordinate system.
- To estimate the plane corresponding to each line-sensor pixel, we introduce a white planar board in the scene with fiducial markers at corners of a rectangle of known dimensions. The helper-camera provides the depth map of the planar board by observing the fiducial markers.

- The projector illuminates a pixel to the board which is observed at the line-sensor, thereby providing one 3D-1D correspondence, where the 3D location is computed by intersection of projector's ray and the board.
- This process is repeated multiple times by placing the board in different poses and depths to obtain more 3D-1D correspondences. Once we obtain sufficiently many correspondences, we fit a plane to the 3D points associated with each pixel to estimate its pre-image.

As a by-product of the calibration procedure, we also measure deviations of the computed depth from the ground truth obtained using the helper-camera. The root-mean-square error (RMSE) over 2.5 million points with depth ranges from 950 mm to 1300 mm (target is out-of-focus beyond this range) was 2.27 mm.

4 Experiments

We showcase the performance of DualSL using different scenes. The scenes were chosen to encompass inter-reflections due to non-convex shapes, materials that produce diffuse and specular reflectances as well as subsurface scattering. Figure 5 shows 3D scans obtained using traditional SL as well as our DualSL prototype. The traditional SL was formed using the helper-camera used for calibration. We used Gray codes for both systems. To facilitate a comparison of the 3D scans obtained from the two SL setups, we represented the depth map as seen in the projector's view, since both systems shared the same projector. Depth maps from both traditional SL and DualSL were smoothened using a 3×3 median filter. We computed the RMSE between the two depth maps for a quantitative characterization of the difference of the two depth maps. Note that, due to differences in view-points, each depth map might have missing depth values at different locations. For a robust comparison, we compute the RMSE only over points where the depth values in both maps were between 500 mm and 1500 mm.

For the chicken and ball scenes (rows 1 and 2 in Fig. 5), both systems get good results and the average difference is smaller than 2 mm. For the box scene (row 3), the average difference is only slightly larger in spite of complex geometry of the scene. We fit planes to four different planar surfaces, and the mean deviation from the fitted planes was 0.45 mm with the average distance to camera being 1050 mm. The porcelain bowl scene (row 4), which has strong inter-reflections, and wax scene (row 5), which exhibits subsurface scattering, have strong global components. The depth maps generated by DualSL in both cases are significantly better than that of the traditional SL. This is because traditional SL illuminates the entire scene, and in contrast, DualSL illuminates a line at a time, thereby reducing the amount of global light. The exact strength of global illumination for a general scene, however, depends on the light transport. For instance, it may be possible to construct scenes where the amount of global light is smaller for conventional SL over DualSL, and vice-versa. However, a formal analysis is difficult because global illumination is scene dependent. Here, the depth map recovered by traditional SL has many "holes" because of missing

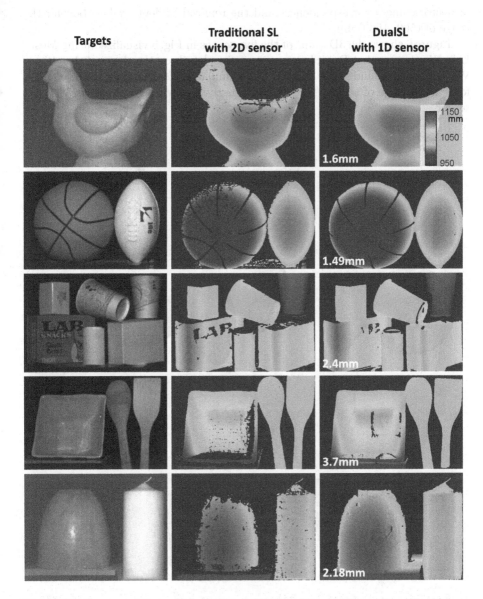

Fig. 5. Depth maps of five scenes obtained using traditional SL and DualSL. Objects in scenes range from simple convex diffuse materials to shiny and translucent materials exhibiting global illumination. Traditional SL is realized by projector and the 2D camera helper here. The left column is a photograph of the target acquired using the 2D camera helper (used only for visualization). The middle and right columns show depth maps obtained by the traditional SL system and DualSL system, respectively. Both depth maps are shown in projector's viewpoint. The number overlaid on DualSL's depth map indicates the average difference between the two depth maps.

projector-camera correspondences and the removal of depth values beyond the range of (500, 1500)mm.

Figure 6 shows the 3D scans of the five scenes in Fig. 5 visualized using Mesh-Lab. We observe that DualSL can capture fine details on the shape of the object. We can thus conclude that DualSL has a similar performance as traditional SL for a wide range of scenes, which is immensely satisfying given the use of a 1D sensor.

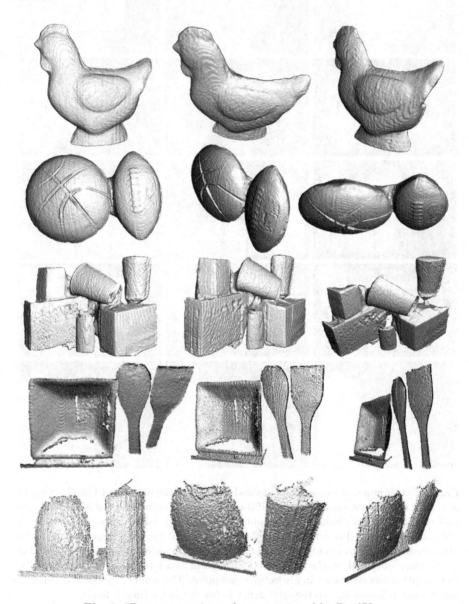

Fig. 6. 3D reconstructions of scenes scanned by DualSL.

5 Discussion

DualSL is a novel SL system that uses a 1D line-sensor to obtain 3D scans with simple optics and no moving components, while delivering a temporal resolution identical to traditional setups. The benefits of DualSL are most compelling in scenarios where sensors are inherently costly. To this end, we briefly discuss the performance of DualSL under ambient and global illumination as well as discuss potential applications of DualSL.

Performance of DualSL under ambient illumination. Performance of SL systems often suffers in the presence of ambient illumination, in part due to potentially strong photon noise. We can measure the effect of ambient illumination using signal-to-noise ratio (SNR), the ratio of the intensity observed at a camera pixel when a scene point is directly illuminated by the projector to the photon noise caused by ambient illumination. The larger the value of SNR, the less is the effect of ambient illumination on the performance since we can more reliably provide thresholds to identify the presence/absence of the direct component. We ignore the presence of global components for this analysis.

The hardware prototype used in this paper uses a DMD-based projector which attenuates a light source, spatially, using a spatial light modulation to create a binary projected pattern. In a traditional SL system, since we read out each camera pixel in isolation, SNR can be approximated as $\frac{P}{\sqrt{A}}$ where P and A are the brightness of the scene point due to the projector and ambient illumination, respectively [10]. Unfortunately, due to integration of light at each line-sensor pixel, SNR of DualSL drops to $\frac{P}{\sqrt{NA}} = \frac{1}{\sqrt{N}}\frac{P}{\sqrt{A}}$ where N is the number of pixels that we sum over. This implies that DualSL is significantly more susceptible to the presence of ambient illumination when we use attenuation-type projectors. This is a significant limitation of our prototype. An approach to address this limitation is to use a scanning laser projector which concentrates all of its light onto a single row of the projector. As a consequence, SNR becomes $\frac{NP}{\sqrt{NA}} = \sqrt{N}\frac{P}{\sqrt{A}}$. In contrast, traditional SL has no gain from using scanning laser projector because it needs projector to illuminate the entire scene.

A more powerful approach is to avoid integrating light and instead use a mirror to scan through scene points in synchrony with a scanning laser projector. Here, we are optically aligning the line-sensor and the illuminated projector pixels to be on epipolar line pairs and is similar to the primal-dual coding system of [17]. This enables acquisition of 3D scans that are highly robust to global and ambient illumination.

Performance of DualSL under global illumination. Global illumination is often a problem when dealing with scenes that have inter-reflections, subsurface- and volumetric-scattering. Similar to ambient illumination, global illumination also leads to loss in performance in decoding at the camera. In a traditional SL system, it is typical that half-the-scene points are illuminated and hence, at any camera pixel, we can expect to receive contributions to the global component from half the scene element. In DualSL, even though we only illuminate one projector-row at a time (and hence, fewer illuminated scene points), each camera pixel integrates light along a scene plane which can significantly increase the amount of global light observed at the pixel. While the results of bowl scene and wax scene in Fig. 5 are promising, a formal analysis of the influence of global illumination on the performance of DualSL is beyond the scope of this paper.

Applications of SWIR DualSL. Imaging through volumetric scattering media often benefits via the use of longer wavelengths. SWIR cameras, which operate in the range of 900 nm to 2.5 μm, are often used in such scenarios (see [24]). The DualSL system design for SWIR can provide an inexpensive alternative to otherwise-costly high-resolution 2D sensors. This would be invaluable for applications such as autonomous driving and fire-fighting operations, where depth sensitivity can be enhanced in spite of fog, smog, or smoke.

High-speed depth imaging using DVS line-sensors. The asynchronous readout underlying DVSs allows us to circumvent the limitations imposed by the readout speed of traditional sensors. Further, the change detection circuitry in DVSs provides a large dynamic range ($\sim$120 dB) that is capable of detecting very small changes in intensity even for scenes under direct sunlight. This is especially effective for SL systems where the goal is simply detecting changes in intensity at the sensor. The MC3D system [15] exploits this property to enable high-speed depth recovery even under high ambient illumination; in particular, the system demonstrated in [15] produces depth maps at a resolution of 128 × 128 pixels, due to lack of commercial availability of higher resolution sensors. In contrast, a DualSL system using the line-sensor in [2] would produce depth maps of 1024 × 1024 pixels at real-time video rates. Further, the DualSL system would also benefit from higher fill-factor at the sensor pixels (80 % versus 8 %).

Active stereo using DualSL. Another interesting modification to the DualSL setup is to enable active stereo-based 3D reconstruction. The envisioned system would have two line-sensors, with its associated optics, and a 1D projector that illuminates one scene plane at a time. By establishing correspondences across the line-sensors, we can enable 3D reconstructions by intersecting the two pre-images of sensor-pixels, which are both planes, with the plane illuminated by the projector. Such a device would provide very high-resolution depth maps (limited by the resolution of the sensors and not the projector) and would be an effective solution for highly-textured scenes.

Acknowledgments. We thank Ms. Chia-Yin Tsai for the help with MeshLab processing. Jian Wang, Aswin C. Sankaranarayanan and Srinivasa G. Narasimhan were supported in part by DARPA REVEAL (#HR0011-16-2-0021) grant. Srinivasa G. Narasimhan was also supported in part by NASA (#15-15ESI-0085), ONR (#N00014-15-1-2358), and NSF (#CNS-1446601) grants.

References

1. Agin, G.J., Binford, T.O.: Computer description of curved objects. IEEE Trans. Comput. **100**(4), 439–449 (1976)
2. Belbachir, A.N., Schraml, S., Mayerhofer, M., Hofstatter, M.: A novel HDR depth camera for real-time 3d 360-degree panoramic vision. In: Proceedings of IEEE Conference on Computer Vision and Pattern Recognition Workshops (CVPRW), pp. 425–432 (2014)
3. Bouguet, J.: Camera calibration toolbox for matlab (2015). http://www.vision. caltech.edu/bouguetj/calib_doc/
4. Brandli, C., Mantel, T.A., Hutter, M., Höpflinger, M.A., Berner, R., Siegwart, R., Delbruck, T.: Adaptive pulsed laser line extraction for terrain reconstruction using a dynamic vision sensor. Front. Neurosci. **7**(EPFL-ARTICLE-200448) (2014)
5. Curless, B., Levoy, M.: Better optical triangulation through spacetime analysis. In: Proceedings of International Conference on Computer Vision (ICCV), pp. 987–994 (1995)
6. Delbruck, T.: Frame-free dynamic digital vision. In: International Symposium on Secure-Life Electronics, Advanced Electronics for Quality Life and Society, pp. 21–26 (2008)
7. Forsen, G.E.: Processing visual data with an automaton eye. In: Pictoral Pattern Recognition (1968)
8. Gehm, M.E., Brady, D.J.: Compressive sensing in the EO/IR. Appl. Opt. **54**(8), C14–C22 (2015)
9. Geng, J.: Structured-light 3d surface imaging: a tutorial. Adv. Opt. Photonics **3**(2), 128–160 (2011)
10. Gupta, M., Yin, Q., Nayar, S.K.: Structured light in sunlight. In: Proceedings of International Conference on Computer Vision (ICCV), pp. 545–552 (2013)
11. iniLabs: Dvs128 specifications (2015). http://inilabs.com/products/ dynamic-and-active-pixel-vision-sensor/davis-specifications/
12. Inokuchi, S., Sato, K., Matsuda, F.: Range imaging system for 3-d object recognition. In: Proceedings of International Conference on Pattern Recognition (ICPR), vol. 48, pp. 806–808 (1984)
13. Lanman, D., Taubin, G.: Build your own 3D scanner: 3D photograhy for beginners. In: ACM SIGGRAPH 2009 Courses, pp. 30–34 (2009)
14. Lichtsteiner, P., Posch, C., Delbruck, T.: A 128× 128 120 db 15 μs latency asynchronous temporal contrast vision sensor. IEEE J. Solid-State Circuits **43**(2), 566–576 (2008)
15. Matsuda, N., Cossairt, O., Gupta, M.: MC3D: motion contrast 3d scanning. In: IEEE International Conference on Computational Photography (ICCP) (2015)
16. Microsoft: Kinect for xbox 360 (2010). https://en.wikipedia.org/wiki/Kinect# Kinect_for_Xbox_360
17. O'Toole, M., Achar, S., Narasimhan, S.G., Kutulakos, K.N.: Homogeneous codes for energy-efficient illumination and imaging. ACM Trans. Graph. **34**(4), 35 (2015)
18. Posch, C., Hofstätter, M., Matolin, D., Vanstraelen, G., Schön, P., Donath, N., Litzenberger, M.: A dual-line optical transient sensor with on-chip precision timestamp generation. In: International Solid-State Circuits Conference, pp. 500–618 (2007)
19. Posdamer, J., Altschuler, M.: Surface measurement by space-encoded projected beam systems. Comput. Graph. Image Process. **18**(1), 1–17 (1982)

20. Proesmans, M., Van Gool, L.J., Oosterlinck, A.J.: One-shot active 3d shape acquisition. In: Proceedings of International Conference on Pattern Recognition (ICPR), pp. 336–340 (1996)
21. Sagawa, R., Ota, Y., Yagi, Y., Furukawa, R., Asada, N., Kawasaki, H.: Dense 3d reconstruction method using a single pattern for fast moving object. In: Proceedings of International Conference on Computer Vision (ICCV), pp. 1779–1786 (2009)
22. Sato, K., Inokuchi, S.: Three-dimensional surface measurement by space encoding range imaging. J. Robotic Syst. **2**, 27–39 (1985)
23. Sen, P., Chen, B., Garg, G., Marschner, S.R., Horowitz, M., Levoy, M., Lensch, H.: Dual photography. ACM Trans. Graph. **24**(3), 745–755 (2005)
24. Sensors Unlimited Inc.: Swir image gallery (2016). http://www.sensorsinc.com/gallery/images
25. Shirai, Y., Suwa, M.: Recognition of polyhedrons with a range finder. In: Proceedings of International Joint Conference on Artificial Intelligence, pp. 80–87 (1971)
26. Srinivasan, V., Liu, H.C., Halioua, M.: Automated phase-measuring profilometry: a phase mapping approach. Appl. Opt. **24**(2), 185–188 (1985)
27. Vuylsteke, P., Oosterlinck, A.: Range image acquisition with a single binary-encoded light pattern. IEEE Trans. Pattern Anal. Mach. Intell. **12**(2), 148–164 (1990)
28. Wang, J., Gupta, M., Sankaranarayanan, A.C.: LiSens – a scalable architecture for video compressive sensing. In: IEEE International Conference on Computational Photography (ICCP) (2015)

Shape Acquisition and Registration for 3D Endoscope Based on Grid Pattern Projection

Ryo Furukawa[1]($\boxtimes$), Hiroki Morinaga[2], Yoji Sanomura[3], Shinji Tanaka[3], Shigeto Yoshida[4], and Hiroshi Kawasaki[2]

[1] Hiroshima City University, Hiroshima, Japan
ryo-f@hiroshima-cu.ac.jp
[2] Kagoshima University, Kagoshima, Japan
{sc110080,kawasaki}@ibe.kagoshima-u.ac.jp
[3] Hiroshima University Hospital, Hiroshima, Japan
{sanomura,colon}@hiroshima-cu.ac.jp
[4] Hiroshima General Hospital of West Japan Railway Company, Hiroshima, Japan
yoshida7@hiroshima-cu.ac.jp

Abstract. For effective endoscopic diagnosis and treatment, size measurement and shape characterization of lesions, such as tumors, is important. For this purpose, 3D endoscopic systems based on active stereo to measure the shape and size of living tissue have recently been proposed. In those works, a large problem is the degree of reconstruction instability due to image blurring caused by the strong subsurface scattering common to internal tissue. To reduce this instability problem, using a coarse pattern for structured light is an option, however it reduces the resolution of the acquired shape information. In this paper, we tackle these shortcomings by developing a new micro pattern laser projector to be inserted in the scope tool channel. There are hardware and software contributions in the paper. First, the new projector uses a Diffractive Optical Element (DOE) instead of a single lens which we proposed to solve the off-focus blur. Second, we propose a new line-based grid pattern with gap coding to counter the subsurface scattering effect. The proposed pattern is a coarse grid pattern so that the grid features are not blurred out by the subsurface scattering. Third, to increase shape resolution of line-based grid pattern, we propose to use a multiple shape data registration technique for the grid-structured shapes, which are acquired sequentially by small motions, is proposed. Quantitative experiments are conducted to show the effectiveness of the method followed by a demonstration using real endoscopic system.

1 Introduction

Endoscopic diagnosis and treatment on digestive tracts has become increasingly accepted methods. For example, in the diagnosis of early-stage gastric tumors, the size of the tumor is one of the most important factors for the choice of treatment. However, this is currently evaluated either by manipulation with forceps or by visual assessment alone, both of which are time consuming and

© Springer International Publishing AG 2016
B. Leibe et al. (Eds.): ECCV 2016, Part VI, LNCS 9910, pp. 399–415, 2016.
DOI: 10.1007/978-3-319-46466-4_24

possible human errors occurring. For this reason, an easy to deploy, accurate tumor size estimation technique is necessary for endoscopic diagnosis systems.

Recently, several papers have proposed 3D endoscope systems to measure the shapes and sizes of living tissue [1–9]. Among them, we have adopted active stereo systems for developing 3D endoscopic systems, because of stability, accuracy and cost effectiveness [5, 7]. These systems use micro-sized pattern projectors with the endoscope cameras, and have successfully reconstructed several *ex vivo* human tumor samples. To implement the micro-sized pattern projector, a micro chip of the pattern and a lens are used to project a focused pattern image on the target surface. One significant limitation of such system is that a lens-based projection method can project a clear pattern only within a narrow depth range. This is because the pattern projector is based on a single lens, and thus, off-focus blurring as well as aberrations in the periphery of the field of view inevitably occur. Another critical problem in an active stereo system for endoscope is the strong subsurface scattering effect, which is common for internal tissue. This not only blurs the projected pattern, making it more difficult to detect, but it also diminishes its brightness. One more important problem is the sparse reconstruction of the system. Since the human body moves dynamically, we are required to scan the target object within a short period of time; such a system is also known as a oneshot scan [10–12]. Usually, the resolution of a oneshot scanning system is low because a certain area of the pattern is required to embed the projector's positional information. Consequently, resolution of oneshot active stereo system for endoscope becomes low.

In this paper, we propose a three approach solution for the aforementioned problems. The first is using a special optical device called Diffractive Optical Element (DOE). Since the DOE is a device that can project sharp patterns regardless of its depth, it solves the narrow depth of field problem. Furthermore, the DOE light efficiency is usually more than 90 %, which helps to maximize the pattern detection accuracy by preserving its visibility. The second is a novel line-based grid pattern, processing gap coding. Since high frequency information is easily lost in the presence of strong scattering effects, low frequency patterns are generally more robust. However, a low frequency pattern is not suitable for encoding rich information. We address this issue by intentionally adding gaps between adjacent lines in the grid pattern, which creates implicit unambiguous higher-level label structures that can be easily detected under strong scattering effects. The third contribution is using a multiple-shape alignment algorithm producing a grid-like shape, which then is reconstructed using the line-based grid pattern. With this method, multiple sparse shapes of the grid patterns are effectively aligned using grid information and merged into a finer shape.

By using our DOE micro pattern projector with a line-based grid pattern, we can achieve an efficient and accurate reconstruction of tissue in metric 3D with a wide depth of field using an ordinary endoscopic system. In the experiments, we show the effectiveness of our technique with several tests using a projector-camera system, and demonstrate the reconstruction of an *ex vivo* tumor sample imaged at several distances from the camera using the endoscopic system.

2   Related Work

For a 3D reconstruction method using endoscopes, techniques using Shape from Shading (SfS) [13–16] have been proposed. However, the SfS techniques often have stringent assumptions concerning the types of images that can be processed, such as the known or uniform diffuse reflection rates of the target surface, thus, the precise size measurement is generally difficult. 3D endoscopes based on binocular stereo [17,18] are actively being researched at the present. For the binocular stereo algorithm, which is a typical passive stereo technique, correspondence problems are often very difficult, especially on textureless surfaces. Visual SLAM has also been also applied on endoscope images [6], but the 3D reconstruction is only up-to-scale. Thus, it cannot be directly applied for measuring real sizes of 3D tissues. As an example of active stereo applications in endoscopy, in work of Grasa et al. [1], a single-line laser scanner attached to the scope head was used to measure tissue shape, however the scope head had to be actuated in a direction parallel to the target, which limited the practical applicability of the technique. Some other vision techniques use special cameras being applied to endoscopes, such as the Shape from Polarization (SfP) [2] which uses an endoscope with a rotating polarizing filter on light source, and ToF sensors [4]. Considering laparoscope systems, computer guided surgery operations have been actively researched, such as Penne et al. [8] or Kunert et al. [9]. However, the 3D system used in a laparoscope is not necessarily small and therefore cannot be used to endoscope. Recently, Furukawa et al. proposed a structured light system for endoscope [5,7], which allows users to update a common endoscope system without any reconfiguration. However, there are several problems with the system and our technique can provide practical solutions to them.

The Structured light based 3D scanning systems have been studied for a several decades and these techniques are well summarized by Salvi et al. [19]. Based on the analysis, the techniques can be largely categorized into two method, the temporal method and the spatial encoding method. Multiple patterns are required for a temporal encoding method [20], whereas just a single static pattern is required for a spatial encoding method. Because of such differences, one of the most important advantages of a spatial encoding method is that it can capture a moving object or, in other words, the sensor can be moved during the scan. Another important benefit is a potential for compact implementation. Note that those two advantages are applicable for endoscopic systems. Based on such advantages, spatial encoding techniques have been intensively studied [11,21–23]. To increase their stability and accuracy, most techniques use color information, however, it is difficult to use multiple colors in endoscopic systems because of space limitations. Koninckx et al. proposed a single color method using parallel lines [24], but it has several limitations in practical usage. Sagawa et al. proposed a single color method using a wave shaped pattern to encode additional information into the phase of the wave [25]. Kinect is another successful implementation using a random dot pattern [12]. However, those patterns are not considered to be useful under strong subsurface scattering environment, and thus, not suitable for endoscopic systems.

Our third contribution is based on a rigid registration algorithm. Rigid registration algorithms estimate translation and rotation of an object from two point sets, with the ICP algorithm [26] and its extension to multiple point sets [27] being the two best-known approaches. Since then, improved techniques have been intensively researched on realtime registration [28], large scale simultaneous registration [29,30] and color compensated registration [31]. However, since they all assume a large overlap of dense shapes, they generally cannot be used whenever the shape is sparse such as a grid based reconstruction [10,11,23]. Recently, an ICP for the sparse point set was proposed [32], however, since the technique is still based on the correspondences of closest points, lines in the same direction are inevitably pulled together, and thus, all the grid based shapes are bundled into a single grid liked shape. Banno *et al.* proposed a method to align the multiple 3D curves which are reconstructed by the light sectioning method into single consistent shape [33], however, they assumed a base shape with holes captured in advance with 3D curves that are aligned with it to fill the holes. Therefore, the technique cannot be applied to the data which consists of independent curves only. Another approach to achieving robust registration of multiple shapes is based on 3D features extracted from input shapes [34–38]. However, stable 3D features are usually extracted only from dense 3D points and cannot be applied to grid based shapes, whose points are sparse and unevenly distributed.

3   DOE Projector for Endoscopy

3.1   System Configuration

A projector-camera system is constructed by installing a micro pattern projector on a standard endoscope as shown in Fig. 1(a). For our system, we used a FujiFilm VP-4450HD system coupled with a EG-590WR scope. The DOE-based pattern projector is inserted in the endoscope through the instrument channel, and the projector protrudes slightly from the endoscope head and emits structured light. The light source of the projector is a green laser module with a wavelength of 517 nm. The laser light is transmitted through a single-mode optical fiber to the head of the DOE projector. In the head, the light is collimated by a grin lens, and go through the DOE. The DOE generates the pattern through diffraction of the laser light.

3.2   DOE Projector for Endoscopy

In the previous work [7], a lens with a mask pattern is used for the pattern projection. From our experience, such an optical system has a generally narrow depth of field, such as approximately an 8 mm depth for a working distance of 40 mm. Another problem with such optical systems is brightness efficiency, which is important since light exposure for the cameras on the endoscopes are low. To solve both problems, we have created a micro-pattern projector consisting of a DOE, a grin lens with single-mode optical fiber and a laser light source as shown

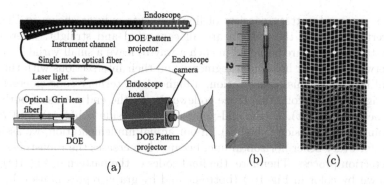

Fig. 1. System configuration: (a) system components, (b) DOE micro projector, (c) the projected pattern (top), and embedded codewords of S colored in red, L in blue, and R in green (bottom). S means edges of the left and the right sides have the same height, L means the left side is higher, and R means the right is higher. (Color figure online)

in Fig. 1(b). The DOE can project a fine, complex pattern at a greater depth range without requiring lenses, and the energy loss is less than 5 %. The actual specifications of the micro pattern projector are as follows. To lead the micro DOE projector into the head of the endoscope through the instrument channel, its dimensions were needed to be 2.8 mm in diameter and 12 mm in length. The working distance, valid depth range and area for the pattern projector are of 30 mm, (-10 mm to $+40$ mm) and 30 mm^2, respectively.

3.3   Design of Projected Pattern

Avoidance of Subsurface Scattering. Since the reflectance conditions inside the body are very different from the ordinary environments for which active scanners are built, we then tailored an original pattern design specifically for the intra-operative environment. One significant casual effect under endoscopic environment is a strong subsurface scattering on the surface of internal organs. In the previous work [7], a grid pattern that consists of waved lines was used. We have found that, under the conditions of strong subsurface scattering, some of the important information of the waved grid patterns, such as the wave curvature, is difficult to be extracted or sometimes is lost completely. To avoid losing important detailed information, we considered a pattern with a larger low-frequency structure. Existing patterns of this kind include sparse dots or a straight line-based pattern with a wide interval. However, sparse dots are difficult to decode with wide baselines and large windows, because the pattern is heavily distorted under such conditions. On the other hand, a simple line-based pattern cannot encode distinctive information efficiently [10]. Instead, we propose a line-based pattern with large intervals with a new encoding technique which is robust against the scattering effect.

Our proposed pattern consists of line segments only as shown in Fig. 1(c). The vertical lines of the pattern are all connected and straight, whereas the horizontal segments are designed in such a way to leave a small variable vertical gap between adjacent horizontal segments and their intersections with the same vertical line. With this configuration, a higher-level ternary code emerges from the design with the following three codewords: S (the end-points of both sides have the same height), L (the end-point of the left side is higher), and R (the end-point of the left side is higher). In our actual implementation, we assign all S code for every other horizontal line, because it increases the robustness of the line detection process. Therefore, the final codes of the pattern of Fig. 1(c) (top) are shown by color in Fig. 1(c) (bottom) and by graph representation in Fig. 3 (left).

Eliminating the Singular Rotation Angle of Pattern. As shown in Fig. 1(a), since a DOE pattern projector cannot be fixed to the head of the endoscope, a rotation angle of the pattern may have some freedom, such as $\pm 30°$. If the rotation angle is near 0 degrees, the epiplor lines, which are drawn on the pattern image of Fig. 1(c), nearly coincide with the horizontal lines and the number of candidate points on the pattern for the intersection on the captured image increases; such a condition increases the ambiguity and results in low reconstruction accuracy. To mitigate the instability at such a singular rotation angle, each set of horizontal line segments in the same column is slightly inclined with a specific degree; e.g., according to a piecewise long wavelength sinusoid as shown in Fig. 1(c).

4   3D Reconstruction

4.1   Detection of Line Patterns

The source image is first geometrically corrected on fisheye lens distortion. Noises in the image are suppressed using Gaussian filters or median filters simultaneously. Figure 2(a) shows an example of an input image. Then, the vertical lines on the captured image are detected because vertical lines projected onto the objects are still connected if the surface of the objects is smooth; remember that the vertical lines are straight whereas the horizontal lines are small segments frequently disconnected. Figure 2(b) shows detected vertical lines.

Next, the horizontal segments connecting the vertical lines are extracted. In this stage, intensities of both sides of the detected vertical lines are traced and the peak values on each side are measured. The position of these peaks are the candidates of end-points of the horizontal segments as shown in Fig. 2(b) as blue dots. From all line segments that connect the candidate end-points, those within a predefined range of lengths are then selected as initial candidates for the horizontal edges as shown in Fig. 2(c) as red lines. Then, to correct for small positional errors of the initial edge candidates, every pixel on the edge is moved to the local peak position along the vertical line from the original pixel. Finally, all

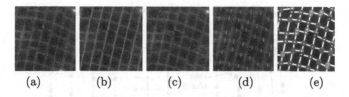

Fig. 2. Example of grid graph detection: (a) source image (a partial region), (b) identified vertical line (violet dots) and candidate end-points (blue dots), (c) initial candidates of the horizontal edges, (d) identified horizontal edges (blue line segments), and (e) detected grid graph with gap codes (colors represent same codes with Fig. 1(c)). (Color figure online)

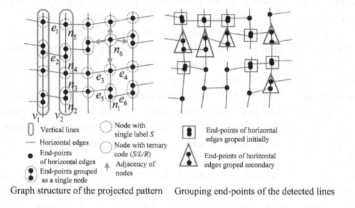

Graph structure of the projected pattern   Grouping end-points of the detected lines

Fig. 3. Grid graph construction: (left) structure of the projected pattern, and (right) grouping end-points of the identified lines.

the distances between the corrected edge candidates are calculated and if there is a pair of edge candidates that are close to each other, the edge candidate with the smaller average intensity is removed. The final determined horizontal edges are shown in Fig. 2(d).

4.2   Constructing Grid Graphs

From the identified line patterns, a grid-graph structure is constructed. The grid graph structure of the proposed pattern is shown in Fig. 3 (left). Note that the vertical lines are first identified (*e.g.*, v_1 and v_2 of the figure), and the horizontal edges are then extracted between them (*e.g.*, e_1 and e_2). Thus, pairs of horizontal edges from both sides of a vertical line may be classified as 'continuous' or 'non-continuous'. Here, 'continuous' horizontal edges do not mean only that they are geometrically continuous as e_3 and e_4. Edges e_5 and e_6 are also considered continuous because their end-points are regarded as a single node n_1. Thus, classifying the continuity of horizontal segments is an important process.

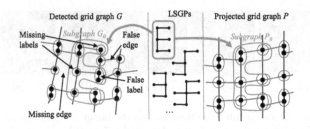

Fig. 4. Matching the detected grid graph and the projected pattern using LSGPs.

As shown in Fig. 3 (left), nodes have ternary $S/L/R$ gap codes. For example, on the vertical line v_2, nodes have S codes at n_3 and n_5, L codes at n_2 and R codes at n_4. Taking this property into account, we first label the nodes from continuous horizontal edges with the label S by selecting those satisfying the small distance threshold between end points of consecutive horizontal segments of the identified lines (end-point groups shown by rectangles in Fig. 3 (right)) Then, the remaining edge pairs with a larger vertical distance between end-points are selected, in which, if the horizontal lines above or below have continuous nodes, then the pair is labeled as belonging to the same horizontal piecewise sinusoid and joined together as a single node (end-point groups shown by triangles in Fig. 3 (right)).

Each node is connected by vertical or horizontal edges with its up, down, left, or right adjacent nodes, such as n_6. Some horizontal edges might have a missing edge because of mis-identification. In this case, the node will only have either a left or a right edge, which may be matched later by looking at other connectivity in the grid graph. Figure 2(e). shows an example of the identified vertical and horizontal patterns with estimated gap codes.

4.3 Finding Correspondences Using Sub-graph Patterns

Let the grid-graph detected be G, and let the pattern of the grid-graph in Fig. 1(c) be P. Note that graph G may lack some edges, or have undesired false edges, missing labels, or false labels of $S/L/R$ as shown in Fig. 4. To match G to P allowing for topological errors, we exploit the notion of local sub-graph patterns (LSGPs). We define the LSGP to be a sub-graph of a grid-graph, which can be used as a template for matching the common local topologies of G to P as shown in Fig. 4. Given a dictionary of LSGPs, G may be matched to P robustly for missing or false edges. By providing multiple LSGPs and trying to match G to P using each of them, matching flexibility can be realized. In our implementation, an LSGP is represented by a path that traces all of its edges. To merge all the matching results of LSGPs, voting is used.

The matching algorithm is as follows. From a node n of G, the path of an LSGP is traced, checking for the existence of missing edges with the sub-graph denoted as G_0. Then, the a corresponding sub-graph P_0 of P is searched, under the condition that the topology of P_0 matches that of G_0, all the nodes of P_0

fulfill epipolar constraints with the corresponding nodes of G_0, and the $S/L/R$ labels of nodes of P_0 and the corresponding nodes G_0 should match to at least some pre-defined agreement ratio. Since our proposed pattern structure has a low number of candidate nodes fulfilling the epipolar constraints (at most 10 depending on the point), the dictionary search can be performed efficiently and with a low degree of ambiguity.

If a P_0 with the above condition is found, all the nodes of P_0 are voted on as candidate matches for the nodes of G_0. The above process is repeated for all the nodes of G with all the pre-defined LSGPs. After each iteration finishes, each node of G is checked if it fulfills the predefined thresholds of minimum number and minimum percentage of votes. If the thresholds are fulfilled, it is matched with the corresponding node of P with the maximum votes.

Once the correspondence of the captured image to the pattern is obtained, the points on the vertical and horizontal lines are reconstructed in 3D using a light-sectioning method.

4.4   Taking Consensus of Vertical and Horizontal Line Positions

In a real system, the calibration of the camera and the projector includes errors. With the existence of calibration errors, vertical and horizontal lines that are reconstructed by a light sectioning method generally do not intersect in 3D space (*i.e.*, they result in skewed positions). The inconsistencies between vertical and horizontal lines are not desirable for obtaining a consistent shape of the target surface.

The direct cause of a inconsistency of the vertical and horizontal lines at an intersection is the displacement of an intersection point from the corresponding epipolar line. Thus, to solve this problem, we propose a deformation of the local segments of both of the detected lines around the intersection in 2D image space so that the intersection is moved strictly onto the epipolar line. This process can be done on each of the intersections after the identified grid-graph is mapped to the corresponding projected grid pattern. Figure 5 shows the approach.

This deformation of the lines is done locally, so that the correction of a grid-graph node does not interfere with the adjacent grid-graph nodes. One more policy about the deformation is to move the points of the lines only in the direction that is vertical to the epipolar line. This deformation can be realized by, first calculating the displacement vectors at each intersection that is vertical to the epipolar lines and move the intersections onto the epipolar lines, and then shift each of the points on the lines with the weighted means of the displacement vectors at the adjacent two nodes in both of the line directions at the point. The weights can be decided using the distances from the two nodes.

4.5   Registration of Reconstructed Grid Patterns

Once the correspondence from the captured image to the pattern is obtained, the points on the vertical and horizontal lines are reconstructed as 3D curves using a light-sectioning method. Since the line intervals between parallel lines

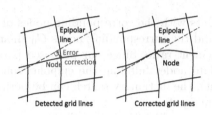

Fig. 5. Correction of position of grid nodes.

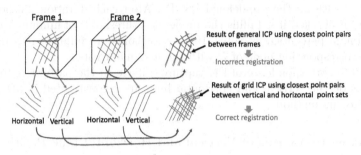

Fig. 6. Process of grid ICP

are wide enough to avoid mis-detection by the subsurface scattering effect, the shapes can be only coarsely reconstructed. To increase the density of the sparse grid shaped 3D points, one solution is to capture the object multiple times by moving the sensor, and then, align and integrate them.

The ICP algorithm is the most used solution to conduct shape alignment between 3D shapes of a static object. The algorithm consists of two steps such as (1) searching for the closest point q_i of the scene object from point p_i, which belongs to the target object, and (2) estimate a rigid transformation R, t by minimizing $\sum_i \|p_i - (R\ q_i + t)\|^2$. Final parameters of R, t are obtained by iterating the two steps until convergence.

However, such a naive ICP algorithm does not work properly on sparse grid shapes, because the closest points from vertical/horizontal lines of the scene object are usually found on the line in same direction as the target shape, note that such incorrect corresponding points are pulled together to minimize the differences to configure an incorrect wrong shape. Noteworthy, if multiple shapes are captured with small translational motions, grid lines tends to be bundled together.

In this paper, we propose a new ICP algorithm to solve this problem. Figure 6 shows the process of our algorithm. We first divide the grid shape into two sets of lines depending on the line directions, *i.e.*, the vertical set and the horizontal set. Then, the closest point q_i^v in the vertical line set from the point p_i^h in the horizontal line set is searched. Similarly, the closest point q_i^h in the horizontal line set from the point p_i^v which belongs to the vertical line set is found. Finally, rigid transformation parameters R, t are estimated by minimizing

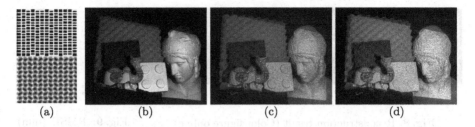

(a)   (b)   (c)   (d)

Fig. 7. Captured images: (a) projected patterns (top is proposed and bottom is wave pattern), (b) measurement scene, (c) a scene projected the wave pattern, and (d) a scene projected the proposed pattern.

$\sum_i \|p_i^h - (R\, q_i^v + t)\|^2 + \sum_j \|p_j^v - (R\, q_j^h + t)\|^2$. Final results are obtained by iterating the aforementioned steps until convergence. Within this scenario, grid lines of the final shapes are evenly distributed realizing dense reconstruction of the object surface.

5   Experiments

5.1   3D Reconstruction Based on Gap-Coded Grid Pattern

To confirm the effectiveness of our gap-coded grid pattern, which is robust to objects with strong subsurface scattering and complicated textures, we prepare the scene with various materials. In addition, to compare our technique with the existing state-of-the-art technique, we reconstruct the same scene using Kinect1 and wave a pattern [7,39], which are also single color and oneshot scanning techniques. Projected patterns are shown in Fig. 7(a). For the ground truth, we also capture the same scene with a time coded technique, *i.e.*, gray code [20]. We use a video projector and a CCD camera for the experiment and the actual captured scene is shown in Fig. 7(b)–(d). Figure 8 shows the reconstructed shapes and the results are summarized in Fig. 9. For the evaluation, we divided the scene with each object as shown in different colors in Fig. 8 and then calculate the value for each segment. From the results, we can confirm that our technique successfully reconstructed the shape with higher density and accuracy than the previous techniques, especially on the strong subsurface scattering object (sponge) and the complicated texture object (camel figurine).

5.2   Evaluation of Grid-Based ICP

Next, we evaluated the grid-based ICP technique by using 15 frames as an input, which are captured with a slight movement of the device. We also used a common ICP for comparison. Figure 10(a) is an example of a reconstructed shape from the first frame. Figure 10(b) is the 3D shape reconstructed with a time-encoded technique. Registration result with the grid-based ICP and a common ICP are shown in Fig. 10(c)(d) and all the results are summarized in Fig. 11. In the figure,

410   R. Furukawa et al.

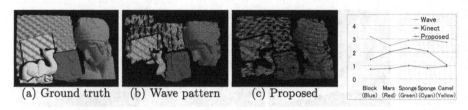

(a) Ground truth   (b) Wave pattern   (c) Proposed

Fig. 8. Reconstruction result (Color figure online)

Fig. 9. RMSE (mm) of wave pattern and proposed method.

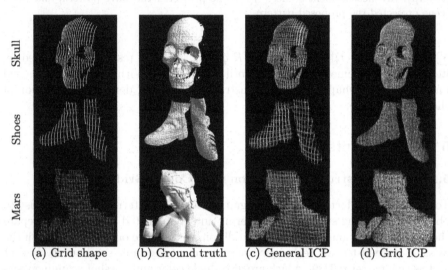

(a) Grid shape   (b) Ground truth   (c) General ICP   (d) Grid ICP

Fig. 10. Registration result

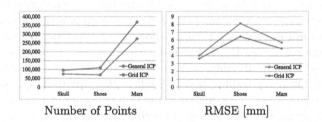

Number of Points   RMSE [mm]

Fig. 11. Registration comparison result

the *Number of Points* are calculated by projecting all the points onto the image plane of the camera and counting their pixels. From the figure and the graph, we can confirm that integrated 3D points with our grid-based ICP are more evenly distributed than that with the general ICP. The RMSE is also improved by 22 % compared to a common ICP.

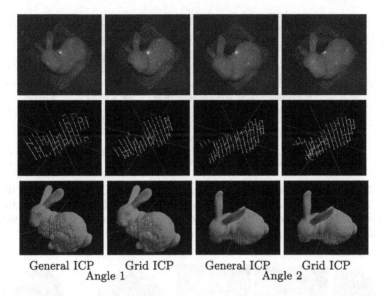

General ICP   Grid ICP   General ICP   Grid ICP
        Angle 1   Angle 2

Fig. 12. Registration of shapes measured by the 3D endoscope. (Top row) Input images, (Middle row) reconstructed 3D points, and (Bottom row) registration results.

5.3   3D Reconstruction Using Endoscope Images

We first evaluated the proposed 3D endoscopic system by measuring a 3D object with a known shape. The target is an output of a 3D printer using the 3D shape model of Stanford bunny object. We used this object because its ground-truth data is available. It is first scanned with the 3D endoscope by moving the object as shown in Fig. 12 (top row), and each of the frames are reconstructed as shown in Fig. 12 (middle row). Finally, those reconstructed frames are registered with both a general ICP algorithm and our grid ICP algorithm, and compared with the ground-truth shape data. The registration results that are fit to the true shape data is shown in Fig. 12 (bottom row). The results show that, in the result shape of the general ICP, the grid lines of multiple frames were pulled together and aggregated, whereas in the result of our grid ICP, the grid lines were uniformly distributed. The RMSEs between the registered 3D shapes and the ground-truth were 1.54 mm for the general ICP, and 1.20 mm for our grid ICP.

To evaluate the system in realistic conditions, a biological specimen extracted from a human stomach in an endoscopy operation is measured, as shown in Fig. 13. We captured the tissue image from different distances about 25 mm and 15 mm. Note that, since the projector is based on DOE, the projected patterns from both images at different distances are sharp enough. Using our proposed algorithm, both images could be nearly reconstructed except for the regions that were affected by bright specular highlights. Our future work will be to avoid the effects of these specular highlights. Other than these points, the correspondence

412   R. Furukawa et al.

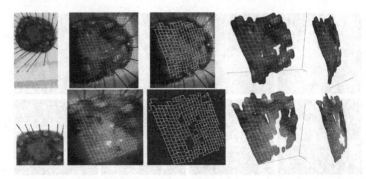

Fig. 13. 3D reconstruction of real tissues from human stomach measured with distance of about 25 mm (top row) and about 15 mm (bottom row). (From left column to right) The appearance of the sample, the captured image, the identified grid graph with gap codes, and the reconstructed shapes (the front and the side).

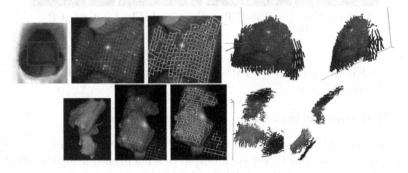

Fig. 14. 3D reconstruction of (top row) the inside of the human mouth (palate), and (bottom row) a piece of intestines of a cattle.

between the detected grid points and the projected pattern were estimated accurately, and the shape of the specimen was successfully reconstructed.

We also measured the inside of the human mouth (palate), and a piece of intestines of a cattle with the endoscopic system and the result were registered with the proposed grid ICP, as shown in Fig. 14. From the figures, we can confirm that shapes are densely reconstructed with our gap-based DOE pattern projector, and grid based ICP technique.

6   Conclusion

We proposed a 3D endoscopic system based on an active stereo, where the pattern projector consists of a DOE that generates a special line based grid pattern. By using a DOE which is free from the blur effect, sharp patterns are projected at wide depth ranges while keeping a strong intensity (usually more than 90 % efficiency). In addition, by using a line based grid pattern, the severely blurred pattern caused by the subsurface scattering effect is also robustly detected and decoded. We also propose a new reconstruction algorithm for the gap coding implemented on the pattern. Since shapes reconstructed from grid pattern are usually sparse, an ICP algorithm specialized for grid patterns is proposed. The potential of the technique was verified by intensive experiment using projector-camera systems and demonstrated by reconstructing the shape of some bio tissues such as the surface of a human palate, or a biological specimen extracted from the stomach of a human subject at various distances from the endoscope. Our future work is to test the system with real diagnosis.

References

1. Grasa, O., Bernal, E., Casado, S., Gil, I., Montiel, J.: Visual slam for handheld monocular endoscope. IEEE Trans. Med. Imaging 33(1), 135–146 (2014)
2. Liao, H.: 3d endoscopic image reconstruction using shape from polarization and central projection model compensation. Int. J. Comput. Assist. Radiol. Surg. 5(1), S281 (2010)
3. Aoki, H., Furukawa, R., Aoyama, M., Hiura, S., Asada, N., Sagawa, R., Kawasaki, H., Tanaka, S., Yoshida, S., Sanomura, Y.: Proposal on 3D endoscope by using grid-based active stereo. In: The 35th Annual International Conference of IEEE EMBC (2013)
4. Köhler, T., Haase, S., Bauer, S., Wasza, J., Kilgus, T., Maier-Hein, L., Feußner, H., Hornegger, J.: ToF meets RGB: novel multi-sensor super-resolution for hybrid 3-D endoscopy. In: Mori, K., Sakuma, I., Sato, Y., Barillot, C., Navab, N. (eds.) MICCAI 2013. LNCS, vol. 8149, pp. 139–146. Springer, Heidelberg (2013). doi:10. 1007/978-3-642-40811-3_18
5. Furukawa, R., Aoyama, M., Hiura, S., Aoki, H., Kominami, Y., Sanomura, Y., Yoshida, S., Tanaka, S., Sagawa, R., Kawasaki, H.: Calibration of a 3d endoscopic system based on active stereo method for shape measurement of biological tissues and specimen. In: EMBC, pp. 4991–4994 (2014)
6. Grasa, O.G., Bernal, E., Casado, S., Gil, I., Montiel, J.: Visual slam for handheld monocular endoscope. IEEE Trans. Med. Imaging 33(1), 135–146 (2014)
7. Furukawa, R., Masutani, R., Miyazaki, D., Baba, M., Hiura, S., Visentini-Scarzanella, M., Morinaga, H., Kawasaki, H., Sagawa, R.: 2-dof auto-calibration for a 3d endoscope system based on active stereo. In: 2015 37th Annual International Conference of the IEEE Engineering in Medicine and Biology Society (EMBC), pp. 7937–7941, August 2015
8. Penne, J., Schaller, C., Engelbrecht, R., Maier-Hein, L., Schmauss, B., Meinzer, H.P., Hornegger, J.: Laparoscopic quantitative 3d endoscopy for image guided surgery. In: Bildverarbeitung für die Medizin, Citeseer, pp. 16–20 (2010)
9. Kunert, W., Storz, P., Kirschniak, A.: For 3d laparoscopy: a step toward advanced surgical navigation: how to get maximum benefit from 3d vision. Surg. Endosc. 27(2), 696–699 (2013)
10. Kawasaki, H., Furukawa, R., Sagawa, R., Yagi, Y.: Dynamic scene shape reconstruction using a single structured light pattern. In: CVPR, 23–28 June, pp. 1–8 (2008)
11. Sagawa, R., Ota, Y., Yagi, Y., Furukawa, R., Asada, N., Kawasaki, H.: Dense 3D reconstruction method using a single pattern for fast moving object. In: ICCV (2009)

12. Microsoft:Xbox 360 Kinect (2010). http://www.xbox.com/en-US/kinect
13. Deguchi, K., Sasano, T., Arai, H., Yoshikawa, Y.: Shape reconstruction from an endoscope image by shape from shading technique for a point light source at the projection. CVIU **66**(2), 119–131 (1997)
14. Visentini-Scarzanella, M., Stoyanov, D., Yang, G.: Metric depth recovery from monocular images using shape-from-shading and specularities. In: ICIP, Orlando, USA, pp. 25–28 (2012)
15. Wu, C., Narasimhan, S., Jaramaz, B.: A multi-image shape-from-shading framework for near-lighting perspective endoscopes. IJCV **86**, 211–228 (2010)
16. Ciuti, G., Visentini-Scarzanella, M., Dore, A., Menciassi, A., Dario, P., Yang, G.Z.: Intra-operative monocular 3d reconstruction for image-guided navigation in active locomotion capsule endoscopy. In: BioRob, pp. 768–774 (2012)
17. Nagakura, T., Michida, T., Hirao, M., Kawahara, K., Yamada, K.: The study of three-dimensional measurement from an endoscopic images with stereo matching method. In: Automation Congress, WAC 2006. World, pp. 1–4, July 2006
18. Stoyanov, D., Scarzanella, M.V., Pratt, P., Yang, G.-Z.: Real-time stereo reconstruction in robotically assisted minimally invasive surgery. In: Jiang, T., Navab, N., Pluim, J.P.W., Viergever, M.A. (eds.) MICCAI 2010. LNCS, vol. 6361, pp. 275–282. Springer, Heidelberg (2010). doi:10.1007/978-3-642-15705-9_34
19. Salvi, J., Batlle, J., Mouaddib, E.M.: A robust-coded pattern projection for dynamic 3D scene measurement. Pattern Recogn. **19**(11), 1055–1065 (1998)
20. Sato, K., Inokuchi, S.: Range-imaging system utilizing nematic liquid crystal mask. In: Proceedings of the International Conference on Computer Vision, pp. 657–661 (1987)
21. Je, C., Lee, S.W., Park, R.-H.: High-contrast color-stripe pattern for rapid structured-light range imaging. In: Pajdla, T., Matas, J. (eds.) ECCV 2004. LNCS, vol. 3021, pp. 95–107. Springer, Heidelberg (2004). doi:10.1007/978-3-540-24670-1_8
22. Zhang, L., Curless, B., Seitz, S.: Rapid shape acquisition using color structured light and multi-pass dynamic programming. In: 3DPVT, pp. 24–36 (2002)
23. Sagawa, R., Kawasaki, H., Furukawa, R., Kiyota, S.: Dense one-shot 3D reconstruction by detecting continuous regions with parallel line projection. In: ICCV, pp. 1911–1918 (2011)
24. Koninckx, T., Gool, L.V.: Real-time range acquisition by adaptive structured light. IEEE Trans. Pattern Anal. Mach. Intell. **28**(3), 432–445 (2006)
25. Sagawa, R., Sakashita, K., Kasuya, N., Kawasaki, H., Furukawa, R., Yagi, Y.: Grid-based active stereo with single-colored wave pattern for dense one-shot 3d scan. In: 2012 Second International Conference on 3D Imaging, Modeling, Processing, Visualization and Transmission (3DIMPVT), pp. 363–370. IEEE (2012)
26. J.Besl, P., D.McKay., N.: A method for registration of 3-d shapes. IEEE Trans. Pattern Anal. Mach. Intell. **14**(2), 239–256 (1992)
27. Neugebauer, P.: Geometrical cloning of 3d objects via simultaneous registration of multiple range image. In: Proceedings of the International Conference Shape Modeling and Applications, pp. 130–139 (1997)
28. Hall-Holt, O., Rusinkiewicz, S.: Stripe boundary codes for real-time structured-light range scanning of moving objects. In: Proceedings of the Eighth IEEE International Conference on Computer Vision, ICCV 2001, vol. 2, pp. 359–366. IEEE (2001)
29. Ooishi, T., Sagawa, R., Nakazawa, A., Kurazume, R., Ikeuchi, K.: Parallel alignment of a large number of range images. In: IEEE Conference 3DIM 2003, pp. 195–202 (2003)

30. Oishi, T., Kurazume, R., Nakazawa, A., Ikeuchi, K.: Fast simultaneous alignment of multiple range images using index images. In: Fifth International Conference on 3-D Digital Imaging and Modeling, 3DIM 2005, pp. 476–483. IEEE (2005)
31. Johnson, A.E., Kang, S.B.: Registration and integration of textured 3d data. Image Vis. Comput. **17**(2), 135–147 (1999)
32. Bouaziz, S., Tagliasacchi, A., Pauly, M.: Sparse iterative closest point. Comput. Graph. Forum **32**(5), 1–11 (2013). Symposium on Geometry Processing
33. Banno, A., Masuda, T., Oishi, T., Ikeuchi, K.: Flying laser range sensor for large-scale site-modeling and its applications in bayon digital archival project. Int. J. Comput. Vision **78**(2–3), 207–222 (2008)
34. Li, H., Hartley, R.: The 3d-3d registration problem revisited. In: Proceedings of the International Conference Computer Vision, pp. 1–8 (2007)
35. Yang, J., Li, H., Jia, Y.: Go-icp: Solving 3d registration efficiently and globally optimally. In: IEEE International Conference Computer Vision, pp. 1457–1464 (2013)
36. Wang, R., Choi, J., Medioni, G.: 3d modeling from wide baseline range scans using contour coherence. In: The IEEE Conference on Computer Vision and Pattern Recognition (CVPR), pp. 4018–4025, June 2014
37. Rusu, R., Blodow, N., Beetz, M.: Fast point feature histograms (FPFH) for 3d registration. In: International Conference Robotics and Automation, pp. 3212–3217, May 2009
38. Rusu, R., Blodow, N., Marton, Z., Beetz, M.: Aligning point cloud views using persistent feature histograms. In: International Conference on Intelligent Robots and Systems, pp. 3384–3391 (2008)
39. Sagawa, R., Sakashita, K., Kasuya, N., Kawasaki, H., Furukawa, R., Yagi, Y.: Grid-based active stereo with single-colored wave pattern for dense one-shot 3D scan. In: 3DIMPVT, pp. 363–370 (2012)

Poster Session 7

Target Response Adaptation
for Correlation Filter Tracking

Adel Bibi[(⊠)], Matthias Mueller[(⊠)], and Bernard Ghanem[(⊠)]

King Abdullah University of Science and Technology (KAUST),
Thuwal, Saudi Arabia
{adel.bibi,matthias.mueller.2,bernard.ghanem}@kaust.edu.sa

Abstract. Most correlation filter (CF) based trackers utilize the circulant structure of the training data to learn a linear filter that best regresses this data to a hand-crafted target response. These circularly shifted patches are only *approximations* to actual translations in the image, which become unreliable in many realistic tracking scenarios including fast motion, occlusion, etc. In these cases, the traditional use of a single centered Gaussian as the target response impedes tracker performance and can lead to unrecoverable drift. To circumvent this major drawback, we propose a generic framework that can adaptively change the target response from frame to frame, so that the tracker is less sensitive to the cases where circular shifts do not reliably approximate translations. To do that, we reformulate the underlying optimization to solve for both the filter and target response *jointly*, where the latter is regularized by measurements made using actual translations. This joint problem has a closed form solution and thus allows for multiple templates, kernels, and multi-dimensional features. Extensive experiments on the popular OTB100 benchmark show that our target adaptive framework can be combined with many CF trackers to realize significant overall performance improvement (ranging from 3 %–13.5 % in precision and 3.2 %–13 % in accuracy), especially in categories where this adaptation is necessary (e.g. fast motion, motion blur, etc.).

Keywords: Correlation filter tracking · Adaptive target design

1 Introduction

Visual object tracking is a classical problem in computer vision. It plays an important role in a plethora of applications, such as robotics, surveillance, and human-computer interaction to name a few. Object tracking can be defined as the task of localizing an object of interest (e.g. by an upright bounding box) in every frame starting from a given patch containing the object in the first frame. The problem is very challenging because the object could undergo a variety of

Electronic supplementary material The online version of this chapter (doi:10.1007/978-3-319-46466-4_25) contains supplementary material, which is available to authorized users.

© Springer International Publishing AG 2016
B. Leibe et al. (Eds.): ECCV 2016, Part VI, LNCS 9910, pp. 419–433, 2016.
DOI: 10.1007/978-3-319-46466-4_25

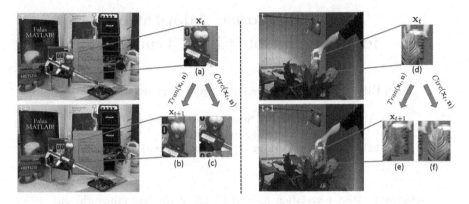

Fig. 1. Shows examples where circular shifts do not represent actual translations. Patches (a) and (b) of video *Lemming* show the object in two consecutive frames, where the target was partially occluded and the occluder is within the filter window. The circular shift corresponding to the actual translation of the object in the next frame is given in patch (c). Note that both the occluder and target are shifted. Circ($\mathbf{x}, \mathbf{n}$), and Tran($\mathbf{x}, \mathbf{n}$) denote $\mathbf{n}$ circular shifts and actual translations applied to the patch $\mathbf{x}$, respectively. Similarly, we show patches (d) and (e) of video *Coke* of two consecutive frames, where fast motion and partial occlusion occur. The corresponding circular shift is given in patch (f). In both examples, translations and their approximations (circular shifts) are quite different. This discrepancy will severely affect the detection step (and in turn the training step) of any CF based tracker at that frame.

transformations making it harder to localize. Typical nuisances that have to be overcome by a successful object tracker include occlusion, in- and out-of-plane rotation, fast motion, illumination changes, etc.

CF based trackers [6,9,11,12,14] have gained much attention lately for their attractive performance both in speed and accuracy. The key idea behind CF trackers is that a learned filter is used to localize the object in the next frame by identifying the location of maximal correlation/convlution response (detection step). Then, it is updated by computing a filter, whose correlation with training templates (most often the current tracking result) closely resembles a hand-crafted target response, usually taken to be a Gaussian centered at the current tracking result (training step) [9–14]. A recent development in this tracking paradigm and the main reason behind its computational efficiency is the use of circulant structure in the training step. In many cases (e.g. when the background is homogenous and no occlusion occurs), the circular shifts of the training templates represent translations in the image domain. This means that the *motion* of a template is inherently accounted for by these circular shifts.

Despite its merits, there are two main drawbacks in the traditional CF tracking paradigm. **(i)** Since the detection step of the tracker might be inaccurate (e.g. due to fast motion, motion blur, etc.), the localization of the object in the next frame is erroneous. Moreover, since the target response is independent of the frame, error will be propagated to the newly computed filter and the

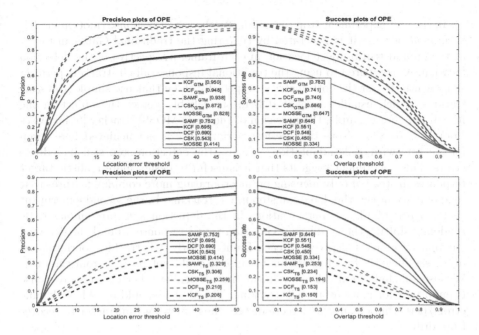

Fig. 2. The first row demonstrates the impressive performance of five CF based trackers (MOSSE$_{GTT}$, DCF$_{GTT}$, CSK$_{GTT}$, KCF$_{GTT}$, and SAMF$_{GTT}$) when the target response is obtained from the ground truth of OTB100 [20]. The second row shows the sensitivity of the tracking results to the target response. By only perturbing the target response by at most 2 pixels, the performance drops significantly. This motivates the importance of designing more robust and effective target response.

tracker becomes at risk of unrecoverable drift. **(ii)** The target response used in the training step is independent of the observed frame and assumes that circular shifts correspond to actual translations, which is not the case in some scenarios (refer to Fig. 1). Obviously, this approximation is not reliable for many tracking nuisances including fast motion, occlusion, and motion blur. Since the target response is not adaptive to the observed frame, the tracker cannot easily recover from errors in the detection step. In this paper, we propose to tackle both drawbacks by jointly solving for the best filter and target response in each frame, where the latter is regularized using actual translation measurements of correlation and not approximated using circular shifts.

As mentioned earlier, the selection of the target response in CF tracking is intimately related to the assumed motion model. Traditionally, this model is simplistic, strict, and prone to drift. Therefore, using/designing a more effective motion model (or equivalently, designing a better target response) is crucial. We justify this observation in Fig. 2 by changing the traditional target response in two different ways and reporting the precision and accuracy results of several CF based trackers in both cases. Note that the traditional detection step is not altered in either case.

In the first experiment (top row of Fig. 2), the target response (motion model) is *optimal* because it is generated by centering the traditional Gaussian target at the ground truth object location in each frame, irrespective of the detection location. As compared to using the traditional response, all CF trackers perform significantly better (in both metrics), especially those that use simple grayscale features, which usually make it difficult to reliably detect the object in the next frame. For example, the precision of the basic MOSSE tracker [6] increases from 14 % to 82 %. Note that perfect performance is not achieved here (even for trackers with scale adaptation) because the detection step still introduces errors. This experiment suggests that it is useful to design more realistic target responses, instead of only focusing on incorporating more complex features that tend only to impact the detection step in CF tracking. In the second experiment (bottom row of Fig. 2), perturbations in the detection step are simulated by randomly shifting the traditional Gaussian target response around the detected location by at most 2 pixels in each frame. Clearly, CF tracking performance drops significantly for all methods because it could not recover from the drift. We also conclude from this experiment that designing a better target response is important for more robust CF tracking. This design should be able to handle errors/perturbations in the detection step, thus, allowing the tracker to recover from drift.

2   Related Work

There have been many advances in the field of object tracking, so we only provide a brief overview of the two main categories of trackers (generative and discriminative) in the literature and focus on those that are most relevant to our proposed framework (CF trackers).

Generative Trackers. They adopt an appearance model to describe a set of target observations. The aim of these trackers is to search for the target that is best represented by the updated generative model. Therefore, learning a representative appearance model that can identify the target, even when it undergoes appearance changes is the main emphasis of these trackers. Examples of this category include incremental tracker (IVT) [18], mean shift tracker [7], L1-min tracker [17], multi-task tracker (MTT) [24], low-rank sparse tracker [23], structural sparse tracker [26], 3D part-based sparse tracker [5], object tracker via structured sparse learning [25], and circulant sparse tracker [22] to name a few.

Discriminative Trackers. They formulate object tracking as a classification problem, where the regions around the previous location of the target are given scores to regress to (e.g. using a classifier to predict background or foreground). Examples of discriminative trackers include multiple instance learning (MIL) [3], ensemble tracking [2], support vector tracking [1], and correlation filter (CF) based trackers like [6,11,12,15].

CF Trackers. Using correlation filters for tracking started with Bolme *et al.* [6], where the formulation was constructed in the frequency domain for efficiency, thus, reaching a runtime of 600–700 FPS. Seminal followup work by Henriques *et al.* [11,12] formulate the problem in the spatial domain, but solved it efficiently in the frequency domain. This is possible by exploiting circulant structure in the optimization. This method (denoted as the kernel correlation filter tracker or KCF [12]) can incorporate both non-linear kernels (e.g. Gaussian) and multi dimensional features (e.g. HOG). Many improvements have recently been made to this popular tracker to address several limiting issues. For instance, the work in [8,15] proposes an adaptive scale version of KCF and also made use of the color names feature. Another approach proposes a multi-template version of KCF [4] by solving a constrained ridge regression problem. Recent work extends KCF to enable part-based tracking [16], where multiple KCF trackers (one for each part) are run independently and the response map of all trackers is computed.

Another variant of CF based trackers changes the objective to spatially focus the filter energy at the center, thus, reducing undesirable boundary effects [9]. Unlike other CF based trackers, their final formulation cannot fully exploit circulant matrix structure into having a closed form element wise solution. Similarly, Galoogahi *et al.* [14] propose a method to deal with the boundary effects of circularly shifted patches by pre-multiplying them with a masking matrix; however, the resulting optimization is also unable to exploit circular structure.

Contributions. To the best of our knowledge, we are the first to investigate the effect of designing an adaptive target response in the context of CF tracking. **(2)** Unlike previous work that fixes the target response for all frames, our proposed method adaptively changes it to account for motion and boundary effects caused by circular shifts. The resulting joint optimization can be solved efficiently by exploiting the underlying circulant structure. **(3)** Extensive experiments on the popular online tracking benchmark OTB100 [20] show that our adaptive target framework can be applied to many CF trackers to improve their performance, while remaining computationally efficient.

3   Correlation Filter Tracking

Similar to other discriminative methods, correlation filters need a set of training examples to learn a filter. In tracking, the first image patch is the only available training example. Other discriminative trackers usually collect positive examples from image patches close to the object in the first frame and negative ones from patches that are farther away. Computational complexity can increase significantly as the number of training patches increases. However, CF based trackers collect dense samples by circularly shifting the patch in the first frame (thus approximating translations) to construct a circulant matrix, which has very desirable properties.

Assuming for simplicity that all the training examples are 1D where $\mathbf{x} \in \mathbb{R}^n$ represents the template in the first frame. Then, $\mathbf{Px} = [x_n, x_1, \ldots, x_{n-1}]$ represents 1 circular shift of $\mathbf{x}$, where $\mathbf{P}$ is a permutation matrix. Concatenating the set of all possible circularly shifted templates forms a circulant matrix that is also referred to as the data matrix. Correlation filtering seeks a filter $\mathbf{w}$ that

424   A. Bibi et al.

minimizes the following ridge regression problem:

$$\underset{\mathbf{w}}{\text{minimize}} \ \|\mathbf{Xw} - \mathbf{y}\|_2^2 + \lambda \|\mathbf{w}\|_2^2 \qquad (1)$$

The data matrix $\mathbf{X} \in \mathbb{R}^{n \times n}$ can either contain the template $\mathbf{x}$ and all its shifts or a kernelized version of them when using circulant structure preserving kernels [12]. Here, $\mathbf{y}$ is the target response, which is usually assumed to be Gaussian centered around the base patch. Equation 1 can be solved in either the primal or the dual domain each with its own pros and cons.

Primal Domain. Here, the filter $\mathbf{w}$ (the primal variable) is computed to solve Eq. 1, which admits a closed form solution in the primal domain given by $\mathbf{w} = (\mathbf{X}^T \mathbf{X} + \lambda \mathbf{I})^{-1} \mathbf{X}^T \mathbf{y}$. Due to the circulant structure of $\mathbf{X}$, it can be diagonalized and the matrix inversion can be done efficiently. The filter solution (in FFT form) is given by $\hat{\mathbf{w}} = \frac{\hat{\mathbf{x}}^* \odot \hat{\mathbf{y}}}{\hat{\mathbf{x}}^* \odot \hat{\mathbf{x}} + \lambda}$, where $\hat{\mathbf{w}}$, $\hat{\mathbf{y}}$, and $\hat{\mathbf{x}}$ are the FFTs of $\mathbf{w}$, $\mathbf{y}$, and $\mathbf{x}$, respectively. The $*$ denotes the complex conjugate and all operations are element wise [12]. The primal formulation also enables the use of multiple templates without changing the solution mechanism much. In this case, Eq. 1 is solved with $\mathbf{X}$ replaced with $\tilde{\mathbf{X}}$, which is the blockwise concatenation of the circulant matrices of all the templates. It can be easily shown [12] that the optimal filter for k templates is given by $\hat{\mathbf{w}} = \frac{\sum_{j=1}^{k} \hat{\mathbf{x}}_j^* \odot \hat{\mathbf{y}}}{\sum_{j=1}^{k} \hat{\mathbf{x}}_j^* \odot \hat{\mathbf{x}}_j + \lambda}$. However, this formulation does not facilitate the use of kernels because the solution is not written as a function of bi-products of the circulant matrices.

Dual Domain. Conversely, Eq. 1 can also be solved in the dual domain, where the solution is $\alpha = (\mathbf{XX}^T + \lambda \mathbf{I})^{-1} \mathbf{y}$. Here, α is the dual variable and it is related to the primal variable through $\mathbf{w} = \mathbf{X}^T \alpha$. The dual formulation admits the solution as a function of bi-products of the circulant data matrix allowing the use of the kernel trick. The dual solution (in FFT form) is $\hat{\alpha} = \frac{\hat{\mathbf{y}}}{\hat{\mathbf{x}}^* \odot \hat{\mathbf{x}} + \lambda}$, where $\hat{\alpha}$ is the FFT of α. Unfortunately, using k templates in the dual domain can no longer be done efficiently because $\mathbf{XX}^T$ is now a matrix with circulant blocks, which has an inversion computational complexity of $n^2 O(k^3)$ compared to $k O(n \log(n))$ in the primal domain.

4 Learning Adaptive Target Responses for CF Tracking

As seen in Fig. 2, exploiting a reliable motion model in CF based tracking (i.e. designing a better target response $\mathbf{y}$) can significantly boost performance. In this paper, we do this by adaptively changing $\mathbf{y}$ in every frame. The peak values of $\mathbf{y}$ not only favor a training template over another based on appearance information, but also based on prior motion information as well. To do this, we solve the following joint optimization:

$$\underset{\mathbf{w}, \mathbf{y}}{\text{minimize}} \ \|\tilde{\mathbf{X}}\mathbf{w} - \mathbf{y}\|_2^2 + \lambda_1 \|\mathbf{w}\|_2^2 + \lambda_2 \|\mathbf{y} - \mathbf{y}_0\|_2^2 \qquad (2)$$

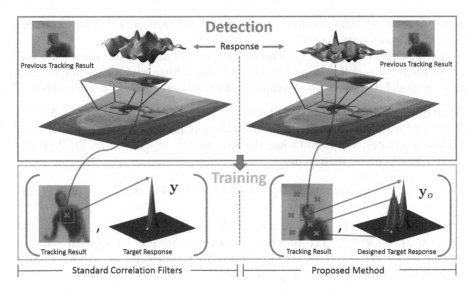

Fig. 3. Shows the pipeline of both standard CF based trackers and our approach. Both involve a detection and training step with a key difference that our approach uses the current detection frame to sample actual translations, which will be used to construct a prior for the target response. In fact, standard CF tracking is a special case of our formulation. When only one translation is sampled around the current tracking result, our approach reduces to the standard CF model.

As compared to the classical CF formulation in Eq. 1, ours does not assume that the target response $\mathbf{y}$ is known apriori, but instead its constructed prior $\mathbf{y}_o$ is known. In what follows, we discuss how $\mathbf{y}_o$ is computed, how Eq. 2 is solved for k templates with $\tilde{\mathbf{X}} \in \mathbb{R}^{kn \times n}$ being a block circulant matrix, and how the single template solution follows directly. We will also provide the new detection equation for the objective in Eq. 2, as well as, an exposition of how our method differs from all other CF based trackers (refer to Fig. 3). All the derivations are done for a 1D example, but they can be easily extended to 2D. More details can be found in the **supplementary material**.

Construction of $\mathbf{y}_o$. In Eq. 2, the target $\mathbf{y}$ is assumed to follow the noise model: $\mathbf{y} = \mathbf{y}_o + \mathbf{n}$, where $\mathbf{y} \in \mathbb{R}^n$ and $\mathbf{y} \sim \mathcal{N}(\mathbf{y}_o, \mathrm{diag}^{-1}(\frac{1}{2\lambda_2}))$. At the first frame, a standard KCF [12] filter is learnt by solving Eq. 1. In the next frame, a fixed number p translations are sampled, at which the previous filter is correlated with the image. These correlations are used to fill the corresponding p entries in $\mathbf{y}_o$. As motivated earlier, this process generates correlation scores for actual translations, which can offset the limiting effects of using their approximations (i.e. circular shifts). We choose $p \ll n$, so the computational burden remains reasonable for our tracking scenario. The rest of the entries in $\mathbf{y}_o$ are computed from the p computed values by Gaussian interpolation. We did experiment with more sophisticated types of interpolation (e.g. bilateral filtering using the image patch as a guide). This resulted in unnoticeable change in performance and an increase in computation cost.

In subsequent frames and to encode motion information, the aforementioned translations are sampled using a standard Kalman filter with a constant velocity motion model. Other motion models can be used here, such as particle filters.

Multiple Template Solution to Eq. 2. Here, $\tilde{\mathbf{X}}^\top = \begin{bmatrix} \mathbf{X}_1^\top & \mathbf{X}_2^\top & \cdots & \mathbf{X}_k^\top \end{bmatrix} \in \mathbb{R}^{kn \times n}$, which is the concatenation of all the circulant matrices generated from all the templates. By introducing the variable $\mathbf{z}^\top = \begin{bmatrix} \mathbf{w}^\top & \mathbf{y}^\top \end{bmatrix}$, Eq. 2 (in its primal form) can be written as:

$$\underset{\mathbf{z}}{\text{minimize}} \ \|\tilde{\mathbf{G}}\mathbf{z}\|_2^2 + \lambda_1\|\mathbf{E}\mathbf{z}\|_2^2 + \lambda_2\|\mathbf{D}\mathbf{z} - \mathbf{y}_o\|_2^2, \tag{3}$$

where $\tilde{\mathbf{G}} = \begin{bmatrix} \tilde{\mathbf{X}} & -\tilde{\mathbf{I}} \end{bmatrix} \in \mathbb{R}^{kn \times 2n}$, $\tilde{\mathbf{I}}^\top = \begin{bmatrix} \mathbf{I} & \cdots & \mathbf{I} \end{bmatrix}$, $\mathbf{E} = \begin{bmatrix} \mathbf{I} & 0 \end{bmatrix} \in \mathbb{R}^{n \times 2n}$, and $\mathbf{D} = \begin{bmatrix} 0 & \mathbf{I} \end{bmatrix} \in \mathbb{R}^{n \times 2n}$. The problem is convex quadratic, so a global solution can be easily derived (refer to **supplementary material** for details of this derivation). In its dual form, Eq. 3 becomes:

$$\underset{\alpha}{\text{minimize}} \ \|\mathbf{D}\tilde{\mathbf{K}}^{-1}\mathbf{D}^T\alpha - \mathbf{y}_o\|_2^2 + \lambda_1\|\mathbf{E}\tilde{\mathbf{K}}^{-1}\mathbf{D}^T\alpha\|_2^2 + \|\mathbf{G}\tilde{\mathbf{K}}^{-1}\mathbf{D}^T\alpha\|_2^2, \tag{4}$$

where α is the dual variable and is related to $\mathbf{z}$ through $\mathbf{z} = \tilde{\mathbf{K}}^{-1}\mathbf{D}^T\alpha$ and $\tilde{\mathbf{K}} = \left(\lambda_1\mathbf{E}^T\mathbf{E} + \mathbf{G}^T\mathbf{G}\right)$. Solving Eq. 4 is straightforward, as it is equivalent to solving the following linear system:

$$\mathbf{D}\tilde{\mathbf{K}}^{-1}\left(\lambda_2\mathbf{D}^T\mathbf{D} + \lambda_1\mathbf{E}^T\mathbf{E} + \mathbf{G}^T\mathbf{G}\right)\tilde{\mathbf{K}}^{-1}\mathbf{D}^T\alpha = \lambda_2\mathbf{D}\tilde{\mathbf{K}}^{-1}\mathbf{D}^T\mathbf{y}_o \tag{5}$$

By using the inverse lemma, the closed form solution to Eq. 5 is:

$$\hat{\alpha}^* = \lambda_2 diag^{-1}(\Upsilon)\left(\frac{\frac{1}{k}\left(\sum_i^k \hat{\mathbf{x}}_{1i}^*\right) \odot \left(\sum_i^k \hat{\mathbf{x}}_{1i}\right) \odot \hat{\mathbf{y}}_0^*}{\sum_i^k(\hat{\mathbf{x}}_{1i}^* \odot \hat{\mathbf{x}}_{1i}) + \lambda_1 - \frac{1}{k}(\sum_i^k \hat{\mathbf{x}}_{1i}^* \odot \sum_i^k \hat{\mathbf{x}}_{1i})} + \frac{\hat{\mathbf{y}}_o^*}{k} \right), \tag{6}$$

where

$$\Upsilon = \left(\frac{\frac{-1}{k}\sum_i^k(\hat{\mathbf{x}}_{1i}^* \odot \hat{\mathbf{x}}_{1i}) + \frac{k+\lambda_2}{k}(\sum_i^k \hat{\mathbf{x}}_{1i}^*) \odot (\sum_i^k \hat{\mathbf{x}}_{1i}) + \frac{\lambda_1(k+\lambda_2)}{k}}{\sum_i^k(\hat{\mathbf{x}}_{1i}^* \odot \hat{\mathbf{x}}_{1i}) + \lambda_1 - \frac{1}{k}(\sum_i^k \hat{\mathbf{x}}_{1i}^*) \odot (\sum_i^k \hat{\mathbf{x}}_{1i})} \right) \odot$$
$$\left(\frac{\frac{1}{k^2}\sum_i^k \hat{\mathbf{x}}_{1i}^* \odot \sum_i^k \hat{\mathbf{x}}_{1i}}{\sum_i^k(\hat{\mathbf{x}}_{1i}^* \odot \hat{\mathbf{x}}_{1i}) + \lambda_1 - \frac{1}{k}(\sum_i^k \hat{\mathbf{x}}_{1i}^*) \odot (\sum_i^k \hat{\mathbf{x}}_{1i})} + \frac{1}{k} \right) \tag{7}$$

Here, $\hat{\mathbf{x}}_{1i}$ denotes the FFT of the first row of $\mathbf{X}_i$ where all the operations are element wise and thus computationally attractive. Moreover, the solution for one single template can be easily found by setting $k = 1$ in Eq. 6 to obtain:

$$\hat{\alpha} = \frac{\left(\frac{\lambda_2}{\lambda_1}(\hat{\mathbf{x}}_1 \odot \hat{\mathbf{x}}_1^*) + \lambda_2\right) \odot \hat{\mathbf{y}}_o}{\frac{\lambda_2}{\lambda_1^2}(\hat{\mathbf{x}}_1 \odot \hat{\mathbf{x}}_1^* \odot \hat{\mathbf{x}}_1 \odot \hat{\mathbf{x}}_1^*) + \frac{1+2\lambda_2}{\lambda_1}(\hat{\mathbf{x}}_1 \odot \hat{\mathbf{x}}_1^*) + (1 + \lambda_2)}, \quad \text{for} \ \ k = 1 \tag{8}$$

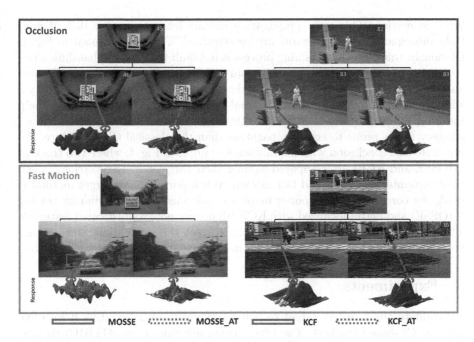

Fig. 4. The first row shows tracking results on occlusion sequences (from left to right: *Coupon* and *Jogging1*) for MOSSE and KCF, along with their adaptive target versions MOSSE$_{AT}$ and KCF$_{AT}$. In the second row, we show similar results for two fast motion sequences (from left to right: *BlurCar2* and *Couple*) for the same trackers.

Detection Formula. The previous solution is used to train the filter $\mathbf{w}$ or the dual variables α. As for the detection, a similar approach is used as in [12], where a circulant data matrix of the test sample $\mathbf{u}$ is considered for detection. The following is the detection formula for a single template case:

$$\mathbf{T}(\mathbf{u}) = \mathbf{U}\mathbf{w} = \mathbf{X}^T\alpha = \frac{1}{\lambda_1}\mathbf{F}diag(\hat{\mathbf{u}} \odot \hat{\mathbf{x}}_1^*)\hat{\alpha}^* \Rightarrow \hat{\mathbf{T}}(\mathbf{u}) = \frac{1}{\lambda_1}\hat{\mathbf{u}}^* \odot \hat{\mathbf{x}}_1 \odot \hat{\alpha}, \qquad (9)$$

where $\hat{\mathbf{T}}$ is the FFT of the detection over all circular shifts of a sample $\mathbf{u}$. It is important to note that when $\lambda_2 \rightarrow \infty$ the soft constraint becomes a hard one, where our formulation reduces back to the original CF tracking formulation with a target response $\mathbf{y}_o$. Therefore, the standard CF tracking framework can be viewed as a special case of our adaptive formulation.

Comparison to CF Based Trackers. As discussed earlier, CF based trackers [6,9,11,12,15], as shown in Fig. 3, exploit two steps: detection and training while the target response used during the training is assumed to be independent of the frame and taken to be Gaussian centered at the window center. This inherently assumes that the detected location of the window is correct.

When errors (even as small as a few pixels) arise in the detection, the target response $\mathbf{y}$ is not centered properly and these errors propagate into the filter estimation. This error propagation usually leads to tracker drift if multiple subsequent detection errors are encountered. This is illustrated in Fig. 2. Obviously, this detection/training process is not fault tolerant and has difficulties recovering from errors. In comparison, our approach assumes that $\mathbf{y}$ is unknown and estimates it at every frame by making use of a target response prior $\mathbf{y}_o$, which exploits correlation values at actual translations in the next frame to help the filter update regress to more realistic target values. As such, our proposed strategy is less prone to error propagation than the classical CF procedure. We illustrate this conclusion with a qualitative example in Fig. 4, where two trackers (MOSSE and KCF) are compared against their target adpative versions, when they encounter occlusion and fast motion. When our adaptive target method is used, the corresponding response maps are less noisy with the simpler tracker (MOSSE) and better localized with KCF (that uses more sophisticated features). The response map is biased towards the correct target location, since actual translations are used in the correlation measurements of the training step.

5   Experiments

We validate our adaptive target response framework by integrating it into five popular CF-based trackers. The experiments are run on the OTB100 dataset [20], which comprises 100 challenging video sequences including all 50 videos from its previous version OTB50 [19]. As compared to other tracking datasets, OTB100 contains a higher percentage of sequences that experience fast motion, motion blur, and occlusion.

Baseline Trackers. They differ in terms of the features used, kernels applied, and their ability to adapt to object scale variations. Particularly, MOSSE [6] uses grayscale features and a linear kernel, while CSK [11] uses the same features but with a gaussian kernel. DCF [12] uses HOG features along with a linear kernel, while KCF [12] uses the same features but with a gaussian kernel. The four aforementioned trackers do not adapt to scale changes, so we choose SAMF [15] to represent CF-based trackers that are scale variant. Note that DSST [8] is another option of this type, but we only include SAMF in our evaluation because it outperforms DSST on OTB100 [20] and their methodology is very similar. Applying our framework to the five baseline trackers gives rise to their adaptive target variants: MOSSE_{AT}, CSK_{AT}, DCF_{AT}, KCF_{AT}, and SAMF_{AT}.

In fact, our framework can be applied to any CF-based tracker, but the aforementioned ones (and most trackers of this type in general) use a formulation that allows for the direct and efficient implementation of our target adaptation. Other trackers, such as SRDCF [9], are included in the evaluation but not modified for target response adaptation because the closed form solutions in Eqs. 6 and 8 do not apply directly to the underlying optimization in these trackers. For example, SRDCF adds spatial regularization to $\mathbf{w}$, which impedes the effective exploitation of circulant structure. Nevertheless, we provide details in the **supplementary material** on how our framework can be extended to include SRDCF and trackers with similar formulations.

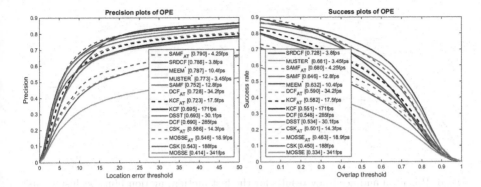

Fig. 5. Precision and accuracy results for five baseline CF trackers, their adaptive target variants, as well as, other state-of-the-art methods. Trackers denoted by * are either not CF trackers or only use a CF tracker as a baseline for a generic framework.

Implementation Details and Parameters. In all our experiments, we use MATLAB on an Intel(R) Xeon(R) 2.67GHz CPU with 32GB RAM. For all the baseline trackers, we use the original parameters provided by the authors. The best regularization parameters λ_1 and λ_2 are selected for each baseline tracker. They are $\{(10^{-1}, 10^{-2}), (10^{-1}, 10^{-4}), (10^{-6}, 10^{-2}), (10^{-3}, 10^{-5}), (10^{-3}, 10^{-2})\}$ for $MOSSE_{AT}$, CSK_{AT}, DCF_{AT}, KCF_{AT}, and $SAMF_{AT}$ respectively. For simplicity and fair comparison, we consider $k = 1$ templates in our experiments for all trackers. The standard update rule for the newly computed filter [6,11,12] is used, where the learning rate is set to $(0.02, 0.01, 0.01, 0.01, 0.015)$ for $MOSSE_{AT}$, CSK_{AT}, DCF_{AT}, KCF_{AT}, and $SAMF_{AT}$ respectively.

As for the number of translations used to form the prior target response $\mathbf{y}_o$, we set $p = 13$ for trackers with grayscale features ($MOSSE_{AT}$ and CSK_{AT}) and $p = 7$ for those with HOG features (DCF_{AT}, KCF_{AT}, and $SAMF_{AT}$). This discrepancy is due to cell size used in HOG (or any other patch based feature). The granularity of each translation is dependent on the cell size of the feature, which is taken to be 4 pixels for HOG. In this case, the minimum translation possible would be 4 pixels, thus, allowing for larger translations with a smaller number of translation samples. For the case of $p = 13$, translations are initialized from the set of $\{0, 3, -3, 5, -5\}$ pixels in a grid fashion, while this set is $\{0, 4\}$ when $p = 7$. Several expirements have been conducted on several choices of p, but it turns out that increasing p beyond 13 have marginal impact on performance. The padding region was set to 2 for all trackers. Moreover, the scaling function of $SAMF_{AT}$ is the same as that of SAMF, where 9 scales are considered with the same step size as the original implementation [15].

Quantitative Results. We run all baseline and adaptive target trackers on OTB100 [20]. Following its standard evaluation strategy, we show the overall precision and accuracy plots of all trackers in Fig. 5. The precision is defined as the average number of frames per video that are at most 20 pixels away from

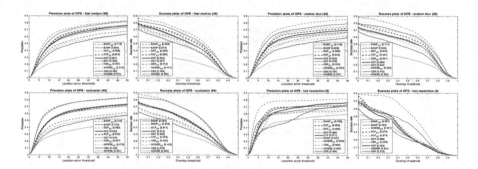

Fig. 6. Precision and accuracy results for the fast motion, motion blur, occlusion, and low resolution categories in OTB100 [20].

the ground truth, while the accuracy is defined as the average number of frames per video where the intersection over union with ground truth is at least 0.5. For a complete comparison, we also show the results of other state-of-the-art trackers including, SRDCF [9], MUSTER [13], MEEM [21], and DSST [8]. All trackers with target adaptation improve in performance, where the improvement ranges from 4 % for sophisticated trackers like SAMF to 15 % for basic ones like MOSSE. It is worthwhile to note that SAMF$_{AT}$ achieves state-of-art performance in precision and is tied with MUSTER for second place right after SRDCF in accuracy. The reason behind this ranking discrepancy between the two metrics is primarily due to the scaling modality used in SAMF. Evidence of this phenomenon also arises in Fig. 2, where SAMF accuracy is worse than its precision, even when the target response is optimal.

In Fig. 6, we show an extensive comparison of the baseline trackers and their adaptive target variants on sequences with attributes (fast motion, motion blur, occlusion, and low resolution) that are expected to benefit the most from our adaptive framework. In fact, the performance of all the baseline trackers improves with target adaptation, some more than others in certain attributes. In general, trackers that use multi-dimensional sophisticated features experience less improvement than those that use grayscale features. For example, since there are more severe object translations in the subset of videos in the motion blur category that do not belong to the fast motion category, the range of improvement in the former category (6 %–24.1 %) is higher than the latter (2.6 %–25.8 %). In the occlusion category, the trackers with grayscale features (MOSSE and CSK) are the only ones with significant improvement (13 % and 7.7 % respectively).

On the other hand, trackers that use sophisticated features and/or non-linear kernels have less improvement (i.e. DCF$_{AT}$, KCF$_{AT}$, and SAMF$_{AT}$). The reason behind this non-uniform improvement among trackers is two-fold. First, the occlusion category comprises about 50 % of the whole OTB dataset, so occlusion videos contain many other attributes (some that do not benefit from target adaptation), thus, making the improvement less obvious. Secondly, more sophisticated features (e.g. HOG) play an important role in making the detection step of the CF

Fig. 7. Shows tracking results comparing five different baseline trackers compared against their target adaptation version over five different videos. The videos from top to bottom are *BlurOwl*, *Human4*, *Freeman4*, *Coke*, and *Woman*. In each row, a different baseline tracker is applied (from top to bottom: SAMF, KCF, DCF, CSK, and MOSSE) along with its adaptive target variant.

tracker more robust to occlusion. The low resolution category witnesses the largest improvements overall. Interestingly, for videos with this attribute, basic trackers like MOSSE and CSK can outperform more established trackers like SAMF, when they exploit target adaptation. In fact, even SAMF improves by 15.7 % here. Since our method makes use of correlation scores from actual translations to bias the target response, the learned filter is better at localizing a smaller object (i.e. whose dimensions are more comparable to its frame-to-frame translation), when compared to traditional CF trackers that only use circular shifts. This is because a standard cosine window is applied to the patch [11,12] which is proportional to object's size. This limits the motion search for the object in standard CF trackers unlike our method that allows for the detection of larger translations.

Qualitative Results. Figure 7 shows qualitative results comparing the five baseline trackers to their target adaptive variants. For the first row (the *BlurOwl* sequence), the target undergoes fast motion along with motion blur. Unlike SAMF, SAMF$_{AT}$ is able to track the object throughout the complete sequence. In the second row (the *Human4* sequence), KCF is unable to keep tracking the target as it undergoes partial occlusion. When the occluder appears inside the filter window, the circular shifts are no longer good approximations of actual translations and the tracker drifts. Similar behaviour arises when the DCF, KCF, and MOSSE trackers are applied to the *Freeman4*, *Coke*, and *Woman* sequences, respectively. In all these sequences, the target adaptive version of each CF tracker is able to consistently maintain the track.

6   Conclusions

In this paper, we propose a generic framework for correlation filter (CF) based trackers to counter the problem of fast motion, motion blur, and occlusion in videos. Our approach efficiently solves for both the filter and target response jointly, whereby the target response is regularized using correlation scores evaluated at sampled translations. Experiments demonstrate significant improvement in performance when our adaptive target framework is applied to many CF trackers. The proposed method is generic and can be incorporated into any CF based tracker. For future work, we aim to investigate more systematic and effective strategies for sampling the translations from frame to frame.

Acknowledgments. This research work was supported by the King Abdullah University of Science and Technology (KAUST) Office of Sponsored Research.

References

1. Avidan, S.: Support vector tracking. IEEE Trans. Pattern Anal. Mach. Intell. **25**, 1296–1311 (2004)
2. Avidan, S.: Ensemble tracking. IEEE Trans. Pattern Anal. Mach. Intell. **29**(2), 261–271 (2007). IEEE
3. Babenko, B., Yang, M.H., Belongie, S.: Visual tracking with online multiple instance learning. In: IEEE Conference on Computer Vision and Pattern Recognition (2009)
4. Bibi, A., Ghanem, B.: Multi-template scale-adaptive kernelized correlation filters. In: IEEE International Conference on Computer Vision Workshops, ICCVW (2015)
5. Bibi, A., Zhang, T., Ghanem, B.: 3d part-based sparse tracker with automatic synchronization and registration. In: IEEE Conference on Computer Vision and Pattern Recognition, CVPR (2016)
6. Bolme, D.S., Beveridge, J.R., Draper, B., Lui, Y.M., et al.: Visual object tracking using adaptive correlation filters. In: IEEE Conference on Computer Vision and Pattern Recognition (2010)
7. Comaniciu, D., Ramesh, V., Meer, P.: Kernel-based object tracking. IEEE Trans. Pattern Anal. Mach. Intell. **17**(8), 790–799 (2003)

8. Danelljan, M., Häger, G., Khan, F., Felsberg, M.: Accurate scale estimation for robust visual tracking. In: British Machine Vision Conference, Nottingham (2014)
9. Danelljan, M., Hager, G., Shahbaz Khan, F., Felsberg, M.: Learning spatially regularized correlation filters for visual tracking. In: IEEE International Conference on Computer Vision (2015)
10. Danelljan, M., Khan, F., Felsberg, M., Weijer, J.: Adaptive color attributes for real-time visual tracking. In: IEEE Conference on Computer Vision and Pattern Recognition (2015)
11. Henriques, J.F., Caseiro, R., Martins, P., Batista, J.: Exploiting the circulant structure of tracking-by-detection with kernels. In: European Conference on Computer Vision (2012)
12. Henriques, J.F., Caseiro, R., Martins, P., Batista, J.: High-speed tracking with kernelized correlation filters. IEEE Trans. Pattern Anal. Mach. Intell. **37**(3), 583–596 (2015)
13. Hong, Z., Chen, Z., Wang, C., Mei, X., Prokhorov, D., Tao, D.: Multi-store tracker (muster): a cognitive psychology inspired approach to object tracking. In: IEEE Conference on Computer Vision and Pattern Recognition (2015)
14. Kiani Galoogahi, H., Sim, T., Lucey, S.: Correlation filters with limited boundaries. In: IEEE Conference on Computer Vision and Pattern Recognition (2015)
15. Li, Y., Zhu, J.: A scale adaptive kernel correlation filter tracker with feature integration. In: European Conference on Computer Vision Workshops (2014)
16. Liu, T., Wang, G., Yang, Q.: Real-time part-based visual tracking via adaptive correlation filters. In: Proceedings of the IEEE Conference on Computer Vision and Pattern Recognition, pp. 4902–4912 (2015)
17. Mei, X., Ling, H.: Robust visual tracking using & # x2113; 1minimization. In: IEEE 12th International Conference on Computer Vision, pp. 1436–1443. IEEE (2009)
18. Poggio, T., Cauwenberghs, G.: Incremental and decremental support vector machine learning. In: Advances in Neural Information Processing Systems (2001)
19. Wu, Y., Lim, J., Yang, M.H.: Online object tracking: A benchmark. In: IEEE Conference on Computer Vision and Pattern Recognition (2013)
20. Wu, Y., Lim, J., Yang, M.H.: Object tracking benchmark. IEEE Trans. Pattern Anal. Mach. Intell. **37**(9), 1834–1848 (2015)
21. Zhang, J., Ma, S., Sclaroff, S.: Meem: Robust tracking via multiple experts using entropy minimization. In: European Conference on Computer Vision (2014)
22. Zhang, T., Bibi, A., Ghanem, B.: In defense of sparse tracking: Circulant sparse tracker. In: IEEE Conference on Computer Vision and Pattern Recognition, CVPR (2016)
23. Zhang, T., Ghanem, B., Liu, S., Ahuja, N.: Low-rank sparse learning for robust visual tracking. In: Fitzgibbon, A., Lazebnik, S., Perona, P., Sato, Y., Schmid, C. (eds.) ECCV 2012. LNCS, vol. 7577, pp. 470–484. Springer, Heidelberg (2012). doi:10.1007/978-3-642-33783-3_34
24. Zhang, T., Ghanem, B., Liu, S., Ahuja, N.: Robust visual tracking via multi-task sparse learning. In: IEEE Conference on Computer Vision and Pattern Recognition (2012)
25. Zhang, T., Ghanem, B., Xu, C., Ahuja, N.: Object tracking by occlusion detection via structured sparse learning. In: IEEE Conference on Computer Vision and Pattern Recognition Workshops, CVPRW (2013)
26. Zhang, T., Liu, S., Xu, C., Yan, S., Ghanem, B., Ahuja, N., Yang, M.H.: Structural sparse tracking. In: IEEE Conference on Computer Vision and Pattern Recognition, CVPR (2015)

Learning Image Matching
by Simply Watching Video

Gucan Long[1,2(✉)], Laurent Kneip[2,3], Jose M. Alvarez[2,4], Hongdong Li[2,3],
Xiaohu Zhang[1], and Qifeng Yu[1]

[1] National University of Defense Technology, Changsha, People's Republic of China
gucan.long@gmail.com
[2] Australian National University, Canberra, Australia
laurent.kneip@anu.edu.au
[3] Australian Centre of Excellence for Robotic Vision, Canberra, Australia
[4] Data61, CSIRO, Canberra, Australia

Abstract. This work presents an unsupervised learning based approach
to the ubiquitous computer vision problem of image matching. We start
from the insight that the problem of frame interpolation implicitly solves
for inter-frame correspondences. This permits the application of analysis-
by-synthesis: we first train and apply a Convolutional Neural Network
for frame interpolation, then obtain correspondences by inverting the
learned CNN. The key benefit behind this strategy is that the CNN for
frame interpolation can be trained in an unsupervised manner by exploiting the temporal coherence that is naturally contained in real-world video
sequences. The present model therefore learns image matching by simply
"watching videos". Besides a promise to be more generally applicable,
the presented approach achieves surprising performance comparable to
traditional empirically designed methods.

Keywords: Image matching · Unsupervised learning · Analysis by
synthesis · Temporal coherence · Convolutional neural network

1 Introduction

We are experiencing a tremendous success of deep learning in almost all research
areas of computer vision. However, for most of the time, deep models are trained
by relying on man-made supervising signals, which are all too often prepared
through a tedious, expensive manual labeling process. Many researchers therefore believe that a more promising paradigm is given by unsupervised learning,
as most of the readily available data simply comes in unlabeled form. This work
contributes to this direction by providing an unsupervised solution to the ubiquitous vision problem of image matching. Specifically, relying on only natural
video sequences, the present model is able to learn the ability of establishing
2D-2D correspondences across consecutive frames.

This work was conducted while G. Long was a visiting student at the ANU, supported by the China Scholarship Council (CSC), and supervised by L. Kneip.

© Springer International Publishing AG 2016
B. Leibe et al. (Eds.): ECCV 2016, Part VI, LNCS 9910, pp. 434–450, 2016.
DOI: 10.1007/978-3-319-46466-4_26

Fig. 1. We train a deep convolutional network for frame interpolation, which can be done without manual supervision by exploiting the temporal coherence that is naturally contained in real-world video sequences. The learned CNN is then used to compute a sensitivity map for each output pixel. This sensitivity map, i.e. the gradients w.r.t. the input, indicates how much each input pixel influences a particular output pixel. The two input pixels (one per input frame) that have the maximum influence are considered as an image correspondence (i.e. a match). Though indirect, the resulting model learns how to perform dense correspondence matching by simply watching video.

Our key insight lies in the understanding that frame interpolation implicitly solves for dense correspondences between the input image pair. It is well known that dense matching can be regarded as a sub-problem of frame interpolation, as the interpolation could be immediately generated by correspondence-based image warping once dense inter-frame matches are available [3]. It then comes as no surprise that if we were able to train a deep neural network for frame interpolation, its application would implicitly also generate knowledge about dense image correspondences. Retrieving this knowledge is known as *analysis by synthesis* [42], a paradigm in which learning is described as the acquisition of a measurement synthesizing model, and inference of generating parameters as model inversion once correct synthesis is achieved. In our context, *synthesis* simply refers to frame interpolation. We then, for the *analysis* part, show that the correspondences can be recovered from the network through gradient back-propagation, which produces sensitivity maps for each interpolated pixel. The procedure is summarized in Fig. 1, explaining how the reciprocal mapping between frame interpolation and dense correspondences is encoded in the forward and backward propagation through one and the same network architecture. We call our approach MIND, which stands for Matching by INverting[1] a Deep neural network.

The key benefit of MIND lies in the fact that the deep convolutional network for frame interpolation can be trained from ordinary video sequences without any man-made ground truth signals. The training data in our case is given by triplets of images, each one consisting of two input images and one output image that represents the ground-truth interpolated frame. A correct example

---

[1] The term of *inverting* is read as *back-propagation* through the given deep neural network.

of a ground truth output image is an image that—when inserted in between the input pair of images—forms a *temporally coherent* sequence of frames. Such temporal coherence is naturally contained in regular video sequences, which allows us to simply use triplets of sequential images from almost arbitrary video streams for training our network. The first and the third frame of each triplet are used as inputs to the network, and the second frame as the ground truth interpolated frame. Most importantly, since the inversion of our network returns frame-to-frame correspondences, it therefore learns how to do image matching without any requirement for manually designed models or expensive ground truth correspondences. In other words, the presented approach learns image matching by simply "watching videos".

The paper is organized as follows. Section 2 reviews relevant prior work. Section 3 explains the present *analysis-by-synthesis* approach, including both the *analysis* part of how MIND works and the *synthesis* part of the deep convolutional architecture for frame interpolation. Section 4 demonstrates the surprising performance for the present purely unsupervised learning approach, which is comparable to several traditional empirically designed methods. Section 5 finally discusses our contribution and provides an outlook onto future work.

2   Related Work

Deep learning meets image matching: Image matching is a classical problem in computer vision. Here we limit the discussion to recent works that address image matching through learning based approaches. Roughly speaking, there exist two lines of research for this topic: the first one consists of making use of features or representations learned by deep neural networks, which are either originally trained for other tasks such as object recognition [13, 26], or specially designed and trained for the purpose of image matching [1, 21, 33]. The second major line of research employs deep neural networks to compute the similarity between image patches [30, 43, 44]. In contrast to our work, the cited contributions mainly address sub-modules of image matching (feature extraction or matching cost computation), rather than providing end-to-end solutions. An exception is given by FlowNet [14], which presents an interesting deep learning based approach for dense optical flow computation. It does however depend on ground truth flow for training the network.

Temporal coherence learning: Unsupervised learning is a broad topic in the field of machine learning. Our discussion here focuses on works that exploit temporal coherence in natural videos, sometimes also called *temporal coherence learning* [4, 29, 41]. As a recent representative work, Wang et al. [39] exploit temporal coherence by visual tracking in videos, and report that the learned representation achieves competitive performance compared to some supervised alternatives. While temporal coherence learning mostly aims at learning features or representations, some recent works on reconstructing and predicting video frames in an unsupervised setting [31] are closely related to our work as well. Srivastava et al. [35] use an encoder LSTM to map input sequences into a fixed length representation, and use the latter for reconstructing the input or even predicting future frames. Goroshin et al. [17] consider videos as one-dimensional, time-parametrized trajectories embedded in a low dimensional manifold. They train deep feature hierarchies that linearize the transformations observed in natural video sequences for the purpose of frame prediction. Though related to our work, these works are not aiming at image matching. It will be interesting to apply our concept of matching by inverting to the above models for temporal coherence learning.

Inversion of artificial neural network: Note that inverting a learned network is traditionally defined as reconstructing the input from the output of an artificial neural network [22]. Mahendran et al. [27] and Dosovitskiy et al. [10] apply this concept to understand what information is preserved by a network. In our context, *inverting a network* means *back-propagation through a learned network in order to obtain the gradient map with respect to the input signals.* Interestingly, the idea has already been introduced in the work of Simonyan et al. [34], emphasizing that the retrieved sensitivity maps may serve to identify image-specific class saliency. Similarly, Bach et al. [2] employ gradient maps as a measure for the contribution of single pixels to nonlinear classifiers, thus helping to explain how decisions are made.

3   Methodology

The *analysis by synthesis* approach for dense image matching is described in this section: we first explain the *analysis* part, i.e. how to obtain correspondences given the trained neural network and the interpolated image. For the *synthesis* part, we describe here the detailed architecture of the deep convolutional network designed for frame interpolation.

3.1   Matching by Inverting a Deep Neural Network

Assuming that we have a well trained deep neural network for frame interpolation in our hand, the core technical question behind our work is how to recover the correspondences between the input pair of images from there. As explained previously, dense correspondence matching may be regarded as a sub-problem of frame interpolation, which is why we should be able to trace back the matches starting from the interpolated frame generated during the forward-propagation through the trained network. Our task then consists of back-tracking each pixel in the output image to exactly one pixel in each of the two input images. Note that this back-tracking does not mean reconstructing input images from the output one. Instead, we only need to find the pixels in each input image which have the maximum influence to each pixel of the output image.

We perform back-tracking by applying a technique similar to the one adopted by Simonyan et al. [34]. For each pixel in the output image, we compute the gradient of its value with respect to each input pixel, thus telling us how much it is under the influence of individual pixels at the input. The gradient is computed based on back-propagation, and leads to sensitivity or influence maps at the input of the network.

From a more formal perspective, our approach may be explained as follows. Let $\mathbf{I}_2 = \mathcal{F}(\mathbf{I}_1, \mathbf{I}_3)$ denote a non-linear function (i.e. the trained deep neural network) that describes the mapping from two input images $\mathbf{I}_1$ and $\mathbf{I}_3$ to an interpolated image $\mathbf{I}_2$ lying approximately at the "center" of the input frames. Thinking of $\mathcal{F}$ as a vectorial mapping, it can be split up into $h \times w$ non-linear sub-functions, each one producing the corresponding pixel in the output image

$$\mathcal{F}(\mathbf{I}_1, \mathbf{I}_3) = \begin{pmatrix} f^{11}(\mathbf{I}_1, \mathbf{I}_3) \cdots f^{1w}(\mathbf{I}_1, \mathbf{I}_3) \\ \vdots \qquad \qquad \vdots \\ f^{h1}(\mathbf{I}_1, \mathbf{I}_3) \cdots f^{hw}(\mathbf{I}_1, \mathbf{I}_3) \end{pmatrix}_{h \times w} . \tag{1}$$

In order to produce the sensitivity maps, we apply back-propagation to compute the Jacobian matrix with respect to each input image individually. The Jacobian with respect to the first image is given by

$$\frac{\partial \mathcal{F}(\mathbf{I}_1, \mathbf{I}_3)}{\partial \mathbf{I}_1} = \begin{pmatrix} \frac{\partial f^{11}(\mathbf{I}_1, \mathbf{I}_3)}{\partial \mathbf{I}_1} \cdots \frac{\partial f^{1w}(\mathbf{I}_1, \mathbf{I}_3)}{\partial \mathbf{I}_1} \\ \vdots \qquad \qquad \vdots \\ \frac{\partial f^{h1}(\mathbf{I}_1, \mathbf{I}_3)}{\partial \mathbf{I}_1} \cdots \frac{\partial f^{hw}(\mathbf{I}_1, \mathbf{I}_3)}{\partial \mathbf{I}_1} \end{pmatrix}_{h \times h \times w \times w} , \tag{2}$$

illustrating that this derivative results in one $h \times w$ matrix for each one of the $h \times w$ pixels at the output. The Jacobian with respect to $\mathbf{I}_3$ is given in a similar way. Let's define the absolute gradients of the output point (i, j) with respect to each one of the input images, and evaluated for the concrete inputs $\hat{\mathbf{I}}_1$ and $\hat{\mathbf{I}}_3$. They are given by

$$\begin{cases} \mathcal{G}_{\mathbf{I}_1}^{i,j}(\hat{\mathbf{I}}_1, \hat{\mathbf{I}}_3) = \mathrm{abs}\left(\frac{\partial f^{ij}(\mathbf{I}_1, \mathbf{I}_3)}{\partial \mathbf{I}_1} \Big|_{\substack{\mathbf{I}_1 = \hat{\mathbf{I}}_1 \\ \mathbf{I}_3 = \hat{\mathbf{I}}_3}} \right) \\ \mathcal{G}_{\mathbf{I}_3}^{i,j}(\hat{\mathbf{I}}_1, \hat{\mathbf{I}}_3) = \mathrm{abs}\left(\frac{\partial f^{ij}(\mathbf{I}_1, \mathbf{I}_3)}{\partial \mathbf{I}_3} \Big|_{\substack{\mathbf{I}_1 = \hat{\mathbf{I}}_1 \\ \mathbf{I}_3 = \hat{\mathbf{I}}_3}} \right) \end{cases}, \tag{3}$$

where abs replaces each entry of a matrix by its absolute value. The gradient maps produced in this way notably represent the seeked sensitivity or influence maps that may now serve in order to derive the coordinates of each correspondence. We notably extract the most responsible point in each gradient map, and connect those two points in order to return the correspondence.

In the spirit of unsupervised learning, we opted for the simplest possible choice, namely taking the coordinates of the maximum entry in $\mathcal{G}_{\mathbf{I}_1}^{i,j}(\hat{\mathbf{I}}_1, \hat{\mathbf{I}}_3)$ and $\mathcal{G}_{\mathbf{I}_3}^{i,j}(\hat{\mathbf{I}}_1, \hat{\mathbf{I}}_3)$, respectively. Let us denote these points with $c_{\mathbf{I}_1}^{ij}$ and $c_{\mathbf{I}_3}^{ij}$. By computing the two gradient maps for each point in the output image and extracting each time the most responsible point, we thus obtain the following two lists of points

$$\begin{cases} \mathcal{C}_{\mathbf{I}_1} = \left\{ c_{\mathbf{I}_1}^{ij} \right\} \\ \mathcal{C}_{\mathbf{I}_3} = \left\{ c_{\mathbf{I}_3}^{ij} \right\} \end{cases}, i = 1, \ldots, h, j = 1, \ldots, w \qquad (4)$$

The set of correspondences $\mathcal{S}$ is then given by combining same-index elements from $\mathcal{C}_{\mathbf{I}_1}$ and $\mathcal{C}_{\mathbf{I}_3}$, eventually resulting in

$$\mathcal{S} = \left\{ s^{ij} \right\}, i = 1, \ldots, h, j = 1, \ldots, w$$
$$= \left\{ \left\{ c_{\mathbf{I}_1}^{11}, c_{\mathbf{I}_3}^{11} \right\}, \ldots, \left\{ c_{\mathbf{I}_1}^{hw}, c_{\mathbf{I}_3}^{hw} \right\} \right\}. \qquad (5)$$

3.2 Deep Neural Network for Frame Interpolation

The architecture of our frame-interpolation network is inspired by *FlowNet-Simple* as presented in Fischer et al. [14]. As illustrated in Fig. 2, it consists of a Convolutional Part and a Deconvolutional Part. The two parts serve as "encoder" and "decoder" respectively, similar to the auto-encoder architecture presented by Hinton and Salakhutdinov [20]. The basic block within the Convolutional Part—denoted Convolution Block—follows the common pattern of the convolutional neural network architecture:

INPUT ->[CONV ->PRELU] * 3 ->POOL ->OUTPUT.

The Parametric Rectified Linear Unit [19] is adopted in our work. Following the suggestions from VGG-Net [9], we set the size of the receptive field of all convolution filters to three—along with a stride and a padding of one—and duplicate [CONV ->PRELU] three times to better model the non-linearity.

The Deconvolution Part consists of Deconvolution Blocks, each one including a convolution transpose layer [38] and two convolution layers. The first one has a receptive field of four, a stride of two, and a padding of one. The pattern of the Deconvolution Block follows:

INPUT ->[CONVT ->PRELU] ->[CONV ->PRELU] * 2 ->OUTPUT.

In order to maintain fine-grained image details in the interpolation frame, we make a copy of the output features produced by Convolution Blocks 2, 3, and 4, and concat them as an additional input to the Deconvolution Blocks 4, 3, and 2, respectively. This concept is illustrated by the side arrows in Fig. 2, and similar ideas have already been used in prior work [11,14]. Recent works [18,36] indicate that the 'side arrows' may also help to better train the deep network.

It is easy to notice that our network is a fully convolutional one, thus allowing us to feed it with images of different resolutions. This is an important advantage, as different data-sets may use different height-to-width ratios. The output blob size for each block in our network is listed in Table 1.

4   Experiments

In this section, we first explain the implementation details behind MIND such as training data and loss function. The examples as proofs of concept for MIND

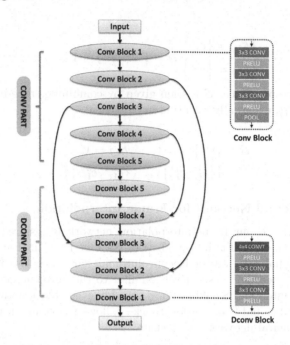

Fig. 2. Architecture of our network. The network takes 2 RGB images as an input to produce the interpolated RGB image. Please note that Dconv Block 4 takes the outputs from both Conv Block 2 and Dconv Block 5 as input. Dconv Block 3 and Dconv Block 2 have a similar input configuration. (Color figure online)

are introduced before a discussion on the generalization ability of the trained CNN. We finally evaluate MIND in terms of quantitative matching performance and compare it to traditional image matching methods.

4.1 Implementation Details

Training data: Quantity and quality of training data are crucial for training a deep neural network. However, our case is particularly easy as we can simply use huge amounts of real-world videos. In this work, we focus on training with the KITTI RAW videos [15] and Sintel videos[2] and show that the resulting learned network performs reasonably well. The network is first trained with the KITTI RAW video sequences which are captured by driving around the city of Karlsruhe, through rural areas and over highways. The dataset contains 56 image sequences with in total 16,951 frames. For each sequence, we take every three consecutive frames (both in forward and backward direction) as a training triplet, where the first and the third image serve as inputs to the network and the second image as the corresponding output. These images are then augmented by vertical flipping, horizontal flipping and a combination of both.

---

[2] Sintel, the Durian Open Movie Project. https://durian.blender.org/.

Table 1. The table lists the output blob size of each block in our network. Note that we stack two RGB images into one input blob, and thus the depth is 6. The output of the network is an RGB image and thus the depth equals to 3. The indicated widths are for the network trained on KITTI. The ones for the Sintel data are easily obtained, the only difference being that the input images are scaled to 256×128 rather than 384×128.

	Input	Conv1	Conv2	Conv3	Conv4	Conv5	Dconv5	Dconv4	Dconv3	Dconv2	Dconv1	Output
Depth	6	96	96	128	128	128	128	128	128	96	96	3
Height	128	64	32	16	8	4	8	16	32	64	128	128
Width	384	192	96	48	24	12	24	48	96	192	384	384

The total number of sample triplets is 133,921. We then fine-tune the network on examples selected from the original Sintel movie. We manually collected 63 video clips with in total 5,670 frames from the movie. After grouping and data augmentation we finally obtain 44,352 sample triplets. Note that, compared to the KITTI sequences which are recorded with relatively uniform velocity, the Sintel sequences represent more difficult training examples in the context of our work, as they contain a lot of fast and artificially rendered motion captured with a frame rate of only 24 fps. A significant portion of the Sintel samples therefore does not contain the required temporal coherence. We will discuss this issue further in Sect. 4.2.

Loss function: Several previous works [17,39] mention that minimizing the L2 loss between the output frame and the training example may lead to unrealistic and blurry predictions. We have not been able to confirm this throughout our experiments, but found that the Charbonnier loss $\rho(x) = \sqrt{(x^2 + \epsilon^2)}$ commonly employed for robust optical flow computation [37] leads to an improvement over the L2 loss. We employ it to train our network, with ϵ set to 0.1.

Training details: The training is performed using Caffe [23] on a machine with two K40c GPUs. The weights of the network are initialized by Xavier's approach [16] and optimized by the Adam solver [24] with a fixed momentum of 0.9. The initial learning rate is set to 1e-3 and then manually tuned down once ceasing of loss reduction sets in. For training on the KITTI RAW data, the images are scaled to 384×128. For training on the Sintel dataset, the images are scaled to 256×128. The batch size is 16. We run the training on KITTI RAW from scratch for about 20 epochs, and then fine-tuned it on the Sintel movie images for 15 epochs. We did not observe over-fitting during training, and terminated the training after 5 days.

Execution time: MIND can be applied to different scenarios (e.g. sparse or dense matching). We focus here on semi-dense image matching in order to obtain a result comparable with other methods. We compute the correspondences across the input images for each corner of a predefined raster grid of 4 pixels width in the interpolated image. Note that MIND currently depends on a large amount of computational resources as it performs back-propagation through the entire network for every pixel that needs to be matched. For an image of size 384×128, each forward pass through our network takes 40 ms on a PC with K40c GPU, and each backward pass takes 158 ms. For each image pair, we need to perform one forward pass to first obtain the interpolation. We then need to perform $384 \times 128/4/4 = 3072$ backward passes to find the correspondences, resulting in a total of about 486 s ($\sim$8 min).

4.2   Qualitative Examples for Interpolation and Matching

We demonstrate here the visual examples as proofs of concept for how the present approach works on both tasks of frame interpolation and image matching.

Fig. 3. Examples of frame interpolation (best viewed in colour). From left to right: example on KITTI, Sintel, ETH Multi-Person Tracking dataset [12] and Bonn Benchmark on Tracking [25], respectively. In each column, the first image is an overlay of the two input frames. The second one is the interpolated image obtained by our network. For the first example, we use the network trained on KITTI itself. For all others, we use the network fine-tuned on Sintel data. (Color figure online)

Examples of frame interpolation: We show the examples of frame interpolation in Fig. 3. The first two columns show the examples on KITTI and Sintel images which are taken from the validation data-sets originally collected for the purpose of monitoring the network training process. It can be seen that the trained CNNs cover the motion correctly for both KITTI and Sintel image pairs. It can furthermore be noticed that some fine-grained details are not preserved well in both examples, despite the special considerations in the architecture of the convolutional network (c.f. Sect. 3.2). Nevertheless, we would like to emphasize that the goal of the present work is not to provide a state-of-the-art frame-interpolation algorithm. As we will see, the preservation of fine-grained image details is in fact not necessarily an indicator for better quality image matching.

And for the goal of image matching, we will see that the preservation of perfect image details is in fact not necessary.

Examples for image matching: Here we present examples to demonstrate how MIND obtains correspondences given the trained CNNs for frame interpolation. The examples taken from KITTI and Sintel videos are shown in Fig. 4. By computing the gradient of manually marked pixels in the interpolated image, MIND successfully obtains correct correspondences between the 2 input images.

It can be seen that the correct correspondences are obtained even in some fast motion areas where fine-grained image details are missed, e.g. the area of the character's shaking hand in the Sintel example.

We further show one failure example taken from Sintel images. In Fig. 5, it can be observed that the interpolation fails as the motion of the small dragon and the character's hand have not been recovered correctly. It then comes as no surprise that MIND fails to extract correct matches for almost all of the selected points. However, it is worth to note that the No.4 match has better quality than others for which the corresponding gradient maps are less distinctive. The matching score/confidence returned by MIND is inspired by this behavior and defined as the ratio between the maximum gradient intensity and the mean gradient intensity within a small area around the maximal gradient location.

As illustrated in Sect. 4.4, the general performance of MIND, especially on KITTI images, is good. The failure example in Fig. 5 indicates an extreme case in the Sintel sequences dominated by fast and highly non-rigid motion in the scene.

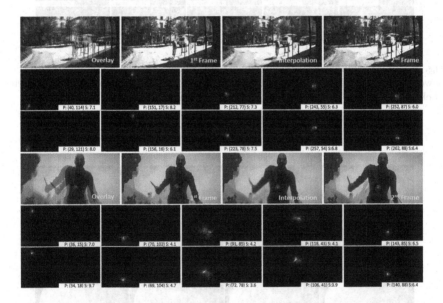

Fig. 4. Two matching examples for image pairs taken from the KITTI RAW video and the Sintel movie clip (best viewed in colour). For each example, the corresponding row of images shows input image 1, the interpolated image, and then input image 2 (from left to right). The red points mark five sample correspondences. The two rows below each example show the gradient/saliency maps for each match (from left to right) in each input image (maps for input image 1 on top, and maps for input image 2 in the bottom). The figures also indicate the coordinates of the maximal gradient location (P) along with the corresponding matching score (S). The matching score is defined as the ratio between the maximum gradient intensity and the mean gradient intensity within a 20×20 area around P. (Color figure online)

4.3   Generalization Ability of the Trained CNN

We first demonstrate the generalization ability of the trained CNN by applying it to images taken from the ETH Multi-Person Tracking dataset [12] and the Bonn Benchmark on Tracking [25], which have not been used for either training or fine-tuning. The results are shown in Fig. 3, from which we can see that the trained CNN again covers the motion correctly. It provides evidence that, by "watching videos", the present CNN is indeed learning the ability to interpolate frames and match images, rather than only "remember" the KITTI or Sintel-like images.

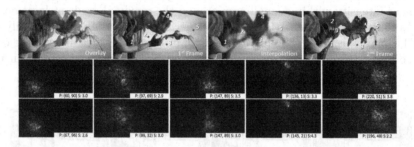

Fig. 5. Failure example of MIND for image pair taken from the Sintel movie clip (best viewed in colour). The gradient/saliency maps (from left to right) are for matches labelled as 1, 2, ..., 5, respectively. (Color figure online)

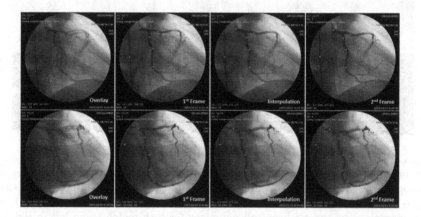

Fig. 6. Examples of MIND on DICOM images. There are two examples shown in different rows. For each example, the columns from left to right show the overlay of the input image-pair, the 1st input image, the interpolation returned by the CNN, and the 2nd input image, respectively. The red points in columns 2, 3 and 4 indicate the matches obtained by MIND. (Color figure online)

The generalization ability is further illustrated by applying MIND to DICOM images of coronary angiogram[3]. As a numerical evaluation of the generalization ability, we compare the CNN based interpolation results to traditional warp based interpolation method [3] using state-of-the-art optical flow, i.e. DeepFlow [40] and a recently proposed phase-based interpolation method [28]. The comparison is similar to the "Ground truth comparisons" outlined in [28]. The averaged SSD (sum of squared distances) for each method is 6.00, 6.23 and 5.55 respectively, suggesting that the trained CNN performs frame interpolation quantitatively well. Two examples are shown in Fig. 6. It can be seen that these images are substantially different from natural ones. Though failing to preserve perfect image details, the CNN, which is trained on natural images, performs impressively well on the DICOM images. The nice generalization ability of the CNN is underlined by results on both frame interpolation and image matching.

4.4   Quantitative Performance of Image Matching

We compare the matches produced by MIND against those of several empirically designed methods: the classical Kanade–Lucas–Tomasi feature tracker [5], HoG descriptor matching [7] (which is widely employed to boost dense optical flow computation), and the more recent DeepMatching approach [40] which relies on a multilayer convolutional architecture and achieves state-of-the-art performance. As observed in [40], comparing different matching algorithms is delicate because they usually produce different numbers of matches for different parts of the image. For the sake of a fair comparison, we adjust the parameters of each algorithm to make them produce as many as possible matches with an as homogeneous as possible distribution across the input images. For DeepMatching, we use the default parameters. For MIND, we extract correspondences for each corner of a uniform grid of 4 pixels width. For KLT, we set the minEigThreshold to 1e-9 to generate as many matches as possible. For HoG, we again set the pixel sampling grid width to 4. We then sort the matches according to suitable metrics[4] and select the same amount of "best" matches for each algorithm. In this way, the 4 algorithms produce the same numbers of matches with similar coverage over each input image.

The comparisons are performed on both KITTI [15] and MPI-Sintel [8] training sets where ground truth correspondences can be extracted from the available ground truth flow fields. We perform all of our experiments on the same image resolution than the one used by our network. On KITTI, the images are scaled to 384×128, and for MPI-Sintel, 256×128. We use the network trained on the

---

[3] The images are taken from a DICOM sample image set: http://www.osirix-viewer. com/datasets/. Alias Name: GRUSELAMBIX.

[4] For DeepMatching, we sort the matches according to the matching score given by the open source code [40]. For KLT, the metric is the error returned by the OpenCV implementation [6]. For HoG, we use the matching score defined in [7]. For MIND, the matching score is defined as the ratio between the maximum gradient intensity and the mean gradient intensity within a 20×20 area around the maximal gradient location.

446   G. Long et al.

Table 2. Matching performance on the KITTI 2012 flow training set. DeepM denotes DeepMatching. Metrics: Average Point Error (APE) (the lower the better), and Accuracy@T (the higher the better). Bold numbers indicate best performance, underlined numbers 2nd best.

	MIND	DeepM	HoG	KLT
APE	4.695	**3.442**	9.680	8.157
Accuracy@5	0.716	**0.835**	0.455	0.702
Accuracy@10	0.915	**0.953**	0.805	0.826
Accuracy@20	0.981	**0.987**	0.929	0.903
Accuracy@30	**0.993**	**0.993**	0.959	0.938

Table 3. Matching performance on the MPI-Sintel training set (Final pass). DeepM denotes DeepMatching. Metrics: Average Point Error (APE) (the lower the better), and Accuracy@T (the higher the better). Bold numbers indicate best performance, underlined numbers 2nd best.

	MIND	DeepM	HoG	KLT
APE	5.838	**3.240**	7.856	8.836
Accuracy@5	0.719	**0.875**	0.688	0.808
Accuracy@10	0.876	**0.951**	0.875	0.864
Accuracy@20	0.948	**0.977**	0.947	0.906
Accuracy@30	0.967	**0.986**	0.964	0.927

KITTI RAW sequences for the matching experiment on the KITTI Flow 2012 training set. We then use the network fine-tuned on Sintel movie clips for the experiments on the MPI-Sintel Flow training set. The 4 algorithms are evaluated in terms of the Average Point Error (APE) and the Accuracy@T. The latter is defined as the proportion of "correct" matches from the first image with respect to the total number of matches [32]. A match is considered correct if its pixel match in the second image is closer than T pixels to ground-truth.

As can be observed in Tables 2 and 3, DeepMatching produces matches with the highest quality in terms of all metrics and on both MPI-Sintel and KITTI sets. Notably, MIND performs very close to DeepMatching on KITTI and outperforms KLT tracking and HoG matching by a considerable amount in terms of Accuracy@10 and Accuracy@20. It is surprising to see that MIND—an unsupervised learning based approach—works so well. The performance on MPI-Sintel however drops a bit due to the difficulty of the contained artificial motion. Though the APE measure indicates better performance than HoG and KLT, it is only safe to conclude that MIND remains competitive in terms of overall performance on MPI-Sintel, which can be seen further in the next section.

4.5   Ability to Initialize Optical Flow Computation

To further understand the matching quality produced by MIND, we replace the DeepMatching part of DeepFlow [40] with MIND to see whether MIND matches are able to boost optical flow performance in a similar way than DeepMatching and HoG or KLT matches. Similar to the evaluation in [40], we feed DeepFlow with matches obtained by each matching method in the previous section. The parameters (e.g. the matching weight) of DeepFlow are tuned accordingly to make best use of the pre-obtained matches. Note that we scale down the input images to 384 × 128 for KITTI and 256 × 128 for MPI-Sintel. We then up-size the obtained flow field to the original resolution by bi-linear interpolation, to the end of comparing results in full resolution.

Table 4. Flow performance on KITTI 2012 flow training set (non-occluded areas). out-x refers to the percentage of pixels where flow estimation has an error above x pixels.

	MIND	DeepM	HoG	KLT	No match
APE	_2.89_	**2.63**	3.06	3.40	3.55
out-2	_17.70 %_	**17.09 %**	17.89 %	18.34 %	18.49 %
out-5	_9.86 %_	**9.18 %**	10.05 %	10.58 %	10.77 %
out-10	_6.45 %_	**5.84 %**	6.66 %	7.20 %	7.40 %

Table 5. Flow performance on MPI-Sintel flow training set. s0-10 is the APE for pixels with motions between 0 and 10 pixels. Similarly for s10-40 and s40+.

	MIND	DeepM	HoG	KLT	No match
APE	5.78	**4.80**	5.46	_5.42_	6.63
s0-10	**2.25**	2.84	3.65	3.22	_2.47_
s10-40	6.26	**6.08**	6.52	6.48	_6.18_
s40+	19.03	18.79	**17.38**	_17.44_	23.16

The results on the KITTI Flow 2012 training set are indicated in Table 4. It can be seen that using the matches obtained by any of the 4 algorithms improves the flow performance compared to the case where we use no matches for initialization. Notably, MIND again reaches closest performance to DeepMatching in terms of all metrics, thus underlining the good matching quality obtained by MIND (better than KLT and HoG and comparable to DeepMatching). Table 5 shows the results obtained on the MPI-Sintel training dataset. As in KITTI, the pre-obtained matches indeed help to improve the optical flow results especially in terms of the APE and s40+ metrics, while flow initialized by DeepMatching remains best overall. The results initialized from MIND matches however rank behind those initialized by HoG or KLT matches, which again suggests the importance of temporal coherence for training our network. The reason why KLT works better than in the evaluation presented in [40] is because we run KLT in the downscaled images rather than the full resolution ones, and this helps KLT to better deal with large displacements.

From the quantitative evaluations of matching and flow performance, it should be concluded that MIND works well on the KITTI Flow training set and achieves comparable performance to the state-of-the-art defined by Deep-Matching. In the MPI-Sintel Flow training set, MIND still obtains comparable performance to the traditional HoG and KLT methods. The latter should still be interpreted as a good result especially considering that the quality of training data for the artificial and perhaps unrealistic Sintel images is insufficient. A closer look into the training data collected from Sintel video suggests that the assumption of temporal coherence does not hold well.

5   Conclusions

We have shown that the present work enables artificial neural networks to learn accurate image matching from only ordinary videos. Though MIND currently does not provide the required computational efficiency for applications in real-world scenarios, it promises a great potential for more natural solutions to further related problems. It is also our hope that the present work helps to promote the concept of *analysis by synthesis* towards a broad acceptance. Our future work focuses on making the present approach more applicable in real-world scenarios, in terms of both computational efficiency and reliability.

Acknowledgment. L. Kneip's research is funded by ARC DECRA grant DE150-101365. The research of L. Kneip and H. Li is also funded by the ARC Centre of Excellence for Robotic Vision CE140100016. All authors gratefully acknowledge the support of the NVIDIA corporation for the donation of Tesla K40 GPUs. G. Long would like to give special thanks to Yuchao Dai, Stephen Gould and Anoop Cherian for the valuable discussions and feedback.

References

1. Agrawal, P., Carreira, J., Malik, J.: Learning to see by moving. arXiv preprint arXiv:1505.01596 (2015)
2. Bach, S., Binder, A., Montavon, G., Klauschen, F., Müller, K.R., Samek, W.: On pixel-wise explanations for non-linear classifier decisions by layer-wise relevance propagation. PloS One **10**(7), e0130140 (2015)
3. Baker, S., Scharstein, D., Lewis, J., Roth, S., Black, M.J., Szeliski, R.: A database and evaluation methodology for optical flow. Int. J. Comput. Vis. **92**(1), 1–31 (2011)
4. Becker, S.: Learning temporally persistent hierarchical representations. In: Advances in Neural Information Processing Systems, pp. 824–830 (1997)
5. Bouguet, J.Y.: Pyramidal implementation of the affine lucas kanade feature tracker description of the algorithm. Intel Corporation **5**(1-10), 4 (2001)
6. Bradski, G., Kaehler, A.: Learning OpenCV: Computer Vision with the OpenCV Library. O'Reilly Media Inc., Sebastopol (2008)
7. Brox, T., Malik, J.: Large displacement optical flow: descriptor matching in variational motion estimation. IEEE Trans. Pattern Anal. Mach. Intell. **33**(3), 500–513 (2011)
8. Butler, D.J., Wulff, J., Stanley, G.B., Black, M.J.: A naturalistic open source movie for optical flow evaluation. In: Fitzgibbon, A., Lazebnik, S., Perona, P., Sato, Y., Schmid, C. (eds.) ECCV 2012. LNCS, vol. 7577, pp. 611–625. Springer, Heidelberg (2012). doi:10.1007/978-3-642-33783-3_44
9. Chatfield, K., Simonyan, K., Vedaldi, A., Zisserman, A.: Return of the devil in the details: delving deep into convolutional nets. arXiv preprint arXiv:1405.3531 (2014)
10. Dosovitskiy, A., Brox, T.: Inverting convolutional networks with convolutional networks. arXiv preprint arXiv:1506.02753 (2015)
11. Eigen, D., Puhrsch, C., Fergus, R.: Depth map prediction from a single image using a multi-scale deep network. In: Advances in Neural Information Processing Systems, pp. 2366–2374 (2014)
12. Ess, A., Leibe, B., Schindler, K., Van Gool, L.: Robust multiperson tracking from a mobile platform. IEEE Trans. Pattern Anal. Mach. Intell. **31**(10), 1831–1846 (2009)
13. Fischer, P., Dosovitskiy, A., Brox, T.: Descriptor matching with convolutional neural networks: a comparison to sift. arXiv preprint arXiv:1405.5769 (2014)
14. Fischer, P., Dosovitskiy, A., Ilg, E., Häusser, P., Hazırbaş, C., Golkov, V., van der Smagt, P., Cremers, D., Brox, T.: Flownet: learning optical flow with convolutional networks. arXiv preprint arXiv:1504.06852 (2015)

15. Geiger, A., Lenz, P., Stiller, C., Urtasun, R.: Vision meets robotics: the KITTI dataset. Int. J. Robot. Res. (IJRR) **32**, 1229–1235 (2013)
16. Glorot, X., Bengio, Y.: Understanding the difficulty of training deep feedforward neural networks. In: International Conference on Artificial Intelligence and Statistics, pp. 249–256 (2010)
17. Goroshin, R., Mathieu, M., LeCun, Y.: Learning to linearize under uncertainty. arXiv preprint arXiv:1506.03011 (2015)
18. He, K., Zhang, X., Ren, S., Sun, J.: Deep residual learning for image recognition. arXiv preprint arXiv:1512.03385 (2015)
19. He, K., Zhang, X., Ren, S., Sun, J.: Delving deep into rectifiers: surpassing human-level performance on imagenet classification. arXiv preprint arXiv:1502.01852 (2015)
20. Hinton, G.E., Salakhutdinov, R.R.: Reducing the dimensionality of data with neural networks. Science **313**(5786), 504–507 (2006)
21. Huang, G., Mattar, M., Lee, H., Learned-Miller, E.G.: Learning to align from scratch. In: Advances in Neural Information Processing Systems, pp. 764–772 (2012)
22. Jensen, C., Reed, R.D., Marks, R.J., El-Sharkawi, M., Jung, J.B., Miyamoto, R.T., Anderson, G.M., Eggen, C.J., et al.: Inversion of feedforward neural networks: algorithms and applications. Proc. IEEE **87**(9), 1536–1549 (1999)
23. Jia, Y., Shelhamer, E., Donahue, J., Karayev, S., Long, J., Girshick, R., Guadarrama, S., Darrell, T.: Caffe: convolutional architecture for fast feature embedding. arXiv preprint arXiv:1408.5093 (2014)
24. Kingma, D., Ba, J.: Adam: a method for stochastic optimization. arXiv preprint arXiv:1412.6980 (2014)
25. Klein, D.A., Schulz, D., Frintrop, S., Cremers, A.B.: Adaptive real-time video-tracking for arbitrary objects. In: IEEE International Conference on Intelligent Robots and Systems (IROS), pp. 772–777, October 2010
26. Long, J.L., Zhang, N., Darrell, T.: Do convnets learn correspondence? In: Advances in Neural Information Processing Systems, pp. 1601–1609 (2014)
27. Mahendran, A., Vedaldi, A.: Understanding deep image representations by inverting them. arXiv preprint arXiv:1412.0035 (2014)
28. Meyer, S., Wang, O., Zimmer, H., Grosse, M., Sorkine-Hornung, A.: Phase-based frame interpolation for video. In: Proceedings of the IEEE Conference on Computer Vision and Pattern Recognition, pp. 1410–1418 (2015)
29. Mobahi, H., Collobert, R., Weston, J.: Deep learning from temporal coherence in video. In: Proceedings of the 26th Annual International Conference on Machine Learning, pp. 737–744. ACM, New York (2009)
30. Park, M.G., Yoon, K.J.: Leveraging stereo matching with learning-based confidence measures. In: Proceedings of the IEEE Conference on Computer Vision and Pattern Recognition, pp. 101–109 (2015)
31. Ranzato, M., Szlam, A., Bruna, J., Mathieu, M., Collobert, R., Chopra, S.: Video (language) modeling: a baseline for generative models of natural videos. arXiv preprint arXiv:1412.6604 (2014)
32. Revaud, J., Weinzaepfel, P., Harchaoui, Z., Schmid, C.: Deep convolutional matching. arXiv preprint arXiv:1506.07656 (2015)
33. Simo-Serra, E., Trulls, E., Ferraz, L., Kokkinos, I., Fua, P., Moreno-Noguer, F.: Discriminative learning of deep convolutional feature point descriptors. In: Proceedings of the International Conference on Computer Vision (ICCV) (2015)

34. Simonyan, K., Vedaldi, A., Zisserman, A.: Deep inside convolutional networks: visualising image classification models and saliency maps. arXiv preprint arXiv:1312.6034 (2013)
35. Srivastava, N., Mansimov, E., Salakhutdinov, R.: Unsupervised learning of video representations using LSTMs. arXiv preprint arXiv:1502.04681 (2015)
36. Srivastava, R.K., Greff, K., Schmidhuber, J.: Highway networks. arXiv preprint arXiv:1505.00387 (2015)
37. Sun, D., Roth, S., Black, M.J.: A quantitative analysis of current practices in optical flow estimation and the principles behind them. Int. J. Comput. Vis. 106(2), 115–137 (2014)
38. Vedaldi, A., Lenc, K.: Matconvnet-convolutional neural networks for MATLAB. arXiv preprint arXiv:1412.4564 (2014)
39. Wang, X., Gupta, A.: Unsupervised learning of visual representations using videos. arXiv preprint arXiv:1505.00687 (2015)
40. Weinzaepfel, P., Revaud, J., Harchaoui, Z., Schmid, C.: Deepflow: large displacement optical flow with deep matching. In: 2013 IEEE International Conference on Computer Vision (ICCV), pp. 1385–1392. IEEE (2013)
41. Wiskott, L., Sejnowski, T.J.: Slow feature analysis: unsupervised learning of invariances. Neural Comput. 14(4), 715–770 (2002)
42. Yildirim, I., Kulkarni, T., Freiwald, W., Tenenbaum, J.B.: Efficient and robust analysis-by-synthesis in vision: a computational framework, behavioral tests, and modeling neuronal representations. In: Annual Conference of the Cognitive Science Society (2015)
43. Zagoruyko, S., Komodakis, N.: Learning to compare image patches via convolutional neural networks. CoRR abs/1504.03641 (2015)
44. Žbontar, J., LeCun, Y.: Computing the stereo matching cost with a convolutional neural network. In: Proceedings of the IEEE Conference on Computer Vision and Pattern Recognition, pp. 1592–1599 (2015)

A Distance for HMMs Based on Aggregated Wasserstein Metric and State Registration

Yukun Chen[1(✉)], Jianbo Ye[1], and Jia Li[2]

[1] College of Information Sciences and Technology,
Pennsylvania State University, University Park, USA
{yzc147,jxy198}@psu.edu
[2] Department of Statistics, Pennsylvania State University, University Park, USA
jol2@psu.edu

Abstract. We propose a framework, named *Aggregated Wasserstein*, for computing a dissimilarity measure or distance between two Hidden Markov Models with state conditional distributions being Gaussian. For such HMMs, the marginal distribution at any time spot follows a Gaussian mixture distribution, a fact exploited to softly match, aka register, the states in two HMMs. We refer to such HMMs as Gaussian mixture model-HMM (GMM-HMM). The registration of states is inspired by the intrinsic relationship of optimal transport and the Wasserstein metric between distributions. Specifically, the components of the marginal GMMs are matched by solving an optimal transport problem where the cost between components is the Wasserstein metric for Gaussian distributions. The solution of the optimization problem is a fast approximation to the Wasserstein metric between two GMMs. The new Aggregated Wasserstein distance is a semi-metric and can be computed without generating Monte Carlo samples. It is invariant to relabeling or permutation of the states. This distance quantifies the dissimilarity of GMM-HMMs by measuring both the difference between the two marginal GMMs and the difference between the two transition matrices. Our new distance is tested on the tasks of retrieval and classification of time series. Experiments on both synthetic data and real data have demonstrated its advantages in terms of accuracy as well as efficiency in comparison with existing distances based on the Kullback-Leibler divergence.

Keywords: Hidden Markov Model · Gaussian Mixture Model · Wasserstein distance

1 Introduction

A hidden Markov model (HMM) with Gaussian emission distributions for any given state is a widely used stochastic model for time series of vectors residing

Electronic supplementary material The online version of this chapter (doi:10.1007/978-3-319-46466-4_27) contains supplementary material, which is available to authorized users.

B. Leibe et al. (Eds.): ECCV 2016, Part VI, LNCS 9910, pp. 451–466, 2016.
DOI: 10.1007/978-3-319-46466-4_27

in an Euclidean space. It has been massively used in the pattern recognition literature, such as acoustic signal processing (e.g. [1–6]) and computer vision (e.g. [7–10]) for modeling spatial-temporal dependencies in data. We refer to such an HMM as Gaussian mixture model-HMM (GMM-HMM) to stress the fact that the marginal distribution of the vector at any time spot follows a Gaussian mixture distribution. Our new distance for HMMs exploits heavily the GMM marginal distribution, which is the major reason we use the terminology GMM-HMM. We are aware that in some literature, Gaussian mixture HMM is used to mean an HMM with state conditional distributions being Gaussian mixtures rather than a single Gaussian distribution. This more general form of HMM is equivalent to an HMM containing an enlarged set of states with single Gaussian distributions. Hence, it poses no particular difficulty for our proposed framework. More detailed remarks are given in Sect. 6.

A long-pursued question is how to quantitatively compare two sequences based on the parametric representations of the GMM-HMMs estimated from them respectively. The GMM-HMM parameters lie on a non-linear manifold. Thus a simple Euclidean distance on the parameters is not proper. As argued in the literature (e.g. [11,12]), directly comparing HMM in terms of the parameters is non-trivial, partly due to the *identifiability* issue of parameters in a mixture model. Specifically, a mixture model can only be estimated up to the permutation of states. Different components in a mixture model are actually unordered even though labels are assigned to them, the permutation of labels having no effect on the likelihood of the model. Some earlier solutions do not principally tackle the parameter identifiability issue and simply assume the components are already aligned based on whatever labels given to them [13]. Other more sophisticated solutions sidestep the issue to use model independent statistics including the KL divergence [14,15] and probability product kernels [16,17]. Those statistics usually cannot be computed easily, requiring Monte Carlo samples or the original sequences [12,18], which can be viewed as one source of Monte Carlo samples.

Sometimes approaches that use the original sequence data may give more reliable results than the Monte Carlo approaches. Yet such approaches require that the original sequences are instantly accessible at the phase of data analysis. Imagine a setting where large volumes of data are collected across different sites. Due to the communication constraints or the sheer size of data, it is possible that one cannot transmit all data to a single site. We may have to work on a distributed platform. The models are estimated at multiple sites; and only the models (much compressed information from the original data) are transmitted to a central site. This raises the need of approaches requiring only the model parameters. Existing methods using only the model parameters typically rely on Monte Carlo sampling (e.g. KL-D based methods [14]) to calculate certain log-likelihood statistics. However, the rate of convergence in estimating the log-likelihoods is $O\left(\left(\frac{1}{n}\right)^{2/d}\right)$ [19,20], where n is the data size and d the dimension. This can be slow for GMM-HMMs in high dimensions, not to mention the time to generate those samples.

In this paper, we propose a non-simulation parameter-based framework named *Aggregated Wasserstein* to compute the distance between GMM-HMMs. To address the state identifiability issue, the framework first solves a registration matrix between the states of two GMM-HMMs according to an optimization criterion. The optimization problem is essentially a fast approximation to the Wasserstein metric between two marginal GMMs. Once the registration matrix is obtained, we compute separately the difference between the two marginal GMMs and the difference between two transition matrices. Finally, we combine the two parts by a weighted sum. The weight can be cast as a trade-off factor balancing the importance between differentiating spatial geometries and stochastic dynamics of two GMM-HMMs.

For an improved estimation of the state registration, we also propose a second approach to calculate the registration matrix based on Monte Carlo sampling. The second approach overcomes certain limitations of the first approach, but at the cost of being more computationally expensive. The second method relies on estimating a mixture weight vector of a special mixture model (explained in our paper), whose rate of convergence is asymptotically $O\left(\sqrt{\frac{\log n}{n}}\right)$ — much faster than the rate of computing log-likelihood based statistics in high dimensions.

We investigate our geometry-driven methods in real world tasks and compare them with the KL divergence-type methods. Practical advantages of our approach have been demonstrated in real applications. By experiments on synthetic data, we also make effort to discover scenarios when our proposed methods outperform the others.

Our contributions. We develop a parameter-based framework with the option of not using simulation for computing a distance between GMM-HMMs. Under such framework, a registration matrix is computed for the states in two HMMs. Two methods have been proposed to compute the registration, resulting in two distances, named *Minimized Aggregated Wasserstein* and *Improved Aggregated Wasserstein*. Both distances are experimentally validated to be robust and effective, often outperform KL divergence-based methods in practice.

The rest of the paper is organized as follows. We introduce notations and preliminaries in Sect. 2. The main framework for defining the distance is proposed in Sect. 3. The second approach based on Monte Carlo to compute the registration between two sets of HMM states is described in Sect. 4. Finally, we investigate the new framework empirically in Sect. 5 based on synthetic and real data.

2   Preliminaries

In Sect. 2.1, we review GMM-HMM and introduce notations. Next, the definition for Wasserstein distance is provided in Sect. 2.2, and its difference from the KL divergence in the case of Gaussian is discussed.

2.1   Notations and Definitions

Consider a sequence $O_T = \{o_1, o_2, ..., o_T\}$ modeled by a GMM-HMM. Suppose there are M states: $S = \{1, ..., M\}$, a GMM-HMM under the stationary condition assumes the following:

1. Each observation $o_i \in O_T$ is associated with a hidden state $s_i \in S$ governed by a Markov chain (MC).

2. $\mathbf{T}$ is the $M \times M$ transition matrix of the MC $\mathbf{T}_{i,j} \overset{\text{def}}{=} P(s_{t+1} = j | s_t = i)$, $1 \le i, j \le M$ for any $t \in \{1, ..., T\}$. The stationary (initial) state probability $\pi = [\pi_1, \pi_2, ..., \pi_M]$ satisfies $\pi \mathbf{T} = \pi$ and $\pi \mathbf{1} = 1$.

3. The Gaussian probabilistic emission function $\phi_i(o_t) \overset{\text{def}}{=} P(o_t | s_t = i)$, $i = 1, ..., M$, for any $t \in \{1, ..., T\}$, is the p.d.f. of the normal distribution $\mathcal{N}(\mu_i, \Sigma_i)$, where μ_i, Σ_i are the mean and covariance of the Gaussian distribution conditioned on state i.

In particular, we use $\mathcal{M}(\{\mu_i\}_{i=1}^M, \{\Sigma_i\}_{i=1}^M, \pi)$ to denote the corresponding mixture of M Gaussions ($\{\phi_1, \phi_2, ..., \phi_M\}$). $\mathcal{M}$'s prior probability of components, aka the mixture weight, coincides with the respective stationary probability π, which is determined by $\mathbf{T}$. Therefore, one can summarize the parameters for a stationary GMM-HMM model via Λ as $\Lambda(\mathbf{T}, \mathcal{M}) = \Lambda(\mathbf{T}, \{\mu_i\}_{i=1}^M, \{\Sigma_i\}_{i=1}^M)$. In addition, the i-th row of the transition matrix $\mathbf{T}$ is denoted by $\mathbf{T}(i,:) \in \mathbb{R}^{1 \times M}$. And the next observation's distribution conditioned on current state i is also a GMM: $\mathcal{M}^{(i)}(\{\mu_i\}_{i=1}^M, \{\Sigma_i\}_{i=1}^M, \mathbf{T}(i,:))$, which we abbreviated as $\mathcal{M}^{(i)}|_{\mathbf{T}(i,:)}$.

2.2   The Wasserstein Distance and the Gaussian Case

In probability theory, Wasserstein distance is a geometric distance naturally defined for any two probability measures over a metric space.

Definition 1 (p-Wasserstein distance). *Given two probability distribution f, g defined on Euclidean space $\mathbb{R}^d$, the p-Wasserstein distance $W_p(\cdot, \cdot)$ between them is given by*

$$W_p(f, g) \overset{\text{def}}{=} \left[\inf_{\gamma \in \Pi(f,g)} \int_{\mathbb{R}^d \times \mathbb{R}^d} \|\mathbf{x} - \mathbf{y}\|^p d\gamma(\mathbf{x}, \mathbf{y}) \right]^{1/p}, \tag{1}$$

where $\Pi(f, g)$ is the collection of all distributions on $\mathbb{R}^d \times \mathbb{R}^d$ with marginal f and g on the first and second factors respectively. In particular, the $\Pi(\cdot, \cdot)$ is often called as the coupling set. The $\gamma^* \in \Pi(f, g)$ that takes the infimum in Eq. (1) is called the optimal coupling.

Remark 1. By Hölder inequality, one has $W_p \le W_q$ for any $p \le q < \infty$. In this paper, we focus on the practice of W_p with $0 < p \le 2$.

While Wasserstein distance between two multi-dimensional GMMs is unsolved, it has a closed formula for two Gaussian $\phi_1(\mu_1, \Sigma_1)$ and $\phi_2(\mu_2, \Sigma_2)$ [21] when $p = 2$:

$$W_2(\phi_1, \phi_2)^2 = \|\mu_1 - \mu_2\|^2 + tr\left(\Sigma_1 + \Sigma_2 - 2\left(\Sigma_1^{1/2}\Sigma_2\Sigma_1^{1/2}\right)^{1/2}\right). \quad (2)$$

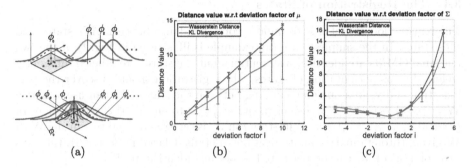

(a)   (b)   (c)

Fig. 1. (a) Experiment scheme for varying μ and varying Σ. A re-estimated $\widehat{\phi}_0$ is denoted as the dashed blue line. (b) (c) Mean estimates of $W_2(\widehat{\phi}_0, \phi_i)$ (blue) and $KL(\widehat{\phi}_0, \phi_i)$ (orange) and their 3σ confidence intervals w.r.t different Gaussian ϕ_i. (b) is for varying μ, and (c) is for varying Σ. (Color figure online)

Remark 2. The formula of Wasserstein distance between two Gaussians does not involve the inverse-covariance matrix, thus admits the cases of singularity. In comparison, KL divergence between two Gaussian $KL(\phi_1, \phi_2)$ could go to infinity if the covariance of ϕ_2 becomes singular.

Remark 3. The Wasserstein distance could also be more statistically robust than KL divergence by comparing the variance of their estimations. To illustrate this point, we conduct two sets of toy experiments. We sample 100 fixed-size batches of points from pre-selected Gaussian ϕ_0, re-estimate each batch's Gaussian parameters $\widehat{\phi}_0 = \mathcal{N}(\widehat{\mu}, \widehat{\Sigma}) \approx \phi_0$, and then calculate $W_2(\widehat{\phi}_0, \phi_i)$ and $KL(\widehat{\phi}_0, \phi_i)$, in which $\{\phi_i\}_{i=1}^{10}$ is a sequence of different Gaussians. We construct ϕ_i by varying μ in the first experiment (See Fig. 1(a) upper plot.) and varying Σ in the second experiment (See Fig. 1(a) bottom plot.). More detailed experiment setup is explained in Appendix A. Figure 1(b) and (c) show the performance of Wasserstein distance and KL divergence on the two toy experiments respectively. Both the estimations and the 3σ confidence intervals are plotted. It is clear that the Wasserstein distances based on estimated distributions have smaller variance and can overall better differentiate $\{\phi_i\}$.

3   The Framework of Aggregated Wasserstein

In this section, we propose a framework to compute the distance between two GMM-HMMs, $\Lambda_1(\mathbf{T}_1, \mathcal{M}_1)$ and $\Lambda_2(\mathbf{T}_2, \mathcal{M}_2)$, where $\mathcal{M}_l$, $l = 1, 2$ are marginal

GMMs with pdf $f_l(x) = \sum_{j=1}^{M_l} \pi_{l,j} \phi_{l,j}(x)$ and $\mathbf{T}_1, \mathbf{T}_2$ are the transition matrices of dimension $M_1 \times M_1$ and $M_2 \times M_2$ (recall notations in Sect. 2). Based on the registration matrix between states in two HMMs, to be described in Sect. 3.1, the distance between Λ_1 and Λ_2 consists of two parts: (1) the difference between $\mathcal{M}_1$ and $\mathcal{M}_2$ (Sect. 3.2); and (2) the difference between $\mathbf{T}_1$ and $\mathbf{T}_2$ (Sect. 3.3).

3.1   The Registration of States

The registration of states is to build a correspondance between Λ_1's states and Λ_2's states. In the simplest case (an example is illustrated in Fig. 2), if the two marginal GMMs are identical distributions but the states are labeled differently (referred to as permutation of states), the registration should discover the permutation and yield a one-one mapping between the states. We can use a matrix $\mathbf{W} = \{w_{i,j}\} \in \mathbb{R}^{M_1 \times M_2}$ whose elements $w_{i,j} \geq 0$ to encode this registration. In particular, $w_{i,j} = \pi_{1,i}(= \pi_{2,j})$ iff state i in Λ_1 is registered to state j in Λ_2. With $\mathbf{W}$ given, through matrix multiplications (details delayed in Sect. 3.3), the rows and columns of $\mathbf{T}_1$ can be permuted to become identical to $\mathbf{T}_2$.

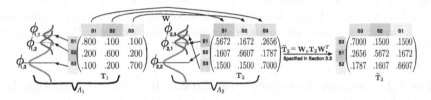

Fig. 2. A simple registration example about how $\mathbf{T}_2$ in Λ_2 is registered towards Λ_1 such that it can be compared with $\mathbf{T}_1$ in Λ_1. For this example, $\mathbf{W}$ encodes a "hard matching" between states in Λ_1 and Λ_2

Generally and more commonly, there may exist no state in Λ_2 having the same emission function as some state in Λ_1, and the number of states in Λ_1 may not equal that in Λ_2. The registration process becomes much more difficult. We resort to the principled optimal transport [22] as a tool to solve this problem and formulate the following optimization problem. Recall Eq. (2) for how to compute $W_2(\phi_{1,i}, \phi_{2,j}))$ and let $0 < p \leq 2$, consider

$$\min_{\mathbf{W} \in \Pi(\pi_1, \pi_2)} \sum_{i=1}^{M_1} \sum_{j=1}^{M_2} w_{i,j} W_2(\phi_{1,i}, \phi_{2,j})^p \tag{3}$$

where

$$\Pi(\pi_1, \pi_2) \overset{\text{def}}{=} \left\{ \mathbf{W} \in \mathbb{R}^{M_1 \times M_2} : \sum_{i=1}^{M_1} w_{i,j} = \pi_{2,j}, j = 1, \ldots, M_2; \right.$$

$$\left. \sum_{j=1}^{M_2} w_{i,j} = \pi_{1,i}, i = 1, \ldots, M_1; \text{ and } w_{i,j} \geq 0, \forall i, j \right\} \tag{4}$$

The rationale behind this is that, two states whose emission functions are geometrically close and in similar shape should be more likely to be matched. The solution $\mathbf{W} \in \Pi(\pi_1, \pi_2)$ of the above optimization is called the *registration matrix* between Λ_1 and Λ_2. And it will play an important role both in the comparison of marginal GMMs and transition matrices of Λ_1 and Λ_2.

The solution of Eq. (3) is an extension of the hard matching between states for the simplest case to the general soft matching when the hard matching is impossible. For the aforementioned simple example (Fig. 2), in which the two Gaussian mixtures are in fact identical thus hard matching is possible, Eq. (3) indeed yields the optimal $\mathbf{W}$ which encodes the correct permutation of states in the two models. In general, there are more than one non-zero elements per row or per column.

3.2   The Distance Between Two Marginal GMMs

Our aim in this subsection is to quantify the difference between Λ_1 and Λ_2's marginal GMMs $\mathcal{M}_1$ and $\mathcal{M}_2$, whose density functions are $f_1(x) = \sum_{j=1}^{M_1} \pi_{1,j} \phi_{1,j}(x)$ and $f_2(x) = \sum_{j=1}^{M_2} \pi_{2,j} \phi_{2,j}(x)$ respectively.

Given the discussion on the advantages of the Wasserstein metric (especially the Gaussian case) in Sect. 2, one may ask *why not to use Wasserstein distance* $W(\mathcal{M}_1, \mathcal{M}_2)$ *directly to measure the dissimilarity between* $\mathcal{M}_1, \mathcal{M}_2$? Unfortunately, there is no closed form formula for GMMs except for the reduced case of single Gaussians. Monte Carlo estimation is usually used. However, similar to the estimation of KL divergence, the Monte Carlo estimation for the Wasserstein distance also suffers from a slow convergence rate. The rate of convergence is as slow as that of KL divergence, i.e., $O\left(\left(\frac{1}{n}\right)^{1/d}\right)$ [23], again posing difficulty in high dimensions. So, instead of estimating the Wasserstein distance itself, we make use of the solved registration matrix $\mathbf{W} \in \Pi(\pi_1, \pi_2)$ and the closed form Wasserstein distance between every pair of Gaussians to quantify the dissimilarity between two marginal GMMs $\mathcal{M}_1$ and $\mathcal{M}_2$:

$$\widetilde{R}_p(\mathcal{M}_1, \mathcal{M}_2; \mathbf{W})^p \stackrel{\text{def}}{=} \sum_{i=1}^{M_1} \sum_{j=1}^{M_2} w_{i,j} W_2(\phi_{1,i}, \phi_{2,j})^p \tag{5}$$

where $\mathbf{W}$ is the solved registration matrix (from Eq. (3)). Note that registration matrix solved by scheme other than Eq. (3) (e.g. the one we will introduce in Sect. 4) can also be plugged into this equation. Since we call $\mathbf{W} \in \Pi(\pi_1, \pi_2)$ the registration matrix, we call $\widetilde{R}_p(\mathcal{M}_1, \mathcal{M}_2; \mathbf{W})^p$ the *registered distance* between $\mathcal{M}_1$ and $\mathcal{M}_2$ at $\mathbf{W}$. The motivation for Eq. (5) is that if the matching weights in $\mathbf{W}$ is acceptable, then it seems natural to aggregate the pairwise distances between the Gaussians in the two mixtures through these weights. We will later prove that $\widetilde{R}_p(\mathcal{M}_1, \mathcal{M}_2; \mathbf{W})$ is a semi-metric (Theorem 2). Next, we present Theorem 1 that states this semi-metric as an upper bound on the true Wasserstein metric.

Theorem 1. *For any two GMMs* $\mathcal{M}_1$ *and* $\mathcal{M}_2$, *let* $\widetilde{R}_p(\cdot, \cdot : \mathbf{W})$ *be defined as Eq.* (5). *If* $\mathbf{W} \in \Pi(\pi_1, \pi_2)$, *we have for* $0 < p \leq 2$

$$\widetilde{R}_p(\mathcal{M}_1, \mathcal{M}_2 : \mathbf{W}) \geq W_p(\mathcal{M}_1, \mathcal{M}_2),$$

where $W_p(\mathcal{M}_1, \mathcal{M}_2)$ *is the true Wasserstein distance between* $\mathcal{M}_1$ *and* $\mathcal{M}_2$ *as defined in Eq.* (1).

Proof. See Appendix B.

For the brevity of notation, if $\mathbf{W}$ is solved from Eq. (3), the resulting distance $\widetilde{R}_p(\mathcal{M}_1, \mathcal{M}_2 : \mathbf{W})$ is denoted by $\widetilde{W}_p(\mathcal{M}_1, \mathcal{M}_2)$.

3.3 The Distance Between Two Transition Matrices

Given the registration matrix $\mathbf{W}$, our aim in this subsection is to quantify the difference between Λ_1 and Λ_2's transition matrices, $\mathbf{T}_1 \in \mathbb{R}^{M_1 \times M_1}$ and $\mathbf{T}_2 \in \mathbb{R}^{M_2 \times M_2}$. Since the *identifiability* issue is already addressed by the registration matrix $\mathbf{W}$, $\mathbf{T}_2$ can now registered towards $\mathbf{T}_1$ by the following transform:

$$\widetilde{\mathbf{T}}_2 \overset{\text{def}}{=} \mathbf{W}_r \mathbf{T}_2 \mathbf{W}_c^T \in \mathbb{R}^{M_1 \times M_1}, \tag{6}$$

where matrix $\mathbf{W}_r$ and $\mathbf{W}_c$ are row-wise and column-wise normalized $\mathbf{W}$ respectively, a.k.a. $\mathbf{W}_r = \text{diag}^{-1}(\mathbf{W} \cdot \mathbf{1}) \cdot \mathbf{W}$ and $\mathbf{W}_c = \mathbf{W} \cdot \text{diag}^{-1}(\mathbf{1}^T \cdot \mathbf{W})$. A simple example of this process is illustrated in the right part of Fig. 2. Likewise, $\mathbf{T}_1$ can also be registered towards $\mathbf{T}_2$:

$$\widetilde{\mathbf{T}}_1 \overset{\text{def}}{=} \mathbf{W}_c^T \mathbf{T}_1 \mathbf{W}_r \in \mathbb{R}^{M_2 \times M_2}. \tag{7}$$

Then, a discrepancy denoted as $D(\mathbf{T}_1, \mathbf{T}_2 : \mathbf{W})$ to measure the dissimilarity of two transition matrices is adopted:

$$D_p(\mathbf{T}_1, \mathbf{T}_2 : \mathbf{W})^p \overset{\text{def}}{=} d_T(\mathbf{T}_1, \widetilde{\mathbf{T}}_2)^p + d_T(\mathbf{T}_2, \widetilde{\mathbf{T}}_1)^p \tag{8}$$

where $\widetilde{\mathbf{T}}_1$ and $\widetilde{\mathbf{T}}_2$ are calculated from Eqs. (6) and (7) (with $\mathbf{W}$ given) respectively and

$$d_T(\mathbf{T}_1, \widetilde{\mathbf{T}}_2)^p \overset{\text{def}}{=} \sum_{i=1}^{M_1} \pi_{1,i} \widetilde{W}_p \left(\mathcal{M}_1^{(i)} |_{\mathbf{T}_1(i,:)}, \mathcal{M}_1^{(i)} |_{\widetilde{\mathbf{T}}_2(i,:)} \right)^p \tag{9}$$

$$d_T(\mathbf{T}_2, \widetilde{\mathbf{T}}_1)^p \overset{\text{def}}{=} \sum_{i=1}^{M_2} \pi_{2,i} \widetilde{W}_p \left(\mathcal{M}_2^{(i)} |_{\mathbf{T}_2(i,:)}, \mathcal{M}_2^{(i)} |_{\widetilde{\mathbf{T}}_1(i,:)} \right)^p \tag{10}$$

We remind that by the notations in Sect. 2.1, $\mathcal{M}_1^{(i)} |_{\mathbf{T}_1(i,:)}$ is the pdf of the next observation conditioned on the previous state being i (likewise for the other similar terms).

3.4   A Semi-metric Between GMM-HMMs —- Minimized Aggregated Wasserstein (MAW)

In summary, the dissimilarity between GMM-HMMs Λ_1, Λ_2 comprises two parts: the first is the discrepancy between the marginal GMMs $\mathcal{M}_1, \mathcal{M}_2$, and the second is the discrepancy between two transition matrices after state registration. A weighted sum of these two terms is taken as the final distance. We call this new distance the *Minimized Aggregated Wasserstein* (MAW) between GMM-HMM models. Let $\mathbf{W}$ be solved from Eq. (3).

$$MAW(\Lambda_1, \Lambda_2) \overset{\text{def}}{=} (1 - \alpha)\widetilde{R}_p(\mathcal{M}_1, \mathcal{M}_2; \mathbf{W}) + \alpha D_p(\mathbf{T}_1, \mathbf{T}_2 : \mathbf{W}) \qquad (11)$$

Choosing α. For the purpose of maximizing the differentiation ability of the distance, α can be determined by maximizing the accuracy obtained by the 1-nearest neighbor classifier on a set of small but representative training GMM-HMMs with ground truth labels.

For clarity, we summarize MAW's computation procedure in Algorithm 1. Theorem 2 states that MAW is a semi-metric. A semi-metric shares all the properties of a true metric (including separation axiom) except for the triangle inequality.

Algorithm 1. Minimized Aggregated Wasserstein (MAW)

Input: $\Lambda_1 \left(\mathbf{T}_1, \mathcal{M}_1 \left(\{\mu_{1,i}\}_{i=1}^{M_1}, \{\Sigma_{1,i}\}_{i=1}^{M_1} \right) \right)$, $\Lambda_2 \left(\mathbf{T}_2, \mathcal{M}_2 \left(\{\mu_{2,i}\}_{i=1}^{M_2}, \{\Sigma_{2,i}\}_{i=1}^{M_2} \right) \right)$
Output: $MAW(\Lambda_1, \Lambda_2) \in \{0\} \cup \mathbb{R}^+$
1: Compute registration matrix $\mathbf{W}$ by Eq. (3) ;
2: Compute $\widetilde{R}_p(\mathcal{M}_1, \mathcal{M}_2; \mathbf{W})$ by Eq. (5)
3: Compute $D_p(\mathbf{T}_1, \mathbf{T}_2)$ by Eqs. (8)–(10)
4: Compute and return $MAW(\Lambda_1, \Lambda_2)$ defined by Eq. (11).

Theorem 2. *MAW defined by Eq.* (11) *is a semi-metric for GMM-HMMs if* $0 < \alpha < 1$.

Proof. See appendix C.

4   Improved State Registration

A clear disadvantage of estimating $\mathbf{W}$ by Eq. (3) and then computing $\widetilde{R}_p(\cdot, \cdot)$ by Eq. (5) is that $\mathbf{W}$ could be sensitive to the parametrization of GMMs. Two GMMs whose distributions are close can be parameterized very differently, especially when the components are not well separated, leading to $\widetilde{W}$ substantially larger than the true Wasserstein metric. In contrast, the real Wasserstein metric W only depends on the underlying distributions, and thus does not suffer from the artifacts caused by the GMM parameterization. In this section, we introduce an improved approach based on Monte Carlo to calculate the registration matrix $\mathbf{W}$ for two GMMs, which can approximate the true Wasserstein metric more accurately than the method specified in Sect. 3.1.

Suppose the Wasserstein distance between two GMMs $\mathcal{M}_1$ and $\mathcal{M}_2$ are presolved such that the inference for their optimal coupling γ^* (referring to Definition 1.) is at hand. We define a new state registration matrix by

$$\mathbf{W}^* = \int \pi(\mathbf{x}; \mathcal{M}_1)^T \cdot \pi(\mathbf{y}; \mathcal{M}_2) d\gamma^*(\mathbf{x}, \mathbf{y}), \qquad (12)$$

where $\pi(\mathbf{x}; \cdot)$ (a column vector) denotes the posterior mixture component probabilities at point $\mathbf{x}$ inferred from a provided GMM. In Appendix D, we provide mathematical properties of $\mathbf{W}^*$, and show that γ^* is also a special mixture model with $M_1 \times M_2$ components whose mixture weights are actually given by vec($\mathbf{W}^*$). Hence a Monte Carlo method to estimate $\mathbf{W}^*$ is hereby given. Two sets ($\{\mathbf{x}_1, \ldots, \mathbf{x}_n\}$ and $\{\mathbf{y}_1, \ldots, \mathbf{y}_n\}$) of equal size i.i.d. samples are generated from $\mathcal{M}_1$ and $\mathcal{M}_2$ respectively. The $\mathbf{W}^*$ is then empirically estimated by

$$\widetilde{\mathbf{W}}_n^* \overset{\text{def}}{=} [\pi(\mathbf{x}_1; \mathcal{M}_1), \ldots, \pi(\mathbf{x}_n; \mathcal{M}_1)] \cdot \Pi_n \cdot [\pi(\mathbf{y}_1; \mathcal{M}_2), \ldots, \pi(\mathbf{y}_n; \mathcal{M}_2)]^T, \quad (13)$$

where $\Pi_n \in \mathbb{R}^{n \times n}$ is the p-th optimal coupling solved for the two samples (essentially a permutation matrix). In practice, we use Sinkhorn algorithm to approximately solve for the optimal coupling [24]. $\widetilde{\mathbf{W}}_n^*$ converges to $\mathbf{W}^*$ with probability 1, as $n \to \infty$. Consequently, the **Improved Aggregated Wasserstein** (IAW) is defined similarly as Eq. (11) with a different $\mathbf{W}$ computed from Eq. (13).

Remark 4 (Convergence Rate). The estimation of $\mathbf{W}^*$ follows the mixture proportion estimation setting [25, 26], whose rate of convergence is $O\left(\sqrt{\dfrac{V_{\widehat{\Pi}} \log n}{n}}\right)$. Here $V_{\widehat{\Pi}} = V_{\widehat{\Pi}}(d, M_1, M_2)$ is the VC dimension of the geometric class induced by the family $\widehat{\Pi}(\mathcal{M}_1, \mathcal{M}_2)$ (See appendix D and [27] for related definitions).

5   Experiments

We conduct experiments to quantitatively evaluate the proposed MAW and IAW. In particular, we set $p = 1$. Our comparison baseline is KL based distance [14] since it is the most widely used one (e.g. [11, 12]). In Sect. 5.1, we use synthetic data to evaluate the sensitivity of MAW and IAW to the perturbation of μ, Σ, and $\mathbf{T}$. Similar synthetic experiments have been done in related work (e.g. [11]). In Sect. 5.2, we compare MAW and IAW with KL using the Mocap data under both retrieval and classification settings.

5.1   Evaluation of Sensitivity to the Perturbation of Parameters

Three sets of experiments are conducted to evaluate MAW and IAW's sensitivity to the perturbation of GMM-HMM parameters ($\{\mu_j\}_{j=1}^M$, $\{\Sigma\}_{j=1}^M$, and $\mathbf{T}$) respectively. In each set of experiments, we have five pre-defined 2-state GMM-HMM models $\left\{\Lambda_j\left(\{\mu_{i,j}\}_{j=1}^2, \{\Sigma_{i,j}\}_{j=1}^2, \mathbf{T}_i\right)\right\}_{i=1}^5$, among which the only difference is GMM means $\{\mu_{i,1}, \mu_{i,2}\}$, GMM covariances $\{\Sigma_{i,1}, \Sigma_{i,2}\}$, or transition matrices $\mathbf{T}_i$. For example, in the 1st experiment, we perturb $\{\mu_{i,1}, \mu_{i,2}\}$ by setting the 5 GMM-HMM's $\{\mu_{i,1}, \mu_{i,2}\}_{i=1}^5$ to be

$$\left\{\left\{\begin{pmatrix}2+i\Delta\mu\\2+i\Delta\mu\end{pmatrix}, \begin{pmatrix}5+i\Delta\mu\cdot\\5+i\Delta\mu\cdot\end{pmatrix}\right\} | i = 1, 2, 3, 4, 5\right\} \tag{14}$$

respectively. $\{\Sigma_{i,1}, \Sigma_{i,2}\}$ of them are all set to be the same: $\left\{\begin{pmatrix}1&0\\0&1\end{pmatrix}, \begin{pmatrix}1&0\\0&1\end{pmatrix}\right\}$.

And the transition matrix of them are also the same: $\begin{pmatrix}0.8&0.2\\0.2&0.8\end{pmatrix}$. $\Delta\mu$ here is a parameter to control the difference between the 5 models. The smaller the value, the 5 models are more similar to each other and the retrieval will be more challenging. We choose $\Delta\mu$ to be $0.2, 0.4, 0.6$, and compare KL, MAW and IAW under each setting. Please refer to Table 1 for detailed experiment setup for the other two experiments. For each model of the five, 10 sequences of dimension 2 and of length 100 are generated. These ten sequences with their later estimated models form a single class. Therefore in total, we have 50 sequences belonging to 5 classes. During the evaluation, we re-estimate each sequence's GMM-HMM parameters using the well known Baum-Welch Algorithm. Then for each sequence's estimated model, we treat it as a query to retrieve other sequences' models using KL, MAW and IAW respectively. The precision recall plot for the retrieval are shown in Fig. 3.

Table 1. Summary of the parameters setup for parameter perturbation experiments. $rand(2)$ here means random matrix of dimension 2 by 2. $Dirichlet(x)$ here means generating samples from Direchlet distribution with parameter x.

Exp. index	deviation step	μ	Σ	$\mathbf{T}$
1	$\Delta\mu = 0.2$, $0.4, 0.6$	$\left\{\begin{pmatrix}2+i\Delta\mu\\2+i\Delta\mu\end{pmatrix}, \begin{pmatrix}5+i\Delta\mu\\5+i\Delta\mu\end{pmatrix}\right\}$ $\|i = 1, 2, 3, 4, 5\}$	$\left\{\begin{pmatrix}1&0\\0&1\end{pmatrix}, \begin{pmatrix}1&0\\0&1\end{pmatrix}\right\}$	$\begin{pmatrix}0.8&0.2\\0.2&0.8\end{pmatrix}$
2	$\Delta\sigma = 0.2$, $0.4, 0.6$	$\left\{\begin{pmatrix}2\\2\end{pmatrix}, \begin{pmatrix}5\\5\end{pmatrix}\right\}$	$\{\{0.2 \cdot exp(i\Delta\sigma \cdot \mathbf{S}),$ $0.2 \cdot exp(i\Delta\sigma \cdot \mathbf{S})\}\|$ $i = 1, 2, 3, 4, 5\},$ $\mathbf{S} = rand(2)$	$\begin{pmatrix}0.8&0.2\\0.2&0.8\end{pmatrix}$
3	$\Delta t = 0.2$, $0.4, 0.6$	$\left\{\begin{pmatrix}2\\2\end{pmatrix}, \begin{pmatrix}5\\5\end{pmatrix}\right\}$	$\left\{\begin{pmatrix}1&0\\0&1\end{pmatrix}, \begin{pmatrix}1&0\\0&1\end{pmatrix}\right\}$	$\{\Delta t \cdot \mathbf{S} + (1 - \Delta t) \cdot \mathbf{T}_i\|$ $\mathbf{T}_i[j,:] \sim Dirichlet(10 \cdot \mathbf{S}[j,:])$ $i = 1, 2, 3, 4, 5\}, \mathbf{S} = \begin{pmatrix}0.8&0.2\\0.2&0.8\end{pmatrix}$

462   Y. Chen et al.

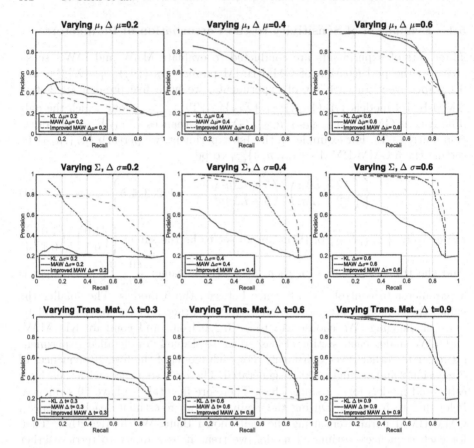

Fig. 3. Precision-recall plot for the study to compare KL, MAW and IAW's sensitivity to the perturbation of GMM-HMM's parameters.

From the first row and third row of Fig. 3, the experiments consistently show that MAW and IAW perform better than KL to differentiate the perturbation of $\{\mu_j\}_{j=1}^M$ and $\mathbf{T}$. From the second row, we can see that for the task of differentiating perturbation of $\{\Sigma\}_{j=1}^M$, KL performs better than IAW, and IAW performs better than MAW. But for the less challenging case, IAW has comparable performance. Note that if we only care about the nearest neighbor query, IAW actually performs better than KL under the perturbation of $\{\Sigma\}_{j=1}^M$. The computation time for MAW and IAW based on our MATLAB implementation are 10 ms and 24 ms (per distance) respectively and that for KL-D based on our C implementation is 5 ms (per distance).[1]

---

[1] Matlab code: https://github.com/cykustcc/aggregated_wasserstein_hmm.

5.2 Motion Capture Data

In this section, we use Carnegie Mellon Motion Capture Dataset (Mocap) to evaluate MAW and IAW and make comparison with KL based approach which [18] takes. To improve the stability of evaluation, we only select motion categories (1) whose sequences contain only 1 motion, and (2) which contain more than 20 sequences. In total, there are 7 motion categories, i.e. *Alaskan vacation, Jump, Story, clean, salsa dance, walk,* and *walk on uneven terrain* that meet this criterion and they contain a total of 337 motion sequences. Since the sequence data is of high dimension (62), following the practice of [18], we split the 62 dimension data to 6 joint-groups[2]. And we conduct both Motion Retrieval based on individual joint-group and Motion Classification using Adaboost on all joint groups. The details of the experiments are specified as follows.

Motion Retrieval. For each motion time series, we first estimate a 3 state GMM-HMM for each joint-group. Then we use it as a query to retrieve GMM-HMMs estimated from other sequences' on the same joint-group data using KL, MAW and IAW respectively. α for MAW and IAW is chosen such that the 1-nearest neighbor classification accuracy on a small set-aside evaluation set is maximized. The precision-recall plot for the motion retrieval is shown in Fig. 4. The curve is averaged over all motion sequences. We can see that MAW and IAW yield consistently better retrieval results on all joints.

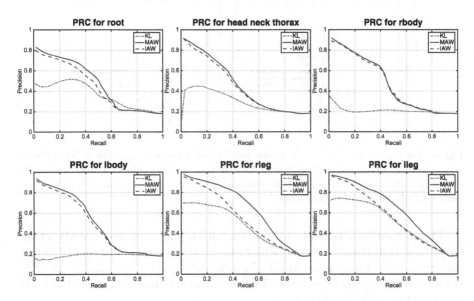

Fig. 4. Precision Recall Plot for Motion Retrieval. The plot for 6 joint-groups, i.e. $root_{12}$, $head\_neck\_thorax_{12}$, $rbody_{12}$, $lbody_{12}$, $rleg_6$, $lleg_6$, are displayed separately.

---

[2] $root_{12}$, $head\_neck\_thorax_{12}$, $rbody_{12}$, $lbody_{12}$, $rleg_6$, $lleg_6$. (The subscript number denotes the dimension of the group).

Motion Classification. First, we split the 337 motion sequences randomly into two sets, roughly half for training and half for testing. In the training phase, for each of the 7 motion categories, we train one GMM-HMM for each individual joint-group using the training data. For each sequence, we also estimate one GMM-HMM for each individual joint-group. And we compute its distance (either KL, MAW or IAW) to all the GMM-HMMs on the same joint-group data from the 7 motion categories. These distance values are treated as features. The dimension of the feature vector of an individual sequence is thus the number of joint-groups multiplied by 7. Finally, we use Adaboost with depth-one decision trees (essentially, each tree is a one-feature thresholder) to obtain a classification accuracy on the test data. We plot the classification accuracy w.r.t the number of iterations for Adaboost in Fig. 5(a). We also split the original data to 27 different joint groups and run the same experiments again. The results show that under both the 6 joint-group scheme and the 27 joint-group scheme, MAW (85.21 % for 6 joint scheme and 95.27 % for 27 joint scheme) and IAW (88.17 % for 6 joint scheme and 94.08 % for 27 joint scheme) achieve considerably better classification accuracy than KL (73.37 % for 6 joint scheme and 88.76 % for 27 joint scheme). The confusion matrices are also drawn in Fig. 7 in the supplement.

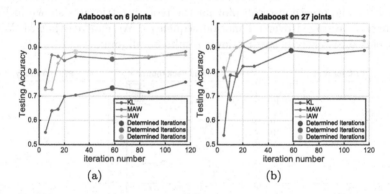

(a)   (b)

Fig. 5. Testing accuracies w.r.t iteration number of Adaboost (number of weak classifiers selected). (a) Motion Classification by Adaboost on 6 joints. (b) Motion Classification by Adaboost on 27 joints. The iteration number means the number of features incrementally acquired in Adaboost.

The computation time of Mocap data with 6 joint groups are MAW 21 ms, IAW 158 ms (1000 samples), and KL-D 8 ms (1000 samples). And that of Mocap data with 27 joint groups are MAW 17 ms, IAW 160 ms (1000 samples), and KL-D 7 ms (1000 samples). Again, the MAW and IAW are implemented in MATLAB, and KL-D is implemented in C.

6   Discussion and Conclusions

Although we focus on GMM-HMM whose emission function is Gaussian in this paper, the same methodology extends readily to:

1. GMM-HMM whose emission function is GMM but *not* single Gaussian. (Each state with GMM emission function consists of k Gaussians can be split into k states. Our current method can be applied directly then.)
2. Other Hidden Markov Models with non-Gaussian state emission functions, provided that a distance between any two state conditional distributions can be computed. For instance, an HMM with discrete emission distributions can be handled by using the Wasserstein metric between discrete distributions.

In conclusion, we have developed the MAW and IAW distances between GMM-HMMs that are invariant to state permutation. These new distances are computationally efficient, especially MAW. Comparisons with the KL divergence have demonstrated clearly stronger retrieval and classification performance. In future, it is interesting to explore how to reasonably group HMMs into a number of clusters based on our proposed MAW and IAW. The HMM clustering has been studied under the context of KL-D [11], and the clustering under Wasserstein distance has been studied for empirical distributions [28].

Acknowledgement. This research is supported by the National Science Foundation under grant number ECCS-1462230.

References

1. Baker, J.K.: The dragon system-an overview. IEEE Trans. Acoust. Speech Signal Process. **23**(1), 24–29 (1975)
2. Cole, R., Hirschman, L., Atlas, L., Beckman, M., Biermann, A., Bush, M., Clements, M., Cohen, J., Garcia, O., Hanson, B., et al.: The challenge of spoken language systems: research directions for the nineties. IEEE Trans. Speech Audio Process. **3**(1), 1–21 (1995)
3. Huang, X.D., Ariki, Y., Jack, M.A.: Hidden Markov Models for Speech Recognition, vol. 2004. Edinburgh University Press Edinburgh, Edinburgh (1990)
4. Nilsson, M., Ejnarsson, M.: Speech recognition using hidden markov model. Department of Telecommunications and Speech Processing, Blekinge Institute of Technology (2002)
5. Young, S., Evermann, G., Gales, M., Hain, T., Kershaw, D., Liu, X., Moore, G., Odell, J., Ollason, D., Povey, D., et al.: The HTK book, vol. 2. Entropic Cambridge Research Laboratory Cambridge (1997)
6. Rabiner, L., Juang, B.H.: Fundamentals of Speech Recognition. Prentice-Hall Inc., Upper Saddle River (1993)
7. Ren, L., Patrick, A., Efros, A.A., Hodgins, J.K., Rehg, J.M.: A data-driven approach to quantifying natural human motion. ACM Trans. Graph. (TOG) **24**(3), 1090–1097 (2005)
8. Bregler, C.: Learning and recognizing human dynamics in video sequences. In: Proceedings of the 1997 IEEE Computer Society Conference on Computer Vision and Pattern Recognition, pp. 568–574. IEEE (1997)
9. Shang, L., Chan, K.P.: Nonparametric discriminant hmm and application to facial expression recognition. In: Conference on Computer Vision and Pattern Recognition (CVPR), pp. 2090–2096. IEEE (2009)

10. Alon, J., Sclaroff, S., Kollios, G., Pavlovic, V.: Discovering clusters in motion time-series data. In: Conference on Computer Vision and Pattern Recognition (CVPR). vol. 1, p. I-375. IEEE (2003)
11. Coviello, E., Chan, A.B., Lanckriet, G.R.: Clustering hidden Markov models with variational hem. J. Mach. Learn. Res. 15(1), 697–747 (2014)
12. Smyth, P., et al.: Clustering sequences with hidden Markov models. In: Advances in Neural Information Processing Systems (NIPS), pp. 648–654 (1997)
13. Levinson, S.E., Rabiner, L.R., Sondhi, M.M.: An introduction to the application of the theory of probabilistic functions of a Markov process to automatic speech recognition. Bell Syst. Tech. J. 62(4), 1035–1074 (1983)
14. Juang, B.H.F., Rabiner, L.R.: A probabilistic distance measure for hidden Markov models. AT&T Tech. J. 64(2), 391–408 (1985)
15. Zhong, S., Ghosh, J.: A unified framework for model-based clustering. J. Mach. Learn. Res. 4, 1001–1037 (2003)
16. Jebara, T., Kondor, R., Howard, A.: Probability product kernels. J. Mach. Learn. Res. 5, 819–844 (2004)
17. Jebara, T., Song, Y., Thadani, K.: Spectral clustering and embedding with Hidden Markov Models. In: Kok, J.N., Koronacki, J., Mantaras, R.L., Matwin, S., Mladenič, D., Skowron, A. (eds.) ECML 2007. LNCS (LNAI), vol. 4701, pp. 164–175. Springer, Heidelberg (2007). doi:10.1007/978-3-540-74958-5_18
18. Lv, F., Nevatia, R.: Recognition and segmentation of 3-D human action using HMM and Multi-class AdaBoost. In: Leonardis, A., Bischof, H., Pinz, A. (eds.) ECCV 2006. LNCS, vol. 3954, pp. 359–372. Springer, Heidelberg (2006). doi:10.1007/11744085_28
19. Lee, Y.K., Park, B.U.: Estimation of Kullback-Leibler divergence by local likelihood. Ann. Inst. Stat. Math. 58(2), 327–340 (2006)
20. Noh, Y.K., Sugiyama, M., Liu, S., du Plessis, M.C., Park, F.C., Lee, D.D.: Bias reduction and metric learning for nearest-neighbor estimation of Kullback-Leibler divergence. In: International Conference on Artificial Intelligence and Statistics (AISTATS), pp. 669–677 (2014)
21. Givens, C.R., Shortt, R.M., et al.: A class of Wasserstein metrics for probability distributions. Michigan Math. J. 31(2), 231–240 (1984)
22. Villani, C.: Topics in Optimal Transportation, vol. 58. American Mathematical Society, Providence (2003)
23. Ramdas, A., Garcia, N., Cuturi, M.: On Wasserstein two sample testing and related families of nonparametric tests. arXiv preprint arXiv:1509.02237 (2015)
24. Cuturi, M.: Sinkhorn distances: lightspeed computation of optimal transport. In: Advances in Neural Information Processing Systems (NIPS), pp. 2292–2300 (2013)
25. Blanchard, G., Lee, G., Scott, C.: Semi-supervised novelty detection. J. Mach. Learn. Res. 11, 2973–3009 (2010)
26. Scott, C.: A rate of convergence for mixture proportion estimation, with application to learning from noisy labels. In: International Conference on Artificial Intelligence and Statistics (AISTATS) (2015)
27. Akama, Y., Irie, K.: Vc dimension of ellipsoids. arXiv preprint (2011). arXiv:1109.4347
28. Ye, J., Wu, P., Wang, J.Z., Li, J.: Fast discrete distribution clustering using Wasserstein barycenter with sparse support, 1–14. arXiv preprint arXiv:1510.00012 (2015)

LIFT: Learned Invariant Feature Transform

Kwang Moo Yi[1]([✉]), Eduard Trulls[1], Vincent Lepetit[2], and Pascal Fua[1]

[1] Computer Vision Laboratory, Ecole Polytechnique Fédérale de Lausanne (EPFL),
Lausanne, Switzerland
{kwang.yi,eduard.trulls,pascal.fua}@epfl.ch
[2] Institute for Computer Graphics and Vision,
Graz University of Technology, Graz, Austria
lepetit@icg.tugraz.at

Abstract. We introduce a novel Deep Network architecture that implements the full feature point handling pipeline, that is, detection, orientation estimation, and feature description. While previous works have successfully tackled each one of these problems individually, we show how to learn to do all three in a unified manner while preserving end-to-end differentiability. We then demonstrate that our Deep pipeline outperforms state-of-the-art methods on a number of benchmark datasets, without the need of retraining.

Keywords: Local features · Feature descriptors · Deep Learning

1 Introduction

Local features play a key role in many Computer Vision applications. Finding and matching them across images has been the subject of vast amounts of research. Until recently, the best techniques relied on carefully hand-crafted features [1–5]. Over the past few years, as in many areas of Computer Vision, methods based in Machine Learning, and more specifically Deep Learning, have started to outperform these traditional methods [6–10].

These new algorithms, however, address only a single step in the complete processing chain, which includes detecting the features, computing their orientation, and extracting robust representations that allow us to match them across images. In this paper we introduce a novel Deep architecture that performs all three steps together. We demonstrate that it achieves better overall performance than the state-of-the-art methods, in large part because it allows these individual steps to be optimized to perform well in conjunction with each other.

K.M. Yi, E. Trulls—Equally contributed.
This work was supported in part by the EU FP7 project MAGELLAN under grant number ICT-FP7-611526.

Electronic supplementary material The online version of this chapter (doi:10.1007/978-3-319-46466-4_28) contains supplementary material, which is available to authorized users.

© Springer International Publishing AG 2016
B. Leibe et al. (Eds.): ECCV 2016, Part VI, LNCS 9910, pp. 467–483, 2016.
DOI: 10.1007/978-3-319-46466-4_28

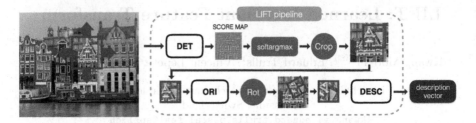

Fig. 1. Our integrated feature extraction pipeline. Our pipeline consists of three major components: the Detector, the Orientation Estimator, and the Descriptor. They are tied together with differentiable operations to preserve end-to-end differentiability. (Figures are best viewed in color.) (Color figure online)

Our architecture, which we refer to as LIFT for Learned Invariant Feature Transform, is depicted by Fig. 1. It consists of three components that feed into each other: the Detector, the Orientation Estimator, and the Descriptor. Each one is based on Convolutional Neural Networks (CNNs), and patterned after recent ones [6,9,10] that have been shown to perform these individual functions well. To mesh them together we use Spatial Transformers [11] to rectify the image patches given the output of the Detector and the Orientation Estimator. We also replace the traditional approaches to non-local maximum suppression (NMS) by the soft argmax function [12]. This allows us to preserve end-to-end differentiability, and results in a full network that can still be trained with back-propagation, which is not the case of any other architecture we know of.

Also, we show *how* to learn such a pipeline in an effective manner. To this end, we build a Siamese network and train it using the feature points produced by a Structure-from-Motion (SfM) algorithm that we ran on images of a scene captured under different viewpoints and lighting conditions, to learn its weights. We formulate this training problem on image patches extracted at different scales to make the optimization tractable. In practice, we found it impossible to train the full architecture from scratch, because the individual components try to optimize for different objectives. Instead, we introduce a problem-specific learning approach to overcome this problem. It involves training the Descriptor first, which is then used to train the Orientation Estimator, and finally the Detector, based on the already learned Descriptor and Orientation Estimator, differentiating through the entire network. At test time, we decouple the Detector, which runs over the whole image in scale space, from the Orientation Estimator and Descriptor, which process only the keypoints.

In the next section we briefly discuss earlier approaches. We then present our approach in detail and show that it outperforms many state-of-the-art methods.

2   Related Work

The amount of literature relating to local features is immense, but it always revolves about finding feature points, computing their orientation, and matching them. In this section, we will therefore discuss these three elements separately.

2.1   Feature Point Detectors

Research on feature point detection has focused mostly on finding distinctive locations whose scale and rotation can be reliably estimated. Early works [13, 14] used first-order approximations of the image signal to find corner points in images. FAST [15] used Machine Learning techniques but only to speed up the process of finding corners. Other than corner points, SIFT [1] detect blobs in scale-space; SURF [2] use Haar filters to speed up the process; Maximally Stable Extremal Regions (MSER) [16] detect regions; [17] detect affine regions. SFOP [18] use junctions and blobs, and Edge Foci [19] use edges for robustness to illumination changes. More recently, feature points based on more sophisticated and carefully designed filter responses [5,20] have also been proposed to further enhance the performance of feature point detectors.

In contrast to these approaches that focus on better engineering, and following the early attempts in learning detectors [21,22], [6] showed that a detector could be learned to deliver significantly better performance than the state-of-the-art. In this work, piecewise-linear convolutional filters are learned to robustly detect feature points in spite of lighting and seasonal changes. Unfortunately, this was done only for a single scale and from a dataset without viewpoint changes. We therefore took our inspiration from it but had to extend it substantially to incorporate it into our pipeline.

2.2   Orientation Estimation

Despite the fact that it plays a critical role in matching feature points, the problem of estimating a discriminative orientation has received noticeably less attention than detection or feature description. As a result, the method introduced by SIFT [1] remains the *de facto* standard up to small improvements, such as the fact that it can be sped-up by using the intensity centroid, as in ORB [4].

A departure from this can be found in a recent paper [9] that introduced a Deep Learning-based approach to predicting stable orientations. This resulted in significant gains over the state-of-the-art. We incorporate this architecture into our pipeline and show how to train it using our problem-specific training strategy, given our learned descriptors.

2.3   Feature Descriptors

Feature descriptors are designed to provide discriminative representations of salient image patches, while being robust to transformations such as viewpoint or illumination changes. The field reached maturity with the introduction of SIFT [1], which is computed from local histograms of gradient orientations, and SURF [2], which uses integral image representations to speed up the computation. Along similar lines, DAISY [3] relies on convolved maps of oriented gradients to approximate the histograms, which yields large computational gains when extracting dense descriptors.

Even though they have been extremely successful, these hand-crafted descriptors can now be outperformed by newer ones that have been learned. These range from unsupervised hashing to supervised learning techniques based on linear discriminant analysis [23,24], genetic algorithm [25], and convex optimization [26]. An even more recent trend is to extract features directly from raw image patches with CNNs trained on large volumes of data. For example, MatchNet [7] trained a Siamese CNN for feature representation, followed by a fully-connected network to learn the comparison metric. DeepCompare [8] showed that a network that focuses on the center of the image can increase performance. The approach of [27] relied on a similar architecture to obtain state-of-the-art results for narrow-baseline stereo. In [10], hard negative mining was used to learn compact descriptors that use on the Euclidean distance to measure similarity. The algorithm of [28] relied on sample triplets to mine hard negatives.

In this work, we rely on the architecture of [10] because the corresponding descriptors are trained and compared with the Euclidean distance, which has a wider range of applicability than descriptors that require a learned metric.

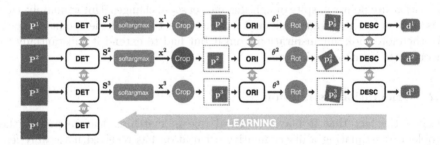

Fig. 2. Our Siamese training architecture with four branches, which takes as input a quadruplet of patches: Patches $\mathbf{P}^1$ and $\mathbf{P}^2$ (blue) correspond to different views of the same physical point, and are used as positive examples to train the Descriptor; $\mathbf{P}^3$ (green) shows a different 3D point, which serves as a negative example for the Descriptor; and $\mathbf{P}^4$ (red) contains no distinctive feature points and is only used as a negative example to train the Detector. Given a patch $\mathbf{P}$, the Detector, the softargmax, and the Spatial Transformer layer Crop provide all together a smaller patch $\mathbf{p}$ inside $\mathbf{P}$. $\mathbf{p}$ is then fed to the Orientation Estimator, which along with the Spatial Transformer layer Rot, provides the rotated patch $\mathbf{p}_\theta$ that is processed by the Descriptor to obtain the final description vector $\mathbf{d}$. (Color figure online)

3 Method

In this section, we first formulate the entire feature detection and description pipeline in terms of the Siamese architecture depicted by Fig. 2. Next, we discuss the type of data we need to train our networks and how to collect it. We then describe the training procedure in detail.

3.1 Problem Formulation

We use image patches as input, rather than full images. This makes the learning scalable without loss of information, as most image regions do not contain keypoints. The patches are extracted from the keypoints used by a SfM pipeline, as will be discussed in Sect. 3.2. We take them to be small enough that we can assume they contain only one dominant local feature at the given scale, which reduces the learning process to finding the most distinctive point in the patch.

To train our network we create the four-branch Siamese architecture pictured in Fig. 2. Each branch contains three distinct CNNs, a Detector, an Orientation Estimator, and a Descriptor. For training purposes, we use quadruplets of image patches. Each one includes two image patches $\mathbf{P}^1$ and $\mathbf{P}^2$, that correspond to different views of the same 3D point, one image patch $\mathbf{P}^3$, that contains the projection of a different 3D point, and one image patch $\mathbf{P}^4$ that does not contain any distinctive feature point. During training, the i-th patch $\mathbf{P}^i$ of each quadruplet will go through the i-th branch.

To achieve end-to-end differentiability, the components of each branch are connected as follows:

1. Given an input image patch $\mathbf{P}$, the Detector provides a score map $\mathbf{S}$.
2. We perform a soft argmax [12] on the score map $\mathbf{S}$ and return the location $\mathbf{x}$ of a single potential feature point.
3. We extract a smaller patch $\mathbf{p}$ centered on $\mathbf{x}$ with the Spatial Transformer layer Crop (Fig. 2). This serves as the input to the Orientation Estimator.
4. The Orientation Estimator predicts a patch orientation θ.
5. We rotate $\mathbf{p}$ according to this orientation using a second Spatial Transformer layer, labeled as Rot in Fig. 2, to produce $\mathbf{p}_\theta$.
6. $\mathbf{p}_\theta$ is fed to the Descriptor network, which computes a feature vector $\mathbf{d}$.

Note that the Spatial Transformer layers are used only to manipulate the image patches while preserving differentiability. They are not learned modules. Also, both the location $\mathbf{x}$ proposed by the Detector and the orientation θ for the patch proposal are treated implicitly, meaning that we let the entire network discover distinctive locations and stable orientations while learning.

Since our network consists of components with different purposes, learning the weights is non-trivial. Our early attempts at training the network as a whole from scratch were unsuccessful. We therefore designed a problem-specific learning approach that involves learning first the Descriptor, then the Orientation Estimator given the learned descriptor, and finally the Detector, conditioned on the other two. This allows us to tune the Orientation Estimator for the Descriptor, and the Detector for the other two components.

We will elaborate on this learning strategy in Sects. 3.3 (Descriptor), 3.4 (Orientation Estimator), and 3.5 (Detector), that is, in the order they are learned.

3.2 Creating the Training Dataset

There are datasets that can be used to train feature descriptors [24] and orientation estimators [9]. However it is not so clear how to train a keypoint detector, and the vast majority of techniques still rely on hand-crafted features. The TILDE detector [6] is an exception, but the training dataset does not exhibit any viewpoint changes.

To achieve invariance we need images that capture views of the same scene under different illumination conditions and seen from different perspectives. We thus turned to photo-tourism image sets. We used the collections from Piccadilly Circus in London and the Roman Forum in Rome from [29] to reconstruct the 3D using VisualSFM [30], which relies of SIFT features. *Piccadilly* contains 3384 images, and the reconstruction has 59k unique points with an average of 6.5 observations for each. *Roman-Forum* contains 1658 images and 51k unique points, with an average of 5.2 observations for each. Figure 3 shows some examples.

We split the data into training and validation sets, discarding views of training points on the validation set and vice-versa. To build the positive training samples we consider only the feature points that survive the SfM reconstruction process. To extract patches that do not contain any distinctive feature point, as required by our training method, we randomly sample image regions that contain no SIFT features, including those that were not used by SfM.

We extract grayscale training patches according to the scale σ of the point, for both feature and non-feature point image regions. Patches **P** are extracted from a $24\sigma \times 24\sigma$ support region at these locations, and standardized into $S \times S$ pixels where $S = 128$. The smaller patches **p** and $\mathbf{p}_\theta$ that serve as input to the Orientation Estimator and the Descriptor, are cropped and rotated versions of these patches, each having size $s \times s$, where $s = 64$. The smaller patches effectively

Fig. 3. Sample images and patches from *Piccadilly* (left) and *Roman-Forum* (right). Keypoints that survive the SfM pipeline are drawn in blue, and the rest in red. (Color figure online)

correspond to the SIFT descriptor support region size of 12σ. To avoid biasing the data, we apply uniform random perturbations to the patch location with a range of 20% (4.8σ). Finally, we normalize the patches with the grayscale mean and standard deviation of the entire training set.

3.3 Descriptor

Learning feature descriptors from raw image patches has been extensively researched during the past year [7,8,10,27,28,31], with multiple works reporting impressive results on patch retrieval, narrow baseline stereo, and matching non-rigid deformations. Here we rely on the relatively simple networks of [10], with three convolutional layers followed by hyperbolic tangent units, l_2 pooling [32] and local subtractive normalization, as they do not require learning a metric.

The Descriptor can be formalized simply as

$$\mathbf{d} = h_\rho(\mathbf{p}_\theta),\tag{1}$$

where $h(.)$ denotes the Descriptor CNN, ρ its parameters, and $\mathbf{p}_\theta$ is the rotated patch from the Orientation Estimator. When training the Descriptor, we do not yet have the Detector and the Orientation Estimator trained. We therefore use the image locations and orientations of the feature points used by the SfM to generate image patches $\mathbf{p}_\theta$.

We train the Descriptor by minimizing the sum of the loss for pairs of corresponding patches $(\mathbf{p}_\theta^1, \mathbf{p}_\theta^2)$ and the loss for pairs of non-corresponding patches $(\mathbf{p}_\theta^1, \mathbf{p}_\theta^3)$. The loss for pair $(\mathbf{p}_\theta^k, \mathbf{p}_\theta^l)$ is defined as the hinge embedding loss of the Euclidean distance between their description vectors. We write

$$\mathcal{L}_{\text{desc}}(\mathbf{p}_\theta^k, \mathbf{p}_\theta^l) = \begin{cases} \left\| h_\rho(\mathbf{p}_\theta^k) - h_\rho(\mathbf{p}_\theta^l) \right\|_2 & \text{for positive pairs, and} \\ \max\left(0, C - \left\| h_\rho(\mathbf{p}_\theta^k) - h_\rho(\mathbf{p}_\theta^l) \right\|_2\right) & \text{for negative pairs,} \end{cases}\tag{2}$$

where positive and negative samples are pairs of patches that do or do not correspond to the same physical 3D points, $\|\cdot\|_2$ is the Euclidean distance, and $C = 4$ is the margin for embedding.

We use hard mining during training, which was shown in [10] to be critical for descriptor performance. Following this methodology, we forward K_f sample pairs and use only the K_b pairs with the highest training loss for back-propagation, where $r = K_f/K_b \geq 1$ is the 'mining ratio'. In [10] the network was pre-trained without mining and then fine-tuned with $r = 8$. Here, we use an increasing mining scheme where we start with $r = 1$ and double the mining ratio every 5000 batches. We use balanced batches with 128 positive pairs and 128 negative pairs, mining each separately.

3.4 Orientation Estimator

Our Orientation Estimator is inspired by that of [9]. However, this specific one requires pre-computations of description vectors for multiple orientations to compute numerically the Jacobian of the method parameters with respect to orientations. This is a critical limitation for us because we treat the output of the detector component implicitly throughout the pipeline and it is thus not possible to pre-compute the description vectors.

We therefore propose to use Spatial Transformers [11] instead to learn the orientations. Given a patch $\mathbf{p}$ from the region proposed by the detector, the Orientation Estimator predicts an orientation

$$\theta = g_\phi(\mathbf{p}), \tag{3}$$

where g denotes the Orientation Estimator CNN, and ϕ its parameters.

Together with the location $\mathbf{x}$ from the Detector and $\mathbf{P}$ the original image patch, θ is then used by the second Spatial Transformer Layer Rot(.) to provide a patch $\mathbf{p}_\theta = \text{Rot}(\mathbf{P}, \mathbf{x}, \theta)$, which is the rotated version of patch $\mathbf{p}$.

We train the Orientation Estimator to provide the orientations that minimize the distances between description vectors for different views of the same 3D points. We use the already trained Descriptor to compute the description vectors, and as the Detector is still not trained, we use the image locations from SfM. More formally, we minimize the loss for pairs of corresponding patches, defined as the Euclidean distance between their description vectors

$$\mathcal{L}_{\text{orientation}}(\mathbf{P}^1, \mathbf{x}^1, \mathbf{P}^2, \mathbf{x}^2) = \left\| h_\rho(G(\mathbf{P}^1, \mathbf{x}^1)) - h_\rho(G(\mathbf{P}^2, \mathbf{x}^2)) \right\|_2, \tag{4}$$

where $G(\mathbf{P}, \mathbf{x})$ is the patch centered on $\mathbf{x}$ after orientation correction: $G(\mathbf{P}, \mathbf{x}) = \text{Rot}(\mathbf{P}, \mathbf{x}, g_\phi(\text{Crop}(\mathbf{P}, \mathbf{x})))$. This complex notation is necessary to properly handle the cropping of the image patches. Recall that pairs $(\mathbf{P}^1, \mathbf{P}^2)$ comprise image patches containing the projections of the same 3D point, and locations $\mathbf{x}^1$ and $\mathbf{x}^2$ denote the reprojections of these 3D points. As in [9], we do not use pairs that correspond to different physical points whose orientations are not related.

3.5 Detector

The Detector takes an image patch as input, and returns a score map. We implement it as a convolution layer followed by piecewise linear activation functions, as in TILDE [6]. More precisely, the score map $\mathbf{S}$ for patch $\mathbf{P}$ is computed as:

$$\mathbf{S} = f_\mu(\mathbf{P}) = \sum_n^N \delta_n \max_m^M (\mathbf{W}_{mn} * \mathbf{P} + \mathbf{b}_{mn}), \tag{5}$$

where $f_\mu(\mathbf{P})$ denotes the Detector itself with parameters μ, δ_n is $+1$ if n is odd and -1 otherwise, μ is made of the filters W_{mn} and biases b_{mn} of the convolution layer to learn, $*$ denotes the convolution operation, and N and M are hyper-parameters controlling the complexity of the piecewise linear activation function.

The main difference with TILDE lies in the way we train this layer. To let $\mathbf{S}$ have maxima in places other than a fixed location retrieved by SfM, we treat this location implicitly, as a latent variable. Our method can potentially discover points that are more reliable and easier to learn, whereas [6] cannot. Incidentally, in our early experiments, we noticed that it was harmful to force the Detector to optimize directly for SfM locations.

From the score map $\mathbf{S}$, we obtain the location $\mathbf{x}$ of a feature point as

$$\mathbf{x} = \text{softargmax}\,(\mathbf{S})\;, \tag{6}$$

where softargmax is a function which computes the Center of Mass with the weights being the output of a standard softmax function [12]. We write

$$\text{softargmax}\,(\mathbf{S}) = \frac{\sum_{\mathbf{y}} \exp(\beta\mathbf{S}(\mathbf{y}))\mathbf{y}}{\sum_{\mathbf{y}} \exp(\beta\mathbf{S}(\mathbf{y}))}\;, \tag{7}$$

where $\mathbf{y}$ are locations in $\mathbf{S}$, and $\beta = 10$ is a hyper-parameter controlling the smoothness of the softargmax. This softargmax function acts as a differentiable version of non-maximum suppression. $\mathbf{x}$ is given to the first Spatial Transformer Layer Crop(.) together with the patch $\mathbf{P}$ to extract a smaller patch $\mathbf{p} = \text{Crop}\,(\mathbf{P}, \mathbf{x})$ used as input to the Orientation Estimator.

As the Orientation Estimator and the Descriptor have been learned by this point, we can train the Detector given the full pipeline. To optimize over the parameters μ, we minimize the distances between description vectors for the pairs of patches that correspond to the same physical points, while maximizing the classification score for patches not corresponding to the same physical points.

More exactly, given training quadruplets $(\mathbf{P}^1, \mathbf{P}^2, \mathbf{P}^3, \mathbf{P}^4)$, where $\mathbf{P}^1$ and $\mathbf{P}^2$ correspond to the same physical point, $\mathbf{P}^1$ and $\mathbf{P}^3$ correspond to different SfM points, and $\mathbf{P}^4$ to a non-feature point location, we minimize the sum of their loss functions

$$\mathcal{L}_{\text{detector}}(\mathbf{P}^1, \mathbf{P}^2, \mathbf{P}^3, \mathbf{P}^4) = \gamma\mathcal{L}_{class}(\mathbf{P}^1, \mathbf{P}^2, \mathbf{P}^3, \mathbf{P}^4) + \mathcal{L}_{pair}(\mathbf{P}^1, \mathbf{P}^2)\;, \tag{8}$$

where γ is a hyper-parameter balancing the two terms in this summation

$$\mathcal{L}_{\text{class}}(\mathbf{P}^1, \mathbf{P}^2, \mathbf{P}^3, \mathbf{P}^4) = \sum_{i=1}^{4} \alpha_i \max\left(0, \left(1 - \text{softmax}\left(f_\mu\left(\mathbf{P}^i\right)\right) y_i\right)\right)^2\;, \tag{9}$$

with $y_i = -1$ and $\alpha_i = 3/6$ if $i = 4$, and $y_i = +1$ and $\alpha_i = 1/6$ otherwise to balance the positives and negatives. softmax is the log-mean-exponential softmax function. We write

$$\begin{aligned}\mathcal{L}_{\text{pair}}(\mathbf{P}^1, \mathbf{P}^2) = \|\; &h_\rho(G(\mathbf{P}^1, \text{softargmax}(f_\mu(\mathbf{P}^1)))) \\ - \;&h_\rho(G(\mathbf{P}^2, \text{softargmax}(f_\mu(\mathbf{P}^2)))) \;\|_2\;.\end{aligned} \tag{10}$$

Note that the locations of the detected feature points $\mathbf{x}$ appear only implicitly and are discovered during training. Furthermore, all three components are tied in with the Detector learning. As with the Descriptor we use a hard mining strategy, in this case with a fixed mining ratio of $r = 4$.

In practice, as the Descriptor already learns some invariance, it can be hard for the Detector to find new points to learn implicitly. To let the Detector start with an idea of the regions it should find, we first constrain the patch proposals $\mathbf{p} = \text{Crop}(\mathbf{P}, \text{softargmax}(f_\mu(\mathbf{P})))$ that correspond to the same physical points to overlap. We then continue training the Detector without this constraint.

Specifically, when pre-training the Detector, we replace $\mathcal{L}_{\text{pair}}$ in Eq. (8) with $\tilde{\mathcal{L}}_{\text{pair}}$, where $\tilde{\mathcal{L}}_{\text{pair}}$ is equal to 0 when the patch proposals overlap exactly, and increases with the distance between them otherwise. We therefore write

$$\tilde{\mathcal{L}}_{\text{pair}}(\mathbf{P}^1, \mathbf{P}^2) = 1 - \frac{\mathbf{p}^1 \cap \mathbf{p}^2}{\mathbf{p}^1 \cup \mathbf{p}^2} + \frac{\max\left(0, \|\mathbf{x}^1 - \mathbf{x}^2\|_1 - 2s\right)}{\sqrt{\mathbf{p}^1 \cup \mathbf{p}^2}}, \tag{11}$$

where $\mathbf{x}^j = \text{softargmax}(f_\mu(\mathbf{P}^j))$, $\mathbf{p}^j = \text{Crop}(\mathbf{P}^j, \mathbf{x}^j)$, $\|\cdot\|_1$ is the l_1 norm. Recall that $s = 64$ pixels is the width and height of the patch proposals.

3.6 Runtime Pipeline

The pipeline used at run-time is shown in Fig. 4. As our method is trained on patches, simply applying it over the image would require the network to be tested with a sliding window scheme over the whole image. In practice, this would be too expensive. Fortunately, as the Orientation Estimator and the Descriptor only need to be run at local maxima, we can simply decouple the detector from the rest to apply it to the full image, and replace the softargmax function by NMS, as outlined in red in Fig. 4. We then apply the Orientation Estimator and the Descriptor only to the patches centered on local maxima.

More exactly, we apply the Detector independently to the image at different resolutions to obtain score maps in scale space. We then apply a traditional NMS scheme similar to that of [1] to detect feature point locations.

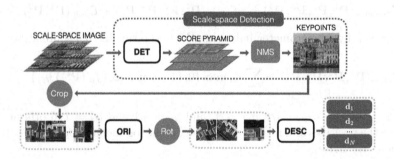

Fig. 4. An overview of our runtime architecture. As the Orientation Estimator and the Descriptor only require evaluation at local maxima, we decouple the Detector and run it in scale space with traditional NMS to obtain proposals for the two other components. (Color figure online)

4 Experimental Validation

In this section, we first present the datasets and metrics we used. We then present qualitative results, followed by a thorough quantitative comparison against a number of state-of-the-art baselines, which we consistently outperform.

Finally, to better understand what elements of our approach most contribute to this result, we study the importance of the pre-training of the Detector component, discussed in Sect. 3.5, and analyze the performance gains attributable to each component.

4.1 Dataset and Experimental Setup

We evaluate our pipeline on three standard datasets:

- The *Strecha* dataset [33], which contains 19 images of two scenes seen from increasingly different viewpoints.
- The *DTU* dataset [34], which contains 60 sequences of objects with different viewpoints and illumination settings. We use this dataset to evaluate our method under viewpoint changes.
- The *Webcam* dataset [6], which contains 710 images of 6 scenes with strong illumination changes but seen from the same viewpoint. We use this dataset to evaluate our method under natural illumination changes.

For *Strecha* and *DTU* we use the provided ground truth to establish correspondences across viewpoints. We use a maximum of 1000 keypoints per image, and follow the standard evaluation protocol of [35] on the common viewpoint region. This lets us evaluate the following metrics.

- Repeatability (Rep.): Repeatability of feature points, expressed as a ratio. This metric captures the performance of the feature point detector by reporting the ratio of keypoints that are found consistently in the shared region.
- Nearest Neighbor mean Average Precision (NN mAP): Area Under Curve (AUC) of the Precision-Recall curve, using the Nearest Neighbor matching strategy. This metric captures how discriminating the descriptor is by evaluating it at multiple descriptor distance thresholds.
- Matching Score (M. Score): The ratio of ground truth correspondences that can be recovered by the whole pipeline over the number of features proposed by the pipeline in the shared viewpoint region. This metric measures the overall performance of the pipeline.

We compare our method on the three datasets to the following combination of feature point detectors and descriptors, as reported by the authors of the corresponding papers: SIFT [1], SURF [2], KAZE [36], ORB [4], Daisy [37] with SIFT detector, sGLOH [38] with Harris-affine detector [39], MROGH [40] with Harris-affine detector, LIOP [41] with Harris-affine detector, BiCE [42] with Edge Foci detector [19], BRISK [43], FREAK [44] with BRISK detector, VGG [26] with SIFT detector, DeepDesc [10] with SIFT detector, PN-Net [28] with SIFT detector, and MatchNet [7] with SIFT detector. We also consider SIFT with Hessian-Affine keypoints [17]. For the learned descriptors VGG, DeepDesc, PN-Net and MatchNet we use SIFT keypoints because they are trained using a dataset created with Difference-of-Gaussians, which is essentially the same as SIFT. In the case of Daisy, which was not developed for a specific detector, we also use SIFT

Fig. 5. Qualitative local feature matching examples of **left:** SIFT and **right:** our method LIFT. Correct matches recovered by each method are shown in green lines and the descriptor support regions with red circles. **Top row:** *Herz-Jesu-P8* of *Strecha*, **second row:** *Frankfurt* of *Webcam*, **third row:** *Scene 7* of *DTU* and **bottom row:** *Scene 19* of *DTU*. Note that the images are very different from one another. (Color figure online)

keypoints. To make our results reproducible, we provide additional implementation details for LIFT and the baselines in the supplementary material.[1]

4.2 Qualitative Examples

Figure 5 shows image matching results with 500 feature points, for both SIFT and our LIFT pipeline trained with *Piccadilly*. As expected, LIFT returns more correct correspondences across the two images. One thing to note is that the two DTU scenes in the bottom two rows are completely different from the photo-tourism datasets we used for training. Given that the two datasets are very different, this shows good generalization properties.

4.3 Quantitative Evaluation of the Full Pipeline

Figure 6 shows the average matching score for all three datasets, and Table 1 provides the exact numbers for the two LIFT variants. LIFT (pic) is trained with *Piccadilly* and LIFT (rf) with *Roman-Forum*. Both of our learned models significantly outperform the state-of-the-art on *Strecha* and *DTU* and achieve

---

[1] Source and models will be available at https://github.com/cvlab-epfl/LIFT.

Table 1. Average matching score for all baselines.

	SIFT	SIFT-HesAff	SURF	ORB	Daisy	sGLOH	MROGH	LIOP	BiCE
Strecha	.283	.314	.208	.157	.272	.207	.239	.211	.270
DTU	.272	.274	.244	.127	.262	.187	.223	.189	.242
Webcam	.128	.164	.117	.120	.120	.113	.125	.086	.166
	BRISK	FREAK	VGG	MatchNet	DeepDesc	PN-Net	KAZE	LIFT-pic	LIFT-rf
Strecha	.208	.183	.300	.223	.298	.300	.250	**.374**	.369
DTU	.193	.186	.271	.198	.257	.267	.213	**.317**	.308
Webcam	.118	.116	.118	.101	.116	.114	.195	.196	**.202**

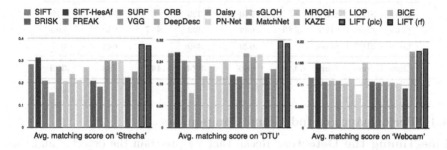

Fig. 6. Average matching score for all baselines.

state-of-the-art on *Webcam*. Note that KAZE, which is the best performing competitor on *Webcam*, performs poorly on the other two datasets. As discussed above, *Piccadilly* and *Roman-Forum* are very different from the datasets used for testing. This underlines the strong generalization capability of our approach, which is not always in evidence with learning-based methods.

Interestingly, on *DTU*, SIFT is still the best performing method among the competitors, even compared to methods that rely on Deep Learning, such as DeepDesc and PN-Net. Also, the gap between SIFT and the learning-based VGG, DeepDesc, and PN-Net is not large for the *Strecha* dataset.

These results show that although a component may outperform another method when evaluated individually, they may fail to deliver their full potential when integrated into the full pipeline, which is what really matters. In other words, it is important to learn the components together, as we do, and to consider the whole pipeline when evaluating feature point detectors and descriptors.

Table 2. Results on *Strecha* for both LIFT models trained on *Piccadilly* and *Roman-Forum*, with the pre-trained and fully-trained Detector.

	Trained on *Piccadilly*		Trained on *Roman-Forum*	
	Rep	M.Score	Rep	M.Score
Pre-trained	.436	.367	.447	.368
Fully-trained	**.446**	**.374**	**.447**	**.369**

Table 3. Results on *Strecha* for both LIFT models trained on *Piccadilly* and *Roman-Forum*, interchanging our components with their SIFT counterparts.

Det.	Ori.	Desc.	Rep.	Trained on *Piccadilly* NN mAP	M.Score	Rep.	Trained on *Roman-Forum* NN mAP	M.Score
SIFT	SIFT	SIFT		.517	.282		.517	.282
SIFT	Ours	SIFT	.428	.671	.341	.428	.662	.338
SIFT	SIFT	Ours		.568	.290		.581	.295
SIFT	Ours	Ours		.685	.344		**.688**	.342
Ours	SIFT	SIFT		.540	.325		.545	.319
Ours	Ours	SIFT	.446	.644	.372	.447	.630	.360
Ours	SIFT	Ours		.629	.339		.644	.337
Ours	Ours	Ours	**.446**	**.686**	**.374**	**.447**	.683	**.369**

4.4 Performance of Individual Components

Fine-Tuning the Detector. Recall that we pre-train the detector and then finalize the training with the Orientation Estimator and the Descriptor, as discussed in Sect. 3.5. It is therefore interesting to see the effect of this finalizing stage. In Table 2 we evaluate the entire pipeline with the pre-trained Detector and the final Detector. As the pair-wise loss term $\tilde{\mathcal{L}}_{\mathrm{pair}}$ of Eq. (11) is designed to emulate the behavior of an ideal descriptor, the pre-trained Detector already performs well. However, the full training pushes the performance slightly higher.

A closer look at Table 2 reveals that gains are larger overall for *Piccadilly* than for *Roman-Forum*. This is probably due to the fact that *Roman-Forum* does not have many non-feature point regions. In fact, the network started to over-fit quickly after a few iterations on this dataset. The same happened when we further tried to fine-tune the full pipeline as a whole, suggesting that our learning strategy is already providing a good global solution.

Performance of Individual Components. To understand the influence of each component on the overall performance, we exchange them with their SIFT counterparts, for both LIFT (pic) and LIFT (rf), on *Strecha*. We report the results in Table 3. In short, each time we exchange to SIFT, we decrease performance, thus showing that each element of the pipeline plays and important role. Our Detector gives higher repeatability for both models. Having better orientations also helps whichever detector or descriptor is being used, and also the Deep Descriptors perform better than SIFT.

One thing to note is that our Detector is not only better in terms of repeatability, but generally better in terms of both the NN mAP, which captures the descriptor performance, and in terms of matching score, which evaluates the full pipeline. This shows that our Detector learns to find not only points that can be found often but also points that can be matched easily, indicating that training the pipeline as a whole is important for optimal performance.

5   Conclusion

We have introduced a novel Deep Network architecture that combines the three components of standard pipelines for local feature detection and description into a single differentiable network. We used Spatial Transformers together with the softargmax function to mesh them together into a unified network that can be trained end-to-end with back-propagation. While this makes learning the network from scratch theoretically possible, it is not *practical*. We therefore proposed an effective strategy to train it.

Our experimental results demonstrate that our integrated approach outperforms the state-of-the-art. To further improve performance, we will look into strategies that allow us to take advantage even more effectively of our ability to train the network as a whole. In particular, we will look into using hard negative mining strategies over the whole image [45] instead of relying on pre-extracted patches. This has the potential of producing more discriminative filters and, consequently, better descriptors.

References

1. Lowe, D.: Distinctive image features from scale-invariant keypoints. IJCV **20**(2), 91–110 (2004)
2. Bay, H., Ess, A., Tuytelaars, T., Van Gool, L.: SURF: speeded up robust features. CVIU **10**(3), 346–359 (2008)
3. Tola, E., Lepetit, V., Fua, P.: A fast local descriptor for dense matching. In: CVPR (2008)
4. Rublee, E., Rabaud, V., Konolidge, K., Bradski, G.: ORB: an efficient alternative to SIFT or SURF. In: ICCV (2011)
5. Mainali, P., Lafruit, G., Tack, K., Van Gool, L., Lauwereins, R.: Derivative-based scale invariant image feature detector with error resilience. TIP **23**(5), 2380–2391 (2014)
6. Verdie, Y., Yi, K.M., Fua, P., Lepetit, V.: TILDE: a temporally invariant learned DEtector. In: CVPR (2015)
7. Han, X., Leung, T., Jia, Y., Sukthankar, R., Berg, A.C.: MatchNet: unifying feature and metric learning for patch-based matching. In: CVPR (2015)
8. Zagoruyko, S., Komodakis, N.: Learning to compare image patches via convolutional neural networks. In: CVPR (2015)
9. Yi, K., Verdie, Y., Lepetit, V., Fua, P.: Learning to assign orientations to feature points. In: CVPR (2016)
10. Simo-Serra, E., Trulls, E., Ferraz, L., Kokkinos, I., Fua, P., Moreno-Noguer, F.: Discriminative learning of deep convolutional feature point descriptors. In: ICCV (2015)
11. Jaderberg, M., Simonyan, K., Zisserman, A., Kavukcuoglu, K.: Spatial transformer networks. In: NIPS (2015)
12. Chapelle, O., Wu, M.: Gradient descent optimization of smoothed information retrieval metrics. Inf. Retrieval **13**(3), 216–235 (2009)
13. Harris, C., Stephens, M.: A combined corner and edge detector. In: Fourth Alvey Vision Conference (1988)

482   K.M. Yi et al.

14. Moravec, H.: Obstacle avoidance and navigation in the real world by a seeing robot rover. Technical report CMU-RI-TR-80-03, Robotics Institute, Carnegie Mellon University, Stanford University, September 1980
15. Rosten, E., Drummond, T.: Machine learning for high-speed corner detection. In: Leonardis, A., Bischof, H., Pinz, A. (eds.) ECCV 2006. LNCS, vol. 3951, pp. 430–443. Springer, Heidelberg (2006). doi:10.1007/11744023_34
16. Matas, J., Chum, O., Martin, U., Pajdla, T.: Robust wide baseline stereo from maximally stable extremal regions. In: BMVC, pp. 384–393, September 2002
17. Mikolajczyk, K., Schmid, C.: An affine invariant interest point detector. In: Heyden, A., Sparr, G., Nielsen, M., Johansen, P. (eds.) ECCV 2002. LNCS, vol. 2350, pp. 128–142. Springer, Heidelberg (2002). doi:10.1007/3-540-47969-4_9
18. Förstner, W., Dickscheid, T., Schindler, F.: Detecting interpretable and accurate scale-invariant keypoints. In: ICCV, September 2009
19. Zitnick, C., Ramnath, K.: Edge foci interest points. In: ICCV (2011)
20. Mainali, P., Lafruit, G., Yang, Q., Geelen, B., Van Gool, L., Lauwereins, R.: SIFER: scale-invariant feature detector with error resilience. IJCV 104(2), 172–197 (2013)
21. Šochman, J., Matas, J.: Learning a fast emulator of a binary decision process. In: Yagi, Y., Kang, S.B., Kweon, I.S., Zha, H. (eds.) ACCV 2007. LNCS, vol. 4844, pp. 236–245. Springer, Heidelberg (2007). doi:10.1007/978-3-540-76390-1_24
22. Trujillo, L., Olague, G.: Using evolution to learn how to perform interest point detection. In: ICPR, pp. 211–214 (2006)
23. Strecha, C., Bronstein, A., Bronstein, M., Fua, P.: LDAHash: improved matching with smaller descriptors. PAMI 34(1), 66–78 (2012)
24. Winder, S., Brown, M.: Learning local image descriptors. In: CVPR, June 2007
25. Perez, C., Olague, G.: Genetic programming as strategy for learning image descriptor operators. Intell. Data Anal. 17, 561–583 (2013)
26. Simonyan, K., Vedaldi, A., Zisserman, A.: Learning local feature descriptors using convex optimisation. PAMI 36, 1573–1585 (2014)
27. Zbontar, J., LeCun, Y.: Computing the stereo matching cost with a convolutional neural network. In: CVPR (2015)
28. Balntas, V., Johns, E., Tang, L., Mikolajczyk, K.: PN-Net: conjoined triple deep network for learning local image descriptors. In: arXiv Preprint (2016)
29. Wilson, K., Snavely, N.: Robust global translations with 1DSfM. In: Fleet, D., Pajdla, T., Schiele, B., Tuytelaars, T. (eds.) ECCV 2014. LNCS, vol. 8691, pp. 61–75. Springer, Heidelberg (2014). doi:10.1007/978-3-319-10578-9_5
30. Wu, C.: Towards linear-time incremental structure from motion. In: 3DV (2013)
31. Paulin, M., Douze, M., Harchaoui, Z., Mairal, J., Perronnin, F., Schmid, C.: Local convolutional features with unsupervised training for image retrieval. In: ICCV (2015)
32. Sermanet, P., Chintala, S., LeCun, Y.: Convolutional neural networks applied to house numbers digit classification. In: ICPR (2012)
33. Strecha, C., Hansen, W., Van Gool, L., Fua, P., Thoennessen, U.: On benchmarking camera calibration and multi-view stereo for high resolution imagery. In: CVPR (2008)
34. Aanaes, H., Dahl, A.L., Pedersen, K.S.: Interesting interest points. IJCV 97, 18–35 (2012)
35. Mikolajczyk, K., Schmid, C.: A performance evaluation of local descriptors. In: CVPR, pp. 257–263, June 2003
36. Alcantarilla, P.F., Bartoli, A., Davison, A.J.: KAZE features. In: Fitzgibbon, A., Lazebnik, S., Perona, P., Sato, Y., Schmid, C. (eds.) ECCV 2012. LNCS, vol. 7577, pp. 214–227. Springer, Heidelberg (2012). doi:10.1007/978-3-642-33783-3_16

37. Tola, E., Lepetit, V., Fua, P.: Daisy: an efficient dense descriptor applied to wide baseline stereo. PAMI **32**(5), 815–830 (2010)
38. Bellavia, F., Tegolo, D.: Improving sift-based descriptors stability to rotations. In: ICPR (2010)
39. Mikolajczyk, K., Schmid, C.: Scale and affine invariant interest point detectors. IJCV **60**, 63–86 (2004)
40. Fan, B., Wu, F., Hu, Z.: Aggregating gradient distributions into intensity orders: a novel local image descriptor. In: CVPR (2011)
41. Wang, Z., Fan, B., Wu, F.: Local intensity order pattern for feature description. In: ICCV (2011)
42. Zitnick, C.L.: Binary coherent edge descriptors. In: Daniilidis, K., Maragos, P., Paragios, N. (eds.) ECCV 2010. LNCS, vol. 6312, pp. 170–182. Springer, Heidelberg (2010). doi:10.1007/978-3-642-15552-9_13
43. Leutenegger, S., Chli, M., Siegwart, R.: BRISK: binary robust invariant scalable keypoints. In: ICCV (2011)
44. Alahi, A., Ortiz, R., Vandergheynst, P.: FREAK: fast retina keypoint. In: CVPR (2012)
45. Felzenszwalb, P., Girshick, R., McAllester, D., Ramanan, D.: Object detection with discriminatively trained part based models. PAMI **32**(9), 1627–1645 (2010)

Learning a Predictable and Generative Vector Representation for Objects

Rohit Girdhar[1]([✉]), David F. Fouhey[1], Mikel Rodriguez[2], and Abhinav Gupta[1]

[1] Robotics Institute, Carnegie Mellon University, Pittsburgh, USA
{rgirdhar,dfouhey,abhinavg}@cs.cmu.edu
[2] MITRE Corporation, McLean, USA
mikel@cs.ucf.edu

Abstract. What is a good vector representation of an object? We believe that it should be generative in 3D, in the sense that it can produce new 3D objects; as well as be predictable from 2D, in the sense that it can be perceived from 2D images. We propose a novel architecture, called the TL-embedding network, to learn an embedding space with these properties. The network consists of two components: (a) an autoencoder that ensures the representation is generative; and (b) a convolutional network that ensures the representation is predictable. This enables tackling a number of tasks including voxel prediction from 2D images and 3D model retrieval. Extensive experimental analysis demonstrates the usefulness and versatility of this embedding.

1 Introduction

What is a good vector representation for objects? On the one hand, there has been a great deal of work on discriminative models such as ConvNets [18,32] mapping 2D pixels to semantic labels. This approach, while useful for distinguishing between classes given an image, has two major shortcomings: the learned representations do not necessarily incorporate the 3D properties of the objects and none of the approaches have shown strong generative capabilities. On the other hand, there is an alternate line of work focusing on learning to generate objects using 3D CAD models and deconvolutional networks [5,19]. In contrast to the purely discriminative paradigm, these approaches explicitly address the 3D nature of objects and have shown success in generative tasks; however, they offer no guarantees that their representations can be inferred from images and accordingly have not been shown to be useful for natural image tasks. In this paper, we propose to unify these two threads of research together and propose a new vector representation (embedding) of objects (Fig. 1).

We believe that an object representation must satisfy two criteria. Firstly, it must be **generative in 3D**: we should be able to reconstruct objects in 3D from it. Secondly, it must be **predictable from 2D**: we should be able to easily infer this representation from images. These criteria are often at odds with each other: modeling occluded voxels in 3D is useful for generating objects but very difficult to predict from an image. Thus, optimizing for only one criterion, as in most past

B. Leibe et al. (Eds.): ECCV 2016, Part VI, LNCS 9910, pp. 484–499, 2016.
DOI: 10.1007/978-3-319-46466-4_29

Fig. 1. (a) We learn an embedding space that has generative capabilities to construct 3D structures, while being predictable from RGB images. (b) Our final model's 3D reconstruction results on natural and synthetic test images. (Color figure online)

work, tends not to obtain the other. In contrast, we propose a novel architecture, the TL-embedding network, that directly optimizes for *both* criteria. We achieve this by building an architecture that has two major components, joined via a 64-dimensional (64D) vector embedding space: (1) An autoencoder network which maps a 3D voxel grid to the 64D embedding space, and decodes it back to a voxel grid; and (2) A discriminatively trained ConvNet that maps a 2D image to the 64D embedding space. By themselves, these represent generative and predictable criteria; by joining them, we can learn a representation that optimizes both.

At training time, we take the 3D voxel map of a CAD model as well as its 2D rendered image and jointly optimize the components. The auto-encoder aims to reconstruct the voxel grid and the ConvNet aims to predict the intermediate embedding. The TL-network can be thought of as a 3D auto-encoder that tries to ensure that the 3D representation can be predicted from a 2D rendered image. At test time, we can use the autoencoder and the ConvNet to obtain a representation for 3D voxels and images respectively in the common latent space. This enables us to tackle a variety of tasks at the intersection of 2D and 3D.

We demonstrate the nature of our learned embedding in a series of experiments on both CAD model data and natural images gathered in-the-wild. Our experiments demonstrate that: (1) our representation is indeed generative in 3D, permitting reconstruction of novel CAD models; (2) our representation is predictable from 2D, allowing us to predict the full 3D voxels of an object from an image (an extremely difficult task), as well as do fast CAD model retrieval from a natural image; and (3) that the learned space has a number of good properties, such as being smooth, carrying class-discriminative information, and allowing vector arithmetic. In the process, we show the importance of our design decisions, and the value of joining the generative and predictive approaches.

2   Related Work

Our work aims to produce a representation that is generative in 3D and predictable from 2D and thus touches on two long-standing and important questions in computer vision: how do we represent 3D objects in a vector space and how do we recognize this representation in images?

Learning an embedding, or vector representation of visual objects is a well studied problem in computer vision. In the seminal work of Olshausen and Field [26], the objective was to obtain a representation that was sparse and could reconstruct the pixels. Since then, there has been a lot of work in this reconstructive vein. For a long time, researchers focused on techniques such as stacked RBMs or autoencoders [12,36] or DBMs [30], and more recently, this has taken the form of generative adversarial models [9]. This line of work, however, has focused on building a 2D generative model of the pixels themselves. In this case, if the representation captures any 3D properties, it is modeled implicitly. In contrast, we focus on explicitly modeling the 3D shape of the world. Thus, our work is most similar to a number of recent exceptions to the 2D end-to-end approach. Dosovitskiy et al. [5] used 3D CAD models to learn a parameterized generative model for objects and Kulkarni et al. [19] introduced a technique to guide the latent representation of a generative model to explicitly model certain 3D properties. While they use 3D data like our work, they use it to build a generative model for 2D images. Our work is complementary: their work can generate the pixels for a chair and ours can generate the voxels (and thus, help an agent or robot to interact with it).

There has been comparatively less work in the 3D generative space. Past works have used part-based models [2,16] and deep networks [20,24,39] for representing 3D models. In contrast to 2D generative models, these approaches acknowledges the 3D structure of the world. However, unlike our work, it does not address the mapping from images to this 3D structure. We believe this is a crucial distinction: while the world is 3D, the images we receive are intrinsically 2D and we must build our representations with this in mind.

The task of inferring 3D properties from images goes back to the very beginning of vision. Learning-based techniques started gaining traction in the mid-2000s [13,31] by framing it as a supervised problem of mapping images of scenes to 2.5D maps. Among a large body of works trying to infer 3D representations from images, our approach is most related to a group of works using renderings of 3D CAD models to predict properties such as object viewpoint [35] or class [34], among others [10,27,33]. Typically, these approaches focus on global 3D properties such as pose in the case of objects, and 2.5D maps in the case of scenes. Our work predicts a much more challenging representation, a voxel map (i.e., including the occluded parts). Related works in 3D prediction include [3,17,38]. Our approach differs from these as it is class agnostic, voxel based and learns a joint embedding that enables various applications beyond 3D prediction.

Our final output is related to CAD model retrieval in the sense that one output of our approach is a 3D model. Many approaches achieve this via alignment [1,14,23] or joint, but non-generative embeddings [21]. In contrast to these works, we take the extreme approach of generating the 3D voxel map from the image. While we obtain coarser results than using an existing model, this explict generative mapping gives the potential to generalize to previously unseen objects.

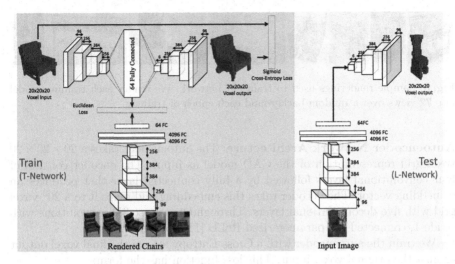

Fig. 2. Our proposed TL-embedding network. **(a) T-network:** At training time, the network takes two inputs: 2D RGB images which are fed into ConvNet at the bottom and 3D voxel maps which are fed into the autoencoder on the left. The output is a 3D voxel map. We apply two losses jointly: a reconstruction loss for the voxel outputs, and a regression loss for the 64-D embedding in the middle. **(b) L-network:** During testing, we remove the encoder part and only use the image as input. The ConvNet predicts the embedding representation and the decoder predicts the voxel. (Color figure online)

3 Our Approach

To reiterate, our goal is to learn a vector representation that is: (a) **generative:** we should be able to generate voxels in 3D from this representation; and (b) **predictable:** we should be able to take a 2D image of an object and predict this representation. Both properties are vital for image understanding tasks.

We propose a novel TL-embedding network (Fig. 2) to optimize both these criteria. The T and L refer to the architecture in the training and testing phase. The top part of the T network is an autoencoder with convolution and deconvolution layers. The encoder maps the 3D voxel map to a low-dimensional subspace. The decoder maps a datapoint in the low-dimensional subspace to a 3D voxel map. The autoencoder forces the embedding to be generative, and we can sample datapoints in this embedding to reconstruct new objects. To optimize the predictable criterion, we use a ConvNet architecture similar to AlexNet [18], adding a loss function that ensures the embedding space is predictable from pixels.

Training this TL-embedding network requires 2D RGB images and their corresponding 3D voxel maps. Since this data is hard to obtain, we use CAD model datasets to obtain voxel maps and render these CAD models with different random backgrounds to generate corresponding image data. We now describe our network architecture and the details of our training and testing procedure.

Fig. 3. Sample renderings used to train our network. We render each training model into 72 views over a random background each epoch of training.

Autoencoder Network Architecture: The autoencoder takes a $20 \times 20 \times 20$ voxel grid representation of the CAD model as input. The encoder consists of four convolutional layers followed by a fully connected layer that produces an embedding vector. The decoder takes this embedding and maps it to a 20^3 voxel grid with five deconvolutional layers. Throughout, we use 3D convolutions with stride 1, connected via parameterized ReLU [11] non-linearities.

We train the autoencoder with a Cross-Entropy loss on the final voxel output against the original voxel input. This loss function has the form:

$$E = -\frac{1}{N} \sum_{n=1}^{N} [p_n \log \hat{p}_n + (1 - p_n) \log(1 - \hat{p}_n)] \qquad (1)$$

where p_n is the target probability (1 or 0) of a voxel being filled, $\hat{p}_n$ is the predicted probability obtained through a sigmoid, and $N = 20^3$.

Mapping 2D Image to Embedding Space: The lower part of the T network learns a mapping from 2D image space to the 64D embedding space. We adopt the AlexNet architecture [18] which has five convolutional layers and two fully connected layers. We add a 64D fc8 layer to the original AlexNet architecture and use a Euclidean loss. We initialize this network with the parameters trained on ImageNet [4] classification task.

One strength of our TL-embedding network is that it can be used to predict a 3D voxel map for a given 2D image. At test time, we remove the encoder part of the autoencoder network and connect the output of the image embedding network to the decoder to obtain this voxel output.

3.1   Training the TL-Embedding Network

We train the network using batches of (image, voxel) pairs. The images are generated by rendering the 3D model and the network is then trained in a three stage procedure. We now describe this in detail.

Data Generation: We use ideas from [35] to render the 3D models for training our network. Some sample renderings are shown in Fig. 3. To prevent the network from overfitting to sharp edges when rendered on a plain background, we render it on randomly selected open room images downloaded from the internet. Following the popular practice [34], we render all the models into 72 views, at three elevations of $15°$, $30°$ and $45°$ and 24 azimuth angles from $0°$ to $360°$, in increments of 15°. We convert the 3D models into 20^3 voxel grid using the voxelizer from [39].

Three-stage Training: Training a TL-embedding network from scratch and jointly is a challenging problem. Therefore, we take a three stage procedure. (1) In the first stage, we train the autoencoder part of the network independently. This network is initialized at random, and trained end-to-end with the sigmoid cross-entropy loss. We train this for about 200 epochs. (2) In the second stage we train the ConvNet to regress to the 64D representation. Specifically, the encoder generates the embedding for the voxel and the image network is trained to regress the embedding. The image network is initialized using ImageNet pre-trained weights. We keep the lower convolutional layers fixed. (3) In the final stage, we finetune the network jointly with both the losses. In this stage, we observe that the prediction loss reduces significantly while reconstruction loss reduces marginally. We also observe that most of the parameter update happens in the autoencoder network, indicating that the autoencoder updates its latent representation to make it easily predictable from images, while maintaining or improving the reconstruction performance given this new latent representation.

Implementation Details: We implement this network using the Caffe [15] toolbox. In the first stage, we initialize all layers of autoencoder network from scratch using $\mathcal{N}(0, 0.01)$ and train with a uniform learning rate of 10^{-6}. Next, we train the image network by initializing fc8 from scratch and remaining layers from ImageNet. We finetune all layers after and including conv4 with a uniform learning rate of 10^{-8}. A lower learning rate is required because the initial prediction loss values are in the range of 500K. The encoder network from the autoencoder is used in testing-phase with its previously learned weights to generate the labels for image network. Finally, we jointly train using both losses, initializing the network using weights learned earlier, and finetuning all layers of autoencoder and all layers after and including conv4 for image network with a learning rate of 10^{-10}. Since our network now has two losses, we balance their values by scaling the autoencoder loss to have approximately same initial value, as otherwise the network tends to optimize for the prediction loss without regard to the reconstruction loss.

Table 1. Reconstruction performance using AP on test data.

	Chair	Table	Sofa	Cabinet	Bed	Overall
Proposed (before Joint)	**96.4**	**97.1**	99.1	**99.3**	**94.1**	**97.6**
Proposed (after Joint)	**96.4**	97.0	**99.2**	**99.3**	93.8	**97.6**
PCA	94.8	96.7	98.6	99.0	91.5	96.8

4 Experiments

We now experimentally evaluate the method. Our overarching goal is to answer the following questions: (1) is the representation we learn generative in 3D?

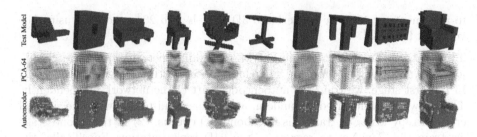

Fig. 4. Reconstructions of *random* test models using PCA and the autoencoder. Predicted voxels are colored and sized by confidence of prediction, from large and red to small and blue in decreasing order of confidence. PCA is much less confident about the extent as well as fine details as compared to our autoencoder. (Color figure online)

(2) can the representation be predicted from images in 2D? In addition to directly answering these questions, we verify that the model has learned a sensible latent representation by ensuring that the latent representation satisfies a number of properties, such as being smooth, discriminative and allowing arithmetic.

We note that our approach has a capability that, to the best of our knowledge, is previous unexplored: it can simultaneously reconstruct in 3D and predict from 2D. Thus, there are no standard baselines or datasets for this task. Instead, we adopt standard datasets for each of the many tasks that our model can perform. Where appropriate, we compare the method with existing methods. These baselines, however, are specialized solutions to only one of the many tasks we can solve and often use additional supervisory information. As the community starts tackling increasingly difficult 3D problems like direct voxel prediction, we believe that our work can be a strong baseline to benchmark progress.

We proceed as follows. We introduce the datasets and evaluation criterion that we use in Sect. 4.1. We first verify that our learned representation models the space of voxels well in a number of ways: that it is reconstructive, smooth, and can be used to distinguish different classes of objects (Sect. 4.2). This evaluates the representation independently of its ability to predict voxels from images. We then verify that our approach can predict the voxels from 2D and show that it outperforms alternate options (Sect. 4.3). Subsequently, we show that our representation can be used to do CAD retrieval from natural images (Sect. 4.4) and is capable of performing 3D shape arithmetic (Sect. 4.5).

4.1 Datasets and Evaluation

We use two datasets for evaluation. The first is a CAD model dataset used to train the TL-embedding and to explore the learned embedding. The second is an in-the-wild dataset used to verify that the approach works on natural images.

CAD Dataset: We use CAD models from the ShapeNet [39] database. This database contains over 220K models organized into 3K WordNet synsets. We take a set of common indoor objects: chair (6778 models), table (8509 models), sofa (3173 models), cabinet (1572 models), and bed (254 models). We split these models randomly into 16228 train and 4058 test objects. All our models are trained with rendered images and voxels from the above train set. We use the test set to quantify our performance and analyze our models.

IKEA Dataset: We quantify the performance of our model on natural indoor images from IKEA Dataset [23] which are labeled with 3D models. Since our approach expects to reconstruct a single object, we test it on cropped images of these objects. These boxes, however, include cluttered backgrounds and pieces of other objects. After cropping these objects out of provided 759 images, we get 937 images labeled with one of provided 225 3D models.

Evaluation Metric: Throughout the paper, we use Average Precision (AP) over the complete test set to evaluate reconstruction performance. We also show per-class APs where applicable to better characterize our model's performance.

4.2   Embedding Analysis

We start by probing our learned representation in terms of 3D voxels. Here, we focus on the autoencoder part of the network – that is, we feed a voxel grid to the network and verify a number of properties: (a) that it can reconstruct the voxels well qualitatively and quantitatively, which verifies that the method works; (b) that it outperforms a linear baseline, PCA, for reconstruction, which further validates the choice of a convolutional autoencoder; and (c) that the learned representation is smooth and carries class-discriminative information, which acts as additional confirmation that the representation is meaningful.

Qualitative Results: First, we show qualitative results: Fig. 4 shows randomly selected reconstructions using the autoencoder and PCA. While a simple linear approach is sufficient to capture the coarse structure, our approach does much better at fine-details (chair legs in col. 6) as well as at getting the extent correct (back of the chair in col. 4). Note also the large amount of low but non-zero probability voxels in the free-space in PCA compared to the auto-encoder.

We next show that the learned space is smooth, by computing reconstructions for linear interpolation between latent representations of randomly picked test models. As Fig. 5(a) shows, the 3D models smoothly transition in structure and most intermediate models are also physically plausible. We also show results exploring the learned space and verifying whether the dimensions are meaningful. One way to do this is to generate new points in the space and reconstruct them. We generate these points by taking the first 32 dimensions from one model and the rest from another. As seen by the difference between the reconstruction and the nearest model in Fig. 5(b), this can generate previously unseen models that combine aspects of each model.

We further attempt to understand the embedding space by clamping all the dimensions of a latent vector but one and scaling the selected dimension by adding a fixed value to it. We show its effect on two dimensions and three models in Fig. 6. Such scaling of these dimensions produces consistent effects across models, suggesting that some learned dimensions are semantically meaningful.

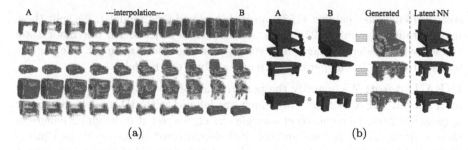

(a)   (b)

Fig. 5. (a) Reconstructions for linear interpolation between two randomly picked latent representations. (b) Evaluating generative ability by combining dimensions from two training models. We show the reconstruction and the nearest neighbor in the training set (over latent features). The difference shows we can generate novel models, such as an armchair with one arm-rest.

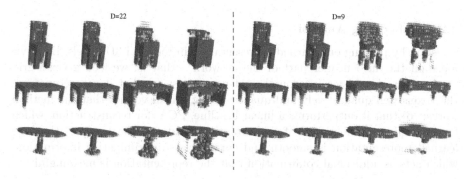

Fig. 6. We evaluate if the dimensions are meaningful by scaling each dimension separately and analyzing the effect on the reconstruction. Some dimensions have a consistent effect on reconstruction across objects. Higher values in dimension 22 lead to thicker legs, and higher values in 9 lead to disappearance of legs.

Quantitative Reconstruction Accuracy: We now evaluate the reconstruction performance quantitatively on the CAD test data and report results in Table 1. Our goal here is to verify that the auto-encoder is worthwhile: we thus compare to PCA using the same number of dimensions. Our method obtains extremely high performance, 97.6 % AP and consistently outperforms PCA, reducing the average error rate by 25 % relative. It can be seen in Table 1 that some categories are easier than others: sofas and cabinets are naturally more easy than beds (including bunk-beds) and chairs. Our method consistently obtains larger gains on challenging objects, indicating the merits of a non-linear representation. We also evaluate the performance of the autoencoder after the joint training. Even after being optimized to be more predictable from image space, we can see that it still preserves the overall reconstruction performance.

CAD Classification: If our representation models 3D well, it should permit us to distinguish different types of objects. We empirically verify this by using our approach *without modifications* as a representation to classify 3D shapes. Note that while adding a classification loss and finetuning might further improve results, it would defeat the purpose of this experiment, which is to see whether the model learns a good 3D representation on its own. We evaluate our representation's performance for a classification task on the Princeton ModelNet40 [28] dataset with standard train-test split from [39]. We train the network on all 40 classes (again: no class information is provided) and then use the autoencoder representation as a feature for 40-way classification. Since our representation is low-dimensional (64D), we expand the feature to include pairwise features and train a linear SVM. Our approach obtains an accuracy of 74.4 %. This is within 2.6 % of [39], a recent approach on voxels that uses class information at representation-learning time, and finetunes the representation discriminatively for the classification experiment. Using a 64D PCA representation trained on ModelNet40 trainset with the same feature augmentation and linear SVM obtains 68.4 %. This shows that our representation is class-discriminative despite not being trained or designed so, and outperforms the PCA.

4.3 Voxel Prediction

We now turn to the task of predicting a 3D voxel grid from an image. We obtain strong performance on this task and outperform a number of baselines, demonstrating the importance of each part of our approach.

Baselines: To the best of our knowledge, there are no methods that directly predict voxels from an image; we therefore compare to a direct prediction method as well an ablation study, where we do not perform joint training. Specifically: (a) *Direct*: finetuning the ImageNet pre-trained AlexNet to predict the 20^3 voxel grid directly. This corresponds to removing the auto-encoder. We tried two strategies for freezing the layers: Direct-conv4 refers to freezing all layers before conv4 and Direct-fc8 refers to freezing all layers except fc8. (b) *Without Joint*: training the T-L network without the final joint fine-tuning (i.e., following only the first two training stages). The direct baselines test whether the auto-encoder's low-dimensional representation is necessary and the without-joint tests whether learning the model to be jointly generative *and* predictable is important.

Qualitative Results: We first show qualitative results on natural images in Fig. 7. Note that our method automatically predicts occluded regions of the object, unlike most work on single image 3D (e.g., [6–8,13,31,37]) that predict a 2.5D shell. For instance, our method predicts all four legs of furniture even if fewer are visible. Our model generalizes well to natural images even though it was trained on CAD models. Note that for instance, the round and rectangular tables are predicted as being round and rectangular, and office chairs on a single post and four-legged chairs can be distinguished. One difficulty with this data is that objects are truncated or occluded and some windows contain multiple objects; our model does well on this data, nonetheless.

Quantitative Results: We now evaluate the approach quantitatively on both datasets. We report results on the CAD dataset in Table 2. Our approach

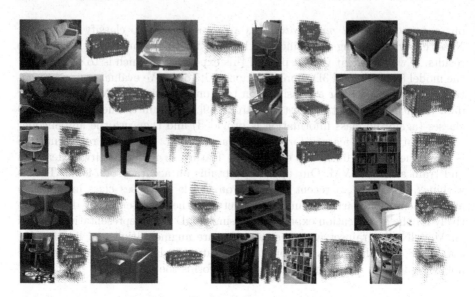

Fig. 7. Reconstruction results on the IKEA dataset. Our model generalizes well to real images, even to bookshelves which our model is not trained on.

Table 2. Average Precision for Voxel Prediction on the CAD test set. The Proposed TL-Network outperforms the baselines on each object.

	Chair	Table	Sofa	Cabinet	Bed	Average
Proposed (with Joint)	**66.9**	**59.7**	**79.3**	**79.3**	**41.9**	**65.4**
Proposed (without Joint)	66.6	57.5	**79.3**	76.5	33.8	62.7
Direct-conv4	40.9	23.7	58.1	44.3	23.1	38.0
Direct-fc8	21.8	15.5	35.6	32.7	18.6	24.8

outperforms all the baselines. Directly predicting the voxels does substantially worse because predicting all the voxels is a very difficult task compared to our embedding space. Not doing joint training produces worse results because the embedding is not forced to be predictable.

The IKEA dataset is more challenging because it is captured in-the-wild, but our approach still produces quantitatively strong performance. While the CAD Dataset models are represented in canonical form, the IKEA models are provided in no consistent orientation. We thus attempt to align each prediction with the ground-truth model by taking the best rigid alignment over permutations, flips and translational alignments (up to 10 %) of the prediction. As Table 3 shows, our approach outperforms the direct prediction by a large margin (38 % compared to 31 %). If we do not correct for translational alignments, we still outperform the baseline (33 % vs 28 %). Directly predicting voxels again performs worse compared to predicting the latent space and reconstructing, validating the idea of using a lower-dimensional representation of objects.

Table 3. Average Precision for Voxel Prediction on the IKEA dataset.

	Bed	Bookcase	Chair	Desk	Sofa	Table	Overall
Proposed	**56.3**	**30.2**	**32.9**	25.8	**71.7**	**23.3**	**38.3**
Direct-conv4	38.2	26.6	31.4	**26.6**	69.3	19.1	31.1
Direct-fc8	29.5	17.3	20.4	19.7	38.8	16.0	19.8

Fig. 8. Predictions on PASCAL 3D+ images using [17] and our method. Our method is better at capturing fine stylistic details, like the straight legs and the hollow back in the first case, a single central leg in the second, and no visible legs in the last.

Comparison with Kar *et al.* [17]: We also compare our method with [17] on PASCAL 3D+ v1.0 [40] dataset for categories that overlap with our training categories (chair and sofa). As Fig. 8 shows, our output is more varied and captures stylistic details better. For quantitative comparison, we voxelize their output and ground truth, and compute the overlap P-R curve with alignment. Since [17] produces a binary non-probabilistic prediction and thus yields only one operating point, we compare via maximum F-1 score instead of AP. After aligning, we outperform their method 0.492 to 0.463.

4.4   CAD Retrieval

We now show results for retrieving CAD models from natural images. Our system can naturally tackle this task: we map each model in the CAD corpus as well as the image to their latent representations, and perform a nearest neighbor search in this embedding space.

We use cosine distance in the latent space for retrieval. This approach is complementary to approaches like [22,23]: these approaches assume the existence of an exact-match 3D model and fits the 3D model into the image. Our approach, on the other hand, does not assume exact match and thus generalizes to retrieving the most similar object to the depicted object (i.e., what is the next-most similar object in the corpus). We show qualitative results in Fig. 9.

We now quantitatively evaluate our approach. For each test window, we rank all 225 CAD models in the corpus by cosine distance. We can then determine two quantities: *(a) Instance match:* at what rank does the exact-match CAD model appear? *(b) Category match:* at what rank does the first model of the same category appear? As a baseline, we render all the 225 models at 30° elevation

Fig. 9. Top CAD model retrievals from natural images from the IKEA dataset.

Table 4. Mean recall @10 of ground truth model in retrievals for our method and baseline described in Sect. 4.4

	Sofa	Chair	Bookcase	Bed	Table	Overall
Proposed	**32.3**	**41.0**	**26.8**	**38.5**	8.0	**29.3**
Fc7-NN	14.6	33.9	23.5	7.7	**17.4**	19.4

and 8 uniformly sampled azimuths from 0° to 360° onto a white background, after scaling and translating each model to a unit square at the origin. We then use ImageNet trained AlexNet's fc7 features over the query image and renderings to perform nearest neighbor search (cosine distance). The first position at which a rendering of a model appears in the retrievals is taken as the position for that model. Note that this is a strong baseline with access to lot more information since it sees images, which are much higher resolution than our 20^3 voxel grids. Moreover, it is significantly slower than our method, as it represents each 3D model using 8 vectors of 4096D each, while our approach uses only a single 64D vector. As shown in Table 4, which reports the mean recall@10 of instance match, we outperform this baseline on all categories except tables/desks because most of the table models are very similar, and fine differentiation between specific models is very hard for a coarse 20^3 voxel representation. We report histograms of these ranks in Fig. 10 per object category. For many categories, the top response is the correct category, and the exact-match model is typically ranked highly. Poor performance tends to result from images containing multiple objects (e.g., a table picture with chairs in it), causing the network to predict the representation for the "wrong" object out of the ambiguous input. We also compare our model with [21] in the supplement available on the project webpage.

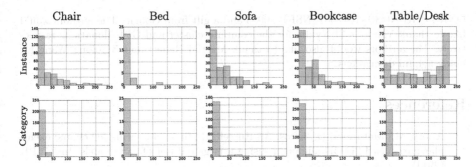

Fig. 10. Histograms over position in retrieval list obtained by our proposed approach (Y axis: #images, X axis: position). First row of histograms is over the position of instance match, and second is over position of category match.

Fig. 11. Results of shape arithmetic. In the first case, adding a cabinet-like-table to a table and removing small 2-leg table results in a table with built-in cabinet. In the second case, adding and removing a similar looking chair with straight and curved edges respectively leads to a table with curved edges.

4.5 Shape Arithmetic

We have shown that the latent space is reconstructive and smooth, that it is predictable, and that it carries class information. We now show some attempts at probing the learned representation. Previous work in vector embedding spaces [25,29] exhibit the phenomena of being able to perform arithmetic on these vector representations. For example, [25] showed that vector(King) - vector(Man) + vector(Woman) results in vector whose nearest neighbor was the vector for Queen. We perform a similar experiment by randomly selecting triplets of 3D models and performing this $a + b - c$ operation on their latent representations. We then use the resulting feature to generate the voxel representation and also find the nearest neighbor in the dataset over cosine distance on this latent representation. We show some interesting triplets in Fig. 11.

Acknowledgments. This work was partially supported by Siebel Scholarship to RG, NDSEG Fellowship to DF and Bosch Young Faculty Fellowship to AG. This material is based on research partially sponsored by ONR MURI N000141010934,

ONR MURI N000141612007, NSF1320083 and a gift from Google. The authors would like to thank Yahoo! and Nvidia for the compute cluster and GPU donations respectively. The authors would also like to thank Martial Hebert and Xiaolong Wang for many helpful discussions.

References

1. Aubry, M., Maturana, D., Efros, A., Russell, B., Sivic, J.: Seeing 3D chairs: exemplar part-based 2D–3D alignment using a large dataset of cad models. In: CVPR (2014)
2. Chaudhuri, S., Kalogerakis, E., Guibas, L., Koltun, V.: Probabilistic reasoning for assembly-based 3D modeling. In: SIGGRAPH (2011)
3. Choy, C.B., Xu, D., Gwak, J., Chen, K., Savarese, S.: 3d–r2n2: a unified approach for single and multi-view 3d object reconstruction. CoRR abs/1604.00449 (2016)
4. Deng, J., Dong, W., Socher, R., Li, L.J., Li, K., Fei-Fei, L.: Imagenet: a large-scale hierarchical image database. In: CVPR, pp. 248–255 (2009)
5. Dosovitskiy, A., Springenberg, J., Brox, T.: Learning to generate chairs with convolutional neural networks. In: CVPR (2015)
6. Eigen, D., Fergus, R.: Predicting depth, surface normals and semantic labels with a common multi-scale convolutional architecture. In: ICCV (2015)
7. Eigen, D., Puhrsch, C., Fergus, R.: Depth map prediction from a single image using a multi-scale deep network. In: NIPS (2014)
8. Fouhey, D.F., Gupta, A., Hebert, M.: Data-driven 3D primitives for single image understanding. In: ICCV (2013)
9. Goodfellow, I., Pouget-Abadie, J., Mirza, M., Xu, B., Warde-Farley, D., Ozair, S., Courville, A., Bengio, Y.: Generative adversarial nets. In: NIPS (2014)
10. Gupta, S., Arbeláez, P.A., Girshick, R.B., Malik, J.: Inferring 3D object pose in RGB-D images. CoRR (2015)
11. He, K., Zhang, X., Ren, S., Sun, J.: Delving deep into rectifiers: surpassing human-level performance on imagenet classification. CoRR abs/1502.01852 (2015)
12. Hinton, G.E., Salakhutdinov, R.R.: Reducing the dimensionality of data with neural networks. Science 313(5786), 504–507 (2006)
13. Hoiem, D., Efros, A.A., Hebert, M.: Recovering surface layout from an image. IJCV 75(1), 151–172 (2007)
14. Huang, Q., Wang, H., Koltun, V.: Single-view reconstruction via joint analysis of image and shape collections. In: SIGGRAPH, vol. 34, no. 4 (2015)
15. Jia, Y., Shelhamer, E., Donahue, J., Karayev, S., Long, J., Girshick, R., Guadarrama, S., Darrell, T.: Caffe: convolutional architecture for fast feature embedding. arXiv preprint arXiv:1408.5093 (2014)
16. Kalogerakis, E., Chaudhuri, S., Koller, D., Koltun, V.: A probabilistic model of component-based shape synthesis. In: SIGGRAPH (2012)
17. Kar, A., Tulsiani, S., Carreira, J., Malik, J.: Category-specific object reconstruction from a single image. In: CVPR (2015)
18. Krizhevsky, A., Sutskever, I., Hinton, G.E.: Imagenet classification with deep convolutional neural networks. In: NIPS, pp. 1097–1105 (2012)
19. Kulkarni, T.D., Whitney, W., Kohli, P., Tenenbaum, J.B.: Deep convolutional inverse graphics network. In: NIPS (2015)
20. Li, Y., Pirk, S., Su, H., Qi, C.R., J., G.L.: FPNN: field probing neural networks for 3d data. CoRR abs/1605.06240 (2016)

21. Li, Y., Su, H., Qi, C.R., Fish, N., Cohen-Or, D., Guibas, L.J.: Joint embeddings of shapes and images via cnn image purification. ACM TOG **34**(6), 1–12 (2015)
22. Lim, J.J., Khosla, A., Torralba, A.: FPM: fine pose parts-based model with 3D CAD models. In: Fleet, D., Pajdla, T., Schiele, B., Tuytelaars, T. (eds.) ECCV 2014. LNCS, vol. 8694, pp. 478–493. Springer, Heidelberg (2014). doi:10.1007/978-3-319-10599-4_31
23. Lim, J.J., Pirsiavash, H., Torralba, A.: Parsing IKEA objects: fine pose estimation. In: ICCV (2013)
24. Maturana, D., Scherer, S.: VoxNet: a 3D convolutional neural network for real-time object recognition. In: IROS (2015)
25. Mikolov, T., Sutskever, I., Chen, K., Corrado, G., Dean, J.: Distributed representations of words and phrases and their compositionality. In: NIPS (2013)
26. Olshausen, B., Field, D.: Emergence of simple-cell receptive field properties by learning a sparse code for natural images. Nature **381**(6583), 607–609 (1996)
27. Peng, X., Sun, B., Ali, K., Saenko, K.: Exploring invariances in deep convolutional neural networks using synthetic images. CoRR (2014)
28. Princeton ModelNet: http://modelnet.cs.princeton.edu/
29. Radford, A., Metz, L., Chintala, S.: Unsupervised representation learning with deep convolutional generative adversarial networks. CoRR abs/1511.06434 (2015)
30. Salakhutdinov, R., Hinton, G.: Deep Boltzmann machines. In: AISTATS, vol. 5 (2009)
31. Saxena, A., Sun, M., Ng, A.Y.: Make3D: learning 3D scene structure from a single still image. TPAMI **30**(5), 824–840 (2008)
32. Simonyan, K., Zisserman, A.: Very deep convolutional networks for large-scale image recognition. CoRR abs/1409.1556 (2014)
33. Stark, M., Goesele, M., Schiele, B.: Back to the future: learning shape models from 3D CAD data. In: BMVC (2010)
34. Su, H., Maji, S., Kalogerakis, E., Learned-Miller, E.G.: Multi-view convolutional neural networks for 3d shape recognition. In: ICCV (2015)
35. Su, H., Qi, C.R., Li, Y., Guibas, L.J.: Render for CNN: viewpoint estimation in images using CNNs trained with rendered 3D model views. In: ICCV (2015)
36. Vincent, P., Larochelle, H., Lajoie, I., Bengio, Y., Manzagol, P.A.: Stacked denoising autoencoders: learning useful representations in a deep network with a local denoising criterion. J. Mach. Learn. Res. **11**, 625–660 (2010)
37. Wang, X., Fouhey, D.F., Gupta, A.: Designing deep networks for surface normal estimation. In: CVPR (2015)
38. Wu, J., Xue, T., Lim, J.J., Tian, Y., Tenenbaum, J.B., Torralba, A., Freeman, W.T.: Single image 3d interpreter network. In: Leibe, B., Matas, J., Sebe, N., Welling, M. (eds.) ECCV 2016, Part VI. LNCS, vol. 9910, pp. 365–382. Springer, Heidelberg (2016)
39. Wu, Z., Song, S., Khosla, A., Yu, F., Zhang, L., Tang, X., Xiao, J.: 3D shapenets: a deep representation for volumetric shapes. In: CVPR (2015)
40. Xiang, Y., Mottaghi, R., Savarese, S.: Beyond pascal: a benchmark for 3d object detection in the wild. In: WACV (2014)

HouseCraft: Building Houses from Rental Ads and Street Views

Hang Chu(✉), Shenlong Wang, Raquel Urtasun, and Sanja Fidler

University of Toronto, Toronto, Canada
{chuhang1122,slwang,urtasun,fidler}@cs.toronto.edu

Abstract. In this paper, we utilize rental ads to create realistic textured 3D models of building exteriors. In particular, we exploit the address of the property and its floorplan, which are typically available in the ad. The address allows us to extract Google StreetView images around the building, while the building's floorplan allows for an efficient parametrization of the building in 3D via a small set of random variables. We propose an energy minimization framework which jointly reasons about the height of each floor, the vertical positions of windows and doors, as well as the precise location of the building in the world's map, by exploiting several geometric and semantic cues from the StreetView imagery. To demonstrate the effectiveness of our approach, we collected a new dataset with 174 houses by crawling a popular rental website. Our experiments show that our approach is able to precisely estimate the geometry and location of the property, and can create realistic 3D building models.

Keywords: 3D reconstruction · 3D scene understanding · Localization

1 Introduction

Significant effort is being invested into creating accurate 3D models of cities. For example, Google and other map providers such as OpenStreetMap are augmenting their maps with 3D buildings. Architects craft such models for urban/property planning, and visualization for their clients. This process typically involves expensive 3D sensors and/or humans in the loop. Automatically creating accurate 3D models of building exteriors has thus become an important area of research with applications in 3D city modeling, virtual tours of cities and urban planning [1–3]. The problem entails estimating detailed 3D geometry of the building, parsing semantically its important facade elements such as windows and doors, and precisely registering the building with the world's map.

Most existing approaches to 3D building estimation typically require LIDAR scans from either aerial [4,5] or ground-level views [2], or video scans [1]. While these approaches have shown impressive results [1,2,6], their use is inherently

Electronic supplementary material The online version of this chapter (doi:10.1007/978-3-319-46466-4_30) contains supplementary material, which is available to authorized users.

© Springer International Publishing AG 2016
B. Leibe et al. (Eds.): ECCV 2016, Part VI, LNCS 9910, pp. 500–516, 2016.
DOI: 10.1007/978-3-319-46466-4_30

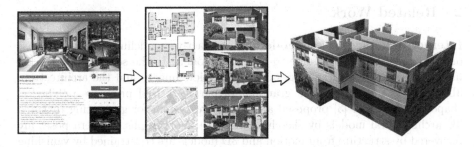

Fig. 1. We exploit rental ads and a small set of (wide-baseline) Google's StreetView images to build realistic textured 3D models of the buildings' exterior. In particular, our method creates models by using only the (approximate) address and a floorplan extracted from the rental ad, in addition to StreetView.

limited to the availability of such sensors. In this paper, our goal is to enable a wider use, where the user can easily obtain a realistic model of her/his house by providing only an approximate address and a floorplan of the building.

Towards this goal, we exploit rental ads which contain both the property's address as well as a floor plan. We convert the address to a rough geo-location, and exploit Google's Geo-Reference API to obtain a set of StreetView images where the property's exterior is visible. A floorplan provides us with an accurate and metric outline of the building's exterior along with information about the position of windows and doors. This information is given in the footprint of the building, and typically the vertical positions (along the height) are not known.

Our approach then reasons jointly about the 3D geometry of the building and its registration with the Google's StreetView imagery. In particular, we estimate the height of each floor, the vertical positions of windows and doors, and the accurate position of the building in the world's map. We frame the problem as inference in a Markov random field that exploits several geometric and semantic cues from the StreetView images as well as the floorplan. Note that the StreetView images have a very wide baseline, and thus relying on keypoint matching across the views would result in imprecise estimation. In our model, we exhaustively explore the solution space, by efficiently scoring our projected building model across all views. Our approach is thus also partially robust to cases where the building is occluded by vegetation.

To demonstrate the effectiveness of our approach, we collected a new dataset with 174 houses by crawling an Australian rental website. We annotated the precise pose of each house with respect to Google's StreetView images, as well as the locations of windows, doors and floors. Our experiments show that our approach is able to precisely estimate the geometry and location of the property. This enables us to reconstruct a realistic textured 3D model of the building's exterior. We refer the reader to Fig. 1 for an illustration of our approach and an example of our 3D rendering. Our dataset and source code will be made available at http://www.cs.toronto.edu/housecraft.

2   Related Work

Interactive image-based modeling: Interactive modeling of buildings use one or more images as a guide to build 3D models. In the seminal work of [7], users are required to draw edges over multi-view images and the architectural 3D model is then built by a grammar of parameterized primitive polyhedral shapes. Sinha et al. [3] proposed an interactive system for generating textured 3D architectural models by sketching multiple photographs. Camera poses are recovered by structure from motion and 3D models are constrained by vanishing point detection. We refer the reader to [8] for a more systematic literature review.

Automatic 3D building modeling: Researchers also attempted to tackle the problem in a fully automatic way. Many approaches made use of LIDAR aerial imagery [4,5] for this purpose. In our review, we focus on approaches that exploit ground-level information. The general idea is to utilize prior knowledge to constrain the target 3D models, such as parallelism, orthogonality, piece-wise planar and vanishing point constraints [1,9–12]. These methods either rely on dense point clouds reconstructed from multiview stereo [1,11] or line segment [9] features that guide the architectural reconstruction. However, line segment based methods are not robust to clutter and occlusion, while multi-view approaches rely on the input to be either a video or a set of images with relatively small motion. Unlike previous approaches, our method requires only on a very sparse set of large-baseline images (typically 3 images per house with average distance between the cameras of 16.7 m). Furthermore, we can handle large occlusion and clutter, such as vegetation and cars in the street.

Facade parsing: Our method is also related to work on facade parsing, which aims at semantic, pixel-level image labeling of the building's facade [13–16]. Hidden structures of building facades are modeled and utilized to tackle this problem, such as repetitive windows, low-rankness and grammar constraints. Compared to these structures, our method exploits the geometry and semantic priors from the floorplan, and can thus work with a much wider range of facades.

Using floorplans for vision: Floorplans contain useful yet inexpensive geometric and semantic information. They have been exploited for 3D reconstruction [17–19] and camera localization [20–22]. However, past methods mainly utilize floorplans for indoor scenes. This is in contrast to our work which aims to exploit floorplans for outdoor image-based modeling. In [23–25], city maps with building contours are used to help localization and reconstruction. City maps differ from floorplans as they do not contain information about windows and doors. To the best of our knowledge, outdoor image-based modeling with floorplans has not been proposed in the literature before. Moreover, due to the rich information available in the floorplans, our 3D parameterized model is very compact with a relative small number of degrees of freedom.

Recently, Arth et al. [25] proposed a camera localization method using 2.5D city maps. Our work differs from theirs in two aspects. First, [25] assumes that the building height is known, e.g., from OpenStreetMaps. For residential houses considered here this information is not available. Second, it assumes that the relative camera height w.r.t. building's base is constant. In our case, reasoning about relative height is necessary due to the difference in elevation between the building and the camera.

Holistic 3D scene understanding: Holistic models reason about semantics and geometry simultaneously, resulting in performance gains. For instance, [26, 27] perform semantic parsing and multi-view reconstruction jointly and [28–30] reason about both depth and semantic labeling from a monocular image. Our approach also reasons about semantic parsing and pose estimation jointly, but constrains the degrees of freedom via floorplan priors.

Fig. 2. The initial building's position and StreetView images. In **(a)**, blue pin shows the geo-reference result, green pins show three nearby StreetView images $S_{1,2,3}$, red lines depict the building contours parsed from the map image. **(b)**: Building's floorplan placed on the map. **(c)** shows StreetView images corresponding to $S_{1,2,3}$ in (a), respectively, overlaid with the virtual house rendered with the initial building position (from (b)) and floor, door, window heights as 1 m, 2 m, 3 m. (Color figure online)

Table 1. Average values of vertical positions computed from GT annotations.

Vertical position	Base	Floor	Door	Upper window	Lower window
Mean value	-2.57 m	3.33 m	2.56 m	0.53 m	1.34 m

3   The SydneyHouse Dataset

We exploit rental ads to obtain our dataset. In this section we first explain data collection and analyze the statistics of our new dataset.

Data Collection: We collected our dataset by crawling an Australian real-estate website[1]. We chose this site because it contains housing information in a formatted layout. We queried the website by using the keyword "Sydney"+"House", and parsed ads for the top 1,007 search results. A rental ad is typically composed of several, mostly indoor photos, a floorplan, as well as meta data information such as the address of the property. In our work we only kept houses for which a floorplan was available (80.8 %). Given the address, we obtained several outdoor street-level photos around the property via Google's Geo-Reference API[2]. In particular, for each rental ad we downloaded a local map around the property using Google Maps (Fig. 2(a)). We then parse the building contours from the map[3], and set the building position as the position of the closest building contour (Fig. 2(b)). This gives us a rough geo-location of the rental property. We then collected Google StreetView images around this location, where we set the camera orientation to always point towards the property of interest. Fig. 2(c) shows that although the building matches the map very well, the property does not align well with the images. Obtaining a more accurate alignment is the subject of our work. We finally discarded ads for which the houses could not be geo-referenced or were not identifiable by the annotators in StreetView imagery (65.3 %). Our final *SydneyHouse* dataset contains 174 houses located in different parts of Sydney. We show examples for house selection in our dataset in the supplementary material.

Ground-truth Annotation: We annotated each house with the vertical positions (e.g., floor height) and its precise location with respect to the geo-tagged imagery. We developed a WebGL based annotation tool that constructs the 3D model of the house given a set of vertical positions. The tool visualizes the projection of the 3D model onto the corresponding StreetView images. The in-house annotators were then asked to adjust the properties until the 3D model is best aligned with the streetview imagery. For each house, we annotate the (1) vertical positions, namely the building's foundation height (w.r.t. camera), (2) each floor's height as well as (3) the door heights, and (4) windows vertical starting and ending positions. We also annotate the floorplan by specifying line segments for walls, windows, and doors, as well as building orientation and scale. On average, the total annotating time for each house was around 20 min.

Statistics: Our dataset consists of 174 houses. On average each house has 1.4 levels, 3.2 windows, 1.7 doors. Average values of vertical positions are in Table 1.

4   Building Houses from Rentals Ads and Street Views

In this section, we show how to create a 3D model of the building exterior given a floor plan and a set of wide-baseline StreetView images. We start by describing

---

[1] http://www.domain.com.au/.

[2] https://www.google.com/maps.

[3] In particular, we use a processing pipeline consisting of color thresholding, connected component analysis, corner detection, and sorting by geodesic distance.

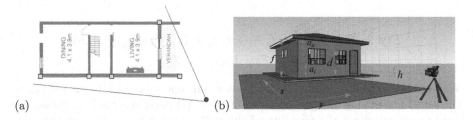

Fig. 3. Visibility and parametrization: (a) shows a floorplan and the visible parts to a given camera, (b) depicts our parametrization of the building and its pose.

our parametrization of the problem in terms of the random variables denoting the building's position and vertical positions. We cast the problem as energy minimization in a Markov Random Field, where inference can be performed efficiently despite a large combinatorial solution space.

4.1 Parameterization and Energy Formulation

Given several geo-tagged StreetView images of a house, $\mathcal{I} = \{\mathcal{I}_i\}_{i=1}^{N}$, and a floorplan $\mathcal{F}$ extracted from the rental ad, our goal is to jointly estimate the 3D layout of the house as well as its accurate geo-location.

A floorplan contains information about the number of floors, the dimensions of the footprint of each floor, and the (2D) location of doors and windows in the footprints. In order to lift the floorplan to 3D, we need to estimate the height of each floor, the building's foundation height as well as the vertical position of each door, window, and possibly a garage gate. Let h be the building's foundation height, where $h = 0$ means that the building sits on a plane having the same height as the camera. Here, h thus simply encodes the vertical offset of the building's support surface from the camera. We parameterize all floors with the same height, which we denote by f. We also assume that all doors (including the garage gates) have the same height, which we denote by d. Further, let $\mathbf{a} = \{a_u, a_l\}$ be the window's vertical starting and ending position.

Our initial estimate of the house's location is not very accurate. We thus parameterize the property's true geolocation with two additional degrees of freedom (x, y), encoding the (2D) position of the house in the map. Note that this parameterization is sufficient as projection errors are mainly due to poor geo-location in Google Maps and not because of inaccurate camera estimates in StreetView. We confirmed this fact while labeling our dataset. Figure 3 visualizes our full parametrization.

Let $\mathbf{y} = \{x, y, h, f, d, \mathbf{a}\}$ be the set of all variables we want to estimate for a house. We formulate the problem as inference in a Markov random field, which encourages the projection of the 3D model to match the image edges, semantics and location of doors and windows in all images. Furthermore, we want to encourage the building to be salient in the image, and its appearance to be different than the one of the background. Our complete energy takes the following form:

$$E(\mathbf{y};\mathcal{I},\mathcal{F}) = E_{\mathrm{edge}}(\mathbf{y};\mathcal{I},\mathcal{F}) + E_{\mathrm{obj}}(\mathbf{y};\mathcal{I},\mathcal{F}) + E_{\mathrm{seg}}(\mathbf{y};\mathcal{I},\mathcal{F})$$
$$+ E_{\mathrm{sal}}(\mathbf{y};\mathcal{I},\mathcal{F}) + E_{\mathrm{app}}(\mathbf{y};\mathcal{I},\mathcal{F}) \tag{1}$$

We note that given a building hypothesis $\mathbf{y}$, our energy scores its projection in the set of StreetView images. Thus, in order to properly score a hypothesis, we need to reason about the visibility of the walls, windows, etc. We compute the visibility with a standard exact 2D visibility reasoning method [31]. Figure 3(a) shows example of visibility reasoning. We refer the reader to suppl. material for details. In the following subsection, we describe the potentials in more detail.

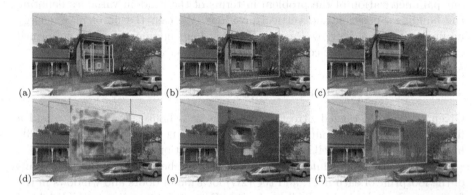

Fig. 4. Feature visualization. (a) Initial building position. All features are computed for a region around the initial building (cyan box in (b)). (b) Detected vertical (blue), horizontal (green), otherwise orientated (red) edges. (c) Detected windows (red) and doors (green). (d) Foreground color potential with foreground and background color sampled from cyan/magenta boxes. (e) Saliency-based foreground segmentation. (f) Semantic segmentation with *building* (red), *sky* (purple), *occlusion* (blue), *other* (yellow). (Color figure online)

4.2   Potentials in Our Energy

Edge Potential: This term encodes the fact that most building facade, window, door and floor boundaries correspond to image edges. We thus define

$$E_{\mathrm{edge}}(\mathbf{y};\mathcal{I},\mathcal{F}) = \sum_{i=1}^{N} \mathbf{w}_{\mathrm{edge}}^{T} \phi_{\mathrm{edge}}(\mathbf{y};\mathcal{I}_{i},\mathcal{F})$$

where N is the number of StreetView images, $\mathbf{w}_{\mathrm{edge}}$ is a vector of learned weights and ϕ_{edge} is a feature vector encoding the distances between the edges of our projected hypothesis and the image edges. We compute distances for different types of building edges, i.e., *vertical, horizontal,* and *all.* When computing the potential, we take into account visibility and exploit distance transforms for efficiency. We use up to four different features per edge type, corresponding to different thresholded distance transforms (i.e., 0.1 m, 0.2 m, 0.4 m). For each edge type, the potential then sums the value of the different distance transforms along the projected visible edges. In particular, we use structured edge [32] to extract the orientated edge map for each image. Figure 4(b) shows an example.

Object Potential: To compute the object potential, we first run an object detector for three classes, i.e. *doors, windows*, and *garage gates*, on StreetView images. This energy term is then designed to encourage agreement between the projection of the model's visible doors, windows, and garage gates, and the detection boxes. We thus define

$$E_{\mathrm{obj}}(\mathbf{y};\mathcal{I},\mathcal{F}) = \sum_{i=1}^{N} \mathbf{w}_{\mathrm{obj}}^{T} \phi_{\mathrm{obj}}(\mathbf{y};\mathcal{I}_i,\mathcal{F})$$

where N is the number of images, $\mathbf{w}_{\mathrm{obj}}$ is a vector of weights and ϕ_{obj} is a feature vector that encodes agreement for each object type. In particular, ϕ_{obj} simply counts the number of pixels for which the projected (visible) object hypothesis and the image detection box agree. We additionally use counts of pixels that are inside the projected object hypothesis, but are not in any detection box, and another count for pixels contained in the detection boxes but not contained inside the object hypothesis. Our feature vector is thus 9-dimensional (three classes and three counting features for each class). We refer the reader to Fig. 4(c) for an illustration. Note that these pixel counts can be computed efficiently with integral geometry [33], a generalization of integral images to non axis-aligned plane homographies. In our work, we rectify the image using the known homography to frontal-parallel view, so that the grid for integral geometry is axis-aligned, thus simplifying the implementation.

Table 2. Object detection performance. Accuracy reported at each stage without taking into account previous errors (objects missed by proposals are excluded for detection).

	Proposal		Detection			
	Precision	Recall	Precision	Recall	F1 score	Overall acc.
Window	10.11 %	63.04 %	34.65 %	76.11 %	47.62	84.10 %
Door	2.32 %	32.50 %	4.41 %	39.29 %	7.93	76.92 %
Garage	7.28 %	49.43 %	32.14 %	81.82 %	46.15	90.87 %

To detect doors, windows and garage gates in the StreetView images we use a pipeline similar to RCNN [34]. We first use edgebox [35] to generate object proposals (most objects are rectangular in the rectified view). In particular, we use only 10 object proposals since a house typically have multiple windows/doors, successfully detecting a few of them is sufficient for our task. We train a convolutional neural network on the region proposals for each class independently, by fine-tuning AlexNet [36] pre-trained on ImageNet [37], which is available in the Caffe's [38] model-zoo. Figure 4(c) shows an example.

Segmentation Potential: This term encodes the fact that we prefer house configurations that agree with semantics extracted from StreetView images. Towards this goal, we take advantage of SegNet [39] and compute semantic segmentation for each StreetView image in terms of four classes: *sky, building, occlusion* and *other*. We define all categories that can occlude a building as *occlusion*, i.e., tree, pole, sign and vehicle. We then define our segmentation potential as

$$E_{\text{seg}}(\mathbf{y}; \mathcal{I}, \mathcal{F}) = \sum_i \mathbf{w}_{\text{seg}}^T \phi_{\text{seg}}(\mathbf{y}; \mathcal{I}_i, \mathcal{F})$$

where $\mathbf{w}_{\text{seg}}$ is a vector of weights and ϕ_{seg} is a feature vector. Each dimension of ϕ_{seg} counts the number of pixels inside the projected building region, that were labeled with one of the categories by the segmentation algorithm. We expect the learning algorithm to learn that the weight for building is positive and the weight for sky and other is negative. Similar to the object potential, this term can be efficiently computed via 2D integral geometry in a rectified frontal-parallel view. Figure 4(d) shows an example.

Table 3. Mean errors of our approach and the baselines. h, f, d, a_l, and a_u denote heights for camera, floor, door, and window, respectively.

	xy/m	IOU	h/cm	f/cm	d/cm	a_l/cm	a_u/cm
Random	9.07	21.04 %	102.8	49.8	45.6	47.0	55.9
Box-reg [40,41]	6.68	33.31 %					
Google	5.01	43.46 %					
Ours	**2.62**	**68.29 %**	**49.7**	**43.1**	**14.1**	**36.9**	**33.6**

Saliency potential: This term encourages the building facade to correspond to salient objects in the scene. In particular, we use [42] to compute a per-pixel saliency score (example depicted in Fig. 4(e)). We then compute our potential by simply summing the salient scores inside the projected building's region. Note that as before we can compute this potential in constant time using integral accumulators.

Appearance potential: This term encourages the image region corresponding to the projected building's facade to have color different than the background. We sample the foreground and background color from image region around, and sufficiently far away, from the initial building position, where background normally corresponds to sky, pavement, grass, and other buildings. We compute per-pixel foreground probability with a kernel density estimator. Our potential is obtained by summing the foreground probability inside the projected facade. Figure 4(f) shows an example.

4.3 Efficient Projection of Building Hypotheses

As shown in Fig. 3(b), given a configuration $\mathbf{y}$, we can lift the floorplan $\mathcal{F}$ to 3D, and project it onto each StreetView image $\mathcal{I}_i$ given the known camera parameters (given by Google's API). Since the camera poses are fixed (we are "moving" the building relative to the camera), we can re-write the model's translation to point $\mathbf{z}$ as: $HK[R|t]\mathbf{z} = HK[R|t](\mathbf{z}_0 + x\triangle\mathbf{z}_x + y\triangle\mathbf{z}_y)$, where H is a homography that rectifies the image to the frontal-parallel view. Here $\mathbf{z}_0$ is a chosen initial point, $(\mathbf{z}_x, \mathbf{z}_y)$ is a chosen discretization of the search space, and (x, y) represents the coordinate of our hypothesis in this space. Since $\mathbf{z}_0$ and $(\mathbf{z}_x, \mathbf{z}_y)$ are fixed for all hypotheses, we can pre-compute $HK[R|t]\mathbf{z}_0$, $HK[R|t]\mathbf{z}_x$, and $HK[R|t]\mathbf{z}_y$, allowing us to avoid matrix multiplication when projecting a new hypothesis $\mathbf{z}$.

Table 4. Impact of the size of the search range on the accuracy of the method. Columns from left to right: xy search range, percentage of ground truth that is within the search range, inference time per house, average error for each variable.

range/m	gt%	time/s	xy/m	h/cm	f/cm	a_l/cm	a_u/cm
5 × 5	19.0 %	**6.22**	3.37	58.1	41.7	41.2	**28.4**
10 × 10	62.1 %	8.58	2.70	**44.0**	43.3	41.5	29.6
15 × 15	88.5 %	12.12	2.66	49.2	42.0	37.1	33.3
20 × 20	96.6 %	19.05	**2.62**	49.7	43.1	36.9	33.6
25 × 25	**97.7 %**	27.16	2.67	46.6	**40.4**	**35.1**	34.2

Table 5. Impact of the height quantization on inference time and accuracy.

quant. thres./m	time/s	xy/m	h/cm	f/cm	a_l/cm	a_u/cm
0.20	19.05	2.62	**49.7**	43.1	36.9	33.6
0.25	16.28	**2.34**	45.7	41.4	26.8	**31.3**
0.35	**12.58**	2.81	51.5	**34.0**	**26.8**	31.9

4.4 Inference

We perform inference by minimizing the energy in Eq. (1) with respect to $\mathbf{y}$. For random variables corresponding to vertical building dimensions, we discretize our solution space by learning a set of prototypes by independently clustering the output space for each random variable. We refer the reader to the suppl.

material for a detailed description of our discretization. It is worth noting that our energy evaluation can be done very efficiently, since all the energy potentials can be computed via integral accumulators. This allows us to perform inference via exhaustive search over the combinatorial space of all prototypes. On average we can evaluate 20.7 k candidates per second on a CPU.

4.5   Learning

We learn the parameters of the model with structured-SVMs [43], using the parallel implementation of [44]. We compute the loss function as the sum of loss functions across all StreetView images. For each individual image, we compute the loss as the intersection-over-union (IOU) between the ground-truth segmentation (implied by the ground-truth layout of the building projected into the image) and the segmentation corresponding to the model's projection. We weigh each class (i.e., building, window, doors/gates) differently. We estimate these weights as well as the slack rescaling term c via cross-validation.

5   Experiments

We first provide implementation details, and then evaluate our approach on our newly collected dataset.

Implementation details. For the building's position, we use a search range of $20\,\mathrm{m} \times 20\,\mathrm{m}$, discretized by $0.25\,\mathrm{m}$. We use k-means clustering with a cluster variance of $0.2\,\mathrm{m}$ for our variable-wise clustering, yielding 5 prototypes for h, 3 for f, 1 for d, 2 for a_l, and 2 for a_u. Thus in total, the number of unique solutions is $81 \times 81 \times 60$, which is roughly 0.4 million possible states.

Table 6. Ablation study of different types of energy terms. The *other* potential includes segmentation, saliency, and appearance. Best result is achieved with all potentials.

Edge	Obj	Other	xy/m	h/cm	f/cm	a_l/cm	a_u/cm
✓			6.42	63.4	47.1	46.7	40.3
	✓		7.24	83.3	52.5	38.0	45.4
		✓	3.50	79.5	41.2	46.7	40.3
✓	✓		5.93	59.7	44.7	37.0	40.9
✓		✓	2.84	53.9	**40.8**	46.7	40.3
	✓	✓	3.18	60.6	46.4	37.1	**33.2**
✓	✓	✓	**2.62**	**49.7**	43.1	**36.9**	33.6

Evaluation. We evaluate our approach on our SydneyHouse dataset. We conduct 6-fold evaluation, where for each test fold, we use 4 folds for training and 1 fold for validation to choose the hyper-parameters. We use grid search to choose the hyper-parameters over the space $c \in \{2^{-4}, 2^{-3}, 2^{-2}, 2^{-1}, 2^{0}, 2^{1}\}$, and $\alpha' = \{0.5, 1, 2\}$, which is the ratio of object IOU to facade IOU in the task loss.

We compare our approach with three baselines. In the first baseline, we randomly generate the building position, with the same xy search range and discretization. We denote this baseline as *random*. In the second baseline, we feed the frontal-parallel facade image to Inception Network [40] and extract features from both global pooling and fully connected layers. We then perform box regression as in [41] to find the optimal building's bounding box, and choose the regularization parameter that yields best results. We use the new box to obtain the building position xy. This baseline is referred to as *box-reg*. In the third baseline referred to as *google*, we obtain building position xy by placing the floorplan to best overlap with the building contour on Google Maps. In all baselines, vertical positions h, f, d, a_u, and a_l are obtained by randomly selecting from the training set. Baselines are repeated 1000 times to get the average performance.

Quantitative results: As shown in Table 3, the box-regression baseline achieves better building position than the random baseline. However, its performance is still poor, due to limited number of training samples. Our method outperforms all baselines by a large margin. To better demonstrate our method's advantage, we also list the frontal facade IOU with the ground truth in Table 3. Note that our approach significantly improves the overlap with the ground truth. For the *google* baseline, we also tried setting vertical dimensions as dataset average and found our method still outperform the baseline significantly.

Object Detection: As shown in Table 2, object proposals detect a fraction of all objects. This is due to the fact that in our multi-view setup, only a few views face the frontal facade perpendicularly, and the rectified images are skewed and blurred in the other views. Doors are more difficult to detect than windows and garage gates as many doors are covered by the porch. Note that we report precision/recall of each stage without taking into account previous errors, i.e., objects that are missed by the proposal are excluded for detection.

Impact of search space discretization: We study the impact of the size of the search range for the building's xy position in Table 4. There is a trade-off between efficiency and efficacy. As we increase the search range, the percentage of ground-truth samples located within the search range increases, and building position accuracy also increases. However, above a certain range the accuracy starts to drop since more ambiguous samples are included. Table 5 shows the impact of different quantization thresholds for the height variables. Supplementary material investigates more discretization choices.

Ablation study: We perform an ablation study of our approach in Table 6. Notice that incorporating more potentials increases the accuracy of our approach. Specifically, we can see that *other* potential, which includes segmentation, saliency, and appearance, helps to estimate the building position xy the most.

(Original)   (Google)   (Ours)   (3D model)

Fig. 5. Qualitative comparison. From left to right: input StreetView image, baseline method, our approach, texture-mapped 3D house model using our result.

The *edge* potentials are more useful for estimating the building foundation height h. The best result is achieved when combining all potentials.

Fig. 6. Our approach demonstrates robustness when the house is occluded. Left: original images (two for each house). Right: our results.

Qualitative results: Figure 5 shows a few qualitative results of our approach and the *google* baseline algorithm. It can be seen that the baseline cannot localize the house precisely in the image due to the mapping and geo-referencing errors. In contrast, our approach is able to provide accurate xy as well as vertical positions (floor/base heights, vertical window and door positions). Figure 6 further shows four examples with partial occlusions caused by trees in one or two viewpoints. Despite occlusion, our approach is still able to accurately estimate the building position and vertical positions.

Fig. 7. Failure modes. Left: original images. Right: our results.

Failure modes: Figure 7 shows a few failure modes. In property 1, our approach fails because the initial building position is too noisy. The ground truth is 16.3 m from the initial position, which exceeds our 20 × 20 search range. Property 2 shows another difficult case, where the building is heavily occluded in the second and third view, the facade has similar color to the sky, and many non-building edges exist. In this case, our method still estimates the building xy position correctly, but fails to estimate the vertical positions.

Timing: We report the efficiency of our method. Computing detection and segmentation features is done on a GPU, while the rest of code is all executed in CPU. Our CPU implementation uses Matlab without parallelization. Training our model takes around 20 min each fold. In inference, our approach takes 19.05 s in total per house, which includes 3.41 s for computing the image features, 8.00 s for rendering all configurations and 7.64 s for inference. Note that in our case both rendering and inference are highly parallelizable, thus allowing for high speed-ups with a more sophisticated implementation.

6 Conclusion

In this paper, we proposed an approach which exploits rentals ads to create realistic textured 3D models of building exteriors. In particular, the property's address is employed to obtain a set of wide-baseline views of the building, while the floor plan is exploited to provide a footprint of the building's facade as well as the location on the floor of doors and windows. We formulated the problem as inference in a Markov random field that exploits several geometric and semantic cues from the StreetView images as well as the floorplan. Our experiments showed that our approach is able to precisely estimate the geometry and location of the property, and can create realistic 3D models of the building exterior.

References

1. Xiao, J., Fang, T., Zhao, P., Lhuillier, M., Quan, L.: Image-based street-side city modeling. ACM Trans. Graph. (TOG) (2009)
2. Pylvanainen, T., Berclaz, J., Korah, T., Hedau, V., Aanjaneya, M., Grzeszczuk, R.: 3d city modeling from street-level data for augmented reality applications. In: 3DIM/3DPVT (2012)
3. Sinha, S.N., Steedly, D., Szeliski, R., Agrawala, M., Pollefeys, M.: Interactive 3d architectural modeling from unordered photo collections. ACM Trans. Graph. (TOG) (2008)
4. Verma, V., Kumar, R., Hsu, S.: 3d building detection and modeling from aerial lidar data. In: CVPR (2006)
5. Zebedin, L., Bauer, J., Karner, K., Bischof, H.: Fusion of feature- and area-based information for urban buildings modeling from aerial imagery. In: Forsyth, D., Torr, P., Zisserman, A. (eds.) ECCV 2008. LNCS, vol. 5305, pp. 873–886. Springer, Heidelberg (2008). doi:10.1007/978-3-540-88693-8_64
6. Wang, L., Neumann, U.: A robust approach for automatic registration of aerial images with untextured aerial lidar data. In: CVPR (2009)

7. Debevec, P.E., Taylor, C.J., Malik, J.: Modeling and rendering architecture from photographs: A hybrid geometry-and image-based approach. In: SIGGRAPH (1996)
8. Musialski, P., Wonka, P., Aliaga, D.G., Wimmer, M., Gool, L., Purgathofer, W.: A survey of urban reconstruction. Comput. Graph. Forum **32**(6), 146–177 (2013)
9. Werner, T., Zisserman, A.: New techniques for automated architectural reconstruction from photographs. In: Heyden, A., Sparr, G., Nielsen, M., Johansen, P. (eds.) ECCV 2002. LNCS, vol. 2351, pp. 541–555. Springer, Heidelberg (2002). doi:10.1007/3-540-47967-8_36
10. Dick, A.R., Torr, P.H., Cipolla, R.: Modelling and interpretation of architecture from several images. IJCV **60**, 111–134 (2004)
11. Sinha, S.N., Steedly, D., Szeliski, R.: Piecewise planar stereo for image-based rendering. In: ICCV (2009)
12. Mičušík, B., Košecká, J.: Multi-view superpixel stereo in urban environments. IJCV **89**, 106–119 (2010)
13. Müller, P., Zeng, G., Wonka, P., Van Gool, L.: Image-based procedural modeling of facades. ACM Trans. Graph. (TOG) **26**(3), 85 (2007)
14. Martinović, A., Mathias, M., Weissenberg, J., Gool, L.: A three-layered approach to facade parsing. In: Fitzgibbon, A., Lazebnik, S., Perona, P., Sato, Y., Schmid, C. (eds.) ECCV 2012. LNCS, vol. 7578, pp. 416–429. Springer, Heidelberg (2012). doi:10.1007/978-3-642-33786-4_31
15. Teboul, O., Simon, L., Koutsourakis, P., Paragios, N.: Segmentation of building facades using procedural shape priors. In: CVPR (2010)
16. Cohen, A., Schwing, A.G., Pollefeys, M.: Efficient structured parsing of facades using dynamic programming. In: CVPR (2014)
17. Furukawa, Y., Curless, B., Seitz, S.M., Szeliski, R.: Reconstructing building interiors from images. In: ICCV (2009)
18. Cabral, R., Furukawa, Y.: Piecewise planar and compact floorplan reconstruction from images. In: CVPR (2014)
19. Ikehata, S., Yang, H., Furukawa, Y.: Structured indoor modeling. In: ICCV (2015)
20. Liu, C., Schwing, A.G., Kundu, K., Urtasun, R., Fidler, S.: Rent3d: floor-plan priors for monocular layout estimation. In: CVPR (2015)
21. Wang, S., Fidler, S., Urtasun, R.: Lost shopping! monocular localization in large indoor spaces. In: ICCV (2015)
22. Chu, H., Ki Kim, D., Chen, T.: You are here: Mimicking the human thinking process in reading floor-plans. In: ICCV (2015)
23. Untzelmann, O., Sattler, T., Middelberg, S., Kobbelt, L.: A scalable collaborative online system for city reconstruction. In: ICCV Workshops (2013)
24. Strecha, C., Pylvänäinen, T., Fua, P.: Dynamic and scalable large scale image reconstruction. In: CVPR (2010)
25. Arth, C., Pirchheim, C., Ventura, J., Schmalstieg, D., Lepetit, V.: Instant outdoor localization and slam initialization from 2.5d maps. TVCG 21(11), 1309–1318 (2015)
26. Savinov, N., Ladicky, L., Hane, C., Pollefeys, M.: Discrete optimization of ray potentials for semantic 3d reconstruction. In: CVPR (2015)
27. Kundu, A., Li, Y., Dellaert, F., Li, F., Rehg, J.M.: Joint semantic segmentation and 3D reconstruction from monocular video. In: Fleet, D., Pajdla, T., Schiele, B., Tuytelaars, T. (eds.) ECCV 2014. LNCS, vol. 8694, pp. 703–718. Springer, Heidelberg (2014). doi:10.1007/978-3-319-10599-4_45
28. Wang, S., Fidler, S., Urtasun, R.: Holistic 3d scene understanding from a single geo-tagged image. In: CVPR (2015)

29. Liu, B., Gould, S., Koller, D.: Single image depth estimation from predicted semantic labels. In: CVPR (2010)
30. Ladický, L., Shi, J., Pollefeys, M.: Pulling things out of perspective. In: CVPR (2014)
31. Teller, S.J., Séquin, C.H.: Visibility preprocessing for interactive walkthroughs. In: SIGGRAPH (1991)
32. Dollár, P., Zitnick, C.L.: Structured forests for fast edge detection. In: ICCV (2013)
33. Schwing, A.G., Hazan, T., Pollefeys, M., Urtasun, R.: Efficient structured prediction for 3D indoor scene understanding. In: Proceedings of the CVPR (2012)
34. Girshick, R., Donahue, J., Darrell, T., Malik, J.: Rich feature hierarchies for accurate object detection and semantic segmentation. In: CVPR (2014)
35. Zitnick, C.L., Dollár, P.: Edge boxes: locating object proposals from edges. In: Fleet, D., Pajdla, T., Schiele, B., Tuytelaars, T. (eds.) ECCV 2014. LNCS, vol. 8693, pp. 391–405. Springer, Heidelberg (2014). doi:10.1007/978-3-319-10602-1_26
36. Krizhevsky, A., Sutskever, I., Hinton, G.E.: Imagenet classification with deep convolutional neural networks. In: NIPS (2012)
37. Russakovsky, O., Deng, J., Su, H., Krause, J., Satheesh, S., Ma, S., Huang, Z., Karpathy, A., Khosla, A., Bernstein, M., Berg, A.C., Fei-Fei, L.: ImageNet large scale visual recognition challenge. IJCV 115(3), 211–252 (2015)
38. Jia, Y., Shelhamer, E., Donahue, J., Karayev, S., Long, J., Girshick, R., Guadarrama, S., Darrell, T.: Caffe: convolutional architecture for fast feature embedding. In: ACM Multimedia (2014)
39. Badrinarayanan, V., Kendall, A., Cipolla, R.: Segnet: A deep convolutional encoder-decoder architecture for image segmentation. arXiv preprint arXiv:1511.00561 (2015)
40. Szegedy, C., Liu, W., Jia, Y., Sermanet, P., Reed, S., Anguelov, D., Erhan, D., Vanhoucke, V., Rabinovich, A.: Going deeper with convolutions. In: CVPR (2015)
41. Ren, S., He, K., Girshick, R., Sun, J.: Faster r-cnn: towards real-time object detection with region proposal networks. In: NIPS (2015)
42. Zhang, J., Sclaroff, S., Lin, Z., Shen, X., Price, B., Mech, R.: Minimum barrier salient object detection at 80 fps. In: ICCV (2015)
43. Tsochantaridis, I., Joachims, T., Hofmann, T., Altun, Y.: Large margin methods for structured and interdependent output variables. JMLR 6, 1453–1484 (2005)
44. Schwing, A.G., Fidler, S., Pollefeys, M., Urtasun, R.: Box in the box: Joint 3d layout and object reasoning from single images. In: Proceedings of the ICCV (2013)

Superpixel-Based Two-View Deterministic Fitting for Multiple-Structure Data

Guobao Xiao[1], Hanzi Wang[1]($\boxtimes$), Yan Yan[1], and David Suter[2]

[1] Fujian Key Laboratory of Sensing and Computing for Smart City,
School of Information Science and Engineering,
Xiamen University, Xiamen, China
x-gb@163.com, wang.hanzi@gmail.com, yanyan@xmu.edu.cn
[2] School of Computer Science, The University of Adelaide, Adelaide, Australia
david.suter@adelaide.edu.au

Abstract. This paper proposes a two-view deterministic geometric model fitting method, termed Superpixel-based Deterministic Fitting (SDF), for multiple-structure data. SDF starts from superpixel segmentation, which effectively captures prior information of feature appearances. The feature appearances are beneficial to reduce the computational complexity for deterministic fitting methods. SDF also includes two original elements, i.e., a deterministic sampling algorithm and a novel model selection algorithm. The two algorithms are tightly coupled to boost the performance of SDF in both speed and accuracy. The key characteristic of SDF is that it can efficiently and deterministically estimate the parameters of model instances in multi-structure data. Experimental results demonstrate that the proposed SDF shows superiority over several state-of-the-art fitting methods for real images with single-structure and multiple-structure data.

Keywords: Deterministic algorithm · Superpixel · Model fitting · Feature appearances

1 Introduction

Geometric model fitting is a challenging problem in computer vision. A major problem in model fitting is how to tolerate numerous outliers, which are ubiquitous in the real-world. RANSAC [1] is one of the most popular fitting methods due to its robustness to outliers. Using the same random sampling technique as RANSAC, many robust fitting methods (e.g., gpbM [2], SCAMS [3], RCG [4] and PEARL [5,6]) have been proposed to improve RANSAC. There are also many robust fitting methods (e.g., SWIFT [7] and T-linkage [8]), developed based on different sampling techniques, during the past few decades. However, these fitting methods cannot guarantee the consistency in their solutions due to their randomized nature. As a consequence, the fitting results may vary if these methods do not sample a sufficient number of subsets.

© Springer International Publishing AG 2016
B. Leibe et al. (Eds.): ECCV 2016, Part VI, LNCS 9910, pp. 517–533, 2016.
DOI: 10.1007/978-3-319-46466-4_31

518   G. Xiao et al.

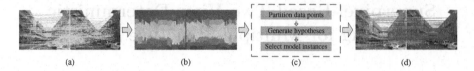

Fig. 1. Overview of the proposed method for homography estimation. (a) An image pair with keypoint correspondences. (b) Superpixel generation (each segment with the same color denotes a superpixel). (c) The procedure of the proposed method. (d) The fitting result according to the estimated model instances (the keypoint correspondences with the same color belong to the inliers of the same model instances). (Color figure online)

Recently, some deterministic methods (e.g., [9–13]) have received much attention for model fitting. In contrast to the unpredictability of non-deterministic fitting methods, these fitting methods can deterministically yield solutions. For example, Li [10] formulated the fitting problem as a mixed integer programming problem and deterministically solve the problem by using a tailored branch-and-bound scheme. Lee et al. [9] employed the maximum feasible subsystem framework to deterministically generate hypotheses for the fitting problem. Litman et al. [11] detected a globally optimal transformation based on inlier rate estimation. Fredriksson et al. [12] proposed a branch and bound approach for the two-view translation estimation problem. Chin et al. [13] formulated the fitting problem as a tree search problem by which globally optimal solutions can be found based on the Astar search algorithm [14].

Although existing deterministic fitting methods (e.g., [9–13]) can guarantee the consistency in their solutions, most of them are computationally expensive, especially for data with few inliers. Moreover, most deterministic methods [10–13] assume that there exists only a single model instance in data, which restricts the application of these methods in the real-world.

In this paper, we aim to solve a harder problem, where the proposed fitting method is used to efficiently and deterministically deal with multiple-structure data. Note that feature appearances contain important prior information, and some works have proposed to introduce feature appearances to model fitting (e.g., [6,15,16]). However, few deterministic fitting methods fully take advantage of feature appearances of keypoint correspondences. Thus, we propose to use prior information of feature appearances to reduce the computational cost of deterministic fitting methods. More specifically, we first obtain grouping cues from superpixels, which can characterize prior information of feature appearances. Then, based on the grouping cues, we propose an efficient and effective method, called Superpixel-based Deterministic Fitting (SDF), for multiple-structure data. The proposed SDF can deterministically generate "high-quality" hypotheses (i.e., the hypotheses mainly include good hypotheses with only a small percentage of bad hypotheses), and efficiently select significant hypotheses as model instances by using a novel model selection algorithm. Figure 1 illustrates the overview of the proposed method for homography estimation.

This paper has three main contributions. First, superpixels are introduced for deterministic model fitting. Superpixels consider spatial homogeneity, and they can provide powerful grouping cues to deterministically deal with model fitting. To the best of our knowledge, it is the first time that superpixels, which capture prior information of feature appearances, are introduced for robust model fitting in an effective manner. Second, a deterministic sampling algorithm is proposed to exploit the grouping cues of superpixels and the corresponding keypoint matching information. With the aid of superpixels, the proposed sampling algorithm can deterministically generate high-quality hypotheses with a low percentage of bad hypotheses. Third, a novel model selection algorithm, which improves the conventional "fit-and-remove" framework by sequentially removing hypotheses rather than keypoint correspondences, is developed to find all model instances in data. The developed model selection algorithm is very efficient and effective since it does not require the generation of new hypotheses in each iteration. Overall, SDF can efficiently and deterministically provide consistent solutions for model fitting. This is significant since most conventional fitting methods are based on randomized nature, and most existing deterministic fitting methods suffer from high computational complexity. Experimental results demonstrate that the proposed SDF can achieve substantial improvements over several recently developed state-of-the-art fitting methods.

2 Introducing Superpixels to Model Fitting

In this section, we aim to obtain prior information of feature appearances, to accelerate deterministic subset sampling for hypothesis generation. The feature appearances can be derived from region consistency, which means that features within the same segments are most likely to be assigned to the same labels [17]. We note that superpixels obtained by an image segmentation method (such as [18,19]) can adhere well to the object boundaries in the image. Moreover, one superpixel has less chance to cut across two or more objects. Thus, superpixels can be used to measure the level of consensus in labeling features for region consistency.

Accordingly, two keypoint correspondences x_i, x_j (a keypoint correspondence x_i consists of a feature pair $\{f_i^1, f_i^2\}$ in two views) have a high possibility of belonging to the inliers of the same structure if two features f_i^k, f_j^k from the k-th view belong to the same superpixel. For example, as shown in Fig. 2 (we use the image pair "Gamebiscuit" from the AdelaideRMF datasets [20]), we perform superpixel segmentation [18] on the image pair and show keypoint correspondences based on the ground truth result of fundamental matrix. We can see that most keypoint correspondences, whose valid features in one view come from the same superpixels, belong to the same structure.

Inspired by the above observations, the keypoint correspondences can be partitioned into a set of groups (i.e., $\mathcal{G}$) (where each group consists of the keypoint correspondences associated to the features within the same superpixel), with the intuition that the keypoint correspondences of a group have a high probability

Fig. 2. An example of superpixels and keypoint correspondences based on the ground truth result of fundamental matrix for an image pair ("Gamebiscuit").

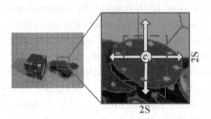

Fig. 3. An example of group combination. c_i is the center of the i-th group in $\mathcal{G}$ and S is the grid interval. The purple dashed box denotes a superpixel size and we perform the combining procedure within a $2S \times 2S$ region (i.e., the blue solid box). (Color figure online)

of belonging to the same structure. This will help to accelerate deterministic subset sampling for hypothesis generation.

3 The Proposed Method

In this section, based on the prior information of feature appearances derived from superpixels (discussed in Sect. 2), we first present a deterministic sampling algorithm for hypothesis generation in Sect. 3.1. Then, in Sect. 3.2, we present a novel "fit-and-remove" framework for model selection. Finally, we summarize the complete fitting method in Sect. 3.3.

3.1 Hypothesis Generation

The prior information of feature appearances can provide powerful grouping cues for hypothesis generation. However, grouping cues cannot be directly used to generate hypotheses. This is caused by two problems: (i) Sampling subsets in small spans may cause degeneration [21] and the keypoint correspondences of a group derived from a superpixel come from a small span; (ii) The keypoint correspondences of a group may contain outliers, which will lead to the failure of estimating a true structure in data.

We propose two strategies to alleviate the above-mentioned problems: For the first problem, we increase the spans of sampled subsets by combining groups in an input group set $\mathcal{G}$. Theoretically, we can combine any two groups in $\mathcal{G}$, but such a strategy is time consuming and will also generate a large number of "bad" groups that consist of keypoint correspondences belonging to different structures. Thus, we propose to only combine groups within a limited region, since the keypoint correspondences of neighboring groups, have a high probability of belonging to the same structure. More specifically, for a group $\mathcal{G}_i \in \boldsymbol{\mathcal{G}}$, we combine it with each of its neighboring group within a limited region to generate a new group $\hat{\mathcal{G}}_{i \cup j}$:

$$\hat{\mathcal{G}}_{i \cup j} = \begin{cases} \mathcal{G}_i \cup \mathcal{G}_j, & if \ \mathcal{G}_j \in \mathcal{N}(\mathcal{G}_i) \ and \ R(l_i, l_j) \leq 2S \times 2S, \\ \mathcal{G}_i \ , & otherwise, \end{cases} \quad (1)$$

where $\mathcal{N}(\mathcal{G}_i)$ is the neighboring group of $\mathcal{G}_i$. l_i and l_j denote the corresponding superpixels of $\mathcal{G}_i$ and $\mathcal{G}_j$, respectively. $R(.,.)$ denotes the combined region of two superpixels in the image. Here, according to the expected superpixel size $(S \times S)$, we compute the grid interval S as [18], i.e., $S = \sqrt{N/M}$, where N and M are the number of pixels and superpixels, respectively. An example of group combination is illustrated in Fig. 3.

In this manner, we can obtain a set of combined groups $\hat{\boldsymbol{\mathcal{G}}}$, where small-size groups are combined, while large-size groups (whose sizes are larger than $2S \times 2S$) are not combined. Although some combined groups may consist of keypoint correspondences belonging to two different structures, the degeneration problem can be effectively alleviated since each group $\hat{\mathcal{G}}_i$ in $\hat{\boldsymbol{\mathcal{G}}}$ includes keypoint correspondences with larger spans.

For the second problem, we only consider the most "promising" keypoint correspondences in a combined group $\hat{\mathcal{G}}_i = \{x_i^j\}_{j=1}^{n_i}$ according to the corresponding matching information. Specifically, for a group $\hat{\mathcal{G}}_i$, by sorting keypoint correspondences according to the corresponding matching score vector $\boldsymbol{s}_i = [s_i^1 \ s_i^2 \ \cdots \ s_i^{n_i}]$ (each score s_i^j is computed according to the SIFT correspondences [22]), we can find a permutation:

$$\boldsymbol{a}_i = [a_i^1 \ a_i^2 \ \cdots \ a_i^{n_i}], \quad (2)$$

where a_i^j is the ranking index of the j-th keypoint correspondence in the i-th group $\hat{\mathcal{G}}_i$. The keypoint correspondences in $\hat{\mathcal{G}}_i$ are sorted in the non-ascending order, i.e.,

$$u < v \Longrightarrow s_i^{a_i^u} > s_i^{a_i^v}, \quad (3)$$

where u and v respectively denote the indices of x_i^u and x_i^v in $\hat{\mathcal{G}}_i$.

Then, for a group $\hat{\mathcal{G}}_i$, we sample the m_0 top sorted keypoint correspondences, i.e., $\{x_i^j\}_{j=a_i^1}^{a_i^{m_0}}$. Here, we only sample the keypoint correspondences with high matching scores to reduce the influence of outliers. This is because a keypoint correspondence with a high matching score has a higher probability to be an inlier of a structure in data [23].

Based on the prior information of feature appearances and the two above-mentioned strategies (i.e., the group combination and the promising keypoint

---

Algorithm 1. The proposed deterministic sampling algorithm for hypothesis generation

---

Input: a set of groups of keypoint correspondences $\mathcal{G}$
1: Combine each group $\mathcal{G}_i \in \mathcal{G}$ with each one $\mathcal{G}_j$ of its neighbors $\mathcal{N}(\mathcal{G}_i)$ within a limited region to generate a new group $\hat{\mathcal{G}}_{i \cup j}$ by Eq. (1).
2: Sort keypoint correspondences in each combined group by Eq. (2).
3: Select the m_0 top sorted keypoint correspondences in the combined group as a sampled subset, which is used to generate a hypothesis θ_i.
Output: The generated hypothesis set θ $(=\{\theta_i\}_{i=1,2,...})$

---

correspondences selection), we propose a deterministic sampling algorithm for hypothesis generation (see Algorithm 1). The proposed sampling algorithm considers both feature appearances and geometric information, and it is also tractable due to its deterministic nature. Therefore, the proposed sampling algorithm can generate reliable and consistent hypotheses for model fitting. For the parameter m_0, i.e., the number of keypoint correspondences we use to generate a hypothesis, we can set it as $p + 2$, where p denotes the minimum size of sampled subsets for computing a unique hypothesis. This is because that the sampled subset with $p + 2$ keypoint correspondences can generate a stable hypothesis, which has been demonstrated in [24]. It is also worth pointing out that the way we sample subsets in the local region will not affect the quality of model hypotheses, because the grouping cues include information of all keypoint correspondences, and the group combination process also allows to sample in a larger region.

We note that PROSAC [15] also employs the most promising keypoint correspondences (measured by the matching information) to generate hypotheses. However, for each hypothesis, the proposed sampling algorithm only selects the most promising keypoint correspondences from a group based on superpixels, which is more "local" than PROSAC (recall that PROSAC samples a subset from all keypoint correspondences). That will help the proposed sampling algorithm to efficiently sample all-inlier subsets, which is more evident on multiple-structure data. Moreover, PROSAC cannot guarantee the consistency of hypotheses due to its randomized nature. In contrast, the proposed sampling algorithm is a deterministic sampling algorithm.

3.2   Model Selection

Given the hypothesis set θ generated by Algorithm 1, the next step is to select model instances for model fitting. For single-structure data, the hypothesis with the largest number of inliers is directly selected as the estimated model instance.

For multiple-structure data, we propose a novel "fit-and-remove" framework, which sequentially selects a hypothesis θ with the largest number of inliers from the hypothesis set, and updates the hypothesis set θ by removing some redundant hypotheses.

In contrast to the traditional "fit-and-remove" framework, the proposed framework removes hypotheses rather than keypoint correspondences and it does not require the generation of new hypotheses during each step. Therefore, it effectively overcomes the limitations of the conventional "fit-and-remove" framework [25], i.e., inaccurate inlier/outlier dichotomy can lead to wrong estimation of the remaining model instances, and repeated hypothesis generation during each step is computationally inefficient as well.

The key step of the proposed framework is how to remove redundant hypotheses. For a selected hypothesis θ_i (e.g., Fig. 4(b)), redundant hypotheses contain bad hypotheses (e.g., Figs. 4(d) and (e)), whose sampled subset consists of outliers or keypoint correspondences from different model instances, and good hypotheses (e.g., Fig. 4(c)), which correspond to the same model instance as θ_i. Therefore, for the selected hypothesis θ_i, we define $h(i,j)$ to determine if a hypothesis θ_j is redundant:

$$h(i,j) = \begin{cases} 1, & if\ \mathbf{Sam}(\theta_j) \cap \mathbf{In}(\theta_i) \neq \emptyset, \\ 0, & otherwise, \end{cases} \tag{4}$$

where $\mathbf{Sam}(\theta_j)$ is the sampled subset of θ_j and $\mathbf{In}(\theta_i)$ is the inlier set of θ_i. $\mathbf{Sam}(\theta_j) \cap \mathbf{In}(\theta_i)$ is used to decide if the sampled subset corresponding to θ_j contains any keypoint correspondence belonging to the inliers of θ_i. Thus, each hypothesis θ_j with $h(i,j) = 1$ will be treated as a redundant hypothesis and removed from the hypothesis set $\boldsymbol{\theta}$.

Note that the proposed framework may fail to remove redundant hypotheses based on some conventional sampling algorithms, e.g., [1,8]. This is because these sampling algorithms will generate a large percentage of bad hypotheses and the sampled subsets consist randomly selected keypoint correspondences.

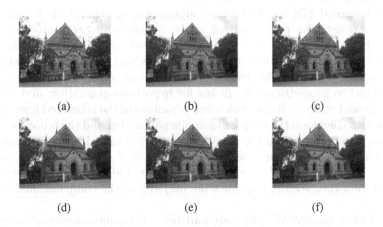

(a)   (b)   (c)

(d)   (e)   (f)

Fig. 4. An example of model selection for homography estimation (only one of the two views is shown): (a) An input image ("Elderhalla") with the ground truth results. (b) The inliers of the first selected hypothesis. (c)–(e) The sampled subsets of three redundant hypotheses. (f) The inliers of the second selected hypothesis.

In contrast, the proposed framework can work well based on the high-quality hypotheses provided by the proposed sampling algorithm (Algorithm 1). Specifically, for a selected hypothesis θ_i, the remaining good hypotheses corresponding to model instances in data include two parts, i.e., the hypotheses $\widehat{\theta}_i$ corresponding to the same model instance as θ_i, and the hypotheses $\widetilde{\theta}_i$ corresponding to the remaining model instances in data. For each iteration, the proposed framework can remove $\widehat{\theta}_i$ while preserving $\widetilde{\theta}_i$. That is, for a hypothesis belonging to $\widehat{\theta}_i$, it can be effectively removed because the keypoint correspondences from its sampled subset have high matching scores and most of these keypoint correspondences more likely belong to the inliers of θ_i. Thus, according to Eq. (4), the hypothesis is one of the redundant hypotheses. In contrast, for a hypothesis belonging to $\widetilde{\theta}_i$, the keypoint correspondences from its sampled subset have a low probability to be the inliers of θ_i and it will not be removed.

3.3   The Complete Method

We summarize the proposed SDF method with all the ingredients developed in the previous sections (see Algorithm 2). We first generate superpixels of an image pair with a selected segmentation algorithm. Here, we perform the SLIC segmentation algorithm [18] (which deterministically generates superpixels by using a variant of the k-means clustering algorithm) to obtain superpixels due to its simplicity and effectiveness. Moreover, it can adhere well to the object boundaries in an image with $O(N)$ complexity (where N is the number of pixels). It is worth pointing out that the performance of the proposed method does not greatly depend on the quality of superpixel segmentation. This is because a model instance in data often corresponds to two or more hypotheses based on the grouping cues derived from different superpixels, and the model instance can be estimated from these hypotheses.

The proposed SDF exploits the grouping cues of superpixels to deterministically estimate the parameters of model instances in multi-structure data. SDF includes two main parts, i.e., a deterministic sampling algorithm and a novel "fit-and-remove" framework for model selection. The proposed deterministic sampling algorithm effectively introduces feature appearances (derived from superpixels) to geometric model fitting for hypothesis generation, and the proposed "fit-and-remove" framework takes advantage of the generated high-quality hypotheses. Therefore, the proposed sampling algorithm and the proposed model selection framework are nicely coupled, and they jointly lead to deterministic fitting results. The computational complexity of SDF is approximately proportional to $O(N)$. Among all the steps of the proposed SDF, the step of superpixel segmentation (i.e., step 1) consumes the majority of the computational time of SDF.

Note that GroupSAC [26] also partitions keypoint correspondences into a set of groups. However, the groups partitioned by the proposed SDF are smaller and more accurate than those partitioned by GroupSAC due to the over-segmentation nature in superpixels. In addition, GroupSAC only works for single-structure data with randomized nature, and its performance greatly

---

Algorithm 2. The superpixel-based two-view deterministic fitting method

---

Input: keypoint correspondences, the inlier scale and the number of model instances
T
1: Perform the superpixel segmentation algorithm [18] on a tested image pair.
2: Partition keypoint correspondences into a set of groups $\mathcal{G}$ based on the segmented superpixels (described in Sect. 2).
3: Deterministically generate hypotheses θ by Algorithm 1.
4: **for** $i = 1$ to T **do**
5:   Select a hypothesis θ_i with the largest number of inliers (based on the input inlier scale) from θ as an estimated model instance.
6:   Find the redundant hypotheses $\vartheta_i(= \{\theta_i^j\}_{j=1,2,...})$ with respect to the selected hypothesis θ_i according to Eq. (4).
7:   Remove the selected hypothesis θ_i and the redundant hypotheses ϑ_i from θ, i.e.,
$\theta \leftarrow \theta \setminus \{\vartheta_i \cup \theta_i\}$.
8: **end for**
Output: The parameters of estimated model instances

---

depends on the quality of image segmentation. In contrast, SDF has significant superiority over GroupSAC since SDF can deterministically deal with multi-structure data.

4 Experiments

In this section, we perform homography estimation and fundamental matrix estimation on single-structure and multiple-structure datasets. We compare the proposed SDF with several state-of-the-art model fitting methods, including PROSAC [15], AStar [13] and T-linkage [8]. PROSAC is evaluated since it also considers feature appearances as dose SDF. AStar is one of the state-of-the-art methods for deterministic fitting. However, AStar only works on single-structure data and thus we do not evaluate it in Sect. 4.1. T-linkage is a representative model fitting method that effectively works on multiple-structure data, but it can not work on single-structure data very well due to the outlier rejection process used. Thus we only use it as the competing method on multiple-structure datasets in Sect. 4.2. In addition, we also run RANSAC as a baseline.

For the parameter settings, we use the same inlier scale on each dataset for all the competing methods and also optimize the other parameters of all the competing methods on each dataset for the best performance. All experiments are run on MS Windows 7 with Intel Core i7-3630 CPU 2.4 GHz and 16 GB RAM.

Datasets. The test datasets consist of 20 image pairs: The first 10 image pairs are single-structure datasets and they are tested in Sect. 4.1. The other 10 image pairs are multiple-structure datasets, which are tested in Sect. 4.2. Images, keypoint correspondences and matching scores are acquired from the

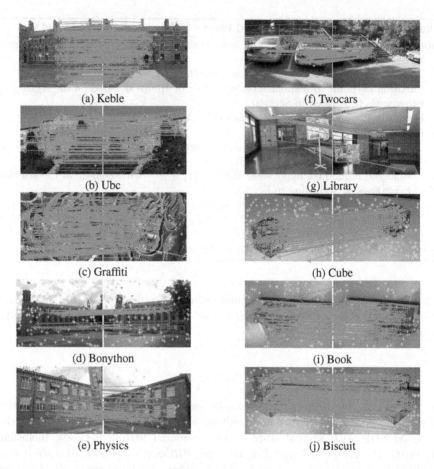

Fig. 5. Fitting results obtained by SDF on 10 image pairs with single-structure data. (a)–(e) show the results obtained by SDF on homography estimation, and (f)–(j) show the results obtained by SDF on fundamental matrix estimation. We do not show the results obtained by the other competing methods due to the space limit.

BLOGS datasets[1], the OXford VGG datasets[2] and the AdelaideRMF datasets[3]. For the image pairs in the BLOGS datasets and the OXford VGG datasets, keypoint correspondences and matching scores are not provided. We detect and match the SIFT keypoints and compute the matching scores using the VLFeat toolbox[4]. The ground truth parameters of structures are provided by the BLOGS datasets and the OXford VGG datasets, based on which, we can manually label the ground truth correspondences. The ground truth keypoint correspondences are provided by the AdelaideRMF datasets.

---

[1] http://www.cse.usf.edu/~sarkar/BLOGS/.

[2] http://www.robots.ox.ac.uk/~vgg/data/.

[3] http://cs.adelaide.edu.au/.

[4] http://www.vlfeat.org/.

Table 1. The Sampson error (and the CPU time in seconds) obtained by the competing methods on single-structure datasets. The best results are boldfaced.

	Homography estimation					Fundamental matrix estimation				
	Keble	Ubc	Graffiti	Bonython	Physics	Twocars	Library	Cube	Book	Biscuit
Inliers (%)	93.85	93.57	69.33	26.26	54.71	61.71	70.37	32.11	56.14	44.24
No. of matches	293	140	212	198	106	128	27	302	187	330
RANSAC	1.71	0.47	1.32	10.76	2.44	0.04	0.01	0.06	0.03	0.14
	(0.29)	(0.31)	(0.30)	(6.45)	(0.43)	(0.10)	(0.07)	(7.38)	(0.19)	(1.30)
PROSAC	1.73	0.46	1.34	9.76	1.46	0.04	0.01	0.06	0.05	0.08
	(0.33)	(0.42)	(0.35)	(6.58)	(0.66)	(0.11)	(0.04)	(8.06)	(0.24)	(1.27)
Astar	**1.69**	0.47	1.31	×	×	**0.03**	0.01	×	×	×
	(15.25)	(1.82)	(7.23)	(> 3600)	(> 3600)	(19.76)	(22.43)	(> 3600)	(> 3600)	(> 3600)
SDF	1.70	**0.45**	**1.28**	**0.32**	**1.45**	**0.03**	**0.00**	**0.05**	**0.01**	**0.04**
	(0.42)	(0.44)	(0.45)	(0.36)	(0.32)	(2.58)	(2.70)	(0.30)	(0.29)	(0.37)

4.1   Single-Structure Data

First, we evaluate the performance of the four fitting methods (i.e., RANSAC, PROSAC, Astar and the proposed SDF) on the 10 image pairs with single-structure data for homography estimation and fundamental matrix estimation. We report the Sampson error as in [11] (we only show the results obtained within 1 h as dose [13]), the computational speed (i.e., the CPU time), the percentage of inliers and the number of keypoint correspondences (matches) on each image pair in Table 1. For RANSAC and PROSAC, we show the average results of 50 repeating experiments due to their randomized nature. For Astar and SDF, we do not repeat experiments due to their deterministic nature. The fitting results obtained by SDF are also shown in Fig. 5.

Homography estimation. From Fig. 5(a)–(e) and Table 1, we can see that all the four methods achieve similar Sampson errors on the image pairs with a high percentage of inliers (i.e., "Keble", "Ubc" and "Graffiti"). However, for the other two image pairs with a low percentage of inliers (i.e., "Bonython" and "Physics"), SDF achieves the lowest Sampson errors. For the computational speed, the methods with the randomized nature (i.e., RANSAC and PROSAC) are faster than SDF on the image pairs with a high percentage of inliers. However, on the image pairs with a low percentage of inliers, SDF is significantly faster. This is because RANSAC and PROSAC cannot generate high-quality hypotheses when data contain a large number of outliers and it is difficult to determine the number of iterations to achieve the desired confidence. Furthermore, SDF shows significant superiority over the other deterministic method (i.e., Astar): Astar takes one order of magnitude more time than SDF on the image pairs with high inlier ratios (i.e., "Keble", "Ubc" and "Graffiti"), and it cannot also yield results within 1 h on the image pairs with low inlier ratios (i.e., "Bonython" and "Physics"). In contrast, SDF obtains results on all image pairs within about 0.32–0.45 s.

Fundamental matrix estimation. From Table 1, we can see that the computational speed of RANSAC and PROSAC increases as the inlier ratio decreases on

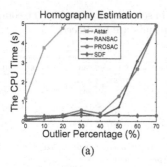
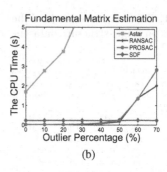

(a)   (b)

Fig. 6. The computational speed of the four methods on two image pairs with different outlier percentages: (a) and (b) show the performance comparison on homography estimation ("Physics") and fundamental matrix estimation ("Book"), respectively.

all the five image pairs. As shown in Fig. 5(f)–(j) and, both methods achieve good results on the image pairs with high inlier ratios (i.e., "Twocars", "Library" and "Book"). However, they are slower than SDF on "Cube" and "Physics" (which have low inlier ratios). Astar achieves low Sampson errors on the image pairs with high inlier ratios, but it cannot yield results within 1 h on the image pairs with high outlier ratios. SDF achieves the lowest Sampson errors on all the five image pairs, and it is much faster than the competing deterministic method (i.e., Astar).

Influence of outlier percentages. We also evaluate the performance of all four methods with different outlier percentages. As shown in Fig. 6, we report the computational speed of the four competing methods on two image pairs with different outlier percentages (the Sampson errors obtained by the four methods are not reported because they are similar). We can see that SDF significantly outperforms the other three methods when the outlier percentage is larger than 50 %. The CPU time of Astar is much higher than that of RANSAC, PROSAC and SDF. The CPU time of RANSAC and PROSAC increases substantially when the outlier percentage is larger than 40 % (for homography estimation) and 50 % (for fundamental matrix estimation). This is because they suffer from the influence of outliers during the process of generating all-inlier subsets. In contrast, the CPU time of SDF has no significant change on both image pairs when the outlier percentage increases, which shows the robustness of SDF to outliers.

Influence of the number of superpixels. Note that, compared with RANSAC and PROSAC, SDF uses an extra parameter for superpixel segmentation, i.e., the number of superpixels (M). Thus, we test the influence of the number of superpixels on the performance of SDF. As shown in Fig. 7, we show the Sampson error and the computational speed of SDF with different numbers of superpixels on six image pairs (three image pairs, i.e., "Keble", "Graffiti" and "Physics", for homography estimation, and the other three image pairs, i.e., "Twocars", "Book" and "Biscuit", for fundamental matrix estimation).

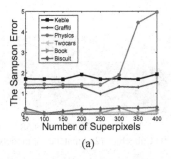

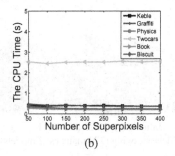

(a)   (b)

Fig. 7. The results of the proposed SDF with different numbers of superpixels on six image pairs.

Table 2. The Sampson error (and the CPU time in seconds) obtained by the competing methods on multiple-structure datasets. The best results are boldfaced.

	Homography estimation					Fundamental matrix estimation				
	D1	D2	D3	D4	D5	D6	D7	D8	D9	D10
RANSAC	1.26	1.12	0.78	3.76	1.55	0.04	0.80	0.41	0.09	4.13
	(1.33)	(57.70)	(11.15)	(3.83)	(3.22)	(20.53)	(21.08)	(23.96)	(37.18)	(27.71)
PROSAC	2.73	1.11	0.87	×	1.48	0.09	0.22	0.29	0.47	6.78
	(2.76)	(33.25)	(19.37)	(> 3600)	(7.84)	(20.92)	(21.39)	(23.92)	(37.81)	(27.97)
T-linkage	**1.02**	**1.09**	0.76	3.75	**1.36**	**0.03**	0.13	0.12	0.11	0.13
	(62.21)	(23.96)	(30.91)	(1508.62)	(233.02)	(45.05)	(22.94)	(31.84)	(53.38)	(33.88)
SDF	1.03	1.11	**0.75**	**3.73**	1.47	**0.03**	**0.11**	**0.10**	**0.07**	**0.04**
	(0.84)	(0.72)	(0.46)	(1.96)	(1.51)	(0.64)	(0.54)	(0.61)	(0.71)	(0.63)

(D1-Oldclassicswing; D2-Elderhalla; D3-Sene; D4-MC3; D5-4B; D6-Cubechips; D7-Breadtoycar; D8-Breadcubechips; D9-Cubebreadtoychips; D10-Breadcartoychips.)

We can see that SDF consistently achieves low Sampson errors on five out of the six image pairs with different numbers of superpixels. However, the Sampson error obtained by SDF dramatically increases on "Physics" when M is larger than 300. The reason behind this is that "Physics" includes few inliers and each group partitioned by SDF includes much less inliers as M becomes larger than 300. In such a case, sampling an all-inlier subset from each group is difficult, and the quality of hypotheses generated by the sampled subsets will affect the fitting results of SDF.

For the computational speed, the result of SDF does not change a lot on all image pairs as M increases. SDF takes more CPU time on "Twocars" than the other five image pairs due to the complex scenario of this image pair (which affects the computational speed of SLIC for superpixel generation). Therefore, we experimentally set the number of superpixels within the range of $[50, 300]$.

4.2   Multiple-Structure Data

In this subsection, we evaluate the performance of the four fitting methods (i.e., RANSAC, PROSAC, T-linkage and SDF) on 10 image pairs with multiple-structure data for homography estimation and fundamental matrix estimation.

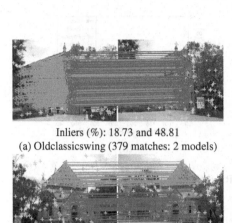

Inliers (%): 18.73 and 48.81
(a) Oldclassicswing (379 matches: 2 models)

Inliers (%):20.07 and 29.58
(f) Cubechips (284 matches: 2 models)

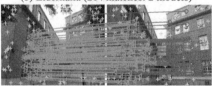

Inliers: 17.76 and 21.50
(b) Elderhalla (214 matches: 2 models)

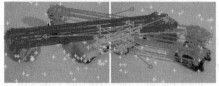

Inliers (%): 20.48, 23.49 and 22.29
(g) Breadtoycar (166 matches: 3 models)

Inliers (%): 18.40 and 34.40
(c) Sene (250 matches: 2 models)

Inliers (%):14.78, 24.78 and 25.22
(h) Breadcubechips (230 matches: 3 models)

Inliers (%): 28.17, 28.17 and 28.17
(d) MC3 (1775 matches: 3 models)

Inliers (%): 11.62, 14.98, 21.71 and 24.77
(i) Cubebreadtoychips (327 matches: 4 models)

Inliers (%): 15.70, 16.09, 17.50 and 29.73
(e) 4B (777 matches: 4 models)

Inliers (%): 9.70, 13.92, 17.30 and 24.47
(j) Breadcartoychips (237 matches: 4 models)

Fig. 8. Fitting results obtained by SDF on 10 image pairs with multiple-structure data. (a)–(e) show the results obtained by SDF on homography estimation, and (f)–(j) show the results obtained by SDF on fundamental matrix estimation. We also report the percentage of inliers for each model instance, the number of model instances and the number of keypoint correspondences (matches) on each image pair. We do not show the results obtained by the other competing methods due to the space limit.

We report the Sampson errors obtained by the competing methods (we only show the results obtained within 1 h) and their computational speed in Table 2. For RANSAC, PROSAC and T-linkage, we show the average results of 50 repeating experiments due to their randomized nature. The fitting results obtained by SDF are also shown in Fig. 8.

Homography estimation. From Fig. 8(a)–(e) and Table 2, we can see that RANSAC achieves low Sampson errors on all five image pairs, but it is much slower than SDF. This is more obvious on the image pairs with low inlier ratios (e.g., SDF is about 80.13 times faster than RANSAC on "Elderhalla"). PROSAC succeeds in fitting four image pairs, but it fails in fitting "MC3" since it cannot sample non-degenerate subsets within 1 h. T-linkage achieves the lowest Sampson errors on 3 out of 5 image pairs, but it suffers from high computational complexity due to a large number of keypoint correspondences used during the agglomerative clustering procedure (e.g., SDF is 769.70 times faster than T-linkage on "MC3"). In contrast, SDF achieves the fastest computational speed among the four fitting methods for all five image pairs: SDF is about 1.58–80.14 times faster than RANSAC, and it is about 3.2 times ~ three order of magnitude faster than PROSAC, and about one to two order of magnitude faster than T-linkage.

Fundamental matrix estimation. From Fig. 8(f)–(j) and Table 2, we can see that both RANSAC and PROSAC need much time to determine the number of iterations to achieve high confidence on all five image pairs. This is because that it is difficult for them to sample all-inlier subsets when a dataset has a high outlier percentage and the estimation needs to sample a large number of subsets. T-linkage achieves lower Sampson errors than RANSAC and PROSAC due to its robustness to outliers. However, SDF achieves the lowest Sampson error for all the five image pairs, and it is much faster than the other three fitting methods (about 32.08–52.37 times faster than RANSAC, and about 32.69–53.25 times faster than PROSAC, and 42.48–75.18 times faster than T-linkage). The results show the effectiveness of SDF for fitting multiple-structure data.

5   Conclusions

In this paper, we propose a simple but effective determinstic fitting method (SDF) that introduces prior information of feature appearance to geometric model fitting. We show that prior information of feature appearance (derived from superpixels) can provide powerful grouping cues for the proposed deterministic sampling algorithm to generate consistent hypotheses, where keypoint correspondences with high matching scores are selected as sampled subsets. The generated hypotheses contain a high percentage of good hypotheses with a small percentage of bad hypotheses. Based on the advantage of the generated hypotheses, a novel fit-and-remove framework is proposed for model selection. SDF effectively combines hypothesis generation and model selection to deterministically deal with the two-view model fitting problems.

Acknowledgments. This work was supported by the National Natural Science Foundation of China under Grants 61472334 and 61571379. David Suter acknowledged funding under ARC DPDP130102524.

References

1. Fischler, M.A., Bolles, R.C.: Random sample consensus: a paradigm for model fitting with applications to image analysis and automated cartography. Comm. ACM **24**(6), 381–395 (1981)
2. Mittal, S., Anand, S., Meer, P.: Generalized projection-based m-estimator. IEEE Trans. PAMI **34**(12), 2351–2364 (2012)
3. Li, Z., Cheong, L.F., Zhou, S.Z.: Scams: simultaneous clustering and model selection. In: CVPR, pp. 264–271 (2014)
4. Liu, H., Yan, S.: Efficient structure detection via random consensus graph. In: CVPR, pp. 574–581 (2012)
5. Isack, H., Boykov, Y.: Energy-based geometric multi-model fitting. IJCV **97**(2), 123–147 (2012)
6. Isack, H., Boykov, Y.: Energy based multi-model fitting & matching for 3d reconstruction. In: CVPR, pp. 1146–1153 (2014)
7. Jaberi, M., Pensky, M., Foroosh, H.: Swift: sparse withdrawal of inliers in a first trial. In: CVPR, pp. 4849–4857 (2015)
8. Magri, L., Fusiello, A.: T-linkage: a continuous relaxation of j-linkage for multimodel fitting. In: CVPR, pp. 3954–3961 (2014)
9. Lee, K.H., Lee, S.W.: Deterministic fitting of multiple structures using iterative maxfs with inlier scale estimation. In: ICCV, pp. 41–48 (2013)
10. Li, H.: Consensus set maximization with guaranteed global optimality for robust geometry estimation. In: ICCV, pp. 1074–1080 (2009)
11. Litman, R., Korman, S., Bronstein, A., Avidan, S.: Inverting ransac: global model detection via inlier rate estimation. In: CVPR, pp. 5243–5251 (2015)
12. Fredriksson, J., Larsson, V., Olsson, C.: Practical robust two-view translation estimation. In: CVPR, pp. 2684–2690 (2015)
13. Chin, T.J., Purkait, P., Eriksson, A., Suter, D.: Efficient globally optimal consensus maximisation with tree search. In: CVPR, pp. 2413–2421 (2015)
14. Hart, P.E., Nilsson, N.J., Raphael, B.: A formal basis for the heuristic determination of minimum cost paths. IEEE Trans. Syst. Sci. Cybern. **4**(2), 100–107 (1968)
15. Chum, O., Matas, J.: Matching with prosac-progressive sample consensus. In: CVPR, pp. 220–226 (2005)
16. Serradell, E., Özuysal, M., Lepetit, V., Fua, P., Moreno-Noguer, F.: Combining geometric and appearance priors for robust homography estimation. In: Daniilidis, K., Maragos, P., Paragios, N. (eds.) ECCV 2010. LNCS, vol. 6313, pp. 58–72. Springer, Heidelberg (2010). doi:10.1007/978-3-642-15558-1_5
17. Kohli, P., Ladick, L., Torr, P.H.S.: Robust higher order potentials for enforcing label consistency. IJCV **82**(3), 302–324 (2009)
18. Achanta, R., Shaji, A., Smith, K., Lucchi, A., Fua, P., Susstrunk, S.: Slic superpixels compared to state-of-the-art superpixel methods. IEEE Trans. PAMI **34**(11), 2274–2282 (2012)
19. Shen, J., Du, Y., Wang, W., Li, X.: Lazy random walks for superpixel segmentation. IEEE Trans. IP **23**(4), 1451–1462 (2014)
20. Wong, H.S., Chin, T.J., Yu, J., Suter, D.: Dynamic and hierarchical multi-structure geometric model fitting. In: ICCV, pp. 1044–1051 (2011)

21. Tran, Q.H., Chin, T.J., Chojnacki, W., Suter, D.: Sampling minimal subsets with large spans for robust estimation. IJCV **106**(1), 93–112 (2014)
22. Lowe, D.G.: Distinctive image features from scale-invariant keypoints. IJCV **60**(2), 91–110 (2004)
23. Brahmachari, A.S., Sarkar, S.: Hop-diffusion monte carlo for epipolar geometry estimation between very wide-baseline images. IEEE Trans. PAMI **35**(3), 755–762 (2013)
24. Tennakoon, R., Bab-Hadiashar, A., Cao, Z., Hoseinnezhad, R., Suter, D.: Robust model fitting using higher than minimal subset sampling. IEEE Trans. PAMI **37**(9), 1–14 (2015)
25. Wang, H., Chin, T.J., Suter, D.: Simultaneously fitting and segmenting multiple-structure data with outliers. IEEE Trans. PAMI **34**(6), 1177–1192 (2012)
26. Ni, K., Jin, H., Dellaert, F.: Groupsac: efficient consensus in the presence of groupings. In: ICCV, pp. 2193–2200 (2009)

Instance-Sensitive Fully Convolutional Networks

Jifeng Dai[1]([✉]), Kaiming He[1], Yi Li[2], Shaoqing Ren[3], and Jian Sun[1]

[1] Microsoft Research, Beijing, China
jifdai@microsoft.com
[2] Tsinghua University, Beijing, China
[3] University of Science and Technology of China, Hefei, China

Abstract. Fully convolutional networks (FCNs) have been proven very successful for semantic segmentation, but the FCN outputs are unaware of object instances. In this paper, we develop FCNs that are capable of proposing instance-level segment candidates. In contrast to the previous FCN that generates one score map, our FCN is designed to compute a small set of *instance-sensitive* score maps, each of which is the outcome of a pixel-wise classifier of a relative position to instances. On top of these instance-sensitive score maps, a simple assembling module is able to output instance candidate at each position. In contrast to the recent DeepMask method for segmenting instances, our method does not have any high-dimensional layer related to the mask resolution, but instead exploits image local coherence for estimating instances. We present competitive results of instance segment proposal on both PASCAL VOC and MS COCO.

1 Introduction

Fully convolutional networks (FCN) [1] have been proven an effective end-to-end solution to semantic image segmentation. An FCN produces a score map of a size proportional to the input image, where every pixel represents a classifier of objects. Despite good accuracy and ease of usage, FCNs are not directly applicable for producing instance segments (Fig. 1 (top)). Previous instance semantic segmentation methods (*e.g.*, [2–5]) in general resorted to off-the-shelf segment proposal methods (*e.g.*, [6,7]).

In this paper, we develop an end-to-end fully convolutional network that is capable of segmenting candidate instances. Like the FCN in [1], in our method *every pixel still represents a classifier*; but unlike an FCN that generates one score map (for one object category), our method computes a set of *instance-sensitive* score maps, where each pixel is a classifier of *relative positions* to an object instance (Fig. 1 (bottom)). For example, with a 3×3 regular grid depicting relative positions, we produce a set of 9 score maps in which, *e.g.*, the map #6

This work was done when Yi Li and Shaoqing Ren were interns at Microsoft Research.

B. Leibe et al. (Eds.): ECCV 2016, Part VI, LNCS 9910, pp. 534–549, 2016.
DOI: 10.1007/978-3-319-46466-4_32

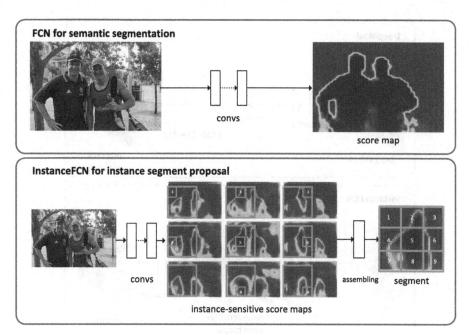

Fig. 1. Methodological comparisons between: (**top**) FCN [1] for semantic segmentation; (**bottom**) our InstanceFCN for instance segment proposal.

in Fig. 1 has high scores on the "right side" of object instances. With this set of score maps, we are able to generate an object instance segment in each sliding window by *assembling* the output from the score maps. This procedure enables a fully convolutional way of producing segment instances.

Most related to our method, *DeepMask* [8] is an instance segment proposal method driven by convolutional networks. DeepMask learns a function that maps an image sliding window to an m^2-d vector representing an $m \times m$-resolution mask (*e.g.*, $m = 56$). This is computed by an m^2-d *fully-connected* (*fc*) layer. See Fig. 2. Even though DeepMask can be implemented in a fully convolutional way (as at inference time in [8]) by recasting this *fc* layer into a convolutional layer with m^2-d outputs, it fundamentally differs from the FCNs in [1] where each output pixel is a *low-dimensional* classifier. Unlike DeepMask, our method has no layer whose size is related to the mask size m^2, and each pixel in our method is a low-dimensional classifier. This is made possible by exploiting *local coherence* [9] of natural images for generating per-window pixel-wise predictions. We will discuss and compare with DeepMask in depth.

On the PASCAL VOC [10] and MS COCO [11] benchmarks, our method yields compelling instance segment proposal results, comparing favorably with a series of proposal methods [6,8,12]. Thanks to the small size of the layer for predicting masks, our model trained on the small PASCAL VOC dataset exhibits good accuracy with less risk of overfitting. In addition, our system also shows

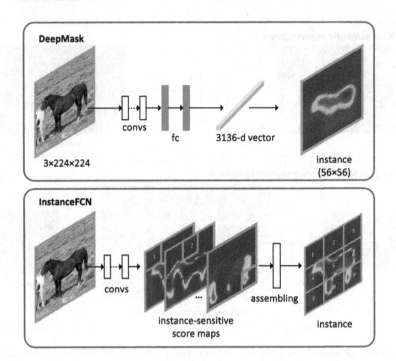

Fig. 2. Methodological comparisons between DeepMask [8] and InstanceFCN for instance segment proposal. DeepMask uses a high-dimensional m^2-d fc layer to generate an instance, $e.g.$, $m = 56$ and $m^2 = 3136$. Our network has no any m^2-d layer.

competitive results for instance semantic segmentation when used with downstream classifiers. Our method, dubbed *InstanceFCN*, shows that segmenting instances can still be addressed by the FCN fashion in [1], filling a missing piece among the broad applications of FCNs.

2   Related Work

The general concept of fully convolutional models dates back to at least two decades ago [13]. For convolutional neural networks (CNNs) [14,15], a sliding window (or referred to as a patch or crop) is not necessarily run on the image domain but instead is run on a feature map, which can be recast into convolutional filters on that feature map. These fully convolutional models are naturally applicable for image restoration problems, such as denoising [16], super-resolution [17], and others [18], where each output pixel is a real-number regressor of intensity values.

Recently FCNs [1] have shown compelling quality and efficiency for semantic segmentation. In [1], each output pixel is a classifier corresponding to the receptive field of the network. The networks can thus be trained end-to-end, pixel-to-pixel, given the category-wise semantic segmentation annotation. But this method can not distinguish object instances (Fig. 1).

Operated fully convolutionally, the Region Proposal Network (RPN) in Faster R-CNN [19] is developed for proposing box-level instances. In an RPN, each pixel of the output map represents a bounding box regressor and an objectness classifier. The RPN does not generate mask-level proposals. In [20], the RPN boxes are used for regressing segmentation masks, conducted by an *fc* layer on Region-of-Interest (RoI) pooling features [21].

3   Instance-Sensitive FCNs for Segment Proposal

3.1   From FCN to InstanceFCN

Although the original FCN [1] for semantic segmentation produces no explicit instance, we can still think of some special cases in which such an FCN can do *a good job* generating an instance. Let's consider an image that contains only one object instance. In this case, the original FCN can produce a good mask about this object category, and because there is only one instance, this is also a good mask about this object instance. In this procedure, the FCN does not have any pre-define filters that are dependent on the mask resolution/size (say, $m \times m$).

Next let's consider an image that contains two object instances that are close to each other (Fig. 1(top)). Although now the FCN output (Fig. 1(top)) does not distinguish the two instances, we notice that the output is indeed *reusable for most pixels*, except for those where one object is conjunct the other — *e.g.*, when the "right side" of the left instance is conjunct the "left side" of the right instance (Fig. 1). If we can discriminate "right side" from "left side", we can still rely on FCN-like score maps to generate instances.

Instance-Sensitive Score Maps. The above analysis motivates us to introduce the concept of *relative positions* into FCNs. Ideally, relative positions are with respect to object instances, such as the "right side" of an object or the "left side" of an object. In contrast to the original FCN [1] where each output pixel is a classifier of an object category, we propose an FCN where each output pixel is *a classifier of relative positions of instances*. For example, for the #4 score map in Fig. 1 (bottom), each pixel is a classifier of being or not being "left side" of an instance.

In our practice, we define the relative positions using a $k \times k$ (*e.g.*, $k = 3$) regular grid on a square sliding window (Fig. 1 (bottom)). This leads to a set of k^2 (*e.g.*, 9) score maps which are our FCN outputs. We call them *instance-sensitive score maps*. The network architecture for producing these score maps can be trained end-to-end, with the help of the following module.

Instance Assembling Module. The instance-sensitive score maps have not yet produced object instances. But we can simply assemble instances from these maps. We slide a window of resolution $m \times m$ on the set of instance-sensitive score maps (Fig. 1 (bottom)). In this sliding window, each $\frac{m}{k} \times \frac{m}{k}$ sub-window directly copies values from the same sub-window in the corresponding score map. The k^2 sub-windows are then put together (according to their relative positions) to assemble a new window of resolution $m \times m$. This is the instance assembled from this sliding window.

This instance assembling module is adopted for both training and inference. During training, this model generates instances from sparsely sampled sliding windows, which are compared to the ground truth. During inference, we densely slide a window on the feature maps to predict an instance segment at each position. More details are in the algorithm section.

We remark that the assembling module is *the only component* in our architecture that involves the mask resolution $m \times m$. Nevertheless, the assembling module has no network parameter to be learned. It is inexpensive because it only has copy-and-paste operations. This module impacts training as it is used for computing the loss function.

3.2   Local Coherence

Next we analyze our method from the perspective of *local coherence* [9]. By local coherence we mean that for a pixel in a natural image, its prediction is most likely the same when evaluated in two neighboring windows. One does not need to completely re-compute the predictions when a window is shifted by a small step.

The local coherence property has been exploited by our method. For a window that slides by one stride (Fig. 3 (bottom)), the same pixel in the image coordinate system will have the same prediction because it is copied from the same score map (except for a few pixels near the partitioning of relative positions). This allows us to conserve a large number of parameters when the mask resolution m^2 is high.

This is in contrast to DeepMask's [8] mechanism which is based on a "sliding fc layer" (Fig. 3 (top)). In DeepMask, when the window is shifted by one stride, the same pixel in the image coordinate system is predicted by two different channels of the fc layer, as shown in Fig. 3 (top). So the prediction of this pixel is in general not the same when evaluated in two neighboring windows.

By exploiting local coherence, our network layers' sizes and dimensions are all independent of the mask resolution $m \times m$, in contrast to DeepMask. This not only reduces the computational cost of the mask prediction layers, but more importantly, reduces the number of parameters required for mask regression, leading to less risk of overfitting on small datasets such as PASCAL VOC. In the experiment section we show that our mask prediction layer can have hundreds times fewer parameters than DeepMask.

3.3   Algorithm and Implementation

Next we describe the network architecture, training algorithm, and inference algorithm of our method.

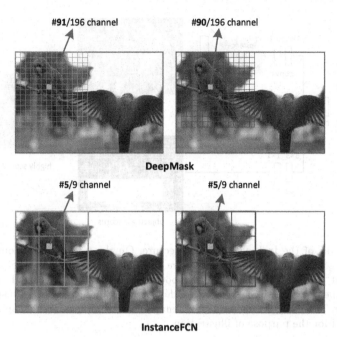

Fig. 3. Our method can exploit image *local coherence*. For a window shifted by one small step (from blue to red), our method can reuse the same prediction from the same score map at that pixel. This is not the case if the masks are produced by a sliding m^2-dimensional fc layer (for illustration $m = 14$ in this figure) (Color figure online).

Network Architecture. As common practice, we use the VGG-16 network [22] pre-trained on ImageNet [23] as the feature extractor. The 13 convolutional layers in VGG-16 are applied fully convolutionally on an input image of arbitrary size. We follow the practice in [24] to reduce the network stride and increase feature map resolution: the max pooling layer pool$_4$ (between conv$_{4\_3}$ and conv$_{5\_1}$) is modified to have a stride of 1 instead of 2, and accordingly the filters in conv$_{5\_1}$ to conv$_{5\_3}$ are adjusted by the "hole algorithm" [24]. Using this modified VGG network, the effective stride of the conv$_{5\_3}$ feature map is $s = 8$ pixels *w.r.t.* the input image. We note that this reduced stride directly determines the resolutions of our score maps from which our masks are copied and assembled.

On top of the feature map, there are two fully convolutional branches, one for estimating segment instances and the other for scoring the instances. For the first branch, we adopt a 1×1 512-d convolutional layer (with ReLU [25]) to transform the features, and then use a 3×3 convolutional layer to generate a set of instance-sensitive score maps. With a $k\times k$ regular grid for describing relative positions, this last convolutional layer has k^2 output channels corresponding to the set of k^2 instance-sensitive score maps. See the top branch in Fig. 4. On top of these score maps, an assembling module is used to generate object instances

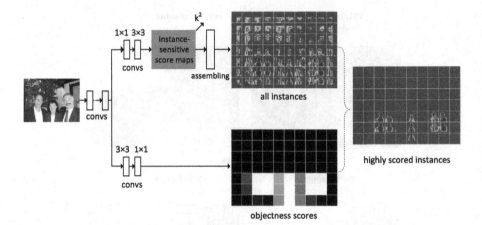

Fig. 4. Details of the InstanceFCN architecture. On the top is a fully convolutional branch for generating k^2 instance-sensitive score maps, followed by the assembling module that outputs instances. On the bottom is a fully convolutional branch for predicting the objectness score of each window. The highly scored output instances are on the right. In this figure, the objectness map and the "all instances" map have been sub-sampled for the purpose of illustration.

in a sliding window of a resolution $m \times m$. We use $m = 21$ pixels (on the feature map with a stride of 8).

For the second branch of scoring instances (bottom in Fig. 4), we use a 3×3 512-d convolutional layer (with ReLU) followed by a 1×1 convolutional layer. This 1×1 layer is a per-pixel logistic regression for classifying instance/not-instance of the sliding window centered at this pixel. The output of this branch is thus an objectness score map (Fig. 4 (bottom)), in which one score corresponds to one sliding window that generates one instance.

Training. Our network is trained end-to-end. We adopt the *image-centric* strategy in [19,21]. The forward pass computes the set of instance-sensitive score maps and the objectness score map. After that, a set of 256 sliding windows are randomly sampled [19,21], and the instances are only assembled from these 256 windows for computing the loss function. The loss function is defined as:

$$\sum_i (\mathcal{L}(p_i, p_i^*) + \sum_j \mathcal{L}(S_{i,j}, S_{i,j}^*)). \tag{1}$$

Here i is the index of a sampled window, p_i is the predicted objectness score of the instance in this window, and p_i^* is 1 if this window is a positive sample and 0 if a negative sample. S_i is the assembled segment instance in this window, S_i^* is the ground truth segment instance, and j is the pixel index in the window. $\mathcal{L}$ is the logistic regression loss. We use the definition of positive/negative samples in [8], and the 256 sampled windows have a positive/negative sampling ratio of 1:1 [19].

Our model accepts images of arbitrary size as input. We follow the scale jittering in [26] for training: a training image is resized such that its shorter side is randomly sampled from $600 \times 1.5^{\{-4,-3,-2,-1,0,1\}}$ pixels. We use Stochastic Gradient Descent (SGD) as the solver. A total of 40k iterations are performed, with a learning rate of 0.001 for the first 32k and 0.0001 for the last 8k. We perform training with an 8-GPU implementation, where each GPU holds 1 image with 256 sampled windows (so the effective mini-batch size is 8 images). The weight decay is 0.0005 and the momentum is 0.9. The first thirteen convolutional layers are initialized by the ImageNet pre-trained VGG-16 [22], and the extra convolutional layers are randomly initialized from a Gaussian distribution with zero mean and standard derivation of 0.01.

Inference. A forward pass of the network is run on the input image, generating the instance-sensitive score maps and the objectness score map. The assembling module then applies densely sliding windows on these maps to produce a segment instance at each position. Each instance is associated with a score from the objectness score map. To handle multiple scales, we resize the shorter side of images to $600 \times 1.5^{\{-4,-3,-2,-1,0,1\}}$ pixels, and compute all instances at each scale. It takes totally 1.5 s evaluating an images on a K40 GPU.

For each output segment, we truncate the values to form a binary mask. Then we adopt non-maximum suppression (NMS) to generate the final set of segment proposals. The NMS is based on the objectness scores and the box-level IoU given by the tight bounding boxes of the binary masks. We use a threshold of 0.8 for the NMS. After NMS, the top-N ranked segment proposals are used as the output.

4 Experiments

4.1 Experiments on PASCAL VOC 2012

We first conduct experiments on PASCAL VOC 2012 [10]. Following [3,4], we use the segmentation annotations from [27], and train the models on the training set and evaluate on the validation set. All segment proposal methods are evaluated by the mask-level intersection-over-union (IoU) between the predicted instances and the ground-truth instances. Following [8], we measure the Average Recall (AR) [28] (between IoU thresholds of 0.5 to 1.0) at a fixed number N of proposals, denoted as "AR@N". In [28], the AR metrics have been shown to be more correlated to the detection accuracy (when used with downstream classifiers [2,21]) than traditional metrics for evaluating proposals.

Ablations on the Number of Relative Positions k^2. Table 1 shows our results using different values of k^2. Our method is not sensitive to k^2, and can perform well even when $k = 3$. Figure 5 shows some examples of the instance-sensitive maps and assembled instances for $k = 3$.

Table 1. Ablation experiments on the numbers of instance-sensitive score maps (*i.e.*, # of relative positions, k^2), evaluated on the PASCAL VOC 2012 validation set.

k^2	AR@10 (%)	AR@100 (%)	AR@1000 (%)
3^2	38.3	49.2	52.1
5^2	_38.9_	_49.7_	52.6
7^2	38.8	_49.7_	_52.7_

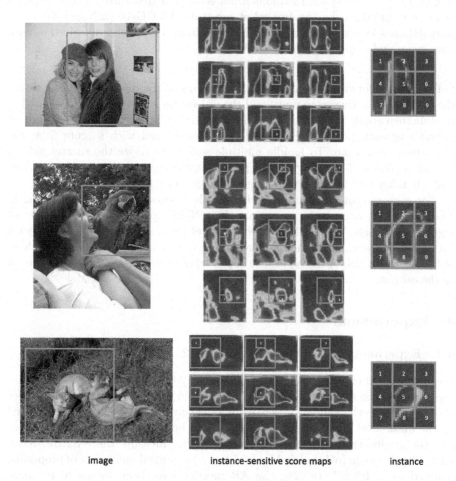

image   instance-sensitive score maps   instance

Fig. 5. Examples of instance-sensitive maps and assembled instances on the PASCAL VOC validation set. For simplicity we only show the cases of $k = 3$ (9 instance-sensitive score maps) in this figure.

Table 1 also shows that our results of $k = 5$ and $k = 7$ are comparable, and are slightly better than the $k = 3$ baseline. Our method enjoys a small gain with a finer division of relative position, but gets saturated around $k = 5$. In the following experiments we use $k = 5$.

Ablation Comparisons with the DeepMask Scheme. For fair comparisons, we implement a DeepMask baseline on PASCAL VOC. Specifically, the network structure is VGG-16 followed by an extra 512-d 1×1 convolutional layer [8], generating a 14×14 feature map as in [8] from a 224×224 image crop. Then a 512-d *fc* layer [8] is applied to this feature map, followed by a 56^2-d *fc* [8] for generating a 56×56-resolution mask. The two *fc* layers under this setting have 53M parameters[1]. The objectness scoring branch is constructed as in [8]. All other settings are the same as ours for fair comparisons. We refer to this model as ~**DeepMask** which means our implementation of DeepMask. This baseline's results are in Table 2.

Table 2 shows the ablation comparisons. As the first variant, we train our model on 224×224 crops as is done in DeepMask. Under this ablative training, our method still outperforms ~DeepMask by healthy margins. When trained on full-size images (Table 2), our result is further improved. The gain from training on full-size images further demonstrates the benefits of our fully convolutional scheme.

It is noteworthy that our method has considerably fewer parameters. Our last k^2-d convolutional layer has only 0.1M parameters[2] (all other layers being the same as the DeepMask counterpart). This mask generation layer has only 1/500 of parameters comparing with DeepMask's *fc* layers. Regressing high-dimensional $m \times m$ masks is possible for our method as it exploits local coherence. We also expect fewer parameters to have less risk of overfitting.

Table 2. Ablation comparisons between ~DeepMask and our method on the PASCAL VOC 2012 validation set. "~DeepMask" is our implementation based on controlled settings (see more descriptions in the main text).

Method	Train	Test	AR@10 (%)	AR@100 (%)	AR@1000 (%)
~DeepMask	crop 224×224	sliding *fc*	31.2	42.9	47.0
Ours	crop 224×224	fully conv.	37.4	48.4	51.4
	fully conv.	fully conv.	**38.9**	**49.7**	**52.6**

Comparisons with State-of-the-Art Segment Proposal Methods. In Table 3 and Fig. 6 we compare with state-of-the-art segment proposal methods: Selective Search (SS) [6], Multiscale Combinatorial Grouping (MCG) [12], ~DeepMask, and Multi-task Network Cascade (MNC) [20]. MNC is a joint multi-stage cascade method that proposes box-level regions, regresses masks from these

---

[1] $512 \times 14 \times 14 \times 512 + 512 \times 56^2 = 53M$.
[2] $512 \times 3 \times 3 \times 25 = 0.1M$.

Table 3. Comparisons with state-of-the-art segment proposal methods on the PASCAL VOC 2012 validation set. The results of SS [6] and MCG [12] are from the publicly available code, and the results of MNC [20] is provided by the authors of [20].

Method	AR@10 (%)	AR@100 (%)	AR@1000 (%)
SS [6]	7.0	23.5	43.3
MCG [12]	18.9	36.8	49.5
~DeepMask	31.2	42.9	47.0
MNC [20]	33.4	48.5	**53.8**
Ours	**38.9**	**49.7**	52.6

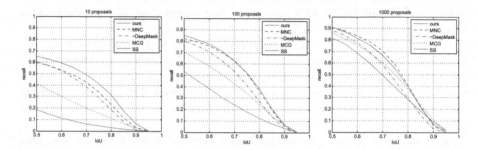

Fig. 6. Recall *vs.* IoU curves of different segment proposals on the PASCAL VOC 2012 validation set. AR is the area under the curves.

Table 4. Semantic instance segmentation on the PASCAL VOC 2012 validation set. All methods are based on VGG-16 except SDS based on AlexNet [15].

Downstream classifier	Proposals	mAP@0.5 (%)	mAP@0.7 (%)
SDS [3]	MCG [7]	49.7	25.3
Hypercolumn [4]	MCG [7]	60.0	40.4
CFM [5]	MCG [7]	60.7	39.6
MNC [20]	MNC [20]	**63.5**	41.5
MNC [20]	**ours**	61.5	**43.0**

regions, and classifies these mask. With a trained MNC, we treat the mask regression outputs as the segment proposals.

Table 3 and Fig. 6 show that the CNN-based methods (~DeepMask, MNC, ours) perform better than the bottom-up segmentation methods of SS and MCG. In addition, our method has AR@100 and AR@1000 similar to MNC, but has 5.5 % higher AR@10. The mask regression of MNC is done by high-dimensional *fc* layers, in contrast to our fully convolutional fashion.

Comparisons on Instance Semantic Segmentation. Next we evaluate the instance semantic segmentation performance when used with downstream

Table 5. Comparisons of instance segment proposals on the first 5k images [8] from the MS COCO validation set. DeepMask's results are from [8].

Segment proposals	AR@10 (%)	AR@100 (%)	AR@1000 (%)
GOP [29]	2.3	12.3	25.3
Rigor [30]	-	9.4	25.3
SS [6]	2.5	9.5	23.0
MCG [7]	7.7	18.6	29.9
DeepMask [8]	12.6	24.5	33.1
DeepMaskZoom [8]	12.7	26.1	36.6
Ours	**16.6**	**31.7**	**39.2**

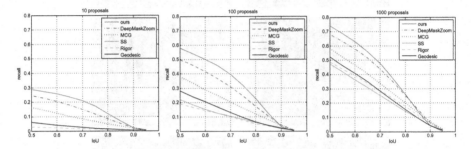

Fig. 7. Recall *vs.* IoU curves on the first 5k images [8] on the MS COCO validation set. DeepMask's curves are from [8].

category-aware classifiers. Following [3,4], we evaluate mean Average Precision (mAP) using mask-level IoU at threshold of 0.5 and 0.7. In Table 4 we compare with: SDS [3], Hypercolumn [4], CFM [5], and MNC [20]. We use MNC's stage 3 as our classifier structure, which is similar to Fast R-CNN [21] except that its RoI pooling layer is replaced with an RoI masking layer that generates features from the segment proposals. We adopt a two-step training: first train our model for proposing segments and then train the classifier with the given proposals. Our method uses $N = 300$ proposals in this comparison.

Table 4 shows that among all the competitors our method has the highest mAP@0.7 score of 43.0 %, which is 1.5 % better than the closest competitor. Our method has the second best mAP@0.5, lower than MNC. We note that MNC is a joint training algorithm which simultaneously learns proposals and category classifiers. Our result (61.5 %) is based on two-step training, and is better than MNC's step-by-step training counterpart (60.2 % [20]).

4.2   Experiments on MS COCO

Finally we evaluate instance segment proposals on the MS COCO benchmark [11]. Following [8], we train our network on the 80k training images

546   J. Dai et al.

DeepMask   InstanceFCN

Fig. 8. Comparisons with DeepMask [8] on the MS COCO validation set. **Left**: Deep-Mask, taken from the paper of [8]. Proposals with highest IoU to the ground truth are displayed. *The missed ground-truth objects (no proposals with IoU > 0.5) are marked by red outlines filled with white.* **Right**: Our results displayed in the same way. (Color figure online)

and evaluate on the first 5k validation images. The results are in Table 5 (Deep-Mask's results are reported from [8]). For fair comparisons, we use the same multiple scales used in [8] for training and testing on COCO. Our method has higher AR scores than DeepMask and a DeepMaskZoom variant [8]. Figures 7, 8 and 9 show the recall *vs.* IoU curves on COCO.

Fig. 9. More examples of our results on the MS COCO validation set, displayed in the same way of Fig. 8 (*the missed ground-truth objects are marked by red outlines filled with white*). (Color figure online)

5   Conclusion

We have presented InstanceFCN, a fully convolutional scheme for proposing segment instances. It is driven by classifying pixels based on their relative positions, which leads to a set of instance-sensitive score maps. A simple assembling module is then able to generate segment instances from these score maps. Our network architecture handles instance segmentation without using any high-dimensional layers that depend on the mask resolution. We expect our novel design of fully convolutional models will further extend the family of FCNs.

References

1. Long, J., Shelhamer, E., Darrell, T.: Fully convolutional networks for semantic segmentation. In: CVPR (2015)

2. Girshick, R., Iandola, F., Darrell, T., Malik, J.: Deformable part models are convolutional neural networks. arXiv preprint arXiv:1409.5403 (2014)
3. Hariharan, B., Arbeláez, P., Girshick, R., Malik, J.: Simultaneous detection and segmentation. In: Fleet, D., Pajdla, T., Schiele, B., Tuytelaars, T. (eds.) ECCV 2014, Part VII. LNCS, vol. 8695, pp. 297–312. Springer, Heidelberg (2014)
4. Hariharan, B., Arbeláez, P., Girshick, R., Malik, J.: Hypercolumns for object segmentation and fine-grained localization. In: CVPR (2015)
5. Dai, J., He, K., Sun, J.: Convolutional feature masking for joint object and stuff segmentation. In: CVPR (2015)
6. Uijlings, J.R., van de Sande, K.E., Gevers, T., Smeulders, A.W.: Selective search for object recognition. IJCV 104(2), 154–171 (2013)
7. Arbeláez, P., Pont-Tuset, J., Barron, J.T., Marques, F., Malik, J.: Multiscale combinatorial grouping. In: CVPR (2014)
8. Pinheiro, P.O., Collobert, R., Dollar, P.: Learning to segment object candidates. In: NIPS (2015)
9. Barnes, C., Shechtman, E., Finkelstein, A., Goldman, D.: Patchmatch: a randomized correspondence algorithm for structural image editing. ACM Trans. Graph. (2009)
10. Everingham, M., Van Gool, L., Williams, C.K., Winn, J., Zisserman, A.: The PASCAL visual object classes (VOC) challenge. IJCV 88(2), 303–338 (2010)
11. Lin, T.-Y., Maire, M., Belongie, S., Hays, J., Perona, P., Ramanan, D., Dollár, P., Zitnick, C.L.: Microsoft COCO: common objects in context. In: Fleet, D., Pajdla, T., Schiele, B., Tuytelaars, T. (eds.) ECCV 2014, Part V. LNCS, vol. 8693, pp. 740–755. Springer, Heidelberg (2014)
12. Agrawal, P., Girshick, R., Malik, J.: Analyzing the performance of multilayer neural networks for object recognition. In: Fleet, D., Pajdla, T., Schiele, B., Tuytelaars, T. (eds.) ECCV 2014, Part VII. LNCS, vol. 8695, pp. 329–344. Springer, Heidelberg (2014)
13. Matan, O., Burges, C.J., Le Cun, Y., Denker, J.S.: Multi-digit recognition using a space displacement neural network. In: NIPS (1992)
14. LeCun, Y., Boser, B., Denker, J.S., Henderson, D., Howard, R.E., Hubbard, W., Jackel, L.D.: Backpropagation applied to handwritten zip code recognition. Neural Comput. 1(4), 541–551 (1989)
15. Krizhevsky, A., Sutskever, I., Hinton, G.E.: Imagenet classification with deep convolutional neural networks. In: NIPS (2012)
16. Jain, V., Seung, S.: Natural image denoising with convolutional networks. In: NIPS (2008)
17. Dong, C., Loy, C.C., He, K., Tang, X.: Learning a deep convolutional network for image super-resolution. In: Fleet, D., Pajdla, T., Schiele, B., Tuytelaars, T. (eds.) ECCV 2014, Part IV. LNCS, vol. 8692, pp. 184–199. Springer, Heidelberg (2014)
18. Eigen, D., Krishnan, D., Fergus, R.: Restoring an image taken through a window covered with dirt or rain. In: ICCV (2013)
19. Ren, S., He, K., Girshick, R., Sun, J.: Faster R-CNN: towards real-time object detection with region proposal networks. In: NIPS (2015)
20. Dai, J., He, K., Sun, J.: Instance-aware semantic segmentation via multi-task network cascades. In: CVPR (2016)
21. Girshick, R.: Fast R-CNN. In: ICCV (2015)
22. Simonyan, K., Zisserman, A.: Very deep convolutional networks for large-scale image recognition. In: ICLR (2015)

23. Russakovsky, O., Deng, J., Su, H., Krause, J., Satheesh, S., Ma, S., Huang, Z., Karpathy, A., Khosla, A., Bernstein, M., et al.: Imagenet large scale visual recognition challenge. arXiv:1409.0575 (2014)
24. Chen, L.C., Papandreou, G., Kokkinos, I., Murphy, K., Yuille, A.L.: Semantic image segmentation with deep convolutional nets and fully connected crfs. In: ICLR (2015)
25. Nair, V., Hinton, G.E.: Rectified linear units improve restricted boltzmann machines (2010)
26. He, K., Zhang, X., Ren, S., Sun, J.: Spatial pyramid pooling in deep convolutional networks for visual recognition. In: Fleet, D., Pajdla, T., Schiele, B., Tuytelaars, T. (eds.) ECCV 2014, Part III. LNCS, vol. 8691, pp. 346–361. Springer, Heidelberg (2014)
27. Hariharan, B., Arbeláez, P., Bourdev, L., Maji, S., Malik, J.: Semantic contours from inverse detectors. In: ICCV (2011)
28. Hosang, J., Benenson, R., Dollár, P., Schiele, B.: What makes for effective detection proposals? TPAMI (2015)
29. Krähenbühl, P., Koltun, V.: Geodesic object proposals. In: Fleet, D., Pajdla, T., Schiele, B., Tuytelaars, T. (eds.) ECCV 2014, Part V. LNCS, vol. 8693, pp. 725–739. Springer, Heidelberg (2014)
30. Humayun, A., Li, F., Rehg, J.: Rigor: reusing inference in graph cuts for generating object regions. In: CVPR (2014)

Domain Adaptive Fisher Vector
for Visual Recognition

Li Niu[1]([✉]), Jianfei Cai[2], and Dong Xu[3]

[1] Interdisciplinary Graduate School,
Nanyang Technological University, Singapore, Singapore
lniu002@ntu.edu.sg
[2] School of Computer Engineering,
Nanyang Technological University, Singapore, Singapore
asjfcai@ntu.edu.sg
[3] School of Electrical and Information Engineering,
University of Sydney, Sydney, Australia
dong.xu@sydney.edu.au

Abstract. In this paper, we consider Fisher vector in the context of domain adaptation, which has rarely been discussed by the existing domain adaptation methods. Particularly, in many real scenarios, the distributions of Fisher vectors of the training samples (*i.e.*, source domain) and test samples (*i.e.*, target domain) are considerably different, which may degrade the classification performance on the target domain by using the classifiers/regressors learnt based on the training samples from the source domain. To address the domain shift issue, we propose a Domain Adaptive Fisher Vector (DAFV) method, which learns a transformation matrix to select the domain invariant components of Fisher vectors and simultaneously solves a regression problem for visual recognition tasks based on the transformed features. Specifically, we employ a group lasso based regularizer on the transformation matrix to select the components of Fisher vectors, and use a regularizer based on the Maximum Mean Discrepancy (MMD) criterion to reduce the data distribution mismatch of transformed features between the source domain and the target domain. Comprehensive experiments demonstrate the effectiveness of our DAFV method on two benchmark datasets.

Keywords: Domain adaptation · Fisher vector

1 Introduction

Constructing global feature representations based on local descriptors of images/videos is a common approach in a multitude of visual recognition tasks. As a commonly used encoding method, Fisher vector [1] encodes both first and second order statistical information of local descriptors *w.r.t.* the generative model (*e.g.*, Gaussian Mixture Model (GMM)) trained based on them, and one Gaussian model in the GMM corresponds to one component in the extracted

© Springer International Publishing AG 2016
B. Leibe et al. (Eds.): ECCV 2016, Part VI, LNCS 9910, pp. 550–566, 2016.
DOI: 10.1007/978-3-319-46466-4_33

Fisher vector. Recently, Fisher vector achieves excellent performance for object recognition [2–5] or human action recognition [6,7]. To extract Fisher vector, we generally train a GMM based on the local descriptors of training samples and extract Fisher vectors for both training and test samples based on the pre-trained GMM. However, the GMM trained on the training samples does not consider the data distribution of test samples properly and thus lacks the generalization ability [8] on the test samples, leading to unsatisfactory recognition performance on the test datasets.

According to the terminology in the field of domain adaptation, the training dataset and the test dataset are referred to as the source domain and the target domain, respectively. When the target domain data are available in the training stage, we can train GMMs based on the mixture of local descriptors from both source domain and target domain. However, even in this case, the generated Fisher vectors of source domain samples and target domain samples may be still considerably different in terms of statistical properties, which is referred to as dataset bias [9]. Instead of training GMMs based on the data from both domains, another approach is to adapt the GMM trained based on the source domain to the target domain [8], or interpolate two GMMs which are trained based on the source domain and the target domain separately [10]. However, these methods did not explicitly consider the domain distribution mismatch between the source domain and the target domain. So they cannot guarantee the extracted Fisher vectors based on the adapted or interpolated GMMs are domain invariant.

In recent works, many domain adaptation approaches [11–20] have been proposed to tackle the domain shift issue between the source domain and the target domain (see Sect. 2 for details). However, none of them is specifically designed for Fisher Vector, since they did not take the generative models (i.e., GMMs) into consideration. Therefore, the excellent performance of Fisher vector for visual recognition [5,7] and the lack of effective domain adaptation methods for Fisher vector motivate our work. By noticing that each Gaussian model in the GMM characterizes the data distribution of a cluster of local descriptors, and some Gaussian models are more likely to capture the common data distribution between the source domain and the target domain, we come out the idea of identifying the common Gaussian models via selecting the corresponding components of Fisher vectors that are more likely to be domain invariant.

Let us take the object recognition and human action recognition tasks as two examples to provide more explanations for domain invariant components. For object recognition, the appearance of images within the same category may be quite different between the source domain and the target domain, which is usually referred to as intra-class difference, while some specific object regions within the category may be relatively consistent. Considering extracting the CNN features of object proposals as local descriptors and encoding them into Fisher vectors based on the pre-trained GMM, we expect to select the components of Fisher vectors corresponding to the Gaussian models from the object proposals which are more consistent across the source domain and the target domain. To validate this point, we present a detailed showcase associated with more discussions in Sect. 5.1. For human action recognition, sometimes the videos in the source domain are captured from the front view while the videos in the target domain are captured from the back view. When using the popular Improved Dense Trajectory (IDT) features as local descriptors in videos, each trajectory represents a local movement of human body, some of which can be observed from both front view and back view while the others can only be observed from one view. After encoding the IDT descriptors in videos into Fisher vectors based on the pre-trained GMM, we want to select the components of Fisher vectors corresponding to the Gaussian models from the trajectories which can be observed from both views.

To this end, we propose our Domain Adaptive Fisher Vector (DAFV) method. Specifically, we learn a transformation matrix to project the Fisher vectors into a lower dimensional latent subspace and consider visual recognition task as a regression problem based on the transformed features. A group lasso based regularizer [21] is employed on the transformation matrix to enforce the components of the transformation matrix corresponding to the selected (resp., unselected) components of Fisher vectors to be associated with large (resp., small) weights. At the same time, we apply the criterion of minimizing the Maximum Mean Discrepancy (MMD) of the transformed features between the source domain and the target domain by using an MMD-based regularizer. In Sect. 3, we briefly provide the background knowledge of Fisher vector. In Sect. 4, we introduce our Domain Adaptive Fisher Vector (DAFV) method in detail and also present a novel solution to the nontrivial optimization problem. In Sect. 5, we conduct extensive experiments on two benchmark datasets Bing-Caltech256 and ACT4^2 to demonstrate the effectiveness of our proposed method.

Our major contributions can be summarized as follows: (1) to the best of our knowledge, domain adaptation method designed for Fisher vectors has been rarely discussed in the previous literature. This is the first work to select domain invariant components of Fisher vectors to reduce the domain distribution mismatch between the source domain and the target domain; (2) we propose a Domain Adaptive Fisher Vector (DAFV) method and develop an effective solution to the proposed formulation; (3) extensive experiments on two benchmark datasets show the effectiveness of our method for selecting domain invariant components.

2   Related Work

Our work is related to using Fisher vector for visual recognition tasks. Fisher vector was first used for image classification in [22] and further improved in [2] with power normalization and L_2 normalization. In [3], Simonyan et al. developed a two-layer deep network based on Fisher vector for large-scale image classification. More recently, with the breakthrough in image representation by using Convolutional Neural Networks (CNN), CNN features of local regions have been used as local descriptors for Fisher vector [4,5,23,24]. Fisher vector was also applied to video action and event recognition [6,25]. Similar to the idea in [3] for image classification, Peng *et al.* proposed stacked Fisher vectors for human action recognition in [7]. All these methods assume the training samples and test samples are with the same data distribution while this assumption does not hold in domain adaptation scenarios.

Our work is related to domain adaptation. The existing domain adaptation methods can be classified into feature-based methods [13–18,26–28], SVM-based methods [12,29–32], instance-reweighting methods [11], dictionary learning methods [19], and low-rank based methods [20,33]. All the above methods are not specifically designed for Fisher vector. Among them, our method is more related to [16] and [17] which also learn a transformation matrix. However, [16,17] are only feature learning methods without considering the property of Fisher vector while our method can select the domain invariant components of Fisher vectors and simultaneously learn the regression matrix.

Finally, our work is also related to adapted or interpolated GMMs. Recently, Bayesian model adaptation has attracted much attention and several approaches have been proposed to adapt the background GMM to each image [34] or each category with very few examples [35]. Then, a more general formulation of Bayesian adaptation was proposed in [8] for image classification. Note that these methods [8,34,35] focus on adapting the background GMM to either a new image or a new category instead of considering the difference between two domains. So the motivation of their methods is intrinsically different from ours. More recently, Kim *et al.* proposed to interpolate a set of GMMs on the manifold in [10], which can be used to learn the interpolation between two GMMs from two domains. Nevertheless, all the above works did not explicitly address the domain shift issue. In contrast, our method explicitly reduces the domain distribution mismatch between two domains. Moreover, the Fisher vectors based on the GMMs learnt by their methods can be readily used to replace the original Fisher vectors in our method to further improve the performance.

3   Fisher Vector

In the remainder of this paper, we denote a matrix/vector by using a upper-case/lowercase letter in boldface (*e.g.*, $\mathbf{A}$ denotes a matrix and $\mathbf{a}$ denotes a vector). We denote an n-dim column vector of all zeros and all ones by using $\mathbf{0}_n, \mathbf{1}_n \in \mathbb{R}^n$, respectively. Note that when the dimension is obvious, we use $\mathbf{0}$ and $\mathbf{1}$ instead of $\mathbf{0}_n$ and $\mathbf{1}_n$ for simplicity. We use $\mathbf{I}$ to denote identify matrix. The superscript $'$ is used to denote the transpose of a matrix or a vector. Moreover, we use $\mathbf{A}^{-1}$ to denote the inverse matrix of $\mathbf{A}$ and $\mathbf{A} \circ \mathbf{B}$ to denote the element-wise product between two matrices $\mathbf{A}$ and $\mathbf{B}$.

Fisher vector is a commonly used encoding method to construct global feature representations from local descriptors. As a combination of generative and discriminative approaches, on one hand, the generation procedure of a set of local descriptors $\mathbf{X} = \{\mathbf{x}_i|_{i=1}^N\}$ (N is the number of local descriptors) is assumed to obey a probability density function $p(\mathbf{X}; \boldsymbol{\theta})$ with parameters $\boldsymbol{\theta}$. On the other hand, the gradients of the log-likelihood *w.r.t.* the model parameters, which describe the contribution of model parameters to the generation procedure of **X** [1], can be used as input features for discriminative methods such as classifiers and regressors. Since each image/video can be treated as a set of local descriptors $\{\mathbf{x}_i|_{i=1}^N\}$, its Fisher vector can be represented as,

$$G_{\boldsymbol{\theta}}^{\mathbf{X}} = \frac{1}{N} \sum_{i=1}^{N} \nabla_{\boldsymbol{\theta}} \log p(\mathbf{x}_i; \boldsymbol{\theta}). \tag{1}$$

For visual recognition tasks, the probability density function $p(\mathbf{X}; \boldsymbol{\theta})$ is usually modeled by Gaussian Mixture Model (GMM) [22,25]. Suppose K is the number of Gaussian models in the GMM, we use model parameters $\boldsymbol{\theta} = \{\pi_1, \boldsymbol{\mu}_1, \boldsymbol{\sigma}_1; \ldots; \pi_K, \boldsymbol{\mu}_K, \boldsymbol{\sigma}_K\}$ to denote the mixture weights, means, and diagonal covariances of GMM, respectively. Based on the definition of Fisher vector (1), the gradients of the log-likelihood *w.r.t.* the model parameters (*i.e.*, means and diagonal covariances) of the k-th Gaussian model can be written as (refer to [22] for the derivation details),

$$\mathcal{G}_{\boldsymbol{\mu},k}^{\mathbf{X}} = \frac{1}{N\sqrt{\pi_k}} \sum_{i=1}^{N} \gamma_i(k)(\frac{\mathbf{x}_i - \boldsymbol{\mu}_k}{\boldsymbol{\sigma}_k}), \tag{2}$$

$$\mathcal{G}_{\boldsymbol{\sigma},k}^{\mathbf{X}} = \frac{1}{N\sqrt{2\pi_k}} \sum_{i=1}^{N} \gamma_i(k)[\frac{(\mathbf{x}_i - \boldsymbol{\mu}_k)^2}{\boldsymbol{\sigma}_k^2} - 1], \tag{3}$$

where $\gamma_i(k)$ is the probability that the i-th local descriptor $\mathbf{x}_i$ belongs to the k-th Gaussian model, which is defined as,

$$\gamma_i(k) = \frac{\pi_k \mathcal{N}(\mathbf{x}_i; \boldsymbol{\mu}_k, \boldsymbol{\sigma}_k)}{\sum_{j=1}^{K} \pi_j \mathcal{N}(\mathbf{x}_i; \boldsymbol{\mu}_j, \boldsymbol{\sigma}_j)}, \tag{4}$$

in which $\mathcal{N}(\mathbf{x}_i; \boldsymbol{\mu}_k, \boldsymbol{\sigma}_k)$ is the probability of $\mathbf{x}_i$ based on the Gaussian distribution of the k-th Gaussian model. Assuming that the dimension of local descriptors is d, then the dimension of the k-th component of Fisher vectors corresponding to the k-th Gaussian model is $2d$ by concatenating (2) and (3). So the final Fisher vector is a $2Kd$-dim vector *w.r.t.* a K-component GMM.

4   Domain Adaptive Fisher Vector

In this section, we introduce our Domain Adaptive Fisher Vector (DAFV) method, in which we select the domain invariant components of Fisher vectors by simultaneously learning a transformation matrix and a regression matrix for visual recognition tasks. In order to make the proposed formulation easier to be optimized, we introduce an intermediate variable and relax our formulation, and then develop an effective algorithm to solve the optimization problem.

4.1 Formulation

Suppose we have n_s source domain samples and n_t target domain samples from C categories. Each sample is represented by a $2Kd$-dim Fisher vector, in which d is the dimension of local descriptors and K is the number of Gaussian models in the GMM. Let us denote $\mathbf{X}^s \in \mathcal{R}^{2Kd \times n_s}$ and $\mathbf{X}^t \in \mathcal{R}^{2Kd \times n_t}$ as the features of source domain samples and target domain samples, and $\mathbf{Y} \in \mathcal{Z}^{C \times n_s}$ as the binary label matrix for the source domain samples. In order to select domain invariant components and simultaneously keep discriminative information, we use the transformation matrix $\mathbf{R} \in \mathcal{R}^{m \times 2Kd}$ to project the original Fisher vector to lower dimensional subspace with m being the dimension of transformed features. We employ the group lasso based regularizer [21] $\|\tilde{\mathbf{R}}\|_{2,1}$ to enforce each column of $\tilde{\mathbf{R}}$ to have either all zero weights or multiple nonzero weights, in which $\tilde{\mathbf{R}} \in \mathcal{R}^{2d \times Km}$ is a reshaped matrix of $\mathbf{R}$ by setting each group of $2d$ entries in each row of $\mathbf{R}$ corresponding to one component in the Fisher vector as one column in $\tilde{\mathbf{R}}$. To be exact, we expect to assign nonzero weights to the selected domain invariant components of Fisher vectors and zero weights to the remaining ones.

To ensure the selected components are domain invariant, we tend to minimize the Maximum Mean Discrepancy (MMD) of transformed features between the source domain and the target domain by using an MMD-based [11] regularizer $\|\frac{1}{n_s}\mathbf{R}\mathbf{X}^s\mathbf{1} - \frac{1}{n_t}\mathbf{R}\mathbf{X}^t\mathbf{1}\|^2$, in which $\frac{1}{n_s}\mathbf{R}\mathbf{X}^s\mathbf{1}$ (*resp.*, $\frac{1}{n_t}\mathbf{R}\mathbf{X}^t\mathbf{1}$) is the mean of transformed features from the source (*resp.*, target) domain, so that the data distribution mismatch between two domains can be reduced. Additionally, inspired by [17], we add a constraint $\mathbf{R}\mathbf{X}\mathbf{H}\mathbf{X}'\mathbf{R}' = \mathbf{I}$ to maximally preserve the data variance, where $\mathbf{X} = [\mathbf{X}^s, \mathbf{X}^t]$ and $\mathbf{H} = \mathbf{I}_n - \frac{1}{n}\mathbf{1}\mathbf{1}'$ with $n = n_s + n_t$.

By denoting $\mathbf{W} \in \mathcal{R}^{C \times m}$ as the regression matrix, we formulate our method by solving the following regression problem:

$$\min_{\mathbf{W},\mathbf{R}} \frac{1}{2}\|\mathbf{W}\mathbf{R}\mathbf{X}^s - \mathbf{Y}\|_F^2 + \frac{\gamma}{2}\|\mathbf{W}\|_F^2 + \lambda\|\tilde{\mathbf{R}}\|_{2,1}$$

$$+\frac{1}{2}\|\frac{1}{n_s}\mathbf{R}\mathbf{X}^s\mathbf{1} - \frac{1}{n_t}\mathbf{R}\mathbf{X}^t\mathbf{1}\|^2 \tag{5}$$

$$\text{s.t. } \mathbf{R}\mathbf{X}\mathbf{H}\mathbf{X}'\mathbf{R}' = \mathbf{I}, \tag{6}$$

in which $\|\mathbf{W}\mathbf{R}\mathbf{X}^s - \mathbf{Y}\|_F^2$ is the regression error, $\|\mathbf{W}\|_F^2$ is the weight decay regularizer to control the complexity of $\mathbf{W}$, γ and λ are two trade-off parameters.

The problem in (5) is not easy to solve due to the constraint in (6). For ease of optimization, we introduce an intermediate variable $\mathbf{S}$ and promote the coherence between $\mathbf{R}$ and $\mathbf{S}$ by adding a coherent regularizer $\|\mathbf{R}\mathbf{S}'\|_F^2$ [36]. With larger $\|\mathbf{R}\mathbf{S}'\|_F^2$, $\mathbf{R}$ is more coherent to $\mathbf{S}$. As a result, the proposed formulation after introducing $\mathbf{S}$ becomes,

$$\min_{\mathbf{W},\mathbf{R},\mathbf{S}} \frac{1}{2}\|\mathbf{WSX}^s - \mathbf{Y}\|_F^2 + \frac{\gamma}{2}\|\mathbf{W}\|_F^2 + \lambda\|\tilde{\mathbf{S}}\|_{2,1}$$

$$+\frac{1}{2}\|\frac{1}{n_s}\mathbf{RX}^s\mathbf{1} - \frac{1}{n_t}\mathbf{RX}^t\mathbf{1}\|^2 - \frac{1}{2}\|\mathbf{RS'}\|_F^2 \qquad (7)$$

$$\text{s.t. } \mathbf{RXHX'R'} = \mathbf{I}. \qquad (8)$$

By replacing $\mathbf{R}$ in $\|\mathbf{WRX}^s - \mathbf{Y}\|_F^2$ and $\|\tilde{\mathbf{R}}\|_{2,1}$ in (5) by $\mathbf{S}$, the subproblem $w.r.t.$ $\mathbf{R}$ in (7) can be easily solved by using eigen decomposition, which will be discussed in detail in the next section.

Another problem is that the dimension of Fisher vector is usually very high. Considering high time-complexity operations such as eigen decomposition, the algorithm will become very time-consuming. To accelerate the algorithm and simultaneously capture the semantic information within each category, we partition each Fisher vector into C uncorrelated parts by training a category-specific GMM with a smaller number of Gaussian models based on the training samples within each category. Then, a set of $\mathbf{W}_c$, $\mathbf{R}_c$, and $\mathbf{S}_c$ is learnt for the components of each Fisher vector corresponding to the c-th GMM. As a result, we have totally C sets of $\mathbf{W}_c \in \mathcal{R}^{C\times\bar{m}}$, $\mathbf{R}_c \in \mathcal{R}^{\bar{m}\times 2\bar{K}d}$, and $\mathbf{S}_c \in \mathcal{R}^{\bar{m}\times 2\bar{K}d}$ for $c = 1,\ldots,C$, in which we denote the number of Gaussian models in each category-specific GMM as $\bar{K}$ ($\bar{K} << K$) and the dimension of the transformed features corresponding to each category-specific GMM as $\bar{m}$ ($\bar{m} << m$). Correspondingly, we partition the training ($resp.$, test) features $\mathbf{X}^s$ ($resp.$, $\mathbf{X}^t$) into $\mathbf{X}_c^s \in \mathcal{R}^{2\bar{K}d\times n_s}$'s ($resp.$, $\mathbf{X}_c^t \in \mathcal{R}^{2\bar{K}d\times n_t}$'s) with each obtained based on the c-th GMM, and denote $\mathbf{X}_c = [\mathbf{X}_c^s, \mathbf{X}_c^t]$. In fact, supervised learning for GMM ($i.e.$, train one GMM per category) has been studied in [37] and proved to be able to preserve the useful discriminative information. To this end, we can relax the problem in (7) as,

$$\min_{\mathbf{W}_c,\mathbf{R}_c,\mathbf{S}_c} \frac{1}{2}\|\sum_{c=1}^{C}\mathbf{W}_c\mathbf{S}_c\mathbf{X}_c^s - \mathbf{Y}\|_F^2 + \frac{\gamma}{2}\sum_{c=1}^{C}\|\mathbf{W}_c\|_F^2 + \lambda\sum_{c=1}^{C}\|\tilde{\mathbf{S}}_c\|_{2,1}$$

$$+\frac{1}{2}\sum_{c=1}^{C}\|\frac{1}{n_s}\mathbf{R}_c\mathbf{X}_c^s\mathbf{1} - \frac{1}{n_t}\mathbf{R}_c\mathbf{X}_c^t\mathbf{1}\|^2 - \frac{1}{2}\sum_{c=1}^{C}\|\mathbf{R}_c\mathbf{S}_c'\|_F^2 \qquad (9)$$

$$\text{s.t. } \mathbf{R}_c\mathbf{X}_c\mathbf{HX}_c'\mathbf{R}_c' = \mathbf{I}, \quad \forall c. \qquad (10)$$

By partitioning a Fisher vector into C uncorrelated parts, we can solve C small-scale subproblems instead of a large-scale problem, which is more efficient. Considering the tradeoff between efficiency and effectiveness, we set $\bar{K}$ as 8 and $\bar{m}$ as 1000 in our experiments. Moreover, another benefit of replacing $\|\tilde{\mathbf{S}}\|_{2,1}$ with $\|\tilde{\mathbf{S}}_c\|_{2,1}$ is that we can guarantee at least one Gaussian model selected from each category-specific GMM, which ensures capturing the semantic information over all categories. Next, we will discuss how to solve the problem in (9).

4.2 Optimization

We solve the problem in (9) by using an alternative optimization approach. Specifically, we alteratively update three sets of variables $\mathbf{W}_c$'s, $\mathbf{S}_c$'s, and $\mathbf{R}_c$'s until the objective value of (9) converges.

Update $\mathbf{W}_c$ when fixing $\mathbf{R}_c$ and $\mathbf{S}_c$: When fixing $\mathbf{R}_c$'s and $\mathbf{S}_c$'s, the problem in (9) reduces to:

$$\min_{\mathbf{W}_c} \frac{1}{2} \| \sum_{c=1}^{C} \mathbf{W}_c \mathbf{S}_c \mathbf{X}_c^s - \mathbf{Y} \|_F^2 + \frac{\gamma}{2} \sum_{c=1}^{C} \|\mathbf{W}_c\|_F^2 \qquad (11)$$

By setting the derivative of (11) *w.r.t.* each $\mathbf{W}_c$ to $\mathbf{0}$, we can derive the close-form solution for each $\mathbf{W}_c$ as,

$$\mathbf{W}_c = (\mathbf{Y} - \sum_{\tilde{c}=1, \tilde{c} \neq c}^{C} \mathbf{W}_{\tilde{c}} \mathbf{S}_{\tilde{c}} \mathbf{X}_{\tilde{c}}^s) \mathbf{X}_c^{s\prime} \mathbf{S}_c' (\mathbf{S}_c \mathbf{X}_c^s \mathbf{X}_c^{s\prime} \mathbf{S}_c' + \gamma \mathbf{I})^{-1}. \qquad (12)$$

We calculate each $\mathbf{W}_c$ when fixing all the other $\mathbf{W}_{\tilde{c}}$ for $\tilde{c} \neq c$ and repeat this process iteratively until the objective value of (11) converges.

Update $\mathbf{R}_c$ when fixing $\mathbf{W}_c$ and $\mathbf{S}_c$: When fixing $\mathbf{W}_c$'s and $\mathbf{S}_c$'s, the problem in (9) can be separated into C independent subproblems with one for each $\mathbf{R}_c$. For ease of optimization, we rewrite the subproblem *w.r.t.* each $\mathbf{R}_c$ by using trace norm as follows,

$$\min_{\mathbf{R}_c} \frac{1}{2} \mathrm{tr}(\mathbf{R}_c \mathbf{X}_c \mathbf{L} \mathbf{X}_c' \mathbf{R}_c') - \frac{1}{2} \mathrm{tr}(\mathbf{R}_c \mathbf{S}_c' \mathbf{S}_c \mathbf{R}_c') \qquad (13)$$

$$\text{s.t.} \quad \mathbf{R}_c \mathbf{X}_c \mathbf{H} \mathbf{X}_c' \mathbf{R}_c' = \mathbf{I}, \qquad (14)$$

where $\mathbf{L}$ is an indicator matrix, in which $L_{ij} = \frac{1}{n_s^2}$ if $i \leq n_s$ and $j \leq n_s$; else $L_{ij} = \frac{1}{n_t^2}$ if $i > n_s$ and $j > n_s$; otherwise, $L_{ij} = -\frac{1}{n_s n_t}$.

By introducing a symmetric matrix $\mathbf{Z}_c$ containing the Lagrangian multipliers for the constraints in (14), we obtain the Lagrangian form of (13) as,

$$\mathcal{L}_{\mathbf{R}_c, \mathbf{Z}_c} = \mathrm{tr}(\mathbf{R}_c(\frac{1}{2}\mathbf{X}_c \mathbf{L} \mathbf{X}_c' - \frac{1}{2}\mathbf{S}_c' \mathbf{S}_c)\mathbf{R}_c') - \mathrm{tr}((\mathbf{R}_c \mathbf{X}_c \mathbf{H} \mathbf{X}_c' \mathbf{R}_c' - \mathbf{I})\mathbf{Z}_c). \qquad (15)$$

By setting the derivative of (15) *w.r.t.* $\mathbf{R}_c$ to $\mathbf{0}$, we arrive at

$$\mathbf{R}_c(\mathbf{X}_c \mathbf{L} \mathbf{X}_c' - \mathbf{S}_c' \mathbf{S}_c) = 2\mathbf{Z}_c \mathbf{R}_c \mathbf{X}_c \mathbf{H} \mathbf{X}_c'. \qquad (16)$$

Multiplying both sides on the right by $\mathbf{R}_c'$, we obtain the solution *w.r.t.* $\mathbf{Z}_c$ as follows,

$$\mathbf{Z}_c = \frac{1}{2}(\mathbf{R}_c(\mathbf{X}_c \mathbf{L} \mathbf{X}_c' - \mathbf{S}_c' \mathbf{S}_c)\mathbf{R}_c')(\mathbf{R}_c \mathbf{X}_c \mathbf{H} \mathbf{X}_c' \mathbf{R}_c')^{-1}. \qquad (17)$$

By substituting (17) back into (15) followed by some simplifications, we derive the dual form of (13) as,

$$\max_{\mathbf{R}_c} \frac{1}{2} \mathrm{tr}((\mathbf{R}_c \mathbf{X}_c \mathbf{H} \mathbf{X}_c' \mathbf{R}_c')^{-1}(\mathbf{R}_c(\mathbf{X}_c \mathbf{L} \mathbf{X}_c' - \mathbf{S}_c' \mathbf{S}_c)\mathbf{R}_c')) \tag{18}$$

Similar to kernel Fisher discriminant analysis [38], the problem in (18) can be solved by eigen decomposition and the rows of $\mathbf{R}_c$ are the $\bar{m}$ leading eigen vectors of $(\mathbf{X}_c \mathbf{H} \mathbf{X}_c')^{-1}(\mathbf{X}_c \mathbf{L} \mathbf{X}_c' - \mathbf{S}_c' \mathbf{S}_c)$.

Update $\mathbf{S}_c$ when fixing $\mathbf{R}_c$ and $\mathbf{W}_c$: When fixing $\mathbf{R}_c$'s and $\mathbf{W}_c$'s, the problem in (9) reduces to the following problem:

$$\min_{\mathbf{S}_c} \frac{1}{2} \| \sum_{c=1}^{C} \mathbf{W}_c \mathbf{S}_c \mathbf{X}_c^s - \mathbf{Y} \|_F^2 + \lambda \sum_{c=1}^{C} \| \tilde{\mathbf{S}}_c \|_{2,1} - \frac{1}{2} \sum_{c=1}^{C} \| \mathbf{R}_c \mathbf{S}_c' \|_F^2 \tag{19}$$

The optimization problem in (19) is non-convex and thus only local optimum can be reached by using gradient descent algorithm. First, we derive the derivative of each term in (19) *w.r.t.* each $\mathbf{S}_c$ separately.

$$\mathbf{J}_1 = \frac{\partial \frac{1}{2} \| \sum_{c=1}^{C} \mathbf{W}_c \mathbf{S}_c \mathbf{X}_c^s - \mathbf{Y} \|_F^2}{\partial \mathbf{S}_c} = \mathbf{W}_c'(\sum_{c=1}^{C} \mathbf{W}_c \mathbf{S}_c \mathbf{X}_c^s - \mathbf{Y})\mathbf{X}_c^{s\prime}, \tag{20}$$

$$\mathbf{J}_2 = \frac{\partial \lambda \| \tilde{\mathbf{S}}_c \|_{2,1}}{\partial \mathbf{S}_c} = \lambda \mathbf{S}_c \circ \mathbf{D}_c, \tag{21}$$

where $\mathbf{D}_c \in \mathcal{R}^{\bar{m} \times 2\bar{K}d}$ is a matrix, in which each entry D_c^{ij} is set as $\frac{1}{\|\mathbf{S}_c^{i,k}\|_2}$ if j belongs to the k-th component, with $\mathbf{S}_c^{i,k}$ denoting the k-th component in the i-th row of $\mathbf{S}_c$.

$$\mathbf{J}_3 = \frac{\partial - \frac{1}{2} \| \mathbf{R}_c \mathbf{S}_c' \|_F^2}{\partial \mathbf{S}_c} = -\mathbf{S}_c \mathbf{R}_c' \mathbf{R}_c. \tag{22}$$

In each iteration, we update each $\mathbf{S}_c$ when fixing all the other $\mathbf{S}_{\tilde{c}}$'s for $\tilde{c} \neq c$ by using the following equation:

$$\mathbf{S}_c \leftarrow \mathbf{S}_c - \eta(\mathbf{J}_1 + \mathbf{J}_2 + \mathbf{J}_3), \tag{23}$$

where η is the learning rate, which is empirically fixed as 0.0001 in our experiments. We repeat this process iteratively until the objective value of (19) converges. The whole algorithm is summarized in Algorithm 1. The objective value of (9) monotonically decreases as the number of iterations increases and usually converges within 20 iterations in our experiments.

In the testing stage, for each test sample $\mathbf{x}^t$ which contains the features $\mathbf{x}_c^t$'s obtained based on each category-specific GMM, we use $\sum_{c=1}^{C} \mathbf{W}_c \mathbf{S}_c \mathbf{x}_c^t$ to obtain the regression values and assign this test sample to the category corresponding to the maximum regression value.

Algorithm 1. Domain Adaptive Fisher Vector (DAFV) Algorithm

1: **Input: $\mathbf{X}_c^s, \mathbf{X}_c^t, \mathbf{Y}, \lambda, \gamma$**
2: Initialize $\mathbf{S}_c$ as the PCA projection matrix on $\mathbf{X}_c$.
3: **repeat**
4:   **repeat**
5:     For c=1,...,C, update $\mathbf{W}_c$ using (12).
6:   **until** The objective of (11) converges.
7:   For c=1,...,C, update $\mathbf{R}_c$ by solving (18).
8:   **repeat**
9:     For c=1,...,C, update $\mathbf{S}_c$ using (23).
10:   **until** The objective of (19) converges.
11: **until** The objective of (9) converges.
12: **Output: $\mathbf{W}_c, \mathbf{S}_c$.**

5 Experiments

In this section, we demonstrate the effectiveness of our Domain Adaptive Fisher Vector (DAFV) approach for object recognition and human action recognition by conducting extensive experiments on two benchmark datasets.

5.1 Object Recognition

Experimental Settings: We use Bing-Caltech256 [39] dataset, which is commonly used to evaluate domain adaption methods for object recognition. Bing-Caltech256 dataset consists of the images from Caltech256 dataset and the images from Bing search engine distributed in 256 categories. Generally, Bing is treated as the source domain and Caltech-256 is treated as the target domain, because Bing images are collected by the search engine without having ground-truth labels and thus not appropriate for being used as test set. Following the setting in [40], we use the first 20 categories and set the number of source (*resp.*, target) domain examples per category to be 50 (*resp.*, 25) based on the train/test split provided in [39].

In order to generate local descriptors for each image, we first use selection search [41] to generate object proposals. Then, we use the output of the 6-th layer of AlexNet [42] as the 4096-dim feature for each proposal with the pretrained model in [43]. After reducing the dimension of proposal features to 200 by using Principle Component Analysis (PCA), we use the proposals from the source domain within each category to train an 8-component Gaussian Mixture Model (GMM), which leads to a total of 160 components for all categories. Finally, we encode each image, which is a bag of 200-dim proposal features, as a $64,000$-dim Fisher vector based on the trained GMMs.
Baselines: We compare our DAFV method with two sets of baselines: domain adaptation baselines and GMM based baselines. We also include Regularized Least Square (RLS) as a baseline. For domain adaptation baselines, we compare our method with feature-based methods GFK [13], SGF [14], SA [15], DIP [16],

TCA [17], LSSA [18], CORAL [28], the SVM-based method DASVM [29], the instance reweighting method KMM [11], the dictionary learning method SDDL [19], and the low-rank based method LTSL [20]. Note that for feature-based methods [13–18], we first obtain the transformed features by employing their methods suggested in the original papers [13–18] and then use the transformed features as input features for RLS.

For GMM based baselines AGMM [8] and EM_RGMM [10], we use different approaches to obtain GMMs, which is explained as follows,

- AGMM [8]: We first train a 160-component GMM by using proposals from the source domain, and then adapt this GMM using the proposals from the target domain. Based on the GMM on the source domain and the adapted GMM, we extract two sets of Fisher vectors for all images from both domains. Based on these two sets of Fisher vectors, we train regressors and obtain the regression values of test images separately, and finally use the average fusion of two sets of regression values for prediction.
- EM_RGMM [10]: We train two 160-component GMMs based on the proposals from the source domain and the target domain, separately. Then, we calculate the interpolated GMM between the two GMMs. Based on the interpolated GMM, we extract Fisher vectors for all images from both domains. Finally, we train regressors and predict the test images based on the extracted Fisher vectors.

Table 1. Accuracies (%) of RLS and GMM based baselines, as well as our DAFV method and its two special cases for object recognition. The best result is denoted in boldface

RLS	AGMM	EM_RGMM	DAFV_sim1	DAFV_sim2	DAFV
73.2	76.8	77.4	75.4	77.8	**79.4**

Table 2. Accuracies (%) of domain adaptation baselines and our DAFV method for object recognition. The best result is denoted in boldface

KMM	DASVM	GFK	SGF	SA	DIP	TCA	LSSA	SDDL	LTSL	CORAL	DAFV
73.6	75.8	73.6	74.4	74.2	71.8	74.8	77.8	62.4	77.6	75.20	**79.4**

Moreover, in order to validate our MMD-based regularizer and group lasso based regularizer, we compare our method with its two simplified versions. Specifically, we remove the group lasso based regularizer $\sum_{c=1}^{C} \|\tilde{\mathbf{S}}_c\|_{2,1}$ in (9) by setting the parameter λ as 0 and refer to this special case as DAFV_sim2. Based on DAFV_sim2, we further remove the MMD-based regularizer $\|\frac{1}{n_s}\mathbf{R}_c\mathbf{X}_c^s\mathbf{1} - \frac{1}{n_t}\mathbf{R}_c\mathbf{X}_c^t\mathbf{1}\|^2$ and denote this special case as DAFV_sim1.

We use accuracy for performance evaluation. Two trade-off parameters γ and λ in (9) are empirically set as 1000 and 10 for our DAFV method. For the baseline methods, we choose their optimal parameters based on their accuracies on the test dataset.

Experimental Results: We report the results of RLS, the GMM based baselines, and our DAFV method including its two special cases in Table 1, from which we observe that AGMM and EM_RGMM achieve better results than RLS, suggesting the benefits of adapting or interpolating GMMs. We also observe that our DAFV method outperforms DAFV_sim2, which validates the effectiveness of selecting some components of Fisher vectors by using group lasso based regularizer. Additionally, DAFV_sim2 outperforms DAFV_sim1, which validates our MMD based regularizer. Finally, our DAFV method outperforms the GMM based baselines, which shows its effectiveness on reducing domain distribution mismatch between the source domain and the target domain.

Moreover, we report the results of domain adaptation baselines in Table 2 and also include the result of our DAFV method for comparison. From Table 2, we observe that the domain adaptation baselines are generally better than RLS reported in Table 1. The results validate the effectiveness of employing different strategies to address the domain shift issue. However, all the domain adaptation baselines are worse than our DAFV method. One possible explanation is that we select the domain invariant components of Fisher vectors, which is designed for Fisher vectors.

Fig. 1. The top object proposals belonging to the selected Gaussian model for the "beer-mug" category from the Bing dataset

Discussion on Domain Invariant Components: As discussed in Sect. 1, the motivation of our DAFV method is that each Gaussian model in the GMM represents the data distribution of a cluster of local descriptors and corresponds to one component in the encoded Fisher vector. Assuming that there exist some Gaussian models representing common distribution shared by both source and target domain, the corresponding components of Fisher vectors should be more domain invariant. The benefit of selecting domain invariant components has been demonstrated in Tables 1 and 2, and now we provide some intuitive examples to illustrate the domain invariant components.

First, recall that we train C category-specific GMMs and $\mathbf{S}_c \in \mathcal{R}^{\bar{m} \times 2\bar{K}d}$ is the transformation matrix corresponding to the c-th GMM. For the c-th category, we compute the L_2 norm for each component in each row of $\mathbf{S}_c$, which corresponds to one Gaussian model in the c-th GMM. Then, we sum the computed values over different rows and choose the component with the maximum value, which corresponds to the selected Gaussian model in the c-th GMM. Because there are probabilities $\gamma_i(k)$'s that the i-th proposal belongs to the k-th Gaussian model (see Sect. 3) when training a GMM, we can easily pick out the top proposals that belong to the cluster corresponding to the selected Gaussian model. Let us take the "beer-mug" category as an example to show the top proposals for the selected Gaussian model in Fig. 1, from which we have an interesting observation that the proposals are all near the handle of beer mug. We conjecture beer mugs from different domains are quite different in shape, color, and pattern of body regions, but the handle regions generally look similar as illustrated in Fig. 1. Intuitively, the handle regions can be used to discriminate beer mugs against the other categories but are less variant across different domains. So the components of Fisher vectors corresponding to the selected Gaussian models are assigned larger weights, which is helpful for improving the performance of object recognition.

5.2   Human Action Recognition

Experimental Settings: We use the ACT4^2 [44] dataset for human action recognition. The ACT4^2 dataset contains videos from 14 categories of human actions, which are captured from 4 camera viewpoints. Following [44], we use a subset with 2648 RGB videos from all 4 viewpoints. We treat one view as the

Table 3. Accuracies (%) of RLS and GMM based baselines, as well as our DAFV method and its two special cases for human action recognition. The best results on each setting are denoted in boldface

Setting	RLS	AGMM	EM_RGMM	DAFV_sim1	DAFV_sim2	DAFV
1->2	69.94	72.36	73.72	71.00	72.96	**74.92**
1->3	44.11	46.07	46.22	45.02	46.68	**48.49**
1->4	77.64	80.21	80.06	81.27	82.33	**83.99**
2->1	74.17	77.95	74.02	77.04	77.64	**79.61**
2->3	67.37	67.52	67.82	69.94	71.00	**72.96**
2->4	60.88	61.03	61.18	60.57	62.24	**63.90**
3->1	52.87	47.89	51.96	51.21	52.87	**55.74**
3->2	66.92	66.92	67.07	69.18	69.94	**71.90**
3->4	40.03	41.69	41.99	41.69	43.20	**45.47**
4->1	71.75	73.72	72.21	68.73	75.98	**76.13**
4->2	46.37	52.27	52.11	49.40	51.96	**53.92**
4->3	37.31	38.97	36.71	38.52	40.03	**41.69**
Avg	59.11	60.55	60.42	60.30	62.24	**64.06**

Table 4. Accuracies (%) of domain adaptation baselines and our DAFV method for human action recognition. The best results on each setting are denoted in boldface

Setting	KMM	DASVM	GFK	SGF	SA	DIP	TCA	LSSA	SDDL	LTSL	CORAL	DAFV
1->2	67.67	59.52	73.11	66.16	72.96	72.21	72.81	73.56	72.96	71.75	72.69	**74.92**
1->3	45.62	35.65	46.37	45.02	45.92	46.37	46.53	44.11	45.02	45.17	46.37	**48.49**
1->4	79.91	74.17	81.72	78.85	80.97	80.51	82.93	82.33	79.00	81.72	81.72	**83.99**
2->1	76.74	68.88	77.95	70.85	75.98	75.38	**79.76**	68.88	75.98	75.68	75.68	79.61
2->3	69.94	55.29	70.54	66.62	69.79	71.60	69.49	65.41	69.94	68.73	71.90	**72.96**
2->4	61.33	56.34	61.48	59.06	62.08	62.84	61.78	62.08	61.33	61.33	61.63	**63.90**
3->1	54.98	48.94	53.78	47.73	54.08	54.53	54.68	50.45	53.47	54.08	53.47	**55.74**
3->2	70.54	62.08	69.94	69.79	67.07	71.00	67.67	64.20	68.88	67.82	67.67	**71.90**
3->4	41.39	32.33	42.60	41.09	42.45	43.20	43.35	40.94	36.40	43.96	43.81	**45.47**
4->1	74.62	67.98	73.11	74.17	73.87	73.87	73.26	66.01	74.47	72.36	73.72	**76.13**
4->2	**54.83**	46.37	49.24	53.02	53.32	51.66	49.85	52.11	47.43	51.66	52.27	53.92
4->3	34.29	36.40	40.03	39.43	38.97	40.33	39.27	39.73	37.61	38.97	40.48	**41.69**
Avg	60.99	53.66	61.66	59.32	61.46	61.96	61.78	59.15	60.21	61.10	61.81	**64.06**

source domain and another different view as the target domain, which results in totally 12 settings.

Following [6], we use the source codes provided in [6] to extract four types of Improved Dense Trajectory (IDT) descriptors (i.e., 30-dim trajectories, 96-dim HOG, 108-dim HOF, and 192-dim MBH). Following [6], we first reduce the dimension of descriptors by a factor of two using PCA. Then, we use the descriptors from the videos in the source domain within each category to train an 8-component GMM, which leads to totally 112 components for all categories. Finally, we encode each video, which is a bag of 213-dim IDT descriptors, as a 47712-dim Fisher vector based on the trained GMMs.

Baselines: We compare our DAFV method with the same baselines as discussed in Sect. 5.1. The only difference is that we train 112-component GMMs for AGMM and EM_RGMM. For the human action recognition task, accuracy is still used for performance evaluation. Our DAFV method employs the same parameters as used for object recognition while optimal parameters of the baseline methods are chosen according to their accuracies on the test dataset.

Experimental Results: We report the experimental results of RLS and GMM based baselines, as well as our DAFV method and its two special cases on 12 settings in Table 3. From the results, we can draw similar conclusions as those for object recognition in Sect. 5.1. In particular, the comparisons among our DAFV method and its two special cases clearly demonstrate the effectiveness of our group lasso based regularizer and the MMD-based regularizer. Moreover, our DAFV method is better than the GMM based baselines on all settings. The results again demonstrate that the recognition performance can be improved by reducing domain distribution mismatch.

Table 4 shows the results of domain adaptation baselines. It can be seen that the average accuracies of the domain adaptation baselines are better than that of RLS reported in Table 3 except DASVM, which indicates the advantage of coping with domain difference by using various methods. While TCA (*resp.*, KMM) is better than our DAFV method on the setting 2->1 (*resp.*, 4->2), our method achieves the best results on 10 out of 12 settings. Moreover, in terms of the average accuracy over 12 settings, our DAFV method is the best, which again demonstrates it is helpful to address the domain shift issue by selecting domain invariant components of Fisher vectors.

6 Conclusion

In this paper, we have proposed a domain adaptation method named Domain Adaptive Fisher Vector (DAFV), which is designed for Fisher vectors. Based on the assumption that some Gaussian models in the GMM can better capture the common data distribution between the source domain and the target domain, our DAFV method is designed to select the domain invariant components of Fisher vectors corresponding to the common Gaussian models and simultaneously solve a regression problem. The effectiveness of our DAFV method for visual recognition has been demonstrated by extensive experiments.

Acknowledgement. This research was partially carried out at the Rapid-Rich Object Search (ROSE) Laboratory, Nanyang Technological University, Singapore. The ROSE Laboratory is supported by the National Research Foundation, Prime Ministers Office, Singapore, under its IDM Futures Funding Initiative and administered by the Interactive and Digital Media Programme Office.

References

1. Jaakkola, T.S., Haussler, D., et al.: Exploiting generative models in discriminative classifiers. In: NIPS (1999)
2. Perronnin, F., Sánchez, J., Mensink, T.: Improving the fisher kernel for large-scale image classification. In: Daniilidis, K., Maragos, P., Paragios, N. (eds.) ECCV 2010, Part IV. LNCS, vol. 6314, pp. 143–156. Springer, Heidelberg (2010)
3. Simonyan, K., Vedaldi, A., Zisserman, A.: Deep Fisher networks for large-scale image classification. In: NIPS (2013)
4. Wei, Y., Xia, W., Huang, J., Ni, B., Dong, J., Zhao, Y., Yan, S.: CNN: Single-label to multi-label (2014). arXiv preprint arXiv:1406.5726
5. Uricchio, T., Bertini, M., Seidenari, L., Bimbo, A.: Fisher encoded convolutional bag-of-windows for efficient image retrieval and social image tagging. In: ICCV (2015)
6. Wang, H., Schmid, C.: Action recognition with improved trajectories. In: ICCV (2013)
7. Peng, X., Zou, C., Qiao, Y., Peng, Q.: Action recognition with stacked fisher vectors. In: Fleet, D., Pajdla, T., Schiele, B., Tuytelaars, T. (eds.) ECCV 2014, Part V. LNCS, vol. 8693, pp. 581–595. Springer, Heidelberg (2014)
8. Dixit, M., Rasiwasia, N., Vasconcelos, N.: Adapted Gaussian models for image classification. In: CVPR (2011)
9. Torralba, A., Efros, A.A.: Unbiased look at dataset bias. In: CVPR (2011)

10. Kim, H.J., Adluru, N., Banerjee, M., Vemuri, B.C., Singh, V.: Interpolation on the manifold of K component GMMs. In: ICCV (2015)
11. Huang, J., Smola, A., Gretton, A., Borgwardt, K., Scholkopf, B.: Correcting sample selection bias by unlabeled data. In: NIPS (2007)
12. Bruzzone, L., Marconcini, M.: Domain adaptation problems: A DASVM classification technique and a circular validation strategy. T-PAMI 32(5), 770–787 (2010)
13. Gong, B., Shi, Y., Sha, F., Grauman, K.: Geodesic flow kernel for unsupervised domain adaptation. In: CVPR (2012)
14. Gopalan, R., Li, R., Chellappa, R.: Domain adaptation for object recognition: an unsupervised approach. In: ICCV (2011)
15. Fernando, B., Habrard, A., Sebban, M., Tuytelaars, T.: Unsupervised visual domain adaptation using subspace alignment. In: ICCV (2013)
16. Baktashmotlagh, M., Harandi, M.T., Lovell, B.C., Salzmann, M.: Unsupervised domain adaptation by domain invariant projection. In: ICCV (2013)
17. Pan, S.J., Tsang, I.W., Kwok, J.T., Yang, Q.: Domain adaptation via transfer component analysis. T-NN 22(2), 199–210 (2011)
18. Aljundi, R., Emonet, R., Muselet, D., Sebban, M.: Landmarks-based kernelized subspace alignment for unsupervised domain adaptation. In: CVPR (2015)
19. Shekhar, S., Patel, V., Nguyen, H., Chellappa, R.: Generalized domain-adaptive dictionaries. In: CVPR (2013)
20. Shao, M., Kit, D., Fu, Y.: Generalized transfer subspace learning through low-rank constraint. IJCV 109(1–2), 74–93 (2014)
21. Yuan, M., Lin, Y.: Model selection and estimation in regression with grouped variables. J. Royal Stat. Soc. Ser. B (Statistical Methodology) 68(1), 49–67 (2006)
22. Perronnin, F., Dance, C.: Fisher kernels on visual vocabularies for image categorization. In: CVPR (2007)
23. Liu, L., Shen, C., Wang, L., van den Hengel, A., Wang, C.: Encoding high dimensional local features by sparse coding based Fisher vectors. In: NIPS (2014)
24. Gong, Y., Wang, L., Guo, R., Lazebnik, S.: Multi-scale orderless pooling of deep convolutional activation features. In: Fleet, D., Pajdla, T., Schiele, B., Tuytelaars, T. (eds.) ECCV 2014, Part VII. LNCS, vol. 8695, pp. 392–407. Springer, Heidelberg (2014)
25. Oneata, D., Verbeek, J., Schmid, C.: Action and event recognition with Fisher vectors on a compact feature set. In: ICCV (2013)
26. Caseiro, R., Henriques, J.F., Martins, P., Batista, J.: Beyond the shortest path: Unsupervised domain adaptation by sampling subspaces along the spline flow. In: CVPR (2015)
27. Kulis, B., Saenko, K., Darrell, T.: What you saw is not what you get: Domain adaptation using asymmetric kernel transforms. In: CVPR (2011)
28. Sun, B., Feng, J., Saenko, K.: Return of frustratingly easy domain adaptation. In: AAAI (2016)
29. Duan, L., Tsang, I.W., Xu, D.: Domain transfer multiple kernel learning. T-PAMI 34, 465–479 (2012)
30. Duan, L., Xu, D., Tsang, I.W., Luo, J.: Visual event recognition in videos by learning from web data. T-PAMI 34, 1667–1680 (2012)
31. Li, W., Niu, L., Xu, D.: Exploiting privileged information from web data for image categorization. In: Fleet, D., Pajdla, T., Schiele, B., Tuytelaars, T. (eds.) ECCV 2014, Part V. LNCS, vol. 8693, pp. 437–452. Springer, Heidelberg (2014)
32. Niu, L., Li, W., Xu, D.: Exploiting privileged information from web data for action and event recognition. In: IJCAI (2016)

33. Jhuo, I.H., Liu, D., Lee, D., Chang, S.F., et al.: Robust visual domain adaptation with low-rank reconstruction. In: CVPR (2012)
34. Zhou, X., Cui, N., Li, Z., Liang, F., Huang, T.S.: Hierarchical Gaussianization for image classification. In: ICCV (2009)
35. Fe-Fei, L., Fergus, R., Perona, P.: A bayesian approach to unsupervised one-shot learning of object categories. In: ICCV (2003)
36. Ramirez, I., Sprechmann, P., Sapiro, G.: Classification and clustering via dictionary learning with structured incoherence and shared features. In: CVPR (2010)
37. Farquhar, J., Szedmak, S., Meng, H., Shawe-Taylor, J.: Improving bag-of-keypoints image categorisation: Generative models and pdf-kernels. Technical report, University of Southampton (2005)
38. Müller, K.R., Mika, S., Rätsch, G., Tsuda, K., Schölkopf, B.: An introduction to kernel-based learning algorithms. T-NN $12(2)$, 181–201 (2001)
39. Bergamo, A., Torresani, L.: Exploiting weakly-labeled web images to improve object classification: a domain adaptation approach. In: NIPS (2010)
40. Hoffman, J., Rodner, E., Donahue, J., Darrell, T., Saenko, K.: Efficient learning of domain-invariant image representations. In: ICLR (2013)
41. Uijlings, J.R., van de Sande, K.E., Gevers, T., Smeulders, A.W.: Selective search for object recognition. IJCV $104(2)$, 154–171 (2013)
42. Krizhevsky, A., Sutskever, I., Hinton, G.E.: Imagenet classification with deep convolutional neural networks. In: NIPS, pp. 1097–1105 (2012)
43. Jia, Y., Shelhamer, E., Donahue, J., Karayev, S., Long, J., Girshick, R., Guadarrama, S., Darrell, T.: Caffe: Convolutional architecture for fast feature embedding (2014). arXiv preprint arXiv:1408.5093
44. Cheng, Z., Qin, L., Ye, Y., Huang, Q., Tian, Q.: Human daily action analysis with multi-view and color-depth data. In: Fusiello, A., Murino, V., Cucchiara, R. (eds.) ECCV 2012. LNCS, vol. 7584, pp. 52–61. Springer, Heidelberg (2012). doi:10.1007/978-3-642-33868-7_6

Deep Robust Encoder Through Locality Preserving Low-Rank Dictionary

Zhengming Ding[1(✉)], Ming Shao[1], and Yun Fu[1,2]

[1] Department of Electrical and Computer Engineering,
Northeastern University, Boston, USA
{allanding,mingshao}@ece.neu.edu
[2] College of Computer and Information Science,
Northeastern University, Boston, USA
yunfu@ece.neu.edu

Abstract. Deep learning has attracted increasing attentions recently due to its appealing performance in various tasks. As a principal way of deep feature learning, deep auto-encoder has been widely discussed in such problems as dimensionality reduction and model pre-training. Conventional auto-encoder and its variants usually involve additive noises (e.g., Gaussian, masking) for training data to learn robust features, which, however, did not consider the already corrupted data. In this paper, we propose a novel Deep Robust Encoder (DRE) through locality preserving low-rank dictionary to extract robust and discriminative features from corrupted data, where a low-rank dictionary and a regularized deep auto-encoder are jointly optimized. First, we propose a novel loss function in the output layer with a learned low-rank clean dictionary and corresponding weights with locality information, which ensures that the reconstruction is noise free. Second, discriminant graph regularizers that preserve the local geometric structure for the data are developed to guide the deep feature learning in each encoding layer. Experimental results on several benchmarks including object and face images verify the effectiveness of our algorithm by comparing with the state-of-the-art approaches.

Keywords: Auto-encoder · Low-rank dictionary · Graph regularizer

1 Introduction

In the recent years, deep learning has attracted considerable interests in computer vision field, as it has achieved promising performance in various tasks, e.g., image classification [1], object detection [2] and face recognition [3]. Generally, deep structure learning tends to extract hierarchical feature representations directly from raw data. Recent representative research works include: deep convolutional neural networks [4], deep neural networks [5], deep auto-encoder [6], and deeply-supervised nets [7].

© Springer International Publishing AG 2016
B. Leibe et al. (Eds.): ECCV 2016, Part VI, LNCS 9910, pp. 567–582, 2016.
DOI: 10.1007/978-3-319-46466-4_34

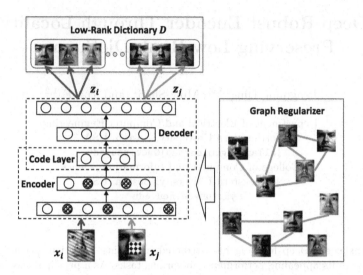

Fig. 1. Illustration of our proposed algorithm. Corrupted data x_i, x_j are the inputs of the deep AE. After encoding and decoding process, the reconstructed x_i, x_j are encouraged to be close to Dz_i, Dz_j on the top, where D is the learned clean low-rank dictionary and z_i, z_j are corresponding coefficients. In addition, graph regularizers are added to the encoder layers to pass on the locality information.

Among different deep structures, auto-encoder (AE) [8] has been treated as robust feature extractors or pre-training scheme in various tasks [9–14]. Conventional AE was proposed to encourage similar or identical input-output pairs where the reconstruction loss is minimized after decoding [8]. Follow-up work with various additive noises in the input layer is able to progressively purify the data, which fulfills the purpose "denoising" against unknown corruptions in the testing data [15]. These works as well as the most recent AE variants, e.g., multi-view AE [13] and bi-shift AE [11], all assume the training data are clean, but can be intentionally corrupted. In fact, real-world data subject to corruptions such as changing illuminations, pose variations, or self-corruption do not meet the assumption above. Therefore, learning deep features from real-world corrupted data instead of intentionally corrupted data with additive noises becomes critical to build robust feature extractor that is generalized well to corrupted testing data. To the best of our knowledge, such AE based deep learning scheme has not been discussed before.

Recently, low-rank matrix constraint has been proposed to learn robust features from corrupted data. Specifically, when data are lying in a single subspace, robust PCA (RPCA) [16] could well recover the corrupted data by seeking a low-rank basis. While low-rank representation (LRR) [17] is designed to recover corrupted data and rule out noises in case of multiple subspaces. Due to these technical merits, low-rank modeling has already been successfully used in different scenarios, e.g., multi-view learning [18], transfer learning [19–21], and dictionary learning [22]. However, fewer works link the low-rank modeling to deep learning framework for robust feature learning.

Inspired by the above facts, we develop a novel algorithm named as Deep Robust Encoder (DRE) with locality preserving low-rank dictionary. The core idea is to jointly optimize deep AE and a clean low-rank dictionary, which can rule out noises and extract robust deep features in a unified framework (Fig. 1). To sum up, our contributions are three folds as follows:

- A low-rank dictionary and deep AE are jointly optimized based on the corrupted data, which can progressively denoise the already corrupted features in the hidden layers so that robust deep AE could be achieved for corrupted testing data.
- The newly designed loss function, which is based on the clean low-rank dictionary and preserved locality information in the output layer, penalizes the corruptions or distortions, meanwhile ensures that the reconstruction is noise free.
- Graph regularizers are developed to guide feature learning in each encoding layer to preserve more geometric structures within the data, in either unsupervised or supervised fashions.

The remaining sections of this paper are organized as follows. In Sect. 2, we present a brief discussion of the related works. Then we propose our novel deep robust encoder in Sect. 3, as well as the solution. Experimental evaluations are reported in Sect. 4, followed by the conclusion in Sect. 5.

2 Related Work

In this section, we mainly discuss the recent related works and highlight the differences between their approaches and ours.

Auto-encoder (AE) has attracted lots of research interests in computer vision fields. It was recently proposed as an efficient scheme for deep structures pretraining and dimensionality reduction [5,8]. Denoising auto-encoder (DAE) generated a robust feature extractor by incorporating artificially random noise to the input data, and then minimized the square loss between reconstructed output and original clean data [15]. Most recently, appealing AE variants have been proposed to handle different learning tasks, e.g., transfer learning [11], domain generalization [12] and multi-view learning [13]. Generally, these variants aim to adapt the knowledge from one domain/view to another by tuning the input or the target data. Different from them, we consider that the real-world data already have been corrupted somehow and we develop an active deep denoising framework to handle the existing corruptions in the training data, which can then be well generalized to the unseen corrupted testing data. However, to the best knowledge, little has been discussed with regard to AE.

Low-rank modeling has demonstrated with appealing performance on robust feature extraction against noisy data. Recently, Robust PCA (RPCA) [16] has been proposed to rule out noises for data lying in a single subspace. Moreover, low-rank representation (LRR) [17] is presented recently to handle real-world noisy data lying in multiple subspaces. It can identify the global subspace structure as well as corruptions. Besides, low-rank modeling has also been adopted in different learning tasks, e.g., generic feature extraction [18], visual domain adaptation [21], robust transfer learning [19], and dictionary learning [22]. In this paper, we also involve the low-rank constraint on the dictionary learning to build a clean and compact basis. Differently, we exploit the low-rank dictionary to reconstruct the outputs of the deep AE with corrupted inputs, instead of the original data [22]. In this way, we could build an active deep denoising framework to generate more robust features from corrupted data. Furthermore, locality-preserving reconstruction helps maintain the geometric structure of the data, which has not been discussed with low-rank dictionary in deep learning before.

3   The Proposed Algorithm

In this section, we first introduce our motivation, and then propose our deep robust encoder through locality preserving low-rank dictionary. Finally, we present an efficient solution to the proposed framework.

3.1   Motivation

Intentional corruptions, e.g., random noises are added artificially while real-world ones are from data itself, e.g., varied lightings or occlusion. Most existing AE and its variants, e.g., DAE, take advantage of different additive noises on the clean data to improve the robustness of deep models. During the deep encoding/decoding process, the perturbed input data are gradually recovered. In this way, the learned deep model is able to tolerate certain corruptions simulated by the additive noises.

However, this raises two problems. First, the robustness of the system completely relies on the formulations of the noises. The richer the noisy patterns are, the better the performance will be. This inevitably increases the computational burden. In the worst case, the learned deep structure may not be well generalized to the unseen testing data. Second, real-world data usually suffer from contaminations of varied sources, and building robust feature extractors to rule out existing noises is more reasonable. In addition, recent advances in low-rank matrix modeling cast a light on denoising for data that are already corrupted. Based on these observations, we propose to jointly learn a deep AE framework and a clean low-rank dictionary to actively mitigate the noises or corruptions within the data (Fig. 2).

3.2   Locality Preserving Low-Rank Dictionary Learning

Suppose training data $X \in \mathbb{R}^{d \times n}$ has n samples and $x_i \in \mathbb{R}^d$ represents the i-th sample. For AE with single hidden layer [5,8], it is usually consisted of two parts,

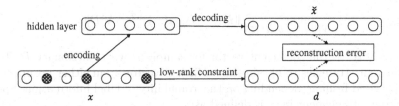

Fig. 2. The AE architecture with low-rank dictionary. A corrupted sample x is correlated to a low-rank clean version d. The AE then maps it to hidden layer (via encoder layer) and attempts to reconstruct x via decoder layer, generating reconstruction $\check{x}$. Finally, reconstruction error can be measured by different loss functions.

encoder and decoder. The encoder, denoted as f_1, attempts to map the input x_i into hidden representations, while the decoder, denoted as f_2, tries to map the hidden representation back to the input x_i. A typical cost function with square loss for AE can be formulated as:

$$\min_{W_1, b_1, W_2, b_2} \sum_{i=1}^{n} \left\| x_i - f_2(f_1(x_i)) \right\|_2^2, \tag{1}$$

where $\{W_1 \in \mathbb{R}^{r \times d}, b_1 \in \mathbb{R}^r\}, \{W_2 \in \mathbb{R}^{d \times r}, b_2 \in \mathbb{R}^d\}$ are the parameters for encoding and decoding, respectively. Specifically, we have $f_1(x_i) = \varphi(W_1 x_i + b_1)$ and $f_2(f_1(x_i)) = \varphi(W_2 f_1(x_i) + b_2)$, where $\varphi(\cdot)$ is an element-wise "activation function", which is usually nonlinear, such as sigmoid function or tanh function. DAE manually involves artificial noise into the input training data so that it aims to train a denoising auto-encoder to remove the random noise.

In reality, however, x_i is usually corrupted already due to environmental factors or noises from the collecting devices. Intuitively, we need to build a network by detecting and removing noise from the corrupted data so that it could better generalize to corrupted testing data. To this end, we propose our robust auto-encoder with low-rank dictionary learning:

$$\min_{W_1, b_1, W_2, b_2, D} \sum_{i=1}^{n} \left\| d_i - f_2(f_1(x_i)) \right\|_2^2 + \lambda \mathrm{rank}(D), \tag{2}$$

where $d_i \in \mathbb{R}^d$ is the i-th column of low-rank $D \in \mathbb{R}^{d \times n}$ and λ is the tradeoff parameter. $\mathrm{rank}(\cdot)$ means the rank operator of a matrix, which encourages to build a clean and compact basis. Generally, the convex surrogate of rank problem, i.e., nuclear norm $\| \cdot \|_*$ will be employed to solve the rank minimization problem [16].

However, similar to the conventional AE and its variants, the point-to-point reconstruction scheme in Eq. (2) only considers one-to-one mapping, which may overfit the data and skip the structure knowledge within the data. To that end, we propose a novel locality preserving low-rank dictionary learning by introducing a new coefficient vector z_i to maintain the locality of each sample x_i throughout the network:

$$\min_{W_1,b_1,W_2,b_2,D} \sum_{i=1}^{n} \|Dz_i - f_2(f_1(x_i))\|_2^2 + \lambda\|D\|_*, \tag{3}$$

where $z_i \in \mathbb{R}^n$ is the coefficient vector for sample x_i w.r.t. dictionary D. There are different strategies to obtain the coefficient vector z_i, in either unsupervised or supervised fashion, depending on the availability of label information. Specifically, the j-th element in z_i is defined as:

$$z_{ij} = \begin{cases} 1, & \text{if } i = j, \\ \exp\left(-\frac{\|x_i - x_j\|^2}{2\sigma^2}\right), & \text{if } x_i \in \mathcal{N}_{k_1}(x_j), \\ 0, & \text{otherwise}, \end{cases} \tag{4}$$

where $x_i \in \mathcal{N}_{k_1}(x_j)$ means x_i is within the k_1 nearest neighbors of x_j. Specifically, we could define the locality-preserving coefficients z_i in two fashions. For unsupervised case, the k_1 nearest neighbors are searched from the whole data, while for supervised case, the k_1 nearest neighbors are searched from the data within the same class to x_i. Actually, we could easily extend semi-supervised scenario. Note σ is a bandwidth for Gaussian kernel (we set $\sigma = 5$ in this paper).

To sum up, our regularized deep auto-encoder transform the original AE's point-to-point reconstruction strategy to our point-to-set reconstruction so that we could preserve more discriminative information. To further guide the locality preserving dictionary learning in the output layer, we propose to couple the discriminant graph regularizers with hidden feature learning during the optimization:

$$\min_{W_1,b_1,W_2,b_2,D} \sum_{i=1}^{n} \|Dz_i - f_2(f_1(x_i))\|_2^2 + \lambda\|D\|_* \\ +\alpha \sum_{j=1}^{n} \sum_{k=1}^{n} s_{jk}(f_1(x_j) - f_1(x_k))^2, \tag{5}$$

where s_{jk} is the similarity between x_j and x_k. α is the balance parameter.

Specifically, s_{jk} can be calculated in unsupervised and supervised fashions as well:

$$s_{jk} = \begin{cases} \exp\left(-\frac{\|x_j - x_k\|^2}{2\sigma^2}\right), & \text{if } x_j \in \mathcal{N}_{k_2}(x_k), \\ 0, & \text{otherwise}, \end{cases} \tag{6}$$

where $x_j \in \mathcal{N}_{k_2}(x_k)$ means x_j is within the k_2 nearest neighbors of x_k. In the same way as z_i, the k_2 nearest neighbors are selected from the whole dataset for unsupervised case, while the k_2 nearest neighbors are selected from the data within the same class to x_j for supervised case.

3.3 Deep Architecture

Considering the learning objective in Eq. (5) as a basic building block, we can train a more discriminant deep model. Existing popular training schemes for deep auto-encoder includes Stacked Auto-Encoder (SAE) [15] and Deep Auto-Encoder [6]. However, as our learning objective/building block is different from theirs, we have a different training scheme for the deep structure.

Assume we have L encoding layers and L decoding layers in our deep structure which minimizes the following loss:

$$
\min_{W_l, b_l, D} \sum_{i=1}^{n} \|Dz_i - \bar{x}_i\|_2^2 + \lambda \|D\|_*
$$
$$
+ \alpha \sum_{l=1}^{L} \sum_{j=1}^{n} \sum_{k=1}^{n} s_{jk} (f_l(x_j) - f_l(x_k))^2, \tag{7}
$$

where $\bar{x}_i$ is the output with a series of encoding and decoding from the input x_i. $\{W_l, b_l\}, (1 \le l \le L)$ are the encoding parameters while $\{W_l, b_l\}, (L+1 \le l \le 2L)$ are the decoding parameters. The third term sums up the graph regularizers from each encoding layer to guide the locality preserving low-rank dictionary learning in the output layer.

3.4   Optimization

Equation (7) is difficult to address because of the non-convexity and non-linearity of the building block formulated in Eq. (5). To this end, we develop an alternating solution to iteratively update the encoding & decoding functions $f_l (1 \le l \le 2L)$ and dictionary D. First we list the low-rank dictionary learning, then provide the regularized deep auto-encoder optimization.

Low-Rank Dictionary Learning. When $f_l (1 \le l \le 2L)$ are fixed, the objective function in Eq. (7) degenerates to a conventional low-rank recovery problem, which can be solved by augmented Lagrange multiplier algorithm [23]. To that end, we first involve a relaxing variable J, and write down its equivalent formulation as:

$$
\min_{D, J} \|\bar{X} - DZ\|_F^2 + \lambda \|J\|_*, \quad \text{s.t.} \ \ D = J,
$$

where $\bar{X} = [\bar{x}_1, \cdots, \bar{x}_n]$ and $Z = [z_1, \cdots, z_n]$. $\|\cdot\|_F^2$ is Frobenius norm of a matrix. Then we derive the corresponding augmented Lagrangian function w.r.t. D, J:

$$
\|\bar{X} - DZ\|_F^2 + \lambda \|J\|_* + \langle R, D - J \rangle + \frac{\mu}{2} \|D - J\|_F^2,
$$

where R is the Lagrange multiplier and $\mu > 0$ is the penalty parameter. $\langle, \rangle$ is the matrix inner product operator. Specifically, we have the following updating rules for D, J one variable at time t:

$$
J_{t+1} = \arg\min_{J} \frac{\lambda}{\mu_t} \|J\|_* + \frac{1}{2} \|J - D_t - \frac{R_t}{\mu_t}\|_F^2, \tag{8}
$$

which can be effectively addressed by the singular value thresholding (SVT) operator [24].

$$
D_{t+1} = \arg\min_{D} \|\bar{X} - DZ\|_F^2 + \langle R_t, D - J_{t+1} \rangle + \frac{\mu_t}{2} \|D - J_{t+1}\|_F^2
$$
$$
= (2\bar{X}Z^\top + \mu_t J_{t+1} - R_t)(2ZZ^\top + \mu_t I_n)^{-1}, \tag{9}
$$

where $I_n \in \mathbb{R}^{n \times n}$ is an identical matrix.

Deep Robust Encoder Learning. When D is fixed, the objective function in Eq. (7) can be reformulated to minimize the following objective function:

$$\mathcal{L} = \sum_{i=1}^{n} \|\bar{x}_i - \bar{d}_i\|_2^2 + \alpha \sum_{l=1}^{L} \sum_{j=1}^{n} \sum_{k=1}^{n} s_{jk}(f_l(x_j) - f_l(x_k))^2,$$

where $\bar{d}_i = Dz_i$. Since the loss function (Eq. (3.4)) is smooth and twice-differentiable, we can still adopt L-BFGS optimizer [25] to deal with this unconstrained problem, whose updating rules at time t are shown as follows:

$$
\begin{cases}
W_{l,t+1} = W_{l,t} - \eta_t H_{l,t} \dfrac{\partial \mathcal{L}}{\partial W_l}|_{W_{l,t}}, \\[2mm]
b_{l,t+1} = b_{l,t} - \eta_t G_{l,t} \dfrac{\partial \mathcal{L}}{\partial b_l}|_{b_{l,t}},
\end{cases}
\tag{10}
$$

in which η_t denotes the learning rate, $H_{l,t}$ and $G_{l,t}$ are the approximations for the inverse Hessian matrices of $\mathcal{L}$ w.r.t. to W_l and b_l, respectively. The detailed formulations and discussions of η_t, $H_{l,t}$ and $G_{l,t}$ are trivial, which can be referred to [25]. In this section, we mainly focus on the derivatives of $\mathcal{L}$ w.r.t. to W_l and b_l.

For the **decoding layers** $(L + 1 \leq l \leq 2L)$, we have:

$$\frac{\partial \mathcal{L}}{\partial W_l} = \sum_{i=1}^{n} \mathcal{F}_{i,l} \mathbf{f}_{i,l-1}^{\top}, \qquad \frac{\partial \mathcal{L}}{\partial b_l} = \sum_{i=1}^{n} \mathcal{F}_{i,l},$$

where $\mathbf{f}_{i,l-1} = f_{l-1}(x_i)$ is the $l\text{-}1^{\text{th}}$-layer hidden layer feature and the updating equations are computed as follows:

$$
\begin{aligned}
\mathcal{F}_{i,2L} &= 2(\bar{x}_i - \bar{d}_i) \odot \varphi'(\mathbf{u}_{i,2L}), \\
\mathcal{F}_{i,l} &= (W_{l+1}^{\top} \mathcal{F}_{i,l+1}) \odot \varphi'(\mathbf{u}_{i,l}).
\end{aligned}
$$

Here the operator $\odot$ denotes the element-wise multiplication, and $\mathbf{u}_{i,l}$ is computed by $\mathbf{u}_{i,l} = W_l \mathbf{f}_{i,l-1} + b_l$.

For the **encoding layers** $(1 \leq l \leq L)$, we have:

$$
\begin{aligned}
\frac{\partial \mathcal{L}}{\partial W_l} &= \sum_{i=1}^{n} \mathcal{F}_{i,l} \mathbf{f}_{i,l-1}^{\top} + \\
&\quad 2\alpha \sum_{p=l}^{L} \sum_{j=1}^{n} \sum_{k=1}^{n} s_{jk}(\mathcal{G}_{jk,p} \mathbf{f}_{j,p-1}^{\top} + \mathcal{G}_{kj,p} \mathbf{f}_{k,p-1}^{\top}), \\
\frac{\partial \mathcal{L}}{\partial b_l} &= \sum_{i=1}^{n} \mathcal{F}_{i,l} + 2\alpha \sum_{p=l}^{L} \sum_{j=1}^{n} \sum_{k=1}^{n} s_{jk}(\mathcal{G}_{jk,p} + \mathcal{G}_{kj,p}),
\end{aligned}
$$

in which $\mathcal{G}_{jk,l}$ and $\mathcal{G}_{kj,l}$ are calculated as follows:

$$
\begin{aligned}
\mathcal{G}_{jk,L} &= (\mathbf{f}_{j,l} - \mathbf{f}_{k,l}) \odot \varphi'(\mathbf{u}_{j,L}), \\
\mathcal{G}_{kj,L} &= (\mathbf{f}_{k,l} - \mathbf{f}_{j,l}) \odot \varphi'(\mathbf{u}_{k,L}), \\
\mathcal{G}_{jk,l} &= (W_{l+1}^{\top} \mathcal{G}_{jk,l+1}) \odot \varphi'(\mathbf{u}_{j,l}), \\
\mathcal{G}_{kj,l} &= (W_{l+1}^{\top} \mathcal{G}_{kj,l+1}) \odot \varphi'(\mathbf{u}_{k,l}).
\end{aligned}
$$

To that end, we can optimize low-rank dictionary and deep auto-encoder iteratively until convergence. The entire procedure of two sub-problems is listed in **Algorithm 1**. Before the alternative updating, the network parameters $f_l(1 \le l \le 2L)$ are initialized through deep auto-encoder with the input and the target as X [6], whilst D is directly set as original data X for initialization.

Algorithm 1. Solution to Problem (7)

Input: $\{X, y\}$, α, λ, $\eta_0 = 0.2, \varepsilon = 10^{-6}, t = 0$,
$\qquad \mu_0 = 10^{-6}, \rho = 1.3, \mu_{\max} = 10^6$, and $t_{\max} = 10^3$.

while not converged **or** $t < t_{\max}$ **do**
  Step 1. Update low-rank dictionary via (8),(9);
  Step 2. Update the deep auto-encoder:
  | **for** $l = 2L, \cdots, 1$ **do**
  | | Compute derivatives $\dfrac{\partial \mathcal{L}}{\partial W_l}, \dfrac{\partial \mathcal{L}}{\partial b_l}$;
  | **end**
  | **for** $l = 1, \cdots, 2L$ **do**
  | | Update W_l, b_l using (10);
  | **end**
  Step 3. Update parameters:
  | $R_{t+1} = R_t + \mu_t(D_{t+1} - J_{t+1})$; $\eta_{t+1} = 0.95 \times \eta_t$;
  | $\mu_{t+1} = \min(\mu_{\max}, \rho\mu_t)$; $t = t + 1$.
  Step 4. Check convergence:
  | $|\mathcal{L}_{t+1} - \mathcal{L}_t| < \varepsilon$, $\|D_{t+1} - J_{t+1}\|_\infty < \varepsilon$.
end

Output: $\{W_l, b_l, D, J\}$.

---

4 Experiments

In this section, we conduct experiments to systematically evaluate our algorithm. First, we present the details of datasets and experimental settings. Then we do self-evaluation on our algorithm and present the comparison results with several state-of-the-art algorithms. Finally, we further testify several properties of the proposed algorithm, e.g., impacts of layer size, parameter analysis.

4.1 Datasets and Experimental Settings

COIL dataset[1] includes 72 views from 100 objects with different illumination conditions (Fig. 3). Each object is captured in equally spaced views, i.e., 5 degrees. In our experiments, we adopt the gray-scale images and resize them to 32×32. We randomly select ten images per object to build the training set, and the rest images as the testing set. We repeat the random selection process 20 times, and report the average performance. In addition, we perform scalability evaluations by gradually involving more categories from 20 to 100. Furthermore,

---

[1] http://www1.cs.columbia.edu/CAVE/software/softlib/coil-100.php.

Fig. 3. Samples of two datasets: COIL-100 (left) and CMU-PIE (right). We show original images and 10 % corrupted ones for COIL-100. For CMU-PIE, the original faces already show large variance with one subject.

Table 1. Recognition results (%) of 4 approaches on different setting of three datasets.

	COIL-100c	PIE-1	PIE-2	PIE-1c	PIE-2c	ALOI-c
AE	74.56 ± 0.38	83.58 ± 0.11	82.79 ± 0.13	74.95 ± 0.14	73.89±0.12	80.98 ± 0.98
LAE	78.32 ± 0.46	85.87 ± 0.16	85.08 ± 0.14	77.82 ± 0.12	76.14 ± 1.45	82.84 ± 1.26
L^2AE-u	79.84 ± 0.64	86.98 ± 0.09	86.45 ± 0.11	79.23 ± 0.11	79.02 ± 0.12	83.42 ± 0.87
L^2AE-s	82.42 ± 0.72	87.67 ± 0.10	87.54 ± 0.12	80.14 ± 0.10	79.96 ± 0.11	86.27 ± 0.75

we also evaluate the robustness of different approaches to noise by adding 10 % random corruption to the original images.

CMU-PIE Face dataset[2] contains 68 subjects under different poses subject to large appearance differences (Fig. 3). In addition, for each pose, there are 21 various illumination conditions. We use face images from 8 different poses to construct various evaluation sets. The sizes of them vary from 2 to 5. Basically, we randomly select 15 images per pose per subject to build the training set while the left as the testing set. The face images are cropped and resized to 64 × 64, and the raw features are used as the inputs.

ALOI dataset[3] consists of 1000 object categories captured from different viewing angles. Specifically, each object has 72 equally spaced views. In this experiments, we select the first 300 objects by following the setting in [26], where the images are transformed to gray-scale and resized to 36 × 48. Furthermore, 10 % pixel corruption is added to testify the robustness of different methods.

Note that previous algorithms, e.g., DAE [15], adopted the "corrupted" data with random noise as the input for training while using the "original" data for testing. However, we assume the data are "already corrupted" and we manage to detect and remove the noise. Thus, we adopt the "same" types of training and testing data without intentional corruptions. Notably, to challenge all comparisons, we introduce additional noises to the datasets that have already been corrupted by poor lighting or arbitrary views. Such practice can be found in previous work [22, 26].

---

[2] http://vasc.ri.cmu.edu/idb/html/face/.
[3] http://aloi.science.uva.nl/.

4.2   Self-evaluation

In this section, we mainly testify if our low-rank dictionary D and locality preserving term $Z = [z_1, \cdots, z_n]$ would facilitate our robust feature learning. Specifically, we define the deep version of Eq.(2) as LAE (Auto-encoder with low-rank dictionary) and deep version of Eq. (3) as L^2AE (Auto-encoder with locality preserving low-rank dictionary). For L^2AE, we have two ways to learn Z, that is, we set $k_1 = k_2 = 5$ for all cases in unsupervised fashion (L^2AE-u), while we set k_1, k_2 as the size of each class for supervised fashion (L^2AE-s). A four-layer scheme is applied for all the comparisons for simplicity. We adopt corrupted COIL-100 and ALOI, while both original and corrupted images of CMU-PIE to testify these algorithms with the baseline, conventional AE [8]. The comparison results are shown in Table 1, where COIL-100c means the 10 % corrupted COIL using 100 objects, PIE-1 and PIE-2 denote the two views cases $\{C02, C14\}, \{C02, C27\}$ with its 10 % corrupted versions PIE-1c and PIE-2c, respectively. ALOI-c represents the 10 % corrupted data.

From the results, we could observe that LAE outperforms the conventional AE, that means jointly learning the low-rank dictionary could boost the deep feature learning of auto-encoder. Furthermore, we witness that our robust AEs with locality preserving low-rank dictionary could achieve better performance than LAE and AE for both unsupervised and supervised settings. That is, locality preserving property could generate more discriminative features for classification.

4.3   Comparison Experiments

We mainly compare with (1) traditional feature extract methods: PCA [27], LDA [28]; (2) low-rank based algorithms: RPCA+LDA [16], LatLRR [29], DLRD [22], LRCS [18], SRRS [26]. Specifically, PCA, LDA, RPCA+LDA, LRCS and SRRS belong to dimensionality reduction algorithms so that we search the optimal dimensionality for each to report the performance. Besides, to further evaluate the effectiveness of our algorithm, DAE [15] is adopted as the baseline. For our algorithm, we have two modes, i.e., unsupervised mode (Ours-I), and supervised mode (Ours-II). Specifically, we set parameters $\alpha = 10^2, \lambda = 10^{-2}$. For DAE and our two modes, we apply a four-layer deep structure. For Ours-I, we set $k_1 = k_2 = 5$ for all cases, while for Ours-II, we set k_1, k_2 as the size of each class. We apply the nearest neighbor classifier (NNC) for all algorithms except DLRD and show experimental results in Tables 2 and 3 and Fig. 4(a).

From Tables 2 and 3 and Fig. 4(a), we could observe our proposed algorithm in two modes outperforms others in most cases, especially for the corruption cases. In the corruption cases, our method has a significant improvement over others on two datasets (about 7 % improvement on corrupted COIL dataset). All the algorithms suffer from additional noises; however, ours can still achieve appealing performance (only 1–2 % performance degradation), which demonstrates the superiority of our method against noises in feature learning.

Z. Ding et al.

Table 2. Recognition results (%) of 9 algorithms on COIL-100 in different evaluation sizes, from 20 to 100 objects, where C1 to C5 denote 20 objects to 100 objects, respectively. Red color denotes the best recognition rates. Blue color denotes the second best.

	PCA	LDA	RPCA+LDA	DLRD	LatLRR	SRRS	DAE	Ours-I	Ours-II
Original images									
C1	86.42 ± 1.11	81.83 ± 2.03	83.26 ± 1.52	89.58 ± 1.04	88.98 ± 0.85	92.03 ± 1.21	87.81 ± 1.43	90.65 ± 1.34	92.63 ± 0.95
C2	83.75 ± 1.12	77.08 ± 1.36	78.39 ± 1.15	85.18 ± 1.10	88.45 ± 0.64	92.51 ± 0.65	84.77 ± 1.25	90.34 ± 1.12	92.21 ± 0.63
C3	81.01 ± 0.92	66.96 ± 1.52	68.93 ± 0.86	82.60 ± 1.06	86.36 ± 0.52	90.82 ± 0.43	80.85 ± 0.65	87.69 ± 0.82	89.83 ± 0.52
C4	80.53 ± 0.78	59.34 ± 1.22	60.73 ± 0.68	81.10 ± 0.58	84.67 ± 0.79	88.75 ± 0.71	79.75 ± 0.61	85.15 ± 0.60	88.96 ± 0.91
C5	82.75 ± 0.59	52.29 ± 0.30	56.44 ± 0.73	79.92 ± 0.93	82.64 ± 0.60	85.12 ± 0.33	78.99 ± 0.48	84.21 ± 0.69	86.02 ± 0.61
Corrupted images with 10 % random noise									
C1	71.43 ± 1.12	47.77 ± 3.06	49.35 ± 1.55	82.96 ± 1.81	81.38 ± 1.25	86.45 ± 1.12	82.37 ± 1.37	89.77 ± 0.94	90.72 ± 1.25
C2	70.22 ± 1.56	45.89 ± 1.12	53.26 ± 1.84	60.46 ± 0.79	81.93 ± 0.92	82.03 ± 1.31	81.13 ± 0.83	89.52 ± 0.66	90.98 ± 0.54
C3	69.80 ± 0.65	36.42 ± 1.12	44.18 ± 2.65	49.88 ± 0.49	80.97 ± 0.45	82.05 ± 0.87	79.61 ± 1.02	86.97 ± 0.62	89.21 ± 0.92
C4	67.84 ± 0.83	27.13 ± 0.95	29.92 ± 0.96	41.52 ± 0.71	77.15 ± 0.72	79.83 ± 0.62	76.23 ± 0.59	84.57 ± 0.52	87.33 ± 0.87
C5	65.68 ± 0.76	16.79 ± 0.34	23.55 ± 0.46	73.82 ± 0.77	73.47 ± 0.62	74.95 ± 0.65	72.15 ± 0.60	83.64 ± 0.44	85.86 ± 0.62

Table 3. Recognition results (%) on CMU-PIE face database, where P1: {C02, C14}, P2: {C02, C27}, P3: {C14, C27}, P4: {C05, C07, C29}, P5: {C05, C14, C29, C34}, P6: {C02, C05, C14, C29, C31}. Red color denotes the best recognition rates. Blue color denotes the second best.

	PCA	LDA	RPCA+LDA	LatLRR	SRRS	LRCS	DAE	Ours-I	Ours-II
Original images									
P1	69.03 ± 0.08	70.46 ± 0.05	74.39 ± 0.08	77.92 ± 0.03	78.27 ± 0.04	87.78 ± 0.02	85.65 ± 0.12	87.97 ± 0.06	88.04 ± 0.08
P2	69.21 ± 0.08	71.32 ± 0.02	75.55 ± 0.12	76.24 ± 0.12	78.74 ± 0.23	86.67 ± 0.01	84.32 ± 0.09	87.61 ± 0.03	87.88 ± 0.06
P3	68.52 ± 0.12	63.51 ± 0.75	75.29 ± 0.09	75.29 ± 0.07	77.45 ± 0.02	87.38 ± 0.19	84.53 ± 0.04	87.87 ± 0.09	88.01 ± 0.06
P4	52.65 ± 0.04	56.53 ± 0.02	61.17 ± 0.12	69.74 ± 0.05	71.44 ± 0.03	74.84 ± 0.04	71.87 ± 0.09	74.08 ± 0.07	75.06 ± 0.13
P5	34.94 ± 0.08	24.07 ± 0.25	38.66 ± 0.08	42.54 ± 0.12	38.86 ± 0.02	44.48 ± 0.03	42.32 ± 0.07	44.42 ± 0.10	45.35 ± 0.09
P6	29.09 ± 0.01	7.06 ± 0.01	31.94 ± 0.12	35.33 ± 0.04	30.16 ± 0.02	36.17 ± 0.01	33.50 ± 0.05	36.42 ± 0.03	36.54 ± 0.04
Corrupted images with 10 % random noise									
P1	64.87 ± 0.32	26.71 ± 0.20	73.07 ± 0.11	73.10 ± 0.07	72.27 ± 0.05	78.98 ± 0.03	77.14 ± 0.11	81.02 ± 0.08	81.54 ± 0.07
P2	66.04 ± 0.08	23.19 ± 0.35	74.28 ± 0.12	73.24 ± 0.32	72.74 ± 0.18	78.67 ± 0.05	76.98 ± 0.06	81.12 ± 0.09	81.48 ± 0.10
P3	65.21 ± 0.04	20.34 ± 0.75	73.92 ± 0.12	73.85 ± 0.12	71.45 ± 0.08	78.38 ± 0.26	77.32 ± 0.09	81.94 ± 0.12	82.31 ± 0.08
P4	50.16 ± 0.04	46.72 ± 0.02	60.18 ± 0.14	58.94 ± 0.09	54.32 ± 0.03	65.84 ± 0.04	70.64 ± 0.08	73.73 ± 0.09	74.83 ± 0.12
P5	31.74 ± 0.08	6.67 ± 0.25	37.65 ± 0.09	39.26 ± 0.12	32.34 ± 0.02	39.48 ± 0.03	40.32 ± 0.09	43.92 ± 0.08	43.81 ± 0.09
P6	27.21 ± 0.01	4.06 ± 0.01	31.34 ± 0.06	32.07 ± 0.03	29.03 ± 0.02	32.57 ± 0.01	33.12 ± 0.09	35.33 ± 0.02	34.59 ± 0.07

In COIL dataset, we can observe that low-rank modeling based methods also achieve very good results compared with DAE, although the latter adds additive noises to train robust deep models. This demonstrates the robustness of low-rank modeling against noisy data. In the CMU-PIE dataset, DAE could achieve very similar performance to low-rank modeling based methods, in both supervised and unsupervised fashions. Similar results can be found from ALOI dataset. On CMU-PIE dataset, our algorithm cannot significantly improve the performance. One reason is that the facial appearances under different views on CMU-PIE dataset are very different. Considering additional illumination variations, this raises a very challenging feature learning problem on real-world dataset. However, our algorithm could still achieve promising performance, even better than a most recent multi-view learning method, LRCS. This further verifies the robustness of our algorithm against noises from real world. Generally, our supervised

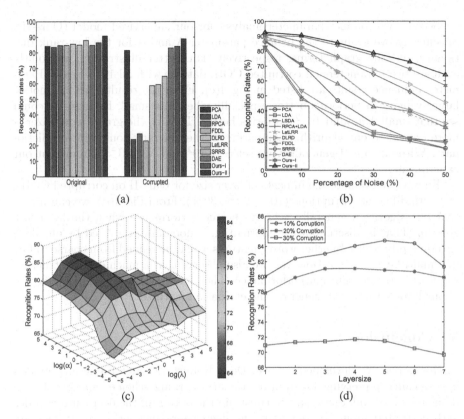

Fig. 4. (a) Recognition results (%) of 9 algorithms on ALOI-300 in original and 10 % corrupted cases. (b) Recognition rates of all comparisons on COIL database with different levels of noise. (c) Parameters analysis on α and λ. (d) The impact of layer size to the recognition performance.

model outperforms unsupervised one in almost all the cases. This demonstrates the importance of discriminative information in classification tasks.

4.4 Property Evaluation

In this section, we further evaluate several properties of our proposed algorithm, e.g., robustness to noise, parameter influence and layer size impact, to achieve a better understanding of the proposed model.

First of all, we evaluate the impacts of different corruption ratios to different algorithms. We evaluate 0 %, 10 %, 20 %, 30 %, 40 %, and 50 % corruptions with 20 objects on COIL dataset, and report results in Fig. 4(b), where our algorithm in two modes consistently outperforms other competitors. This demonstrates that our proposed algorithm can build a more robust feature extractor, especially for data with large corruption. Therefore, our algorithm could work efficiently in real-world applications with various noise.

Second, we conduct parameter analysis for our supervised model (Ours-II). Specifically, we evaluate the balance parameter λ and α for the low-rank dictionary and the graph terms, respectively. For better illustration, we jointly evaluate two parameters on corrupted COIL dataset with all 100 objects. Parameter influence results are listed in Fig. 4(c). From the results, we can notice larger value of α performs better especially when λ is small. Besides, we could see that small λ around 10^{-2} performs better. That is, the graph regularizer is more critical to our algorithm comparing to the low-rank constraint on dictionary. Without loss of generality, we set $\alpha = 10^2$ and $\lambda = 10^{-2}$ throughout our experiments.

Finally, we evaluate the impacts of layer size for Ours-II on corrupted COIL-100 with different corruptions (10 %, 20 %, 30 %). From Fig. 4(d), we can notice that our algorithm generally achieves better performance when the layer size goes up. That is, discriminative information is hopefully recovered by our deep encoding procedure. In other words, features would be refined from coarse to fine in a multi-layer fashion. However, we also observe that a much deeper structure would ruin the recognition performance. Therefore, in the experiments, we use a four-layer structure to generate the evaluation features.

5   Conclusion

In this paper, we developed a novel Deep Robust Encoder framework guided by a locality preserving low-rank dictionary learning scheme. Specifically, we designed a low-rank dictionary to constrain the output of the deep auto-encoder with corrupted input. In this way, the deep neural networks would generate more robust features by detecting noise from the corrupted data. Moreover, coefficient vectors z_i were maintained through the networks so that each output sample would be reconstructed by the most similar data samples in the dictionary with different weights. Furthermore, graph regularizers were developed to couple each layer's encoding to preserve more geometric structure. In experiments, we achieved more effective features for classification and results on several benchmarks demonstrated our method's superiority over other methods.

Acknowledgment. This research is supported in part by the NSF CNS award 1314484, ONR award N00014-12-1-1028, ONR Young Investigator Award N00014-14-1-0484, and U.S. Army Research Office Young Investigator Award W911NF-14-1-0218.

References

1. Donahue, J., Jia, Y., Vinyals, O., Hoffman, J., Zhang, N., Tzeng, E., Darrell, T.: Decaf: a deep convolutional activation feature for generic visual recognition. In: International Conference on Machine Learning, pp. 647–655 (2014)
2. Szegedy, C., Toshev, A., Erhan, D.: Deep neural networks for object detection. In: Neural Information Processing Systems, pp. 2553–2561 (2013)

3. Taigman, Y., Yang, M., Ranzato, M., Wolf, L.: Deepface: closing the gap to human-level performance in face verification. In: IEEE Conference on Computer Vision and Pattern Recognition, pp. 1701–1708. IEEE (2014)
4. Krizhevsky, A., Sutskever, I., Hinton, G.E.: Imagenet classification with deep convolutional neural networks. In: Neural Information Processing Systems, pp. 1097–1105 (2012)
5. Bengio, Y.: Learning deep architectures for ai. Found. Trends Mach. Learn. 2(1), 1–127 (2009)
6. Le, Q.V., Ngiam, J., Coates, A., Lahiri, A., Prochnow, B., Ng, A.Y.: On optimization methods for deep learning. In: International Conference on Machine Learning, pp. 265–272 (2011)
7. Lee, C.Y., Xie, S., Gallagher, P., Zhang, Z., Tu, Z.: Deeply-supervised nets. In: International Conference on Artificial Intelligence and Statistics, pp. 562–570 (2015)
8. Hinton, G.E., Salakhutdinov, R.R.: Reducing the dimensionality of data with neural networks. Science 313(5786), 504–507 (2006)
9. Hinton, G.E., Krizhevsky, A., Wang, S.D.: Transforming auto-encoders. In: Honkela, T., Duch, W., Girolami, M., Kaski, S. (eds.) ICANN 2011. LNCS, vol. 6791, pp. 44–51. Springer, Heidelberg (2011). doi:10.1007/978-3-642-21735-7_6
10. Droniou, A., Sigaud, O.: Gated autoencoders with tied input weights. In: International Conference on Machine Learning, pp. 154–162 (2013)
11. Kan, M., Shan, S., Chen, X.: Bi-shifting auto-encoder for unsupervised domain adaptation. In: IEEE International Conference on Computer Vision, pp. 3846–3854 (2015)
12. Ghifary, M., Bastiaan Kleijn, W., Zhang, M., Balduzzi, D.: Domain generalization for object recognition with multi-task autoencoders. In: IEEE International Conference on Computer Vision, pp. 2551–2559 (2015)
13. Wang, W., Arora, R., Livescu, K., Bilmes, J.: On deep multi-view representation learning. In: International Conference on Machine Learning, pp. 1083–1092 (2015)
14. Xia, C., Qi, F., Shi, G.: Bottom-up visual saliency estimation with deep autoencoder-based sparse reconstruction. IEEE Trans. Neural Netw. Learn. Syst. 27(6), 1227–1240 (2016)
15. Vincent, P., Larochelle, H., Lajoie, I., Bengio, Y., Manzagol, P.A.: Stacked denoising autoencoders: learning useful representations in a deep network with a local denoising criterion. J. Mach. Learn. Res. 11, 3371–3408 (2010)
16. Wright, J., Ganesh, A., Rao, S., Peng, Y., Ma, Y.: Robust principal component analysis: exact recovery of corrupted low-rank matrices via convex optimization. In: Neural Information Processing Systems, pp. 2080–2088 (2009)
17. Liu, G., Lin, Z., Yan, S., Sun, J., Yu, Y., Ma, Y.: Robust recovery of subspace structures by low-rank representation. IEEE Trans. Pattern Anal. Mach. Intell. 35(1), 171–184 (2013)
18. Ding, Z., Fu, Y.: Low-rank common subspace for multi-view learning. In: IEEE International Conference on Data Mining, pp. 110–119. IEEE (2014)
19. Shao, M., Kit, D., Fu, Y.: Generalized transfer subspace learning through low-rank constraint. Int. J. Comput. Vis. 109(1–2), 74–93 (2014)
20. Ding, Z., Shao, M., Fu, Y.: Deep low-rank coding for transfer learning. In: Twenty-Fourth International Joint Conference on Artificial Intelligence, pp. 3453–3459 (2015)
21. Jhuo, I.H., Liu, D., Lee, D., Chang, S.F., et al.: Robust visual domain adaptation with low-rank reconstruction. In: IEEE Conference on Computer Vision and Pattern Recognition, pp. 2168–2175. IEEE (2012)

22. Ma, L., Wang, C., Xiao, B., Zhou, W.: Sparse representation for face recognition based on discriminative low-rank dictionary learning. In: IEEE Conference on Computer Vision and Pattern Recognition, pp. 2586–2593. IEEE (2012)
23. Lin, Z., Chen, M., Ma, Y.: The augmented lagrange multiplier method for exact recovery of corrupted low-rank matrices. arXiv preprint (2010). arXiv:1009.5055
24. Cai, J.F., Candès, E.J., Shen, Z.: A singular value thresholding algorithm for matrix completion. SIAM J. Optim. **20**(4), 1956–1982 (2010)
25. Liu, D.C., Nocedal, J.: On the limited memory bfgs method for large scale optimization. Math. Program. **45**(1–3), 503–528 (1989)
26. Li, S., Fu, Y.: Learning robust and discriminative subspace with low-rank constraints. IEEE Trans. Neural Netw. Learn. Syst. PP(99), 1–13 (2015)
27. Turk, M., Pentland, A.: Eigenfaces for recognition. J. Cogn. Neurosci. **3**(1), 71–86 (1991)
28. Belhumeur, P.N., Hespanha, J.P., Kriegman, D.J.: Eigenfaces vs. fisherfaces: recognition using class specific linear projection. IEEE Trans. Pattern Anal. Mach. Intell. **19**(7), 711–720 (1997)
29. Liu, G., Yan, S.: Latent low-rank representation for subspace segmentation and feature extraction. In: IEEE International Conference on Computer Vision, pp. 1615–1622 (2011)

Pattern Mining Saliency

Yuqiu Kong[1], Lijun Wang[2], Xiuping Liu[1], Huchuan Lu[2(✉)], and Xiang Ruan[3]

[1] Department of Mathematical Sciences,
Dalian University of Technology, Dalian, China
jinghongkyq@mail.dlut.edu.cn, xpliu@dlut.edu.cn
[2] Department of Electrical Engineering,
Dalian University of Technology, Dalian, China
wlj@mail.dlut.edu.cn, lhchuan@dlut.edu.cn
[3] Tiwaki Corporation, Tiwaki, Japan
ruanxiang@gmail.com

Abstract. This paper presents a new method to promote the performance of existing saliency detection algorithms. Prior bottom-up methods predict saliency maps by combining heuristic saliency cues, which may be unreliable. To remove error outputs and preserve accurate predictions, we develop a pattern mining based saliency seeds selection method. Given initial saliency maps, our method can effectively recognize discriminative and representative saliency patterns (features), which are robust to the noise in initial maps and can more accurately distinguish foreground from background. According to the mined saliency patterns, more reliable saliency seeds can be acquired. To further propagate the saliency labels of saliency seeds to other image regions, an Extended Random Walk (ERW) algorithm is proposed. Compared with prior methods, the proposed ERW regularized by a quadratic Laplacian term ensures the diffusion of seeds information to more distant areas and allows the incorporation of external classifiers. The contributions of our method are complementary to existing methods. Extensive evaluations on four data sets show that our method can significantly improve accuracy of existing methods and achieves more superior performance than state-of-the-arts.

Keywords: Saliency detection · Pattern mining · Random walk

1 Introduction

Saliency detection is a fundamental problem that has found wide applications in various computer vision tasks, such as object recognition [1], image segmentation [2] and visual tracking [3]. As a pre-processing step, saliency detection facilitates more sensible assignments of limited processing resource to prominent regions, thus allows more sophisticated subsequent processing stages. Though

Electronic supplementary material The online version of this chapter (doi:10. 1007/978-3-319-46466-4_35) contains supplementary material, which is available to authorized users.

© Springer International Publishing AG 2016
B. Leibe et al. (Eds.): ECCV 2016, Part VI, LNCS 9910, pp. 583–598, 2016.
DOI: 10.1007/978-3-319-46466-4_35

much research effort has been made [4–9], it is still a very challenging task to design a saliency model with high performance in real complex scenes.

In their seminal work [10], Itti *et al.* point out that human visual system is sensitive to high-contrast regions and propose to detect saliency by measuring local contrast in multi-scales across different feature channels, including intensity, color, orientation, *etc.* Since then, contrast prior is widely studied and adopted by a variety of saliency models [11–14] from either local or global view. For local methods [10–12,15], saliency is characterized by regional center-surround contrast. Although these methods can highlight salient pixels along object boundaries, they often fail in discovering inner regions of salient objects. Due to the lack of global information, unsatisfactory results are achieved under cluttered scenes. In contrast, global methods [4,13,14] estimate saliency by considering feature contrast over the entire image and thus are more capable of locating salient objects precisely. Since detailed local information is ignored, they have very limited discriminative power to uniformly capture salient objects from background with similar appearance.

Instead of computing local contrast or blindly comparing similarity over the entire image, some saliency methods [6,16,17] propose to explore the boundary prior, *i.e.*, by regarding image boundaries as background and propagating their labels to detect salient foreground. These methods are effective in certain scenarios. Though unlike contrast based models, which suffer from failures in detecting object inner regions or separating foreground from background distractors, these methods also have their own drawbacks. Firstly, boundary prior is mainly utilized in a trivial and heuristic manner, such that salient objects appearing at image boundary will be incorrectly labeled as background. Secondly, most of these methods mainly rely on low-level handcrafted features, which are incapable for high-level cognition and understanding, thus insufficient to highlight semantic objects from complex scenarios. To incorporate high-level concepts, other methods [11,18–20] explore task-driven strategies, which involve supervised learning on image data with pixel-wise annotations. However, obtaining massive amount of manually-labeled data is very expensive and time consuming.

In order to address the above issues of existing methods, we seek an alternative approach for saliency detection. Our first contribution is a novel salient seeds selection method. Saliency maps predicted by combining heuristic saliency cues can sometimes be very noisy, *i.e.*, the saliency maps shown in Fig. 1(b). To improve accuracy of these initial saliency maps, we apply a pattern mining algorithm to recognize saliency rules (feature patterns) which are frequently depicted by foreground regions in the initial saliency map and rarely carried by background regions. Based on these saliency rules, a sufficient number of reliable saliency seeds can be effectively detected (See Fig. 1(c)), which can significantly remove the inaccurate prediction of the initial saliency maps (See Fig. 1(d)). Our second contribution is an Extended Random Walk (ERW) algorithm which incorporates quadratic Laplacian term and an external classifier into traditional approach and achieves significant performance improvement in terms of propagation ability. By exploiting the proposed ERW algorithm, the label information

(a)   (b)   (c)   (d)   (e)

Fig. 1. Intermediate results of the proposed saliency detection algorithm. Brighter pixels indicate higher saliency values. (a) Original images. (b) Saliency maps generated by CB [5] which is used as initial maps. (c) Saliency seeds detected by pattern mining algorithm. (d) The final saliency map via propagating saliency seeds. (e) Ground truth.

of saliency seeds is diffused to more distant areas, which ensures the final saliency map of our model to be more accurate. Taking saliency maps generated by existing methods as initial maps, our algorithm is able to promote the precision of these maps with a considerable margin. Extensive evaluations on four benchmark data sets demonstrate that the promoted results achieve favorable performance against state-of-the-art methods.

2   Related Work

Saliency detection can be conducted by either bottom-up computational models or top-down data driven methods. Most bottom-up methods detect salient regions by combining heuristic saliency cues, such as contrast prior [11–14] and boundary prior [6,16,17]. Recently, [8] proposes boundary connectivity to measure the background probability of regions. Although the heuristic saliency cues based methods perform well for images with simple scene, they may fail to capture the true salient regions when the image background is complex or the appearance between objects and background is similar.

Different from bottom-up methods, top-down approaches [11, 19–21] are able to automatically learn saliency models in a supervised manner from large number of training samples. While these methods are shown to be more robust in handling complex scenarios, their generalization abilities heavily rely on training data. Moreover, the training process is very computational expensive. In contrast, [9] learns an unique multi-kernel boosting classifier for each input image supervised by an initial saliency map. However, the inaccuracy of initial map will contaminate the saliency labels of training samples and inevitably degrade the performance of the classifier. Different from the above methods, we employ a pattern mining algorithm to detect the common feature patterns of salient regions for each image based on its initial map. The pattern mining algorithm is more robust to noisy initial maps. As a result, the mined patterns can more reliably characterize salient regions and facilitate reliable saliency seeds selection.

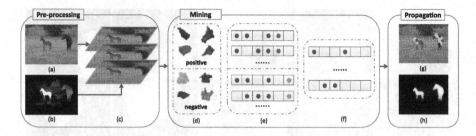

Fig. 2. Framework of the proposed algorithm. (a) Input image. (b) Initial maps generated by other methods. (c) SLIC segmentation results. (d) Sample pool. (e) Transaction database. (f) Saliency rules. (g) Selected saliency seeds. (h) Final saliency map.

Recently, label propagation based saliency detection methods have attracted growing interest from the community. The performance of these methods strongly rely on the quality of the saliency seeds as well as the propagation ability. Some existing methods [6,16,17,22] heuristically treat image boundary as background seeds and use different propagation methods to determine the saliency degree of other image regions. For instance, [17] constructs a graphical model with superpixels as nodes and predicts their saliency according to the hitting time at the equilibrium state. A geodesic distance is defined in [6] to measure the similarity of an image region to the image boundary The proposed method also explores the label propagation scheme for saliency detection. Instead of simply using image boundaries as background seeds, we adopt a pattern mining algorithm to detect more reliable saliency seeds. Compared with random walk based saliency methods [17,23–25], the ERW algorithm incorporates a quadratic Laplacian energy term to explicitly enforce both extensiveness and smoothness of label propagation. In addition, external classifier integrated in ERW algorithm can enable more accurate label assignment.

3   Pattern Mining Algorithm

Pattern mining algorithm is firstly studied for market basket analysis and recently applied in computer vision tasks [26,27]. Given the massive customer transaction database, the aim is to learn the association rules, which indicate the probability of customers buying certain items based on the items they have already bought. In this section, we introduce the terminology and basic concept of pattern mining algorithm.

Frequent itemset. Denote a set of M items as $I = \{i_1, i_2, ..., i_M\}$. A transaction T is a subset of I, namely $T \subseteq I$. A transaction database $D = \{T_1, T_2, ..., T_N\}$ consists of N different transactions. $A \subseteq I$ is called a frequent itemset if A is frequently occurred as a fraction of transactions $T \in D$. The frequency can be described by the support value of A:

$$supp(A) = \frac{|\{T | T \in D, A \subseteq T\}|}{N} \in [0, 1]. \tag{1}$$

If $supp(A) > t_{min}$, A is a frequent itemset, where t_{min} is a pre-defined threshold.

Association rule. An association rule $A \rightarrow p$ describes the situation where item p presents in transactions which contain itemset A. The support value of a rule is defined as:

$$supp(A \rightarrow p) = supp(A \cup \{p\}) = \frac{|\{T | T \in D, A \cup \{p\} \subseteq T\}|}{|D|} \quad (2)$$

The quality of an association rule $A \rightarrow p$ can be evaluated by a confidence value:

$$conf(A \rightarrow p) = \frac{supp(A \rightarrow p)}{supp(A)} = \frac{|\{T | T \in D, A \cup \{p\} \subseteq T\}|}{|\{T | T \in D, A \subseteq T\}|}. \quad (3)$$

The association rules with high confidence are regarded as representative rules.

4 Seeds Detection Based on Pattern Mining

In this section, we give details of how to detect sufficient and reliable saliency seeds using pattern mining algorithm. The outline is illustrated in Fig. 2. Given an initial map generated by existing method, we first construct a sample pool (Fig. 2(d)) consisting of both foreground and background regions. A transaction database (Fig. 2(e)) is then created by collecting feature patterns of all the samples in the sample pool. To obtain saliency rules (Fig. 2(f)) that can accurately discriminate foreground from background, we apply an efficient pattern mining algorithm to the transaction database. Finally, the saliency seeds (Fig. 2(g)) can be selected according to the acquired saliency rules.

Feature extraction. Given the input image and the corresponding initial saliency map, we first oversegment the image from three different scales and

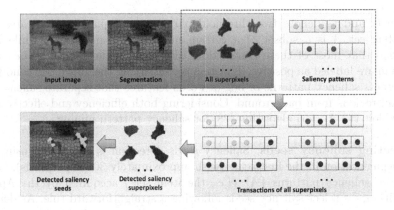

Fig. 3. Detailed process of seeds detection.

obtain a set of superpixels $S = \{s_1, s_2, ..., s_N\}$, serving as the sample pool. By thresholding the saliency maps with a threshold t_0, the image is segmented into foreground and background regions. Superpixels within foreground regions are labeled as positive samples, whereas those within background are labeled as negative samples. Our method can also take multiple initial saliency maps as input by labeling sample superpixels according to each initial map, respectively.

We exploit the bag-of-words representation to character each superpixel considering both global context and local appearance information. Specifically, we apply K-means algorithm to cluster all the superpixels in the RGB color space and obtain a set of cluster centriods W which serves as the visual vocabulary, with each centriod as a visual word. Each superpixel is assigned with the visual word (*i.e.* its cluster centroid) indexed by $w_i \in \{1, 2, ..., |W|\}$, where $|W|$ denotes the total number of visual words. Note that the visual vocabulary contains the global context information of the input image. We then represent each superpixel sample s_i from a local view using the bag-of-words feature which contains three components: its visual word index w_i, the visual word indexes of its K nearest neighbors, and its class label (either *pos* or *neg*).

Mining saliency patterns. Pattern mining theories are explored to identify discriminative patterns of bag-of-words features that can accurately distinguish foreground from background. To this end, we regard the set of visual words W as the overall item set with each visual word as an item. Furthermore, the bag-of-words feature of each superpixel can be treated as a transaction with $K + 2$ items, where the first $K + 1$ items are visual words and the last is the label (*pos* or *neg*). The bag-of-words features of all the superpixel samples in the sample pool then creat a transaction database. As a result, to identify discriminative patterns of visual words is then equivalent to find a collection of item sets $\{A\}$ that satisfy the following two conditions:

$$supp(A) > t_1, \tag{4}$$

$$conf(A \rightarrow pos) > t_2, \tag{5}$$

where t_1 and t_2 denote two threshold parameters. Equation 4 indicates that the item set A is a subset of a certain number of transactions, while Eq. 5 enforces that most of these transactions also contain the item *pos*, *i.e.*, most of them are labeled as positive. The item set satisfying the above two conditions represents saliency patterns of bag-of-words features that separate salient foreground regions from background. Considering both efficiency and effectiveness, we exploit the Apriori algorithm [28] for saliency pattern mining.

Detecting saliency seeds. Saliency seeds detection is conducted using the oversegmentation in the first scale (with approximately 300 superpixels). Given a set of saliency patterns $\{A\}$ (*i.e.*, the item sets) accquired by the Apriori algorithm, we select saliency seeds following a straightforward rule. As demonstrated in Fig. 3, a superpixel is selected as a saliency seed only if a subset of its bag-of-words feature belongs to the saliency pattern set $\{A\}$. As illustrated

(a)   (b)   (c)   (d)   (e)

Fig. 4. Examples of seeds detection results. (a) Original images. (b) Initial maps generated by method CA [4]. (c) Saliency seeds detected by pattern mining algorithm. (d) The final saliency map. (e) Ground truth.

in Fig. 4, with accurate saliency patterns, we can select a sufficient number of reliable saliency seeds with the mined saliency rules. The prediction error of the initial maps can then be significantly removed.

5 Saliency Propagation

We propose an Extended Random Walk (ERW) algorithm on graphic model with superpixels as nodes. Given the selected saliency seeds, the final saliency map of the input image is achieved by propagating the seeds information to other image regions. Both the reliable saliency seeds and the proposed ERW algorithm ensure to more accurately render the final saliency map.

Graph construction. The saliency propagation procedure is also conducted using the oversegmentation of the input image in the first scale. Given the set of superpixels $S = \{s_1, s_2, ..., s_{N_1}\}$, we construct an undirected graph $G = (V, E)$ with node set V and edge set E, where each node represents a superpixel and is connected to its 2-ring neighbors [16] with undirected edges. The weight matrix $W \in R^{N_1 \times N_1}$ measures the similarity and adjacency relationship between each pair of nodes, with each element $w_{ij} = \exp(-\|g(s_i - g(s_j)\|/2\sigma^2)$, if $j \in \mathcal{N}(i)$, and other positions are 0, where $g(s_i)$ denotes the feature of node s_i and $\mathcal{N}(i)$ indicates the nodes connected to s_i. The Laplacian matrix can be computed by $L = D - W$, where $D = diag(d_1, d_2, ..., d_{N_1})$ is degree matrix with $d_i = \sum_j w_{ij}$.

Extended Random Walk. Let $\mathcal{L}$ denote a labeled node set consisting of all the mined saliency seeds, and $\mathbf{f} = [f_1, f_2, ..., f_{N_1}]^T$ denote the label vector of all the nodes, where f_i is fixed to 1 if $s_i \in \mathcal{L}$, and f_i is initialized to 0 otherwise. Label propagation aims to infer the labels of all the nodes based on the saliency seeds. In this work, we propose an Extended Random Walk algorithm for label propagation by minimizing the following energy function

$$\arg\min_{\mathbf{f}} \frac{1}{2}\sum_{i,j} w_{ij}(f_i - f_j)^2 + \frac{\alpha}{2}\sum_{i=1}^{N_1}(d_i f_i - \sum_{j\in\mathcal{N}(i)} w_{ij}f_j)^2 + \frac{\beta}{2}\sum_{i=1}^{N_1}(f_i - y_i)^2, \qquad (6)$$

$$\text{s.t. } f_i = 1, \ \forall s_i \in \mathcal{L},$$

where weight w_{ij} measures the similarity of s_i and s_j; $d_i = \sum_j w_{ij}$ is the degree of node s_i; y_i denotes the output of an external classifier and adopts the mean saliency value of node s_i in initial saliency map; α, β are trade-off parameters.

The first term of Eq. 6 is the traditional random walk formulation which enforces label consistency of nodes with strong affinity. The second term is the quadratic Laplacian. To gain more comprehensive interpretation, we minimize the Laplacian term with respect to $\mathbf{f}$ by setting its derivative to zero and obtain the following solution:

$$f_i = \frac{1}{d_i}\sum_{j\in\mathcal{N}(i)} w_{ij}f_j + \frac{1}{d_i^2}\sum_{j\in\mathcal{N}(i)} w_{ij}\left(\sum_{h\in\mathcal{N}(j)} w_{jh}(f_j - f_h)\right). \qquad (7)$$

Apparently, the value of f_i is influenced not only by its direct neighbors $j \in \mathcal{N}(i)$, but also by its neighbors' context $h \in \mathcal{N}(j)$. As a consequence, the seeds information can be more extensively propagated to distant nodes than traditional first-order laplacian diffusion (i.e., the first term of Eq. 6). The third term incorporates the prior knowledge provided by the initial saliency maps into the random walk algorithm, and penalizes saliency predictions that significantly differ from saliency priors. As illustrated in Fig. 5, initialized by the same saliency seed, the proposed ERW algorithm with strong propagation ability achieves more accurate predictions than the traditional method in a challenging setting.

To solve the energy function in Eq. 6, we first re-order the label vector as $\mathbf{f} = [\mathbf{f}_l^T \ \mathbf{f}_u^T]^T$ and the external classifier as $\mathbf{y} = [\mathbf{y}_l^T \ \mathbf{y}_u^T]^T$, where l indicates the labeled nodes set and u corresponds to unlabeled nodes set. The energy minimization problem can then be re-written in the following matrix form

$$\mathbf{f}^* = \arg\min_{\mathbf{f}} \frac{1}{2}\mathbf{f}^T L\mathbf{f} + \frac{\alpha}{2}\mathbf{f}^T L^2\mathbf{f} + \frac{\beta}{2}(\mathbf{f} - \mathbf{y})^T(\mathbf{f} - \mathbf{y}) \qquad (8)$$

$$\text{s.t. } \mathbf{f}_l = 1,$$

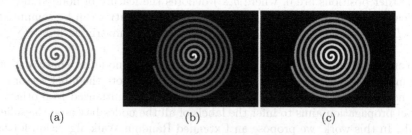

(a)   (b)   (c)

Fig. 5. (a) Input image and the red pentagram is saliency seeds. (b) Saliency map detected by random walk algorithm. (c) Saliency map detected by random walk with quadratic Laplacian term.

where $L = \begin{bmatrix} L_{ll} & L_{lu} \\ L_{ul} & L_{uu} \end{bmatrix}$ is Laplacian matrix. By setting the derivative of Eq. 8 to zero, the final saliency values of unlabeled nodes are computed as

$$\mathbf{f}_u = M_{uu}^{-1}(-M_{ul}\mathbf{f}_l + \beta\mathbf{y}_u), \tag{9}$$

where $M = L + \alpha L^2 + \beta I$, and I is identity matrix.

Integration. In this paper, we employ the mean CIELab color feature and the Local Binary Pattern (LBP) feature to characterize each superpixel. The above label propagation is independently conducted in the two feature spaces. Color feature is effective when the salient object depicts a distinct color appearance against background. In contrast, the texture feature will be more discriminative when the target object have similar color but different texture compared with background (See the second example of Fig. 8). Based on these observations, we integrate these two feature representations by linearly combining two prediction results to generate the final saliency map,

$$S_f = \lambda S_1 + (1 - \lambda)S_2. \tag{10}$$

where S_1 and S_2 are saliency maps computed in two feature spaces and λ is a weight parameter to balance these two maps. In our experiments, we empirically set $\lambda = 0.5$ to weight these two features.

In this section, we conduct experimental evaluations of the proposed pattern mining based saliency detection method (named as PM) against state-of-the-art methods on benchmark data sets. The contributions of different components of the proposed methods (*i.e.*, seeds selection method and the ERW algorithm) are also analyzed. More results can be found in supplementary material[1].

6   Experiments

6.1   Parameter Setting

In our experiments, we find that the proposed method is insensitive to most of the parameters. Therefore, all the parameters are empirically set through cross-validation and fixed through all the data sets. The threshold t_0 for constructing sample pool is set to 0.5. The size of visual vocabulary $|W|$ is set to 300. The bag-of-words feature for each sample is computed using $K = 20$ nearest neighbors. The thresholds t_1 and t_2 for pattern mining are set to 90% and 20%, respectively. The parameter σ to compute weight matrix is set to 10. The trade-off parameters of the ERW algorithm are set as $\alpha = 0.5$ and $\beta = 0.01$, respectively. The proposed method is implemented in MATLAB, and runs at 4 seconds per image on a PC with a 3.4 GHz CPU. The source code will be made publicly available (see Footnote 1).

---

[1] http://ice.dlut.edu.cn/lu/index.html.

6.2   Data Sets and Evaluation Metrics

We evaluate the proposed algorithm on four benchmark data sets. The MSRA-5000 dataset [11] contains 5000 images with complex scenes; The SOD dataset [29] consists of 300 images; The ECSSD dataset [30] incorporates 1000 images and the Pascal-S dataset [31] is composed of 850 images. The later three data sets are very challenging, since most images have cluttered background or more than one salient object.

Precision-Recall curves, F-measure and the mean absolute error (MAE) are employed to evaluate the performance of each detection model, where F-measure is the weighted harmonic mean of precision and recall value, and MAE is the average pixel-wise difference between saliency map and its ground truth.

6.3   Quantitative Analysis

Performance of the proposed framework. We choose 12 existing saliency detection algorithms as baseline methods, including ITTI [10], GBVS [32], CA [4], CB [5], LR [33], DSR [7], UFO [34], HS [30], wCO [8], HDCT [19], BL [9] and RR [25]. Two evaluations are conducted: single model promotion and joint promotion. For single model promotion, we apply the proposed algorithm to promote the performance of each baseline method by taking its predicted saliency map as the initial saliency map. The promoted method is denoted by -PM (*e.g.*, CA-PM denotes the promoted model of baseline CA). For joint promotion, we apply our method to jointly promote a set of baselines (*i.e.*, SET1={CA,CB,LR} and SET2={DSR,UFO,wCO}), by taking their predicted saliency maps as initial maps (See Sect. 4).

Figure 6 compares the P-R curves of the baseline models and their promoted methods on four data sets. Table 1 shows the F-measures and MAE scores, where the baseline results of different methods are shown in the columns of "BS", and the corresponding promoted results are displayed in the columns of "PM". As shown in Fig. 6, our method can effectively promote all the baseline results and achieve state-of-the-art performance regardless of the accuracy of initial maps. The results further verifies that the proposed method has a strong generalization ability across a wide range of baseline methods and is very robust to the noisy prediction of initial maps Especially, initialized by eye fixation results (*e.g.*, ITTI/GBVS), the proposed method is capable to promote their performance with a considerable margin.

In addition, the joint promotion on a set of baselines achieves consistently higher performances than the corresponding single model promotion in most data sets. This may be attributed to the fact that more samples can be acquired for pattern mining in the joint promotion case. However, sometimes labels of samples from different methods may be inconsistent which causes confusion for the pattern mining procedure. Thus the final detection results may be affected by this circumstance.

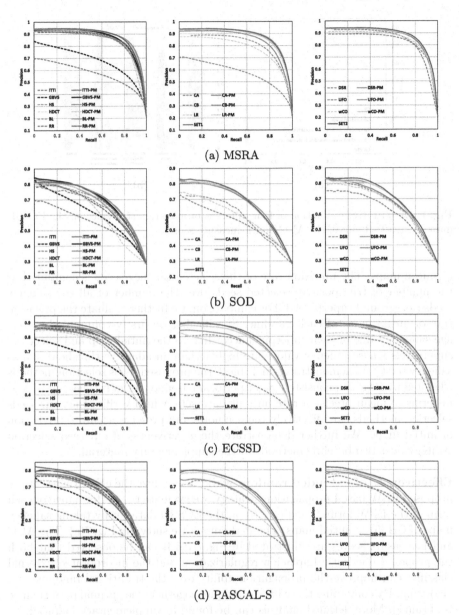

Fig. 6. P-R curve of the state-of-the-art algorithms and their promoted results by our proposed algorithm(PM) on four datasets.

Validation of pattern mining based seeds detection. Saliency seeds plays a very critical role in our saliency algorithm. To verify the effectiveness of the proposed seeds selection method, we report the mean precision rate of the saliency seeds selected by our method by taking saliency maps of each baseline method

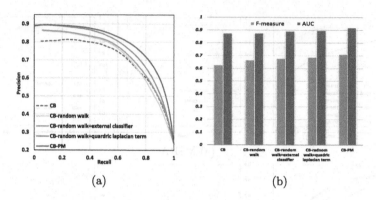

(a)   (b)

Fig. 7. Quantitative evaluation of four different propagation strategies on the ECSSD data set. (a) P-R curve. (b) AUC and F-measure scores.

as initial maps. The precision rate of the selected saliency seeds is computed as the number of true positive selected seeds over the number of all the saliency seeds (foreground superpixels). For comparison, we further evaluate the precision rate of initial maps of each baseline. Specifically, we firstly compute the average saliency value of each superpixel according to the initial map and select the superpixels whose saliency values are higher than an adaptive threshold [35] as saliency seeds. As demonstrated in Table 2, the proposed seeds selection methods (denoted by PM) can consistently outperform baseline methods (denoted by BS) in terms of mean precision rate on four data sets, which verifies that our seeds selection methods can effectively remove noise and preserve accurate prediction of initial maps. We further demonstrate the effectiveness of our seed selection strategy over two baseline methods in the supplementary material.

Effectiveness of extended random walk. To analyze the effectiveness of the proposed ERW based propagation strategy, we evaluate the performance of each term of the ERW formulation (Eq. 6) on the ECSSD data set by taking saliency maps of CB [5] as initial maps. The P-R curves are shown in Fig. 7(a). The AUC and F-measure scores are illustrated in Fig. 7(b). It can be observed that both the proposed quadratic Laplacian regularization and the incorporated external classifier can improve the propagation ability over the traditional random walk algorithm. By combining these two techniques together, the optimal performance is obtained. More detailed analysis can be found in supplementary material.

6.4   Qualitative Analysis

Figure 8 illustrates some example saliency maps generated by baseline methods and the corresponding (jointly) promoted results. In the first example, the appearance between salient object and image background is unconspicuous in color space. Due to the adopted LBP texture feature, our algorithm can accurately capture the foreground object. The background regions in the second

Table 1. F-measures and MAE scores of baseline methods and their promoted methods on MSRA, SOD, ECSSD and PASCAL-S data sets. The promoted results are marked as blue if they out-perform their baseline methods. If the jointly promoted results (SET1, SET2) are higher than the corresponding single promotion, the scores are marked as red.

Method	Metric	MSRA		SOD		ECSSD		PASCAL-S	
		BS	PM	BS	PM	BS	PM	BS	PM
ITTI	F-measure	0.515	0.779	0.433	0.573	0.428	0.664	0.391	0.568
	MAE	0.249	0.151	0.307	0.259	0.290	0.203	0.296	0.234
GBVS	F-measure	0.608	0.792	0.508	0.593	0.549	0.684	0.496	0.589
	MAE	0.227	0.150	0.292	0.257	0.263	0.203	0.273	0.230
CA	F-measure	0.537	0.779	0.447	0.563	0.429	0.653	0.402	0.552
	MAE	0.250	0.149	0.313	0.259	0.310	0.210	0.301	0.237
CB	F-measure	0.737	0.815	0.490	0.592	0.626	0.711	0.511	0.590
	MAE	0.185	0.128	0.294	0.250	0.240	0.185	0.269	0.220
LR	F-measure	0.694	0.803	0.484	0.584	0.562	0.695	0.476	0.581
	MAE	0.221	0.138	0.308	0.257	0.274	0.195	0.287	0.228
DSR	F-measure	0.784	0.814	0.596	0.615	0.690	0.721	0.554	0.590
	MAE	0.117	0.123	0.234	0.239	0.171	0.161	0.214	0.218
UFO	F-measure	0.775	0.810	0.548	0.594	0.644	0.698	0.549	0.579
	MAE	0.146	0.128	0.257	0.248	0.205	0.187	0.232	0.224
HS	F-measure	0.767	0.814	0.521	0.600	0.635	0.693	0.528	0.594
	MAE	0.162	0.124	0.283	0.247	0.228	0.185	0.264	0.209
wCO	F-measure	0.796	0.816	0.598	0.606	0.676	0.698	0.596	0.612
	MAE	0.111	0.120	0.245	0.225	0.178	0.161	0.201	0.192
HDCT	F-measure	0.773	0.820	0.561	0.594	0.644	0.694	0.532	0.583
	MAE	0.144	0.121	0.244	0.243	0.192	0.183	0.232	0.210
BL	F-measure	0.784	0.815	0.577	0.601	0.683	0.713	0.571	0.609
	MAE	0.169	0.125	0.267	0.246	0.217	0.182	0.249	0.217
RR	F-measure	0.807	0.815	0.567	0.590	0.698	0.716	0.587	0.607
	MAE	0.126	0.124	0.265	0.255	0.185	0.162	0.231	0.204
SET1	F-measure	-	0.811	-	0.598	-	0.708	-	0.597
	MAE	-	0.136	-	0.237	-	0.179	-	0.206
SET2	F-measure	-	0.823	-	0.614	-	0.717	-	0.620
	MAE	-	0.121	-	0.222	-	0.158	-	0.195

example depict different features which causes failure in the most existing methods. Our model succeeds to highlight the entire salient object even with inaccurate initial maps, which attributes to the robustness of our seeds selection methods against noisy initial maps. When there exists small scale noise in the

Table 2. Precision rate of saliency seeds on the MSRA, SOD, ECSSD and PASCAL-S data sets.

	ITTI		CA		CB		LR		DSR		UFO		SET1
	BS	PM	BS	PM	BS	PM	BS	PM	BS	PM	BS	PM	
MSRA	.536	.843	.549	.876	.806	.893	.733	.890	.878	.891	.860	.895	.891
SOD	.519	.708	.515	.751	.637	.776	.569	.752	.731	.772	.686	.764	.780
ECSSD	.488	.749	.469	.774	.714	.828	.610	.812	.810	.811	.746	.829	.835
PASCAL-S	.468	.680	.479	.697	.637	.734	.565	.723	.687	.729	.688	.730	.744
	GBVS		HS		wCO		HDCT		BL		RR		SET2
	BS	PM	BS	PM	BS	PM	BS	PM	BS	PM	BS	PM	
MSRA	.568	.855	.821	.890	.844	.888	.828	.889	.815	.891	.859	.889	.898
SOD	.525	.712	.672	.778	.714	.748	.705	.756	.696	.761	.677	.751	.793
ECSSD	.525	.767	.723	.816	.750	.809	.751	.806	.734	.815	.775	.804	.832
PASCAL-S	.514	.709	.645	.719	.680	.720	.665	.723	0.651	.728	.686	.721	.750

background (such as the third example), most saliency models detect yellow flowers as salient regions, while our algorithm is effective in suppressing the response of noise regions. In the case that saliency object presents various features as is shown in the last example (the cattle with dark brown and light brown hair),

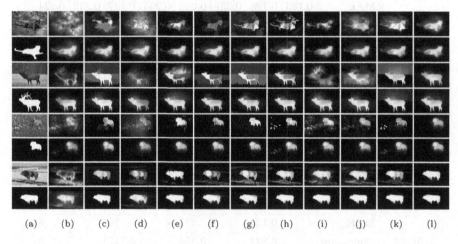

(a)   (b)   (c)   (d)   (e)   (f)   (g)   (h)   (i)   (j)   (k)   (l)

Fig. 8. Saliency maps of four examples. Every two rows correspond to one example. In each example, saliency maps at the first row of (b)-(k) are generated by existed saliency models and the second row present their promoted results. (l) is the jointly boosted results generated by SET1 and SET2, respectively. From left to right: (a) input image and its ground truth (b) CA [4] (c) CB [5] (d) LR [33] (e) DSR [7] (f) UFO [34] (g) HS [30] (h) wCO [8] (i) HDCT [19] (j) BL [9] (k) RR [25] (l) SET1 and SET2. Our model is able to highlight foreground uniformly and suppress the response of cluttered background.

some initial saliency maps fail to highlight the entire object uniformly. Based on pattern mining algorithm, our method is able to detect saliency seeds with a variety of features. Thus all saliency regions can be consistently detected by the proposed method.

7 Conclusions

In this paper, we propose a novel saliency detection model based on pattern mining algorithm. Given an initial saliency map generated by any existing method, our method can effectively recognize discriminative and representative saliency patterns. According to these saliency patterns, sufficient and reliable saliency seeds are detected. Subsequently, we propose an Extended Random Walk (ERW) algorithm to further propagate saliency labels of saliency seeds to other image regions. Compared with prior methods, ERW constrained by a quadratic Laplacian term allows the propagation of saliency seeds to more distant areas and incorporates external classifiers at the same time. Quantitative and qualitative experiments on four benchmark data sets demonstrate that our method is able to improve the performance of existing algorithms and performs favorably against the state-of-the-arts.

Acknowledgement. The work is supported by the National Natural Science Foundation of China under Grant 61370143, 61262050, 61528101 and 61472060.

References

1. Yang, L., Zheng, N., Yang, J., Chen, H.: A biased sampling strategy for object categorization. In: ICCV (2009)
2. Rahtu, E., Kannala, J., Salo, M., Heikkilä, J.: Segmenting salient objects from images and videos. In: Daniilidis, K., Maragos, P., Paragios, N. (eds.) ECCV 2010, Part V. LNCS, vol. 6315, pp. 366–379. Springer, Heidelberg (2010)
3. Mahadevan, V., Vasconcelos, N.: Saliency-based discriminant tracking. In: CVPR (2009)
4. Goferman, S., Zelnik-Manor, L., Tal, A.: Context-aware saliency detection. In: CVPR (2010)
5. Jiang, H., Wang, J., Yuan, Z., Liu, T., Zheng, N., Li, S.: Automatic salient object segmentation based on context and shape prior. In: BMVC (2011)
6. Wei, Y., Wen, F., Zhu, W., Sun, J.: Geodesic saliency using background priors. In: Fitzgibbon, A., Lazebnik, S., Perona, P., Sato, Y., Schmid, C. (eds.) ECCV 2012, Part III. LNCS, vol. 7574, pp. 29–42. Springer, Heidelberg (2012)
7. Li, X., Lu, H., Zhang, L., Ruan, X., Yang, M.H.: Saliency detection via dense and sparse reconstruction. In: ICCV (2013)
8. Zhu, W., Liang, S., Wei, Y., Sun, J.: Saliency optimization from robust background detection. In: CVPR (2014)
9. Tong, N., Lu, H., Ruan, X., Yang, M.H.: Salient object detection via bootstrap learning. In: CVPR (2015)
10. Itti, L., Koch, C., Niebur, E.: A model of saliency-based visual attention for rapid scene analysis. TPAMI **20**(11), 1254–1259 (1998)

11. Liu, T., Sun, J., Zheng, N.N., Tang, X., Shum, H.Y.: Learning to detect a salient object. In: CVPR (2007)
12. Xie, Y., Lu, H., Yang, M.H.: Bayesian saliency via low and mid level cues. TIP **22**(5), 1689–1698 (2013)
13. Achanta, R., Hemami, S., Estrada, F., Süsstrunk, S.: Frequency-tuned salient region detection. In: CVPR (2012)
14. Cheng, M., Zhang, G., Mitra, N.J., Huang, X.H., S.: Global contrast based salient region detection. In: CVPR (2011)
15. Klein, D.A., Frintrop, S.: Center-surround divergence of feature statistics for salient object detection. In: ICCV (2011)
16. Yang, C., Zhang, L., Lu, H., Yang, M.: Saliency detection via graph-based manifold ranking. In: CVPR (2013)
17. Gopalakrishnan, V., Hu, Y., Rajan, D.: Random walks on graphs for salient object detection in images. TIP **19**(12), 3232–3242 (2010)
18. Jiang, H., Wang, J., Yuan, Z., Wu, Y., Zheng, N., Li, S.: Salient object detection: A discriminative regional feature integration approach. In: CVPR (2013)
19. Kim, J., Han, D., Tai, Y.W., Kim, J.: Salient region detection via high-dimensional color transform. In: CVPR (2014)
20. Lu, S., Mahadevan, V., Vasconcelos, N.: Learning optimal seeds for diffusion-based salient object detection. In: CVPR (2014)
21. Wang, L., Lu, H., Ruan, X., Yang, M.H.: Deep networks for saliency detection via local estimation and global search. In: CVPR (2015)
22. Li, N., Sun, B., Yu, J.: A weighted sparse coding framework for saliency detection. In: CVPR (2015)
23. Chang, K.Y., Liu, T.L., Chen, H.T., Lai, S.H.: Fusing generic objectness and visual saliency for salient object detection. In: ICCV (2011)
24. Jiang, B., Zhang, L., Lu, H., Yang, C., Yang, M.H.: Saliency detection via absorbing markov chain. In: ICCV (2013)
25. Li, C., Yuan, Y., Cai, W., Xia, Y., Feng, D.D.: Robust saliency detection via regularized random walks ranking. In: CVPR (2015)
26. Fernando, B., Fromont, E., Tuytelaars, T.: Effective use of frequent itemset mining for image classification. In: Fitzgibbon, A., Lazebnik, S., Perona, P., Sato, Y., Schmid, C. (eds.) ECCV 2012, Part I. LNCS, vol. 7572, pp. 214–227. Springer, Heidelberg (2012)
27. Li, Y., Liu, L., Shen, C., van den Hengel, A.: Mid-level deep pattern mining. In: CVPR (2015)
28. Agrawal, R., Srikant, R.: Fast algorithms for mining association rules in large databases. In: VLDB (1994)
29. Movahedi, V., Elder, J.H.: Design and perceptual validation of performance measures for salient object segmentation. In: POCV, pp. 49–56 (2010)
30. Yan, Q., Xu, L., Shi, J., Jia, J.: Hierarchical saliency detection. In: CVPR (2013)
31. Li, Y., Hou, X., Koch, C., Rehg, J., Yuille, A.: The secrets of salient object segmentation. In: CVPR (2014)
32. Schölkopf, B., Platt, J., Hofmann, T.: Graph-based visual saliency. In: NIPS (2007)
33. Shen, X.S., Wu, Y.: A unified approach to salient object detection via low rank matrix recovery. In: CVPR (2012)
34. Jiang, P., Ling, H., Yu, J., Peng, J.: Salient region detection by ufo: Uniqueness, focusness and objectness. In: ICCV (2013)
35. Otsu, N.: A threshold selection method from gray-level histograms. SMC **9**(1), 62–66 (1979)

Streaming Video Segmentation via Short-Term Hierarchical Segmentation and Frame-by-Frame Markov Random Field Optimization

Won-Dong Jang[✉] and Chang-Su Kim

School of Electrical Engineering, Korea University, Seoul, Korea
wdjang@mcl.korea.ac.kr, changsukim@korea.ac.kr

Abstract. An online video segmentation algorithm, based on short-term hierarchical segmentation (STHS) and frame-by-frame Markov random field (MRF) optimization, is proposed in this work. We develop the STHS technique, which generates initial segments by sliding a short window of frames. In STHS, we apply spatial agglomerative clustering to each frame, and then adopt inter-frame bipartite graph matching to construct initial segments. Then, we partition each frame into final segments, by minimizing an MRF energy function composed of unary and pairwise costs. We compute the unary cost using the STHS initial segments and the segmentation result at the previous frame. We set the pairwise cost to encourage similar nodes to have the same segment label. Experimental results on a video segmentation benchmark dataset, VSB100, demonstrate that the proposed algorithm outperforms state-of-the-art online video segmentation techniques significantly.

Keywords: Video segmentation · Online segmentation · Streaming segmentation · Agglomerative clustering · Graph matching

1 Introduction

Segmentation, the task of partitioning data into disjoint subsets based on the underlying data structure, is one of the most fundamental problems in computer vision. For image segmentation, contour-based algorithms [1,2] have achieved great success recently. As the state-of-the-art contour detector [3] presents comparable performance to the human visual system, the contour-based image segmentation can provide more promising performance. On the other hand, video segmentation is the process to divide a video into volumetric segments. It is applicable to a wide variety of vision applications, such as action recognition, scene classification, video summarization, content-based video retrieval, and 3D reconstruction. However, video segmentation still remains a challenging problem due to object and camera motion, occlusion, and contour ambiguities. To overcome these issues, many attempts have been made.

Video segmentation algorithms can be categorized into offline or online ones. Offline algorithms [4–10] divide a video into segments by processing all frames

© Springer International Publishing AG 2016
B. Leibe et al. (Eds.): ECCV 2016, Part VI, LNCS 9910, pp. 599–615, 2016.
DOI: 10.1007/978-3-319-46466-4_36

at once. On the other hand, online (or streaming) algorithms [11–13] extract segments sequentially from the first to the last frames. Note that the offline algorithms can achieve more accurate segmentation by exploiting the entire information in a video jointly, but they require huge memory space for a long video. Thus, the online algorithms, which use regular memory space regardless of the duration of a video, can be used more versatilely in practical applications.

We propose a novel online video segmentation algorithm. The proposed algorithm consists of two steps: short-term hierarchical segmentation (STHS) and Markov random field (MRF) optimization. In the first pass, STHS generates initial segments sequentially, by sliding a short window of frames, to identify newly appearing segments effectively. It attempts to prevent the propagation of erroneous segments by processing each frame independently of the previous segmentation results. In the second pass, we define an MRF energy function for obtaining the final segmentation result of each frame, which consists of unary and pairwise costs. The unary cost takes into account the segmentation result at the previous frame and the initial STHS result at the current frame. The pairwise cost is computed based on node affinities. Then, we achieve temporally coherent and spatially accurate video segmentation by minimizing the energy function. Experimental results demonstrate that the proposed algorithm outperforms the state-of-the-art conventional algorithms in [11–13] on the video segmentation benchmark (VSB) dataset [14]. To summarize, this paper has three main contributions.

- Development of STHS, which combines spatial agglomerative clustering and temporal bipartite graph matching to detect newly appearing objects and achieve initial video segmentation reliably.
- Proposal of the MRF optimization scheme, which refines the initial segmentation results and yield temporally coherent and spatially accurate segments.
- Remarkable performance achievement on the VSB dataset, which consists of challenging video sequences.

2   Related Work

2.1   Offline Video Segmentation

An offline video segmentation algorithm processes all frames in a video simultaneously. Corso et al. [4] developed a graph-based video segmentation algorithm using a hierarchical structure. Grundmann et al. [5] also proposed a hierarchical algorithm, which merges similar superpixels sequentially in a spatiotemporal graph. Galasso et al. [7] first applied the spectral clustering [15] to the video segmentation problem. Galasso et al. [14] assessed video segmentation algorithms by introducing a benchmark dataset, called VSB100. Khoreva et al. [8] introduced learning-based must-link constraints, which enforce two nodes to belong to the same cluster during spectral clustering. Also, Khoreva et al. [9] trained a classifier to determine affinities between superpixels, and selected edges to construct a sparse efficient graph. Yi and Pavlovic [10] proposed an MRF model, whose node potentials are obtained from the results of [5]. Yu *et al.* [16] introduced a parametric graph partitioning method to identify and remove between-cluster edges. While these offline algorithms provide promising segmentation results, they often demand huge memory space to process all frames simultaneously. Thus, they may fail to segment long video clips.

2.2 Online Video Segmentation

An online (or streaming) video segmentation algorithm sequentially partitions from the first to the last frames in a video sequence. To segment a frame, it uses only a few (usually less than 10) previous and subsequent frames. Vazquez-Reina *et al.* [17] proposed an online algorithm, which sequentially divides video frames into partitions by selecting optimal hypothesis flows of superpixels. Xu *et al.* [11] applied the hierarchical image segmentation algorithm in [18] to two consecutive frames to propagate segment labels temporally. Also, online super-voxel algorithms have been proposed to yield regularly sized spatiotemporal segments [19,20]. Recently, Galasso *et al.* [12] reduced the full graph for a video, by re-assigning edge weights, and achieved streaming segmentation by performing the clustering on the reduced graph. Moreover, Li *et al.* [13] decomposed an affinity matrix into low-rank ones to represent relations among supervoxels efficiently and applied the normalized cuts to the low-rank matrices.

2.3 Video Object Segmentation

Many attempts have been made to separate salient objects from the background in a video. Shi and Malik [21] clustered motions using the normalized cuts. Brox and Malik [22] exploited long-term point trajectories to determine object tracks. Ochs and Brox [6] converted sparse point trajectories into dense regions to yield pixel-wise object annotations. Ochs and Brox [23] employed the spectral clustering on point trajectories to delineate objects. Also, several algorithms [24–26] have been proposed to achieve video object segmentation using object proposal techniques. They first generate object proposals in all frames and then delineate objects by determining proposal tracks. Oneata *et al.* [27] developed a video object proposal algorithm by generating supervoxels. Wang *et al.* [28] adopted saliency detection techniques to segment a primary object. Giordano *et al.* [29] segmented moving objects by observing temporal consistency of sequential super-pixels. Taylor *et al.* [30] analyzed occluder-occluded relations to ensure temporal consistency of objects. Jang *et al.* [31] minimized an energy function by performing the alternate convex optimization to discover a primary object sequentially. However, these video object segmentation algorithms may fail to segment temporally static or small objects, since they focus on moving, salient, and relatively large objects in general.

3   Proposed Algorithm

We propose a novel online video segmentation algorithm. The input is a set of consecutive video frames, and the output is a set of the corresponding pixel-wise

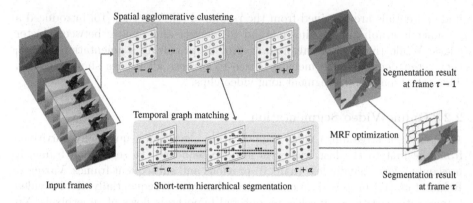

Fig. 1. Overview of the proposed algorithm. To partition the current frame τ, we apply the short-term hierarchical segmentation (STHS) to a window of frames from $\tau - \alpha$ to $\tau + \alpha$. Then, we obtain the final segmentation result at frame τ, by minimizing an MRF energy function, based on the initial STHS result and the previous segmentation result at frame $\tau - 1$

segment label maps. All pixels in a spatiotemporal segment are assigned the same label.

Figure 1 shows an overview of the proposed algorithm. First, we apply STHS to a short window of frames in order to segment the current frame initially. STHS merges spatially similar superpixels in each frame into clusters, and then links temporally coherent clusters. For the spatial and temporal merging, we adopt agglomerative clustering and bipartite graph matching, respectively. Second, we obtain final segment labels at the current frame τ, by minimizing an MRF energy function that consists of unary and pairwise costs. The unary cost is defined using the initial STHS result and the previous segmentation result at frame $\tau - 1$, and the pairwise cost encourages similar nodes to have the same label. We perform this process sequentially from the first to the last frames to achieve streaming video segmentation.

3.1 Feature Extraction

For each frame τ, we estimate both forward and backward optical flows using [32]. Also, we over-segment each frame into superpixels using the mean-shift algorithm [33]. For the mean-shift, we fix the parameters of spatial bandwidth and range bandwidth to 9 and 5, respectively, and set the minimum superpixel area to 0.1% of the number of pixels in a frame. We extract three types of features: color feature, motion feature, and boundary feature. Let us describe these three features subsequently.

Color is a fundamental feature for image and video segmentation. We first represent each superpixel with a histogram of LAB colors. Each dimension is quantized into 20 bins independently. Also, we extract bag-of-words (BoW) features in the LAB and RGB color spaces, respectively. We generate the BoW using the K-means algorithm, where K equals 300 for both LAB and RGB spaces. By aggregating the encoded words in each superpixel, we obtain the LAB and RGB BoW histograms. Thus, to obtain the color feature $\mathbf{h}^c$ of a superpixel, we concatenate the LAB histogram, the LAB BoW histogram, and the RGB BoW histogram. Consequently, the dimension of a color feature is 660, $\mathbf{h}^c \in \mathbb{R}^{660 \times 1}$.

Unlike image segmentation, video segmentation can exploit motion features, as well as color features. Motion features are complementary to color features, since they can distinguish similarly colored regions that move differently. To encode motion characteristics, we construct a BoW, by employing both backward and forward optical flows and setting K to 100. We represent each superpixel with the backward and forward optical flow BoW histograms, respectively. Then, we construct the motion feature $\mathbf{h}^m$ by cascading the two histograms. Therefore, the dimension of a motion feature is 200, $\mathbf{h}^m \in \mathbb{R}^{200 \times 1}$. In the first frame, the backward optical flow BoW histogram is unavailable, and thus copied from the forward one. Similarly, in the last frame, the forward histogram is copied from the backward one.

A good segment should be enclosed by a reliable boundary. Hence, we adopt a boundary feature to differently characterize superpixels that have strong boundaries between them. More specifically, we use results of the contour-based segmentation algorithms in [1,34], which generate segments with reliable boundaries. Let us consider segment labels as encoded words on each pixel. Then, we can obtain a histogram of the segment labels for each superpixel. Notice that the number of bins varies according to the number of segment labels. In this work, to exploit multiple levels of segmentation granularity, we generate three segmentation maps with thresholds 0.1, 0.3, and 0.5, respectively. Figure 2 shows segmentation results of [1] according to the thresholds. As the threshold increases, segments are divided by stronger boundaries only. We cascade the three label histograms to obtain the boundary feature $\mathbf{h}^b$ of a superpixel. When two superpixels have different boundary features, there are a strong boundary between them. Notice that we use [34] for a faster version of the proposed algorithm.

We construct the LAB, RGB, and optical flow BoW features using the 40 training sequences in the VSB100 dataset [14]. We normalize each feature $\mathbf{h}^c$, $\mathbf{h}^m$, or $\mathbf{h}^b$ to make its l_2-norm to 1, i.e. $\sum_i h_i^2 = 1$.

(a) Input frame   (b) UCM   (c) UCM> 0.1   (d) UCM> 0.3   (e) UCM> 0.5

Fig. 2. Examples of various segmentation results using an ultrametric contour map (UCM) [1]. As the threshold increases, segments are separated by stronger boundaries only

3.2   Short-Term Hierarchical Segmentation

In general, offline algorithms delineate newly appearing objects more effectively than online ones do, since they consider all frames at once. It is hard to find new objects using the current and previous frames only. Therefore, we develop STHS that performs initial segmentation of frame τ, by sliding a short window of frames from $\tau - \alpha$ to $\tau + \alpha$, where α is set to 7. In other words, STHS consider the subsequent α frames, as well as the current and previous α frames, to identify object appearance more effectively. In general, the future frames are used in the streaming video segmentation algorithms [7,11,35]. Also, within the entire segmentation algorithm in Fig. 1, STHS helps to alleviate the propagation of segmentation errors in the previous frames, by providing an initial segmentation result, which is independent of the previous segmentation results. Figure 3 visualizes the efficacy of STHS in comparison with the spatial clustering, which uses the current frame only. It is observable that STHS describes the appearing man from the right more concisely with fewer segments.

STHS consists of spatial agglomerative clustering and temporal graph matching techniques. In the spatial clustering, all color, motion, and boundary features are used to merge superpixels in each frame. On the other hand, only color features are used in the temporal graph matching between frames, since motion and boundary features are not temporally coherent.

For each frame t in the short-term window $\tau - \alpha \leq t \leq \tau + \alpha$, we adopt the simple agglomerative clustering [36] to merge the most similar pair of clusters iteratively. First, we define a graph $G^{(t)} = (V^{(t)}, E^{(t)})$ for frame t, where $V^{(t)} = \{x_1, \ldots, x_N\}$ is the set of nodes and $E^{(t)} = \{e_{ij}\}$ is the set of edges. The superpixels become the nodes. If two superpixels x_i and x_j share a boundary, they are connected by edge e_{ij}. Note that these graphs $\{G^{(1)}, \ldots, G^{(T)}\}$ are also used in the MRF optimization in Sect. 3.3, where T denotes the number of frames in an input video. To perform the agglomerative clustering at frame t, we initially regard superpixels $\{x_1, \ldots, x_N\}$ as individual clusters $\{c_1, \ldots, c_N\}$. We measure the distances between these clusters by

$$d(c_i, c_j) = \begin{cases} d_{\chi^2}(x_i, x_j) & \text{if } e_{ij} \in E^{(t)}, \\ \infty & \text{otherwise,} \end{cases} \tag{1}$$

where d_{χ^2} denotes the chi-square distance between x_i and x_j in the feature space. We use the color feature $\mathbf{h}^c$, motion feature $\mathbf{h}^m$, and boundary feature $\mathbf{h}^b$ by concatenating them. We normalize the concatenated feature again. Then, we iteratively merge the two clusters c_i and c_j that yield the minimum distance. The mergence yields a new cluster c_n. The distance between the new cluster c_n and an existing cluster c_k is updated by

$$d(c_n, c_k) = \min\{d(c_i, c_k), d(c_j, c_k)\} \tag{2}$$

according to the single link algorithm [36]. We terminate the merging when the minimum distance is higher than a threshold γ. Notice that this threshold γ controls the segmentation granularity. Finally, we reassign the cluster indices

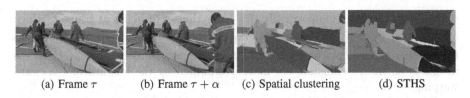

| (a) Frame τ | (b) Frame $\tau + \alpha$ | (c) Spatial clustering | (d) STHS |

Fig. 3. Efficacy of STHS in comparison with the spatial clustering. The newly appearing man at frame τ is depicted by yellow boundaries. While the spatial agglomerative clustering divides the man into unnecessarily many segments, STHS represents him concisely with fewer segments by exploiting the information in the future frame $\tau + \alpha$

from 1 to the number of clusters. Let $c_u^{(t)}$ denote the resultant uth cluster at frame t.

After the intra-frame agglomerative clustering, we link the clusters temporally in the short-term window. To this end, we perform the temporal matching between two frames, t and $t + 1$, sequentially for $\tau - \alpha \le t \le \tau + \alpha - 1$. We first construct a bipartite graph $G^{(t,t+1)} = (U^{(t)}, U^{(t+1)}, E^{(t,t+1)})$, where $U^{(t)} = \{c_1^{(t)}, \dots, c_N^{(t)}\}$ is the set of nodes at frame t. The clusters, produced by the intra-frame agglomerative clustering, become the nodes. $E^{(t,t+1)} = \{e_{uv}^{(t,t+1)}\}$ is the set of inter-frame edges. Node $c_u^{(t)}$ at frame t is connected to node $c_v^{(t+1)}$ by edge $e_{uv}^{(t,t+1)}$, if at least one pixel within $c_u^{(t)}$ is mapped to a pixel within $c_v^{(t+1)}$ according to the forward or backward optical flow. Then, edge $e_{uv}^{(t,t+1)}$ is assigned an affinity weight, given by

$$
w_{uv}^{(t,t+1)} = \begin{cases} \eta(c_u^{(t)}, c_v^{(t+1)}) & \text{if } e_{uv}^{(t,t+1)} \in E^{(t,t+1)}, \\ 0 & \text{otherwise,} \end{cases} \tag{3}
$$

where η is a similarity function between the two clusters. It is defined as

$$
\eta(c_u^{(t)}, c_v^{(t+1)}) = \eta_c(c_u^{(t)}, c_v^{(t+1)}) \times \eta_o(c_u^{(t)}, c_v^{(t+1)}) \tag{4}
$$

where η_c and η_o are color and overlap similarities, respectively. We measure the color similarity by

$$
\eta_c(c_u^{(t)}, c_v^{(t+1)}) = \exp\left(-d_{\chi^2}(c_u^{(t)}, c_v^{(t+1)})\right) \tag{5}
$$

in which d_{χ^2} denotes the chi-square distance between the color features for the two clusters. As mentioned previously, for the inter-frame matching, we do not use the motion and boundary features due to their inter-frame irrelevance. We compute the overlap similarity by

$$
\eta_o(c_u^{(t)}, c_v^{(t+1)}) = \frac{1}{2}\left(\frac{|\mathcal{P}_u^{(t)} \cap \overleftarrow{\mathcal{P}}_v^{(t+1)}|}{\max_k |\mathcal{P}_k^{(t)} \cap \overleftarrow{\mathcal{P}}_v^{(t+1)}|} + \frac{|\overrightarrow{\mathcal{P}}_u^{(t)} \cap \mathcal{P}_v^{(t+1)}|}{\max_k |\overrightarrow{\mathcal{P}}_u^{(t)} \cap \mathcal{P}_k^{(t+1)}|}\right) \tag{6}
$$

where $\mathcal{P}_u^{(t)}$ is the set of pixels that belongs to cluster $c_u^{(t)}$. Also, $\overrightarrow{\mathcal{P}}_u^{(t)}$ is the set of pixels at frame $t + 1$, which are mapped from the pixels in $\mathcal{P}_u^{(t)}$ by the forward optical flow vectors. Symmetrically, $\overleftarrow{\mathcal{P}}_v^{(t+1)}$ is the set of pixels at frame t, which are mapped from $\mathcal{P}_u^{(t+1)}$ by the backward vectors. The operator $|\cdot|$ returns the number of elements in a set. Note that a higher similarity $\eta_o(c_u^{(t)}, c_v^{(t+1)})$ is assigned, as the two clusters are more overlapped by the forward or backward warping.

To represent temporal matching results, we define a matching variable $\mu_{uv}^{(t,t+1)}$, which equals 1 if $c_u^{(t)}$ is matched to $c_v^{(t+1)}$, and 0 otherwise. To determine the set of matching variables $\mathcal{M} = \{\mu_{uv}^{(t,t+1)}\}$, we maximize the objective function

$$\max_{\mathcal{M}} \sum_{t=\tau-\alpha}^{\tau+\alpha-1} \sum_{u \in U^{(t)}} \sum_{v \in U^{(t+1)}} \mu_{uv}^{(t,t+1)} \times w_{uv}^{(t,t+1)} \tag{7}$$

subject to the constraints

$$\sum_{v \in U^{(t+1)}} \mu_{uv}^{(t,t+1)} \leq 1, \quad \mu_{uv}^{(t,t+1)} \in \{0,1\}. \tag{8}$$

This constrained maximization can be easily solved by performing the greedy bipartite matching from $t = \tau - \alpha$ to $t = \tau + \alpha - 1$ sequentially. In other words, for each cluster at frame t, we match it to the cluster at frame $t+1$ that is connected with the highest affinity. However, to reflect occlusion scenarios, if all affinities between cluster $c_u^{(t)}$ and clusters at frame $t+1$ are smaller than a threshold, we do not match $c_u^{(t)}$ to any cluster at frame $t+1$ and $\sum_{v \in U^{(t+1)}} \mu_{uv}^{(t,t+1)} = 0$. After the temporal matching, we assign an identical label to the set of clusters that are connected according to the matching variables. Finally, the label of a cluster becomes the initial segment labels of all superpixels that the cluster includes. Let $s_i^{(t)}$ denote the initial segment that includes superpixel x_i at frame t. Notice that, in the following process, we only use the initial segment results at frame τ.

Figure 4 exemplifies the temporal matching of inter-clusters. The temporal matching assigns segment labels in a temporally coherent manner, and groups

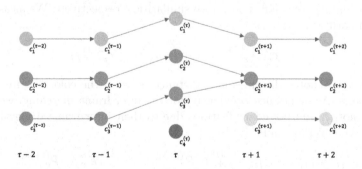

Fig. 4. An example of the temporal graph matching with $\alpha = 2$. Each circle denotes a cluster. The clusters in an identical color have the same label. $c_4^{(\tau)}$ is not matched to any cluster at frame $\tau + 1$. While $c_2^{(\tau)}$ and $c_3^{(\tau)}$ are not merged in the intra-frame clustering, they are assigned the same label after the temporal matching

Algorithm 1. Short-Term Hierarchical Segmentation (STHS)

Input: Superpixels in a window of frames from $\tau - \alpha$ to $\tau + \alpha$
1: **for** frame $t = \tau - \alpha$ to $\tau + \alpha$ **do**
2:     Set each superpixel as an individual cluster
3:     Compute the distance between each pair of neighboring superpixels   ▷ (1)
4:     **repeat**
5:         Find a cluster pair of the minimum distance
6:         Merge the two clusters into a new cluster
7:         Update the distances between the new cluster and the existing clusters ▷
            (2)
8:     **until** the minimum distance is higher than γ
9: **end for**
10: **for** frame $t = \tau - \alpha$ to $\tau + \alpha - 1$ **do**
11:     Construct a bipartite graph for the clusters in two consecutive frames t and
            $t + 1$ ▷ (3)
12:     Perform the inter-frame matching between clusters   ▷ (7)
13: **end for**
14: Assign an identical label to each set of connected clusters
Output: Initial segment label of each superpixel in the window of frames

---

some clusters in a frame that are not merged in the agglomerative clustering. Thus, by employing STHS, we can detect newly appearing segments and also group distant superpixels that compose the same segment. Algorithm 1 summarizes the proposed STHS scheme.

3.3   MRF Optimization

Next, we partition the current frame τ into segments by employing the initial segments, which are obtained by STHS. To this end, we develop an MRF optimization scheme. We use the graph $G^{(\tau)} = (V^{(\tau)}, E^{(\tau)})$, which is already constructed for the intra-frame agglomerative clustering in Sect. 3.2. The node set $V^{(\tau)} = \{x_1^{(\tau)}, \ldots, x_N^{(\tau)}\}$ consists of the superpixels at frame τ. We define a variable $y_i^{(\tau)}$ to indicate the label of node $x_i^{(\tau)}$. By combining unary and pairwise costs, the MRF energy function is defined as

$$\mathcal{E}(\mathbf{y}^{(\tau)}) = \sum_{i \in V^{(\tau)}} \psi(x_i^{(\tau)}, y_i^{(\tau)}) + \lambda \times \sum_{(i,j) \in E^{(\tau)}} \phi(x_i^{(\tau)}, x_j^{(\tau)}, y_i^{(\tau)}, y_j^{(\tau)}) \qquad (9)$$

where λ controls the relative importance between the unary and pairwise costs. The unary cost is given by

$$\psi(x_i^{(\tau)}, l) = -\log p(l \mid x_i^{(\tau)}) \qquad (10)$$

$$= -\log \frac{\theta_s(x_i^{(\tau)}, l) + \theta_t(x_i^{(\tau)}, l)}{\sum_k (\theta_s(x_i^{(\tau)}, k) + \theta_t(x_i^{(\tau)}, k))} \qquad (11)$$

where $p(l \,|\, x_i^{(\tau)})$ is the probability that node $x_i^{(\tau)}$ belongs to the lth segment. In other words, the unary cost $\psi(x_i^{(\tau)}, l)$ gets lower, as node $x_i^{(\tau)}$ is more likely to be labeled as l. In (11), θ_s and θ_t are the STHS similarity function and the temporal consistency function, respectively.

Although STHS provides robust initial segmentation results, they are not harmonized with the labels at the previous frame $\tau - 1$. Hence, for each initial segment at the current frame τ, we check if it is consistent with each label l at frame $\tau - 1$. More specifically, we compute the STHS similarity function $\theta_s(x_i^{(\tau)}, l)$ by

$$\theta_s(x_i^{(\tau)}, l) = \begin{cases} \eta(z_l^{(\tau-1)}, s_i^{(\tau)}) & \text{if } \max_k \eta(z_k^{(\tau-1)}, s_i^{(\tau)}) > \beta, \\ 0 & \text{otherwise,} \end{cases} \quad (12)$$

where η is the similarity function in (4), and the threshold β is 0.5. Also, $z_l^{(\tau-1)}$ denotes the segment that has label l at frame $\tau - 1$. If the initial segment $s_i^{(\tau)}$ including superpixel $x_i^{(\tau)}$ is similar to the segment $z_l^{(\tau-1)}$, the function $\theta_s(x_i^{(\tau)}, l)$ yields a high value. Moreover, we generate new labels to consider newly appearing segments. Specifically, if $\max_k \eta(z_k^{(\tau-1)}, s_i^{(\tau)}) \leq \beta$, we declare that $s_i^{(\tau)}$ is not harmonized with any existing label at the previous frame. For this inharmonic initial segment, we assign a new label $\hat{l}$ and set the STHS similarity by $\theta_s(x_i^{(\tau)}, \hat{l}) = 1$. Note that we regard all initial segments at the first frame as inharmonic.

To enforce temporal coherence of inter-frame segments, we adopt the temporal consistency function $\theta_t(x_i^{(\tau)}, l)$ in the unary cost in (11), which is given by

$$\theta_t(x_i^{(\tau)}, l) = \exp\left(-d_{\chi^2}(\overleftarrow{x}_i^{(\tau)}, x_i^{(\tau)})\right) \times \frac{|\mathcal{Z}_l^{(\tau-1)} \cap \overleftarrow{\mathcal{X}}_i^{(\tau)}|}{\max_k |\mathcal{Z}_k^{(\tau-1)} \cap \overleftarrow{\mathcal{X}}_i^{(\tau)}|} \quad (13)$$

where $\overleftarrow{x}_i^{(\tau)}$ denotes the superpixel at frame $\tau - 1$, which is warped from $x_i^{(\tau)}$ by the backward optical flow vectors, and $\overleftarrow{\mathcal{X}}_i^{(\tau)}$ is the set of pixels in $\overleftarrow{x}_i^{(\tau)}$. Also, $\mathcal{Z}_l^{(\tau-1)}$ is the set of pixels within the lth segment at frame $\tau - 1$. The chi-square distance $d_{\chi^2}(\overleftarrow{x}_i^{(\tau)}, x_i^{(\tau)})$ is computed using only the color features. Note that $\theta_t(x_i^{(\tau)}, l)$ yields a higher value when the color matching error is smaller and the warped area $\overleftarrow{\mathcal{X}}_i^{(\tau)}$ has a bigger overlap with the lth segment $\mathcal{Z}_l^{(\tau-1)}$. Thus, the temporal consistency function helps to propagate the segment labels at the previous frame to the current frame.

To encourage neighboring nodes with similar features to have the same segment label, we define the pairwise cost in (9) by

$$\phi(x_i^{(\tau)}, x_j^{(\tau)}, y_i^{(\tau)}, y_j^{(\tau)}) = \begin{cases} \exp(-d_{\chi^2}(x_i^{(\tau)}, x_j^{(\tau)})) & \text{if } y_i^{(\tau)} \neq y_j^{(\tau)}, \\ 0 & \text{otherwise,} \end{cases} \quad (14)$$

where d_{χ^2} is computed using all the color, motion, and boundary features.

We employ the graph-cut algorithm [37] to minimize the MRF energy function in (9). Consequently, we obtain the segment label of each superpixel at the current frame. This segmentation result is recorded for segmenting the next frame.

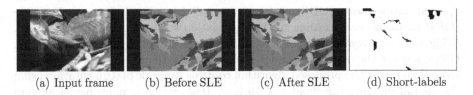

(a) Input frame   (b) Before SLE   (c) After SLE   (d) Short-labels

Fig. 5. An example of the short-label elimination (SLE). Noisy labels with short durations are depicted in black in (d). They are erased, and the corresponding superpixels are re-labeled using the neighboring labels in (c). The frames are from "Chameleons"

3.4 Short-Label Elimination

In general, an online segmentation algorithm may produce noisy segments, which have short temporal durations. To suppress such noise, we develop the short-label elimination scheme. At frame τ, we check the temporal duration of each segment at frame $\tau - \epsilon$, where $\epsilon = 10$. If the duration is shorter than ϵ, we erase the labels of the corresponding superpixels. To re-label these erased superpixels, we apply the MRF optimization scheme again. For a non-erased superpixel, its unary cost is set to 0 for the original label, and 1 for the other labels. For an erased superpixel, its unary cost is set to 1 for all labels. Also, we use the same pairwise cost in (14). Then, we minimize the energy function using the graph-cut algorithm. Consequently, the erased superpixels are labeled consistently with the neighboring superpixels. Figure 5 shows an example of the short-label elimination.

4 Experimental Results

We test the proposed video segmentation algorithm on the VSB100 dataset [14], which consists of 40 training videos and 60 test videos. The spatial resolution of these video sequences are between 960×720 and 1920×1080. The ground-truth is annotated for every 20th frame by four subjects. The VSB100 sequences are very challenging due to motion blur, jerky camera motion, occlusion, object deformation, and ambiguous object boundaries. For efficient computation, we test the proposed algorithm after resizing video frames by a factor of 0.5 in both x and y directions. We use the same parameters for all experiments, unless otherwise specified.

We use two performance metrics, boundary precision-recall (BPR) and volume precision-recall (VPR), which were introduced in [14]. BPR measures the qualities of segmentation boundaries in the precision-recall framework after the bipartite graph matching between computer-generated boundaries and the ground-truth boundaries. VPR assesses volumetric qualities of segmentation by computing the maximal overlap between computer-generated segments and the ground-truth segments. For both BPR and VPR, we calculate the average precision (AP), which is the area under the precision-recall curve. We report the optimal dataset scale (ODS) performance and the optimal segmentation scale (OSS) performance according to the aggregation strategy of F-measure scores. While ODS aggregates the scores of all sequences at a fixed segmentation scale, OSS discovers the optimal scale for each sequence. Hence, OSS yields a higher score than ODS. The proposed algorithm controls the scale of segmentation using the spatial merging threshold $\gamma \in \{0.1, \ldots, 0.6\}$, which is more practical than specifying the number of segments. Figure 6 visualizes segmentation results of the proposed algorithm according to the scale parameter γ. As γ increases, more superpixels are merged, resulting in coarser segments. In addition, we count the number of segments (NCL) and compute the average length (μ) and the standard deviation (δ) of segment durations in ODS. We analyze running times of the proposed algorithm and the conventional methods [5–7,9,11] by seconds per frame (SPF) for "Arctic Kayak" sequence at 640×360 resolution. We test the methods on a PC with a 3.0 GHz CPU.

(a) Input frame   (b) Ground-truth   (c) $\gamma = 0.1$ (d) $\gamma = 0.2$ (e) $\gamma = 0.4$

Fig. 6. Segmentation results of the proposed algorithm in various scales according to the parameter γ. As γ increases, the proposed algorithm generates coarser segments. The frames are from "Fish Underwater"

Table 1 compares the performance of the proposed algorithm on the VSB100 dataset with those of 12 conventional algorithms: nine offline methods [4–10,12,14] and three online methods [11–13]. The scores of the conventional algorithms are from [9,10,12,13]. The oracle method links the per-frame UCM segments [1] optimally using the ground-truth data as specified in [14]. We see that the proposed algorithm surpasses the conventional online video segmentation algorithms in terms of both BPR and VPR. Especially, in terms of VPR ODS, the proposed algorithm provides a 20 % gain, compared with the state-of-the-art online algorithm [12]. Moreover, the proposed algorithm even outperforms most offline video segmentation algorithms and provides comparable performances to the state-of-the-art offline algorithms [9,10]. In addition, we develop a faster version, which shortens the overall running time from 176.1 to 18.6 by employing lighter optical flow estimator, [32] without matching, and faster contour detector [34]. The faster version reduces the running time by 89 %, while sacrificing a small BPR-AP score only. The faster version of the proposed algorithm is faster than all conventional methods.

Table 1. Comparison of video segmentation performances on the VSB100 [14]. The best and the second best results are boldfaced and underlined, respectively

Algorithm	BPR			VPR			Length	NCL	Time
	ODS	OSS	AP	ODS	OSS	AP	$\mu(\delta)$	μ	SPF
Human	0.81	0.81	0.67	0.83	0.83	0.70	83.24(40.04)	11.90	-
Oracle [14]	0.61	0.67	0.61	0.65	0.67	0.68	-	118.56	-
A. Offline segmentation algorithms									
Corso et al. [4]	0.51	0.53	0.37	0.51	0.52	0.38	70.67(48.39)	25.83	-
Grundmann et al. [5]	0.47	0.54	0.41	0.52	0.55	0.52	51.83(39.91)	117.90	**26.8**
Ochs and Brox [6]	0.17	0.17	0.06	0.25	0.25	0.12	87.85(38.83)	3.73	<u>268.9</u>
Galasso et al. [7]	0.51	0.56	0.45	0.45	0.51	0.42	80.17(37.56)	8.00	425.6
Galasso et al. [14]	0.61	0.65	<u>0.59</u>	0.59	0.62	0.56	25.50(36.48)	258.05	-
Galasso et al. [12]	0.62	0.66	0.54	0.55	0.59	0.55	61.25(40.87)	80.00	-
Khoreva et al. [8]	0.61	0.64	0.51	0.58	0.61	0.58	60.48(43.19)	50.00	-
Khoreva et al. [9]	**0.64**	**0.70**	**0.61**	<u>0.63</u>	<u>0.66</u>	<u>0.63</u>	83.41(35.27)	50.00	416.2
Yi and Pavlovic [10]	<u>0.63</u>	<u>0.67</u>	0.57	**0.65**	**0.67**	**0.64**	35.76(38.72)	168.93	-
B. Online segmentation algorithms									
Xu et al. [11]	0.38	0.46	0.32	0.45	0.48	0.44	59.27(47.76)	26.58	<u>39.2</u>
Galasso et al. [12]	0.61	**0.67**	<u>0.52</u>	0.55	0.59	0.53	73.31(40.33)	15.63	-
Li et al. [13]	0.54	0.58	0.40	0.53	0.60	0.46	-	-	-
Proposed	<u>0.63</u>	0.66	**0.53**	**0.66**	**0.68**	**0.62**	36.61(31.19)	133.22	176.1
Proposed (Faster ver.)	**0.63**	<u>0.66</u>	0.51	**0.66**	**0.68**	**0.62**	37.01(31.27)	140.97	**18.6**

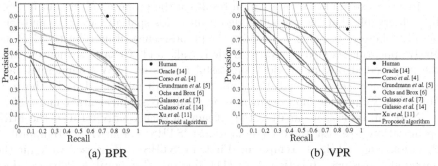

(a) BPR   (b) VPR

Fig. 7. Comparison of the precision-recall curves of the proposed algorithm and the conventional algorithms [4–7,11,14]

Figure 7 shows the precision-recall curves of BPR and VPR. We compare the proposed algorithm with the conventional algorithms [4–7,11,14], whose results are available in the benchmark [14]. Among them, only the proposed algorithm and [11] are online ones, and the others are offline ones. The curves of the proposed algorithm are mostly higher than those of the conventional algorithms.

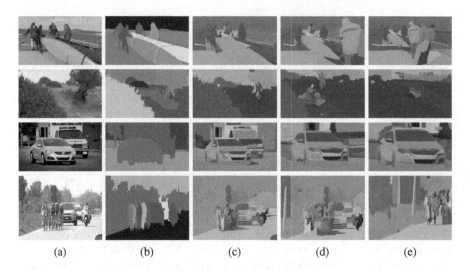

(a)   (b)   (c)   (d)   (e)

Fig. 8. Qualitative results of the proposed segmentation algorithm. (a), (b), and (c) show the input frame, the ground-truth, and the computed results at the same frames, respectively. (d) and (e) illustrate more segmentation results at different frames. From top to bottom, the frames are from "Arctic Kayak," "Gokart," "VW Commercial," and "Bicycle Race" in the VBS100 dataset [14]

Furthermore, the proposed algorithm partly outperforms the oracle method, which uses the ground-truth data.

Figure 8 exemplifies segmentation results of the proposed algorithm in OSS. It is observable that the proposed algorithm yields spatially accurate and temporally coherent segments. Especially, the proposed algorithm robustly identifies newly appearing segments on the "Arctic Kayak" and "Gokart" sequences. Also, the proposed algorithm provides successful results on "VW Commercial" and "Bicycle Race," even though there are fast camera motions. Due to the page limitation, we provide more segmentation results as supplementary materials.

Next, in Table 2, we analyze the efficacy of each energy term in the MRF optimization. We test three configurations: 'STHS + Pairwise,' 'Temporal + Pairwise,' and 'STHS + Temporal.' First, in 'STHS + Pairwise,' we omit the temporal consistency function θ_t in (11). Second, 'Temporal + Pairwise' does not perform STHS and ignores the STHS similarity function θ_s in (11). Third, in 'STHS + Temporal,' we omit the pairwise cost in the MRF optimization. Note that the omission of the temporal consistency function in 'STHS + Pairwise' leads to worse VPR scores. Since the proposed STHS plays an essential role in handling newly appearing segments and alleviating the propagation of erroneous segmentation labels, 'Temporal + Pairwise' presents the worst scores. Also, the omission of the pairwise term in 'STHS + Temporal' leads to the performance degradation. However, since we consider spatial affinities in STHS, the degradation is relatively small.

Table 2. The segmentation performance of the proposed algorithm using various experimental configurations

	BPR			VPR			Length	NCL
Experimental setting	ODS	OSS	AP	ODS	OSS	AP	$\mu(\delta)$	μ
Proposed algorithm	0.63	0.66	0.53	0.66	0.68	0.62	36.61(31.19)	133.22
A. Combination of energy functions								
STHS + Pairwise	0.62	0.66	0.55	0.64	0.66	0.59	34.02(28.69)	119.45
Temporal + Pairwise	0.57	0.61	0.45	0.61	0.64	0.55	65.64(40.38)	39.02
STHS + Temporal	0.62	0.65	0.52	0.65	0.67	0.62	35.43(30.26)	125.68
B. Post processing (short-label elimination)								
Without post processing	0.63	0.66	0.52	0.66	0.68	0.62	13.54(23.49)	345.83

To analyze the effectiveness of the short-label elimination, we measure the performance of the proposed algorithm without the post processing. As reported in Table 2, the short-label elimination extends the average duration of segments and decreases the number of segments, by eliminating noisy segments. It does not increase BPR and VPR significantly, since the noisy segments are too small to affect on the quantitative results.

5   Conclusions

We proposed a novel online video segmentation algorithm. To identify newly appearing segments effectively, we introduced the STHS technique, which generates initial segments by sliding a window of frames. We first employed the spatial agglomerative clustering for each frame, and then performed the temporal bipartite graph matching across frames. Moreover, we defined the MRF energy function, which consists of the unary and pairwise costs. We computed the unary cost to exploit the initial STHS result and the previous segmentation result, and the pairwise cost to encourage similar superpixels to have the same label. Experimental results on the VSB100 dataset [14] showed that the proposed algorithm outperforms the state-of-the-art online video segmentation algorithms [11–13] significantly.

Acknowledgement. This work was supported partly by the National Research Foundation of Korea (NRF) grant funded by the Korea government (MSIP) (No. NRF-2015R1A2A1A10055037), and partly by the MSIP, Korea, under the ITRC support program supervised by the Institute for Information & communications Technology Promotion (No. IITP-2016-R2720-16-0007).

References

1. Arbelaez, P., Maire, M., Fowlkes, C., Malik, J.: Contour detection and hierarchical image segmentation. IEEE Trans. Pattern Anal. Mach. Intell. **33**(5), 898–916 (2011)
2. Yu, Y., Fang, C., Liao, Z.: Piecewise flat embedding for image segmentation. In: ICCV, pp. 1368–1376 (2015)
3. Xie, S., Tu, Z.: Holistically-nested edge detection. In: ICCV, pp. 1395–1403 (2015)
4. Corso, J.J., Sharon, E., Dube, S., El-Saden, S., Sinha, U., Yuille, A.: Efficient multilevel brain tumor segmentation with integrated bayesian model classification. IEEE Trans. Med. Imaging **27**(5), 629–640 (2008)
5. Grundmann, M., Kwatra, V., Han, M., Essa, I.: Efficient hierarchical graph-based video segmentation. In: CVPR, pp. 2141–2148 (2010)
6. Ochs, P., Brox, T.: Object segmentation in video: a hierarchical variational approach for turning point trajectories into dense regions. In: ICCV, pp. 1583–1590 (2011)
7. Galasso, F., Cipolla, R., Schiele, B.: Video segmentation with superpixels. In: Lee, K.M., Matsushita, Y., Rehg, J.M., Hu, Z. (eds.) ACCV 2012, Part I. LNCS, vol. 7724, pp. 760–774. Springer, Heidelberg (2013)
8. Khoreva, A., Galasso, F., Hein, M., Schiele, B.: Learning must-link constraints for video segmentation based on spectral clustering. In: Jiang, X., Hornegger, J., Koch, R. (eds.) CPR 2014. LNCS, vol. 8753, pp. 701–712. Springer, Heidelberg (2014)
9. Khoreva, A., Galasso, F., Hein, M., Schiele, B.: Classifier based graph construction for video segmentation. In: CVPR, pp. 951–960 (2015)
10. Yi, S., Pavlovic, V.: Multi-cue structure preserving MRF for unconstrained video segmentation. In: ICCV, pp. 3262–3270 (2015)
11. Xu, C., Xiong, C., Corso, J.J.: Streaming hierarchical video segmentation. In: Fitzgibbon, A., Lazebnik, S., Perona, P., Sato, Y., Schmid, C. (eds.) ECCV 2012, Part VI. LNCS, vol. 7577, pp. 626–639. Springer, Heidelberg (2012)
12. Galasso, F., Keuper, M., Brox, T., Schiele, B.: Spectral graph reduction for efficient image and streaming video segmentation. In: CVPR, pp. 49–56 (2014)
13. Li, C., Lin, L., Zuo, W., Yan, S., Tang, J.: SOLD: sub-optimal low-rank decomposition for efficient video segmentation. In: CVPR, pp. 5519–5527 (2015)
14. Galasso, F., Nagaraja, N., Cardenas, T., Brox, T., Schiele, B.: A unified video segmentation benchmark: annotation, metrics and analysis. In: CVPR, pp. 3527–3534 (2013)
15. Ng, A.Y., Jordan, M.I., Weiss, Y.: On spectral clustering: analysis and an algorithm. Adv. Neural Inf. Process. Syst. **2**, 849–856 (2002)
16. Yu, C.P., Le, H., Zelinsky, G., Samaras, D.: Efficient video segmentation using parametric graph partitioning. In: ICCV, pp. 3155–3163 (2015)
17. Vazquez-Reina, A., Avidan, S., Pfister, H., Miller, E.: Multiple hypothesis video segmentation from superpixel flows. In: Daniilidis, K., Maragos, P., Paragios, N. (eds.) ECCV 2010, Part V. LNCS, vol. 6315, pp. 268–281. Springer, Heidelberg (2010)
18. Felzenszwalb, P.F., Huttenlocher, D.P.: Efficient graph-based image segmentation. Int. J. Comput. Vis. **59**(2), 167–181 (2004)
19. Chang, J., Wei, D., Fisher, J.: A video representation using temporal superpixels. In: CVPR, pp. 2051–2058 (2013)
20. Reso, M., Jachalsky, J., Rosenhahn, B., Ostermann, J.: Temporally consistent superpixels. In: ICCV, pp. 385–392 (2013)

21. Shi, J., Malik, J.: Motion segmentation and tracking using normalized cuts. In: ICCV, pp. 1154–1160 (1998)
22. Brox, T., Malik, J.: Object segmentation by long term analysis of point trajectories. In: Daniilidis, K., Maragos, P., Paragios, N. (eds.) ECCV 2010, Part V. LNCS, vol. 6315, pp. 282–295. Springer, Heidelberg (2010)
23. Ochs, P., Brox, T.: Higher order motion models and spectral clustering. In: CVPR, pp. 614–621 (2012)
24. Lee, Y.J., Kim, J., Grauman, K.: Key-segments for video object segmentation. In: ICCV, pp. 1995–2002 (2011)
25. Ma, T., Latecki, L.J.: Maximum weight cliques with mutex constraints for video object segmentation. In: CVPR, pp. 670–677 (2012)
26. Zhang, D., Javed, O., Shah, M.: Video object segmentation through spatially accurate and temporally dense extraction of primary object regions. In: CVPR, pp. 628–635 (2013)
27. Oneata, D., Revaud, J., Verbeek, J., Schmid, C.: Spatio-temporal object detection proposals. In: Fleet, D., Pajdla, T., Schiele, B., Tuytelaars, T. (eds.) ECCV 2014, Part III. LNCS, vol. 8691, pp. 737–752. Springer, Heidelberg (2014)
28. Wang, W., Shen, J., Porikli, F.: Saliency-aware geodesic video object segmentation. In: CVPR, pp. 3395–3402 (2015)
29. Giordano, D., Murabito, F., Palazzo, S., Spampinato, C.: Superpixel-based video object segmentation using perceptual organization and location prior. In: CVPR, pp. 4814–4822 (2015)
30. Taylor, B., Karasev, V., Soatto, S.: Causal video object segmentation from persistence of occlusions. In: CVPR, pp. 4268–4276 (2015)
31. Jang, W.D., Lee, C., Kim, C.S.: Primary object segmentation in videos via alternate convex optimization of foreground and background distributions. In: CVPR, pp. 696–704 (2016)
32. Weinzaepfel, P., Revaud, J., Harchaoui, Z., Schmid, C.: DeepFlow: large displacement optical flow with deep matching. In: ICCV, pp. 1385–1392 (2013)
33. Comaniciu, D., Meer, P.: Mean shift: a robust approach toward feature space analysis. IEEE Trans. Pattern Anal. Mach. Intell. 24(5), 603–619 (2002)
34. Dollár, P., Zitnick, C.L.: Fast edge detection using structured forests. IEEE Trans. Pattern Anal. Mach. Intell. 37(8), 1558–1570 (2015)
35. Li, F., Kim, T., Humayun, A., Tsai, D., Rehg, J.M.: Video segmentation by tracking many figure-ground segments. In: ICCV, pp. 2192–2199 (2013)
36. Theodoridis, S., Koutroumbas, K.: Pattern Recognition, 3rd edn. Academic Press, Orlando (2006)
37. Boykov, Y., Veksler, O., Zabih, R.: Efficient approximate energy minimization via graph cuts. IEEE Trans. Pattern Anal. Mach. Intell. 20(12), 1222–1239 (2001)

Learning to Learn: Model Regression Networks for Easy Small Sample Learning

Yu-Xiong Wang$^{(\boxtimes)}$ and Martial Hebert

Robotics Institute, Carnegie Mellon University, Pittsburgh, USA
{yuxiongw,hebert}@cs.cmu.edu

Abstract. We develop a conceptually simple but powerful approach that can learn novel categories from few annotated examples. In this approach, the experience with already learned categories is used to facilitate the learning of novel classes. Our insight is two-fold: (1) there exists a *generic, category agnostic* transformation from models learned from few samples to models learned from large enough sample sets, and (2) such a transformation could be effectively learned by high-capacity regressors. In particular, we automatically learn the transformation with a deep model regression network on a large collection of model pairs. Experiments demonstrate that encoding this transformation as prior knowledge greatly facilitates the recognition in the small sample size regime on a broad range of tasks, including domain adaptation, fine-grained recognition, action recognition, and scene classification.

Keywords: Small sample learning · Transfer learning · Object recognition · Model transformation · Deep regression networks

1 Motivation

Over the past decade, large-scale object recognition has achieved high performance levels due to the integration of powerful machine learning techniques with big annotated training data sets [38,51,52,62,79,83,84]. In practical applications, however, training examples are often expensive to acquire or otherwise scarce [30]. Visual phenomena follow a long-tail distribution, in which a few sub-categories are common while many are rare with limited training data even in the big-data setting [105,106]. More crucially, current recognition systems assume a set of categories known a priori, despite the obviously dynamic and open nature of the visual world [12,32,64,96].

Such scenarios of learning *novel categories from few examples* pose a multitude of open challenges for object recognition in the wild. For instance, when operating in natural environments, robots are supposed to recognize unfamiliar objects after seeing only few examples [50]. Humans are remarkably able to grasp a new category and make meaningful generalization to novel instances from just a short exposure to a single example [30,81]. By contrast, typical machine learning tools require tens, hundreds, or thousands of training examples and often break down for small sample learning [7,40].

© Springer International Publishing AG 2016
B. Leibe et al. (Eds.): ECCV 2016, Part VI, LNCS 9910, pp. 616–634, 2016.
DOI: 10.1007/978-3-319-46466-4_37

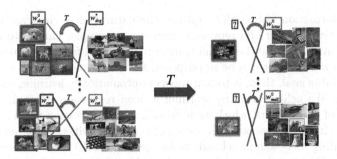

Fig. 1. Our main hypothesis is that there exists a generic, category agnostic transformation T from classifiers $\mathbf{w}^0$ learned from few annotated samples (represented as blue) to the underlying classifiers $\mathbf{w}^*$ learned from large sets of samples (represented as red). We estimate the transformation T by learning a deep regression network on a large collection of model pairs, i.e., a model regression network. For a novel category/task (such as scene classification and fine-grained object recognition), we introduce the learned T to construct the target model and thus facilitate its generalization in the small sample size regime (Color figure online)

In this paper, we explore a novel *learning to learn* approach that leverages the knowledge gained when learning models in large sample sets to facilitate recognizing novel categories from few samples. From a discriminative machine learning perspective, object recognition is basically a process that learns an object category classifier to separate annotated positive and negative examples in a feature space. We assume a *fixed, discriminative* feature space, which is reasonable especially considering the recent learned feature representations via deep convolutional neural networks. We now take the model such as SVM classifiers and make important modification. The central issue can be reduced to the following: How to estimate a classifier that would be learned from a large set of samples (on the order of hundreds or thousands of) based on its corresponding classifier learned from few annotated samples (as few as one and up to a hundred)?

Our main hypothesis is that there exists a *generic, category agnostic* transformation from small-sample models to the underlying large-sample models. This hypothesis is validated empirically in Sect. 4. Intuitively, a model can be viewed as a separating hyperplane in the feature space.[1] Small training examples already constrain the search space by pointing to an initial hyperplane not far from the desired hyperplane produced by a large training set. When gradually introducing additional examples, the initial hyperplane is progressively subject to a series of transformations until it converges as illustrated in Fig. 1.

We suspect that this transformation, or at least certain components of it, is fairly generic. In a machine learning context, a learner needs to be biased in some way for it to generalize well [9,30,40,81]. Consequently, there might exist some systematic bias from a small-sample model to its large-sample version. In essence,

---

[1] A kernel model can be viewed as a separating hyperplane in the lifted feature space.

this transformation potentially captures the natural intra-class variability in a discriminative manner and represents how sparse samples change to a category cluster. Hence, we view the model transformation as a form of shared structure and, when available, it can be re-purposed for novel categories.

A desirable goal, then, is to find ways of automatically learning such a transformation. We achieve this by learning a deep regression network on a large collection of model pairs, which we term as a *model regression network*. The network explicitly regresses between the small-sample classifiers (as input) and their corresponding large-sample classifiers (as ground-truth) on a variety of known categories. The deep learning framework enables us to learn the transformation without imposing strong priors. Now, for a novel category/task, we introduce the learned transformation to construct the target model and thus facilitate its generalization in the small sample size regime.

Our approach is inspired by the recent observation in deep learning based object recognition that features extracted from deep convolutional neural networks trained on a large set of particular object categories exhibit attractive transferability [4,20,76,104]. They could thus serve as universal feature extractors for novel categories/tasks. Our key insights then are that such generality would also hold on a model level and that it would be learnable in a similar fashion as on the feature level. This is also suggested by the duality perspective between the feature space and the classifier space [91]. Eventually, the transformation can be also viewed to be imposed on features but parametrized in a model fashion.

Our contribution is three-fold: First, we show how to construct a training "model set" by generating a large collection of model pairs that are learned from small and large sample sets respectively on various categories (Sect. 3.1). Second, we show how a model regression network, based on deep neural networks and this training model set, is learned and a generic transformation between these two types of models is identified by the regressor (Sects. 3.2 and 3.3). Finally, we show how our regression network is used to facilitate the recognition of novel categories from few samples, leading to significantly improved performance on a broad range of tasks, including domain adaptation, fine-grained recognition, action recognition, and scene classification (Sects. 3.4 and 4).

2 Related Work

It remains a fundamental challenge to understand how to recognize novel categories from few examples for both humans and machines. This line of research is generally addressed in the fields of one/few-shot learning [26], inductive transfer or transfer learning [70], multi-task learning [14], learning to learn [86], and meta-learning [82]. Because of high-dimensionality of feature spaces, successful generalization from small training samples typically requires strong and appropriately tuned "inductive biases" using additional available information [9,40].

A natural source of information comes from additional data via "data manufacturing" [7] in various ways. For instance, (1) obtain more examples of categories of interest from large amounts of unlabeled data as in semi-supervised learning [15,107] and active learning [73], (2) augment the available examples by performing simple image transformations including jittering and noise injection as commonly used in deep learning [16,22,52], (3) borrow examples from other relevant categories [61], (4) introduce Universum examples (i.e., unlabeled examples that do not belong to the concerned classes) for max-margin regularization [98], and (5) synthesize new virtual examples, either rendered explicitly with computer graphics techniques or created implicitly through compositional representations [18,21,66,67,71,106]. These approaches can significantly improve recognition performance if a generative model that accounts for the underlying, natural intra-class variability is known. Unfortunately, such a model is usually unavailable [7] and the generation of additional real or artificial examples often requires substantial effort.

In a broad sense, learning novel categories is addressed by exploiting and transferring knowledge gained from familiar categories [14,70,72,77,86,87]. This is to imitate the human ability of adapting previously acquired experience when performing a new task [74]. In particular, inter-class transfer [40] and cross-generalization [7] are achieved by discovering shared feature representations: (1) captured by linear or nonlinear feature transformations [1,14,31,48,63,85,94], (2) obtained by feature selection [27,59,60] or regularization [37], (3) described by similarities between novel classes and familiar classes [8], (4) encoded as a distance metric by metric learning [10,11,29,75,92,100] or kernel learning [40], and (5) learned by boosting approaches [69,89,101]. Recently, there has been growing interest in learning deep convolutional neural networks in fully supervised, semi-supervised, or unsupervised fashions to extract generic features and then to transfer them to different tasks [19,22,33,35,46,49,52,65,83,95,99].

Another type of knowledge transfer focuses on modeling (hyper-)parameters that are shared across domains, typically in the context of generative statistical modeling [25,58,78]. A variational Bayesian framework is first developed by incorporating previously learned classes into the prior and combining with the likelihood to yield a new class posterior distribution [25,26]. Gaussian processes [57,78] and hierarchical Bayesian models [81] are also employed to allow transferring in a non-parametric Bayesian way. The recently proposed hierarchical Bayesian program learning utilizes the principles of compositionality and causality to build a probabilistic generative model of visual objects [54–56]. In addition, adaptive SVM and its variants present SVM-based model adaptation by combining classifiers learned on related categories [2,3,23,47,53,88,97,102]. Other approaches transfer the knowledge across different modalities [6,32,36]. Despite many notable successes, it is still unclear what kind of underlying structures are shared across a wide variety of categories and are useful for transfer.

Different from the previous work, we propose a plausible alternative for transferring inter-class structure from a model perspective. This paper is the first to show that there exists certain generic, category agnostic transformation between small-sample and large-sample models on a wide spectrum of categories. In addition, such a transformation could be effectively learned by high-capacity regressors, such as deep neural networks, in a model-level big-data setting. Our approach could also be seen as an alternative parametric way of doing model distillation that relies on the connection between different models [5,13,41].

3 Model Regression Networks

We are given a fixed, discriminative feature space $\mathcal{X}$ of dimensionality d, such as the current deep convolutional neural network features.[2] For an object category c of interest, we generate a model or classifier $h(\mathbf{x})$ that discriminates between its positive and negative instances $\mathbf{x} \in \mathcal{X}$. We consider, for example, the linear SVM classifier commonly used for object recognition tasks, which is a separating hyperplane in the feature space. The classifier $h(\cdot)$ can then be represented as a weight vector $\mathbf{w}$ belonging to the model parameter space $\mathcal{W}$.

Let $\mathbf{w}^0$ indicate a classifier learned from few annotated samples *without any additional information*. Let $\mathbf{w}^*$ indicate the corresponding *underlying* classifier learned from a large set of annotated samples of the same category. Our goal is to generate $\mathbf{w}$ (or equivalently, $h(\cdot)$) that generalizes well from these few training examples, i.e., to make $\mathbf{w}$ as close as to the desired $\mathbf{w}^*$. The key assumption is that there exists a generic non-linear transformation $\widetilde{T} : \mathcal{W} \to \mathcal{W}$ for a broad range of categories, so that for $\mathbf{w}^0$ and $\mathbf{w}^*$ in any category c, we have $\mathbf{w}^* \approx \widetilde{T}(\mathbf{w}^0)$. That is, there is a set of large-sample models and $\widetilde{T}$ is the projection into that set (with $\mathbf{w}^*$ being a fixpoint of $\widetilde{T}$). Once the transformation $\widetilde{T}$ is available, we could easily improve the classifier generalization.

Inspired by recent progress in deep learning, it is possible to estimate this transformation $\widetilde{T}$ from a large set of known categories. A straightforward approach then is to learn a regression function T parameterized by Θ based on a large collection of "annotated" model pairs $\left\{ \left(\mathbf{w}_j^0, \mathbf{w}_j^* \right) \right\}_{j=1}^{J}$ from these categories. That is, $\mathbf{w}_j^* \approx T\left(\mathbf{w}_j^0, \Theta \right)$ for any small-sample model $\mathbf{w}_j^0$ and its large-sample model $\mathbf{w}_j^*$ learned on the same category. We employ multi-layer neural networks as regressors, which are well-known to learn complex, non-linear functions with minimal human design. By doing so, we avoid an explicit description of the space of transformations. We then use the obtained transformation in learning models for novel categories.

3.1 Generation of Model Pairs

We start from large amounts of labeled data from a variety of categories, denoted as $\{(\mathbf{x}_i, y_i)\}_{i=1}^{L}$. Here $\mathbf{x}_i \in \mathbb{R}^d$ is the ith data sample in the feature space $\mathcal{X}$, $y_i \in \{1, \ldots, C\}$ is the corresponding label, and C is the number of categories. Different from conventional recognition systems that directly learn from the data and label pairs, we learn on a model level. To this end, we produce a collection of model pairs $\left\{ \left(\mathbf{w}_j^0, \mathbf{w}_j^* \right) \right\}_{j=1}^{J}$ as our *training model set* using the original training

---

[2] Notation: We use boldface letters for vectors and matrices and italicized capital letters for transformation functions. For notational simplicity, $\mathbf{x}$ already includes a constant 1 as the last element and thus $\mathbf{w}$ includes the bias term.

data set $\{(\mathbf{x}_i, y_i)\}_{i=1}^L$. Each model is generated as a binary classifier focused on separating a single category from all the remaining categories in a manner inspired by the one-vs.-all strategy in multi-class classification.

Specifically, for each category c, we first learn $\mathbf{w}^{c,*}$ from a large sample set. We treat $\mathbf{w}^{c,*}$ as the *ground-truth model*. Let the positive examples $\{\mathbf{x}_i^{c,pos}\}_{i=1}^{L_c}$ be all the data points of category c, where L_c is the total number of samples whose labels are c. We obtain negative examples $\{\mathbf{x}_i^{c,neg}\}_{i=1}^M$ by randomly sampling M data points from other categories not in category c. We train a binary SVM classifier $\mathbf{w}^{c,*}$ on the training set $\mathcal{P}^c = \{(\mathbf{x}_i^{c,pos}, +1)\}_{i=1}^{L_c} \cup \{(\mathbf{x}_i^{c,neg}, -1)\}_{i=1}^M$.

We now learn the small-sample model $\mathbf{w}^{c,0}$ for category c. Consistent with the few-shot scenario that consists of few positive examples, we randomly sample $N \ll L_c$ data points $\{\mathbf{x}_i^{c,pos}\}_{i=1}^N$ out of the L_c positive examples of category c. We train a binary SVM classifier $\mathbf{w}^{c,0}$ on the reduced training set $\mathcal{Q}^c = \{(\mathbf{x}_i^{c,pos}, +1)\}_{i=1}^N \cup \{(\mathbf{x}_i^{c,neg}, -1)\}_{i=1}^M$.

Note that we have many ways of choosing the small sample set for a given $\mathbf{w}^{c,*}$ to learn $\mathbf{w}^{c,0}$. This indicates that we could repeat the sampling procedure S times, leading to S small-sample models $\left\{\mathbf{w}_j^{c,0}\right\}_{j=1}^S$ learned from different small-sample sized training subset $\left\{\mathcal{Q}_j^c\right\}_{j=1}^S$ of $\mathcal{P}^c$. Since they correspond to the unique ground-truth model, we thus obtain a series of model pairs for category c as $\left\{\left(\mathbf{w}_j^{c,0}, \mathbf{w}^{c,*}\right)\right\}_{j=1}^S$. Including the learned model pairs from all the C categories, we generate the desired training model set $\left\{\left(\mathbf{w}_j^0, \mathbf{w}_j^*\right)\right\}_{j=1}^J$, where $J = S \times C$. Due to sub-sampling, the size of the training model set could be potentially large, with many orders of magnitude larger than the number of categories.

3.2 Regression Network

Given the training model set $\left\{\left(\mathbf{w}_j^0, \mathbf{w}_j^*\right)\right\}_{j=1}^J$ with one to one model correspondence, we aim to learn a mapping: $\mathbf{w}^0 \to \mathbf{w}^*$. We parametrize the transformation as a regression function $T\left(\mathbf{w}^0, \Theta\right)$, such that $\mathbf{w}^* \approx T\left(\mathbf{w}^0, \Theta\right)$. We simply use the square of the Euclidean distance to quantify the quality of the approximation. For each model $\mathbf{w}_j^0$, we have the corresponding small sample set $\mathcal{Q}_j = \left\{\left(\mathbf{x}_i^j, y_i^j\right)\right\}_{i=1}^{M+N}$ used to learn the model as well. To make the regression more robust, we include the performance on these samples as an additional loss, which is standard in the transfer learning approaches with model parameter sharing [97,102]. Our final loss function then is

$$L(\Theta) = \sum_{j=1}^J \left\{ \frac{1}{2} \left\|\mathbf{w}_j^* - T\left(\mathbf{w}_j^0, \Theta\right)\right\|_2^2 + \lambda \sum_{i=1}^{M+N} \left[1 - y_i^j \left(T\left(\mathbf{w}_j^0, \Theta\right)^T \mathbf{x}_i^j\right)\right]_+ \right\}. \quad (1)$$

The second term represents the data fitting on the training samples. Here, the performance loss is measured by a hinge loss, and it could be other types of losses such as a logistic loss as well.

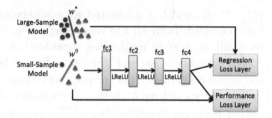

Fig. 2. The architecture of our model regression network. Given a model $\mathbf{w}^0$ learned from few samples as input, it is passed though four fully-connected layers with leaky ReLU. On the loss layer, a model regression loss and a classification performance (e.g., hinge) loss on the training data is minimized jointly

Consistent with recent work, we use a multi-layer feed-forward neural network as the regression function for its high capacity. As shown in Fig. 2, our regression network consists of $F = 4$ fully-connected layers where the fth layer applies a non-linear transformation G, which is an affine transformation followed by a non-linear activation function. We use leaky ReLU. For the purpose of regression capacity, the number of units in the first two layers is larger than the dimensionality of the input classifier weight vectors. The desired transformation T is then represented as a series of transformations G layer by layer.

3.3   Implementation Details

For the feature space, consistent with recent work, we use the Caffe Alexnet convolutional neural network (CNN) feature pre-trained on ILSVRC 2012 [20,45, 52]. All the weights of the CNN are frozen to those learned on ILSVRC without fine-tuning on any other datasets. For each image, we extract the feature on the center 224×224 crop of the 256×256 resized image. It is a $d = 4{,}096$-dim feature vector $fc6$ taking from the penultimate hidden layer of the network, unless otherwise specified.

To generate the training model set, we use the ILSVRC 2012 training data set for purpose of reproducibility. There are 1,000 object categories with 600 to 1,300 images per category and 1.2 million images in total. We use Liblinear [24] to train linear SVM models $\mathbf{w}^0$ and $\mathbf{w}^*$. For each category, using all the positive images and randomly sampled negative images, we train $\mathbf{w}^*$ with the optimal SVM regularization parameter obtained by 10-fold cross-validation. We then randomly sample $N = 1, 2, \ldots, 9, 10, 15, 20, \ldots, 100$ positive images. For each N, we repeat random sub-sampling $S = 5$ times, and use different SVM regularization parameters from $10^{\{-2, -1, 0, 1, 2\}}$ to train the SVM model $\mathbf{w}^0$ from few samples. These are essentially valid ways of doing "data augmentation" [52] for training the regression network, which mimic in practice how $\mathbf{w}^0$ changes. Hence, the number of the generated model pairs is 700 for each category, and the size of the training model set is 700,000. Finally, we randomly split the set with 685 model pairs as training and the remaining 15 pairs as validation per category.

We then use Caffe [45] to train our model regression network on the generated training model set and the corresponding training data set. The number of units from $fc1$ to $fc4$ are 6144, 5120, 4097, and 4097, respectively. We use 0.01 as the negative slope for leaky ReLU. λ is set to 1. We implement the loss function as two loss layers in Caffe, with one loss layer focusing on the model regression accuracy and the other focusing on the performance loss on the training data. We train the network using standard SGD and batch normalization [44].

3.4 Learning Target Models for Novel Categories

We now consider recognizing a novel category from a small labeled training set $\{(\mathbf{x}_i, y_i)\}_{i=1}^{K}$, where $\mathbf{x}_i \in \mathbb{R}^d$ is a data sample and $y_i \in \{-1, 1\}$ is the corresponding label. By leveraging the obtained generic model transformation T as informative prior knowledge, we aim to infer the target model $\mathbf{w}$ that generalizes better than the one produced only from the few training examples. We use a coarse-to-fine procedure that learns the target model in three steps: initialization, transformation, and refinement.

Initialization. In this first step, we directly learn the target model $\mathbf{w}^0$ on the small training sample set $\{(\mathbf{x}_i, y_i)\}_{i=1}^{K}$.

Transformation. Using $\mathbf{w}^0$ as input to our learned model regression network, after forward propagation, we obtain the output model $T\left(\mathbf{w}^0, \Theta\right)$. This thus encodes the prior knowledge about $\mathbf{w}$ being preferable.

Refinement. We then introduce $T\left(\mathbf{w}^0, \Theta\right)$ as biased regularization into the standard SVM max-margin formulation to retrain the model by minimizing

$$R\left(\mathbf{w}\right) = \frac{1}{2}\left\|\mathbf{w} - T\left(\mathbf{w}^0, \Theta\right)\right\|_2^2 + \eta \sum_{i=1}^{K}\left[1 - y_i\left(\mathbf{w}^T\mathbf{x}_i\right)\right]_+. \tag{2}$$

Equation (2) is similar to the standard SVM formulation, with the only difference being the bias towards $T\left(\mathbf{w}^0, \Theta\right)$ instead of 0. η is the regularization parameter used to control the trade-off between the regularization term and data fitting term. We thus obtain an intermediate solution with a decision boundary close to the regressed classifier while separating the labeled examples well.

4 Experimental Evaluation

In this section, we explore the use of our learned model regression network on a number of supervised learning tasks with limited data, including domain adaptation, fine-grained recognition, action recognition, and scene classification. We begin with a sanity check of the regression network for the 1,000 training categories on the ILSVRC validation data set. We then evaluate the network

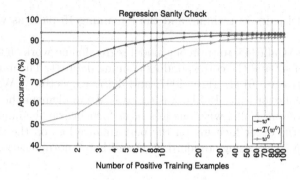

Fig. 3. Performance sanity check of the model regression network by comparing small-sample models $\mathbf{w}^0$, large-sample models $\mathbf{w}^*$ (learned on thousands of examples), and regressed models $T(\mathbf{w}^0)$ on the held-out ILSVRC validation data set. X-axis: number of positive training examples. Y-axis: average binary classification accuracy. Our network effectively identifies a generic model transformation

for one-shot domain adaptation and compare with state-of-the-art adaptation approaches. We further evaluate our approach for novel fine-grained, action, and scene categories. Finally, we present experimental results evaluating the impact of different feature spaces and model types.

4.1   Sanity Check

Our model regression network is learned from the 1,000 categories on the ILSVRC training data set. As a sanity check, the first question to answer is whether the learned transformation indeed improves generalization of the small-sample models for these categories. To answer this question, we evaluate the models on the held-out ILSVRC validation data set, which contains the same 1,000 categories with 50 images per category and has no overlap with the ILSVRC training data.

Consistent with the way the models are generated, we evaluate them in a binary classification scenario. For each category, we construct a test set consisting of all these 50 positive images and 50 randomly sampled negative images from other categories. We compare the three types of models: small-sample models $\mathbf{w}^0$, large-sample models $\mathbf{w}^*$ (as ground-truth), and regressed models $T(\mathbf{w}^0)$ (without the refinement step). We evaluate how performance varies with the number of positive training examples N when used to learn $\mathbf{w}^0$. We average the classification accuracy over the models corresponding to the same N but with different sampled training data and SVM regularization parameters. Figure 3 summarizes the average performance over the 1,000 categories.

As expected, Fig. 3 shows that $T(\mathbf{w}^0)$ significantly improves the generalization of $\mathbf{w}^0$. In the one-shot learning case, there is a notable 20 % performance improvement of $T(\mathbf{w}^0)$ over $\mathbf{w}^0$, whose performance is only a little bit higher than chance (50 % for binary classification). With increased number of training

Table 1. Performance comparison between our model transformation with state-of-the-art approaches that adapt other types of prior knowledge gained on the ILSVRC source domain in manners of data, feature, model parameter, and joint fine-tuning for one-shot learning on the Webcam domain of the Office dataset

Source prior knowledge type	Method	Acc (%)
NA	SVM (target only) [43]	62.28
Data	SVM (source only) [43]	53.51
	SVM (source and target) [43]	56.68
Feature	GFK [34]	65.16
	SA [28]	59.30
	Daumé III [17]	59.21
	MMDT [42]	59.21
Model parameter	PMT [2]	66.30
	Late fusion (Max) [43]	59.59
	Late fusion (Lin. Int. Avg) [43]	60.64
Joint	Fine-tuning [43]	61.13
Model transformation	Model regression network (Ours)	**68.47**

examples, the performance of $T(\mathbf{w}^0)$ gradually converges to that of $\mathbf{w}^*$ trained on thousands of examples. This verifies the existence of a generic transformation from small-sample to large-sample models for these 1,000 categories, which is effectively identified by our model regression network. In the following experiments, we will show that the learned transformation applies to other novel categories as well.

4.2 One-Shot Adaptation

Our approach can be viewed as transferring certain prior knowledge gained from the source domain (ILSVRC) to new tasks. It is thus interesting to compare different types of prior knowledge, including those on data, feature, and model parameter levels. To this end, we provide a comprehensive evaluation in the scenario of domain adaptation, in which the target images come from the same set of source categories but are drawn from a different distribution. Due to the common categories between source and target domains, this experimental setup allows us to best identify the possible shared domain structure and compare with state-of-the-art adaptation approaches without learning additional category correspondence, which turns to be another difficult problem.

Datasets and Tasks. We evaluate on the Office dataset [80], a standard domain adaptation benchmark for multi-class object recognition. The Office dataset is a collection of 4,652 images from three distinct domains: Amazon, DSLR, and Webcam. We use Webcam as the target domain since it was shown to be the most challenging shifted domain [43]. Of the 31 categories in the dataset, 16 overlap with the categories presented in the 1,000-category ILSVRC. We focus on these common classes as our target (i.e., 16-way classification), as is customary in [43]. Following a similar experimental setup in [43], 1 labeled training and 10 test images per category are randomly selected on Webcam. We report average multi-class accuracy over 20 random train/test splits in Table 1.

Baselines. In addition to the SVM (target only) baseline that directly trains SVM classifiers on the target data, we compare against four other types of baselines that transfer prior knowledge on the ILSVRC source domain gained in manners of data, feature, model parameters, and joint fine-tuning. **Type I data level**: SVM classifiers trained on only source data and both source and target data, respectively. **Type II feature level**: geodesic flow kernel (GFK) [34], subspace alignment (SA) [28], Daumé III [17], and max-margin domain transforms (MMDT) [42], which seek common feature spaces using learned feature embedding, augmentation, or transformation. **Type III model parameter level**: projective model transfer (PMT) [2] and late fusion [43], which adapt the parameters of the pre-trained source classifier to construct the target classifier. **Type IV joint level**: fine-tune the weights of the pre-trained CNN on the 16-way target classification task. These results are reported from [43].

Table 1 shows that our model transformation provides an alternative, competitive way to encode the shared structure and prior knowledge. It is on par with or outperforms other types of prior knowledge and adaption approaches. Notably, ours achieves significantly better performance than fine-tuning, the standard transfer strategy for CNNs, in this one-shot learning scenario. Fine-tuning requires a considerable amount of labeled target data and actually reduces performance in the very sparse label regime.

4.3   Learning Novel Categories

We now evaluate whether our learned model regression network facilitates the recognition of novel categories from few samples. For multi-class classification on the target datasets, we test how performance varies with the number of training samples per category. Following the standard practice, we train linear SVMs in a one-vs.-all fashion with default settings in Liblinear [24]. After obtaining the regressed models, we then incorporate them to retrain each one-vs.-all classifier.

Datasets and Tasks. We evaluate on standard benchmark datasets for fine-grained recognition: Caltech-UCSD Birds (CUB) 200-2011 [93] and Oxford 102 Flowers [68], for action recognition (compositional semantic recognition): Stanford-40 actions [103], and for scene classification: MIT-67 [90]. We follow the standard experimental setups (e.g., the train/test splits) for these datasets: **CUB**200-2011 contains 11,788 images of 200 bird species; 5,994 images are used for training (29 or 30 images per class) and 5,794 for testing. 102 **Flowers** contains 102 flower classes and each class consists of 40–258 images; 10 images per class are used as training data and the rest are used as test data. **Stanford-40** contains 9,532 images of humans performing 40 actions with 180–300 images per action class; 100 images per class are used as training data and the rest are used as test data. **MIT-67** contains 15,620 images spanning 67 indoor scene classes; the provided split for this dataset consists of 80 training and 20 test images per class. In our experiments, due to the lack of published protocols for small-sample learning, we randomly generate the small-sample version of training images as shown in Fig. 4 and use all the same test images for testing.

Baselines. Due to the CNN training procedure, the original models directly learned from target samples can be viewed as transfer learning with feature sharing. We also include the transfer learning baseline with model parameter sharing on Stanford-40 and MIT-67, which transfers the 1,000 ILSVRC category models using [88]. Moreover, we report an additional CNN fine-tuning baseline on MIT-67, which is the best fine-tuning result we have achieved following [39].

Figure 4 summarizes the average performance over 10 random splits on these datasets. The performance of the model transfer is similar to the original models learned from few samples due to the dissimilarity between source and target tasks. In our case of limited target data, the standard fine-tuning approach leads to degraded performance due to over-fitting. The models refined by our regression network, however, significantly outperform them for a broad range of novel categories. Our approach has particularly large performance boosts in one-shot learning scenarios. For example, there is a nearly 15 % boost on MIT-67.

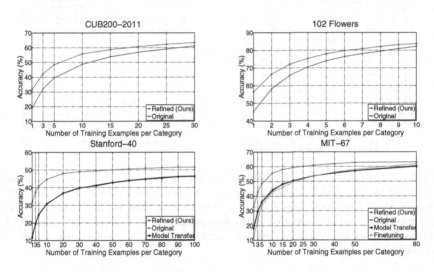

Fig. 4. Performance comparison between models learned from few samples and models refined by our model regression network for fine-grained recognition, action recognition, and scene classification on four benchmark datasets. For completeness, we also include additional baselines of transfer learning with model parameter sharing and CNN fine-tuning on certain datasets. The Alexnet CNN is used as the feature space. X-axis: number of training examples per class. Y-axis: average multi-class classification accuracy. Since they benefit from the learned generic model transformation, ours significantly outperform all the baselines for small sample learning

4.4 Evaluation of Different Feature Spaces

In the previous experiments, we used the Alexnet CNN as the feature. To test the robustness of our model regression network to the choice of the feature space, here we evaluate two additional features: the more powerful VGG19 CNN [83] $fc7$, pre-trained on ILSVRC 2012, and the unsupervised CNN [95] $fc6$, pre-trained on YouTube videos. We keep the other design choices the same (e.g., the way of generating the training model set and the regression network structure). In a similar way as before, we train our network and evaluate the recognition performance on the target tasks with few samples. Figure 5 validates the benefit of our approach in different feature space settings. Importantly, it shows that the data used to estimate the model transformation (ILSVRC) is not necessarily the same as the data used to learn the feature representation (YouTube).

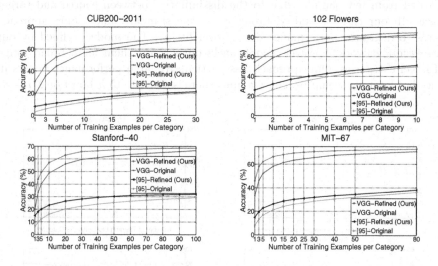

Fig. 5. Feature space evaluation between models learned from few samples and models refined by our model regression network on these four benchmark datasets. The stronger VGG CNN [83], pre-trained on ILSVRC, and the unsupervised CNN [95], pre-trained on YouTube, are used as the feature space, respectively. Ours show consistent performance improvements over the original models for small sample learning in different feature spaces

4.5 Evaluation of Different Types of Classification Models

In the previous experiments, we focused on SVM classifiers. In fact, the models do not need to come from max-margin classifiers and could be other set of weights learned in different fashions. To verify this, we test a widely used alternative classifier, logistic regression, and keep the other design choices the same (e.g., the way of generating the training model set and the regression network

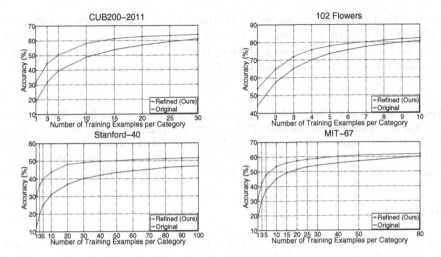

Fig. 6. Model type evaluation between models learned from few samples and models refined by our model regression network on these four benchmark datasets. We evaluate the logistic regression as the model of interest. The robust performance shows generic transformations for different types of models

structure). Naturally, we change the hinge loss to the logistic loss. In a similar way as before, we train our network and evaluate the recognition performance on the target tasks with few samples as shown in Fig. 6. Combining with Fig. 4, the logistic regression demonstrates comparable performance to SVM, and the refined logistic regression classifiers generalize better as well.

5   Conclusions

Even though it has long been believed that learning algorithms should be able to induce general functions not only from examples but also from experience as humans, it is still unclear what types of knowledge are shared across tasks and crucial for transfer. In this work we proposed a conceptually simple but power-ful approach to address the problem of small sample learning in this context of learning to learn. Our approach is based on the insight that there exists a generic, category agnostic transformation T from small-sample models to the underly-ing large-sample models. In addition, such a transformation could be effectively learned by high-capacity regressors on a large collection of model pairs and could be later used as informative prior for learning novel categories. This work opens up several interesting questions and could be explored further. While we focused on the existence of the transformation here, it would be interesting to design the best network architecture and other types of regressors (e.g., kernelized ridge regression) to learn the transformation. Also, we have assumed that the trans-formation T is independent of the sample size whereas, in general, one would envision that T would change when the number of samples increases dramatically all the way to $T =$ identity for very large training sample sets. Finally, while we assumed a fixed representation, it would be interesting to extend this approach for use of a loss to inform modification of features as well.

Acknowledgments. We thank Liangyan Gui, David Fouhey, and Deva Ramanan for valuable and insightful discussions. This work was supported in part by ONR MURI N000141612007 and U.S. Army Research Laboratory (ARL) under the Collaborative Technology Alliance Program, Cooperative Agreement W911NF-10-2-0016. We also thank NVIDIA for donating GPUs and AWS Cloud Credits for Research program.

References

1. Amit, Y., Fink, M., Srebro, N., Ullman, S.: Uncovering shared structures in multiclass classification. In: ICML (2007)
2. Aytar, Y., Zisserman, A.: Tabula rasa: model transfer for object category detection. In: ICCV (2011)
3. Aytar, Y., Zisserman, A.: Enhancing exemplar SVMs using part level transfer regularization. In: BMVC (2012)
4. Azizpour, H., Razavian, A.S., Sullivan, J., Maki, A., Carlsson, S.: From generic to specific deep representations for visual recognition. In: CVPR Workshops (2015)
5. Ba, J., Caruana, R.: Do deep nets really need to be deep? In: NIPS (2014)
6. Ba, J., Swersky, K., Fidler, S., Salakhutdinov, R.: Predicting deep zero-shot convolutional neural networks using textual descriptions. In: ICCV (2015)
7. Bart, E., Ullman, S.: Cross-generalization: learning novel classes from a single example by feature replacement. In: CVPR (2005)
8. Bart, E., Ullman, S.: Single-example learning of novel classes using representation by similarity. In: BMVC (2005)
9. Baxter, J.: A Bayesian/information theoretic model of learning to learn via multiple task sampling. Mach. Learn. **28**(1), 7–39 (1997)
10. Bellet, A., Habrard, A., Sebban, M.: A survey on metric learning for feature vectors and structured data. arXiv preprint arXiv:1306.6709 (2013)
11. Ben-David, S., Schuller, R.: Exploiting task relatedness for multiple task learning. In: Schölkopf, B., Warmuth, M.K. (eds.) COLT/Kernel 2003. LNCS (LNAI), vol. 2777, pp. 567–580. Springer, Heidelberg (2003)
12. Bendale, A., Boult, T.: Towards open world recognition. In: CVPR (2015)
13. Buciluǎ, C., Caruana, R., Niculescu-Mizil, A.: Model compression. In: KDD (2006)
14. Caruana, R.: Multitask learning. Mach. Learn. **28**(1), 41–75 (1997)
15. Chapelle, O., Schölkopf, B., Zien, A.: Semi-supervised Learning. Adaptive Computation and Machine Learning. The MIT Press, Cambridge (2006)
16. Chatfield, K., Simonyan, K., Vedaldi, A., Zisserman, A.: Return of the devil in the details: delving deep into convolutional nets. In: BMVC (2014)
17. Daumé III, H.: Frustratingly easy domain adaptation. In: ACL (2007)
18. Denton, E.L., Chintala, S., Szlam, A., Fergus, R.: Deep generative image models using a laplacian pyramid of adversarial networks. In: NIPS (2015)
19. Doersch, C., Gupta, A., Efros, A.A.: Unsupervised visual representation learning by context prediction. In: ICCV (2015)

20. Donahue, J., Jia, Y., Vinyals, O., Hoffman, J., Zhang, N., Tzeng, E., Darrell, T.: Decaf: a deep convolutional activation feature for generic visual recognition. In: ICML (2014)
21. Dosovitskiy, A., Springenberg, J.T., Brox, T.: Learning to generate chairs with convolutional neural networks. In: CVPR (2015)
22. Dosovitskiy, A., Springenberg, J.T., Riedmiller, M., Brox, T.: Discriminative unsupervised feature learning with convolutional neural networks. In: NIPS (2014)
23. Duan, L., Tsang, I.W., Xu, D., Chua, T.S.: Domain adaptation from multiple sources via auxiliary classifiers. In: ICML (2009)
24. Fan, R.E., Chang, K.W., Hsieh, C.J., Wang, X.R., Lin, C.J.: LIBLINEAR: a library for large linear classification. JMLR 9, 1871–1874 (2008)
25. Fei-Fei, L., Fergus, R., Perona, P.: A Bayesian approach to unsupervised one-shot learning of object categories. In: ICCV (2003)
26. Fei-Fei, L., Fergus, R., Perona, P.: One-shot learning of object categories. TPAMI 28(4), 594–611 (2006)
27. Ferencz, A., Learned-Miller, E.G., Malik, J.: Building a classification cascade for visual identification from one example. In: ICCV (2005)
28. Fernando, B., Habrard, A., Sebban, M., Tuytelaars, T.: Unsupervised visual domain adaptation using subspace alignment. In: ICCV (2013)
29. Fink, M.: Object classification from a single example utilizing class relevance metrics. In: NIPS (2005)
30. Fink, M.: Acquiring a new class from a few examples: learning recurrent domain structures in humans and machines. Ph.D. thesis, The Hebrew University of Jerusalem (2011)
31. Fleuret, F., Blanchard, G.: Pattern recognition from one example by chopping. In: NIPS (2005)
32. Fu, Y., Sigal, L.: Semi-supervised vocabulary-informed learning. In: CVPR (2016)
33. Girshick, R., Donahue, J., Darrell, T., Malik, J.: Rich feature hierarchies for accurate object detection and semantic segmentation. In: CVPR (2014)
34. Gong, B., Shi, Y., Sha, F., Grauman, K.: Geodesic flow kernel for unsupervised domain adaptation. In: CVPR (2012)
35. Goroshin, R., Bruna, J., Tompson, J., Eigen, D., LeCun, Y.: Unsupervised learning of spatiotemporally coherent metrics. In: ICCV (2015)
36. Gupta, S., Hoffman, J., Malik, J.: Cross modal distillation for supervision transfer. In: CVPR (2016)
37. Hariharan, B., Girshick, R.: Low-shot visual object recognition. arXiv preprint arXiv:1606.02819 (2016)
38. He, K., Zhang, X., Ren, S., Sun, J.: Deep residual learning for image recognition. In: CVPR (2016)
39. Held, D., Thrun, S., Savarese, S.: Robust single-view instance recognition. In: ICRA (2016)
40. Hertz, T., Hillel, A.B., Weinshall, D.: Learning a kernel function for classification with small training samples. In: ICML (2006)
41. Hinton, G., Vinyals, O., Dean, J.: Distilling the knowledge in a neural network. In: NIPS Workshops (2014)
42. Hoffman, J., Rodner, E., Donahue, J., Darrell, T., Saenko, K.: Efficient learning of domain-invariant image representations. In: ICLR (2013)
43. Hoffman, J., Tzeng, E., Donahue, J., Jia, Y., Saenko, K., Darrell, T.: One-shot adaptation of supervised deep convolutional models. In: ICLR Workshops (2014)
44. Ioffe, S., Szegedy, C.: Batch normalization: accelerating deep network training by reducing internal covariate shift. In: ICML (2015)

45. Jia, Y., Shelhamer, E., Donahue, J., Karayev, S., Long, J., Girshick, R., Guadarrama, S., Darrell, T.: Caffe: convolutional architecture for fast feature embedding. In: ACM MM (2014)
46. Joulin, A., van der Maaten, L., Jabri, A., Vasilache, N.: Learning visual features from large weakly supervised data. In: ECCV (2016)
47. Kienzle, W., Chellapilla, K.: Personalized handwriting recognition via biased regularization. In: ICML (2006)
48. Kim, J., Collomosse, J.: Incremental transfer learning for object recognition in streaming video. In: ICIP (2014)
49. Koch, G., Zemel, R., Salakhutdinov, R.: Siamese neural networks for one-shot image recognition. In: ICML Workshops (2015)
50. Krause, E.A., Zillich, M., Williams, T.E., Scheutz, M.: Learning to recognize novel objects in one shot through human-robot interactions in natural language dialogues. In: AAAI (2014)
51. Krishna, R., Zhu, Y., Groth, O., Johnson, J., Hata, K., Kravitz, J., Chen, S., Kalanditis, Y., Li, L.J., Shamma, D.A., Bernstein, M., Fei-Fei, L.: Visual genome: connecting language and vision using crowdsourced dense image annotations. arXiv preprint arXiv:1602.07332 (2016)
52. Krizhevsky, A., Sutskever, I., Hinton, G.E.: Imagenet classification with deep convolutional neural networks. In: NIPS (2012)
53. Kuzborskij, I., Orabona, F., Caputo, B.: From N to N+1: multiclass transfer incremental learning. In: CVPR (2013)
54. Lake, B.M., Salakhutdinov, R., Gross, J., Tenenbaum, J.B.: One shot learning of simple visual concepts. In: CogSci (2011)
55. Lake, B.M., Salakhutdinov, R., Tenenbaum, J.B.: One-shot learning by inverting a compositional causal process. In: NIPS (2013)
56. Lake, B.M., Salakhutdinov, R., Tenenbaum, J.B.: Human-level concept learning through probabilistic program induction. Science 350(6266), 1332–1338 (2015)
57. Lawrence, N.D., Platt, J.C., Jordan, M.I.: Extensions of the informative vector machine. In: Winkler, J.R., Niranjan, M., Lawrence, N.D. (eds.) Deterministic and Statistical Methods in Machine Learning. LNCS (LNAI), vol. 3635, pp. 56–87. Springer, Heidelberg (2005)
58. Lee, S.I., Chatalbashev, V., Vickrey, D., Koller, D.: Learning a meta-level prior for feature relevance from multiple related tasks. In: ICML (2007)
59. Levi, K., Fink, M., Weiss, Y.: Learning from a small number of training examples by exploiting object categories. In: CVPR Workshops (2004)
60. Levi, K., Weiss, Y.: Learning object detection from a small number of examples: the importance of good features. In: CVPR (2004)
61. Lim, J.J., Salakhutdinov, R., Torralba, A.: Transfer learning by borrowing examples for multiclass object detection. In: NIPS (2011)
62. Lin, T.-Y., Maire, M., Belongie, S., Hays, J., Perona, P., Ramanan, D., Dollár, P., Zitnick, C.L.: Microsoft COCO: common objects in context. In: Fleet, D., Pajdla, T., Schiele, B., Tuytelaars, T. (eds.) ECCV 2014, Part V. LNCS, vol. 8693, pp. 740–755. Springer, Heidelberg (2014)
63. Miller, E.G., Matsakis, N.E., Viola, P.A.: Learning from one example through shared densities on transforms. In: CVPR (2000)
64. Misra, I., Wang, Y.-X., Hebert, M.: Learning object models from few examples. In: SPIE Unmanned Systems Technology XVIII (2016)
65. Misra, I., Zitnick, C.L., Hebert, M.: Shuffle and learn: unsupervised learning using temporal order verification. In: ECCV (2016)

66. Movshovitz-Attias, Y.: Dataset curation through renders and ontology matching. Ph.D. thesis, Carnegie Mellon University (2015)
67. Movshovitz-Attias, Y., Yu, Q., Stumpe, M.C., Shet, V., Arnoud, S., Yatziv, L.: Ontological supervision for fine grained classification of street view storefronts. In: CVPR (2015)
68. Nilsback, M.E., Zisserman, A.: Automated flower classification over a large number of classes. In: ICVGIP (2008)
69. Opelt, A., Pinz, A., Zisserman, A.: Incremental learning of object detectors using a visual shape alphabet. In: CVPR (2006)
70. Pan, S.J., Yang, Q.: A survey on transfer learning. TKDE **22**(10), 1345–1359 (2010)
71. Park, D., Ramanan, D.: Articulated pose estimation with tiny synthetic videos. In: CVPR (2015)
72. Patricia, N., Caputo, B.: Learning to learn, from transfer learning to domain adaptation: a unifying perspective. In: CVPR (2014)
73. Patterson, G., Van Horn, G., Belongie, S., Perona, P., Hays, J.: Tropel: crowdsourcing detectors with minimal training. In: HCOMP (2015)
74. Pinker, S.: How the mind works. Ann. N. Y. Acad. Sci. **882**(1), 119–127 (1999)
75. Quattoni, A., Collins, M., Darrell, T.: Transfer learning for image classification with sparse prototype representations. In: CVPR (2008)
76. Razavian, A.S., Azizpour, H., Sullivan, J., Carlsson, S.: CNN features off-the-shelf: an astounding baseline for recognition. In: CVPR Workshops (2014)
77. Rodner, E.: Visual transfer learning: informal introduction and literature overview. arXiv preprint arXiv:1211.1127 (2012)
78. Rodner, E., Denzler, J.: One-shot learning of object categories using dependent gaussian processes. In: Goesele, M., Roth, S., Kuijper, A., Schiele, B., Schindler, K. (eds.) Pattern Recognition. LNCS, vol. 6376, pp. 232–241. Springer, Heidelberg (2010)
79. Russakovsky, O., Deng, J., Su, H., Krause, J., Satheesh, S., Ma, S., Huang, Z., Karpathy, A., Khosla, A., Bernstein, M., Berg, A.C., Fei-Fei, L.: ImageNet large scale visual recognition challenge. IJCV **115**(3), 211–252 (2015)
80. Saenko, K., Kulis, B., Fritz, M., Darrell, T.: Adapting visual category models to new domains. In: Daniilidis, K., Maragos, P., Paragios, N. (eds.) ECCV 2010, Part IV. LNCS, vol. 6314, pp. 213–226. Springer, Heidelberg (2010)
81. Salakhutdinov, R., Tenenbaum, J., Torralba, A.: One-shot learning with a hierarchical nonparametric Bayesian model. In: ICML Workshops (2012)
82. Santoro, A., Bartunov, S., Botvinick, M., Wierstra, D., Lillicrap, T.: One-shot learning with memory-augmented neural networks. In: ICML (2016)
83. Simonyan, K., Zisserman, A.: Very deep convolutional networks for large-scale image recognition. In: ICLR (2015)
84. Szegedy, C., Liu, W., Jia, Y., Sermanet, P., Reed, S., Anguelov, D., Erhan, D., Vanhoucke, V., Rabinovich, A.: Going deeper with convolutions. In: CVPR (2015)
85. Thrun, S., Mitchell, T.M.: Learning one more thing. In: IJCAI (1995)
86. Thrun, S., Pratt, L.: Learning to Learn. Springer Science & Business Media, New York (2012)
87. Tommasi, T.: Learning to learn by exploiting prior knowledge. Ph.D. thesis, École Polytechnique Fédérale de Lausanne (2013)
88. Tommasi, T., Orabona, F., Caputo, B.: Learning categories from few examples with multi model knowledge transfer. TPAMI **36**(5), 928–941 (2014)
89. Torralba, A., Murphy, K.P., Freeman, W.T.: Sharing visual features for multiclass and multiview object detection. TPAMI **29**(5), 854–869 (2007)

90. Torralba, A., Quattoni, A.: Recognizing indoor scenes. In: CVPR (2009)
91. Vapnik, V.N.: Statistical Learning Theory. Wiley, New York (1998)
92. Vinyals, O., Blundell, C., Lillicrap, T., Kavukcuoglu, K., Wierstra, D.: Matching networks for one shot learning. arXiv preprint arXiv:1606.04080 (2016)
93. Wah, C., Branson, S., Welinder, P., Perona, P., Belongie, S.: The Caltech-UCSD Birds-200-2011 dataset. Technical report, California Institute of Technology (2011)
94. Wan, J., Ruan, Q., Li, W., Deng, S.: One-shot learning gesture recognition from RGB-D data using bag of features. JMLR **14**(1), 2549–2582 (2013)
95. Wang, X., Gupta, A.: Unsupervised learning of visual representations using videos. In: ICCV (2015)
96. Wang, Y.-X., Hebert, M.: Model recommendation: generating object detectors from few samples. In: CVPR (2015)
97. Wang, Y.-X., Hebert, M.: Learning by transferring from unsupervised universal sources. In: AAAI (2016)
98. Weston, J., Collobert, R., Sinz, F., Bottou, L., Vapnik, V.: Inference with the universum. In: ICML (2006)
99. Weston, J., Ratle, F., Mobahi, H., Collobert, R.: Deep learning via semi-supervised embedding. In: ICML (2008)
100. Wolf, L., Hassner, T., Taigman, Y.: The one-shot similarity kernel. In: ICCV (2009)
101. Wolf, L., Martin, I.: Robust boosting for learning from few examples. In: CVPR (2005)
102. Yang, J., Yan, R., Hauptmann, A.: Adapting SVM classifiers to data with shifted distributions. In: ICDM Workshops (2007)
103. Yao, B., Jiang, X., Khosla, A., Lin, A.L., Guibas, L., Fei-Fei, L.: Human action recognition by learning bases of action attributes and parts. In: ICCV (2011)
104. Yosinski, J., Clune, J., Bengio, Y., Lipson, H.: How transferable are features in deep neural networks? In: NIPS (2014)
105. Zhu, X., Anguelov, D., Ramanan, D.: Capturing long-tail distributions of object subcategories. In: CVPR (2014)
106. Zhu, X., Vondrick, C., Fowlkes, C.C., Ramanan, D.: Do we need more training data? IJCV **119**(1), 76–92 (2016)
107. Zhu, X.: Semi-supervised learning literature survey. Technical report, University of Wisconsin-Madison (2005)

Shape from Water: Bispectral Light Absorption for Depth Recovery

Yuta Asano[1], Yinqiang Zheng[2(✉)], Ko Nishino[3], and Imari Sato[1,2]

[1] Department of Information Processing,
Tokyo Institute of Technology, Meguro, Japan
asano.y.ac@m.titech.ac.jp
[2] Digital Content and Media Sciences Division,
National Institute of Informatics, Tokyo, Japan
{yqzheng,imarik}@nii.ac.jp
[3] Department of Computer Science, Drexel University, Philadelphia, USA
kon@drexel.edu

Abstract. This paper introduces a novel depth recovery method based on light absorption in water. Water absorbs light at almost all wavelengths whose absorption coefficient is related to the wavelength. Based on the Beer-Lambert model, we introduce a bispectral depth recovery method that leverages the light absorption difference between two near-infrared wavelengths captured with a distant point source and orthographic cameras. Through extensive analysis, we show that accurate depth can be recovered irrespective of the surface texture and reflectance, and introduce algorithms to correct for nonidealities of a practical implementation, including tilted light source and camera placement and non-ideal bandpass filters. We construct a coaxial bispectral depth imaging system using low-cost off-the-shelf hardware and demonstrate its use for recovering the shapes of complex and dynamic objects in water. Experimental results validate the theory and practical implementation of this novel depth recovery paradigm, which we refer to as shape from water.

Keywords: Depth recovery · Light absorption · Multispectral imaging

1 Introduction

Three-dimensional geometry recovery has been one of the central focuses of research in computer vision from its inception due to the fundamental role 3D geometry may play in almost all applications. These research efforts have culminated in the establishment of a handful of distinct principles for modern shape recovery methods, including triangulation, time of flight, and shape-from-X where X can be shading, texture, focus, and other surface or image formation properties. The fundamental but often neglected assumption of these different approaches is that the light, either actively or passively shed on the object surface including environmental illumination, can be measured unaltered between the surface and the camera. Although there are some works that study shape

© Springer International Publishing AG 2016
B. Leibe et al. (Eds.): ECCV 2016, Part VI, LNCS 9910, pp. 635–649, 2016.
DOI: 10.1007/978-3-319-46466-4_38

recovery of objects in non-air medium where this assumption does not hold (e.g., participating medium like dilute milk), their focus is on undoing the adversarial optical perturbations such as scattering to apply the same recovery principals that were designed for objects in clear air. In other words, the medium is treated as an unwanted nuisance that violates the assumed geometry recovery principle.

Can we instead exploit whatever may happen to the light as it travels from the surface to the camera for shape recovery? If we can, what advantages would it give us? In the past, scattering has been modeled to restore clear day scene appearance from images taken in bad weather conditions (e.g., fog), in whose process the scene depth can also be recovered. This, however, is limited to accidental imaging in bad weather conditions, and cannot be used as a general shape recovery method. In this paper, we focus on light absorption in the infrared spectrum as a light propagation characteristic that encodes depth. When light travels through a homogeneous isotropic medium, it usually gets absorbed at some wavelengths. The light absorption is dictated by the Beer-Lambert law, which denotes the absorption at a certain wavelength to be proportional to the length of the light travel path and to the absorption coefficient of the medium [12]. This suggests that we may recover the distance of a surface point to the camera by measuring the amount of light absorption that takes place between the surface and the camera. In other words, we may recover depth of an object by measuring the light path distance (i.e., optical depth) from the camera of the medium in between.

In this paper, we focus on water as the medium for a few important reasons. In addition to the fact that water is a familiar liquid that we can easily find in our daily lives, geometry recovery in water in itself finds applications in many areas of science such as oceanography, geography, and biology, as well as engineering including underwater surveillance and navigation. Furthermore, multi-spectral light propagation in water is mostly dominated by absorption and scattering plays little effect as long as the water is sufficiently clear, which would otherwise compound the optical length computation. Few past methods have directly applied the depth recovery principals in air to underwater scenarios, and have found light absorption to adversely affect the results [2]. We instead take advantage of light absorption in water and establish shape from water as a novel shape recovery approach.

We propose a novel shape recovery method based on monochromatic images captured at two different infrared wavelengths, which we refer to as the bispectral principle of depth recovery. The key idea is to exploit the difference in the amount of light absorption that takes place at two distinct wavelength and cancel out light interaction effects, including those due to surface texture and reflectance, other than that proportional to the optical length to the object surface. Figure 1 shows an example of recovering a textureless, specular object which would be a challenging object for conventional depth recovery methods.

We thoroughly analyze the theory including its limitations as well as practical accuracy of the proposed method. In particular, we examine the effect of reflectance spectrum difference of the object at the two working wavelengths,

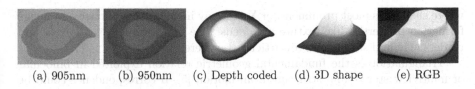

(a) 905nm   (b) 950nm   (c) Depth coded   (d) 3D shape   (e) RGB

Fig. 1. Shape from water based on bispectral light absorption. (a) and (b) show the scene at 905 nm and 950 nm, after normalizing the illumination and camera and filter sensitivity functions. The intensity difference between (a) and (b) is due to the difference of water absorption at these two wavelengths which we exploit to recover the depth. The color coded depth is shown in (c), and the recovered 3D shape is given in (d). (e) shows the target object for this example: a textureless ceramic object with strong specularity.

and develop a criterion to properly choose the two wavelengths so as to maximize the difference of the absorption coefficient and minimize the dependence on material spectral reflectance. We also propose correction algorithms to handle those factors arising from practical implementation limitations of our bispectral principle, including the effects of tilting the light source and/or the camera with respect to the water surface and the effects of nonideal spectral bandpass filters.

We build a co-axial bispectral imaging system using low-cost off-the-shelf hardware as a prototype implementation for single exposure, real-time shape from water. The system consists of two monochromatic cameras equipped with near-infrared bandpass filters, aligned on the same optical axis with a half beam splitter. We envision use of shape from water with a bispectral imaging system immersed in water, but for practical reasons, all experiments are done with a water tank and the co-axial system placed outside of it. Experimental results validate the theory of our bispectral light absorption depth imaging principle, and demonstrate its advantages over conventional approaches.

Our major contributions can be summarized as follows.

– We introduce light absorption as a means to depth sensing in computer vision.
– We derive the bispectral light absorption principle for depth recovery and apply it to water leading to shape from water.
– We thoroughly analyze the theory and practical implications of shape from water.
– We construct a low-cost co-axial bispectral imaging system and demonstrate its use for dense shape recovery of complex and dynamic objects in water.

Taken together, for the first time, we introduce a new shape recovery method based on light absorption in water and its working prototype that achieves shape recovery of complex, dynamic objects.

2   Related Works

Most popular shape recovery methods can be categorized based on the underlying shape or depth probing principles: triangulation, time of flight, and shape-from-X where shading is most prominent for X but may include other surface and image formation properties like texture and focus. The literature for each is vast and readers may find suitable survey articles elsewhere.

Triangulation is the fundamental geometric relation exploited in binocular or multiview stereo, and structure from motion [5]. If correspondence could be reliably established, sparse or even dense 3D shape can be recovered. The fundamental limitation of triangulation is that sufficient (unique) texture must be found on the surface to establish those correspondences. Structured active light can mitigate this limitation [1] by essentially putting texture on the surface, by actively projecting visible or infrared light patterns.

Time of flight, the travel time of a light pulse to hit a surface and come back to the source, directly encodes the distance of the surface from the source [4]. Coherent light (e.g., laser) can be used for long-distance depth sensing, while infra-red light has been recently used for short-distance measurements (e.g., Kinect 2). Accurate measurement of time of flight is challenging due to the very high speed of light and can limit the resolution of the depth image.

Shape-from-X refers to shape recovery methods that exploit specific surface or image formation properties. Among the many radiometric cues, shading so far has been one of the most popular. Shape-from-shading [17] and photometric stereo [16] model the surface brightness change to infer its gradients (i.e., surface normals) from which the shape can be recovered. In contrast to triangulation-based methods, texture as well as complex reflectance (i.e., non-Lambertian surfaces) become nuisances that hinder the applicability of these methods.

In this paper, we introduce a novel bispectral depth imaging principle based on light absorption. It clearly differs from triangulation and other shape-from-X, especially shading, methods in that it neither requires feature correspondence nor known or simplistic surface reflectance. Unlike time-of-flight methods, it recovers depth by measuring pixel intensity difference, in contrast to light travel time, which obviates the need of often expensive hardware for accurate temporal measurement.

Shape recovery in non-air medium has been studied in the past. Narasimhan et al. [10] apply light stripe range scanning and photometric stereo to objects in participating media. They model sub-surface scattering and account for it to recover object geometry in murky water (e.g., dilute milk). Light scattering has also been studied in computer vision for other participating media such as fog [3,6,7,9,11,13,14] in which depth can be recovered in the process of removing the light propagation effects on the appearance (i.e., defogging). Our depth recovery principle is similar to such approaches in that it actively exploits the light propagation characteristics in the medium to decode the optical length and thus depth. Our focus is, however, light absorption, not scattering.

A number of underwater depth recovery methods have been introduced in the past. For example, Tomohiko et al. [15] used multiview stereo to reconstruct underwater objects, and their focus was on accounting for the refractive effect of water and the shape of the interfacing layer (glass wall of the container here). Murez et al. [8] applied photometric stereo to underwater objects, and tried to handle the scattering problem due to water turbidity. Dancu et al. [2] evaluated the performance of various time-of-flight sensors to reconstruct underwater objects, and found that these sensors do not work for slightly deep water, because of severe infrared light absorption of water.

3   Light Absorption in Water

Let us first review the basics of light absorption in water. When light travels in water, it gets absorbed at some wavelengths. The absorption curve in Fig. 2(a) shows how light will be attenuated as it travels through water (with 6 mm depth here), in the wavelength range from 400 nm to 1400 nm. From this curve, we can observe that water rarely absorbs visible light, which explains why water appears transparent to human eyes. In contrast, it clearly absorbs infrared light from 900 nm to 1400 nm.

As illustrated in Fig. 2(b), at a given wavelength λ, the Beer-Lambert law [12] accurately expresses light absorption as the relation between incident light intensity I_0 and outgoing attenuated intensity I

$$I = I_0 e^{-\alpha(\lambda)l}, \tag{1}$$

in which l represents the light path length in millimeter (mm), $\alpha(\lambda)$ denotes the wavelength dependent absorption coefficient in mm^{-1}, and $e^{-\alpha(\lambda)l}$ is the natural exponential of $-\alpha(\lambda)l$.

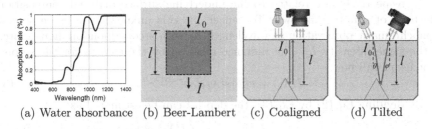

(a) Water absorbance   (b) Beer-Lambert   (c) Coaligned   (d) Tilted

Fig. 2. (a) shows the water absorption curve in the range from 400 nm to 1600 nm. (b) shows the setup of the Beer-Lambert law. (c) and (d) illustrate our bispectral depth imaging in the coaligned and tilted configuration, respectively.

4   Bispectral Light Absorption for Depth Recovery

We will exploit the wavelength dependence of light absorption for depth recovery of objects immersed in water. We assume that the camera is orthographic and the incident light rays to the object surface are parallel coming from an infinitely distant point source. Yet, we do not make assumptions on the surface reflectance such as Lambertian or diffuse plus specular, except that the geometric and spectral characteristics of the reflectance are separable. This is a very mild assumption that assumes that the reflectance function $f(\omega, \lambda) = r(\omega)s(\lambda)$ can be factorized into its geometric properties (e.g., incident and exitant light angles), $r(\omega)$, and spectral characteristics (i.e., color), $s(\lambda)$, which applies to most real-world surfaces. The only exceptions are when the surface geometry intricacies are comparable to light wavelength in scale (e.g., CD-ROM). Most importantly, we envision an imaging system fully immersed in the water, in which the consideration of water surface is unnecessary, but for all practical necessity, we place the camera and light source outside the water. As we assume directional light and orthographic cameras and use sufficiently close wavelengths, we may safely ignore the effects of light refraction at the water surface.

4.1 Bispectral Depth Imaging

As illustrated in Fig. 2(c), we first consider an ideally coaligned light-camera configuration, in which both the optical axis of the camera and the directional light are perpendicular to the planar water surface. Monochromatic light of wavelength λ_1 and intensity I_0 reaches an opaque scene point with water depth l. After being reflected back from the scene point, the intensity of the light received by the camera is

$$I(\lambda_1) = r(\omega)s(\lambda_1)I_0 e^{-2\alpha(\lambda_1)l}, \tag{2}$$

in which $2l$ denotes light travel distance which is twice as long as the water depth l.

The geometric and spectral characteristics of surface reflectance, $r(\omega)$ and $s(\lambda_1)$, respectively, are related to the underlying surface material composition which is, of course, unknown. To cancel out this unknown, we use a second monochromatic observation at wavelength λ_2 with a corresponding light source of the same intensity I_0. The radiance received by the camera for the second light beam will be

$$I(\lambda_2) = r(\omega)s(\lambda_2)I_0 e^{-2\alpha(\lambda_2)l}. \tag{3}$$

By dividing Eq. (2) by Eq. (3), the depth l can be estimated as

$$l = \frac{1}{2(\alpha(\lambda_2) - \alpha(\lambda_1))} \ln\left(\frac{I(\lambda_1)}{I(\lambda_2)}\frac{s(\lambda_2)}{s(\lambda_1)}\right). \tag{4}$$

It is interesting to note that the geometric factor of the reflectance function $r(\omega)$ has been eliminated, no matter how complex it is. Provided that we can choose two wavelengthes such that the reflectance spectrum values at these two wavelengthes are almost identical, i.e., $s(\lambda_1) \simeq s(\lambda_2)$, the approximate depth can be recovered,

$$l \simeq \frac{1}{2(\alpha(\lambda_2) - \alpha(\lambda_1))} \ln\frac{I(\lambda_1)}{I(\lambda_2)}. \tag{5}$$

Equation (5) stays at the core of our bispectral depth recovery principle, which allows us to estimate depth simply by measuring the pixel intensity difference at two properly chosen wavelengths, without knowing any information of the arbitrarily general reflectance function of the scene point material.

4.2   Depth Accuracy and Surface Reflectance

Let us first analyze the relative depth error Δl with respect to the relative difference Δs between $s(\lambda_1)$ and $s(\lambda_2)$, which is defined as $\Delta s = s(\lambda_1)/s(\lambda_2)$-1.

According to Eqs. (4) and (5), the relative depth error Δl can be calculated by

$$\Delta l = \frac{\ln\left(\frac{I(\lambda_1)}{I(\lambda_2)}\frac{s(\lambda_2)}{s(\lambda_1)}\right) - \ln\frac{I(\lambda_1)}{I(\lambda_2)}}{\ln\left(\frac{I(\lambda_1)}{I(\lambda_2)}\frac{s(\lambda_2)}{s(\lambda_1)}\right)} = \frac{\ln(1+\Delta s)}{\ln(1+\Delta s) - \ln\frac{I(\lambda_1)}{I(\lambda_2)}}. \tag{6}$$

Figure 3(a) shows relative depth error plotted against relative reflectance difference for varying intensity ratios $I(\lambda_1)/I(\lambda_2)$. From these curves, we can observe that the estimated depth becomes less sensitive to the reflectance spectrum difference, as the intensity ratio steps away from one (i.e., the difference between the two wavelengths becomes larger). This suggests a criterion for choosing the two wavelengths for bispectral depth recovery. Specifically, we should choose two wavelengths whose water absorption coefficients' difference is maximized, while the corresponding reflectance spectrum difference is minimized.

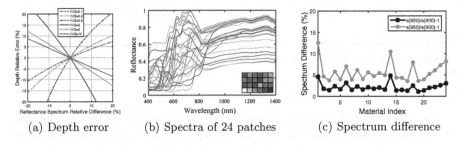

(a) Depth error   (b) Spectra of 24 patches   (c) Spectrum difference

Fig. 3. (a) shows relative depth error with respect to the reflectance spectrum difference, under varying intensity ratios. (b) shows the spectra of the 24 patches on the color checker in the range from 400 nm to 1400 nm. The reflectance spectrum difference for spectral pairs of 900 nm and 920 nm, as well as 900 nm and 950 nm for each patch spectrum is shown in (c). (Color figure online)

As shown in Fig. 2(a), the amount of light absorption in water changes quickly in the range between 900 nm and 1000 nm. Surprisingly, we empirically find that the reflectance spectra of a great variety of materials tend to be flat (i.e., spectrally white) in this range.

We start our investigation by examining the spectra of the standard color checker board, as shown in Fig. 3(b), from which we can clearly observe that the spectral variance for all patches drastically reduces in the range longer than 900 nm. As shown in Fig. 3(c), although there are a few patches with larger difference, the average relative spectrum difference for 900 nm and 950 nm is 5.7 %, which will further reduce to 2.1 % for the spectral pair of 900 nm and 920 nm.

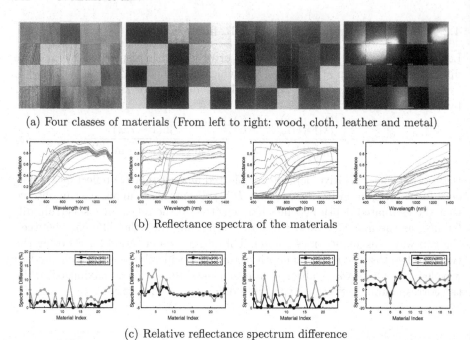

(a) Four classes of materials (From left to right: wood, cloth, leather and metal)

(b) Reflectance spectra of the materials

(c) Relative reflectance spectrum difference

Fig. 4. A reflectance spectra database in the Vis-NIR range from 400 nm to 1400 nm. We empirically find that the spectral reflectance difference for two close near-infrared wavelengths is usually negligible.

We have also collected several other classes of common materials, including wood, cloth, leather and metal, as shown in Fig. 4(a). There are 24 different materials in each class, except metal which has only 18. We measure their reflectance spectra and evaluate the reflectance spectrum difference for wavelength pairs of 900 nm and 920 nm, as well as 900 nm and 950 nm. The average relative spectrum difference of these four classes for the bispectral pair 900 nm and 950 nm is 3.8 %, 2.1 %, 6.0 % and 11.1 %, respectively. For the bispectral pair 900 nm and 920 nm, the corresponding average difference reduces to 1.4 %, 1.1 %, 1.9 % and 5.0 %. Although the scale of our database is limited, the evaluation result suggests that the reflectance spectrum difference is usually very small for two close near-infrared wavelengths.

5 Practical Shape from Water

We derive algorithms for shape from water with practical setups based on the bispectral depth recovery principle. In particular, we propose two algorithms that correct distorted depth estimates resulting from nonidealities in the imaging setup.

5.1   Non-collinear/Perpendicular Light-Camera Configuration

Until now, we have considered the collinear light-camera configuration, in which both the optical axis of the orthographic camera and the directional light are perpendicular to the water level. In practice, the light rays and/or the camera might be slightly tilted from the water surface, due to practical requirements of the system setup. Here, we will show that, if the depth of a single point is given, the depth distortion can be corrected.

As illustrated in Fig. 2(d), the tilt angles in water for the illuminant and the camera are denoted by θ and ψ, respectively. Note that, the refractive ratio of water is almost constant in the near-infrared range. Therefore, we can assume that these two angles do not change at the two working wavelengths. The light path length is stretched to $l(\frac{1}{\cos\theta} + \frac{1}{\cos\psi})$, rather than $2l$. Similar to Eq. (5), now the depth can be calculated by

$$l(\frac{1}{\cos\theta} + \frac{1}{\cos\psi}) \simeq \frac{1}{\alpha(\lambda_2) - \alpha(\lambda_1)} \ln\frac{I(\lambda_1)}{I(\lambda_2)}, \qquad (7)$$

from which we can observe that, if the depth of a single point is provided, the distortion factor $(\frac{1}{\cos\theta} + \frac{1}{\cos\psi})$ can be easily estimated.

5.2   Nonideal Narrow-Band Filters

When implementing a bispectral imaging system for shape from water, it is preferable to use a wide-band illuminant and two narrow-band filters in front of the camera. Until now, we have implicitly assumed that the response function of the filters is a delta function (i.e., perfect narrow-band), which is hard to achieve in practice.

Let us denote the spectral response functions of two nonideal narrow-band filters each centered at λ_1 and λ_2 with $\beta_1(\lambda)$ and $\beta_2(\lambda)$, respectively. If the band-pass filters are sufficiently narrow, we can assume that the reflectance spectrum of the scene point is flat between the two wavelengths. The imaging equation Eq. (2) becomes

$$I(\lambda_1) = r(\omega)s(\lambda_1)I_0 \int_0^\infty \beta_1(\lambda)e^{-2\alpha(\lambda)l}d\lambda. \qquad (8)$$

A similar equation can be established for Eq. (3). The depth l can be corrected by solving the following equation

$$I(\lambda_1) \int_0^\infty \beta_2(\lambda)e^{-2\alpha(\lambda)l}d\lambda = I(\lambda_2) \int_0^\infty \beta_1(\lambda)e^{-2\alpha(\lambda)l}d\lambda, \qquad (9)$$

using standard one-dimensional zero-finding techniques. Note that we do not explicitly consider the illumination spectrum and the camera spectral sensitivity function, since they can be merged into the spectral response function of the filters.

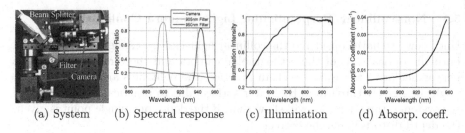

(a) System	(b) Spectral response	(c) Illumination	(d) Absorp. coeff.

Fig. 5. (a) shows our co-axial bispectral imaging system, and (b) the spectral response functions of the camera and the two filters. (c) is the spectrum of the incandescent illuminant. (d) is the calibrated water absorption coefficient.

6   Co-Axial Bispectral Imaging System and Experiment Results

We built a co-axial bispectral imaging system for shape from water. The system uses co-axial cameras to simultaneously capture the scene in two wavelengths, recording bispectral image pairs at video-rate. From the image sequence, we may recover the geometry of complex and dynamic objects immersed in water.

6.1   System Configuration and Calibration

As shown in Fig. 5(a), the co-axial bispectral imaging system consists of a beam splitter and two grayscale cameras (POINTGREY GS3-U3-41C6NIR), which can sense NIR light albeit with limited spectral sensitivity. We use two narrow band-pass filters centered at 905 nm and 950 nm, whose spectral response curves are shown in Fig. 5(b). For the illumination, we use an incandescent lamp with sufficient irradiance in the NIR range, as shown in Fig. 5(c). We synchronize the two cameras, and carefully adjust the position of the beam splitter to capture spatially-aligned bispectral image pairs of the same scene.

The water absorption coefficient needs to be known for shape from water, which can be estimated easily beforehand. We use a spectrophotometer and a standard white target for calibration. By immersing the white target into water at a known depth, we can calculate the water absorption coefficient from the Beer-Lambert law. Figure 5(d) illustrates the calibrated absorption coefficient for different wavelengths.

6.2   Depth and Shape Accuracy

We use planar plates with different materials for depth accuracy evaluation. We put the plates in water and measure the water depth by a ruler for ground truth. We vary the water depth from 10 mm to 40 mm. At each depth, we capture two images with our co-axial bispectral system and estimate the depth using Eq. (5). To evaluate the effectiveness of our algorithms in Sect. 5, we also correct the depth further by using Eqs. (7) and (9).

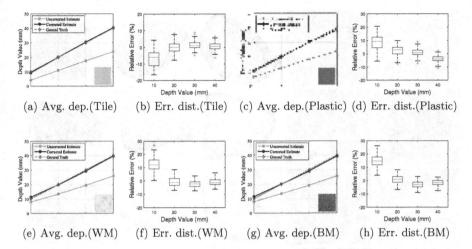

(a) Avg. dep.(Tile)   (b) Err. dist.(Tile)   (c) Avg. dep.(Plastic) (d) Err. dist.(Plastic)

(e) Avg. dep.(WM)   (f) Err. dist.(WM)   (g) Avg. dep.(BM)   (h) Err. dist.(BM)

Fig. 6. Depth estimation error for four planar plates, including cyan tile, red plastic board, white marble (WM) and black marble (BM). (Color figure online)

As shown in Fig. 6, we use four plates for experiments, including a piece of cyan tile, a red plastic board, a piece of white and black marble. On each plate, we randomly choose 121 points (pixels), and calculate the average depth for these points. To evaluate the spatial consistency of the depth estimate at each depth, we draw the distribution of the relative error of the corrected depth for these 121 points in Fig. 6(b,d,f,h). The values between the 25 and 75 percentiles are shown as a box with a horizontal line at the mean value. The red crosses indicate data beyond 1.5 times the inter-percentile range.

From Fig. 6, we can observe that the correction algorithms play a critical role in improving the estimation accuracy. With correction, the average depth estimates are very close to the ground truth, usually within a relative error of 3%. However, the average depth error is clearly higher at 10 mm depth. The main reason for this is that we measure the ground truth with a ruler, which introduced errors at this distance. As for the spatial consistency of the depth estimates, we can observe that the corrected depth at the measured 121 points is sufficiently consistent with each other, even when the plate assumes spatially varying textures (e.g., the marble plate).

6.3   Complex Static and Dynamic Objects

We apply shape from water to objects with complex reflectance and dynamically moving objects whose shape deforms. Since the ground truth shape is difficult to capture for these objects, we qualitatively evaluate the recovered geometry.

Figure 7 shows the recovery results of several opaque objects with varying color, texture, and reflectance properties. We can observe that our system and method work well for textureless objects with strong specularities. The surface reflectance and geometry of the seashell and rock in the first and second row

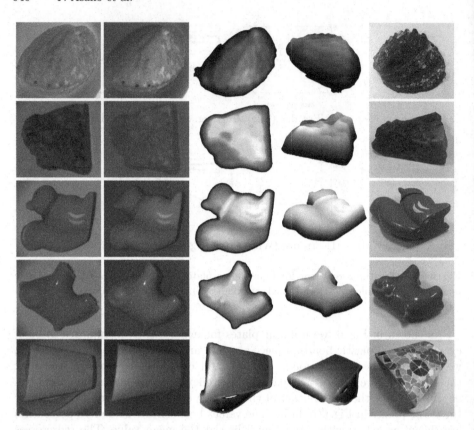

Fig. 7. Shape recovery of objects with complex geometry, texture, and reflection properties. For each row, from left to right, the input images at 905 nm and 950 nm, the depth coded 3D shape, the virtually shaded shape and the RGB appearance of the object are shown. (Color figure online)

of Fig. 7 are particularly complicated, and would pose significant challenges to other shape recovery methods. The results clearly show that shape from water, as the theory shows, is insensitive to such intricacies. This property is verified again by the compelling results for the colorful cups in the last row of Fig. 7. We also note that artifacts due to specularities sometimes occur (fourth row), which is attributed to camera saturation, rather than the method itself.

Figure 8 shows the recovery results of some even more challenging objects with translucence. The recovered shape looks compelling, when compared it with its corresponding RGB appearance.

Our co-axial shape from water system is suited to capture dynamic scenes. As shown in Fig. 9, we demonstrate this by recovering the geometry of a moving hand in water.

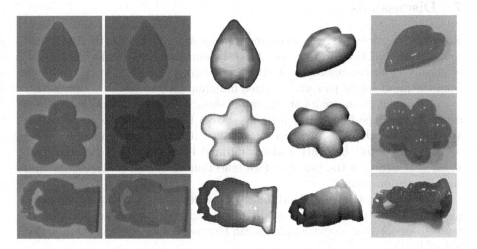

Fig. 8. Shape recovery of translucent objects.

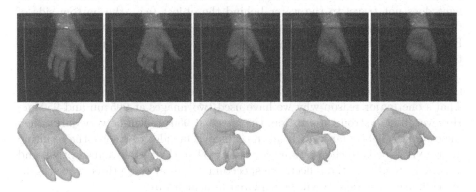

Fig. 9. Action capturing of a moving hand in water.

Fig. 10. Recovery of a transparent glass object. From left to right are the RGB image (a side view of the glass at 905 nm in the corner shows that the glass is also transparent under NIR light), 3D shape from a laser scanner, RGB image of the same object with painting, 3D shape from a laser scanner with painting, and 3D shape from our method without painting. (Color figure online)

7   Discussions

Bispectral depth recovery in its current form is not able to directly handle environment illumination. In practice, it can be eliminated by taking another pair of images under the environment illumination only, and subtracting them away from the input image pair under mixed illumination.

Surface reflection occurs at the water surface, which will lead to erroneous depth for a shape-from-water imaging system situated outside water surface. We have found that this problem can be alleviated by simply taking one image without any object but only a black, infrared light absorbing, material in the water that captures the water surface reflection alone and subtracting it from the observation pairs.

Similar to most existing depth imaging principles and techniques, our principle is vulnerable to interreflection, often not negligible for concave surfaces, and tends to smooth out shape details, as can be observed for the statue in the third row of Fig. 8.

Shape reconstruction of transparent objects is challenging for contact-free depth imaging. For shape from water, if the material happens not to absorb near-infrared light, which is actually the case for many kinds of glasses, and the light does not travel to the water behind the object (e.g., the bottom side of the object is opaque), we can safely recover the surface geometry, as shown in Fig. 10. Note that the 3D laser scanner can not correctly capture the shape of the glass surface, unless it is uniformly painted.

The analysis in Sect. 4.2 implies that choosing two wavelengths with drastically different absorption coefficients would benefit depth recovery accuracy. That's one major reason why we have used two images at 905 nm and 950 nm. However, due to strong absorption, the image at 950 nm will be very dark, when the object is slightly far away from the camera. One idea to resolve the resulting poor SNR issue is to choose three shorter wavelengths with less absorption, and assume instead that the reflectance spectrum values at these three wavelengths are collinear. The details will be explored in near future.

8   Conclusions

In this paper, we introduced shape from water, a novel depth recovery method based on light absorption in water. Shape from water builds on the newly derived bispectral depth sensing principle based on the idea of leveraging the light absorption difference between two near-infrared wavelengths to estimate depth regardless of the surface reflectance. We constructed a co-axial bispectral depth imaging system using low-cost off-the-shelf hardware to capture bispectral image pairs for shape from water at video-rate. Experimental results show that shape from water can recover accurate geometry of objects with complex reflectance and dynamically deforming shapes.

Acknowledgments. This research was supported in part by the Ministry of Education, Science, Sports and Culture Grant-in-Aid for Scientific Research on Innovative Areas.

References

1. Batlle, J., Mouaddib, E., Salvi, J.: Recent progress in coded structured light as a technique to solve the correspondence problem: a survey. Pattern Recogn. **31**(7), 963–982 (1998)
2. Dancu, A., Fourgeaud, M., Franjcic, Z., Avetisyan, R.: Underwater reconstruction using depth sensors. In: SIGGRAPH Asia Technical, Briefs, pp. 1–4 (2014)
3. Fattal, R.: Single image dehazing. Proc. ACM SIGGRAPH **27**, 1–9 (2008)
4. Hansard, M., Lee, S., Choi, O., Horaud, R.: Time-of-Flight Cameras: Principles, Methods and Applications. Springer, Heidelberg (2012)
5. Hartley, R., Zisserman, A.: Multiple View Geometry in Computer Vision, 2nd edn. Cambridge University Press, Cambridge (2003)
6. He, K., Sun, J.X.T.: Single image haze removal using dark channel prior. In: Proceedings of IEEE International Conference on Computer Vision and Pattern Recognition, vol. 1 (2009)
7. Kratz, L., Nishino, K.: Factorizing scene albedo and depth from a single foggy image. In: IEEE International Conference on Computer Vision, pp. 1701–1708 (2009)
8. Murez, Z., Treibitz, T., Ramamoorthi, R., Kriegman, D.: Photometric stereo in a scattering medium. In: ICCV, pp. 3415–3423 (2015)
9. Narasimhan, S.G., Nayar, S.K.: Vision and the atmosphere. Int. J. Comp. Vis. **48**(3), 233–254 (2002)
10. Narasimhan, S., Nayar, S., Sun, B., Koppal, S.: Structured light in scattering media. In: IEEE International Conference on Computer Vision (2005)
11. Nishino, K., Kratz, L., Lombardi, S.: Bayesian defogging. Int. J. Comput. Vis. **98**(2), 232–255 (2012)
12. Reinhard, E., Khan, E.A., Akyuz, A.O., Johnson, G.: Color Imaging: Fundamentals and Applications. CRC Press, Boca Raton (2008)
13. Schechner, Y.Y., Narasimhan, S.G., Nayar, S.K.: Instant dehazing of images using polarization. In: Proceedings of IEEE International Conference on Computer Vision and Pattern Recognition, vol. 1, pp. 325–332, June 2001
14. Tan, R.T.: Visibility in bad weather from a single image. In: Proceedings of IEEE International Conference on Computer Vision and Pattern Recognition, pp. 1–8, June 2008
15. Tomohiko, Y., Nobuhara, S., Matsuyama, T.: 3D shape from silhouettes in water for online novel-view synthesis. IPSJ Trans. Comput. Vis. Appl. **5**, 65–69 (2013)
16. Woodham, R.: Photometric method for determining surface orientation from multiple images. Opt. Eng. **19**(1), 191139 (1980)
17. Zhang, R., Tsai, P., Cryer, J., Shah, M.: Shape-from-shading: a survey. IEEE TPAMI **21**(8), 690–706 (1999)

Learning Dynamic Hierarchical Models
for Anytime Scene Labeling

Buyu Liu[1,2](✉) and Xuming He[1,2](✉)

[1] The Australian National University, Canberra, Australia
{buyu.liu,xuming.he}@anu.edu.au
[2] Data61, CSIRO, Canberra, Australia

Abstract. With increasing demand for efficient image and video analysis, test-time cost of scene parsing becomes critical for many large-scale or time-sensitive vision applications. We propose a dynamic hierarchical model for anytime scene labeling that allows us to achieve flexible trade-offs between efficiency and accuracy in pixel-level prediction. In particular, our approach incorporates the cost of feature computation and model inference, and optimizes the model performance for any given test-time budget by learning a sequence of image-adaptive hierarchical models. We formulate this anytime representation learning as a Markov Decision Process with a discrete-continuous state-action space. A high-quality policy of feature and model selection is learned based on an approximate policy iteration method with action proposal mechanism. We demonstrate the advantages of our dynamic non-myopic anytime scene parsing on three semantic segmentation datasets, which achieves 90 % of the state-of-the-art performances by using 15 % of their overall costs.

1 Introduction

A fundamental and intriguing property of human scene understanding is its efficiency and flexibility, in which vision systems are capable of interpreting a scene at multiple levels of details given different time budgets [1,2]. Despite much progress in the pixel-level semantic scene parsing [3–6], most efforts are focused on improving the prediction accuracy with complex structured models [7,8] and learned representations [9–11]. Such computation-intensive approaches often lack the flexibility in trade-off between efficiency and accuracy, making it challenging to apply them to large-scale data analysis or cost-sensitive applications.

In order to improve the efficiency in scene labeling, a common strategy is to develop active inference mechanisms for the structured models used in this task [12,13]. This allows users to adjust the trade-off between efficiency and accuracy for a *given* model, which is learned using a separate procedure with unconstrained test-time budget. However, this may lead to a sub-optimal performance for the cost-sensitive tasks.

Electronic supplementary material The online version of this chapter (doi:10.1007/978-3-319-46466-4_39) contains supplementary material, which is available to authorized users.

© Springer International Publishing AG 2016
B. Leibe et al. (Eds.): ECCV 2016, Part VI, LNCS 9910, pp. 650–666, 2016.
DOI: 10.1007/978-3-319-46466-4_39

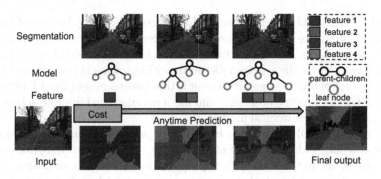

Fig. 1. Overview of our approach. We propose to incrementally increase model complexity in terms of used image features and model structure. Our approach generates high-quality prediction at any given cost.

A more appealing approach is to learn a model representation *for* Anytime performance, which can stop its inference at any cost budget and achieve an optimal prediction performance under the cost constraint [14]. While such learned representations have shown promising performance in anytime prediction, most work address the unstructured classification problems and focus on efficient feature computation [2,15,16]. Only recent work of Grubb et al. [17] proposes an anytime prediction method for scene parsing, which relies on learning a representation for individual segments. Nevertheless, to achieve coherent scene labeling, it is important to learn a representation that also encodes the relations between scene elements (e.g., segments).

In this work, we tackle the anytime scene labeling problem by learning a family of structured models that captures long-range dependency between image segments. Labeling with structured models, however, involves both feature computation *and* inference cost. To enable anytime prediction, we propose to generate scene parsing from spatially coarse to fine level and with increasing number of image features. Such a strategy allows us to control both feature computation cost *and* the model structure which determines the inference cost.

Specifically, we design a hierarchical model generation process based on growing a segmentation tree for each image. Starting from the root node, this process gradually increases the overall model complexity by either splitting a subset of leaf-node segments or adding new features to label predictors defined on the leaf nodes. At each step, the resulting model encodes the structural dependency of labels in the hierarchy. For any cost budget, we can stop the generation process and produce a scene labeling by collecting the predictions from leaf nodes. An overview of our coarse-to-fine scene parsing is shown in Fig. 1. We note that a large variety of hierarchical models can be generated with different choices of node splitting and feature orders.

To achieve aforementioned Anytime performance, we seek a policy of generating the hierarchical models which produce high-quality or optimal pixel-level label predictions for any given test budget. We follow the anytime setting in [15,16], in which the test-time budget is *unknown* during model learning. Instead of learning a greedy strategy, we formulate the anytime scene labeling as a sequential decision making problem, and define a finite-horizon Markov Decision Process (MDP). The MDP maximizes the average label accuracy improvement per unit cost (or the average 'speed' of improvement if the cost is time) over a range of cost budgets as a surrogate for the anytime objective, and has a parametrized discrete action space for expanding the hierarchical models.

We solve the MDP to obtain a high-quality policy by developing an approximate least square policy iteration algorithm [18]. To cope with the parametrized action space, we propose an action proposal mechanism to sample a pool of candidate actions, of which the parameters are learned based on several greedy objectives and on different subsets of images. We note that the key properties of our learned policy are *dynamic*, which generates an image-dependent hierarchical representation, and *non-myopic*, which takes into account the potential future benefits in a sequence of predictions.

We evaluate our dynamic anytime parsing method on three publicly available semantic segmentation benchmarks, CamVid [19], Stanford Background [20] and Siftflow [21]. The results show that our approach is favorable in terms of anytime scene parsing compared to several state-of-the-art representation learning strategies, and in particular we can achieve 90 % of the state-of-the-art performances within 15 % of their total costs.

2   Related Work

Semantic scene labeling has become a core problem in computer vision research [3]. While early efforts tend to focus on structural models with hand-crafted features, recent work shift towards deep convolutional neural network based representation with significant improvement on prediction accuracy [4,6,10]. Hierarchical models, such as dynamic trees [22], segmentation hierarchies [23–26] and And-Or graphs [27], have adopted for semantic parsing. However, in general, those methods are expensive to deploy due to complex model inference or costly features.

Most of prior work on efficient semantic parsing focus on the active inference, which assumes redundancy in pre-learned models and achieves efficiency by allocating resource to an informative subset of model components. Roig et al. [12] use perturb-and-MAP inference model to select informative unary potentials to compute. Liu and He [28] actively select most-rewarding subgraphs for video segmentation. In [29], a local classifier is learned to select views for multi-view semantic labeling. Unlike these methods, we explicitly learn a representation for achieving strong performance at any test-time budget.

Learning anytime representation has been extensively explored for unstructured prediction problems (e.g., classification) [15,16]. Karayev et al. [2] learn an anytime representation for object and scene recognition, focusing on dynamic feature selection under a total budget. Weiss and Taskar [13] develop a reinforcement learning framework for feature selection in structured models. In contrast, we consider both feature computation and model inference cost. More importantly, we incorporate the cost in an MDP reward which encourages anytime property. Unlike [2], the test-time budget is explicitly unknown during learning in our setting. Perhaps the most related work is [17], which learns a segment-based anytime representation consisting of a selection function and a boosted predictor for individual segments. Their policy of segment and feature selection is trained in a greedy manner based on [16] and a single strategy is applied to all the images. By contrast, we build a structured hierarchical model on segmentation trees and learn an image-adaptive policy.

More generally, cost-sensitive learning and inference have been widely studied in learning and vision literature under various different contexts, including feature selection [30], learning classifier cascade by empirical risk minimization [31,32] or Wald's sequential ratio test [33], model selection [34,35], prioritized message passing inference [36], object detection [37], and activity recognition [38]. However, few approaches have been designed for optimizing the anytime prediction performance [14], or considering both feature and inference costs. We note that while the MDP framework has been extensively used in those methods, our formulation of discrete-continuous MDP is tailored for anytime scene parsing.

Unfolding and learning inference in graphical models has been explored in various inference machines [26,39]. Nevertheless, such methods usually use a greedy approach to learn the messages or model predictions. [40] use reinforcement learning to obtain a dynamic deep network model, but they do not address the structured prediction problem. Lastly, we note that, although some search-based structured prediction methods [41,42] are capable of terminating inference and generating outputs at any time, they usually do not consider feature computation cost and are not optimized for anytime performance.

3   Anytime Scene Labeling with a Hierarchical Model

We aim to learn a structured model representation with anytime performance property for semantic scene labeling. As structured prediction involves both feature computation and inference, we need a flexible representation that allows us to control the cost of feature and inference computation. To this end, we first introduce a family of hierarchical models based on image segmentation trees in Sect. 3.1, which is capable of incrementally increasing its complexity in terms of used image features and model structure.

We then formulate the anytime scene labeling as a sequential feature and model selection process in this model family with a cost-sensitive labeling loss in Sects. 3.2 and 3.3. Based on an MDP framework, our goal is to learn an optimal selection policy to generate a sequence of hierarchical models from a set of annotated images. In Sect. 4, we develop an iterative procedure to solve the policy learning problem approximately.

3.1   Coarse-to-Fine Scene Parsing with a Segmentation Hierarchy

We now introduce a flexible hierarchical representation for semantic parsing that enables us to control the test-time complexity. To achieve effective semantic labeling, we want to design a model framework capable of incorporating rich image features, modeling long-range dependency between regions and achieving anytime property. To this end, we adopt a coarse-to-fine scene labeling strategy, and consider a family of hierarchical models built on image segmentation trees, which has a simplified form of the Hierarchical Inference Machine (HIM) [26].

Specifically, given an image I, we construct a sequence of segmentation trees by recursively partitioning the image using graph-based algorithms [43,44]. We then develop a sequence of hierarchical models that predict label marginal distributions on the leaf nodes of the segmentation trees. Formally, let the semantic label space be $\mathcal{Y}$. We start from an initial segmentation tree T^0 with a single node and a marginal distribution $Q^0 = \{q^0\}$ on the node, which can be uniform or a global label prior. We incrementally grow the tree and update the prediction of marginal distributions on the leaf nodes by two update operators described in detail below, which generates a sequence of hierarchical models for labeling, denoted by $\mathcal{M}^1, \cdots, \mathcal{M}^T$, where T is the total number of steps.

At each step t, the hierarchical model $\mathcal{M}^t$ consists of a tree T^t and a set of predicted label distributions on the tree's leaf nodes, Q^t. More concretely, we denote the leaf nodes of T^t as $\mathcal{B}^t = \{b_1, \cdots, b_{N_t}\}$ where N_t is the number of leaf nodes. We associate each leaf-node segment b_i with a label variable y_i^t indicating its dominant label assignment. Let the label distributions $Q^t = \{q_i^t\}_{i=1}^{N_t}$, where q_i^t is the current label marginals at node b_i. We generate the next hierarchical model $\mathcal{M}^{t+1}$ by applying the following two update operators.

Split-inherit update. We choose a subset of leaf-node segments and split them into finer scale segments in the segmentation tree. The selection criterion is based on the entropy of the node marginals $H(q_i^t)$, and all the nodes with $H(q_i^t) > \theta_t$ will split into their children [17]. θ_t is a parameter of the operator and $\theta_t \in \mathbb{R}$. The new leaf-node segments inherit the marginal distributions of their parents.

$$q_i^{t+1}(k) = q_{pa(i)}^t(k), \quad k \in \mathcal{Y}, \ i \in \mathcal{B}^{t+1} \tag{1}$$

where $\mathcal{B}^{t+1}$ is the new leaf node set and $pa(i)$ indicates the parent node of i in the new tree T^{t+1}. We denote the parameter space of the operator as Θ.

Local belief update. For the newly generated leaf nodes from splitting, we improve their marginal distributions by adding more image cues or context information from their parents. Specifically, we extract a set of input features x_i from segment b_i, and adopt a boosting-like strategy: Using a weak learner taking the image feature x_i and the marginal of its parent $q_{pa(i)}^t$ as input [26], we update the marginals of leaf nodes as follows,

$$q_i^{t+1}(k) \propto q_i^t(k) \exp\left(\alpha_t h_k^t(f_i^t(j))\right), \quad k \in \mathcal{Y}, \quad f_i^t = [x_i, q_{pa(i)}^t] \tag{2}$$

where $f_i^t(j)$ is the j-th feature used in the weak learner; $h_t = [h_t^1, ..., h_t^{|\mathcal{Y}|}]$ and α_t are the newly added weak learners and their coefficient, respectively. We denote the weak learner space as $\mathcal{H}$ and $\alpha_t h_t \in \mathcal{H}$.

By applying a sequence of these update operators to the segmentation tree from its root node, we can generate a dynamically growing hierarchical models

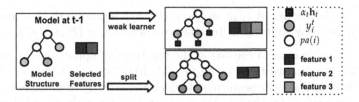

Fig. 2. Example of operators at step t. We choose either to add weak learners or split a subset of leaf nodes, which leads to gradually increasing model complexity.

for scene labeling (see Fig. 2 for an illustration). We refer to the resulting structured models as the *Dynamic Hierarchical Model* (DHM). We use 'dynamic' to indicate that our model generation process can vary from image to image or given different choices of the operators, which is not predetermined by greedy learning as in [26]. Using DHM as our representation for anytime scene labeling has several advantages. First, a DHM is capable of generating a sequence of model predictions with incrementally increasing cost as every update operator can be computed efficiently. In addition, it utilizes multiscale region grouping to create models from coarse to fine level, leading to gradually increasing model complexity. Furthermore, it has a flexible structure to select image features by weak learners and to capture long-range dependency between segments, which is critical to achieve the state-of-the-art performance for any test-time budget.

3.2 Anytime Scene Labeling by Cost-Sensitive DHM Generation

Given the dynamic hierarchical scene models defined in Sect. 3.1, we now formulate the anytime scene labeling as a cost-sensitive DHM generation problem. Specifically, we want to find a model generation strategy, which selects an sequence of image-dependent update operators, such that the incrementally built hierarchical models achieve good performance (measured by average labeling accuracy) at all possible test-time cost budgets. To address this sequential selection problem, we model the cost-sensitive model generation as a Markov Decision Process (MDP) that encourages good anytime performance with a cost-sensitive reward function. By solving this MDP, we are able to find a policy of selection that yields a sequence of hierarchical models with high-quality anytime performance.

Concretely, we first model an episode of coarse-to-fine DHM generation as an MDP with finite horizon. This MDP consists of a tuple $\{\mathcal{S}, \mathcal{A}, T(\cdot), R(\cdot), \gamma\}$, which defines its state space, action space, state transition, reward function and a discounting factor, respectively.

State: At time t, the state $s_t \in \mathcal{S}$ represents the current segment set corresponding to the leaf nodes of the segmentation tree and the label marginal distributions on the leaf nodes. As in Sect. 3.1, we denote the leaf-node segment set and the corresponding marginal label distributions as $\mathcal{B}^t = \{b_i\}_{i=1}^{N_t}$ and $\mathcal{Q}^t = \{\mathbf{q}_i^t\}_{i=1}^{N_t}$ respectively. We also introduce an indicator vector $Z^t \in \{0,1\}^{N_t}$ to describe an active set of leaf-nodes at t, in which $Z^t(k) = 1$ indicates the leaf node b_k is newly generated by splitting. Altogether, we define $s_t = \{\mathcal{B}^t, \mathcal{Q}^t, Z^t\}$.

Action: The action set $\mathcal{A}$ consists of the two types of update operators defined in Sect. 3.1. We denoted them by $\{u_s(\theta), u_b(\alpha \mathbf{h})\}$. For $a_t = u_s(\theta_t)$, we choose to split a subset of leaf-node segments of which the entropy of predicted marginal distributions are greater than θ_t. For $a_t = \alpha_t \mathbf{h}_t$, we apply the local belief update to the active nodes in Z^t using the weak learner $\alpha_t \mathbf{h}_t \in \mathcal{H}$. Note that the action space $\mathcal{A}$ is a discrete-continuous space $\Theta \cup \mathcal{H}$ due to their parameterization.

State Transition: The state transition $T(s_{t+1}|s_t, a_t)$ is a deterministic function in our MDP. For $a_t = \theta_t$, it expands the tree and generates a new set of leaf-node segments $\mathcal{B}^{t+1}$ with inherited marginals $\mathcal{Q}^{t+1}$ as defined in Eq. (1). The new active regions are the newly generated leaf-nodes from splitting, denoted by Z^{t+1}. The action $a_t = \alpha_t \mathbf{h}_t$ keeps the tree structure and active regions unchanged, such that $\mathcal{B}^{t+1} = \mathcal{B}^t$ and $Z^{t+1} = Z^t$; while it only updates the node marginals $\mathcal{Q}^{t+1}$ according to Eq. (2).

Reward Function and γ: The reward function R defines a mapping from (s_t, a_t) to rewards in $\mathbb{R}$ and γ is a discount factor that determines the lookahead in selection actions. For the anytime learning problem, we design a reward function that is cost-sensitive and encourages the sequence of generated models can achieve good labeling accuracies across a range of possible cost budgets. The details of the reward function and γ will be discussed in the next subsection.

3.3 Defining Reward Function

We now define a reward function that favors a coarse-to-fine dynamic hierarchical model generation with anytime performance. To this end, we first describe the action costs of the MDP, which compute the overall cost of model prediction. We then introduce a labeling loss for our hierarchical models, based on which the cost-sensitive reward and the value function of the MDP are defined.

Action Cost: The action cost represents the cost of scene labeling using a hierarchical model, which consists of feature extraction cost c_{f_t} for computing feature set f_t (from the entire image or specific regions), region split cost c_r for pooling features for newly split regions, total weak learner cost c_{h_t} for applying the weak learner $\alpha_t \mathbf{h}_t$ to predict labels. For each action a_t, we define the action cost $c(a_t)$ as $c_{h_t} + c_{f_t}$ if $a_t = u_b$, or c_r if $a_t = u_s$. In this work, we use the CPU time used in a_t as a surrogate for the computation cost while any other type of costs can also be applied.

Labeling loss of DHMs: Given a hierarchical model represented by s_t, we introduce a loss function measuring the scene labeling performance. Particularly, we adopted an entropy-based labeling loss function defined as follows,

$$\mathcal{L}(s_t, \hat{\mathbf{Y}}|I) = -\sum_{i \in \mathcal{B}^t} w_i \mathbf{p}_i^T \log(\mathbf{q}_i^t) - \alpha \sum_{i \in \mathcal{B}^t} w_i \mathbf{p}_i^T \log(\mathbf{p}_i), \tag{3}$$

where $\mathbf{p}_i$ is the ground-truth label distribution in region $b_i \in \mathcal{B}^t$, derived from the ground-truth labeling $\hat{\mathbf{Y}}$, and w_i denotes its normalized size. The first term is the cross-entropy between the marginals and the ground-truth while the second term penalizes the regions with mixed labels. These two terms reflect the label prediction and image partition quality respectively and we further introduce a weight α to control their balance. Intuitively, the loss favors a model with a sensible image segmentation and a good prediction for the segment labels. A larger α prefers to learn predictors after reaching fine levels in hierarchy while a small value may lead to stronger predictors at all levels.

Cost-sensitive reward: To achieve the anytime performance, an ideal model generation sequence will minimize the labeling loss as fast as possible such that it can obtain high quality scene labeling for a full range of cost budgets. Following this intuition, we define the reward for action a_t as the labeling loss improvement between s_{t+1} and s_t normalized by the cost of a_t [16]. Formally, we define the reward as,

$$R(s_t, a_t | I) = \frac{1}{c(a_t)} \left[\mathcal{L}(s_t, \hat{\mathbf{Y}} | I) - \mathcal{L}(s_{t+1}, \hat{\mathbf{Y}} | I) \right] \tag{4}$$

where $c(a_t)$ summarizes all the computation cost in the action a_t.

Policy and value function: A policy of the MDP is a function mapping from a state to an action, $\pi(s) : \mathcal{S} \to \mathcal{A}$. The value function of the MDP at state s_t under policy π is the total accumulated reward defined as,

$$V_\pi(s_t) = \sum_{\tau=t}^{T} \gamma^{\tau-t} R(s_\tau, \pi(s_\tau) | I) \tag{5}$$

where T is the number of actions taken and s_0 is the initial state. Our goal is to find an optimal policy π^* that maximizes the expected value function over the image space for any state s_t. We will discuss how to learn such a policy using a training set in the following section. We note that our objective describes a weighted average speed of labeling performance improvement (c.f. (4), (5)), and γ controls how greedy the policy would be. When $\gamma = 0$, the optimal policy maximizes a myopic objective as in [16]. We choose $\gamma > 0$ so that our policy also considers potential future benefit (i.e., fast improvement in later stages).

4   Learning Anytime Scene Labeling

To learn anytime scene labeling, we want to seek a policy π^* to maximize the expected value function for any state s_t in a MDP framework. Given a training set $\mathcal{D} = \{I^{(m)}, \hat{\mathbf{Y}}^{(m)}\}_{m=1}^{M}$ with M images, the learning problem is defined as,

$$\pi^*(s_t) = \operatorname*{argmax}_{\pi} E_{\mathcal{D}}[V_\pi(s_t)] = \operatorname*{argmax}_{\pi} \frac{1}{M} \sum_{m=1}^{M} \sum_{\tau=t}^{T} \gamma^{\tau-t} R(s_\tau, \pi(s_\tau) | I^m), \; \forall t \tag{6}$$

where $E_{\mathcal{D}}$ is the empirical expectation on the dataset $\mathcal{D}$. The main challenge in solving this MDP is to explore the parametrized action space $\mathcal{A}$ due to its discrete-continuous nature and high-dimensionality. In this work, we design an action generation strategy that proposes a finite set of effective parameters for the actions. We then use the proposed action pool as our discrete action space and develop a least square policy learning procedure to find a high quality policy.

4.1 Action Proposal Generation

To cope with the parameterized actions, we discretize the parameter space $\Theta \cup \mathcal{H}$ by generating a finite set of effective and diversified parameter values. Our discretization uses a greedy learning criterion to generate a sequence of actions with instantiated parameters based on the training set $\mathcal{D}$.

Specifically, we start from s_0 for all the training images, and generate a sequence of actions and states (which corresponds to a sequence of hierarchical models) as follows. At step t, we first discretize Θ by uniformly sample the 1D space. For the weak learner space $\mathcal{H}$, we generate a set of weak learners by minimizing the following regression loss as in the Greedy Miser method [45]:

$$\alpha_t, \mathbf{h}_t = \arg\min_{\alpha, \mathbf{h}} \sum_{i \in D^t} w_i \| \mathbf{p}_i - \mathbf{q}_i^{t-1} - \alpha \mathbf{h}(\mathbf{f}_i^t) \|^2 + \lambda(c_{h_t} + c_{f_t}) \tag{7}$$

where $D^t = \{i | Z_m^t(i) = 1, m = 1, \ldots, M\}$ is the set of all active nodes at step t in all M images, and $\mathbf{p}_i$ and $\mathbf{q}_i^{t-1}$ are the ground-truth marginal and the previous marginal prediction on node i respectively. The second term regularizes the loss with the cost of applying the weak learner and a weight parameter λ controls its strength. We obtain several weak learner $\alpha_t \mathbf{h}_t$ by varying the value of λ. From these discretized actions, denoted by $\mathcal{A}_s^t$, we then select a most effective action using our reward function, $a_t^0 = \arg\max_{a_t \in \mathcal{A}_s^t} E_D[R(s_t, a_t | I)]$. We continue this process until step T based on a held-out validation set, and $\{a_t^0\}_{t=1}^T$ is a sampled action sequence.

To increase the diversity of our discrete action candidates, we also apply the same action proposal generation method to different subsets of images. The image subsets are formed by K-means clustering and we refer the reader to the supplementary for the details. Finally we combine all the generated discrete action sequences as our action candidates to form a new discrete action space $\mathcal{A}^d$, which is used for learning our policy.

4.2 Least-Square Policy Iteration for Solving MDP

In order to find a high-quality policy π_d^* on $\mathcal{A}^d$, we adopt an approximate least-square policy iteration approach and learn a parametrized Q-function [13,18], which can be generalized to the test scenario. Specifically, we use a linear function to approximate the Q-function, and the approximate Q and corresponding policy can be written as

$$\hat{Q}(s_t, a_t) = \eta^T \phi(s_t, a_t), \tag{8}$$

$$\pi_d(s_t) = \arg\max_{a_t \in \mathcal{A}^d} \hat{Q}(s_t, a_t) \tag{9}$$

where $\phi(s_t, a_t)$ is the meta-feature of the model computed from the current state s_t and action a_t. η is the linear coefficient to be learned. We will discuss the details of our meta-feature in Sect. 5.1.

Our least-square policy iteration procedure includes the following three steps, which starts from an initial policy π_d^0 and iteratively improves the policy.

A. Policy initialization. We initialize the policy π_d^0 by a greedy action selection that optimizes the average immediate reward on the training set at each time step. Specifically, at each t, we choose $\pi_d^0(s_t) = \arg\max_{a_t \in \mathcal{A}^d} E_D[R(s_t, a_t|I)]$.

B. Policy evaluation. Given a policy π_d^n at iteration n, we execute the policy for each training example to generate a trajectory $\{(s_t^m, a_t^m)\}_{m=1}^M$. We then compute the value function of the policy recursively based on $Q_\pi(s_t, a_t) = R(s_t, a_t|I) + \gamma Q_\pi(s_{t+1}, a_{t+1})$. As in [13], we only consider the non-negative contribution of Q_π, which allows early stop if the reward is no longer positive,

$$Q_\pi(s_t^m, a_t^m) = R(s_t^m, a_t^m) + \gamma[Q_\pi(s_{t+1}^m, a_{t+1}^m)]_+ \tag{10}$$

C. Policy improvement. Given a set of trajectories $\{(s_t^m, a_t^m)\}_{m=1}^M$ and the corresponding Q-function value $\{Q_\pi(s_t^m, a_t^m)\}_{m=1}^M$, we update the linear approximate $\hat{Q}$ by solving the following least-square regression problem:

$$\min_\eta \beta \|\eta\|^2 + \frac{1}{TM} \sum_m \sum_t \left(\eta^T \phi(s_t^m, a_t^m) - Q_\pi(s_t^m, a_t^m)\right)^2 \tag{11}$$

where the iteration index n is omitted here for clarity. Denote the solution as η^*, we can compute the new updated policy $\pi_d^{n+1}(s_t) = \arg\max_{a_t} \eta^* \phi(s_t, a_t)$. We also add a small amount of uniformly distributed random noise to the updated policy as in [2]. We perform policy evaluation (Step B) and improvement iteration (Step C) several times until the segmentation performance does not change in a held-out validation set.

During the test, we apply the learned policy π_d to an test image, which produces a trajectory $\{(s_0, a_0), (s_1, a_1), \ldots, (s_T, a_T)\}$. The state sequence defines a coarse-to-fine scene labeling process based on the generated hierarchical models. For any given cost budget, we can stop the scene labeling process and use the leaf-node marginal label distributions (i.e., taking the most likely label) to make a pixel-wise label prediction for the entire image. More detailed discussion of the test-time procedure can be found in the supplementary.

5   Experiments

We evaluate our method on three publicly available datasets, including CamVid [19], Standford Background [20] and Siftflow [21]. We focus on CamVid [19] as it provides more complex scenes with multiple foreground object classes of various scales. We refer the reader to supplementary material for the details of datasets.

5.1   Implementation Details

Feature set and action proposal: We extract 9 different visual features (Semantics using Darwin [46], Geometric, Color and Position, Texture, LBP, HoG, SIFT and hyper-column feature [4,5]). In action proposal, the weak learner $\alpha_t \mathbf{h}_t$ is learned as in Sect. 4.1 using [45]. To propose multiple weak learners with a variety of costs, we also learn p weak learners sequentially where p is set to 5,10 and 20 empirically and use them as action candidates. As for split action, we discretize Θ into $\{0, 0.3, 0.6, 1\}$ and we generate a 8-layer hierarchy using [43] as in [17]. In our experiment, we use grid search method and choose the set of hyper-parameters that gives us the optimal pixel-level prediction.

The cost of each feature type measures the computation time for an entire image. We note that this cost can be further reduced by efficient implementation of local features. The segmentation time is taken into account as an initial cost during the evaluation in order to have a fair comparison with existing methods. More details on cost computation can be found in the supplementary materials.

Policy learning features: We design three sets of features for $\phi(s_t, a_t)$. The first are computed from marginal distributions on all regions, consisting of the average entropy, the average entropy gap between previous marginal estimation and current marginals, two binary vectors of length 9 to indicate which feature set has been used and which unseen feature set will be extracted respectively, and one vector for the statistics of difference in current marginal probabilities of the top two predictions. The second are region features on active leaf nodes, including the normalized area of active regions in current image, the average entropy of active regions and the average entropy gap between previous and current prediction in active regions. The third layer features consist of the distribution of all regions in hierarchies and the distribution of active regions in hierarchies. More details on policy learning features can be found in the supplementary material.

5.2   Baseline Methods

We compare our approach to two types of baselines as below. We also report the state-of-the-art performances on three datasets.

- Non-anytime CRF-based methods using the full feature set: (1) A fully-connected CRF (DCRF) model [47] whose data term is learned on finest layer of segmentation trees; (2) A Hierarchical Inference Machine (HIM) implemented by following the algorithm in [26]; (3) A pixel-level dense CRF model with superpixel higher-order terms (H-DCRF) as in [48]. They prove to be strong baselines for scene labeling tasks.
- Three strong anytime baselines, including a Static-Myopic (S-M), a Random Selection (RS) and a static-myopic feature selection (F-SM) anytime model. The static-myopic method (S-M) learns a fixed sequence of actions by maximizing immediate rewards on training set (cf. $\{a_t^0\}_{t=1}^T$ in Sect. 4.1). The random selection method (RS) uses our action pool and randomly takes

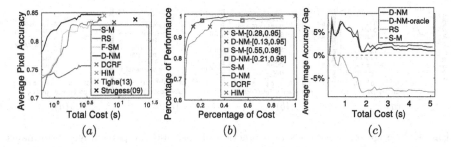

Fig. 3. (a): Average pixel accuracy vs. cost; (b): percentage of performance vs. percentage of cost; (c): average per-image accuracy gap vs. total cost in CamVid. Our D-NM consistently outperforms S-M in all figures and achieves full performance using about 50 % total cost. Moreover, it outperforms all anytime baselines consistently and achieves better performance w.r.t. non-anytime state-of-the-art.

an action at each step. The feature selection method (F-SM) uses the DCRF above as its model and greedily selects features that maximize the immediate rewards. We note that the baselines utilize some state-of-the-art feature selection methods such as [16,45], and our RS baseline is built on the learned high-quality action pool.

5.3 Results

We report the results of our experiments on anytime scene labeling in three parts: (1) overall comparison with the baselines and the state-of-the-art methods on CamVid. (2) detailed analysis of anytime property on CamVid. (3) results on Stanford Background and Siftflow datasets.

Overall performance on CamVid. We first show the quantitative results of our method and compare with state-of-the-art methods in Fig. 3.(a) and Table 1. We compute the accuracy and Intersection-Over-Union(IOU) score of semantic segmentation on CamVid. Note that here we report the performance of anytime methods at the time budget of T_{DCRF}, which is the average prediction time of DCRF. In Table 1, we can see that our method achieves better performance than DCRF in terms of per-pixel accuracy and IOU score, and DCRF is a strong baseline since it uses the full feature set. Our per-pixel accuracy is comparable to the HIM, which uses the most complex model and full feature set, while we achieve similar performance with about 50 % of its computation cost (See below for details). In addition, we outperform all the rest of state-of-the-art methods [17,49], especially in terms of average per-class accuracy (5.4 % to 9 % absolute gap). Moreover, we achieve similar or slightly better performance w.r.t. the methods that use additional information such as Structure-from-Motion(SfM) of video sequence [19,50] or pre-trained object detectors [51].

We conduct comparisons on the anytime performance of our methods and baselines in Fig. 3(a) and (b). We introduce a plot (b) showing all the performance and cost values w.r.t the HIM and its prediction cost since it is the state-of-the-art

662   B. Liu and X. He

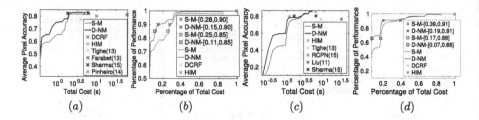

(a)   (b)   (c)   (d)

Fig. 4. Average pixel accuracy as a function of cost and the percentage performance vs. percentage of cost in SBG (a,b) and Siftflow (c,d), respectively. D-NM achieves similar performance with less cost. Cost of related work is from [52].

Table 1. Performance comparison on CamVid. D-NM outperforms [17,49], especially in average class accuracy. Our results are comparable to [19,50,51] that use additional information. We achieve a performance similar to HIM and DCRF with less cost.

CamVid	Tighe [49]	SIM [17]	Video [19]	Detector [51]	Video [50]	DCRF	H-DCRF	HIM	D-NM (ours)
Pixel	83.3	81.5	69.1	83.2	83.8	83.2	83.9	84.5	**84.7**
Class	51.2	54.8	53.0	59.6	59.2	59.8	60.0	**60.5**	60.2
IOU	NA	NA	NA	**49.3**	49.2	46.3	48.4	**49.3**	48.8

and most costly. Specifically, Fig. 3(b) shows the percentage of average pixel-level accuracy vs. percentage of total cost curves of our methods and baselines w.r.t the HIM. We note that this illustration is invariant to the specific values of prediction cost/time, and shows how the accuracy improves with increasing cost.

We first show comparison of our method with all the anytime and non-anytime baselines in Fig. 3(b), which also highlights two sets of intermediate results. Our dynamic policy D-NM achieves the 90 % of performance using only around 10 % cost and outperforms the S-M consistently. Specifically, D-NM achieves similar performance with around half S-M test-time cost (13 % and 21 % vs. 28 % and 55 %). Moreover, D-NM achieves the full performance of HIM with around 50 % total cost while S-M saturates at a lower accuracy. We refer the reader to the supplementary material for examples of our anytime output with specific actions.

Anytime property analysis on CamVid. We analyze the anytime property of our method by comparing to three different baselines. First, we validate the importance of encoding model complexity in anytime prediction model by comparing with F-SM (fixed model with feature selection). Second, we evaluate the effectiveness of policy learning by comparing with RS (random search on the same action space). Results of these two comparisons can be viewed in Fig. 3(a). Finally, we explore the effectiveness of action space exploration by generating the oracle results of D-NM on CamVid test set in Fig. 3(c).

Figure 3(a) shows that the D-NM outperforms all baselines consistently and generates superior results under the same cost. RS is almost always the worst and far below D-NM, which shows our policy learning is important and effective to achieve better trade-offs between accuracy and cost. F-SM is slightly above

S-M at the beginning and always below D-NM. Moreover, due to the limited representation power of its fixed model, F-SM quickly stabilizes at a lower performance. This demonstrates the benefits of joint feature and model selection in our method. We also visualize results of other methods (crossings) and show that we can achieve better performance more efficiently. These results evidence that our method can learn a better representation for anytime scene parsing. Detailed averaged IOU score and labeling loss as a function of cost, area-under-average-accuracy table can be viewed in supplementary materials.

Table 2. Semantic segmentation results on Stanford background dataset. We can achieve better performance w.r.t state-of-the-art methods.

SBG	RCPN [53]	Tighe [49]	Gould [20]	Farabet [9]	Pinheiro [54]	Sharma [52]	H-DCRF	S-M	D-NM (ours)
Pixel	81.8	77.5	76.4	81.4	80.2	82.3	82.6	81.7	**83.0**
IOU	61.3	NA	NA	NA	NA	64.5	**64.7**	61.4	**64.7**

Figure 3(c) shows the average per-image accuracy gap w.r.t the S-M method as a function of total cost. We note that D-NM always achieves superior performance to the S-M. We also visualize the oracle performance of D-NM. D-NM-oracle is always above S-M, which proves the effectiveness of action space exploration. Also, the early stop of oracles shows that more features or complex models will not introduce further segmentation improvement. Our D-NM is only slightly below D-NM-oracle, which shows the effectiveness of policy learning.

Table 3. Semantic segmentation results on Siftflow dataset. We can achieve comparable/better performance w.r.t. state-of-the-art methods.

Siftflow	RCPN [53]	Yang [55]	Pinheiro [54]	Liu [21]	Tighe [49]	FCN [4]	Farabet [9]	Sharma [52]	H-DCRF	S-M	D-NM (ours)
Pixel	79.6	79.8	77.7	76.7	77.0	85.7	78.5	80.8	**85.8**	**85.8**	85.8
IOU	26.9	NA	NA	NA	NA	**36.7**	NA	30.7	**36.7**	35.8	**36.7**

Stanford Background. Results on Stanford Background dataset [20] are shown in Table 2. D-NM outperforms existing work in terms of pixel-level accuracy and IOU score. We visualize the anytime property in top row of Fig. 4. Figure 4(a) shows that D-NM achieves the state-of-the-art performance (crossings) more efficiently while S-M stops at a lower performance. Figure 4(b) highlights two sets of intermediate results and shows that D-NM generates similar results with about half of the S-M cost (11 % and 15 % vs. 25 % and 28 %).

Siftflow. We report our results on Siftflow dataset [21] in Table 3. Again, D-NM achieves the state-of-the-art in terms of pixel level accuracy and IOU score. Figure 4(c) shows its anytime performance curves and Fig. 4(d) also highlights two sets of intermediate results. We can see that D-NM achieves the state-of-the-art performance (crossings) more efficiently, and produces similar accuracy with much less cost.

6   Conclusion

In this paper, we presented a dynamic hierarchical model for anytime semantic scene segmentation. Our anytime representation is built on a coarse-to-fine segmentation tree, which enables us to select both discriminative features and effective model structure for cost-sensitive scene labeling. We developed an MDP formulation and an approximated policy iteration method with an action proposal mechanism for learning the anytime representation. The results of applying our method to three semantic segmentation datasets show that our algorithm consistently outperforms the baseline approaches and the state-of-the-arts. This suggests that our learned dynamic non-myopic policy generates a more effective representation for anytime scene labeling.

Acknowledgement. DATA61 (formerly NICTA) is funded by the Australian Government through the Department of Communications and the Australian Research Council through the ICT Centre for Excellence Program. We thank NVIDIA Corporation for the donation of GPUs used in this research.

References

1. Hegdé, J.: Time course of visual perception: coarse-to-fine processing and beyond. Progress Neurobiol. (2008)
2. Karayev, S., Fritz, M., Darrell, T.: Anytime recognition of objects and scenes. In: CVPR (2014)
3. Gould, S., He, X.: Scene understanding by labeling pixels. CACM (2014)
4. Long, J., Shelhamer, E., Darrell, T.: Fully convolutional networks for semantic segmentation. In: CVPR (2015)
5. Hariharan, B., Arbeláez, P., Girshick, R., Malik, J.: Hypercolumns for object segmentation and fine-grained localization. In: CVPR (2015)
6. Dai, J., He, K., Sun, J.: Convolutional feature masking for joint object and stuff segmentation. In: CVPR (2015)
7. He, X., Zemel, R.S., Carreira-Perpiñán, M.: Multiscale conditional random fields for image labeling. In: CVPR (2004)
8. Yao, J., Fidler, S., Urtasun, R.: Describing the scene as a whole: joint object detection, scene classification and semantic segmentation. In: CVPR (2012)
9. Farabet, C., Couprie, C., Najman, L., LeCun, Y.: Learning hierarchical features for scene labeling. In: PAMI (2013)
10. Chen, L.C., Papandreou, G., Kokkinos, I., Murphy, K., Yuille, A.L.: Semantic image segmentation with deep convolutional nets and fully connected CRFs. In: ICLR (2015)
11. Simonyan, K., Zisserman, A.: Very deep convolutional networks for large-scale image recognition. CoRR abs/1409.1556 (2014)

12. Roig, G., Boix, X., Nijs, R.D., Ramos, S., Kuhnlenz, K., Gool, L.V.: Active MAP inference in CRFs for efficient semantic segmentation. In: ICCV (2013)
13. Weiss, D., Taskar, B.: Learning adaptive value of information for structured prediction. In: NIPS (2013)
14. Zilberstein, S.: Using anytime algorithms in intelligent systems. AI Magazine (1996)
15. Xu, Z., Kusner, M., Huang, G., Weinberger, K.Q.: Anytime representation learning. In: ICML (2013)
16. Grubb, A., Bagnell, D.: SpeedBoost: anytime prediction with uniform near-optimality. In: AISTATS (2012)
17. Grubb, A., Munoz, D., Bagnell, J.A., Hebert, M.: SpeedMachines: anytime structured prediction. In: Learning with Test-time Budgets Workshop on ICML (2013)
18. Lagoudakis, M.G., Parr, R.: Least-squares policy iteration. In: JMLR (2003)
19. Brostow, G.J., Shotton, J., Fauqueur, J., Cipolla, R.: Segmentation and recognition using structure from motion point clouds. In: Forsyth, D., Torr, P., Zisserman, A. (eds.) ECCV 2008. LNCS, vol. 5302, pp. 44–57. Springer, Heidelberg (2008). doi:10. 1007/978-3-540-88682-2_5
20. Gould, S., Fulton, R., Koller, D.: Decomposing a scene into geometric and semantically consistent regions. In: ICCV (2009)
21. Liu, C., Yuen, J., Torralba, A.: Nonparametric scene parsing via label transfer. PAMI (2011)
22. Slorkey, A., Williams, C.K.: Image modeling with position-encoding dynamic trees. PAMI (2003)
23. Socher, R., Lin, C.C., Manning, C., Ng, A.Y.: Parsing natural scenes and natural language with recursive neural networks. In: ICML (2011)
24. Lempitsky, V., Vedaldi, A., Zisserman, A.: Pylon model for semantic segmentation. In: NIPS (2011)
25. Russell, C., Kohli, P., Torr, P.H., et al.: Associative hierarchical crfs for object class image segmentation. In: ICCV (2009)
26. Munoz, D., Bagnell, J.A., Hebert, M.: Stacked hierarchical labeling. In: Daniilidis, K., Maragos, P., Paragios, N. (eds.) ECCV 2010. LNCS, vol. 6316, pp. 57–70. Springer, Heidelberg (2010). doi:10.1007/978-3-642-15567-3_5
27. Zhu, S.C., Mumford, D.: A Stochastic Grammar of Images. Now Publishers Inc., Hanover (2007)
28. Liu, B., He, X.: Multiclass semantic video segmentation with object-level active inference. In: CVPR (2015)
29. Riemenschneider, H., Bódis-Szomorú, A., Weissenberg, J., Gool, L.: Learning where to classify in multi-view semantic segmentation. In: Fleet, D., Pajdla, T., Schiele, B., Tuytelaars, T. (eds.) ECCV 2014. LNCS, vol. 8693, pp. 516–532. Springer, Heidelberg (2014). doi:10.1007/978-3-319-10602-1_34
30. He, H., Daumé III., H., Eisner, J.: Dynamic feature selection for dependency parsing. In: EMNLP (2013)
31. Wang, J., Bolukbasi, T., Trapeznikov, K., Saligrama, V.: Model selection by linear programming. In: Fleet, D., Pajdla, T., Schiele, B., Tuytelaars, T. (eds.) ECCV 2014. LNCS, vol. 8690, pp. 647–662. Springer, Heidelberg (2014). doi:10.1007/ 978-3-319-10605-2_42
32. Trapeznikov, K., Saligrama, V.: Supervised sequential classification under budget constraints. In: AISTATS (2013)
33. Sochman, J., Matas, J.: Waldboost-learning for time constrained sequential detection. In: IEEE Computer Society Conference on Computer Vision and Pattern Recognition (CVPR 2005). IEEE (2005)

34. Weiss, D., Sapp, B., Taskar, B.: Dynamic structured model selection. In: ICCV (2013)
35. Benbouzid, D., Busa-Fekete, R., Kégl, B.: Fast classification using sparse decision DAGs. In: ICML (2012)
36. Jiang, J., Moon, T., Daumé III., H., Eisner, J.: Prioritized asynchronous belief propagation. In: Inferning Workshop on ICML (2013)
37. Wu, T., Zhu, S.C.: Learning near-optimal cost-sensitive decision policy for object detection. In: ICCV (2013)
38. Amer, M.R., Xie, D., Zhao, M., Todorovic, S., Zhu, S.-C.: Cost-sensitive top-down/bottom-up inference for multiscale activity recognition. In: Fitzgibbon, A., Lazebnik, S., Perona, P., Sato, Y., Schmid, C. (eds.) ECCV 2012. LNCS, vol. 7575, pp. 187–200. Springer, Heidelberg (2012). doi:10.1007/978-3-642-33765-9_14
39. Ross, S., Munoz, D., Hebert, M., Bagnell, J.A.: Learning message-passing inference machines for structured prediction. In: CVPR (2011)
40. Denoyer, L., Gallinari, P.: Deep sequential neural network. In: Workshop Deep Learning NIPS (2014)
41. Doppa, J.R., Fern, A., Tadepalli, P.: Structured prediction via output space search. JMLR (2014)
42. Zhang, Y., Lei, T., Barzilay, R., Jaakkola, T.: Greed is good if randomized: new inference for dependency parsing. In: EMNLP (2014)
43. Felzenszwalb, P.F., Huttenlocher, D.P.: Efficient graph-based image segmentation. IJCV (2004)
44. Grundmann, M., Kwatra, V., Han, M., Essa, I.: Efficient hierarchical graph-based video segmentation. In: CVPR (2010)
45. Xu, Z., Weinberger, K., Chapelle, O.: The greedy miser: learning under test-time budgets. In: ICML (2012)
46. Gould, S.: DARWIN: A framework for machine learning and computer vision research and development. JMLR (2012)
47. Krähenbühl, P., Koltun, V.: Efficient inference in fully connected CRFs with gaussian edge potentials. In: NIPS (2011)
48. Vineet, V., Warrell, J., Torr, P.H.: Filter-based mean-field inference for random fields with higher-order terms and product label-spaces. Int. J. Comput. Vis. (2014)
49. Tighe, J., Lazebnik, S.: Superparsing - scalable nonparametric image parsing with superpixels. IJCV (2013)
50. Sturgess, P., Alahari, K.: Combining appearance and structure from motion features for road scene understanding. In: BMVC (2009)
51. Floros, G., Rematas, K., Leibe, B.: Multi-class image labeling with top-down segmentation and generalized robust p^n potentials. In: BMVC (2011)
52. Sharma, A., Tuzel, O., Jacobs, D.W.: Deep hierarchical parsing for semantic segmentation. In: CVPR (2015)
53. Sharma, A., Tuzel, O., Liu, M.Y.: Recursive context propagation network for semantic scene labeling. In: NIPS (2014)
54. Pinheiro, P., Collobert, R.: Recurrent convolutional neural networks for scene labeling. In: ICML (2014)
55. Yang, J., Price, B., Cohen, S., Yang, M.H.: Context driven scene parsing with attention to rare classes. In: CVPR (2014)

Semantic 3D Reconstruction of Heads

Fabio Maninchedda[1]($\boxtimes$), Christian Häne[2], Bastien Jacquet[3],
Amaël Delaunoy[1], and Marc Pollefeys[1,4]

[1] ETH Zurich, Zurich, Switzerland
fabiom@inf.ethz.ch
[2] UC Berkeley, Berkeley, USA
[3] Kitware SAS, Villeurbanne, France
[4] Microsoft, Redmond, USA

Abstract. We present a novel approach that jointly reconstructs the
geometry of a human head and semantically segments it into labels
such as skin, hair and eyebrows. In order to get faithful reconstructions
from data captured in uncontrolled environments, we propose to adapt a
recently introduced implicit volumetric surface normal based shape prior
formulation. Shape prior based approaches critically rely on an accurate
alignment between the data and the prior to succeed. To this end, we
propose an automatic alignment procedure for the used shape prior formulation. We evaluate our alignment procedure thoroughly and show
head reconstruction results on challenging datasets.

Keywords: Face · Head · Semantic · Multi-label · Shape prior ·
Alignment

1 Introduction

Reconstruction of human faces and heads is an ongoing topic in computer vision
and related areas. There is much interest due to the wide field of applications
and the inherent difficulty of the problem. Use cases are for example content
generation for movie production, computer games, virtual make over, physical
manufacturing of figurines, i.e. 3D printing, and many more. Due to the wide
range of applications many different capturing technologies are utilized in practice. When generating content for movies, high quality capturing setups that
facilitate a very accurate geometry acquisition are the natural choice [2]. However, this is expensive and needs expert knowledge during the capturing process.
In this paper we focus on less constrained scenarios, such as a person taking a 3D
selfie [32] or a person capturing a 3D head model of another person by using a

---

C. Häne, B. Jacquet and A. Delaunoy—Work done while authors were at the Department of Computer Science, ETH Zurich.

Electronic supplementary material The online version of this chapter (doi:10.
1007/978-3-319-46466-4_40) contains supplementary material, which is available to
authorized users.

© Springer International Publishing AG 2016
B. Leibe et al. (Eds.): ECCV 2016, Part VI, LNCS 9910, pp. 667–683, 2016.
DOI: 10.1007/978-3-319-46466-4_40

hand held camera. Therefore, there is little control over the conditions in which the images are taken. They can be badly exposed, blurry and are generally of lower quality than with a dedicated capturing setup. A common way to address these issues is to use shape priors [7,13,23].

For many applications also semantic labels are of interest. In video games the hair of characters can be physically simulated in real time. Being able to generate a semantically segmented 3D model would directly facilitate such a simulation on user generated content. Similarly, for 3D printing different semantic labels could be manufactured with different materials. For augmented reality the head could be augmented with a hat which would interact with the hair, but not affect the shape of the head. For such applications not only the visible surfaces, such as skin or hair, need to be modeled but also the hidden, invisible surfaces, for example the surface between skin and hair needs to be estimated convincingly. In this paper, we show that this can be achieved by posing the reconstruction of human heads as a volumetric multi-label segmentation problem [15] together with a multi-label shape prior [14]. When using shape priors one has to establish the correspondence between the input data and the shape prior and eventually recover a good alignment between them. To this end, we propose a novel alignment procedure that allows us to align the implicit volumetric shape prior of [14] fully automatically to the input data. In previous work the alignment for this type of shape prior was done manually.

1.1   Related Work

Using synchronized, high resolution multi-camera systems in controlled environments with good lighting, high quality face models can be acquired by stereo matching [2,8]. An extension [3], estimates facial hair as separate layer. A skin surface is always present underneath the hair, however it is only a pseudo surface which is not meant to be a plausible reconstruction of the unobserved surface.

In uncontrolled environments where data is captured with lower resolution, face reconstruction is often achieved by fitting a blend shape to the images. A classical way is to generate a statistical shape model (of faces) [4,23,26], which is fitted into the input data. First, facial landmarks [10,17,27,28] are extracted, which are then used to register the input images to the shape model. Using such a blend shape model with additional refinements, [12,16] focus on reconstructing dynamic face models. Even though realistic reconstructions are obtained using a low-dimensional statistical shape model, they generally do not capture instance specific shape variations, such as big moles. Also for 3D reconstruction of hair methods that exploit the specific structure of hair were proposed [22,34]. Most of the methods focus on reconstructing either the face or the hair. In this work, we reconstruct complete, printable, 3D models of human *heads* similar to [8]. While [8] uses a similar capturing setup as [2], we tackle the challenging problem of working with images captured using a hand-held camera, e.g. a mobile phone or a compact camera. We achieve this with volumetric multi-label formulation.

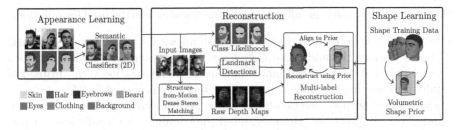

Fig. 1. Overview of our method.

Volumetric 3D reconstruction dates back to [6]. A voxel space is labeled into *free space* and *occupied space*. Regularizing the input data by penalizing the surface area was proposed in [20,36] for the discrete graph-based and the spatially continuous (variational) formulation, respectively. Continuous formulations for multi-label segmentation have been proposed in [5,37,38]. Instead of using a single *occupied space* label, [15] proposed to use multiple semantic classes to segment the occupied space. This continuously inspired method, penalizes transitions between different labels anisotropically and can therefore include priors on the direction of the surfaces. The idea of using anisotropic surface area penalization in the continuous setting [15], was extended in [14] to describe 3D object shape priors, learned from training data, in form of an implicit normal direction based shape prior. This leads to a very powerful object shape prior, however the alignment between the prior and the input data is assumed to be given as input.

1.2 Contributions

Our main contributions are the following:

- We present a system which reconstructs and semantically segments human heads from images captured with standard hand-held cameras in uncontrolled environments. In contrast to previous systems we do not only reconstruct the geometry of the head but also acquire a semantic segmentation into classes such as skin, hair, beard and eyebrows. This includes a plausible reconstruction of the unobserved surfaces (e.g. skin underneath hair). Moreover, our system is able to recover instance specific shape details which are typically lost when using a low-dimensional statistical shape model.
- We propose an automatic alignment procedure for the implicit shape prior formulation of [14], which was considered as an input in the original publication and hence done manually. Our key insight is that despite the volumetric nature of the shape prior we can formulate the alignment as an optimization over the surface. We propose an optimization scheme which alternates between optimizing for the geometry and the alignment. Despite the non-convexity of the optimization we can robustly infer the geometry and the alignment. This part is detailed in Sect. 4.1.

Moreover, we propose generalizations and modifications to the used formulations:

- In Sect. 3.2 we present a data term which allows for thin layers of semantic classes without the additional complexity of ray potentials [29,30]. The idea is to represent parts of the input data in the regularization term, instead of fully representing the data cost as unary terms as proposed in [15].
- The implicit normal direction based shape prior, discretizes the normals regularly over all directions. However, often the training data locally suggest just one single or very few predominant directions with little variation. We propose to detect and exploit this for a more efficient formulation, as explained in Sect. 3.3.

1.3 Overview

Figure 1 illustrates our reconstruction pipeline. In the training part of the method, we train an image based semantic classifier and the volumetric shape prior. From the input images camera poses and depth maps are computed through structure from motion and subsequent dense matching. For each of the images pixel-wise semantic likelihoods are obtained by running the trained semantic classifier. An approximate alignment of the input data to the shape prior is based on detecting landmarks around the eyes, nose and mouth in the input data. The core of our method is an optimization with respect to both the geometry and the alignment.

2 Optimization Problem

Our method is based on a volumetric multi-label problem, formulated as a convex optimization that does usually not include an alignment. We propose to include the alignment into the formulation leading to an energy which is convex with respect to the labeling and non-convex with respect to the alignment. The actual choices for the unary cost and the regularization term will be detailed in Sect. 3, they are based on pixel-wise semantic classifications and depth maps.

Mathematically, we have a voxel space Ω, understood as discretization of a subset of $\mathbb{R}^3$. Each voxel gets assigned a label $\ell \in \mathcal{L}$. Indicator variables $x_s^i \in [0,1]$, indicate if label i is assigned at voxel s. In addition to the original formulation, we propose to include a similarity transform $\mathcal{T}$ into the optimization problem. The transform $\mathcal{T} : \mathbb{R}^3 \to \mathbb{R}^3$, is defined as $y \mapsto \alpha R y + t$, with a positive scaling factor $\alpha > 0$, a rotation matrix R and a translation vector t.

$$E(\mathbf{x}, \mathcal{T}) = \sum_{s \in \Omega} \left(\sum_i \rho_s^i(\mathcal{T}) x_s^i + \frac{1}{\alpha^2} \sum_{i,j:i<j} \phi_s^{ij}(\mathcal{T}, x_s^{ij} - x_s^{ji}) \right) \tag{1}$$

$$\text{s. t. } x_s^i = \sum_j (x_s^{ij})_k, \quad x_s^i = \sum_j (x_{s-e_k}^{ji})_k, \quad \sum_i x_s^i = 1, \quad x_s^i \geq 0, \quad x_s^{ij} \geq 0.$$

Next, we intuitively explain the meaning of the formulation. A thorough derivation of the basic formulation without the alignment is given in [38]. The first
line defines the objective of the minimization problem. It is split into two parts:
the unary term and the regularization term. The values $\rho_s^i(\mathcal{T})$ define the cost for
assigning a label i to a voxel s. The second part is a spatially varying anisotropic
regularization term $\phi_s^{ij}(\cdot, \cdot) \to \mathbb{R}^+$, which is derived in the continuum and discretized afterwards [9]. It assigns a cost to a surface between labels i and j in
voxel s with a surface normal pointing into the direction of $x_s^{ij} - x_s^{ji} \in [-1, 1]^3$.
The functions $\phi_s^{ij}(\cdot, \cdot)$ need to be convex and positively 1-homogeneous in their
second argument. The variables $x_s^{ij} \in [0, 1]^3$ describe how much the assignment
of label i changes to label j in the direction in which they point. In order to
allow for arbitrary convex non-metric smoothness terms the x_s^{ij} need to be non-
negative, which limits the possible directions they can point to. This is resolved
by using $x_s^{ij} - x_s^{ji}$, which allows for arbitrary directions, for details see [38]. The
first two constraints, are called marginalization constraints. They connect the x_s^i
and x_s^{ij} variables. k indexes the components of the vector and e_k denotes the k-th
canonical basis vector, i.e. $e_1 = (1, 0, 0)^T$. Intuitively, these constraints describe
that if label i is assigned to voxel s and label j in a neighboring voxel then the
x_s^{ij} variables need to reflect such a transition. Next, the normalization constraint
enforces that one label is assigned. Finally, all the x_s need to be non-negative.

As mentioned above we included the similarity transform $\mathcal{T}$ into the original
convex multi-label formulation. $\mathcal{T}$ transforms the input data into the coordinate
frame of the shape prior. The smoothness term is dependent on the transformation $\mathcal{T}$ because it includes parts of the data cost. The normalization of the
smoothness term with respect to α^2 ensures that a change in scaling does not
change the cost of the surface. This is crucial for the optimization of the alignment as we will see in Sect. 4.1.

3   Choices for ρ and ϕ

The key difficulty that needs to be tackled, when defining the unary cost and the
regularization term, is thin layers of semantic classes such as eyebrows in front
of the skin. It has already been pointed out in [29,30] that this is problematic
when using the data term of [15] (c.f. Fig. 2). The solution given in [29,30] is a
formulation which represents the dataterm as a potential over viewing rays. They
propose a purely discrete graph-based scheme [30] and a continuous (variational)
formulation [29]. Both versions introduce the additional complexity that also the
assignment to additional per-voxel variables for each viewing ray that crosses a
specific voxel needs to be determined during the optimization, which makes the
optimization problem much more complex. This can be resolved using a coarse-
to fine scheme in the discrete setting but remains a problem for the continuous
setting. To this end, we propose an alternative representation in the continuous
setting which does not add any additional variables. Our solution can be seen as
an alternative to ray potentials in cases where the only feature that is needed is
the representation of thin layers of semantic classes.

Fig. 2. Unary term for a ray going through the eyebrow next to the skin layer of an example reconstruction (Left) data term of [15]. (Right) our proposed data term. Both sides illustrate the weight added to the voxels along the ray for the class eyebrow by the unary term. (Left) The per-pixel semantic cost σ, is entered into the last voxel of the uncertainty region. In this case eyebrow is visible in the image but the weight ends up inside the skin layer due to the very little thickness of the semantic class eyebrow, which leads to artifacts in the reconstruction. (Right) in our proposed data term the weight σ is moved to the regularization term. The unary term only captures the geometric information about free and occupied space. This resolves the artifacts in the reconstruction.

3.1 Unary Term

We only include the information from the depth maps in the per voxel unary term and represent the likelihood of the semantic class in the surface regularization term. The rationale behind this is the following. The semantic classifier only gives a likelihood for which semantic label should be closest to the camera along the ray, but not where along the ray this transition from free space to occupied space happens. The depth measurement roughly tells us the region where we expect the transition. If we now decrease the smoothness cost of a transition from free space to the desired semantic label in that region, then our formulation prefers to place the observed semantic class as the transition from free to occupied space but does not affect a potential additional transition from one semantic label to another one just behind it (c.f. Fig. 2).

The unary cost $\rho_s^i(\mathcal{T})$ contains the information from the depth maps. There is one free space label $i = 0$ and several occupied space labels $i > 0$. Therefore, we have $\rho_s^i(\mathcal{T}):=\rho_s(\mathcal{T})$, $\forall i > 0$ and $\rho_s^0(\mathcal{T}):=0$. We denote the non-zero unary cost that a single depth map contributes to voxel s by $\rho_s(\mathcal{T})'$, the complete unary cost is formed by summing over all the depth maps. Further, z_s is the depth of voxel s and $\hat{z}_s(\mathcal{T})$ is the depth at the depth map position to which the voxel s projects to with the alignment transformation $\mathcal{T}$. Using the assumption that in front of an observed depth we expect *free space* in a region γ and behind the observed depth *occupied space*, we set the unary cost to

$$\rho_s(\mathcal{T})' = \begin{cases} \beta & \text{if } z_s - \hat{z}_s(\mathcal{T}) \in [0, \gamma] \\ -\beta & \text{if } z_s - \hat{z}_s(\mathcal{T}) \in [-\gamma, 0). \end{cases} \tag{2}$$

3.2 Data Dependent Regularization Term

The regularization term $\phi_s^{ij}(\mathcal{T}, n)$ describes the cost of a transition between label i and j with normal direction n. We derive our novel regularization term based on the underlying probabilities. $\leftrightarrow_s$ denotes that there is a surface at location s, $\leftrightarrow_s^{ij}$ denotes the existence of a surface between label i and j at location s and n_s^{ij} indicates that a surface with normal n between label i and j is present at location s. Finally, we denote the per pixel knowledge about the semantic labels as Γ and also need a dependency on the alignment transformation $\mathcal{T}$. We start by stating the probability of a surface element as

$$P(n_s^{ij}|\mathcal{T},\Gamma) := P(n_s^{ij}|\leftrightarrow_s^{ij})P(\leftrightarrow_s^{ij}|\leftrightarrow_s,\mathcal{T},\Gamma)P(\leftrightarrow_s). \qquad (3)$$

The probability is modeled as a Bayesian network and factored into three parts. The rightmost term $P(\leftrightarrow_s)$ captures the probability of observing a surface at voxel s. $P(\leftrightarrow_s^{ij}|\leftrightarrow_s,\mathcal{T},\Gamma)$ is the probability to have a surface between two specific labels i and j given there is a surface. This part includes the knowledge about the per pixel semantic labels Γ in the input images and hence is dependent on the alignment $\mathcal{T}$. $P(n_s^{ij}|\leftrightarrow_s^{ij})$ takes into account the surface orientation and is essentially capturing the implicit normal direction based shape prior. In the following we will explain how we approximate the above model in our energy formulation. To simplify the notation for the rest of this section we will consider the alignment $\mathcal{T}$ to be fixed and drop it from the equations. The mathematical formulation [38] allows any convex positively 1-homogeneous function as function $\phi_s^{ij}(\cdot)$. To find a function which fulfills these properties and approximates the above model well, we rewrite it in its dual form in terms of a Wulff shape [9]. Every convex positively 1-homogeneous function can be written as

$$\phi_s^{ij}(x) = \max_{p \in \mathcal{W}_s^{ij}} \{p^T x\}. \qquad (4)$$

$\mathcal{W}_s^{ij}$ is the Wulff shape. It defines the regularizer and can be any closed convex shape which contains the origin. Any convex shape can be written as intersection of half spaces. [14] proposes to use a discrete set of normal directions $n \in \mathcal{S} \subset \mathbb{S}^2$ to form a discretized Wulff shape $\mathcal{W}_{\mathcal{H}_s^{ij}}$ by intersecting the half spaces $h_s^{n,ij} \in \mathcal{H}_s^{ij}$. The distance of the half space boundary to the origin at voxel s with normal n for the boundary between i and j is denoted as $d_s^{n,ij}$. Looking at the probabilistic meaning of the energy formulation and assuming all the half spaces $\mathcal{H}_s^{ij}$ share a boundary with $\mathcal{W}_{\mathcal{H}_s^{ij}}$, it follows that

$$P(n_s^{ij}|\Gamma) = \exp\left(-\phi_s^{ij}(n_s^{ij})\right) = \exp\left(-\max_{p \in \mathcal{W}_{\mathcal{H}_s^{ij}}}(p^T n_s^{ij})\right) = \exp\left(-d_s^{n,ij}\right) \qquad (5)$$

and hence using the model of Eq. 3 leads to

$$d_s^{n,ij} := -\log(P(n_s^{ij}|\leftrightarrow_s^{ij})) - \log(P(\leftrightarrow_s^{ij}|\leftrightarrow_s,\Gamma)) - \log(P(\leftrightarrow_s)). \qquad (6)$$

The resulting Wulff shape is a convex approximation to the original probability model. In cases where the assumption that all the half spaces $\mathcal{H}_s^{ij}$ share a boundary with $\mathcal{W}_{\mathcal{H}_s^{ij}}$ does not hold, the cost of unlikely transitions can be underestimated. However, for the most likely directions and hence most relevant directions the approximation will model the true likelihood exactly (c.f. [14]).

In order to use Eq. 6 we also need to approximate the probabilities. $P(n_s^{ij}|\leftrightarrow_s^{ij})$ is estimated from training data, given as a collection of surface meshes, by building a histogram over the training data's normals [14]. The term $P(\leftrightarrow_s^{ij}|\leftrightarrow_s, \mathcal{T}, \Gamma)$ is dependent on the input data and hence changes with the per image classifications Γ and the alignment $\mathcal{T}$. Computing the convex shape as the intersection of the half spaces is computationally demanding (computation of a 3D convex hull on the dual points using point plane duality [25]). Directly inserting the above term would require such a computation whenever the alignment changes. Hence, we want to only do this during the training of the shape prior. To achieve this, we follow the often used approach of weighting the regularization term by the input data.

We fix the structure of the Wulff shape at the training stage by dropping the dependence on the input data. To bring the lost information back to the model we scale the Wulff shape with a weight w_s^{ij}, giving an approximation of Eq. 6:

$$\tilde{d}_s^{n,ij} := w_s^{ij}(\mathcal{T}, \Gamma)\left(-\log(P(n_s^{ij}|\leftrightarrow_s^{ij})) - \log(P(\leftrightarrow_s^{ij}|\leftrightarrow_s)) - \log(P(\leftrightarrow_s))\right). \quad (7)$$

This is in analogy to, image segmentation, where often the regularization term is weighted by the input image gradient magnitude.

3.3 Training Data Dependent Parametrization of the Wulff Shapes

A disadvantage of the discretized Wulff shape approach is that a complex Wulff shape composed of the intersection of many half spaces needs to be stored for all the voxels which contained training data (for the other voxels a strong isotropic cost is used). However, often most of the training data normals point in a very similar direction and therefore it is not necessary to store such a complex Wulff shape. To this end, we propose to cluster the input training data and whenever all the training normals lie in up to three clusters we replace them with a surrogate Wulff shape which serves as a faithful approximation (c.f. Fig. 3). For multiple clusters the intersection of multiple surrogate Wulff shapes is used. Using a soft clustering where 95 % of the normals closest to the cluster center with a maximal deviation of 10° are considered, we obtained 74.6 % of voxels with 1 cluster, 10.6 % with 2 clusters and 6.3 % with 3 clusters. Note, that in these cases we do not need to compute a Wulff shape based on half spaces and

1 cluster
2 clusters
3 clusters
General Wulff shape

Fig. 3. (Left) 2D illustration of a discretized Wulff shape, where all the training data lies close to a single direction. (Middle) our approximation of the general shape with a surrogate parametric Wulff shape composed out of a spherical sector with an attached spherical cap. (Right) Slice through the volumetric shape prior that indicates the type of Wulff shape used at each place.

hence can directly fit the surrogate Wulff shape into the original training data, which circumvents the discretization of the directions (see supplementary material for more details). Furthermore, when using the prosed clustering approach the memory requirements are reduced by a factor of 3.75 in our implementation.

4   Optimization

The critical part in most algorithms exploiting shape priors is to establish the correspondence between the input data and the shape prior. One of our main contributions is to equip [14] with an automatic alignment procedure. Our optimization strategy alternates between optimizing for the geometry and optimizing for the alignment. The geometry is optimized first, therefore an initialization for the alignment needs to be determined beforehand. We follow the often used strategy of detecting landmark positions, such as points around the eyes and nose. Determining these positions in multiple images allows us to get an estimate of the head pose [7, 10]. There is no direct correspondence between the triangulated landmark positions and the implicit volumetric shape prior, as the shape prior is based on many training shapes, and hence the landmark positions end up at slightly different positions in the volume. Our shape prior is trained from shapes that are sampled from a statistical shape model. Therefore, we register the triangulated landmark positions to the ones of the mean shape of the statistical model.

4.1   Optimization with Respect to the Alignment

The energy from Eq. 1 is convex in the variables $\mathbf{x}$, which describe the geometry and labeling, but it is non-convex in the alignment $\mathcal{T}$. It is important to note that for the alignment, only the observed geometry can be used. This means surfaces which are purely filled in by the prior should ideally not be taken into account for the alignment. This can be surfaces which are simply not observable in the input data such as a transition between hair and skin or areas which are filled in by the prior where data is missing. Taking all this into account is important to get a good alignment that can be robustly inferred.

Before we further discuss the optimization we detail the rationale behind the way the alignment transformation is introduced into the formulation. Generally, there are two different ways for defining the alignment, either the input data is at a fixed position and the shape prior gets transformed or the shape prior is at a fixed position and the input data gets transformed. The former one has the disadvantage that the shape prior would not be fixed and hence would need to be adapted for different alignments, by either recomputing or interpolating. Both of these choices add additional computational effort. Therefore, we keep the shape prior at a fixed position and align the input data into the volume of the prior. In this way only the unary cost of the energy and the scaling factors of the data dependent regularization need to be adjusted when the alignment changes. This can be done very efficiently on the GPU in a few seconds by re-evaluating the per voxel data costs using the new alignment transformation. For the alignment with respect to the scaling factor α we need to ensure that a rescaling does not change the energy proportionally to the surface area. Otherwise, the optimization would just try to shrink the object to a reconstruction with 0 surface area and hence no regularization cost. Therefore we normalize the smoothness term with respect to the scaling factor α. In the following derivation we will see that this factor cancels out from the optimization with respect to the alignment.

Given that the convex optimization algorithm which is commonly used to optimize the continuously inspired multi-label assignment problems, the first order primal-dual algorithm [24], essentially executes gradient descent and ascent steps with subsequent proximity operations, it would be tempting to include additional gradient steps in each iteration that account for the alignment. However, this comes with problems and disadvantages. The optimization of the alignment would be an additional update over the volume, we argue that the alignment can be optimized on a surface level and hence more efficiently. Besides the gradient steps that would need to be executed over the volume, a change in alignment also means that the data cost changes due to the dependence on the alignment transformation T and hence would need to be re-evaluated for the whole volume in each iteration. Additionally, including the alignment update in this straight forward manner would mean that the convergence guarantees that the convex optimization algorithm offers are lost. Therefore, we propose an optimization strategy that addresses these issues by alternating between optimizing for the geometry and aligning the reconstructed surface to the prior.

For the alignment we only take into account the meaningful surfaces, namely the ones which are visible and hence originate from a transition between *free space* and *occupied space*. To avoid bad local minima, we execute the alignment before full convergence and only take into account surfaces which are already present by thresholding the magnitude of the transition gradient x_s^{ij}. We ran an experiment where we optimize for the alignment every 25, 50, 100, 250 and 500 iterations and then measure the distance to the mean shape of the statistical model to evaluate the alignment quality. As shown in Fig. 4 the alignment converges quickly when the alignment is performed often, the longer the interval between the alignments the slower the convergence. If the alignment is performed after many iterations the optimization gets stuck in a bad extremal point. Please note that the geometry at every alignment step is different and therefore the average distance for a better alignment can be higher when more geometry is reconstructed. With these points in mind, we propose to already run the alignment as soon as some geometry is reconstructed and only let the reconstruction converge once the alignment does not change any more. To additionally make the alignment more robust we start the reconstruction with a weak shape prior which only captures the strongest features of the shape and gradually change the prior after each alternation to the desired one for the reconstruction. When directly starting with the final shape prior the experiment given in Fig. 4(a) does not manage to find the right alignment in 3 out of the 5 runs. Taking into account all this leads to an algorithm which robustly finds an accurate alignment

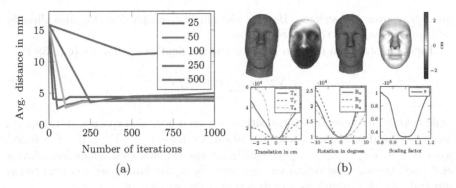

(a)   (b)

Fig. 4. (a) Plot of average distance from mean face for different alignment intervals during the optimization. The optimized model is aligned every 25, 50, 100, 250 and 500 iterations for a total of 1000 iterations. (b) Alignment to the shape prior as described in Sect. 4.1. Top: Visualization of signed alignment error in centimetres. From left to right: face before alignment, error visualization on mean face before alignment, aligned face, error visualization on mean face after alignment. Bottom: Energy function plot of translation, rotation and scale components of seven degree of freedom alignment.

between the input data and the shape prior fully automatically starting from an initial rough estimate of the alignment. Next, we detail our alignment with respect to the surface.

Recall that label 0 denotes free space and labels $i > 0$ occupied space labels (skin, hair, beard, eyebrows and clothing, respectively). The goal is to minimize energy Eq. 1 with respect to the alignment $\mathcal{T}$ but only taking into account visible surfaces, e.g. occupied space $\leftrightarrow$ free space transitions. We observe that as soon as we keep the reconstruction fixed, meaning the function that maps given input data to the reconstruction, a change in the alignment transformation $\mathcal{T}$ transforms the input data and hence also the solution for the x_s^i and x_s^{ij} with the same transformation. To make this dependency explicit in the notation we write $\tilde{x}_s^i(\mathcal{T})$ and $\tilde{x}_s^{ij}(\mathcal{T})$, to denote the assignments for the x_s^i and x_s^{ij} that we get for a fixed reconstruction under the alignment transformation $\mathcal{T}$. In terms of energy this means that the unary term is constant under a change of the alignment transformation $\mathcal{T}$ (note that here we ignore the effects of the discretization, which also agrees with the continuous origin of the formulation). The remaining energy for the alignment optimization step reads as

$$E(\mathcal{T}) = \sum_{s \in \Omega, i > 0} \frac{1}{\alpha^2} \phi_s^{0,i}(\mathcal{T}, \tilde{x}_s^{0,i}(\mathcal{T}) - \tilde{x}_s^{i,0}(\mathcal{T})). \tag{8}$$

Besides the dependency of the fixed reconstruction on $\mathcal{T}$ also the smoothness term $\phi_s^{0,i}$ is dependent on $\mathcal{T}$. This is due to the semantic part of the data cost which is included in the smoothness term. For the alignment this is not of big importance as its influence is minimal and it does not add significant complexity to the optimization. In the following we will transform the above energy as an energy over the surface. Besides the smaller complexity this also directly addresses issues with the discretization.

First, we state the relation between the gradient of x_s^i and x_s^{ij} (c.f. [38]):

$$\nabla x_s^i = \sum_j x_s^{ji} - x_s^{ij}. \tag{9}$$

Only taking into account the transitions between occupied space and free space, and ignoring discretization and relaxation, we have $x_s^{ji} = x_s^{ij} = 0$, $\forall j > 0$ and we arrive at $\nabla x_s^i = x_s^{0,i} - x_s^{i,0}$. Considering the original continuous formulation and again ignoring the relaxation, meaning the x_s^i are binary, we can rewrite the integral over the volume as an integral over the surface [9]

$$E(\mathcal{T}) = \int_\Omega \frac{1}{\alpha^2} \phi_s^{0,i}(\mathcal{T}, \nabla \tilde{x}_s^i(\mathcal{T})) ds = \int_{\partial \mathcal{F}^i} \frac{1}{\alpha^2} \phi_s^{0,i}(\mathcal{T}, n_s^i(\mathcal{T})) dA, \tag{10}$$

with n_s^i a unit length normal direction on the boundary between free space and label i ($\partial \mathcal{F}^i = \{s : x_s^{0,i} - x_s^{i,0} > 0\}$) at position s. This relation enables us to define the surface regularization in terms of the volume on the left hand side and in terms of an integral over the surface on the right hand side.

Before we explain the alignment over the discrete surface we need to make a remark on how to extract it from the volume. The surface cannot be extracted through thresholding the x_s^i because the entire information about the surface normal direction would get lost. To preserve the surface orientation accurately it is common to extract the surface using marching cubes [21] directly on the non-thresholded x_s^i variables. The output of marching cubes is a triangular mesh representing the surface. We denote the set of all triangles of occupied label i by $\mathbb{T}^i$. The triangle normal and surface area are denoted by $n_t^i(\mathcal{T})$ and $A_t^i(\mathcal{T})$, respectively. The transformation $\mathcal{T}$ also maps the triangle t to a position s in the volume. In the continuous setting this would mean the smoothness term varies at different positions on the triangle. However in practice the smoothness term is only defined on a discrete voxel grid, therefore we use a single constant smoothness term for each triangle which is extracted from the volumetric shape prior by trilinearly interpolating the smoothness cost of the neighboring voxels to the centroid of the triangle. We denote this term by $\phi_t^i(\mathcal{T}, n_t^i(\mathcal{T}))$. Finally, we state the regularization term in its surface formulation over the triangle mesh:

$$E_{\text{mesh}}(\mathcal{T}) = \sum_{i:i>0,t\in\mathbb{T}^i} \phi_t^i(\mathcal{T}, n_t^i(\mathcal{T})) \frac{A_t^i(\mathcal{T})}{\alpha^2} = \sum_{i:i>0,t\in\mathbb{T}^i} \phi_t^i(\mathcal{T}, n_t^i(\mathcal{T})) A_t^i(\mathcal{I}). \tag{11}$$

In the second equation we used that a transformation $\mathcal{T}$ changes the surface area with the square of the scaling factor α. By inserting the identity transformation $\mathcal{I}$, the term α^2 cancels out from the fraction. Leading to the desired property that the alignement part of the energy is independent from the surface area.

For minimizing Eq. 11, we use the gradient descent based, L-BFGS line search approach, implemented in the Ceres solver [1]. In order to start with a weak shape prior which gradually gets stronger, the prior is weakened by increasing $-\log P(\leftrightarrow_s)$

by a constant and scaling the data term. This corresponds to adding non-informative random training data to all voxels.

We present a qualitative and quantitative evaluation of the alignment in Fig. 4(b). The first part shows the signed distance to the mean face before and after refinement of the initial coarse alignment. We recover translation, rotation and scale parameters that lead to a very satisfactory alignment. The mean face used as a reference for the evaluation is close to the location of the best alignment due to the fact that all head models in the shape prior have been aligned to the mean shape. The second part shows plots of our alignment energy. To this end, we took a fixed geometry and plot the energy with respect to the seven dimensions of the similarity transform. We observe that for each of the dimensions the energy has one single local minimum and looks very smooth. It is important to note that we can easily handle translations of 2.5 cm, rotations of 10 degrees in yaw, pitch and roll and scale variations of 20 %. Typical errors of landmark detectors lie well within those bounds [10].

5   Experimental Evaluation

Our input data are images of faces captured using a mobile phone or a compact camera. The typical dataset size is between 15 and 100 images, with a resolution of 640×480 pixels. This is depending on whether only frontal images are taken by the person her- or himself or another person is taking pictures all around.

We use two sets of training data. To train the shape prior we use geometric models of heads. This data is derived by randomly sampling 100 human heads from the statistical model of [23]. To train an image based semantic classifier we labeled 80 training images (labels: skin, hair, eyebrows, eyes, beard, clothing and background). We only used the beard label for persons wearing a beard. The eye label is only used to filter the depth maps which are typically unreliable in the eye region (these are often non-rigid during capture, e.g. tracking the camera). We trained a per-pixel semantic classifier using the publicly available code from [19]. The camera poses are estimated using structure-from-motion [32,35] using SIFT features from [33]. The depth maps are computed with the publicly available plane-sweeping stereo matching implementation [13]. We use the landmark detector of [28] and our optimization is implemented in C++.

We present our results in Fig. 5. For more datasets and additional comparisons (patch-based multi view stereo [11] + Poisson surface reconstruction [18]) we refer the reader to the supplementary material. We compare our reconstructions to a state-of-the-art depth map fusion method and a state-of-the-art method for fitting statistical shape models. In the depth map fusion comparison we fuse the depth maps with the TV-Flux fusion from [36], which in our implementation corresponds to regularizing the same unary term that we are using for our multi-label reconstructions with a total variation (TV) prior. In the statistical shape model comparison we fit the model of [23] into our raw input data (depth maps and semantic labels). This leads to a reconstruction of the skin label only. Our proposed approach computes a full semantically annotated reconstruction of the head. Both shape prior formulations manage to overcome the defects

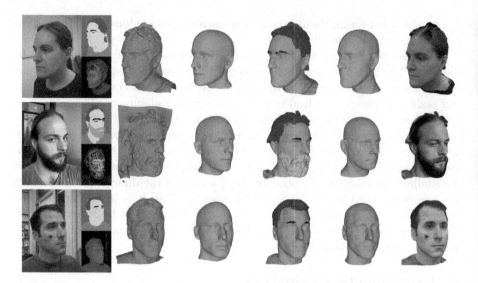

Fig. 5. From left to right: Input image; Input labels and depth; Depth map fusion (TV-Flux fusion from [36]); Statistical model of [23] fitted into our raw input data; Our semantic reconstruction; Our result *skin* class; Our model textured.

in the shapes of the observed geometry. The mole (simulated with a raisin) on the cheek of the person in the last row of Fig. 5 cannot be captured with the low dimensional shape model of [23], therefore it is completely invisible in the respective result. Using our method the mole gets correctly reconstructed even tough such shape details are not represented in the shape prior. One of the key advantages of the implicit shape prior over fitting a low dimensional statistical shape model, is that a deviation from the prior is possible if the data suggests it. In terms of semantic segmentation we are able to fuse the per image semantic classifications, which might be inconsistent in different images, to one single semantic segmentation which is consistent over the whole dataset. Additionally, the semantic segmentation is directly attached to the geometry. In summary, our method is able to reconstruct shape details, at the same time utilizes a strong shape prior for ambiguous input data, recovers hidden surfaces, and extracts one single consistent semantic segmentation for the whole dataset.

6   Conclusion

In this work we introduced a system that fully automatically computes a semantic 3D reconstruction of heads from images. The key novelty of the system is a fully automatic alignment of the shape prior to the input data. Our system reconstructs multiple semantic classes such as skin, hair, beard, clothing, and even handles thin layers of semantic classes such as eyebrows. We demonstrate the applicability of our method to challenging real-world data taken in uncontrolled environments. In future work, we plan to include the capability to handle glasses, potentially using connectivity priors [31]. Further generalizing the alignment to a non rigid transform to a space closer to the mean shape of a statistical shape model might lead to stronger implicit shape priors which are able to hallucinate more complex surfaces than the skin underneath the hair.

Acknowledgment. This project is supported by Grant 16703.1 PFES-ES of CTI Switzerland and the Swiss National Science Foundation under Project Nr. 143422.

References

1. Agarwal, S., Mierle, K., Others: Ceres solver. http://ceres-solver.org
2. Beeler, T., Bickel, B., Beardsley, P., Sumner, B., Gross, M.: High-quality single-shot capture of facial geometry. ACM Trans. Graph. (ToG) **29**(4), 40 (2010)
3. Beeler, T., Bickel, B., Noris, G., Marschner, S., Beardsley, P., Sumner, R.W., Gross, M.: Coupled 3D reconstruction of sparse facial hair and skin. ACM Trans. Graph. (ToG) **31**(4), 117 (2012)
4. Brunton, A., Salazar, A., Bolkart, T., Wuhrer, S.: Review of statistical shape spaces for 3D data with comparative analysis for human faces. Comput. Vis. Image Underst. (CVIU) **128**, 1–17 (2014)
5. Chambolle, A., Cremers, D., Pock, T.: A convex approach to minimal partitions. SIAM J. Imaging Sci. **5**(4), 1113–1158 (2012)
6. Curless, B., Levoy, M.: A volumetric method for building complex models from range images. In: International Conference on Computer graphics and interactive techniques (SIGGRAPH) (1996)
7. Dame, A., Prisacariu, V.A., Ren, C.Y., Reid, I.: Dense reconstruction using 3D object shape priors. In: Conference on Computer Vision and Pattern Recognition (CVPR) (2013)
8. Echevarria, J.I., Bradley, D., Gutierrez, D., Beeler, T.: Capturing and stylizing hair for 3D fabrication. ACM Trans. Graphics (ToG) **33**(4), 125 (2014)
9. Esedoglu, S., Osher, S.J.: Decomposition of images by the anisotropic Rudin-Osher-Fatemi model. Commun. Pure Appl. Math. **57**(12), 1609–1626 (2004)
10. Fanelli, G., Dantone, M., Gall, J., Fossati, A., Van Gool, L.: Random forests for real time 3D face analysis. Int. J. Comput. Vis. (IJCV) **101**(3), 437–458 (2013)
11. Furukawa, Y., Ponce, J.: Accurate, dense, and robust multi-view stereopsis. IEEE Trans. Pattern Anal. Mach. Intell. (TPAMI) **32**(8), 1362–1376 (2010)
12. Garrido, P., Valgaerts, L., Wu, C., Theobalt, C.: Reconstructing detailed dynamic face geometry from monocular video. ACM Trans. Graph. (ToG) **32**(6), 158 (2013)
13. Häne, C., Heng, L., Lee, G.H., Sizov, A., Pollefeys, M.: Real-time direct dense matching on fisheye images using plane-sweeping stereo. In: International Conference on 3D Vision (3DV) (2014)
14. Häne, C., Savinov, N., Pollefeys, M.: Class specific 3D object shape priors using surface normals. In: IEEE Conference on Computer Vision and Pattern Recognition (CVPR) (2014)
15. Häne, C., Zach, C., Cohen, A., Angst, R., Pollefeys, M.: Joint 3D scene reconstruction and class segmentation. In: IEEE Conference on Computer Vision and Pattern Recognition (CVPR) (2013)
16. Ichim, A.E., Bouaziz, S., Pauly, M.: Dynamic 3D avatar creation from hand-held video input. ACM Trans. Graph. (ToG) **34**(4), 45 (2015)

17. Jourabloo, A., Liu, X.: Pose-invariant 3D face alignment. In: International Conference on Computer Vision (ICCV) (2015)
18. Kazhdan, M., Bolitho, M., Hoppe, H.: Poisson surface reconstruction. In: Eurographics Symposium on Geometry Processing (SGP) (2006)
19. Ladicky, L., Russell, C., Kohli, P., Torr, P.H.: Associative hierarchical random fields. IEEE Trans. Pattern Anal. Mach. Intell. (TPAMI) 36(6), 1056–1077 (2014)
20. Lempitsky, V., Boykov, Y.: Global optimization for shape fitting (2007)
21. Lorensen, W.E., Cline, H.E.: Marching cubes: a high resolution 3D surface construction algorithm. In: Conference on Computer Graphics and Interactive Techniques (SIGGRAPH) (1987)
22. Luo, L., Li, H., Paris, S., Weise, T., Pauly, M., Rusinkiewicz, S.: Multi-view hair capture using orientation fields. In: Conference on Computer Vision and Pattern Recognition (CVPR) (2012)
23. Paysan, P., Knothe, R., Amberg, B., Romdhani, S., Vetter, T.: A 3D face model for pose and illumination invariant face recognition (2009)
24. Pock, T., Chambolle, A.: Diagonal preconditioning for first order primal-dual algorithms in convex optimization. In: International Conference on Computer Vision (ICCV) (2011)
25. Preparata, F.P., Shamos, M.: Computational Geometry: An Introduction. Springer, New York (1985)
26. Prisacariu, V.A., Segal, A.V., Reid, I.: Simultaneous monocular 2D segmentation, 3D pose recovery and 3D reconstruction. In: Lee, K.M., Matsushita, Y., Rehg, J.M., Hu, Z. (eds.) ACCV 2012, Part I. LNCS, vol. 7724, pp. 593–606. Springer, Heidelberg (2013)
27. Ren, S., Cao, X., Wei, Y., Sun, J.: Face alignment at 3000 FPS via regressing local binary features. In: IEEE Conference on Computer Vision and Pattern Recognition (CVPR) (2014)
28. Saragih, J.M., Lucey, S., Cohn, J.F.: Deformable model fitting by regularized landmark mean-shift. Int. J. Comput. Vis. (IJCV) 91(2), 200–215 (2011)
29. Savinov, N., Häne, C., Ladicky, L., Pollefeys, M.: Semantic 3D reconstruction with continuous regularization and ray potentials using a visibility consistency constraint. In: Conference on Computer Vision and Pattern Recognition (CVPR) (2016)
30. Savinov, N., Ladicky, L., Häne, C., Pollefeys, M.: Discrete optimization of ray potentials for semantic 3D reconstruction. In: Conference on Computer Vision and Pattern Recognition (CVPR) (2015)
31. Stühmer, J., Schröder, P., Cremers, D.: Tree shape priors with connectivity constraints using convex relaxation on general graphs. In: International Conference on Computer Vision Proceedings (ICCV) (2013)
32. Tanskanen, P., Kolev, K., Meier, L., Camposeco, F., Saurer, O., Pollefeys, M.: Live metric 3D reconstruction on mobile phones. In: International Conference on Computer Vision (ICCV) (2013)
33. Vedaldi, A., Fulkerson, B.: VLFeat: an open and portable library of computer vision algorithms (2008). http://www.vlfeat.org/
34. Wei, Y., Ofek, E., Quan, L., Shum, H.Y.: Modeling hair from multiple views. ACM Trans. Graphics (TOG) 24(3), 816–820 (2005)
35. Wu, C.: VisualSFM: a visual structure from motion system (2011). http://ccwu.me/vsfm/
36. Zach, C.: Fast and high quality fusion of depth maps. In: International Symposium on 3D Data Processing, Visualization and Transmission (3DPVT) (2008)

37. Zach, C., Häne, C., Pollefeys, M.: What is optimized in tight convex relaxations for multi-label problems? In: IEEE Conference on Computer Vision and Pattern Recognition (CVPR) (2012)
38. Zach, C., Häne, C., Pollefeys, M.: What is optimized in convex relaxations for multilabel problems: Connecting discrete and continuously inspired map inference. IEEE Trans. Pattern Anal. Mach. Intell. (TPAMI) 36(1), 157–170 (2014)

Human Attribute Recognition
by Deep Hierarchical Contexts

Yining Li$^{(\boxtimes)}$, Chen Huang, Chen Change Loy, and Xiaoou Tang

Department of Information Engineering, The Chinese University
of Hong Kong, Hong Kong, China
{ly015,chuang,ccloy,xtang}@ie.cuhk.edu.hk

Abstract. We present an approach for recognizing human attributes in unconstrained settings. We train a Convolutional Neural Network (CNN) to select the most attribute-descriptive human parts from all poselet detections, and combine them with the whole body as a pose-normalized deep representation. We further improve by using *deep hierarchical contexts* ranging from human-centric level to scene level. Human-centric context captures human relations, which we compute from the nearest neighbor parts of other people on a pyramid of CNN feature maps. The matched parts are then average pooled and they act as a similarity regularization. To utilize the scene context, we re-score human-centric predictions by the global scene classification score jointly learned in our CNN, yielding final scene-aware predictions. To facilitate our study, a large-scale WIDER Attribute dataset(Dataset URL: http://mmlab.ie.cuhk.edu.hk/projects/WIDERAttribute) is introduced with human attribute and image event annotations, and our method surpasses competitive baselines on this dataset and other popular ones.

1 Introduction

Accurate recognition of human attributes such as gender and clothing style can benefit many applications such as person re-identification [1–4] in videos. However, this task still remains challenging in unconstrained settings where images of people exhibit large variation of viewpoint, pose, illumination and occlusion. Consider, for example, Fig. 1 where inferring the attributes "formal suits" and "sunglasses" from only the target person is very difficult, due to the occlusion and low image quality respectively. Fortunately, we have access to the *hierarchical* contexts—from the neighboring similar people to the global image scene wherein the target person appears. Leveraging such contextual cues makes attributes much more recognizable, *e.g.* being aware of a funeral event, we would be more confident about people wearing "formal suits". We build on this intuition to develop a robust method for unconstrained human attribute recognition.

Electronic supplementary material The online version of this chapter (doi:10.1007/978-3-319-46466-4_41) contains supplementary material, which is available to authorized users.

B. Leibe et al. (Eds.): ECCV 2016, Part VI, LNCS 9910, pp. 684–700, 2016.
DOI: 10.1007/978-3-319-46466-4_41

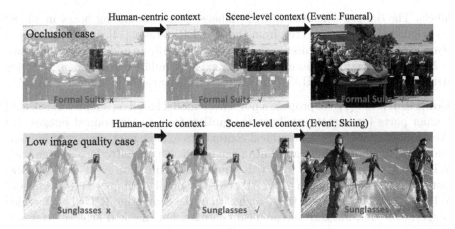

Fig. 1. WIDER Attribute - example images to motivate the use of hierarchical contexts for robust attribute recognition for the target person (red box): the human-centric context and scene-level context help resolve visual ambiguities due to occlusion and low image quality (low resolution/blurring). (Color figure online)

Our method is inspired by recent attribute models using parts, such as Poselets [5], Deformable Part Model (DPM) [6] and window-specific parts [7]. These methods are robust against pose and viewpoint variations. They are also capable of localizing attribute clues at varying scales (*e.g.* small glasses vs. the full body). State-of-the-art studies [8–10] improve by learning CNN features from detected part regions instead of using low-level features, and finally combine them into a pose-normalized deep representation for attribute recognition. The deep part features have also been used in [11,12] for fine-grained categorization tasks. Our method is based on deep parts too, inheriting the aforementioned benefits and end-to-end training.

Our major difference with respect to prior methods lies in the use of *deep hierarchical contexts*. The hierarchical contexts are called 'deep' because they are selected and represented in layers of our deeply trained model. Specifically, at the human-centric level, we compute the nearest neighbor fields between parts of the target person and contextual persons on a pyramid of CNN feature maps. Then we pool all the matched parts together as a multi-scale similarity regularization of our CNN, which proves effective in reducing attribute recognition ambiguities in challenging cases. At the scene level, we fuse our human-centric predictions with the global scene classification score that is jointly learned in CNN, which are finally mapped to scene-aware attribute predictions. We notice that R*CNN [10] also exploits context for human attribute recognition. But this model is limited to using unspecified and potentially insufficient contextual cues from only some bottom-up region proposal [13]. In contrast, we utilize semantically organized contexts from both related human parts and the entire image scene.

To facilitate the study of deep hierarchical contexts, we introduce a large-scale WIDER Attribute dataset with 14 human attribute labels and 30 event class labels. The dataset consists of 57,524 labeled person bounding boxes in 13,789 event-labeled images collected from the WIDER dataset [14]. It is a new large-scale human attribute dataset with both human attribute and scene annotations. It has more human attribute labels than existing public datasets, e.g. Berkeley Attributes of People [5], HAT [15], CRP [16], PARSE-27k [17] and PETA [41].

Contributions: (1) We propose a novel deep model based on adaptively selected human parts for human attribute recognition from unconstrained images. (2) We propose to use deep hierarchical contexts to exploit joint context of humans and scene for more robust attribute recognition. (3) We introduce a large-scale WIDER Attribute dataset with rich human attribute and event class annotations. Our method obtains a mean AP of 81.3 % for all attributes on the test set of WIDER Attribute dataset, 0.8 % higher than the competing R*CNN [10] which suggests the usefulness of hierarchical contexts. Our method achieves state-of-the-art performance on other popular datasets too.

2   Related Work

Attribute Recognition. Attributes have been used as an intermediate representation to describe object properties [18,19] or even unseen object categories [20]. For attributes of people, early works rely on frontal faces only and predict a limited number of attributes. For example, Haar features extracted from the face region can be fed into the SVM [21] and AdaBoost [22] classifiers for gender and race recognition. Kumar *et al.* proposed using the predicted face attributes for face recognition [23] and visual search [24]. More recent works study the problem of recognizing a larger set of attributes, such as gender, hairstyle, and clothing style, from the whole human body image with large variation of viewpoint, pose, and appearance. Part-based methods are the state-of-the-art family of methods nowadays because they can decompose the input image into parts that are pose-specific and allow to combine evidence from different locations and scales. Successful part models include Poselets [5], DPM [6] and window-specific parts [7]. Recent deep part models [8–10] improve attribute recognition performance by training deep CNNs from part regions. Nevertheless, most part models only concern for the target person region, thus miss the opportunity to leverage rich contexts to reduce the attribute recognition ambiguities in challenging cases. An exception is R*CNN [10] that exploits context from adaptive region proposals. Our experiments will show that it is weaker than using hierarchical contextual cues from human-centric relations to global scene event.

Nearest-Neighbor Learning. One of our goals in using hierarchical contexts is to capture human relations or similarities by computing nearest neighbor parts between people. Finding nearest neighbors to define image similarities has a long history for vision tasks like image classification [25,26]. For bird sub-category classification, Zhang *et al.* [27] further proposed a similarity function for poselet neighbor matching. In comparison, our part matching is more adaptive, and is performed at online and multi-scale feature maps in a deep model. A recent deep learning method [28] for multilabel image annotation also inherits the idea of nearest neighbor matching, and pools the neighbor features for robustness. Our method is related in neighbor pooling, but operates at score level and between different objects on the feature maps of one input image rather than between feature maps of different images, thus can be seen as a self-similarity regularization during CNN training.

Scene Contexts. Oliva and Torralba [29] have studied the role of context in object recognition, and analyzed a rich collection of contextual associations of objects with their scene. Object detection also frequently exploits scene contexts. DPM [30] re-scores each detected object by taking into account the scores of all other classes in an image, thus the object co-occurrences in scenes. Choi et al. [31] re-scored by learning the object co-occurrence and spatial priors in a hierarchical tree structure[1]. Mottaghi et al. [32] exploited the object class contexts in both local region and global scene. However, our exploited hierarchical contexts are not limited to only object class relations, but also cover the entire background scene. In this respect, our method is closely related to those works e.g. [33,34] that use global scene features. This line of work is attractive for not anchoring context analysis to any specific regions or individual objects within a scene, thus has a complete information coverage and also lower computation complexity than e.g. the local model [35] that needs to additionally compute an adaptive local contextual region. In our work, to prevent global scene context from enforcing strong properties on some less related objects, we only treat the global scene features as complementary signals and map them into scene classification scores in our CNN, conditioned on which we make probabilistic scene-aware predictions.

3   Human Attributes from Deep Hierarchical Contexts

The proposed human attribute recognition method is part-based, and learns pose-normalized deep feature representations from localized parts in a deep ConvNet. Combining the human parts and deep learning lends us robustness when dealing with unconstrained human images with large variation. We adapt Fast R-CNN [36] to process multiple regions, and the CNN feature maps and attribute scoring modules are trained end-to-end by back-propagation and stochastic gradient descent. This is in contrast to the deep methods in [8,9] that optimize an additional linear SVM for prediction. Figure 2 provides the overview of our network architecture.

Given an input image, each person in it is associated with one bounding box hypothesis and a set of human part detections. The input image and its Gaussian pyramid are passed through the network to obtain multi-scale convolutional feature maps. Then we branch out four attribute scoring paths using different

---

[1] The term 'Hierarchical Context' is used in this paper to denote the tree-structured organization of object classes in a scene. We use the same term but with a different meaning of (human) object-object and object-scene contextual relations at two semantic levels, which is also more complete in the coverage of image information.

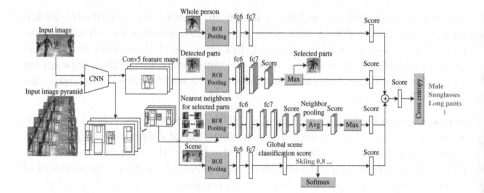

Fig. 2. Network architecture for unconstrained human attribute recognition using deep hierarchical contexts. Given an input image, we compute its Gaussian pyramid and pass them all through the CNN to obtain multi-scale feature maps. From the feature maps we extract features for four sets of bounding box regions: the whole target person, a target's chosen parts (for clarity we only show 3 selected out of 5 detected), nearest neighbor parts from the image pyramid and global image scene. The latter two correspond to hierarchical contexts: human-centric and scene-level contexts. After scoring the four region sets (see texts), we sum up all the scores as the final attribute score.

bounding box regions on the feature maps. On the first two paths, we respectively use the target person's bounding box and part boxes to cover the full scale body and local parts. This representation is widely adopted in many studies [8–10]. We incorporate deep hierarchical contexts on the third and fourth paths. Specifically, the human-centric context is selected from the nearest neighbor parts of other people on the deep feature pyramid; the scene-level context is mapped to the scene classification score as prior probability for re-scoring human attributes in a scene-aware manner. Details will be provided in the following subsections.

3.1 Preliminaries

We first describe backgrounds of the Fast R-CNN framework before delving into our model details. We choose the VGG16 [37] network pre-trained on ImageNet classification [38] for its excellent performance. Fast R-CNN follows the paradigm of generating region proposals first and then classifying them with learned features and classifiers. To ensure computational efficiency, the intense convolutions are only performed at image-level to obtain global *conv5* feature maps, which are reused for each region by ROI Pooling. The ROI Pooling layer functions by superimposing a fixed 7×7 spatial grid over a bounding box region, then performing max pooling within each grid cell to extract a fixed length feature vector from *conv5* feature maps. The feature vector is subsequently passed through two fully connected layers *fc6* and *fc7* to generate prediction scores.

Our task is human centric. We thus adopt the whole person bounding box and Poselet [39] detected regions as region proposals. To detect poselets, strong poselet activations are first localized on the input image in a multi-scale sliding

Fig. 3. Left: example poselet detections on the HAT [15] dataset. Right: example HAT image with only one bounding box annotation (red box) for a person. The yellow and green dashed boxes denote the detections of poselets and new people respectively. (Color figure online)

window fashion. Then following [40], we refine the activation scores by considering the spatial context of each. The refined poselet activations are finally clustered to form consistent person hypotheses. On datasets like HAT [15] and our proposed WIDER Attribute, there may not exist a bounding box annotation for every person in one image. So we associate to an unannotated person the person hypothesis and its related poselets when the hypothesis confidence is above a threshold [40]. We use these new detections to explore human-centric context. For those already annotated people with ground truth bounding boxes, we empirically associate to them the closest poselets whose person hypotheses sufficiently overlap (with IoU larger than 0.6) with them. If such poselets do not exist, we simply associate the nearby poselets that overlap with the ground truth bounding boxes by at least 50 %. Figure 3 shows example detections of poselets on an annotated person, and new detections of poselets and bounding boxes on unannotated people.

3.2 Enriching Human Cues with Deep Hierarchical Contexts

Our goal is to recognize a set of human attributes $\{a \in A\}$ for all the people in an unconstrained image I. Suppose for a target person's bounding box b in I, we have detected a set of parts $\{s \in S\}$. We frame the attribute recognition problem in a probabilistic framework, and estimate the likelihood of the presence of attribute a on the target person given a set of his/her measurements V. We take into account **Human Cues** from both human body b and parts S, and also contextual cues from the remaining background regions in I. Thus we consider measurements $V = \{b, S, N(s_a^*), I\}$, where $N(s_a^*)$ and I are the **Hierarchical Contexts** that will be detailed later.

We evaluate for each attribute a the conditional probability function given measurements V:

$$P(a \mid V) = P(a \mid b, S, N(s_a^*), I)$$
$$\propto P(b, S, N(s_a^*), I \mid a) = P(b \mid a) \cdot P(S \mid a) \cdot P(N(s_a^*) \mid a) \cdot P(I \mid a), \quad (1)$$

where we assume uniform distribution for the prior probability $P(a)$ that is hence omitted, and assume conditional independence between different image measurements. Equation 1 can be equivalently solved in a log-linear model. We implement this model in CNN by directly learning a score function $Score(a; \cdot)$ for each attribute a, and the learned score corresponds to the log probability after normalization. Then we can simply write the attribute score as the sum of four terms:

$$Score(a; b, S, N(s_a^*), I) = \underbrace{\boldsymbol{w}_{a,b}^T \cdot \boldsymbol{\phi}(b; I)}_{person\ bounding\ box} + \underbrace{\max_{s \in S} \boldsymbol{w}_{a,s}^T \cdot \boldsymbol{\phi}(s; I)}_{attribute-specific\ parts}$$

$$+ \underbrace{\frac{1}{|N(s_a^*)|} \sum_{s \in N(s_a^*)} \boldsymbol{w}_{a,s}^T \cdot \boldsymbol{\phi}(s; I)}_{human-centric\ context} + \underbrace{\boldsymbol{w}_{a,sc}^T \cdot \boldsymbol{W}_{sc} \cdot \boldsymbol{\phi}(I)}_{scene-level\ context}. \tag{2}$$

where $\boldsymbol{\phi}(b; I)$ is the extracted $fc7$ features from region b in image I, while $\boldsymbol{w}_{a,\cdot}$ are the scoring weights of attribute a for different regions.

The scoring terms for person bounding box b and parts $\{s \in S\}$ form the basis of our model, and are shown on the upper two paths in Fig. 2. Their sum can be regarded as a pose-normalized deep representation at score level. Such score fusion is found to be more effective than feature fusion (*e.g.* in [8]) in our task, because the latter would generate a very large feature vector from the many parts and overfits easily. In our CNN, the scoring weights and feature vectors are jointly learned for all attributes $a \in A$.

Note for the part set S, we select the most informative part s for each attribute a by a *max* score operation, and only add the maximum to the final attribute score. This is because human attribute signals often reside in different body parts, so not all parts should be responsible for recognizing one particular attribute. For example, the head part can hardly be used to infer the "long pants" attribute. Through the max pooling of part scores, we are now able to capture those distributed attribute signals from the rich part collection.

The third and fourth terms capture deep hierarchical contexts in case the target person contains insufficient information, *e.g.* when he/she appears at a very small scale or occluded (Fig. 1).

Human-centric context. Let $s_a^* = \arg\max_{s \in S} \boldsymbol{w}_{a,s}^T \cdot \boldsymbol{\phi}(s; I)$ be the person's highest scoring part that best describes attribute a, and $N(s_a^*)$ be its part neighbor set searched by computing Euclidean distance between the $fc7$ features of detected parts in the same image. We exploit $N(s_a^*)$ as the *human-centric context* to capture human relations,

Each part neighbor found in human-centric context is scored by the part weights $\boldsymbol{w}_{a,s}$, and then average pooled (see also Fig. 2, third path). By doing so, we hope to accumulate more stable or even stronger signals of attributes from the nearest neighbor fields between contextual people. Indeed, recognizing "sunglasses" from an occluded or low resolution face can become much clearer when considering a lot of similarly looking faces around. Here we choose to define similarities in terms of the human parts instead of whole body because people usually appear quite different globally but very similar at local parts. So it is more reasonable to only transfer the good knowledge locally rather than globally

Part neighbors specific to the" Long Hair" attribute   Part neighbors specific to the" Long Paints" attribute

Fig. 4. Example nearest neighbors found for a human part that best describes a particular attribute. In each image, we show the target person's bounding box in red, the attribute-specific part in green, and the part neighbors in yellow. We also show the average images of the found neighbor clusters, which strengthen the signal of attribute. (Color figure online)

from surrounding people. In our approach, the local part matching is made easier by using (1) poselet-based body parts that are pose-specific and well-aligned to match, (2) a compact poselet selection $\{s_a^*\}$ for each person which reduces the computational burden of online neighbor matching.

In practice, our part matching is performed on the CNN feature maps of a Gaussian pyramid of input image (with three scales in our implementation). Such a multi-scale neighbor set $N(s_a^*)$ is able to cover a broader range of part similarities. Its size $K = |N(s_a^*)|$ is determined by experiments. Note we match parts from all detected people including himself in one image. This guarantees our approach can still work on images with only one person. In this case, the use of human-centric context is actually a self-similarity regularization among multi-scale features of the same person.

Figure 4 illustrates some examples of the found part neighbors and their average images. It is observed that the part patterns are strengthened from their multi-scale versions as well as similar patterns from other people. This makes attributes emerge more clearly and their recognition less ambiguous in challenging cases.

Scene-level context. The scene-level context is further exploited by the fourth term in Eq. 2 (see also Fig. 2, fourth path). We propose to reuse the entire scene feature $\phi(I)$ holistically, without the need for explicitly identifying helpful objects or regions within a scene as in [35]. Obviously our method is computationally more appealing, but the downside is that some irrelevant information contained in the global feature $\phi(I)$ may confuse the recognition of attributes.

Therefore, we "filter" $\phi(I) \in \mathbb{R}^D$ by converting it to the scene classification score via $W_{sc} \in \mathbb{R}^{|C| \times D}$, where C refers to all the considered scene types. This way, only the scene-related high level information is preserved, while other variables are marginalized over during the conversion. Then we use the scene score to provide the prior probability for most likely human attributes in the scene, and re-score each attribute a via $w_{a,sc} \in \mathbb{R}^{|C|}$ in a scene-aware manner. This factorization is actually equivalent to applying the Bayes' rule to split the scene conditional probability function $P(a \mid I)$ in two factors:

$$P(a \mid I) = \sum_{c \in C} P(a \mid c, I) \cdot P(c \mid I), \tag{3}$$

where the latent variable of scene type c is introduced.

Accordingly, the attribute score is learned in our CNN via the total scoring weights $w_{a,sc}^T \cdot W_{sc}$. Note in some atypical cases, even the mere scene type can be misleading. When a total mismatch exists between the human attributes and background scene (e.g. suitmen on a basketball court), the pure person characteristics is what our model should focus on. So we do not always expect the scene context to have strong re-scoring effects. In our CNN, the weightings between the human- and scene-induced scores are automatically learned in their respective scoring weights.

3.3   Learning Details

We train our CNN together with the four scoring paths from an ImageNet initialization. As shown in Fig. 2, the whole network is trained end-to-end using a *cross entropy* loss over independent logistics to output multi-attribute predictions. Since the first three scoring paths all take human regions as input, we tie their *fc6* and *fc7* layers to reduce the parameter space (but the scoring weights for the whole person and body parts are separated). The fourth path's fully connected layers are not tied with others as they capture semantics of the global scene. Particularly, we attach right after the scene's *fc7* layer a *softmax* scene classification loss, in order to jointly learn the scene context priors.

During training, we augment the data by using bounding boxes of both human body and human parts that have no more than 10 % horizontal and vertical shift from the ground truth. We consider one image per mini-batch, and input with bounding boxes of the whole body and $|S| = 30$ poselet detections for each person. We set the learning rate to 10^{-5}, the momentum to 0.9, and train for 40 K iterations. The running time depends on the person number in one image. On average, training takes about 1 s for all persons in one image per iteration, while testing takes about 0.5 s per image on a NVIDIA Titan X GPU.

4   Datasets

4.1   Existing Human Attribute Datasets

We summarized a few popular human attribute datasets in Table 1. The Berkeley Attributes of People [5] dataset is the most widely used human attribute database. It consists of 2003 training, 2010 validation and 4022 test images, and a total of 17628 bounding boxes and 9 attribute labels such as "is male" and "has hat". Although this dataset is challenging for its wide human variation in pose, viewpoint and occlusion, the number of images is rather small and each is cropped from the original high resolution image and centered at a person's

Table 1. Statistics of the proposed WIDER Attribute dataset and comparison with existing human attribute datasets ('trunc.' denotes truncation; 'fg.' denotes fine-grained).

Dataset	Images	Boxes	Boxes/Img	Attributes	Attribute labels	Scene labels
Berkeley [5]	8,035	17,628	2.2 trunc	9	72,315	-
HAT [15]	9,344	19,872	2.1	27 fg	536,544	-
CRP [16]	20,999	27,454	1.3	4 fg	109,816	-
PARSE-27k [17]	9887	~27,000	2.7	10 fg	~270,000	-
WIDER Attribute	13,789	57,524	4.2	14	805,336	13,789

full body, leaving only limited background scene and people (likely truncated). This is not suitable to exploit contexts in our method to attain its full capacity. But we still detect poselets from the few and potentially incomplete neighboring people as described in Sect. 3.1. We treat them as a localized human-centric context to see if they can help in this case.

We also use a larger dataset of HAT [15] with 9344 human images from Flickr that show a considerable variation in pose and resolution. The images are not cropped and of the original full resolution. There are totally 19872 persons with annotated bounding boxes, about 2 full persons per image on average, which is more suitable than Berkeley dataset for our context-based method. To make full use of the human-centric context, we further detect new person bounding boxes and related poselets in HAT images following Sect. 3.1. There are 27 attribute labels for each person, but some refer to human actions (e.g. "standing", "sitting", "running") and some are overly-fine-grained (e.g.6 age attributes of "baby", "kid", "teen", "young", "middle aged" and "elderly"). We follow the train-val-test split of 3500, 3500 and 2344 images and employ all 27 attributes in our experiments to facilitate comparison.

There are two other video-based human attributes datasets, namely Caltech Roadside Pedestrians (CRP) [16] dataset and PARSE-27k [17] dataset. We summarize these datasets in our supplementary material. We do not employ the two datasets in our experiments since they are either small in terms of images (attributes), or limits (even disables) the exploitation of human-centric context in one image. Also they lack the scene labels to exploit global scene context.

4.2 WIDER Attribute Dataset

We introduce a large-scale WIDER Attribute dataset to overcome all the aforementioned drawbacks of existing public datasets. Our dataset is collected from the 50574 WIDER images [14] that usually contain many people and huge human variations (see Fig. 5). We discard those images full of non-human objects or low quality humans that are hardly attribute-recognizable, ending up with 13789 images. Then we annotate a bounding box for each person in these images, but no more than 20 people (with top resolutions) in a crowd image, resulting in 57524 boxes in total and 4+ boxes per image on average. For each bounding box, we label 14 distinct human attributes (no subcategories as in CRP [16] and PARSE-27k [17]),

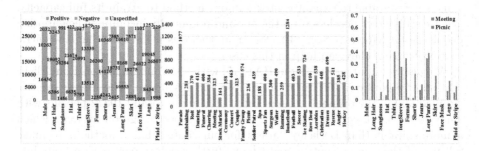

Fig. 5. Thirty examples of WIDER Attribute images, each from an image event class.

Fig. 6. Statistics of the number of attribute labels (Left), event class labels (Middle), and event-specific attribute labels (Right) on WIDER Attribute dataset.

resulting in a total of 805336 labels. The label statistics are shown in Table. 1 and Fig. 6 (Left). Note that we allow missing annotation since not every attribute can be specified for every person. For example, in the presence of face occlusion, one cannot sensibly label a valid "sunglasses" attribute.

We split our dataset into 5509 training, 1362 validation and 6918 test images. The large quantities of images and human labels permit us to study the benefit of human-centric context. To explore the scene-level context, we further label each image into 30 event classes. Figure 6 (Middle and Right) illustrates the image event distribution and two event-specific attribute distributions. We observe strong correlations between image event and the frequent human attributes in it, *e.g.* "longsleeve" and "formal" are frequent in *meeting*, while "tshirt" is frequent in *picnic*. Such correlations motivate our attribute re-scoring scheme conditioned on scene classification.

Figure 5 shows example images of events. In many cases, humans are small and their attributes are hard to recognize without referring to contexts, *e.g.* in *ceremony*. In other cases where only one person appears in an image (*e.g. angler*) or the person is inconsistent with the background and stands out on his own (*e.g.* a formally dressed man on the *basketball* court), our model should learn to weigh more on the target human features over human-centric or scene-level contexts. The new WIDER Attribute dataset forms a well-suited testbed for a full examination of using hierarchical contexts.

5 Experiments

We evaluate our method on the test sets of the Berkeley Attributes of People [5] and HAT [15] datasets, where there are many results to compare. We also use the test set of the proposed WIDER Attribute dataset to compare with the baselines that do not fully exploit the joint context of humans and scene. It would be interesting to see the performance of our method when extended to the video datasets of CRP [16] and PARSE-27k [17]. However, these datasets hinder the use of human-centric context as mentioned in Sect. 4.1 and have no scene labels. Hence they are not well-suited for the context where our method is used, and we leave their experiments to future work. We measure performance with the average precision (AP) for each human attribute and the mean average precision (mAP) over all attributes.

Table 2 shows the results on Berkeley dataset where our method is compared against all CNN-based state-of-the-arts. Both PANDA [8] and ACNH [17] achieve relatively low mAPs with 5-layer networks. With a well trained 16-layer network, R-CNN [36] improves the performance for nearly all the attributes, using the holistic human body region only. R*CNN [10] and Gkioxari *et al.* [9] further improve by adding a secondary contextual region and three human parts respectively.

Our baseline that combines the human body and selected attribute-descriptive parts achieves a mean AP of 90.8 %. By searching a different number of parts $K = |N(s_a^*)|$ from other people, our human-centric contextual model obtains consistent gains across attributes, especially those located at small

Table 2. AP on the test set of the Berkeley Attributes of People [5] dataset. Note PANDA [8] and ACNH [17] use 5-layer CNNs while others use 16-layer CNNs. Our baseline combines the human body and attribute-descriptive parts at score level. Our human-centric contextual models further pool scores from $K = 1$ or 2 nearest neighbor parts. Part neighbors searched from single-scale (ss) CNN maps are also evaluated.

AP(%)	Male	Long Hair	Glasses	Hat	Tshirt	LongSleeves	Shorts	Jeans	Long Pants	mAP
PANDA [8]	91.7	82.7	70.0	74.2	49.8	86.0	79.1	81.0	96.4	79.0
ACNH [17]	87.8	81.5	48.8	75.3	64.1	88.1	87.1	89.5	98.1	80.0
R-CNN [36]	91.8	88.9	81.0	90.4	73.1	90.4	88.6	88.9	97.6	87.8
R*CNN [10]	92.8	88.9	82.4	92.2	74.8	91.2	92.9	89.4	97.9	89.2
Gkioxari *et al.* [9]	92.9	90.1	77.7	93.6	72.6	93.2	93.9	**92.1**	98.8	89.5
Ours (baseline)	94.1	90.8	86.8	94.4	76.1	92.9	94.0	90.2	98.2	90.8
Ours ($K = 1$)	**95.0**	**92.4**	**89.3**	95.7	**79.1**	**94.3**	93.7	91.0	99.2	**92.2**
Ours ($K = 2$)	94.8	91.8	88.4	**95.8**	76.6	94.1	**95.4**	91.5	**99.3**	92.0
Ours ($K = 1$, ss)	94.3	91.5	88.0	94.6	77.7	93.9	93.7	90.0	98.7	91.4
Ours ($K = 2$, ss)	94.2	91.3	88.0	94.8	77.6	93.9	92.9	90.2	98.7	91.3

Table 3. Comparing mAP on the test set of the HAT [15] dataset. Note ACNH [17] uses a 5-layer CNN while other deep methods use 16-layer CNNs.

Methods	DSR [15]	EPM [42]	Joo *et al.* [7]	EPM+Context [42]	ACNH [17]	EPM+VGG16 [42]
mAP(%)	53.8	58.7	59.3	59.7	66.2	69.6
Methods	R-CNN [36]	R*CNN [10]	Ours (baseline)	Ours ($K = 1$)	Ours ($K = 2$)	Ours ($K = 5$)
mAP(%)	76.3	76.4	76.7	77.6	**78.0**	77.8

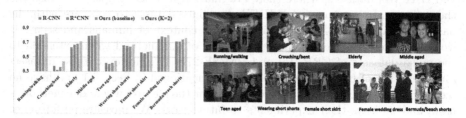

Fig. 7. Visualizing the AP and example image for some hard human attributes in the HAT [15] dataset.

scales *e.g.* "glasses". We attain the highest mean AP of 92.2 % when $K = 1$. This indicates that, even in the case of cropped Berkeley images with rather limited context (2 neighboring people on average with large truncation), the local use of human context can at least help and will not degrade the performance on single-person images. But we found no more gains with more than $K = 1$ part neighbors. When the part neighbors are searched at a single scale (ss) of CNN feature maps instead of their Gaussian pyramid, a performance drop is observed which shows the importance of seeking multi-scale part similarity. In the following experiments, we always use three scales in a pyramid due to the good tradeoff between performance and computational speed.

Table 3 reports the performance in mean AP of our approach and other competitive methods on the HAT dataset. Our method outperforms all others based on CNN or not (the first four). Note the Expanded Parts Model (EPM) [42] uses the immediate context around a person, but only achieves 59.7 % mean AP. Its combination with deep VGG16 features significantly improves to 69.6 % mean AP. We finetune the state-of-the-art R-CNN [36] and R*CNN [10] on this dataset, obtaining substantial margins over others. Whereas our adaptive deep-part and whole body-based baseline performs slightly better. More gains are obtained from using human-centric context, with the best mean AP of 78.0 % using $K = 2$ human part neighbors. This is reasonable considering the HAT dataset contains richer human contexts in full resolution images.

Figure 7 compares the competitive methods with our baseline and best-performing methods in terms of AP of some hard attributes. It is evident that our used human-centric context offers especially large gains for the hard attributes that current competing methods do badly on, *e.g.* "crouching/bent", "teen aged" and "female short skirt". These are the attribute categories that have large pose variation and have small-sized or limited number of human samples.

Table 4. Comparing mAP on the test set of the WIDER Attribute dataset. All methods use 16-layer CNNs. Our full method exploits the scene-level context besides human-centric context. Here 'scene no cl.' means directly using scene features with no scene label conversions to re-score human attributes.

Methods	R-CNN [36]	R*CNN [10]	Ours (baseline)	Ours ($K = 1$)
mAP(%)	80.0	80.5	80.5	80.7
Methods	Ours ($K = 5$)	Ours (scene + $K = 5$)	Ours (scene no cl. + $K = 5$)	
mAP(%)	80.9	**81.3**	81.1	

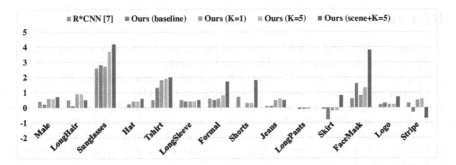

Fig. 8. Visualizing the absolute gains of competing methods over R-CNN [36] in terms of AP(%) on the test set of WIDER Attrbiute

The WIDER Attribute dataset contains richer contexts of humans and event labels. We compare our deep hierarchical context-based method with the state-of-the-art R-CNN [36] and R*CNN [10] in Table 4. Our method performs consistently better for most attributes, achieving the best mean AP of 81.3 % when we use $K = 5$ human part neighbors. The reason is that there are more people (about 4 on average) in the full image of the WIDER Attribute dataset. Our performance also benefits from the use of scene-aware attribute re-scoring, as can be observed from the mAP value difference. We further compare with the result from a direct attribute scoring using global scene features, which is worse than our proposed scheme. Figure 8 shows our absolute improvements in AP over competing methods to validate our advantages. In the supplementary material, the scene classification results as well as more detailed attribute recognition results will be included.

6   Conclusion

We propose a new method for unconstrained human attribute recognition, built on the simple observation that context can unveil more clues to make recognition easier. To this end, we not only learn to score the human body and attribute-specific parts jointly in a deep CNN, but also learn two scoring functions that capture deep hierarchical contexts. Specifically, collaborative part modeling among humans and global scene re-scoring are performed to respectively capture human-centric and scene-level contexts. We introduce a large-scale WIDER Attribute dataset to enable the exploitation of such hierarchical contexts. Our method achieves state-of-the-art results on this dataset and popular ones as well. We believe our method can be easily extended to the video datasets and other tasks such as human pose estimation.

Acknowledgement. This work is partially supported by SenseTime Group Limited.

References

1. Layne, R., Hospedales, T.M., Gong, S.: Person re-identification by attributes. In: British Machine Vision Conference, pp. 1–11 (2012)
2. Liu, C., Gong, S., Loy, C.C.: On-the-fly feature importance mining for person re-identification. Pattern Recogn. **47**(4), 1602–1615 (2014)
3. Su, C., Yang, F., Zhang, S., Tian, Q., Davis, L.S., Gao, W.: Multi-task learning with low rank attribute embedding for person re-identification. In: Proceedings of the IEEE International Conference on Computer Vision, pp. 3739–3747 (2015)
4. Gong, S., Cristani, M., Yan, S., Loy, C.C.: Person Re-Identification, vol. 1. Springer, London (2014)
5. Bourdev, L., Maji, S., Malik, J.: Describing people: poselet-based attribute classification. In: IEEE International Conference on Computer Vision, pp. 1543–1550 (2011)
6. Zhang, N., Farrell, R., Iandola, F., Darrell, T.: Deformable part descriptors for fine-grained recognition and attribute prediction. In: IEEE International Conference on Computer Vision, pp. 729–736 (2013)
7. Joo, J., Wang, S., Zhu, S.C.: Human attribute recognition by rich appearance dictionary. In: IEEE International Conference on Computer Vision, pp. 721–728 (2013)
8. Zhang, N., Paluri, M., Ranzato, M., Darrell, T., Bourdev, L.D.: PANDA: pose aligned networks for deep attribute modeling. In: IEEE Conference on Computer Vision and Pattern Recognition, pp. 1637–1644 (2014)
9. Gkioxari, G., Girshick, R., Malik, J.: Actions and attributes from wholes and parts. In: IEEE International Conference on Computer Vision, pp. 2470–2478 (2015)
10. Gkioxari, G., Girshick, R., Malik, J.: Contextual action recognition with R*CNN. In: IEEE International Conference on Computer Vision, pp. 1080–1088 (2015)
11. Zhang, N., Donahue, J., Girshick, R., Darrell, T.: Part-based R-CNNs for fine-grained category detection. In: European Conference on Computer Vision, pp. 834–849 (2014)
12. Branson, S., Horn, G.V., Belongie, S., Perona, P.: Bird species categorization using pose normalized deep convolutional nets. In: British Machine Vision Conference (2014)
13. Uijlings, J.R.R., van de Sande, K.E.A., Gevers, T., Smeulders, A.W.M.: Selective search for object recognition. Int. J. Comput. Vision **104**(2), 154–171 (2013)
14. Xiong, Y., Zhu, K., Lin, D., Tang, X.: Recognize complex events from static images by fusing deep channels. In: IEEE Conference on Computer Vision and Pattern Recognition, pp. 1600–1609 (2015)
15. Sharma, G., Jurie, F.: Learning discriminative spatial representation for image classification. In: British Machine Vision Conference, pp. 1–11 (2011)

16. Hall, D., Perona, P.: Fine-grained classification of pedestrians in video: benchmark and state of the art. In: IEEE Conference on Computer Vision and Pattern Recognition, pp. 5482–5491 (2015)

17. Sudowe, P., Spitzer, H., Leibe, B.: Person attribute recognition with a jointly-trained holistic CNN model. In: IEEE International Conference on Computer Vision Workshop, pp. 329–337 (2015)

18. Farhadi, A., Endres, I., Hoiem, D., Forsyth, D.: Describing objects by their attributes. In: IEEE Conference on Computer Vision and Pattern Recognition, pp. 1778–1785 (2009)

19. Huang, C., Change Loy, C., Tang, X.: Unsupervised learning of discriminative attributes and visual representations. In: Proceedings of the IEEE Conference on Computer Vision and Pattern Recognition, pp. 5175–5184 (2016)

20. Lampert, C.H., Nickisch, H., Harmeling, S.: Learning to detect unseen object classes by between-class attribute transfer. In: IEEE Conference on Computer Vision and Pattern Recognition, pp. 951–958 (2009)

21. Moghaddam, B., Yang, M.H.: Learning gender with support faces. IEEE Trans. Pattern Anal. Mach. Intell. 24(5), 707–711 (2002)

22. Shakhnarovich, G., Viola, P.A., Moghaddam, B.: A unified learning framework for real time face detection and classification. In: IEEE International Conference on Automatic Face & Gesture Recognition, pp. 16–26 (2002)

23. Kumar, N., Berg, A.C., Belhumeur, P.N., Nayar, S.K.: Attribute and simile classifiers for face verification. In: IEEE International Conference on Computer Vision, pp. 365–372 (2009)

24. Kumar, N., Belhumeur, P., Nayar, S.: FaceTracer: a search engine for large collections of images with faces. In: European Conference on Computer Vision, pp. 340–353 (2008)

25. Boiman, O., Shechtman, E., Irani, M.: In defense of nearest-neighbor based image classification. In: IEEE Conference on Computer Vision and Pattern Recognition, pp. 1–8 (2008)

26. McCann, S., Lowe, D.G.: Local naive bayes nearest neighbor for image classification. In: IEEE Conference on Computer Vision and Pattern Recognition, pp. 3650–3656 (2012)

27. Zhang, N., Farrell, R., Darrell, T.: Pose pooling kernels for sub-category recognition. In: IEEE Conference on Computer Vision and Pattern Recognition, pp. 3665–3672 (2012)

28. Johnson, J., Ballan, L., Li, F.: Love thy neighbors: Image annotation by exploiting image metadata. In: IEEE International Conference on Computer Vision, pp. 4624–4632 (2015)

29. Oliva, A., Torralba, A.: The role of context in object recognition. Trends Cogn. Sci. 11(12), 520–527 (2007)

30. Felzenszwalb, P.F., Girshick, R.B., McAllester, D., Ramanan, D.: Object detection with discriminatively trained part-based models. IEEE Trans. Pattern Anal. Mach. Intell. 32(9), 1627–1645 (2010)

31. Choi, M.J., Lim, J.J., Torralba, A., Willsky, A.S.: Exploiting hierarchical context on a large database of object categories. In: IEEE Conference on Computer Vision and Pattern Recognition, pp. 129–136 (2010)

32. Mottaghi, R., Chen, X., Liu, X., Cho, N.G., Lee, S.W., Fidler, S., Urtasun, R., Yuille, A.: The role of context for object detection and semantic segmentation in the wild. In: IEEE Conference on Computer Vision and Pattern Recognition, pp. 891–898 (2014)

33. Russell, B., Torralba, A., Liu, C., Fergus, R., Freeman, W.T.: Object recognition by scene alignment. In: Advances in Neural Information Processing Systems, pp. 1241–1248 (2007)
34. Torralba, A.: Contextual priming for object detection. Int. J. Comput. Vision 53(2), 169–191 (2003)
35. Li, C., Parikh, D., Chen, T.: Extracting adaptive contextual cues from unlabeled regions. In: IEEE International Conference on Computer Vision, pp. 511–518 (2011)
36. Girshick, R.: Fast R-CNN. In: IEEE International Conference on Computer Vision, pp. 1440–1448 (2015)
37. Simonyan, K., Zisserman, A.: Very deep convolutional networks for large-scale image recognition. In: International Conference on Learning Representations (2015)
38. Krizhevsky, A., Sutskever, I., Hinton, G.E.: Imagenet classification with deep convolutional neural networks. In: Advances in Neural Information Processing Systems, pp. 1097–1105 (2012)
39. Bourdev, L., Malik, J.: Poselets: body part detectors trained using 3D human pose annotations. In: IEEE International Conference on Computer Vision, pp. 1365–1372 (2009)
40. Bourdev, L., Maji, S., Brox, T., Malik, J.: Detecting people using mutually consistent poselet activations. In: European Conference on Computer Vision, pp. 168–181 (2010)
41. Deng, Y., Luo, P., Loy, C.C., Tang, X.: Pedestrian attribute recognition at far distance. In: Proceedings of the 22nd ACM international conference on Multimedia, pp. 789–792. ACM (2014)
42. Sharma, G., Jurie, F., Schmid, C.: Expanded parts model for semantic description of humans in still images. IEEE Trans. Pattern Anal. Mach. Intell. (2016)

Person Re-identification via Recurrent Feature Aggregation

Yichao Yan[1(✉)], Bingbing Ni[1], Zhichao Song[1], Chao Ma[1], Yan Yan[2], and Xiaokang Yang[1]

[1] Shanghai Jiao Tong University, Shanghai, China
{yanyichao,nibingbing,5110309394,chaoma,xkyang}@sjtu.edu.cn
[2] University of Michigan, Ann Arbor, USA
tom.yan.555@gmail.com

Abstract. We address the person re-identification problem by effectively exploiting a globally discriminative feature representation from a sequence of tracked human regions/patches. This is in contrast to previous person re-id works, which rely on either single frame based person to person patch matching, or graph based sequence to sequence matching. We show that a progressive/sequential fusion framework based on long short term memory (LSTM) network aggregates the frame-wise human region representation at each time stamp and yields a sequence level human feature representation. Since LSTM nodes can *remember and propagate* previously accumulated good features and *forget* newly input inferior ones, even with simple hand-crafted features, the proposed recurrent feature aggregation network (**RFA-Net**) is effective in generating highly discriminative sequence level human representations. Extensive experimental results on two person re-identification benchmarks demonstrate that the proposed method performs favorably against state-of-the-art person re-identification methods.

Keywords: Person re-identification · Feature fusion · Long short term memory networks

1 Introduction

Person re-identification (re-id) deals with the problem of re-associating a specific person across non-overlapping cameras. It has been receiving increasing popularity [1] due to its important applications in intelligent video surveillance.

Existing methods mainly focus on addressing the single-shot person re-id problem. Given a probe image of one person taken from one camera, a typical scenario for single-shot person re-id is to identify this person in a set of gallery images taken from another camera. Usually, the identification results are based on ranking the similarities of the probe-gallery pairs. The performance of person re-id is measured by the rank-k matching rate if the correct pair hits the retrieved top-k ranking list. To increase the matching rate, state-of-the-art approaches either employ discriminative features in representing persons

© Springer International Publishing AG 2016
B. Leibe et al. (Eds.): ECCV 2016, Part VI, LNCS 9910, pp. 701–716, 2016.
DOI: 10.1007/978-3-319-46466-4_42

or apply distance metric learning methods to increase the similarity between matched image pairs. Numerous types of features have been explored to represent persons, including global features like color and texture histograms [2,3], local features such as SIFT [4] and LBP [5], and deep convolutional neural network (CNN) features [6,7]. In the meantime, a large number of metric learning approaches have been applied to person re-id task, such as LMNN [8], Mahalanobis distance metric [9], and RankSVM [10]. Despite the significant progress in recent years, the performance achieved by these methods do not fulfill the real-application requirement due to the following reasons. First, images captured by different cameras undergo large amount of appearance variations caused by illumination changes, heavy occlusion, background clutter, or human pose changes. More importantly, for real surveillance, persons always appear in a video rather than in a single-shot image. These single-shot based methods fail to make full use of the temporal sequence information in surveillance videos.

Several algorithms have been proposed to tackle the multi-shot person re-id problem, i.e., to match human instances in the sequence level (these human patch sequences are usually obtained by visual detection and tracking). To exploit the richer sequence information, existing methods mainly resort to: (1) key frame/fragment representation [11]; (2) feature fusion/encoding [12–14] and (3) spatio-temporal appearance model [15]. Despite their favorable performance on recent benchmark datasets [11,16], we have the following observations on their limitations. First, key frame/fragment representation based algorithms [11] often assume the discriminative fragments to be located in the local minima and maxima of Flow Energy Profile [11], which may not be accurate. During the final matching, since only one fragment is selected to represent the whole sequence, richer information contained by the rest of the sequences is not fully utilized. Second, feature fusion/encoding methods [12–14] take bag-of-words approach to encode a set of frame-wise features into a global vector, but ignore the informative spatio-temporal information of human sequence. To overcome these shortages, the recently proposed method [15] employs the spatially and temporally aligned appearance of the person in a walking cycle for matching. However, such approach is extremely computationally inefficient and thus inappropriate for real applications. It is therefore of great importance to explore a more effective and efficient scheme to make full use of the richer sequence information for person re-id.

The fundamental challenge of multi-shot person re-id is how to systematically aggregate both the frame-wise appearance information as well as temporal dynamics information along the human sequence to generate a more discriminative sequence level human representation. To this end, we propose a recurrent feature aggregation network (**RFA-Net**) that builds a sequence level representation from a temporally ordered sequence of frame-wise features, based on a typical version of recurrent neural network, namely, Long Short-Term Memory network [17]. Figure 1 shows an overview of the difference between our method and previous approaches. The proposed feature aggregation framework possesses various advantages. First, it allows discriminative information of frame-wise data

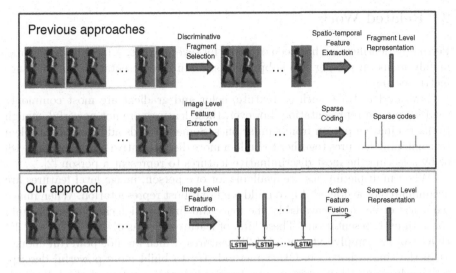

Fig. 1. Pipeline of the proposed recurrent feature aggregation network for multi-shot person re-id with comparison to previous methods. The top part depicts two common used methods for multi-shot person re-id, *i.e.*, to choose a most discriminative fragment for matching, or to use sparse coding method to enhance feature representation. The bottom part gives an illustration of our approach, frame-wise features are input into a feature aggregation (LSTM) network, and the output vector of the network builds the sequence level representation

to propagate along the temporal direction, and discriminative information could be accumulated from the first LSTM node to the deepest one, thus yielding a highly discriminative sequence level human representation. Second, during feature propagation, this framework can *prevent* non-informative information from reaching the deep nodes, therefore it is robust to noisy features (due to occlusion, tracking/detection failure, or background clutter etc.). Third, the proposed fusion network is simple yet efficient, which is able to deal with sequences with variable length.

The main contributions of this work lie in that we present a recurrent feature aggregation network to address the multi-shot person re-id problem. The proposed network jointly takes the feature fusion and spatio-temporal appearance model into account and makes full use of the temporal sequence information for multi-shot person re-id. With the use of the proposed network, hand-crafted low-level features can be augmented with temporal cues and significantly improve the accuracy of person re-id. Extensive experiments on two publicly available benchmark datasets demonstrate that the proposed person re-id method performs favorably against state-of-the-arts algorithms in terms of effectiveness and efficiency.

2   Related Work

Person re-identification has been explored for several years. A large body of works mainly focus on solving two subproblems: feature representation and distance metric learning.

Low-level features such as texture, color and gradient are most commonly used for person representation, however, these features are not powerful enough to discriminate a person from similar ones. Some methods address this problem by combining features together to build a more discriminative representation [18] or by selecting the most discriminative features to represent a person [2].

When multiple images are available for one person, image level features are accumulated or averaged [14] to build a more robust representation. When image sequences or videos are available, the space-time information can be used to build space-time representations. These kind of features such as 3D SIFT [19] and 3D HOG [20] are simply extensions of 2D features, which are not powerful enough as in the single-shot case. Other methods try to build more powerful descriptors, such as in [21], interest points descriptors are accumulated along the time space to capture appearance variability. Different color-based features combined with a graph based approach was proposed in [22]. This method tries to learn the global geometric structure of the people and to realize comparison of the video sequences. Many other methods also exploit image sequences to enhance feature description [23,24]. Wang et al. [11] presented a model to automatically select the most discriminative video fragments and simultaneously to learn a video ranking function for person re-id. Karanam et al. [14] proposed a Local Discriminant Analysis approach that is capable of encoding a set of frame-wise features representing a person into a global vector. Liu et al. recently proposed a spatio-temporal appearance representation method [15], and feature vectors that encode the spatially and temporally aligned appearance of the person in a walking cycle are extracted. These methods are usually feature-sensitive, designing complex/good features or combining several features together may achieve good performance, while only using simple features would lead to significant performance drop [11]. In contrast to these methods, the method we proposed is simple and effective, i.e., it could learn to aggregate very simple features (LBP and color information) into a highly discriminative representation.

A large number of metric learning as well as ranking algorithms have been proposed to solve the person re-id problem. Mahalanobis distance metric [9] is most commonly used in person re-id. Boosting was applied to Mahalanobis distance learning by Shen et al. [25]. Person re-id was formulated as a learning-to-rank problem in [26]. Zheng et al. have also formulated person re-id as a relative distance comparison (RDC) problem [27]. Although an efficient distance metric learning algorithm can model the transition in feature space between two camera views and thus enhance the re-identification performance, it will be no longer necessary if the features possess high discriminativeness. As demonstrated by our experiments, our feature representation will still generate promising results when only a simple metric (cosine distance) is applied.

Deep learning based methods [6,7] have also been applied to person re-id to simultaneously solve feature representation and metric learning problem. A typical structure of this approach consists of two parts. The first part is a feature learning network, usually a convolutional neural network or other kinds of networks. The feature pairs extracted from the first step are then fed into several metric learning layers to predict weather a pair of images belong to the same person. Usually the networks have simple structure and can be trained end-to-end. However, this kind of approaches use image pairs to learn feature representation and distance metric, which is unable to consider the space-time information in video sequences, this makes it more suitable for single-shot problem. Moreover, deep learning based methods are easy to overfit on small database. In contrast, our method adopts a simple LSTM network to learn space-time information, which is more efficient than the deep learning based models. We also realize two contemporary works [28,29].

3 Sequential Feature Aggregation for Person Re-identification

3.1 Overview

As mentioned above, previous single-shot based re-id methods rely on the information extracted from a single image, which is insufficient to identify the person in a gallery of images. For multi-shot person re-id, on one hand, methods based on graph matching to calculate the similarity between sequences are computationally complex and sensitive to outliers (e.g., false human detections). On the other hand, methods based on pooling frame-level features into a sequence level representation usually cannot well model the temporal change of human appearance, e.g., human dynamics. Therefore, in this work, we aim to aggregate both image level features and human dynamics information into a discriminative sequence level representation. More specifically, our sequential feature aggregation scheme is based on a recurrent neural network (e.g., LSTMs). Frame-wise human features are sequentially fed into this network and discriminative/descriptive information is propagated and accumulated through the LSTM nodes, and yielding final sequence level human representation. Accordingly, both the frame-wise human appearance information and human dynamics information are properly encoded.

3.2 Sequential Feature Aggregation Network

Network Architecture. Motivated by the success of recurrent neural networks (RNNs) in temporal sequence analysis, we employ a LSTM network as our feature aggregation network prototype. A LSTM network maintains the information of the previous time stamp and uses it to update the current state sequentially, therefore it is a powerful tool to deal with sequential data. With a LSTM network, information could be propagated from the first LSTM node to the last one, and this information aggregation mechanism is very useful for our given

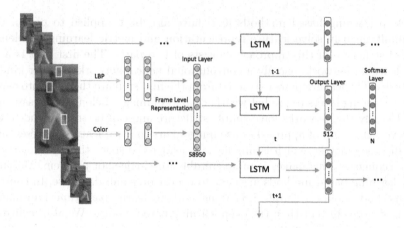

Fig. 2. Details of the network structure. LBP and color features are first extracted from overlapping rectangular image patches, and then concatenated as frame level representation. This representation as well as the previous LSTM outputs are input to the current LSTM node, the output of the LSTM is further connected to a softmax loss layer for error calculation and gradient backpropagation (Color figure online)

task, *i.e.*, to fuse the frame-wise features to a sequence level feature representation. In other words, the output of the last LSTM nodes contains aggregated discriminative information of the sequence. Each LSTM node of the feature aggregation network contains input nodes, hidden nodes and output nodes, as illustrated in Fig. 2. The input features, denoted as $\{\mathbf{x}_t\}_{t=1:T}$, could be either deep CNN features or simply hand crafted features. In this work, we use simple hand crafted features. This is because although deep CNN features are more prevailing recently, to train a valid CNN model requires large amount of data. Unfortunately, existing person re-id databases are mostly with small size, and the learned deep CNN features inevitably suffer from over-fitting. The dimensionality of the input feature vector of each time stamp is 58950. Although in many other applications, stack of LSTM nodes are used for better network representation capability, our proposed network employs only one layer of LSTM nodes (*i.e.*, no stack) with 512 hidden units, as our experimental results show that it is sufficient for our re-id task and deeper models or more hidden units do not bring too much performance gain.

Frame Level Representation. For each human bounding box, we use both color and texture features to represent human appearance features, which have proven to be effective for the task of person re-id [18,30]. These features are naturally complementary to each other, because texture features are usually extracted from gray-scale images, while color features could capture the chromatic patterns within an image. Particularly, we use Local Binary Patterns (LBP) [5], HSV and Lab color channels to build an image frame level person representation, as have been used by many previous works [31,32]. All images are resized to the size of

128×64 before feature extraction. Features are extracted from 16×8 rectangular patches, with a spatial overlap of 8 and 4 pixels, vertically and horizontally. For each patch, we compute the histogram of LBP codes from gray scale representation. The mean values of HSV and Lab color channels are also computed. All these patch level features are concatenated to build an image frame level representation, *i.e.*, for each rectangular patch, the dimension is 262 $(256 + 6)$, and the dimensionality of the input feature is 58950 $(262*225)$ for each time stamp. The output of the LSTM unit at each time stamp is a 512-dimensional vector.

Network Training. The sequence of image level feature vectors are input to a LSTM network for progressive/sequential feature fusion. The network is trained as a classification problem of N classes (N is the number of persons), *i.e.*, we aim to classify the feature vectors which belong to the same person into the same class. In particular, each LSTM node includes three gates, (*i.e.* the input gate $\mathbf{i}$, the output gate $\mathbf{o}$ and the forget gate $\mathbf{f}$) as well as a memory cell. At each time stamp t (in our case, t indicates the order in the sequence), given the input $\mathbf{x}_t$ and the previous hidden state $\mathbf{h}_{t-1}$, we update the LSTM network as follows:

$$\mathbf{i}_t = \sigma(\mathbf{W}_i \mathbf{x}_t + \mathbf{U}_i \mathbf{h}_{t-1} + \mathbf{V}_i \mathbf{c}_{t-1} + \mathbf{b}_i) \tag{1}$$

$$\mathbf{f}_t = \sigma(\mathbf{W}_f \mathbf{x}_t + \mathbf{U}_f \mathbf{h}_{t-1} + \mathbf{V}_f \mathbf{c}_{t-1} + \mathbf{b}_f) \tag{2}$$

$$\mathbf{c}_t = \mathbf{f}_t \cdot \mathbf{c}_{t-1} + \mathbf{i}_t \cdot \tanh(\mathbf{W}_c \mathbf{x}_t + \mathbf{U}_c \mathbf{h}_{t-1} + \mathbf{b}_c) \tag{3}$$

$$\mathbf{o}_t = \sigma(\mathbf{W}_o \mathbf{x}_t + \mathbf{U}_o \mathbf{h}_{t-1} + \mathbf{V}_o \mathbf{c}_t + \mathbf{b}_o) \tag{4}$$

$$\mathbf{h}_t = \mathbf{o}_t \cdot \tanh(\mathbf{c}_t) \tag{5}$$

where σ is the sigmoid function and $\cdot$ denotes the element-wise multiplication operator. $\mathbf{W}_*$, $\mathbf{U}_*$ and $\mathbf{V}_*$ are the weight matrices, and $\mathbf{b}_*$ are the bias vectors. The memory cell $\mathbf{c}_t$ is a weighted sum of the previous memory cell $\mathbf{c}_{t-1}$ and a function of the current input. The weights are the activations of forget gate and input gate respectively. Therefore, intuitively, the network can learn to propagate/accumulate the good features to the deeper nodes of the network and forget noisy features in the meantime. The output of the LSTM hidden state $\mathbf{h}_t$ serves as the fused image level feature representation vector, which is further connected to a softmax layer. The output of the N-way softmax is the prediction of the probability distribution over N different identities.

$$y_i = \frac{\exp(y_i')}{\sum_{k=1}^{N} \exp(y_i')}, \tag{6}$$

where $y_j' = \mathbf{h}_t \cdot \mathbf{w}_j + b_j$ linearly combines the LSTM outputs. The network is learned by minimizing $-\log y_k$, where k is the index of the true label for a given input. Stochastic gradient descent is used with gradients calculated by back-propagation.

As only two sequences are available for a single person, and the length of the sequences are variable. To increase training instances and to make the model applicable for sequences of variable length, we randomly extract subsequences of fixed length L for training. L can be determined according to the nature of the dataset, we fix $L = 10$ in our experiments, considering the tradeoff between the amount of training instances and the information contained within each subsequence.

Network Implementation Details. In the proposed framework, the LSTM networks are trained/tested using the implementation of Donahue *et al.* [33] based on *caffe* [34]. The LSTM layer contains 512 output units, and a dropout layer is placed after it to avoid over-fitting. The weights of the LSTM layer is initialized from a uniform distribution in $[-0.01, 0.01]$. The training phase lasts for 400 epoches. As mentioned above, there is only a single LSTM layer to learn, therefore, we start with small learning rate 0.001 and after 200 epoches it decreases to 0.0001. The training procedure will terminate after another 200 epoches. We train the network on a Titan X GPU card, and a whole training duration is about 8 h for a dataset of 400 image sequences.

3.3   Person Re-identification

Once the feature aggregation network is trained, the sequence level representation can be obtained as follows. First, the testing sequence of a human patches is input to the aggregation network, then the LSTM outputs of each time stamp are concatenated to form the sequence level human feature representation for re-id purpose. The LSTM network we trained contains 10 time stamps, and from each time stamp we can extract a 512-dimensional feature vector. Therefore the total length of the sequence level representation is $5120(512 \times 10)$, denoted as $\mathbf{s}_i$ for the i-th human sequence sample. In our test phase, since the lengths of the human sequences are varying, the representations of K randomly selected subsequences (we assume the length of the sequence is larger than 10) are averaged to build the final sequence level representation. There are two benefits from this scheme. First, noisy information can be further diluted while discriminative information can be retained. Second, influences of different poses and walking circles are decreased.

After we get the person representation, we can apply a simple metric or distance metric learning methods to measure the similarity of two input instances. In this paper, we employ the RankSVM [10] method to measure the similarity as in [26]. In the meantime, a non supervised method (cosine distance metric) is also applied as a baseline metric. Experiments show that this simple combination works well in our re-id task. Consider the sequence level features $\{(\mathbf{s}_i^a, \mathbf{s}_i^b)\}_{i=1}^N$, where $\mathbf{s}_i^a$ and $\mathbf{s}_i^b$ denote the sequence level features of the i-th person from camera a and b. Suppose images from camera a are probe images and images from camera b are galleries. The cosine distance of a probe-gallery pair is represented as

$$d_{ij} = \frac{\mathbf{s}_i^a \cdot \mathbf{s}_j^b}{\|\mathbf{s}_i^a\| \, \|\mathbf{s}_j^b\|}, \tag{7}$$

where the $\|\cdot\|$ denotes the L_2 norm of the vector. Note that we do not use any complex metric learning technique. For a probe $\mathbf{s}_i^a$, the distances of all the pairs $\{d_{ij}\}_{i=1}^N$ are ranked in ascending order. If the distance of the true probe-gallery pair is ranked within the k top matched samples, it is counted in the top-k matching rate.

To train the RankSVM model, probe-gallery pairs with ground-truth labels are used for training. There is a single positive instance for a person, denoted as $\mathbf{s}_i^+ = |\mathbf{s}_i^a - \mathbf{s}_i^b|$. The negative instances consist of non-matching pairs: $\mathbf{s}_{ij}^- = |\mathbf{s}_i^a - \mathbf{s}_j^b|$, for all $j \neq i$. Consider a linear function $F(\mathbf{s}) = \mathbf{w} \cdot \mathbf{s}$, we wish to learn a weight vector such that:

$$\forall j \neq i : F(\mathbf{s}_i^+) > F(\mathbf{s}_{ij}^-). \tag{8}$$

The solution can be obtained using the SVM solver by minimizing following objective function:

$$\frac{1}{2}\mathbf{w} \cdot \mathbf{w} + C \sum \xi_{ij}$$
$$s.t. \; \forall j \neq i : \mathbf{w} \cdot \mathbf{s}_i^+ \geq \mathbf{w} \cdot \mathbf{s}_{ij}^- + 1 - \xi_{ij} \tag{9}$$
$$\forall (i,j) : \xi_{ij} \geq 0.$$

Once the RankSVM model is trained, it can be used to give the similarity rankings out of a set of probe-gallery pairs, $i.e.$, to fullfill the re-id task.

4 Experiments

In this section, we present extensive experimental evaluations and in-depth analysis of the proposed method in terms of effectiveness and robustness. We also quantitatively compare our method with the state-of-the-art multi-shot re-id methods. Algorithmic evaluations are performed on the following two person re-id benchmarks:

iLIDS-VID dataset. The iLIDS-VID dataset contains of 600 image sequences for 300 people in two non-overlapping camera views. Each image sequence consists of frames of variable length from 23 to 192, with an average length of 73. This dataset was created at an airport arrival hall under a multi-camera CCTV network, and the images were captured with significant background clutter, occlusions, and viewpoint/illumination variations, which makes the dataset very challenging.

PRID 2011 dataset. The PRID 2011 dataset includes 400 image sequences for 200 people from two camera. Each image sequence has a variable length consisting of 5 to 675 image frames, with an average number of 100. The images were captured in an uncrowded outdoor environment with relatively simple and clean background and rare occlusion; however, there are significant viewpoint and illumination variations as well as color inconsistency between the two views.

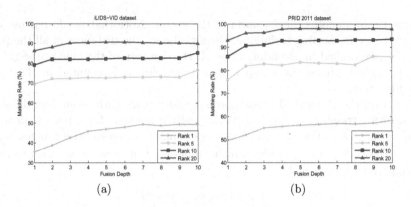

(a)   (b)

Fig. 3. Rank-1,5,10 and 20 person re-id matching rates based on different *fusion depth* on (a) iLIDS-VID and (b) PRID 2011 datasets

Following [11], the sequence pairs with more than 21 frames are used in our experiments.

Evaluation settings. Following [11], the whole set of human sequence pairs of both datasets is randomly split into two subsets with equal size, *i.e.*, one for training and the other for testing. The sequence of the first camera is used as probe set while the gallery set is from the other one. For both datasets, we report the performance of the average Cumulative Matching Characteristics (CMC) curves over 10 trials.

4.1   Effectiveness of Recurrent Feature Aggregation Network

To evaluate the effectiveness of the proposed recurrent feature aggregation network (**RFA-Net**), we extract the learned feature representation from each LSTM node of our network and evaluate the person re-id matching rate on the testing set. The results on both datasets are illustrated in Fig. 3. From Fig. 3, we have two observations. First, the matching rate increases consistently when the features are extracted from *deeper* LSTM nodes of our network. And the accumulated sequence level person representation (last node output) outperforms single frame level representation (first node output) for about 10 % on both datasets. This demonstrates that the proposed network is able to aggregate discriminative information from frame level towards a more discriminative sequence level feature representation. Second, we note that the rank-1 matching rate increases (with respect to the network depth) faster than others, which shows that the rank-1 matching performance relies more on the feature representation.

Based on the same type of visual features (*i.e.*, Color&LBP), we further compare our method with state-of-the-art matching method for person re-id. The compared methods are as follows. (1) Baseline method: the averagely pooled feature representation (*i.e.*, Color&LBP) of each frame in the person sequence combined with RankSVM [10] based matching method; (2) Sequence matching method: the two person sequences are matched by the Dynamic Time Wrapping

Table 1. Performance of different methods based on Color&LBP feature

Dataset	iLIDS-VID				PRID 2011			
Rank R	R=1	R=5	R=10	R=20	R=1	R=5	R=10	R=20
Color&LBP [31]+RSVM	23.2	44.2	54.1	68.8	34.3	56.0	65.5	77.3
Color&LBP+DTW [35]	9.3	21.7	29.5	43	14.6	33	42.6	47.8
Color&LBP+DVR [11]	34.5	56.7	67.5	77.5	37.6	63.9	75.3	89.4
Color&LBP+**RFA-Net**+Cosine	44.5	71.9	82.0	**90.1**	54.9	84.2	**93.7**	**98.4**
Color&LBP+**RFA-Net**+RSVM	**49.3**	**76.8**	**85.3**	90.0	**58.2**	**85.8**	93.4	97.9

(DTW) [35] method; and (3) Discriminative feature selection method: the Discriminative Video Ranking (DVR) [11] method which selects the most discriminative fragments for person matching. The comparison results on both datasets are summarized in Table 1. For our method, we perform experiment by using the simple cosine distance metric or the learned distance based on RankSVM and report both results. Note that for the rank-1 matching rate, our method outperforms the baseline method and the Discriminative Video Ranking (DVR) based method for more than 60 %. We further notice that even without metric learning, our method still achieves a rather good performance, which well demonstrates the discriminativeness of our learned sequence level representation, *i.e.*, our propose network is capable of fusing frame level human features into a more discriminative human sequence level feature representation. Also, based on recurrent scheme, our network implicitly encodes human dynamics. In contrast, the comparing methods which are only based on frame level feature matching (or even discriminative feature selection) do not possess good discriminative capability.

4.2   Robustness of Recurrent Feature Aggregation Network

As there exist a large amount of color/illumination change as well as occlusion and background clutter, a good re-id method should be robust to these noise. Here, we evaluate the robustness of our method by adding noise to human patch sequences to be matched. For the test image sequences in each dataset, part of the images are replaced by noise images, which are randomly selected from the other dataset (e.g., the noise for PRID 2011 dataset are images from iLIDS-VID dataset). Then we extract feature vectors from the noise contaminated images for person re-id. As shown in Table 2, although the performance suffers from the noise, our method still achieves 29.8 % and 44.7 % rank-1 matching rate on the two datasets when up to 50 % images (frames) are contaminated, which is remarkable. We also notice that the rank-10 and rank-20 matching rates just decree slightly compared to the corresponding noise-free sequences. This demonstrates that despite large amount of noises, our feature representation still remains good discriminativeness. This is because that LSTM network is capable of *propagating* discriminative features to deeper LSTM nodes as well as *forgetting* irrelevant information (*i.e.*, noises) during propagation. Therefore the aggregated sequence level representation is highly discriminative.

Table 2. Performance of our method in existence of noises

Dataset	iLIDS-VID				PRID 2011			
Rank R	R=1	R=5	R=10	R=20	R=1	R=5	R=10	R=20
Noise Level: 0%	49.3	76.8	85.3	90.0	58.2	85.8	93.4	97.9
Noise Level: 10%	43.4	70.6	81.5	88.9	52.3	83.2	91.4	97.5
Noise Level: 30%	40.0	67.4	77.5	87.0	51.4	81.1	90.5	96.9
Noise Level: 50%	29.8	60.5	71.9	81.5	44.7	75.2	85.6	95.5

Table 3. Performance of our method choosing different number of subsequences

Dataset	iLIDS-VID				PRID 2011			
Rank R	R=1	R=5	R=10	R=20	R=1	R=5	R=10	R=20
No. of subsequences: 1	33.1	60.9	73.0	82.9	45.6	73.0	84.7	94.3
No. of subsequences: 5	43.9	70.7	80.7	89.2	52.4	81.6	91.7	97.3
No. of subsequences: 10	**49.3**	**76.8**	**85.3**	**90.0**	**58.2**	**85.8**	**93.4**	97.9
No. of subsequences: 15	47.8	72.2	82.4	89.7	57.9	83.4	92.8	**98.0**

4.3 Effectiveness of Feature Averaging

We also evaluate the performance of our method when different numbers of subsequences are selected in the test phase. Choosing a single subsequence is similar to single-shot case, *i.e.*, the feature of a randomly selected fragment is used for matching. Therefore to be more discriminative, we first randomly select several subsequences from the input human sequence and average the subsequence level human features (based on our recurrent feature aggregation network) over several subsequences. The results are shown in Table 3. As expected, averaging several subsequences significantly enhance the performance because it makes the feature vector more robust to pose/illumination changes for representing a person, *i.e.*, noise is also diluted by this scheme. We also notice that the performance does not have much difference when the number of subsequences is 10 and 15. This is because 10 subsequences are already sufficient to well represent human dynamics.

4.4 Comparison to the State-of-the-Art

In this section, our method is compared with the state-of-the-art multi-shot person re-id approaches. We choose three methods for comparison and the results are shown in Table 4. From the results, we see that our method has outperformed the Discriminative Video Ranking (DVR) [36] for more than 20% on rank-1 matching rate. This is due to the fact that instead of selecting just one discriminative video fragment, we randomly select several subsequences in the video, which makes our feature more discriminative. Our method also achieves

Table 4. Performance of our method compared against state-of-the-art methods

Dataset	iLIDS-VID				PRID 2011			
Rank R	R=1	R=5	R=10	R=20	R=1	R=5	R=10	R=20
3D Hog&Color+DVR [36]	39.5	61.1	71.7	81.0	40.0	71.7	84.5	92.2
DVDL [14]	25.9	48.2	57.3	68.9	40.6	69.7	77.8	85.6
STFV3D [15]	37.0	64.3	77.0	86.9	21.6	46.4	58.3	73.8
STFV3D+KISSME [37]	44.3	71.7	83.7	**91.7**	**64.1**	**87.3**	89.9	92.0
Color&LBP+**RFA-Net**+Cosine	44.5	71.9	82.0	90.1	54.9	84.2	**93.7**	**98.4**
Color&LBP+**RFA-Net**+RSVM	**49.3**	**76.8**	**85.3**	90.0	58.2	85.8	93.4	97.9

better performance than the dictionary learning method DVDL [14], which discriminatively trained viewpoint invariant dictionaries. However, DVDL is unable to encode temporal information into the dictionaries. In our case, LSTM effectively solves this problem. Spatio-temporal Fisher vector (STFV3D) [15] generates a spatio-temporal body-action model that consists of a series of body-action units, which are represented by Fisher vectors built upon low-level features that combines color, texture and gradient information. This representation aligns the spatio-temporal appearance of a person globally and thus displays high discriminativeness when combines with a metric learning method (KISSME [37]). Compared to this method, our approach is simple and does not need to consider the temporal alignment problem. Even though, we still achieves comparable results to STFV3D+KISSME. In addition, the impressive performance of STFV3D+KISSME is largely due to the effectiveness of the metric learning method. Thus, using no metric learning leads to a large performance drop for this method. On the other hand, our method does not necessarily require a metric learning method to enhance performance. Even using a simple cosine distance metric, it still achieves impressive results on both datasets. This demonstrates that the feature we learned is very discriminative itself.

4.5 Matching Examples

In this section, we discuss about some matching examples in our experiments, as shown in Fig. 4. Here, four typical failure re-identification examples and a successful example are illustrated, where each row displays one. The first column in the figure consists of probe sequences, the second corresponds to their correct matching pairs and the third one contains the top matching sequence generated by our method. The top two rows show the failure examples from iLIDS-VID datasets, where the first failure is largely due to color inconstancy and occlusion. In the second case, the persons in last two sequences nearly have the same pose and they wear clothes of similar color, which make it difficult for a texture and color based feature to discriminate. In fact, these two sequence have very close similarity scores. The next two failure cases are similar, which are illustrated in the third and fourth row. The matching failure is caused by similar local

714 Y. Yan et al.

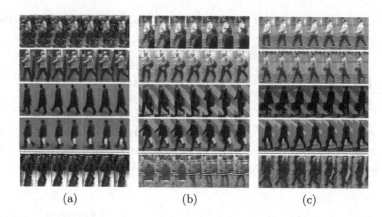

(a)   (b)   (c)

Fig. 4. Matching examples. (a) probe sequence, (b) Correct match, (c) Rank-1 matching sequence. The first four rows correspond to failure examples using features accumulated to the 10th LSTM node. The bottom row illustrates an example that fails to match the correct sequence when using the features from the first LSTM node, but correctly matches the probe sequence when using the features accumulated to the 10th LSTM node

information such as black briefcase in and white bag in hand, which makes it difficult to identify the correct match. These failure examples demonstrate that both color and local features have their limitations, using or combing more features has great opportunity to enhance the performance of our system.

An interesting example is displayed in the bottom row, where the third column corresponds to the rank-1 matching sequence using the features extracted from the first LSTM node. The failure is due to the occlusion, pose change and color inconsistency in the gallery sequence. However, when features are accumulated to the deeper (10th) LSTM nodes, our system correctly matches the probe sequence with the corresponding gallery sequence, which well demonstrate the effectiveness of our feature aggregation method. In addition, notice that all the examples displayed here are also difficult for humans to identify. The performance of our method using simple texture and color features is remarkable.

5 Conclusions

In this paper, we proposed a novel recurrent feature aggregation framework for person re-identification. In contrast to existing multi-shot person re-id methods that use complex feature descriptors or design complex matching metric, our method is capable of learning discriminative sequence level representation from simple frame-wise features. Experimental results show that features learned by this recurrent network not only possess high discriminativeness, and also show great robustness to noise. Even using simple texture and color features as input, the performance of the proposed method is better/comparable to the state-of-the-art methods.

Acknowledgements. The work was supported by State Key Research and Development Program (2016YFB1001003), NSFC (61527804, 61521062, 61502301), STCSM (14XD1402100), the 111 Program (B07022) and China's Thousand Youth Talents Plan.

References

1. Bedagkar-Gala, A., Shah, S.K.: A survey of approaches and trends in person re-identification. Image Vis. Comput. **32**(4), 270–286 (2014)
2. Farenzena, M., Bazzani, L., Perina, A., Murino, V., Cristani, M.: Person re-identification by symmetry-driven accumulation of local features. In: CVPR, pp. 2360–2367 (2010)
3. Gray, D., Tao, H.: Viewpoint invariant pedestrian recognition with an ensemble of localized features. In: Forsyth, D., Torr, P., Zisserman, A. (eds.) ECCV 2008, Part I. LNCS, vol. 5302, pp. 262–275. Springer, Heidelberg (2008)
4. Lowe, D.G.: Distinctive image features from scale-invariant keypoints. IJCV **60**(2), 91–110 (2004)
5. Ojala, T., Pietikäinen, M., Mäenpää, T.: Multiresolution gray-scale and rotation invariant texture classification with local binary patterns. TPAMI **24**(7), 971–987 (2002)
6. Li, W., Zhao, R., Xiao, T., Wang, X.: Deepreid: deep filter pairing neural network for person re-identification. In: CVPR, pp. 152–159 (2014)
7. Ahmed, E., Jones, M.J., Marks, T.K.: An improved deep learning architecture for person re-identification. In: CVPR, pp. 3908–3916 (2015)
8. Weinberger, K.Q., Blitzer, J., Saul, L.K.: Distance metric learning for large margin nearest neighbor classification. In: NIPS, 1473–1480 (2005)
9. Roth, P.M., Hirzer, M., Köstinger, M., Beleznai, C., Bischof, H.: Mahalanobis distance learning for person re-identification. In: Gong, S., Cristani, M., Yan, S., Loy, C.C. (eds.) Person Re-Identification. ACVPR, pp. 247–267. Springer, Heidelberg (2014)
10. Chapelle, O., Keerthi, S.S.: Efficient algorithms for ranking with svms. Inf. Retrieval **13**(3), 201–215 (2010)
11. Wang, T., Gong, S., Zhu, X., Wang, S.: Person re-identification by video ranking. In: Fleet, D., Pajdla, T., Schiele, B., Tuytelaars, T. (eds.) ECCV 2014, Part IV. LNCS, vol. 8692, pp. 688–703. Springer, Heidelberg (2014)
12. Zheng, L., Shen, L., Tian, L., Wang, S., Wang, J., Tian, Q.: Scalable person re-identification: A benchmark. In: ICCV, pp. 1116–1124 (2015)
13. Zheng, L., Shen, L., Tian, L., Wang, S., Bu, J., Tian, Q.: Person re-identification meets image search. CoRR abs/1502.02171 (2015)
14. Karanam, S., Li, Y., Radke, R.J.: Person re-identification with discriminatively trained viewpoint invariant dictionaries. In: ICCV, pp. 4516–4524 (2015)
15. Liu, K., Ma, B., Zhang, W., Huang, R.: A spatio-temporal appearance representation for viceo-based pedestrian re-identification. In: ICCV, pp. 3810–3818 (2015)
16. Hirzer, M., Beleznai, C., Roth, P.M., Bischof, H.: Person re-identification by descriptive and discriminative classification. In: Heyden, A., Kahl, F. (eds.) SCIA 2011. LNCS, vol. 6688, pp. 91–102. Springer, Heidelberg (2011)
17. Hochreiter, S., Schmidhuber, J.: Long short-term memory. Neural Comput. **9**(8), 1735–1780 (1997)
18. Ma, B., Su, Y., Jurie, F.: Bicov: a novel image representation for person re-identification and face verification. In: BMVC, pp. 1–11 (2012)

19. Scovanner, P., Ali, S., Shah, M.: A 3-dimensional sift descriptor and its application to action recognition. In: ICME, pp. 357–360 (2007)
20. Kläser, A., Marszalek, M., Schmid, C.: A spatio-temporal descriptor based on 3d-gradients. In: BMVC, pp. 1–10 (2008)
21. Hamdoun, O., Moutarde, F., Stanciulescu, B., Steux, B.: Person re-identification in multi-camera system by signature based on interest point descriptors collected on short video sequences. In: ICDSC, pp. 1–6 (2008)
22. Truong Cong, D.N., Achard, C., Khoudour, L., Douadi, L.: Video sequences association for people re-identification across multiple non-overlapping cameras. In: Foggia, P., Sansone, C., Vento, M. (eds.) ICIAP 2009. LNCS, vol. 5716, pp. 179–189. Springer, Heidelberg (2009)
23. Gheissari, N., Sebastian, T.B., Hartley, R.I.: Person reidentification using spatiotemporal appearance. In: CVPR, pp. 1528–1535 (2006)
24. Xu, Y., Lin, L., Zheng, W., Liu, X.: Human re-identification by matching compositional template with cluster sampling. In: ICCV, pp. 3152–3159 (2013)
25. Shen, C., Kim, J., Wang, L., van den Hengel, A.: Positive semidefinite metric learning using boosting-like algorithms. J. Mach. Learn. Res. 13, 1007–1036 (2012)
26. Prosser, B., Zheng, W., Gong, S., Xiang, T.: Person re-identification by support vector ranking. In: BMVC, pp. 1–11 (2010)
27. Zheng, W., Gong, S., Xiang, T.: Reidentification by relative distance comparison. TPAMI 35(3), 653–668 (2013)
28. McLaughlin, N., Martinez del Rincon, J., Miller, P.: Recurrent convolutional network for video-based person re-identification. In: CVPR (June 2016)
29. Haque, A., Alahi, A., Fei-Fei, L.: Recurrent attention models for depth-based person identification. In: CVPR (June 2016)
30. Zhao, R., Ouyang, W., Wang, X.: Unsupervised salience learning for person re-identification. In: CVPR, pp. 3586–3593 (2013)
31. Hirzer, M., Roth, P.M., Köstinger, M., Bischof, H.: Relaxed pairwise learned metric for person re-identification. In: Fitzgibbon, A., Lazebnik, S., Perona, P., Sato, Y., Schmid, C. (eds.) ECCV 2012, Part VI. LNCS, vol. 7577, pp. 780–793. Springer, Heidelberg (2012)
32. Jing, X., Zhu, X., Wu, F., You, X., Liu, Q., Yue, D., Hu, R., Xu, B.: Super-resolution person re-identification with semi-coupled low-rank discriminant dictionary learning. In: CVPR, pp. 695–704 (2015)
33. Donahue, J., Hendricks, L.A., Guadarrama, S., Rohrbach, M., Venugopalan, S., Saenko, K., Darrell, T.: Long-term recurrent convolutional networks for visual recognition and description. In: CVPR (2015)
34. Jia, Y., Shelhamer, E., Donahue, J., Karayev, S., Long, J., Girshick, R., Guadarrama, S., Darrell, T.: Caffe: Convolutional architecture for fast feature embedding (2014). arXiv preprint arXiv:1408.5093
35. Simonnet, D., Lewandowski, M., Velastin, S.A., Orwell, J., Turkbeyler, E.: Reidentification of pedestrians in crowds using dynamic time warping. In: Fusiello, A., Murino, V., Cucchiara, R. (eds.) ECCV 2012. LNCS, vol. 7583, pp. 423–432. Springer, Heidelberg (2012). doi:10.1007/978-3-642-33863-2_42
36. Wang, T., Gong, S., Zhu, X., Wang, S.: Person re-identification by discriminative selection in video ranking. CoRR abs/1601.06260 (2016)
37. Köstinger, M., Hirzer, M., Wohlhart, P., Roth, P.M., Bischof, H.: Large scale metric learning from equivalence constraints. In: CVPR, pp. 2288–2295 (2012)

Biconvex Relaxation for Semidefinite Programming in Computer Vision

Sohil Shah[1(✉)], Abhay Kumar Yadav[1], Carlos D. Castillo[1], David W. Jacobs[1], Christoph Studer[2], and Tom Goldstein[1]

[1] University of Maryland, College Park, MD, USA
sohilas@umd.edu, {jaiabhay,djacobs,tomg}@cs.umd.edu,
carlos@umiacs.umd.edu
[2] Cornell University, Ithaca, NY, USA
studer@cornell.edu

Abstract. Semidefinite programming (SDP) is an indispensable tool in computer vision, but general-purpose solvers for SDPs are often too slow and memory intensive for large-scale problems. Our framework, referred to as biconvex relaxation (BCR), transforms an SDP consisting of PSD constraint matrices into a specific biconvex optimization problem, which can then be approximately solved in the original, low-dimensional variable space at low complexity. The resulting problem is solved using an efficient alternating minimization (AM) procedure. Since AM has the potential to get stuck in local minima, we propose a general initialization scheme that enables BCR to start close to a global optimum—this is key for BCR to quickly converge to optimal or near-optimal solutions. We showcase the efficacy of our approach on three applications in computer vision, namely segmentation, co-segmentation, and manifold metric learning. BCR achieves solution quality comparable to state-of-the-art SDP methods with speedups between 4× and 35×.

1 Introduction

Optimization problems involving either integer-valued vectors or low-rank matrices are ubiquitous in computer vision. Graph-cut methods for image segmentation, for example, involve optimization problems where integer-valued variables represent region labels [1–4]. Problems in multi-camera structure from motion [5], manifold embedding [6], and matrix completion [7] all rely on optimization problems involving matrices with low rank constraints. Since these constraints are non-convex, the design of efficient algorithms that find globally optimal solutions is a difficult task.

For a wide range of applications [6,8–12], non-convex constraints can be handled by *semidefinite relaxation* (SDR) [8]. In this approach, a non-convex optimization problem involving a vector of unknowns is "lifted" to a higher dimensional convex problem that involves a positive semidefinite (PSD) matrix, which then enables one to solve a SDP [13]. While SDR delivers state-of-the-art

---

S. Shah and A.K. Yadav—The first two authors contributed equally to this work.

B. Leibe et al. (Eds.): ECCV 2016, Part VI, LNCS 9910, pp. 717–735, 2016.
DOI: 10.1007/978-3-319-46466-4_43

performance in a wide range of applications [3,4,6–8,14], the approach significantly increases the dimensionality of the original optimization problem (i.e., replacing a vector with a matrix), which typically results in exorbitant computational costs and memory requirements. Nevertheless, SDR leads to SDPs whose global optimal solution can be found using robust numerical methods.

A growing number of computer-vision applications involve high-resolution images (or videos) that require SDPs with a large number of variables. General-purpose (interior point) solvers for SDPs do not scale well to such problem sizes; the worst-case complexity is $O(N^{6.5} \log(1/\varepsilon))$ for an $N \times N$ problem with ε objective error [15]. In imaging applications, N is often proportional to the number of pixels, which is potentially large.

The prohibitive complexity and memory requirements of solving SDPs exactly with a large number of variables has spawned interest in fast, non-convex solvers that avoid lifting. For example, recent progress in phase retrieval by Netrapalli et al. [16] and Candès et al. [17] has shown that non-convex optimization methods provably achieve solution quality comparable to exact SDR-based methods with significantly lower complexity. These methods operate on the original dimensions of the (un-lifted) problem, which enables their use on high-dimensional problems. Another prominent example is max-norm regularization by Lee et al. [18], which was proposed for solving high-dimensional matrix-completion problems and to approximately perform max-cut clustering. This method was shown to outperform exact SDR-based methods in terms of computational complexity, while delivering acceptable solution quality. While both of these examples outperform classical SDP-based methods, they are limited to very specific problem types, and cannot handle more complex SDPs that typically appear in computer vision.

1.1 Contributions

We introduce a novel framework for approximately solving SDPs with positive semi-definite constraint matrices in a computationally efficient manner and with small memory footprint. Our proposed bi-convex relaxation (BCR), transforms an SDP into a biconvex optimization problem, which can then be solved in the original, low-dimensional variable space at low complexity. The resulting biconvex problem is solved using a computationally-efficient AM procedure. Since AM is prone to get stuck in local minima, we propose an initialization scheme that enables BCR to start close to the global optimum of the original SDP—this initialization is key for our algorithm to quickly converge to an optimal or near-optimal solution. We showcase the effectiveness of the BCR framework by comparing to highly-specialized SDP solvers for a selected set of problems in computer vision involving image segmentation, co-segmentation, and metric learning on manifolds. Our results demonstrate that BCR enables high-quality results while achieving speedups ranging from 4× to 35× over state-of-the-art competitor methods [19–23] for the studied applications.

2   Background and Relevant Prior Art

We now briefly review semidefinite programs (SDPs) and discuss prior work on fast, approximate solvers for SDPs in computer vision and related applications.

2.1   Semidefinite Programs (SDPs)

SDPs find use in a large and growing number of fields, including computer vision, machine learning, signal and image processing, statistics, communications, and control [13]. SDPs can be written in the following general form:

$$
\begin{aligned}
&\underset{\mathbf{Y} \in \mathcal{S}_{N \times N}^{+}}{\text{minimize}} \quad \langle \mathbf{C}, \mathbf{Y} \rangle \\
&\text{subject to} \quad \langle \mathbf{A}_i, \mathbf{Y} \rangle = b_i, \quad \forall i \in \mathcal{E}, \\
&\phantom{\text{subject to}} \quad \langle \mathbf{A}_j, \mathbf{Y} \rangle \leq b_j, \quad \forall j \in \mathcal{B},
\end{aligned} \tag{1}
$$

where $\mathcal{S}_{N \times N}^{+}$ represents the set of $N \times N$ symmetric positive semidefinite matrices, and $\langle \mathbf{C}, \mathbf{Y} \rangle = \text{tr}(\mathbf{C}^T \mathbf{Y})$ is the matrix inner product. The sets $\mathcal{E}$ and $\mathcal{B}$ contain the indices associated with the equality and inequality constraints, respectively; $\mathbf{A}_i$ and $\mathbf{A}_j$ are symmetric matrices of appropriate dimensions.

The key advantages of SDPs are that (i) they enable the transformation of certain non-convex constraints into convex constraints via semidefinite relaxation (SDR) [8] and (ii) the resulting problems often come with strong theoretical guarantees.

In computer vision, a large number of problems can be cast as SDPs of the general form (1). For example, [6] formulates image manifold learning as an SDP, [12] uses an SDP to enforce a non-negative lighting constraint when recovering scene lighting and object albedos, [24] uses an SDP for graph matching, [5] proposes an SDP that recovers the orientation of multiple cameras from point correspondences and essential matrices, and [7] uses low-rank SDPs to solve matrix-completion problems that arise in structure-from-motion and photometric stereo.

2.2   SDR for Binary-Valued Quadratic Problems

Semidefinite relaxation is commonly used to solve binary-valued labeling problems. For such problems, a set of variables take on binary values while minimizing a quadratic cost function that depends on the assignment of pairs of variables. Such labeling problems typically arise from Markov random fields (MRFs) for which many solution methods exist [25]. Spectral methods, e.g., [1], are often used to solve such binary-valued quadratic problems (BQPs)—the references [2,3] used SDR inspired by the work of [4] that provides a generalized SDR for the max-cut problem. BQP problems have wide applicability to computer vision problems, such as segmentation and perceptual organization [2,19,26], semantic segmentation [27], matching [3,28], surface reconstruction including photometric stereo and shape from defocus [11], and image restoration [29].

BQPs can be solved by lifting the binary-valued label vector $\mathbf{b} \in \{\pm 1\}^N$ to an N^2-dimensional matrix space by forming the PSD matrix $\mathbf{B} = \mathbf{b}\mathbf{b}^T$, whose non-convex rank-1 constraint is relaxed to PSD matrices $\mathbf{B} \in S^+_{N \times N}$ with an all-ones diagonal [8]. The goal is then to solve a SDP for $\mathbf{B}$ in the hope that the resulting matrix has rank 1; if $\mathbf{B}$ has higher rank, an approximate solution must be extracted which can either be obtained from the leading eigenvector or via randomization methods [8,30].

2.3 Specialized Solvers for SDPs

General-purpose solvers for SDPs, such as SeDuMi [31] or SDPT3 [32], rely on interior point methods with high computational complexity and memory requirements. Hence, their use is restricted to low-dimensional problems. For problems in computer vision, where the number of variables can become comparable to the number of pixels in an image, more efficient algorithms are necessary. A handful of special-purpose algorithms have been proposed to solve specific problem types arising in computer vision. These algorithms fit into two classes: (i) convex algorithms that solve the original SDP by exploiting problem structure and (ii) non-convex methods that avoid lifting.

For certain problems, one can exactly solve SDPs with much lower complexity than interior point schemes, especially for BQP problems in computer vision. Ecker *et al.* [11] deployed a number of heuristics to speed up the Goemans-Williamson SDR [4] for surface reconstruction. Olsson *et al.* [29] proposed a spectral subgradient method to solve BQP problems that include a linear term, but are unable to handle inequality constraints. A particularly popular approach is the SDCut algorithms of Wang *et al.* [19]. This method solves BQP for some types of segmentation problems using dual gradient descent. SDCut leads to a similar relaxation as for BQP problems, but enables significantly lower complexity for graph cutting and its variants. To the best of our knowledge, the method by Wang *et al.* [19] yields state-of-the-art performance—nevertheless, our proposed method is at least an order of magnitude faster, as shown in Sect. 4.

Another algorithm class contains non-convex approximation methods that avoid lifting altogether. Since these methods work with low-dimensional unknowns, they are potentially more efficient than lifted methods. Simple examples include the Wiberg method [33] for low-rank matrix approximation, which uses Newton-type iterations to minimize a non-convex objective. A number of methods have been proposed for SDPs where the objective function is simply the trace-norm of $\mathbf{Y}$ (i.e., problem (1) with $\mathbf{C} = \mathbf{I}$) and without inequality constraints. Approaches include replacing the trace norm with the max-norm [18], or using the so-called Wirtinger flow to solve phase-retrieval problems [17]. One of the earliest approaches for non-convex methods are due to Burer and Montiero [34], who propose an augmented Lagrangian method. While this method is able to handle arbitrary objective functions, it does not naturally support inequality constraints (without introducing auxiliary slack variables). Furthermore, this approach uses convex methods for which convergence is not well understood and is sensitive to the initialization value.

While most of the above-mentioned methods provide best-in-class performance at low computational complexity, they are limited to very specific problems and cannot be generalized to other, more general SDPs.

3   Biconvex Relaxation (BCR) Framework

We now present the proposed *biconvex relaxation (BCR)* framework. We then propose an alternating minimization procedure and a suitable initialization method.

3.1   Biconvex Relaxation

Rather than solving the general SDP (1) directly, we exploit the following key fact: any matrix $\mathbf{Y}$ is symmetric positive semidefinite if and only if it has an expansion of the form $\mathbf{Y} = \mathbf{X}\mathbf{X}^T$. By substituting the factorization $\mathbf{Y} = \mathbf{X}\mathbf{X}^T$ into (1), we are able to remove the semidefinite constraint and arrive at the following problem:

$$
\begin{aligned}
\underset{\mathbf{X} \in \mathbb{R}^{N \times r}}{\text{minimize}} \quad & \operatorname{tr}(\mathbf{X}^T \mathbf{C} \mathbf{X}) \\
\text{subject to} \quad & \operatorname{tr}(\mathbf{X}^T \mathbf{A}_i \mathbf{X}) = b_i, \quad \forall i \in \mathcal{E}, \\
& \operatorname{tr}(\mathbf{X}^T \mathbf{A}_j \mathbf{X}) \leq b_j, \quad \forall j \in \mathcal{B},
\end{aligned}
\tag{2}
$$

where $r = \operatorname{rank}(\mathbf{Y})$.[1] Note that any symmetric semi-definite matrix $\mathbf{A}$ has a (possibly complex-valued) square root $\mathbf{L}$ of the form $\mathbf{A} = \mathbf{L}^T \mathbf{L}$. Furthermore, we have $\operatorname{tr}(\mathbf{X}^T \mathbf{A} \mathbf{X}) = \operatorname{tr}(\mathbf{X}^T \mathbf{L}^T \mathbf{L} \mathbf{X}) = \|\mathbf{L}\mathbf{X}\|_F^2$, where $\|\cdot\|_F$ is the Frobenius (matrix) norm. This formulation enables us to rewrite (2) as follows:

$$
\begin{aligned}
\underset{\mathbf{X} \in \mathbb{R}^{N \times r}}{\text{minimize}} \quad & \operatorname{tr}(\mathbf{X}^T \mathbf{C} \mathbf{X}) \\
\text{subject to} \quad & \mathbf{Q}_i = \mathbf{L}_i \mathbf{X}, \quad \|\mathbf{Q}_i\|_F^2 = b_i, \quad \forall i \in \mathcal{E}, \\
& \mathbf{Q}_j = \mathbf{L}_j \mathbf{X}, \quad \|\mathbf{Q}_j\|_F^2 \leq b_j, \quad \forall j \in \mathcal{B}.
\end{aligned}
\tag{3}
$$

If the matrices $\{\mathbf{A}_i\}$, $\{\mathbf{A}_j\}$, and $\mathbf{C}$ are themselves PSDs, then the objective function in (3) is convex and quadratic, and the inequality constraints in (3) are convex—non-convexity of the problem is only caused by the equality constraints. The core idea of BCR explained next is to relax these equality constraints. Here, we assume that the factors of these matrices are easily obtained from the underlying problem structure. For some applications, where these factors are not readily available this could be a computational burden (worst case $\mathcal{O}(N^3)$) rather than an asset.

In the formulation (3), we have lost convexity. Nevertheless, whenever $r < N$, we achieved a (potentially large) dimensionality reduction compared to the

---

[1] Straightforward extensions of our approach allow us to handle constraints of the form $\operatorname{tr}(\mathbf{X}^T \mathbf{A}_k \mathbf{X}) \geq b_k, \forall k \in \mathcal{A}$, as well as complex-valued matrices and vectors.

original SDP (1). We now relax (3) in a form that is biconvex, i.e., convex with respect to a group of variables when the remaining variables are held constant. By relaxing the convex problem in biconvex form, we retain many advantages of the convex formulation while maintaining low dimensionality and speed. In particular, we propose to approximate (3) with the following *biconvex relaxation* *(BCR)*:

$$
\underset{\mathbf{X},\mathbf{Q}_i, i \in \{\mathcal{B} \cup \mathcal{E}\}}{\text{minimize}} \ \operatorname{tr}(\mathbf{X}^T \mathbf{C} \mathbf{X}) + \frac{\alpha}{2} \sum_{i \in \{\mathcal{E} \cup \mathcal{B}\}} \|\mathbf{Q}_i - \mathbf{L}_i \mathbf{X}\|_F^2 - \frac{\beta}{2} \sum_{j \in \mathcal{E}} \|\mathbf{Q}_j\|_F^2
$$
$$
\text{subject to} \quad \|\mathbf{Q}_i\|_F^2 \le b_i, \quad \forall i \in \{\mathcal{B} \cup \mathcal{E}\},
$$
(4)

where $\alpha > \beta > 0$ are relaxation parameters (discussed in detail below). In this BCR formulation, we relaxed the equality constraints $\|\mathbf{Q}_i\|_F^2 = b_i$, $\forall i \in \mathcal{E}$, to inequality constraints $\|\mathbf{Q}_i\|_F^2 \le b_i$, $\forall i \in \mathcal{E}$, and added negative quadratic penalty functions $-\frac{\beta}{2}\|\mathbf{Q}_i\|$, $\forall i \in \mathcal{E}$, to the objective function. These quadratic penalties attempt to force the inequality constraints in $\mathcal{E}$ to be satisfied exactly. We also replaced the constraints $\mathbf{Q}_i = \mathbf{L}_i \mathbf{X}$ and $\mathbf{Q}_j = \mathbf{L}_j \mathbf{X}$ by quadratic penalty functions in the objective function.

The relaxation parameters are chosen by freezing the ratio α/β to 2, and following a simple, principled way of setting β. Unless stated otherwise, we set β to match the curvature of the penalty term with the curvature of the objective i.e., $\beta = \|\mathbf{C}\|_2$, so that the resulting bi-convex problem is well-conditioned.

Our BCR formulation (4) has some important properties. First, if $\mathbf{C} \in \mathcal{S}_{N \times N}^+$ then the problem is biconvex, i.e., convex with respect to $\mathbf{X}$ when the $\{\mathbf{Q}_i\}$ are held constant, and vice versa. Furthermore, consider the case of solving a constraint feasibility problem (i.e., problem (1) with $\mathbf{C} = \mathbf{0}$). When $\mathbf{Y} = \mathbf{X}\mathbf{X}^T$ is a solution to (1) with $\mathbf{C} = \mathbf{0}$, the problem (4) assumes objective value $-\frac{\beta}{2}\sum_j b_j$, which is the global minimizer of the BCR formulation (4). Likewise, it is easy to see that any global minimizer of (4) with objective value $-\frac{\beta}{2}\sum_j b_j$ must be a solution to the original problem (1).

3.2 Alternating Minimization (AM) Algorithm

One of the key benefits of biconvexity is that (4) can be globally minimized with respect to $\mathbf{Q}$ or $\mathbf{X}$. Hence, it is natural to compute approximate solutions to (4) via alternating minimization. Note the convergence of AM for biconvex problems is well understood [35,36]. The two stages of the proposed method for BCR are detailed next.

Stage 1: Minimize with respect to $\{\mathbf{Q}_i\}$. The BCR objective in (4) is quadratic in $\{\mathbf{Q}_i\}$ with no dependence between matrices. Consequently, the optimal value of $\mathbf{Q}_i$ can be found by minimizing the quadratic objective, and then reprojecting back into a unit Frobenius-norm ball of radius $\sqrt{b_i}$. The minimizer of the quadratic objective is given by $\frac{\alpha}{\alpha - \beta_i}\mathbf{L}_i\mathbf{X}$, where $\beta_i = 0$ if $i \in \mathcal{B}$ and $\beta_i = \beta$ if $i \in \mathcal{E}$. The projection onto the unit ball then leads to the following

---

Algorithm 1. AM for Biconvex Relaxation

1: **inputs:** $\mathbf{C}$, $\{\mathbf{L}_i\}$, b_i, α, and β, **output:** $\mathbf{X}$
2: Compute an initializer for $\mathbf{X}$ as in Sect. 3.3
3: Precompute $\mathbf{M} = \left(\mathbf{C} + \alpha \sum_{i \in \{\mathcal{E} \cup \mathcal{B}\}} \mathbf{L}_i^T \mathbf{L}_i\right)^{-1}$
4: **while** not converged **do**
5: $\quad \mathbf{Q}_i \leftarrow \frac{\mathbf{L}_i \mathbf{X}}{\|\mathbf{L}_i \mathbf{X}\|_F} \min\left\{\sqrt{b_i}, \frac{\alpha}{\alpha - \beta_i}\|\mathbf{L}_i \mathbf{X}\|_F\right\}$
6: $\quad \mathbf{X} \leftarrow \mathbf{M}\left(\sum_{i \in \{\mathcal{E} \cup \mathcal{B}\}} \mathbf{L}_i^T \mathbf{Q}_i\right),$
7: **end while**

---

expansion–reprojection update:

$$\mathbf{Q}_i \leftarrow \frac{\mathbf{L}_i \mathbf{X}}{\|\mathbf{L}_i \mathbf{X}\|_F} \min\left\{\sqrt{b_i}, \frac{\alpha}{\alpha - \beta_i}\|\mathbf{L}_i \mathbf{X}\|_F\right\}. \tag{5}$$

Intuitively, this expansion–reprojection update causes the matrix $\mathbf{Q}_i$ to expand if $i \in \mathcal{E}$, thus encouraging it to satisfy the relaxed constraints in (4) with equality.

Stage 2: Minimize with respect to X. This stage solves the least-squares problem:

$$\mathbf{X} \leftarrow \underset{\mathbf{X} \in \mathbb{R}^{N \times r}}{\text{argmin}} \ \text{tr}(\mathbf{X}^T \mathbf{C} \mathbf{X}) + \frac{\alpha}{2} \sum_{i \in \{\mathcal{E} \cup \mathcal{B}\}} \|\mathbf{Q}_i - \mathbf{L}_i \mathbf{X}\|_F^2. \tag{6}$$

The optimality conditions for this problem are linear equations, and the solution is

$$\mathbf{X} \leftarrow \left(\mathbf{C} + \alpha \sum_{i \in \{\mathcal{E} \cup \mathcal{B}\}} \mathbf{L}_i^T \mathbf{L}_i\right)^{-1} \left(\sum_{i \in \{\mathcal{E} \cup \mathcal{B}\}} \mathbf{L}_i^T \mathbf{Q}_i\right), \tag{7}$$

where the matrix inverse (one-time computation) may be replaced by a pseudo-inverse if necessary. Alternatively, one may perform a simple gradient-descent step with a suitable step size, which avoids the inversion of a potentially large-dimensional matrix.

The resulting AM algorithm for the proposed BCR (4) is summarized in Algorithm 1.

3.3 Initialization

The problem (4) is biconvex and hence, a global minimizer can be found with respect to either $\{\mathbf{Q}_i\}$ or $\mathbf{X}$, although a global minimizer of the joint problem is not guaranteed. We hope to find a global minimizer at low complexity using the AM method, but in practice AM may get trapped in local minima, especially if the variables have been initialized poorly. We now propose a principled method for computing an initializer for $\mathbf{X}$ that is often close to the global optimum of the BCR problem—our initializer is key for the success of the proposed AM procedure and enables fast convergence.

The papers [16,17] have considered optimization problems that arise in phase retrieval where $\mathcal{B} = \varnothing$ (i.e., there are only equality constraints), $\mathbf{C} = \mathbf{I}$ being the identity, and $\mathbf{Y}$ being rank one. For such problems, the objective of (1) reduces to tr($\mathbf{Y}$). By setting $\mathbf{Y} = \mathbf{xx}^T$, we obtain the following formulation:

$$\underset{\mathbf{x} \in \mathbb{R}^N}{\text{minimize}} \; \|\mathbf{x}\|_2^2 \quad \text{subject to} \; \mathbf{q}_i = \mathbf{L}_i\mathbf{x}, \quad \|\mathbf{q}_i\|_2^2 = b_i, \quad \forall i \in \mathcal{E}. \tag{8}$$

Netrapali *et al.* [16] proposed an iterative algorithm for solving (8), which has been initialized by the following strategy. Define

$$\mathbf{Z} = \frac{1}{|\mathcal{E}|} \sum_{i \in \mathcal{E}} b_i \mathbf{L}_i^T \mathbf{L}_i. \tag{9}$$

Let $\mathbf{v}$ be the leading eigenvector of $\mathbf{Z}$ and λ the leading eigenvalue. Then $\mathbf{x} = \lambda\mathbf{v}$ is an accurate approximation to the true solution of (8). In fact, if the matrices $\mathbf{L}_i$ are sampled from a random normal distribution, then it was shown in [16,17] that $\mathbb{E}\|\mathbf{x}^\star - \lambda\mathbf{x}\|_2^2 \to 0$ (in expectation) as $|\mathcal{E}| \to \infty$, where $\mathbf{x}^\star$ is the true solution to (8).

We are interested in a good initializer for the general problem in (3) where $\mathbf{X}$ can be rank one or higher. We focus on problems with equality constraints only—note that one can use slack variables to convert a problem with inequality constraints into the same form [13]. Given that $\mathbf{C}$ is a symmetric positive definite matrix, it can be decomposed into $\mathbf{C} = \mathbf{U}^T\mathbf{U}$. By the change of variables $\widetilde{\mathbf{X}} = \mathbf{UX}$, we can rewrite (1) as follows:

$$\underset{\mathbf{X} \in \mathbb{R}^{N \times r}}{\text{minimize}} \; \|\widetilde{\mathbf{X}}\|_F^2 \quad \text{subject to} \; \langle \widetilde{\mathbf{A}}_i, \widetilde{\mathbf{X}}\widetilde{\mathbf{X}}^T \rangle = b_i, \quad \forall i \in \mathcal{E}, \tag{10}$$

where $\widetilde{\mathbf{A}}_i = \mathbf{U}^{-T}\mathbf{A}_i\mathbf{U}^{-1}$, and we omitted the inequality constraints. To initialize the proposed AM procedure in Algorithm 1, we make the change of variables $\widetilde{\mathbf{X}} = \mathbf{UX}$ to transform the BCR formulation into the form of (10). Analogously to the initialization procedure in [16] for phase retrieval, we then compute an initializer $\widetilde{\mathbf{X}}_0$ using the leading r eigenvectors of $\mathbf{Z}$ scaled by the leading eigenvalue λ. Finally, we calculate the initializer for the original problem by reversing the change of variables as $\mathbf{X}_0 = \mathbf{U}^{-1}\widetilde{\mathbf{X}}_0$. For most problems the initialization time is a small fraction of the total runtime.

3.4 Advantages of Biconvex Relaxation

The proposed framework has numerous advantages over other non-convex methods. First and foremost, BCR can be applied to general SDPs. Specialized methods, such as Wirtinger flow [17] for phase retrieval and the Wiberg method [33] for low-rank approximation are computationally efficient, but restricted to specific problem types. Similarly, the max-norm method [18] is limited to solving trace-norm-regularized SDPs. The method of Burer and Montiero [34] is less specialized, but does not naturally support inequality constraints. Furthermore, since BCR problems are biconvex, one can use numerical solvers with guaranteed convergence. Convergence is guaranteed not only for the proposed AM least-squares method in Algorithm 1 (for which the objective decreases monotonically), but also for a broad range of gradient-descent schemes suitable to find solutions to biconvex problems [37]. In contrast, the method in [34] uses augmented Lagrangian methods with non-linear constraints for which convergence is not guaranteed.

4   Benchmark Problems

We now evaluate our solver using both synthetic and real-world data. We begin with a brief comparison showing that biconvex solvers outperform both interior-point methods for general SDPs and also state-of-the-art low-rank solvers. Of course, specialized solvers for specific problem forms achieve superior performance to classical interior point schemes. For this reason, we evaluate our proposed method on three important computer vision applications, i.e., segmentation, co-segmentation, and manifold metric learning, using public datasets, and we compare our results to state-of-the-art methods. These applications are ideal because (i) they involve large scale SDPs and (ii) customized solvers are available that exploit problem structure to solve these problems efficiently. Hence, we can compare our BCR framework to powerful and optimized solvers.

4.1   General-Form Problems

We briefly demonstrate that BCR performs well on general SDPs by comparing to the widely used SDP solver, SDPT3 [32] and the state-of-the-art, low-rank SDP solver CGDSP [38]. Note that SDPT3 uses an interior point approach to solve the convex problem in (1) whereas the CGDSP solver uses gradient-descent to solve a non-convex formulation. For fairness, we initialize both algorithms using the proposed initializer and the gradient descent step in CGDSP was implemented using various acceleration techniques [39]. Since CGDSP cannot handle inequality constraints we restrict our comparison to equality constraints only.

Experiments: We randomly generate a 256×256 rank-3 data matrix of the form $\mathbf{Y}_{\text{true}} = \mathbf{x}_1\mathbf{x}_1^T + \mathbf{x}_2\mathbf{x}_2^T + \mathbf{x}_3\mathbf{x}_3^T$, where $\{\mathbf{x}_i\}$ are standard normal vectors. We generate a standard normal matrix $\mathbf{L}$ and compute $\mathbf{C} = \mathbf{L}^T\mathbf{L}$. Gaussian matrices $\mathbf{A}_i \in \mathbb{R}^{250 \times 250}$ form equality constraints. We report the relative error in the recovered solution $\mathbf{Y}_{\text{rec}}$ measured as $\|\mathbf{Y}_{\text{rec}} - \mathbf{Y}_{\text{true}}\|/\|\mathbf{Y}_{\text{true}}\|$. Average runtimes for varying numbers of constraints are shown in Fig. 1a, while Fig. 1b plots the average relative error. Figure 1a shows that our method has the best runtime of all the schemes. Figure 1b shows convex interior point methods do not recover the correct solution for small numbers of constraints. With few constraints, the full lifted SDP is under-determined, allowing the objective to go to zero. In contrast, the proposed BCR approach is able to enforce an additional rank-3 constraint, which is advantageous when the number of constraints is low.

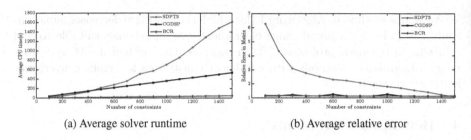

(a) Average solver runtime   (b) Average relative error

Fig. 1. Results on synthetic data for varying number of linear constraints.

4.2 Image Segmentation

Consider an image of N pixels. Segmentation of foreground and background objects can be accomplished using graph-based approaches, where graph edges encode the similarities between pixel pairs. Such approaches include normalized cut [1] and ratio cut [40]. The graph cut problem can be formulated as an NP-hard integer program [4]

$$\underset{\mathbf{x}\in\{-1,1\}^N}{\text{minimize}} \ \mathbf{x}^T \mathbf{L} \mathbf{x}, \tag{11}$$

where $\mathbf{L}$ encodes edge weights and $\mathbf{x}$ contains binary region labels, one for each pixel. This problem can be "lifted" to the equivalent higher dimensional problem

$$\underset{\mathbf{X}\in S_{N\times N}^+}{\text{minimize}} \ \text{tr}(\mathbf{L}^T \mathbf{X}) \quad \text{subject to} \ \text{diag}(\mathbf{X}) = \mathbf{1}, \quad \text{rank}(\mathbf{X}) = 1. \tag{12}$$

After dropping the non-convex rank constraint, (12) becomes an SDP that is solvable using convex optimization [2,14,28]. The SDP approach is computationally intractable if solved using off-the-shelf SDP solvers (such as SDPT3 [32] or other interior point methods). Furthermore, exact solutions cannot be recovered when the solution to the SDP has rank greater than 1. In contrast, BCR is computational efficient for large problems and can easily incorporate rank constraints, leading to efficient spectral clustering.

BCR is also capable of incorporating annotated foreground and background pixel priors [41] using linear equality and inequality constraints. We consider the SDP based segmentation presented in [41], which contains three grouping constraints on the pixels: $(\mathbf{t}_f^T \mathbf{P} \mathbf{x})^2 \geq \kappa \|\mathbf{t}_f^T \mathbf{P} \mathbf{x}\|_1^2$, $(\mathbf{t}_b^T \mathbf{P} \mathbf{x})^2 \geq \kappa \|\mathbf{t}_b^T \mathbf{P} \mathbf{x}\|_1^2$ and $((\mathbf{t}_f - \mathbf{t}_b)^T \mathbf{P} \mathbf{x})^2 \geq \kappa \|(\mathbf{t}_f - \mathbf{t}_b)^T \mathbf{P} \mathbf{x}\|_2^2$, where $\kappa \in [0,1]$. $\mathbf{P} = \mathbf{D}^{-1}\mathbf{W}$ is the normalized pairwise affinity matrix and $\mathbf{t}_f$ and $\mathbf{t}_b$ are indicator variables denoting the foreground and background pixels. These constraints enforce that the segmentation respects the pre-labeled pixels given by the user, and also pushes high similarity pixels to have the same label. The affinity matrix $\mathbf{W}$ is given by

$$W_{i,j} = \begin{cases} \exp\left(-\dfrac{\|\mathbf{f}_i - \mathbf{f}_j\|_2^2}{\gamma_f^2} - \dfrac{d(i,j)^2}{\gamma_d^2}\right), & \text{if } d(i,j) < r \\ 0, & \text{otherwise,} \end{cases} \tag{13}$$

where $\mathbf{f}_i$ is the color histogram of the ith super-pixel and $d(i,j)$ is the spatial distance between i and j. Considering these constraints and letting $\mathbf{X} = \mathbf{Y}\mathbf{Y}^T$, (12) can be written in the form of (2) as follows:

$$
\begin{aligned}
\underset{\mathbf{Y}\in\mathbb{R}^{N\times r}}{\text{minimize}} \quad & \mathrm{tr}(\mathbf{Y}^T\mathbf{L}\mathbf{Y}) \\
\text{subject to} \quad & \mathrm{tr}(\mathbf{Y}^T\mathbf{A}_i\mathbf{Y}) = 1, \quad \forall i = 1,\ldots,N \\
& \mathrm{tr}(\mathbf{Y}^T\mathbf{B}_2\mathbf{Y}) \geq \kappa\|\mathbf{t}_f^T\mathbf{P}\mathbf{x}\|_1^2, \ \mathrm{tr}(\mathbf{Y}^T\mathbf{B}_3\mathbf{Y}) \geq \kappa\|\mathbf{t}_b^T\mathbf{P}\mathbf{x}\|_1^2 \\
& \mathrm{tr}(\mathbf{Y}^T\mathbf{B}_4\mathbf{Y}) \geq \kappa\|(\mathbf{t}_f - \mathbf{t}_b)^T\mathbf{P}\mathbf{x}\|_1^2, \ \mathrm{tr}(\mathbf{Y}^T\mathbf{B}_1\mathbf{Y}) = 0.
\end{aligned}
\tag{14}
$$

Here, r is the rank of the desired solution, $\mathbf{B}_1 = \mathbf{1}\mathbf{1}^T$, $\mathbf{B}_2 = \mathbf{P}\mathbf{t}_f\mathbf{t}_f^T\mathbf{P}$, $\mathbf{B}_3 = \mathbf{P}\mathbf{t}_b\mathbf{t}_b^T\mathbf{P}$, $\mathbf{B}_4 = \mathbf{P}(\mathbf{t}_f-\mathbf{t}_b)(\mathbf{t}_f-\mathbf{t}_b)^T\mathbf{P}$, $\mathbf{A}_i = \mathbf{e}_i\mathbf{e}_i^T$, $\mathbf{e}_i \in \mathbb{R}^n$ is an elementary vector with a 1 at the ith position. After solving (14) using BCR (4), the final binary solution is extracted from the score vector using the swept random hyperplanes method [30].

We compare the performance of BCR with the highly customized BQP solver SDCut [19] and biased normalized cut (BNCut) [20]. BNCut is an extension of the Normalized cut algorithm [1] whereas SDCut is currently the most efficient and accurate SDR solver but limited only to solving BQP problems. Also, BNCut can support only one quadratic grouping constraint per problem.

Experiments: We consider the Berkeley image segmentation dataset [42]. Each image is segmented into super-pixels using the VL-Feat [43] toolbox. For SDCut and BNCut, we use the publicly available code with hyper-parameters set to the values suggested in [19]. For BCR, we set $\beta = \lambda/\sqrt{|\mathcal{B} \cup \mathcal{E}|}$, where λ controls the coarseness of the segmentation by mediating the tradeoff between the objective and constraints, and would typically be chosen from $[1, 10]$ via cross validation. For simplicity, we just set $\lambda = 5$ in all experiments reported here.

We compare the runtime and quality of each algorithm. Figure 2 shows the segmentation results while the quantitative results are displayed in Table 1. For all the considered images, our approach gives superior foreground object segmentation compared to SDCut and BNCut. Moreover, as seen in Table 1, our solver is $35\times$ faster than SDCut and yields lower objective energy. Segmentation using BCR is achieved using only rank 2 solutions whereas SDCut requires rank 7 solutions to obtain results of comparable accuracy.[2] Note that while BNCut with rank 1 solutions is much faster than SDP based methods, the BNCut segmentation results are not on par with SDP approaches.

4.3   Co-Segmentation

We next consider image co-segmentation, in which segmentation of the same object is jointly computed on multiple images simultaneously. Because co-segmentation

---

[2] The optimal solutions found by SDCut all had rank 7 except for one solution of rank 5.

728   S. Shah et al.

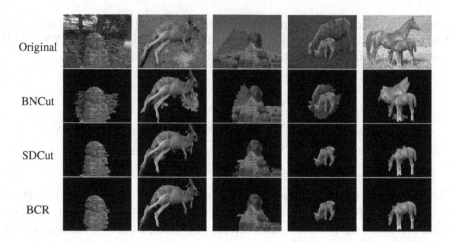

Fig. 2. Image segmentation results on the Berkeley dataset. The red and blue marker indicates the annotated foreground and background super-pixels, respectively. (Color figure online)

Table 1. Results on image segmentation. Numbers are the mean over the images in Fig. 2. Lower numbers are better. The proposed algorithm and the best performance are highlighted.

Method	BNCut	SDCut	BCR
Time (s)	**0.08**	27.64	0.97
Objective	10.84	6.40	**6.34**
Rank	1	7	2

Table 2. Co-segmentation results. The proposed algorithm and the best performance is highlighted.

Dataset		Test Cases			
		horse	face	car-back	car-front
Number of images		10	10	6	6
Variables in BQPs		4587	6684	4012	4017
Time (s)	LowRank	2647	1614	724	749
	ISDCut	220	274	180	590
	BCR	**18.8**	**61.8**	**46.7**	**44.7**
Objective	LowRank	4.84	4.48	5.00	4.17
	SDCut	5.24	4.94	4.53	4.27
	BCR	**4.64**	**3.29**	**4.36**	**3.94**
Rank	LowRank	18	11	7	10
	SDCut	3	3	3	3
	BCR	**2**	**2**	**2**	**2**

involves multiple images, it provides a testbed for large problem instances. Co-segmentation balances a tradeoff between two criteria: (i) color and spatial consistency within a single image and (ii) discrimination between foreground and background pixels over multiple images. We closely follow the work of Joulin *et al.* [26], whose formulation is given by

$$\text{minimize}_{\mathbf{x}\in\{\pm1\}^N} \mathbf{x}^T\mathbf{A}\mathbf{x} \quad \text{subject to } (\mathbf{x}^T\delta_i)^2 \le \lambda^2, \quad \forall i = 1,\ldots,M, \quad (15)$$

where M is the number of images and $N = \sum_{i=1}^{M} N_i$ is the total number of pixels over all images. The matrix $\mathbf{A} = \mathbf{A}_b + \frac{\mu}{N}\mathbf{A}_w$, where $\mathbf{A}_w$ is the intra-image affinity matrix and $\mathbf{A}_b$ is the inter-image discriminative clustering cost matrix computed using the χ^2 distance between SIFT features in different images (see [26] for a details).

To solve this problem with BCR, we re-write (15) in the form (2) to obtain

$$\underset{\mathbf{X} \in \mathbb{R}^{N \times r}}{\text{minimize}} \quad \text{tr}(\mathbf{X}^T \mathbf{A} \mathbf{X})$$

$$\text{subject to:} \quad \text{tr}(\mathbf{X}^T \mathbf{Z}_i \mathbf{X}) = 1, \quad \forall i = 1, \ldots, N \qquad (16)$$

$$\text{tr}(\mathbf{X}^T \boldsymbol{\Delta}_i \mathbf{X}) \leq \lambda^2, \quad \forall i = 1, \ldots, M,$$

where $\boldsymbol{\Delta}_i = \delta_i \delta_i^T$ and $\mathbf{Z}_i = \mathbf{e}_i \mathbf{e}_i^T$. Finally, (16) is solved using BCR (4), following which one can recover the optimal score vector $\mathbf{x}_p^*$ as the leading eigenvector of $\mathbf{X}^*$. The final binary solution is extracted by thresholding $\mathbf{x}_p^*$ to obtain integer-valued labels [21].

Experiments: We compare BCR to two well-known co-segmentation methods, namely low-rank factorization [21] (denoted LR) and SDCut [19]. We use publicly available code for LR and SDCut. We test on the Weizman horses[3] and MSRC[4] datasets with a total of four classes (horse, car-front, car-back, and face) containing $6 \sim 10$ images per class. Each image is over-segmented to $400 \sim 700$ SLIC superpixels using the VLFeat [43] toolbox, giving a total of around $4000 \sim 7000$ super-pixels per class. Relative to image segmentation problems, this application requires 10× more variables.

Qualitative results are presented in Fig. 3 while Table 2 provides a quantitative comparison. From Table 2, we observe that on average our method converges $\sim 9.5\times$ faster than SDCut and $\sim 60\times$ faster than LR. Moreover, the optimal objective value achieved by BCR is significantly lower than that achieved by both

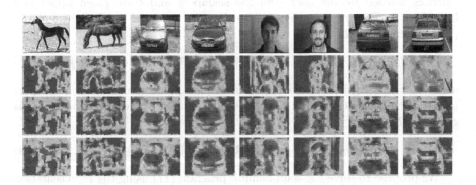

Fig. 3. Co-segmentation results on the Weizman horses and MSRC datasets. From top to bottom: the original images, the results of LR, SDCut, and BCR, respectively.

---

[3] www.msri.org/people/members/eranb/.
[4] www.research.microsoft.com/en-us/projects/objectclassrecognition/.

SDCut and LR methods. Figure 3 displays the visualization of the final score vector $\mathbf{x}_p^*$ for selected images, depicting that in general SDCut and BCR produce similar results. Furthermore, the optimal BCR score vector $\mathbf{x}_p^*$ is extracted from a rank-2 solution, as compared to rank-3 and rank-7 solutions needed to get comparable results with SDCut and LR.

4.4 Metric Learning on Manifolds

Large SDPs play a central role in manifold methods for classification and dimensionality reduction on image sets and videos [22,23,44]. Manifold methods rely heavily on covariance matrices, which accurately characterize second-order statistics of variation between images. Typical methods require computing distances between matrices along a Riemannian manifold—a task that is expensive for large matrices and limits the applicability of these techniques. It is of interest to perform dimensionality reduction on SPD matrices, thus enabling the use of covariance methods on very large problems.

In this section, we discuss dimensionality reduction on manifolds of SPD matrices using BCR, which is computationally much faster than the state-of-the-art while achieving comparable (and often better) performance. Consider a set of high-dimensional SPD matrices $\{\mathbf{S}_1, \ldots, \mathbf{S}_n\}$ where $\mathbf{S}_i \in S_{N \times N}^+$. We can project these onto a low-dimensional manifold of rank $K < N$ by solving

$$\begin{aligned}
\underset{\mathbf{X} \in S_{N \times N}^+, \eta_{ij} \geq 0}{\text{minimize}} \quad & \text{tr}(\mathbf{X}) + \mu \sum_{i,j} \eta_{ij} \\
\text{subject to} \quad & \mathbb{D}_X(\mathbf{S}_i, \mathbf{S}_j) \leq u + \eta_{ij}, \quad \forall (i,j) \in \mathcal{C} \\
& \mathbb{D}_X(\mathbf{S}_i, \mathbf{S}_j) \geq l - \eta_{ij}, \quad \forall (i,j) \in \mathcal{D}
\end{aligned} \tag{17}$$

where $\mathbf{X}$ is a (low-dimensional) SPD matrix, $\mathbb{D}_X$ is Riemannian distance metric, and η_{ij} are slack variables. The sets $\mathcal{C}$ and $\mathcal{D}$ contain pairs of similar/dissimilar matrices labeled by the user, and the scalars u and l are given upper and lower bounds. For simplicity, we measure distance using the log-Euclidean metric (LEM) defined by [22]

$$\mathbb{D}(\mathbf{S}_i, \mathbf{S}_j) = \| \log(\mathbf{S}_i) - \log(\mathbf{S}_j) \|_F^2 = \text{tr}\big((\mathbf{R}_i - \mathbf{R}_j)^T (\mathbf{R}_i - \mathbf{R}_j)\big), \tag{18}$$

where $\mathbf{R}_i = \log(\mathbf{S}_i)$ is a matrix logarithm. When $\mathbf{X}$ has rank K, it is a transformation onto the space of rank K covariance matrices, where the new distance is given by [22]

$$\mathbb{D}_X(\mathbf{S}_i, \mathbf{S}_j) = \text{tr}\big(\mathbf{X}(\mathbf{R}_i - \mathbf{R}_j)^T (\mathbf{R}_i - \mathbf{R}_j)\big). \tag{19}$$

We propose to solve the semi-definite program (17) using the representation $\mathbf{X} = \mathbf{Y}\mathbf{Y}^T$ which puts our problem in the form (2) with $\mathbf{A}_{ij} = (\mathbf{R}_i - \mathbf{R}_j)^T(\mathbf{R}_i - \mathbf{R}_j)$. This problem is then solved using BCR, where the slack variables $\{\eta_{ij}\}$ are removed and instead a hinge loss penalty approximately enforces the inequality constraints in (4). In our experiments we choose $u = \rho - \xi\tau$ and $l = \rho + \xi\tau$, where ρ and τ are the mean and standard deviation of the pairwise distances between

$\{S_i\}$ in the original space, respectively. The quantities ξ and μ are treated as hyper-parameters.

Experiments: We analyze the performance of our approach (short BCRML) against state-of-the-art manifold metric learning algorithms using three image set classification databases: ETH-80, YouTube Celebrities (YTC), and YouTube Faces (YTF) [45]. The ETH-80 database consists of a 10 image set for each of 8 object categories. YTC contains 1,910 video sequences for 47 subjects from YouTube. YTF is a face verification database containing 3,425 videos of 1,595 different people. Features were extracted from images as described in [22]. Faces were cropped from each dataset using bounding boxes, and scaled to size 20×20 for the ETH and YTC datasets. For YTF we used a larger 30×30 scaling, as larger images were needed to replicate the results reported in [22].

We compare BCR to three state-of-the-art schemes: LEML [22] is based on a log-Euclidean metric, and minimizes the logdet divergence between matrices using Bregman projections. SPDML [23] optimizes a cost function on the Grassmannian manifold while making use of either the affine-invariant metric (AIM) or Stein metric. We use publicly available code for LEML and SPDML and follow the details in [22,23] to select algorithm specific hyper-parameters using cross-validation. For BCRML, we fix α to be $1/\sqrt{|\mathcal{C} \cup \mathcal{D}|}$ and μ as $\alpha/2$. The ξ is fixed to 0.5, which performed well under cross-validation. For SPDML, the dimensionality of the target manifold K is fixed to 100. In LEML, the dimension cannot be reduced and thus the final dimension is the same as the original. Hence, for a fair comparison, we report the performance of BCRML using full target dimension (BCRML-full) as well as for $K = 100$ (BCRML-100).

Table 3 summarizes the classification performance on the above datasets. We observe that BCRML performs almost the same or better than other ML algorithms. One can apply other algorithms to gain a further performance boost after projecting onto the low-dimensional manifold. Hence, we also provide a

Table 3. Image set classification results for state-of-the-art metric learning algorithms. The last three columns report computation time in seconds. The last 3 rows report performance using CDL-LDA after dimensionality reduction. Methods using the proposed BCR are listed in bold.

Method	ETH-80	YTC	YTF	Train (s)	Test (s)	Total (s)
AIM	89.25 ± 1.69	62.77 ± 2.89	59.82 ± 1.63	-	5.189	1463.3
Stein	89.00 ± 2.42	62.02 ± 2.71	57.56 ± 2.17	-	3.593	1013.3
LEM	90.00 ± 2.64	62.06 ± 3.04	59.78 ± 1.69	-	1.641	462
SPDML-AIM [23]	91.00 ± 3.39	65.32 ± 2.77	61.64 ± 1.46	3941	0.227	4005
SPDML-Stein [23]	90.75 ± 3.34	66.10 ± 2.92	61.66 ± 2.09	1447	**0.024**	1453.7
LEML [22]	92.00 ± 2.18	62.13 ± 3.13	60.92 ± 1.95	93	1.222	437.7
BCRML-full	92.00± 3.12	64.40 ± 2.92	60.58 ± 1.75	189	1.222	669.7
BCRML-100	92.25 ± 3.78	64.61 ± 2.65	**62.42 ± 2.14**	45	0.291	127
CDL-LDA [44]	**94.25 ± 3.36**	72.94 ± 1.81	N/A	-	1.073	302.7
LEML+CDL-LDA [22]	94.00 ± 3.57	73.01 ± 1.67	N/A	93	0.979	369
BCRML-100+CDL-LDA	93.75 ± 3.58	**73.48 ± 1.83**	N/A	45	0.045	**57.7**

performance evaluation for LEML and BCRML using the LEM based CDL-LDA recognition algorithm [44]. The last three columns of Table 3 display the runtime measured on the YTC dataset. We note that BCRML-100 trains roughly 2× faster and overall runs about 3.5× faster than the next fastest method. Moreover, on testing using CDL-LDA, the overall computation time is approximately 5× faster in comparison to the next-best performing approach.

5   Conclusion

We have presented a novel biconvex relaxation framework (BCR) that enables the solution of general semidefinite programs (SDPs) at low complexity and with a small memory footprint. We have provided an alternating minimization (AM) procedure along with a new initialization method that, together, are guaranteed to converge, computationally efficient (even for large-scale problems), and able to handle a variety of SDPs. Comparisons of BCR with state-of-the-art methods for specific computer vision problems, such as segmentation, co-segmentation, and metric learning, show that BCR provides similar or better solution quality with significantly lower runtime. While this paper only shows applications for a select set of computer vision problems, determining the efficacy of BCR for other problems in signal processing, machine learning, control, etc. is left for future work.

Acknowledgements. The work of S. Shah and T. Goldstein was supported in part by the US National Science Foundation (NSF) under grant CCF-1535902 and by the US Office of Naval Research under grant N00014-15-1-2676. The work of A. Yadav and D. Jacobs was supported by the US NSF under grants IIS-1526234 and IIS-1302338. The work of C. Studer was supported in part by Xilinx Inc., and by the US NSF under grants ECCS-1408006 and CCF-1535897.

References

1. Shi, J., Malik, J.: Normalized cuts and image segmentation. Pattern Anal. Mach. Intell. IEEE Trans. **22**(8), 888–905 (2000)
2. Keuchel, J., Schno, C., Schellewald, C., Cremers, D.: Binary partitioning, perceptual grouping, and restoration with semidefinite programming. IEEE Trans. Pattern Anal. Mach. Intell. **25**(11), 1364–1379 (2003)
3. Torr, P.H.: Solving markov random fields using semi definite programming. Artif. Intell. Stat. **2**, 900–907 (2003)
4. Goemans, M.X., Williamson, D.P.: Improved approximation algorithms for maximum cut and satisfiability problems using semidefinite programming. J. ACM (JACM) **42**(6), 1115–1145 (1995)
5. Arie-Nachimson, M., Kovalsky, S.Z., Kemelmacher-Shlizerman, I., Singer, A., Basri, R.: Global motion estimation from point matches. In: 2012 Second International Conference on 3D Imaging, Modeling, Processing, Visualization and Transmission (3DIMPVT), pp. 81–88. IEEE (2012)
6. Weinberger, K.Q., Saul, L.K.: Unsupervised learning of image manifolds by semidefinite programming. Int. J. Comput. Vis. **70**(1), 77–90 (2006)

7. Mitra, K., Sheorey, S., Chellappa, R.: Large-scale matrix factorization with missing data under additional constraints. In: Advances in Neural Information Processing Systems (NIPS), pp. 1651–1659 (2010)
8. Luo, Z.Q., Ma, W.K., So, A.M.C., Ye, Y., Zhang, S.: Semidefinite relaxation of quadratic optimization problems. IEEE Signal Process. Mag. **27**(3), 20–34 (2010)
9. Lasserre, J.B.: An explicit exact SDP relaxation for nonlinear 0-1 programs. In: Aardal, K., Gerards, B. (eds.) IPCO 2001. LNCS, vol. 2081, pp. 293–303. Springer, Heidelberg (2001). doi:10.1007/3-540-45535-3_23
10. Boyd, S., Vandenberghe, L.: Semidefinite programming relaxations of non-convex problems in control and combinatorial optimization. In: Paulraj, A., Roychowdhury, V., Schaper, C.D. (eds.) Communications, Computation, Control, and Signal Processing, pp. 279–287. Springer, Heidelberg (1997)
11. Ecker, A., Jepson, A.D., Kutulakos, K.N.: Semidefinite programming heuristics for surface reconstruction ambiguities. In: Forsyth, D., Torr, P., Zisserman, A. (eds.) ECCV 2008. LNCS, vol. 5302, pp. 127–140. Springer, Heidelberg (2008). doi:10.1007/978-3-540-88682-2_11
12. Shirdhonkar, S., Jacobs, D.W.: Non-negative lighting and specular object recognition. In: Tenth IEEE International Conference on Computer Vision, ICCV 2005. vol. 2, pp. 1323–1330. IEEE (2005)
13. Vandenberghe, L., Boyd, S.: Semidefinite programming. SIAM Rev. **38**(1), 49–95 (1996)
14. Heiler, M., Keuchel, J., Schnörr, C.: Semidefinite clustering for image segmentation with a-priori knowledge. In: Kropatsch, W.G., Sablatnig, R., Hanbury, A. (eds.) DAGM 2005. LNCS, vol. 3663, pp. 309–317. Springer, Heidelberg (2005). doi:10.1007/11550518_39
15. Shen, C., Kim, J., Wang, L.: A scalable dual approach to semidefinite metric learning. In: 2011 IEEE Conference on Computer Vision and Pattern Recognition (CVPR), pp. 2601–2608. IEEE (2011)
16. Netrapalli, P., Jain, P., Sanghavi, S.: Phase retrieval using alternating minimization. In: Advances in Neural Information Processing Systems (NIPS), pp. 2796–2804 (2013)
17. Candès, E.J., Li, X., Soltanolkotabi, M.: Phase retrieval via wirtinger flow: theory and algorithms. Inf. Theor. IEEE Trans. **61**(4), 1985–2007 (2015)
18. Lee, J.D., Recht, B., Srebro, N., Tropp, J., Salakhutdinov, R.R.: Practical large-scale optimization for max-norm regularization. In: Advances in Neural Information Processing Systems, pp. 1297–1305 (2010)
19. Wang, P., Shen, C., van den Hengel, A.: A fast semidefinite approach to solving binary quadratic problems. In: The IEEE Conference on Computer Vision and Pattern Recognition (CVPR), June 2013
20. Maji, S., Vishnoi, N.K., Malik, J.: Biased normalized cuts. In: IEEE Conference on Computer Vision and Pattern Recognition (CVPR), pp. 2057–2064. IEEE (2011)
21. Journée, M., Bach, F., Absil, P.A., Sepulchre, R.: Low-rank optimization on the cone of positive semidefinite matrices. SIAM J. Optim. **20**(5), 2327–2351 (2010)
22. Huang, Z., Wang, R., Shan, S., Li, X., Chen, X.: Log-euclidean metric learning on symmetric positive definite manifold with application to image set classification. In: Proceedings of the 32nd International Conference on Machine Learning (ICML-15), pp. 720–729 (2015)
23. Harandi, M.T., Salzmann, M., Hartley, R.: From manifold to manifold: geometry-aware dimensionality reduction for SPD matrices. In: Fleet, D., Pajdla, T., Schiele, B., Tuytelaars, T. (eds.) ECCV 2014. LNCS, vol. 8690, pp. 17–32. Springer, Heidelberg (2014). doi:10.1007/978-3-319-10605-2_2

24. Bai, X., Yu, H., Hancock, E.R.: Graph matching using spectral embedding and alignment. In: International Conference on Pattern Recognition (ICPR). vol. 3, pp. 398–401. IEEE (2004)

25. Wang, C., Komodakis, N., Paragios, N.: Markov random field modeling, inference & learning in computer vision & image understanding: a survey. Comput. Vis. Image Underst. 117(11), 1610–1627 (2013)

26. Joulin, A., Bach, F., Ponce, J.: Discriminative clustering for image co-segmentation. In: Proceedings of the Conference on Computer Vision and Pattern Recognition (CVPR) (2010)

27. Wang, P., Shen, C., van den Hengel, A.: Efficient SDP inference for fully-connected CRFs based on low-rank decomposition. In: The IEEE Conference on Computer Vision and Pattern Recognition (CVPR), June 2015

28. Schellewald, C., Schnörr, C.: Probabilistic subgraph matching based on convex relaxation. In: Rangarajan, A., Vemuri, B., Yuille, A.L. (eds.) EMMCVPR 2005. LNCS, vol. 3757, pp. 171–186. Springer, Heidelberg (2005). doi:10.1007/11585978_12

29. Olsson, C., Eriksson, A.P., Kahl, F.: Solving large scale binary quadratic problems: Spectral methods vs. semidefinite programming. In: IEEE Conference on Computer Vision and Pattern Recognition, CVPR 2007, pp. 1–8. IEEE (2007)

30. Lang, K.: Fixing two weaknesses of the spectral method. Adv. Neural Inf. Process. Syst. (NIPS) 16, 715–722 (2005)

31. Sturm, J.F.: Using sedumi 1.02, a matlab toolbox for optimization over symmetric cones. Optim. Methods Softw. 11(1–4), 625–653 (1999)

32. Toh, K.C., Todd, M., Tutuncu, R.: Sdpt3 - a matlab software package for semidefinite programming. Optim. Methods Softw. 11, 545–581 (1998)

33. Okatani, T., Deguchi, K.: On the wiberg algorithm for matrix factorization in the presence of missing components. Int. J. Comput. Vis. 72(3), 329–337 (2007)

34. Burer, S., Monteiro, R.D.: A nonlinear programming algorithm for solving semidefinite programs via low-rank factorization. Math. Programm. 95(2), 329–357 (2003)

35. Duchi, J.C., Singer, Y.: Efficient online and batch learning using forward backward splitting. J. Mach. Learn. Res. 10, 2899–2934 (2009)

36. Douglas, J., Gunn, J.E.: A general formulation of alternating direction methods. Numer. Math. 6(1), 428–453 (1964)

37. Xu, Y., Yin, W.: A block coordinate descent method for regularized multiconvex optimization with applications to nonnegative tensor factorization and completion. SIAM J. Imaging Sci. 6(3), 1758–1789 (2013)

38. Zheng, Q., Lafferty, J.: A convergent gradient descent algorithm for rank minimization and semidefinite programming from random linear measurements. In: Neural Information Processing Systems (NIPS) (2015)

39. Goldstein, T., Studer, C., Baraniuk, R.: A field guide to forward-backward splitting with a FASTA implementation. arXiv eprint abs/1411.3406 (2014)

40. Wang, S., Siskind, J.M.: Image segmentation with ratio cut. IEEE Trans. Pattern Anal. Mach. Intell. 25, 675–690 (2003)

41. Yu, S.X., Shi, J.: Segmentation given partial grouping constraints. Pattern Anal. Mach. Intell. IEEE Trans. 26(2), 173–183 (2004)

42. Martin, D., Fowlkes, C., Tal, D., Malik, J.: A database of human segmented natural images and its application to evaluating segmentation algorithms and measuring ecological statistics. In: Proceedings of the 8th Int'l Conference Computer Vision, vol. 2, pp. 416–423, July 2001

43. Vedaldi, A., Fulkerson, B.: Vlfeat: An open and portable library of computer vision algorithms (2012) (2008)
44. Wang, R., Guo, H., Davis, L.S., Dai, Q.: Covariance discriminative learning: A natural and efficient approach to image set classification. In: 2012 IEEE Conference on Computer Vision and Pattern Recognition (CVPR), pp. 2496–2503. IEEE (2012)
45. Wolf, L., Hassner, T., Maoz, I.: Face recognition in unconstrained videos with matched background similarity. In: 2011 IEEE Conference on Computer Vision and Pattern Recognition (CVPR), pp. 529–534. IEEE (2011)

Image Co-segmentation Using Maximum Common Subgraph Matching and Region Co-growing

Avik Hati$^{(\boxtimes)}$, Subhasis Chaudhuri, and Rajbabu Velmurugan

Electrical Engineering Department,
Indian Institute of Technology Bombay, Mumbai, India
{avik,sc,rajbabu}@ee.iitb.ac.in

Abstract. We propose a computationally efficient graph based image co-segmentation algorithm where we extract objects with similar features from an image pair or a set of images. First we build a region adjacency graph (RAG) for each image by representing image superpixels as nodes. Then we compute the maximum common subgraph (MCS) between the RAGs using the minimum vertex cover of a product graph obtained from the RAG. Next using MCS outputs as the seeds, we iteratively co-grow the matched regions obtained from the MCS in each of the constituent images by using a weighted measure of inter-image feature similarities among the already matched regions and their neighbors that have not been matched yet. Upon convergence, we obtain the co-segmented objects. The MCS based algorithm allows multiple, similar objects to be co-segmented and the region co-growing stage helps to extract different sized, similar objects. Superiority of the proposed method is demonstrated by processing images containing different sized objects and multiple objects.

Keywords: Maximum common subgraph · Region co-growing

1 Introduction

Co-segmentation is the problem of segmenting objects with similar features from more than one image (see Fig. 1) or from multiple frames in a video. The objects of common interest in multiple images are detected as co-segmented objects [1], [2], [3]. Image foreground segmentation without supervision is a difficult problem. If an additional image containing a similar foreground is provided, both images can be segmented simultaneously with a higher accuracy using co-segmentation. Co-segmentation can also be used to detect objects of common

Partial financial supports from Bharti Centre for Communication in IIT Bombay and K.N Bajaj Chair Professorship are gratefully acknowledged.

Electronic supplementary material The online version of this chapter (doi:10. 1007/978-3-319-46466-4_44) contains supplementary material, which is available to authorized users.

B. Leibe et al. (Eds.): ECCV 2016, Part VI, LNCS 9910, pp. 736–752, 2016.
DOI: 10.1007/978-3-319-46466-4_44

(a)   (b)   (c)   (d)   (e)   (f)   (g)   (h)   (i)   (j)

Fig. 1. Illustration of the co-segmentation problem. (a–e) Images retrieved by a child from the internet, when asked to provide pictures of a tiger, and (f–j) common object quite apparent from the given set of images (Color figure online)

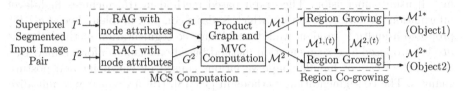

Fig. 2. Block diagram of the proposed co-segmentation algorithm. Input image pair I^1 and I^2 is represented as region adjacency graphs (RAGs) G^1 and G^2 that are used to obtain the maximum common subgraph (MCS) that gives the initial matched regions $\mathcal{M}^1$ and $\mathcal{M}^2$ in I^1 and I^2. These are iteratively (index-(t)) co-grown to obtain the final matched regions $\mathcal{M}^{1*}$ and $\mathcal{M}^{2*}$. In order to grow the region $\mathcal{M}^1$ in I^1, the region $\mathcal{M}^2$ is needed to find the match and similarly $\mathcal{M}^2$ requires $\mathcal{M}^1$ to grow (Color figure online)

interest in a set of crowd sourced images. A related topic in this area is image co-saliency. Co-saliency measures the saliency of co-occurring objects in multiple images. Image segmentation using co-segmentation is, in principle, different from object segmentation using co-saliency as the segmented object need not be the salient object in both images.

The co-segmentation methods in [1], [4], [5], [6] incorporate the foreground similarity of an image pair in their Markov Random Field model based optimization problem. Rother *et al.* [1] first introduced co-segmentation of an image pair using histogram matching through graph cuts. Mukherjee *et al.* [4] used a similar method by replacing l_1-norm in the cost function of [1] by l_2-norm. But the optimization problem in both methods is computationally intensive. Hochbaum and Singh [5] rewarded foreground histogram consistency, instead of minimizing foreground histogram difference [1], [4] to simplify the optimization. They also use prior information about foreground and background colors. The methods in [1], [4], [5], [6] perform well only for exactly same object on different background.

There has been some work on simplifying the co-segmentation problem by including user interaction for segmentation [7], [8]. Recent works focus on co-segmenting more than two images as it has more applications. Joulin *et al.* [9] formulated co-segmentation as a two-class clustering problem using a discriminative clustering method. They extended this work for multiple classes in [10] by incorporating spectral clustering. As their kernel matrix is defined for all possible pixel pairs of all images, the complexity goes up rapidly with the number of images. Mukherjee *et al.* [11] proposed a scale invariant co-segmentation method. Vicente *et al.* [12] used proposal object segmentations to train a random forest regressor for co-segmentation. This method relies heavily on the accuracy of individual segmentation outputs as it is assumed that one segment contains the complete object. Kim *et al.* [13] used anisotropic diffusion to optimize the number and location of image segments. As all the images are segmented into an equal number of clusters, over-segmentation may become an issue in a set of different types of images. Furthermore, this method cannot co-segment heterogeneous objects. An improvement to this has been proposed in [14] using supervision. The graph based method in [15] includes high-level information like object detection, which is also a complex problem. Lee *et al.* [16] proposed a multiple random walk based image co-segmentation method. Tao *et al.* [17] proposed a co-segmentation method based on shape conformability. But this method cannot handle shape variations caused by viewpoint and posture changes. The co-segmentation methods in [3], [18], [19] use saliency to initialize their methods.

Recently co-saliency based methods [20], [21], [22], [23], [24], [25], [26], [27] have also been used for co-segmentation. These methods detect common, salient objects by combining (i) individual image saliency outputs and (ii) pixel or superpixel feature distances among the images. Liu *et al.* [26] used hierarchical segmentation and Tan *et al.* [25] used a bipartite graph to compute feature similarity. Cao *et al.* [24] combined outputs of multiple saliency detection methods. Objects with high saliency value may not necessarily have common features while considering a set of images, hence these saliency guided methods do not always detect similar objects across images correctly. Also a good saliency detection method introduces additional complexity to the co-segmentation algorithm. Our solution to the co-segmentation problem is independent of saliency or any prior knowledge or pre-processing.

In this paper, we propose a novel foreground co-segmentation algorithm using an efficient graph matching based approach. We set up the problem as a maximum common subgraph (MCS) computation problem. We find a solution to MCS of two RAGs obtained from an image pair and then perform region co-growing to obtain the complete co-segmented objects.

In a standard MCS problem, node attributes are matched exactly for a pair of graphs. But in natural images, there can be some changes in features (e.g. color, texture, size) of similar objects or regions. So in our approach, node attributes do not need to match exactly. This necessitates selecting a threshold for node matching. The MCS algorithm matching allows multiple similar objects to be co-segmented. Region co-growing allows objects of different size to be detected. We show that an efficient use of the MCS algorithm followed by region co-growing can co-segment high resolution images without increasing computations.

We present the co-segmentation algorithm initially for two images in Sects. 2 and 3. We extend it for multiple images in Sect. 4. We show comparative results in Sect. 5 and conclude in Sect. 6.

2   Co-segmentation for Two Images

In the co-segmentation problem for two images, we are interested in finding the objects of interest that are present in both the images and have similar features. The flow of the proposed co-segmentation algorithm is shown in Fig. 2. First we segment each image (Fig. 3(a),(e)) into superpixels using SLIC method [28] and represent each image as a graph by representing the superpixels as nodes. Superpixel segmentation allows a coarse level description of the image through a limited number (N) of nodes of the graph. An increase in N increases the computation in graph matching drastically. So, we use superpixels instead of pixels as nodes. Moreover, each superpixel contains pixels from a single object and is homogeneous in feature and helps in retaining the shape of an object boundary. As an image is a group of connected components, we build a region adjacency graph (RAG) for each image where every spatially contiguous superpixel (node) pair is connected by an edge.

2.1   Image Representation as Attributed RAGs

We build two RAGs $G^1 = (\mathcal{V}^1, E^1)$ and $G^2 = (\mathcal{V}^2, E^2)$ corresponding to images I^1 and I^2, respectively (see Fig. 4(a) for illustration of MCS matching problem). Here $\mathcal{V}^i = \{v_k^i\}$ and $E^i = \{e_{kl}^i\}$ for $i = 1, 2$ denote the set of nodes and edges, respectively. In each graph G^i, an edge exists between a pair of nodes (superpixels) if they are spatial neighbors of each other. One can assign several features to each node. We use two features: (i) CIE Lab mean color and (ii) rotation invariant histogram of oriented gradient (HoG) of the pixels within the corresponding superpixel. The use of HoG feature is motivated by the fact that multiple superpixels can have similar mean color in spite of being completely different in color, and HoG features are useful to capture the image texture. To co-segment similar objects with different orientation, we use rotation invariant HoG of each superpixel. If an image is rotated, the gradient direction of every pixel is also changed by the same angle. Hence, the histogram (of gradients of a superpixel) will be shifted as a function of the rotation angle. In order to achieve rotation invariance, we circularly shift the computed HoG with respect to the location of the maximum histogram value. We compute the feature similarity ($\mathcal{S}_f(\cdot)$) between nodes v_k^1 in G^1 and v_l^2 in G^2 as a weighted sum of the corresponding color and HoG feature similarities denoted as $\mathcal{S}_c(\cdot)$ and $\mathcal{S}_h(\cdot)$, respectively as

$$\mathcal{S}_f \left(v_k^1, v_l^2 \right) = 0.5\,\mathcal{S}_c \left(v_k^1, v_l^2 \right) + 0.5\,\mathcal{S}_h \left(v_k^1, v_l^2 \right). \tag{1}$$

Here a normalized Euclidean distance measure is used for computing the feature distance. Normalization is done with respect to the maximum pairwise distance between all nodes. The similarity measure $\mathcal{S}_f(\cdot)$ is defined as the additive inverse of the computed normalized distance. We then obtain the MCS between the two RAGs to obtain the common objects as explained next.

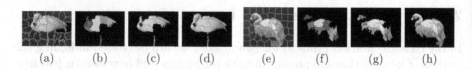

(a)   (b)   (c)   (d)   (e)   (f)   (g)   (h)

Fig. 3. Illustration of co-segmentation of an image pair. ((a),(e)) Input images and their SLIC segmentation. ((b),(f)) The matched nodes i.e., superpixels across images (shown in same color) obtained from the MCS computation and the corresponding ((c),(g)) object regions in the images. ((d),(h)) Co-segmented objects obtained after performing region co-growing on the initially matched regions in ((c),(g)) (Color figure online)

2.2   MCS Computation from RAGs

To solve the co-segmentation problem of an image pair, we need superpixel correspondences from one image to the other and match the superpixels within the objects of similar features across images. The computational complexity is $O((|G^1| + |G^2|)^3)$ assuming a minimum cost many-to-many matching algorithm [29]. Without any prior information about the objects, this matching becomes exhaustive and may result in many disconnected segments as matched regions. Each of these segments may be a group of superpixels or even a single superpixel and such matching may not be meaningful. To obtain a meaningful match, wherein the connectivity among the superpixels are maintained, we use a graph based approach to jointly segment the complete objects from an image pair. Thus our objective is to obtain the maximum common subgraph (MCS) that represents the co-segmented objects. The MCS corresponds to the common subgraphs M^1 in G^1 and M^2 in G^2. It may be noted that, in general, $M^1 \neq M^2$ as the common object in both the images need not undergo identical superpixel segmentation, and hence many-to-one matching must be permitted, unlike in a standard MCS finding algorithm. The computation time depends on the number of nodes in the graph, and this explains why we use the superpixel segmentation first as it cuts down the number of nodes drastically. Further to reduce the complication arising from many-to-one node matching, we assume that upto a maximum of p nodes in one image may match to a single node in the other image, based on a similarity measure. Following the work of Madry [30], it is possible to show that the computation complexity reduces to $O((p(|G^1| + |G^2|))^{10/7})$ when the matching is restricted to a maximum of p nodes only.

To find the MCS, we build two product graphs H^{12} and H^{21} (ideally known as vertex product graph) from the RAGs G^1 and G^2 based on their inter-image (superpixel) feature similarities (see Eq. (1)). A node in a product graph [31] is denoted as a 2-tuple (v_k^1, v_l^2) with $v_k^1 \in G^1$ and $v_l^2 \in G^2$. We call it a product node to differentiate it from single image nodes. As motivated in Sect. 1, node features do not need to match exactly for natural images. So, we select a threshold t_G ($0 \leq t_G \leq 1$) for matching. For a fixed $v_k^1 \in \mathcal{V}^1$, let $\mathcal{U}_k^2$ be the ordered list of nodes $\{v_l^2\}$ in $\mathcal{V}^2$ such that $\{\mathcal{S}_f(v_k^1, v_l^2)\}_{\forall l}$ are in descending order of magnitude. We define the set of product nodes $\mathcal{H}^{12}$ of the product graph H^{12} as

$$\mathcal{H}^{12} = \bigcup_{\forall k} \left\{ \left(v_k^1, u_l \in \mathcal{U}_k^2\right)_{l=1,2,\dots p} | \mathcal{S}_f \left(v_k^1, u_l\right) > t_G \right\} \qquad (2)$$

Similarly, we compute $\mathcal{H}^{21}$ by keeping $\mathcal{V}^2$ as reference. It is interesting to note that allowing one node in one graph to match to p nodes in the other graph leads to $\mathcal{H}^{12} \neq \mathcal{H}^{21}$, resulting in $M^1 \neq M^2$ (i.e. not commutative) as noted earlier. A large value of t_G restricts the matching to only a few candidate superpixels, and yet allowing certain amount of inter-image variations in the common objects. A small value of p ensures a fast computation during subgraph matching, still allowing the soft matches to be recovered during the region co-growing phase in Sect. 2.3. Thus the product graph size as well as the possibility of spurious matching reduces. For example, the size of the product graph for many-to-many matching is $O(|G^1||G^2|)$, and the choice of p in the matching process reduces the size to $O(p(|G^1| + |G^2|))$, while the additional use of the threshold t_G makes it $O(\alpha p(|G^1| + |G^2|))$ with $0 < \alpha \ll 1$. This reduces the computation drastically.

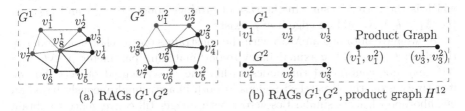

(a) RAGs G^1, G^2 (b) RAGs G^1, G^2, product graph H^{12}

Fig. 4. Illustration of maximum common subgraph computation. (a) Two RAGs G^1 and G^2 are obtained from images I^1 and I^2, respectively. The set of nodes $\mathcal{M}^1$, $\mathcal{M}^2$ and edges in the maximum common subgraphs M^1 and M^2 of G^1 and G^2, respectively, are highlighted (*in blue*). (b) Illustration of requirement of condition **C.2** of edge assignment in Sect. 2.2. Let the product nodes in the product graph obtained from the RAGs G^1, G^2 be $\left(v_1^1, v_1^2\right)$ and $\left(v_3^1, v_3^2\right)$ due to the constraint defined in Eq. (2). They are connected by an edge according to condition **C.2** although condition **C.1** is not satisfied. It is easy to derive that the nodes in the MCS are $\left(v_1^1, v_1^2\right)$ and $\left(v_3^1, v_3^2\right)$. This shows that multiple disconnected but similar objects can be co-segmented (Color figure online)

In H^{12}, we add an edge between two product nodes $\left(v_{k_1}^1, v_{l_1}^2\right)$ and $\left(v_{k_2}^1, v_{l_2}^2\right)$ with $k_1 \neq k_2 \wedge l_1 \neq l_2$ if
C.1. $e_{k_1 k_2}^1 \in G^1 \wedge e_{l_1 l_2}^2 \in G^2$, or **C.2.** $e_{k_1 k_2}^1 \notin G^1 \wedge e_{l_1 l_2}^2 \notin G^2$,
where $\wedge$ stands for the logical AND operation. As edges in the product graph H^{12} represent matching, the edges in its complement graph H_C^{12} and the product nodes which they are incident on represent non-matching. These product nodes are essentially the minimum vertex cover (MVC) of H_C^{12}. The MVC of a graph is the smallest set of vertices required to cover all the edges in that graph [32]. So, the set of product nodes ($\mathcal{M}^{12}$) other than this MVC represents the *left* matched product nodes, known as the maximal clique of H^{12} in the literature [31] (i.e. the reference graph G^1 being matched to G^2). Similarly, we obtain the *right* matched product nodes $\mathcal{M}^{21}$ from H^{21} (i.e. the reference graph G^2 being matched to G^1).

Let $\mathcal{M} \triangleq \mathcal{M}^{12} \cup \mathcal{M}^{21}$, and $\mathcal{M}^1 \subseteq \mathcal{V}^1$ and $\mathcal{M}^2 \subseteq \mathcal{V}^2$ be the set of nodes (see Fig. 3(b),(f)) in the corresponding common subgraphs M^1 in G^1 and M^2 in G^2, respectively, with

$$\mathcal{M}^1 = \{v_k^1 | (v_k^1, v_l^2) \in \mathcal{M}\} \quad \text{and} \quad \mathcal{M}^2 = \{v_l^2 | (v_k^1, v_l^2) \in \mathcal{M}\}, \qquad (3)$$

and they correspond to the matched regions (nodes) in I^1 and I^2, respectively (see Fig. 3(c),(g)). Note M^1 and M^2 are induced subgraphs. Here $|\mathcal{M}^1|$ and $|\mathcal{M}^2|$ need not be equal due to reasons mentioned earlier. The maximum common subgraphs for the example graphs G^1 and G^2, respectively, are highlighted in Fig. 4(a). Condition **C.1** alone cannot perform co-segmentation of multiple objects, if present, that are not connected to each other. The addition of condition **C.2** helps to achieve this. We illustrate this using an example. In Fig. 4(b), let the disconnected nodes v_1^1 and v_3^1 in G^1 be similar to the disconnected nodes v_1^2 and v_3^2 in G^2, respectively. Here use of condition **C.1** alone will co-segment either (i) v_1^1 and v_1^2 or (ii) v_3^1 and v_3^2, but not both. But using both conditions, we will be able to co-segment both (i) v_1^1 and v_1^2 and (ii) v_3^1 and v_3^2 which is the correct result. In the case of product nodes $\left(v_k^1, v_{l_1}^2\right)$ and $\left(v_k^1, v_{l_2}^2\right)$ (i.e. $k_1 = k_2$), we add an edge if $e_{l_1 l_2}^2$ exists.

As we have obtained an MCS with the constraints on the choice of similarity threshold t_G and the maximal many-to-one matching parameter p, $\mathcal{M}^1$ and $\mathcal{M}^2$ may not contain all the nodes within the co-segmented objects. So, we iteratively grow these matched regions in both images simultaneously based on neighborhood feature similarities across both images till convergence to obtain the complete co-segmented objects as explained next.

2.3 Region Co-growing

In the MCS algorithm of Sect. 2.2, our goal is to keep the product graph size small to reduce the computation even if the subgraphs obtained at the MCS output do not cover the complete objects. We do so by using a relatively large value of t_G and a small value of p. If two superpixels do match, it is expected to find matching of superpixels in their neighborhoods when the object is partially recovered. We can perform region co-growing on the regions $\mathcal{M}^1$ and $\mathcal{M}^2$ obtained from the MCS matching algorithm using them as seeds to obtain the complete objects. So, even if an image pair contains common objects of different size (and number of superpixels), they are completely detected after region co-growing. Moreover, obtaining an MCS with a small number of nodes followed by region co-growing is computationally less intensive than solving for a large product graph.

As we are interested in co-segmentation, we jointly and iteratively grow $\mathcal{M}^1$ and $\mathcal{M}^2$. Here our objective is to find nodes, in the *neighborhood of already matched regions (nodes)* in one image, having high feature similarity to the *already matched regions (nodes)* in the other image. We use these neighborhood nodes for region growing. Let $\mathcal{N}_{\mathcal{M}^i}$ denote the set of neighbors of $\mathcal{M}^i$, with $\mathcal{N}_{\mathcal{M}^i} = \bigcup_{v \in \mathcal{M}^i} \{u \in \mathbb{N}(v)\}$ for $i = 1, 2$, where $\mathbb{N}(\cdot)$ denotes neighborhood. In every iteration-t, we append a certain set of neighbors $\mathcal{N}_{s_2}^{(t)} \subseteq \mathcal{N}_{\mathcal{M}^2}^{(t)}$ to $\mathcal{M}^{2,(t)}$ if they

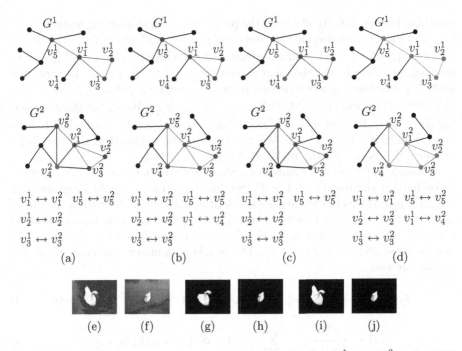

$$v_1^1 \leftrightarrow v_1^2 \quad v_5^1 \leftrightarrow v_5^2 \qquad v_1^1 \leftrightarrow v_1^2 \quad v_5^1 \leftrightarrow v_5^2 \qquad v_1^1 \leftrightarrow v_1^2 \quad v_5^1 \leftrightarrow v_5^2 \qquad v_1^1 \leftrightarrow v_1^2 \quad v_5^1 \leftrightarrow v_5^2$$

$$v_2^1 \leftrightarrow v_2^2 \qquad v_2^1 \leftrightarrow v_2^2 \quad v_1^1 \leftrightarrow v_4^2 \qquad v_2^1 \leftrightarrow v_2^2 \qquad v_2^1 \leftrightarrow v_2^2 \quad v_1^1 \leftrightarrow v_4^2$$

$$v_3^1 \leftrightarrow v_3^2 \qquad v_3^1 \leftrightarrow v_3^2 \qquad v_3^1 \leftrightarrow v_3^2 \qquad v_3^1 \leftrightarrow v_3^2$$

(a)   (b)   (c)   (d)

(e)   (f)   (g)   (h)   (i)   (j)

Fig. 5. Illustration of region co-growing. (a) The set of nodes $\mathcal{M}^1$ and $\mathcal{M}^2$ at the MCS outputs of the graphs G^1 and G^2, with v_1^1, v_2^1, v_3^1, v_5^1 match v_1^2, v_2^2, v_3^2, v_5^2, respectively. The nodes in MCSs are $\mathcal{M}^{1,(t)}$ and $\mathcal{M}^{2,(t)}$ (*blue*) at $t = 1$. To grow $\mathcal{M}^{2,(t)}$, we compare feature similarities of each node, e.g. v_4^2 (*red*), in the neighborhood of $\mathcal{M}^{2,(t)}$ to all the nodes in $\mathcal{M}^{1,(t)}$. (b) $\mathcal{M}^{2,(t+1)}$ (*green*) has been obtained by growing $\mathcal{M}^{2,(t)}$ and v_4^2 has been included in the set due to high feature similarity with v_1^1. (c) To grow $\mathcal{M}^{1,(t)}$, we compare feature similarities of each node, e.g. v_4^1 (*red*), in the neighborhood of $\mathcal{M}^{1,(t)}$ to all the nodes in $\mathcal{M}^{2,(t)}$. (d) The set of matched nodes (*purple*) after iteration-1 of region growing, assuming no match has been found for v_4^1. Effectiveness of region co-growing is illustrated in (e–j). ((e),(f)) Input images. ((g),(h)) The object regions in the images obtained from the MCS algorithm. As the two objects are of different size, the larger object (of image (e)) is not completely detected. ((i),(j)) Co-segmented objects are completely obtained after performing region growing on the initially matched regions (Color figure online)

have high inter-image feature similarity to the nodes in $\mathcal{M}^{1,(t)}$. Similarly, we append a certain set of neighbors $(\mathcal{N}_{s_1}^{(t)} \subseteq \mathcal{N}_{\mathcal{M}^1}^{(t)})$ of $\mathcal{M}^{1,(t)}$ to it. The matched region sets are updated as shown in the program.

We compute the weighted feature similarity $\mathcal{S}'_f(v_k^1, v_l^2)$ between a node v_k^1 in $\mathcal{M}^{1,(t)}$ and a node v_l^2 in $\mathcal{N}_{\mathcal{M}^2}^{(t)}$ as a function of (i) their feature similarity $\mathcal{S}_f(v_k^1, v_l^2)$ of Eq. (1) and (ii) the average feature similarity between their neighbors $(\mathcal{N}_{v_k^1}$ and $\mathcal{N}_{v_l^2})$ that are already in the set of matched regions i.e., in $\mathcal{M}^{1,(t)}$ and $\mathcal{M}^{2,(t)}$, respectively. Thus the similarity measure for region growing has an additional measure of neighborhood similarity compared to the measure used for graph matching in Sect. 2.2. We illustrate the proposed region co-growing method using Fig. 5. In Fig. 5(a), to compute the weighted feature similarity $\mathcal{S}'_f(v_1^1, v_4^2)$ between a matched node $v_1^1 \in \mathcal{M}^1$ and an unmatched neighboring node $v_4^2 \in \mathcal{N}_{\mathcal{M}^2}$ while growing $\mathcal{M}^2$, we consider their feature similarity $\mathcal{S}_f(v_1^1, v_4^2)$ and the feature similarity between the respective (matched) neighboring node pairs $(v_3^1 \in \mathcal{M}^1 \cap \mathcal{N}_{v_1^1}$, $v_3^2 \in \mathcal{M}^2 \cap \mathcal{N}_{v_4^2})$ and $(v_5^1 \in \mathcal{M}^1 \cap \mathcal{N}_{v_1^1}, v_5^2 \in \mathcal{M}^2 \cap \mathcal{N}_{v_4^2})$. We ignore the neighboring nodes $v_2^1 \in \mathcal{M}^1$ and $v_1^2 \in \mathcal{M}^2$ assuming they have not been matched to each other. Similarly while growing $\mathcal{M}^1$, we compute the weighted feature similarity between $v_4^1 \in \mathcal{N}_{\mathcal{M}^1}$ and the nodes in $\mathcal{M}^2$ (see Fig. 5(c)).

If a node in G^i has less number of *already matched neighbors*, it is more likely to be part of the background in I^i. So, less importance should be given to it even if it has relatively high feature similarities with the nodes within the object in I^j. In Fig. 5(a), the unmatched node $v_4^2 \in \mathcal{N}_{\mathcal{M}^2}$ has three matched neighboring nodes v_1^2, v_3^2 and v_5^2, whereas in Fig. 5(c), the unmatched node $v_4^1 \in \mathcal{N}_{\mathcal{M}^1}$ has one matched neighboring node v_1^1. The weighted similarity measure $\mathcal{S}'_f(v_k^1, v_l^2)$ is computed as

$$\mathcal{S}'_f(v_k^1, v_l^2) = \omega_{\mathcal{N}}\mathcal{S}_f\left(v_k^1, v_l^2\right) + (1 - \omega_{\mathcal{N}})\left(1 - (Q)^{|U_1||U_2|}\right) \text{, where} \quad (4)$$

$$Q = \frac{1}{|U_1||U_2|}\sum_{u_1 \in U_1, u_2 \in U_2}(1 - \mathcal{S}_f(u_1, u_2))\mathbb{1}(u_1, u_2) . \quad (5)$$

Here $\omega_{\mathcal{N}}$ is an appropriately chosen weight, $U_1 = \mathcal{N}_{v_k^1} \cap \mathcal{M}^{1,(t)}, U_2 = \mathcal{N}_{v_l^2} \cap \mathcal{M}^{2,(t)}$, $|\cdot|$ indicates cardinality and the indicator function $\mathbb{1}(u_1, u_2) = 1$ if the MCS matching algorithm yields a match between nodes u_1 and u_2 and $\mathbb{1}(u_1, u_2) = 0$ otherwise. The first term in Eq. (4) is the feature similarity, as defined earlier in Eq. (1), between the two nodes in consideration, v_k^1 and v_l^2. The second term is a measure of inter-image feature similarity among neighbors of v_k^1 and v_l^2. As desired, this value increases as the number of neighbors that have *already been matched* increases.

```
Region co-growing program
  begin
    repeat until convergence
```
$\mathcal{N}_{s_1}^{(t)} := \bigcup_{v_l^2 \in \mathcal{M}^{2,(t)}}\{v_k^1 \in \mathcal{N}_{\mathcal{M}^1}^{(t)}|\mathcal{S}_f'(v_k^1, v_l^2) > t_G\};$

$\mathcal{N}_{s_2}^{(t)} := \bigcup_{v_k^1 \in \mathcal{M}^{1,(t)}}\{v_l^2 \in \mathcal{N}_{\mathcal{M}^2}^{(t)}|\mathcal{S}_f'(v_k^1, v_l^2) > t_G\};$
```
    Region growing in G¹:  M^{1,(t+1)} := M^{1,(t)} ∪ N_{s_1}^{(t)};
    Region growing in G²:  M^{2,(t+1)} := M^{2,(t)} ∪ N_{s_2}^{(t)};
  end.
```

The region co-growing algorithm converges when $\mathcal{M}^{1,(t)} = \mathcal{M}^{1,(t-1)}$, $\mathcal{M}^{2,(t)} = \mathcal{M}^{2,(t-1)}$. We use $\mathcal{M}^{1*} \triangleq \mathcal{M}^{1,(t)}$ and $\mathcal{M}^{2*} \triangleq \mathcal{M}^{2,(t)}$ (see Fig. 2) to extract common objects completely from I^1 and I^2, respectively (also see Fig. 3(d),(h)). The example in Fig. 5(e–j) shows that region growing helps to completely detect common objects of different size. The larger object has been partially detected from MCS (Fig. 5(g)) and is fully recovered after region co-growing (Fig. 5(i)).

Relevance Feedback. The weight $\omega_{\mathcal{N}}$ in Eq. (4) is used to compute the similarity $\mathcal{S}'_f(v_1, v_2)$ between a pair of nodes from G^1 and G^2 during region co-growing from two constituent similarity measures. Instead of using heuristics, we use relevance feedback [33] to quantify the importance of the neighborhood information and find $\omega_{\mathcal{N}}$. It has been used by Rui *et al.* [34], among many others, to find optimal weights while combining different features for various applications.

2.4 Common Background Elimination

In the co-segmentation problem, we are interested in common foreground segmentation and not in common background segmentation. If an image pair contains background regions with similar features such as the sky or water body, the co-segmentation algorithm, as described so far, will also include the background regions as part of the co-segmented objects. Moreover, inclusion of similar background nodes will unnecessarily increase the size of product graph. We use the method of Zhu *et al.* [35] to obtain an estimate of the probability of a superpixel belonging to the background to eliminate it while building the product graphs and region co-growing. This method is briefly described next.

As we normally capture images keeping the objects of interest at the center of the image, the superpixels at the image boundary are more likely to be part of the background. In addition to the boundary superpixels, some superpixels not at the image boundary will also belong to the background and they have features similar to the boundary superpixels $(\mathcal{B})$. The boundary connectivity $\mathcal{C}_{\mathcal{B}}(v_i)$ of a superpixel v_i is defined as the fraction of its cumulative similarity to all superpixels in the image present at the image boundary. The probability of a superpixel v_i belonging to the background is given by [35] $\mathcal{P}_{\mathcal{B}}(v_i) = 1 - \exp\left(-\frac{1}{2}(\mathcal{C}_{\mathcal{B}}(v_i))^2\right)$. We compute this probability for all superpixels in images I^1 and I^2 independently, and discard the superpixels that have $\mathcal{P}_{\mathcal{B}}(v_i) > t_{\mathcal{B}}$, where $t_{\mathcal{B}}$ is a threshold, while constructing the graphs G^1 and G^2.

3 Pyramidal Image Co-segmentation

With an increase in image size for a well textured scene, the number of superpixels increases and the graph size becomes larger. To maintain the computational efficiency of the proposed co-segmentation algorithm for high resolution images, we use a pyramidal representation of images. We compute the maximum common subgraph at the coarsest level as it contains the least number of superpixels (nodes). This reduces the computation of the MCS matching algorithm. Then we perform region co-growing at every finer level in the pyramid. This avoids any localization error that might have occurred if both MCS computation and

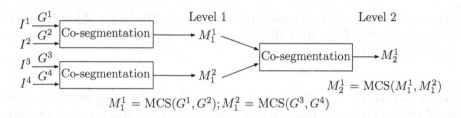

$$M_1^1 = \mathrm{MCS}(G^1, G^2); M_1^2 = \mathrm{MCS}(G^3, G^4)$$

Fig. 6. Illustration of image co-segmentation method for the case of four images. Input images I^1–I^4 are represented as graphs G^1–G^4. Co-segmentation of I^1 and I^2 yields MCS M_1^1. Co-segmentation of I^3 and I^4 yields MCS M_1^2. Co-segmentation of M_1^1 and M_1^2 yields MCS M_2^1 that represents the co-segmented objects in images I^1–I^4. Here, M_l^j denotes the j-th subgraph at level l

region co-growing are performed at the coarsest level and that output is resized to the input image size.

Let the input image pair I^1 and I^2 be successively downsampled (by 2) P times with I_P^1 and I_P^2 being the coarsest level image pairs, and let $I_1^1 = I^1$ and $I_1^2 = I^2$. We segment the set of downsampled images into superpixels of same sizes. So, I_P^1 and I_P^2 contain the least number of superpixels. Let $\mathcal{M}_P^1$ and $\mathcal{M}_P^2$ be the set of matched superpixels in I_P^1 and I_P^2 obtained from the MCS matching algorithm. To find the matched superpixels in I_{P-1}^i, we map every superpixel in $\mathcal{M}_P^i$ to certain superpixels in I_{P-1}^i based on the co-ordinates of the pixels inside the superpixels. A superpixel $v \in \mathcal{M}_P^i$ is mapped to a superpixel $u \in I_{P-1}^i$ if u has the highest overlap with the twice-scaled co-ordinates of pixels of v among all superpixels in $\mathcal{M}_P^i$. Then we perform region co-growing on the mapped superpixels in I_{P-1}^1 and I_{P-1}^2 as discussed in Sect. 2.3 and obtain the matched superpixel sets $\mathcal{M}_{P-1}^1$ in I_{P-1}^1 and $\mathcal{M}_{P-1}^2$ in I_{P-1}^2. We repeat this process for subsequent levels and obtain the final matched superpixel sets $\mathcal{M}_1^1$ and $\mathcal{M}_1^2$ that constitute the co-segmented objects in I_1^1 and I_1^2, respectively.

4   Co-segmentation of Multiple Images

Here we extend the proposed co-segmentation method to multiple images, instead of finding matches over just an image pair. This is more relevant in analyzing crowd sourced images in an event or a touristic location. If we try to obtain the MCS of K number of images simultaneously, the size of the product graph grows drastically $\left(O\left(p^{K-1}|G^1|^{K-1}\right)\right.$, assuming same cardinality of every graph for simplicity) making the proposed algorithm incomputatble. We propose a different scheme to convert this into an algorithm dealing with $K - 1$ separate product graph pairs of size $O(\alpha p(|G^1| + |G^2|))$ using a hierarchical scheme involving pair-wise co-segmentation over a binary tree structured organization of the constituent images (see Fig. 6).

To co-segment a set of K images I^1, I^2, ..., I^K, we perform $L = \lceil \log_2 K \rceil$ levels of co-segmentation. Let G^1, G^2, ..., G^K denote the graphs of the respective input images and M_l^j denotes the j-th subgraph at level l. We independently compute the co-segmentation outputs of image pairs (I^1, I^2), (I^3, I^4), ...,

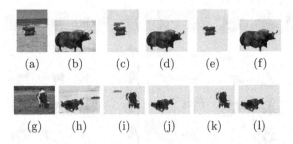

(a)   (b)   (c)   (d)   (e)   (f)

(g)   (h)   (i)   (j)   (k)   (l)

Fig. 7. Illustration of image co-segmentation from four images. Co-segmentation of the image pair in ((a),(g)) yields outputs ((c),(i)), and the pair in ((b),(h)) yields outputs ((d),(j)). These outputs are co-segmented to obtain the final outputs ((e),(f),(k),(l)). Notice how small background regions present in ((c),(i)) have been removed in ((e),(k)) after the second round of co-segmentation (Color figure online)

(I^{K-1}, I^K). Let M_1^1, M_1^2, ..., $M_1^{K/2}$ be the resulting subgraphs for pairwise co-segmentation at level $l = 1$ in Fig. 6. Then we again compute MCS of each pair (M_1^1, M_1^2), (M_1^3, M_1^4), ..., $(M_1^{K/2-1}, M_1^{K/2})$ and then obtain the corresponding co-segmentation map M_2^1, M_2^2, ... for $l = 2$. We repeat this process until we obtain the final co-segmentation map M_L^1 at level $l = L$. Figure 6 shows the block diagram when considering co-segmentation for four images $(L = 2)$.

The advantage with this approach is that the computational complexity greatly reduces after the first level of operation as $|M_l^j| \ll |G^i|$ in any level l and the graph size reduces at every subsequent level. We need to perform co-segmentation at most $K - 1$ times for K input images i.e., the complexity increases linearly with the number of images to be co-segmented. Also if at any level any MCS is null, we can stop the algorithm and conclude that there is no common object over the image set. It may be noted that due to non-commutativity, as the MCS output of two graphs at any level corresponds to two different matched regions, we may choose any of them for the next level of co-segmentation. Figure 7 shows an example of co-segmentation for four images. Co-segmentation outputs M^1, M^2 in (c),(i) and M^3, M^4 in (d),(j) at level $l = 1$ are obtained from input image pairs I^1, I^2 in (a),(g) and I^3, I^4 in (b),(h), respectively. Final co-segmented objects are in (e),(k),(f),(l).

5   Experimental Results

Choice of parameters: For an $N_1 \times N_2$ image (in the coarsest level), we experimentally choose the number of superpixels to be $N = \min(100, 0.004 N_1 N_2)$. This limits the size of the graph to be under 100. The maximal many-to-one matching is limited to $p = 2$ as a trade-off between the size of the product graph and possible reduction in seeding the co-segmentation process before region co-growing. We have adaptively chosen the inter-image feature similarity threshold t_G in Eq. (2) to ensure that the size of the product graphs, H^{12} and H^{21}, is at most 40–50 due to computational restrictions. In Sect. 2.4, we have set the threshold

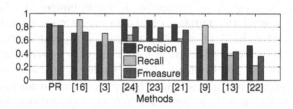

Fig. 8. Visual comparison of result of image co-segmentation. Co-segmentation outputs obtained from the image pairs in (a,b), (c,d), (e,f), (g,h), (i,j) and (k,l) of Row A using [22], [21], [23], [13], [3], [24], [16] and the proposed method (**PR**) are shown in Rows B–H and Row I, respectively. Ground-truth data are shown in Row J (Color figure online)

Fig. 9. Comparison of precision, recall and F-measure values of the proposed method (**PR**) with [16], [3], [24], [23], [21], [9], [13], [22] on the image pair dataset [21] (Color figure online)

for background probability as $t_\mathcal{B} = 0.75 \max(\{\mathcal{P}_\mathcal{B}(v_i), \forall v_i \in I\})$ to discard the possible background superpixels in the proposed co-segmentation algorithm.

Results: We have tested our algorithm with images selected from five datasets. Results for MSRC dataset [3] and the image pair dataset [21] are provided here. Results for the iCoseg dataset [7], the flower dataset [36] and the Weizmann horse dataset [37] are in the supplementary material. We first visually analyze results of some of the existing methods and compare with the results of the proposed method (PR) on images containing a single object (Fig. 8(a)–(h)) as well as

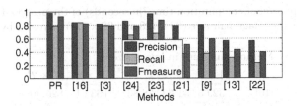

Fig. 10. Comparison of mean precision, recall and F-measure values of the proposed method (**PR**) with [16], [3], [24], [23], [21], [9], [13], [22] on images selected from 'cow', 'duck', 'dog', 'flower' and 'sheep' classes in the MSRC dataset [3] (Color figure online)

multiple objects (Fig. 8(i)–(l)). We show visual comparison of our result with the methods [22], [21], [23], [13], [3], [24], [16] in Fig. 8 (Rows B–H, respectively) and results demonstrate the superior performance of PR (Row I). For the input image pair in Fig. 8(i),(j), the methods in [22], [13], [3] detect only one of the two common objects (shown in Rows B, E, F). Most of the outputs of [22], [21], [23], [13] (shown in Rows B–E) contain discontiguous and spurious objects. Further, in most cases the common objects are either under-segmented or over-segmented. Although the method of Rubinstein *et al.* [3] yields contiguous objects, they very often fail to detect any object from both images (Row F in Fig. 8(a),(c),(e),(h)). However, the proposed method yields the entire object as a single entity with very little over or under-segmentation.

The quality of the proposed co-segmentation output is also quantitatively measured using precision, recall and F-measure, as used in earlier works e.g., [21]. These metrics are computed by comparing the segmentation output mask with the ground-truth provided in the database. Precision is the ratio of the number of correctly detected object pixels to the number of detected object pixels. This penalizes for classifying background pixels as object. Recall is the ratio of the number of correctly detected object pixels to the number of ground-truth pixels. This penalizes for not detecting all pixels of the object. F-measure is the weighted harmonic mean (we use weight $= 0.3$) of precision and recall. We compare these measures of the proposed method with those of methods in [16], [3], [24], [23], [21], [9], [13], [22] on the image pair dataset [21] (Fig. 9) and the MSRC dataset [3] (Fig. 10). Results show that the proposed method outperforms others. Moreover our precision and recall values are very close, as it should be, and yet being very high. This indicates that the proposed method reduces both false positives and false negatives. While the methods in [23], [24] (Fig. 9) also have high precision values, the recall rate is significantly inferior to the proposed method. Method [16] has a good recall measure, but the precision is quite low. In order to compare the computation time of the proposed method, we execute the competing methods also on the same system. Table 1 shows that the proposed method is significantly faster than existing methods [16], [3], and the advantage is more noticeable when the image size increases.

Table 1. Comparison of computation time (in seconds) of the proposed method (**PR**) with [16], [3], as the image pair size (86 × 128 and 98 × 128) increases by shown factors

Method	Increase in image size				
	1×1	2×2	$2^2 \times 2^2$	$2^3 \times 2^3$	$2^4 \times 2^4$
[16]	32.65	51.63	78.83	163.61	820.00
[3]	1.80	6.00	25.20	107.40	475.80
PR	1.54	2.08	2.94	5.69	13.90

6 Conclusions

In this paper, we have proposed a novel and computationally efficient image co-segmentation algorithm based on the concept of maximum common subgraph matching. Performing region co-growing on a small number of nodes (seeds) obtained as the MCS output and incorporating them in a pyramidal co-segmentation makes the proposed method computationally very efficient. The proposed method can handle variation in shape, size, orientation and texture in the common object among constituent images. It can also deal with presence of multiple common objects, unlike some existing methods.

References

1. Rother, C., Minka, T., Blake, A., Kolmogorov, V.: Cosegmentation of image pairs by histogram matching - incorporating a global constraint into MRFs. In: Proceedings of CVPR, vol. 1, pp. 993–1000 (2006)
2. Rubio, J.C., Serrat, J., López, A., Paragios, N.: Unsupervised co-segmentation through region matching. In: Proceedings of CVPR, pp. 749–756 (2012)
3. Rubinstein, M., Joulin, A., Kopf, J., Liu, C.: Unsupervised joint object discovery and segmentation in internet images. In: Proceedings of CVPR, pp. 1939–1946, June 2013
4. Mukherjee, L., Singh, V., Dyer, C.: Half-integrality based algorithms for cosegmentation of images. In: Proceedings of CVPR, pp. 2028–2035, June 2009
5. Hochbaum, D., Singh, V.: An efficient algorithm for co-segmentation. In: Proceedings of ICCV, pp. 269–276, September 2009
6. Vicente, S., Kolmogorov, V., Rother, C.: Cosegmentation revisited: models and optimization. In: Daniilidis, K., Maragos, P., Paragios, N. (eds.) ECCV 2010, Part II. LNCS, vol. 6312, pp. 465–479. Springer, Heidelberg (2010)
7. Batra, D., Kowdle, A., Parikh, D., Luo, J., Chen, T.: iCoseg: Interactive co-segmentation with intelligent scribble guidance. In: Proceedings of CVPR, pp. 3169–3176, June 2010
8. Collins, M., Xu, J., Grady, L., Singh, V.: Random walks based multi-image segmentation: Quasiconvexity results and GPU-based solutions. In: Proceedings of CVPR, pp. 1656–1663, June 2012
9. Joulin, A., Bach, F., Ponce, J.: Discriminative clustering for image co-segmentation. In: Proceedings of CVPR, pp. 1943–1950, June 2010

10. Joulin, A., Bach, F., Ponce, J.: Multi-class cosegmentation. In: Proceedings of CVPR, pp. 542–549, June 2012
11. Mukherjee, L., Singh, V., Peng, J.: Scale invariant cosegmentation for image groups. In: Proceedings of CVPR, pp. 1881–1888, June 2011
12. Vicente, S., Rother, C., Kolmogorov, V.: Object cosegmentation. In: Proceedings of CVPR, pp. 2217–2224, June 2011
13. Kim, G., Xing, E., Fei-Fei, L., Kanade, T.: Distributed cosegmentation via submodular optimization on anisotropic diffusion. In: Proceedings of ICCV, pp. 169–176, November 2011
14. Kim, G., Xing, E.: On multiple foreground cosegmentation. In: Proceedings of CVPR, pp. 837–844, June 2012
15. Meng, F., Li, H., Liu, G., Ngan, K.N.: Object co-segmentation based on shortest path algorithm and saliency model. IEEE Trans. Multimedia 14(5), 1429–1441 (2012)
16. Lee, C., Jang, W.D., Sim, J.Y., Kim, C.S.: Multiple random walkers and their application to image cosegmentation. In: Proceedings of CVPR, pp. 3837–3845, June 2015
17. Tao, W., Li, K., Sun, K.: Sacoseg: Object cosegmentation by shape conformability. IEEE Trans. Image Process. 24(3), 943–955 (2015)
18. Jerripothula, K., Cai, J., Meng, F., Yuan, J.: Automatic image co-segmentation using geometric mean saliency. In: Proceedings of ICIP, pp. 3277–3281, October 2014
19. Chen, M., Velasco-Forero, S., Tsang, I., Cham, T.J.: Objects co-segmentation: propagated from simpler images. In: Proceedings of ICASSP, pp. 1682–1686 (2015)
20. Chang, K.Y., Liu, T.L., Lai, S.H.: From co-saliency to co-segmentation: An efficient and fully unsupervised energy minimization model. In: Proceedings of CVPR, pp. 2129–2136, June 2011
21. Li, H., Ngan, K.N.: A co-saliency model of image pairs. IEEE Trans. Image Process. 20(12), 3365–3375 (2011)
22. Chen, H.T.: Preattentive co-saliency detection. In: Proceedings of ICIP, pp. 1117–1120, September 2010
23. Fu, H., Cao, X., Tu, Z.: Cluster-based co-saliency detection. IEEE Trans. Image Process. 22(10), 3766–3778 (2013)
24. Cao, X., Tao, Z., Zhang, B., Fu, H., Feng, W.: Self-adaptively weighted co-saliency detection via rank constraint. IEEE Trans. Image Process. 23(9), 4175–4186 (2014)
25. Tan, Z., Wan, L., Feng, W., Pun, C.M.: Image co-saliency detection by propagating superpixel affinities. In: Proceedings of ICASSP, pp. 2114–2118, May 2013
26. Liu, Z., Zou, W., Li, L., Shen, L., Meur, O.: Co-saliency detection based on hierarchical segmentation. IEEE Signal Process. Lett. 21(1), 88–92 (2014)
27. Li, Y., Fu, K., Liu, Z., Yang, J.: Efficient saliency-model-guided visual co-saliency detection. IEEE Signal Process. Lett. 22(5), 588–592 (2015)
28. Achanta, R., Shaji, A., Smith, K., Lucchi, A., Fua, P., Susstrunk, S.: SLIC superpixels compared to state-of-the-art superpixel methods. IEEE Trans. Pattern Anal. Mach. Intell. 34(11), 2274–2282 (2012)
29. Colannino, J., Damian, M., Hurtado, F., Langerman, S., Meijer, H., Ramaswami, S., Souvaine, D., Toussaint, G.: Efficient many-to-many point matching in one dimension. Graphs Comb. 23(1), 169–178 (2007)
30. Madry, A.: Navigating central path with electrical flows: from flows to matchings, and back. In: IEEE Annual Symposium on FOCS, pp. 253–262 (2013)
31. Koch, I.: Enumerating all connected maximal common subgraphs in two graphs. Theor. Comput. Sci. 250(1), 1–30 (2001)

32. Cormen, T.H., Stein, C., Rivest, R.L., Leiserson, C.E.: Introduction to Algorithms, 2nd edn. McGraw-Hill Higher Education, New York (2001)
33. Manning, C.D., Raghavan, P., Schütze, H.: Introduction to Information Retrieval. Cambridge University Press, New York (2008)
34. Rui, Y., Huang, T., Ortega, M., Mehrotra, S.: Relevance feedback: a power tool for interactive content-based image retrieval. IEEE Trans. Circ. Syst. Video Technol. 8(5), 644–655 (1998)
35. Zhu, W., Liang, S., Wei, Y., Sun, J.: Saliency optimization from robust background detection. In: Proceedings of CVPR, pp. 2814–2821, June 2014
36. Nilsback, M.E., Zisserman, A.: A visual vocabulary for flower classification. In: Proceedings of CVPR, vol. 2, pp. 1447–1454 (2006)
37. Borenstein, E., Ullman, S.: Combined top-down/bottom-up segmentation. IEEE Trans. Pattern Anal. Mach. Intell. 30(12), 2109–2125 (2008)

End-to-End Localization and Ranking
for Relative Attributes

Krishna Kumar Singh$^{(\boxtimes)}$ and Yong Jae Lee

University of California, Davis, USA
krsingh@ucdavis.edu

Abstract. We propose an end-to-end deep convolutional network to simultaneously localize and rank relative visual attributes, given only weakly-supervised pairwise image comparisons. Unlike previous methods, our network jointly learns the attribute's features, localization, and ranker. The localization module of our network discovers the most informative image region for the attribute, which is then used by the ranking module to learn a ranking model of the attribute. Our end-to-end framework also significantly speeds up processing and is much faster than previous methods. We show state-of-the-art ranking results on various relative attribute datasets, and our qualitative localization results clearly demonstrate our network's ability to learn meaningful image patches.

Keywords: Relative attributes · Ranking · Localization · Discovery

1 Introduction

Visual attributes are mid-level representations that describe semantic properties (e.g., 'furry', 'natural', 'short') of objects and scenes, and have been explored extensively for various applications including zero-shot learning [1–3], image retrieval [4–6], fine-grained recognition [7–9], and human computer interaction [10]. Attributes have been studied in the binary [7,11]—describing their presence or absence—and relative [3,12]—describing their relative strength—settings.

Recent work on visual attributes have shown that local representations often lead to better performance compared to global representations [9,11,13]. These methods use pre-trained part detectors to bring the candidate object parts into correspondence to model the attribute, with the assumption that there is at least one well-defined part that corresponds to the attribute. However, this assumption does not always hold; for example, the exact spatial extent of the attribute bald head can be ambiguous, which means that training a bald head detector itself can be difficult. Furthermore, since the part detectors are trained independently of the attribute, their learned parts may not necessarily be useful for modeling the attribute. Finally, these methods are designed for binary attributes and are not applicable for relative attributes; however, relative attributes have been shown to be equally or more useful in many settings [3,12].

© Springer International Publishing AG 2016
B. Leibe et al. (Eds.): ECCV 2016, Part VI, LNCS 9910, pp. 753–769, 2016.
DOI: 10.1007/978-3-319-46466-4_45

Recently, Xiao and Lee [14] proposed an algorithm that overcomes the above drawbacks by automatically *discovering* the relevant spatial extent of relative attributes given only weakly-supervised (i.e., image-level) pairwise comparisons. The key idea is to transitively connect "visual chains" that localize the same visual concept (e.g., object part) across the attribute spectrum, and then to select the chains that together best model the attribute. The approach produces state-of-the-art performance for relative attribute ranking. Despite these qualities, it has three main limitations due to its pipeline nature: (1) The various components of the approach, including the feature learning and ranker, are not optimized jointly, which can lead to sub-optimal performance; (2) It is slow due to time-consuming intermediate modules of the pipeline; (3) In order to build the visual chains, the approach assumes the existence of a visual concept that undergoes a gradual visual change along with the change in attribute strength; however, this does not always hold. For example, for the `natural` attribute for outdoor scenes, there are various visual concepts (e.g., forests and mountains) that are relevant but not consistently present across the images.

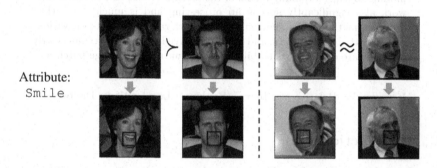

Fig. 1. Given pairwise relative attribute strength comparisons (i.e., greater/less than (left) or similar (right)), our goal is to automatically localize the most informative image regions corresponding to the visual attribute. For example, the mouth region is the most informative for the attribute `smile`. To this end, we train an end-to-end network that discovers the image regions and uses them for relative attribute ranking.

To address these issues, in this paper, we propose an end-to-end deep convolutional network that simultaneously learns to rank and localize relative attributes. Our setting is the same as in [14]: we are given only weakly-supervised image-level pairwise attribute comparisons, but no supervision on where in each image the attribute is present nor what the attribute looks like. Thus, the main challenge is to automatically localize the relevant regions in each image pair simultaneously, such that an accurate relative ranking of the attribute for each image pair can be produced. We tackle this challenge by designing a new architecture that combines a localization network with a ranking network, and optimize a pairwise image ranking loss. In this way, our approach learns to focus on the regions in each image that are optimal for attribute ranking. Furthermore, our network is optimized end-to-end, and jointly learns an attribute's features, localization, and ranker, which mutually benefit each other. This end-to-end framework also significantly speeds up processing. Finally, unlike [14], we do not assume that the attribute must be conditioned on the same visual concept across the attribute spectrum. Instead, our network is free to identify discriminative patterns in each image that are most relevant for attribute ranking (e.g., for the **natural** attribute, localizing trees for forest images and buildings for city images). We demonstrate that all of these lead to improved performance over standard pipeline approaches.

Briefly, our method works as follows: we train a Siamese network [15] with a pairwise ranking loss, which takes as input a pair of images and a weak-label that compares the relative strength of an attribute for the image pair. A Siamese network consists of two identical parallel branches with shared parameters, and during testing, either branch can be used to assign a ranking score to a single image. Each branch consists of a localization module and a ranking module. The localization module is modeled with spatial transformer [16] layers, which discover the most relevant part of the image corresponding to the attribute (see Fig. 1 for examples of localized patches). The output patch of the localization module is then fed into the ranking module for fine-grained attention for ranking.

Contributions. To our knowledge, this is the first attempt to learn an end-to-end network to rank and localize relative attributes. To accomplish this, we make two main contributions: (1) a new deep convolutional network that learns to rank attributes given pairwise relative comparisons, and (2) integrating the spatial transformer into our network to discover the image patches that are most relevant to an attribute. We demonstrate state-of-the-art results on the LFW-10 [13] face, UT-Zap50K [17] shoe, and OSR [18] outdoor scene datasets.

2   Related Work

Visual attributes. Visual attributes serve as an informative and compact representation for visual data. Earlier work relied on hand-crafted features like SIFT and HOG to model the attributes [1–3,6,19–23]. More recent work use deep convolutional networks to learn the attribute representations, and achieve superior performance [9,24–26]. While these approaches learn deep representations for *binary* attributes, we instead learn deep representations for *relative* attributes. Concurrent work [27] also trains a deep CNN for the relative setting; however, it does not perform localization as we do.

Attribute localization. Learning attribute models conditioned on local object parts or keypoints have shown to produce superior performance for various recognition tasks [8,9,11,13,14,28]. Most existing work rely on pre-trained part/keypoint detectors or crowd-sourcing to localize the attributes [8,9,11,20, 28,29]. Recently, Xiao and Lee [14] proposed a method to automatically *discover* the spatial extent of relative attributes. Since it does not rely on pre-trained detectors, it can model attributes that are not clearly tied to object-parts (e.g., **open** for shoes). However, the approach consists of several sequential independently-optimized modules in a pipeline system. As a result, it can be suboptimal and slow. In contrast, we propose to localize the attributes and train the attribute models *simultaneously* in an end-to-end learning framework. Similar to [14], our approach automatically discovers the relevant attribute regions, but is more accurate in ranking and faster since everything is learned jointly.

Attention modeling. Attention models selectively attend to informative locations in the visual data to process at higher resolution. The key idea is to neglect irrelevant regions (like background clutter) and instead focus on the important regions that are relevant to the task at hand. Earlier work on bottom-up saliency (e.g., [30,31]) focus on interesting regions in the image, while high-level object proposal methods (e.g., [32-35]) generate candidate object-like regions. Recent work use deep networks for attention modeling in various tasks including fine-grained classification [36,37], image caption generation [38], and image generation [39,40]. In particular, Spatial Transformer Networks [16] spatially transform the input image to focus on the task-relevant regions, and have shown to improve performance on digit and fine-grained bird recognition. In our work, we show how to integrate spatial transformer layers into a deep *pairwise ranking* network in order to automatically localize and rank relative attributes for faces, shoes, and outdoor scenes, in the more challenging ranking setting.

3 Approach

Given pairs of training images, with each pair ordered according to relative strength of an attribute, our goal is to train a deep convolutional network that learns a function $f : \mathbb{R}^M \to \mathbb{R}$ to simultaneously discover where in each image the attribute is present and rank each image (with M pixels) according to predicted attribute strength. Importantly, the only supervision we have are the pairwise image comparisons; i.e., there is no supervision on where in each image the attribute is present nor prior information about the visual appearance of the attribute.

3.1 Input

For training, the input to our network is an image pair (I_1, I_2) and a corresponding label L for a given attribute (e.g., smile) indicating whether the image pair belongs to set E or Q. $(I_1, I_2) \in E$ means that the ground-truth attribute strengths of I_1 and I_2 are similar to each other, while $(I_1, I_2) \in Q$ means that the ground-truth attribute strength of I_1 is greater than that of I_2. (If attribute strength of I_1 is less than that of I_2, we simply reorder the two as $(I_2, I_1) \in Q$.)

For testing, the input is a single image I_{test}, and our network uses its learned function f (i.e., network weights) to predict the attribute strength $v = f(I_{test})$.

3.2 Architecture

Figure 2 shows the overall architecture of our network. We have a Siamese network [41], which takes as input an image pair (I_1, I_2) along with its label L,

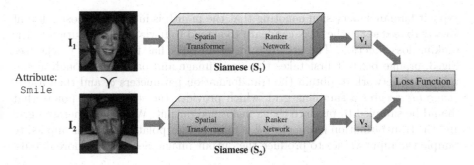

Fig. 2. Overall architecture of our network. It takes as input a pair of images (I_1, I_2) and a label denoting the images' relative ordering according to ground-truth attribute strength (here, I_1 is more smiling than I_2). Each image is fed into a Siamese network, which consists of a Spatial Transformer Network (STN) and a Ranker Network (RN). The Siamese networks output the predicted attribute scores v_1 and v_2 for the images, which are used by the loss function to update the network's parameters.

and outputs two scalar values $v_1 = f(I_1)$ and $v_2 = f(I_2)$, which are fed into our loss function. A Siamese network consists of two identical branches S_1 and S_2 with shared parameters. Each branch consists of a **Spatial Transformer Network** (STN) and a **Ranker Network** (RN). The STN is responsible for localizing the relevant image patch corresponding to the visual attribute, while the RN is responsible for generating a scalar value v that denotes the input image's attribute strength. During testing, only one of the branches is used to produce the attribute strength v for the input test image.

Spatial Transformer Network (STN). Intuitively, in order to discover the regions in each training image pair that are relevant to the attribute, we could apply a ranking function to various pairs of regions (one region from each image in the pair), and then select the pair that leads to the best agreement with the ground-truth pairwise rankings. STNs [16] provide an elegant framework for doing so. An STN learns an explicit spatial image (or feature map) transformation for each image that is optimal for the task at hand [16]. It has two main advantages: (1) fully-differentiable and can be trained with backpropagation; and (2) can learn to translate, crop, rotate, scale, or warp an image without any explicit supervision for the transformation. By attending to the most relevant image regions, the STN allows the ensuing computation to be dedicated to those regions. In [16], STNs were shown to learn meaningful transformations for digit classification and fine-grained bird classification.

In this work, we incorporate an STN as part of our end-to-end ranking system, in order to discover the region-of-interest for each relative attribute. The STN's output can then be fed into the ensuing Ranker network, easing its task. For example, for attribute `visible-teeth`, it will be easier to optimize the ranking function if the Ranker network receives the mouth region. While there is no explicit human supervision denoting that the mouth is in fact the most relevant for `visible-teeth`, the STN can learn to attend to it via its contribution to the ranking loss function. The architecture of an STN has three main blocks (see Fig. 3, orange box): it first takes the input image and passes it through a convolutional network to obtain the transformation parameters θ, and then a *grid generator* creates a sampling grid, which provides the set of input points that should be sampled to produce the transformed output. With the generated grid and the transformation parameters θ, a bilinear interpolation kernel is applied to sample the input values to produce the output image. See [16] for more details.

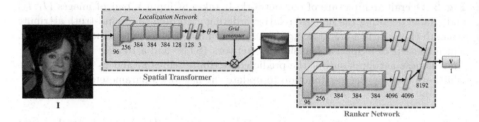

Fig. 3. Illustration of one Siamese network branch. The input image I goes through the spatial transformer network (STN), which generates the transformation parameters θ. The transformation is applied to image I to localize the most relevant region corresponding to the attribute. In this example, the attribute is `smile`, so the STN localizes the mouth. Next, the ranker network computes and combines the features of the STN output and image I to compute the attribute strength v. (Color figure online)

In our STN, we have three transformation parameters $\theta = [s, t_x, t_y]$, representing isotropic scaling s and horizontal and vertical translation t_x and t_y.[1] The transformation is applied as an inverse warp to generate the output image:

$$\begin{pmatrix} x_i^{in} \\ y_i^{in} \end{pmatrix} = \begin{bmatrix} s & 0 & t_x \\ 0 & s & t_y \end{bmatrix} \begin{pmatrix} x_i^{out} \\ y_i^{out} \\ 1 \end{pmatrix}, \tag{1}$$

where x_i^{in} and y_i^{in} are the input image coordinates, x_i^{out} and y_i^{out} are the output image coordinates, and i indexes the pixels in the output image.

The convolutional network of our STN has six convolutional layers and two fully-connected layers (see Fig. 3, orange box). The first five layers are equivalent to those of AlexNet [42]. After the max-pooling layer of the 5th convolutional layer (i.e., `pool5`), we add a convolutional layer consisting of 128 filters of size 1×1 to reduce feature dimensionality. After the convolutional layer, we add two fully-connected layers; the first takes in 4608 values as input and outputs 128 values, while the second takes the 128 values as input and outputs the final 3 transformation parameters (i.e., scale, vertical and horizontal translation). We

---

[1] More complex transformations (e.g., affine, thin plate spline) are possible, but we find this transformation to be sufficient for our datasets.

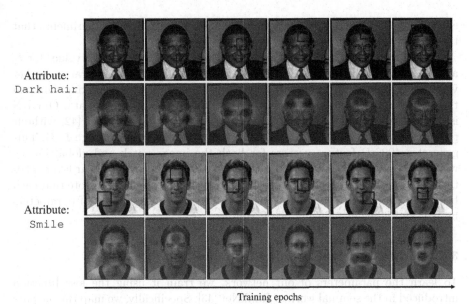

Fig. 4. The localization behavior of the STN during training of our network. For each attribute, the first row shows the output of the STN for the same image across different training epochs. The second row shows the distribution of the STN outputs for all the training images across different training epochs (we overlay the heatmap onto an example image). Notice how the STN output initially has high variance but then gradually converges to the top of the head for dark-hair and the mouth for smile. (Color figure online)

find these hyperparmeters to provide a good balance of high enough capacity to learn the transformation while minimizing overfitting.

Figure 4 shows the change in the STN output over the training epochs of our network. For each attribute, the first row shows an example image with the STN's localized patch in the red box, while the second row shows the distribution of the STN's output over the entire training data overlaid onto the example image (this visualization works because the face images in LFW-10 are roughly aligned). The STN is initially unsure of the attribute's location and thus has high spatial variance. It then proceeds to search over the various regions in each image and converges to the top of the head for dark-hair and to the mouth for smile.

Ranker Network (RN). The RN takes the output of the STN (i.e., an image patch) and the original image as input, and computes and combines their features to generate a scalar attribute strength v as output (see Fig. 3, blue box). The key idea of combining the two inputs is to provide the ranker with both the high-resolution image patch that is focused on the visual attribute as well as the entire image to provide global context. We demonstrate in our experiments that the two sources of information are indeed complementary.

For image pair $(I_1, I_2) \in E$, the RN will learn to generate similar values for I_1 and I_2, while for image pair $(I_1, I_2) \in Q$ the RN will learn to generate a higher value for I_1 than I_2. Ultimately, the RN will learn a global ranking function that tries to satisfy all such pairwise constraints in the training data. Our RN is a Siamese network [41], with each branch consisting of AlexNet [42] without the last fully connected classification layer (i.e., all layers up through fc7). This generates 4096-D feature vectors for both the image patch and global image, which are concatenated to produce the final 8192-D feature. A linear layer takes the 8192-D feature to generate a final single value v for the image. Note that each branch of the RN has shared weights, which reduces the number of parameters by half and helps in reducing overfitting.

3.3   Localization and Ranking Loss Function

To learn the parameters of our network, we train it using the loss function introduced in the seminal work of RankNet [43]. Specifically, we map the outputs v_1 and v_2 (corresponding to I_1 and I_2), to a probability P via a logistic function $P = e^{(v_1 - v_2)}/(1 + e^{(v_1 - v_2)})$, and then optimize the standard cross-entropy loss:

$$Rank_{loss}(I_1, I_2) = -L \cdot log(P) - (1 - L) \cdot log(1 - P), \tag{2}$$

where if $(I_1, I_2) \in Q$ then $L = 1$, else if $(I_1, I_2) \in E$ then $L = 0.5$. This loss function enforces $v_1 > v_2$ when I_1 has a higher ground-truth attribute strength than I_2, and enforces $v_1 = v_2$ when I_1 and I_2 have similar ground-truth attribute strengths. As described in [43], a nice property of this loss function is that it asymptotes to a linear function, which makes it more robust to noise compared to a quadratic function, and handles input pairs with similar ground-truth attribute strengths in a principled manner as it becomes symmetric with minimum value at 0 when $L = 0.5$.

In our initial experiments, we found that large magnitudes for the translation parameters of the STN can lead to its output patch going beyond the input image's boundaries (resulting in a black patch with all 0-valued pixels). One reason for this is because for any similar pair $(I_1, I_2) \in E$, its ranking loss can be minimized when the STN produces identical patches for both I_1 and I_2. This makes learning difficult because the resulting gradient direction of the ranking loss with respect to the transformation parameters becomes uninformative, since the same black patch will be produced in all nearby spatial directions. To handle this, we introduce a simple loss that updates the transformation parameters to bring the STN's output patch back within the image boundaries if it goes outside:

$$ST_{loss}(I) = (C_x - s \cdot t_x)^2 + (C_y - s \cdot t_y)^2, \tag{3}$$

where t_x and t_y are horizontal and vertical translation, respectively, s is isotropic scaling, and C_x and C_y are the center x and y pixel-coordinates of the input image I, respectively. ST_{loss} is simply the squared distance of the center coordinates of the output patch from the input image's center, and is differentiable. The loss increases as $(s \cdot t_x, s \cdot t_y)$ moves farther away from the image center, so the output patch will be forced to move back toward the image. Importantly, we do not apply this loss if the output patch's center coordinates are within the image's boundaries (i.e., this loss does not bias the STN to produce regions that are near the image center).

Putting Eqs. 2 and 3 together, our final loss function is:

$$Loss = \frac{1}{N} \sum_i (1-\lambda_1^i)(1-\lambda_2^i) \cdot Rank_{loss}(I_1^i, I_2^i) + \lambda_1^i \cdot ST_{loss}(I_1^i) + \lambda_2^i \cdot ST_{loss}(I_2^i), \quad (4)$$

where N is the total number of training image pairs, i indexes over the training pairs, $\lambda_1^i=1$ ($\lambda_2^i=1$) if the center coordinates of the STN's output patch of I_1^i (I_2^i) falls outside of the image's boundaries. We optimize Eq. 4 with backpropagation to learn the entire network's weights f. Note that the gradient computed for ST_{loss} is only backpropagated through the STN and does not affect the RN. If both $\lambda_1^i=\lambda_2^i=0$ (the STN's output patches for both I_1^i and I_2^i are within their image boundaries), then the gradient computed for $Rank_{loss}$ is backpropagated through the entire network (i.e., both the RN and STN are updated).

4 Results

In this section, we analyze our network's attribute localization and ranking accuracy through both qualitative and quantitative results.

Datasets. LFW-10 [13]: It consists of 10 face attributes (bald-head, dark-hair, eyes-open, good-looking, masculine-looking, mouth-open, smile, visible-teeth, visible-forehead, and young). There are 1000 training images and 1000 test images, with 500 pairs per attribute for both training and testing. We use the same train-test split used in [13].

UT-Zap50K-1 [17]: It consists of 4 shoe attributes (open, pointy, sporty and comfort). There are 50,025 shoe images, and 1388 training and 300 testing pairs per attribute. We use the train-test splits provided by [17].

OSR [18]: It consists of outdoor scene attributes (natural, open, perspective, large-objects, diagonal-plane, and close-depth). There are 2688 images, and we use the same train/test split as in [3,17].

Implementation Details. We train a separate network for each visual attribute. We initialize the STN and RN weights with those of AlexNet [42] pre-trained on ImageNet classification up through conv5 and fc7, respectively. We first train our network without the global image; i.e., the RN only receives the output of the STN to generate the attribute score v. We then retrain the entire network—in which we use both the STN output and the global image to train the RN—with the STN weights initialized with the initially learned weights. We find that this setup helps the STN localize the attribute more accurately, since initially the STN is forced to find the optimal image region without being able to rely on the global image when predicting the attribute strength.

For training, we use a mini-batch size of 25 image pairs for SGD, and train the network for 400, 200, and 15 epochs for LFW-10, UT-Zap50K, and OSR, respectively. We set the learning rate for the RN and STN to be 0.001 and 0.0001, respectively, and fix momentum to 0.9. Also, we set the relative learning rate for the scale parameter to be one-tenth of that of the translation parameters, as we find scaling to be more sensitive and can transform the image drastically. We initialize the scale to be 1/3 of the image size for LFW-10 and 1/2 for UT-Zap50K and OSR, based on initial qualitative observations. Translation is initialized randomly for all datasets. We use random crops of size 227 × 227 from our 256 × 256 input image during training, and average the scores for 10 crops (4 corners plus center, and same with horizontal flip) during testing.

Baselines. We compare against the state-of-the art method of Xiao and Lee [14], which uses a pipeline system to discover the spatial extent of relative attributes and trains an SVM ranker to rank the images. We report the method's results obtained by combining the features computed over the global image and discovered patches, which produce the best accuracy.

We also compare against [13], which computes dense SIFT features on keypoints detected using a supervised facial keypoint detector [44] to train an SVM ranker, and [3], which trains an SVM ranker with global image features. For [3], we compare against the results reported using CNN (pre-trained AlexNet pool5) features in [14]. Finally, we compare against the local learning method of [17]. We report its numbers generated using GIST+color-histogram features.

4.1   Qualitative Results of Localized Attributes

We first visualize our attribute localization results. In Fig. 5, we show the results for the face attributes on the LFW-10 test images. Each row corresponds to a face attribute, and the red box in each image indicates the output of the STN. The images in each row are uniformly sampled after sorting them according to the attribute strength predicted by our network. We can see that our network localizes the relevant regions for the various face attributes. For example, it localizes the mouth region for mouth-open, smile, and visible-teeth; the top of the head for bald-head and dark-hair; near the eyes for eyes-open; and the forehead for visible-forehead. For more global attributes like good-looking, masculine-looking, and young, there is no definite answer but our network tends to localize larger portions of the face.

In Fig. 6, we show the results for the shoe attributes on the UT-Zap50K-1 test images. Again, our network localizes the relevant regions for the different shoe attributes. It localizes the heel for comfort; the toe end for pointy; and the top opening for open. Finally, our network is able to produce accurate image rankings using the localized image parts, as shown in both Figs. 5 and 6. For

Fig. 5. Qualitative results on LFW-10 test images. Each row corresponds to an attribute, with the images uniformly sampled according to predicted attribute strength. In each image, the STN localization is depicted in the red box. It corresponds to meaningful regions for each localizable attribute (e.g., top of the head for bald-head and dark-hair; forehead for visible-forehead; mouth for mouth-open, smile and visible-teeth; eyes for eyes-open). For more global attributes like good-looking, masculine-looking, and young, there is no definite answer, but our method tends to focus on larger areas that encompass the eyes, nose, and mouth. Finally, the ranking obtained by our method is accurate for all attributes. (Color figure online)

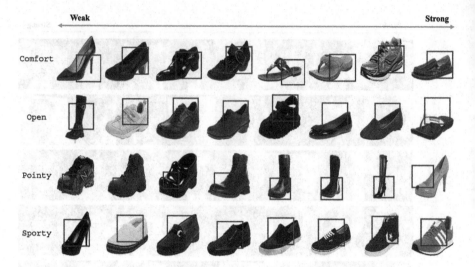

Fig. 6. Qualitative results on UT-Zap50K-1 test images. The STN localizes the relevant image regions: toe end for **pointy**, heel for **comfort**, top opening for **open**, and area around the laces for **sporty**. Our method's ranking is also accurate for each attribute.

example, we can see the progression of light-to-dark hair for **dark-hair**, and closed-to-open shoes for **open**.

Table 1. Attribute ranking accuracy on LFW-10. On average, we outperform all previous methods, and achieve the best accuracy for 7 out of 10 attributes. These results show the advantage of our end-to-end network, which simultaneously learns to localize and rank relative attributes.

	BH	DH	EO	GL	ML	MO	S	VT	VF	Y	Mean
Parikh & Grauman [3]+CNN	78.10	83.09	71.43	68.73	95.40	65.77	63.84	66.46	81.25	72.07	74.61
Sandeep et al. [13]	82.04	80.56	83.52	68.98	90.94	82.04	85.01	82.63	83.52	71.36	81.06
Xiao & Lee [14]	83.21	88.13	82.71	**72.76**	93.68	88.26	**86.16**	86.46	**90.23**	75.05	84.66
Ours	**83.94**	**92.58**	**90.23**	71.21	**96.55**	**91.28**	84.75	**89.85**	87.89	**80.81**	**86.91**

Overall, these qualitative results demonstrate that our method is able to produce accurate localizations.

4.2 Quantitative Results for Attribute Ranking

We next evaluate quantitative ranking accuracy. We report the percentage of test image pairs whose relative attribute ranking is predicted correctly.

Table 1 shows the results on LFW-10. First, the baseline method of [3] uses a global representation instead of a local one to model the attributes and produces

Table 2. Attribute ranking accuracy on UT-Zap50K-1. The shoe images are well-aligned, centered, and have clear backgrounds, so all methods obtain very high accuracy and results are nearly saturated.

	Open	Pointy	Sporty	Comfort	Mean
Parikh and Grauman [3]+CNN	94.37	93.97	95.40	95.03	94.69
Yu and Grauman [17]	90.67	90.83	92.67	92.37	91.64
Xiao and Lee [14]	**95.03**	94.80	96.47	95.60	95.47
Ours	94.87	**94.93**	**97.47**	**95.87**	**95.78**

the lowest accuracy. The state-of-the-art method of Xiao and Lee [14] outperforms the baseline method of [13] because it automatically discovers the relevant regions of an attribute without relying on pretrained keypoint detectors whose detected parts may be irrelevant to the attribute. Still, across all attributes, we improve on average by 2.25 % absolute over the method of Xiao and Lee [14], and produce the best results on seven attributes. This shows the benefit of our end-to-end network, which learns the attribute features, localization, and ranker jointly. In contrast, the method of Xiao and Lee [14] optimizes each step independently, which leads to sub-optimal results.

Table 2 shows the results on UT-Zap50K-1. For this dataset, our improvement over the baselines is marginal because the shoe images are so well-aligned, centered, and have clear backgrounds. Consequently, all baselines obtain very high accuracy and the results are nearly saturated. Thus, following [14], we perform a cross-dataset experiment on the more challenging Shoes-with-Attribute [5] dataset, whose shoe images are not as well-aligned and have more variation in style and scale. Shoes-with-Attribute has three overlapping attributes with UT-Zap50K-1 (open, pointy, and sporty) with 140 annotated image pairs per attribute. We take our models trained on UT-Zap50K-1, and test on Shoes-with-Attribute in order to evaluate cross-dataset generalization ability. Table 3 shows the results. We get a significant boost of 4.88 % absolute over the method of Xiao and Lee [14]. This demonstrates that our joint training of the attribute features, localization, and ranker lead to more robustness to appearance and scale variations, compared to training them independently.

Table 3. Attribute ranking accuracy on Shoe-with-Attribute using the models trained on UT-Zap50K-1. We significantly outperform the previous state-of-the-art (Xiao and Lee [14]) on this more challenging dataset, which demonstrates our network's cross-dataset generalization ability.

	Open	Pointy	Sporty	Mean
Parikh & Grauman [3]+CNN	77.10	72.50	71.56	73.72
Xiao & Lee [14]	80.15	**82.50**	88.07	83.58
Ours	**89.31**	**82.50**	**93.58**	**88.46**

Table 4. Attribute ranking accuracy on OSR. We outperform previous methods.

	Natural	Open	Perspective	Size-Large	Diagonal	Depth-Close	Mean
Parikh & Grauman [3]	95.03	90.77	86.73	86.23	86.50	87.53	88.80
Parikh & Grauman [3]+CNN	98.02	94.52	93.04	94.04	95.00	95.25	94.98
Li et al. [45]	95.24	92.39	87.58	88.34	89.34	89.54	90.41
Yu and Grauman [17]	95.70	94.10	90.43	91.10	92.43	90.47	92.37
Ours	**98.89**	**97.20**	**96.31**	**95.98**	**97.64**	**96.10**	**97.02**

Finally, Table 4 shows the results on OSR, which contains very different looking images for the same relative attribute (e.g., forest vs. city images for **natural**). We compare against the previous state-of-the-art local learning method of Yu and Grauman [17], the relative forest method of [45], and global image-based method of [3]. We obtain an overall accuracy of 97.02 %, which is better than all baselines. More importantly, this result shows our advantage over the method of Xiao and Lee [14], which is not applicable to this dataset, since it requires a visually consistent concept (e.g., the same object) for an attribute to build its visual chains. In contrast, our method can handle drastically different visual concepts for the same attribute (e.g., forest image with trees being more **natural** than city image with buildings) since the STN only needs to localize the most relevant region in each image without requiring that the concept be present in other images.

4.3   Ablation Study

We study the contribution that the global image versus the output region of the STN has on ranking performance. For this, we train and compare two baseline networks: (1) the RN is trained with only the global image as input (**Global image**), i.e., we do not have the STN as part of the network; and (2) the RN is trained with only the STN output region as input without the global image (**STN output**). For both baseline networks, the final linear layer uses the newly-learned 4096-D feature output of the RN to generate the attribute strength v.

Table 5 shows quantitative ranking accuracy of these baseline networks on LFW-10. Overall, the STN output baseline outperforms the Global image baseline. It performs especially well for attributes that are conditioned on small facial parts like **eyes-open**, **mouth-open**, and **visible-teeth**. This is mainly because the Global image baseline needs to process the entire input image, which means that small object parts like the eyes or mouth have very low resolution, and thus, cannot receive the fine-grained attention that they need. In contrast, the STN can attend to those small informative parts, and provide a high-resolution (cropped-out) image for the RN to learn the ranking function. Finally, the third row in Table 5 shows the result of our full model, i.e., combining both the global input image and STN output to train the RN. Our full model produces the best accuracy for eight out of the 10 attributes, which shows that the global contextual information from the input image and the fine-grained information from the localized STN output are complementary. The boost is especially significant for

Table 5. Ablation study on LFW-10 comparing the contribution of the global input image (1st row) and the STN's localized output region (2nd row) for attribute ranking. Our combined model (3rd row) produces the best performance, showing that the information present in the global image and STN output are complementary.

	BH	DH	EO	GL	ML	MO	S	VT	VF	Y	Mean
Global image	**84.31**	90.21	82.71	69.97	94.83	80.20	80.79	79.38	85.55	77.19	82.51
STN output	78.10	89.32	**93.23**	66.56	95.4	**91.28**	84.46	88.62	85.55	73.77	84.63
Combined	83.94	**92.58**	90.23	**71.21**	**96.55**	**91.28**	**84.75**	**89.85**	**87.89**	**80.81**	**86.91**

mid-sized and global attributes like dark-hair, visible-forehead, and young, likely because they require both fine-grained information of specific parts as well as more global contextual information of the entire face.

4.4   Computational Speed Analysis

Finally, we analyze the computational speed of our network. Our approach is significantly faster than the related baseline method of Xiao and Lee [14]. Since that method has to process a sequence of time-consuming modules including feature extraction, nearest neighbor matching, iterative SVM classifier training to build the visual chains, and training an SVM ranker to rank the chains, it takes $\sim$10 h to train one attribute model on LFW-10 using a cluster of 20 CPU nodes with 2 cores each. In contrast, our end-to-end network only takes $\sim$3 h to train one attribute model using a single Titan X GPU. For testing, our approach takes only 0.011 s per image compared to 1.1 s per image for [14].

5   Discussion

We presented a novel end-to-end deep network that combines a localization module with a ranking module to jointly localize and rank relative attributes. Our qualitative results showed our network's ability to accurately localize the meaningful image patches corresponding to an attribute. We demonstrated state-of-the-art attribute ranking performance on benchmark face, shoe, and outdoor scene datasets. One limitation of our approach is that it can only localize one image part for a visual attribute. However, for certain attributes there can be multiple relevant parts. We would like to explore this issue further either by having multiple spatial transformers or directly predicting pixel-level relevance.

Acknowledgements. This work was supported in part by an Amazon Web Services Education Research Grant and GPUs donated by NVIDIA.

References

1. Palatucci, M., Pomerleau, D., Hinton, G., Mitchell, T.: Zero-shot learning with semantic output codes. In: NIPS (2009)

2. Lampert, C.H., Nickisch, H., Harmeling, S.: Learning to detect unseen object classes by between-class attribute transfer. In: CVPR (2009)
3. Parikh, D., Grauman, K.: Relative attributes. In: ICCV (2011)
4. Siddiquie, B., Feris, R.S., Davis, L.S.: Image ranking and retrieval based on multi-attribute queries. In: CVPR (2011)
5. Kovashka, A., Parikh, D., Grauman, K.: Whittlesearch: image search with relative attribute feedback. In: CVPR (2012)
6. Kovashka, A., Grauman, K.: Attribute adaptation for personalized image search. In: ICCV (2013)
7. Kumar, N., Berg, A.C., Belhumeur, P.N., Nayar, S.K.: Attribute and simile classifiers for face verification. In: ICCV (2009)
8. Duan, K., Parikh, D., Crandall, D., Grauman, K.: Discovering localized attributes for fine-grained recognition. In: CVPR (2012)
9. Zhang, N., Paluri, M., Ranzato, M., Darrell, T., Bourdev, L.: PANDA: pose aligned networks for deep attribute modeling. In: CVPR (2014)
10. Branson, S., Wah, C., Schroff, F., Babenko, B., Welinder, P., Perona, P., Belongie, S.: Visual recognition with humans in the loop. In: Daniilidis, K., Maragos, P., Paragios, N. (eds.) ECCV 2010, Part IV. LNCS, vol. 6314, pp. 438–451. Springer, Heidelberg (2010)
11. Bourdev, L., Maji, S., Malik, J.: Describing people: poselet-based approach to attribute classification. In: ICCV (2011)
12. Shrivastava, A., Singh, S., Gupta, A.: Constrained semi-supervised learning using attributes and comparative attributes. In: Fitzgibbon, A., Lazebnik, S., Perona, P., Sato, Y., Schmid, C. (eds.) ECCV 2012, Part III. LNCS, vol. 7574, pp. 369–383. Springer, Heidelberg (2012)
13. Sandeep, R.N., Verma, Y., Jawahar, C.V.: Relative parts: distinctive parts for learning relative attributes. In: CVPR (2014)
14. Xiao, F., Lee, Y.J.: Discovering the spatial extent of relative attributes. In: ICCV (2015)
15. Chopra, S., Hadsell, R., LeCun, Y.: Learning a similarity metric discriminatively, with application to face verification. In: CVPR (2005)
16. Jaderberg, M., Simonyan, K., Zisserman, A., Kavukcuoglu, K.: Spatial transformer networks. In: NIPS (2015)
17. Yu, A., Grauman, K.: Fine-grained visual comparisons with local learning. In: CVPR (2014)
18. Oliva, A., Torralba, A.: Modeling the shape of the scene: a holistic representation of the spatial envelope. In: IJCV (2001)
19. Farhadi, A., Endres, I., Hoiem, D., Forsyth, D.: Describing objects by their attributes. In: CVPR (2009)
20. Kumar, N., Berg, A., Belhumeur, P., Nayar, S.: Attribute and simile classifiers for face verification. In: ICCV (2009)
21. Farhadi, A., Endres, I., Hoiem, D.: Attribute-centric recognition for cross-category generalization. In: CVPR (2010)
22. Rastegari, M., Farhadi, A., Forsyth, D.: Attribute discovery via predictable discriminative binary codes. In: Fitzgibbon, A., Lazebnik, S., Perona, P., Sato, Y., Schmid, C. (eds.) ECCV 2012, Part VI. LNCS, vol. 7577, pp. 876–889. Springer, Heidelberg (2012)
23. Saleh, B., Farhadi, A., Elgammal, A.: Object-centric anomaly detection by attribute-based reasoning. In: CVPR (2013)
24. Chung, J., Lee, D., Seo, Y., Yoo, C.D.: Deep attribute networks. In: NIPS Workshop on Deep Learning and Unsupervised Feature Learning (2012)

25. Escorcia, V., Niebles, J.C., Ghanem, B.: On the relationship between visual attributes and convolutional networks. In: CVPR (2015)

26. Shankar, S., Garg, V.K., Cipolla, R.: Deep-carving: Discovering visual attributes by carving deep neural nets. arXiv:1504.04871 (2015)

27. Souri, Y., Noury, E., Adeli-Mosabbeb, E.: Deep relative attributes. arXiv:1512.04103 (2015)

28. Kumar, N., Belhumeur, P.N., Nayar, S.K.: FaceTracer: a search engine for large collections of images with faces. In: Forsyth, D., Torr, P., Zisserman, A. (eds.) ECCV 2008, Part IV. LNCS, vol. 5305, pp. 340–353. Springer, Heidelberg (2008)

29. Kiapour, M.H., Yamaguchi, K., Berg, A.C., Berg, T.L.: Hipster wars: discovering elements of fashion styles. In: Fleet, D., Pajdla, T., Schiele, B., Tuytelaars, T. (eds.) ECCV 2014, Part I. LNCS, vol. 8689, pp. 472–488. Springer, Heidelberg (2014)

30. Itti, L., Baldi, P.F.: A principled approach to detecting surprising events in video. In: CVPR (2005)

31. Gao, D., Mahadevan, V., Vasconcelos, N.: The discriminant center-surround hypothesis for bottom-up saliency. In: NIPS (2007)

32. Alexe, B., Deselaers, T., Ferrari, V.: What is an object? In: CVPR (2010)

33. Carreira, J., Sminchisescu, C.: Constrained parametric min-cuts for automatic object segmentation. In: CVPR (2010)

34. Uijlings, J., Sande, K., Gevers, T., Smeulders, A.: Selective search for object recognition. IJCV 104(2), 154–171 (2013)

35. Zitnick, C.L., Dollár, P.: Edge boxes: locating object proposals from edges. In: Fleet, D., Pajdla, T., Schiele, B., Tuytelaars, T. (eds.) ECCV 2014, Part V. LNCS, vol. 8693, pp. 391–405. Springer, Heidelberg (2014)

36. Mnih, V., Heess, N., Graves, A., Kavukcuoglu, K.: Recurrent models of visual attention. In: NIPS (2014)

37. Xiao, T., Xu, Y., Yang, K., Zhang, J., Peng, Y., Zhang, Z.: The application of two-level attention models in deep convolutional neural network for fine-grained image classification. In: CVPR (2015)

38. Xu, K., Ba, J., Kiros, R., Courville, A., Salakhutdinov, R., Zemel, R., Bengio, Y.: Show, attend and tell: Neural image caption generation with visual attention. arXiv:1502.03044 (2015)

39. Gregor, K., Danihelka, I., Graves, A., Wierstra, D.: Draw: A recurrent neural network for image generation. arXiv:1502.04623 (2015)

40. Tang, Y., Srivastava, N., Salakhutdinov, R.R.: Learning generative models with visual attention. In: NIPS (2014)

41. Chopra, S., Hadsell, R., LeCun, Y.: Learning a similarity metric discriminatively with application to face verification. In: CVPR (2005)

42. Krizhevsky, A., Sutskever, I., Hinton, G.E.: Imagenet classification with deep convolutional neural networks. In: NIPS (2012)

43. Burges, C.J., Shaked, T., Renshaw, E., Lazier, A., Deeds, M., Hamilton, N., Hullender, G.: Learning to rank using gradient descent. In: ICML (2005)

44. Zhu, X., Ramanan, D.: Face detection, pose estimation, and landmark localization in the wild. In: CVPR (2012)

45. Li, S., Shan, S., Chen, X.: Relative forest for attribute prediction. In: Lee, K.M., Matsushita, Y., Rehg, J.M., Hu, Z. (eds.) ACCV 2012, Part I. LNCS, vol. 7724, pp. 316–327. Springer, Heidelberg (2013)

Efficient Large Scale Image Classification via Prediction Score Decomposition

Duy-Dinh Le[1,2]($\boxtimes$), Tien-Dung Mai[1], Shin'ichi Satoh[2],
Thanh Duc Ngo[1], and Duc Anh Duong[1]

[1] University of Information Technology, VNU-HCM, Ho Chi Minh City, Vietnam
{duyld,dungmt,thanhnd,ducda}@uit.edu.vn
[2] National Institute of Informatics, 2-1-2 Hitotsubashi, Chiyoda-ku, Tokyo, Japan
{ledduy,satoh}@nii.ac.jp

Abstract. There has been growing interest in reducing the test time complexity of multi-class classification problems with large numbers of classes. The key idea to solve it is to reduce the number of classifier evaluations used to predict labels. The state-of-the-art methods usually employ the label tree approach that usually suffers the well-know error propagation problem and it is difficult for parallelization for further speedup. We propose another practical approach, with the same goal of using a small number of classifiers to achieve a good trade-off between testing efficiency and classification accuracy. The proposed method analyzes the correlation among classes, suppresses redundancy, and generates a small number of classifiers that best approximate the prediction scores of the original large number of classes. Different from label-tree methods in which each test example follows a different traversing path from the root to a leaf node and results in a different set of classifiers each time, the proposed method applies the same set of classifiers to all test examples. As a result, it is much more efficient in practice, even in the case of using the same number of classifier evaluations as the label-tree methods. Experiments on several large datasets including ILSVRC2010-1K, SUN-397, and Caltech-256 show the efficiency of our method.

Keywords: Large scale classification · Label tree · Matrix decomposition

1 Introduction

Multi-class classification, which is the problem of classifying one example with a predefined set of classes, is one of the fundamental problems of computer vision. The availability of large-scale datasets, such as ImageNet [9], SUN [37], and Caltech-256 [17], that have many training and testing examples and many classes has posed significant challenges in computational issues.

Electronic supplementary material The online version of this chapter (doi:10.1007/978-3-319-46466-4_46) contains supplementary material, which is available to authorized users.

B. Leibe et al. (Eds.): ECCV 2016, Part VI, LNCS 9910, pp. 770–785, 2016.
DOI: 10.1007/978-3-319-46466-4_46

One of the challenges that has attracted growing attention is *how to discriminate a large number of classes*. The complexity in test time grows linearly with the number of classes when using the standard one-versus-all (OvA) approach [1,31], and this is prohibitive for large-scale datasets used in practical applications. *The key idea to solve this problem is to reduce the number of classifiers evaluated for each testing example.*

The Error Correcting Output Codes (ECOC) based approaches [2,8,12–14, 30,39,40] combines multi binary classifiers to solve the multi-class classification problem. Given a testing example, the set of bit predictors is applied to obtain a code, and the second stage involves assignment the class whose codeword is the closest to the code. The computational complexity of ECOC is linear to the number of binary classifier evaluations (i.e. code length). In the case of a large number of classes, learning an efficient coding matrix is challenging and problem-dependent. Furthermore, good coding matrix does not ensure good classification [8].

The tree-based approaches [4–7,10,16,18,24,25,27,33,36,38] use a hierarchical label tree to organize a predefined set of classes. In the testing process, an example is classified by traversing the tree from the root node to a leaf node. Since the number of classifiers at each node is much smaller than the number of original classifiers of OvA methods, in the ideal case, label tree methods achieve sub-linear complexity. To achieve high accuracy, methods have been proposed for optimization of the overall tree loss through building the tree structure and learning classifiers at nodes. Although these methods are considered to be state of the art in large-scale image classification [4,10,16,24,33], they still have drawbacks such as *(i) error propagation problem where errors made at an internal node are propagated through the tree and yield misclassification, and (ii) difficulty in parallelization for further speed-up because the set of classifiers used in the evaluation of a testing example is not known in advance.*

In this paper, we propose a novel method for solving the multi-class classification problems with large numbers of classes that does not use a tree structure. To achieve a good trade-off between testing efficiency and classification accuracy, at the first stage, our method analyzes the correlation among classes, suppresses redundancy, and generates a small number of fixed classifiers (*pseudo-classifiers*) that best approximate the prediction scores of the original large number of classes. Because there are errors in the approximated scores, it does not guarantee good classification accuracy if directly using for prediction. At the second stage, a verification process is used to handle this situation. Specifically, a set of the candidate labels is selected using the top k scores, and the k corresponding OvA classifiers are applied to recompute the scores for final decision.

Our contribution is two-fold:

- We propose a novel framework for the multi-class classification problem that is easy to balance between accuracy and speed. Approximated scores can be computed extremely fast using a small number of pseudo-classifiers and can be further speed-up using parallel computing. The verification stage only requires several OvA classifier evaluations to significantly improve classification accuracy.

Our method has potential in practice because it is very fast, requires less memory space, is easy to implement, and only has one parameter (number of pseudo-classifiers) to tune for the balance.
- We conducted comprehensive experiments showing that the proposed method can achieve better state-of-the-art performance and yet is much more efficient in terms of actual testing time compared with existing methods.

2   Related Work

Computational efficiency is one of the most important considerations in large-scale image classification in which the number of classes is also large. The standard methods, such as one-versus-all [31], and DAG (directed acyclic graph) [29], treat the label space as flat, and therefore, their time complexity as far as testing goes is linearly proportional to the number of classes, which is prohibitive in practical applications.

2.1   Label Tree Approach

The label-tree approach is a popular approach to reduce the time complexity of testing to a sub-linear value. It works by creating a hierarchical structure in the label space.

Label-tree methods [4,10,16,24,33] involve two issues: *(i) learning the tree structure and (ii) learning the classifier weights for each internal node and the labels of the leaf nodes.* Learning the label tree parameters requires finding the classifier weights for each node and the labels for the leaf nodes. The label embedding tree proposed by S. Bengio et al. [4] learns the tree structure by applying spectral clustering to a confusion matrix generated by OvA classifiers in order to split the classes into disjoint subsets. The node classifiers are then learned jointly by optimizing the overall tree loss. However, for large numbers of classes, it suffers from drawbacks: *(i) learning OvA classifiers in order to generate the confusion matrix is costly, (ii) splitting the classes into disjoint subsets is difficult because the assumption of separability of classes usually fails, and (iii) it might generate an unbalanced tree that leads to a sub-optimal testing time.*

In the fast and balanced tree proposed by J. Deng et al. [10], these drawbacks are avoided by performing the splitting process and learning process jointly and by allowing overlaps among the subsets of child nodes. The relaxed hierarchy proposed by T. Gao and D. Koller [16] is an alternative solution based on max-margin optimization in which a subset of confusing classes is allowed to be ignored at each node. This method shares the same idea as the method proposed by Marszalek and C. Schmid [27], but has significant improvements over it. Recently, Liu et al. [24] proposed the probabilistic label tree, which outperforms existing methods. The key idea here is to define the label tree as a probabilistic model and use maximum likelihood optimization to learn the parameters.

2.2 ECOC Approach

ECOC-based methods [2,8,12,14,30] mainly involve designing an optimal coding matrix that requires a small number of bits for efficiency, good row and column separation for robustness, and high accurate bit predictors. Sparse random codes and random codes described in [2,12] require a large number of bit predictors ($15.log(C)$ and $10.log(C)$ respectively where C is the number of classes) to achieve reasonable accuracy. However, it is shown in [31], the accuracy of these methods is worse than that of the OvA approach. Spectral ECOC [39] is based on spectral decomposition on the normalized Laplacians of the similarity graph of the classes. The resulting eigenvectors are used to define partitions. Because it uses one-versus-one (OvO) classifiers to generate the similarity matrix, it is not scalable for classification problems with large number of classes. Recently, Sparse Output Coding (SpOC) [40] is a new encoding and decoding scheme that learns coding matrix and bit predictor separately but still has good balance between error-correcting ability and bit prediction accuracy. However, it uses a predefined class taxonomy to build semantic relatedness matrix for the both stages. It is unknown what happens if this prior knowledge is removed.

2.3 Other Complementary Approaches

There are other approaches proposed for solving the problem of large scale image classification [3,19,23,26,32]. Most of them adopt the OvA approach due to its competitive performance and its easy parallelization on multi-cores or machines. For example, a method for fast feature extraction and SVM learning for OvA classifiers is described in [23]. The studies described in [1,3,19,26] aim to achieve better accuracy than OvA methods by simultaneously learning shared characteristics common to the classes and minimizing classification loss using trace-norm. Sparselets introduced in [32] is another approach that learns shared intermediate representation for multi-class object detection with deformable part models using sparse reconstruction of object models. *The main contributions of the studies described above are scalable learning methods for large datasets with good generalization ability, hence they are complementary with our proposed method.*

Another approach [21] is based on attribute based learning. The idea is to analyze visual correlations between classes instead of manual human efforts to design attribute classifiers and relations between classes and attributes for classification.

Recently, methods to speeding up evaluation of Convolutional Neural Networks (CNN) [11,20] using low-rank approximation were proposed. However, much attention was paid to convolutional layers, i.e. lower layers used for feature extraction, rather than fully connected layers; and the approximations are performed after the network has been fully trained.

3 Preliminaries

Suppose that N images whose feature vectors are $v_i, i = 1, \cdots, N$, are to be classified into C classes $c_j, j = 1, \cdots, C$. We will use v_i to denote a feature vector or image interchangeably. We want to generate an N by C response matrix[1] R, where $r_{(i,j)}$ corresponds to the "response" of the i-th image for the j-th class. The response can be a binary value, $r_{(i,j)} = +1$, if v_i belongs to c_j (-1 otherwise) or it can be a score, $r_{(i,j)} \geq 0$, if v_i belongs to c_j (< 0 otherwise).

There are a number of ways to train multi-class classifiers; however, one standard way to obtain the responses for a given set of images is to train C classifiers, $f_j(\cdot)$, $j = 1, \cdots, C$, based on the OvA strategy [31], and then to obtain the responses, $r_{(i,j)} = f_j(v_i)$. For multi-class classification (i.e., one-out-of-C classes classification), v_i can be classified into the class c_j whose $f_j(v_i)$ is maximum. For multiple binary classification results, v_i can be classified into classes whose responses are positive.

Now let us consider a smaller number of classifiers, namely, L classifiers $g_k(v)$, $k = 1, \cdots, L$, where $L \ll C$. Let's assume that f can be sufficiently approximated as $f(v) \approx f'(g_1(v), g_2(v), \cdots, g_L(v))$. *If the cost of evaluating f' is significantly cheaper than that of g_k, and the cost of f_j is almost the same as that of g_k, we can expect that the above approximation will yield significant cost reductions.*

4   Proposed Method

4.1   Overview of the Method

We propose a two-stage method for solving the multi-class classification problem. The key idea is to use an extremely fast method for filtering process to find a set of candidate labels, then use robust OvA classifiers for the verification process to get the correct label. At first, a matrix decomposition based technique is used to find a small number of classifiers that best approximate the prediction scores of the original large number of classes. Because there is no guarantee that using the approximated scores directly minimizes classification loss, only the top k scores are used to select a set of k candidate labels. Then a verification process is carried out by applying k OvA classifiers corresponding to the candidate labels to recompute the scores for the final decision.

The first stage uses the same set of fixed classifiers (*pseudo-classifiers*) to all test examples, leading to be extremely fast in testing process and reasonable performance. Meanwhile the second stage is used to further improve the accuracy by applying a small number of OvA classifiers. By this way, a good trade-off between testing efficiency and classification accuracy is achieved easily.

4.2   Fast Classification via Prediction Score Decomposition

Let us factorize the N by C response matrix R into an N by L matrix A and an L by C matrix B, namely, $R = AB$. By letting $a_{(i,k)} = g_k(v_i)$, A can be regarded as classification results of N images for L classifiers, and the final response R

---

[1] We use score matrix and response matrix interchangeably.

Algorithm 1. Training

Input:
1:    – R: score matrix of N training images.
2:    – S: the feature vectors of the training images.
Output:
3:    – $\tilde{W}$: the eigenvectors corresponding to the L largest eigenvalues.
4:    – Σ: the eigenvalues corresponding to the L largest eigenvalues.
5:    – V: the right singular vectors corresponding to the L largest eigenvalues.
6: Obtain $\tilde{S}$ by using the training feature vectors formed with (9).
7: Obtain $P = \tilde{S}RR^T\tilde{S}^T$ and $Q = \tilde{S}\tilde{S}^T$.
8: Solve the generalized eigenvalue problem $Pw = \lambda Qw$ and obtain $\lambda_1 \geq \lambda_2 \geq \cdots \geq \lambda_L$ and $\tilde{W} = [\tilde{w}_1 \cdots \tilde{w}_L]$ keeping the eigenvectors corresponding to the L largest eigenvalues. Let $\Sigma = diag(\lambda_1, \cdots, \lambda_L)^{1/2}$.
9: Obtain $U = \tilde{S}^T\tilde{W}$.
10: Obtain $V = ((U\Sigma)^+R)^T$.

---

can be obtained by multiplying B. One way to perform this decomposition is to use singular value decomposition (SVD for short):

$$R \approx U\Sigma V^T \tag{1}$$

where U and V are composed of left and right singular vectors corresponding to the L largest singular values, and we can set $A = U$ and $B = \Sigma V^T$. In doing so, R can be approximated in the MSE sense. This implies f' to be a linear combination of g_k. Given this singular value decomposition, we can use $U = [u_1 u_2 \cdots u_L]$ to train functions g_k that well approximate u_k, namely, $g_k(v_i) \approx u_{(i,k)}$ via regression. However, this process results in a two-stage approximation; namely, in the first stage, R is approximated by singular value decomposition, and following that, each $g_k(\cdot)$ is fit to $u_{(\cdot,k)}$ by regression. The pseudo-classifier $g_k(\cdot)$ obtained in this way may not be optimal. Instead, we will jointly optimize the decomposition of R and the regressor for $g_k(\cdot)$ in a single step. Therefore, cost of training the regressors is reduced and improved accuracy is expected.

Let's revisit SVD.

$$R = U\Sigma V^T \tag{2}$$
$$RR^T = U\Sigma V^T V\Sigma U^T = U\Sigma^2 U^T \tag{3}$$
$$RR^T U = U\Sigma^2. \tag{4}$$

Instead of obtaining U directly by singular value decomposition, we take into account that U is the result of performing regression on the feature vectors of the images. To do so, we will pose the original problem as an eigenvalue problem,

$$RR^T u = \lambda u \tag{5}$$
$$u^T RR^T u = u^T \lambda u = \lambda \tag{6}$$

where u is an eigenvector and λ is the corresponding eigenvalue. The first eigenvector corresponding to the largest eigenvalue can be obtained by maximizing

(6), and the following eigenvalues and eigenvectors are iteratively obtained using the above process along with Gram-Schmidt orthonormalization.

Now we consider u as regression result, namely, $u_{(i,k)} \approx g_k(v_i)$. We further assume linear regression:

$$g_k(v_i) = \langle w_k, v_i \rangle + b_k \tag{7}$$

$$= [w_k \, b_k][v_i \, 1]^T \overset{\text{def}}{=} \tilde{w}_k \tilde{v}_i. \tag{8}$$

By defining the matrix of features:

$$\tilde{S} = \begin{bmatrix} v_1 \, v_2 \cdots v_N \\ 1 \; 1 \; \cdots \; 1 \end{bmatrix} \tag{9}$$

we want $u \approx \tilde{S}^T \tilde{w}$. Substituting this into (6), the problem becomes:

$$\text{maximize } \tilde{w}^T \tilde{S} R R^T \tilde{S}^T \tilde{w} \tag{10}$$

$$\text{such that } \tilde{w}^T \tilde{S} \tilde{S}^T \tilde{w} = 1 \tag{11}$$

We can use the Lagrange multipliers method to solve it.

$$J = \tilde{w}^T \tilde{S} R R^T \tilde{S}^T \tilde{w} - \lambda(\tilde{w}^T \tilde{S} \tilde{S}^T \tilde{w} - 1) \tag{12}$$

$$\frac{\partial L}{\partial \tilde{w}} = 2 \tilde{S} R R^T \tilde{S}^T \tilde{w} - 2\lambda \tilde{S} \tilde{S}^T \tilde{w} = 0 \tag{13}$$

$$\tilde{S} R R^T \tilde{S}^T \tilde{w} = \lambda \tilde{S} \tilde{S}^T \tilde{w}. \tag{14}$$

The above can be regarded as a generalized eigenvalue problem $Pw = \lambda Qw$, where $P = \tilde{S} R R^T \tilde{S}^T$ and $Q = \tilde{S} \tilde{S}^T$. Obviously P and Q are Hermitian and Q is positive semi-definite. Therefore, the eigenvalues λ are real. Let us assume that we have obtained the eigenvalues λ_i and eigenvectors $\tilde{w}_i$ where $\lambda_1 \geq \lambda_2 \geq \cdots$. From the properties of the generalized eigenvalue problem, the $\tilde{w}_i$ are Q-orthogonal, namely, $\tilde{w}_i Q \tilde{w}_j = 0$ where $i \neq j$. Since

$$\tilde{w}_i^T \tilde{S} \tilde{S}^T \tilde{w}_j = (\tilde{S}^T \tilde{w}_i)^T (\tilde{S}^T \tilde{w}_j) \tag{15}$$

$$= u_i^T u_j = 0 \tag{16}$$

this ensures the orthogonal relationship among u_i. In addition, due to (11), u_i are orthonormal. Therefore, by selecting $\tilde{w}_i$ corresponding to the L largest λ_i, we can obtain u_i that optimally approximate R, while at the same time $\tilde{w}_i$ defines the optimal regressors.

Let us consider such $\tilde{w}_i, i = 1, \cdots, L$. We can obtain $\tilde{W} = [\tilde{w}_1 \cdots \tilde{w}_L]$. Accordingly, U can be obtained as

$$U = \tilde{S}^T \tilde{W}. \tag{17}$$

In theory, V can be obtained through an eigenvalue decomposition of $R^T R$. However, due to the estimation error of linear regression in U, the resultant V

Algorithm 2. Classification
___
Input:
1: $-$ S_{tg}: the feature vectors of the target images.
2: $-$ $\tilde{W}$: the eigenvectors corresponding to the L largest eigenvalues.
3: $-$ Σ: the eigenvalues corresponding to the L largest eigenvalues.
4: $-$ V: the right singular vectors corresponding to the L largest eigenvalues.
Output:
5: $-$ R_{tg}: score matrix of the target images.
6: Obtain $\tilde{S}_{tg}$ by using (9).
7: Calculate the estimated response as $R_{tg} = \tilde{S}_{tg}^T \tilde{W} \Sigma V^T$.
8: Output the classification results (multi-class classification using the max operator or multiple binary classification using thresholding) from R_{tg}.

---

obtained by the above method may not be in right correspondence with U. So, we obtain V using the relationship $R \approx U\Sigma V^T$, where $\Sigma = diag(\lambda_1, \cdots, \lambda_L)^{1/2}$:

$$V = ((U\Sigma)^+ R)^T \tag{18}$$

where X^+ is Moore-Penrose pseudoinverse $X^+ = (X^T X)^{-1} X^T$.

The algorithms for training and classification are summarized in Algorithms 1 and 2.

4.3 Verification by OvA Classifiers

Given the estimated score matrix $R_{tg} \in \mathbb{R}^{N \times C}$ returned from Algorithm 2, each row r_i is corresponding scores of C classifiers for test example v_i, i.e. $r_{i,j} = f_j(v_i), (j = 1, .., C, i = 1, .., N)$. The simplest way to predict label is directly to use these scores: $y_i = \underset{j=1,..,C}{\mathrm{argmax}}\ r_{i,j}$. However, there might be errors in estimated scores that affect classification accuracy, a verification process is needed.

Specifically, a set of candidate labels $C^* = \{c_1, c_2, ..., c_k\}$ corresponding to top k scores is selected. Then the new scores are re-computed $r_{i,j}^* = f_j(v_i), j \in C^*$. The final decision is $y_i = \underset{j \in C^*}{\mathrm{argmax}}\ r_{i,j}^*$.

5 Experiments

5.1 Datasets

We evaluated our algorithms on several large datasets that are widely used in experiments for large-scale image classification [4,10,16,24], including the ILSVRC2010-1K [9], SUN-397 [37], and Caltech-256 [17]. ILSVRC2010-1K has 1.2M images in 1 K classes for training, 50 K images for validation, and 150 K images for testing. SUN-397 has 108,754 images in 397 classes. Caltech-256 has 29,780 images in 256 classes. With SUN-397 dataset and Caltech-256 dataset, we used 50 % for training, 25 % for validation, and the rest 25 % for testing. We used the same feature settings as in [10,24] for fair comparison. Specifically, for each image, we used the VLFeat toolbox [34] to extract dense SIFT features from the image. The features were encoded using the LLC coding strategy described in [35], with a codebook having 10,000 visual words, and the image was encoded using a two-level spatial pyramid [22] with 1×1 and 2×2 grids. This resulted in a feature vector with approximately 50,000 dimensions. *Experiments on CNN features and a larger dataset ImageNet-10K are reported in the Supplementary Material.*

5.2   Results

Accuracy Comparison. Table 1 compares the classification accuracy (we use top-1 average per class accuracy) on ILSVRC2010-1K dataset ($C = 1,000$ classes) of our system with those of two state-of-the-art label-tree methods including Fast-Balanced Tree [10] and Probabilistic Tree [24]. We use the same fashion as described in [24] for comparison. Specifically, the columns of Table 1 represent different tree structures. The tree denoted by $T_{m,n}$ has m children per node when branching and n levels, not including the root node. Test speedup S_{te} is the OvA test cost divided by the label tree test cost (measured as the average number of dot products used to classify each example) as defined in [10].

Similar to [24], to make a fair comparison, we adjusted the number of pseudo-classifiers to achieve a similar test time (i.e. the average number of dot-products to classify each example). Specifically, one example is the tree config $T_{32,2}$, to achieve the test speedup $S_{te} = 10.42$, the average number of classifiers to apply for each example is $L_{T_{32,2}} = \frac{C}{S_{te}} = \frac{1,000}{10.42} = 96$. The accuracy of our method is reported via two configs. The first one (Ours-[L_1]) does not use the verification step and the second one (Ours-[$L_2 + k$]) uses the verification step with the number of OvA classifiers of $k = 5$. Because the number of classifier evaluations is fixed in advance in this comparison, for example $L_{T_{32,2}} = 96$, in the case of the first one, $L_1 = L_{T_{32,2}} = 96$ pseudo-classifiers is used, while the second one uses only $L_2 = L_{T_{32,2}} - k = 91$ pseudo-classifiers.

In addition, the accuracy of ECOC-based methods is also reported. We used the ECOC library provided by [13] to generate the coding matrix for Random Dense Output Coding ($RDOC$) and Random Sparse Output Coding ($RSOC$) [2] with the number of bit predictors being equal to the number of pseudo-classifiers in the second config (L_2). As for *SpectralECOC* [39], we used confusion matrix for computing eigen vectors because the original method used OvO classifiers that are not scalable for large number of classes. The verification step ($k = 5$) is used for these ECOC methods. The accuracy of the method based on attribute learning [21] and the accuracy of multi-class classification using OvA classifiers trained with LIBLINEAR [15] (1K-OvA(LIBLINEAR)) are also reported for reference. The results in Table 1 show that:

– The classification accuracy of our method (Ours-[$L2 + k$]) is significantly better than that of other state of the art methods. The method Ours-[$L2 + k$] improves the accuracy over the method Ours-[$L1$] from $25\% - T_{32,2}$ to

Table 1. Classification accuracy comparison of our method and other state of the art methods on ILSVRC2010-1K dataset ($C = 1,000$ classes). We adopt the notion $T_{m,n}$ of the label-tree methods [10,24] for different tree configurations. Given $T_{m,n}$ and S_{te}, the number of pseudo-classifiers (L_1 and L_2 in our method corresponding to without/with using the verification step) and the number of bit predictors (ECOC-based methods) are adjusted to reach the target number of classifiers of $L = \frac{C}{S_{te}}$. The same verification process is applied for ECOC-based methods with the number of OvA classifiers of $k = 5$ as with Ours-$[L2 + k]$.

Method	Flat		$T_{32,2}$ $(L = 96)$		$T_{10,3}$ $(L = 56)$		$T_{6,4}$ $(L = 32)$	
	Acc%	S_{te}	Acc%	S_{te}	Acc%	S_{te}	Acc%	S_{te}
Fast-Balanced Tree [10]			11.9	10.3	8.92	18.20	5.62	31.3
Probabilistic Tree [24]			21.38	10.42	20.54	17.85	17.02	31.25
$RDOC$ [2]			3.35	10.42	2.15	17.86	1.28	31.25
$RSOC$ [2]			3.48	10.42	2.18	17.86	1.34	31.25
$SpectralECOC$ [39]			7.18	10.42	5.57	17.86	4.25	31.25
Attribute-based learning [21]			12.13	10.42	8.07	17.86	5.81	31.25
Ours-$[L_1]$			20.31	10.42	16.96	17.86	11.67	31.25
Ours-$[L_2 + k]$			**25.38**	10.42	**23.32**	17.86	**17.88**	31.25
1K-OvA(LIBLINEAR)	26.01	1						

$53\% - T_{6,4}$ showing that the verification process is helpful. Furthermore, its accuracy is very close to that of 1K-OvA(LIBLINEAR) while the number of classifiers is more than ten times smaller.

- The classification accuracy of our method (Ours-$[L1]$) without using the verification step is significantly better than that of Fast-Balanced Tree method [10] and quite comparable with that of the Probabilistic Tree method [24] if using sufficient large number of pseudo-classifiers as shown in $T_{32,2}$. As shown in Fig. 2, our method needs at least 100 pseudo-classifiers to achieve reasonable classification accuracy.

We implemented a variant of the label tree proposed by Bengio et. al [4] for comparison. The tree structure was learned by applying spectral clustering [28] on the confusion matrix similar to [4]. However, for each node, given a label set associated with that node, we trained multi-class classifiers using OvA strategy. The resulting tree, which we call Label Tree-$R1$, is similar to the tree using $Relaxation(1)$ described in [4] in which node classifiers are optimized independently. The methods such as Fast-Balanced Tree [10] and Probabilistic Tree [24] do not report the classification accuracy on the datasets of SUN-397 and Caltech-256. Therefore, only the accuracy of Label Tree-$R1$ is reported for comparison. *Observation and conclusion from the result (shown in Tables 2 and 3) of these two datasets are the same as that of ILSVRC2010-1K dataset.*

Effect of the Number of OvA Classifiers in the Verification Stage.
Figure 1 shows effect of the number of OvA classifiers k used for the verification

Table 2. Classification accuracy comparison of our method and other state of the art methods on SUN-397 dataset ($C = 397$ classes).

Method	Flat Acc%	S_{te}	$T_{20,2}$ ($L = 40$) Acc%	S_{te}	$T_{8,3}$ ($L = 25$) Acc%	S_{te}	$T_{5,4}$ ($L = 19$) Acc%	S_{te}
Label Tree-$R1$ [4]			29.24	9.98	23.97	15.81	21.49	20.34
$RDOC$ [2]			17.89	9.98	12.14	15.81	8.96	20.34
$RSOC$ [2]			19.52	9.98	13.55	15.81	9.84	20.34
$SpectralECOC$ [39]			29.56	9.98	24.47	15.81	17.61	20.34
Ours-$[L_1]$			36.52	9.98	31.26	15.81	27.27	20.34
Ours-$[L_2 + k]$			**49.01**	9.98	**45.37**	15.81	**40.49**	20.34
397-OvA(LIBLINEAR)	50.99	1						

stage. The accuracy is improved when using more number of OvA classifiers. The config Ours-$[L_2 + k]$ where $L_2 = 200$ and $k = 5$ outperforms 1K-OvA classifiers. It should be noted that the verification stage is necessary only if top-1 accuracy is required (for fair comparison with label tree methods). The top-5 accuracy of Ours-$[L_1]$ is equal to that of Ours-$[L_2 + k]$ ($k = 5$).

Effect of the Number of Pseudo-classifiers. As described in the training algorithm in Sect. 4.2, our method needs to train OvA classifiers using training images and apply these classifiers to validation images to obtain matrix R from which pseudo-classifiers are generated. Figure 2 shows the relationship between the classification accuracy and the number of pseudo-classifiers used for approximation the classification scores for ILSVRC2010-1K dataset. It also shows the relationship between the number of images used in training OvA classifiers and the number of validation images used to obtain matrix R. We tested with different situations TrainnT-ValnV, where $nT = 100, 300$ is the number of training images per class and $nV = 30, 50$ is the number of validation images per class. The results indicate that the number of training images has influence to the final performance, while the number of validation images has no influence. A reasonable classification accuracy can be achieved with using 100 pseudo-classifiers.

Real Processing Time. Prior studies in measurement of testing efficiency only consider the number of average dot products M to classify each example (for estimating S_{te}). We argue that M does not reflect the true test time and thus real processing time is more appropriate for practical evaluation. The fact is that tree-based methods rely on a hierarchical structure, meaning that the selection of the classifier used in each level of the tree depends on the decisions of the classifiers used in the previous level of the tree. Therefore, the total cost includes not only the cost of dot-product operators when applying linear classifiers to the test example, but also the cost of switching classifiers when traversing down child nodes.

Table 3. Classification accuracy comparison of our method and other state of the art methods on Caltech-256 dataset ($C = 256$ classes).

Method	Flat		$T_{16,2}$ ($L = 32$)		$T_{7,3}$ ($L = 20$)		$T_{4,4}$ ($L = 16$)	
	Acc%	S_{te}	Acc%	S_{te}	Acc%	S_{te}	Acc%	S_{te}
Label Tree-$R1$ [4]			32.32	8.00	27.76	12.80	25.81	16.00
$RDOC$ [2]			26.77	8.00	21.15	12.80	18.47	16.00
$RSOC$ [2]			26.80	8.00	20.98	12.80	17.89	16.00
$SpectralECOC$ [39]			27.38	8.00	21.30	12.80	16.77	16.00
Ours-$[L_1]$			33.38	8.00	25.45	12.80	22.08	16.00
Ours-$[L_2 + k]$			**45.38**	8.00	**36.59**	12.80	**30.27**	16.00
256-OvA(LIBLINEAR)	50.95	1						

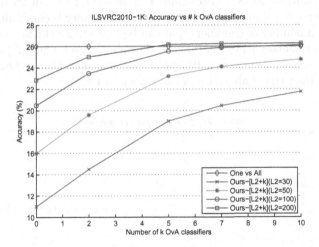

Fig. 1. Effect of the verification stage.

One advantage of our method in the case of Ours-$[L_1]$ is the same set of pseudo-classifiers is applied to all test examples, meaning that it is merely performed by matrix multiplying operator (see formula 7). Therefore, it is extremely fast to select candidate classes for the verification step. Figure 3 shows comparison of the processing time (measured by wall-clock time in seconds) of our method and that of the Label Tree-$R1$ method for $T_{32,2}$ (note that the processing time of the Label Tree-$R1$ method is also representative for other label tree methods). In our implementation, we assume all classifiers can be loaded in memory once. We measure the processing time of the methods for different values $numTest$, that is the number of test examples can be loaded into the memory at a certain time. As for the Label Tree-$R1$ method, we only count the processing time of dot-product operators and ignore other costs such as loading classifiers at each level. The results indicate that the testing speed of our method is significantly better than that of the Label Tree-$R1$ method. For example, for the case $numTest = 50,000$, with the similar $S_{te} = 10.4$ (i.e. the similar average number of dot products to classify each example), our method requires 3.4 s to return the classification result, while the Label Tree-$R1$ method using $T_{32,2}$ requires 267.5 s.

Given a target accuracy, as shown in Fig. 1 there are two ways to achieve it that are (i) increasing the number of pseudo-classifiers L_1 if using Ours-$[L_1]$ and (ii) increasing the number of OvA classifiers k if using Ours-$[L_2 + k]$.

The former way yields extremely fast classification process for a set of test images because the same set of classifiers is applied by one matrix multiplying operator. For example, given the target accuracy of 21.38 % of the Probabilistic Tree [24] of T32,2, Ours-$[L1]$ needs $L_1 = 200$ pseudo-classifiers to achieve 22.85 %, but 15 times faster. Similarly, for T6,4, it needs $L_1 = 100$ pseudo-classifiers to achieve 20.48 % (Probabilistic Tree is 17.2 %), but 25 times faster.

The latter way is more appropriate when the memory is constrained, leading to the limited number of classifiers that can be loaded into the memory. Given a target number of classifier evaluations, as shown in Table 1, Ours-$[L_2+k]$ achieves the best classification accuracy. Its speed is slower than that of Ours-$[L_1]$, but much faster than that Label Tree-$R1$ as shown in Fig. 3.

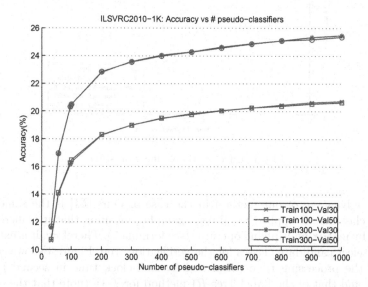

Fig. 2. The relationship between the classification accuracy and the number of pseudo-classifiers used for approximation the classification scores for ILSVRC2010-1K dataset. We tested with different situations TrainnT-ValnV, where $nT = 100, 300$ is the number of training images per class and $nV = 30, 50$ is the number of validation images per class. The classification accuracy significantly increases when the number of training images per class changes from 100 to 300. However, it does not change much when the number of validation images per class changes from 30 to 50 when the number of training images per class is fixed.

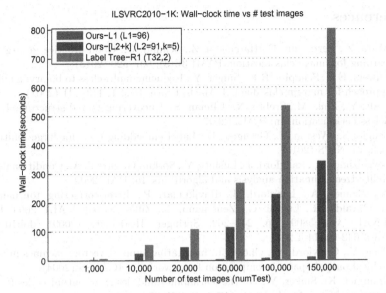

Fig. 3. Real processing time between our method and the Label Tree-$R1$ method for $T_{32,2}$ (that is representative for label tree methods). Our method uses the same set of pseudo-classifiers all the times, so it only needs matrix multiplication operator (as shown in formula 7) to calculate the classification scores for a set of test examples. Meanwhile, the Label Tree-$R1$ method uses different sets of classifiers for each example, so it is much slower than our method. For example, for the case $N = 50,000$, with the similar $S_{te} = 10.4$ (i.e. the similar average number of dot products to classify each example), our method requires 3.4 s to return the classification result, while the Label Tree-$R1$ method using $T_{32,2}$ requires 267.5 s (78 times slower).

6 Conclusion

We presented a novel method for multi-class classification in the case of a large number of classes. Our method can find a small set of pseudo-classifiers that best approximate the scores of the original classes. Furthermore, it is easy to implement, and one can simply adjust the accuracy or efficiency of the trade-off by specifying the number of pseudo-classifiers. Comprehensive experiments on large datasets such as ILSVRC2010-1K, SUN-397, and Caltech-256 showed that our method achieves state-of-the-art classification accuracy and is more efficient in terms of testing time than other methods.

Acknowledgment. This research is funded by Vietnam National University Ho Chi Minh City (VNU-HCM) under grant number B2015-26-01.

References

1. Akata, Z., Perronnin, F., Harchaoui, Z., Schmid, C.: Good practice in large-scale learning for image classification. PAMI 36(3), 507–520 (2013)
2. Allwein, E.L., Schapire, R.E., Singer, Y.: Reducing multi-class to binary: a unifying approach for margin classifiers. J. Mach. Learn. Res. 1, 113–141 (2001)
3. Amit, Y., Fink, M., Srebro, N., Ullman, S.: Uncovering shared structures in multiclass classification. In: ICML (2007)
4. Bengio, S., Weston, J., Grangier, D.: Label embedding trees for large multi-class task. In: NIPS (2010)
5. Beygelzimer, A., Langford, J., Lifshits, Y., Sorkin, G., Strehl, A.: Conditional probability tree estimation analysis and algorithms. In: UAI (2009)
6. Beygelzimer, A., Langford, J., Ravikumar, P.: Error-correcting tournaments. In: Gavaldà, R., Lugosi, G., Zeugmann, T., Zilles, S. (eds.) ALT 2009. LNCS (LNAI), vol. 5809, pp. 247–262. Springer, Heidelberg (2009). doi:10.1007/978-3-642-04414-4_22
7. Chen, Y., Crawford, M., Ghosh, J.: Integrating support vector machines in a hierarchical output space decomposition framework. In: IGARSS (2004)
8. Crammer, K., Singer, Y.: On the learnability and design of output codes for multiclass problems. Mach. Learn. 47(2–3), 201–233 (2002)
9. Deng, J., Dong, W., Socher, R., Li, L., Li, K., Fei-Fei, L.: Imagenet: a large-scale hierarchical image database. In: CVPR (2009)
10. Deng, J., Satheesh, S., Berg, A., Fei-Fei, L.: Fast and balanced: efficient label tree learning for large scale object recognition. In: NIPS (2011)
11. Denton, E.L., Zaremba, W., Bruna, J., Lecun, Y., Fergus, R.: Exploiting linear structure within convolutional networks for efficient evaluation. In: NIPS (2014)
12. Dietterich, T.G., Bakiri, G.: Solving multi-class learning problems via error-correcting output codes. J. Artif. Intell. Res. 2, 263–286 (1995)
13. Escalera, S., Pujol, O., Radeva, P.: Error-correcting ouput codes library. J. Mach. Learn. Res. 11, 661–664 (2010)
14. Escalera, S., Tax, M., Pujol, O., Radeva, P.: Subclass problem-dependent design for error-correcting output codes. PAMI (2008)
15. Fan, R.E., Chang, K.W., Hsieh, C.J., Wang, X.R., Lin, C.J.: Liblinear: a library for large linear classification. J. Mach. Learn. Res. 8, 1871–1874 (2008)
16. Gao, T., Koller, D.: Discriminative learning of relaxed hierarchy for large-scale visual recognition. In: ICCV (2011)
17. Griffin, G., Holub, A., Perona, P.: Caltech-256 object category dataset. Technical report, California Institute of Technology (2007)
18. Griffin, G., Perona, P.: Learning and using taxonomies for fast visual categorization. In: CVPR (2008)
19. Harchaoui, Z., Douze, M., Paulin, M., Dudik, M., Malick, J.: Large-scale image classification with trace-norm regularization. In: CVPR (2012)
20. Jaderberg, M., Vedaldi, A., Zisserman, A.: Speeding up convolutional neural networks with low rank expansions. In: BMVC (2014)
21. Kusakunniran, W., Satoh, S., Zhang, J., Wu, Q.: Attribute-based learning for large scale object classification. In: ICME (2013)
22. Lazebnik, S., Schmid, C., Ponce, J.: Beyond bags of features: spatial pyramid matching for recognizing natural scene categories. In: CVPR (2006)
23. Lin, Y., Lv, F., Zhu, S., Yang, M., Cour, T., Yu, K., Cao, L., Huang, T.: Large-scale image classification: fast feature extraction and svm training. In: CVPR (2011)

24. Liu, B., Sadeghi, F., Tappen, M., Shamir, O., Liu, C.: Probabilistic label trees for efficient large scale image classification. In: CVPR (2013)
25. Liu, S., Yi, H., Chia, L.T., Rajan, D.: Adaptive hierarchical multi-class svm classifier for texture-based image classification. In: ICME (2005)
26. Loeff, N., Farhadi, A.: Scene discovery by matrix factorization. In: Forsyth, D., Torr, P., Zisserman, A. (eds.) ECCV 2008. LNCS, vol. 5305, pp. 451–464. Springer, Heidelberg (2008). doi:10.1007/978-3-540-88693-8_33
27. Marszałek, M., Schmid, C.: Constructing category hierarchies for visual recognition. In: Forsyth, D., Torr, P., Zisserman, A. (eds.) ECCV 2008. LNCS, vol. 5305, pp. 479–491. Springer, Heidelberg (2008). doi:10.1007/978-3-540-88693-8_35
28. Ng, A., Jordan, M., Weiss, Y.: On spectral clustering: Analysis and an algorithm. In: NIPS (2002)
29. Platt, J.C., Cristianini, N., Shawe-taylor, J.: Large margin dags for multi-class classification. In: NIPS (2000)
30. Pujol, O., Radeva, P., Vitrià, J.: Discriminant ECOC: A heuristic method for application dependent design of error correcting output codes. PAMI (2006)
31. Rifkin, R., Klautau, A.: In defense of one-vs-all classification. J. Mach. Learn. Res. 5, 101–141 (2004)
32. Song, H.O., Girshick, R., Zickler, S., Geyer, C., Felzenszwalb, P., Darrell, T.: Generalized sparselet models for real-time multiclass object recognition. PAMI (2013)
33. Sun, M., Huang, W., Savarese, S.: Find the best path: an efficient and accurate classifier for image hierarchies. In: ICCV (2013)
34. Vedaldi, A., Fulkerson, B.: VLFeat - an open and portable library of computer vision algorithms. In: ACM International Conference on Multimedia (2010)
35. Wang, J., Yang, J., Yu, K., Lv, F., Huang, T., Gong, Y.: Locality-constrained linear coding for image classification. In: CVPR (2010)
36. Xia, S., Li, J., Xia, L., Ju, C.: Tree-structured support vector machines for multiclass classification. In: Liu, D., Fei, S., Hou, Z., Zhang, H., Sun, C. (eds.) ISNN 2007. LNCS, vol. 4493, pp. 392–398. Springer, Heidelberg (2007). doi:10.1007/978-3-540-72395-0_50
37. Xiao, J., Hays, J., Ehinger, K., Oliva, A., Torralba, A.: Sun database: large-scale scene recognition from abbey to zoo. In: CVPR (2010)
38. Yuan, X., Lai, W., Mei, T., Hua, X., Wu, X., Li, S.: Automatic video genre categorization using hierarchical svm. In: ICIP (2006)
39. Zhang, X., Liang, L., Shum, H.: Spectral error correcting output codes for efficient multiclass recognition. In: ICCV (2009)
40. Zhao, B., Xing, E.P.: Sparse output coding for large-scale visual recognition. In: CVPR (2013)

Stochastic Dykstra Algorithms for Metric Learning with Positive Definite Covariance Descriptors

Tomoki Matsuzawa[1], Raissa Relator[2], Jun Sese[2], and Tsuyoshi Kato[1(✉)]

[1] Faculty of Science and Engineering, Gunma University, Maebashi, Japan
katotsu@cs.gunma-u.ac.jp
[2] The Artificial Intelligence Research Center, AIST, Tokyo, Japan

Abstract. Recently, covariance descriptors have received much attention as powerful representations of set of points. In this research, we present a new metric learning algorithm for covariance descriptors based on the Dykstra algorithm, in which the current solution is projected onto a half-space at each iteration, and runs at $O(n^3)$ time. We empirically demonstrate that randomizing the order of half-spaces in our Dykstra-based algorithm significantly accelerates the convergence to the optimal solution. Furthermore, we show that our approach yields promising experimental results on pattern recognition tasks.

Keywords: Covariance descriptor · Metric learning · Convex optimization · Stochastic optimization · Dykstra algorithm

1 Introduction

Learning with example objects characterized by a set of several points, instead of a single point, in a feature space is an important task in computer vision and pattern recognition. Recently, the covariance descriptor [1–4] has received much attention as a powerful representation of a set of points. The performance of categorizing covariance descriptors depends on the metric that is used to measure the distances between them. To compare covariance descriptors, a variety of distance measures such as affine invariant Riemannian metric [5], Stein metric [6], J-divergence [7], Frobenius distance [1], and Log-Frobenius distance [8], have been discussed in existing literature. Some of them are designed from their geometrical properties, but some are not. Many of these distance measures are expressed in the form

$$D_{\Phi}(X_1, X_2) := \|\Phi(X_1) - \Phi(X_2)\|_F^2, \tag{1}$$

where Φ is some function that maps a symmetric positive definite matrix to a square matrix with the same size. If $\Phi(X) := \mathrm{logm}(X)$, where $\mathrm{logm}(X)$

Electronic supplementary material The online version of this chapter (doi:10.1007/978-3-319-46466-4_47) contains supplementary material, which is available to authorized users.

B. Leibe et al. (Eds.): ECCV 2016, Part VI, LNCS 9910, pp. 786–799, 2016.
DOI: 10.1007/978-3-319-46466-4_47

takes the principal matrix logarithm of a strictly positive definite matrix X, the Log-Frobenius distance [8] is obtained. Setting $\Phi(X) := X^p$ gives the Power-Frobenius distance [1], while $\Phi(X) := \mathbf{chol}(X)$, where $\mathbf{chol}(\cdot)$ produces the Cholesky decomposition of X such that $X = \mathbf{chol}(X)\mathbf{chol}(X)^\top$, yields the Cholesky-Frobenius distance [9]. These metrics are pre-defined before the employment of machine learning algorithms, and are not adaptive to the data to be analyzed. Meanwhile, for categorization of vectorial data, supervised learning for fitting metrics to the task has been proven to significantly increase the performance of the distance-based classifier [10–12].

In this paper, we introduce a parametric distance measure between covariance descriptors and present novel metric learning algorithms to determine the parameters of the distance measure function. The learning problem is formulated as the Bregman projection onto the intersections of half-spaces. This kind of problem can be solved by the Dykstra algorithm [13,14], which chooses a single half-space in a cyclic order and projects a current solution to the half-space. We developed an efficient technique for projection onto a single half-space. Furthermore, we empirically found that selecting the half-space stochastically, rather than in a cyclic order, dramatically increases the speed of converging to an optimal solution.

Related work. Jayasumana et al. [1] defined a positive definite kernel among covariance descriptors based on the two facts that the exponential of any conditional negative definite kernel is positive definite, and that the distance function given in the form of (1) is a conditional negative definite kernel. A disadvantage of using such a kernel is that the feature space derived from the kernel is not always given explicitly. Some approaches perform dimensionality reduction [15–17] by finding some informative subspace or learning a more discriminant lower dimensional space. However, in these methods, some information may be discarded when projecting into a lower dimensional subspace.

Vamulapalli and Jacobs [3] introduced a supervised metric learning approach for covariance descriptors. They vectorized the matrix logarithms of the covariance descriptors to apply existing metric learning methods to the vectorizations of matrices. The dimensionality of the vectorizations is $n(n+1)/2$ when the size of the covariance matrices are $n \times n$. Thus, the size of the Mahalanobis matrix is $n(n+1)/2 \times n(n+1)/2$, which is computationally prohibitive when n is large.

Our approach is a generalization of the distance measure of Huang et al. [2], which is based on the Log-Euclidean metric, with their loss function being a special case of our formulation. They also adopted the cyclic Dykstra algorithm for learning the Mahalanobis-like matrix. Their main finding is that projection onto a half-space can be obtained analytically. However, having misused the Woodbury matrix inversion formula and thereby deriving a wrong closed-form solution, their claim does not hold. Therefore, their algorithm has no theoretical guarantee of converging to the optimal solution. In this paper, their update rule is corrected by presenting a new technique that projects a current solution to a single half-space within $O(n^3)$ computational time.

Yger and Sugiyama [4] devised a different formulation of metric learning. They introduced the congruent transform and measures distances between the transformations of covariance descriptors. An objective function based on the kernel target alignment [18] is employed to determine the transformation parameters. Compared to their algorithm, our algorithm has the capability to monitor the upper bound of the objective gap, i.e. the difference between the current objective and the minimum. This implies that the resultant solution is ensured to be ϵ-suboptimal if the algorithm's convergence criterion is set such that the objective gap upper bound is less than a very small number ϵ. Since Yger and Sugiyama [4] employed a gradient method for learning the congruent transform, there is no way to know the objective gap.

Contributions. Our contributions of this paper can be summarized as follows.

- For metric learning on positive semidefinite cone, we developed a new algorithm based on the Dykstra algorithm, in which the current solution is projected onto a half-space at each iterate, and runs at $O(n^3)$ time (Fig. 1).
- We empirically found that randomizing the order of half-spaces in our Dykstra-based algorithm significantly accelerates the convergence to the optimal solution. Especially, the proposed approach enables the use of an *almost hard margin* (weak regularization), although the classical approach can attain an optimum within a practical time only when a strong regularization is chosen.
- We present an upper-bound for the objective gap which provides a stopping criterion and ensures the optimality of the solution.
- We show that our approach yields promising experimental results on pattern recognition tasks.

2 Our Metric Learning Problem

We introduce the following dissimilarity measure for covariance descriptors $X_1, X_2 \in \mathbb{S}_+^n$:

$$D_{\Phi}(X_1, X_2; W) := \langle W, (\Phi(X_1) - \Phi(X_2))(\Phi(X_1) - \Phi(X_2))^\top \rangle, \qquad (2)$$

where $W \in \mathbb{S}_+^n$ is the parameter of this function. Therein, $\mathbb{S}_+^n$ and $\mathbb{S}_{++}^n$ are the sets of $n \times n$ positive semi-definite matrices and strictly positive semi-definite matrices, respectively. We shall also use $\mathbb{R}_+^n$ and $\mathbb{R}_{++}^n$ to denote the sets of n-dimensional real vectors with non-negative and strictly positive entries, respectively.

Theorem 1. *If W is strictly positive definite and Φ is bijective, then the dissimilarity measure $D_{\Phi}(\cdot, \cdot; W) : \mathbb{S}_+^n \times \mathbb{S}_+^n \to \mathbb{R}$ is a distance metric.*

The proof of Theorem 1 is given in Section A.1. To determine the value of the parameter matrix W, we pose a constrained optimization problem based on the idea of ITML [10]. We now consider a multi-class categorization problem.

Suppose we are given $(\boldsymbol{X}_1, \omega_1), \ldots, (\boldsymbol{X}_\ell, \omega_\ell)$ as a training dataset, where $\boldsymbol{X}_i$ is the covariance descriptor of the i-th example, and ω_i is its class label. From the ℓ examples, K index pairs $(i_1, j_1), \ldots, (i_K, j_K)$ are selected, and each pair is given the following constraint:

$$D_{\boldsymbol{\Phi}}(\boldsymbol{X}_{i_k}, \boldsymbol{X}_{j_k}; \boldsymbol{W}) \begin{cases} \leq b_{\mathrm{ub}}\xi_k, & \text{if } \omega_{i_k} = \omega_{j_k}, \\ \geq b_{\mathrm{lb}}\xi_k, & \text{if } \omega_{i_k} \neq \omega_{j_k}, \end{cases} \tag{3}$$

where the two constants b_{ub} and b_{lb} are the upper-bound of the distances between any two examples in the same class and the lower-bound of the distances between any two examples in different classes, respectively, when $\xi_k = 1$. Now let us define $(y_k, b_k) := (+1, b_{\mathrm{ub}})$ for k such that $\omega_{i_k} = \omega_{j_k}$, and $(y_k, b_k) := (-1, b_{\mathrm{lb}})$ for $\omega_{i_k} \neq \omega_{j_k}$. Under the constraint (3), we wish to find $\boldsymbol{W}$ and ξ_k such that $\boldsymbol{W}$ is not much deviated from the identity matrix and ξ_k is close to one. From this motivation, we pose the following problem:

$$\min \quad \mathrm{BD}_\varphi((\boldsymbol{W}, \boldsymbol{\xi}), (\boldsymbol{I}, \boldsymbol{1})),$$

$$\mathrm{wrt} \quad \boldsymbol{W} \in \mathbb{S}^n_{++}, \quad \boldsymbol{\xi} = [\xi_1, \ldots, \xi_K]^\top \in \mathbb{R}^K_{++},$$

$$\text{subject to} \quad \forall k \in \mathbb{N}_K, \quad y_k D_{\boldsymbol{\Phi}}(\boldsymbol{X}_{i_k}, \boldsymbol{X}_{j_k}; \boldsymbol{W}) \leq y_k b_k \xi_k, \tag{4}$$

where $\mathrm{BD}_\varphi(\cdot, \cdot) : (\mathbb{S}^n_{++} \times \mathbb{R}^K_{++}) \times (\mathbb{S}^n_{++} \times \mathbb{R}^K_{++}) \to \mathbb{R}_+$ is the *Bregman divergence*. Only if $(\boldsymbol{W}, \boldsymbol{\xi}) = (\boldsymbol{I}, \boldsymbol{1})$ will the divergence $\mathrm{BD}_\varphi((\boldsymbol{W}, \boldsymbol{\xi}), (\boldsymbol{I}, \boldsymbol{1}))$ become zero, and the value of divergence becomes larger if $(\boldsymbol{W}, \boldsymbol{\xi})$ is more deviated from $(\boldsymbol{I}, \boldsymbol{1})$. The definition of the Bregman divergence contains a seed function $\varphi : \mathbb{S}^n_{++} \times \mathbb{R}^K_{++} \to \mathbb{R}$ which is assumed to be continuously differentiable and strictly convex. For some φ, the Bregman divergence is defined as

$$\mathrm{BD}_\varphi(\boldsymbol{\Theta}, \boldsymbol{\Theta}_0) = \varphi(\boldsymbol{\Theta}) - \varphi(\boldsymbol{\Theta}_0) - \langle \nabla\varphi(\boldsymbol{\Theta}_0), \boldsymbol{\Theta} - \boldsymbol{\Theta}_0 \rangle, \tag{5}$$

for $\boldsymbol{\Theta}, \boldsymbol{\Theta}_0 \in \mathbb{S}^n_{++} \times \mathbb{R}^K_{++}$, where $\langle \cdot, \cdot \rangle$ used here denotes the inner-product defined simply as,

$$\forall(\boldsymbol{W}_1, \boldsymbol{\xi}_1), \forall(\boldsymbol{W}_2, \boldsymbol{\xi}_2) \in \mathbb{S}^n_{++} \times \mathbb{R}^K_{++},$$
$$\langle (\boldsymbol{W}_1, \boldsymbol{\xi}_1), (\boldsymbol{W}_2, \boldsymbol{\xi}_2) \rangle = \langle \boldsymbol{W}_1, \boldsymbol{W}_2 \rangle + \angle \boldsymbol{\xi}_1, \boldsymbol{\xi}_2 \rangle. \tag{6}$$

This implies that the quantities of the deviations of the solution $(\boldsymbol{W}, \boldsymbol{\xi})$ from $(\boldsymbol{I}, \boldsymbol{1})$ depend on the definition of the seed function. In this study, the seed function is assumed to be the sum of two terms:

$$\varphi(\boldsymbol{W}, \boldsymbol{\xi}) := \varphi_{\mathrm{r}}(\boldsymbol{W}) + \sum_{k=1}^K c_k \varphi_{\mathrm{l}}(\xi_k), \tag{7}$$

where c_k is a positive constant that trades off the importance of regularization versus that of losses. Larger c_k yields a harder margin. The first term in the definition of the seed function is defined as $\varphi_{\mathrm{r}} : \mathbb{S}^n_{++} \to \mathbb{R}$, where $\varphi_{\mathrm{r}}(\boldsymbol{W}) := -\log\det(\boldsymbol{W})$. Meanwhile, for the second term containing $\varphi_{\mathrm{l}} : \mathbb{R}_{++} \to \mathbb{R}$, we considered the following three functions:

$$\varphi_{\mathrm{is}}(\xi_k) := -\log(\xi_k), \qquad \varphi_{\mathrm{l2}}(\xi_k) := \frac{1}{2}\xi_k^2, \qquad \varphi_{\mathrm{e}}(\xi_k) := (\log\xi_k - 1)\xi_k. \tag{8}$$

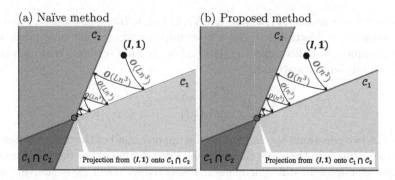

Fig. 1. Dykstra algorithm chooses a half-space in each iterate to project a current solution to the half-space. This study devised a new technique that performs the exact projection with $O(n^3)$ computation, where naïve method requires $O(Ln^3)$ computation, where L is defined in Sect. 4.

The Bregman divergences generated from the three seed functions φ_{is}, φ_{l2}, and φ_e, respectively, are referred to as *Itakura-Saito Bregman Divergence* (**ISBD**), *L2 Bregman Divergence* (**L2BD**), and *Relative Entropy Bregman Divergence* (**REBD**), where ISBD is equal to the objective function employed by Huang et al. [2].

3   Stochastic Variants of Dykstra Algorithm

We introduce the Dykstra algorithm [13,14] to solve the optimization problem (4). The original Dykstra algorithm [14] was developed as a computational method that finds the Euclidean projection from a point onto the intersection of half-spaces. This Dykstra algorithm can also be applied to finding the projection onto the interaction of multiple convex sets, although in this paper we focus on the interaction of half-spaces with the aim of utilizing the Dykstra algorithm for solving our metric learning problem. Censor & Reich [13] extended the Dykstra algorithm to finding the *Bregman projection* from a point $\boldsymbol{x}_0$ to the intersection $\mathcal{C}$, defined by

$$\underset{x \in \mathcal{C}}{\operatorname{argmin}} \operatorname{BD}_\varphi(\boldsymbol{x}, \boldsymbol{x}_0). \tag{9}$$

In each iterate, the Dykstra algorithm chooses a single half-space in a cyclic order to project the current solution onto the half-space (Fig. 1). The Dykstra algorithm is guaranteed to converge to a minimum linearly.

In available literature related to stochastic gradient descent methods and the variants [19–22] that minimize the regularized loss averaged over a set of examples, it is empirically shown that, rather than choosing an example in a cyclic order, example selection in a stochastic order dramatically speeds up the convergence to the optimal solution.

Motivated by these facts, this study proposes the use of stochastic selection of half-spaces in the Dykstra algorithm, herein termed as the *stochastic Dykstra algorithm*. Altogether, there are three ways to select half-spaces: **Cyclic**: A half-space is selected in a cyclic order at each iteration. **Rand**: A half-space is chosen randomly at each iteration. **Perm**: Prior to selection, the order of the K half-spaces are permuted randomly at the beginning of each epoch. Hereinafter, we assume to employ the "Rand" option, although replacing this option with one of the remaining two is straightforward.

If we define the k-th half-space $\mathcal{C}_k$ as $\mathcal{C}_k := \{x \mid \langle a_k, x \rangle \leq b_k\}$, it can be shown, from Lagrangean theory, that computing the Bregman projection from a point x_0 to its boundary $\mathrm{bd}(\mathcal{C}_k)$ is equivalent to solving the following saddle point problem:

$$\max_{\delta} \min_{x} \mathrm{BD}_{\varphi}(x, x_0) + (\langle a_k, x \rangle - b_k)\delta \tag{10}$$

where $\delta \in \mathbb{R}$ is the Lagrangean multiplier.

Algorithm 1. Stochastic Dykstra Algorithm.

1: **begin**
2:   $\forall k \in \mathbb{N}_K : \alpha_k := 0$;
3: **for** $t = 1, 2, \ldots$ **do**
4:     Pick k randomly from $\{1, \ldots, K\}$;
5:     Solve the following saddle point problem and let $\delta_{t-1/2}$ be the solution of δ:

$$\max_{\delta} \min_{x} \mathrm{BD}_{\varphi}(x, x_{t-1}) + \delta_t(\langle a_k, x \rangle - b_k); \tag{11}$$

6:     $\delta_t := \max(\delta_{t-1/2}, -\alpha_k)$; $\alpha_k := \alpha_k + \delta_t$;
7:     $x_t = \nabla\varphi^*(\nabla\varphi(x_{t-1}) - \delta_t a_k)$;
8: **end for**
9: **end.**

This fact enables us to rewrite the Dykstra algorithm with Rand option for finding the Bregman projection from a point x_0 to the intersection of $\mathcal{C}_1, \ldots, \mathcal{C}_K$, as described in Algorithm 1, where φ^* is the convex conjugate [23] of the seed function φ. When applying Algorithm 1 to our metric learning problem (4), the most crucial step is Step 5, which solves the saddle point problem (11). In this study, a fast computational technique for this step was devised, with details presented in the next section.

4 Efficient Projection Technique

We first show that solving the optimization problem (4) is equivalent to finding a Bregman projection from a point $(I, 1) \in \mathbb{S}_{++}^n \times \mathbb{R}_{++}^K$ onto the intersection of multiple half-spaces, followed by introducing a new fast technique for solving the sub-problem (11).

Let A_k be a positive semi-definite matrix expressed as

$$A_k := (\boldsymbol{\Phi}(\boldsymbol{X}_{i_k}) - \boldsymbol{\Phi}(\boldsymbol{X}_{j_k}))(\boldsymbol{\Phi}(\boldsymbol{X}_{i_k}) - \boldsymbol{\Phi}(\boldsymbol{X}_{j_k}))^\top \qquad (12)$$

for $k \in \mathbb{N}_K$, to define a half-space

$$\mathcal{C}_k := \left\{ (\boldsymbol{W}, \boldsymbol{\xi}) \in \mathbb{S}_{++}^n \times \mathbb{R}_{++}^K \mid y_k \langle A_k, \boldsymbol{W} \rangle - y_k b_k \xi_k \le 0 \right\}. \qquad (13)$$

Then, it can be shown that the intersection of K half-spaces $\bigcap_{k=1}^K \mathcal{C}_k$ is the feasible region of the optimization problem (4). This implies that the Dykstra algorithm can be applied to solve problem (4). Hereinafter, we assume A_k is strictly positive definite. By setting $A_k \leftarrow A_k + \epsilon I$, with ϵ as a small positive constant, this assumption can be satisfied readily.

Next we present an efficient technique for Step 5 in Algorithm 1 that projects $(\boldsymbol{W}_{t-1}, \boldsymbol{\xi}_{t-1}) \in \mathbb{S}_{++}^n \times \mathbb{R}_{++}^K$ onto the k-th half-space $\mathcal{C}_k$, where $(\boldsymbol{W}_{t-1}, \boldsymbol{\xi}_{t-1}) \in \mathbb{S}_{++}^n \times \mathbb{R}_{++}^K$ is the model parameter after the $(t-1)$-th iteration. Performing the projection is equivalent to finding the saddle point of the function $Q : \mathbb{S}_{++}^n \times \mathbb{R}_{++}^K \times \mathbb{R} \to \mathbb{R}$ defined as

$$Q(\boldsymbol{W}, \boldsymbol{\xi}, \delta) := \mathrm{BD}_\varphi((\boldsymbol{W}, \boldsymbol{\xi}), (\boldsymbol{W}_{t-1}, \boldsymbol{\xi}_{t-1})) + \delta y_k (\langle A_k, \boldsymbol{W} \rangle - b_k \xi_k). \qquad (14)$$

Lemma 1. *Let $\xi_{k,t-1}$ be the k-th entry in the vector $\boldsymbol{\xi}_{t-1}$. The value of the function $J_t : \mathbb{R} \to \mathbb{R}$ defined by*

$$J_t(\delta) := \langle A_k, (\boldsymbol{W}_{t-1}^{-1} + \delta y_k A_k)^{-1} \rangle - b_k \nabla \varphi_l^*(\nabla \varphi_l(\xi_{t-1}) + \delta y_k b_k / c_k), \qquad (15)$$

is zero at the solution δ of the saddle point of Q. The solution δ must satisfy the strictly positive definiteness:

$$\boldsymbol{W}_{t-1}^{-1} + \delta y_k A_k \succ \boldsymbol{O}, \qquad (16)$$

and the feasibility of the slack variables:

$$\exists \xi_{k,t-1/2} \quad s.t. \quad \nabla \varphi_l(\xi_{k,t-1/2}) = \nabla \varphi_l(\xi_{k,t-1}) - \delta y_k b_k / c_k. \qquad (17)$$

The proof is given in Section A.2. There is no closed-form solution found for this projection problem. Hence, some numerical method such as the Newton-Raphson method is necessary for solving the nonlinear equation $J_t(\delta) = 0$. If one tries to compute the value of $J_t(\delta)$ naïvely, it will require an $O(n^3)$ computational cost because $J_t(\cdot)$ involves computation of the inverse of an $n \times n$ matrix. If we suppose the numerical method assesses the value of the scalar-valued function $J_t(\cdot)$ L times, the naïve approach will take $O(Ln^3)$ computational time to find the solution of the nonlinear equation $J_t(\delta) = 0$. Furthermore, the positive definiteness condition in (16) and the feasibility condition in (17) must be checked.

The proposed technique for finding the saddle point is given as follows. Let $d_1, \ldots, d_n$ be the eigenvalues of $A_k^{-1/2} \boldsymbol{W}_{t-1}^{-1} A_k^{-1/2}$ with $d_1 \ge \cdots \ge d_n$. Then, we get

$$J_t(\delta) = \sum_{i=1}^n \frac{1}{d_i + y_k \delta} - b_k \nabla \varphi_l^* \left(\nabla \varphi_l(\xi_{t-1}) + \frac{\delta y_k b_k}{c_k} \right), \qquad (18)$$

which implies that assessment of $J_t(\delta)$ can be done within $O(n)$ computational cost after $d_1, \ldots, d_n$ are obtained (Derivation of (18) is given in Section A.4. Combining it with the fact that it takes $O(n^3)$ time to get the n scalars $d_1, \ldots, d_n$, the solution can be computed in $O(n^3 + Ln)$ time (See Section A.6 for details). Define $\delta_b := c_k / (b_k \xi_{k,t-1})$. The interval of $y_k \delta$ satisfying (16) and (17) is given as $(-d_n, \delta_b)$ for ISBD, and $(-d_n, +\infty)$ for L2BD and REBD (See Section A.5 for detailed discussion). Thus, our theoretical results are summarized in the following theorem.

Theorem 2. *The saddle point of $Q(\boldsymbol{W}, \boldsymbol{\xi}, \delta)$ can be found within $O(n^3 + Ln)$ time, where L is the number of times a numerical method assesses the value of $J_t(\cdot)$. Moreover, a unique solution exists.*

A brief proof of this theorem has been shown above, but the complete description of the proof is given in Sections A.3–A.7. Since $L \in O(n^2)$ in a typical setting, we can say that each update can be done in $O(n^3)$ computation.

Convex Conjugate Functions: Our algorithm requires the derivative of the convex conjugate function of a seed function φ_l. The convex conjugates of the seed functions generating ISBD, L2BD, and REBD are given, respectively, as

$$\varphi_{is}^*(g) = \begin{cases} +\infty, & \text{for } g \geq 0, \\ -1 - \log(-g), & \text{for } g < 0, \end{cases} \tag{19}$$

$$\varphi_{12}^*(g) := \frac{1}{2}g^2, \qquad\qquad \varphi_e^*(g) := \exp(g). \tag{20}$$

These derivatives are expressed as

$$\nabla\varphi_{is}^*(g) = \frac{1}{g}, \qquad \nabla\varphi_{12}^*(g) = g, \qquad \nabla\varphi_e^*(g) = \exp(g). \tag{21}$$

Stopping Criterion: Here we discuss how to determine if the solution is already optimal and when to terminate the algorithm. While running the algorithm, $(\boldsymbol{W}_t, \boldsymbol{\xi}_t)$ may violate some of constraints. Denote the index set of the violated constraints by $\mathcal{I}_{\text{vio}} := \{k \in \mathbb{N}_K \mid (\boldsymbol{W}_t, \boldsymbol{\xi}_t) \notin \mathcal{C}_k\}$ and let us define $\bar{\boldsymbol{\xi}}_t \in \mathbb{R}_{++}^K$ so that the k-th entry is given by $\bar{\xi}_{h,t} := \frac{1}{b_h}\langle \boldsymbol{W}_t, \boldsymbol{A}_h\rangle$ for $h \in \mathcal{I}_{\text{vio}}$ and $\bar{\xi}_{h,t} := \xi_{h,t}$ for $h \notin \mathcal{I}_{\text{vio}}$. Note that $(\boldsymbol{W}_t, \bar{\boldsymbol{\xi}}_t)$ is a feasible solution, and $\bar{\boldsymbol{\xi}}_t = \boldsymbol{\xi}_t$ when $(\boldsymbol{W}_t, \boldsymbol{\xi}_t)$ is feasible. The objective gap after iteration t is bounded as follows:

$$\text{BD}_\varphi((\boldsymbol{W}_t, \bar{\boldsymbol{\xi}}_t), (\boldsymbol{I}, 1)) - \text{BD}_\star \leq \sum_{h \in \mathcal{I}_{\text{vio}}} c_h\left(\varphi_l(\bar{\xi}_{h,t}) - \varphi_l(\xi_{h,t}) - \nabla\varphi_l(1)(\bar{\xi}_{h,t} - \xi_{h,t})\right)$$

$$- \sum_{h=1}^{K} \alpha_h y_h \left(\langle \boldsymbol{A}_h, \boldsymbol{W}_t\rangle - b_h \xi_{h,t}\right), \tag{22}$$

Table 1. Computational times.

n	5	10	50	100	500
Proposed (sec)	**20.93**	**15.55**	**13.24**	**20.04**	**234.64**
Naïve (sec)	21.95	17.84	51.48	184.69	4166.01
# of Epochs	18.5	12.3	8.5	10.3	9.0

Table 2. Average accuracies (%) of the Proposed Method when using different losses and different mapping functions for pattern recognition.

(a) Brodatz

	Eye	REBD	L2BD	ISBD
Id	73.08	**79.55**	79.29	79.33
Log	79.29	**80.27**	80.18	79.96
Sqrt	76.88	80.94	80.89	**81.12**
Chol	78.71	82.77	**82.90**	82.72

(b) ETH-80

	Eye	REBD	L2BD	ISBD
Id	66.98	76.93	**77.99**	76.79
Log	94.40	96.12	**96.35**	96.12
Sqrt	88.26	88.96	**89.32**	88.74
Chol	90.88	91.64	**91.85**	90.83

Algorithm 2. Proposed Metric Learning Algorithm with Covariance Descriptors.

Require: $A_1, \ldots, A_K$, b, c, φ, ϵ.
Ensure: ϵ-approximate solution of (W, ξ).
1: **begin**
2: $\forall k \in \mathbb{N}_K : \alpha_k := 0$; $W_0 = I$; $\xi = 1_K$;
3: **for** $t = 1, 2, \ldots$ **do**
4:     Pick k randomly from $\{1, \ldots, K\}$;
5:     Find the saddle point of the function $L(W, \xi, \delta)$ by solving the nonlinear equation
        $J_t(\delta) = 0$ using (18), where the solution must satisfy $y_k \delta \in (-d_n, \delta_b)$ for ISBD,
        and $y_k \delta \in (-d_n, +\infty)$ for L2BD and REBD, where $\delta_b = c_k / (b_k \xi_{k,t-1})$. Let $\delta_{t-1/2}$
        be the solution of δ:
6:     $\delta_t := \max(\delta_{t-1/2}, -\alpha_k)$; $\alpha_k := \alpha_k + \delta_t$;
7:     $W_t := (W_{t-1} + \delta_t y_k A_k)^{-1}$; $\xi_k := \nabla \varphi^* (\nabla \varphi(\xi_k) + \delta_t y_k b_k / c_k)$;
8:     **if** (RHS of (22)) $\leq \epsilon$ **then** terminate the algorithm;
9: **end for**
10: **end**

---

where BD$_*$ denotes the minimal objective value. Then this upper-bound of the objective gap can be used for the stopping criterion of the Dykstra algorithm.

From the above discussion, our metric learning algorithm for covariance descriptors is summarized as Algorithm 2.

5   Experiments

We conducted experiments to assess the convergence speed of our optimization algorithms, the total computational time for learning, and the generalization performance for pattern recognition.

5.1   Convergence Behavior of Optimization Algorithms

We examined our algorithms for assessment of convergence speed. Artificial datasets were generated as follows. Fifty matrices $F_k \in \mathbb{R}^{n \times n}$ $(k = 1, \ldots, K$ where $K = 50)$ were generated in which each entry was drawn from the uniform distribution in the interval $[-0.5, 0.5]$. Then, we set $A_k := F_k F_k^\top$. The values of the variables y_k were randomly chosen from $\{\pm 1\}$ with same probabilities. We set $b = 1$ and $c = 1/(\lambda K)$, and exhaustively tested Cyclic, Perm, and Rand with $\lambda = 10^{-2}, 10^{-3}, 10^{-4}$ and $n = 10, 50, 100$.

Figure 2 illustrates the convergence behavior of the cyclic Dykstra algorithm and the two stochastic Dykstra algorithms with various λ and n values. Here, one epoch corresponds to projecting onto a single half-space K times. ISBD was employed as the objective function for learning the metric W. In most of the settings, the two stochastic Dykstra algorithms converged faster than the cyclic algorithm. Especially when regularization is weak (e.g. $\lambda = 10^{-4}$), the cyclic algorithm was too slow to use it in practice, but the stochastic version can attain an accurate solution whichever regularization constant is chosen. From the fact that the convergence performances of Rand and Perm do not differ a lot, only the experimental results using Perm are reported hereinafter.

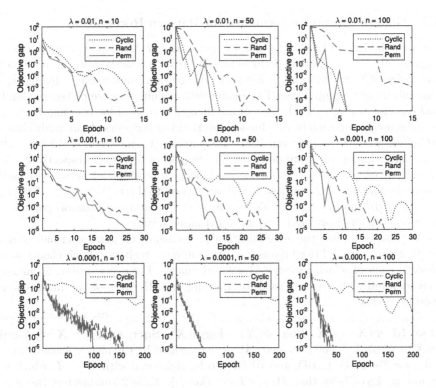

Fig. 2. Convergence behavior of the algorithms using different settings.

T. Matsuzawa et al.

Table 3. Mean recognition accuracies (%) with standard deviations.

	Euclid	Ours	V&J [3]	Huang et al. [2]
Brodatz	79.29 ± 1.04	$\mathbf{82.90 \pm 1.18}$	65.63 ± 2.18	79.33 ± 1.59
ETH-80	94.40 ± 0.55	$\mathbf{96.35 \pm 0.49}$	93.40 ± 1.02	96.09 ± 0.44

5.2 Total Computational Time for Learning

Table 1 details the computational times for metric learning of W, comparing the proposed projection technique (Sect. 4) with the naïve method, where the proposed technique takes $O(n^3 + Ln)$ time for a single projection, whereas the naïve method requires $O(Ln^3)$ time. The experimental settings in Table 1 are similar to those in Fig. 2. For Table 3, we tested the data with $n = 5, 10, 50, 100, 500$. The runtimes were measured on a Linux machine with Intel(R) Core(TM) i7 (3.6 GHz) CPU and 32-GB memory. We repeated the experiments five times, and the average computational times are reported in Table 1. The proposed technique was faster than the naïve method in all cases, and significant improvements were achieved for larger n.

5.3 Generalization Performance for Pattern Recognition

We used the Brodatz texture dataset containing 112 different texture images to examine the generalization performance for texture classification. Each image has a size of 640×640 and gray-scaled. Images were individually divided into four sub-images of equal size. Two of the four sub-images were picked randomly and used for testing, and the rest of the images were used for training. For each training image and each testing image, covariance descriptors of randomly chosen 20 images were extracted from 128×128 patches. Then, $4,480 (= 112 \times 2 \times 20)$ covariance descriptors were obtained for training and testing, respectively. For evaluation of generalized performance, k-nearest neighbor classifier was used, where the number of the nearest neighbors was set to three. We set $K = 100 \times n_c$. Following [10], we set $b_{ub} = 0.05$, and $b_{lb} = 0.95$. The regularization parameter λ was chosen by cross-validation within training dataset.

We also examined the generalization performance for generic visual categorization using the ETH-80 dataset containing $n_c = 8$ classes. Each class has 10 objects, each of which includes 41 colored images. For every object, 20 images were randomly chosen and used for training, and the rest of the images were used for testing.

One covariance matrix is obtained from each image. We tried four types of Φ: Id: $\Phi(X) = X$, Log: $\Phi(X) = \text{logm}(X)$, Sqrt: $\Phi(X) = X^{1/2}$, Chol: $\Phi(X) = \text{chol}(X)$. The parameter W is determined by the metric learning algorithms with ISBD, L2BD, and REBD, to be compared with $W = I$, which we denote as **Eye**. Note that $D_\Phi(\cdot, \cdot; I) = D_\Phi(\cdot, \cdot)$. Table 2 summarizes the average accuracies over ten repeated experiments. Whichever Φ was used, supervised metric learning improved the generalization performance both for texture classification and for generic visual categorization. For texture classification, the Cholesky decomposition-based mapping $\mathbf{chol}(\cdot)$ achieved the best accuracy, while the matrix logarithm-based mapping $\mathbf{logm}(\cdot)$ obtained the highest accuracy for generic image categorization.

We compared the proposed method with two existing metric learning methods of Huang et al. [2] and Vemulapalli and Jacobs [3]. We used Huang et al.'s implementation available from their web site. Their update rule does not guarantee the convergence of the algorithm, and their paper does not present a stopping criterion. To compare our methods with Vemulapalli and Jacobs's method, we implemented their method in Matlab. We performed the principal component analysis after vectorization so that their degree of freedom coincides with ours and Huang et al.'s. As shown in Table 3, our metric learning algorithm achieved significant improvements in accuracy from existing distances (1) and its performance surpassed those of the two existing metric learning methods.

The computational times for learning W using the Brodatz and ETH-80 datasets, respectively, were 76.24 and 6.96 s averaged over ten trials, and the number of epochs are 10 and 7. Meanwhile, using Huang et al.'s Matlab code took 41.87 and 13.6 s, respectively, and 249 and 1047.6 epochs for the two datasets. From these results, Huang et al.'s method seems faster than the proposed method, but it should be emphasized that their method does not possess optimality. In fact, using the same constant values, the objective gaps obtained from their method were 0.0113 and 0.943 in average, whereas in our implementation, the algorithm is designed to terminate when the upper bound of the objective gap becomes less than ϵ, where ϵ was set to 10^{-3}.

6 Conclusions

In this paper, we have devised several objective functions for metric learning on positive semidefinite cone, all of which can be minimized by the Dykstra algorithm. We have introduced a new technique that performs each update efficiently. We have empirically demonstrated that the stochastic versions of the Dykstra algorithm are much faster than the original algorithm and the generalization performance for pattern recognition is significantly improved. A strong advantage of our algorithm is the existence of a stopping criterion that guarantees the sub-optimality, although a gradient method is often employed for non-linear optimization. Numerical comparison to the gradient approach is left to future work.

References

1. Jayasumana, S., Hartley, R., Salzmann, M., Li, H., Harandi, M.T.: Kernel methods on the Riemannian manifold of symmetric positive definite matrices. In: CVPR, pp. 73–80. IEEE (2013)
2. Huang, Z., Wang, R., Shan, S., Li, X., Chen, X.: Log-euclidean metric learning on symmetric positive definite manifold with application to image set classification. In: ICML, pp. 720–729 (2015)

3. Vemulapalli, R., Jacobs, D.W.: Riemannian metric learning for symmetric positive definite matrices. arXiv:1501.02393 (2015)
4. Yger, F., Sugiyama, M.: Supervised logeuclidean metric learning for symmetric positive definite matrices. arXiv:1502.03505 (2015)
5. Pennec, X., Fillard, P., Ayache, N.: A Riemannian framework for tensor computing. Int. J. Comput. Vis. 66(1), 41–66 (2006)
6. Sra, S.: A new metric on the manifold of kernel matrices with application to matrix geometric means. In: Advances in Neural Information Processing Systems, pp. 144–152 (2012)
7. Wang, Z., Vemuri, B.C.: An affine invariant tensor dissimilarity measure andits applications to tensor-valued image segmentation. In: Proceedings of the 2004 IEEE Computer Society Conference on Computer Vision and Pattern Recognition, vol. 1, pp. I–228. IEEE (2004)
8. Arsigny, V., Fillard, P., Pennec, X., Ayache, N.: Log-Euclidean metrics for fast and simple calculus on diffusion tensors. Magnetic Resonance Med. 56(2), 411–421 (2006)
9. Dryden, I.L., Koloydenko, A., Zhou, D.: Non-Euclidean statistics for covariance matrices, with applications to diffusion tensor imaging. Ann. Appl. Stat. 1102–1123 (2009)
10. Davis, J.V., Kulis, B., Jain, P., Sra, S., Dhillon, I.S.: Information-theoretic metric learning. In: ICML, pp. 209–216. ACM (2007)
11. Kato, T., Nagano, N.: Metric learning for enzyme active-site search. Bioinformatics 26(21), 2698–2704 (2010)
12. Relator, R., Nagano, N., Kato, T.: Using Bregman divergence regularized machine for comparison of molecular local structures. IEICE Trans. Inf. Syst. 1, E99-D (2016)
13. Censor, Y., Reich, S.: The Dykstra algorithm with Bregman projections. Comm. Appl. Anal. 2, 407–419 (1998)
14. Dykstra, R.L.: An algorithm for restricted least squares regression. J. Am. Stat. Assoc. 78(384), 837–842 (1983)
15. Sivalingam, R., Morellas, V., Boley, D., Papanikolopoulos, N.: Metric learning for semi-supervised clustering of region covariance descriptors. In: Third ACM/IEEE International Conference on Distributed Smart Cameras, (ICDSC 2009) (2009)
16. Tosato, D., Farenzena, M., Spera, M., Murino, V., Cristani, M.: Multi-class classification on riemannian manifolds for video surveillance. In: Daniilidis, K., Maragos, P., Paragios, N. (eds.) ECCV 2010. LNCS, vol. 6312, pp. 378–391. Springer, Heidelberg (2010). doi:10.1007/978-3-642-15552-9_28
17. Horev, I., Yger, F., Sugiyama, M.: Geometry-aware principal component analysis for symmetric positive definite matrices. In: Proceedings of the Fourth Asian Conference on Machine Learning (ACML2015), vol. 45. JMLR Workshop and Conference Proceedings, Hong Kong, China, pp. 1–16, 20–22 November 2015
18. Cristianini, N., Shawe-Taylor, J., Elisseeff, A., Kandola, J.S.: On kernel-target alignment. In: Dietterich, T.G., Becker, S., Ghahramani, Z., (eds.) NIPS, pp. 367–373. MIT Press (2001)
19. Bottou, L.: Large-scale machine learning with stochastic gradient descent. In: Lechevallier, Y., Saporta, G., (eds.) COMPSTAT 2010, pp. 177–187. Springer, Heidelberg (2010)
20. Johnson, R., Zhang, T.: Accelerating stochastic gradient descent using predictive variance reduction. In: Advances in Neural Information Processing Systems 26, Proceedings of a meeting held 5–8 December 2013, Lake Tahoe, Nevada, United States, pp. 315–323 (2013)

21. Roux, N.L., Schmidt, M., Bach, F.R.: A stochastic gradient method with an exponential convergence rate for finite training sets. In Pereira, F., Burges, C., Bottou, L., Weinberger, K., (eds.) Advances in Neural Information Processing Systems, vol. 25, pp. 2663–2671. Curran Associates, Inc. (2012)
22. Shalev-Shwartz, S., Singer, Y., Srebro, N., Cotter, A.: Pegasos: primal estimated sub-gradient solver for SVM. Math. Program. **127**(1), 3–30 (2011)
23. Boyd, S., Vandenberghe, L.: Convex Optimization. Cambridge University Press, New York (2004)

MeshFlow: Minimum Latency Online Video Stabilization

Shuaicheng Liu[1]([✉]), Ping Tan[2], Lu Yuan[3], Jian Sun[3], and Bing Zeng[1]

[1] University of Electronic Science and Technology of China, Chengdu, China
{liushuaicheng,eezeng}@uestc.edu.cn
[2] Simon Fraser University, Burnaby, Canada
pingtan@sfu.ca
[3] Microsoft Research Asia, Beijing, China
{luyuan,jiansun}@microsoft.com

Abstract. Many existing video stabilization methods often stabilize videos off-line, i.e. as a postprocessing tool of pre-recorded videos. Some methods can stabilize videos online, but either require additional hardware sensors (e.g., gyroscope) or adopt a single parametric motion model (e.g., affine, homography) which is problematic to represent spatially-variant motions. In this paper, we propose a technique for online video stabilization with only *one* frame latency using a novel *MeshFlow* motion model. The MeshFlow is a spatial smooth sparse motion field with motion vectors only at the mesh vertexes. In particular, the motion vectors on the matched feature points are transferred to their corresponding nearby mesh vertexes. The MeshFlow is produced by assigning each vertex an unique motion vector via two median filters. The path smoothing is conducted on the *vertex profiles*, which are motion vectors collected at the same vertex location in the MeshFlow over time. The profiles are smoothed adaptively by a novel smoothing technique, namely the *Predicted Adaptive Path Smoothing* (PAPS), which only uses motions from the past. In this way, the proposed method not only handles spatially-variant motions but also works online in real time, offering potential for a variety of intelligent applications (e.g., security systems, robotics, UAVs). The quantitative and qualitative evaluations show that our method can produce comparable results with the state-of-the-art off-line methods.

Keywords: Online video stabilization · MeshFlow · Vertex profile

1 Introduction

Most existing video stabilization methods stabilize videos offline [1–5], where the videos have already been recorded. These methods post-process shaky videos by estimating and smoothing camera motions for the stabilized results. Typically, to stabilize the motion at each time instance, they require not only camera motions in the past but also camera motions in the future for high quality stabilization. There is an increasing demand of online video stabilization, where the video

© Springer International Publishing AG 2016
B. Leibe et al. (Eds.): ECCV 2016, Part VI, LNCS 9910, pp. 800–815, 2016.
DOI: 10.1007/978-3-319-46466-4_48

is stabilized on the spot during capturing. For example, a robot or drone often carries a wireless video camera so that a remote operator is aware of the situation. Ideally, the operator wants to see the video stabilized as soon as it appears on the monitor for immediate responses. Offline stabilization are not suitable for this application, though they produce strongly stabilized results.

Online stabilization is challenging mainly for two reasons. Firstly, the camera motion estimation is difficult. Some online stabilization methods use gyroscope [6,7] for realtime motion estimation. However, gyro-based methods can only capture rotational motion, leaving translational motion untouched. High quality video stabilization requires handling of spatially-variant motion, which is often due to parallax and camera translation, a common problem in general scenes with depth changes. Spatially-variant motion is complicated. It cannot be represented by a single homography [1,3]. Recent methods [4,5,8] divide the video frame into several regions. However, this strategy is computationally expensive and hinders realtime applications. Enforcing spatial-temporal coherence during camera motion smoothing further complicates this approach.

Secondly, successful camera motion filtering often requires future frames. Some online video stabilization methods [9–11] use the single homography model and buffer some future frames. For example, the method of [10] requires a minimum of one second delay. The temporal buffer is needed to adaptively set the smoothing strength so as to avoid artifacts caused by excessive smoothing. Reducing this buffer for future frame will significantly deteriorate the results.

We design an online video stabilization method with minimum latency by solving the two aforementioned challenges. Our method only requires past motions for high quality motion filtering. We propose a novel motion model, *MeshFlow*, which is a spatially smooth sparse motion field with motion vectors defined only at the mesh vertexes. It can be regarded as a down-sampled dense flow. Specifically, we place a regular 2D mesh on the video frame. We then track image corners between consecutive frames, which yields a motion vector at each feature location. Next, these motion vectors are transferred to their corresponding nearby mesh vertexes, such that each vertex accumulates several motions from its surrounding features. The MeshFlow is a sparse 2D array of motion vectors consisting of motions at all mesh vertices.

With regards to the camera motion smoothing, we design a filter to smooth the temporal changes of the motion vector at each mesh vertex. This filter is applied to each mesh vertex. Thus, it can naturally deal with the spatially-variant motion. The uniqueness of this filter is that it mainly requires previous motions for strong stabilization. This is achieved by predicting an appropriate smoothing strength according to the camera motion at previous frames. In this way, it can achieve adaptive smoothing to avoid excessive cropping and wobble distortions. We call this filter *Predicted Adaptive Path Smoothing* (PAPS).

In summary, the main contribution of the paper consists of: (1) a computationally efficient motion model, MeshFlow, for spatially-variant motion representation; and (2) an adaptive smoothing method PAPS, designed for the new model for online processing with only one frame latency. We evaluate our method on various challenging videos and demonstrate its effectiveness in terms of both visual quality and efficiency.[1]

2 Related Work

According to the adopted motion model, video stabilization methods can be categorised into 3D [8,12,13], 2D [1,3,14], and 2.5D [2,15] approaches. The 3D methods estimate camera motions in 3D space for stabilization. Beuhler et al. [16] stabilized videos under projective 3D reconstruction. Liu et al. [8] applied Structure from Motion (SfM) to the video frames and used content preserving warps for novel view synthesis. Zhou et al. [13] introduced 3D plane constraints for improved warping quality. Smith et al. [17] and Liu et al. [5] adopted light field camera and Kinect camera, respectively, in acquiring of 3D structures. Methods [6,7] and [18] used gyroscope to estimate 3D rotations. Some 2.5D approaches relax the full 3D requirement to some partial 3D information that is embedded in long feature tracks. Goldstein and Fattal [15] used "epipolar transfer" to enhance the length of feature tracks while Liu et al. [2] smoothed feature tracks in subspace so as to maintain the 3D constraints. Later, the subspace approach is extended for stereoscopic videos [19]. All these methods either conducted expensive and brittle 3D reconstruction or required additional hardware sensors for stabilization. In contrast, our method is a sensor-free approach that neither recoveries the 3D structures nor relies on long feature tracks.

The 2D methods use a series of 2D linear transformations (e.g., affines, homographies) for motion estimation and smooth them for stabilized videos [1,20–22]. Grundmann et al. [3] employed cinematography rules for camera path design. Later, they extended their approach by dividing a single homography into homography array [14] such that the rolling shutter distortions could be well compensated. Wang et al. [4] divided frames into triangles and smoothed feature trajectories with a spatial-temporal optimization. Liu et al. [5] smoothed bundled paths for spatially-variant motions. Bai et al. [23] extended the bundled-paths by introducing user interactions. Liu et al. [24] proposed to replace the smoothing of feature tracks with the smoothing of pixel profiles and showed several advantages over smoothing of traditional feature tracks. Inspired from [24], we propose to smooth vertex profiles, a sparse version of pixel profiles, for an improved robustness and efficiency, which facilitates an online system with spatially-variant motion representation.

3 MeshFlow

In this section, we introduce the MeshFlow motion model. Figure 1 shows a comparison between the SteadyFlow [24] and our MeshFlow. Compared with the SteadyFlow, which calculates dense optical flow and extracts *pixel profiles* at all pixel locations for stabilization, our MeshFlow is computationally more efficient.

---

[1] Project page: http://www.liushuaicheng.org/eccv2016/index.html.

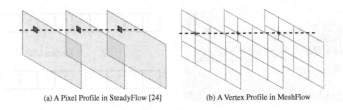

(a) A Pixel Profile in SteadyFlow [24]   (b) A Vertex Profile in MeshFlow

Fig. 1. (a) Pixel profiles [24] collect motion vectors at the same pixel location in SteadyFlow over time for all pixel locations. Motions of SteadyFlow come from dense optical flow. (b) Vertex profiles only collect motion vectors in MeshFlow at mesh vertexes. Motions of MeshFlow come from feature matches between adjacent frames.

We only operate on a sparse regular grid of *vertex profiles*, such that the expensive optical flow can be replaced with cheap feature matches. For one thing, they are similar because they both encode strong spatial smoothness. For another, they are different as one is dense and the other is sparse. Moreover, the motion estimation methods are totally different. Next, we show how to estimate spacial coherent motions at mesh vertexes.

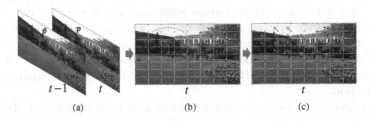

(a)   (b)   (c)

Fig. 2. (a) A pair of matched features (red dots) between frame t and $t-1$. (b) The arrow indicates the motion of the feature point at frame t. (c) The motion is propagated to the nearby vertexes. (Color figure online)

3.1 Motion Propagation

We match image features between neighboring frames. Figure 2 shows an example. Suppose $\{p, \hat{p}\}$ is the p-th matched feature pair, with p at frame t and $\hat{p}$ at frame $t-1$ (p and $\hat{p}$ denote the image coordinates of features). The motion v_p at feature location p can be computed as: $v_p = p - \hat{p}$ (see the dashed arrow in Fig. 2(a)). The mesh vertexes nearby the feature p should have a similar motion as v_p. Therefore, we define an eclipse that is centered at p (dashed circle in Fig. 2(b)) and assign v_p to the vertexes within the eclipse (see Fig. 2(c)). Specifically, we detect FAST features [25] and track them by KLT [26] to the adjacent frame. We place a uniform grid mesh with 16×16 regular cells onto each frame.[2]

---

[2] We draw this mesh as 8×8 in all figures for the purpose of clearer illustration.

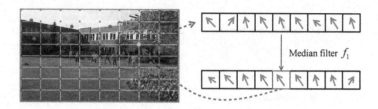

Fig. 3. A grid accumulates multiple motion vectors from several nearby features. We assign each grid a unique motion vector by applying median filter f_1 to the candidates. (Color figure online)

The eclipse covers 3×3 cells. Notably, according to literatures (such as works on visual SLAM [27,28]) and our own experiments, FAST and KLT are known as the most efficient way compared with other options (e.g., SURF, ORB etc.).

3.2 Median Filters

All matched features propagate their motions to their nearby mesh vertexes. Therefore, a vertex may receive multiple motion vectors. Figure 3 illustrates an example, where red dots denote feature points and a vertex (yellow dot) receives several motions. We propose to use a median filter f_1 to filter the candidates. The filter response is assigned to the vertex. The median filter is frequently used in optical flow estimation and has been treated as the secret of a high quality flow estimation [29]. Here, we borrow the similar idea for sparse motion regularization.

After applying f_1 to all vertexes, we obtain a sparse motion field as illustrated in the left part of Fig. 4. This motion field resembles the SteadyFlow, except that it is only defined at sparse mesh vertices. This sparsity is the key to make the spatially-variant motion estimation computationally lightweight. The motion field needs to be smooth spatially for stabilization [24]. However, due to various reasons, such as false feature matches and dynamic objects, the motion field is noisy (yellow arrows in the left part of Fig. 4). We propose to use another median filter f_2 (covers 3×3 cells) to remove the noises, producing a spatially-smooth sparse motion filed, MeshFlow, as shown in the right part of Fig. 4.

The two median filters provide the essential spatial smoothness to MeshFlow. The strong spatial smoothness is particularly important in flow-based stabilization [24]. Motion compensation on "noise flows" (inconsistent flows) often causes render artifacts on discontinuous boundaries [24]. Therefore, the SteadyFlow estimates dense raw optical flow [30] and upgrades it to a dense smooth flow by regularizing small vibrations and excluding large inconsistencies (i.e., flow on dynamic objects). Here, the two median filters achieve a similar effect: the first filter emphasizes on removing small noises and the second one concentrates on rejecting large outliers. More discussions are provided in Sect. 5.

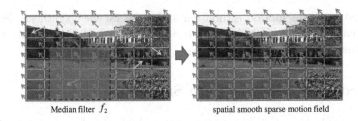

Median filter f_2 spatial smooth sparse motion field

Fig. 4. A second median filter f_2 is applied to enforce spatial smoothness (Color figure online)

3.3 Vertex Profiles Generation

A vertex profile is generated by collecting all motion vectors at a vertex position in MeshFlow sequentially over time. It is a one-dimensional array consisting of motion vectors of all frames. Repeating the same procedure for all vertexes provides vertex profiles.

3.4 Robust Estimation

The robustness of MeshFlow estimation can be improved by several operations.

Rich features. We hope to have rich features to cover the entire video frame densely and uniformly such that every grid can receive several motion vectors. When selecting good feature points for tracking [26], a global threshold on corner response often produces few features in poorly textured regions (e.g., ground, sky), because the threshold is biased by other highly textured areas [14]. Therefore, we divide the image into small regions and adopt a local threshold.

Outlier rejection. Classical methods for outlier rejection, such as fitting a global homography model by RANSAC [31], is not applicable in our application, because we want to retain motions which do not reside in a global linear space. We divide the image into 4×4 sub-images and reject outliers with a local homography fitting by RANSAC. Large motion deviations caused by false matches or dynamic objects can be rejected successfully while small variations due to depth changes and rolling shutter effects [32,33] can be well maintained. A similar approach is reported in [5]. Notably, both median filters and the RANSAC are critical for the robust outlier removal. The former works locally while the latter reject outliers in a more global fashion.

Pre-warping. Before MeshFlow estimation, we use a global homography F_t, estimated using all matched features, to transform features $\hat{p}$ from frame $t - 1$ to frame t. Clearly, F_t induces a global motion vector field V_t for all vertexes. The local residual motions are calculated as $\tilde{v}_p = p - F_t\hat{p}$. The MeshFlow is first estimated from these residual motions. Then, the final MeshFlow motion is an addition of the global and the local motions: $v_p = V_t + \tilde{v}_p$. A similar idea is adopted in [5] for motion estimation and in [8] for view synthesis. For some extreme cases where no features are detected, (e.g., a purely white wall), vertexes are assigned with the global motion V_t.

4 Predicted Adaptive Path Smoothing (PAPS)

A vertex profile represents the motion of its neighboring image regions. We can smooth all the vertex profiles for the smoothed motions. We begin by describing an offline filter, and then extend it for online smoothing.

4.1 Offline Adaptive Smoothing

We can consider a vertex profile as the local camera path C_i. All vertex profiles aggregate to multiple camera paths $\mathbf{C}$ that covers the whole frame. We want to obtain the optimized paths $\mathbf{P}$. As the MeshFlow itself enforces strong spatial coherence, we do not enforce any additional spatial constraints during smoothing. That is, each vertex profile is smoothed independently, like the SteadyFlow [24].

For an aesthetic path optimization, we want to avoid excessive cropping as well as annoying distortions after stabilization. This can be achieved by leveraging the temporal smoothness and the similarity of the original paths:

$$\mathcal{O}(\mathbf{P}(t)) = \sum_t (\|\mathbf{P}(t) - \mathbf{C}(t)\|^2 + \lambda_t \sum_{r \in \Omega_t} w_{t,r} \|\mathbf{P}(t) - \mathbf{P}(r)\|^2) \qquad (1)$$

where $\mathbf{C}(t) = \sum_t \mathbf{v}(t)$ is the camera path at time t $\left(\mathbf{v}(t)\right.$ represents the MeshFlow at time t, $\mathbf{v}(0) = \mathbf{0}\left.\right)$. The first term encourages the stabilized video staying close to the original camera path so as to avoid excessive cropping and distortions. The second term enforces temporal smoothness. Ω_t denotes a temporal smoothing radius, $w_{t,r}$ is a Gaussian weight which is set to $exp(-\|r-t\|^2/(\Omega_t/3)^2)$, and λ_t balances two terms. The energy function is quadratic and can be minimized by the sparse linear solver. Similar to approaches [5,24], we solve it iteratively by a Jacobi-based solver.

The adaptive weight λ_t for each frame is the most important component in Eq. 1. Adaptive controlling the strength of smoothness can effectively suppress some artifacts (e.g., large cropping, wobbling). It is a tradeoff between stability and some side-effects. If all λ_t is set to 0, the optimized path is equal to the original path such that the output video is identical to the input video with no cropping and wobbling. In general, smaller λ_t leads to less copping and wobbling.

The method in [5] adopted an iterative refinement approach to search the optimal value of λ_t for each frame. They proposed to evaluate the cropping and wobbling numerically. Suppose that we have the values of cropping and wobbling respect to all frames after the optimization by setting all $\lambda_t = 1$. Then, we check these values at each frame to see if they satisfy some pre-requirements. For example, at least 80 % of visual content must be maintained after cropping. For any frame that does not satisfy the requirements, λ_t is decreased by a step and the optimization is re-run for a second time. The procedure is iterated until all frames satisfying the requirements. This dynamic parameter adjustment can find the optimal values of λ_t but is not efficient obviously. Notably, $w_{t,r}$ in [5] is a bilateral weight which leads to a quicker convergence than a Gaussian weight.

Though the above method is proven to be effective, it is designed for offline applications. It requires both previous and future frames. The iterative refinement for λ_t is impractical for the online scenario. Therefore, we propose to predict a reasonable value of λ_t rather than applying iterative adjustment.

4.2   Predict λ_t

We want to use the current camera motion to predict a suitable λ_t. Therefore, we need to find some indicators. Designing good indicators is non-trivial. By extensively experiments, we suggest two empirically good indicators, *translational element* T_v and *affine component* F_a, both extracted from a global homography F between adjacent frames.

Translational element measures the velocity of the current frame. It is calculated as $T_v = \sqrt{(v_x^2 + v_y^2)}$, where v_x and v_y represent motions in x and y directions in F, respectively. If we oversmooth frames under high velocity, the motion compensation often leads to large empty regions (black borders), resulting in excessive cropping. In iterative adjustment of λ_t, the cropping can only be evaluated afterwards. The translational element allows the cropping being evaluated beforehand.

Affine Component is computed by the ratio of the two largest eigenvalues of the affine part of the homography. A single homography can not describe the spatially-variant motion. For scenes with large depth variations, an estimated homography is highly distorted [34]. The distortion can be measured by its affine part. A similar idea is reported in [5] for distortion evaluation.

To reveal the relationship between the two proposed indicators and λ_t, we collect 200 videos with various camera motions and scene types from publicly available data sets [2,3,5,8,14,15]. We run the iterative adjustment algorithm for λ_t on these videos and record the corresponding values. In particular, the two indicators might be correlated. To better sketch their independent impact to λ_t, we use videos with quick camera motions to train the translational element while videos contain large depth variations are adopted for affine component.

The result is plotted in Fig. 5. Note that F_t is normalized by the image width and height. By observing the distributions, we fit two linear models:

$$\lambda_t' = -1.93 * T_v + 0.95 \qquad (2)$$

$$\lambda_t'' = 5.83 * F_a + 4.88 \qquad (3)$$

The final value of λ_t is chosen as $max(min(\lambda_t', \lambda_t''), 0)$. A lower λ_t can satisfy both requirements. Notably, the translational element and affine component are

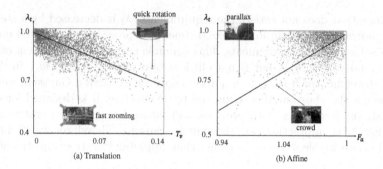

(a) Translation   (b) Affine

Fig. 5. (a) The plot of λ_t and values of translational elements T_v using 50 videos with quick camera motions (e.g., quick rotation, fast zooming). (b) The plot of λ_t and values of affine component F_a using another 50 videos containing large depth variations.

two indicators that we found empirically, which works well in practice. There might be some other alternatives. For example, more sophisticated method could be attempted for distortion evaluation, such as applying SfM to explicitly evaluate depth variations. Here, we keep our method simple and effective. Given λ_t for every frame, we run Eq. 1 to smooth vertex profiles. The optimization of Eq. 1 is efficient and can be further accelerated by the parallel computing.

4.3   Online Smoothing

The aforementioned approach is offline, though it can run in real time. Note that, processing an already captured video in a real time speed (e.g., 100 fps) is not identical to online stabilization. The online processing not only requires the real time speed, but also constrains the usage of future frames. Figure 6 shows our system setting. The green rectangle shows the current frame being displayed to the audiences. The red rectangle shows the incoming frame, which is about to show (turn into green) in the next run. The white rectangles are the past frames.

We define a buffer to hold previous frames. At the beginning, the buffer size is small, it increases gradually to a fixed size frame by frame and becomes a moving window that holds the latest frames and drops the oldest ones. *Each time*, we smooth the motions in the buffer by minimizing over the following energy:

$$\mathcal{O}(\mathbf{P}^{(\xi)}(t)) = \sum_{t \in \Phi} \left(\left\| \mathbf{P}^{(\xi)}(t) - \mathbf{C}(t) \right\|^2 + \lambda_t \sum_{t \in \Phi, r \in \Omega_t} w_{t,r} \left\| \mathbf{P}^{(\xi)}(t) - \mathbf{P}^{(\xi)}(r) \right\|^2 \right)$$
$$+ \beta \sum_{t \in \Phi} \left\| \mathbf{P}^{(\xi)}(t-1) - \mathbf{P}^{(\xi-1)}(t-1) \right\|^2 \tag{4}$$

where Φ denotes the buffer. When an incoming frame arrives, we run the optimization of Eq. 4 (except the first two frames). The ξ indexes the optimization at each time. For each ξ, we obtain $\mathbf{P}^{(\xi)}(t)$ for all frames in the buffer. Only

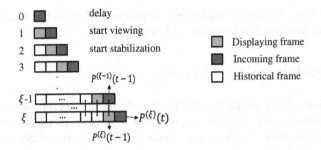

Fig. 6. The system is delayed at the time 0. At the time 1, we begin to display. The stabilization is started at the time 3 when there is at least one historical frame. The ξ indexes the optimization conducted at each time. The third term in Eq. 4 enforces similarities between paths in the current optimization ξ and paths obtained in the previous optimization $\xi - 1$, which is indicated by the dashed lines. (Color figure online)

the result of the last one will be used to warp the incoming frame. All frames prior to that have already been stabilized and displayed. We can not change the paths of the displayed frames. We can only change the path of the current frame. Therefore, we add a third term to encourage the paths obtained at the current optimization ξ, up to $\mathbf{P}^{(\xi)}(t-1)$, to be similar to their previous optimized solutions obtained at the optimization $\xi - 1$, i.e. $\mathbf{P}^{(\xi-1)}(t-1)$. The dashed line in Fig. 6 shows the paths enforced with similarity constraints. The β is a balancing weight which is set to 1.

Notably, Eq. 4 does not need any future motions (not even one) for optimization. However, our system has a one frame latency. Because no matter how fast the optimization runs, it occupies some time. In other words, the user is viewing a frame, at the mean time, the next incoming frame (the newest frame) is being processed simultaneously at the background. Any frames beyond the newest frame haven't been captured yet. The system is online as long as the processing time is less than the displaying time. For example, a video with framerate 30 fps. Its displaying time is 33.3 ms per frame. The processing time should be faster than 33.3 ms per frame for online performance. Curiously, if we enforce 0 frame latency, the processing time approaches 0, which is theoretically impossible. In practice, one frame latency is hard to be observed.

Equation 4 is quadratic. Similarly to Eq. 1, we optimize it by a Jacobi-based solver. The optimization is efficient. In our implementation, the buffer size is set to 40 frames. If a video has framerate about 30–50 fps, we roughly hold one second of past motions in the memory.

4.4 View Synthesis

After each optimization, the last frame in the buffer is warped towards the stabilized position, i.e. $\mathbf{P}^{(\xi)}(t)$, by a sparse update motion field for mesh vertices. The update motion is computed as, $\mathbf{U} = \mathbf{P} - \mathbf{C}$. Specifically, every vertex has an update motion vector. Therefore, we obtain an update motion mesh, i.e. a vector per mesh vertex. The image content is warped according to the mesh warp [35]. Notably, the warping can be computed in parallel as well.

5 Discussions and Validation

In this section, we would like to validate the effectiveness of our proposed motion model in several aspects. When comparing with previous methods, we would like to exclude 3D methods [8,13,16] and single homography-based 2D methods [1,3, 20,21], because the former requires computationally expensive 3D reconstruction and is fragile for consumer videos while the latter can not represent spatially-variant motion and renders limited stability. Therefore, we focus on 2D or 2.5D methods which can handle spatially-variant motions. In general, these methods can be classified into three categories, smoothing long feature tracks [2,4,15], smoothing multiple 2D models [5,14,23] and smoothing dense flows [24].

If long feature tracks are provided (normally, average track length longer than 50 frames), the underlying 3D structure can be extracted from the tracks [2,19], and smoothing feature tracks gives strong results. However, long feature tracks are hard to obtain in consumer videos. Both the track length and the number of tracks drop quickly when there are quick camera swings, rotations or zoomings. For the robustness, our model does not rely on long feature tracks.

The second category proposes to smooth multiple parametric models estimated between neighboring frames for stabilization. The advantage is that they only require simple feature matches between two consecutive frames. Therefore, the robustness is largely improved. The drawback is that estimating these more advanced models are computationally expensive. They are not fast enough to achieve real-time performance.

The SteadyFlow belongs to the third category. It shows that the pixel profiles can well approximate the long feature tracks, which densely cover the entire video both spatially and temporally. While a feature track might start or end at any frame of the video, all pixel profiles begin at the first frame and end at the last frame, which is a much desired property for smoothing. Our MeshFlow resembles the SteadyFlow, and our vertex profiles resemble the pixel profiles. Our vertex profiles are a sparse version of pixel profiles. The SteadyFlow estimates pixel profiles by computing dense optical flow between neighboring frames. Then, the discontinuous motions in the flow, (e.g., motions on the boundary of different depth layers or on dynamic moving objects), are excluded by an iterative flow refinements, yielding a spatially smooth optical flow. We argue that the SteadyFlow overkills the problem. We can estimate sparse smooth flows by feature matches. Figure 7 shows a comparison between the SteadyFlow and the MeshFlow. We choose a dynamic video with a moving foreground. We show the raw optical flow calculated by [30] (Fig. 7(a)), the SteadyFlow (Fig. 7(b)) and our MeshFlow, interpolated into dense flow for visual comparison (Fig. 7(c)). As can be seen, our MeshFlow is quite similar to the SteadyFlow. The MeshFlow enjoys the merits of the SteadyFlow while the computation is much cheaper.

(a) raw optical flow [30]   (b) SteadyFlow [24]   (c) our interpolated Meshflow

Fig. 7. (a) The raw optical flow calculated by [30]. (b) The SteadyFlow [24]. (c) Our MeshFlow interpolated into a dense field for visual comparison.

6   Experiments

We run our method on a laptop with 2.3 GHz CPU and 4G RAM. For frames with resolution 720 × 480, our un-optimized code can process a frame in 20 ms, without any acceleration of parallel computing. Specifically, we spend 6 ms, 1 ms, 10 ms and 3 ms to extract features, estimate MeshFlow, smooth vertex profiles and rendering frames, respectively.

6.1   Online Video Stabilization

We tried our method on various video sources. Figure 8 shows some examples. In each column, we show a capturing device and a sample video frame. The first example is a video captured by a general hand-held webcam. The second example is a micro UAV with real-time video transmissions. It often suffers from turbulence during the flight due to its small size and light weight, rendering videos with lots of vibrations and strong rolling shutter effects. The third example is a sport camera. It captures videos under wide view angles, which are transmitted through wifi in real-time. We show that our method can handle wide view angle lens as well. The last example is a tablet with the videos captured by its build-in camera. For all these examples, we show a side by side comparison which demonstrate original frames and the prompt stabilized results.

Fig. 8. Our experiments on various devices. Each column shows a capturing device and the corresponding sample frame.

6.2   Compare with Previous Methods

To compare our method with the previous methods, we slightly modify our programme to make it work on existing pre-captured videos. To imitate online processing, at each frame, our program reads in a frame from the video and processes it immediately, then saves it before processing the next frame. To evaluate the quality, we follow the approach of [5] which introduces three objective metrics: *cropping ratio*, *distortion* and *stability*. For a good result, these metrics should be close to 1. For completeness, we briefly introduce these metrics.

Cropping ratio measures the remaining area after cropping away black boundaries. A larger ratio means less cropping and hence better video quality. A homography B_t is fitted at each frame between input and output video. The cropping ratio for each frame can be extracted from the scale component of the homography. We average all ratios from all frames to yield the cropping ratio.

Distortion score is estimated from the anisotropic scaling of B_t, which can be computed by the ratio of the two largest eigenvalues of the affine part of B_t. The idea is borrowed for λ_t prediction in Sect. 4.2. Each frame has a distortion score, among which we choose the worst one as the final score for the whole video.

Stability score estimates the smoothness of the final video. Slightly different from the method in [5], we use the vertex profiles extracted from the stabilized video for evaluation. We analyze each vertex profile in the frequency domain. We take a few of the lowest frequencies (2nd to 6th) and calculate the energy percentage over full frequencies (DC component is excluded). Averaging from all profiles gives the final score.

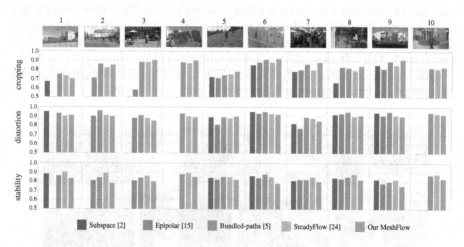

Fig. 9. Comparison with 10 publicly available videos in terms of three metrics.

We choose 10 publicly available videos and compare our method with the methods [2,5,15] and [24] in terms of the objective metrics. The result is reported in Fig. 9. The stabilized videos of these methods are either collected from their project pages or provided by the corresponding authors. For videos that we do not find the result, we leave it blank.

It is slightly unfair for our method to compare with these offline approaches. We show that we can produce comparable quality. In general, our stability is slightly lower compared with the other methods. Because we only use the previous 40 frames for stabilization. We can buffer more previous frames for improved stability if they can fit into the memory. If some latency is allowed [9], we can even obtain future frames for improvements. The first several frames of the video have a relatively lower stability compared with other frames, as they are stabilized with a even smaller buffer. Specifically, the first frame is not stabilized and we begin to stabilize when there are at least three frames in the buffer. The stability increases gradually when more and more frames are hold in the buffer.

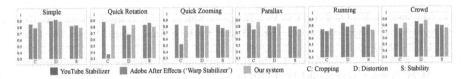

Fig. 10. Comparison with two offline video stabilization systems on datasets [5].

We further compare our method with two well-known commercial offline systems on a publicly available video data sets [5]. The two systems are Youtube Stabilizer developed according to methods [3,14] and Warp Stabilizer at Adobe After Effects built upon method [2]. The data sets group videos into several categories according to different scene types and camera motions, including (1) Simple, (2) Quick rotation, (3) Quick Zooming, (4) Large Parallax, (5) Crowd and (6) Running. The result is reported in Fig. 10. Similarly, it is not that fair to compare our method with these offline systems. We show our method is effective and robust to many challenging consumer videos.

7   Limitations

Our method can not handle videos containing large near-range foreground objects [36]. This is the common challenge faced by many previous methods [2,3,5,8,14,15,24]. Our method may also fail when features are insufficient for motion estimation under some extreme cases. Other types of features can be attempted for improvements [37,38].

8   Conclusions

We have presented a new motion model, *MeshFlow*, for online video stabilization. The MeshFlow is a sparse and spatially smooth motion field with motion vectors only located at mesh vertices. By smoothing *vertex profiles*, motion vectors collected at mesh vertexes in MeshFlow over time, we can stabilize videos with spatially variant motion. Moreover, a *Predicted Adaptive Path Smoothing* (PAPS) is proposed to shift the method online with minimum latency. The experiment shows that our method is comparable with the state-off-the-art offline methods. The effectiveness is further validated by different capturing devices, which demonstrates potentials for practical applications.

Acknowledgements. This work is supported by National Nature Science Foundation of China (61502079 and 61370148). Ping Tan is supported by the NSERC Discovery Grant 31-611664, the NSERC Discovery Accelerator Supplement 31-611663.

References

1. Matsushita, Y., Ofek, E., Ge, W., Tang, X., Shum, H.: Full-frame video stabilization with motion inpainting. IEEE Trans. Pattern Anal. Mach. Intell. **28**, 1150–1163 (2006)
2. Liu, F., Gleicher, M., Wang, J., Jin, H., Agarwala, A.: Subspace video stabilization. ACM Trans. Graphics **30**(1), 4 (2011)
3. Grundmann, M., Kwatra, V., Essa, I.: Auto-directed video stabilization with robust l1 optimal camera paths. In: Proceedings of CVPR, pp. 225–232 (2011)
4. Wang, Y., Liu, F., Hsu, P., Lee, T.: Spatially and temporally optimized video stabilization. IEEE Trans. Vis. Comput. Graph. **19**, 1354–1361 (2013)
5. Liu, S., Yuan, L., Tan, P., Sun, J.: Bundled camera paths for video stabilization. ACM Trans. Graphics **32**(4), 78 (2013)
6. Karpenko, A., Jacobs, D.E., Baek, J., Levoy, M.: Digital video stabilization and rolling shutter correction using gyroscopes. In: Stanfor. Comput. Scie. Tech. Rep. CSTR 2011–03 (2011)
7. Bell, S., Troccoli, A., Pulli, K.: A non-linear filter for gyroscope-based video stabilization. In: Fleet, D., Pajdla, T., Schiele, B., Tuytelaars, T. (eds.) ECCV 2014. LNCS, vol. 8692, pp. 294–308. Springer, Heidelberg (2014). doi:10.1007/978-3-319-10593-2_20
8. Liu, F., Gleicher, M., Jin, H., Agarwala, A.: Content-preserving warps for 3D video stabilization. ACM Trans. Graphics **28**, 44 (2009)
9. Yang, J., Schonfeld, D., Chen, C., Mohamed, M.: Online video stabilization based on particle filters. In: Proceedings of ICIP, pp. 1545–1548 (2006)
10. Bae, J., Hwang, Y., Lim, J.: Semi-online video stabilization using probabilistic keyframe update and inter-keyframe motion smoothing. In: Proceedings of ICIP, pp. 5786–5790 (2014)
11. Jiang, W., Wu, Z., Wus, J., Yu, H.: One-pass video stabilization on mobile devices. In: Proceedings of Multimedia, pp. 817–820 (2014)
12. Liu, S., Wang, Y., Yuan, L., Bu, J., Tan, P., Sun, J.: Video stabilization with a depth camera. In: Proceedings of CVPR, pp. 89–95 (2012)
13. Zhou, Z., Jin, H., Ma, Y.: Plane-based content-preserving warps for video stabilization. In: Proceedings of CVPR, pp. 2299–2306 (2013)
14. Grundmann, M., Kwatra, V., Castro, D., Essa, I.: Calibration-free rolling shutter removal. In: Proceedings of ICCP, pp. 1–8 (2012)
15. Goldstein, A., Fattal, R.: Video stabilization using epipolar geometry. ACM Trans. Graphics **31**(5), 126 (2012)

16. Buehler, C., Bosse, M., McMillan, L.: Non-metric image-based rendering for video stabilization. In: Proceedings of CVPR, vol. 2, pp. 609–614 (2001)
17. Smith, B., Zhang, L., Jin, H., Agarwala, A.: Light field video stabilization. In: Proceedings of ICCV, pp. 341–348 (2009)
18. Ovrén, H., Forssén, P.E.: Gyroscope-based video stabilisation with auto-calibration. In: Proceedings of ICRA, pp. 2090–2097 (2015)
19. Liu, F., Niu, Y., Jin, H.: Joint subspace stabilization for stereoscopic video. In: Proceedings of ICCV, pp. 73–80 (2013)
20. Chen, B., Lee, K., Huang, W., Lin, J.: Capturing intention-based full-frame video stabilization. Comput. Graph. Forum 27(7), 1805–1814 (2008)
21. Gleicher, M., Liu, F.: Re-cinematography: improving the camera dynamics of casual video. In: ACM Conference on Multimedia, pp. 27–36 (2007)
22. Morimoto, C., Chellappa, R.: Evaluation of image stabilization algorithms. In: Proceedings of ICASSP, vol. 5, pp. 2789–2792 (1998)
23. Bai, J., Agarwala, A., Agrawala, M., Ramamoorthi, R.: User-assisted video stabilization. Comput. Graph. Forum 33(4), 61–70 (2014)
24. Liu, S., Yuan, L., Tan, P., Sun, J.: Steadyflow: spatially smooth optical flow for video stabilization. In: Proceedings of CVPR, pp. 4209–4216 (2014)
25. Trajković, M., Hedley, M.: Fast corner detection. Image Vis. Comput. 16(2), 75–87 (1998)
26. Shi, J., Tomasi, C.: Good features to track. In: Proceedings of CVPR, pp. 593–600 (1994)
27. Zou, D., Tan, P.: Coslam: collaborative visual SLAM in dynamic environments. IEEE Trans. Pattern Anal. Mach. Intell. 35(2), 354–366 (2013)
28. Klein, G., Murray, D.: Parallel tracking and mapping for small AR workspaces. In: Proceedings of ISMAR, pp. 225–234 (2007)
29. Sun, D., Roth, S., Black, M.: Secrets of optical flow estimation and their principles. In: Proceedings of CVPR, pp. 2392–2399 (2010)
30. Liu, C.: Beyond pixels: exploring new representations and applications for motion analysis. Ph.D. thesis, MIT (2009)
31. Fischler, M.A., Bolles, R.C.: Random sample consensus: a paradigm for model fitting with applications to image analysis and automated cartography. Commun. ACM 24(6), 381–395 (1981)
32. Liang, C.K., Chang, L.W., Chen, H.H.: Analysis and compensation of rolling shutter effect. IEEE Trans. Image Process. 17(8), 1323–1330 (2008)
33. Baker, S., Bennett, E., Kang, S.B., Szeliski, R.: Removing rolling shutter wobble. In: Proceedings of CVPR, pp. 2392–2399 (2010)
34. Hartley, R., Zisserman, A.: Multiple View Geometry in Computer Vision, 2nd edn. Cambridge University Press, New York (2003)
35. Igarashi, T., Moscovich, T., Hughes, J.: As-rigid-as-possible shape manipulation. ACM Trans. Graph. 24(3), 1134–1141 (2005)
36. Liu, S., Xu, B., Deng, C., Zhu, S., Zeng, B., Gabbouj, M.: A hybrid approach for near-range video stabilization. IEEE Trans. Circ. Syst. Video Technol. PP(99), 1 (2016). http://ieeexplore.ieee.org/xpl/articleDetails.jsp?arnumber=7457352
37. Zhou, H., Zou, D., Pei, L., Ying, R., Liu, P., Yu, W.: StructSLAM: visual SLAM with building structure lines. IEEE Trans. Veh. Technol. 64(4), 1364–1375 (2015)
38. Li, S., Yuan, L., Sun, J., Quan, L.: Dual-feature warping-based motion model estimation. In: Proceedings of the IEEE International Conference on Computer Vision, pp. 4283–4291 (2015)

Large-Scale Training of Shadow Detectors with Noisily-Annotated Shadow Examples

Tomás F. Yago Vicente$^{(\boxtimes)}$, Le Hou, Chen-Ping Yu,
Minh Hoai, and Dimitris Samaras

Computer Science Department, Stony Brook University, Stony Brook, USA
{tyagovicente,lehhou,cheyu,minhhoai,samaras}@cs.stonybrook.edu

Abstract. This paper introduces training of shadow detectors under the large-scale dataset paradigm. This was previously impossible due to the high cost of precise shadow annotation. Instead, we advocate the use of quickly but imperfectly labeled images. Our novel label recovery method automatically corrects a portion of the erroneous annotations such that the trained classifiers perform at state-of-the-art level. We apply our method to improve the accuracy of the labels of a new dataset that is 20 times larger than existing datasets and contains a large variety of scenes and image types. Naturally, such a large dataset is appropriate for training deep learning methods. Thus, we propose a semantic-aware patch level Convolutional Neural Network architecture that efficiently trains on patch level shadow examples while incorporating image level semantic information. This means that the detected shadow patches are refined based on image semantics. Our proposed pipeline can be a useful baseline for future advances in shadow detection.

Keywords: Shadow detection · Large scale shadow dataset · Noisy labels

1 Introduction

Shadows are ubiquitous in images of natural scenes. On one hand, shadows provide useful cues about the scene including object shapes [28], light sources and illumination conditions [23,30,31], camera parameters and geo-location [19], and scene geometry [21]. On the other hand, the presence of shadows in images creates difficulties for many computer vision tasks from image segmentation to object detection and tracking. In all cases, being able to automatically detect shadows, and subsequently remove them or reason about their shapes and sizes would usually be beneficial. Moreover, shadow-free images are of great interest for image editing, computational photography, and augmented reality, and the first crucial step is shadow detection.

Shadow detection in single images is a well studied, but still challenging problem. Early work focused on physical modeling of the illumination and shadowing phenomena. Such approaches, e.g., illumination invariant methods [8,9],

© Springer International Publishing AG 2016
B. Leibe et al. (Eds.): ECCV 2016, Part VI, LNCS 9910, pp. 816–832, 2016.
DOI: 10.1007/978-3-319-46466-4_49

only work well for high quality images [24]. In contrast, for consumer-grade photographs and web quality images, the breakthrough in performance came with statistical learning approaches [12,17,24,49]. These approaches learn the appearance of shadows from images with ground-truth labels. The first sizable database with manually annotated shadows was the UCF shadow dataset [49], followed, soon after, by the UIUC shadow dataset [12]. These publicly available datasets with pixel-level annotations have led to important advances in the field. They enabled both systematic quantitative and qualitative evaluation of detection performance, as opposed to the prior practice of qualitative evaluation on a few selected images. In the past few years, several novel shadow detection methods (e.g., [14,43]), gradually advanced state-of-the-art performance in these datasets, to the point of saturation. However, shadow detection is still far from being solved. Due to their limited sizes, UIUC is biased by certain type of images such as objects in close range shots, whereas UCF is biased towards scenes with darker shadows. Thus their generality is limited, and as expected, cross-dataset performance (e.g., training on UIUC and testing on UCF) degrades significantly [13,44]. In order to facilitate the development of robust classifiers, a much larger and more general dataset is needed. However, creating a large shadow dataset would require enormous amount of effort, primarily for obtaining pixel-level annotation.

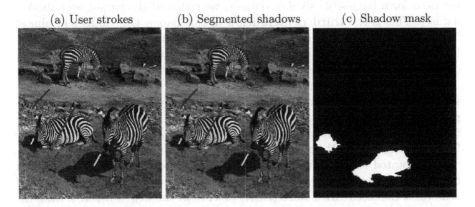

(a) User strokes   (b) Segmented shadows   (c) Shadow mask

Fig. 1. Lazy labeling for shadow annotation [44]. (a) White strokes for shadows, red stokes for negative areas. (b) Automatically segmented shadow regions. (c) Corresponding annotation mask. (Color figure online)

Fortunately, pixel-level annotation might not be required after all, given the recently introduced *lazy labeling* approach [44]. Instead of pixel selection or boundary tracing, lazy labeling allows annotators to use a few brush strokes to roughly label a shadow image, as illustrated in Fig. 1. Lazy labeling significantly reduces annotation time, so now 3–4 images can be easily annotated per minute. The drawback of lazy labeling is that the obtained annotation can be noisy.

However, it is possible to recover the true value for a large portion of such noisy labels so that the noisy annotated shadow images are still useful [44].

In this work, we introduce an efficient framework for learning shadow detection from a large collection of noisy annotations. Our **first contribution** is the extension of our previous work [44] to yield a scalable kernelized method for noisy label recovery. Noisy label recovery is posed as an optimization problem, seeking to minimize the sum of squared leave-one-out errors for a Kernel Least Squares SVM [40]. Since the leave-one-out error is most meaningful for similar data instances, we propose to group similar images into small clusters and perform label recovery for each cluster independently. Hence, our method can be used for large-scale noisy label recovery. Our **second contribution** is a novel stacked Convolutional Neural Network (CNN) based method for structured shadow prediction that takes advantage of the wealth of cleaned-up data. Given a large dataset, we expect to learn not only local shadow cues, but also the discriminative global context. Our *semantics-aware* stacked CNN architecture combines an image level Fully Connected Network (FCN) and a patch-based CNN (patch-CNN). We train the FCN for semantically aware shadow prediction. We use the outputs of the FCN together with the corresponding input RGB images to train the patch-CNN from a random initialization. Thus, the output of the FCN functions as an image-level shadow prior that is further refined by the more local appearance focus of the patch-CNN. To validate our approach while addressing the need for a large-scale shadow dataset, we collected the largest ever shadow dataset. This is the **third contribution** of this paper. Our dataset of almost 5000 images covers a wide range of scenes and is 20 times bigger than UCF [49], bringing shadow detection to the large-data paradigm, and increasing the utility of deep learning approaches.

We first validate our model trained on the newly collected training set performing shadow detection on the UCF test set. Experimental results show comparable performance to state of the art methods [14,43] trained on the UCF training set. This is remarkable as our training set does not overlap with the UCF dataset, proving the generality of our trained model and dataset. We carefully annotated shadow masks for 700 images to serve as a new benchmark for shadow detection. The test set covers a wide range of scenes. Our method achieves a Balanced Error Rate (BER) of 11 % in the new test set, setting the baseline for future comparisons. We observe that our label recovery method correctly retrieves most of the shadows missed by human annotators. Experiments training our network model with cleaned annotations show an improvement in classification performance by 9.1 %, thus proving the effectiveness of our label recovery framework. The dataset is available to the public at http://www3.cs. stonybrook.edu/~cvl/dataset.html.

2   Previous Work

A number of shadow detection methods have been developed in recent years. Guo *et al.* [12] proposed to model long-range interaction between pairs of regions of the same material, with two types of pairwise classifiers: same illumination condition and different illumination condition. Then, they combined the pairwise classifier and a shadow region classifier with a CRF. Similarly, Vicente et al. [45] proposed an MRF that combines a unary region classifier with a pairwise classifier and a shadow boundary classifier. These approaches achieved good shadow detection results, but required expensive ground-truth annotation. Khan et al. [14] were the first to use deep learning for shadow detection. They combined a CNN for shadow patches and a CNN for shadow boundaries with a CRF, achieving state-of-the-art results at the time. Vicente et al. [43] optimized a multi-kernel model for shadow detection based on leave-one-out estimates, obtaining even better shadow predictions than [14]. More recently, Shen et al. [35] proposed a CNN for structured shadow edge prediction.

Label noise, also known as class noise, may severely degrade classification performance [10,50]. Numerous methods seek robustness to noisy labels [6,22,27, 39]. For instance, Stempfel and Ralaivola [38] deal with training a binary Support Vector Machine (SVM) when the probability of flipping a label is constant and only depends on the true class. For this, they replace the objective functional by a uniform estimate of the corresponding noise-free SVM objective. This becomes a non-convex problem that can be solved with Quasi-Newton BFGS. Biggio et al. [3] compensate noise in the labels by modifying the SVM kernel matrix with a structured matrix modeling the noise. This approach only models random flips with fixed probability per class and adversarial flips. That is, for a set number of labels to be flipped, the adversary tries to maximize the classification error. These methods are designed to be unaffected by label noise rather than to be effective in using noisy labels for training. Moreover, these methods focus on asymptotic behavior with unlimited training data. The label recovery method described in this paper is built on our previous work [44], addressing the scalability issues to handle a large amount of training samples.

3   Noisy Label Recovery with Kernel Least Squares SVM

In this section, we describe a method for noisy label recovery. We pose it as an optimization problem, where the labels of some training examples can be flipped to minimize the sum of squared leave-one-out errors. Our formulation is based on the fact that the leave-out-out error of kernel LSSVM is a linear function of the labels. Our method extends our previous work [44] by introducing a kernelized algorithm for noisy label recovery that allows the use of non-linear kernels, which have been shown to be important for shadow detection [43]. Our framework for recovering noisy annotation is based on Least-Squares Support Vector Machine (LSSVM) [33,41]. LSSVM has a closed-form solution, and once the solution of the LSSVM has been computed, the solution for a reduced training set obtained by removing any training data point can be found efficiently. This enables reusing training data for further calibration, e.g., [15,16], and for noisy label recovery.

Given a training set of n data points $\{\mathbf{x}_i\}_{i=1}^n$[1] and associated binary labels $\{y_i\}_{i=1}^n$, LSSVM optimizes the following:

$$\underset{\mathbf{w},b}{\text{minimize}} \ \lambda ||\mathbf{w}||^2 + \sum_{i=1}^n s_i (\mathbf{w}^T \phi(\mathbf{x}_i) + b - y_i)^2. \tag{1}$$

For high dimensional data (i.e., $\phi(\mathbf{x}_i)$ is large), it is more efficient to obtain the solution for $(\mathbf{w}, b)$ via the representer theorem, which states that $\mathbf{w}$ can be expressed as a linear combination of training data, i.e., $\mathbf{w} = \sum_{i=1}^n \alpha_i \phi(\mathbf{x}_i)$. Let $\mathbf{K}$ be the kernel matrix, $k_{ij} = \phi(\mathbf{x}_i)^T \phi(\mathbf{x}_j)$. The objective function becomes:

$$\underset{\boldsymbol{\alpha},b}{\text{minimize}} \ \lambda \boldsymbol{\alpha}^T \mathbf{K} \boldsymbol{\alpha} + \sum_{i=1}^n s_i (\mathbf{k}_i^T \boldsymbol{\alpha} + b - y_i)^2 \tag{2}$$

Here s_i is the instance weight, allowing the assignment of different weights to different training instances. Let $\overline{\boldsymbol{\alpha}} = [\boldsymbol{\alpha}, b], \overline{\mathbf{K}} = [\mathbf{K}; \mathbf{1}_n^T], \mathbf{R} = \begin{bmatrix} \lambda\mathbf{K} & \mathbf{0}_n \\ \mathbf{0}_n^T & 0 \end{bmatrix}$. Then Eq. (2) is equivalent to minimizing $\lambda \overline{\boldsymbol{\alpha}}^T \mathbf{R} \overline{\boldsymbol{\alpha}} + \sum_{i=1}^n s_i (\overline{\mathbf{k}}_i^T \overline{\boldsymbol{\alpha}} - y_i)^2$. This is an unconstrained quadratic program, and the optimal solution can be found by setting the gradient to zero. That is to solve:

$$(\mathbf{R} + \overline{\mathbf{K}} diag(\mathbf{s}) \overline{\mathbf{K}}^T) \overline{\boldsymbol{\alpha}} = \overline{\mathbf{K}} diag(\mathbf{s}) \mathbf{y} \tag{3}$$

Let $\mathbf{C} = \mathbf{R} + \overline{\mathbf{K}} diag(\mathbf{s}) \overline{\mathbf{K}}^T, \mathbf{d} = \overline{\mathbf{K}} diag(\mathbf{s}) \mathbf{y}$. The solution for kernel LSSVM is: $\overline{\boldsymbol{\alpha}} = \mathbf{C}^{-1} \mathbf{d}$. Now suppose we remove the training data $\mathbf{x}_i$, let $\mathbf{C}_{(i)}, \mathbf{d}_{(i)}, \overline{\boldsymbol{\alpha}}_{(i)}$ be the corresponding values when removing $\mathbf{x}_i$. We have $\overline{\boldsymbol{\alpha}}_{(i)} = \mathbf{C}_{(i)}^{-1} \mathbf{d}_{(i)}$. Note that, even though we remove $\mathbf{x}_i$ from the training data, we can still write $\mathbf{w}$ as the linear combination of $\phi(\mathbf{x}_1), \cdots, \phi(\mathbf{x}_n)$ without excluding the term $\phi(\mathbf{x}_i)$. The matrices $\mathbf{K}, \overline{\mathbf{K}}, \mathbf{R}$ remain the same, and the only change is the removal of $s_i (\mathbf{k}_i^T \boldsymbol{\alpha} + b - y_i)^2$ from the objective function. Thus we have $\mathbf{C}_{(i)} = \mathbf{C} - s_i \overline{\mathbf{k}}_i \overline{\mathbf{k}}_i^T$ and $\mathbf{d}_{(i)} = \mathbf{d} - y_i s_i \overline{\mathbf{k}}_i$. Using the Sherman-Morrison formula, we have:

$$\mathbf{C}_{(i)}^{-1} = (\mathbf{C} - s_i \overline{\mathbf{k}}_i \overline{\mathbf{k}}_i^T)^{-1} = \mathbf{C}^{-1} + \frac{\mathbf{C}^{-1} s_i \overline{\mathbf{k}}_i \overline{\mathbf{k}}_i^T \mathbf{C}^{-1}}{1 - s_i \overline{\mathbf{k}}_i^T \mathbf{C}^{-1} \overline{\mathbf{k}}_i} \tag{4}$$

Using the above equations to develop $\overline{\boldsymbol{\alpha}}_{(i)} = \mathbf{C}_{(i)}^{-1} \mathbf{d}_{(i)}$, and let $\mathbf{M} = \mathbf{C}^{-1} \overline{\mathbf{K}}$ and $\mathbf{H} = \mathbf{M}^T \overline{\mathbf{K}}$, we obtain the following formula for the LOO weight vector:

$$\overline{\boldsymbol{\alpha}}_{(i)} = \overline{\boldsymbol{\alpha}} + \frac{(\overline{\boldsymbol{\alpha}}^T \overline{\mathbf{k}}_i - y_i) s_i}{1 - s_i h_{ii}} \mathbf{m}_i$$

---

[1] Bold uppercase letters denote matrices (e.g., $\mathbf{K}$), bold lowercase letters denote column vectors (e.g., $\mathbf{k}$). $\mathbf{k}_i$ represents the ith column of the matrix $\mathbf{K}$. k_{ij} denotes the scalar in the row j^{th} and column i^{th} of the matrix $\mathbf{K}$ and the jth element of the column vector $\mathbf{k}_i$. Non-bold letters represent scalar variables. $\mathbf{1}_n \in \Re^{n \times 1}$ is a column vector of ones, and $\mathbf{0}_n \in \Re^{n \times 1}$ is a column vector of zeros.

The LOO error can therefore be computed efficiently: $\overline{\alpha}_{(i)}^T \overline{\mathbf{k}}_i - y_i = \frac{\overline{\alpha}^T \overline{\mathbf{k}}_i - y_i}{1 - s_i h_{ii}}$.
Substituting $\overline{\alpha} = \mathbf{M} diag(\mathbf{s}) \mathbf{y}$ into the above, the leave-one-out error becomes:

$$\frac{\overline{\mathbf{k}}_i^T \mathbf{M} diag(\mathbf{s}) \mathbf{y} - y_i}{1 - s_i h_{ii}} \tag{5}$$

Let $\mathbf{P} = diag(\mathbf{s}) \mathbf{H}$ and recall that $\mathbf{H} = \mathbf{M}^T \overline{\mathbf{K}}$. The leave-one-out error can be shown to be: $\frac{\mathbf{p}_i^T \mathbf{y} - y_i}{1 - p_{ii}}$. Let $\mathbf{e}_i$ be the ith column of the identity matrix of size n, and let $\mathbf{a}_i = \frac{\mathbf{p}_i - \mathbf{e}_i}{1 - p_{ii}}$, then the leave-one-out error becomes $\mathbf{a}_i^T \mathbf{y}$. Because the vector $\mathbf{a}_i$ only depends on the data, the leave-one-out error is a linear function of the label vector $\mathbf{y}$.

Let $\mathcal{P}, \mathcal{N}$ be the indexes of (noisy) positive and negative training instances respectively, i.e. $\mathcal{P} = \{i | y_i = 1\}$ and $\mathcal{N} = \{i | y_i = 0\}$. We pose noisy label recovery as the optimization problem that minimizes the sum of squared leave-one-out errors:

$$\underset{y_i \in \{0,1\}}{\text{minimize}} \sum_{i=1}^{n} (\mathbf{a}_i^T \mathbf{y})^2, \text{s.t.} \sum_{i \in \mathcal{P}} y_i \geq \alpha |\mathcal{P}| \quad \text{and} \quad \sum_{i \in \mathcal{N}} y_i \leq (1 - \beta) |\mathcal{N}|. \tag{6}$$

In the above $|\mathcal{P}|, |\mathcal{N}|$ are the original number of positive and negative training instances respectively, and α, β are parameters of the formulation ($0 \leq \alpha, \beta \leq 1$). The constraint of the above optimization problem requires that the proportion of original positive training instances that remains positive must be greater than or equal to α. It also limits the proportion of flipped negative data points to be at most $1 - \beta$. If $\alpha = \beta = 1$, none of the training labels can be flipped.

4 Large-Scale Noisy Label Recovery

The presence of label noise is known to deteriorate the quality of training data. To address this problem, we use the method described in Sect. 3. However, this method requires solving a binary quadratic program in which the number of variables is the same as the number of image regions. This full-scale optimization problem is too big for the optimization algorithm developed in our previous work [44]. To circumvent this issue, we propose here a simple but effective approach. We divide images into clusters of similar images, and perform label recovery for each cluster independently. This approach is motivated by the fact that our label recovery algorithm is based on optimizing the leave-one-out errors. Perhaps the wrong label of a region can be corrected because the region is similar to other regions with correct labels. As such, for label recovery, dissimilar regions do not have much impact on each other. Hence, it makes sense to recover labels within clusters of similar images.

The ability to perform label recovery in smaller clusters leads to large-scale label recovery. Using our approach, we can recover the labels of hundreds of thousands of image regions. This approach allows us to consider superpixels rather than larger regions as in our previous work [44]. We oversegment images using Linear Spectral Clustering [48]. The oversegmentation minimizes frequent inaccuracies in shadow segmentation where small shadow areas "leak" into large non-shadow regions. After all shadows are well known to confound segmentation.

For image clustering, we use a modified version of the Parametric Graph Partitioning method (PGP) [46], which has been shown to work well for image and video segmentation [47]. Here we use PGP instead of the more popular k-means clustering because PGP does not require setting the number of clusters. The details of the image clustering algorithm are provided below (Fig. 2).

Fig. 2. Examples of clusters of similar shadow images.

Image clustering details. We aim to create clusters of images that depict similar scenes and therefore similar shadows (the appearance of shadows depends on scene properties, including illumination, the color, and the texture of materials). For feature representation, we use GIST [29], and the a and b components of the Lab color space. We compute histograms of a and b from the shadow areas and their surroundings. For this, we use the initial annotated shadow mask and dilate it with an area ratio of 3:2 (shadow vs non shadow). We used a 30-bin histogram for the a and b features separately, and the original 512-bin histogram for the GIST feature.

PGP [46] groups data into clusters by finding and removing between-cluster edges from a weighted graph, where the graph nodes are the data points and the edges define neighborhood relationships where the pair-wise similarity distances are the edge weights. Given the graph, a two-component Weibull Mixture Model is fitted over the edge weights. Then, we use the cross-point of the two Weibull components as the critical value that represents the cut-off between the within-cluster edge weights and the between-cluster edge weights. After the critical value is computed, the edges with weights higher than the critical value are identified as between-cluster edges and removed, with the subsequent disjoint sets of sub-graphs as the final clustering result.

For the shadow image clustering problem, initial neighborhood relationships are not explicitly defined. Therefore, we construct the data graph by linking data nodes with their k nearest neighbors. Each node represents an image. We use Earth Mover's Distance (EMD) as the distance metric for the a and b color histograms, and Euclidean (L_2) distance for the GIST features. Given the three similarity distances per node pair, we normalize the EMD and L_2 distance values to have zero mean and unit variance, perform PCA, and take the first principal

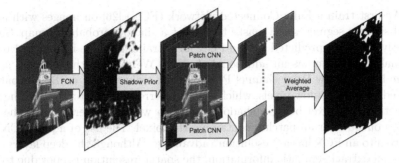

Fig. 3. The proposed pipeline for shadow segmentation. An FCN takes an RGB image and outputs an image level shadow prior map. Then a patch level CNN with structured output takes the RGBP (P is the image level shadow Prior channel) image and outputs a local shadow prediction map. Finally, the probability of each pixel being a shadow pixel is computed by averaging results from different patches.

component as the combined similarity distance for constructing the k nearest neighbor data graph.

Once the clusters are computed by applying PGP on the graph. We add a post-processing step to enforce the size of each cluster to be between $n_{min} = 10$ to $n_{max} = 60$ images. We iteratively merge small clusters (with less than n_{min} images) into the closest cluster. That is, the cluster that has the member with the lowest combined similarity distance to a member of the small cluster. Finally, we re-apply PGP to the clusters with sizes larger than n_{max} until the sizes of all resulting clusters fall within the desired range.

5   Shadow Segmentation Using Stacked-CNN

Most previous methods for shadow detection are based on classification of image regions using local color and texture cues. This approach, however, ignores global semantic information, which is useful for disambiguation. For example, without reasoning about global semantics, a dark cloud in the sky might be misclassified as a shadow region. In this section, we describe a semantics-aware patch level CNN, a method that combines global semantics with local cues for shadow detection.

Our method is based on the combination of two neural networks. Combining multiple neural networks has been successfully used in many applications [5,18,20,32,34,37]. One approach is to train multiple neural networks separately then combine their predictions [5,18,37]. Another approach is to combine the feature maps of neural networks instead of the final predictions [20]. These approaches, however, require the networks to share the same input/output structure and learning objective. Instead we propose to stack two CNNs into a single stream, as shown in Fig. 3. The two networks can have heterogeneous input/output representation and learning objectives.

We first train a Fully Connected Network (FCN) [26] on images with annotated shadow segmentation masks to predict a shadow probability map. Subsequently, the map predicted by the FCN for a training image is attached to the
original RGB image as an additional channel. We refer to this channel as the
image level shadow Prior channel P. Finally we train a CNN on RGBP patches
to predict local shadow pixels, which will be referred to as patch-CNN. The final
prediction of a pixel being a shadow pixel is a weighted average over the prediction outputs for all patches containing this pixel. The use of a patch-CNN in
addition to an FCN has a "resolution" advantage. Although the deep layers of an
FCN can extract semantic information, the spatial resolution is poor due to several max-pooling and down-sampling operations. Therefore, a local patch-CNN is
necessary to refine the segmentation result. Furthermore, the patch-CNN learns
from millions of training samples, leading to a more robust shadow classifier.
By including the image level shadow prior channel in the input, we incorporate
semantic information into the patch-CNN to generate improved shadow masks
as shown in Fig. 4.

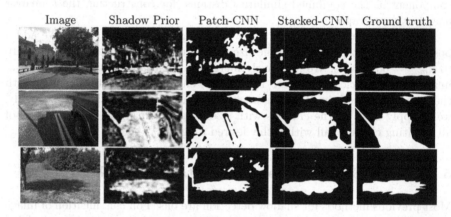

Fig. 4. Shadow segmentation examples. Qualitative results using patch-CNN on
RGB images, and on RGBP (P is the image level shadow prior) images (stacked-CNN).
The stacked-CNN achieves the best results by incorporating both semantic and subtle
local texture and color information. For example, in the first image, although the color
and texture of the tree is shadow-like, we can exclude the tree pixels thanks to the
FCN generated shadow prior.

Semantic FCN details. We train a FCN [26] on images of various sizes to
generate the image level shadow prior. We use the VGG-16 network [36], a CNN
trained on a large scale object classification dataset, to initialize the semantic
FCN. We fine-tune the semantic FCN using the given shadow masks. Because the
initial FCN was trained for object classification, the resulting shadow probability
maps contain semantic information.

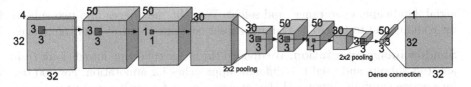

Fig. 5. Patch-CNN with structured output. The input is a 32 × 32 RGBP (RGB + image level shadow Prior) image, the output is a 32 × 32 shadow probability map.

Patch-CNN details. We build a patch level CNN with structured output for local shadow segmentation, as shown in Fig. 5. The loss function is the average negative log-likelihood of the prediction of every pixel. We extract image patches for training in three ways. Twenty-five percent of the patches are extracted at random image locations to include patches of various textures and colors. Fifty percent are extracted on Canny edges [4] to include hard-to-classify boundaries. Twenty-five percent are extracted at shadow locations to guarantee a minimum percent of positive instances. This results in an overall balanced number of shadow pixels and non-shadow pixels in the training batches for stochastic gradient descent. During testing, we feed all overlapping patches of each image to the patch-CNN. Thus every pixel has a maximum of 32 × 32 = 1024 predicted values from different patches. We use a weighted average to fuse multiple predictions. More precisely, suppose there are n patches containing the pixel, the distances between the pixel and the center of those patches are $d_1, d_2, \ldots, d_n$, and the predicted shadow probabilities are $p_1, p_2, \ldots, p_n$ respectively. Then the fused shadow probability is taken as: $p = (\sum_i G(d_i; \sigma)p_i) / \sum_i G(d_i; \sigma)$, where $G(d_i; \sigma)$ is a zero-mean Gaussian with variance σ^2. In our experiments we use $\sigma^2 = 8$.

6   A Large-Scale Shadow Dataset

We have collected a new shadow dataset, one that is significantly larger and more diverse than the existing datasets [12,49], and use lazy annotation [44] to quickly annotate the images. In this section we describe the details.

Image collection. To compile our dataset, we collected almost 5,000 images containing shadows. A quarter of the images came from the MS COCO dataset [25]. The rest were collected from the web. This image collection is significantly larger than the existing UCF [49] and UIUC [12] datasets, which contain less than 400 images combined. This image collection is also more diverse than existing datasets, which consist of images from a few specific domains (e.g., close shots of objects predominate in UIUC, whereas the majority images in UCF are scenes with darker shadows and objects). The image collection covers a wide range of scenes including urban, beach, mountain, roads, parks, snow, animals, vehicles, and houses. It also contains different picture types including aerial, landscape, close range, and selfies. We split the images into two subsets for training and testing. The training subset contains about 85 % of the images.

Shadow image annotation. We divided the image collection into disjoint train and test subsets and used two different approaches for annotation. For 700 test images, we carefully annotated the images, aiming for pixel accuracy to ensure the validity of numerical evaluation. We will refer to this test set as **SBU-Test**. For training images, we used *lazy labeling* to quickly annotate a large set of images. For lazy labeling, we drew a few strokes on shadow areas and a few other strokes on non-shadow areas. These strokes were used as shadow and non-shadow seeds for geodesic convexity image segmentation [11]. Figure 1 illustrates this procedure. With lazy labeling, we were able to annotate the dataset quickly, at the rate of 3 to 4 images per minute. However, the obtained annotation was noisy. In particular, there were many "dirty negatives" — shadow regions that were incorrectly labeled as negative. This was due to misclassification of shadow regions or poor segmentation (image regions contain both shadow and non-shadow pixels). Dirty negatives are more prevalent than "dirty positives". Since we focused on drawing strokes on major shadow areas, the chosen shadow areas were generally well segmented. The final dataset contains images with shadow labels that have been "cleaned" using the method described in Sect. 3. Hereafter, we refer to the dataset with noisy labels as **SBU-Train-Noisy** and the dataset with recovered labels as **SBU-Train-Recover**.

7   Experiments

We conducted experiments to evaluate our shadow detection method, the generalization ability of the proposed training dataset, and the effectiveness of the noisy shadow label recovery approach. Our newly collected dataset, SBU-Train-Recover contains 4085 training images. The dataset contains no images from existing shadow UCF and UIUC datasets.

For performance evaluation we compared the predicted shadow masks with the high quality annotation masks, measuring classification error rates at pixel level. The main performance metric is the Balanced Error Rate (BER). We avoid an overall error metric because shadow pixels are considerably less than non-shadow pixels, hence classifying all pixels as non-shadow would yield a low overall error.

CNN training details. We apply data augmentation: for the FCN training, we downsample the training images by six different factors: 1.0, 0.9, 0.8, 0.7, 0.6, 0.5 and perform left-right flip. For the patch-CNN training, we store original images in memory and randomly extract patches on the fly. Patches are randomly rotated and flipped. We use the implementation of the FCN provided by Long *et al.* [26]. We implement the patch-CNN using Theano [1,2]. The total training time of the stacked-CNN is approximately 10 h on a single Titan X GPU.

7.1   Shadow Segmentation Method Evaluation

We evaluate our shadow segmentation method on the UCF dataset [49]. We trained and tested on the original UCF dataset (255 images), using the split given by Guo *et al.* [12]. Measuring performance in terms of BER, our proposed method (stacked-CNN) performs comparably to several state-of-the-art methods[2]. Table 1 (left) shows that our method achieves lower BER than Convnets+CRF [14], and the kernel optimization method (LooKOP+MRF) [43]. We also evaluate separately the different components of our architecture. As can be seen in Table 1 (right), the proposed stacked-CNN outperforms both the FCN and the patch-CNN. The 12 % reduction in BER compared to the patch-CNN confirms the benefits of using the FCN result as an image level shadow prior in our stacked-CNN architecture.

Table 1. Evaluation of shadow detection on UCF [49]. All methods are trained and tested on UCF training and test subsets. Our method stacked-CNN achieves better performance than state-of-the-art methods.

Method	BER Sha. Non.	Method	BER Sha. Non.
Convnets+CRF [14]	17.7 27.5 7.9	FCN	13.4 17.3 15.3
LooKOP+MRF [43]	13.2 20.0 6.4	Patch-CNN on RGB	13.3 9.8 16.8
Stacked-CNN (ours)	**11.6** 10.4 12.8	Stacked-CNN	**11.6** 10.4 12.8

Table 2. Experiments across datasets. Training on our dataset generalizes well on the UCF testing set, while the model trained on the UCF training set does not

Training Set	Methods	UCF Test			SBU-Test		
		BER	Sha.	Non-sha	BER	Sha.	Non-sha
UCF Train	LooKOP+MRF [43]	13.2	20.0	6.4	-	-	-
UCF Train	Stacked-CNN	**11.6**	10.4	12.8	13.9	13.1	14.7
SBU-Train-Recover	Stacked-CNN	13.0	9.0	17.1	**11.0**	9.6	12.5

7.2   Experiments with the SBU Datasets

We first evaluate the generalization ability of a classifier trained on our proposed dataset. We train the stacked-CNN on SBU-Train-Recover and test on UCF. As can be seen from Table 2, the stacked-CNN trained on SBU-Train-Recover achieves lower error than LooKOP+MRF [43] trained on UCF. Furthermore, training on SBU-Train-Recover slightly decreases the performance of the stacked-CNN as compared to training on UCF. This suggests that our stacked-CNN

---

[2] [35] cannot be directly compared because it used an extended version of the UCF dataset that is not publicly available.

Image   Trained on UCF   Trained on LSSD   Ground truth

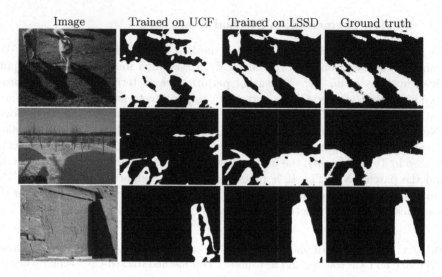

Fig. 6. Comparison of Stacked-CNN trained on UCF and SBU-Train-Recover. A stacked-CNN trained on a larger dataset shows improved shadow segmentation compared to a stacked-CNN trained on the UCF training set. Because SBU-Train-Recover contains a variety of scenes, the classifier trained on it is more robust on a general test set.

classifier trained on SBU-Train-Recover generalizes well to a totally different dataset. We also evaluate the performance of our proposed method on the newly collected testing set (SBU-Test). Our stacked-CNN achieves 11.0 % BER. In Fig. 6 we show qualitative results comparing the performance of out stacked-CNN trained on UCF and SBU-Train-Recover datasets.

7.3   Noisy Label Recovery Performance

For label recovery, PGP clusters SBU-Train-Noisy into 224 subsets of 10–60 images. To perform label recovery we allow up to 5 % negative and up to 1 % positive labels to be flipped ($\alpha = 0.99$, $\beta = 0.95$). We use our label recovery framework with $\mathcal{X}^2$ kernel as shadow region classifier. We choose the scaling parameter of the $\mathcal{X}^2$ kernel that minimizes the leave-one-out error on the noisy training set. We oversegment the training images into superpixels using Linear Spectral Clustering [48]. For each superpixel we compute intensity, color and texture features. We use 30 bin histograms for each of the channels of the CIELab color space. For texture, we use texton histograms. We run the full MR8 [42] filter bank on the input images and on the image density map [7]. Textons from density maps were shown to work well for shadow detection [7]. We cluster the filter responses, sampling 2,000 locations per image (balancing shadow and non shadow pixels), to build two 128-word dictionaries. Our method is able to flip labels and correct some annotation mistakes. Figure 7 shows examples of label recovery. New shadow boundaries are depicted in cyan.

Table 3. Label recovery influence on CNNs. We show the BER of the FCN, the patch-CNN, and the stacked-CNN trained on SBU-Train-Noisy and SBU-Train-Recover, and tested on the UCF testing set and SBU-Test.

Labels	FCN		Patch-CNN		Stacked-CNN	
	UCF test	SBU-Test	UCF test	SBU-Test	UCF test	SBU-Test
SBU-Train-Noisy	20.0	17.7	14.1	12.6	14.0	12.1
SBU-Train-Recover	**16.5**	**13.0**	**13.6**	**12.0**	**13.0**	**11.0**

(a) Noisy Annotation   (b) Recovered Shadows   (c) Cleaned-up Annotation

Fig. 7. Recovery from noisy annotations. Example of shadow region label recovery. (a) Original shadow annotation depicted with red boundaries. (b) Recovered shadows depicted with blue boundaries. (c) Resulting cleaned-up shadow annotation: shadow boundaries depicted in red. (Color figure online)

Since we could not quantitatively evaluate the proposed label recovery in a direct way, we measured the influence of training with noisy versus recovered labels in terms of classification performance. To expedite these experiments, we resized the training input images and corresponding shadow masks (for recovered and noisy) to be no bigger than 650 by 480 pixels. Then, we retrained our models using both recovered and noisy labels.

In Table 3, we compare the performance of the FCN, the patch-CNN, and the stacked-CNN when trained on SBU-Train-Noisy and SBU-Train-Recover and tested on the UCF testing set and the proposed SBU-Test. As can be seen, the models trained with recovered labels outperform models trained with noisy labels. Using recovered labels reduces the error rate of the stacked-CNN by 7 % and 9 % respectively, when testing in UCF and SBU-Test. Similarly, label recovery reduces the error rate of the FCN by 17.5 % and 26.5 %.

8 Conclusions

We have proposed a novel method for large-scale label recovery of noisily annotated shadow regions. This allowed us to create a new shadow dataset that is 20 times bigger than existing datasets. This dataset is well suited for deep-learning, and we proposed a novel deep learning framework to take advantage of the new dataset. Our deep learning architecture operates at the local patch level, but it can incorporate the global semantics. This leads to a shadow classifier that performs well across different datasets. We expect this new dataset to become the benchmark for large scale shadow detection.

Acknowledgments. Partially supported by NSF IIS-1161876, FRA DTFR5315-C00011, the Stony Brook SensonCAT, the Subsample project from DIGITEO Institute, France. The authors would like to thank Amazon for providing EC2 credits and NVIDIA for donating GPUs.

References

1. Bastien, F., Lamblin, P., Pascanu, R., Bergstra, J., Goodfellow, I.J., Bergeron, A., Bouchard, N., Bengio, Y.: Theano: new features and speed improvements. In: NIPS Workshop (2012)
2. Bergstra, J., Breuleux, O., Bastien, F., Lamblin, P., Pascanu, R., Desjardins, G., Turian, J., Warde-Farley, D., Bengio, Y.: Theano: a CPU and GPU math expression compiler. In: SciPy (2010)
3. Biggio, B., Nelson, B., Laskov, P.: Support vector machines under adversarial label noise. In: ACML (2011)
4. Canny, J.: A computational approach to edge detection. IEEE Trans. Pattern Anal. Mach. Intell. **6**, 679–698 (1986)
5. Ciresan, D., Meier, U., Schmidhuber, J.: Multi-column deep neural networks for image classification. In: CVPR (2012)
6. Crammer, K., Lee, D.D.: Learning via Gaussian herding. In: NIPS (2010)
7. Ecins, A., Fermller, C., Aloimonos, Y.: Shadow-free segmentation in still images using local density measure (2014)
8. Finlayson, G., Hordley, S., Lu, C., Drew, M.: On the removal of shadows from images. IEEE Trans. Pattern Anal. Mach. Intell. **28**(1), 59–68 (2006)
9. Finlayson, G., Drew, M., Lu, C.: Entropy minimization for shadow removal. Int. J. Comput. Vis. **85**(1), 35–57 (2009)
10. Frenay, B., Verleysen, M.: Classification in the presence of label noise: a survey. IEEE Trans. Neural Netw. Learn. Syst. **25**(5), 845–869 (2014)
11. Gulshan, V., Rother, C., Criminisi, A., Blake, A., Zisserman, A.: Geodesic star convexity for interactive image segmentation (2010)
12. Guo, R., Dai, Q., Hoiem, D.: Single-image shadow detection and removal using paired regions (2011)
13. Guo, R., Dai, Q., Hoiem, D.: Paired regions for shadow detection and removal (2012)
14. Hameed Khan, S., Bennamoun, M., Sohel, F., Togneri, R.: Automatic feature learning for robust shadow detection (2014)
15. Hoai, M.: Regularized max pooling for image categorization (2014)

16. Hoai, M., Zisserman, A.: Improving human action recognition using score distribution and ranking (2014)
17. Huang, X., Hua, G., Tumblin, J., Williams, L.: What characterizes a shadow boundary under the sun and sky? (2011)
18. Ji, S., Xu, W., Yang, M., Yu, K.: 3D convolutional neural networks for human action recognition. PAMI 35(1), 221–231 (2013)
19. Junejo, I.N., Foroosh, H.: Estimating geo-temporal location of stationary cameras using shadow trajectories. In: Forsyth, D., Torr, P., Zisserman, A. (eds.) ECCV 2008. LNCS, vol. 5302, pp. 318–331. Springer, Heidelberg (2008)
20. Karpathy, A., Toderici, G., Shetty, S., Leung, T., Sukthankar, R., Fei-Fei, L.: Large-scale video classification with convolutional neural networks. In: CVPR (2014)
21. Karsch, K., Hedau, V., Forsyth, D., Hoiem, D.: Rendering synthetic objects into legacy photographs. ACM Trans. Graph. 30(6), 157 (2011)
22. Khardon, R., Wachman, G.: Noise tolerant variants of the perceptron algorithm. J. Mach. Learn. Res. 8, 227–248 (2007)
23. Lalonde, J.F., Efros, A., Narasimhan, S.: Estimating natural illumination from a single outdoor image (2009)
24. Lalonde, J.-F., Efros, A.A., Narasimhan, S.G.: Detecting ground shadows in outdoor consumer photographs. In: Daniilidis, K., Maragos, P., Paragios, N. (eds.) ECCV 2010. LNCS, vol. 6312, pp. 322–335. Springer, Heidelberg (2010)
25. Lin, T.-Y., et al.: Microsoft COCO: common objects in context. In: Fleet, D., Pajdla, T., Schiele, B., Tuytelaars, T. (eds.) ECCV 2014. LNCS, vol. 8693, pp. 740–755. Springer, Heidelberg (2014)
26. Long, J., Shelhamer, E., Darrell, T.: Fully convolutional networks for semantic segmentation. In: CVPR (2015)
27. Natarajan, N., Dhillon, I.S., Ravikumar, P.K., Tewari, A.: Learning with noisy labels. In: NIPS (2013)
28. Okabe, T., S.I., Sato, Y.: Attached shadow coding: estimating surface normals from shadows under unknown reflectance and lighting conditions (2009)
29. Oliva, A., Torralba, A.: Modeling the shape of the scene: a holistic representation fo the spatial envelope. Int. J. Comput. Vis. 42(3), 145–175 (2001)
30. Panagopoulos, A., Samaras, D., Paragios, N.: Robust shadow and illumination estimation using a mixture model (2009)
31. Panagopoulos, A., Wang, C., Samaras, D., Paragios, N.: Simultaneous cast shadows, illumination and geometry inference using hypergraphs. IEEE Trans. Pattern Anal. Mach. Intell. 35(2), 437–449 (2013)
32. Park, E., Han, X., Berg, T.L., Berg, A.C.: Combining multiple sources of knowledge in deep cnns for action recognition. In: WACV (2016)
33. Saunders, C., Gammerman, A., Vovk, V.: Ridge regression learning algorithm in dual variables (1998)
34. Sharkey, A.J.: Combining Artificial Neural Nets: Ensemble and Modular Multi-net Systems. Springer Science & Business Media (2012)
35. Shen, L., Chua, T.W., Leman, K.: Shadow optimization from structured deep edge detection (2015)
36. Simonyan, K., Zisserman, A.: Very deep convolutional networks for large-scale image recognition. CoRR (2014)
37. Simonyan, K., Zisserman, A.: Two-stream convolutional networks for action recognition in videos (2014)
38. Stempfel, G., Ralaivola, L.: Learning SVMs from sloppily labeled data. In: Alippi, C., Polycarpou, M., Panayiotou, C., Ellinas, G. (eds.) ICANN 2009. LNCS, vol. 5768, pp. 884–893. Springer, Heidelberg (2009). doi:10.1007/978-3-642-04274-4_91

39. Stempfel, G., Ralaivola, L.: Learning kernel perceptrons on noisy data using random projections. In: Hutter, M., Servedio, R.A., Takimoto, E. (eds.) ALT 2007. LNCS, vol. 4754, pp. 328–342. Springer, Heidelberg (2007)

40. Suykens, J.A.K., Gestel, T.V., Brabanter, J.D., Moor, B.D., Vandewalle, J.: Least Squares Support Vector Machines. World Scientific, Singapore (2002)

41. Suykens, J.A.K., Vandewalle, J.: Least squares support vector machine classifiers. Neural Process. Lett. 9(3), 293–300 (1999)

42. Varma, M., Zisserman, A.: Classifying images of materials: achieving viewpoint and illumination independence. In: Heyden, A., Sparr, G., Nielsen, M., Johansen, P. (eds.) ECCV 2002. LNCS, vol. 2352, pp. 255–271. Springer, Heidelberg (2002)

43. Yago Vicente, T.F., Hoai, M., Samaras, D.: Leave-one-out kernel optimization for shadow detection (2015)

44. Yago Vicente, T.F., Hoai, M., Samaras, D.: Noisy label recovery for shadow detection in unfamiliar domains (2016)

45. Yago Vicente, T.F., Yu, C.P., Samaras, D.: Single image shadow detection using multiple cues in a supermodular MRF (2013)

46. Yu, C.P., Hua, W.Y., Samaras, D., Zelinsky, G.: Modeling clutter perception using parametric proto-object partitioning. In: NIPS (2013)

47. Yu, C.P., Le, H., Zelinsky, G., Samaras, D.: Efficient video segmentation using parametric graph partitioning. In: ICCV (2015)

48. Zhengqin, L., Jiansheng, C.: Superpixel segmentation using linear spectral clustering (2015)

49. Zhu, J., Samuel, K., Masood, S., Tappen, M.: Learning to recognize shadows in monochromatic natural images (2010)

50. Zhu, X., Wu, X.: Class noise vs. attribute noise: a quantitative study. Artif. Intell. Rev. 22(3), 177–210 (2004)

RNN Fisher Vectors for Action Recognition and Image Annotation

Guy Lev[1,2], Gil Sadeh[1], Benjamin Klein[1(✉)], and Lior Wolf[1]

[1] The Blavatnik School of Computer Science, Tel Aviv University, Tel Aviv, Israel
beni.klein@gmail.com
[2] IBM Research, Haifa, Israel

Abstract. Recurrent Neural Networks (Rnns) have had considerable success in classifying and predicting sequences. We demonstrate that Rnns can be effectively used in order to encode sequences and provide effective representations. The methodology we use is based on Fisher Vectors, where the Rnns are the generative probabilistic models and the partial derivatives are computed using backpropagation. State of the art results are obtained in two central but distant tasks, which both rely on sequences: video action recognition and image annotation. We also show a surprising transfer learning result from the task of image annotation to the task of video action recognition.

Keywords: Action recognition · Image annotation · Fisher vectors · Recurrent Neural Networks

1 Introduction

Fisher Vectors have been shown to provide a significant performance gain on many different applications in the domain of computer vision [1–4]. In the domain of video action recognition, Fisher Vectors and Stacked Fisher Vectors [2] have recently outperformed state-of-the-art methods on multiple datasets [2,5]. Fisher Vectors (FV) have also recently been applied to word embedding (e.g. word2vec [6]) and have been shown to provide state of the art results on a variety of NLP tasks [7], as well as on image annotation and image search tasks [8].

In all of these contributions, the FV of a set of local descriptors is obtained as a sum of gradients of the log-likelihood of the descriptors in the set, with respect to the parameters of a probabilistic mixture model that was fitted on a training set in an unsupervised manner. Despite being richer than the mean vector pooling method, Fisher Vectors based on a probabilistic mixture model are invariant to order. This makes them less appealing for annotating, for example, video, in which the sequence of events determines much of the meaning.

This work presents a novel approach for FV representation of sequences using a Recurrent Neural Network (RNN). The RNN is trained to predict the next

Electronic supplementary material The online version of this chapter (doi:10. 1007/978-3-319-46466-4_50) contains supplementary material, which is available to authorized users.

B. Leibe et al. (Eds.): ECCV 2016, Part VI, LNCS 9910, pp. 833–850, 2016.
DOI: 10.1007/978-3-319-46466-4_50

element of a sequence given the previous elements. Conveniently, the gradients needed for the computation of the FV are extracted using the available back-propagation infrastructure.

The new representation is sensitive to ordering and, therefore, mitigates the disadvantage of using the standard Fisher Vector representation. It is applied to two different and challenging tasks: video action recognition and image annotation by sentences.

Several recent works have proposed to use an RNN for sentence representation [9–12]. The Recurrent Neural Network Fisher Vector (RNN-FV) method differs from these works in that a sequence is represented by using derived gradient from the RNN as a vector representation, instead of using a hidden or an output layer of the RNN.

The paper explores training an RNN regressor to predict the vector representation of the next element of a sequence given the previous ones (i.e. treating it as a regression task). In the image annotation and image search tasks, word embeddings are used for representing words. In the video action recognition task, the VGG [13] Convolutional Neural Network (CNN) is used to extract features from the frames of the video and the RNN is trained to predict the embedding of the next frame given the previous ones. Similarly, C3D [14] features of sequential video sub-volumes are used with the same training technique.

Although the image annotation and video action recognition tasks are quite different, a surprising boost in performance in the video action recognition task was achieved by using a transfer learning approach from the image annotation task. Specifically, the VGG image embedding of a frame is projected using a linear transformation which was learned on matching images and sentences by the Canonical Correlation Analysis (CCA) algorithm [15].

The proposed RNN-FV method achieves state-of-the-art results in action recognition on the HMDB51 [16] and UCF101 [17] datasets. In the image annotation and image search tasks, the RNN-FV method is used for the representation of sentences and achieves state-of-the-art results on the Flickr8K dataset [18] and competitive results on other benchmarks.

2   Previous Work

Action Recognition. As in other object recognition problems, the standard pipeline in action recognition is comprised of three main steps: feature extraction, pooling and classification. Many works [19–21] have focused on the first step of extracting local descriptors. Laptev et al. [22] extend the notion of spatial interest points into the spatio-temporal domain and show how the resulting features can be used for a compact representation of video data. Wang et al. [23,24] used low-level hand-crafted features such as histogram of oriented gradients (HOG), histogram of optical flow (HOF) and motion boundary histogram (MBH).

Recent works have attempted to replace these hand-crafted features by deep-learned features for video action recognition due to its wide success in the image domain. Early attempts [25–27] achieved lower results in comparison to hand-crafted features, proving that it is challenging to apply deep-learning techniques on videos due to the relatively small number of available datasets and complex motion patterns. More recent attempts managed to overcome these challenges and achieve state of the art results with deep-learned features. Simonyan et al. [28] designed two-stream ConvNets for learning both the appearance of the video frame and the motion as reflected by the estimated optical flow. Du Tran et al. [14] designed an effective approach for spatiotemporal feature learning using 3-dimensional Con-vNets.

In the second step of the pipeline, the pooling, Wang et al. [29] compared different pooling techniques for the application of action recognition and showed empirically that the Fisher Vector encoding has the best performance. Recently, more complex pooling methods were demonstrated by Peng et al. [2] who proposed Stacked Fisher Vectors (SFV), a multi-layer nested Fisher Vector encoding and Wang et al. [5] who proposed a trajectory-pooled deep-convolutional descriptor (TDD). TDD uses both a motion CNN, trained on UCF101, and an appearance CNN, originally trained on ImageNet [30], and fine-tuned on UCF101. Fernando et al. [31] suggested to capture the temporal ordering of a particular video by training a linear ranking machine on the frames of that video. The parameters of the ranking machine are used as the video representation for action recognition. In parallel to our work, Nagel et al. [32] proposed using event Fisher Vectors for encoding a visual stream. They considered two different generative models beyond the Gaussian Mixture Model. The first is the Student's-t mixture model which has heavy tails but is not sensitive to the order of the elements in the sequence. The second is the Hidden Markov Model which can capture the temporal ordering of the elements in the sequence. Our work is using a Fisher Vector which is defined on a Recurrent Neural Network model.

Image Annotation and Image Search. In the past few years, the state-of-the-art results in image annotation and image search have been provided by deep learning approaches [8,33–41]. A typical system is composed of three important components: (i) Image Representation, (ii) Sentence Representation, and (iii) Matching Images and Sentences. The image is usually represented by applying a pre-trained CNN on the image and taking the activations from the last hidden layer.

There are several different approaches for the sentence representation; Socher et al. [33] used a dependency tree Recursive Neural Network. Yan et al. [34] used a TF-IDF histogram over the vocabulary. Klein et al. [8] used word2vec [6] as the word embedding and then applied Fisher Vector based on a Hybrid Gaussian-Laplacian Mixture Model (HGLMM) in order to pool the word2vec embeddings of the words in a given sentence into a single representation. Ma et al. [41] proposed a matching CNN (m-CNN) that composes words to different semantic fragments and learns the inter-modal relations between the image and the composed fragments at different levels.

Since a sentence can be seen as a sequence of words, many works have used a Recurrent Neural Network (RNN) in order to represent sentences [12,35–37,40]. To address the need for capturing long term semantics in the sentence, these works mainly use Long Short-Term Memory (LSTM) [42] or Gated Recurrent Unit (GRU) [43] cells. Generally, the RNN treats a sentence as an ordered sequence of words, and incrementally encodes a semantic vector of the sentence, word-by-word. At each time step, a new word is encoded into the semantic vector, until the end of the sentence is reached. All of the words and their dependencies will then have been embedded into the semantic vector, which can be used as a feature vector representation of the entire sentence. Our work also uses an RNN in order to represent sentences, but takes the derived gradient from the RNN as features, instead of using a hidden or an output layer of the RNN. In parallel to our work, Gordo et al. [44] proposed using the gradient representation of CNNs for images.

A number of techniques have been proposed for the task of matching images and sentences. Klein et al. [8] used CCA [15] and Yan et al. [34] introduced a Deep CCA in order to project the images and sentences into a common space and then performed a nearest neighbor search between the images and the sentences in the common space. Kiros et al. [37], Karpathy et al. [35], Socher et al. [33] and Ma et al. [41] used a contrastive loss function trained on matching and unmatching pairs of (image, sentence) in order to learn a score function for a given pair. Mao et al. [36] and Vinyals et al. [40] learned a probabilistic model for inferring a sentence given an image and, therefore, are able to compute the probability that a given sentence will be created by a given image and used it as the score.

Related Work. [45,46] have also proposed methods incorporating advanced pooling techniques within the CNN and backpropagation infrastructure.

2.1   Baseline Pooling Methods

In this section, we describe two baseline pooling methods that can represent a multiset of vectors as a single vector. The notation of a multiset is used to clarify that the order of the vectors does not affect the representation, and that a vector can appear more than once. Both methods can be applied to sequences. However, the resulting representation will be insensitive to ordering.

Mean Vector. This pooling method takes a multiset of vectors, $X = \{x_1..x_N\} \in \mathbb{R}^D$, and computes its mean: $v = \frac{1}{N} \sum_{i=1}^{N} x_i$. Clearly, the vector v that results from the pooling is in $\mathbb{R}^D$.

Fisher Vector of a GMM. Given a multiset of vectors, $X = \{x_1..x_N\} \in \mathbb{R}^D$, the standard FV [47] is defined as the gradient of the log-likelihood of X with respect to the parameters of a pre-trained Diagonal-Covariance Gaussian Mixture Model (GMM). In [4], Perronnin et al. introduced two normalizations of the FV which improved its performance. It is worth noting that the linear structure of the GMM FV pooling would not be preserved in the RNN model, where the probability of an element in the sequence depends on all the previous elements.

3   RNN-Based Fisher Vector

The pooling methods described above share a common disadvantage: insensitivity to the order of the elements in the sequence. A way to tackle this, while keeping the power of gradient-based representation, would be to replace the Gaussian model by a generative sequence model that takes into account the order of elements in the sequence. A desirable property of the sequence model would be the ability to calculate the gradient (with respect to the model's parameters) of the likelihood estimate by this model to an input sequence.

In this section, we show that such a model can be obtained by training an RNN regressor to predict the embedding of the next element in a sequence, given the previous elements. Having this, we propose, for the first time, the RNN-FV: A Fisher Vector that is based on such an RNN sequence model.

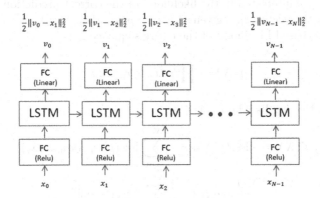

Fig. 1. RNN structure and loss function (in red), as was trained for the action recognition task. The RNN is trained to predict the next element of the sequence, given the previous ones. The gradient of the loss function (which can be seen as likelihood), with respect to the RNN's weights, constitutes the unnormalized RNN-FV. (Color figure online)

Given a sequence of vectors S with N vector elements $x_1, ..., x_N \in \mathbb{R}^D$, we convert it to the input sequence $X = (x_0, x_1, ..., x_{N-1})$, where $x_0 = x_{start}$. This special element is used to denote the beginning of the input sequence, and we use $x_{start} = 0$ throughout this paper. The RNN is trained to predict, at each time step i, the next element x_{i+1} of the sequence, given the previous elements $x_0, ..., x_i$. Therefore, given the input sequence, the target sequence would be: $Y = (x_1, x_2, ...x_N)$. The training data and the training process are application dependent, as described in Sect. 4 for action recognition and in Sect. 5 for image annotation. There are several regression loss functions that can be used. Here, we consider the following loss function:

$$Loss(y, v) = \frac{1}{2}\|y - v\|^2 \tag{1}$$

where y is the target vector and v is the predicted vector.

After the RNN training is done, and given a new sequence S, the derived sequence X is fed to the RNN. Denote the output of the RNN at time step i

($i = 0, ..., N - 1$) by $RNN(x_0, ..., x_i) = v_i \in \mathbb{R}^D$. The target at time step i is x_{i+1} (the next element in the sequence), and the loss is:

$$Loss(x_{i+1}, v_i) = \frac{1}{2}\|x_{i+1} - v_i\|^2 \tag{2}$$

The RNN can be seen as a generative model, and the likelihood of any vector x being the next element of the sequence, given $x_0, ..., x_i$, can be defined as:

$$p(x|x_0, ..., x_i) = (2\pi)^{-D/2} \exp\left(-\frac{1}{2}\|x - v_i\|^2\right) \tag{3}$$

Here, we are interested in the likelihood of the correct prediction, i.e., in the likelihood of the vector x_{i+1} given $x_0, ..., x_i$: $p(x_{i+1}|x_0, ..., x_i)$.
The RNN-based likelihood of the entire sequence X is:

$$p(X) = \prod_{i=0}^{N-1} p(x_{i+1}|x_0, ..., x_i) \tag{4}$$

The negative log likelihood of X is:

$$\mathcal{L}(X) = -\log(p(X)) = -\sum_{i=0}^{N-1} \log(p(x_{i+1}|x_0, ..., x_i))$$

$$= \frac{ND}{2}\log(2\pi) + \frac{1}{2}\sum_{i=0}^{N-1}\|x_{i+1} - v_i\|^2 \tag{5}$$

In order to represent X using the Fisher Vector scheme, we have to compute the gradient of $\mathcal{L}(X)$ with respect to our model's parameters. With RNN being our model, the parameters are the weights W of the network. By (2) and (5), we get that $\mathcal{L}(X)$ equals the loss that would be obtained when X is fed as input to the RNN, up to an additive constant. Therefore, the desired gradient can be computed by backpropagation: we feed X to the network and perform forward and backward passes. The obtained gradient $\nabla_W \mathcal{L}(X)$ would be the (unnormalized) RNN-FV representation of X. Notice that this gradient is *not* used to update the network's weights as done in training - here we perform backpropagation *at inference time*. Other loss functions may be used instead of the one presented in this analysis. Given a sequence, the gradient of the RNN loss may serve as the sequence representation, even if the loss is not interpretable as a likelihood. Figure 1 illustrates the RNN structure and the loss function that we used for the action recognition task.

3.1   Normalization of the RNN-FV

It was suggested by [47] that normalizing the FVs by the Fisher Information Matrix is beneficial. We approximated the diagonal of the Fisher Information Matrix (FIM), which is usually used for FV normalization. Note, however, that we did not observe any empirical improvement due to this normalization, and our experiments are reported without it.

4 Action Recognition Pipeline

The action recognition pipeline contains the underlying appearance features used to encode the video, the sequence encoding using the RNN-FV, and an SVM classifier on top. The entire pipeline is illustrated in Fig. 2. In this section, we discuss each step of the pipeline.

4.1 Visual Features

The RNN-FV is capable of encoding the sequence properties, and as underlying features, we rely on video encodings that are based on single frames or on fixed length blocks of frames.

VGG. Using the pre-trained 19-layer VGG convolutional network [13], we extract a 4096-dimensional representation of each video frame. The VGG pipeline is used, namely, the original image is cropped in ten different ways into 224 by 224 pixel images: the four corners, the center, and their x-axis mirror image. The mean intensity is then subtracted in each color channel and the resulting images are encoded by the network. The average of the 10 feature vectors obtained is then used as the single image representation. In order to speed up the method, the input video was sub-sampled, and one in every 10 frames was encoded. Empirically, we noticed that recognition performance was not harmed by this sub-sampling. To further reduce run-time, the data dimensionality was reduced via PCA to 500D. In addition, L2 normalization was applied to each vector. All PCAs in this work were trained for each dataset and each training/test split separately, using only the training data.

CCA. Using the same VGG representation of video frames as mentioned above and the code of [8][1], we represented each frame by a vector as follows: we considered the common image-sentence vector space obtained by the CCA algorithm, using the best model (GMM+HGLMM) of [8] trained on the COCO dataset [48]. We mapped each frame to that vector space, getting a 4096-dimensional image representation. As the final frame representation, we used the first (i.e. the principal) 500 dimensions. For our application, the projected VGG representations were L2 normalized. The CCA was trained for an unrelated task of image to sentence matching, and its success, therefore, suggests a new application of transfer learning: from image annotation to action recognition.

C3D. While the representations above encode single frames, the C3D method [14] splits the video into sub-volumes that are encoded one by one. Following the recommended settings, we applied the C3D pre-trained 3D convolutional neural network in order to extract a 4096D representation of each 16-frame blocks. The blocks are sampled with an 8 frame stride. Following feature extraction, PCA dimensionality reduction (500D) and L2 normalization were applied. Notice that while we used the available pretrained C3D network, our results are not comparable to [14]'s highest reported performance which was

---

[1] Available at www.cs.tau.ac.il/~wolf/code/hglmm.

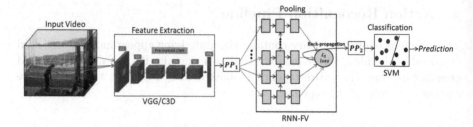

Fig. 2. Our general action recognition pipeline is composed of 6 steps: (a) Input Data - we use subsampled video frames or frame blocks as input to our system. (b) Feature Extraction - we extract features from the frames/frame-blocks using VGG/C3D pretrained CNN. (c) Post-Processing (PP_1) - PCA/CCA dimension reduction and L_2 normalization are performed. (d) Pooling - the extracted sequential features are fed into the RNN, then backpropagation is performed to obtain the partial derivatives with respect to the weights of the last fully-connected layer. (e) Post-Processing (PP_2) - PCA dimension reduction is performed, followed by power normalization and L_2 normalization. (f) Classification - the final representation is fed into a linear multi-class SVM classifier which predicts the estimated action label.

reached using an ensemble of 3 C3D networks (to our knowledge, the other two networks were not released) combined with idt [49].

4.2 Network Structure

Our RNN model (illustrated in Fig. 1) consists of three layers: a 200D fully-connected layer with Leaky-Relu activation ($\alpha = 0.1$), a 200D Long Short-Term Memory (LSTM) [42] layer, and a 500D linear fully-connected layer. Our network is trained as a regressor with the mean square error (MSE) loss function. Weight decay and dropouts were also applied. An improvement in recognition performance was noticed when the dropout rate was enlarged, up to a rate of 0.95, due to its ability to ensure the discriminative characteristics of each weight and hence also of each partial derivative in the gradient.

4.3 Training and Classification

We train the RNN to predict the next element in our video representation sequence, given the previous elements, as described in Sect. 3. In our experiments, we use only the part of gradient corresponding to the weights of the last fully-connected layer. Empirically, we saw no improvement when using the partial derivatives with respect to the weights of other layers. In order to obtain a fixed size representation, we average the gradients over all time steps. The gradient representation dimension is $500 \times 201 = 100500$, which is the number of weights in the last fully-connected layer. We then apply PCA to reduce the representation size to 1000D, followed by power and L2 normalization.

Video classification is performed using a linear SVM with a parameter $C = 1$. Empirically, we noticed that the best recognition performance is obtained very quickly and hence early stopping is necessary. In order to choose an early stopping point, we use a validation set. Some of the videos in the dataset are actually segments of the same original video, and are included in the dataset as different samples. Care was taken to ensure that no such similar videos are in both the training and validation sets, in order to guarantee that high validation accuracy will ensure good generalization and not merely over-fitting.

After each RNN epoch, we extract the RNN-FV representation as described above, train a linear SVM classifier on the training set and evaluate the performance on the validation set. The early stopping point is chosen at the epoch with the highest recognition accuracy on the validation set. After choosing our model this way, we train an SVM classifier on all training samples (training + validation samples) and report our performance on the test set.

5   Image-Sentence Retrieval

In the image-sentence retrieval tasks (image annotation and image search), vector representations are extracted separately for the sentences and the images. These representations are then mapped into a common vector space, where the two are being matched. [8] have presented a similar pipeline for GMM-FV. We replace this representation with RNN-FV.

A sentence, being an ordered sequence of words, can be represented as a vector using the RNN-FV scheme. Given a sentence with N words $w_1, ..., w_N$, (where w_N is considered to be the period, namely a w_{end} special token), we treat the sentence as an ordered sequence $S = (w_0, w_1, ..., w_{N-1})$, where $w_0 = w_{start}$. An RNN is trained to predict, at each time step i, the next word w_{i+1} of the sentence, given the previous words $w_0, ..., w_i$. Therefore, given the input sequence S, the target sequence would be: $(w_1, w_2, ...w_N)$. The training data may be any large set of sentences. These sentences may be extracted from the dataset of a specific benchmark, or, in order to obtain a generic representation, any external corpus, e.g., Wikipedia, may be used.

As observed in the action recognition case, we did not benefit from extracting partial derivatives with respect to the weights of the hidden layers, and hence we only use those of the output layer as our representation.

The input to the network is the word's embedding, a 300D vector in our case, followed by an LSTM layer of size 100. The output layer is a fully-connected one, where the (300 dimensional) word embedding of the next word is predicted. We use no activation function at the output layer.

For matching images and text, each image is represented as a 4096-dimensional vector extracted using the 19-layer VGG, as described in Sect. 4.1. The regularized CCA algorithm [50], where the regularization parameter is selected based on the validation set, is used to match the the VGG representation with the sentence RNN-FV representation. In the shared CCA space, the cosine similarity is used in order to score (image, sentence) pairs.

We explored several configurations for training the RNN. **RNN training data** We employed either the training data of each split in the respective benchmark, or the 2010-English-Wikipedia-1M dataset made available by the Leipzig

Table 1. Pooling technique comparison: mean-pooling (MP), GMM-FV, RNN-FV, and their combinations with Temporal-Pyramid-Pooling (TPP), as evaluated on HMDB51 and UCF101 datasets. Three types of sequential features are used: VGG-PCA, VGG-CCA, and C3D. Additionally, a combination of descriptors (C3D + VGG) is evaluated, including a combination with idt GMM-FV [49]. All combinations are performed with early fusion. The table reports recognition average accuracy (higher is better).

HMDB51						
Method	MP	MP+TPP	GMM-FV	GMM-FV+TPP	RNN-FV	RNN-FV+TPP
VGG-PCA	42.16	46.14	36.8	38.54	45.62	47.38
VGG-CCA	43.05	47.19	39.61	41.5	46.14	46.01
C3D	51.2	54.01	45.82	48.54	52.88	53.51
C3D + VGG-CCA	37.1	56.23	50.19	52.16	54.33	55.77
C3D + VGG-CCA + idt	58.48	63.70	64.68	61.00	67.71	64.99
UCF101						
Method	MP	MP+TPP	GMM-FV	GMM-FV+TPP	RNN-FV	RNN-FV+TPP
VGG-PCA	75.51	77.34	76.53	77.12	79.29	81.56
VGG-CCA	77.49	78.68	76.84	77.95	79.49	80.83
C3D	81.05	81.72	80.04	80.10	82.33	82.81
C3D + VGG-CCA	65.55	87.85	86.73	87.11	88.01	88.09
C3D + VGG-CCA + idt	89.02	92.16	93.22	91.80	94.08	93.67

Corpora Collection [51]. This dataset contains 1 million sentences randomly sampled from English Wikipedia. **Word embedding** A word was represented either by word2vec, or by a "CCA word embedding" obtained as follows: (1) Each word was represented by the GMM+HGLMM FV representation of [8]. (2) These word representations were projected to the common image-sentence CCA space trained by [8] (on the respective dataset). (3) To reduce dimensionality, the first (i.e. the principal) 300 dimensions (out of 4096) of the mapped word representations were used. We made sure to match the training split according to the benchmark tested. **Sentence sequence direction** We explored both the conventional left-to-right sequence of words and the reverse direction.

We also explored using an RNN-FV which is based on a classifier RNN instead of a regressor. This design creates two challenges. The first is dimensionality: the size of the softmax layer equals the size of the dictionary, which is typically large. As a result, $\nabla_W \mathcal{L}(X)$ has a high dimensionality. The second issue is with generalization capability: since the softmax layer is fixed, a network cannot handle a sentence containing a word that does not appear in its training data. The RNN-FV regressor outperformed the RNN-FV classifier, and our experiments are reported without it.

6   Experiments

We evaluated the effectiveness of the various pooling methods on two important yet distinct application domains: action recognition and image textual annotation and search. As mentioned, applying the FIM normalization (Sect. 3.1) did not seem to improve results. Another form of normalization we have tried, is to normalize each dimension of the gradient by subtracting its mean and dividing by its standard deviation. This also did not lead to an improved performance. Two normalizations that were found to be useful are the Power Normalization and the L2 Normalization, which were introduced in [52]. Both are employed, using a constant $\alpha = 1/2$. In addition to the experimental details provided in this section, further technical details and comparisons with baselines are given in the supplementary material.

6.1 Action Recognition

Our experiments were conducted on two large action recognition benchmarks. The UCF101 [17] dataset consists of 13,320 realistic action videos, collected from YouTube, and divided into 101 action categories. We use the three splits provided with this dataset in order to evaluate our results and report the average accuracy over these splits. The HMDB51 dataset [16] consists of 6766 action videos, collected from various sources, and divided into 51 action categories. Three splits are provided as an official benchmark and are used here. The average accuracy over these splits is reported.

We compare the performance of the RNN-FV to the baselines of mean-pooling and GMM-FV when combined with Temporal-Pyramid-Pooling (TPP) in order to validate that it is able to better capture temporal ordering information, as shown in Table 1. Three sets of features, as described in Sect. 4.1, are used: VGG coupled with PCA, VGG projected by the image to sentence matching CCA, and C3D.

As can be seen in Table 1, the RNN-FV pooling outperformed the other pooling methods by a sizable margin. Another interesting observation is that with VGG frame representation, CCA outperformed PCA consistently in all pooling methods. Not shown is the performance obtained when using the activations of the RNN as a feature vector. These results are considerably worse than all pooling methods. Notice that the representation dimension of Mean pooling is 500 (like the features we used), the GMM-FV dimension is $2 \times k \times 500$, where k is the number of clusters in the GMM (this parameter was chosen according to performance on a validation set) and the RNN-FV dimension is 1000.

Table 2 compares our proposed RNN-FV method, combining multiple features together, with recently published methods on both datasets. The combinations were performed using early fusion, i.e., we concatenated the normalized low-dimensional gradients of the models and train multi-class linear SVM on the combined representation. We also tested the combination of our two best models with idt [49] and got state of the art results on both benchmarks. Interestingly, comparable results were obtained even when training the RNN on one dataset and testing on the other, proving that our RNN-FV representation is generic and not dataset specific.

844   G. Lev et al.

Table 2. comparison to the state of the art on UCF101 and HMDB51. In order to obtain the best performance, we combine, similar to all other contributions, multiple features. We also present a result where idt [49] is combined, similar to all other top results (Multi-skip extends idt). This adds motion based information to our method.

Method	HMDB51	UCF101
idt [49]	57.2	85.9
idt + high-D encodings [53]	61.1	87.9
Two-stream CNN (2 nets) [28]	59.4	88
Multi-skip Feature Stacking [54]	65.4	89.1
C3D (1 net) [14]	–	82.3
C3D (3 nets) [14]	–	85.2
C3D (3 nets) + idt [14]	–	90.4
TDD (2 nets) [5]	63.2	90.3
TDD (2 nets) + idt [5]	65.9	91.5
stacked FV [2]	56.21	–
stacked FV + idt [2]	66.78	–
RNN-FV(C3D + VGG-CCA)	54.33	88.01
RNN-FV(C3D + VGG-CCA) + idt	**67.71**	**94.08**

6.2 Image-Sentence Retrieval

The effectiveness of RNN-FV as sentence representation is evaluated on the bidirectional image and sentence retrieval task. We perform our experiments on three benchmarks: Flickr8K [18], Flickr30K [58], and COCO [48]. The datasets contain $8,000$, $30,000$, and $123,000$ images respectively. Each image is accompanied by 5 sentences describing the image content, collected via crowdsourcing.

The Flickr8k dataset is provided with training, validation, and test splits. For Flickr30K and COCO, no training splits are given, and the splits by [8] are used. There are three tasks in this benchmark: image annotation, in which the goal is to retrieve, given a query image, the five ground truth sentences; image search, in which, given a query sentence, the goal is to retrieve the ground truth image; and sentence similarity, in which the goal is, given a sentence, to retrieve the other four sentences describing the same image. Evaluation is performed using Recall@K, namely the fraction of times that the correct result was ranked within the top K items. The median and mean rank of the first ground truth result are also reported. For the sentence similarity task, only the mean rank is reported.

As mentioned in Sect. 5, we explored RNN-FV based on several RNNs. The first RNN is a generic one: it was trained with the Wikipedia sentences as training data and word2vec as word embedding. In addition, for each of the three datasets, we trained three RNNs with the dataset's training sentences as training data: one with word2vec as word embedding; one with the "CCA word embedding" derived from the semantic vector space of [8], as explained in Sect. 5; and one with

Table 3. Image annotation, image search and sentence similarity results on the Flickr8k, Flickr30k and COCO datasets. Shown are the recall rates at 1, 5, and 10 retrieval results (higher is better). Also shown are the median and mean rank of the first ground truth (lower is better). We compare the results of the previous work to variants of our RNN-FV. The 'wiki' notation indicates that the RNN was trained on Wikipedia and not on the sentences of the specific dataset. Models notated by 'w2v' employ word2vec, while the other models ('cca') use the CCA word embedding (as explained in Sect. 5). 'rvrs' models were trained on reversed sentences. We also report results of combinations: 'cca' and 'reverse' models; 'cca' and the best model (GMM+HGLMM) of [8] ('MM-ENS'); 'cca', 'reverse' and [8]; All RNN-FV models; All RNN-FV models and [8]. The RTP method [57] utilizes additional information that is not accessible to the other methods: manual annotations of bounding boxes in the images, which were collected via crowdsourcing.

| | | Image Annotation | | | | | Image Search | | | | | Sentence |
		r@1	r@5	r@10	median rank	mean rank	r@1	r@5	r@10	median rank	mean rank	mean rank
Flickr8k Previous	SDT-RNN [33]	6.0	22.7	34.0	23.0	NA	6.6	21.6	31.7	25.0	NA	NA
	DFE [35]	12.6	32.9	44.0	14.0	NA	9.7	29.6	42.5	15.0	NA	NA
	RVP [38]	11.7	34.8	48.6	11.2	NA	11.4	32.0	46.2	11.0	NA	NA
	DVSA [39]	16.5	40.6	54.2	7.6	NA	11.8	32.1	44.7	12.4	NA	NA
	SC-NLM [37]	18.0	40.9	55.0	8.0	NA	12.5	37.0	51.5	10.0	NA	NA
	DCCA [34]	17.9	40.3	51.9	9.0	NA	12.7	31.2	44.1	13.0	NA	NA
	NIC [40]	20.0	NA	61.0	6.0	NA	19.0	NA	64.0	5.0	NA	NA
	m-RNN [55]	14.5	37.2	48.5	11.0	NA	11.5	31.0	42.4	15.0	NA	NA
	m-CNN [41]	24.8	53.7	67.1	5.0	NA	20.3	47.6	61.7	5.0	NA	NA
	MeanVector [8]	22.6	48.8	61.2	6.0	28.7	19.1	45.3	60.4	7.0	27.0	12.5
	GMM-FV [8]	28.4	57.7	70.1	4.0	20.1	20.6	48.6	64.2	6.0	21.8	10.8
	MM-ENS [8]	31.0	59.3	73.7	4.0	18.4	21.3	50.1	64.8	5.0	21.0	10.5
Flickr8K Ours	wiki,w2v	29.3	57.8	70.8	4.0	21.4	19.8	48.5	62.9	6.0	25.2	10.0
	w2v	27.4	57.9	70.5	4.0	22.7	20.4	49.1	63.4	6.0	25.5	10.4
	cca	30.9	60.1	73.1	4.0	19.4	20.7	48.7	63.8	6.0	29.2	11.3
	cca,rvrs	29.1	57.3	71.7	4.0	18.4	20.8	48.5	62.9	6.0	30.2	12.5
	cca + rvrs	30.8	59.8	72.9	4.0	18.2	21.8	49.6	64.4	6.0	27.3	11.2
	cca + [8]	**32.9**	**61.7**	**74.9**	3.0	16.8	22.0	51.5	66.5	5.0	20.7	9.4
	cca + rvrs + [8]	32.1	60.7	74.8	3.0	**16.5**	22.1	51.4	66.5	5.0	21.4	9.5
	all rnn-fv models	29.9	60.7	73.4	4.0	17.9	22.4	52.7	67.2	5.0	20.9	8.7
	all rnn-fv models + [8]	31.6	61.2	74.3	3.0	17.4	**23.2**	**53.3**	**67.8**	5.0	**19.4**	**8.5**
Flickr30k Previous	SDT-RNN [33]	9.6	29.8	41.1	16.0	NA	8.9	29.8	41.1	16.0	NA	NA
	DFE [35]	14.2	37.7	51.3	10.0	NA	10.2	30.8	44.2	14.0	NA	NA
	RVP [38]	12.1	27.8	47.8	11.0	NA	12.7	33.1	44.9	12.5	NA	NA
	DVSA [39]	22.2	48.2	61.4	4.8	NA	15.2	37.7	50.5	9.2	NA	NA
	SC-NLM [37]	23.0	50.7	62.9	5.0	NA	16.8	42.0	56.5	8.0	NA	NA
	DCCA [34]	16.7	39.3	52.9	8.0	NA	12.6	31.0	43.0	15.0	NA	NA
	NIC [40]	17.0	NA	56.0	7.0	NA	17.0	NA	57.0	7.0	NA	NA
	LRCN [56]	NA	NA	NA	NA	NA	17.5	40.3	50.8	9.0	NA	NA
	RTP [57](manual annotations)	37.4	63.1	74.3	NA	NA	26.0	56.0	69.3	NA	NA	NA
	m-RNN [55]	35.4	63.8	73.7	3.0	NA	22.8	50.7	63.1	5.0	NA	NA
	m-CNN [41]	33.6	64.1	74.9	3.0	NA	26.2	56.3	69.6	4.0	NA	NA
	MeanVector [8]	24.9	52.5	64.4	5.0	27.3	20.5	46.4	59.3	6.8	32.3	16.2
	GMM-FV [8]	33.0	60.8	72.0	3.0	19.0	23.9	51.7	64.9	5.0	24.8	15.0
	MM-ENS [8]	35.0	62.1	73.8	3.0	17.4	25.1	52.8	66.1	5.0	23.7	14.1
Flickr30k Ours	wiki,w2v	32.9	59.6	72.1	3.0	18.5	23.9	52.0	65.2	5.0	26.0	15.2
	w2v	32.0	59.5	71.4	3.0	17.2	23.4	51.7	65.2	5.0	24.5	14.1
	cca	33.6	60.5	73.0	3.0	15.7	24.5	52.5	66.3	5.0	27.7	16.9
	cca,rvrs	32.8	61.9	72.7	3.0	17.4	24.4	51.2	64.6	5.0	28.9	16.1
	cca + rvrs	33.6	62.4	73.4	3.0	15.5	25.0	53.6	66.9	5.0	26.2	15.5
	cca + [8]	35.1	63.3	74.2	3.0	15.3	26.4	54.9	68.6	4.0	21.7	13.4
	cca + rvrs + [8]	35.1	63.5	74.5	3.0	**15.0**	26.5	55.2	68.5	4.0	22.0	13.5
	all rnn-fv models	34.7	62.7	72.6	3.0	15.6	26.2	55.1	69.2	4.0	21.2	12.8
	all rnn-fv models + [8]	35.6	62.5	74.2	3.0	**15.0**	**27.4**	55.9	**70.0**	4.0	**20.0**	**12.2**
COCO Previous	DVSA [39]	38.4	69.9	80.5	1.0	NA	27.4	60.2	74.8	3.0	NA	NA
	m-RNN [55]	41.0	73.0	83.5	2.0	NA	29.0	42.2	77.0	3.0	NA	NA
	m-CNN [41]	**42.8**	73.1	84.1	2.0	NA	**32.6**	**68.6**	**82.8**	3.0	NA	NA
	STV [12]	33.8	67.7	82.1	3.0	NA	25.9	60.0	74.6	4.0	NA	NA
	MeanVector [8]	33.2	61.8	75.1	3.0	14.5	24.2	56.4	72.4	4.0	14.7	14.3
	GMM-FV [8]	39.0	67.0	80.3	2.0	11.2	24.2	59.3	76.0	4.0	11.3	12.4
	MM-ENS [8]	39.4	67.9	80.9	2.0	10.4	25.2	59.9	76.7	4.0	11.0	12.9
COCO Ours	wiki,w2v	37.7	70.5	81.0	2.0	9.9	26.6	61.1	76.9	4.0	10.9	11.9
	w2v	39.9	71.5	81.3	2.0	10.5	26.9	61.8	77.4	4.0	11.4	12.1
	cca	40.9	**75.0**	**84.9**	2.0	8.2	30.2	65.0	80.4	3.0	11.1	13.2
	cca,rvrs	41.3	71.5	83.7	2.0	**8.1**	28.9	64.5	79.9	3.0	11.3	12.6
	cca + rvrs	40.8	73.4	84.1	2.0	8.2	30.4	65.5	80.9	3.0	10.7	12.3
	cca + [8]	40.7	72.3	83.5	2.0	9.1	28.1	64.1	79.8	3.0	10.2	11.5
	cca + rvrs + [8]	40.2	72.7	84.2	2.0	8.6	29.0	64.8	80.2	3.0	10.1	11.5
	all rnn-fv models	40.8	71.9	83.2	2.0	8.9	29.6	64.8	80.5	3.0	9.7	10.6
	all rnn-fv models + [8]	41.5	72.0	82.9	2.0	9.0	29.2	64.7	80.4	3.0	**9.5**	10.2

the CCA word embedding, and with feeding the sentences in reverse order. The
RNN is using an LSTM layer of size 100. We did not observe a benefit in using
more LSTM units. We used the part of the gradient corresponding to all 30,300
weights of the output layer (including one bias per word-embedding dimension).
In the case of the larger COCO dataset, due to the computational burden of the
CCA calculation, we used PCA to reduce the gradient dimension from 30,300 to
20,000. PCA was calculated on a random subset of 300,000 sentences (around
50 %) of the training set. We also tried PCA dimension reduction to a lower
dimension of 4,096, for all three datasets. We observed no change in performance
(Flickr8K) or slightly worse results (Flickr30K and COCO).

Table 3 shows the results of the different RNN-FV variants compared to the
baselines and to the current state of the art methods. The baselines, Mean Vector
and GMM-FV, appear in the table as previous work of [8]. We also report results
of combinations of models. Combining was done by averaging the image-sentence
(or sentence-sentence) cosine similarities obtained by each model.

First, we notice the competitive performance of the model trained on
Wikipedia sentences, which demonstrates the generalization power of the RNN-
FV, being able to perform well on data different than the one which the RNN
was trained on. Training using the dataset's sentences only slightly improves
results, and not always. Improved results are obtained when using the CCA
word embedding instead of word2vec. It is interesting to see the result of the
"reverse" model, which is on a par with the other models. It is somewhat complementary to the "left-to-right" model, as the combination of the two yields somewhat improved results. Finally, the combination of RNN-FV with the best model
(GMM+HGLMM) of [8] outperforms the current state of the art on Flickr8k,
and is competitive on the other datasets.

7   Conclusions

This paper introduces a novel FV representation for sequences that is derived
from RNNs. The proposed representation is sensitive to the element ordering in
the sequence and provides a richer model than the additive "bag" model typically
used for conventional FVs.

The RNN-FV representation surpasses the state-of-the-art results for video
action recognition on two challenging datasets. When used for representing
sentences, the RNN-FV representation achieves state-of-the-art or competitive
results on image annotation and image search tasks. Since the length of the sentences in these tasks is usually short and, therefore, the ordering is less crucial,
we believe that using the RNN-FV representation for tasks that use longer text
will provide an even larger gap between the conventional FV and the RNN-FV.

A transfer learning result from the image annotation task to the video
action recognition task was shown. The conceptual distance between these two
tasks makes this result both interesting and surprising. It supports a human
development-like way of training, in which visual labeling is learned through
natural language, as opposed to, e.g., associating bounding boxes with nouns.

While such training was used in computer vision to learn related image to text tasks, and while recently zero-shot action recognition was shown [59,60], NLP to video action recognition transfer was never shown to be as general as presented here.

Acknowledgments. This research is supported by the Intel Collaborative Research Institute for Computational Intelligence (ICRI-CI).

References

1. Simonyan, K., Parkhi, O.M., Vedaldi, A., Zisserman, A.: Fisher vector faces in the wild. In: Proceedings BMVC, vol. 1. 7 (2013)
2. Peng, X., Zou, C., Qiao, Y., Peng, Q.: Action recognition with stacked fisher vectors. In: Fleet, D., Pajdla, T., Schiele, B., Tuytelaars, T. (eds.) ECCV 2014. LNCS, vol. 8693, pp. 581–595. Springer, Heidelberg (2014). doi:10.1007/978-3-319-10602-1_38
3. Chatfield, K., Lempitsky, V., Vedaldi, A., Zisserman, A.: The devil is in the details: an evaluation of recent feature encoding methods. In: British Machine Vision Conference (2011)
4. Perronnin, F., Liu, Y., Sánchez, J., Poirier, H.: Large-scale image retrieval with compressed fisher vectors. In: 2010 IEEE Conference on Computer Vision and Pattern Recognition (CVPR), pp. 3384–3391. IEEE (2010)
5. Wang, L., Qiao, Y., Tang, X.: Action recognition with trajectory-pooled deep-convolutional descriptors. arXiv preprint (2015). arXiv:1505.04868
6. Mikolov, T., Sutskever, I., Chen, K., Corrado, G.S., Dean, J.: Distributed representations of words and phrases and their compositionality. Adv. Neural Inf. Process. Syst. **28**, 3111–3119 (2013)
7. Lev, G., Klein, B., Wolf, L.: In defense of word embedding for generic text representation. In: Biemann, C., Handschuh, S., Freitas, A., Meziane, F., Métais, E. (eds.) NLDB 2015. LNCS, vol. 9103, pp. 35–50. Springer, Heidelberg (2015). doi:10.1007/978-3-319-19581-0_3
8. Klein, B., Lev, G., Sadeh, G., Wolf, L.: Associating neural word embeddings with deep image representations using fisher vectors. In: Proceedings of the IEEE Conference on Computer Vision and Pattern Recognition, pp. 4437–4446 (2015)
9. Sutskever, I., Vinyals, O., Le, Q.V.: Sequence to sequence learning with neural networks. In: Advances in Neural Information Processing Systems, pp. 3104–3112 (2014)
10. Bahdanau, D., Cho, K., Bengio, Y.: Neural machine translation by jointly learning to align and translate. arXiv preprint (2014). arXiv:1409.0473
11. Palangi, H., Deng, L., Shen, Y., Gao, J., He, X., Chen, J., Song, X., Ward, R.: Deep sentence embedding using the long short term memory network: Analysis and application to information retrieval. arXiv preprint (2015). arXiv:1502.06922
12. Kiros, R., Zhu, Y., Salakhutdinov, R., Zemel, R.S., Torralba, A., Urtasun, R., Fidler, S.: Skip-thought vectors. arXiv preprint (2015). arXiv:1506.06726
13. Simonyan, K., Zisserman, A.: Very deep convolutional networks for large-scale image recognition. CoRR abs/1409.1556 (2014)
14. Tran, D., Bourdev, L., Fergus, R., Torresani, L., Paluri, M.: Learning spatiotemporal features with 3d convolutional networks. arXiv preprint (2014). arXiv:1412.0767

15. Hotelling, H.: Relations between two sets of variates. Biometrika **17**, 321–377 (1936)
16. Kuehne, H., Jhuang, H., Garrote, E., Poggio, T., Serre, T.: HMDB: a large video database for human motion recognition. In: Proceedings IEEE International Conference on Computer Vision (2011)
17. Soomro, K., Zamir, A.R., Shah, M.: UCF101: A dataset of 101 human action classes from videos in the wild. In: CRCV-TR-12-01, November 2012
18. Hodosh, M., Young, P., Hockenmaier, J.: Framing image description as a ranking task: Data, models and evaluation metrics. J. Artif. Intell. Res. (JAIR) **47**, 853–899 (2013)
19. Laptev, I., Marszalek, M., Schmid, C., Rozenfeld, B.: Learning realistic human actions from movies. In: Proceedings IEEE Conference on Computer Vision Pattern Recognition, pp. 1–8 (2008)
20. Wang, H., Klaser, A., Schmid, C., Liu, C.: Action recognition by dense trajectories. In: Proceedings IEEE Conference on Computer Vision Pattern Recognition, pp. 3169–3176 (2011)
21. Kliper-Gross, O., Gurovich, Y., Hassner, T., Wolf, L.: Motion interchange patterns for action recognition in unconstrained videos. In: Fitzgibbon, A., Lazebnik, S., Perona, P., Sato, Y., Schmid, C. (eds.) ECCV 2012. LNCS, vol. 7577, pp. 256–269. Springer, Heidelberg (2012). doi:10.1007/978-3-642-33783-3_19
22. Laptev, I.: On space-time interest points. Int. J. Comput. Vis. **64**(2), 107–123 (2005)
23. Wang, H., Schmid, C.: Action Recognition with improved trajectories. In: International Conference on Computer Vision, October 2013
24. Wang, H., Kläser, A., Schmid, C., Liu, C.L.: Dense trajectories and motion boundary descriptors for action recognition. Int. J. Comput. Vis. **103**(1), 60–79 (2013)
25. Taylor, G.W., Fergus, R., LeCun, Y., Bregler, C.: Convolutional learning of spatio-temporal features. In: Daniilidis, K., Maragos, P., Paragios, N. (eds.) ECCV 2010. LNCS, vol. 6316, pp. 140–153. Springer, Heidelberg (2010). doi:10.1007/978-3-642-15567-3_11
26. Ji, S., Xu, W., Yang, M., Yu, K.: 3d convolutional neural networks for human action recognition. Pattern Anal. Mach. Intell. IEEE Trans. **35**(1), 221–231 (2013)
27. Karpathy, A., Toderici, G., Shetty, S., Leung, T., Sukthankar, R., Fei-Fei, L.: Large-scale video classification with convolutional neural networks. In: 2014 IEEE Conference on Computer Vision and Pattern Recognition (CVPR), pp. 1725–1732. IEEE (2014)
28. Simonyan, K., Zisserman, A.: Two-stream convolutional networks for action recognition in videos. Adv. Neural Inf. Process. Syst. **25**, 568–576 (2014)
29. Wang, X., Wang, L.M., Qiao, Y.: A comparative study of encoding, pooling and normalization methods for action recognition. In: Lee, K.M., Matsushita, Y., Rehg, J.M., Hu, Z. (eds.) ACCV 2012. LNCS, vol. 7726, pp. 572–585. Springer, Heidelberg (2013). doi:10.1007/978-3-642-37431-9_44
30. Chatfield, K., Simonyan, K., Vedaldi, A., Zisserman, A.: Return of the devil in the details: Delving deep into convolutional nets. arXiv preprint (2014). arXiv:1405.3531
31. Fernando, B., Gavves, E., Oramas, J.M., Ghodrati, A., Tuytelaars, T.: Modeling video evolution for action recognition. In: Proceedings of the IEEE Conference on Computer Vision and Pattern Recognition, pp. 5378–5387 (2015)
32. Nagel, M., Mensink, T., Snoek, C.G.: Event fisher vectors: robust encoding visual diversity of visual streams. Identity **27**(27.2), 22–28 (2015)

33. Socher, R., Le, Q., Manning, C., Ng, A.: Grounded compositional semantics for finding and describing images with sentences. In: NIPS Deep Learning Workshop (2013)

34. Mikolajczyk, F.Y.K.: Deep correlation for matching images and text (2015)

35. Karpathy, A., Joulin, A., Fei-Fei, L.: Deep fragment embeddings for bidirectional image sentence mapping. arXiv preprint (2014). arXiv:1406.5679

36. Mao, J., Xu, W., Yang, Y., Wang, J., Yuille, A.: Deep captioning with multimodal recurrent neural networks (m-rnn). arXiv preprint (2014). arXiv:1412.6632

37. Kiros, R., Salakhutdinov, R., Zemel, R.S.: Unifying visual-semantic embeddings with multimodal neural language models. Trans. Assoc. Comput. Linguist. 2(10), 351–362 (2015)

38. Chen, X., Zitnick, C.L.: Learning a recurrent visual representation for image caption generation. arXiv preprint (2014). arXiv:1411.5654

39. Karpathy, A., Fei-Fei, L.: Deep visual-semantic alignments for generating image descriptions. Technical report, Computer Science Department, Stanford University (2014)

40. Vinyals, O., Toshev, A., Bengio, S., Erhan, D.: Show and tell: A neural image caption generator. arXiv preprint (2014). arXiv:1411.4555

41. Ma, L., Lu, Z., Shang, L., Li, H.: Multimodal convolutional neural networks for matching image and sentence. arXiv preprint (2015). arXiv:1504.06063

42. Hochreiter, S., Schmidhuber, J.: Long short-term memory. Neural Comput. 9(8), 1735–1780 (1997)

43. Chung, J., Gulcehre, C., Cho, K., Bengio, Y.: Empirical evaluation of gated recurrent neural networks on sequence modeling. arXiv preprint (2014). arXiv:1412.3555

44. Gordo, A., Gaidon, A., Perronnin, F.: Deep fishing: Gradient features from deep nets. In: Proceedings of the British Machine Vision Conference 2015, BMVC 2015, Swansea, UK, September 7–10, 2015, pp. 111.1–111.12 (2015)

45. Arandjelovic, R., Gronat, P., Torii, A., Pajdla, T., Sivic, J.: Netvlad: Cnn architecture for weakly supervised place recognition. In: The IEEE Conference on Computer Vision and Pattern Recognition (CVPR), June 2016

46. Lin, T.Y., RoyChowdhury, A., Maji, S.: Bilinear cnn models for fine-grained visual recognition. In: Proceedings of the IEEE International Conference on Computer Vision, pp. 1449–1457 (2015)

47. Perronnin, F., Dance, C.: Fisher kernels on visual vocabularies for image categorization. In: IEEE Conference on Computer Vision and Pattern Recognition, CVPR 2007. pp. 1–8. IEEE (2007)

48. Lin, T.-Y., Maire, M., Belongie, S., Hays, J., Perona, P., Ramanan, D., Dollár, P., Zitnick, C.L.: Microsoft COCO: common objects in context. In: Fleet, D., Pajdla, T., Schiele, B., Tuytelaars, T. (eds.) ECCV 2014. LNCS, vol. 8693, pp. 740–755. Springer, Heidelberg (2014). doi:10.1007/978-3-319-10602-1_48

49. Wang, H., Schmid, C.: Action recognition with improved trajectories. In: 2013 IEEE International Conference on Computer Vision (ICCV), pp. 3551–3558. IEEE (2013)

50. Vinod, H.: Canonical ridge and econometrics of joint production. J. Econometrics 4(2), 147–166 (1976)

51. Quasthoff, U., Richter, M., Biemann, C.: Corpus portal for search in monolingual corpora. In: Proceedings of the Fifth International Conference on Language Resources and Evaluation, vol. 17991802 (2006)

52. Perronnin, F., Sánchez, J., Mensink, T.: Improving the fisher kernel for large-scale image classification. In: Daniilidis, K., Maragos, P., Paragios, N. (eds.) ECCV 2010. LNCS, vol. 6314, pp. 143–156. Springer, Heidelberg (2010). doi:10.1007/978-3-642-15561-1_11

53. Peng, X., Wang, L., Wang, X., Qiao, Y.: Bag of visual words and fusion methods for action recognition: Comprehensive study and good practice. arXiv preprint (2014). arXiv:1405.4506

54. Lan, Z., Lin, M., Li, X., Hauptmann, A.G., Raj, B.: Beyond gaussian pyramid: Multi-skip feature stacking for action recognition. arXiv preprint (2014). arXiv:1411.6660

55. Mao, J., Xu, W., Yang, Y., Wang, J., Yuille, A.L.: Explain images with multimodal recurrent neural networks. arXiv preprint (2014). arXiv:1410.1090

56. Donahue, J., Hendricks, L.A., Guadarrama, S., Rohrbach, M., Venugopalan, S., Saenko, K., Darrell, T.: Long-term recurrent convolutional networks for visual recognition and description. arXiv preprint (2014). arXiv:1411.4389

57. Plummer, B.A., Wang, L., Cervantes, C.M., Caicedo, J.C., Hockenmaier, J., Lazebnik, S.: Flickr30k entities: Collecting region-to-phrase correspondences for richer image-to-sentence models. In: Proceedings of the IEEE International Conference on Computer Vision, pp. 2641–2649 (2015)

58. Hodosh, P., Hockenmaier, J.: From image descriptions to visual denotations: New similarity metrics for semantic inference over event descriptions. Trans. Assoc. Comput. Linguist. 2, 67–78 (2014)

59. Jain, M., van Gemert, J.C., Mensink, T., Snoek, C.G.M.: Objects2action: classifying and localizing actions without any video example. In: Proceedings of the IEEE International Conference on Computer Vision, Santiago, Chile, December 2015

60. Xu, X., Hospedales, T.M., Gong, S.: Semantic embedding space for zero-shot action recognition. CoRR abs/1502.01540 (2015)

CDT: Cooperative Detection and Tracking for Tracing Multiple Objects in Video Sequences

Han-Ul Kim$^{(\boxtimes)}$ and Chang-Su Kim

School of Electrical Engineering, Korea University, Seoul, South Korea
hanulkim@mcl.korea.ac.kr, changsukim@korea.ac.kr

Abstract. A cooperative detection and model-free tracking algorithm, referred to as CDT, for multiple object tracking is proposed in this work. The proposed CDT algorithm has three components: object detector, forward tracker, and backward tracker. First, the object detector detects targets with high confidence levels only to reduce spurious detection and achieve a high precision rate. Then, each detected target is traced by the forward tracker and then by the backward tracker to restore undetected states. In the tracking processes, the object detector cooperates with the trackers to handle appearing or disappearing targets and to refine inaccurate state estimates. With this detection guidance, the model-free tracking can trace multiple objects reliably and accurately. Experimental results show that the proposed CDT algorithm provides excellent performance on a recent benchmark. Furthermore, an online version of the proposed algorithm also excels in the benchmark.

Keywords: Joint detection and tracking · Multiple object tracking · Object detection · Model-free tracking · Online multi-object tracking

1 Introduction

The objective of multiple object tracking (MOT) is to estimate the states (or bounding boxes) of as many objects as possible in a video sequence and trace them temporally. Especially, tracking specific objects, such as pedestrians and cars, has drawn attention for its various applications, including surveillance systems and self-driving cars. For this purpose, many tracking-by-detection algorithms [1–19] have been proposed to yield promising performance. The tracking-by-detection approach decomposes MOT into two subproblems: object detection and data association. It first detects objects in each frame and then links the detection results to form trajectories across frames. With the recent success of object detection techniques [20–23], this approach has several advantages over model-free tracking, which does not assume a specific object and instead traces the bounding box of an arbitrary object, manually annotated in the first frame. Specifically, the tracking-by-detection approach is more robust against object appearance variation and model drift, and it can identify emerging or disappearing objects in a video sequence more easily.

© Springer International Publishing AG 2016
B. Leibe et al. (Eds.): ECCV 2016, Part VI, LNCS 9910, pp. 851–867, 2016.
DOI: 10.1007/978-3-319-46466-4_51

MOT, however, still remains a challenging problem in case of crowded or cluttered scenes. A complicated scene causes more detection failures, which are either undetected objects (false negatives) or spurious detection (false positives). The poor detection, in turn, decreases the accuracy of data association. To compensate for detection failures, many MOT algorithms [1–12,14] focus on the global data association. Given detection results in all frames, they design a cost function to formulate the data association as an optimization problem and then determine optimal trajectories by minimizing the cost function. By considering detection results in all frames simultaneously, they can alleviate adverse effects of detection failures. Notice that an alternative approach for achieving accurate MOT is to improve the quality of object detection directly. But, contrary to the data association that has been investigated intensively, relatively little efforts have been made for this straightforward approach in the MOT community.

In this work, we attempt to improve the detection quality, by combining an object detector with a model-free tracker. We first collect detection results with high confidence levels only to decrease the number of false positives. However, there is a trade-off between precision and recall, and reducing false positives increases undetected objects. To restore the undetected objects, we conduct model-free tracking in the forward and backward directions sequentially. In general, a model-free tracker and an object detector have different strengths and weaknesses. For instance, a model-free tracker can temporally trace missing states of a target object from its initial state, but it is vulnerable to model drift and may fail to identify the appearance or disappearance of a target reliably, which can be easily handled by an object detector. Therefore, we propose the cooperative detection and tracking (CDT) algorithm, in which an object detector and a model-free tracker cooperate to complement each other. Specifically, the detector initiates the tracker, by providing initial states of targets, and informs of the termination conditions for the tracking. Also, the detector is utilized to refine the tracking results. Experimental results demonstrate that the proposed CDT algorithm improves the quality of object detection and excels on a recent MOT benchmark [24]. Moreover, by omitting the backward tracking, the proposed algorithm can operate online.

The rest of this paper is organized as follows: Sect. 2 reviews related work. Section 3 presents the proposed CDT algorithm. Section 4 analyzes the performance of the proposed algorithm. Finally, Sect. 5 draws conclusions.

2   Related Work

2.1   Multiple Object Tracking

Many MOT algorithms, including [1–12], adopt global (or batch) data association techniques. Specifically, a batch of frames are taken as input, objects are detected in these frames, and the association among the detected results is formulated as the minimization of a cost function. Then, the optimal trajectories are determined to minimize the cost function. Some algorithms formulate the data association as a relatively simple problem, such as linear programming relaxation [1,7] and minimum-cost flow [3–5,11], for which the global minimum can be computed plausibly. Other algorithms consider more complicated problems to represent real world scenarios more faithfully, which are however too complex to find the global optimum. Thus, they instead find locally optimal solutions, by employing quadratic boolean programming [2], continuous or discrete-continuous energy minimization [9,12], generalized clique graph [8,10], and maximum weight-independent set [6].

Recently, Bae and Yoon [13] proposed the notion of tracklet confidence to handle fragmented trajectories and adopted online learning to discriminate target appearance during the data association. To reduce the dependency on erroneous detection results, Leal-Taixé et al. [14] proposed interaction feature strings, which encode pedestrians' interactions. Milan et al. [15] developed a unified framework of tracking and segmentation to exploit low-level image features more effectively. Xiang et al. [16] formulated the online MOT problem as decision making in a Markov decision process. Rezatofighi et al. [17] reformulated the joint probabilistic data association (JPDA) [25] technique to make it computationally tractable. Similarly, Kim et al. [18] revisited another classic solution, multiple hypothesis tracker (MHT) [26], and adopted an online discriminative appearance model using a deep convolutional neural network. Choi [19] introduced the aggregated local flow descriptor to encode the relative motion pattern between two objects and proposed a near-online MOT algorithm. Also, Wang et al. [27] proposed the target-specific metric learning to represent target appearance faithfully. Moreover, their algorithm utilizes a motion cue for accurate tracking and shows excellent results in the MOT benchmark [24].

2.2 Object Detection

Recently, deep convolutional neural networks have made impressive progress in object detection. Girshick et al. [20] proposed the R-CNN detector using a deep convolutional neural network to classify object proposals. To prevent the overfit due to a small dataset, they introduced a domain-specific fine-tuning method, improving the detection performance dramatically. To accelerate the processing speed of R-CNN, He et al. [21] presented the architecture to compute a convolutional feature map of an entire image prior to the spatial pyramid pooling. However, it cannot fine-tune the convolutional layers. Girshick [22] proposed the Fast R-CNN, which is an end-to-end trainable system with shared convolutional layers. In these detectors [20–22], separate region proposal methods [28–30] are required, which cause computational bottlenecks. To overcome this issue, Shaoqing [23] introduced the region proposal network to extract proposals from a convolutional feature map directly.

2.3 Model Free Tracking

For model-free tracking, we adopt a discriminative approach that uses a classifier to estimate targets states. Thus, we briefly review discriminative trackers only.

Avidan [31] used an offline-trained classifier to track a target, but the classifier may provide wrong results when an object changes its appearance. In [32,33], online learning techniques have been developed to adjust to variations in object appearance. These techniques, however, may update appearance models unreliably with falsely labeled samples. Grabner *et al.* [34] attempted to reduce the impacts of false labels, by training a classifier with labeled samples in the first frame and unlabeled samples in subsequent frames. Babenko *et al.* [35] adopted the multiple instance learning to deal with the ambiguity in the foreground labeling. Hare *et al.* [36] employed the structured support vector machine [37] to avoid a heuristic for assigning binary labels to samples. Henriques *et al.* [38] introduced a correlation filter to track an object and performed the filtering efficiently in the Fourier domain.

3   Proposed Algorithm

The proposed CDT algorithm consists of three components: object detector, forward tracker, and backward tracker. The first component detects targets in a video using a conventional detector [22]. It selects only the detection results with high scores to provide reliable information to the other components. The second component traces the detection results forwardly in the time domain to restore undetected states of the targets. To this end, we adopt a model-free tracker that is guided by the object detector. The third component conducts the backward tracking to recover more missing states and refine the target trajectories.

3.1   Object Detection

We adopt an end-to-end trainable object detector, called Fast R-CNN [22]. However, other detectors, *e.g.* [20,21,23], also can be used instead of Fast R-CNN.

Training: We employ the pre-trained Fast R-CNN detector with the VGG16 model [39], trained with the PASCAL VOC dataset. Since the MOT challenge dataset [24] is for pedestrian detection, we replace the softmax layer to consider only two classes (pedestrian or non-pedestrian). We use the selective search [29] to generate region proposals. To fine-tune the detector on the MOT challenge dataset, we adopt the mini-batch sampling in [22].

Detection: Given a video, we generate region proposals using [29]. Then, the detector measures the score for each proposal and chooses only the proposals whose scores are greater than a high threshold $\theta_{high} = 0.99$. A lot of objects remain undetected due to the high threshold θ_{high}. However, the impacts of undetected objects are less severe than those of false positives, since our CDT system includes a model-free tracker to trace temporally the states of a target object from its initial state. When a target is detected, we regard it as an initial state. Then, we can restore undetected target states by performing the model-free tracking. To summarize, since precision is more important than recall, we adopt the high threshold θ_{high} to provide reliable information to the tracker.

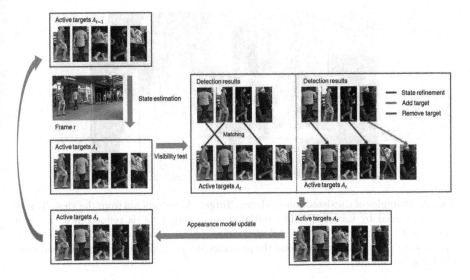

Fig. 1. Illustration of the forward tracking process.

3.2 Forward Tracking

As mentioned above, many target states remain undetected. To restore these missing states, we carry out model-free tracking forwardly in the time domain. During the tracking, the object detector cooperates with the model-free tracker to achieve accurate tracking. Figure 1 illustrates the forward tracking. Let $\mathcal{A}_t$ be the active target list to record detected target states and their appearance models in frame t. Given active targets in $\mathcal{A}_{t-1}$ in the previous frame $t-1$, the forward tracker estimates their states in the current frame t. Then, guided by the object detector, the tracker checks the visibility of each active target to remove disappearing or occluded targets. The detector also helps to improve the initial state estimation of the tracker. To this end, we perform the matching between tracked target states and detection results, and update a target state when its corresponding detection result is more reliable. Also, an unmatched detection result is regarded as a new target and added to the active target list $\mathcal{A}_t$. Finally, the appearance model of each active target is updated.

State Estimation: Let $\mathbf{x}_{i,t-1} = (\mathbf{c}, w, h) \in \mathcal{A}_{t-1}$ denote the state of the ith active target in frame $t-1$, where $\mathbf{c}$, w, and h are the location, width, and height of the target. Given the previous state $\mathbf{x}_{i,t-1}$, we estimate its current state $\mathbf{x}_{i,t}$ using a discriminative tracker and put it into the active target list $\mathcal{A}_t$. We set a square search region with center $\mathbf{c}$ and side length $\sqrt{wh}$. Then, we sample candidate states within the search region using the sliding window method. To describe the contents in each candidate $\mathbf{x}$, we encode it into a feature vector $\phi(\mathbf{x})$. Similarly to [40], the candidate window is decomposed into 64 non-overlapping

Fig. 2. Examples of the detection guidance. Target 'A' disappears from the view. Target 'B' is occluded by target 'C.' The initial state of target 'D' is refined into the cyan box. Target 'E' newly appears. All these disappearance, occlusion, refinement, and appearance cases are handled using the guidance information from the object detector. (Color figure online)

patches and each patch is described by a 24-dimensional RGB histogram and a 31-dimensional HOG histogram [41]. We then concatenate all patch features to construct $\phi(\mathbf{x})$. We determine the current state $\mathbf{x}_{i,t}$ to yield the highest score,

$$\mathbf{x}_{i,t} = \arg\max_{\mathbf{x}} \mathbf{w}_i^T \phi(\mathbf{x}) \qquad (1)$$

where $\mathbf{w}_i$ is the appearance model of the ith target.

Detection Guidance: During the tracking, the tracker is guided by the object detector. Let us consider target 'A' in Fig. 2, which is disappearing from the view. Note that the goal of object detection is to identify the existence of an object. Thus, we can easily handle the disappearing case by computing the detection score. Specifically, we check the detection score for each active target in $\mathcal{A}_t$ and remove targets, whose scores are lower than a threshold θ_{low}, from $\mathcal{A}_t$. The low threshold θ_{low} is fixed to 0.5, since we consider only two classes and a lower score than 0.5 indicates that the estimated state contains no pedestrian.

In Fig. 2, targets 'B' and 'C' illustrate an occlusion case, which also causes an invisible target. To find occlusion, we compute the intersection-over-union (IoU) overlap ratio between each pair of active targets. We declare that an occlusion case occurs, when the overlap ratio is larger than a threshold $\theta_{\text{iou}} = 0.3$. Then, we compare the detection scores of the two targets and determine that the target with a lower score is occluded. We exclude the occluded target from $\mathcal{A}_t$.

Another task of the detection guidance is to refine the initial estimation of the tracker for each active target. An object may experience scale variation. In this case, the tracker may provide an inaccurate result, since it does not consider scale variation in this work. To correct such inaccuracy, we utilize the detection results in Sect. 3.1. More specifically, we first determine which detection result should be used for the target state refinement. The matching cost $c(\mathbf{x}, \mathbf{z})$ between a target state $\mathbf{x}$ and a detection result $\mathbf{z}$ is defined as

$$c(\mathbf{x}, \mathbf{z}) = \begin{cases} \|\phi(\mathbf{x}) - \phi(\mathbf{z})\|^2 & \text{if } \Delta(\mathbf{x}, \mathbf{z}) \geq \theta_{\text{iou}}, \\ \infty & \text{otherwise,} \end{cases} \tag{2}$$

where $\Delta(\mathbf{x}, \mathbf{z})$ denotes the IoU overlap ratio. We determine the optimal matching between the initial tracking results and the detection results using the Hungarian algorithm [42]. For instance, target 'D' becomes closer to the camera in Fig. 2, in which the initial estimation of the tracker and the corresponding detection result are depicted by blue and cyan boxes, respectively. In this example, the detection result represents the target more faithfully. In general, given an initial target state and the matching detection result, we compare their detection scores. If the detection result yields a higher score, then it replaces the initial state. Finally, when a detection result is unmatched, e.g. target 'E' in Fig. 2, we regard it as a new target and insert it into the active target list $\mathcal{A}_t$.

Appearance Model Update: After determining the state of each target in $\mathcal{A}_t$, we update its appearance model. We model the target appearance using the structured support vector machine (SSVM) [36,37], which yields excellent performance in a recent model-free tracking benchmark [43]. To update the appearance model of the ith target, we sample 81 bounding boxes around the current object location and extract their feature vectors. SSVM constrains that the bounding box $\mathbf{x}_{i,t}$ should yield a larger score than a nearby box $\mathbf{x}$ by a margin, which decreases as the IoU overlap ratio between the two boxes increases. Specifically, the appearance model $\mathbf{w}_i$ is trained to minimize an objective function,

$$\mathbf{w}_i = \arg\min_{\mathbf{w}} \frac{1}{2}\|\mathbf{w}\|^2 + \beta \sum_{\mathbf{x}} \max\{0, (1 - \Delta(\mathbf{x}_{i,t}, \mathbf{x})) - \mathbf{w}^T(\phi(\mathbf{x}_{i,t}) - \phi(\mathbf{x}))\} \tag{3}$$

where β is 10. We use the LaRank algorithm [36,44] for the minimization.

3.3 Backward Tracking

Figure 3 illustrates the entire process of the proposed CDT algorithm. First, the object detector collects reliable detection results. Once an object is detected, it becomes an active target and the forward tracker estimates its missing states after the activation. Moreover, the detector cooperates with the tracker to improve the estimation. For example, in Fig. 3, the estimated states are replaced by the detection results at t_5 and t_7 to localize the target more accurately. The forward tracking stops when the target disappears due to occlusion or out-of-view. After the forward tracking, the states in $t_1 \sim t_2$ still remain undetected and should be estimated. Therefore, we further perform the backward tracking.

Suppose that the forward tracking starts at t_s and ends at t_{e+1}. Then, the backward tracking is activated at t_e. First, it refines the trajectory, obtained by the forward tracking, backwardly from t_e to t_s. Second, the backward tracking restores missing states backwardly from t_s until its termination.

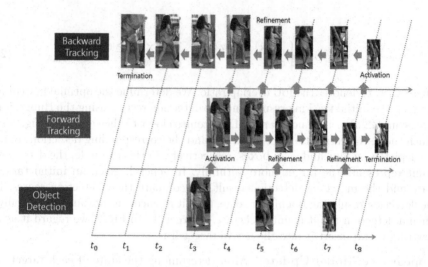

Fig. 3. Illustration of the target tracking. A pedestrian is first detected at t_3 and becomes an active target. From t_4, the forward tracker estimates its states. At t_5 and t_7, the tracker refines the estimated states using the detection results. The forward tracking terminates at t_8 due to the occlusion. Given the state at t_7, the backward tracker estimates new states at t_6 and t_5 to refine the trajectory. However, these states are rejected since the original states yield higher detection scores. On the contrary, a new state is accepted at t_4. Moreover, the backward tracking restores undetected states at t_2 and t_1, and then stops at t_0.

Existing State Refinement: Given the target state $\mathbf{x}_{i,t+1}$ in the subsequent frame $t + 1$, the backward tracker traces its state $\mathbf{x}_{i,t}$ in the current frame t. It compares the detection score of $\mathbf{x}_{i,t}$ with that of the forward tracking result. Then, the state with a higher score is selected as the final tracking result. In Fig. 3, the forward result is replaced by the backward result at t_4.

Missing State Restoration: The backward tracking process from t_s is identical with the forward tracking process in Sect. 3.2, but the temporal direction is reversed. Moreover, we check the IoU overlap ratio of the estimated state with the other active states, which are already estimated by the forward tracker, to prevent duplicated estimation. Specifically, we only accept an estimated state $\mathbf{x}_{i,t}$ and update its appearance model $\mathbf{w}_i$, when the maximum IoU overlap ratio between $\mathbf{x}_{i,t}$ and the other active states is smaller than θ_{iou}. Otherwise, we regard $\mathbf{x}_{i,t}$ as duplication and terminate its backward tracking.

4   Experimental Results

We assess the proposed CDT algorithm on the MOT challenge benchmark [24], which consists of 22 sequences with different view points, camera motions, and weather conditions. They are divided into 11 training sequences and 11 test sequences, and annotations are available for the training sequences only.

We use the F1-score to quantify the detection performance of the proposed algorithm, which is a harmonic mean between precision and recall. We also employ various evaluation metrics in the benchmark [24] to compare the proposed and conventional algorithms: the number of false positives (FP), the number of false negatives (FN), the number of ID switches (IDS), multiple object tracking accuracy (MOTA), multiple object tracking precision (MOTP), mostly tracked targets (MT), and mostly lost targets (ML).

4.1 Analysis on Validation Sequences

Unlike the training sequences, the annotations for the test sequences are not released. Therefore, as done in [16], we partition the 11 training sequences into two subsets 'training' and 'validation' to analyze the proposed algorithm. Table 1 lists the contents in each subset. We use the five 'training' sequences to fine-tune the object detector and the six 'validation' ones for the evaluation.

Figure 4(a) is the precision-recall curve of the object detector. In the proposed MOT system, the high detection threshold $\theta_{high} = 0.99$ is used to detect reliable objects only. Therefore, the operating point is selected from the high-precision, low-recall part of the curve, resulting in the F1-score of 0.549. In the forward tracking, the model-free tracker detects missing objects and increases the recall rate, at the cost of a relatively small reduction in the precision rate. Thus, after the forward tracking, the F1-score is increased to 0.623. Similarly, the backward tracking further improves the detection performance and the final F1-score becomes 0.646, which corresponds to 17.7 % improvement in comparison with the original F1-score. Figure 4(b) presents the F1-scores on each sequence after the object detection, the forward tracking, and the backward tracking. Each component of the proposed algorithm leads to better results on all sequences with no exception. As mentioned in Sect. 3.2, the tracker is guided by the detector in our CDT system. It is worth pointing out that the cooperation in the opposite direction is also carried out; the experimental results in Fig. 4 indicate that the detection performance itself is improved with the assistance of the tracker.

Table 1. Training and validation sequences for performance analysis.

Training	TUD-Stadtmitte, ETH-Bahnhof, ADL-Rundle-6, PETS09-S2L1, KITTI-13
Validation	TUD-Campus, ETH-Sunnyday, ETH-Pedcross2, ADL-Rundle-8, KITTI-17, Venice-2

Next, to quantify the performance gain achieved by each algorithmic part, Table 2 compares the MOT results using various settings. Settings 'A' and 'B' denote the results after the forward tracking: 'A' does not perform the state refinement using the detection guidance, while 'B' does. Setting 'C' and 'D' denote the results after the backward tracking: 'C' does not conduct the state

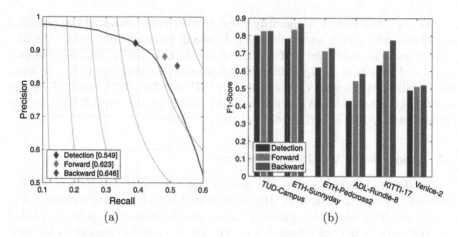

(a)   (b)

Fig. 4. (a) The precision-recall curve of the object detection. The blue diamond point is selected with the high threshold $\theta_{high} = 0.99$ by the object detector. Then, the detection performance is improved by the forward tracker and then by the backward tracker. A number within brackets is the F1-score after each component. (b) The F1-scores on each validation sequence after each component. (Color figure online)

Table 2. MOT results of the proposed CDT algorithm on the validation sequences with various settings. Settings 'A' and 'B' denote the results after the forward tracking, and settings 'C' and 'D' after the backward tracking. Settings 'A' and 'C' do not perform the state refinement, while settings 'B' and 'D' do.

Setting	MOTA↑	MOTP↑	MT↑	ML↓	FP↓	FN↓	IDS↓
A: Forward w/o	26.8	67.1	12.8	28.2	3,160	13,457	293
B: Forward	40.8	72.5	22.2	27.8	1,516	11,964	180
C: Backward w/o	42.1	72.1	32.1	26.5	2,119	11,072	184
D: Backward	42.4	72.2	32.5	26.5	2,077	11,050	178

refinement, while 'D' does. Comparing 'A' with 'B,' we see that the state refinement significantly increases the MOTA score by 14 points in the forward tracking. Notice that a refined state also helps to estimate the target states in subsequent frames. In other words, correcting a tracking error not only improves the state in the current frame but also prevents model-drift. Thus, it contributes to the extraction of a longer trajectory of a target, thereby increasing the MT score from 12.8 to 22.2. The comparison between 'C' and 'D' shows that the state refinement also improves the performance of the backward tracking. It improves the MOTA, MOTP, MT scores and reduces false positives, false negatives, ID switches. The comparison between 'B' and 'C' demonstrates the impacts of the state estimation in the backward tracking. It restores a lot of missing target states and improves the performance.

Fig. 5. Comparison of active targets after (a) the object detection, (b) the forward tracking, and (c) the backward tracking. From top to bottom, the sequences "ADL-Rundle-8," "ETH-Pedcross2," "ETH-Sunnyday," "KITTI-17," and "Venice-2" are used.

Figures 5(a), (b), and (c) compare active targets after the object detection, the forward tracking, and the backward tracking, respectively. The number of states, provided by the object detector, is relatively small, but it is increased by the forward tracker and then by the backward tracker. For instance, the object with ID 19 in "ADL-Rundle-8" is missing in the detection stage. However, it is already active in the previous frame and its state is accurately estimated by the forward tracker. Similarly, the object with ID 22 in "ADL-Rundle-8" is restored by the backward tracker. The results on the other sequences also confirm that the forward and backward trackers restore missing states effectively.

4.2   Additional Tests on Validation Sequences

Table 3 shows the results of the proposed algorithm on the validation sequences with different object proposal methods. SS denotes the default mode, in which the detector uses the selective search [29] to generate proposals. On the other hand, ACF indicates that it employs the published detection results in the benchmark [24] as proposals. It can be observed that, even when we use the published detection results, the proposed algorithm provides similar performance. Compared with SS, ACF [45] provides more reliable results for small scale objects and improves the performance on the "Venice-2" sequence. In contrast, SS is more effective on the "ETH-Pedcross2" sequence, where ACF fails to detect objects that are very high and thus touch the top and bottom boundaries of images.

Table 3. The results of the proposed algorithm on the validation sequences with different object proposals. SS denotes that the selective search [29] is used for generating object proposals, while ACF [45] means that the published detection results in the MOT benchmark [24] are used as the proposals.

Sequences	Proposal	MOTA↑	MOTP↑	MT↑	ML↓	FP↓	FN↓	IDS↓
TUD-Campus	SS	67.1	73.8	62.5	0.0	27	87	4
	ACF	71.0	74.2	62.5	0.0	13	87	4
ETH-Sunnyday	SS	72.1	74.4	70.0	3.3	297	202	20
	ACF	66.0	77.6	40.0	23.3	129	494	9
ETH-Pedcross2	SS	53.6	74.3	25.5	32.3	402	2,435	69
	ACF	28.4	74.4	10.5	63.9	162	4,302	23
ADL-Rundle-8	SS	34.9	69.7	32.1	25.0	683	3,695	41
	ACF	38.2	74.0	28.5	28.5	449	3,714	30
KITTI-17	SS	58.3	70.8	11.1	0.0	64	211	10
	ACF	60.8	71.5	11.1	0.0	45	217	6
Venice-2	SS	29.2	70.8	23.1	42.3	604	4,420	34
	ACF	41.5	75.1	34.6	42.3	116	4,042	23
Average	SS	42.4	72.2	32.5	26.5	2,077	11,050	178
	ACF	39.9	74.8	20.9	47.4	914	12,856	95

The performance of an MOT algorithm depends strongly on its object detector. Therefore, Table 4 compares the proposed algorithm with the conventional algorithms in [17,18], by employing an identical detector. In this test, all algorithms employ the detector in Sect. 3.1. We obtain the results of the conventional algorithms using their published codes and default parameters. Overall, the proposed algorithm provides the best performance. JPDA [17] yields relatively poor performance, since it does not consider the appearance of targets. Thus, it cannot handle complex scenes, in which it is difficult to identify objects from the

Table 4. Performance comparison with the same detector.

Algorithm	MOTA↑	MOTP↑	MT↑	ML↓	FP↓	FN↓	IDS↓
MHT [18]	39.9	74.7	18.8	38.9	616	13,180	70
JPDA [17]	27.2	72.2	14.1	42.3	2,970	13,625	220
Proposed	42.4	72.2	32.5	26.5	2,077	11,050	178

Table 5. Performance improvements when we use the MHT [18] algorithm for the post-processing.

Algorithm	MOTA↑	MOTP↑	MT↑	ML↓	FP↓	FN↓	IDS↓
Proposed	42.4	72.2	32.5	26.5	2,077	11,050	178
Proposed+MHT	44.6	73.2	36.3	27.0	2,045	10,639	112

Table 6. MOT results on each test sequence.

Sequences	MOTA↑	MOTP↑	MT↑	ML↓	FP↓	FN↓	IDS↓
TUD-Crossing	70.0	73.3	61.5	0.0	73	229	29
PETS09-S2L2	47.7	70.4	21.4	19.0	502	4,429	113
ETH-Jelmoli	48.2	75.0	60.0	11.1	758	529	26
ETH-Linthescher	60.5	76.4	43.7	24.4	1,425	1,963	138
ETH-Crossing	59.0	81.5	30.8	30.8	169	221	21
AVG-TownCentre	45.5	68.5	28.3	27.4	653	3,127	117
ADL-Rundle-1	26.0	70.1	21.9	28.1	1,697	5,146	47
ADL-Rundle-3	43.3	75.4	29.5	13.6	1,168	4,517	84
KITTI-16	44.7	69.3	23.5	0.0	232	690	19
KITTI-19	45.7	72.8	30.6	9.7	884	1,946	72
Venice-1	32.3	70.9	29.4	41.2	527	2,538	18
Average	44.5	72.9	34.7	22.1	8,088	25,335	684

motion information only. The recent state-of-the-art MHT [18] uses the convolutional neural network (CNN) features to exploit the appearance information and outperforms JPDA. However, it suffers from missing states in the detection stage and produces a lot of false negatives. In contrast, the proposed algorithm restores undetected states effectively, reducing the false negatives.

As mentioned previously, the tracking-by-detection approach decomposes the MOT problem into two subproblems: object detection and data association. The proposed algorithm focuses on improving the detection quality, but its performance can be also improved by adopting a sophisticated data association technique. Table 5 shows the improvements on the validation sequences when we use MHT [18] for the data association. In this test, using the results of the proposed algorithm as initial detection results, we employ MHT as a post-processing

Table 7. Comparison of the proposed CDT algorithm with conventional algorithms on the test sequences. The best and the second best scores are boldfaced and underlined, respectively.

Algorithm	MOTA↑	MOTP↑	MT↑	ML↓	FP↓	FN↓	IDS↓
TSML-CDE [27]	**49.1**	**74.3**	<u>30.4</u>	26.4	**5,204**	25,460	637
NOMT [19]	33.7	71.9	12.2	44.0	7,762	32,547	442
MHT [18]	32.4	71.8	16.0	43.8	9,064	32,060	<u>435</u>
MDP [16]	30.3	71.3	13.0	38.4	9,717	32,422	680
JPDA [17]	23.8	68.2	5.0	58.1	6,373	40,084	**365**
MotiCon [14]	23.1	70.9	4.7	52.0	10,404	35,844	1,018
SegTrack [15]	22.5	71.7	5.8	63.9	7,890	39,020	697
DCO [12]	19.6	71.4	5.1	54.9	10,652	38,232	521
CEM [9]	19.3	70.7	8.5	46.5	14,180	34,591	813
RMOT [46]	18.6	69.6	5.3	53.3	12,473	36,835	684
SMOT [47]	18.2	71.2	2.8	54.8	8,780	40,310	1,148
TC-ODAL [13]	15.1	70.5	3.2	55.8	12,970	38,538	637
DP-NMS [5]	14.5	70.8	6.0	40.8	13,171	34,814	4,537
Proposed	<u>44.5</u>	72.9	**34.7**	**22.1**	8,088	**25,335**	684
Proposed-online	42.8	<u>73.3</u>	23.8	<u>25.1</u>	5,494	28,997	668

scheme for the data association. Notice that the post-processing improves the MOTA score by 2.2 points, by reducing the number of tracking failures (FP, FN, and IDS). From a different point of view, we see in Tables 4 and 5 that the proposed algorithm increases the MOTA score of the MHT algorithm [18] by 4.7 points, by providing more reliable detection results.

4.3 Comparative Evaluation on Test Sequences

For the evaluation on test sequences, we fine-tuned the object detector using all 11 training and validation sequences in Table 1, and submitted our results to the MOT challenge website [24]. Note that the post-processing in Sect. 4.2 was not employed. Table 6 lists the results of the proposed CDT algorithm on each test sequence.

Table 7 compares the proposed algorithm with conventional trackers. In terms of MOTA, the proposed algorithm outperforms the recent trackers in [16–19] significantly, while providing a comparable score to the state-of-the-art tracker TSML-CDE [27]. Furthermore, the proposed algorithm provides the best performance in terms of MT, ML, and FN scores. Note that a lot of target states remain undetected in the detection stage, since the object detector focus on decreasing the number of false positives. Nevertheless, the proposed algorithm successfully restores these missing states and reduces the FN score considerably. Also, the proposed algorithm yields the outstanding performance in the trajectory quality metrics (MT, ML). These results indicate the effectiveness of the detection guidance in the model-free tracking. Even though the proposed CDT algorithm does not perform explicit global data association, the cooperation between the object detector and the model-free tracker enables to build long reliable trajectories.

By removing the backward tracker, the proposed algorithm can operate as an online tracker, since the object detector and the forward tracker are causal components. Thus, we consider it as the online version of the proposed algorithm. Table 7 presents the performance of the online version as well. The online version still outperforms the recent trackers [16–19] by considerable margins.

5   Conclusions

We proposed a novel MOT algorithm, called CDT. The proposed CDT algorithm first collects detection results with high confidence levels only to reduce spurious detection. Then, the proposed algorithm conducts model-free tracking in the forward direction and then in the backward direction to restore undetected states. For accurate tracking, the model-free trackers are guided by the object detector, in order to identify emerging or disappearing objects in a video and refine inaccurate state estimates. Experimental results demonstrated that the proposed CDT algorithm provides excellent performance on the MOT benchmark [24].

Acknowledgments. This work was supported partly by the National Research Foundation of Korea (NRF) grant funded by the Korea government (MSIP) (No. NRF-2015R1A2A1 A10055037), and partly by the MSIP, Korea, under the ITRC support program supervised by the Institute for Information & communications Technology Promotion (No. IITP-2016-R2720-16-0007).

References

1. Jiang, H., Fels, S., Little, J.J.: A linear programming approach for multiple object tracking. In: CVPR (2007)
2. Leibe, B., Schindler, K., Gool, L.V.: Coupled detection and trajectory estimation for multi-object tracking. In: ICCV (2007)
3. Zhang, L., Li, Y., Nevatia, R.: Global data association for multi-object tracking using network flows. In: CVPR (2008)
4. Berclaz, J., Fleuret, F., Turetken, E., Fua, P.: Multiple object tracking using k-shortest paths optimization. TPAMI **33**(9), 1806–1819 (2011)
5. Pirsiavash, H., Ramanan, D., Fowlkes, C.C.: Globally-optimal greedy algorithms for tracking a variable number of objects. In: CVPR (2011)
6. Brendel, W., Amer, M., Todorovic, S.: Multiobject tracking as maximum weight independent set. In: CVPR (2011)
7. Wu, Z., Thangali, A., Sclaroff, S., Betke, M.: Coupling detection and data association for multiple object tracking. In: CVPR (2012)
8. Roshan Zamir, A., Dehghan, A., Shah, M.: GMCP-Tracker: global multi-object tracking using generalized minimum clique graphs. In: Fitzgibbon, A., Lazebnik, S., Perona, P., Sato, Y., Schmid, C. (eds.) ECCV 2012, Part II. LNCS, vol. 7573, pp. 343–356. Springer, Heidelberg (2012)

9. Milan, A., Roth, S., Schindler, K.: Continuous energy minimization for multitarget tracking. TPAMI **36**(1), 58–72 (2014)
10. Dehghan, A., Assari, S.M., Shah, M.: GMMCP tracker: Globally optimal generalized maximum multi clique problem for multiple object tracking. In: CVPR (2015)
11. Lenz, P., Geiger, A., Urtasun, R.: FollowMe: efficient online min-cost flow tracking with bounded memory and computation. In: ICCV (2015)
12. Milan, A., Schindler, K., Roth, S.: Multi-target tracking by discrete-continuous energy minimization. In: TPAMI (2016)
13. Bae, S.H., Yoon, K.J.: Robust online multi-object tracking based on tracklet confidence and online discriminative appearance learning. In: CVPR (2014)
14. Leal-Taixé, L., Fenzi, M., Kuznetsova, A., Rosenhahn, B., Savarese, S.: Learning an image-based motion context for multiple people tracking. In: CVPR (2014)
15. Milan, A., Leal-Taixé, L., Schindler, K., Reid, I.: Joint tracking and segmentation of multiple targets. In: CVPR (2015)
16. Xiang, Y., Alahi, A., Savarese, S.: Learning to track: online multi-object tracking by decision making. In: ICCV (2015)
17. Rezatofighi, S.H., Milan, A., Zhang, Z., Shi, Q., Dick, A., Reid, I.: Joint probabilistic data association revisited. In: ICCV (2015)
18. Kim, C., Li, F., Ciptadi, A., Rehg, J.M.: Multiple hypothesis tracking revisited. In: ICCV (2015)
19. Choi, W.: Near-online multi-target tracking with aggregated local flow descriptor. In: ICCV (2015)
20. Girshick, R., Donahue, J., Darrell, T., Malik, J.: Rich feature hierarchies for accurate object detection and semantic segmentation. In: CVPR (2014)
21. He, K., Zhang, X., Ren, S., Sun, J.: Spatial pyramid pooling in deep convolutional networks for visual recognition. In: Fleet, D., Pajdla, T., Schiele, B., Tuytelaars, T. (eds.) ECCV 2014, Part III. LNCS, vol. 8691, pp. 346–361. Springer, Heidelberg (2014)
22. Girshick, R.: Fast R-CNN. In: ICCV (2015)
23. Ren, S., He, K., Girshick, R., Sun, J.: Faster R-CNN: Towards real-time object detection with region proposal networks. In: NIPS (2015)
24. Leal-Taixé, L., Milan, A., Reid, I., Roth, S., Schindler, K.: MOTChallenge 2015: Towards a benchmark for multi-target tracking (2015). https://motchallenge.net. Accessed 8 March 2016
25. Fortmann, T., Bar-Shalom, Y., Scheffe, M.: Sonar tracking of multiple targets using joint probabilistic data association. IEEE J. Ocean. Eng. **8**(3), 173–184 (1983)
26. Reid, D.: An algorithm for tracking multiple targets. TAC **24**(6), 843–854 (1979)
27. Wang, B., Wang, G., Chan, K.L., Wang, L.: Tracklet association by online target-specific metric learning and coherent dynamics estimation. TPAMI **PP**(99), 1 (2016)
28. Zitnick, C.L., Dollár, P.: Edge boxes: locating object proposals from edges. In: Fleet, D., Pajdla, T., Schiele, B., Tuytelaars, T. (eds.) ECCV 2014, Part V. LNCS, vol. 8693, pp. 391–405. Springer, Heidelberg (2014)
29. Uijlings, J., van de Sande, K., Gevers, T., Smeulders, A.: Selective search for object recognition. IJCV **104**(2), 154–171 (2013)
30. Arbelaez, P., Pont-Tuset, J., Barron, J., Marques, F., Malik, J.: Multiscale combinatorial grouping. In: CVPR (2014)
31. Avidan, S.: Support vector tracking. TPAMI **26**(8), 1064–1072 (2004)
32. Grabner, H., Grabner, M., Bischof, H.: Real-time tracking via on-line boosting. In: BMVC (2006)

33. Avidan, S.: Ensemble tracking. TPAMI **29**(2), 261–271 (2007)

34. Grabner, H., Leistner, C., Bischof, H.: Semi-supervised on-line boosting for robust tracking. In: Forsyth, D., Torr, P., Zisserman, A. (eds.) ECCV 2008, Part I. LNCS, vol. 5302, pp. 234–247. Springer, Heidelberg (2008)

35. Babenko, B., Yang, M.H., Belongie, S.: Robust object tracking with online multiple instance learning. TPAMI **33**(8), 1619–1632 (2011)

36. Hare, S., Saffari, A., Torr, P.H.S.: Struck: Structured output tracking with kernels. In: ICCV (2011)

37. Tsochantaridis, I., Joachims, T., Hofmann, T., Altun, Y.: Large margin methods for structured and interdependent output variables. JMLR **6**, 1453–1484 (2005)

38. Henriques, J.F., Caseiro, R., Martins, P., Batista, J.: High-speed tracking with kernelized correlation filters. TPAMI **37**(3), 583–596 (2015)

39. Simonyan, K., Zisserman, A.: Very deep convolutional networks for large-scale image recogntion. In: ICLR (2015)

40. Kim, H.U., Lee, D.Y., Sim, J.Y., Kim, C.S.: SOWP: spatially ordered and weighted patch descriptor for visual tracking. In: ICCV (2015)

41. Felzenszwalb, P., Girshick, R., McAllester, D., Ramanan, D.: Object detection with discriminatively trained part-based models. TPAMI **32**(9), 1627–1645 (2010)

42. Kuhn, H.W.: The hungarian method for the assignment problem. Nav. Res. Logist. Quart. **2**(1–2), 83–97 (1955)

43. Wu, Y., Lim, J., Yang, M.H.: Object tracking benchmark. TPAMI **37**(9), 1834–1848 (2015)

44. Bordes, A., Bottou, L., Gallinari, P., Weston, J.: Solving multiclass support vector machines with LaRank. In: ICML (2007)

45. Dollar, P., Appel, R., Belongie, S., Perona, P.: Fast feature pyramids for object detection. TPAMI **36**(8), 1532–1545 (2014)

46. Yoon, J.H., Yang, M.H., Lim, J., Yoon, K.J.: Bayesian multi-object tracking using motion context from multiple objects. In: WACV (2015)

47. Dicle, C., Camps, O.I., Sznaier, M.: The way they move: Tracking multiple targets with similar appearance. In: ICCV (2013)

MARS: A Video Benchmark
for Large-Scale Person Re-Identification

Liang Zheng[1,3], Zhi Bie[1], Yifan Sun[1], Jingdong Wang[2],
Chi Su[4], Shengjin Wang[1(✉)], and Qi Tian[3]

[1] Tsinghua University, Beijing, China
liangzheng06@gmail.com, wgsgj@tsinghua.edu.cn
[2] Microsoft Research, Beijing, China
[3] UTSA, San Antonio, USA
[4] Peking University, Beijing, China

Abstract. This paper considers person re-identification (re-id) in videos. We introduce a new video re-id dataset, named Motion Analysis and Re-identification Set (MARS), a video extension of the Market-1501 dataset. To our knowledge, MARS is the largest video re-id dataset to date. Containing 1,261 IDs and around 20,000 tracklets, it provides rich visual information compared to image-based datasets. Meanwhile, MARS reaches a step closer to practice. The tracklets are automatically generated by the Deformable Part Model (DPM) as pedestrian detector and the GMMCP tracker. A number of false detection/tracking results are also included as distractors which would exist predominantly in practical video databases. Extensive evaluation of the state-of-the-art methods including the space-time descriptors and CNN is presented. We show that CNN in classification mode can be trained from scratch using the consecutive bounding boxes of each identity. The learned CNN embedding outperforms other competing methods considerably and has good generalization ability on other video re-id datasets upon fine-tuning.

Keywords: Video person re-identification · Motion features · CNN

1 Introduction

Person re-identification, as a promising way towards automatic VIDEO surveillance, has been mostly studied in pre-defined IMAGE bounding boxes (bbox). Impressive progress has been observed with image-based re-id. However, rich information contained in video sequences (or tracklets) remains under-explored. In the generation of video database, pedestrian detectors [11] and offline trackers [7] are readily available. So it is natural to extract tracklets instead of single (or multiple) bboxes. This paper, among a few contemporary works [25,29,36,38,41], makes initial attempts on video-based re-identification.

The dataset and codes are available at http://www.liangzheng.com.cn.

© Springer International Publishing AG 2016
B. Leibe et al. (Eds.): ECCV 2016, Part VI, LNCS 9910, pp. 868–884, 2016.
DOI: 10.1007/978-3-319-46466-4_52

With respect to the "probe-to-gallery" pattern, there are four re-id strategies: image-to-image, image-to-video, video-to-image, and video-to-video. Among them, the first mode is mostly studied in literature, and previous methods in image-based re-id [5,24,35] are developed in adaptation to the poor amount of training data. The second mode can be viewed as a special case of "multi-shot", and the third one involves multiple queries. Intuitively, the video-to-video pattern, which is our focus in this paper, is more favorable because both probe and gallery units contain much richer visual information than single images. Empirical evidences confirm that the video-to-video strategy is superior to the others (Fig. 3).

Currently, a few video re-id datasets exist [4,15,28,36]. They are limited in scale: typically several hundred identities are contained, and the number of image sequences doubles (Table 1). Without large-scale data, the scalability of algorithms is less-studied and methods that fully utilize data richness are less likely to be exploited. In fact, the evaluation in [43] indicates that re-id performance drops considerably in large-scale databases.

Moreover, image sequences in these video re-id datasets are generated by hand-drawn bboxes. This process is extremely expensive, requiring intensive human labor. And yet, in terms of bounding box quality, hand-drawn bboxes are biased towards ideal situation, where pedestrians are well-aligned. But in reality, pedestrian detectors will lead to part occlusion or misalignment which may have a non-ignorable effect on re-id accuracy [43]. Another side-effect of hand-drawn box sequences is that each identity has one box sequence under a camera. This happens because there are no natural break points inside each sequence. But in automatically generated data, a number of tracklets are available for each identity due to miss detection or tracking. As a result, in practice one identity will have multiple probes and multiple sequences as ground truths. It remains unsolved how to make use of these visual cues.

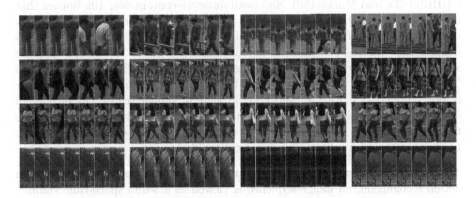

Fig. 1. Sample tracklets in MARS. The first three rows each corresponds to an identity, and tracklets in each column belong to different cameras. The last row presents four examples of false detection and tracking results. Images are shown every 6 frames

In light of the above discussions, it is of importance to (1) introduce large-scale and real-life video re-id datasets and (2) design effective methods which fully utilizes the rich visual data. To this end, this paper contributes in collecting and annotating a new person re-identification dataset, named "Motion Analysis and Re-identification Set" (MARS) (Fig. 1). Overall, MARS is featured in several aspects. First, MARS has 1,261 identities and around 20,000 video sequences, making it the largest video re-id dataset to date. Second, instead of hand-drawn bboxes, we use the DPM detector [11] and GMMCP tracker [7] for pedestrian detection and tracking, respectively. Third, MARS includes a number of distractor tracklets produced by false detection or tracking result. Finally, the multiple-query and multiple-ground truth mode will enable future research in fields such as query re-formulation and search re-ranking [45].

Apart from the extensive tests of the state-of-the-art re-id methods, this paper evaluates two important features: (1) motion features including HOG3D [18] and the gait [13] feature, and (2) the ID-disciminative Embeddings (IDE) [46], which learns a CNN descriptor in classification mode. Our results show that although motion features achieve impressive results on small datasets, they are less effective on MARS due to intensive changes in pedestrian activity. In contrast, the IDE descriptor learned on the MARS training set significantly outperforms the other competing features, and demonstrates good generalization ability on the other two video datasets after fine-tuning.

2   Related Work

Re-id dataset review. Most previous studies of person re-id are based on image datasets. The most commonly used one is VIPeR [12], which consists of 632 identities and 1,264 images. Datasets with similar scale include RAiD [6], i-LIDS [47], *etc.* Recently, two large-scale image datasets are released, *i.e.*, CUHK03 [23] and Market1501 [43]. Both datasets contain over 10k bboxes that are generated by DPM detector. The Market1501 dataset further adds 500k distractor bboxes of false detection results. Results of the large-scale datasets demonstrate that re-id accuracy drops considerably with the increase in database size, thus calling for scalable re-id methods. In video re-id (Table 1), iLIDS-VID [36] and PRID-2011 [15] contain several hundred identities and twice the number of box sequences. 3DPES [3] and ETH [32] are of similar scales. On such small datasets, the scalability of methods cannot be fully evaluated. Considering the trend of large scale in vision, the re-id community is in need of scalable video re-id datasets which reflect more practical problems.

Motion features in action recognition and person re-identification. In action recognition, an image sequence is viewed as a 3-dim space-time volume. Space-time features can be extracted based on the space-time interest points [9,21,37]. These methods generate compact representation of an image sequence using the sparse interest points, which are sensitive to variations such as viewpoint, speed, scale, *etc* [17]. An improved version associates with space-time

Table 1. Comparing MARS with datasets in videos [3, 15, 32, 36] and images [12, 23, 43]

Datasets	MARS	iLIDS	PRID	3DPES	ETH	CUHK03	VIPeR	Market
#identities	1,261	300	200	200	146	1,360	632	1,501
#tracklets	20,715	600	400	1000	146	-	-	-
#BBoxes	1,067,516	43,800	40k	200k	8580	13,164	1,264	32k
#distractors	3,248	0	0	0	0	0	0	2,793
#cam./ID	6	2	2	8	1	2	2	6
Produced by	DPM+GMMCP	hand	hand	hand	hand	hand	hand	DPM
Evaluation	mAP &CMC	CMC	CMC	CMC	CMC	CMC	CMC	mAP

volume based representations [30]. Popular descriptors include HOG3D [18], 3D-SIFT [33], *etc*, which can be viewed as extensions of their corresponding 2-dim versions. In person re-id, few works focus on motion features because it is challenging to discriminate pedestrians solely by motion. Among the few, Wang *et al.* [36] employ the HOG3D descriptor with dense sampling after identifying walking periodicity. Nevertheless, [36] has only been tested on two small video datasets without further validation on large-scale settings. In this paper, we mostly follow [36] in the video description part, and show that this strategy has some flaws in dealing with practical video data.

CNN in person re-id. In person re-id, the study of CNN [1, 8, 23, 40] has only recently launched due to the small scale of re-id datasets. These works formulate person re-id as a ranking problem. Image pairs [1, 23, 40] or triplets [8] are defined as input to CNN, instead of single training images. Such design avoids the shortage of training images per identity by generating quadratically/cubically enlarged training sets. Then, with such input data, the network is designed to have parallel convolutional layers, max pooling layers, as well as fully connected layers to learn an optimized metric. In video-based re-id, McLaughlin *et al.* [29] propose a variant of the recurrent neural network to incorporate time flows, an idea that is later adopted by [38]. In this paper, since each pedestrian has a number of training data (from image sequences), we are capable of training a classification network [16]. In this scenario, each single image is represented by a feature vector, which will greatly accelerate online process by nearest neighbor search or ANN algorithms.

3 MARS Dataset

3.1 Dataset Description

In this paper, we introduce the MARS (Motion Analysis and Re-identification Set) dataset for video-based person re-identification. It is an extension of the Market-1501 dataset [43]. During collection, we placed six near-synchronized cameras in the campus of Tsinghua university. There were five $1,080 \times 1920$ HD cameras and one 640×480 SD camera. MARS consists of 1,261 different pedestrians whom are captured by at least 2 cameras.

For tracklet generation, we first use the DPM detector [11] to detect pedestrians. Then, the GMMCP tracker [7] is employed to group overlapping detection results in consecutive frames and fill in missing detection results. As output, a total of 20,715 image sequences are generated. Among them, 3,248 are distractor tracklets produced due to false detection or tracking results, which is close to practical usage. Overall, the following features are associated with MARS.

First, as shown in Table 1, compared with iLIDS-VID and PRID-2011, MARS has a much larger scale: 4 times and 30 times larger in the number of identities and total tracklets, respectively.

Second, the tracklets in MARS are generated automatically by DPM detector and GMMCP tracker, which differs substantially from existing datasets: the image sequences have high quality guaranteed by human labor. The detection/tracking error enables MARS to be more realistic than previous datasets. Moreover, in MARS, to produce "smooth" tracklets, we further apply average filtering to the bbox coordinates to reduce localization errors. As we will show in Sect. 5.3, tracklet smoothing improves the performance of motion features.

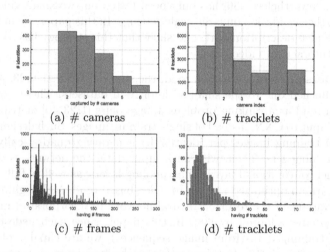

(a) # cameras   (b) # tracklets

(c) # frames   (d) # tracklets

Fig. 2. Statistics of the MARS dataset. (a): the number of identities captured by 1–6 cameras. (b): the numbers of tracklets in each camera. (c): the distribution of the number of frames in the tracklets. (d): the distribution of the number of tracklets belonging to the pedestrians

Third, in MARS, each identity has 13.2 tracklets on average. For each query, an average number of 3.7 cross-camera ground truths exist; each query has 4.2 image sequences that are captured under the same camera, and can be used as auxiliary information in addition to the query itself. As a result, MARS is an ideal test bed for algorithms exploring multiple queries or re-ranking methods [45]. Figure 2 provides more detailed statistics. For example, most IDs are captured by 2–4 cameras, and camera-2 produces the most tracklets. A large number of tracklets contain 25–50 frames, and most IDs have 5–20 tracklets.

3.2   Evaluation Protocol

In the MARS dataset, we stick to the cross-camera search mode as in previous datasets [12,23,43], *i.e.*, query and gallery are captured by different cameras. Each identity will have one probe under each camera. Since each identity may have multiple tracklets under a camera, the representative probe image is randomly selected from them, resulting in 2,009 probes. The MARS dataset is evenly divided into train and test sets, containing 631 and 630 identities, respectively, and this partition is fixed. The dataset is large, so we fix the train/test partitioning instead of repeating random partitioning for 10 or 20 times [12,23]. Then, given a query image sequence, all gallery items are assigned a similarity score. We then rank the gallery according to their similarity to the query. In our system, since a query has multiple ground truths, regular CMC curve (Cumulative Matching Characteristic, representing the expectation of the true match being found within the first n ranks) does not fully reflect the true ranking results, so we resort to both CMC and mAP as the evaluation metric [43]. The Average Precision (AP) is calculated based on the ranking result, and the mean Average Precision (mAP) is computed across all queries which is viewed as the final re-id accuracy. CMC is a pragmatic measurement focusing on retrieval precision, while mAP considers precision and recall and is useful for research purpose (Table 1).

Table 2. Three important features evaluated in the baseline

Features	Dim	Description
CNN	1,024	Using AlexNet [20], the three fully convolutional layers have 1,024, 1,024, and 631 blobs. Trained on MARS, fine-tuned on PRID and iLIDS. Using FC7 (after RELU) for testing.
HOG3D [18]	2,000	Motion feature. Detecting walking cycles by FEP [36]. HOG3D feature extracted from $8 \times 8 \times 6$ or $16 \times 16 \times 6$ patches and quantized using a codebook of size 2,000.
GEI [13]	2,400	Gait feature. Detecting walking cycles by FEP [36]. Pedestrian segmentation using code from [26]. Resulting maps within a cycle are resized to 80×30 and averaged to obtain the feature

4   Important Features

4.1   Motion Features

The **HOG3D** [18] feature has been shown to have competitive performance in action recognition [22]. In feature extraction, given a tracklet, we first identify walking cycles using Flow Energy Profile (FEP) proposed in [36]. For bboxes aligned in a cycle, we densely extract HOG3D feature in $8 \times 8 \times 6$ (or $16 \times$

16 × 6) space-time patches, with 50 % overlap between adjacent patches. The feature dimension of each space-time patch is 96. Since videos with different time duration have different numbers of the dense space-time tubes, we encode the local features into a Bag-of-Words (BoW) model. Specifically, a codebook of size 2,000 is trained by k-means on the training set. Then, each 96-dim descriptor is quantized to a visual word defined in the codebook. So we obtain a 2,000-dim BoW vector for an arbitrary-length video. We do not partition the image into horizontal stripes [43] because this strategy incurs larger feature dimension and in our preliminary experiment does not improve re-id accuracy.

The **Gait Energy Image (GEI)** [13] is widely applied in gait recognition. In GEI extraction, we also first find walking cycles using FEP. Then, for bboxes within a cycle, we segment each bbox into foreground (pedestrian) and background using the code released by Luo *et al.* [26]. The resulting binary images within a cycle are averaged to yield the GEI of the tracklet. In our experiment, the size of GEI is 80 × 30, which is reshaped into a column as the final vector.

After feature extraction, we learn a metric on the training set using several metric learning schemes such as Kissme [19] and XQDA [24], due to their efficiency and accuracy.

4.2 CNN Features

The Convolutional Neural Network (CNN) has achieved state-of-the-art accuracy in a number of vision tasks. In person re-identification, current CNN methods [1,8,23,40] take positive and negative image pairs (or triplets) as input to the network due to the lack of training data per identity. In this paper, we employ the ID-discriminative Embedding (IDE) [46] using CaffeNet [20] to train the re-id model in classification mode. More sophisticated networks [14,34] may yield higher re-id accuracy.

During training, images are resized to 227 × 227 pixels, and along with their IDs (label) are fed into CNN in batches. Through five convolutional layers with the same structure as the CaffeNet [20], we define two fully connected layers each with 1,024 blobs. The number of blobs in the 8th layer is equal to the number of training identities which in the case of MARS is 631. The total number of training bboxes on MARS is 518k.

In testing, since re-id is different from image classification in that the training and testing identities do not overlap, we extract probe and gallery features using the CNN model before metric learning steps. Specifically, we extract the FC7 features for all bboxes in an input tracklet. Then, max/average pooling is employed to generate a 1,024-dim vector for an tracklet of arbitrary length (A comparison between the two pooling methods can be accessed in Sect. 5). Finally, metric learning is leveraged as in image-based re-id. In Sect. 5.4, we will demonstrate that IDE descrptors learned through person classification can be effectively used in re-id.

When transferring the CNN model trained on MARS to other video re-id datasets, we fine-tune the MARS-learned CNN model on the target datasets. In experiment, we find that fixing parameters in the convolutional layers typically

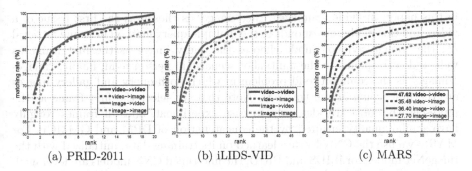

(a) PRID-2011   (b) iLIDS-VID   (c) MARS

Fig. 3. Comparison of four re-id strategies on three datasets. CNN features trained/fine-tuned on the corresponding datasets are used. We adopt XQDA for metric learning (Kissme yields very similar performance with XQDA). Numbers in the legend of (c) MARS are mAP results. Clearly, the video-to-video mode is superior

results in compromised accuracy, so in practice, all the 7 CNN layers including the convolutional and fully connected layers are fine tuned. The Last fully connected layer (FC8) is trained from scratch.

5   Experiments

5.1   Datasets

We use three datasets, *i.e.*, PRID-2011 [15], iLIDS-VID [36], and MARS. For the former two, we use the Cumulative Match Characteristics (CMC) curve for evaluation, which is averaged over ten train/test partitions. We use the same partition rule as [36]. For MARS, a fixed partitioning is used (our preliminary experiments show that different paritions yield stable and consistent results), and mAP and CMC are both reported.

PRID-2011 dataset contains 400 image sequences of 200 pedestrians under two cameras. Each image sequence has a length of 5 to 675 frames. Following [36], sequences with more than 21 frames from 178 persons are used. So the probe and gallery both have 89 identities.

iLIDS-VID dataset is a newly released dataset consisting of 300 identities and each has 2 image sequences, totaling 600 sequences. The length of image sequences varies from 23 to 192, with an average number of 73. This dataset is more challenging due to environment variations. The test and training set both have 150 identities.

5.2   Why Do We Prefer Video-Based Re-Identification?

This paper mentioned four re-id modes in the Sect. 1. In this section, we will evaluate their performance and gain insights in the reason why video re-id should be preferred. Among the four modes, "video->video" is what we have described in this paper; in "video->image", the "image" is chosen as the first frame of a video, and this mode corresponds to the multiple-query method in image retrieval [2]; the "image->video" mode chooses the query image as the first frame as well, and corresponds to the multi-shot scenario in person re-id; finally, "image->image" is the common re-id problem in which both query and gallery images are the first frame of the tracklets. Note that we select the first frame as the representative of a tracklet only to ease experiment, and all frames roughly have similar quality ensured by the concatenation of DPM and GMMCP. For MARS, we use the CNN feature learned on its training data, initialized with the ImageNet model; for iLIDS and PRID, the fine-tuned CNN models are leveraged, initialized by ImageNet and MARS, respectively. Max pooling is used for MARS and PRID, and averge pooling for iLIDS, to aggregate bbox features. We use XQDA [24] in metric learning.

We observe from Fig. 3 that the video-to-video re-id strategy significantly outperforms the other three, while the image-to-image mode exhibits the worst performance. On MARS, for example, video-based re-id exceeds image-based re-id by +19.92 % in mAP. The video-to-image and image-to-video modes also have considerable improvment over using single images only, but are inferior to video re-id. On MARS, "image->video" outperforms "video->image" probably because the former has richer visual cues and a finer distance metric can be learned. Previous studies on person re-identification mostly focus on the image-to-image mode, while this paper argues that the generation of tracklets instead of single images will be both more natural and higher accuracy can be expected. Our results lay a groundwork for the argument: other things being equal, video re-id consistently improves re-id accuracy and should be paid more emphasis on.

5.3 Evaluation of Motion Features

As described in Sect. 4.1, we use HOG3D and Gait Energy Image (GEI) features for motion representation. Results are presented in Fig. 4 and Table 4.

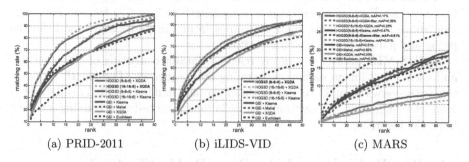

(a) PRID-2011   (b) iLIDS-VID   (c) MARS

Fig. 4. CMC curves of HOG3D and GEI features on three video re-id datasets. HOG3D with $8 \times 8 \times 6$ and $16 \times 16 \times 6$ sampling strategies are presented. For MARS, "filter" denotes average filtering to smoothen consecutive bboxes

Performance of HOG3D and GEI. In Fig. 4 and Table 4, we observe that HOG3D and GEI feature both yield decent accuracy on iLIDS-VID and PRID-2011 datasets. Specifically, for HOG3D, the rank-1 accuracy is 21.68% and 16.13% on PRID-2011 and iLIDS-VID datasets, respectively; for GEI, the rank-1 accuracy is 19.00% and 10.27%, respectively. Our implementation is competitive with [36]: matching rate is relatively lower in low ranks, but higher in larger ranks (see Fig. 6 for clear comparison). Therefore, on the two small datasets, both features have competitive performance, and HOG3D is slightly superior.

On the MARS dataset, however, the performance of HOG3D and GEI both drops considerably. The rank-1 accuracy of HOG3D is 2.61% with Kissme, and mAP is 0.81%; for GEI, rank-1 accuracy and mAP are 1.18% and 0.40%, respectively. For the two features, both precision (rank-1) and recall (mAP) are low on MARS. **The reason why motion features have poor performance on MARS is two-fold.** On one hand, a larger dataset will inevitably contain many pedestrians sharing similar motion feature with the probe, and it is challenging to discriminate different persons based on motions. On the other hand, since MARS is captured by six cameras, motion of the same identity may undergo significant variations due to pedestrian pose change (see Fig. 7 for visual results), so the motion-based system may miss the same pedestrian under motion variations. For example, a walking person with frontal and side views will have large intra-class variability, let alone considering persons standing still with hardly any motion at all.

Impact of tracklet smoothing. In MARS, consecutive bboxes in the tracklets may not be smooth due to detection errors. To correct this, we employ the average filtering to smoothen bboxes within each tracklet. In our experiment, we use a window of size 5, and across the 5 bboxes, compute the average coordinates of the upper left point as well as the frame width and height, which is taken as the smoothed bbox of the frame in the middle. Features are then extracted using the smoothed tracklets. In Fig. 4(c), we find that, the smoothing strategy yields some marginal improvement for HOG3D feature (mAP increases from 0.47% to 0.81%). For GEI, the segmentation method [26] already corrects this artifact, so the improvement is limited (not shown, because it overlaps with other lines).

In summary, on PRID-2011 and iLIDS-VID datasets, motion features such as HOG3D and GEI are effective for two reasons: both datasets have relatively small scales; image sequences in both datasets do not undergo significant variances. On the MARS dataset, our observation goes that motion features have much lower accuracy. In comparison with PRID-2011 and iLIDS-VID datasets, MARS has much more tracklets, and the tracklets have more intensive variations in viewpoint, pose, *etc.* Intra-class variance is large, while inter-class variance can be small, making it challenging for effective usage of motion features. Figure 7 presents re-id examples in which motion feature fails.

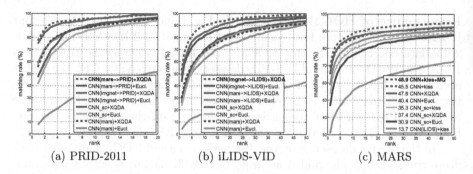

(a) PRID-2011   (b) iLIDS-VID   (c) MARS

Fig. 5. CMC curves on three video re-id datasets with the IDE feature. "(mars->PRID)" represents CNN model pre-trained on MARS and fine-tuned on PRID. "sc" means training from scratch. "(mars)" and "(iLIDS)" indicate that the model is trained on MARS or iLIDS and then directly transferred to the target set. Kissme and XQDA are used as distance metric; otherwise, Euclidean (Eucl.) distance is used. "MQ" denotes multiple queries

Table 3. Method comparisons on three datasets. "Self" means training IDE on the target dataset set. "MARS" denotes directly transferring MARS-learned model to the target dataset. "Self pretrained on MARS" stands for fine-tuning IDE on a MARS-initialized model. "avg" means using average pooling, or otherwise, max pooling. All models are first initialized with the ImageNet model. Red and blue numbers indicate average pooling compromises and improves accuracy, respectively

Train. Set	Metric	PRID-2011				iLIDS-VID				MARS			
		1	5	10	20	1	5	10	20	1	5	20	mAP
Self	Eucl.	58.2	82.7	90.6	98.2	40.5	70.0	78.9	84.7	58.7	77.1	86.8	40.4
	avg.	-1.1	-0.7	-0.4	-0.2	+3.1	+1.9	+2.5	+2.7	+1.3	+0.8	+1.1	+2.0
	Kiss.	66.3	88.5	93.9	98.2	47.6	76.1	86.1	92.5	65.0	81.1	88.9	45.6
	avg.	+0.2	-1.6	-1.1	-0.4	+1.2	-0.5	+1.1	+0.1	-0.2	-0.1	-0.5	+1.6
	XQDA	74.8	92.1	95.7	99.1	53.3	79.1	87.2	94.3	65.3	82.0	89.0	47.6
	avg.	+2.0	-1.8	-0.2	-0.4	+1.7	+2.3	+2.5	+0.8	-0.7	-0.6	+0.1	-0.1
MARS	Eucl.	7.6	24.6	39.0	51.8	2.9	9.9	14.7	23.0	-	-	-	-
	avg.	-0.3	-1.1	-1.2	-1.1	+1.0	+3.1	+2.8	+3.9				
	XQDA	55.5	83.6	89.3	95.4	24.3	56.3	66.9	79.3	-	-	-	-
	avg.	-2.1	-3.3	-0.2	-0.2	+5.7	+4.1	+2.0	+0.4				
Self pretrained on MARS	Eucl.	58.9	93.5	95.7	99.3	25.9	44.4	57.2	71.5	-	-	-	-
	avg.	+2.2	+2.5	+2.5	+0.4	-0.9	-1.9	+0.9	-0.3				
	XQDA	77.3	93.5	95.7	99.3	47.1	76.7	85.6	93.3	-	-	-	-
	avg.	-3.6	-0.9	-1.1	-0.9	+1.1	-0.4	-1.2	-1.1				

5.4   Evaluation of the CNN Feature

Training from scratch vs. fine-tuning on ImageNet. For the three datasets, CNN modesl are either trained from scratch or fine-tuned on ImageNet-pretrained models. In Fig. 5, we observe that fine-tuning on the ImageNet model consistently outperforms training from scratch. On MARS, fine-tuning brins about +9.5 % and 10.2 % improvement when Euclidean or XQDA distances are used, respectively. Situation on iLIDS and PRID is simila. In the following experiments, we always employ ImageNet-initilized models, if not specified.

Comparison with motion features. In Fig. 6 and Table 4, direct comparisons are made available between the two feature types. On PRID and iLIDS, "CNN+XQDA" exceeds "HOG3D+XQDA" by 55.6 % and 46.9 % in rank-1 accuracy, respectively. On MARS, the performance gap is 65.7 % and 48.5 % in rank-1 and mAP, respectively. On all the three datasets, CNN outperforms the motion features by a large margin, validating the effectiveness of appearance models.

Generalization ability of MARS. We conduct two experiments to study the relationship between MARS and the two small datasets. First, we directly transfer the CNN model trained on MARS to iLIDS and PRID. In Figs. 5(a) and (b), and Table 3, we directly extract features with the MARS-trained model for iLIDS and PRID. We find that re-id accuracy with Euclidean distance is pretty low. This is expected because the data distribution of MARS is different from that of iLIDS and PRID. Metric learning then improves accuracy to a large extent. Our second experiment is fine-tuning a CNN model on the target set using MARS-pretrained models (Self pretrained on MARS). On both dataset, fine-tuning yields improvement over direct model transfer. On PRID, we achieve rank-1 accuracy = 77.3, which is higher than fine-tuning from ImageNet. On iLIDS, fine-tuning from MARS is lower than ImageNet by ~4 % in rank-1 accuracy. This demonstrates that data distribution of PRID is close to MARS, while iLIDS seems to be more different. We note that MARS was captured in summer while the other two depicts scenes in colder seasons, and that PRID and MARS are both outdoor datasets, while iLIDS is an indoor one.

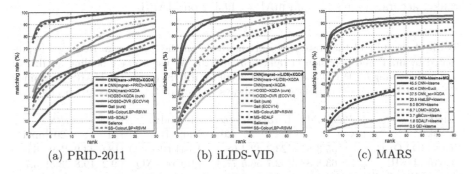

(a) PRID-2011   (b) iLIDS-VID   (c) MARS

Fig. 6. Comparison with state-of-the-art methods on three video re-id datasets. Numbers before each method name in (c) denote the mAP(%). "(ours)" and "ECCV14" denote result implemented by ourselves and borrowed from [36], respectively

Max pooling vs. avg pooling. In this paper, bbox features within a tracklet are combined into a fixed-length vector using max/average pooling. Now we compare the performance of the two pooling methods. Results are summarized in Table 3, in which max pooling is used if not specified. We observe that max pooling is generally better on PRID and MARS, while for iLIDS, average pooling seems to be superior. One possible explanation is that max pooling helps to find local salient features, which is desirable under large illuminations changes like in iLIDS. Other pooling options are worth exploiting, such as the $\mathcal{L}_p$—norm pooling [44], the fisher vector encoding [31], etc.

Multiple queries (MultiQ). In MARS, multiple tracklets for the same ID exist within the same camera as mentioned in Sect. 3.1. They contain rich information as the pedestrian may have varying poses within each tracklet. Following [46], we re-formulate each probe by max-pooling the tracklets within the same camera. Results are presented in Fig. 6(c) and Table 4. With multiple queries, we improve the rank-1 accuracy from 65.0 % to 68.3 % (+3.3 %).

5.5   Comparison with State-of-the-arts

In Table 4 and Fig. 6, we compare our results with the state-of-the-art methods. On PRID-2011 and iLIDS-VID datasets, five descriptors are compared, *i.e.*, HOG3D [18], color, color+LBP, SDALF [10], Salience [42], and BoW [43]. Three metric learning methods, *i.e.*, DVR [36], XQDA [24], and Kissme [19] are evaluated. We observe that the CNN descriptor is superior to these methods, obtaining rank-1 accuracy = 77.3 % and 53.0 % on PRID and iLIDS, respectively.   Comparing with recent video re-id works, the best known rank-1 accuracy is 70 % and 58 % on PRID and iLIDS, respectively, both reported in [29]. So this paper sets a new state of the art on PRID, and is 5 % lower on iLIDS. On the MARS dataset, results of another set of features are presented, *i.e.*, HistLBP [39], gBiCov [27], LOMO [24], BoW [43], and SDALF [10]. We report rank-1 accuracy = 68.3 % and mAP = 49.3 % on MARS.

Table 4. Results of the state-of-the-art methods on the 3 datasets. Accuracy is presented by mAP and precision in rank 1, 5, and 20. We use average pooling for iLIDS, and max pooling for PRID and MARS. Except for iLIDS, we use the MARS-pretrained CNN model. ImageNet initialization is always employed. Best results are in blue

Methods	PRID-2011			iLIDS-VID			Methods	MARS			
Rank R	1	5	20	1	5	20	Rank R	1	5	20	mAP
HOG3D+DVR	28.9	55.3	82.8	23.3	42.4	68.4	HistLBP+XQ.	18.6	33.0	45.9	8.0
Color+DVR	41.8	63.8	88.3	32.7	56.5	77.4	gBiCov+XQ.	9.2	19.8	33.5	3.7
ColorLBP+DVR	37.6	63.9	89.4	34.5	56.7	77.5	LOMO+XQ.	30.7	46.6	60.9	16.4
SDALF+DVR	31.6	58.0	85.3	26.7	49.3	71.6	BoW+Kissme	30.6	46.2	59.2	15.5
Salience+DVR	41.7	64.5	88.8	30.9	54.4	77.1	SDALF+DVR	4.1	12.3	25.1	1.8
BoW+XQDA	31.8	58.5	81.9	14.0	32.2	59.5	HOG3D+Kiss.	2.6	6.4	12.4	0.8
GEI+Kiss.	19.0	36.8	63.9	10.3	30.5	61.5	GEI+Kiss.	1.2	2.8	7.4	0.4
HOG3D+XQDA	21.7	51.7	87.0	16.1	41.6	74.5	CNN+XQDA	65.3	82.0	89.0	47.6
CNN+Kiss	69.9	90.6	98.2	48.8	75.6	92.6	CNN+Kiss.	65.0	81.1	88.9	45.6
CNN+XQDA	77.3	93.5	99.3	53.0	81.4	95.1	+MQ	68.3	82.6	89.4	49.3

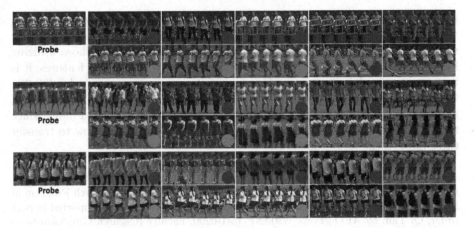

Fig. 7. Sample re-id results of three probes. For each probe, the first and the second row display ranking results obtained by HOG3D and CNN features, respectively. Green and red discs denote the same and different person with the probe, respectively

In Fig. 7, three sample re-id results are shown. Our observation is that a large number of pedestrians share similar motion, a phenomenon that is less-studied on small datasets. The usage of motion features therefore tends to find pedestrians with similar activities. In contrast, by replacing motion features with the CNN feature, We find the CNN embedding is effective in dealing with image variances and yields superior results to motion features.

6 Conclusions

This paper advocates using video tracklets in person re-identification. Attempts are made in constructing a realistic video re-id dataset, named "MARS". This dataset is four times larger than previous video re-id datasets, and is collected with automatic detector and tracker. Moreover, MARS dataset is featured by multi-query, multi-ground truth, and over 3,000 distractor tracklets produced by false detection and tracking results. These characteristics make MARS an ideal test bed for practical re-id algorithms. We employ two motion features as well as the Convolutional Neural Networks to learn a discriminative embedding in the person subspace. Our experiments reveal that motion features that were previously proved successful on small datasets turn out to be less effective under realistic settings with complex background, occlusion, and various poses. Instead, given the large amount of training data in video datasets, the learned CNN feature outperforms motion features and a number of state-of-the-art image descriptors to a large margin, and has good generalization ability on other video datasets.

Multiple research directions are made possible with MARS. For example, it is important to design view-invariant motion features that can deal with view changes in real-life datasets. Since each tracklet has multiple frames, another feasible topic is video pooling which aims to find discriminative information within video frames. Moreover, when classic CNNs can be trained on the rich visual data, a number of CNN variants can be explored such as those utilizing human parts. While this paper finds it less effective to use motion features, it is interesting to exploit the temporal cues in addition to appearance models [29,38]. Our preliminary results have revealed some moderate improvement using LSTM, and further experiment is needed to extend the temporal models. Finally, since there exists a number of tracking datasets, it remains unknown how to transfer these data to the target domains.

Acknowledgement. We thank Zhun Zhong and Linghui Li for providing some benchmarking results. This work was supported by Initiative Scientific Research Program of Ministry of Education under Grant No. 20141081253. This work was supported in part to Dr. Qi Tian by ARO grants W911NF-15-1-0290, Faculty Research Gift Awards by NEC Laboratories of America and Blippar, and National Science Foundation of China (NSFC) 61429201.

References

1. Ahmed, E., Jones, M., Marks, T.K.: An improved deep learning architecture for person re-identification. In: CVPR (2015)
2. Arandjelovic, R., Zisserman, A.: Multiple queries for large scale specific object retrieval. In: BMVC (2012)
3. Baltieri, D., Vezzani, R., Cucchiara, R.: 3dpes: 3d people dataset for surveillance and forensics. In: ACM Workshop on Human Gesture and Behavior Understanding (2011)
4. Bialkowski, A., Denman, S., Sridharan, S., Fookes, C., Lucey, P.: A database for person re-identification in multi-camera surveillance networks. In: DICTA (2012)
5. Chen, D., Yuan, Z., Hua, G., Zheng, N., Wang, J.: Similarity learning on an explicit polynomial kernel feature map for person re-identification. In: CVPR (2015)
6. Das, A., Chakraborty, A., Roy-Chowdhury, A.K.: Consistent re-identification in a camera network. In: Fleet, D., Pajdla, T., Schiele, B., Tuytelaars, T. (eds.) ECCV 2014. LNCS, vol. 8690, pp. 330–345. Springer, Heidelberg (2014). doi:10.1007/978-3-319-10605-2_22
7. Dehghan, A., Assari, S.M., Shah, M.: Gmmcp tracker: Globally optimal generalized maximum multi clique problem for multiple object tracking. In: CVPR (2015)
8. Ding, S., Lin, L., Wang, G., Chao, H.: Deep feature learning with relative distance comparison for person re-identification. Pattern Recogn. **48**(10), 2993–3003 (2015)
9. Dollár, P., Rabaud, V., Cottrell, G., Belongie, S.: Behavior recognition via sparse spatio-temporal features. In: 2nd Joint IEEE International Workshop on Visual Surveillance and Performance Evaluation of Tracking and Surveillance (2005)
10. Farenzena, M., Bazzani, L., Perina, A., Murino, V., Cristani, M.: Person re-identification by symmetry-driven accumulation of local features. In: CVPR (2010)
11. Felzenszwalb, P.F., Girshick, R.B., McAllester, D., Ramanan, D.: Object detection with discriminatively trained part-based models. Pattern Anal. Mach. Intell. IEEE Trans. **32**(9), 1627–1645 (2010)
12. Gray, D., Brennan, S., Tao, H.: Evaluating appearance models for recognition, reacquisition, and tracking. In: Proceedings IEEE International Workshop on Performance Evaluation for Tracking and Surveillance, vol. 3 (2007)

13. Han, J., Bhanu, B.: Individual recognition using gait energy image. Pattern Anal. Mach. Intell. IEEE Trans. **28**(2), 316–322 (2006)
14. He, K., Zhang, X., Ren, S., Sun, J.: Deep residual learning for image recognition. In: CVPR (2016)
15. Hirzer, M., Beleznai, C., Roth, P.M., Bischof, H.: Person re-identification by descriptive and discriminative classification. In: Image Analysis, pp. 91–102 (2011)
16. Jia, Y., Shelhamer, E., Donahue, J., Karayev, S., Long, J., Girshick, R., Guadarrama, S., Darrell, T.: Caffe: Convolutional architecture for fast feature embedding. In: ACM Multimedia, pp. 675–678 (2014)
17. Ke, Y., Sukthankar, R., Hebert, M.: Volumetric features for video event detection. Int. J. Comput. Vis. **88**(3), 339–362 (2010)
18. Klaser, A., Marszałek, M., Schmid, C.: A spatio-temporal descriptor based on 3d-gradients. In: BMVC (2008)
19. Kostinger, M., Hirzer, M., Wohlhart, P., Roth, P.M., Bischof, H.: Large scale metric learning from equivalence constraints. In: CVPR, pp. 2288–2295 (2012)
20. Krizhevsky, A., Sutskever, I., Hinton, G.E.: Imagenet classification with deep convolutional neural networks. In: NIPS (2012)
21. Laptev, I.: On space-time interest points. Int. J. Comput. Vis. **64**(2–3), 107–123 (2005)
22. Li, W., Wang, X.: Locally aligned feature transforms across views. In: CVPR (2013)
23. Li, W., Zhao, R., Xiao, T., Wang, X.: Deepreid: Deep filter pairing neural network for person re-identification. In: CVPR, pp. 152–159 (2014)
24. Liao, S., Hu, Y., Zhu, X., Li, S.Z.: Person re-identification by local maximal occurrence representation and metric learning. In: CVPR (2015)
25. Liu, K., Ma, B., Zhang, W., Huang, R.: A spatio-temporal appearance representation for video-based pedestrian re-identification. In: CVPR, pp. 3810–3818 (2015)
26. Luo, P., Wang, X., Tang, X.: Pedestrian parsing via deep decompositional network. In: ICCV (2013)
27. Ma, B., Su, Y., Jurie, F.: Covariance descriptor based on bio-inspired features for person re-identification and face verification. IVC **32**(6), 379–390 (2014)
28. Martinel, N., Micheloni, C., Piciarelli, C.: Distributed signature fusion for person re-identification. In: ICDSC (2012)
29. McLaughlin, N., Martinez del Rincon, J., Miller, P.: Recurrent convolutional network for video-based person re-identification. In: CVPR (2016)
30. Poppe, R.: A survey on vision-based human action recognition. Image Vis. Comput. **28**(6), 976–990 (2010)
31. Sánchez, J., Perronnin, F., Mensink, T., Verbeek, J.: Image classification with the fisher vector: Theory and practice. IJCV **105**(3), 222–245 (2013)
32. Schwartz, W.R., Davis, L.S.: Learning discriminative appearance-based models using partial least squares. In: SIBGRAPI (2009)
33. Scovanner, P., Ali, S., Shah, M.: A 3-dimensional sift descriptor and its application to action recognition. In: ACM Multimedia (2007)
34. Simonyan, K., Zisserman, A.: Very deep convolutional networks for large-scale image recognition. arXiv preprint (2014). arXiv:1409.1556
35. Su, C., Yang, F., Zhang, S., Tian, Q., Davis, L.S., Gao, W.: Multi-task learning with low rank attribute embedding for person re-identification. In: CVPR (2015)
36. Wang, T., Gong, S., Zhu, X., Wang, S.: Person re-identification by video ranking. In: Fleet, D., Pajdla, T., Schiele, B., Tuytelaars, T. (eds.) ECCV 2014. LNCS, vol. 8692, pp. 688–703. Springer, Heidelberg (2014). doi:10.1007/978-3-319-10593-2_45

37. Willems, G., Tuytelaars, T., Gool, L.: An efficient dense and scale-invariant spatio-temporal interest point detector. In: Forsyth, D., Torr, P., Zisserman, A. (eds.) ECCV 2008. LNCS, vol. 5303, pp. 650–663. Springer, Heidelberg (2008). doi:10.1007/978-3-540-88688-4_48

38. Wu, L., Shen, C., Hengel, A.V.D.: Deep recurrent convolutional networks for video-based person re-identification: An end-to-end approach. arXiv preprint (2016). arXiv:1606.01609

39. Xiong, F., Gou, M., Camps, O., Sznaier, M.: Person re-identification using kernel-based metric learning methods. In: Fleet, D., Pajdla, T., Schiele, B., Tuytelaars, T. (eds.) ECCV 2014. LNCS, vol. 8695, pp. 1–16. Springer, Heidelberg (2014). doi:10.1007/978-3-319-10584-0_1

40. Yi, D., Lei, Z., Liao, S., Li, S.Z.: Deep metric learning for person re-identification. In: ICPR, pp. 34–39 (2014)

41. You, J., Wu, A., Li, X., Zheng, W.S.: Top-push video-based person re-identification. In: CVPR (2016)

42. Zhao, R., Ouyang, W., Wang, X.: Unsupervised salience learning for person re-identification. In: CVPR (2013)

43. Zheng, L., Shen, L., Tian, L., Wang, S., Wang, J., Tian, Q.: Scalable person re-identification: a benchmark. In: CVPR (2015)

44. Zheng, L., Wang, S., Liu, Z., Tian, Q.: Lp-norm idf for large scale image search. In: CVPR (2013)

45. Zheng, L., Wang, S., Tian, L., He, F., Liu, Z., Tian, Q.: Query-adaptive late fusion for image search and person re-identification. In: CVPR (2015)

46. Zheng, L., Zhang, H., Sun, S., Chandraker, M., Tian, Q.: Person re-identification in the wild. arXiv preprint (2016). arXiv:1604.02531

47. Zheng, W.S., Gong, S., Xiang, T.: Associating groups of people. In: BMVC, vol. 2, p. 6 (2009)

Author Index